W. E. B. Du Bois

ALSO BY DAVID LEVERING LEWIS

King: A Biography

Prisoners of Honor:
The Dreyfus Affair

District of Columbia:
A Bicentennial History

When Harlem Was in Vogue

Harlem Renaissance:
Art of Black America (contributor)

The Race to Fashoda: European Colonialism
and African Resistance in the
Scramble for Africa

W. E. B.
Du Bois

BIOGRAPHY OF A RACE

1868-1919

David Levering Lewis

A JOHN MACRAE BOOK
HENRY HOLT AND COMPANY NEW YORK

Henry Holt and Company, Inc.
Publishers since 1866
115 West 18th Street
New York, New York 10011

Henry Holt ® is a registered
trademark of Henry Holt and Company, Inc.

Published in Canada by Fitzhenry & Whiteside Ltd.,
195 Allstate Parkway, Markham, Ontario L3R 4T8.

Library of Congress Cataloging-in-Publication Data

Lewis, David L.
W.E.B. Du Bois—biography of a race, 1868–1919 / David Levering Lewis.—1st ed.
p. cm.
Includes bibliographical references and index.
1. Du Bois, W. E. B. (William Edward Burghardt), 1868–1963.
2. Afro-Americans—Biography. 3. Afro-Americans—Civil rights.
4. Afro-Americans—History—1877–1964. 5. Civil rights movements—United States—History. I. Title.
E185.97.D73L48 1993
973′.0496073′0092—dc20 93-16617
[B] CIP

ISBN 0-8050-2621-5

Henry Holt books are available for special promotions and premiums.
For details contact: Director, Special Markets.

First Edition—1993

Designed by Claire Naylon Vaccaro

Printed in the United States of America
All first editions are printed on acid-free paper.∞

5 7 9 10 8 6 4

For Ruth Ann

CONTENTS

CONTENTS

ACKNOWLEDGMENTS

AT AGE twelve I stood beside my father one day in August 1948 as he spoke with W.E.B. Du Bois on the campus of Wilberforce University. I cannot recall the answer I gave when the latter asked what my plans were for life, but it certainly could not have anticipated what I would say to him today about the plan my life has followed for the past eight years. Research for this biography began in 1985. Since that time, it has often almost seemed that the problem of the twentieth century for me was far less the problem of the color line than it was the problem of W.E.B. Du Bois. The voyage through his ninety-five years has been long, challenging, and fascinating, extending over three continents into twenty-eight archives and research libraries containing ninety-nine collections, and into the lives of some 150 people. Yet with the completion of this volume, the writing of the life is only half done. The opposite hurtles of fatigue and obsession inherent in biography, thus far avoided, still stand in the road ahead. If luck holds, however, the splendid support and counsel of friends and colleagues and the exceptional cooperation of a great variety of professionals will continue to safeguard me from both dangers.

Because those to whom I owe large and lasting debts for having made this first volume possible are so numerous, I hope I may be forgiven for deciding that the most fitting manner in which to record my appreciation is simply to list them below without the comment each so richly merits. To Ron Bailey, therefore, and Esme Bhan, Philip Butcher, and James Celarier; Paul Clemens, David Donald, and Gabrielle Edgcomb; Paula Giddings, Louis Harlan, and Kenneth Janken; August Meier, John McCormick, and

Wilson Moses; Marc Pachter, Lila Parrish, Carol Preece, and Claudia Tate—all of whom read portions of this sprawling manuscript—eternal gratitude for criticism and suggestions, absolution from responsibility for all errors and deficiencies, and please stand by. Portions of what was read by these friends and professional acquaintances were written with the fellowship support of the Guggenheim Foundation, the Woodrow Wilson International Center for Scholars, and the creative and exceptionally generous research support of the department of history and the administration of Rutgers University, notably due to Edward Bloustein (president, deceased), Kenneth Wheeler, former provost, Richard L. McCormick, history chair and former faculty of arts and sciences dean; Rudolph Bell, current chair of the department of history; and Maryann Holtsclaw, without whom the Rutgers ship of history would have been, for all the luster of its navigators, rudderless. In the category of particular acknowledgments must also be included Richard Newman, formerly of the New York Public Library, who passed along much Du Boisiana and many astute hints in the early stages of this volume that were invaluable; my research assistants Chad Birely and Florice Whyte Kovan, and my graduate students Kimn Carlton-Smith, now a peer, and Martin Summers, still under sentence of dissertation.

The vibrant companionship and steady discernment of Ruth Ann Stewart, to whom this volume is dedicated, have sustained me in the highs and lows of living and writing. Her patient affection, her take-charge resiliency, and the untold hours she devoted to critical readings have meant far more to me than I can adequately or discreetly convey. Without her, there would be no biography. Our children, Allison, Jason, and Allegra, have shown remarkable understanding and affection year after year as this project enveloped our lives and often rendered me unaware of the routine of daily life. Perhaps now ways can be found to repay their precocious forbearance. Henry Holt and Company published *The Negro* in 1915, Du Bois's fifth work of nonfiction, and John Macrae, possessed of a rare knack for getting authors to borrow his own editorial blue pencil, has believed in and supported this biography as if some special bond subsisted between Holt and Du Bois. Although he hadn't bargained on a one-volume life turning into a two-volume one, Jack's measured enthusiasm never faltered. Nor did that of the meticulous Amy Robbins, Holt's tireless former associate editor, whose urgings to be clear and simple went only moderately against the grain. Once again to Claire Smith of Harold Ober Associates my gratitude for guidance in coping with the real world.

Acknowledgments

Abiding gratitude is expressed for advice or assistance to the following persons, with apologies in advance for the inadvertence of omissions: Kathleen Adams; Adele Alexander; Lee Alexander; Maya Angelou; Herbert Aptheker; Paul Ariani; Edward Beliaev; Emma Bell; Gila Bercovitch; John Bracey; Randall Burkett; Barbara Chase-Riboud; John Henrik Clarke; Willie Coleman; Claire Collier; Charles Cooney; Maceo Dailey; William L. Dawson; Robert Demariano; St. Clair Drake; Martin Duberman; Rachel Davis Du Bois; Walter Fisher; John Hope Franklin; Jacqueline Goggin; Leroy Graham; David Graham-Du Bois; Carol Grant; Jeffrey Green; Betty Gubert; Jessie P. Guzman; Debra Newman Ham; Grace Towns Hamilton; Faire Hart; Robert Hill; Wendell P. Holbrook; Harley Holden; Mr. and Mrs. John Hope 2d; Beth Howse; James Hudson; Irene C. Hypps; Karen Jefferson; Margaret Jerrido; William Jordan; Roger D. Joslyn; Mrs. Alfred A. Knopf; Theodore Kornweibel; Diana Latachenier; Robert and Sarah Lee; Josephine Harreld Love; Bettye Lovejoy; Fritz Malval; J. David Miller; Robert Morris; Emil P. Moschella; Albert Murray; Ethel Ray Nance; Kathy Nicastro; Stephen Ostrow; Paul Partington; Dovey Patrick; Edward Paul; Robert Paynter; Benjamin Quarles; Michael Raines; Arnold Rampersad; Priscilla Ramsey; T. Allen Ramsey; Naomi Richmond; James Rose; Kenneth Rose; Irving Rosenberg; Lucy Aiken Rucker; Elliott Rudwick; Everett H. Sanneman, Jr.; Morris U. Schappes; Linda Seidman; Veoria Shivery; Ann Allen Shockley; Steven Sklarow; Jeffrey Stewart; Edward Spingarn; Alan Stone; William Strickland; Charles M. Sullivan; Mae Miller Sullivan; John Taylor; Paul Thornell; Bazolene Usher; Carolyn Wedin; Dorothy Porter Wesley; Denise Williams; Du Bois Williams; Sondra Kathryn Wilson; C. Vann Woodward; Melanie Yollis; Pauline Young.

I wish to thank most sincerely the staffs of the following libraries and research institutions: The Amistad Research Center, Tulane University; The Beinecke Library, Yale University; Special Collections, Robert W. Woodruff Library, Clark-Atlanta University; The Oral History Office Research Collection, Nicholas Murray Butler Library, Columbia University; Special Collections, The Du Sable Museum, Chicago; Fisk University Library, Fisk University; Special Collections, Collis P. Huntington Memorial Library, Hampton University; The Houghton Library, Harvard University; The Library of America; Special Collections, Manuscript Division, The Library of Congress; Black Studies Reference Division, The Martin Luther King, Jr., Memorial Library of the District of Columbia; Special Collections, Soper Library, Morgan State University; Moorland-Spingarn Research Center, Howard University; National Archives; Rare Books and

Manuscripts Division, The New York Public Library; Nathan Pusey Library, Harvard University; Rockefeller Archive Center, Pocantico Hills, North Tarrytown, New York; The Schomburg Center for Research in Black Culture, The New York Public Library; Archives and Special Collections, Hollis Burke Frissell Library, Tuskegee University; Special Collections and Archives, University Library, University of Massachusetts at Amherst; Archives of the Trustees, University of Pennsylvania; Records Management Division, Federal Bureau of Investigation, U.S. Department of Justice.

—David Levering Lewis
Washington, D.C., and New Brunswick, N.J.
April 30, 1993

Find out just what any people will quietly submit to and you have found out the exact measure of injustice and wrong which will be imposed upon them, and these will continue until they are resisted with either words or blows, or with both.

—Frederick Douglass
"West Indian Emancipation"
4 August 1857

Genius . . . means little more than the faculty of perceiving in an unhabitual way.

—William James
The Principles of Psychology
(1890)

1.
Postlude to the Future

THE ANNOUNCEMENT of W.E.B. Du Bois's death came just after Odetta finished singing, a mighty trumpet of a voice that had accompanied the nonviolent civil rights movement from early days. Roy Wilkins, executive secretary of the National Association for the Advancement of Colored People (NAACP), broke the news in his precise Midwestern voice that always reminded you of a proper Protestant pastor or one of the older men behind the counter at Brooks Brothers. From late morning into mid-afternoon, the scalding sun and suffocating clamminess had exacted their toll from more than 250,000 men, women, and young people who crowded the length of the Reflecting Pool of the nation's capital in response to the charge of Asa Philip Randolph, the moving force behind the March On Washington. Tall, white-maned, and as ebony as an African chief's walking stick, Randolph, the grand old man of civil rights, had summoned Americans to Washington that twenty-eighth day of August, 1963, in all their professional, social, and ethnic variety to act, as he said in his cathedral baritone, as "the advance guard of a massive moral revolution for jobs and freedom."[1]

Before Wilkins's brief, epochal announcement, speaker after speaker had stepped up to the altar of microphones to music and song by Joan Baez; Peter, Paul, and Mary; Pete Seeger; Marian Anderson; and Mahalia Jackson. As the sun blazed down, the marchers witnessed a who's who of America's civil rights, religious, and labor leadership. Eugene Carson Blake of the National Council of Churches, with a speech too dry for this evangelical occasion, was followed by young John Lewis of the Student

Nonviolent Coordinating Committee (SNCC), whose speech in its original draft, threatening to lay waste to the white South, had brought down upon his militant head the collective wrath of the civil rights elders and Cardinal Patrick O'Boyle of the Washington archdiocese. Lewis finally agreed to soften his words, but not by much, and the crowd cheered when he intoned, "Listen, Mr. Kennedy, listen, Mr. Congressman, listen, fellow citizens—the black masses are on the march for jobs and freedom, and we must say to the politicians that there won't be a 'cooling-off' period." The United Automobile Workers' ebullient Walter Reuther almost matched Lewis's cautionary rhetoric, telling a nation on guard against Soviet imperialism that it could not "defend freedom in Berlin, so long as we deny freedom in Birmingham." Then came Floyd McKissick of the Congress of Racial Equality (CORE) to read James Farmer's powerful speech. Had Farmer not insisted on staying in jail in Plaquemine, Louisiana, his baritone delivery would surely have made eyes water and pulses rise even more than the intense McKissick succeeded in doing. Whitney Young, Jr., the handsome, gregarious new head of the National Urban League (NUL), was more at home in the boardrooms of corporate donors than in trying to stir crowds, and his too-rapidly read message showed it.[2] When Matthew Ahmann of the National Conference for Interracial Justice (NCIJ) used up his ten minutes in moral generalities, the thermometer stood at eighty-two humid degrees and attention spans evaporated.

Now Roy Wilkins was at the microphone, to be followed by Rabbi Joachim Prinz of the American Jewish Congress. But instead of beginning his prepared address straightaway, he opened by saying that he was the bearer of news of solemn and great significance. Dr. W.E.B. Du Bois was dead. He had died in his sleep around midnight, on the twenty-seventh, in Ghana, the country of his adopted citizenship. "Regardless of the fact that in his later years Dr. Du Bois chose another path," Wilkins told the suddenly still crowd, "it is incontrovertible that at the dawn of the twentieth century his was the voice calling you to gather here today in this cause." The NAACP head asked for silence, and a moment almost cinematic in its poignancy passed over the marchers. Saddened, though unsurprised by Wilkins's announcement, Rachel Davis Du Bois ("the mother of intercultural education") wondered aloud at that moment if Du Bois's spirit, "now free from his body, in some mysterious way might have hovered in our midst." Unrelated by ties of blood or marriage to the legendary old icon, she had known and loved him deeply much of her life. Jim Aronson, another white Du Bois stalwart, would write in *The Guardian*, a socialist weekly, of an aged, black woman in the crowd weeping, " 'It's like Moses. God had written that he should never enter the promised land.' "[3] Aronson left unsaid what all who had known him at the end understood, that Du Bois had finally concluded that this weeping woman's promised land was a cruel, receding mirage for people of color. And so he had chosen to live out his last days in West Africa.

Legendary Dr. Du Bois (for few had ever dared a more familiar direct address) appeared to have timed his exit for maximum symbolic effect. Someone had told the actor Sidney Poitier and the writers James Baldwin and John Killens the news while they were standing with several others in the lobby of Washington's Willard Hotel early that morning. " 'The Old Man died.' Just that. And not one of us asked, 'What old man?' " Killens recalled.[4] In a real sense, Du Bois was seen by hundreds of thousands of Americans, black and white, as the paramount custodian of the intellect that so many impoverished, deprived, intimidated, and desperately striving African-Americans had either never developed or found it imperative to conceal. His chosen weapons were grand ideas propelled by uncompromising language. Lesser mortals of the race—heads of civil rights organizations, presidents of colleges, noted ministers of the Gospel—conciliated, tergiversated, and brought back from white bargaining tables half loaves for their people. Never Du Bois. Not for him the tea and sympathy of interracial conferences or backdoor supplications, hat in hand and smile fixed, in patient anticipation of greater understanding or guilt-ridden, one-time-only concessions. From an Olympus of scholarship and opinion, he waved his pen and, as he wrote later, attempted "to explain, expound and exhort; to see, foresee and prophesy, to the few who could or would listen." Many, many listened, and one who did, Percival Prattis, the aggressive editor of the influential Pittsburgh *Courier*, wrote proudly at the time of the Old Man's McCarthy-era trial as a foreign agent, "They could not look at him and call me inferior."[5]

Born in Massachusetts in the year of Andrew Johnson's impeachment and dead ninety-five years later in the year of Lyndon Johnson's installation, William Edward Burghardt Du Bois cut an amazing swath through four continents (he was a Lenin Peace Prize laureate and his birthday was once a national holiday in China), writing sixteen pioneering or provocative books of sociology, history, politics, and race relations. In his eighties, he found time to finish a second autobiography and produce three large historical novels, complementing the two large works of fiction he wrote in the first two decades of the twentieth century. The first African-American to win a Harvard doctorate, he claimed later that it was a consolation for having been denied the few additional months needed to take a coveted doctorate in economics from the University of Berlin. The premier architect of the civil rights movement in the United States, he was among the first to grasp the international implications of the struggle for racial justice, memorably proclaiming, at the dawn of the century, that the problem of the twentieth century would be the problem of the color line.

Du Bois was one of the founders of the NAACP and the fearless editor of its monthly magazine, *The Crisis*, from whose thousands of heated pages scholarship, racial propaganda, visionary pronouncements, and majestic indignation thundered and flashed across Afro-America and beyond for a quarter of a century. In its peak year, the magazine reached one hundred thousand devoted subscribers. Professor, editor, and propagandist, he was also once a candidate for the U.S. Senate, and, at least until the last decade of his Promethean life, civil rights role model to an entire race. In its transcendence of place, time, and, ultimately, even of race, his fabulous life encompassed large and lasting meanings. Always controversial, he espoused racial and political beliefs of such variety and seeming contradiction as to often bewilder and alienate as many of his countrymen and women, black and white, as he inspired and converted. Nearing the end, Du Bois himself conceded mischievously that he would have been hailed with approval if he had died at fifty. "At seventy-five my death was practically requested."[6]

Wilkins was into his speech now, mincing no words about the "sugar water" of civil rights proposals of the Kennedy administration. As the ovation for the NAACP secretary died down, Mahalia Jackson electrified the great crowd with "I've Been 'Buked and I've Been Scorned." A few minutes later, at 3:40 P.M. on that catalytic August day, Martin Luther King, Jr., the new shepherd of the 'buked and scorned, soared into one of the noblest speeches in the history of the American republic. Meanwhile, in Accra, Ghana, preparations for the elaborate state funeral were already well along that Wednesday, before the planet's network-television eyes turned away from the March On Washington at 4:30 P.M. Osagyefo President Kwame Nkrumah of the Republic of Ghana had commanded that the farewell for his friend and teacher, the Father of Pan-Africa, be movingly splendid. The Osagyefo was the second African to take command of a state south of the Sahara (even seasoned Africa watchers routinely forgot that the leader of the Sudan had assumed his duties in January 1956, more than a year before Nkrumah); his title was a self-created one derived from the

Akan language, roughly meaning "Redeemer." With 300 million pounds sterling in its treasury and the most educated population in the sub-Sahara, Ghana's ruler advertised his republic of seven million as the lodestar of black Africa, the beacon for independence and unity throughout the continent. The state funeral for W. E. B. Du Bois on Thursday afternoon, August 29, 1963, was meant to celebrate and symbolize Ghana's claim to Pan-African leadership.

The body lay in state in the spacious, white bungalow at 22 First Circular Road. It was a long barge of a house, a gift of the Ghana government, moored gently in Shirley Graham-Du Bois's flourishing garden. This was the second Mrs. Du Bois, musicologist, novelist, playwright, former American Communist Party (CPUSA) activist, now in her fifty-seventh year of tempestuous willpower and talented improvisation. A handsome African-American woman of fair complexion and features strongly imprinted by Native American ancestry, her take-charge personality, piercing eyes, and prominent nose made her seem even handsomer and taller than her five feet two inches.[7] From 10:00 A.M. until 2:00 P.M. on the twenty-ninth, Shirley Graham-Du Bois had received those coming to pay final respects. Efua Sutherland, a tall, cocoa-brown woman of great beauty, arrived to console and stayed to help with the last-minute oversights of such occasions. She was the director of the Ghana Drama Society and had brought William Branch, a young black American actor and free-lance journalist with her. Branch's coverage of the funeral in Harlem's *Amsterdam News* would be a trove of detail. A broad spectrum of the diplomatic corps (but no one from the embassy of the United States), officials of the Ghana government, representatives from state-supported academic and cultural organizations, and many people from the large resident African-American community came to offer condolences, to express what the widow's husband had meant to the world, to Ghana, or simply to themselves, and to gaze silently for a few seconds upon the remains in the bronze casket. Du Bois lay deep in his burnished vessel, bronzed flesh encased in bronzed metal, cravated and light-suited, his features even more refined in death, the finely spheroidal cranium and trimmed Wilhelmine mustache and goatee completing the effect of assured apotheosis.[8]

The script for the last rites called for a triple ceremony of leave-taking: first, in the bungalow, largely among close family friends and a few persons of position in government, diplomacy, and the burgeoning cultural community of the capital; a second, public and photographed, on the grounds of the compound beneath a thatched, stone-pillared gazebo that had been completed too late for the deceased to enjoy in the evenings; and a final march and symbolic fanfare among thousands by the ocean. Shortly after two, a general's signal sent a detachment of infantry in full dress to enter the rear of the bungalow. Shirley Graham-Du Bois stood silently, comforted by Efua Sutherland and others, as the soldiers entered in lockstep, closed the lid of the coffin, and removed it to the red-carpeted gazebo. The coffin, resting on a silver catafalque, was reopened. Four soldiers in crimson jackets, heads bowed, rifles reversed, stood beside each pillar. Above the body lying in serene repose, a Chinese lantern glowed and, occasionally, swayed slightly.[9]

By then, the grounds of the bungalow were packed with the grieving and the curious. Men, women, and children of all classes—market women, cabinet ministers, and Europeans—reverently filed past the bier. The easy fellowship of the day was underscored by a pennanted Rolls-Royce gliding up to disgorge Prime Minister Hastings Banda of Nyasaland, an energetic little man who self-importantly acknowledged greetings as he bounded through the crowd into the gazebo. President Nkrumah was convinced that such freewheeling contact with his own people was too dangerous. A bomb in a potted plant in a far-north place called Kulungugu had nearly killed him the year before. Shortly before 3:00 P.M., therefore, the commissioner of police ordered the compound cleared. Fellowship gave way to maximum-security autocracy in a wail of sirens and backfiring motorcycles as a behemoth Russian ZIL limousine arrived. (There were only three of these machines in the country—Nkrumah's, the Du Boises', and the Soviet ambassador's, whose country's gift they were.) The leader of Ghana, a trim, slight man with a polished forehead, descended briskly, wearing his customary frown of deep concentration. He was dressed in a black, impeccably tailored version of the Nehru jacket, now his signature on state occasions.

As Nkrumah strode down the red carpet to the gazebo, Mrs. Graham-Du Bois, in black dress and veiled hat, descended the steps of the bungalow to greet him. She leaned slightly upon the chief of state's left arm as they approached the casket together. Nkrumah stood head bowed for three minutes. Then, solemnly, he placed his right hand upon Du Bois and allowed something of the moment's deep emotion to play across his face. Shirley Graham-Du Bois followed, repeating the gesture, her tender expression of the moment before giving way to one of ineffable grief. The stillness was broken by what the *Evening News* described as the chanting of a "state linguist" (the witch doctor of mocking Europeans) pouring a traditional libation upon the ground and asking God in Akan "to lead Africa's son into the next world." The newspapers tell us that "at that precise moment," rain fell in sheets, an unmistakable sign to Ghanaians that the gods had granted Du Bois citizenship in their world. Nkrumah briskly returned to his limousine, under an attendant's umbrella. As he drove away, the rain stopped as suddenly as it had come.[10]

Precisely on the hour, the chief of the defense staff of the Ghanaian army and the commissioner of police presented themselves to Mrs. Graham-Du Bois. Saluting crisply, they informed her that the caisson and military honor guard stood ready to transport her husband from the Cantonments Residential Area (once the preserve of the occupying British) to the grounds of the Old Government Printing Office on 28th February Road. Army pallbearers began sealing the coffin, lacing the red, gold, and green colors of Ghana around it, then hoisted it atop a howitzer gun carriage drawn by a black Land Rover. On the one-mile drive to the staging area, Shirley sat deep in the rear plush of the ZIL that had given her husband so many hours of pleasure and contemplation. Following several cars back with Efua Sutherland, William Branch wondered to himself how his own country's officials could behave so pettily, as the cortege passed the American embassy and he caught sight of its staring personnel and the Stars and Stripes at full staff in front.[11] Within a few minutes, they reached the Old Government Printing Office where the funeral parade would assemble.

Thus it was that a few minutes after 3:00 P.M., in keeping with the punctuality always insisted upon by Nkrumah, the bronze casket began the final leg of its ceremonious journey. To Nkrumah—who approved as the American title of his life story, *Ghana: The Autobiography of Kwame Nkrumah*—a sense of history and of occasion were second nature. "Arrangements for the Burial of Dr. W.E.B. Du Bois" were intended to advertise abroad and to enhance at home, with solemnity and pageantry, the reality of an African nationhood still being consolidated.[12] "O God, Our Help in Ages Past" filled the heated air as the trombones and tubas of the Central Army Band followed behind the ZIL and the slow-moving caisson. Next came two double columns of elite infantry in gold-braided tunics of crimson—rifle stocks reversed and cradled in underarm position—executing the distinctive, ceremonial glide, the famous Slow March, learned from British drillmasters. The three-thirty sun spangled off medals won during the Ghana army's participation in the United Nations peacekeeping action in the former Belgian Congo. The *shh-wutt-shh-wutt* of the Slow March and the mournful notes of the band funneled through the great arch at Black Star Square, where several thousand hushed onlookers watched from bleachers under skies now blown blue and clear of clouds.

Castle Osu, old Christiansborg, sits on a spit of land less than fifty yards from the Atlantic, one of the half dozen stone holding-pens built along the coast by Portuguese, Danish, and Dutch slave traders. For the Europeans, the gold of the old Gold Coast had become, by the beginning of the sixteenth century, not mineral but animal. Few sacks of gold dust were ever stored in Portugal's infamous São Jorge d'El Mina Castle ("the Mine") one hundred miles west southwest of Accra. Instead, a ghastly collaboration had come to pass as the smart, corner-cutting Fanti people of the coast leapt at the opportunity to enter into the European spiderweb market of rum, cloth, trinkets, firearms, and chattels gradually interlacing four continents. For four hundred years, African slave magnates fed several million black men, women, and children to El Mina, Christiansborg, and the other grim, dank coastal entrepots from Senegal to Angola that supplied the rapacious Atlantic slave trade. Between ten and fifteen million people are estimated to have been shipped out of Africa between 1450 and 1860, and millions of them surely came from the Gold Coast.[13] But all this was now understood to be part of a history best left to historians. For the people of postcolonial Ghana, Castle Osu symbolized, in its reincarnation as the residence of their head of state, the reassertion of sovereignty and the resolve to become players on the modern world stage.

So, with fitting ceremony, the people of Ghana took their Pan-African Moses down to the sea, to entomb him just outside the white walls of looming Castle Osu. The *Ghanaian Times* would wax conventionally metaphorical the following morning about "that enigma of a fighter, that phenomenon of a sage, sleep[ing] the long sleep in a spot that symbolizes his true return to the home of his ancestors."[14] Yet his burial in the soil of Ghana meant much more than that, as Nkrumah certainly knew and intended his people to appreciate over time. It implied mitigation of African peoples for collusion in slavery—not through alibi or justification but through a recognition that, in selling Du Bois's ancestors into bondage, the Africans who had profited were, in reality, no more free than those who ended up on auction blocks. The message of Karl Marx delivered by Du Bois to all Africans, as to the rest of the less-developed world, was that the market economy perfected in northern Europe always made the weak weaker—and most of the strong weaker.

Du Bois had shaped and launched upon the rising tide of twentieth-century nationalisms the idea of the solidarity of the world's darker peoples, of the glories in the forgotten African past, of the vanguard role destined to be played by Africans of the diaspora in the destruction of European imperialism, and, finally, as he grew older but more radical, of the inevitable emergence of a united and socialist Africa. Master of seductive syntheses of scholarship and prophecy, only Du Bois would have serenely foretold, but a few months into the din of the guns of August 1914, that "a belief in humanity means a belief in colored men" and that the "future world will, in all reasonable probability, be what colored men make it." In what were virtually his last words of warning, he had written that a "body of local private capitalists, even if they are black, can never free Africa; they will simply sell it into new slavery to old masters overseas."[15] Du Boisian Pan-Africanism, then, meant enormously more than the ethnic romanticism of roots traced and celebrated. It signified the militant, anticapitalist solidarity of the darker world.

Standing before the starkly white walls of Castle Osu, Ghanaian ambassador plenipotentiary Michael Dei Anang read Du Bois's "Last Message to the World," composed six years earlier in the deceased's Brooklyn home. As he read, eight bareheaded officers threaded ropes underneath the gleaming casket in preparation for its final descent. Speaking through Dei Anang's clipped British accent, the old sage told the world that he had "loved people and my play, but always I have been uplifted by the thought that what I have done will live long and justify my life; that what I have done ill or never finished can now be handed on to others for endless days to be finished, perhaps better than I could have done."[16] Among the honorary pallbearers was an unusually tall, gaunt, and handsome African-American whose priestly bearing and ideological fervor had earned him the rare honor of intimate collaborator and de facto editor of the Great Man's last large undertaking, the *Encyclopaedia Africana*, funded by Nkrumah's government through the Ghana Academy of Sciences. Alphaeus Hunton, once professor of literature at Howard University, intended to devote the remainder of his life to this monumental work whose creator was being lowered into the ground to the bugled notes of the Last Post.

Wreaths were laid, first for the president and Mrs. Graham-Du Bois, and, one by protocol one, by portly Chief Justice Sir Arku Korsah; towering Liberian ambassador George Flamma Sherman; bespectacled chief of the ruling Convention People's Party (CPP), N. A. Welbeck; writer Julian Mayfield, representing the African-American community; and, finally, by a phalanx of army officers for national, continental, and foreign organizations. The president's farewell message was read over Ghana Broadcasting that night a few hours after Martin Luther King described his incandescent dream in another time zone. The Osagyefo must have been deeply moved when writing his speech. It was plain yet vibrant, and as the Ghana Broadcasting announcer read of shared experiences and plans, something of Nkrumah's sense of personal loss entered his own voice. "I knew him in the United States and even spoke on the same platform with him," Nkrumah boasted of his days as a university student in America. (Du Bois had had to be rather carefully reminded of the occasion years later.) The greatest scholar the Negro race had produced became a "real friend and father to me," Nkrumah continued. He had asked Dr. Du Bois to "come to Ghana to pass the evening of his life with us." The president's radio apostrophe ended after a few more phrases with a perfect summation: "Dr. Du Bois is a phenomenon. May he rest in peace."[17]

During the next few days, the newspapers would tally the impressive cable traffic—from J. B. Bernal of the World Peace Council, Gus Hall of the American Communist Party, Chief Awolowo of Nigeria, Cheddi Jagan of British Guiana, Jomo Kenyatta of Kenya, Ahmad Ben Bella of Algeria, Kim Il Sung of North Korea. Walter Ulbricht of the now dismantled German Democratic Republic wished that "the memory of Dr. Du Bois—an outstanding fighter for the liberation and prosperity of Africans—continue to live in our hearts." The cables from Mao Tse-tung and Chou En-lai were lengthy but less formulistic than most of the others, reflecting the political and personal camaraderie that had been so much advertised during the Du Boises' two sojourns in China. Chou En-lai's farewell fittingly summed up the course and meaning of his friend's near hundred-year odyssey as "one devoted to struggles and truth-seeking for which he finally took the road of thorough revolution. His unbending will and his spirit of uninterrupted revolution are examples for all oppressed peoples." Expressing his sense of loss, premier Nikita Khrushchev wrote Shirley Graham that her husband's "shining memory" would stay forever "in the hearts of the Soviet people." The day after the state funeral, the *Ghanaian Times* carried a moving front page editorial under the Akan headline, "NANTSEW YIE!" (Farewell!). The following day, the rains came again, heavily and steadily.[18]

2.
Mary Silvina's Great Barrington

WILLIE DU BOIS, as his family and the townspeople knew him, was born on Church Street in Great Barrington, Massachusetts, on February 23, 1868, a Sunday. On Saturday, the town had celebrated George Washington's birthday. The birth certificate reads William E. Duboise, "colored," issue of Alfred Duboise and Mary (no maiden name given), whose February 5 nuptials in the nearby village of Housatonic the previous year had been duly noted in the *Berkshire Courier*. The town clerk very likely spelled the father's name as he heard it pronounced—*Dewboys* rather than the Gallic *Dew-Bwah*. There is no way of knowing if Alfred Du Bois, whose birthplace is given as San Domingo, Hayti, was the clerk's informant. *Dewboys* may have been what Alfred's people had found it handiest to be called, as generations of them roved back and forth from the Caribbean and through New York, Connecticut, and Massachusetts. Like Franklin Roosevelt, Leonard Bernstein, and other problematically named Americans, Alfred's son would unfailingly insist upon the "correct" pronunciation of his surname. "The pronunciation of my name is *Due Boyss*, with the accent on the last syllable," he would patiently explain to the uninformed.[1]

Most of what is known about these years comes from Du Bois himself, whose compelling prose re-creations of the town, the times, the races, and of his own family and himself are landmarks in American letters. He was to leave his hometown at age seventeen, returning during the following fourscore years only infrequently, and always for brief stays. Fifteen years after leaving, the village prodigy had transformed himself, almost beyond recognition, into a cosmopolitan traveler and distinguished scholar. But the importance of the Great Barrington period, its imprint upon all that Willie Du Bois grew to be, was deep, and certainly singular. His sense of identity or belonging was spun out between the poles of two distinct racial groups—black and white—and two dissimilar social classes—lower and upper—to form that double consciousness of being he would famously describe at age thirty-five in *The Souls of Black Folk*. Because he sedulously invented, molded, and masked this village world to suit his egocentric, if inspired, purposes of personal and racial affirmation, a sojourn there needs to be leisurely and probing enough to recover the Great Barrington that its most famous citizen knew and yet did not wish to know or have known. There were family matters of which he was deeply ashamed, others that made him angrier than he could admit to himself. For Willie Du Bois, the Berkshire period was variously Edenic fable, racial definition, and psychic trapdoor.

Great Barrington is the last town of any size in the wedge of western Massachusetts just before reaching the New York state line and the Hudson River, twenty-four miles beyond. Albany is northwest, about forty-five miles away. The town lies high and clear-aired in the dip of two mountain ranges, the Berkshires to the east (one of them resembling Mount Greylock, thirty miles to the north, the hump-backed inspiration for Melville's *Moby-Dick*), and the Taconic chain to the west with nearby vaulting Mount Everett. For a few blocks, Great Barrington nestles along the west bank of the Housatonic as it winds south out of the Berkshire Valley across Connecticut, finally emptying into Long Island Sound at Bridgeport. Berkshire historian Charles Taylor, one of Willie's earliest mentors, discovered the first European mention of the Housatonic when Major John Talcott's Connecticut troops "pursued a party of fugitive Indians into this region" in August 1676, at the close of King Philip's War, "overtaking them on the banks of the Housatonic, inflicting severe chastisement on them." The site of that chastisement was not far from the house where Willie was born. The Housatonic turns up again in a 1694 entry in Reverend Benjamin Wadsworth's journal. Accompanying the Massachusetts and Connecticut commissioners to a pow-wow with the chiefs of the Iroquois Confederacy at Albany, Wadsworth, a Bostonian and future president of Harvard College, records his progress through a "howling wilderness" in which they took "lodgings, about sundown, in ye woods, at a place called Ousetonuck, formerly inhabited by Indians." Two wars against the French, King William's and Queen Anne's, more or less secured English claims below Lake Ontario, including the Berkshire region, by the early eighteenth century.

On April 24, 1724, twenty Muhhekunnucks (as the European chronicler called the local tribe) affixed X's at Westfield to a deed conveying their lands along the Housatonic to one Colonel John Stoddard and captains John Ashley, Henry Dwight, and Luke Hitchcock for 460 pounds of powder, 3 barrels of cider, and 30 quarts of rum.[2]

But as Anglo-American Deweys, Ingersolls, Kelloggs, and Phelpses came to claim and clear western Massachusetts, they found that the Hudson Valley Dutch—Burghardts, Hollenbecks, and Van Deusens—were also arriving or often already in place. Among the welter of documents generated by these longstanding colonial disputes was the 1741 petition to the Massachusetts General Court of one Coenraet Borghghardt for restitution of the very same property Colonel Stoddard and his friends had acquired from the Muhhekunnucks. The disputed acreage encompassed much of the western part of the township that would be incorporated in 1761, without a name, but soon to become known as Great Barrington.[3] By then, the Dutchman and his family were among the undisputed proprietors on the plain stretching west from Great Barrington across gentle Green River to Egremont Village. This same Coenraet Borghghardt, Coonrad Borghardt, or Conraed/Conrad Burghardt (the first of the Berkshire Burghardts) soon came into possession of a slave boy named Tom, born in West Africa, probably in the early 1730s, and sold by Dutch slavers in New York. During four days in October 1780, Tom served as a private in Captain John Spoor's company, whose regimental commander was a Colonel John Ashley. The regiment mustered and hurried (too late) to lift the British siege of forts Ann and George, for which service Tom probably won his freedom. Tom Burghardt died in Great Barrington, about six years after the cause for which he had apparently been willing, however briefly, to give his life triumphed at the Battle of Yorktown. Nothing more is known about him except that he had a wife (who may have also been born in West Africa) and that there were begats aplenty from his line.[4]

One son, Jacob or Jack, born about 1760, fathered at least six children, one of whom, Othello, was Willie Du Bois's maternal grandfather. When Captain Daniel Shays's indebted farmers and veterans, driven by hard money and harsh courts to sedition, marched through the Housatonic Valley on their way to seize the arsenal at Springfield in February 1787, Jack Burghardt may have played a small part in Great Barrington's biggest drama of the century. Either he joined Shays's men or stood solidly with the forces of order under Colonel John Ashley at Sheffield (both of which incompatible distinctions his great-grandson claimed at different times). Willie

Du Bois also found a sketchy place for his maternal great-grandfather in the War of 1812.[5]

Handsome, free, and heir to a fair amount of good farmland near South Egremont Village, Jack, after the death of his first wife, Violet, became the young husband of Elizabeth Freeman sometime in early 1790. A Berkshire woman of such exceptional achievements that she was to live on, inspirationally, in Harriet Martineau's *Retrospect of Western Travel*, "Mum Bett" (as she was affectionately known to black and white throughout the state) helped to deliver a mortal blow to slavery in the Bay State, in 1783, by suing her abusive Sheffield mistress, Colonel John Ashley's wife, and winning her freedom and thirty shillings' damages before the county court in Great Barrington. Later, when Shays and his rebels appeared at Stockbridge, Mum Bett hid her employers' family silver and bluffed the men from the door. Her watercolor portrait at the State Historical Society confirms Elizabeth Freeman's legendary grit and intelligence, inviting conjecture about what her life can have meant to the great-grandson by marriage who mentions her proudly ("a rather celebrated figure") in two autobiographical works.[6]

As with much else to do with early Burghardt history, Du Bois has left several confusing and contradictory accounts of the "little black Bantu" ancestor who sang a sad West African tune, still heard at the fireside of his childhood:

> Do bana coba, gene me, gene me!
> Do bana coba, gene me, gene me!
> Ben d'nuli, ben d'le.

Willie never learned the meaning of her song, the exact origin and translation of which have continued to defy linguists. Perhaps the best hypothesis suggests that it was a Wolof song from Senegambia about confinement or captivity: "*gene me, gene me* [gene ma, gene ma]!"—"get me out, get me out!" In two remembrances of his Burghardt kin—*Darkwater* (1920) and the *Autobiography* (1968)—it is great-great-grandfather Tom's unnamed mate who "clasped her knees and rocked and crooned" the African song. In *Dusk of Dawn* (1940), it is Jack's Violet, mother of the six surviving Burghardts, who pines for Africa.[7] Violet seems a more likely candidate, but it was the influence of the song, rather than the singer, that finally mattered to Willie. It was his one truly palpable tie to that African homeland he would spend an academic and political lifetime trying to interpret and shape. "Africa is, of course, my fatherland," he would write sixteen years after spending a few months during 1923 in Monrovia, Liberia. "What is it between us that constitutes a tie which I can feel better than I can explain?"[8] Violet's song had been the earliest prompting of a very New England and supremely intellectual great-grandson to try to discern a few true notes of a remote, vestigial, and mysterious heritage.

There were 3,920 people living in Great Barrington at the end of the Civil War, three years before Du Bois was born. At least one of them, a lanky lawyer named Joyner, admitted to being a Democrat. Two years before Willie's birth, Congress had overridden Andrew Johnson's vetoes in order to pass the first civil rights act and to establish the Freedmen's Bureau, the first federal poverty program. In March 1867, alarmed by the return to Congress of the very colonels who had so recently stacked arms at Appomattox and who now protested paying off the war debt at its face value in gold, and further outraged by Ku Klux Klan violence and flagrant Black Codes reimposing slavery in the South in all but name, the Republicans rushed through the first Reconstruction Act. Ten southern states were placed under military rule until new state constitutions, drafted with full participation by the former slaves, were ratified along with the proposed Fourteenth Amendment, which southern white legislators had just unwisely rejected. Five months after Mary Silvina Burghardt Du Bois brought Willie into the world, the lengthy Fourteenth Amendment was ratified by state constitutional conventions throughout the South, with some 260 African-American convention delegates voting, and incorporated into the Constitution of the United States. Less than two years elapsed before ratification of the Fifteenth Amendment, definitively guaranteeing the franchise to black Americans. Until the experiment crafted by the "radical" Republicans expired as a result of racial hostility, scandal, economic exploitation, and sectional rapprochement, the "reconstructed" South would survive biracial state legislatures and even send two African-American senators and twenty representatives to Congress.[9]

Western Massachusetts applauded what then seemed patent evidence of Christian progress, racial uplift, and partisan political wisdom. Remote as the citizens of Great Barrington were from the commencing potlatch of the Gilded Age, the clangor of titanic industrial growth and raucous political corruption nevertheless reached upward into the Berkshires as muted, if distinct, echoes. Coming hard on the heels of the "Whiskey Ring" scandal (bogus liquor-tax certificates) and the Credit Mobilier (dummy railroad-construction companies) vacuuming of federal treasury millions during Ulysses S. Grant's inattentive administration, the disastrous Panic of 1873 seems to have rattled the business confidence of more than a few of Great Barrington's citizens, and even Willie's relatives felt the economic effects briefly. By and large, though, the towns of western Massachusetts missed most of the turbulence of the century's closing decades, and were content to have it so. But the region was host to several cultural energies of singular power and significance. Nathaniel Hawthorne wrote *The House of the Seven Gables* in nearby Lenox, and his friend Herman Melville created *Moby-Dick* outside the town of Pittsfield, where Oliver Wendell Holmes spent summers with his family.[10] Great Barrington would eventually come to boast about the years an undistinguished young lawyer named William Cullen Bryant spent there.

Approaching the town from Stockbridge to the northeast, old U.S. 7 pretzels to the iron Great Bridge at the Housatonic, then straightens and broadens past a cemetery into Main Street, unpaved until the end of the century, and runs arrow-straight past yet another cemetery, southwestward to Green River, and onto Egremont Plain. Great Barrington's few thousands lived in summer under a canopy of elms over Main Street and on streets that sloped east to the Housatonic River or rose west and petered out in mountain trails. In the short daylight of frozen winters, people found their way home by the glow of Main Street's revolutionary naphtha lamps, installed in 1871 and among the first in America. But until a special town meeting addressed the peril in the mid-'80s, Jared Lewis grumbled in the *Berkshire Courier* that horses cantering to and from Main Street across the two iron bridges often shied and plunged "through the large openings at the sides." Most visitors were familiar with the town's outstanding feature, David Leavitt's barn at Brookside—the largest barn in America when it was completed in 1854. Horace Greeley had come to see it and its large water-powered wheel for a story in the New York *Tribune*.[11]

The town was made of wood in the 1860s, except for St. James Episcopal Church, haughty in its Romanesque blue limestone. The brick town hall went up in 1876, along with the brownstone shaft monument to Great Barrington's Civil War dead, the 251 officers and men of the 57th Regiment, many of whom fell in the Battle of the Wilderness. Main Street's First Congregational Church, where Willie Du Bois and his relatives often worshipped, the *Berkshire Courier* building, Madame L'Hommedieu's millinery shop, Hollister's grocery store, the bakery, and even the new National Mahaiwe Bank were wooden. In 1882, the Congregational Church rose in blue limestone from its ashes, as did a number of structures destroyed by fire that year. The fire of October 1892, a six-hour conflagration leaving nothing standing on either side of Railroad Street, completed the transition from wood to brick and stone. The place would still have been recognizable to William Cullen Bryant, who combined the town clerkship with poetry until 1825, not quite immortalizing Green River "as it glides along/ Through its beautiful banks in a trance of song."[12]

Great Barrington's sense of itself became somewhat self-consciously Anglo-Saxon Protestant and Republican in the 1860s—Dutch families like the Burghardts became Burgetts and joined the Episcopal faith—due to the growing numbers of Irish Catholics and Czechoslovaks arriving to work in the textile and paper mills in Housatonic Village, about four miles north of the town. The Russell brothers, John and Asa, had incorporated Monument Mills there in 1850, taking advantage of the Housatonic's waterpower, as well as the eight-year-old Berkshire Railroad line. In 1875, they added on a soaring bell tower and a four-story brick building. When Willie Du Bois graduated from high school ten years later, Monument Mills was the town's largest employer, its 350 workers turning out 330,000 Marseilles quilts and 2,700,000 pounds of "plain and fancy double twist cotton warps" annually. A history of the mill ranked it as "by far the largest mill in South Berkshire," although diminutive when compared to the textile juggernauts of Lowell in the northeast and Adams in the northwest corner of the state. Housatonic Village was also the home of Owen Paper Mill, the second-largest employer. Van Deusenville, several miles away, turned out pig iron.[13]

From Du Bois's recollections and a culling of town-hall records, a reasonable estimate would fix the number of African-American families in the region at less than thirty. Most were Burghardts, with a smattering of Crawfords, Freemans, and Pipers, although a small influx of freed slaves from the South was just beginning. A few of them, like the Thomas Burghardt who worked for the Kellogg family, were substantial property owners. With rare exception if any, Great Barrington's African-Americans stayed away from the mills. Not only did industry-wide policy keep them out, most of them did their best to affect the same superior attitude of their white Protestant neighbors toward the Catholic newcomers who had no choice but to work in the mills. Mill work was long, hard, low-paying, and regimented. The old African-American families that ventured out of farming preferred personal service, and, at least until the 1870s, tended to have the pick of gentler jobs as domestics, barbers, stewards, and coachmen. Dr. C. T. Collins had opened his hotel in 1854, heralding the prosperous summer resort trade that was making Great Barrington, along with Lee and Stockbridge, favored retreats of New York and Connecticut's new leisure classes.[14]

Willie recalled "several hotel cooks and waiters" in the family who were in charge of dining rooms, "did well and were held in high esteem"—in high esteem, perhaps, but not as equals. "The color line was manifest," Willie has written, "and yet not absolutely drawn." Black and white Great Barrington coexisted civilly, even affectionately, but the two seldom commingled except on Sundays and in town meetings. And even when African-American citizens were present, town meetings were, with rare exception, the business of white men. The white churches, probably with some shame and much haggling, were even beginning to encourage their black parishioners to go elsewhere. By the late 1870s, although Willie and some of his immediate family continued to worship in the Congregational Church (previous generations had been Episcopalian), the religious and social life of the black community found its pulse in the little African Methodist Episcopal Zion (AME Zion) Church founded by freedmen and women from the South.[15]

There were actually three Great Barringtons, and the white newcomers were pressing against the door of domestic service, a challenge coming just as the Burghardt farms on Egremont Plain were less able to compete with produce shipped by river and rail from great distances. Economic historian Christopher Clark notes that Berkshire Valley "dependence on imported foodstuffs as well as other goods" was well advanced by the 1870s. Three of Jack Burghardt's sons, Othello, Ira, and Harlow, struggled along on the plain beyond Green River in neat houses set back from the main road within easy walking distance of each other. Harlow seems to have held on best. His property transactions in the town hall Registry of Deeds show a fair amount of profit from land sales during the period, including a December 19, 1868, transaction for eighty dollars.[16] Othello had the least gumption, or so thought his demanding grandson. "Uncle Tello," as Willie called his mother's father, was said to be too fond of the medicine prescribed for a hip injury, and left much of the running of things to his capable wife, Sarah or Sally, a handsome, tan woman from Hillsdale, New York. The federal census tracks Othello Burghardt's occupational vagaries decade by decade: 1850, whitewasher; and 1860, laborer; until that for 1870 finds him with "no occupation" at eighty, in a nimbus of pipe tobacco by the fireside.[17]

But whether energetic or indolent, this black yeomanry was grappling with large, impersonal forces, and as Great Barrington's established white families began to prosper, its black ones, Willie Du Bois's among them, were sliding into subsistence. The black families clung fiercely to basic moral values—churchgoing, work, wedlock, and legitimate births. "The speech was an idiomatic New England tongue, with no African dialect," Willie says. "The family customs were New England, and the sex mores." None of them had gone much beyond learning the alphabet, and few of them saw the need for more formal education.[18] Hemmed in by a racially exclusive industrialism, the whitening of domestic work, and their own deep conservatism, they were like Uncle Tello, stuporous by his fireside, atrophying, or, like cousin John Burghardt, determined not to be licked and moving on. But if the rising tide of development threatened some with drowning, in the crucial area of public education it promised a lift for all those with enough motivation. Before Willie Du Bois's first birthday, Great Barringtonians voted two thousand dollars to create a public high school. Until then, only private institutions like the Bostwick, Kellogg, Simmons, and Sedgwick schools for the affluent offered training beyond the early grades.[19] A plain, rectangular building went up next to the old wooden elementary schoolhouse in 1869, the town's second brick structure after the Episcopal Church. It would be Willie Du Bois's salvation.

The real world Tom Burghardt's faltering descendants made for themselves appears much transformed in the mythopoeic prose of Tom's illustrious great-great-grandson. In those lyrical memoirs, whether *Darkwater, A Pageant of Seven Decades*, *Dusk of Dawn*, or the *Autobiography*, we are drawn to participate in a chronicle of epic sweep, at once familial, racial, national, global, and prophetic. Enchantingly, heroically, they employ the language of the saga. Each alludes to the author's portentous birth "by a golden river in the shadow of two great hills, five years after the Emancipation Proclamation." The place of birth is idyllic and the circumstances neither rich nor poor but suited in their modesty to the author's large destiny. In local-color accents redolent of Washington Irving, Great Barrington is fairly faithfully pictured as "a little New England town nestled shyly in its valley with something of Dutch cleanliness and English reticence." The house of his birth is "quaint, with clapboards running up and down, neatly trimmed." There is a "rosy front yard" to frolic in and "unbelievably delicious strawberries in the rear." Elsewhere, we read of "a rather nice little cottage . . . furnished with some comfort."[20]

Whereupon the chords of destiny begin to sound ever fuller. His "own people were part of a great clan." "These Burghardts lived on South

Egremont Plain for near 200 years." The founding ancestor's relationship to his master, Coenraet Borghghardt, is subtly altered. "Sullen in his slavery," Tom Burghardt had come through the western pass from the Hudson "*with* his Dutch captor," rather than brought there *by* him. Tom's four days of service in Captain Spoor's company becomes an enlistment "to serve for three years" in the War of Independence.[21] By the time of the *Autobiography,* Tom's son Jack definitely decides his place is with Daniel Shays against the forces of monopoly capital. From Jack and Violet are born "a mighty family, splendidly named: Harlow and Ira, Chloe, Lucinda, Maria, and Othello!" Du Bois's exclamation point is like an arpeggio notation for successive chords about the "ancestral home on Egremont Plain," that "sturdy, small and old-fashioned" dwelling, "the house of my grandfather Othello." Here, ten more shoots of the mighty family burst forth from broken-hipped Othello and the once-attractive Sally, now "thin, yellow, and hawk-faced"—one of them, Mary Silvina, Willie Du Bois's mother, sometime in 1831. Hers is a dulcet movement: "Mother was dark shining bronze, with smooth skin and lovely eyes; there was a tiny ripple in her black hair; and she had a heavy, kind face."[22] In the surviving photograph, she is an erect, dark-skinned woman with sad eyes, a strong chin, and rather voluptuous lips.

Where and how Mary Silvina met Alfred Du Bois elude the historian and genealogist, at least for the present. Alfred may have made his way to Great Barrington in 1867, "small and beautiful of face and feature, just tinted with the sun, his wavy hair chiefly revealing his kinship to Africa." His people were free people of color, descended from Dr. James Du Bois of Poughkeepsie, New York, a wealthy physician of French Huguenot origins. James Du Bois's family had chosen the cause of George III over that of George Washington, receiving as reward from the British crown extensive lands in the Bahamas. A few years later, the Du Boises and their cousins, the Gilberts, had spread their plantation holdings to Haiti. On the island of Long Cay in the Bahamas, James sired at least three sons and a daughter of his slave mistresses. He took two of the children, probably the lightest in complexion, Alexander and John, with him when he returned to New York about 1812, enrolling them in Connecticut's exclusive Cheshire School for Boys. James Du Bois died, unexpectedly, not long afterward, and his Creole sons found themselves disowned by their white relatives and forced to give up boarding school for skilled labor. John resigned himself to his marginal lot, dying in December 1830 in his late twenties in Fair Haven, Connecticut. Alexander was apprenticed to a shoemaker but bolted to become a small merchant in New Haven. Marrying there in 1823, he and Sarah Marsh Lewis had several children by 1830, only one of whom, Augusta, survived into adulthood.[23]

The enigmatic Alfred Du Bois was born in Haiti, where Alexander had gone alone to try to salvage what he could of a once considerable patrimony, no later than 1833. When Alexander returned to the United States soon after Alfred's birth, he left the boy and his mother behind. Whether estranged or not, he and Sarah in New Haven were still legally married; Alexander understandably elected to come back to the city and his tobacco shop without Haitian dependents. When and how Alfred left Haiti remains conjectural, but by the time he appears in the 1860 census he may have been plying the trades of barber and cook or waiter in upstate New York for several years. Perhaps, as Willie speculates, his father came through the western pass from New York to try his luck in the valley of the Housatonic. An adoring son deploys Homeric imagery for the roving young god's advent, announcing that, "Alfred, my father, must have seemed a splendid vision in that little valley under the shelter of those mighty hills."[24] Yet Willie almost surely came to suspect years later that his father was something more than a well-meaning, romantic rakehell, "indolent, kind, unreliable," who came and soon departed from the valley and his family, only to die shortly thereafter.[25]

The suspicion is unavoidable that he knew more, if only subconsciously, considering the number of factual inconsistencies, surprising in a historian, as well as the nervousness apparent in some of the writing. Had Alfred been married before he took Mary Silvina to live "by the golden river"? In *Dusk of Dawn*, Du Bois "imagined not," and in the *Autobiography* denies even the "hint" of it, speculations absent from the earlier *Darkwater*. Although Alfred certainly never marched with the splendid black Massachusetts 54th Infantry Regiment during the Civil War, as some have supposed, he wears a private's uniform in his sole extant, undated photograph. The five-feet-six sloe-eyed soldier looks from under a dented kepi somewhat vacantly into the camera, his elbow-length cape mushrooming around narrow shoulders. Had he truly enlisted somewhere (possibly as a white man), the son wondered, and, if so, what had he done? Willie abandons the puzzle with an uncharacteristic shrug, deciding that the dazzling "Alfred never actually did much of anything." But what happened to Alfred after 1869 or early 1870? Although Willie was not then even two years old, somehow he writes later of "last remember[ing] urgent letters for us to come to New Milford," Connecticut. Yet if Alfred died as a barber or a preacher somewhere in Connecticut soon thereafter, as his son says in several places, then the final words about Alfred in the *Autobiography* are surprisingly inconsistent: "I never saw him, and know not where or when he died."[26]

In fact, as probate court documents in Bristol County, Massachusetts, disclose, Alfred Du Bois was almost certainly alive in Meriden, Connecticut, as late as 1887, which is hardly surprising, considering the eighty-four years enjoyed by his own father, Alexander, and the ninety-five allotted to his son, Willie. Whether or not Alfred married again and had offspring in New Milford or Meriden is unknown, but it is virtually certain that he committed bigamy when he and Mary Silvina Burghardt presented themselves to be married by Reverend Amos E. Lawrence in February 1867. At various times from 1858 through 1862, he was a baker, barber, and waiter in Albany, New York, giving the federal census taker his age as twenty-eight in 1860, and that of his presumed wife, Hannah, as twenty-one. Their household also contained a white woman named Catherina Dillman, "servant," age twenty, probably a paying boarder or possibly even part of a ménage à trois. Two years later, before disappearing permanently from the city directory, Alfred Du Bois was a waiter at the exclusive Delavan House, site of the titanic Erie Railroad battle five years later among Commodore Vanderbilt, Daniel Drew, and Jay Gould.[27]

"Gay and carefree," in the son's debonair description, "refusing to settle long at any one place or job," Alfred eventually left Hannah, who is last seen struggling on alone as a washerwoman in the 1866 Albany directory.[28] By then, he had also deserted from his Civil War unit, Company D, 20th Regiment, United States Colored Troops (New York). Having signed up at Amenia, New York, for a three-year term, he mustered in at Poughkeepsie on January 23, 1864. Private Alfred Du Bois gave his age as thirty and Connecticut, rather than Haiti, as his birthplace. Although his son would have been surprised to learn of actual service with Union forces at Port Hudson, Louisiana, Alfred's record was predictably feckless. The Records of the Adjutant General of the United States reveal the unimpressive truth. Laid up in Port Hudson General Hospital with bouts of diarrhea and dysentery in early April, then assigned there as a medical attendant after recovering, he was listed as absent without leave in August after being ordered to rejoin his regiment. On February 7, 1865, Alfred was "dropped as a deserter," eight weeks before Appomattox.[29] For some reason, Willie gave his father's age as forty-two when he appeared in Great Barrington, although the town-hall registry makes him, as well as his bride, only thirty-four. Mary Silvina would actually have been nearer thirty-six, if her son and her death certificate are correct. Alfred would have been no more than thirty-seven, and probably a year or so younger, having been born after 1831. The son's mistake could explain his readiness to believe that Alfred had died in the early 1870s.[30]

With his indeterminate color and Franco-Haitian background, a moral chameleon like Alfred would have found the hothouse atmosphere of occupied New Orleans full of potential. Maybe a stint as a physician (only a step up from barbering then), perhaps the bagging of a rich widow (the war had made many), or, possibly, scheming to make himself useful to the city's rising mulatto politicians detained him for a time. Equally likely, he may have returned to wander over the familiar terrain of upstate New York on the lookout for a grubstake. No evidence having been found to substantiate any of these plausible speculations, this is an opportune point to return, amid these speculations, to the where and how of Alfred and Mary's meeting. As crucial as she is to Willie Du Bois's life, Mary Silvina is never more than a shaded figure, hovering, always approaching, but never to be beheld in the high noon of abundant evidence. "She gave one the impression of infinite patience," her son recalled almost eighty years after her death, "but a curious determination was concealed in her softness." Rebelliousness, perhaps, more than determination?[31]

His mother had not always been the reticent homebody Willie remembered. He recalled dimly that she may have gone to New York City once, but he left that intriguing possibility unexplored.[32] Again, however, as with his father, Willie may very well have heard things—family gossip, rumors among the townspeople, or, perhaps, simply intuited meanings from what went unsaid—to suspect that his mother had lived a fuller, more complicated life in her youth. She had transgressed Burghardt family tradition in the most fundamental way. Modest farmers and semiskilled laborers, proud people who clung to respectability even as fate pushed them toward the margin, the black Burghardts had been New England to the core in culture and values. "There was only one illegitimate child throughout the family in my grandfather's and the two succeeding generations," Willie would boast. But that one exception was Mary Silvina herself, whose firstborn, Adelbert, the family claimed to be the issue of a "romance" with John Burghardt, a first cousin—a "love affair" broken up "on account of consanguinity."[33] Adelbert was the half brother about whom Willie was never quite able to write comfortably—or even correctly, consistently rendering his name as Idelbert. The fact that Adelbert's illegitimate birth in

1862 is unreported either at Great Barrington or South Egremont Village town halls suggests that Mary Silvina had left home. There is no Mary in Othello's household on the 1860 census for Great Barrington. Nor is she reported there on the 1865 interim census, although Adelbert, listed as three years old, is.[34]

Adelbert Burghardt himself could of course have thrown light on the circumstances of his birth, as well as something of his mother's character. It seems certain that his younger brother, an investigator *sans pareil* in other matters, somehow never made sufficient effort to learn everything he could. Adelbert's real father was not likely to have been John Burghardt, a dentist in the town. That the affair with the cousin was a probable fabrication appears to be confirmed by Adelbert, who insisted that he was born in Connecticut and later that his father was a man named Charles Craigg or Craig. A black man named Charles Craig worked in the home of Artemis and Judith Bigelow, wealthy white citizens of Great Barrington. Craig, who must have come to the town after 1860, would have been forty-one or forty-two when Adelbert was born. The 1870 census lists his profession as coachman, the line of work Du Bois's older brother would follow.[35] The "rather silent" Mary Silvina, then, could, and probably did, tell her younger son much about the promise and peril of worlds beyond settled and tidy Great Barrington.

She had wrenched free of Burghardt provincialism in her late teens, very likely defying family commands to fit into the grooved drudgery of low-paying domestic work and a humdrum labor pact that too often passed for marriage among the people she knew. The new Housatonic mills where she could have earned a little more money and had weekends free were closed to her because of race and tradition. Mary Silvina had enough intelligence and initiative, and maybe enough of the double-edged imagination that drove an increasing number of working-class women, to risk all—virtue, family, and health—on the main chance of the cities. If she ever saw New York City, as Willie believed, she may not have worked there for any length of time; more likely she was hired for kitchen work in large hotels in the towns along the upper Hudson and the Connecticut portion of the Housatonic. Salesclerking, the toniest occupation available to women of Mary Silvina's class and skills—native-born "American girls" who spoke pure English—was for whites only. There should also have been stints as a maid in private homes.

Clearly, she was a woman with a past that proper New England townspeople would have called, if not scarlet, certainly pink. She would have been no stranger to dance halls or amusement parks, permissive places young working women flocked to, indulging in styles of dress and sexual mores decades ahead of anything yet imagined in their hometowns. The possibility exists, of course, that, in reaction to her early experiences, Mary Silvina's sober, sensitive Great Barrington personality bore scant resemblance to the woman known to her peers in New York and Connecticut. It is more reasonable to believe, however, that the two women were intimately related—that Willie's mother was never a wild or wanton person. A certain sensitivity is hinted at in the name Adelbert. There is her deep aversion to alcohol, no doubt grounded in too many observations of painful drunkenness. By the time she met Alfred, probably somewhere in upstate New York, she was in her mid-thirties and compromised, although far from being a creature pummelled in the way of other poor working women, white and black, whom industrializing America was degrading in ever-larger numbers.[36] Living on the edge of a working woman's urban abyss, but coming early and leaving before too late, she narrowly escaped the classic fate of Stephen Crane's *Maggie: A Girl of the Streets* or Theodore Dreiser's *Sister Carrie*. Alfred Du Bois was not the stunning cavalier described by his son, but to Mary Silvina, in her circumstances and given her yearnings, this short, debonair, "light mulatto" war veteran with the French surname and the rarefied pedigree must have seemed a unique catch.

3.
Berkshire Prodigy

"So with some circumstance," Du Bois trumpeted in *Darkwater*, "having finally gotten myself born, with a flood of Negro blood, a strain of French, a bit of Dutch, but, thank God! no 'Anglo-Saxon,' I come to the days of my childhood." The house where he was born was one of two on Church Street belonging to Thomas Jefferson McKinley, an enterprising ex-slave who worked as a coachman for the Humphrey family, sold vegetables, and quietly accumulated considerable real estate. "Old Jeff," as the townspeople called him, had come north out of Louisiana about 1863, after being sold "down the Mississippi" by his North Carolina master. Later, he escaped and served in some menial capacity with the Southern Berkshire Company of the 49th Massachusetts Infantry Regiment at Port Hudson, Louisiana. Alfred and Mary lived next door to McKinley, on the north side of Church Street, just a few yards from the Housatonic, at what is today number 51. Both houses were torn down about 1900, and M. T. Cavanaugh's plumbing supply roughly marks the spot today, ninety years later. The house was, as Willie described it, sturdy, neat, large enough, with fair-sized front and back yards, and convenient to Main Street. Their lives together should have been off to a good start.[1]

The collapse of Mary Silvina's marriage came quickly. Before the baby was two years old, she had had to give up the house by the Housatonic and leave him with Othello and Sarah in their house on the South Egremont road. Willie always believed that the "black Burghardts" had made Alfred feel so unwelcome that he took his barber's tools elsewhere, fully expecting that Mary Silvina and the new baby would shortly follow. Not only were the black Burghardts seen as clannish rustics, deeply hostile to all that was different or new, Du Bois almost bitterly accuses his mother's people of color prejudice. These "black Burghardts didn't like it [marriage to Alfred], because he was too white," he insisted, "and he had a lot of extra manners which they weren't used to. . . . At any rate, they practically drove him away." When a historian from Columbia University's Oral History Project delicately probed the subject the year before Du Bois left for Ghana, reproach gave way to raw indictment, exposing the festering wound inflicted by a father's absence upon a still-tortured son. To the interviewer's question about whether his father "didn't just run away," Du Bois's agitated denial was, "No . . . I know, from testimony from other parts of the family, that they made it just as uncomfortable for Alfred as they could." Then, reflecting upon the doleful implications of in-group color prejudice, Du Bois added, "I don't suppose it was simply a matter of color. It was a matter of culture." In the son's final ordering of blame, Alfred was absolved because he "came from a different world."[2]

And yet, subconsciously, he must always have wondered. The family's brooding conspiracy of silence about Alfred was deeply unsettling. He watched as his mother "sank into depression." If Willie asked her very little about Alfred because he knew "instinctively that this was a subject which hurt" too much even to mention, how much of his reticence also came from knowing instinctively that his father had caused much of the pain? That he was not illegitimate like his older brother meant a great deal to a sensitive boy born into the last generation of Victorians and growing up in a typical New England town.[3] The stigma of bastardy on top of poverty and blackness in a fishbowl community of whites must have been an appalling threat to the Burghardts. Star-crossed love with a first cousin was supposed to repair Mary Silvina's transgression, although the extent to which the fiction was actually believed is doubtful. But the stigma of spousal desertion remained. Willie would have needed to believe Mary Silvina when she told him that Alfred had intended for them to follow him to Connecticut, and that he had waited and hoped until his death. But as this, too, was a fiction, undoubtedly it retained its hold over mother and son only to the degree that it remained unexamined and accepted on faith. What boy would choose to believe that his father had deserted him when the romantic myth of the well-intentioned cavalier allowed the blame to be shifted to jealous, rustic clansmen?

Reading these formative years through Willie's reconstructions of them in mature life raises doubts about how much is a faithful record of his mother's thoughts and how much is his own elaboration. Adelbert's version is certainly very different. According to Willie, his older brother was "silent"—a cipher, evanescent, and conveniently unavailable. His virtual absence from Willie's autobiographies—aside from two or three sentences—makes us neglect to probe the nature of their relationship. Adelbert must have had to care for his little brother when they lived on Egremont Plain. Five years older than his sibling, he might have instructed Willie in his first game of marbles or put a healing gob of spittle on a small cut. Willie, of course, had no memory of that strangely confused night when some of his Burghardt cousins—the Jackson boys, George, Henry, and Samuel—fired pistols from the riverbank near the Church Street house, throwing Alfred into frenzied packing and a precipitous exit from Great Barrington. Although Adelbert said long afterward that what was merely a rustic prank had been mistaken for a deadly plot—"for some reason [he] thought they were after him"—Alfred certainly had reason to think he was escaping from angry Burghardts who had found out about the Albany Hannah or some other indecent chapter in his life. Apparently, Adelbert never told Willie about the details of this night until long after they reached adulthood. And there was more he could have told. Seventy-seven years later, living on public welfare in Brooklyn, he sent word to his now famous brother that he wanted to share information about the family. The gigantic collection of Du Bois papers is silent about the response, if any, Adelbert received.[4] Were there things about his family (especially his father) Willie sensed early on that it was better not to know for the sake of the family past he preferred to invent? In any case, Alfred Du Bois appears to have shot out of Mary's and Willie's lives like a rocket.

Othello—"Uncle Tello"—died when Willie was only five, and family fortunes went steadily downward from then on. In *Darkwater*, the most passionate but least candid of his autobiographical writings, Du Bois says of these times, nevertheless, "They were very happy." Almost a score of years afterward, he still insisted his childhood had been idyllic. He could "remember no poverty, although our family was certainly poor." The town and its surroundings "were a boy's paradise. . . . My family were pleasant and miscellaneous." Yet Sarah was forced to sell the property on Egremont Plain immediately in settlement of debts, moving with Mary Silvina and her two grandsons into central Great Barrington, where Inez, the daughter of Mary Silvina's brother, James, probably continued to live with them. For a time, they lived above the Sumner estate stables south of Main Street, which Willie remembered as affording "infinite pleasure" because of the wide yard and the lane leading to the public school grounds. As needy as Sarah and Mary must have been for lodging and domestic work, Willie suggests that "this nearness to school induced mother to choose this home."[5] Adelbert's half brother fails to say whether Mary Silvina was also concerned about her older son's education. Presumably, Adelbert was already working as a waiter to help the family.

Willie says that the home above the stables gave way, with Sarah's death in about 1875, to a sojourn in Railroad Street. Living there would have undermined the emotional resiliency of most boys of average abilities. Willie, who was anything but average, lost no time in learning how to survive the unacceptable fate of the Railroad Street years. It was a feat of sublimation, willpower, and brains. Railroad intersects Main at its midpoint, then runs west up a mild gradient where several buildings in its path force a sharp L turn, after which it follows for a short, parallel distance what were, in Willie's day, the old Housatonic Railroad tracks. To local Comstocks, Railroad Street was two blocks of perdition, a foul causeway of ruin through three or four saloons, gambling dens, and at least one house of prostitution. A miasma of tobacco and reek of alcohol saturated the narrow street, as mill workers, day laborers, and more than a few less-respectable old settlers stumbled into and out of it. The indelible social taint of the street was such that, long after George Briggs invested his saloon profits in a respectable and successful business, Willie said the townspeople "never forgot his former calling." Mary Silvina rented a dilapidated house at the top of Railroad Street, hard by the tracks. They shared it with a white family, the Millers, even more destitute than themselves. Mrs. Miller was nearly insane.[6]

In his Columbia oral-history transcript, Willie remembers having liked the Railroad Street house because he "could see the engines." But even then, at ninety-two, this must surely have been reflexive bravura about a milieu circumscribed by immiseration, dementia, and deformity. Mary Silvina's nerves tell us the truth about the family's fall from grace, even if, humanly enough, her son never quite could. A paralytic stroke, suffered soon after renting the soot-covered house by the tracks, impaired her left leg or arm, or both. James, her barbering brother, and her sisters "always stood by," and many of the townspeople gave them necessities and found light chores that Mary Silvina could do without taxing herself.[7] Adelbert sent small sums from odd jobs in Albany. Willie pitched in, finding work after school. Most school days, he headed down Main after four to meet his mother, taking whatever bundles she was carting home and offering a supporting shoulder as they hobbled into Railroad Street. They were a regular feature of town life, occasioning well-intentioned remarks about their mutual devotion. Willie was always "a little surprised because people said how nice I was to my mother." "I just grew up that way. We were companions," said he, pure and simple.[8]

The companionship of cellmates is a harsh image, and yet it would be serviceably close to the truth. By nature laconic, Mary Silvina said almost nothing these days, shutting up memories of improvident loves and spoiled womanhood inside herself. She had responded with a venturesome woman's love to Alfred's trompe-l'oeil world of breeding and enterprise. There in Railroad Street—almost the end of the line for her—disabled, and further disabled by education, class, gender, and race, Mary Silvina invested what was left of herself in Willie. Her specific do's and don'ts were few, he said: with the ravages at their doorstep as a constant reminder, Willie must never touch liquor (which he didn't until student days in Germany); loose women and games of chance for money were never to be indulged; and she forbade smoking (a command he violated "a little bit, but not very much"). Otherwise, Mary Silvina followed a policy of noninterference in Willie's conduct. Unlike many parents of her generation, she made no attempt to train him out of left-handedness. But though taciturn, she had a way of making her displeasure unmistakable, and when that happened, if Willie "got the idea that anything that I did displeased her, then I just didn't do it, that's all."[9] What gave Mary Silvina the greatest of all pleasures was her younger son's performance in school. It was not only a means by which a dutiful son could please his mother; Willie gradually saw that academic achievement was his ticket out of Railroad Street.

Even before his scholastic abilities became apparent, he sensed that he was something of a curiosity to the white townspeople because of his light color and the long locks that changed to a crinkly texture by the time he was four; and he was well aware of their interest by the time he entered public elementary school. But if his being physically different "riveted attention" upon him, he was fortunate in long being able to ignore Great Barrington's muted racism (even when he dimly recognized it). First came an awareness of class distinctions. A restraint of displayed affluence muted Great Barrington's income disparities, making the lot of the deprived socially less onerous. The mill-owning Russell family's unostentatious frame house was distinguished from that of Johnny Morgan's storeowning parents by quantity of Victorian plush in furnishings, rather than by dramatic differences of scale and inventory. Gradually, Willie realized nonetheless that "most of the colored persons . . . including my own folk, were poorer than the well-to-do whites." If he couldn't say exactly why this was so while he was growing up ("There was no real discrimination on account of color"), he could see that the mudsill Irish served, like black people in the contemporary South, to deflect stigma from others who would have shared a place at the bottom. "I cordially despised the poor Irish and South Germans," he confessed, adding that "none of the colored folk I knew were so poor, drunken and sloven."[10]

However poor, drunken, and sloven, the Irish and Bavarians and Czechs were as white as their Anglo-Saxon detractors, a trump card that Willie and his people could never find in the deck of assimilation. *Darkwater* would insist that his adolescence was spent securely among white mates, that he "annexed the rich and well-to-do" as his natural companions, and was "very much one of them," even at "the center and sometimes the leader of the town gang of boys." Not when they played the new game of baseball, however; he confessed to being not very good at it. Never once, interestingly, does Willie mention that he was shorter and skinnier than most of his peers. Yet, much as he felt he "belonged" and disdained the foul-mouthed, rock-throwing immigrant youngsters who ridiculed his proper airs and sometimes called him "nigger," Willie's troubling sense that he was somehow different grew, at first imperceptibly, then gnawingly. Puberty and high school brought the feeling to a climax.[11]

One, perhaps two, African-American teenagers had taken a year or more of high school, but no Burghardt had ever gone beyond an elementary education. They saw no need of it, says Willie. Mary Silvina did. "My mother rather insisted on it," Willie recalled. By now, at age twelve, he "began to recognize that in some way, for some reason—I wasn't clear at all about it—I sort of had to justify myself." Part of the reason must have been Mary Silvina. Her boy had the stamina of the best of her people and the quickness of the Du Boises, and it would have been in her nature to do all that she could to save him from an obscure existence as one more upstanding, prosaic Great Barrington Burghardt. She must have resigned herself to her son's success coming too late to improve her lot: Mary Silvina would already be in her late fifties when Willie reached manhood—aged in the enervated way of working-class females, her once-sturdy frame crippled and crumbling. But Willie deserved the chance to make a place for himself beyond the Berkshires; and his success would be her redemption.

But first they had to escape Railroad Street. Fortunately, some of the town's prominent citizens had begun to take more than passing interest in the family ("a sort of overseeing custody," Willie wrote later)—especially in Willie.[12] In an act of supreme commitment to his future, silent Mary Silvina led them out of Railroad Street to a prim, small house behind the property of the Cass family back in Church Street, just a few diagonal paces from the rear of the First Congregational Church on Main and within sight of the Housatonic. Willie tells us that the river was golden-colored because of pollution from the paper mill upstream. Mary Silvina's brother, the barber James, boarded with them, which helped. The house Dr. Cass rented to them was without plumbing or electricity, like most of the houses of the period, but it had two rooms and a pantry on the ground floor and two bedrooms above. Willie now had his own room, a "luxury [he] never dreamed was so rare," an admission bourgeois enough to be excised, eighty-one years later, from the Russian-language edition of his *Autobiography*.[13] From the neat house with its breathing space and relative quiet, he walked every day up to Main Street to the brick school building facing the town hall.

FOUR YEARS of hard, resourceful, stellar labors rolled by while he and his mother lived in the Cass home. Willie mowed lawns, distributed tea from the new A&P chain, tossed the hefty *Springfield Republican* onto front porches, chopped wood on weekends for the spinster Smith sisters, stoked Madame L'Hommedieu's millinery shop stove every morning for twenty-five cents a week, and fetched free milk from old Mr. Taylor's cows on lower Main. Charles Taylor, who died soon after volume one of his *History of Great Barrington* was published in 1883, "impressed [Willie] greatly." Very likely, the old scholar talked shop with the young scholar; but the fact that African-Americans are invisible in Taylor's rich chronicle tells us much about the times, the milieu, and the races. Willie was certainly not invisible, though, as he scurried from home to school to chores and back. As the hard slog to survive ground down his mother and the other Burghardts, it had the reverse effect on him. While Mary Silvina persevered, limping and sighing, and Uncle Jim came home from Railroad Street "walking very straight because of liquor," and the Casses learned not always to expect the monthly rent, Willie developed a compensating sense of adolescent self that would become more portentous and embracing in the coming years. "I very early got the idea," he told the interviewer from Columbia, "that what I was going to do was to prove to the world that Negroes were just like other people."[14]

He had told himself that race, in the large sense of generalized and dismissive attitudes about his people, had played no part in his elementary school experience. Had he not become the "favorite" of "stern and inflexible" Miss Cross, his first primary teacher? Had he not been cheered on by the leading citizens as he advanced year after year—the sole black boy in the school—more quickly than most of his white classmates? Had he not always felt welcome in the homes of even his wealthy classmates and frequently been complimented by their parents for setting a good example? In the early, innocent, Horatio Alger years, then, Willie believed that the differences between people were the result of industry or ability—and sometimes physical courage. "Trounced" once by a burly white lad during recess, "honor" had been preserved by fighting and suffering manfully before onlooking classmates.[15] The shanty Irish "preferred" to live as they did, he concluded, just as most of the black Burghardts now lacked the acumen to keep up. Mike Gibbons was better at marbles than he, but Mike was a dummy at Latin. Art Benham drew awfully good pictures but was a slouch when it came to putting his feelings into words. Secure in his playground sociology, in which class and race had more to do with character than with economics, Willie had acquired a rugged individualist's understanding of social mobility and been greatly reassured until he reached his teens.[16]

With that flare for drama in language in which he has few equals, Willie pinpoints, in *The Souls of Black Folk*, the exact moment in his ten-year-old life, a spring day in 1878, when the theorems of playground sociology were, supposedly, forever shattered:

> I remember well when the shadow swept across me. I was a little thing, away up in the hills of New England, where the dark Housatonic winds between Hoosac and Taghkanic to the sea. In a wee wooden schoolhouse, something put it into the boys' and girls' heads to buy gorgeous visiting-cards—ten cents a package—and exchange. The exchange was merry, till one girl, a tall newcomer, refused my card—refused it peremptorily, with a glance. Then it dawned upon me with a certain suddenness that I was different from the others; or like, mayhap, in heart and life, and longing, but shut out from their world by a vast veil.[17]

A permanent, anchoring sense of Du Bois's racial identity *could* have come from a single such traumatic rebuff in the "wee wooden schoolhouse." Interracial companionship has always been one of the first casualties of approaching puberty. The incident must have occurred, and his account of it is certainly psychologically plausible; yet sympathetic skepticism is advisable whenever Du Bois advances a concept or proposition by way of autobiography. Often, the truth is not in the facts but in the conceptual or moral validity behind them. In the case of the sweeping shadow and separating veil, there are several versions and equivalents.

In one, the lacerating moment is replaced by a Chinese water torture of small and subtle insults. "Very gradually—I cannot now distinguish the steps," *Darkwater*, angriest of the memoirs, says, "though here and there I remember a jump or a jolt—but very gradually I found myself assuming quite placidly" that race mattered greatly. And how is the placid recognition of racism on one page of *Darkwater* to be squared with the unambiguous racial assault on his ego when local girls spurn him?—"Then I flamed! I lifted my chin and strode off to the mountains, where I viewed the world at my feet and strained my eyes across the shadow of the hills." Another account seems to place the conversion experience of the cards in the brick high school, and the offending newcomer may have been Agnes O'Neil, whom Willie dismisses in the *Autobiography* as a gorgeous dresser "whose ancestors nobody knew . . . otherwise she was negligible." In this version, it was then that he "began to feel the pressure of the 'veil of color'; in little matters at first and then in larger," after entering high school.[18]

Whatever the personal dynamics of racial self-discovery were, by his thirteenth birthday Willie came to have an informed idea of what being a black male meant even in the relatively tolerant New England. "There were some days of secret tears." He became painfully aware of the local whites who "actually considered . . . brown skin a misfortune"; some "even thought it a crime." One of them, a Church Street neighbor, nearly sent him to the large reform school in eastern Massachusetts for stealing grapes from the yard of a wealthy citizen. Judge Justin Dewey, Jr., of the county court, who huffed out of the Congregational Church into the Episcopal over a matter involving communion wine cups, was of the opinion that a smart, poor, spirited black boy would be much improved learning a trade under lock and key. After considerable hubbub and firm opposition from the high school principal, Frank Hosmer, the judge settled for a crotchety admonition. It was the close call historically awaiting all black males in American society, putting Willie on notice of his fragility and isolation, and driving him much closer to despair than his game, euphuistic prose ever revealed. There were many times when he soared above Great Barrington in order to keep "them" from deflating his spirits, pitying his "pale companions" and telling himself that he "felt not so much disowned and rejected as rather drawn up into higher spaces and made part of a mightier mission."[19]

Frank Alvin Hosmer had more than an inkling of the social and emotional gamut Willie Du Bois had to run, and he did his best to guide him through it, but without obvious favoritism or condescension. Hosmer's was an old, moderately distinguished New England family with strong Congregational ties. Service, uplift, and reform were bred deep in it. After graduating from Amherst, he came to Great Barrington to teach, becoming principal of the public high school—"G.B.H.S."—in the late 1870s. In 1890, he took over the editorship of the *Berkshire Courier* but answered the call to Hawaii after a year to take the presidency of the missionary college at Oahu. When the American sugar planters and missionaries overthrew Queen Liliuokalani two years later, electing Sanford Ballard Dole, another Bay State Congregationalist, to the presidency of the Provisional Government of Hawaii, Frank Hosmer served on the Advisory Council. About 1900, he came back to the mainland, successfully ran for the Massachusetts legislature, and, always ready to serve, died, according to *The New York Times*, "from overwork in [the] Red Cross" in May 1918. Yankee families like Hosmer's had manned the battalions of American Missionary Association (AMA) teachers and Freedmen's Bureau personnel fanning out over the defeated South to take charge of the ex-slaves—what one historian has aptly called "soldiers of light and love," who, with limited understanding of their wards and less sense of humor, set out to inculcate an austere gospel, a stern work ethic, and an enabling literacy.[20]

By the time Willie entered high school, the end of the military occupation of the South—Reconstruction—was just four years old, bringing with it, in the infamous Compromise of 1877, the inevitable dismantling of what most white people in the former Confederacy furiously denounced as the alien political and social experiment in black empowerment. For better or worse, Yankee stewardship of the republic's newest citizens was in its final phase. Formal disfranchisement, in naked violation of the Fifteenth Amendment, had not yet come about, nor had institutionalized "Jim Crow"—banning of black people from commercial establishments and public places and herding them into the last seats and rickety add-ons in trains and streetcars. That would begin in earnest a decade later, with the revision of Mississippi's constitution. In the 1880s, however, it was still possible for northern "friends" to believe that there would be room in the "redeemed" South for "wise" and "patient" exercise of civil rights, provided African-Americans found intelligent, upright leaders of their own race. Principal Hosmer believed in the prospect of fair-minded race relations in the South, and, as was true of many other leading Congregationalists, he was always on the lookout for African-American leadership talent. Without knowing it at the time, Willie began his audition with Hosmer before the end of the first year.

Later, he would understand just how fortuitous Hosmer's influence upon his life had been. In 1880s America, not even the sons of millowners (and no daughters) took college education as a matter of course. Willie recalled that maybe two others in his graduating class of thirteen were heading for college. He knew well that the doors to higher education were "barred with ancient tongues" and that his best hope for steady work in the future, paying enough to support himself and his ailing mother, was by way of vocational courses offered at Great Barrington High. Willie's supercharged ambition at first failed to grasp the value a college education might have for a colored man. That realization came from Hosmer: "He suggested, quite as a matter of fact, that I ought to take the college preparatory course."[21] There was no way Mary Silvina's weekend work at farmer Beckwith's, Uncle Jim's barbering, the unraveling Burghardt clan's fitful help, and all Willie's odd jobs could afford the college-course textbooks on Greek, Latin, algebra, and geometry. Hosmer spoke to Louis Russell's mother, second wife of Farley Russell the millowner, who agreed to buy them. Louis Russell was a frail, friendly boy, not too bright, who attended the town's private secondary school, the exclusive Sedgwick Institute now run by the Van Lennups. Willie helped him with his lessons, and, perhaps, as Mrs. Russell had hoped, became one of the awkward boy's closest companions. Charles Church, independent-minded heir to the paper-mill fortune and another Van Lennup student, hobnobbed with them. These were friendships that support Will's insistence that he "was thrown with the upper rather than the lower social classes and protected in many ways."[22]

The picture of a mischievous Willie, assigned to a front seat in Miss Ida Roraback's class in order to be watched, rings false, even though schoolmate Mary Crissey's recollections have to be taken seriously. Mary was a good student, but nearly ninety years had elapsed when reporter John La Fontana of the *Berkshire Courier* asked her what she remembered about Du Bois. The single surviving mention of him in the school records notes a perfect attendance record. Then there is Willie's distress over the lackluster scholastic performance of the only other black student to attend GBHS (who "did not excel the whites as I was used to doing" and washed out quickly). He was probably too competitive for prankishness, too "grimly determined to make them sweat for it!" whenever any of his white mates topped him in academics. Still, he was sociable enough. Mary Crissey and Sabra Taylor liked him, and since there were no dances at GBHS to trouble the racially squeamish, Willie felt he could be friendly without fear of complications.[23] Fat Ned Kelly, future town clerk, and unsmart George Beebee, GBHS's best dresser, were boon companions to go skinny-dipping with in Green River or for hiking up into the Mountains of the Moon. George and Willie were closer, opposites attracted to one another, with Willie, wearing hand-me-down clothes tenderly restitched by Mary Silvina, helping handsome, natty George with his studies. George Beebee became a prosperous physician. Willie and Mary Dewey, the hanging judge's daughter, seem to have been on amicable terms, even though she ran rings around him in math.[24]

Today's educators would find the learning environment at GBHS rigid and limited, with no-nonsense Ida Roraback and the school's other female teacher beating time with their pointers to Latin declensions and rote declamations from Underwood's *Primer of English Literature* and Greenleaf's *Algebra*, while Frank Hosmer presided over the complexities of Xenophon's *Anabasis*, Virgil's *Georgics*, and William Jevons's *Theory of Political Economy* in the higher grades. But Hosmer was progressive for his day, with a vision of Great Barrington's own sons and daughters enriching cultural life through such newfangled activities as plays at the town hall and a school paper. Sir Walter Scott's *Lady of the Lake* (without Willie) and *Old John Brown Had a Little Indian* (with Willie) were hits, filling Main Street with the buckboards of farming families come to town hungry for entertainment. Willie and a red-haired classmate, Art Benham, as gifted and unattractive as George Beebee was slow and handsome, coedited the school newspaper, *The Howler*, during its very short life. Hosmer even suggested the adoption of a snappy cap emblazoned with G.B.H.S. (ridiculed, says Willie, as "Great Big Hosmer Speculation") to promote esprit de corps and present a tonier face to the Sedgwick Institute swells.[25]

AS FOR Willie, Hosmer continued to influence his intellectual growth. Some of those titles on Johnny Morgan's shelves, in what passed for the town's bookstore, must have been suggested by Hosmer. Thanks to Morgan, a chatty Welshman, Willie was welcome to read cover to cover each weekend the new *Puck* and *Judge* illustrateds before they were put on sale. But Willie was there every day after school, as well, unobtrusively browsing in a corner the books he had no money to buy. One fall day—it was early in his sophomore year—he saw a deluxe edition of Macaulay's five-volume

History of England. He "wanted it fiercely." Fondness for this nonpaying customer had grown to the point where Morgan made what was then a radical proposal: purchase on the installment plan at twenty-five cents a week—the weekly wage from Madame L'Hommedieu's. Willie accepted, carting his five volumes proudly off to Church Street just before Christmas to devour them.

This supremely smug Whig history of the British Isles had sold more than one hundred thousand copies before its author's death in 1859 stopped the series at volume five. For Thomas Babington Macaulay, civilization (by definition, Anglo-Saxon) was like a precisely engineered clock whose mainspring, the Parliament at Westminster, had (ever since the rout of monarchical privilege in the Glorious Revolution of 1688) kept the works ticking over as perfectly as the Newtonian God did the cosmos. A few historians already deplored Macaulay's Eminent Victorian narrowmindedness, as well as his sociopolitical point of view, which was, said the biographer Lytton Strachey, "distinct enough, but . . . without distinction." Fourteen-year-old Willie was unaware of such cutting-edge criticisms, of course; but in his enthusiasm for Macaulay's matchless narrative powers—of such metered verisimilitude that Macaulay's Seige of Derry and Battle of Killiecrankie were recited from memory in cultured parlors on both sides of the Atlantic—he found common ground even with the detractors ("no one has ever surpassed Macaulay," the caustic Strachey conceded). Hosmer and Johnny Morgan had introduced their young protégé to a style of writing perhaps best characterized as Westminster Abbey vivid—whose phrases, spliced by commas, would swell in his inner ear decades after GBHS.[26]

Fortunately for his readers, Macaulay's influence is altogether absent from Willie's regular notices in the New York *Globe* during this time. Willie had been the Great Barrington distributor of the weekly for more than a year before his first piece appeared in April 1883. Founded in 1881 by Timothy Thomas Fortune, a Byronically handsome African-American who once seemed destined to inherit the mantle of the great Frederick Douglass, the immensely popular *Globe* spoke for the forward-looking members of the race.[27] Fortune hailed originally from Jacksonville, Florida, where his father, Emmanuel, had served in the Reconstruction legislature and battled the Klan. Fortune was named after his Irish grandfather, and, as if to prove an era's stereotype, his meteoric career as author, journalist, and founder of protest organizations was to be brawling, hard-drinking, and, in the end, a tragedy of brilliance and courage misspent. He was one of the first African-American men outside his own family whom

Willie Du Bois admired.[28] No paper trace of his thoughts survives, but Willie must have hoped that writing might open the door to a career, and T. Thomas Fortune was surely delighted to find another free contributor.

Between April 10, 1883, and May 16, 1885, no less than twenty-four articles and notices, signed "W.E.D.," appeared in the *Globe* and the *Freeman*, its successor. They are remarkably revealing. First, they make it possible for us to realign the tilted picture in the autobiographical writings of a somewhat uprooted, mock-patrician, teenage Du Bois. Second, they catch for us the embryonic distinct voice of the future prophet of African-American advancement and protest. The *Autobiography* was composed during the last full decade of his life, when Willie was already well within the fold of the American Communist Party, and yet, paradoxically, it contains the most bourgeois treatment of the Great Barrington period. There, he writes of having "the social heritage not only of a New England clan but Dutch taciturnity," and rather superciliously notes the existence of " 'contrabands,' " those newcomers, "a little uncouth" but "hardworkers and so jolly," who "astonished us by forming a little Negro Methodist Zion Church, which we sometimes attended." A similar superior tone is heard in *Dusk of Dawn* when, as he leaves Great Barrington for the South, we hear that once or twice already he "had had swift glimpses of the colored world."[29]

He had had more than glimpses, and the AME Zion Church turns out not to have been "sometimes attended" but a place of important and continual social reference for him. He filed regular reports to the *Globe* and *Freeman* detailing the church's busy doings—the AME Zion Sewing Society's monthly supper at the home of Mr. Jason Cooley (April 10); the well-attended quarterly-meeting services, attracting worshippers from Lee and Stockbridge (May 29); the Sewing Society's monthly supper and a debate ("Ought the Indian to Have Been Driven Out of America?") between Messrs. Crosby and Du Bois (June 26); and, in the last report for 1883 (December 26), the startling news that fifteen-year-old Willie is secretary of the Zion Sewing Society.[30] For a precocious teenage boy who found baseball uninteresting and relations with girls of both races problematic, service as secretary of a sewing circle must have had compensations. Whether or not those compensations were ever sexual (introducing a brittle young male to forbidden delights among sultry AME Zion wives and widows) is unknown, though unlikely. The principal benefit may well have been in affording Willie the experience of guiding an adult group's activities. That the group was mainly of women may also have resonated in some deep recess of his sexual identity—in that part of the male core where proclivities deemed to be feminine by Victorian society reside. In any case, the Zion Sewing Society was the first in a lifetime of similar activities in which collaboration with women proved crucial to Willie's advancement.

Instead of the Sleepy Hollow peopled by taciturn Burghardts, Willie's newspaper dispatches introduce us to a larger, livelier African-American community, with himself in the midst of its joyous church services, sewing circle, Sons of Freedom, and hayriding picnics to Lake Buell. Rather quickly, also, his pieces in the New York weekly evolve from straightforward reporting to uplifting commentary, occasionally just on the cusp of scolding. "The best thing that could be done for the colored people" would be the creation of a literary society, he advises, regretting that "there was not much interest manifested." "By the way," he interjects in the middle of one sewing circle piece, "I did not notice many colored men at the town meeting last month." He notes the local indifference to the forthcoming National Convention of Colored Men in Louisville, Kentucky, to protest the 1883 Supreme Court decision invalidating the Civil Rights Act of 1875. But he applauds recent concern about the lack of "business men among us." A September 1883 piece—probably the lengthiest—has all the didactic urgency that future readers of *The Crisis* would come to expect. There had been a humiliating reminder that year of black people's subordinate position in New England civic life when two men of the town—one a white Democrat, the other a black Republican—were finalists for the position of nightwatchman. A committee of Republicans chose the Democrat, an improbability that led Willie to summon the race to action: "The colored men of Great Barrington hold the balance of power, and have decided the election of many officers for a number of years."[31]

How Willie Du Bois actually began to see himself in these teen years, rather than how he portrayed that consciousness of racial self years later, assumed sharper contours during the summer before his last year at GBHS. During July and early August 1883, he went to visit the grandfather he had never seen, Alexander Du Bois, Alfred's elegant, iron-willed father, now a retired merchant and ship's steward in New Bedford, Massachusetts. Annie M. Freeman, Alexander's third wife, persuaded the eighty-year-old patriarch that, before it was too late, an inspection of Alfred's son was right and proper.[32] Annie Freeman's letter must have stimulated long dormant hopes in Mary Silvina. Suddenly, there was a chance that Alexander Du Bois could give her son some of the advantages she had believed possible through Alfred. Either she scraped together the money or Alexander sent it, and Willie was off on the Housatonic Railroad to Bridgeport for the first extended trip of his life.

There were missed connections: first, the train to New Haven; then, after exchanging tickets and going to Hartford, the early train to Providence. There were memorable sights: the frescoed capitol building at Hartford, where Willie entered his "illustrious name" into the registry; beautiful coastal scenery, grand resorts, and steamships along the Providence route. There was emotion and nostalgia: a Burghardt relative doted on him in her "nice little cottage" in Providence. There was entertainment: a grand picnic at Onset Point, followed by a Martha's Vineyard outing to hear a famous female elocutionist. There was a new navy blue suit, bought by an uncle in Amherst. All of it he recorded in a wonderfully observant "Dear Mam" letter to Mary Silvina shortly after reaching New Bedford. Telling her of the Hartford stopover, he wrote:

> I looked into the chamber of the House of representatives. It is very nice. The chairs & desk are arranged in a semicircle. The chairmans [sic] seat is in the middle. In front are seats for the clerks & at the side for reporters. There is an elevator which anybody can go up & down in when they wish to. The whole building is frescoed splendidly. On the outside there are niches for statues. There is a picture gallery in the state library room. I cannot tell you 1/2 what I saw there. I did not go up in the dome fearing that the train would leave me. When I came down to the depot & finding that I had a little time left I took a walk up a street near by. When I got back to the depot the train was *gone*, & news agent told me there was no other to providence train that afternoon. imagine my situation![33]

Other things happened that impressionable summer. Heading home by way of Providence again, Will was swept into the British Emancipation Day festivities on August 1, mounted by the United Order of Odd Fellows at Rocky Point on Narragansett Bay. "Ten thousand Negroes of every hue and bearing" from three states came to celebrate the 1833 manumission by Parliament of the slaves of the West Indies. Willie saw the "whole gorgeous gamut of the American Negro world; the swaggering men, the beautiful girls, the laughter and gaiety, the unhampered self-expression"—more people of color than he had ever imagined could be found together in one spot. In *Dusk of Dawn* and the *Autobiography* Willie remembered stopping in Albany with Adelbert and seeing his first electric streetlights; but this was actually an experience from a later trip.[34] None of his experiences that summer, however, quite matched Grandfather Alexander.

Meeting Grandfather Alexander was one of the turning points of Willie's young life. "Mad, very mad," because nobody met him at the depot, he found his grandfather's home at 93 Acushnet Street about a half mile off—a white house with green shutters and a "yard full of flower gardens [sic]." "Grandma," Alexander's wife, "is about my color and taller than I thought." He found Alexander short, thickset, and erect. "He says very little but speaks civily [sic]" when spoken to, Willie reported to Mary Silvina. Grandmother Annie maneuvered adroitly between them, taking Willie on walks, presenting him to New Bedford's quality "colored folk," and interpreting Alexander's cryptic moods. "Grandma says by and bye he'll talk more." But grandfather never once mentioned Alfred, as far as the available record reveals. He told his grandson almost nothing of his own past (Annie, who had known Alfred, must have, though), but Alexander's library, his silver plate, silk waistcoats, and oenophile conceits filled the silences between them, leaving his grandson with an evening's ineffaceable sense of the importance of stately manners and breeding. With impressionable Willie looking on, Alexander entertained New Bedford's leading colored citizen, Mr. Freedom, with lace tablecloth and cut-glass decanter displayed. More than seventy years after Mr. Freedom's visit, Willie described the scene:

> They sat down and talked seriously; finally my grandfather arose, filled the wine glasses and raised his glass and touched the glass of his friend, murmuring a toast. I had never before seen such a ceremony; I had read about it in books, but in Great Barrington both white and black avoided ceremony. To them it smacked of pretense. . . . The black Burghardts indulged in jokes and backslapping. I suddenly sensed in my grandfather's parlor what manners meant and how people of breeding behaved and were able to express what we in Great Barrington were loath to give act to, or unable. I never forgot that toast.[35]

What Willie knew about his paternal ancestry and when are difficult to determine precisely: the quest would still be under way when he was in his eighties, drawing him to island pinpoints in the Bahamas.[36] Long before then, however, and very probably a few months after Alexander Du Bois's death in December 1887, he learned the essentials of the story about his father's people. Grandfather Alexander bequeathed to him all that was left of the Du Bois memory—cryptic leatherbound diaries, whose fragmentary hieroglyphs and tantalizing allusions Willie would decode by the time he reached his twenty-first year. Fabulous encounters and one or two painful secrets were embedded in the strata of his grandfather's past, and Willie would always harbor an almost desperate need to unearth them, cleaning and carefully restoring them to a gloss in the museum of his mind. Grandfather Alexander was more than a little remarkable; as a man of color in antebellum America, he was, as President Nkrumah would say of his grandson, a phenomenon.

Alexander's movements during the 1820s and early 1830s are now impossible to reconstruct, despite his grandson's creative attempt to do so in the *Autobiography*. Certainly, he cannot have departed in 1821 for ten years in Haiti, as Du Bois believed, on account of his marriage two years later in New Haven to Sarah Marsh Lewis (both were twenty), who bore a daughter, Augusta, within the year.[37] With almost equal certainty, his diary places him in Haiti during 1829, midpoint in the ambitious, repressive presidency of Jean-Pierre Boyer, an educated mulatto ruler who fled into French exile in 1843. Under Boyer, Haiti, the French-speaking western third of the island of Hispaniola, brutally conquered Santo Domingo, the Spanish-speaking eastern portion, devastated the Spanish Creole elite, doubled the size of the army, and bound the peasantry to perpetual tillage on the great mulatto plantations. In this way, Haiti maximized its coffee and sugar exports to a United States whose southern parts verged on apoplexy over this black republic's continued existence. Machiavellian politics, rampant corruption, and brutal repression kept Haiti, chronically primed to explode along seams of class and color, docile.[38]

To strengthen his regime, Boyer offered land to free people of color in the northern cities of the United States. The president's New York agent was instructed to sell "fifty thousand weights" of coffee so that "such individuals of the African race, who groaning in the United States under the weight of prejudice and misery" might be resettled "under Haitian beneficence." That venerable Philadelphia divine, Richard Allen, founder and bishop of the first organized church among his people in America, the African Methodist Episcopal (of which the Zion was an offshoot), assumed chairmanship of the Society for Promoting the Emigration of Free Persons to Hayti. More than two thousand came during 1824–25, quickly found the Haitian peasants darkly suspicious, the agents of the enterprise embezzlers or incompetents, the land useless, living conditions deadly, and President Boyer prey to second thoughts.[39]

As Du Bois guessed, his grandfather was a strong candidate for involvement in this experiment. It would have been a compelling reason for a proud, free man of color with unique ties to the Caribbean to leave New Haven, either in some organizational capacity or as a solitary pioneer counting on inherited connections in the island republic. Then, as the resettlement scheme unraveled, personal relationships soured, and Boyer's policies only aggravated what they were designed to correct, Alexander left Haiti sometime between 1833 and 1834. Back in New Haven, at 23 Washington Street, he resumed his grocery business and, briefly, life with Sarah Marsh. When Sarah died in July 1834, Alexander buried her in the family plot in Grove Street Cemetery behind Yale College. He remarried the following year. The grocery flourished well enough, even though Alexander was also chief steward on ships plying between New Haven and New York. His energies were divided among the store, the ships, and being treasurer of St. Luke's, the Episcopal church he angrily helped form about 1842, after Trinity Parish made African-Americans unwelcome.[40] Twenty-one-year-old Alexander Crummell led the Trinity Parish walkout, serving as de facto pastor of St. Luke's, a mainspring of Free Negro advocacy. Rivetingly eloquent, the first of his race ordained in the Episcopal faith, the tall, lithe Crummell gloried in his black color as much as in his abundant learning. Until Willie became Dr. William Edward Burghardt Du Bois of Harvard and Berlin, incomparably surpassing them, Crummell of New York's Oneida Institute and Cambridge University was among the half dozen most carefully educated persons of his race in the United States. Alexander's records for 1840 enumerate collection-tray receipts for stirring public lectures in New Haven by Crummell, whose ideas the grandson would applaud in the ennobling Crummell portrait in *The Souls of Black Folk*.[41]

There is a ten-year hiatus in Alexander's diaries. When they resume, he is living in Springfield, Massachusetts, possessed of an estate with a declared value of four thousand dollars. Mary Emily Jacklyn, the second New Haven wife, twenty when they married in 1835, had produced in fecund sequence, between 1836 and 1842, Henrietta, Henry, Helen, Harriet, and John, the last two recorded by the 1850 census as being in the Springfield home. Grandfather had become a gentleman farmer, residing in town and paying seasonal visits to the farm, and was still an occasional communicant in the New Haven church during this roiling decade of increasing antislavery agitation, sectional strife, and John Brown's last-straw martyrdom.[42] At St. Luke's, Reverend James Theodore Holly was installed as the church's first official black rector in 1856. Freeborn in Washington, D.C., Holly's considerable capacities had won him appointment as clerk to Lewis Tappan, New York's leading white abolitionist, and priestly orders in the Episcopal Church in 1855. Within weeks, Holly had discovered his life's passion during an exploratory visit to Haiti. Upon his return, he poured his emigrationist convictions into a famous printed sermon on *The Capacity of the Negro Race for Self Government*. Amid the shipwreck of state, the incoming President Lincoln, a much-troubled advocate of voluntary removal of Africans from North America, encouraged in his endeavors the British abolitionist James Redpath, a one-man dynamo of publicity and fund-raising, official agent of Haiti, and director, with Holly's dedicated assistance, of the Haytian Bureau of Emigration in Boston.[43]

Now, as the South departed the Union and months of fecklessness at Washington ensued, African-American leadership stampeded to Holly's cause. The existence of the Confederate States of America meant slavery forever. Frederick Douglass uttered words in January 1861 that totally contradicted the combative injunctions of a lifetime: "Whatever the future may have in store for us, it seems plain that inducements offered . . . to remain here are few, feeble, and very uncertain." At Holly's invitation, Douglass and his daughter stood ready to embark for Haiti with more than a hundred St. Luke's parishioners that May, deciding against sailing only after news of Fort Sumter, on April 12. Alexander Du Bois was one of the leaders of this St. Luke's exodus, although clearly conflicted about it. "Have thoughts of leaving the vessel," a May 9 diary entry confessed, "but want resolution to do so." Commitments had been made; he felt "ashamed to back out, will wait a day or two longer, but feel like one rushing to his fate." Grandfather reached Port-au-Prince on June 3: "Jackasses, Negroes, mud, water, soldiers, universal filth." Another entry concluded that "the people have retrograded since I last saw them in 1829. . . . Even the very animals appear dwarfed."[44]

To say that history had cursed Haiti since Alexander Du Bois's last visit was not an exaggeration. After Boyer had come Faustin-Élie Soulouque, former slave and hardened veteran of Haiti's wars against France. President Soulouque became Emperor Faustin I, after surprising and liquidating his overconfident mulatto supporters in 1849. A scorched-earth invasion of the now-independent Dominican Republic and ten years of carnage within Haiti blanketed the island until Soulouque's overthrow.

Haiti's new president, Nicolas-Fabre Geffrard, securely connected to the pigmentocracy although dark-skinned himself, was closer to being a statesman than any of that country's nineteenth-century rulers. Recognition by the United States of Haiti's existence had occurred on his watch in 1861. He summoned Redpath and Holly's Haitian Bureau into existence, imposed paper reforms in the ministries, and appointed as his minister of education the enlightened, aggressive François-Élie Du Bois. Grandfather was received at the palace, the day following his arrival, by President Geffrard and his Du Bois relative, with whom he sailed on a government steamer to the town of St. Marc. However Holly and his immigrants sized up their settlement east of Port-au-Prince, Alexander decided that the experiment was hopeless. Securing passage on a British merchant ship, he wrote in his diary that he "felt happy to arrive [and] . . . more than happy to leave. God grant that I may see Massachusetts again." He sailed on June 8. Some profit must have come from the venture, though, because on July 12 he and his new partner, one Thomas, leased a shop on Springfield's Main Street "at $150 a year."[45]

If Frank Hosmer had made it possible for Willie to find a way out of an impoverished, limited present to a transformed future, Grandfather Alexander made it possible for him to transform the past. The name Du Bois was no longer merely a formal patronymic but the link in a vital, rich, fairly exalting chain of being. The old man of grave manners and stoic perseverance brought Willie into communion with the spirits of the clan, enabling him for the first time to feel truly sprung from the Huguenot seed of that seventeenth-century seigneur, Chrétien Du Bois, and ultimately from the primordial Geoffroi Du Bois who sailed with William the Conqueror. The black Burghardts retained his respect—even affection—in a formal way, but in occasional moments of unguardedness Willie's psychic affinity, after the New Bedford summer of 1883, was less with great-grandfather Jake and his Bantu wife in their Berkshire hollows than with Grandfather Alexander and his transoceanic universe of Norman knights, Caribbean notables, and black abolitionists. What an inspiration for a fatherless young man, this grandfather who always "held his head high, took no insults, made few friends. He was not a 'Negro'; he was a man!"[46]

Yet, for all its glamor and even some distinction, the pedigree must have presented the young Du Bois with a formidable problem, a Medea's robe of a gift, as potentially harmful as it was appealing. Whether or not Annie Freeman, Alexander's widow, finally told her step-grandson that Alfred, his father, was alive (or had recently been) in Meriden, Connecticut, is impossible to know, but he must have begun to suspect it. He would have suspected that the meaning of a poem about illicit love, composed during Alexander's second voyage to Haiti, explained much about the old man's estrangement from Alfred:

> *It may be right, perchance tis wrong*
> *To love without the priestly ken,*
> *Such things are often known among*
> *The disappointed Sons of Men.*[47]

Since Alfred was not born in New Haven, and nothing suggests that Alexander took Sarah Marsh to Haiti in the 1820s, he must have been born out of wedlock—of "love without the priestly ken," a product of Haitian venture number one.

Several scenarios suggest themselves: Alfred may have come to the United States either with his father's help or on his own as a very young man (after the death in 1834 of Sarah Du Bois, perhaps); Alexander, dour and outwardly moral, may have found his son's presence an intolerable reminder of a failed economic and domestic experiment; conversely, Alfred may have resented his situation with such bitterness that none of his father's amends was acceptable. In any case, an illegitimate Alfred fathered an illegitimate son, by virtue of his bigamy, deserted his family, lived on for at least a decade after disappearing, and very likely married a third time. Here was the downside of the Du Bois lineage, the corrosive, humiliating part of the heritage (or so Willie would have felt in his late-Victorian marrow) for which his particular predicament of color and class could find no other solution than in transcendence through ability, aplomb, and carefully calibrated amnesia.

Transcendence was already well along by his senior year of high school. Johnny Morgan encouraged him to try writing for the *Springfield Republican*, the most influential newspaper outside New York City and the largest newspaper in western Massachusetts, and he did, becoming its occasional Great Barrington correspondent that year and the next. "The Housatonic Festival," September 26, 1884, "From Our Special Correspondent," must be one of his three or four (unsigned) lost articles. Readers of the *Globe* had read his piece on the topping off the year before of the rebuilt First Congregational Church. Only the granite walls of the church had withstood the fire leaping out of the basement furnace room one Saturday evening in early March 1882. Communicants and fellow townspeople had immediately rallied to rebuild the steepled structure on its 139-year-old foundations. More than one hundred thousand dollars were contributed by the Hopkins family alone—descendants of the renowned Reverend Samuel Hopkins, the church's doctrinally exigent first pastor. The splendid new 3,594-pipe organ, built by the firm of Hilborne L. Roosevelt, was so massive that the Hopkinses had to provide additional funds to construct a loft for it at the rear of the church. Willie and Mary Silvina attended the dedicatory service on September 21, 1883. The six-hundred-plus audience was mammoth for Great Barrington, with persons coming from as far away as Springfield. The organist for the occasion, Albert A. Stanley of Providence, Rhode Island, was one of New England's finest; his recital that evening on the Roosevelt organ would live on in the collective memory of the town, the round chords of Sodermann, Delibes, and Mendelssohn's "Spring Song" reverberating from the new walls of what was now one of New England's most imposing tabernacles. Great Barrington's First Congregational Church was simply the "handsomest church in the county, and compares with any in the State," Willie's *Globe* dispatch boasted.

Willie's religious beliefs at this time were superficially orthodox and anchored in the rigorous Calvinism of New England Congregationalism. The First Congregational Church's Articles of Faith had remained steadfast in their "Hopkinsian" rigor—a rigor proceeding virtually arrow-straight from the tenets of the great divine, the Reverend Jonathan Edwards, and his Yale disciple Samuel Hopkins, through the teachings of Professor Edwards A. Park of Andover Theological Seminary to Evarts Scudder, the admired pastor whose twenty-eight-year tenure (1867–1895) would be the second longest since the church's founding in 1743: the divine authority of the Bible was to be interpreted literally; man's nature was sinful; salvation was possible solely through sanctification by Christ; and the wicked were to roast everlastingly in Hell. Mary Silvina is recorded as having been formally admitted to membership in Reverend Scudder's congregation in 1878. Prior to that time, the family tradition had been to attend the Episcopal Church a few blocks farther along Main Street, but First Congregational was closer and its pastor was friendlier. It is extremely doubtful that Mary Silvina would have harbored any reservations about the theological literalism at First Congregational. As for Willie, participation in the church's Sunday school was, like his role among the AME Zion parishioners, another opportunity to shine. He savored the building's lavish, sunlit appointments made possible in large part by the largesse of Mrs. Mark Hopkins and of Timothy, her adopted son who lived on a ducal estate in

Menlo Park, California. "The new Sunday School building was my chief pride and joy," Willie fondly remembered long afterward. "The carpet, the chairs, the tables, were all new, and the teachers were inspired to new efforts with their growing classes."

Willie was, as he himself put it, "quite in his element" as he "led in discussions, with embarrassing questions." He showed off in Greek, being "proudly able to read: '*He alethia eleutherosi humas*' (The truth shall make you free)," and he may well have been more of a nuisance to his fellow Sunday school communicants than the awesome interlocutor he fancied himself. He became "both popular and a little dreaded," he says, as he served up "long disquisitions" on the Hebrew scriptures. What his genuine religious beliefs were, though, is unclear. Such was his precocity that Willie would have been intrigued by almost any well-reasoned, controversial idea. Although the dynamic Reverend Scudder set himself uncompromisingly athwart the liberal theological currents just beginning to waft through Congregationalism, his vigilance proved barely adequate to the task even in his own church. Judge Dewey was as progressive in theological matters as he was irascible. The Articles of Faith were outmoded, he maintained, for which Scudder denounced him from the pulpit. One Sunday morning in 1881, nevertheless, Judge Dewey had revealed to the Great Barrington Bible Society that, based on his readings of the latest criticism, he now believed that God's message was not absolute but progressive—that that which "is later is higher" than the earliest revelations of the Old Testament. It was even suggested that non-Christians might not be damned for all eternity. The clangorous dispute over the substituting of Welch's unfermented grape juice for communion wine caused Judge Dewey to storm out of First Congregational into the Episcopal (temporarily) and left a deep trace in Willie's memory.[48]

Great Barrington, then, was being penetrated by ecumenical and relativistic notions at the very time Willie was beginning to examine the teachings of his Congregational faith. It seems plausible to conjecture that, while his formal religious beliefs stayed well within the circle of orthodoxy, Willie's fierce dislike of narrow, intolerant religious thinking (soon to manifest itself in college) was nurtured in the church ferment along Main Street. Within a few years after the memorable 1883 dedication ceremony for the grand church building, he would hold theological beliefs that would have scandalized Reverend Scudder; but Willie's ethical beliefs would remain, in their Calvinist essence, as firm as the dolomite from the Hopkins quarry used to rebuild Scudder's church. The promise of salvation would lie in the social sciences, not the Bible; damnation lay in store for those who led unexamined lives or who squandered their talents; above all, inner strength and quiet resolve he deemed to be attributes possessed by the elect.

Whatever his bedrock beliefs at the time, Willie knew that the church could help promote him in life, and his Sunday school enthusiasms were largely a vehicle to further that eventuality, just as his affiliation with the AME Zion congregation advanced his social side. Neither the god of Moses nor the redeeming Christ appears to have spoken deeply to Mary Silvina's brainy, self-absorbed son. On the other hand, the prose of the King James Version registered powerfully, complementing the influence of Macaulay. It may have been a case of medium over message—of the way in which the Lord and His servants spoke, rather than of what they said.

Meanwhile, schoolwork went along dazzlingly. The records for the high school years are lost or destroyed, but memories of Willie's academic rage to succeed persist even today among some of the townspeople. There were seven boys and six girls in the graduation class. The evening ceremony was held at the town hall on June 27, 1884, a Friday, followed by a reception at GBHS. The *Berkshire Courier* reported that there were declamations interspersed with music by the Germania Orchestra of Pittsfield after the opening prayer by Reverend C. W. Mallory of Housatonic. It must have been a long evening, with the program preliminaries, music, and thirteen finest-hour recitations. Salutatorian James Parker offered a spirited "Defense of Andrew Johnson," followed by Mary Frein's celebration of Berkshire beauty, and a little later Minnie Ford's clever, warmly applauded speech about the pleasures of reading. Looking "somewhat drawn" but proud, Mary Silvina, and probably Uncle James and other Burghardts, heard Willie deliver an oration on Wendell Phillips, the conscience of New England abolitionism. It was the success of the evening, the *Berkshire Courier* reporter judging that "William E. Dubois [sic] a colored lad who has had good standing" gave an excellent oration and "provoked repeated applause." George Beebee's Longfellow recitation and valedictorian Abbie Joyner's "Knownothingism" were somewhat upstaged.[49]

Phillips had died recently, the "gatling gun" mind described by Van Wyck Brooks slowing down, but its sweeping arc blasting away at capitalism until the end. Phillips had become more radical, isolated from the compromisers who announced in 1870, as they dissolved the Abolitionist Movement, that the Fifteenth Amendment was all African-Americans needed to forge ahead. Fellow Brahmins, like Charles Sumner and Charles Francis Adams, who rallied to Horace Greeley's insurgent Liberal Republican party because the Grant presidency was corrupt, because the Bourbon South promised to behave if left alone with its "Negroes," and because the votes of western farmers and southern planters were said to be had in exchange for lower tariffs—they and all these rationalizations earned Phillips's eloquent, withering contempt. "Our work is not done," he had lectured the Garrisons and the Whittiers when the American Anti-Slavery Society was dismantled, "we probably never shall live to see it done." Moral righteousness impelled him from the rights of former slaves and women to greenbackism and unionism. In his seventies, he became a paladin of socialism. "We affirm as a fundamental principle," Phillips wrote in *The Labor Question*, "that labor, the creator of wealth, is entitled to all it creates."[50]

Although neither the speaker nor anyone in the audience could then have possibly guessed, the public career of Wendell Phillips uncannily prefigured that of William Edward Burghardt Du Bois. Even though the Phillips that evening was not Phillips the economic radical but Phillips the abolitionist stalwart, it was more than hindsight when Willie wrote much later of being fascinated by "his life and work and [taking] a long step toward a wider conception" of what he was going to do because of Phillips's example. Looking back on that graduation summer, it can now be seen just how relevant Phillips's double message of racial and economic justice was. Just three weeks after his town-hall oration, Willie could have read the enormously popular James G. Blaine's letter of acceptance of the Republican party's presidential nomination in the *Springfield Republican*. Blaine of Maine, the "Plumed Knight," former secretary of state and twice candidate for the presidency, pledged, if elected, to uphold the 1877 bargain with the Bourbon South. "It would be a great calamity," the letter stated, "to change these influences under which southern commonwealths are learning to vindicate civil rights and adapting themselves to the conditions of political tranquility and industrial progress." New England humanitarianism was then running at low tide, as dark alarms about troublesome European immigrants prompted contrite, collusive sympathy for the white South on the part of erstwhile abolitionists turned businessmen.[51]

There had been talk of Williams College during his graduation year, but Willie dreamed of going to Harvard. That he was going to go to college had been "settled in [his] own mind" ever since Hosmer steered him into the preparatory curriculum.[52] The problem was not just money, however. The money might be earned or borrowed. There was the care of failing Mary Silvina. She wanted college for Willie as much as he did, but the loyal, humane thing for him to do was to stay in Great Barrington working to help support her. He was only sixteen, anyway. College could wait another year or two. Meantime, unlike many boys his age in an era of early marriages, Willie seems to have been undistracted from his goal by the opposite sex. For a sensitive, well-behaved male of sixteen, and in that time and place, his innocence of the opposite sex was not all that unusual. Except for a single, coy reference in the *Autobiography* to a "lovely little plump, brown girl who appeared out of nowhere, and smiled at me demurely," girls had significance solely as classmates or relatives in the Great Barrington narratives.[53] Willie's class consciousness and the town's attitude toward interracial courtship compounded a boy's otherwise difficult-enough life after puberty. But he was not only innocent of girls, he seems to have been wholly uninvolved. The closeness of mother and son could have been an underlying cause or effect of that innocence. He was, after all, her world, her future, her vindication. Her son knew Latin, even Greek. He was her marvel. Her brilliant Willie was certainly not going to consort with plump, smiling brown girls if Mary Silvina could help it. Watchful indulgence and subtle imperatives tied him to her in a mutual dependency.

Yet it seems not too psychologically speculative to detect latent resentment on Willie's part. Gnawing suspicions (possibly even a few hard facts) about the reasons for his father's disappearance led him to cling to paternal mythology—to gild Alfred's portrait—and to blame Mary Silvina for removing him from their lives. After all, it was she who had acquiesced in the Burghardt clan's putative opposition to their going to Connecticut. At bottom, she had deserted his father and was largely responsible, therefore, for their demeaning material predicament in Great Barrington. Undereducated and infirm, Mary Silvina, his "good chum," was now an albatross, although the more this cruel, disloyal thought insinuated itself, the more evasive, ambivalent, and wretched Willie's feelings for her must have become. He knew that she lived almost entirely to see him prosper in the world, that she would die for him if need be. But if his mother were to die, then it surely followed that his life would make sense only if he repayed her sacrifice with extraordinary success—a success in which no other woman would ever be included as a full participant. In "The Damnation of Women," a midlife essay of great emotion and feminist conviction, Willie would write of the sad truth and pain behind these shaping Berkshire years. "Only at the sacrifice of intelligence and the chance to do their best work can the majority of modern women bear children," he lamented.[54] Pondering what his "good chum" mother and his "pretty, brown" cousin Inez represented, Willie tells us that they "existed not for themselves, but for men." He owed them a great deal, indeed.

Suddenly, Mary Silvina was gone, dead of an apoplectic stroke and buried in the last week in March 1885. For all the tender words of affection and comradeship, Willie's grief is oddly formal, repressed, intellectualized. In both *Darkwater* and the *Autobiography* he writes of relief, of "choking gladness" to see her at last at peace, and gives the wrong year for her death. "Of my own loss," he tells us, he had then "little realization. That came only in after years. Now it was the choking gladness and solemn feel of wings!" He may have been shaken to the core by his mother's death, manfully holding in his grief as a stoic New England teenager ought to, until emotions could burst through in some private corner after her burial. On the other hand, feeling frankly relieved as he did at her release from wearying debility, yet feeling guilty, too, because Mary Silvina's death ended his own suffocating calvary and flashed a green light to his future, Willie may not have known, in the whipsaw of such conflict, which emotional chord to sound. What gave the appearance of extreme control may have been in reality a state of emotional paralysis—a failure to grieve and a freezing up of oedipal disengagement. Whatever her death really meant to him, the timing was perfect. One more obstacle to Harvard College had fallen. Finally, he was free to begin redefining himself.[55]

Aunt Minerva, one of Mary Silvina's sisters, took him in, and the African-American community, about which he says always as little as possible, came to his rescue. J. Carlisle Dennis, a steward recently arrived from San Francisco with the widow of railroad prince Mark Hopkins, having ascended almost overnight to the pinnacle of local "colored" society, broadcast the community's pride in "young Willie Du Bois," writing as J. C. D. in his July 8 letter to the *Globe* about the overly modest scholar:

> Du Bois entered school under many disadvantages; being his widowed mother's only support, he was compelled to perform odd jobs between school hours for the friendly neighbors. By persistent, industrious effort he has accomplished the results hoped for . . . and is considered by all who know him to be one of the most promising young colored men of the times. Du Bois is the youngest of his class, being only sixteen.[56]

Dennis was a relatively young man and, like Willie, possessed of ability and pretensions. They liked each other, and Dennis, as chief steward to Mrs. Mark Hopkins, was in a position to be uniquely helpful. Mary

Frances Hopkins was a Great Barrington Kellogg whose considerable wealth had been a hefty factor in the Gilded Age rise and railroad predations of her deceased husband. Now she was back from California, conferring with bankers, architects, and builders in her Victorian on Main Street. Her castellated mansion of blue dolomite and fourteen rare pink marble columns rose throughout the spring of 1885, a McKim, Mead & White version of the Chenonceaux chateau. In all her deliberations, Dennis, debonair and slightly swarthy, stood by her side. And as the vast pile of masonry rose, thanks to Dennis, Willie Du Bois sat in a shed keeping time on the army of laborers at the "fabulous wage" of a dollar a day. Dennis may have been, as Willie believed, Mrs. Hopkins's lover, although, given their age difference and her eventual marriage to her decorator, Edward Searles, who was almost surely homosexual, the truth of the story might be quite different. "Searles had the glamour and the clothes of an English gentleman," the timekeeper recalls, "and soon the whole direction and control of the Hopkins fortune passed into his hands." Willie's friend Dennis is said to have committed suicide. But Searles (whose name attaches to this day to the castle) came from Methuen, Massachusetts, not from England; and he was not an architect but a very saucy interior decorator. Our timekeeper, however, remembers talking "with the contractors," poring "over the plans and specifications and even came in some contact with the distinguished English architect, Searles."[57] The Searles Castle experience was one Willie liked to recount, and his embellishments reflected two lifelong predilections—for illustration over accuracy and his prominence in events.

Searles Castle rose and Leavitt's gigantic barn burned down that summer. The *Springfield Republican* carried Willie's eyewitness account of the fire, his farewell dispatch from Great Barrington. He would be gone before the town's next momentous happening, the first practical demonstration in America of the alternating-current lighting system in March 1886. But he was not going to Harvard. The reconstructed Harvard of President Charles W. Eliot had admission standards that were probably just a cut above what had been offered at GBHS. Money remained a big problem, even with his timekeeper windfall. And there was the racial factor, the distinct lack of enthusiasm among so many otherwise kindly, charitable white people for helping even a brilliant "Negro" to attend the nation's leading college. Hosmer got busy just as Willie began the job at the castle, finding an ally in the principal of the private school, Edward Van Lennup. They were joined by Reverend Scudder and Reverend C. C. Painter, another Congregationalist brother and former official of the Federal Indian

Bureau. Through their efforts, four Congregational churches pledged twenty-five dollars each for four years to underwrite Willie's education at Fisk University, a Congregational school for Negroes in Nashville, Tennessee.[58]

Willie disguised his disappointment masterfully. His Burghardt relatives supposedly grumbled about his going South. He says he did not. For him, it was a great adventure into the unknown, sort of an educational safari among the fascinating and barbarous—"the South of slavery, rebellion, and black folk." He would finally meet other people of color like himself. They were still a mystery, these vibrant people, Willie reminds us again. With the exception of the Providence Emancipation Day picnic and the Hampton Institute quartet that had "thrilled [him] to tears" in the First Congregationalist Church not long ago, what did he know of The Negro? And so he was "glad to go to Fisk." In a sense, he represented the new thrust of New England uplift. African-Americans in the South "needed trained leadership. I was sent to furnish it." Harvard was not lost—the thought never occurred to him—merely adjourned. Meanwhile, the "age of miracles" had begun.[59]

4.

The Age of Miracles

Fisk and Josie's World

Even though he always minimized the role that Great Barrington's African-American community had played in his growing up, Willie's knowledge of the larger world of black people—and especially of southern black people—was as indirect and negligible as he said it was. Western Massachusetts was an incomparably kinder place, racially, in which to grow up than the lynch-law backwaters and scabrous townships that were home to most of the young men and women who came to Fisk University. The mighty clan of Burghardts along with the immigrants pouring into the AME Zion church went about their interracial lives with a relaxed deference, modest ambition, and subdued group awareness—in stark contrast to the cagey anger, professional strivings, and racial chauvinism common to many of the southerners Willie was to meet. The South was alien and mysterious—a place of dread for black people in the North. Yet the year's wait to go off to college, the repressed, half-examined feelings Mary Silvina's death provoked, the heady responsibilities and contacts in connection with Searles Castle, the subtle social exclusions—that veil he later described so poignantly—all made Willie eager for the South, for a group of young people of his "own race," and for an end to the "spiritual isolation" in which he was living.[1]

Fisk Free Colored School had opened on the site of the Union army hospital in south Nashville in early 1866, three American Missionary Association officers pledging on their own authority the four-thousand-dollar down payment for twenty low, narrow, windowless frame buildings jammed into a small rectangle near Chattanooga depot. Two hundred ex-slaves, men, women, and children, came to learn to read, write, and count on the first day. By February, six hundred clamored for instruction. A year later, a thousand a day were being spelled by the dedicated men and women of the AMA and the Tennessee department of the Freedmen's Bureau, headed by General Clinton Bowen Fisk, a former colonel of a regiment of Negro troops. Ragged and mostly jobless, they advanced upon Nashville like a leaderless army from great distances and remote places to master the rudimentary knowledge that, denied on pain of corporal punishment until then, every one of them knew held the key to the white man's power. Webster's *Blue-Backed Speller*, McGuffey's *Reader*, Davis's *Primary Arithmetic*, and General Fisk's *Plain Counsels for Freedmen* were talismans of far greater immediacy and import to these men, women, and children than recent and pending amendments of the federal constitution. "Those were wonderful days, directly after the war," ex-slave Booker Taliaferro Washington recalled. "Suddenly, as if at the sound of a trumpet, a whole race that had been slumbering for centuries . . . awoke and started off one morning for school."[2]

In August 1867 principal John Ogden, former lieutenant of the 2nd Wisconsin Cavalry, renamed the school Fisk University, ambitiously laying on coeducational instruction above the primary grades. A Congregationalist warrior captured and interned in Tennessee until the end of the Civil War, Ogden was typical of the best of the Freedmen's Bureau—selfless, commanding, appalled by social evil, and unabashedly visionary about the capacities of the ex-slaves. During his three years at Fisk, he established a school of theology to prepare the first generation of black Congregationalist preachers. He set on course a model high school and a "normal" school to train teachers to man the South's sketchy public school systems, the first graduates—twelve in number—going forth in 1869. When Reverend Barnas Sears, general agent for the new southern-oriented Peabody Fund, visited that year, he was pleased to recommend eight hundred dollars for Ogden's institution in preference to Berea College, another Kentucky AMA school, praising Fisk as "the best normal school" he had seen. Fisk's masters discreetly noted, however, the implications for Fisk of the fact that Berea had prejudiced the Peabody agent by actively encouraging the enrollment of black students.[3]

When Ogden left the "university" in 1870, its academic prospects were as bright as its financial health was dim, despite careful economizing and sporadic philanthropy. The situation was saved by another Congregationalist warrior, George L. White, veteran of bloody Gettysburg and Chancellorsville and former staff officer to General Fisk, who served as the school's pugnacious business manager. Something of an amateur musician, White listened spellbound whenever he happened upon groups of students relaxing in songs from slavery times. It was his decision that Fisk should literally sing itself into permanence. Going forth from their first autumn 1871 success in Reverend Henry Ward Beecher's influential Plymouth Congregational Church in Brooklyn (hidden in a loft so that white parishioners heard their voices before seeing their faces), the school's Jubilee Singers enthralled audiences in Boston (Johann Strauss joyously tossed his hat in the air), London, Paris, Berlin, and much of Europe, with presidents, prime ministers, and royals vying for their presence at special occasions. "I heard them sing once," Mark Twain wrote an English friend, "and I would walk seven miles to hear them sing again."[4] Known informally as "Beecher's Nigger Minstrels," these eleven poised, handsome men and women called themselves after that jubilant, momentous day at war's end when slaves received news of their freedom. *Jubilee Songs: As Sung by the Jubilee Singers of Fisk University,* Theodore Seward's best-selling compilation, appeared in 1872. These were the "Sorrow Songs" Du Bois would write of in his pioneering essay. The enormous popularity of the new "Negro spirituals" enabled White's students to earn on several tours more than ninety thousand dollars, enough to cover the college's debts, buy a new campus site north of the city, and erect Jubilee Hall, a massive, bell-towered, all-purpose Victorian structure of grey brick.[5]

Thirteen years and one principal later, Willie Du Bois came to the nation's most famous college for the uplift of his people. Erastus Milo Cravath was now president, a towering, bearded authority figure out of the Old Testament, whose upstate New York parents had been "conductors" on the Underground Railroad before moving to Oberlin, Ohio, where young Cravath received his divinity degree. Intellectually, President Cravath appears to have been somewhat slow, finding his way, Willie said, in "intricate and involved" sentences that usually fatigued student listeners until the approach of the inevitable inspirational conclusion. Former chaplain to the 101st Regiment of Ohio Volunteers, President Cravath unfailingly greeted students with a sweeping military salute.[6] With one admired African-American exception, the faculty of fifteen, like former regimental chaplain Cravath himself, was white, northern, deeply religious, overwhelmingly Congregationalist, and of impeccable abolitionist credentials. As admission standards steadily rose in the two decades after Fisk's founding, the number of students fell, stabilizing at about 450 by 1885. Ably assisted by his dean, former University of Michigan Greek scholar Adam K. Spence, President

Cravath had almost achieved his goal of transforming Fisk University into a solid liberal arts college, among the best, in fact, in a part of the nation where antebellum standards attained in higher education had never been especially rigorous. Cravath and Spence were set upon quickly and uncompromisingly, making Fisk the flagship school of AMA higher education. When the department of college studies enrolled four full-time degree candidates as early as 1871, the first such students among the twenty-odd new southern colleges for African-Americans, that ambition bounded forward.[7]

Now that the federal troops were gone with the Compromise of 1877, those who spoke for the "redeemed" South deplored such higher education experiments at Fisk, Atlanta University, Talladega, and other lonely enclaves of black schooling as worse than misguided. Their mean-spirited objections were far different from the qualms of Ralph Waldo Emerson, who exclaimed when handed its first catalog, "Atlanta University? There is no institution in this country that comes anywhere near being a university except Harvard"—adding upon reflection, "and that does not really deserve the title."[8] The new social and economic order emerging in the Bourbon South was based on racial subservience. Higher education—Latin, philosophy, science, and history—was denounced as an academic perversion inimical to that order. But Fisk ignored the doubters and defamers. Superintended by pious Dean Spence, the college curriculum made no formal concessions either to the cultural deficits of its students, who were the first of their race born out of slavery, or to the second-class citizenship awaiting them in the emerging apartheid of an angry white South. "If the Negro is inferior to whites, give him superior training," Adam Spence would twit white southerners didactically; "if he is superior, give him inferior training; but if equal, give him the same."[9]

Spence and his colleagues were giving students Greek, Latin, French, and German, theology, natural sciences, music, moral philosophy, and history when Willie arrived in September 1885, entering the sophomore class at the age of seventeen because of his superior northern secondary education. Professors like Dean Spence's Michigan-trained brother-in-law Frederick A. Chase, who taught chemistry and physics "in a funny little basement," Helen Morgan from Oberlin, the first woman appointed full professor in a coeducational institution in the country (she chose Fisk over Vassar as the place of her life's work in Latin), and Henry S. Bennett, another Oberlinian, who taught German and served as college pastor (a Quaker suspected of having a sense of humor), made the learning experience in the college's small classes tonic and memorable. "Splendid" Dean Spence (Du Bois's words), who bore an uncanny physical resemblance to fellow Scot Andrew Carnegie, taught them to "know what the Greek language meant," and President Cravath, in chapel and class, saw to their souls and morals as solicitously as his own parents had ministered to fugitive slaves on the last leg of their flight to Canada.[10] Except for Atlanta University, its Congregationalist rival, no other four-year institution in the South was so adequately committed to and as consistently successful in producing African-American versions of New England ladies and gentlemen—Black Puritans or Afro-Saxons, as they were sometimes half mockingly called.[11]

Willie Du Bois plunged into this world with gusto. In the first place, he arrived with a sense of mission almost as exalted as that of his AMA teachers. As the train out of New York's Grand Central Terminal dropped below the Mason-Dixon Line past West Virginia and Kentucky, his fascination and excitement mounted at each whistle-stop as speech became slower, skin colors proliferated across the spectrum from alabaster to burnt cork, and the complex etiquette of race relations became increasingly flammable. Willie says nothing about accommodations aboard his train, but segregation in interstate travel was already being imposed. Tennessee, in fact, had been the first state to enact race separation laws in travel and public accommodation. That had been in 1881, and two years later, by its fateful invalidation of the Civil Rights Act of 1875 in all matters state and local, the Supreme Court of the United States handed 90 percent of the African-American population over to the discretionary mercies of southern legislatures and courts.[12] Not unlikely, then, when his future roommate during the three years at Fisk clambered aboard at Bowling Green, Kentucky, neatly dressed, friendly Otho Porter joined Willie in a Jim Crow car. But if so, this first brush with segregation failed to dampen the exhilaration, novelty, and sense of predestination Willie felt upon entering "the land of slaves" and seeing for the first time his crooning great-grandmother's Africa, transplanted and thriving, and bound to him from then on "by new and exciting and eternal ties."[13]

Fisk brought a three-year high that began in earnest the evening of the first day on campus. Moving into the new men's dormitory named after the explorer David Livingstone, a grey brick building on five acres of magnolias, he met, one after another, persons of a class and bearing amazing to him. They strode about confidently, most of them modishly dressed, speaking to people they met with an easy gaze and ready tongue. Even so, most of them came from conditions close to poverty, whether genteel or hardworking; some, like studious Margaret Murray, from homes where a single, breadwinning mother stroked seven sacrificial days a week in the river of domestic service. Willie remembered "coarse-looking Sherrod, poor and slow," who, like roommate Porter, went on to become a successful physician in Mississippi.[14] The sons and daughters of slaves and slave masters, few of them displayed servile traits because, to the extent advantages flowed from it, they were beneficiaries of the slave system. Few came directly from farming backgrounds, and the parents of those who did owned more than a few acres. Their fathers were preachers, barbers, undertakers, and caterers, and, as often, the privileged domestic and sole doctor or pharmacist in a small town. These students hailed from the South's cities—from Birmingham, Nashville, Louisville, Galveston—and from its medium-sized towns—Sparta, Pine Bluff, Waycross. Their contact with white people had usually been far more restricted than Willie's and seldom social in character—formalized, governed in the workplace and forum by an inviolable etiquette. Whereas Willie's intellectual and social growth had depended upon and led him into ever-closer contact with Great Barrington's white community, the educational and social advancement of his Fisk classmates had largely depended on the extent to which they had been insulated from local whites. They had learned their algebra and sentence diagramming in one-room schoolhouses and academies in church basements whose academic standards were a far cry from those at GBHS.

But not all were poor, especially those in the highly selective college department. Dancing off a pinhead of privilege, the sons and daughters of affluent Afro-America came to Fisk, as they did to Atlanta, Talladega, Howard, Lincoln, and a handful of other colleges, in such numbers that, although never in the majority, they set the tone and defined the institutional character—a tone and character that, although curiously imitative of the cavalier and lady of the Old South, had no truck with antebellum values when it came to racial rights. Willie was bedazzled by the likes of Ransom C. Edmondson and his younger brother, elegant sons of a white planter; by the unnamed relative of a future U.S. president, chauffeured to campus daily; by studious Thomas J. Calloway, a Washingtonian who carried himself like a senator and became a lifelong friend; by the high-strutting Frank Smith, much older and madly popular with the coeds.[15] Mulattoes seemed to be everywhere, walking indictments of the concupiscence, hypocrisy, and paradox at the core of all master-slave societies: "Lots and lots of mulattoes of that sort, some of whom were financed by their fathers, and some of them were financed by the fact that as mulattoes they got the better jobs." One of them, lanky Henry Hugh Proctor from Tennessee, future pastor of Atlanta's select First Congregational Church, remembered Willie and the rainbow student population in the autobiography he chose to call, significantly, *Between White and Black*. But whether racially mixed or, like "big, black, earnest" C. O. Hunter and others, more African in appearance, Willie admired all of them. "Such airs, and colored men at that," he pinched himself.[16]

"Who Are We?" the Fisk *Herald* would ask the year following Du Bois's editorship of the college's literary magazine. "We are not the Negro from whom the chains of slavery fell a quarter of a century ago, assuredly not." Rather, they now comprised an elite, confident, leadership class. "It can be truly said that we who have learned what the privileges and responsibilities of citizenship are, have no desire to see the South ruled simply by majorities. At the same time," the editorial challenged, "it need not be expected that we will contend for anything less than our actual deserts in the function of government." The South's white supremacy had not yet made a complete mockery of such sentiments in the mid-1880s. An occasional African-American still went to the House of Representatives from Alabama, North Carolina, and Virginia. Notwithstanding poll taxes, multiple ballot boxes, literacy tests, arcane regulations, and blatant intimidation, 130,344 African-American men were still registered voters in Louisiana, as were tens of thousands in Alabama, Mississippi, and Georgia. The southern white assault on voting rights claimed to be color blind, supposedly designed to trim from the voting rolls only those who by education and citizenship were deemed incompetent to participate in democracy. Approximately one third of Georgia's white voters and one fourth of Virginia's were expunged from the rolls in the mid-1880s.[17] Many more black people would of course be eliminated in this scheme in which voting was a class privilege rather than a civil right. Yet the young men who matriculated at Fisk and Atlanta and Howard tended to delude themselves that a franchise supposedly based on education and property would remain open to them and their class. Two decades later, Fisk man Du Bois would build a movement on the betrayal of the civil rights of the African-American elite.

The southerners were just as curious about this rare northerner among them, so uncommonly smart that he was admitted to the sophomore class. "Coming out of New England there was something about him no other seemed to possess," Henry Proctor thought. He was at least a year younger than most of the college-course freshmen, and several years junior to the normal-school and theology-department students, which made him appear tender in the extreme. Willie's Yankee upbringing had lumped the gift of gab, a distinguishing trait of southerners black and white, with such follies as idleness and gambling. In another year, he would palaver with the best, but in the fall of 1885 he was far from being the "lively, jovial chap, a speaker of great magnetism," that Proctor said he became. Between the lines of the memoirs, we can detect just a trace of social awkwardness and sexual intimidation. Unable to dissemble, to shoot the bull, he suffered the terrible dormitory ridicule of the teenager who fails to hide the fact that he is still a virgin. Livingstone Hall jeered in disbelief when he had to confess his ignorance of "the physical difference between men and women."[18] Then his dormitory mates took pity, and would have helped correct the deficiency speedily if Willie had been willing.

Meantime, he gazed longingly at those female classmates he had met during his first evening in the Jubilee Hall refectory. G. M. McClellan, another sophomore, had led him to the dining hall. Thirty years later, McClellan recalled being surprised by Willie's reaction to the food—"the comment was unusual. You praised the food."[19] But more than food impressed Willie. His memory of that evening's supper he carried to his grave, retrieving this "never-to-be-forgotten marvel" of the moment when he sat "opposite two of the most beautiful beings God ever revealed to the eyes of seventeen." One of them, Lena Calhoun, was the great-aunt of Lena Horne, who would enchant a middle-aged Du Bois almost as much as her comely forebear. "The Calhoun family was a family of mulattoes with money," Willie would animatedly tell the Columbia Oral History Project interviewer at ninety-two, "and she was beautifully dressed—oh, a perfectly lovely girl."[20] He learned quickly that debonair Frank Smith had already staked his claim there. But there was no shortage of marvels at Jubilee Hall.

Fisk swarmed with intelligent, attractive women (then and much later), with Sissie Dorsey (a "golden fairy"), Mattie Nichol ("dark cream"), Alice Vassar of the beautiful voice, and stately, competitive Margaret Murray, Booker T. Washington's future third wife, who would annoy Willie when he forgot his lines in rhetoric class. For the first time in his life, he was thrown together with women from "good" social backgrounds—women of color with delicate manners and fine minds. He must have wondered if Mary Silvina could have been like them had she been less deprived as a girl and more fortunate as a wife. Several years stood between the Great Barrington innocent and the man who would acquire the confident ease with women that made him an impressive suitor. For the present, Fisk coeds merely smiled, bantered, and told him how smart he seemed. But if they preferred the company of a Frank Smith, it was a wonderful comfort to Willie to know that it was not because of race. No Fisk woman would ever refuse his card because he was black. His profound relief and delight at having finally reached at Fisk a safe harbor of feelings could still burst out long afterward, as in this cathartic passage from *Darkwater*:

> Consider, for a moment, how miraculous it all was to a boy of seventeen, just escaped from a narrow valley: I willed and lo! my people came dancing about me,—riotous in color, gay in laughter, full of sympathy, need, and pleading; darkly delicious girls—'colored' girls—sat beside me and actually talked to me while I gazed in tongue-tied silence or babbled in boastful dreams. Boys with my own experiences and out of my own world, who knew and understood, wrought out with me great remedies.[21]

Yet even in this ideal environment, he would never be able to make friends easily, especially with men. Younger and less schooled by life than his dorm mates, it was a question not so much of shyness, although he always offered it by way of apology, but of insecurity masquerading as arrogance. Willie had reached full height more than two inches below the five-feet-eight average for men of his day. It was a feature almost no one readily noticed about him in later years, offset as it was by imposing personality and carriage (not once in eighty years of ink does he mention it), yet, whatever its psychological impact, the fact is that Du Bois usually found himself physically looking up to men whose intelligence he frequently looked down upon. So, as he sauntered to class, he cultivated a mordant sense of humor and a conversational brevity that was decidedly spiky. Sometimes he went a little too far. A sarcastic remark caused big C. O. Hunter to twist Willie's arm, warning him, "Don't you do that again!" Willie says he didn't.[22]

In the often strange ways of group acceptance, an almost fatal illness helped Willie's adjustment at Fisk. In October, typhoid fever flattened him. Perhaps, as he claims, "the whole school hung on the bulletins," but there is no reason to doubt that his recovery brought cheers in the dining hall and a boost in popularity. His performance a few days later on the college English examination won more attention, even though Willie remained permanently nettled that he placed second after Mary Bennett, daughter of the professor of German—"a girl and a white one at that," he noted ungenerously.[23] Up and about, he joined the college church, volunteering to teach Sunday school. Sunday classes with Willie in the little chapel in Livingstone Hall were likely to have turned more on expository showmanship than on instructive piety, although his Great Barrington respect for the tenets of Congregationalism was still solid. There was some annoyance about the Sunday school involvement, however, that was soon to have profound consequences for his beliefs. Looming in the background was "Pops" Miller, a much older student upon whose ungainly figure and invidious mind Willie would heap epithets that anticipate by more than three decades his imprecations on Marcus Garvey.[24] Miller, always alert to possible impieties, kept his eyes especially peeled for Willie.

The course of events defies clear reconstruction, but when Willie and several others were overheard planning a dance, "Pops" Miller became convinced that his darkest suspicions of the Devil's work were valid. Much hubbub ensued, with appeals to the faculty, citation of Pauline scripture ("I have never had much respect for Paul since"), and huffy renunciation of Sabbath duties by the recent typhoid victim. In other accounts, the dancing controversy is upstaged by a more philosophical turning point in Willie's abandonment of organized religion. In one of them, he claimed to have been disgusted by charges of heresy lodged against a New York Episcopal priest whose book on religion and politics was used at Fisk. In another, the expulsion of a nationally prominent Presbyterian divine because of heterodoxy was the cause. Then, maybe, it was the affront to Willie's logic by George Frederick Wright's *The Logic of Christian Evidences* (1880), "a book we were compelled to read." He never got the story quite straight, but, in any case, his disgust with organized religion was such that he "just stopped and refused to teach Sunday School any more."[25] But not before writing a dutifully pious letter in February to Reverend Scudder and the Great Barrington congregation, rejoicing in his religious activities, the prayers that might "help guide [him] in the path of Christian duty," the "forty conversions" at revival, and the arrival on campus of world-famous evangelist Dwight L. Moody.[26]

Thus began an intellectual journey that would end, after a very short time, in serene agnosticism. No dark night of the soul or Promethean defiance of Heaven seized Willie, as far as can be ascertained. In what seems almost an emotional replay of his mother's death, he calmly adjusted, outwardly at least, to the departure of another central force in his life. But had God ever been central in the sense of a spiritual anchor, rather than simply an appropriate feature of his internal life—familiar architecture like the blue dolomite Congregational Church on Main Street? He says that, until the Fisk controversy, he had never questioned his religious convictions. "Its theory had presented no particular difficulties: God ruled the world, Christ loved it, and men did right, or tried to." For a life whose exceptional course had been steered by self-control, intelligence, enormous psychic reserves, and strategic relationships, Willie's need for a personal deity who intervened and judged was objectively minimal by the time he finished college. Frank Hosmer and J. Carlisle Dennis had proven rather more helpful than God. In the future, as in the private reflections of his early years, later collected as *Prayers for Dark People*, or in the magisterial "Credo," Willie would rhetorically invoke the Deity, just as the witness of the Nazarene frequently served him as a powerful literary device.[27] While his ethical standards always remained exemplary, he began to think of God as ceremonial and largely unavailable for duty as a counselor. Total loss of conventional faith would have to wait for Harvard. Answering the query of a Cuban priest many years later, Du Bois provided an unambiguous reply: "[If] you mean by 'God' a vague Force which, in some uncomprehensible way, dominates all life and change, then I answer, Yes; I recognize such Force, and if you wish to call it God, I do not object."[28]

But while his religious faith shriveled in the hot breath of hypocrisy and intolerance, Willie rapidly acquired a faith in his race that was quasi-religious. A letter written to Reverend Scudder in February 1886 revealed that he was finding his existential anchor at Fisk, growing in self-esteem among people who didn't "despise [his] . . . color," and learning how to be a "Negro" in the fullest sense. And there was real wonderment, as he looked about him in the Fisk chapel, that "they are all my people; that this great assembly of youth and intelligence are the representatives of a race which twenty years ago was in bondage." Visions of his classmates forming the vanguard of African-American progress, with himself in the lead pointing the way, danced in his head. In *Darkwater*, the memoir closest in time to the Fisk experience, as well as in the closing-years *Autobiography*, Willie's reanimation of his 1880s' mood borders on the delusional (even making allowance for epic prose). He is "captain of [his] soul and master of fate." He wills "and lo!" his people "came dancing about [him]—riotous in color, gay in laughter, full of sympathy." He prophesies for the race an early arrival in the Promised Land: "Through the leadership of men like myself and my fellows we were going to have these enslaved Israelites out of the still enduring bondage in short order."[29]

The first year at Fisk taught Willie a good deal about bondage. He had experiences no amount of reading in the North could ever have equaled. First came the barbaric violence as pandemic to the South as kudzu. Lynching of African-Americans, soon to reach such volume as to become one of the region's pastimes, was beginning its steady, ghoulish rise. He saw the buckshot tracings by which a leading white Nashville editor had been fatally splattered for some crusading offense. Many fellow students went about armed when they left campus to go into the city. The most cautious public interracial contacts could detonate in a second, while casual interaction involved risks only the most instructed and dexterous were advised to undertake. Accidentally brushing a white woman in town, Willie had instinctively doffed his hat in apology, only to have her explode in red-faced expletives. "From that day to this," *Darkwater* insists, he "never knowingly raised [his] hat to a Southern white woman." The South was still unready to strip his people completely of the rights 180,000 of them had served in the Civil War to win and that the Fourteenth and Fifteenth Amendments were supposed to guarantee perpetually. But it was plain to see that that elimination was almost as certain as the sharecroppers' deepening indebtedness. "There is scarcely one public relation in the South," wrote the sympathetic Louisiana novelist George Washington Cable, in 1885, "where the Negro is not arbitrarily and unlawfully compelled to hold toward the white man the attitude of an alien, a menial, and a probable reprobate, by reason of race and color."[30]

If they were going to be his life's work, Willie needed to spend time among those African-Americans who were unlikely ever to see the inside of a Fisk classroom—among real peasants in the rural backcountry. Instead of returning home at the end of the sophomore year, then, he set out on a Saturday in late June to walk the Lebanon Pike. It took him past Andrew Jackson's sprawling estate just outside Nashville, east in the direction of Knoxville and the Cumberland Mountains, until he came to Lebanon, seat of Wilson County. After a back-slapping week at the Lebanon Teachers' Institute (morning classes for white candidates, afternoon for black), he passed the primitive examination to become an elementary school teacher. R. C. McMillan, county superintendent, signed his certificate on June 27, qualifying Willie to teach first grade at a monthly salary to be negotiated with the local commissioner of schools. Then, in the rough and tumble of negotiating, Willie forfeited the small-town post he wanted to an older candidate by dawdling self-satisfied over dinner. Horseplay and shared watermelon were no passkey to the job network his Lebanon colleagues were plugged into, he discovered. "The county teachers looked at me askance and knew of no vacant schools in their vicinity."[31]

He traveled, all told, no more than fifty miles from Nashville, but measured by the distance from civilization, Willie found himself entering a zone where time had stopped the day after the day of jubilee—he "touched the very shadow of slavery."[32] Wilson County, Tennessee, would remain in his memory bank for a lifetime, influencing a prose to which he was beginning to give a mythic spin, his conception of what he would later call the black proletariat, and, most profoundly, his gestating, romantic ideas about African-American "racial traits." Some of the keenest writing would come out of this summer experience, authentic and graphic—emotional in a personal, as opposed to its usual heroic, sense. The freshest examples of it are "The Hills of Tennessee" and "How I Taught School" in the October and December issues, respectively, of the *Herald*, the student magazine. Although Willie never allows his emotions to be caught off guard if he can help it, and despite the striving for narrative embellishment, these pieces come as close as any to revealing an unbuttoned eighteen-year-old Du Bois. We see him eight miles south of Lebanon on a horse "with a gait like a churn handle," birds dancing jigs on the treetops; eventually taking the train to Silver Springs, then sauntering along "slowly eating the ripened plums by the wayside," unsuccessful but unruffled as he finds the one-room schoolhouses along the road already supplied with teachers.

Suddenly, a mile or so on the approach to Watertown, then a Cumberland Plateau hamlet of seven homes, Wilson L. Waters's feed store, and a brand new railroad depot, Josie sprang into the road with a sunlit smile and a barrage of questions. Josie (her family name was Dowell) was wiry, dark-skinned, about twenty years old, and physically plain, but every inch alive. She and he had never seen the likes of each other before. As they strolled down the road together in mutual fascination, she told him of the schoolhouse over the hill just beyond Alexandria, a "land of 'varmints' and rattlesnakes" to Willie then, but today a sleepy, attractive town where visitors are still not much more common than a century ago.[33] Presenting himself to the local school commissioner, a pleasant, white college fellow who readily appointed him at twenty-eight dollars a month, Willie could still be surprised in *The Souls of Black Folk* that his acceptance of a dinner invitation meant eating alone after the commissioner and his family—"even then fell the awful shadow of the Veil." Josie's four-room place in a scraggly clearing deep in the woods became home for the summer, with its illiterate, indolent but solid, kindly father, its brood of children, and Mrs. Dowell, depicted by Willie as "strong, bustling, and energetic, with a quick, restless tongue, and an ambition to live 'like folks.' "[34]

Old Colonel Wheeler's log storage barn served as the windowless schoolhouse for a wriggling mass of fifteen Dowells, Burkes, Lawrences, Neills, and Hickmans, ranging from age six to twenty-year-old Josie and "Fat" Reuben, most of whom made up in earnestness what they lacked in the rudiments of learning. *The Souls of Black Folk* and the *Autobiography* describe a progressive-education idyll that summer—the "fine faith" his charges reposed in him, their spelling together, singing, picking flowers, and "listening to stories of the world beyond the hill." But the *Herald's* earlier "How I Taught School" is less idyllic, more reminiscent of prim, lovely Charlotte Forten's Civil War *Diary*, a hand-wringing classic by another African-American northerner on a mission of educational uplift in the backward South. The first "colored teacher who has dropped in among these hills," Willie knew the local white people had him under a magnifying glass, on the alert for they knew not exactly what alien mischief; so he did his jaunty best to please, and pretty well succeeded, although Fiskites read that he had "to swallow some large lumps of 'sassiness,' and even now some of the old farmers say they'll be 'de-dad-jimmed ef they like sich a biggety nigger.' "[35] An elderly, respected abecedarian named Uncle Mose swore by the 1857 Webster speller, making his unhappiness with the newfangled revised edition loudly manifest in the classroom. Threading his way between purist Uncle Mose and dad-jimming farmers, by summer's end Willie caught "faint and transient glimpses of the dawn in the struggling minds of my pupils." Josie, nervous, always in motion, led the class. The *Herald* piece closed with Willie vowing he "wouldn't take $200 for [his] summer's experience, and [he] wouldn't experience it again for $2000."[36]

But he did. He was back in Alexandria the following summer at thirty dollars a month, back in this hardscrabble Eden of postbellum innocence, as a lodger again with Josie's people. The experience builds in lyricism now. Josie and her family and the Burkes and the Neills and Fat Reuben and the others are made symbolic: of agricultural toil sliding into peonage; of white farmers and black laborers in a symbiosis of fatal inefficiency; of transforming urban energies doused and drowned by one-crop economies. There is wasted learning and wasted love, self-hatred, lethargy, decay, and miscegenated rape. The struggles of the little people of the South were to be captured in all their fabulous afflictions, as in this sample threnody from *The Souls of Black Folk*:

> I would visit Mun Eddings, who lived in two very dirty rooms, and ask why little Lugene, whose flaming face seemed ever ablaze with the dark-red hair uncombed, was absent all last week, or why I missed so often the inimitable rags of Mack and Ed. Then the father, who worked Colonel Wheeler's farm on shares, would tell me how the crops needed the boys; and the thin, slovenly mother, whose face was pretty when washed, assured me that Lugene must mind the baby. 'But we'll start them again next week.' When the Lawrences stopped, I knew that the doubts of the old folks about book-learning had conquered again, and so, toiling up the hill . . .[37]

The heroic futility of the two summers weighed upon him. He saw written across the faces deep in Wilson County the rebuked destinies of the black people who came singing, praying, and aspiring out of slavery, and who were sinking into "listless indifference, or shiftlessness, or reckless bravado." But if the aspirations sputtered, the praying continued in jerry-built tabernacles with a "pythian madness" Willie describes wonderfully. And what was sung were the "sorrow songs" in their unmannered, slurred-diction purity which no Jubilee Singers concert ever truly captured.[38] There is no question but that he grew fond of the people in Wilson County, that they came to have meaning for him, transcending symbolism and sociology. The intensity of his prose when he describes these two summers attests to the personal impact of the Alexandria sojourns.

Ten years passed before Du Bois saw Alexandria again. When he did, he remembered that nobody had believed then in "Doc" Burke's heroic efforts to buy the seventy-five acres he worked like a robot. " 'White folks would get it all,' " people said. He remembered, too, rocking on Josie's porch, helping himself to a basket of peaches while her mother boasted of Josie's savings for college, her sewing machine, and her wages from the "big house." But ten years later, Josie was dead (" 'We've had a heap of trouble since you've been away,' " her mother said), and the seventy-five acres Doc Burke had finally bought left him deeper in debt. That trade-off of material progress for loss of innocence that humanists are wont to underscore, Willie saw everywhere, in the flight to Nashville and Knoxville of the young men, in the six-room house the Burkes were building, the store-bought shoes worn by the wives, the new Wheeler schoolhouse with large blackboard and windows. "Death and marriage had stolen youth and left age and childhood there," he reflected. He departed after this third visit wondering how to "measure progress there where the dark face of Josie lies?"[39] Willie might have been somewhat encouraged could he have known that his teaching would be remembered a century later in Watertown and Alexandria among African-American families, and that some of them—the Dowells and Burkes in particular—would prosper in real estate and undertaking.[40]

He probably never returned again to Alexandria, but in "My Character," an astonishingly confessional chapter in the *Autobiography*, Willie in his mid-eighties disclosed for the first time a sexual watershed in his life. He slept with Josie's mother. Although we can decode her identity from a cryptic paragraph, it is impossible to know which summer it happened. But his senior year, if not the year before, there was no more ribbing about virginity in Livingstone Hall. Finally, something had happened that enabled him to overcome his mentally incestuous bonding with Mary Silvina. Great Barrington's taboo on interracial romance had retarded Willie's sexual maturity, certainly; and the perceived social deficiencies of the women of his own race in the town greatly compounded the problem. But there was surely another, deeper factor at play. If there was at least one young woman of suitable credentials anywhere in the area—in nearby Lee or Pittsfield or, somewhat farther, in Springfield—whom a high school graduate and news reporter could have courted, Willie seems never to have dated her. Mary Silvina was the woman in his life until the fateful summer in the Tennessee backcountry. Until then, Willie saw in women of his own kind and milieu—nice ones—too much of his ambiguously cherished mother.

The world was full of women who could have instructed him in the pleasures of the flesh, yet there are indications that he found himself in a double bind. Psychologists would be alert to the subconscious castration complex that afflicts males who figuratively violate the paternal taboo against possession of the mother. In Willie's exact, startling words in the *Autobiography*, as he "tried to solve the contradiction of virginity and motherhood," he found himself faced with the "other contradiction of prostitution and adultery." Josie's mother solved a dilemma that was social as well as sexual. Sex with a woman who was totally opposite to the imperative, venerated image of the mother—with a whore—although wrong in the eyes of society and religion, offered escape from impotence. That the old man would recall the young man's loss of virginity as a violent encounter in which he was exploited by an experienced peasant woman ("literally raped") suggests a tangle of Freudian pathologies. "Then, as a teacher in the rural districts of East Tennessee, I was literally raped by the unhappy wife who was my landlady."[41] In Willie's mind, then, the violence of a "rape" was the necessary act of his liberation. Innocent victim, henceforth he would go roaring into sexual conquests convinced that he was never the initiator because he always saw himself on his back in a dark bedroom, his "unhappy landlady" flexing and groaning on top of him. Henceforth, sex was something the Devil in others made him do.

It always annoyed Rayford Whittingham Logan, one of his closest future collaborators, whenever Du Bois insisted (as he often did) that he had embraced his racial identity only at Fisk. "Henceforward I was a Negro," Du Bois would proclaim, and then soar into a grand vision of his place in the race, knowing full well that Anglo-Saxon America was objectively blind by custom and law to intermediate racial categories. Logan always said that Du Bois's claim of belated racial self-discovery was a polemical contrivance to give greater punch to his writings about race relations. To claim that his identity as a Negro was in some sense the exercise of an option, an existential commitment, was to define Willie's celebration of and struggle for his people as an act of the greatest nobility and philanthropy. He was a Negro not because he had to be—was born immutably among them—but because he had embraced the qualities of that splendid race and the moral superiority of its cause. With the country beginning to fill up with Slavic and southern European immigrants for whom, like the earlier Irish, the surest touchstone of citizenship was distance between themselves and Americans of African ancestry, pretending to be racially indeterminate was an invitation to physical battery or even institutional commitment. You were either white or black; there was no Creole or mestizo (with the problematic exception of Louisiana), and mulatto was largely a census term that was shortly to be abandoned.[42]

Willie acknowledged this fact, and yet he knew better than to believe it completely because, although only white and black Americans formally existed (Native Americans were invisible and Asians excluded), the veil of color had always been porous. The subtle and not-so-subtle advantages of light skin were a social reality, however varied and complex the manifestations, South and North.[43] What is of more delicate and indubitable importance is that Willie's feelings about race in these early years were more labile or tangled, not to say conflictive, than his public professions revealed. Grandfather Alexander's death in his junior year not only brought a small legacy of four hundred dollars, it brought him those diary entries flashing over Franco-Caribbean roots like far-off lightning, enhancing a lordly sense of self. Willie's racial shape in his last year at Fisk was still congealing, and it would always be an alloy, never entirely pure. Rayford Logan was right about the debater's point, but he elected to pass over the deeper significance of the racial-identity claim that sociologist E. Franklin Frazier, another protégé of the mature Du Bois, grasped: that Willie's ambivalence endowed him with a resilient superiority complex, and that that complex convinced Willie himself, as well as many others, that his lifelong espousal of the "Darker World" was an optional commitment based above all upon principles and reason, rather than a dazzling advocacy he was born into. In an interview recorded for Folkways Records shortly before leaving for Ghana, Du Bois would speak precisely and revealingly about racial belonging, telling his interlocutor that it had been during the Fisk period that he had become "quite willing to be a Negro and to work with the Negro group."[44]

This developing sense of mission was fully evident in his senior year. Fisk was basic training for combat, and Fiskites were to provide the officer corps. If he had not yet coined his most famous term, the concept of the "talented tenth" must already have been gestating in "The New Negro," a lost essay submitted to *Century Magazine*, probably in his senior year.[45] "An Open Letter to the Southern People," another 1887 unpublished offering, would have pleased Mary Silvina. It championed the prohibition of liquor while explaining that African-Americans throughout the South voted with the wets in recent state referenda because of ignorance and their suspicions about the better classes of white people—themselves to blame through direct neglect of public education and indirect encouragement of mob rule. His open letter would also have enormously pleased the principal of the new industrial school at Tuskegee, Alabama, Booker T. Washington, in its plea for humane southern solutions to southern problems: "Let us then, recognizing our common interests (for it is unnecessary to speak of our dependence upon you), work for each other's interest, casting behind us unreasonable demands on the one hand, and unreasonable prejudice on the other." But it was Willie's nature always to couple conciliation with admonition, which this piece did with supreme clairvoyance. "The South will not always be solid," he wrote, "and in every division the Negro will hold the balance of power."[46]

He had got himself on the *Herald* as editor in charge of student publications exchanges his first year, barely a month after recovery from the typhoid attack. A typical exchanges-editor comment (this one about Lincoln University's *Register*) archly noted that "good advice is acceptable even if it comes from sophomoric effusions." Which could not be said for Nashville's Roger Williams University *Record* because, "from its tone," Willie judged it to be published "by the faculty and not the students."[47] Entirely to his liking, on the other hand, was the Greensboro College *Message* containing a "first rate woman's rights argument." By December

1886, Willie was *Herald* literary editor and in November 1887 editor-in-chief, with Tom Calloway as business manager, the first of many years ahead in which "T. J." Calloway would serve Willie in this role. Along with running the college magazine, he devoted himself to public speaking, writing a philosophical essay on forensics, and becoming, according to his own estimate, "an impassioned orator," although reason rather than passion was what most audiences would remember him for.[48] He was an enraptured member of little Dean Spence's Mozart Society, never missing rehearsals for the religious oratorios, marveling at Ed Bailey's tenor, and amused as the frock-coated dean waved his hands in the air. "Our race, but a quarter of a century removed from slavery, can master the greatest musical compositions," Willie clucked editorially.[49]

The *Herald* was where he made his mark, though. Turning its brittle pages to Willie's "Editorial" and "Editorial Toothpick" columns reveals a mind constantly running ahead, sometimes too rapidly for the information it contained. Ebullitions in the Balkans are commented upon as well as, closer to home, the duty of the nation to protect the rights of patriotic Fisk students. He plows through the new one-volume edition of George Washington Williams's *History of the Negro Race in America from 1619 to 1880*, rejoicing that "at last we have a historian," and an African-American historian at that. He bids a highly complimentary farewell to T. Thomas Fortune, retiring editor of the New York *Freeman* (the old *Globe*), the man who had started Willie on his amateur journalism career.[50] His enthusiastic feminism (striking in a young Negro male of his Victorian cast) is reiterated in an editorial on the Women's Christian Temperance Union meeting in Nashville—"the Age of Women is surely dawning." In that same vein, the issues for December 1887 through January and March 1888 carried "Tom Brown at Fisk," the editor's first extended sortie into fiction. The three-chapter short story's protagonist is a woman, a Fisk student teacher named Ella Boyd, marking the appearance of the female protagonist as an autobiographical device Willie would employ in the ambitious novels *The Quest of the Silver Fleece* and *Dark Princess*. As in the novels, Tom, the male figure in the *Herald* story, is something of a lovable, morally innocent stumblebum decisively aided by quick-witted, complex women as he copes with life's realities.[51] For reasons better left to later exploration, he preferred the company of intelligent women in fiction as in real life.

Like Great Barrington African-Americans, Fisk students receive their due of lecturing and admonishment. The "Editorial Toothpick" for March 1888 informs readers that Thomas Carlyle, the fulminating Scots historian and essayist (Willie spelled the name Carlisle), having once reproved a student who "had no plans laid for his future life," would find at Fisk "several weeks of profitable employment at the same business." What was wrong with them? Why wasn't there a Fisk student "at Leipsic [sic], or a Fisk metaphysician at Berlin? Aren't we smart enough?" Willie certainly thought he was. His discovery of Carlyle had an influence on his prose more enduring than Macaulay's. Macaulay's smug, practical Whig temperament was a pale inspiration next to the High Tory prejudices Carlyle expressed through effulgent adjectives and magnificent invective. The *Herald's* editor was undoubtedly ignorant of Carlyle's infamous fulminations against blacks in "The Nigger Question" as incapable of surviving outside slavery. Immersion in the Scotsman's works—*On Heroes, Hero-Worship, and the Heroic in History* and the slashing, egocentric *Sartor Resartus*—would come in the Harvard years, but he was already wading in the waters of authoritarian romanticism.[52] Fan mail from one *Herald* reader brought portentous thanks for "words of encouragement . . . toward a life that shall be an honor to the Race." Yet Willie was also capable of lighter, more common concerns. He once even made fun of his own editorial pretensions, confessing that his "demeanor even surpasses in superciliousness the far-famed senior prep."[53]

For all his usual twenty-year-old gravitas, Willie Du Bois may actually have become fairly popular by the end of his Fisk education. He was a new man in his confident, verbally magnetic dealings with female classmates. Pert Maria Benson from Nashville, who went on to teach at Tuskegee, admired him. His regular date was an attractive coed whom he never identified other than as Nellie. As she was Willie's first sweetheart, she may have been the recipient of a fair amount of bravado and lack of consideration. They corresponded once or twice after leaving Fisk, and, in a rare mention of her soon thereafter, Willie says that they have broken up "from no fault" of his, although, in the same remarkable circular letter, he alludes to his "*penchant* for hurting other peoples' feelings."[54] Henry Proctor and Willie were the same age and amiable rivals in debating, but Proctor was to spend six years getting his bachelor's degree due to the miserable schooling of his Fayetteville, Tennessee, youth. By the time they met again in Atlanta at the turn of the century, Yale Divinity graduate Proctor was one of the African-American lights of Congregationalism, a powerful speaker, opinion maker, and staunch Republican with a girth matching that of William Howard Taft, his favorite president.[55] As for others in the class of '88, Willie's relationship with them seems to have been more collegial than intimate. He felt that they "little understood each other," but they did share a bond of common experience strong enough to keep a senior year vow to write. Two years after graduating from Fisk, one of his self-absorbed circular letters to his classmates alluded to a "light-heartedness of other days," but all indications are that, while nineteen-year-old Willie was by turns congenial and sarcastic, he was decidedly too earnest to be thought of as lighthearted.[56]

Surviving school records for these years are sparse in detail. Dean Spence, Fisk's gatekeeper in Greek and French, in fact kept only impressionistic comments about students, in Willie's case the notation forwarded to Harvard that he was "one of my best." Math professor Herbert Wright judged his work to be "of a very high order." Grave President Cravath concurred. "An unusually quick, active mind," he advised the Harvard admissions committee. Professor Helen Morgan's description of Willie's work in Latin was as detailed as it was enthusiastic, speaking of Willie's "manliness, faithfulness to duty and earnestness in study." Morgan's careful comments track her student through the twenty-first book of Livy, "5/5ths of the Odes of Horace, 3 satires, 3 of the shorter Epistles, and the entire Ars Poetica, and the Agricola of Tacitus." That Morgan, the favorite of most Fisk students, thought highly of Du Bois the man as well as the scholar serves as something of an indication of a personality more serious than arrogant. This was the point science professor Chase wanted to make in his Harvard reference letter, warning the committee, "If his application should be accepted I should fear that he might give you the impression of being somewhat conceited."[57]

In June 1888, five graduating seniors posed for their class photograph; a sixth, the aristocratic Ransom Edmondson, was absent, but his diploma was subsequently granted. The three women, Leonora Bowers of Galveston, Texas, Maria Benson of Nashville, and Mary Stewart of Oswego, New York, stand corsetted and coiffed, looking with unsmiling directness into the tripod camera. L. A. Tindall of Aberdeen, Mississippi, sits in Prince Albert coat and polished boots looking slightly away with a hint of preoccupation on his handsome face. Willie also sits. He and the camera meet eye to eye in a pleasantness that seems out of character. Out of range, someone who may have hoped they were going to have a future together—the "Nellie" or "Nell" of his twenty-fifth birthday reminiscences—waited, proudly holding Willie's diploma. A short time earlier, each had stepped before the interested and proud commencement audience of faculty, students, and local citizens, a sprinkling of white people included, to say something in a manner befitting the world awareness and polish of Fisk University's thirteenth college graduation class. Willie chose "Bismarck . . . my hero," and, incidentally, also one of Carlyle's.

Bismarck had made a nation "out of bickering peoples." The Second Reich should be a model for African-Americans "marching forth with strength and determination under trained leadership." Willie fully shared the German statesman's impatience with outmoded tradition and cumbersome institutions. African-Americans had achieved much in the quarter-century since the end of slavery, but if they were to become a cohesive, modern people then they must submit to strenuous discipline and scientific culture. "The life of this powerful Chancellor illustrates the power and purpose, the force of an idea," Willie told his audience. "It shows what a man can do if he will." Here, the young orator introduced a sage caveat about expediency and power, for his admiration of his subject was not entirely slavish. Bismarck's success carried with it "a warning lest we sacrifice a lasting good to temporary advantage; lest we raise a nation and forget the people, become a Bismarck and not a Moses. To one object of his life Bismarck sacrificed even truth and liberty. No lie ever stood between him and success; no popular right ever hindered that ruthless hand of iron."[58]

In later years, Willie felt compelled to explain his choice of commencement theme. Not only was Bismarck the architect of an empire banged together on battlefields, held together by Junkers and industrial magnates and aggrandized through diplomatic chicanery, he was convener, moreover, of the European banquet at which whole sides of Africa were served up. Fisk was a "good college," with its curriculum proudly conventional in the best traditions of the New England faculty. Willie's textbooks in ethics and logic propagated philosophical idealism as the only true doctrine worthy of an educated Christian. John Stuart Mill, Auguste Comte, and Herbert Spencer were profaners—"infected throughout" by heresies in Immanuel Kant's *Critique of Pure Reason*—wrote the Scots divine and Princeton president James McCosh in his authoritative *Laws of Discursive Thought* (1870). Nor did the supposedly modern *The Science of Mind* (1881) by John Bascom advance beyond putting a gloss upon the cumulative materialist evidences disclosed by the physical sciences. The new heterodoxies of political and economic thought were not so much opposed as unknown. Certainly, it never occurred to Dean Spence to add the just-translated first volume of *Das Kapital* to the college's supplementary reading list. Consequently, Willie's estimable racial motives hadn't saved him from falling into the abyss between his "education and the truth in the world," as he put it, adding confessionally (deleted from the Russian edition of the *Autobiography*) that he was "blithely European and imperialist in outlook, democratic as democracy was conceived in America."[59]

If the irony of the Iron Chancellor being extolled by the future father of Pan-Africanism has been severely noted by critics, it is relevant to mention for historical context that one of Willie's four classmates spoke to the theme "Anglo-Saxon Influence." Fisk students were emphatically men and women of their Victorian times, and as Willie left the South proclaiming himself now fully a "Negro" and dedicated to the cause of racial uplift, he carried with this commitment an elitist, literary conception of what that meant, equally exemplified by the writings of Thomas Carlyle and their heroic rendering of historic personalities as by the heavy, deadly plottings of Bismarck the Junker.[60]

5.

The Age of Miracles

"At but not of Harvard"

DU BOIS'S MOOD—W.E.B. Du Bois's mood (Willie is no more)—ran to euphoria during the next twelve years, and never more so than in the fall of 1888 on his way to Harvard. Repeatedly, those years would be recaptured and revised in fine-tuned memoirs that expertly combined truth with license: *Darkwater* (1920); "A Pageant in Seven Decades: 1868–1938" (1938); *Dusk of Dawn* (1940); and the *Autobiography* (1968). Life was promising, exhilarating. Obstacles existed merely to test his mettle and be overcome. "I willed and lo! I was walking beneath the elms of Harvard—the name of allurement, the college of my youngest, wildest visions. I needed money, scholarships and prizes fell into my lap." When, within the full, quick, first Harvard year, nostalgic letters came from Fisk classmates telling of disappointments in love and career, he gently chided them for their "more or less unconscious mocking of the world," commending to them the remedy of "all-absorbing life work." He found bitterness unworthy, for now he loved "the great throbbing heart of the world" as he never loved it before. In *Darkwater* (so furious at the world yet so pleased with himself), Du Bois cakewalks through Harvard in a single paragraph of breathless compression. "Commencement came and standing before governor, president, and grave, gowned men," he is a comet flashing on to glory but not before telling them "certain astonishing truths, waving my arms and breathing fast!" Without "thought of modest hesitation" he forces a supercilious philanthropy headed by a former president of the United States to capitulate before his onslaught for a fellowship, then sails confidently for Europe.[1]

Later, as his rage with American apartheid evolved into what many saw as racial chauvinism and then into a special brand of Marxism, Du Bois wrote divergent scripts for his Harvard incarnations. The Grateful Outsider yielded center stage to the Imperial Self, with shadings of given details subtly manipulated until autobiographical discordances tend to pass unnoticed. As the Grateful Outsider, he "asked nothing of Harvard but the tutelage of teachers and the freedom of the library." If most of his white classmates were merely civil in the lecture hall and unaware of his very existence in the Yard, the loss was theirs; he had his " 'island within' and it was fair country." If the glee club rejected a rare attempt to join in the social life of the college and to share his fine singing voice, ultimately it meant little because he was a prized member of Boston's vital African-American community. If he sang the college song, it was merely because he "liked the music, and not from any pride in the Pilgrims." He was, he said, "in Harvard but not of it," yet he made certain to make an impression on his professors sufficient to merit welcome among them in the august Philosophical Club.[2]

The Imperial Self was less impressed by his Harvard world. The possibility that his social conduct had been governed by an "inferiority complex" (conceded in *Dusk of Dawn*) was dismissed in the *Autobiography* as having nothing to do with "unhappiness or resentment." He had simply been exceptional among African-Americans of his generation in embracing "voluntary race segregation," although he approved of geology professor Nathaniel Southgate Shaler's classroom expulsion of a white southerner who objected to sitting next to him.[3] Ruminating in the *Massachusetts Review* at ninety-two, Du Bois remembered Harvard as an endured experience charged with frivolity, snobbishness, and conservatism—merely adequate to the intellectual needs of a sojourner preoccupied with the predestined part he was to play in the larger world. Grades meant less than knowledge. No " 'snap' " courses for him; he was there "to enlarge my grasp of the meaning of the universe." "Of course, [he] wanted friends," but because of his uncompromising racial philosophy, he "could not seek them."[4] Despite his self-imposed segregation and boilerplate "brusquerie," he joined the Foxcraft Club, was a Philosophical Club regular, and even allowed himself to notice a few classmates destined to cut large swaths beyond Harvard—Herbert Croly, Augustus Hand, Robert Herrick, and two or three others. He recalled reading Kant's *Critique of Pure Reason* with George Santayana in the philosopher's rooms, and William James was a social friend who gave Du Bois advice about a career. All in all the place was useful, and Du Bois departed Cambridge of the opinion that he "did not find better teachers at Harvard, but teachers better known" than at Fisk.[5]

But the road to and through Harvard was not so easy in reality. Getting there, surviving its Anglo-Saxon Protestant environment in which Catholics and Jews were condescended to almost as much as African-Americans, winning its academic prizes, and graduating cum laude was not the snap Du Bois made it out to be.[6] It detracts not at all from his unique intelligence and nobly defined goals to rewrite the Harvard years in less-inflated prose, to winch Du Bois down from a pedestal of successive triumphs onto the bed of his own contingent and very human success story. It was a story he discarded in the interests of constructing the myth of the Imperial Self that he believed his people needed in order to take themselves as seriously as he took himself. This was his ego's learning decade, the ten or more years when the life and destiny of Africans in America merged inseparably with his own. But the transformation, though remarkably quick and thorough, proceeded unevenly, and, occasionally, even faltered. It took Du Bois time and considerable effort to become himself.

Despite the dreams revealed in the *Herald* and the seemingly providential good fortune reported in the memoirs, his future after Fisk had been anything but assured. Curiously enough, the academic standards at Harvard and Fisk may not have been as incommensurable as it might seem reasonable to suppose today, given the imported Ivy League faculties and the minuscule social class from which the southern liberal arts colleges recruited their best students. Still, for a young African-American even of Du Bois's manifest brilliance to pass from a two-decades-old missionary school to the 252-year-old empyrean of white collegiate training in America was an extraordinary ascension. As part of President Charles W. Eliot's ongoing plan to transform what had been a diploma-granting club for New England and, particularly, Back Bay scions into a university where national leadership in all the professions was forged, Harvard began opening its doors to exceptional male representatives of immigrant groups, as well as a few African-Americans. President Eliot's inaugural address had expressed the view that "only after generations of civil freedom and social equality" would the intellectual capacities of women for higher education be determined. Harvard was ready, however, to risk admitting even the poorest men, "provided that with their poverty . . . they bring capacity, ambition and purity." Richard T. Greener, who was to spend his foreign-service career languishing in Vladivostok, had been the first of the African-Americans, graduating from Harvard College in 1870.[7] Wagering that

Eliot's enlightened admission policy made his educational ambitions realizable, Du Bois had declined President Cravath's offer of a scholarship to Hartford Theological Seminary and written to Harvard in October 1887.[8]

Harvard and Yale traditionally required African-American baccalaureates to repeat a portion of their undergraduate training, a requirement frequently imposed on white graduates of undistinguished colleges. Money was a problem; probably he couldn't raise more than $150 a year. What did Harvard suggest he do about it? his letter of inquiry asked. Across the top of this straightforward appeal, Secretary Frank Bolles penned the suggestion that Du Bois might apply for a Price Greenleaf stipend, "if strongly recommended by faculty of Fisk." In addition to the strong Fisk recommendations, Frank Hosmer underscored that the applicant was destined for important service, "one of those who should be assisted in obtaining a thorough preparation for his work." Uncle James Burghardt wrote in trembling hand to certify that his nephew was "unable of himself, or with such aid as I can give him, to meet his necessary expenses at Harvard College." Two hundred fifty dollars in Price Greenleaf support still left Du Bois short by at least an equal amount.[9] A chance conversation with a student in the Fisk Preparatory School, one Fortson, raised the possibility of summer work waiting tables in a Minnesota resort hotel. Fortson thought that he, Du Bois, T. J. McClellan, his Livingstone Hall roommate, Du Bois's friend Tom Calloway, and perhaps two others from Fisk could save enough from tips to pay a good portion of their expenses the following year. After two summers' work there, Fortson had reached the impressive rank of second waiter.[10]

The significance of the stint at Lake Minnetonka lay not so much in the money Du Bois and his companions netted that summer, although had he headed east without part of it, he might well have had to postpone life in Cambridge for another year. But the experience would have been of passing significance were it not that, once again with Du Bois, the incidental or routine was freighted with dramatic personal and racial meaning. As he recounted the Lake Minnetonka period, drunken vulgarity abounded—corpulent, red-faced businessmen and a good number of sporting-crowd types caromed the hallways with easy women—and hotel patrons treated the staff like faceless peons, while, in retaliation, the staff creamed off the best food for itself. In that world of servility, Du Bois grandly declared, he declined to be more than an uncorrupted observer. He made no tips at Lake Minnetonka. Rudely summoned to a table once, he left the astonished diner waiting with hand raised. For all Du Bois knew, "he may be beckoning yet."[11] Du Bois claimed that, according to their original plan, he left the hotel at the end of the season to drum up singing concerts for Fortson and the others in Minneapolis, St. Paul, Madison, Milwaukee, and Chicago, an undertaking sharply testing his mother wit and diplomacy but one that succeeded in the end in earning money. Finally, Minnetonka had been "on the whole a rather disillusioning experience."[12]

The memoirs tinker with the Lake Minnetonka summer: they had never intended to be waiters because of inexperience, only busboys; the others had waited tables, but he "could not or would not learn"; the glee-club gambit, with himself as advance agent—"executive planner"—had been stage two of a well-thought-out plan.[13] But when he wrote a detailed circular letter the following year to Fisk classmates (who would have learned from the others about the graduation summer), he said "work at Lake Minnetonka was pleasant," that he had found time to read Longfellow's "Hiawatha," "fancying that the 'Githchie Gumee' lay before me." Du Bois, who was justly proud of his voice, revealed that he had joined Calloway, McClellan, and the others in regular hotel parlor concerts "which sometimes netted and sometimes didn't." If he never got tips waiting table, it may well have been more because of inexperience than disdain of serving. Finally, the advance-agent "plan" is revealed to have been desperate improvisation after the management "startled" Fortson's recruits with the August warning that, due to slow business, the hotel would close early. And if Du Bois then "seemed the most available advance agent," it was probably because, useless in the dining room, his fellows urged the role upon him.[14] Without the revealing Fisk circular letter, the Lake Minnetonka summer would remain as Du Bois presented it in his published writings, a financial exigency in which his abilities ultimately saved the day. Whatever the truth of that summer experience, his presentation effectively screens from us the finesse with which he retouched the quotidian details of life in order to produce the desired image of impregnable racial pride.

IT WAS a rainy September day when Du Bois arrived in Cambridge with less than the fifty dollars he had started off with. (At Syracuse, New York, a young con man had boarded the train and, after a rapid exchange of bills, a sleepy, chagrined Du Bois had been left ten dollars poorer.) Reporting to the bursar, he was dumbfounded to learn that the Price Greenleaf fellowship money would not be available until later in the semester. The thirty dollars outstanding from the glee clubbers ("the boodle," he called it) was a few weeks away from being remitted, and meanwhile Harvard required a partial tuition payment up front. He managed to borrow seventy-five dollars but failed to find someone in Boston who would stand him to the four-hundred-dollar loan he needed to cover the semester's expenses. His slim cash reserves dwindled a few more precious dollars each day. Was it Frank Hosmer and the Congregationalists of Great Barrington who saved him with a loan requiring of him no security? Probably.[15] Help also came from his Cambridge landlady, Mrs. Mary Taylor, who allowed him to owe the rent. John and Mary Taylor, solid working-class people, were African-Americans originally from Nova Scotia, whose two-story frame house, still standing a century later, at 20 Flagg Street a few blocks from the Yard, was home to Du Bois during his four years of undergraduate and graduate study.[16] He took his meals at Memorial Hall, the large dining facility where students of moderate means boarded. That first year was, he said in the circular letter, the "tightest place" of his life.

But he was in, with 281 others of the class of '90—only the sixth African-American admitted to the college since Richard Greener.[17] Many of those who matriculated at Harvard during the closing years of the nineteenth century looked back on those days as a golden age. By Du Bois's time, the increasingly unfettered system of course electives—President Eliot's gamble—was a widely acclaimed, proven curriculum, immensely popular with undergraduates. The philosophy of growth through choice had even extended to spiritual matters in 1886, when compulsory daily chapel attendance was abolished. The threat of a national university being established in Washington now fifteen years behind it, Harvard monopolized the role, increasingly matching a varied student body to a varied curriculum. "The poorest and the richest students are equally welcome here," the reforming president boasted. If membership in the Dickie, Fly, or Porcellian clubs mattered greatly to many of his classmates, and if Cabots, Endicotts, Mathers, and Wentworths passed him under the elms, Du Bois's own presence and that of Clement Garnett Morgan, the other African-American in his class, underscored the college's steady enrollment of men who were neither Brahmins nor prized solely because of family wealth. Du Bois had arrived never even having heard of Phi Beta Kappa, "and of such important social organizations as the Hasty Pudding Club, [he] knew nothing."[18]

Hutchins Hapgood from Chicago ('92) was typical of this newer generation of students who affected complete indifference to membership in exclusive clubs, an attitude fully shared by his old-line Boston classmate, Robert Morss Lovett, who believed that most undergraduates "were unconcerned with it." They shared the tonic sentiment that, as Lovett crooned, "this period was a golden age in the history of Harvard," that, as Hapgood's brother Norman crooned, "if there could be a place intellectually more attractive," his imagination could not formulate it. All of which agreed with Du Bois's own age-of-miracles euphoria. Haughty Oswald Garrison Villard, class of '93, the European-educated son of one of America's richest families and grandson of abolitionist William Lloyd Garrison, said pithily that Harvard was "entirely satisfied with itself. It had reason to be."[19] Villard himself was headed for a history degree and graduate work under Albert Bushnell Hart, ownership of a major newspaper, and a lifetime of civil misunderstandings with upperclassman Du Bois.

Although Du Bois was later among those who, like Henry Brooks Adams, George Santayana, and the sociologist Robert Ezra Park, argued persuasively that Harvard was too satisfied with itself, he and they praised the faculty.[20] Professor Nathaniel Shaler's introduction to geology (Natural History 4) was steadily popular, apparently because the Kentucky-bred scientist's vast learning overflowed the narrows of his discipline and swept students into much of the knowledge of the cosmos. Old Professor Francis James Child's English department acquired bespatted, cane-twirling, and entertainingly eccentric Barrett Wendell in 1880, a founder in his college days of the *Harvard Lampoon* and future author of *A Literary History of America*. There were Harvard men, Du Bois among them, who recounted well into dotage the rites and rigors of Wendell's English 12, in which enrollments sometimes reached two hundred.[21] Hardly a year passed during the 1880s but that President Eliot approved an appointment that would achieve legendary or near-legendary proportions. The year Du Bois came, Child brought George Lyman Kittredge, his prize student, then teaching at Exeter Academy, into the department, where his scholarship became the national touchstone for the study of Shakespeare. The field of fine arts was presided over by the scholarship of the exquisite Charles Eliot Norton.

The economics department, where Charles Francis Dunbar tended the votive candles to laissez-faire and free trade, would evoke Du Bois's dismissive comments in later years about "dying Ricardian economics," but the bedrock course, Political Economy 1, under recently arrived Frank William Taussig, never admitted a moment's doubt in the minds of students about the immutable laws of free enterprise. "Stinker" Taussig's 1911 textbook, *Principles of Economics*, would put a high gloss on the rough and ready practices of the nation's business and financial elites, becoming the canon for almost a generation.[22] Sociology was still a novel import (the enormously influential William Graham Sumner had taught the first course in it at Yale), and Harvard would eventually lag behind the new University of Chicago, then two years away from creation, and Columbia for a number of years.[23] Even so, under kindly Francis Greenwood Peabody, Plummer Professor of Christian Morals, Harvard men were prodded to consider what the social classes owed each other and what the causes and social implications of extreme wealth and poverty were. For Du Bois, whose admiration for Peabody would be helpfully reciprocated years afterward, such concerns were hardly the curious mental excursions most classmates found them. If Oswald Villard wrote his father that Harvard was "like sitting in a club window and watching the world go by," Du Bois expected much more in the way of real-world knowledge from the science of economics. Yet even he remained too much the convert of Bismarckian statecraft and Carlylian willpower to be inclined to draw radical conclusions about inequities in the "Triumphant Democracy" just then being gloriously described by Andrew Carnegie. "What the white world was doing, its goals and ideals," he criticized as deficient only in the degree to which they excluded people like himself.[24]

History, the department in which he would eventually take his advanced degrees, impressed him as distinguished but somewhat dull. Herbert Croly, Du Bois's classmate who was in and out of Harvard over a fourteen-year period before being awarded a bachelor's, found, as did Robert Lovett and others, that professors Edward Perkins Channing and Silas MacVane covered material easily found in the textbooks. The short, round, smooth-shaven Channing's course in early American institutions ticked along year after year while his near-genius was to flower only much later, yielding the prodigious six-volume *History of the United States (1905–25)*. MacVane's History 2, Constitutional Government in England and America, was now a husk of what it had been under the opinionated originality of Henry Adams. Its newest member, Albert Hart, would catapult the department into the twentieth century but was just then introducing his close-reading techniques of original documents in U.S. history, which Du Bois found, despite Hart's dryness, more and more interesting.[25] But none of the other departments and no other professor interested him more than philosophy and William James.

For Harvard men drawn to the humanities, the philosophy department usually proved irresistible. Sociology might flourish incomparably at Chicago, schools of history develop national sway at Johns Hopkins and Columbia, but Harvard remained synonymous with philosophy until the

Great War, the cradle and preceptor of its American incarnation. Harvard's senior light, Francis Bowen, Alford Professor of Natural Religion, Moral Philosophy and Civil Polity, now a year from retiring, had mentored Chauncey Wright, Charles Sanders Peirce, George Herbert Palmer, and William James himself, the latter two well embarked upon their legendary teaching careers when Du Bois arrived.[26] The delicate, hirsute Palmer, whose recent courtship of the president of Wellesley had given innocent spice to gossip in the Yard, was an engrossing classroom lecturer with more of a Platonic bias than a coherent philosophy. Philosophy 4, his always heavily subscribed, two-semester course, inaugurated what Palmer called "self-realization ethics," broad-gauge inquiry, independent of theology, into the means of approaching the ideal in personal and social conduct. For Palmer, Harvard's elective system was but the latest refinement in mankind's everlasting experiment in self-realization. "Our Father in Heaven had been using the elective system long before we discovered it," he reminded college men.[27]

William James was an altogether different phenomenon. All energy in a well-built frame, a somewhat disorganized lecturer, he was notably available for advice and brainstorming, even for that era when professional solicitude toward students was the natural relationship, rather than the sometimes unavoidable one of later generations. His Logic and Psychology course played to packed lecture halls, with James encouraging fascinated students to talk him through proofs of the existence of the Deity, to argue over the nature of sensations and consciousness, the need for practical personal and social solutions ("live options"), the optimal balance between science and faith—all of it soon leading to the groundbreaking *Principles of Psychology* (1890) and *The Will to Believe* (1897). The empirical and psychological essentials of the Jamesian philosophy were already unmistakable, although the term "pragmatism" was a few years away from general currency. It was a lumping of philosophical temperaments into "tough-minded" and "tender-minded" categories, the testing of the "cash value" of ideas by demanding to know what concrete difference their being true makes in the real world, and an insistence that society must accommodate the plural, unsettling, competing interests of individuals ("Individualism is fundamental").[28] For James, arguments for the existence of God and the pursuit of ethics depended in the final analysis not on logic or evidence but on belief. "The question of having moral beliefs at all or not having them," he asserted, "is decided by our will." But it was the man, as much as the ideas, that made James's discipline much more appealing to Du Bois than the area of political science in which he had intended to concentrate.

The philosophy department's other monument (the "John L. Sullivan of philosophy," a student called him) was Josiah Royce from the mining town of Grass Valley, California, such an odd-looking man, with bowling-pin torso and pointed head fringed with red hair, that Mrs. Royce would startle Du Bois speechless at a student reception with the aside, " 'Funny-looking man, isn't he?' "[29] Royce was the academy's pillar of Philosophical Idealism, as certain of his ontological proof of the existence of the Absolute and of the grounding of morals in reciprocity as James was conditional and experimental in his ethical and theological beliefs. "All reality," *The Religious Aspect of Philosophy* (1885) affirmed, "must be present to the Unity of Infinite Thought." Summing up the argument with apposite metaphor, one modern academic critic wrote that Royce's "Absolute is the melody, we are the notes." Depression and insomnia in the wake of completing *The Religious Aspect of Philosophy*, followed by a major history of California, along with a forgettable novel about that state, required Royce to take leave during the spring of 1888 for a cruise to Australia. He returned in time for Du Bois's first semester, "as fresh as a new born babe," James said.

Du Bois wrote of Royce's influence in general rather than specific or personal terms because his actual course work and contact with the philosopher must have been minimal. Perhaps the muted influence had something to do with the fact that Royce was a disaster in his dealings with students outside the classroom. Absorbed in Olympian contemplations, rolling out of his house with Mrs. Royce hurrying behind waving his clip-on tie, the future professor of History of Philosophy was usually incapable of holding an informal conversation. He knew so much about the Absolute, Santayana wickedly said, "that he has forgotten what individual consciousness is like." In terms of intellectual temperament, though, Royce's Hegelianism, with its insistence upon Absolute Truth behind the universe, the evolving unity of mankind, the Kantian certainty that humanity sensed the need to be loyal to the highest morals, and even his vague concern about race relations might have seemed to have had irresistible appeal for Du Bois—more so than Jamesian pragmatism.[30]

As Royce receded for Du Bois, Santayana stepped forward. Santayana had lived with his Boston Sturgis mother during his undergraduate years, spending summers in Spain with his reclusive father, a former governor in the Spanish Philippines who had retired to Avila. A founder of the *Lampoon* and the *Harvard Monthly*, Santayana had graduated Phi Beta Kappa and summa cum laude in 1886. In September 1888, encouraged by James, he returned to Cambridge from European graduate studies to complete his doctorate, entering the philosophy department as instructor the following year. President Eliot's espousal of academic electives by no means extended to elective sex, and he brooded over the possibility that James's Spanish-born recruit was "abnormal." Santayana's senior colleague, Palmer, worried more about his teaching, which he thought to be lacking in the young philosopher's first years. It was Santayana's hint of decadence and his disengaged and stylish approach that won students. The affectation of indifference was much in vogue among men of the college, and the cold, brilliant, skeptical young instructor with a "curious Latin beauty about him physically" (he was not yet bald when Hutchins Hapgood first saw him) excited interest, loyalty, and the titillating, cerebral homoeroticism often just below the surface in all-male environments.[31] Max Eastman found him "dangerously fascinating." Santayana's empiricism was of the radical kind, in which an idea was no more true than a sensation was demonstrably real—beyond the undeniable fact that they were both the stuff of conscious existence.

This was not how Du Bois saw philosophy. However shaken in his religious faith and skeptical of moral abstractions, he was an idealist by temperament, always believing that it was possible, somehow, to get from the world's welter—observed phenomena—to the bedrock of principles—upper-case Truth. Once again, philosophical principles were less important in the instructor-student bond than the personality of the philosopher. Well connected socially, but not an authentic Puritan, the snobbish, swarthy Santayana, though infinitely more at home in the Cambridge milieu than it was possible for Du Bois to be, was still subtly, slightly an outsider. Royce was the peerless authority on Kant, but when Du Bois and Santayana read the *Critique of Pure Reason* together ("he and I alone, in an upper room") as undergraduate and graduate scholars, the undergraduate's lifelong memory of that experience may have been enhanced by a fleeting moment when each man recognized in the other something of his own anomalous situation.[32] Du Bois, along with Croly, the Hapgoods, and Lovett, took the first courses taught by Santayana. Over the next decade or so, they would be followed by Bronson Cutting, Witter Bynner, T. S. Eliot, Conrad Aiken, Max Eastman, Van Wyck Brooks, Robert Frost, and Alain Locke.[33]

A euphoric confidence made Du Bois remarkably casual about competing with classmates who had already absorbed two years of Harvard. He "burned no midnight oil," he wrote. Instead, he followed a precise routine of work that would have impressed Kant. Harvard residence halls in Du Bois's day had no running water; Hemenway Gymnasium was the place to take a hot shower at the start of the day: "Rising at 7:15 and breakfast. Work from 8–12:30. Lunch. Work from 1–4. From 4–5 I go to the gymnasium. 5–5:30 I take a breathing spell. 5:30–7, dinner and daily paper. 7–10:30 study or lectures or social visits, etc." This was to be pretty much the itinerary for the remainder of his life, minus trips to the gymnasium. It was a regimen that produced good results, especially in the sciences, where he racked up A's in Chemistry 3, under H. B. Hill; in Natural History 4a, a half-year laboratory course under Harris; and in Natural History 8, under Shaler and Davis. The second-semester course, Political Economy 9, Constitutional and Legal History of England to the 16th Century, under Charles Gross, yielded an A–, Du Bois's comprehensive, analytical, and very detailed "Report on the German Railway System" signaling his rapidly maturing scholarly prowess. His senior-year performance in History 13, Constitutional and Political History of the United States, was superlative, earning a final A+ from the demanding Albert Hart.[34]

The weak spot in the first year, surprisingly, was English composition—almost his "Waterloo at Harvard." He received the first failing grade of his life on a paper ("I was aghast"). English C, Forensics, under Messrs. Thompson and Baker, was the one compulsory course still required of all degree candidates, the reasonable rationale being that while they might elect their subjects, all Harvard men must be able to write about them in the Queen's English. The sheer number of Tuesday and Thursday assignments necessitated parceling the essays out to any number of faculty members in and out of the department. The luck of the draw put Du Bois's essay in the merciless hands of the just-arrived George Kittredge, who exploded in "Egad!"s at the top and bottom of it, only simmering down to pen lengthier marginalia after scolding the author for not writing "upon regular forensic paper with margins for comments."[35]

The topic of the offending essay, which Du Bois mistakenly remembered as a rebuttal of a magazine piece by an Alabama senator, was in fact a nineteen-page cartwheeling counterattack upon Louisiana Senator James B. Eustis's article in the October *Forum* claiming that the granting of the franchise to African-Americans had been a mistake. If African-Americans were naturally inferior rather than historically disadvantaged, then how explain, Du Bois asked, that the senator's distant ancestors had "preferred to squat in the caves and fens of Northern Europe rather than to come out into the glorious noontide of the most wonderful of the world's ages, since they had had 'equal advantages with the [Greek] race' "? Not even the forceful reasoning and apt historical parallels (evoking a surprised "fine writing" from Kittredge on page five), could save this essay. Although his stirring appeals to history and democracy foretold the themes of Du Bois's several books about Africa (and Africa in the mind of Europe), what Kittredge saw in that December 3 effort was E work—failure, and a just admonition that "By trying to put too much into one sentence, you confuse your ideas." The final C in English C, a two-semester course, damaged his class ranking, but it also spurred Du Bois to do better in English D under Thompson and Baker as a senior (a final B), and risk Barrett Wendell's English 12 in his first year of graduate studies.[36]

According to Du Bois, he was "repeatedly a guest in the house of William James." There is circumstantial confirmation for the claim not only in a vividly recalled trip the two of them made to Roxbury one day in 1892 to visit the deaf-mute Helen Keller at the Perkins Institute for the Blind but also in the exchange of letters after Du Bois left Harvard. James's penchant for unusual personalities was well known to his colleagues, later provoking from Palmer the mild censure that his cultivation of the "underdog, and his insistence on keeping the door open for every species of human experiment, sometimes brought James into alliance with causes his social set looked on with disfavor." Santayana, one of those exotic personalities himself, spoke archly of James's fondness for "lame ducks and neglected possibilities." In Du Bois's case, James might have been particularly predisposed to befriend a young Negro from the Berkshires because of his own brother's service as an officer with the 54th Infantry Regiment, the famous black Massachusetts unit Wilky James had fought with and survived at Fort Wagner.[37] James was indisputably Du Bois's passport to the Harvard Philosophical Club, founded about 1878 and a collateral descendant of what had been in the early 1870s probably the most fecund intellectual circle in the United States, the amorphous Metaphysical Club.

The Philosophical Club, unlike the Metaphysical Club and its immediate successors, was closed to amateurs outside the university, and so reflected the growing professionalization of knowledge at the close of the nineteenth century. The club kept no records, so, aside from a brief note from James to Du Bois about a "philosophical supper on Saturday, Feb 14th," we have only Du Bois's claim that he was something of a regular, (going "very methodically").[38] But even if only an occasional invitee, the impact upon a serious, socially isolated undergraduate of philosophizing with Palmer, Royce, James, and Santayana can be imagined. But James had a realistic opinion of the value of philosophy as a livelihood—as a general rule, don't try it. When he had advised Santayana as an undergraduate not to become a philosopher, he probably did so as a test of commitment. This same advice to Du Bois proved a turning point in a life. No man without independent means, certainly not a man dedicating his life to programmatic uplift of a disadvantaged race, should become a philosophy professor, James told Du Bois in his senior year, advice Professor Chase at Fisk had also volunteered. But until then, admiration for the "keen analysis of William James, Josiah Royce, and young George Santayana" drew Du Bois deeper into what he eventually saw as the "lovely but sterile land of philosophic speculation."[39]

Du Bois was taken seriously (whatever neo-abolitionist motives were at play) because he took the life of the mind so seriously. Harvard professors were, as he keenly appreciated, "glad to receive a serious student, to whom extra-curricular activities were not of paramount importance." His philosophy professors recognized the exceptional depth of his interest, his quest for truth and the ethics derived from it. At Fisk, philosophy had essentially been presented as another way of grappling with theological concerns—all Platonic ideals and incontrovertible moral facts; reason was the handmaiden of revelation. At Harvard, Du Bois began to understand the limitations of such traditional philosophizing, as the distinctions and conflicts between what James called "tender-minded" idealism (belief in absolutes) and "tough-minded" realism (reliance upon science) became much clearer. If the gentle, pious Palmer had served as his initial conductor, Du Bois's philosophical instruction would have resumed at the juncture where Cravath and Spence had left it. Because Palmer was on sabbatical leave during academic year 1888–89, however, Philosophy 4 was taught by James, who hurried into the Yard from his New Hampshire summer retreat having, he confessed to a friend, only begun "systematic reading in that line three weeks ago."[40]

Using "that dear old duffer" James Martineau's *Types of Ethical Theory* as the textbook (Martineau was an English Unitarian who searched for nonbiblical justification for belief in God), James's lecture notes suggest a road map being drawn up as the conductor charged freewheelingly into new, occasionally divergent, directions.[41] On the one hand, he marshaled his extensive knowledge of medicine and neurology to show how much that was supposedly rational in reality sprang from psychological and even physiological energies. No belief or act, he said, was to be exempted from rigorous scientific scrutiny; nothing that ran against the grain of practical implementation was to be accepted solely on appeal to tradition or emotion. Yet, on the other hand, James would come to assert the validity of religious experience and the reality of God—the "reality of the unseen"—on intuitive grounds that without them men and women experience "a sense that there is *something wrong about us* as we naturally stand." Social Darwinism, with its Spencerian "laws" of efficient, organic social integration through the universal mechanism of "survival of the fittest," was then ascendant in philosophy. Partly in reaction to such cosmic dogma, as well as reflecting his own muscular temperament, James celebrated freewheeling willpower and real-world advantages as the ultimate sources and sanctions of ethical conduct. In a famous parody of Spencer's arcane definition of evolution, James said that evolution was "a change from a nohowish, untalkaboutable, all alikeness to a somehowish and in general talkaboutable, not-all-alikeness by continuous stick-to-getherations and something elsifications." In its effort to mediate between the "tender" and the "tough," Jamesian pragmatism was the very antithesis of system and, to its critics, even of coherence. Santayana, who tracked his senior colleague's arguments, respected his "masculine directness, his impressionistic perceptions" but finally decided, waspishly, that James "started without caring where he went. In fact, he got nowhere."[42]

Wherever James was heading, Du Bois's left-handed lecture notes indicate that he gave clear instructions at the Philosophy 4 starting post that first week. "Man spontaneously *believes* and spontaneously *acts*," he told the class. "But as acts and beliefs multiply they grow inconsistent. To escape *bellum omnium contra omnes* (the war of all against all), reasonable principles, fit for all to agree upon, must be sought." It was this search, according to James, that constituted philosophy, with its two subdivisions of science ("the principles of *fact* or what *is*, whether good or bad") and ethics ("what is good or bad, whether it be or be not)."[43] The learned President Cravath had certainly entertained no such experimental and consensual view of moral philosophy; the novelty of James's approach was enormously exciting. Du Bois confronted the ancient problem of justifying what ought to be from what is, of finding a bridge between the normative and the descriptive, with such laserlike intensity that he must have hoped to pierce the conundrum in Gore Hall, the college's uncrowded library, or in the upstairs room in Flagg Street. "While I think a Science of Ethics possible," one of his Philosophy 4 blue books hypothesized, "I cannot see the way to it clearly."[44]

By the end of the second semester, though, he believed he might be about to crack one of philosophy's great perennials—justification of moral conduct through empirical observation. The result was a fifty-two-page handwritten essay, "The Renaissance of Ethics: A Critical Comparison of Scholastic and Modern Ethics." Despite a few solecisms and much dense writing, eliciting from James marginal comments such as "obscurely put," and "a little too compact to be clear," Du Bois's offering made a favorable impression on his idol. As a history of ideas, the third-year student's essay demonstrated enormous learning; as a treatise on ethics dependent upon logical clarity, however, some portions of it are as impenetrable as others are engrossing.[45] The essay audaciously dismissed modern metaphysics "from Kant to Royce" as no better than that of the "scientific" Scholastics Peter Abelard and William of Occam because, in becoming alienated from science, it had abandoned the splendid goal of the unity of knowledge. But there was error aplenty on the "tough" side, Du Bois continued. Having liberated itself from metaphysics after the seventeenth century, science had forged ahead via discovery and invention to make sense of the physical realm, yet it had chosen to abjure the higher objective of the unity of knowledge. The study of ethics had added to the confusion by becoming decoupled from both metaphysics and science.

Du Bois proceeded to formulate a way out for James and himself. It was through duty. The "fundamental question of the Universe, for ages, past, present, and to come" involved duty, he contended. Not, however, the duty of the *summum bonum*, the highest good, "as Scholastic and most Moslem ethical philosophers would say." Du Bois defined duty in relativist terms as the obligation to know "how much better is the best that can be than the worst?" eliciting "Good! first rate!" from James.[46] "The Renaissance of Ethics" asserted that "the whole purpose of duty hangs upon the Cause and Purpose of this great drama we call life," and to understand "duty we must know Ends." But knowledge of ends brought Du Bois squarely up against the dilemma that had led to the separation of metaphysics and science in the first place. Put another way, the problem was simply the logical impossibility of moving from the realm of matter (or what is) to the realm of spirit (or what ought to be). Determined to make modern ethics do a better job of guiding social and individual conduct, Du Bois foundered in a large patch of conceptual yeast for several bewildering pages. Emerging from his expository ordeal, he could do no better than to lay down a rule that "a man must have a life-work on the fulfilling of which depends his hope of the life to come." With James observing "too oracular and ambiguous," and "all becomes obscure here," Du Bois's essay pressed doggedly onward: "The fact that a science of ethics today is not possible for lack of facts upon which to base it ought not to hinder ethical conduct." Ethical science will come slowly, fallibly, Du Bois contended, if the "cornerstone of the world structure," guided by science, becomes "first the what, then the why—underneath the everlasting Ought."[47]

Without yet realizing it, Du Bois, for all his admiration of William James and his debt to him in the realm of ideas ("my friend and guide to clear thinking"), showed in "The Renaissance of Ethics" that the wills to believe of Du Bois and James diverged sharply. The instructor was reconciled to making the best of things in a world of unprovable ultimates. The student was unwilling to concede the future to trial and error leading to everlasting trial and error—to, as James is quoted as saying in Du Bois's lecture notes, living " 'under the sword of the future.' " For all its complexity and confusion, Du Bois's essay was also intriguingly similar to solutions to the perennial matter-mind puzzle worked out in Marx's *Kapital* and, especially, Friedrich Engels's then-untranslated, polemical *Anti-Duhring*. Had Marx and Engels been part of the Harvard bibliography of the day, James's student could have discovered that Philosophy 4 brought him close to the epistemology upon which the new dialectical materialism rested. Because mind was immanent in nature, Marx and Engels maintained that the structure and laws of the world became revealed through manipulation (engagement) of the forces of nature. Essentially, "The Renaissance of Ethics" waveringly arrived at the same conclusion: ethical imperatives arose out of the interaction of mind and matter as both became transformed and purposive through willpower.[48]

The marginalia accompanying James's grade (A) pronounced "The Renaissance of Ethics" a "very original thesis, full of independent thought and vigorous [sic] expressed," but it was also the work of a man "who is yet feeling his way to clearness and has a great deal of extrication still to perform on his ideas." Finally, James asserted his bedrock conviction about the unbridgeable chasm between facts and ethical beliefs. "To me, that is impossible—we can only trust in its ends being what we sympathize with." The "extrication" James commended was never quite achieved, and this engrossing essay Du Bois filed away with his papers, deciding many years later, curiously, to turn it over to Yale University library. If anything, the philosophical distance between James and Du Bois would grow as the latter soon became committed to a program of finite investigation, incremental accumulation of data, and confidence that that unity of knowledge and discovery of truth, behind or beyond mere contingency of which he wrote in his Philosophy 4 essay, was, with perseverance and intellect, possible. But by the end of his first year, Du Bois had progressed far beyond the vague transcendentalism of Great Barrington and the elaborate moral tautologies of Nashville. Thanks to James, he had been guided "out of the sterilities of scholastic philosophy to realist pragmatism"—or so he believed.[49]

At this distance, James's imprint on Du Bois is somewhat less distinct than some recent students of ideas have believed. In a general sense, the professor's extolling of a pluralistic society, robust espousal of democracy, opposition to imperialism, and hostility to religious and racial intolerance shaped his student's views of politics and society—especially as these positions were accompanied by a natural aristocrat's flattering accessibility and unconcern for posturing. James's ideas and demeanor contrasted strikingly with those of such popular professors as Shaler, Wendell, or Charles Eliot Norton, each of whom variously displayed an aversion to the rise of popular culture and majority rule. Wendell would serve up his cultural and political credo soon after Du Bois left Harvard in *The Privileged Classes*, a work of exquisite snobbery. But to what extent, if at all, the insights in James's *Principles of Psychology* were the source of Du Bois's own special insights into what he would describe as the double nature of the African-American psyche remains highly ambiguous. Du Bois probably did hear James expound on the neurological and epiphenomenal nature of mind; certainly he would have read his favorite professor's groundbreaking book soon after publication, in which suggestive terms such as "alternating selves" and "primary and secondary consciousness" appeared. Through James, he may have had his awareness of the already large body of medical and psychological literature about schizophrenia heightened. The very term Du Bois was to employ in his most famous work, *The Souls of Black Folk*—"double consciousness"—had been used to characterize mental disturbance in a case study in which James was a consultant. That said (and with more to be said later), the irreducible fact that Du Bois's existence, like that of other men and women of African descent in America, amounted to a lifetime of being "an outcast and a stranger in mine own house," as he would write, was a psychic purgatory fully capable by itself of nurturing a concept of divided consciousness, whatever the Jamesian influences.[50]

It was easier for Du Bois to get good grades than it was to find money to stay in Harvard. It seemed he was not going to last out the year without it. Prospects for getting the legacy that would come with the settlement of Grandfather Alexander's estate were still dim ("for lack of exact data concerning my father's death," he revealed). Winning the fifty-dollar Boylston

Prize for oratory would help considerably, and Fisk debating experience was a considerable asset.[51] Du Bois would be competing against the other African-American in Harvard College, Clement Morgan, who was almost ten years older than himself. Morgan was the son of Virginia slaves who had taken him to Washington, D.C., during the Civil War, where he eventually completed secondary education at the excellent M Street "Colored" public high school. After four years of teaching and barbering in St. Louis, he came east, investing his savings, while still barbering, in a Boston Latin School education. In the fall of 1886, twenty-seven-year-old Morgan was admitted to Harvard College. He and Du Bois took to each other, remaining somewhat close friends and civil rights allies until Morgan's death in 1929. "A pleasant, unassuming person," Morgan was "fairly well received" by his classmates, Du Bois recalled.[52] Morgan's academic record was not as strong as Du Bois's; he was by no means an intellectual, but when it came to the spoken word it was said that few, if any, of his classmates could excel him. In the second semester, 1889, Morgan and Du Bois made history in the college theater by taking first and second Boylston Prizes, respectively. Presumably, Du Bois adhered to the theory of forensics, carefully developed at Fisk, which called for blending "every gesture and position" so well that the audience forgot the speaker "in contemplation of his ideas"; but what he said however has been lost beyond retrieval.[53]

What was significant was that Du Bois made his classmates much more aware of his presence, although they were probably not especially charmed by it. Unlike the affable Morgan, or the wealthy William Monroe Trotter, a cocky Bostonian about to enter Harvard, Du Bois was never capable of mixing comfortably with his white classmates. The few efforts he made left bruises. There was the glee club rejection his first year and mention of other club rebuffs. He would have given his eyeteeth to write for the *Harvard Monthly* but was certain that the editors "were not interested in [his] major interests." He did take meals regularly at the nonexclusive Foxcroft Club, and very occasionally he stopped to chat with Hutchins Hapgood, Augustus Hand, or Robert Herrick in the Yard. He claimed in the *Autobiography* that he was closest to Robert Morss Lovett, a future *New Republic* editor, of all the white undergraduates who were invariably taken aback by what seemed to them gratuitous *hauteur*. Lovett, a freshman, had met Du Bois in Shaler's class. After the upper classman's Boylston celebrity, Lovett had sought his friendship, and the two of them hiked as far as the dunes of Quincy several times. Fifty years later, Lovett believed that he had not bothered to think of Du Bois "as a Negro until the double victory of himself and Morgan called attention to the preeminence of that race in one aspect of eloquence." Lovett's relationship, such as it was at the time, was exceptional. Du Bois, for his part, was so quick to anticipate condescension that chance interracial encounters usually fizzled.[54]

From the post–civil rights perspective of the late twentieth century, his spiky relations with white peers may appear to have been symptomatic of a morbid hypersensitivity. Harvard was more of a mirage than an oasis of racial benevolence, but the Anglo-Saxon Protestant goodwill of its president and much of the faculty was high-mindedly genuine. The place was saturated by snobbery, certainly, with some of the most egregious acts of social and racial superciliousness committed by professors rather than students. Yet, as the Harvard experiences of Morgan and Trotter testify (as well as those of other African-Americans in eastern colleges), cordial relations, if not many deep friendships, did develop. Moreover, to a significant degree difficult to measure, Du Bois's behavior at Harvard should also be understood as a defensiveness stemming from tensions of class and culture, rather than solely from racial sensitivities. He was not unique in his feelings of being something of an outsider. Entering Harvard as an undergraduate after three years at Emporia College in Kansas, Vernon Lane Parrington, class of 1893, was sharply disconcerted by the snobbery of the Yard. "I could have made friends had I tried," the future progressive historian snapped in a manner reminiscent of Du Bois, "but I didn't try, being as proud and independent as I was poor." Thirteen years later, Walter Lippmann would arrive from New York, impeccably educated and equipped with a small library, a dozen tailored suits, and two tennis rackets, only to be astonished to find, says his biographer, that he couldn't "scale the social peaks at Harvard as easily as at Sachs [School for Boys]."[55]

And yet, the fact that he was a young black man endowed with such acute social insight did make Du Bois's lot a great deal harder than that experienced by other outsiders who were white—religion, economic background, or small-town formation notwithstanding. He saw himself as driven into lonely defensiveness by the times. He was not one to be deceived by surface civility or to turn a resigned or placatory face to institutional discrimination. Indignation—constant, intellectualized, and eloquently verbalized—must have been regarded by him as the only face worthy of being presented to a white society whose philanthropy was at best incidental and capricious, and at worst serving increasingly to segregate and emasculate his race. The new northern wisdom in race relations counseled the sons and daughters of the abolitionists that it was unrealistic to expect

African-Americans to measure up fully to obligations of citizenship, that it was both kinder and more expedient to entrust them to solutions devised by the white South. During Du Bois's graduation year, the Mississippi legislature had rewritten the state's constitution to eliminate the black voter. The decade of the nineties would see a rash of articles and books about the "Negro Problem," a few of them compassionate but the majority arraigning the race as the cause of its own suffering. Some, like the inflammatory fiction (*The Leopard's Spots*) of the unstable Baptist preacher Thomas Dixon, Jr., and the merciless findings (*Race Traits and Tendencies of the American Negro*) of the Prudential insurance statistician Dr. Frederick L. Hoffmann, virtually prescribed the race's extinction. Nor had Du Bois to await the incoming tide of Negrophobic titles in order to gauge the erosion of national support for his people. Edwin Lawrence Godkin, the transplanted Anglo-Irish editor, had already repeatedly sounded the retreat of northern white liberalism throughout the seventies and eighties in the pages of *The Nation*.[56]

And from the pen of kindly old Nathaniel Shaler, the same professor who had expelled from his class the southern boor who refused to sit next to Du Bois, had come a widely read *Atlantic Monthly* piece, in 1884, predicting the relapse into barbarism of African-Americans now removed from the tutelage of their slave masters. Fifteen years later, although not so certain of Shaler's hypothesis, Albert Hart's *The Southern South* concluded that the experience of the race in the North "leads rather to negative than to positive conclusions as to their intellectual and moral power." If Du Bois seemed paranoid, he had reason to believe his enemies were everywhere and numerous. Harvard must have nurtured those biting, bitter insights that would explode a few years later in the pages of *Atlantic Monthly, Dial, The Outlook*, and, like a supernova, in *The Souls of Black Folk*. " 'How does it feel to be a problem?', they say," one such essay would parody. " 'I know an excellent colored man in my town; or, I fought at Mechanicsville; or Do not these Southern outrages make your blood boil?' At these I smile, or am interested, or reduce the boiling to a simmer, as the occasion may require." Du Bois's state of mind in his senior year is revealed in a letter to George Washington Cable, the white novelist and racial liberal who had relocated to Massachusetts from his native Louisiana. Cable's denunciation of the "New South" gospel being effectively propagated in the North by southern white supremacists was widely reported in the newspapers. "In the midst of so much confusion and misapprehension," Du Bois wrote on February 23, 1890, "the clear utterance and moral heroism of one man, is doubly welcome to the young Negro who is building a Nation."[57]

Fortunately, there was a world beyond Harvard. The Boylston Prize competition gave its two winners the idea of offering public readings in Connecticut and Massachusetts that summer for money. Well received in Great Barrington, luck stayed with them as they traveled through eastern Massachusetts. Du Bois and Morgan returned to Cambridge with about two hundred dollars between them, and, to his relief, Du Bois found himself awarded a three-hundred-dollar Matthews Scholarship. Before the end of the year, he would reenter the Boylston competition, determined not to "take less than a first prize," which he would. His money problems well in hand, he drew up a list of advance courses, demanding even for a confident senior who was regarded by many of his classmates as a "grind."[58] There was Francis Peabody's Philosophy 11, Ethics of Social Reform, meeting Tuesday and Thursday. Peabody's religiously tinged social-reform ideas Du Bois found somewhat quaint, but the Boston Brahmin's racial integrity impressed him. English D, Forensics, met on the same days as Ethics of Social Reform. History 13, Constitutional and Political History of the United States, met under Hart on Tuesday, Thursday, and Saturday; Political Economy 1, with MacVane and Taussig, early Monday, Wednesday, and Friday; Philosophy 6, Earlier French Philosophy from Descartes to Leibniz and German Philosophy from Kant to Hegel, under Santayana Monday, Wednesday, and Friday at 11:00 A.M.; and Philosophy 2, Logic and Psychology, under James on Monday, Wednesday, and Friday at noon. His work under Peabody, Hart, and MacVane and Taussig was excellent, a string of A's.[59]

Du Bois graduated cum laude on June 25, 1890, with a concentration in philosophy. The class of 1890 majority had already broken dramatically with the traditional Brahmin monopoly of class offices by selecting Clement Morgan as class-day orator that year. Morgan played his part to the hilt in the finest nineteenth-century rhetorical style, establishing a tradition for a number of years in white colleges and universities of selecting African-Americans as class orators. The selection of Du Bois as one of the six student commencement orators was intended as another signal of the university's evolution into a national institution (Greener had been the first African-American to hold the honor).[60] As President Eliot and his platform guests, Mrs. Grover Cleveland, the governor of Massachusetts, and the Episcopal bishop of New York among others, watched, a slender student mounted the platform in Sanders Theatre with an almost unmistakable self-possession and began his memorized address, "Jefferson Davis as Representative of Civilization." As Du Bois shifted quickly into high gear, it was as though the audience had been instantly hitched to a fast, new-model locomotive. Astonished applause exploded when he finished in less than ten minutes.[61]

The Fisk commencement speech served as model, the president of the Confederacy substituting for the chancellor of the Second Reich. Modern conditions, Du Bois urged, desperately called for a new model to complement the millennial primacy of the Strong Man as represented by Davis. "Under whatever guise . . . as race, or as nation, his life can only logically mean . . . the advance of a part of the world at the expense of the whole," he explained; or, clearly echoing Royce, "the overwhelming sense of the I, and the consequent forgetting of the Thou." As counterforce to the Teutonic Strong Man, he proposed the Submissive Man, of whom there was no better incarnation than the Negro. "The Teutonic met civilization and crushed it," the Sanders Theatre Teutons heard. "The Negro met civilization and was crushed by it." Jefferson Davis must be checked by the "cringing slave," the blond beast by the Christlike Negro, the people of rugged individualism and private gain by a people animated by an idea of "submission apart from cowardice, laziness or stupidity, such as the world never saw before." Du Bois foretold a better world emerging from the dialectical struggle between Strong Man and Submissive Man, ending his commencement speech with the supplication, "You owe a debt to humanity for this Ethiopia of the Outstretched Arm."[62]

Bishop Potter of New York trotted out of the auditorium enthusiastic about Du Bois's "brilliant and eloquent address." " 'Here is what an historic race can do if they have a clear field, a high purpose, and a resolute will,' " he was quoted as saying in the Boston *Herald*. *The Nation* said the young scholar handled his "difficult and hazardous subject with absolute good taste, great moderation, and almost contemptuous fairness." The periodical *Kate Field's Washington* hailed the speech as "a ten-strike" and dubbed Du Bois "star of the occasion," polishing off its enthusiasm with an amazingly prescient judgment, to be fulfilled forty-five years later: "No history of the Civil War will be worth reading, saving as fiction, until . . . the spirit of [Horace] Greeley and Du Bois inspires its writer." Leonora Bowers spoke for a growing number of African-Americans that Du Bois was beginning to inspire, writing in her Fisk circular letter of being proud "to be able to tell persons that he was a classmate of mine." If "Jefferson Davis as Representative of Civilization" was fully as bold and brilliant as its commentators claimed, it remained entangled, nevertheless, in nineteenth-century racialist conceptions that would bedevil its author for many years afterward. It also showed a normally pugnacious Du Bois calibrating his message to flatter as carefully as any address ever given by Booker T. Washington before a white audience.[63]

About three months before his graduation fame, Du Bois had petitioned the Harvard Academic Council for scholarship assistance to pursue the Ph.D. in social science, with a view, he wrote, "to the ultimate application of its principles to the social and economic rise of the Negro people." The topic of his dissertation was already clearly enough formulated to share with Fisk classmates in the lengthy November circular letter—"The Suppression of the African Slave Trade in America," although the preposition *to* would soon supplant *in*. Philosophy, his first love, had receded. Although he was probably right to follow James's recommendation against philosophy as a career because of practical considerations, there may have been another, albeit secondary, reason. "He used to give me A's and even A-plus," the *Autobiography* is quick to observe. In fact, after the A− in Philosophy 4, grades in his major field dropped to B during the senior year: B+ in James's Logic and Psychology; B from Santayana in Earlier French Philosophy. Compared to the superlative undergraduate record of Santayana or Ralph Barton Perry (shortly to join the department), Du Bois's performance in philosophy was merely impressive, and an impecunious African-American scholar who was merely impressive as a philosopher would have been merely a modest contributor to the struggles of his emergent people, thus depriving them of the cogent guidance he could render in the needier fields of the social sciences.[64]

Whether racism, subtle or unconscious, played any part in his instructors' evaluations is a question that must be raised, even though, from what is known, it cannot be adequately answered. Hart and Shaler published deeply disturbing views on the alleged racial retardation of African-Americans, but Du Bois's history and science grades were uniformly excellent. Nor are there any revealing asides from the philosophers in either published or private sources. Du Bois is not mentioned in anything written by Santayana, unless it is implicit in the reference to James's "love of lame ducks and neglected possibilities." James lauded Du Bois publicly a few years later and gave him a letter of introduction to his brother Henry in England. Finally, and most instructively, Du Bois never made such a charge. It seems not unfair, then, to suggest that Du Bois may have abandoned philosophy on the grounds of aptitude, as well as practicality.[65]

The Academic Council was so impressed by his proposal that it surprised Du Bois by awarding him a Henry Bromfield Rogers Memorial Fellowship of $450 almost immediately for graduate study in social science the following year. Albert Hart had recommended him as showing "distinct ability." At about the same time, a bearer of one of New England's most distinguished names, James Bradley Thayer, recent successor of Oliver Wendell Holmes to the Weld Professorship of Law, had written an unsolicited letter endorsing Du Bois's candidacy. A former pupil, now president of Atlanta University, had brought Du Bois's merits to Thayer's attention. Thayer suggested that Harvard might owe "some special favorable consideration" in light of the "benevolent and patriotic ends" to which Du Bois proposed to dedicate his life.[66]

WITH WHAT was left of his four-hundred-dollar inheritance from Grandfather Alexander and the guarantee of a graduate stipend, and "feeling rich and tired," for the first time in his life Du Bois spent a summer trying to learn to relax. Consequently, as he wrote his Fisk friends, he didn't have "a very pleasant time," although he says he ate more than enough and made lots of friends. Exactly what he did that graduation summer, and with whom, is mostly a blank. It is significant, though, that he spent time with brother Adelbert in Albany, New York, and somehow (at least briefly) even "had a good time there."[67] Whatever he did, he must have been generally enjoying himself more than his Fisk letter admitted. By now, there were socially prominent persons in Boston's African-American community who found it simply unthinkable that a Harvard Man, and especially an overnight sensation (even one as occasionally snappish as Du Bois), should remain in prickly isolation in Flagg Street, the Philosophical Club, or the college library. He knew something of this society already, very probably thanks to the affable Clement Morgan; but from the chronology of social high moments beginning to unfold after his graduation, it's improbable that, while he was an undergraduate, Du Bois was as much at the center of Boston's affluent African-American activities as he remembered half a century afterward in *Dusk of Dawn*. Even without burning late-night oil, his undergraduate academic regimen left only so much time for amusement. And an impecunious, supersensitive Du Bois, bearing a negligible Great Barrington pedigree, would have been disinclined to risk his ego among what was then the most preening, self-satisfied collection of black folk in America. Becoming an integral part of Boston's ancient, inbred African-American community during his first year of graduate studies was as transforming in its own way as the Harvard curriculum. Once accepted into it, he found an enclave where he was welcome "without reservations and annoying distinctions."[68]

Among the city's nearly six thousand African-Americans no more than a few dozen families possessed real influence or wealth in the eyes of white Boston. And even they were beginning to lose their footing in the early 1890s as the swift, post-Reconstruction tide of southern accommodation, immigrant competition, and reordered social priorities of the new corporate order rolled in. The days when Boston's chief merchant tailor, principal wigmaker, and prestige stationer were African-Americans, when Cambridge's exclusive Agassiz Grammar School was headed by gracious Maria Baldwin and Boston's Lying-in Hospital benefited from the resident expertise of Dr. Samuel Courtney of Harvard Medical School were already fading. The Progressive journalist Ray Stannard Baker wrote his investigative "color line" series on the North in 1907 when hardly anything more than a shell remained of it, but when Du Bois knew it in the faint afterglow of New England abolitionism, affluent black Boston was still healthy.[69]

That society was presided over by aristocratic Mrs. Josephine St. Pierre Ruffin, whose Virginia-freeborn husband, George Lewis Ruffin, an 1869 graduate of Harvard Law School, the first of his race, was briefly an elected member of the Massachusetts legislature and judge of the Boston Municipal Court at the time of his death in 1886. Mrs. Ruffin's roots branched into France, England, and Africa. She was a *très grande dame* and as white of complexion as it was possible to be and still be called a "Negro." Once, when a sympathetic Back Bay clubwoman confessed an abiding interest in Mrs. Ruffin's race, the latter asked grandly, "Which race?" She and her beautiful daughter "Birdie" held weekly court in Charles Street where high and mighty freeborn families—Grimkés, Pindells, Trotters, and others—regularly attended. There were literary evenings salted with the poetry of Browning (whose antecedents were widely believed to be "mixed") and musicales featuring Brahms or the Chevalier de St. Georges (about whose mixed antecedents there was no question).[70]

But Josephine Ruffin, with her beehive of white hair and grand ways, was more than a society hostess. Her politics were militant suffragette. She numbered among her white acquaintances Julia Ward Howe and Lucy Stanton. She thrust herself at the center of the national women's club movement, representing a network of African-American clubwomen at national conclaves, whether the ladies from the South liked it or not. She raised such a couth ruckus about full acceptance at the 1900 Milwaukee

General Federation of Women's Clubs that the *Chicago Tribune* called for her to be gaveled into silence: "Mrs. Ruffin belongs among her own people . . . among us she can create nothing but trouble."[71] Just as Du Bois was being welcomed into the Charles Street circle, Josephine Ruffin began publishing the *Courant*, a weekly newspaper of women's rights, civil rights, and informed opinion circulating far beyond Boston and soon to carry some of Du Bois's earliest literary effusions.[72] Nowhere does Du Bois suggest that Mrs. Ruffin's feminist politics influenced his own precocious views about the rights of women. Mary Silvina's son had already arrived at them independently by then, yet the distinguished personalities and articulate opinions he met in Charles Street may well have quickened and sharpened the positive views he had come to hold.

One thing Charles Street definitely sharpened was his amorous eye. Nellie, the young woman he dated during his senior year at Fisk, was now a slightly sad memory. Du Bois even admitted he felt just "a little ashamed" of the way he had treated her, although he claimed they parted as friends. He blamed his faithlessness on an "old habit of universal love-making," presumably dating from the summers in backcountry Tennessee. He was interested in Geraldine ("Deenie") Pindell, a quintessential mulatto with wispy blond hair and blue eyes whose noted uncle had led the successful fight in the 1850s to integrate Boston's public schools. They dated occasionally, but dapper Monroe Trotter from Hyde Park posed a clear and present danger destined to be fulfilled in marriage.[73] Then Maud Cuney from Galveston, Texas, entered the Charles Street circle.

She was in her early twenties, a "tall, imperious brunette, with gold-bronze skin, brilliant eyes and coils of black hair." Her father was irrepressible Norris Wright Cuney, until his political destruction and death in 1896 one of the most skillful, powerful African-American politicians in the United States. Republican national committeeman from Texas after 1884, Cuney delivered his people's vote with the expert flair of a broncobuster, for which his considerable reward was a presidential appointment as collector of customs at Galveston port. Maud's Levantine good looks came from both parents, her fine musical talent from her mother, and her head-high perseverance undoubtedly from her father. When Du Bois met her she was just beginning the pianoforte studies at the New England Conservatory of Music that would lead to an arduous career as teacher, folklorist, and music historian. Later, she would study under Emil Ludwig, a pupil of Anton Rubinstein. Her arrival in the fall of 1891 had occasioned something of a scandal when the school authorities unsuccessfully tried to exclude her from the conservatory's dormitory because of her race. She and Du Bois would remain much more than friends through the years of her companionable marriage to a well-connected black Bostonian until her death in 1936. "Du" (Maud's endearment) fell in love with her almost on sight, escorting her to Harvard social affairs and (he claims) asking her to marry.[74]

He found happiness with Maud in the Boston African-American community, release from the pressures and challenge to seek more than marginal social presence in white Cambridge. Yet there were, if not exceptions to the rule of ethnic clannishness, such temporary exemptions in the Yard as Clement Morgan and Monroe Trotter. Trotter entered the college in 1891, after being elected senior class president of his white high school and graduating with highest honors. He stood third in his Harvard class of 376 at the end of his first year. Domiciled in College House, active in the Wendell Phillips Club, organizer of the small but nettlesome Total Abstinence Club, first African-American junior Phi Beta Kappa, notorious about Cambridge as a speeding cyclist, Trotter made his Brahmin classmates notice, respect, and, to a degree far greater than Du Bois had ever conceived possible, accept him. Du Bois was practically bowled over by his confident gregariousness. He would "like to have known him and spoken to him," but the young Boston man scarcely appeared to notice the solitary Du Bois. "Colored students must not herd together, just because they were colored," Trotter told him, dashing off with his white friends and companions. "And they liked him," Du Bois recalled, just a bit wistfully. But then Trotter was nonpareil, inheriting a $20,000 fortune his freshman year from his father, the improbable James Monroe, Civil War lieutenant in the 55th Massachusetts, prominent Democrat in a race of reverent Republicans, and successor after the venerated Frederick Douglass to the plum appointment under Grover Cleveland of recorder of deeds of the District of Columbia.[75]

The Trotter family was remarkable among the remarkable families Du Bois got to know, like the Grimkés of overwhelmingly white Hyde Park, neighbors of the Trotters and also break-rank Democrats. The Grimké family patriarch, Archibald Henry, was the slave son of South Carolinian Henry Grimké (brother of Angelina and Sarah of abolitionist renown); he was Harvard Law School's second African-American graduate, a newspaper publisher, a prosperous law partner, and, under Grover Cleveland, the resourceful consul to the Dominican Republic.[76] At some point, Du Bois rediscovered a distant Boston cousin, apparently related through a marriage tie of Mary Silvina's sister, Lucinda. Eliza Ann Gardiner was a churchwoman of some means, active in the affairs of the AME Zion denomination, and frequently provided Sunday meals to her earnest young relative. Du Bois never forgot meeting in her home the spellbinding AME Zion orator and southern college president, Joseph Charles Price, who until his early death in 1893 was perhaps the only serious rival of Booker T. Washington for the mantle of paramount race spokesperson.[77]

With the remaining money from Grandfather Alexander's estate, Du Bois made quite a splash in Charles Street. His mood was expressed in another letter to Fisk classmates, where he spoke of sporting a "young but promising mustache," and of his rather crass intention to "get me a little wife" in three or four years. He accompanied a group on excursions in the bay, boating on the Charles, and round-robin visits to the handful of African-American students at other New England colleges. One of those visits was to attend the 1892 graduation of two Amherst men, William H. Lewis and George Forbes, classmates of Calvin Coolidge. Lewis, one of the best footballers in the Ivy League, joined Clement Morgan at Harvard Law the following year, played center for the university, kept up his friendship with Du Bois, Forbes, and Trotter until he had to choose between them and Booker T. Washington, and eventually became assistant attorney general of the United States under President Taft. The beautiful Elizabeth Baker went from Wellesley with Du and Maud, Monroe and Deenie, and the others to Amherst on that proud day, meeting Lewis, her future husband, for the first time.[78] In an issue of the *Crimson* from these days, Du Bois claimed there was a note about himself, the high-strutting scholar, and his Maud. All of these women appear to have had complexions light enough to permit them, had they wished, to "pass" for white. In fact, one of them attended Vassar under concealed racial identity. According to Du Bois, their light complexions ultimately proved a bar to his marrying one of them. "As a sheer matter of taste," he wrote later, "I wanted the color of my group to be visible"—a curious boast in light of his marriage to a woman whose physical characteristics were as racially ambiguous as the women in the Charles Street circle.[79] Gilding his prose as usual, he summed up Josephine Ruffin's realm beyond the Yard as the place where college-bred African-Americans "met and ate, danced and argued and planned a new world."[80]

Popular and comfortable as he was, it would have been out of character if Du Bois hadn't decided that the culture and civic-mindedness of Boston's black blue bloods needed improving. One Thanksgiving night, therefore, a cooperative (though not much entertained) audience sat through a performance of Aristophanes' *Birds* in Charles Street AME

Church. Distressed by how little his exclusive circle influenced the lives of the vast majority of Boston's African-Americans, who failed abysmally in his eyes to capitalize their considerable advantages, the Harvard graduate student sacrificed his "limited leisure" on another occasion to say a word "to the Negroes of Boston."[81] Far more than a word, "Does Education Pay?" his address to the city's National Colored League in early March 1891, ran to the equivalent of eighteen printed pages in Mrs. Ruffin's *Courant*. Harvard president Eliot was about to become a household name because of the "five-foot shelf of books" he would urge Americans to acquire in the service of broader intellectual culture. That evening Du Bois proposed a reading list in black history spanning the millennia 900 B.C. to A.D. 1900. He identified public institutions for cultural enhancement, illustrated the impact of science and philosophy on daily life, gently demolished the alibis and prejudices clung to by hardworking folk, foretold the inevitable decline of a race that lived an unexamined life, acknowledged his debt to Mary Silvina ("what I am is hers"), and repeatedly enjoined his audience to "get a liberal education." Booker T. Washington and his ideas in backwoods Alabama about vocational education were then barely known, but in his essay "Does Education Pay?" Du Bois anticipated the nub of their differences. "Never make the mistake of thinking that the object of being a man is to make a carpenter," he told Bostonians; "the object of being a carpenter is to be a man."[82]

Returning to Cambridge late one night from Boston shortly before graduation, Du Bois had had a memorable, chance encounter on a streetcar with another Harvard man. " 'There's nothing in which I am particularly interested!' " the latter blurted out after a few minutes' talk about careers. More than astonished, Du Bois wrote that he was "almost outraged to meet any human being of the mature age of 22 who did not have his life all planned before him." The anecdote sets the stage for Du Bois's final two years of precisely planned scholarship at Harvard. Bromfield Rogers fellows were required to submit annual progress reports. In Du Bois's case, there were two of them because he held the fellowship for a second year. Although he maintained the cordial relationship with James and was still attending Philosophical Club dinners, there were to be no more philosophy courses as he concentrated on history and political economy under Hart, Channing, and Taussig.[83] Half his time was spent in special research for History 20E under Hart for what would finally become the monumental *Suppression of the African Slave Trade to the United States of America, 1638–1870*; the balance was distributed over political economy, Roman law, early German history and institutions, and English 12. What the extant blue books and bound essays reveal is a common thread of robust analysis, a gutsy readiness on Du Bois's part to reshape large quantities of knowledge to make them fit into new conceptual containers. Undogmatic, intuitive, skeptical, his intellectual powers as a graduate student were arresting.[84]

Du Bois had done excellent undergraduate work under Taussig in political economy. When he wrote about Taussig's courses in the Marxist *Autobiography*, he may have been somewhat chagrined by how well he had done. There is more than a hint in his undergraduate work of the Harvard man's customary reverence for the iron laws of David Ricardo, English free trade, and of brutal, arcane "wages-fund" theory (funds for workers' wages after employers take their profits); but if he really suspected at that time that Harvard was becoming "rich and reactionary" because of men like Taussig, Du Bois's "The Free Coinage Controversy," an undergraduate paper written for Political Economy 1, was a plutocrat's delight, roundly denouncing as sophistry, dishonesty, and jingoism the popular platform of debt-ridden Populists and Silver Democrats that called for coinage of silver at a ratio of sixteen to every one ounce of gold. Not only did he plump for the gold standard in his Taussig essay, he deplored as "ignorant lawlessness" disruptions to business like those of the wave of railroad strikes in 1886.[85] The Texas railroad strikes beginning in March against Jay Gould's line had spread quickly into Missouri, Arkansas, and Kansas. Freight had come to a dead standstill throughout the Southwest. The ensuing violence in the industrial and rail center of East St. Louis, Illinois, seemed to many Americans to prefigure the long-dreaded civil war of labor against capital. The Knights of Labor, ballooning to seven-hundred-thousand strong, campaigned for an eight-hour workday and a national contract labor law. In May, the Knights supported the workers striking the McCormick Reaper Works in Chicago.

By late June 1886, the specter of a militant and mighty working class assailing the citadels of capital caused alarm among the Goulds, Carnegies, Morgans, and Pullmans, presenting them with splendid opportunities for provocation and repression. Haymarket, on June 28, was a turning point, and Du Bois appears to have applauded the swift, callous retribution of the forces of order after an anarchist's bomb, tossed from the packed crowd in the square, killed seven Chicago policemen. As Du Bois finished his graduate studies in 1892, the titanic struggle to reshape and consolidate the American economy—the Search for Order to some historians or, perhaps more validly, the Triumph of Conservatism to others—began in bloody earnest with the Pinkerton carnage at the Homestead steelworks near Pittsburgh and in the copper mines at Coeur d'Alene, Idaho. Social insurrection loomed beyond Harvard Yard during most of the 1890s, as the political contest for control of the national economy became increasingly savage between corporate power and labor.[86]

There is some evidence that Du Bois grew less sanguine about the automatic corrections supposedly built into market forces. Academic questions about capital, labor, rent, value, and wages took on real-world trenchancy with the 1890 collapse of the powerful British banking firm of Baring Brothers. Severe depression racked the land, fusing angry farmers in the South and West, along with remnant Grangers, greenbackers, Knights of Labor, silverites, and utopian followers of Edward Bellamy and Henry George, into a voting hoard almost overnight. Secular evangelicals with tangy names like "Sockless Jerry" Simpson, "Bloody Bridles" Waite, and "Pitchfork Ben" Tillman fulminated against banks, railroads, tariffs, industrialists, immigrants, and much more, while others like Mary Elizabeth Lease circuit-rode among Kansas farmers exhorting them to "raise less corn and more hell." As Du Bois settled into his graduate studies, bankers, businessmen, and leaders of the two national parties rubbed their eyes as this organized mass (southern black and white people joining at the ballot box) captured four Senate and fifty House seats in the fall elections of 1890. Two years later, the People's party, speaking through the indignant voices of Tom Watson, Ignatius Donnelly, and others at Omaha, Nebraska, called for the nationalization of railroads, telegraphs, and telephones, a graduated income tax, an eight-hour workday, all the silver that could be coined, federal loans to farmers backed by crops stored in federal granaries, and with much else radical, secret ballots, direct election of senators, and immigration restriction. To the forces of order, populism was a scaffold rather than a political platform.[87]

Du Bois expressed his unease cautiously, abstractly, by grappling with the value to be placed on labor and the commodities it produced. Under Taussig, and in other departments of political economy at well-endowed universities, the subject was formulated with a theoretical exactitude in which the sacrifice of workers' wages to employers' profits was the first postulate of economic sanity and growth. Profligacy, overpopulation, unemployment, and starvation awaited those workers who temporarily forced more out of the economy than the iron law of wages allowed. Du Bois makes clear straightaway his dissatisfaction with supposed laws governing wages. "A Constructive Critique of Wage-Theory," a 158-page, handwritten entry for the prestigious Toppan Prize his first year, appears to have been too venturesome for the judges, who may also have found it almost as opaque in spots. Corrected spellings and other signs of haste mar an ambitiously expanded political economy paper. From his readings of John Stuart Mill and David Ricardo, Du Bois announced that he had developed a theory of wages, which, after checking "different wage-theories to see if any resembled mine," he now believed to be unique. Although his essay managed to be by turns both precise and murky, what Du Bois essentially seemed to be proposing by his "hierarchy of wants" was society's obligation to moderate profit as the sole engine for the distribution of wealth, an idea that would have been in keeping with the humane values expressed in the Jefferson Davis speech.[88]

The paper may not have made any contribution to economic theory, but his concern was a significant reflection of Du Bois's imaginative need for theoretical formulations in which humanist justifications prevailed. "Critique of Wage-Theory" was also interesting because the two pages devoted to the labor theory of surplus value—sandwiched between equally careful encapsulations of Walter Bagehot, Stanley Jevons, Alfred Marshall, and Sidney Webb—show that Du Bois knew far more about Marxist economic theory at Harvard than he subsequently let on.[89] Du Bois would be gone before the ravaging Panic of 1893, which gave populism such credibility and force that the custodians of the status quo believed they were looking into the maw of doom, but his disdain for the movement as revealed in his undergraduate economics essay almost surely would have remained, given his deep-seated elitism. A proper colored gentleman, he admits to having felt a twinge of sentiment when the Anglo-Saxon world paused to observe the Diamond Jubilee of Queen Victoria, now empress of India, and to having cheered the European explorers, soldiers, and missionaries bringing Christianity, civilization, and commerce to darker peoples. The linkage to the "race problem" in America had simply not yet occurred to him.[90] On the other hand, this long, dense "Critique of Wage-Theory" groped for a formulation of the wages problem less Darwinian than the prevailing one, more benign and community-oriented. The essay was much more a reflection of its author's aristocratic proclivities than of any will to affirm Socialist principles. Vulgar wealth troubled him greatly, but so did vulgar democracy.[91]

The same gift for imaginative analysis characterized his work under Hart. When it came time to impart meaning to a documentary welter of bills of sale, criminal codes, statutes, and statistics, Du Bois's imagination was invariably active, as in "Contributions to the Negro Problems," an essay handed in to Hart probably during the second semester of 1891. Anticipating interpretations that were only to gain credibility in the late 1960s, he argued against the scholarly presumption that slavery had come about partly because the "repulsion between the whites and the blacks is instinctive." The documents, he insisted, tended to prove that ideological racism "only appeared after a long period of artificial fostering by the laws of the land." The ability to leap from evidence to reinterpretation was something Hart encouraged in his prize graduate student, although he himself was anything but imaginative. "He was dry as dust, so far as that's concerned," Du Bois said later. A recent doctorate from the University of Freiburg, Hart's forte was research methodology. His imprint upon the study of history in early twentieth-century America was unmatched, as the growing corps of Ph.D.s trained by him under the new seminar method rose through tenure to positions of command in departments throughout the country. Unlike John Fiske or Frederick Jackson Turner, historians given to sweeping deductions, Hart cautiously threaded his way through a thicket of particulars. To find out what had actually happened in history, he drummed into his students the sanctity of primary sources and of careful scrutiny of documents.[92]

But there were two Harts: the walrus-mustached Hart whose graduate seminars were conducted in strictest conformity to German historiographic rigor; and the other in whom the Puritan conviction of the North's moral and economic rectitude in the Civil War was unalterably fixed. God and history were with the Union. Slavery was a wrong that "affected the social and economic life of the people," his widely read "Why the South was Defeated in the Civil War" announced in the *New England Magazine*. For all his scientific methodology, Du Bois's principal professor remained an old-fashioned moralist for whom character was the key determinant—the "inner man not the outer"—in social change.[93] Hart was troubled, therefore, by his beliefs about the prospects of black people in America. If the antebellum South had been nothing but irremediable decadence behind a showy facade, another of Hart's *a priori* convictions—elaborated after months of southern travel in a popular book on the subject (*The Southern South*, 1910)—was that the Negro was a moral and social cripple. Yet his abolitionist optimism and social-science scrupulosity kept him from becoming a misanthropic racist. He remained a *liberal* racist, reading virtually everything written by both races on the South and the Negro, factoring in the cultural, economic, and political debits of slavery, and the significance of such exceptional minds as the historian George Washington Williams's and his own student Du Bois's before deciding that "the supposed inferiority of the negro is not a foregone conclusion." In the case of Du Bois, Hart concluded almost immediately that the presumption of inferiority did not apply, although he seems never to have made up his mind as to just what that meant, writing confidentially much later that Du Bois was "living proof . . . that a mulatto may have as much power and passion as any white man."[94]

"Harvard and the South," another argumentative Du Bois piece that may have been written for Peabody's course, was a fascinating blend of the economic determinism and sociological evangelism typical of the Gilded Age, two strains uppermost in Du Bois's thinking. The South's peculiar civilization cannot be explained by theories of psychology or climate. At its core, Du Bois says, was a "vast economic mistake" based on oligarchy and planned underdevelopment. Where there is industrial growth, "parallel evolution of political rights and social prosperity has been the striking feature of modern history," but the New South of Henry Grady was the exception—a modern feudalism in which profit-taking is maximized by denying all black people their rights and most white people their dignity.[95] A practice shot at a large future target was to be heard in his warning of the "catastrophe" certain to result from "giving the future leaders of the Negro people ten hours at the plow and one at the spelling book." Du Bois's facile solution was to have Harvard educate the South's best white and black minds in the most advanced principles of sociology, while a system of university education should be established below the Mason-Dixon Line for the benefit of the elites of both races.[96]

Hart was sufficiently impressed by Du Bois's master's thesis on the Atlantic slave trade to arrange for him to present it to the American Historical Association (AHA) meeting in Washington, D.C., in December 1891. Arguing that the North's colluding with the South in nonenforcement of the constitutional ban on importing slaves after 1808 created an economic monster that nearly devoured the republic, Du Bois attributed the staggering increase in the South's slave population to an uninterrupted influx of smuggled Africans—a major flaw that would be carried over into his book on the subject published four years later. His mistake was based on reasonable deduction and was unsuspected by virtually all contemporary historians.[97] In "The Enforcement of the Slave Trade Laws," his AHA paper, the twenty-two-year-old scholar held the respectful attention of the distinguished seniors as he traced the fatal consequences of the moral compromise brokered at the very moment of the American republic's creation. Moral turpitude had been transformed into economic determinism, Du Bois argued. "If slave labor was an economic god," he concluded with a memorable turn of phrase, "then the slave trade was its strong right arm."[98]

Much later scholarship would demonstrate that the slavocracy slaked its labor hunger in the 1840s and 1850s through natural population increases over time, rather than by illegal importation of slaves, but Du Bois's larger economic account of institutional impotence on the part of the North was highly valuable for the times. The reporter for the New York *Independent* pronounced the paper one of the three best at the conference: "here was an audience of white men listening to a black man—listening, moreover, to a careful, cool, philosophical history of the laws which have not prevented the enslavement of his race." It was all so extraordinary, the reporter decided, that Americans need not "worry about the future of our country in the matter of race distinctions."[99] The bestowal of the Master of Arts degree in June 1892 must have come almost as an anticlimax.

In addition to mastering history, Du Bois had worked with almost equal diligence to perfect a prose style that became the signature of his ideas and opinions so completely that it is somewhat surprising to discover that it was not innate. The generally clear and frequently vivid writings from the early Harvard period are marred only here and there by a misspelling or malapropism, due largely to haste; but they tended to be more eloquent than elegant, more descriptive than metaphorical. Determined to acquire a literary style to carry his message, he enrolled in Wendell's English 12 in his first year of graduate studies. The class met three times a week, with Jefferson B. Fletcher assisting Wendell in grading the fifty-odd, half-sheet themes written daily and due each meeting. Undergraduates found the robust, red-bearded Wendell a "character," and took to imitating his speech and squirarchical mannerisms. Du Bois thought Wendell was British because of his "Oxford accent"—but the accent, like the spats, cane, and cape, were affectations. Wendell's waspish friend Santayana called him one of Harvard's "stray souls," who longed for an American aristocracy, was an excellent teacher, fastidious about style, and witty but with a mind, like his speech, "explosive and confused."[100]

But if the master of Harvard's most famous undergraduate course was colorful, his literary tastes were distinctly conventional. A stickler for "manliness" and good form, what he called "rum and decorum," there was no place in his canon for the likes of the "indecent" Guy de Maupassant or the "eccentric" Walt Whitman. Good writing, like good politics, meant fidelity to what was "Reputable, National, and Present"—no vulgarity, slang, neologisms, or technical accretions need apply. Du Bois quickly caught Wendell's attention with a snappy piece titled "Something About Me," which the professor read aloud, to Du Bois's immense pleasure. "In early youth a great bitterness entered my life and kindled a great ambition," the piece concluded candidly. "I wanted to go to college because others did. I came and graduated and am now in search of a Ph.D. and bread. I believe, foolishly perhaps but sincerely, that I have something to say to the world and I have taken English twelve in order to say it well."[101]

Not all of Du Bois's themes were so well received, though. "Autumn Leaves" was painstaking—"commonplace"—and one about a visit from two Fisk friends was "a bit crude." Another, "Frightened," was dismissed as "flippant." "The American Girl" sinned badly against Wendell's canon of taste. William Dean Howells had sparked considerable comment a few years earlier when he had explored the topic of the American girl in *Atlantic Monthly* but in a far different vein from the Harvard graduate student. What provoked Du Bois can only be guessed at (some incident reminding him of the visiting-card episode in the "wee wooden schoolhouse"?), but he handed Wendell and Fletcher a tirade beginning, "When I wish to meet the American hog in its native simplicity; when I wish to realize the world-pervading presence of the Fool; when I wish to be reminded that whatever rights some have I have none . . . I seek the company of the American girl." Holding this piece at a distance, Wendell commented acidly, "Such truculence as yours is thoroughly injudicious. Nothing could more certainly induce an average reader to disagree."

By the second semester, Du Bois's themes were earning comments such as "fairly interesting" for "Historical Conference," "vivacious" for "Wedding Reception," "realistic, amusing" for "Debating Club," and "good description" for "Dekalb County."[102] All in all, he got what he bargained for from Wendell's course. The gauche images and pleonasms were much less in evidence. A certain ornateness and gravity took hold, while punctuation and spelling vastly improved. The Du Boisian prose style, noble, metaphorical, reaching backward to classical models rather than forward into experimentation, began to crystallize. Old-fashioned and high-toned, it was saved from the stiltedness that slavish fidelity to Wendell would have induced by its flashing insights and magisterial indignation. His immersion in the works of Carlyle had yielded a rhythm and prose ideal for expressing insights and outrage. *The French Revolution*, Carlyle's dazzling, Calvinist history of divine chastisement and human agency, would remain near at hand. Certain as to what he wanted to say, Du Bois now had the literary form in which to convey it to the world.

What more could Harvard offer him? Even as he petitioned the trustees for permission to expand his master's into a doctorate, he was orchestrating a campaign to win a fellowship for study in Europe. Although there is nothing on the subject in the correspondence, he must have been told, at least informally, that Harvard's Walker Travelling Fellowship was unavailable, otherwise he certainly would have applied. But there was another option, although in the year and a half since a friend had first mentioned it to him during a card game, prospects had seesawed maddeningly. Handed a Boston *Herald* clipping dated November 2, 1890, Du Bois read that the president of the John F. Slater Fund for the Education of Negroes had offered to underwrite the European education of "any young colored man in the South whom we find to have a talent for art or literature." In a speech at Johns Hopkins University, Rutherford B. Hayes, the president who had dismantled Reconstruction and now presided over the million-dollar Slater benefaction, had added that it was very doubtful such a Negro existed. "Hitherto," said Hayes (in what was surely a dismissive reference to Du Bois's friend Morgan), "their chief and almost only gift has been that of oratory." Du Bois had rushed at the challenge; "No thought of modest hesitation occurred to me." Two days after the *Herald* story appeared, he sent a detailed letter announcing that he was just what the Slater Fund was looking for.[103] That he would also be leaving Maud Cuney behind, if the fund eventually recognized his claim, was the bittersweet price of destiny.

6.
LEHRJAHRE

W. E. BURGHARDT Du Bois's ambitions and John F. Slater's money intersected at a point in American history roughly equidistant between the espousal by the ruling classes of a fading creed of Christian uplift and their heartfelt embrace of a social gospel based on greed. Slater, of Norwich, Connecticut, knew that his splendid success in business owed as much to cheap cotton as to the Lord's benevolence. So that the least of God's creatures might also aspire to better themselves, he set aside the imposing sum of $1 million in 1882 for "uplifting the lately emancipated population of the Southern states and their posterity, by conferring on them the blessings of Christian education." His was the second of the great early philanthropies whose significant or principal concern was the education of the former slaves and their descendants. Between 1867 and 1869, the even more pious Episcopal financier George Foster Peabody, of New York and London, endowed a fund bearing his name with more than $2 million for "intellectual, moral, or industrial education" in the "more destitute portions of the Southern and Southwestern states."[1]

Although there was rich potential in its human capital, the South would have to educate its people first in order to make optimal use of that capital. This was a staggering challenge to a hierarchical social order whose prosperity before the Civil War had been made to depend upon an illiterate black labor force and a white yeomanry only barely able to read its Bibles. African slavery had made the antebellum South a unique social, political, and economic form of capitalism in North America and Europe. The consequences of tenant agriculture, single-crop economy, and racial segregation continued to make the region unique and too poor to pay its own way into the postwar world of industry, political democracy, social services, and public education. Consequently, southern white leaders looked upon the education of their people as no more achievable than the Second Coming, and about as imminent. And, whether possible or not, they asked themselves if it was even desirable. It was a bedeviling quandary for the Bourbon rulers of the Redeemed South—redeemed from "Negro rule"—as to how much education the poor white people should have. The ideal minimum of instruction to be risked on the former slaves was an even greater dilemma. "Education has but one tendency: to give higher hopes and aspirations," a North Carolina newspaper warned. "We want the negro to remain here, just about as he is—with mighty little change."[2]

But whatever the eventual answers to such sensitive, vexatious questions, would the tax rates ever be anywhere near adequate? Alabama, as a typical case, devoted nearly 50 percent of its state budget to public education during the 1890s, which only amounted to a lamentable $4.50 per year per pupil. The average annual per-pupil expenditure in the South during the 1890s was less than two dollars. In the North it was almost twenty. But if the North-South gap in public expenditures was great, a comparable gap grew with each passing year between public money spent for the education of white and black children below the Mason-Dixon Line. By 1900, the average was twice as much for white children, and in the following decade the disparity would widen cruelly. The Peabody and Slater funds, along with the Daniel Hand Fund, the Southern Education Board (SEB), the Anna T. Jeanes Fund, and others soon called into existence by the desperate state of affairs, found themselves disbursing thousands of dollars each year to train teachers and prop up public schools. Christian noblesse not unmixed with guilt created these benefactions; but the kingdom of mammon was never far from sight. The distant but paramount goal was a literate labor force adjusted to the rhythm and discipline of modernizing agriculture and industry, which the business associates of the Peabodys and Slaters hoped to bring to the South.[3]

After the late 1880s, these philanthropies in effect assumed what should have been the last-resort role of the federal government. Like an incandescent bulb at its brightest before dying, the Republican administration of Benjamin Harrison had flashed federal attention upon the South's special problems, lighting up the plight of the Negro in particular. "When is he in fact to have those full civil rights which have so long been his in law?" asked the president in his first annual message to Congress in 1889. Responding to their leader, as well as to what survived of the finer ideals of the Grand Old Party, Senator Henry W. Blair of New Hampshire and young Representative Henry Cabot Lodge of Massachusetts introduced legislation in early 1890 that threatened (or so it seemed) the new racial understanding between white North and white South. Eloquent, learned even, Blair was the Senate's authority on education. His bill (approved twice before in the Senate) provided for eight years of federal subsidies to states where the percentage of illiterates was unusually high in comparison to the national norm. Federal funding would come from the surplus generated by the high Republican tariff on imports.

Although the Blair Education Bill realistically bowed to the South's segregated educational system, it caused considerable offense by requiring state governors to certify annually to the secretary of the interior that no racial discrimination existed in the expenditure of monies for public education. Still, as one fifth of the region's white school-age children was unable to read and write, more southern politicians than not favored the bill. The time had not yet come when it was suicidal for white officials to endorse gains for African-Americans in order to add to those already benefiting their own people. The Blair Bill met its final death in 1890 primarily due to the pact between northern Republicans, who were opposed to federal dollars going to southern illiterates, and midwestern farmers and southern populists for whom the high tariff was anathema.[4] Lobbed into the House later that year, Lodge's so-called Force Bill included the threat of federal supervision of elections whenever a prescribed percentage of local voters petitioned Washington. Cynics who claimed to have suspected all along a ploy by Republican business and financial interests to blackmail the farming South into a deal for a factory-protecting tariff were not surprised to see Lodge's bill, barely voted through in the House, expire the following January in Senate horsetrading among high-tariff easterners, "home rule" southerners, and cheap-money westerners.[5]

With these reverses, the afterglow of abolitionism and Reconstruction was to be extinguished in Washington for more than fifty years. Whatever tremors reached Du Bois at Harvard, he cannot really have felt at that moment the shifting regional and racial plates deep beneath the surface of the nation's political culture, catastrophic realignments that would soon flatten the futures of many millions of African descent and make even of him a near-casualty. Such was his high Tory sense of civil rights, in fact, that he saw no need for the Lodge Bill, writing serenely to Fortune's New

York *Age* that "when you have the right sort of black voters, you will need no election laws. The battle of my people must be a moral one, not a legal or physical one." Although Booker T. Washington was beginning to voice such sentiments from the rostrum, Carlyle was far more likely to have been Du Bois's civics preceptor at the time. In any case, the twenty-two-year-old graduate student's views were in accord with the new order in race relations that was hurriedly being codified and implemented throughout the South, lest some new political agenda above the Mason-Dixon Line inaugurate another rash of meddling bills or even awaken the Supreme Court to a democratic construing of the Fourteenth and Fifteenth Amendments. Mississippi took the lead, even as Congress was heatedly debating the federal education and election legislation. Meeting in Jackson in a constitutional convention in mid-August 1890, 130-odd white Democrats and planter Isaiah T. Montgomery of all-black Mound Bayou Township, lone survivor of what had once been a significant political presence, voted in the "Mississippi Plan." A two-dollar poll tax, a literacy test, disqualification for petty crimes, and duty to recite from memory and interpret upon request the clauses in the new state constitution effectively disfranchised all but a handful of African-Americans and several thousand poor white people as well.[6]

This was the fast-developing reality when Du Bois's application reached Slater Fund president Rutherford B. Hayes—an application supported, Du Bois said, with letters "from every person I knew in the Harvard Yard and places outside." Despite his claim to have become thoroughly and irrevocably "a Negro" at Fisk, in the fall of 1890 when he mailed his first Slater Fund letters, Du Bois clearly thought of himself both as the embodiment of his race as well as something ambiguously superordinate. "I omitted stating that I am, in blood, about one half or more Negro, and the rest French and Dutch," the April 1891 postscript to his second letter read. "I wish to lay my case before you," Du Bois stated crisply.[7] Surely he had no idea that, in the estimation of the former U.S. president, the Slater Fund was obliged to subordinate the merits of his application to weighty issues of national policy on race relations. Those weighty issues were to be reviewed at two of the most fateful gatherings ever assembled to thrash out the "Negro Problem," the first and second Mohonk Conferences on the Negro Question, deliberating in upstate New York during the first week in June of 1890 and 1891. Hayes, whose idea they were (seven previous Lake Mohonk conferences had focused on the American Indian), presided.[8]

Among the throng of concerned men and women accommodated in

the Smiley brothers' rambling hotel with its manicured lawns planing to the lake were some of America's most influential educators and molders of opinion. They were exclusively white, Protestant, and, in the main, male, and, some of them, opulently hypocritical. The education of "that other weaker race"—"our brothers in black," said Hayes, quoting the South's leading paternalist, Methodist Bishop Atticus Haygood of Atlanta, as he opened the 1890 conclave—was the urgent matter of the hour. Unfortunately, Hayes conceded, "the recent adverse action of the Senate admonishes us, that we may no longer look with confidence for government aid." Responsibility for the southern Negro now devolved upon the men and women at Mohonk. "Having deprived them of their labor, liberty, and manhood, and grown rich and strong while doing it," the dismantler of Reconstruction admitted, "we have no excuse for neglecting them."[9]

A minority of the Mohonkers attending the first conference had arrived, like the grandson of John Jay, with a presumption that what African-Americans mainly needed was plenty of general education, not special education different in nature from that administered to whites. That was how Miss Elizabeth Botume saw the matter, speaking with emotion of her days at war's end among the freedmen and freedwomen at Port Royal, South Carolina. Yet the absence of one of the white South's most knowledgeable and honest authorities on race relations was ominous. Ex-Confederate cavalryman and novelist of Creole Louisiana Cable not only boycotted Mohonk on the grounds that the conference was designed to reach a predetermined agreement about higher education for the Negro, the author of *The Silent South* also alerted Booker T. Washington and other race leaders of the conspiracy. Washington answered Cable's warning letter by confessing that he had "thought it a little strange that no invitation came to me," adding (mistakenly) that "the exclusion of colored men will in large degree cripple the influence" of any recommendations issued by the conference.[10] William Sanders Scarborough, the learned African-American professor of classics at Afro-America's first college, Wilberforce University, protested the exclusion in the widely circulated *Arena* magazine, charging that there was "a great deal of insincerity on the part of many so-called advocates of the race." Any who doubted the reasonableness of Scarborough's suspicions had only to hear the explanation offered by the lordly Congregationalist divine, Lyman Abbott: "A patient is not invited to the consultation of the doctors on his case."[11]

By the time the second Mohonk Conference assembled, the old optimism of Yankee schoolmarms and Union officers–turned-professors in

AMA "universities" was dismissed as a harmful extravagance. Those waning voices that still appealed for broad training and social justice for the Negro were met with increasing impatience at Mohonk. Albion Tourgee, southern expatriate, folklorist, and jurist; Malcolm MacVicar, New York bishop and Baptist Home Mission Society secretary of education; William Torrey Harris, U.S. commissioner of education; and several others were opposed by educational "realists" like Merrill E. Gates of Rutgers, Andrew Dickson White of Cornell, Oliver Otis Howard of Howard, and, above all, by Hampton Institute's founder and redoubtable drillmaster of colored peoples, General Samuel Chapman Armstrong. Commissioner Harris and Reverend MacVicar protested that the best races were those receiving the best education. The African-American was, "in every sense that you and I claim to be, a man," cried MacVicar. Judge Tourgee, exercising a renegade white southerner's prerogative to represent the Negro race, flayed as hypocrites those whose very fortunes were built upon the supposed shiftlessness of black people. Tourgee momentarily stirred the conscience of the assembly by declaring that this reviled people had "accomplished more in twenty-five years . . . than any people on the face of the earth ever before achieved." Far more, he said, "than the 'poor whites' of the South, the landless cropper-class." A professor from Charlotte, North Carolina, rose to suggest "when we speak of industrial education, we should emphasize the word 'education.' "[12]

Moved but unpersuaded, the Mohonkers were brought back to earth by Cornell president White's practiced pose of objectivity. The recent past was riven by injustices, yet history could not be rewritten. The South must be allowed to solve its race problem as it saw best, White pleaded, even at the constitutional price of disfranchising millions of its citizens. Lyman Abbott, pastor of Brooklyn's venerable Plymouth Church, the ruling voice of Congregationalism and editor of what was shortly to become the influential *Outlook*, shared his considerable knowledge of the race problem at the Second Mohonk Conference. After a recent visit to North Carolina where he had "studied it for two days and a half," Abbott assured the doubters that "taking the South as a whole . . . prejudices are disappearing and a sincere, earnest desire for the very best and largest education of the colored people is coming." Had not Reverend R. H. Allen, D.D., secretary of the Presbyterian Board, and several other reconstructed slaveholding southerners, testified with evangelical zeal and anecdotal felicity to the newfound racial understanding in the South? "History affords no instance in which one race has redeemed another race," Abbott admonished.[13]

Underlying their indecision and their subsequent retreat from the educational model they themselves—and hosts of relatives—had carried messianically to the South was a much larger reservation in the minds of Mohonkers. The national philosophy of education had been under review and revision for more than two decades. Practical training, vocational instruction, industrial education—there were a number of terms for it—was praised by a swelling chorus as the right way to nurture the minds of the great majority of Americans. Educators carefully read the writings of Johann Pestalozzi, Philipp von Fellenberg, and Friedrich Froebel, the European philosophers whose advocacy of industrial and vocational education had become a conquering ideology in post–Civil War America. It was said that the dawning Machine Age called for a quick-response citizenry with intelligences unfettered by antiquarian and nonutilitarian knowledge. To the genuinely progressive advocates, the new theories meant breaking out of stodgy instruction based on abstractions, rote memory, useless languages, and hoary fables; it anticipated the emphasis on spontaneity and learning-by-doing that informed the coming instrumentalism and progressive education reforms of John Dewey and his followers.[14] To many others—the more conservative faction—the new philosophy held the key to the social control of working-class men and women, the construction of an educational regime designed to equip them with the technical competency necessary to function obediently and narrowly in the new industrial order. Vocational and industrial training would act as a safety valve in a turbulent democracy. Many of them saw the German technical high schools as the model to emulate.

The application of vocational education to the African-American was cause for great excitement and even more mischief. Again, the genuinely progressive—the nonpaternalists—saw it as a breakthrough, an affordable, academically sufficient, and economically productive solution to the South's intractable problems. As originally conceived, therefore, vocationalism was not a bogus substitute to be foisted on black people but an education as appropriate for them as for most white people. But there were other theorists, public figures, and politicians who looked upon vocationalism as a way to avoid an increasingly resented and vexing burden. This new thinking about educating African-Americans naturally appealed to them, and for them, the laboratory at Hampton Institute in Virginia had demonstrated that the experiment could work perfectly without any threat to the South's socioeconomic order. Ex-Confederate general and New South railroad magnate Thomas Muldrop Logan had seen that clearly some fifteen years before the two conferences at Lake Mohonk, reassuring his Richmond business colleagues that after African-Americans had been trained to perform "efficiently their part in the social economy, his [sic] caste allotment of social duties might prove advantageous to southern society, as a whole, on the principle of a division of labor applied to races."[15]

At the Mohonk conferences, then, a new and dubious educational paradigm edged out an idealistic old one. Having commanded African-American soldiers in the Civil War, and now training their sons and daughters in tidewater Virginia, Samuel Armstrong was hailed as an oracle. Hawaiian-born, sternly handsome, he was one of the leaders of industrial education in the country, the most persuasive exponent of the Froebelian ideal of harmonious development of "head, heart, and hand." With Yankee grit he had founded and structured Hampton Normal and Agricultural Institute in 1868 so that Negroes and Indians could learn the lessons of humility, cleanliness, thrift, and, above all, the love of the white race that his prize pupil Booker T. Washington was about to exemplify to a reassured world. "Labor is a great moral and educational force," the general observed on the first morning of the first conference. "The Negroes are a laboring people." Slavery had diminished the value of work, unfortunately, because, like the American Indians, African-Americans had "had it forced upon them." "The great thing" was to give them "an idea of the dignity of labor, that is to change their standpoint," as Armstrong had done at Hampton. Resting his case in a peroration of Victorian cant—"The Negro is back in the iron age; the white race is in its golden age; and idleness is equally the curse of both"—the general regained his seat to thunderous applause.[16]

In the end, the Mohonkers came to agree that facilities for industrial education were to be increased in the South, "not only in the trades," as Resolution One announced, "but especially in improved agriculture, and for the girls in household duties that [are] fit for home-making and housekeeping." Resolution Three conceded the principle of higher education "open to the most capable Negroes," but no one left Lake Mohonk in doubt as to the new emphasis upon rudimentary education "of heart and hand," intended to turn out subservient farmers, cooks, seamstresses, maids, carpenters, and masons. Having ceded their franchise to the white South, the spirit of Mohonk began the surrender of the best educational future of African-Americans.[17]

These and similar impending developments were in the air when Rutherford Hayes eventually replied to Du Bois at the beginning of May

1891. By then, the Slater Fund files contained letters from other ambitious, well-educated young men of color, or their white sponsors, inquiring about the widely publicized fellowship Hayes had promised at Johns Hopkins. With the Second Mohonk Conference convening in a few weeks, the last thing the ex-president needed were reports in the southern press about a brilliant black Harvard student headed for Europe and one of the finest prospective educations attained by an American citizen, all thanks to the Slater Fund. Most assuredly a Du Bois fellowship was not the appropriate symbol for a policy of training of "heart and hand." Conceivably, Hayes may even have been troubled by the hypocrisy in replying that the news reports were mistaken, that, in any case, "the plan had been given up," and that he recognized that Du Bois was a candidate "who might otherwise have been given attention."[18]

No less a figure than Confederate warrior and Alabama legislator Jabez Lamar Curry, now general agent of both the Peabody and the Slater funds, had wondered, when his opinion was sought, whether Du Bois's "persuasive" endorsements didn't make his case "exceptionally meritorious." Professor Francis Peabody, distantly related to the fund founder, thought Hayes should appreciate that Du Bois's "color is in no way involved" in his brilliant record. "It merely indicates that he is among the most satisfactory students of the last few years." Taussig, the economics professor, wrote that Du Bois was "as good a candidate for the sort of aid he requests as the Trustees . . . are ever likely to come across. Not only this, but an excellent candidate *per se.*" Dean Charles Dunbar of the Faculty of Arts and Sciences informed the fund that Harvard regarded Du Bois "as a young man of exceptional capacity, of independent mind, fixed purposes and of strong resolution." That old Kentucky gentleman Nathaniel Shaler commended Du Bois and his "rather Shemitic [sic]" type of mind as "decidedly the best specimen of his race we have had in our classes."[19]

When the Slater Fund president opened Du Bois's third letter, dated May 25, he saw that he had a manifesto on his hands. Among the many thousands of such letters Du Bois would write during his combative career, this one to Hayes was among the most significant for his race; for him personally, it was perhaps the most important since his appeal for a stipend to attend Harvard College. He knew that its perceived impertinence could fatally mark him in the eyes of the philanthropic mighty or would jolt them into evaluating his case solely on its merits. "The outcome of the matter" was as he expected, he informed Hayes. He had never doubted that the fund's "search in vain for men to educate" was insincere. Moreover, he was "perfectly capable of fighting alone for an education" if the trustees declined to help him. But the twenty-two-year-old graduate student proceeded to tell the sixty-nine-year-old former American president that what he had done was inexcusable:

> . . . The injury you have—unwittingly I trust—done the race I represent, and am not ashamed of, is almost irreparable. You went before a number of keenly observant men who looked upon you as an authority in the matter, and told them in substance that the Negroes of the United States either couldn't or wouldn't embrace a more liberal opportunity for advancement. . . . When now finally you receive three or four applications for the fulfillment of that offer, the offer is suddenly withdrawn, while the impression remains. . . . I think you owe an apology to the Negro people.

Winding down, Du Bois sardonically related several previous, unsuccessful attempts to secure help from self-proclaimed white patrons of his race. "I find men willing to help me thro' cheap theological schools, I find men willing to help me use my hands before I have got my brains in working order, I have an abundance of good wishes on hand, but I never found a man willing to help me get a Harvard Ph.D."[20]

Du Bois's shock tactics caused the prospects for his academic advancement to improve virtually overnight as a chagrined Hayes encouraged him to reapply the following year. Fund trustee Daniel Coit Gilman, the president of Johns Hopkins, seems to have favored Du Bois, probably for the same reasons motivating Jabez Curry, namely that "negroes as a race need the directive intelligence of characterful leaders."[21] In the closing months of his two-year graduate fellowship, then, Du Bois knocked on the Slater Fund door again—this time more discreetly. Trusting that Hayes would pardon his importunity, he carefully elaborated his educational plans for a year of study abroad, again reminding the fund that the question of his future was of more than "merely personal interest." The two, with Gilman, finally met in early April 1892, in New York City at the old Astor House, where the full terms of the fellowship were discussed. Du Bois left "walking on air." In a fashionable store window his eye caught a stylish dress shirt priced at three dollars—four times as much as he had ever paid for a shirt. He bought it. On the morning of April 13, Hayes noted in his diary that he and Gilman had decided to give the Harvard student $750 at 5 percent interest, half in cash outright, with the balance advanced against a personal note. A friendly card from Du Bois that morning prompted Hayes's diary entry, "Very glad to find that he is sensible, sufficiently religious, able, and a fair speaker."[22] About one thing, the Slater Fund president was surely correct: Du Bois was very able indeed.

AS THE aging, slow *Amsterdam* sailed for Europe in mid-July, Du Bois allowed himself to savor pure exhilaration. Seven years ago to the month, he had been a privileged wage earner on the Hopkins estate, praying mightily that ability and luck would finally get him off to a small southern college. Three years ago, the Fisk graduate had scrambled for tips in the Minnesota lake country in order to make at least a year at Harvard possible. Although he registered as a nonresident candidate for the doctorate under Hart and Channing for the academic year 1892–93, Du Bois was already contemplating a breakthrough even more impressive than a Harvard Ph. D. Harvard's degree, after all, was regarded in about the same light by the leading German universities as his Fisk bachelor's had been by Harvard.[23] To return to the United States with a coveted Heidelberg or Berlin doctorate would be the ultimate seal of professional standing, a personal triumph and a racial marker. He entered upon this third installment of the Age of Miracles "in a trance," telling himself over and over, " 'It's not real; I must be dreaming!' "[24] Still, he remained on his guard and politely aloof from the *Amsterdam*'s other passengers, no doubt spending a good deal of time reviewing German grammar in his cabin. In a wash of sunlight the sprawl of Rotterdam came into view on the morning of August 1, 1892.

The travel notes he began taking are about what we would expect of Du Bois—detailed, cogent, opinionated. Rotterdam was bustling, a multinational port so completely yoked to trade that it spoke English, French, and German even to itself, but little Dutch. Holland, an "extremely well-ordered mud-puddle," was pleasant enough, but because of Dutch "phlegm" Du Bois was forced to spend a full week in Rotterdam waiting for his Baring Brothers bank draft to clear.[25] Secure in his habit of standing "on the outside of the American world, looking in," he was unprepared to discover that culturally, even physically, he fit none of the preconceptions that most continental Europeans held of American Negroes—a race less than a generation out of slavery, overwhelmingly southern, peasant, and minimally literate. Aboard the little steamer wending up the Rhine was a Dutch mother and her three daughters, two of them adult and attractive. Once or twice when the steamer docked, he held back until they left the boat before strolling down the gangplank to see one of the towns. He felt awkward, choreographing his every move so as to avoid one of those small scandals he had learned to expect whenever men and women of the two races commingled in America. But at Düsseldorf, the first city in Germany, the more attractive daughter made him join them, and Du Bois found himself chattering away in German.

What they actually saw is unrecorded. Düsseldorf was a densely populated industrial and chemical center, the Pittsburgh of Imperial Germany, fed by the Ruhr's inexhaustible ore deposits. Having digested every detail in his Baedeker, Du Bois would have wanted to see the ruins of Frederick Barbarossa's palace, had there been time enough. The medieval Lambertuskirche, with its famous crooked tower, would have drawn the steamer's passengers. When the family finally got off at Cologne, he and they had become friends in three languages and a dozen or more songs. The massive thirteenth-century defensive wall circumscribing the ancient cathedral city had been torn down little more than ten years before, to be replaced by the encircling roadways of the Ringstrasse. The modern city now surged outward from the Ringstrasse like some vital fluid released by its tourniquet into a network of railway arteries. Germany's oldest chamber of commerce nurtured the city's prosperity. All of this Du Bois knew from his Baedeker reading as he and the Dutch family hurried through the Hohe Strasse to the Innenstadt, the heart of Cologne, tilting their heads upward to marvel at the soaring towers of the largest Gothic church in northern Europe. The Rathaus and the Romanesque Querstolzenhaus they would have seen as they passed, but the splendid reward of their excursion was the illumined interior of Cologne Cathedral with its massive gold shrine to the Magi and the fourteenth-century "Adoration of the Magi," the great triptych over the altar. Seven years later, Du Bois would remember gratefully waving goodbye to the family there "in the solemn arched aisles."[26]

Then, after disembarking at Frankfurt, came Eisenach, an old town, once the seat of the landgraves of Thuringia, more recently the birthplace of Johann Sebastian Bach, and one of Germany's most historic. Ringing the base of a mountain overwhelmed by long, looming Schloss Wartburg, Hermann I's twelfth-century castle, Eisenach gave the appearance of one of the kaiser's future battle cruisers at rest in the Thuringian forest. Du Bois planned to spend seven weeks in intensive German-language conversation there, living in the pension of Herr Doktor Johannes Marbach, the rector of the Wartburg, and his family.[27] As he wrote to his old Sunday school in care of Edward Van Lennup, physically the town reminded Du Bois of Great Barrington, "if the hills were thrown in somewhat wilder confusion, our shingles turned into red tiles, and our streets crooked a bit." Martin Luther had found shelter in the Wartburg after the Diet of Worms had ordered his exile. Incognito as Junker Georg, he had stamped his volcanic personality ineffaceably into the culture by translating for the first time the Greek New Testament into German. This bit of history Du Bois related to the Great Barrington Sunday school, adding to it a jarring fact of equal historic weight by tracing the Wartburg's age far beyond the time "when your great-great-grandfathers stole my great-great-grandfather and brought him a slave to America."[28] This was an early instance of seemingly unconnected turning points in history tied together didactically—the signature of Du Boisian racial discourse.

He found Eisenach glorious, worshipping in the simple church in the square where Luther had preached, mastering the libretto of *Tannhäuser* (Richard Wagner's opera set in the Wartburg), strolling and picnicking in the woods with the Marbach family and some of the other boarders, and, hoping Mary Silvina would have condoned it, learning to drink a great deal of beer in the August evenings. Out of range of his American demons, he seemed to grow lighter, almost playful, and more accessible with each week. Eisenach had begun to modify "profoundly my outlook on life," Du Bois always insisted, awakening in him "something of the possible beauty and elegance of life." He began to escape "extremes of . . . racial provincialism" in the company of the three or four other boarders, all of them European. Blue-eyed, raven-haired Dora, one of the Marbachs' two daughters, was happy to help him become "more human."[29] She paired herself with him on their chaperoned forays, to church and concerts, and prompted him to invite her to the town's very formal annual ball.

Five years later at Hampton Institute, the spell of that Eisenach evening would still be with Du Bois as he recalled publicly the little social in the brilliantly lit, well-ventilated hall. A young white woman of good character had placed herself in his arms to be twirled about the floor, and did so naturally and joyously, with the serene approval of pouter-pigeon mothers and bewhiskered fathers looking on. A good dancer, he showed off a bit. But when it was the turn of the women to ask the men to dance, the hoary ghost of the old visiting-card business in Great Barrington haunted him just for an instant, and he "drew back." He need not have, "for [his] card was filled for every dance." Three magical hours passed gliding from daughters to mothers until it was time to sit at tables groaning with food and drink. It was an epiphany of liberation. He had had many good times in life, Du Bois would tell his Hampton Institute audience, "but not one to which I look back with more genuine pleasure and satisfaction."[30] Later, he serenaded Dora in his fine baritone and perfect German, and she fell in love with her Willy.

The arrival of a white American professor and his wife from the Far West suddenly deflated Pension Marbach's *Gemütlichkeit*. Mrs. Far West Professor hurried Frau Marbach aside to educate the family about the frightful peril to a daughter who consorted with Negroes. There was general relief after the couple's departure, but in their wake came a certain awkwardness—just enough to make Du Bois feel "a little sensitive," and almost spoiling the most perfect summer of his life. Dora was unconcerned, however, and asked him to marry her. She would follow him to America " '*gleich!*' " (straightaway), she said. In *Dusk of Dawn* he would write rather flatly of telling her "she would not be happy." Besides, he added, he "had work to do."[31] What he did not tell her was that his own racial pride was as much a bar to intermarriage as the prejudices of the departed Americans from the Far West. Yet, sixty years later, he would confess to his second wife that he had fallen in love with Dora, and leaving her had been painful. Taking consolation in the proverb "*Es war so schön gewessen/Es hat nicht sollen sein*" (It would have been so lovely/It could not be), he went on his promising way. He and the Marbachs exchanged a few letters, but he never saw Dora again after leaving Eisenach on the second Saturday in October 1892. As she is not mentioned in the list he later made of sexual conquests, Du Bois appears to have behaved honorably, according to the contemporary code of courtship.[32]

GERMAN UNIVERSITY lectures began the last week of October. Du Bois had decided to present himself for admission to the Friedrich-Wilhelm III Universität at Berlin, familiarly known as the University of Berlin, the largest in the Second Reich. Founded in 1809 by Wilhelm von Humboldt, the Prussian minister of education, Berlin was the parvenu among the continent's great universities, such as Bologna, Paris, Prague, or Heidelberg. Almost two decades shy of celebrating its first century when Du Bois enrolled, its excellence was already legendary in that short time. The fiery Romantic Johann Gottlieb Fichte had been the first rector, returning grimly from sanctuary in Copenhagen after Napoleon's retreat in 1807 to deliver *Reden an die deutsche Nation* (*Addresses to the German Nation*), his cultural marching orders to the German people. Alluding to the virtues Tacitus had praised in them, Fichte told the Germans that they had a special mission to redeem human culture. His influence was still far from slight in Du Bois's time. Professors Gustav von Schmoller and Adolf Wagner were among the modernizing exponents of the *Vernunftstaat*, the rational state presiding over a planned economy, as proposed by Fichte in his 1800 book *Der geschlossene Handelsstaat* (*The Closed Commercial State*).[33] Georg W. F. Hegel in the first chair of philosophy had drawn hundreds to his lectures, including the young Karl Marx, while Arthur Schopenhauer, competitively scheduling his at the same hour, had succumbed to depression in a near-empty hall. The study of history at Berlin took on scientific pretensions under Leopold von Ranke that would never entirely be effaced, however much later generations of historians tried to moderate them. One of its most illustrious graduates, Max Weber, received a temporary lectureship during Du Bois's second year, before leaving for a sociology professorship at Freiburg.[34] For Du Bois, no other German university held the cachet of Friedrich-Wilhelm.

On the morning of October 17, wedging himself among some two hundred fellow Americans jabbering about football, Du Bois was almost giddy. He had just arrived from Weimar and Leipzig. Now he and the others waited in the long hallway to be presented, one hundred at a time, to the "Rector Magnificus" and faculty deans. As they quick-marched into the famous room 33, Du Bois heard himself announced in German as a "most ornamented young man," whereupon Rudolf Virchow, the white-haired little rector, officially welcomed him to the university as a member of the philosophical faculty, handing him an embossed, folio-sized document that he now had to present to what seemed an endless array of high-collared administrators, as well as to those professors whose lectures he wished to attend.[35] After much shuffling of papers and ceremony, he left the former palace registered for a daunting six lecture courses of twenty hours a week, among them Heinrich von Treitschke's Politics and Adolf Wagner's Political Economy, plus independent research for Professor Schmoller's economics seminar. He fairly floated down the Unter den Linden, past Frederick the Great's huge equestrian statue, the elegant State Opera House, and the Brandenburg Gate on the way to number 130A Oranienstrasse two miles away, where, for eight dollars a month, an elderly, motherly landlady provided morning coffee and an upstairs room warmed by a colossal, "nicely ornamented" tile stove.[36]

German professors were not in the habit of coddling students after the fashion of some of their American counterparts. Berlin students could do as much or as little as they chose, as one professor told an American who asked about the required study load. This sort of autonomy suited the inner-directed Du Bois perfectly. Unlike Hutchins Hapgood, another Harvard man who ran into him "apparently having a good time," Du Bois made sure the good times didn't compromise a good German education, as they did that of Hapgood and a number of other Americans at the university.[37] He sized up his professors with a superior graduate student's mixture of awe and perspicacity. Wagner, a tall man with a fringe of brown hair reaching to his collar, had a "face rather stern but still kindly." At Wagner's mention of Bismarck on the first day, there was a five-minute "rub-a-dub-dub" of student disapproval, but Du Bois omits to say whether he joined in. Rudolf von Gneist was the only professor with wide knowledge of Anglo-Saxon institutions. Von Treitschke, however, claimed to know a great deal about virtually everything. A huge man with a full, iron-gray beard, he arrived twenty minutes late consistently, lumbering into the hall in a dark cutaway and charging, stone deaf, into his lectures at breakneck speed, which sorely tested Du Bois's command of the language.

Taking lodging with a German family rather than in one of the "American" boarding houses (where he might not have been welcome), mimicking the German student's strut, and cultivating Kaiser Wilhelm's mustache under his fine nose, Du Bois felt exceptionally free, more liberated in these years than he would ever feel again. Asking the Slater Fund to renew his fellowship the following year, he would make the point that to the African-American, "even more than to the white, is the contact with European culture of inestimable value in giving him a broad view of men and affairs."[38] So thin as almost to be diaphanous now, the veil of race was still there, largely because, although Du Bois had learned to lift it, it was not in his psychic makeup to remove it completely because it allowed a lonely young intellectual to glorify his own race in order to better combat the glorification of race by others.[39]

The surviving Oranienstrasse diary notebooks have an unmistakable feel of lonely sublimation about them, frequently lubricated by the grape. An occasional name bobs to the surface of a narrative rich in travel and culture—Du Bois's English classmate John Dollar, a girlfriend named Amalie, two or three others.[40] Otherwise, his notebooks read like a pageant to which only Du Bois has been invited. He "kept up [his] older habit of travelling alone."[41] He took solitary strolls along Friedrichstrasse, through parks, and along canals. He sat alone in cafés with a newspaper over a coffee. There were recorded visits to a prostitute in Potsdam, and slightly tipsy late-night compositions in his uncarpeted room. These comprise a large portion of the notebooks, presenting a young man as decoupled from society in Berlin as he had been in Boston during his first year or more, although much less tightly wound. One such entry, undated and untitled, but surely written during his first term at the University of Berlin, was remarkably Gothic. A woman stands by a window, "her hair flying, her gown almost tattered, and in her eye the look of a wild fierce doe at bay." A story without beginning or ending, this fragment offers no clue to the nature of the tragedy enveloping the man and woman in their darkened bedroom: "He said not a word but with his eyes bent on the floor slowly yet resolutely the murderous words rose in her throat till she gasped in agony, the sweat rolled down her cheeks but mingled with no tears; tighter yet tighter she grasped the knife in the folds of her dress—she bent forward—his hand was now extended: a piteous look of despair."[42] There must have been some traumatic memory deep within Du Bois that found expression in this sketch's extravagant imagery and unpunctuated narration. Perhaps those shadowy figures are Alfred and Mary Silvina reenacting a crisis in their son's subconscious.

Another piece, a short story written on an early December evening and headed "Plot for a Story," was about a white orphan boy, "X" from Great Barrington, who grows up to make a success of a dry goods business in Boston, thanks partly to his fiancée's father. Over the objections of his white workers, he hires an attractive, intelligent African-American female as chief accountant. The dry goods prince was another early prototype for male protagonists in Du Bois's fiction—uncomplicated, credulous men whose intellectual and political aptitudes were nurtured by extraordinary women. The character of the new secretary, portentously identified only as "Z" (for the Zora of his first novel?), was informed by Du Bois's nascent feminism. Propping up X after the nervous collapse he suffers after his fiancée's desertion, she expands his business to the point where his admiration turns to love. Z refuses his marriage proposal, undertaking instead his instruction in what would today be called Third World studies. "She was born in the South and attempted teaching," but as if anticipating her creator's concept of the Talented Tenth, Z saw the need "of a leading aristocracy to raise her people." But before the dry goods prince can invest in her business schemes to "help civilize Africa," his white workers strike, forcing him to fire Z. X marries his new bookkeeper, raises a family, and years later, while vacationing at Narragansett, notices the headwaiter's wife and child. "It is Z. They look and part forever."[43] Apart from its psychological import, "Shattered Ideals" (its subtitle) is intriguing for the alliance depicted between educated white wealth and visionary black intelligence—a politics of global racial progress that Du Bois seems fascinated by and whose fiercest enemy is the myopic white working class.

No one could make a virtue of loneliness better than Du Bois. On Wednesday evening, February 22, 1893, a case in point, he returned to Oranienstrasse from a Schubert concert and drew up elaborate plans for his twenty-fifth birthday the next day. The night was bleak and he was homesick. After writing letters to Great Barrington relatives, he held a "curious . . . little ceremony" at midnight of Greek wine, oil, song, candles, and prayer to the Zeitgeist. "The second quarter-century of my life" would not only bring great personal achievement, he wrote in his diary, it held great significance for the world. Deadly serious about this pivot point, he laid out solemn plans for the next day. They were to be executed with clockwork precision: rising at 7:00 A.M. for breakfast; reflection, poetry, and song until 9:30 ("Steal Away Jesus," "America the Beautiful"); a stroll until 11:00; a museum until 1:00 P.M.; lunch "with Einderhof over a bottle of Rudesheimer and cigarettes"; 3:00 to 6:00, coffee in Potsdam ("saw a pretty girl"); Schmoller's seminar, 6:00–7:00; and so forth. "The program was very pleasantly carried out," he reported to himself. "I go to bed after one of the happiest days of my life."[44]

There was more to come later that night. Agitated, probably lightheaded from the wine, he rose in an exalted mood, dedicated his library to the memory of Mary Silvina, then confided his darkest fears and wildest aspirations to his notebook. "Night—grand and wonderful. I am glad I am living," the stream of consciousness entry began:

> I rejoice as a strong man to run [win?] a race, and I am strong—is it egotism—is it assurance—or is it the silent call of the world spirit that makes me feel that I am royal and that beneath my scepter a world of kings shall bow. The hot dark blood of that [a] black forefather—born king of men—is beating at my heart, and I know that I am either a genius or a fool. O I wonder what I am—I wonder what the world is—I wonder if life is worth the striving. . . . I do know: be the truth what it may, I will seek it on the pure assumption that it is worth seeking—and Heaven nor Hell, God nor Devil shall turn me from my purpose till I die. . . . There is a grandeur in the very hopelessness of such a life—life? and is life all?[45]

He knew, too, that the life most fulfilled was the most beautiful—"beautiful as a dark passionate woman, beautiful as a golden hearted school girl." His thoughts on beauty became more specific, more intense, running to the women he claimed to have loved—"loves, how many and how dear, she the beautiful whom I worshipped, Ollie the loving [lonely?], Dicky the timid, Jenny the meek, Nellie the wavery child." He struck a note of self-indulgent regret about Amalie, the Berlin shop girl who had been swept up in the physical intensity of their love—"(perhaps) life-ruin of Amalie which is cruel"—but what could he, who followed a course exactly opposite St. Paul's, do about it?[46]

His pen raced on. He grasped one existential truth: his own "best development is now one and the same with the best development of the world." Temporarily liberated from the "hard iron hands of America," he would bring to perfection his quarter-century "apprenticeship" as he sprinted toward professional service to the world. The notebook entry closed on a Tamburlainian high: "These are my plans: to make a name in [social?] science, to make a name in literature and thus to raise my race. Or perhaps to raise a visible empire in Africa thro' England, France or Germany. I wonder what will be the outcome? Who knows? I will go unto the king—which is not according to the law and if I perish—I PERISH." Du Bois's seemingly borderline thoughts that night were a manifestation of his particular genius, as well as of the Sturm und Drang literary tradition he and many German students of his generation relished in Goethe's *Sorrows of Young Werther*.[47] Laying the notebook aside, he finally went to bed.

The solitary existence Du Bois led among the Germans (and the psychological insights to be gleaned from it) ought not to be overdrawn. Financial resources being scant and his studies intensely absorbing, opportunities for casual friendships were decidedly limited. Moreover, psychological motives aside, the social-science career upon which he was embarked demanded, in his judgment, that he reinforce the habit of systematic observation and generalization of even the most trivial or transitory phenomena. He was neither humorless nor misanthropic, but it offended his Puritan upbringing and, much worse, struck him as racially treasonable not to yoke virtually every experience to purposes that could be considered intellectually and socially redeeming. His seriousness of purpose was but a more rigorous version of the uplift ideology men and women of his generation and presumed class subscribed to. A unique glimpse of a serious and politely impatient Du Bois in Berlin would come half a century later when a Chicago attorney wrote to ask if they hadn't met when both were students at the university. Alfred Eisenstaedt was positive Du Bois had called at the offices of *Das Kleine Journal* in response to an ad for German lessons in exchange for English. Du Bois had given the young German law student a tutorial on American race relations that had left him stupefied. Studying Du Bois's photo in Benjamin Brawley's *History of the American Negro*,

Eisenstaedt recognized the man who had "so deeply touched" him with a description of the Negro problem that "even today I remember these facts."[48] But there had been no exchange of language lessons after all, the Chicago attorney recalled, "I guess because the American student would have liked to discuss at once the German law and I was at that time only in the beginning of my study."[49]

Du Bois's social behavior was constrained, ultimately, by factors that no amount of attempted gregariousness could really have overcome. There were numerous instances in which European culture and racial identity grappled with each other—instances in which he became acutely aware at some level of a conflict between culture and destiny. A case in point was the kaiser prancing on horseback through the Brandenburg Gate at the head of his "white and golden troops," with Du Bois "thrilled at the sight" and stroking his pointed mustaches. As Wilhelm II gleamed and clanked down the Linden, Du Bois sensed "that dichotomy which all my life has characterized my thought," he recalled much later; "how far can love for my oppressed race accord with love for the oppressing country? And when these loyalties diverge," where could his soul come to rest?[50] When von Treitschke, a volcanic bigot of encyclopedic learning, suddenly erupted in class one morning, apropos of nothing in particular, "*Die Mulattin[en] sind niedrig*! *Sie fuhlen sich niedrig*" (Mulattoes are inferior! They feel themselves inferior), Du Bois insisted the remark was neither directed toward himself nor particularly upsetting. The lumbering Prussian historian was probably not even aware that there was a mulatto in the lecture hall, Du Bois thought, nor did his classmates seem to make the connection. Besides, von Treitschke often deplored the influence of Jews and criticized the German government outrageously. "His outlook is that of the born aristocrat who has something of the Carlyle contempt of levelling democracy," Du Bois decided. Yet, for all his interpretive generosity, the mulatto from Great Barrington would hardly have missed the personal relevance of von Treitschke's invidious remark.[51]

BUT IF he could never totally belong to Germany and to Europe, he intended to make certain he fully understood why. Until Bismarck's devious diplomacy and Helmuth von Moltke's military strategy made the Hohenzollern Reich possible after a few weeks of summer war in 1870, Germany had been a culture in search of a nation. By population, three fifths of the formidable new fatherland was Prussian, as was in spirit if not numbers its monocled officer corps and fustian civil service.[52] Du Bois's notebook caught the Prussian ethos, as he saw it, just weeks after settling in at the university. "German ideals from king to lower orders appear at first sight to be clad in spurs and shoulder straps," he wrote. Berlin moved in a "half military stride." What he saw impelled him to draw an unfavorable comparison of the German federal system to the American. The USA was a "boundlessly optimistic state founded on individual freedom," whereas Germany, for all its order, efficiency, high culture, and social welfare institutions, was a "restlessly pessimistic state founded on obedience."[53] Yet even as he recorded these quick, harsh impressions, Germany was in its second year of liberal reforms under Bismarck's able successor, chancellor Leo von Caprivi, an unlikely Prussian aristocrat who boasted of owning no land, and whose policies legalized the Socialist party, created arbitration courts in industry, and imposed lower agricultural tariffs on the flabbergasted Junkers of Silesia and Pomerania. Caprivi even dared to contemplate abolishing the three-class electoral system of the oligarchic Prussian legislature, or Diet.[54]

Nevertheless, Du Bois saw the Prussian reality; Caprivi's was the Germany of the enlightened poet Heinrich Heine, a version destined not to prevail. In Wilhelm II, German emperor and Prussian king, Prussia had a ruler who pandered to its autocratic, martial inclinations, a monarch whose own father once snapped, "Look at my son—the complete Guards officer."[55] But how true were these generalizations for Germany beyond Prussia, for Bavaria with its quirky Wittelsbach dynasty or the cities along the Rhine where the spirit of '48 survived? The Christmas vacation before that portentous twenty-fifth birthday, Du Bois had set off with two other Berlin colleagues, a German-American and the Englishman John Dollar, on a Baedeker tour, heading first for Goethe's Weimar, then southwest to Frankfurt, Mannheim, Heidelberg, and the Pfalz region. The route from Weimar to Frankfurt passed near Eisenach, but Dora was not on the itinerary. They stayed from Christmas to the New Year in a tiny village off the map somewhere near Neustadt, in an atmosphere of wine-soused sociability, where Du Bois set about comparing the mores and living standards of some twenty peasant families who treated him "like a prince!" with those of Tennessee backcountry African-Americans. Schmoller, his principal professor, had suggested this topic, which was intended to be the focus of Du Bois's proposed German doctoral thesis. In Neustadt, the trio was housed for a week by a family whose head had driven the first troop train into France during the Franco-Prussian War. Du Bois remembered fondly the "fine, homely" daughter who "did everything to make us comfortable."[56]

The German-American was a decent enough fellow, but, after Strasbourg and Stuttgart—when the cultural diet thickened with the Raphaels and Titians in Munich's glorious Alte Pinakothek and became positively academic at Nuremberg, Albrecht Dürer's hometown—he dropped out with relief (his education had "left no visible results," Du Bois decided).[57] The sole male friendship of his German period began with Dollar on the Christmas vacation tour. He thought they got on "famously together" because they were such opposites. Dollar was "coldly and conventionally British" and "constitutionally afraid of women." When he and Dollar roved back to Berlin by way of Prague and Dresden, Du Bois made the most of his introduction to German painting, sculpture, and architecture. Eventually, his knowledge of European masterworks would be distilled into the richly detailed paper he would read to his first students at Wilberforce University, "The Art and Art Galleries of Modern Europe." His report to the Slater Fund itemized a frugal total of eighty dollars.[58]

From mid-March to mid-April, when the second semester commenced, Du Bois and Baedeker (but no Dollar) were on the road again. Applying for renewal of his Slater stipend, he explained to Gilman of Johns Hopkins that he could save money by surrendering his Oranienstrasse lodgings and spending the spring break at Kassel. He traveled there by heading first to the old Hanseatic cities of Lübeck, Hamburg, and Bremen, then south to make the obligatory *Harzreise*, the walk through the Harz Mountains and up the Brocken, the peak on which, German mythology holds, the Walpurgis Night revels take place on April 30. His travel notes mentioned a "dear girl who met and loved me" in Kassel, possibly Amalie but probably someone else; but in any case another woman who serviced his large and enlarging appetite for sex.[59] The notes were silent, however, about another matter. That spring excursion brought a racial experience so shattering that he would never write about it. His mood had been one of bubbling well-being on a Friday morning as he left Berlin from the Stettin Bahnhof at dawn aboard the Lübeck express, alone as usual. "Floods of the sweetest yellow sunshine" bathed his compartment. Lakes and marshes flitted by. He sang quietly a favorite passage from his favorite symphony, Beethoven's ninth: *"Aller Menschen werden Bruder."* "So wonderful," he exulted in the diary, "so wonderful—I could sing it over the wide grey-green fields—over the green pine forests—over the great north world reawakening today into a sweet new life of toil and gladness."[60]

The mood began to falter in Lübeck soon after leaving his small hotel that evening. At first, there were the little girls "who rode for one station and giggled" at his dark face as he traveled on the streetcar. He was utterly unprepared for the Saturday-morning experience in the town market. "Heavens, but these Lubeckers are curious." He was "used to curiosity on a pretty large scale" but not like this. Suddenly, they were pursuing him, men, women, and children, staring, gesticulating, chattering—the page in his diary became a tablet of almost indecipherable strokes. "These children, o God these children—how they do stare and what can a man do when children stare?" Anger welled up in Du Bois, "anger, and a general feeling of forlornness and homesickness that is terrible." By the time he boarded the express for Bremen, the diary had composed itself, yet, for a page or so, Du Bois showed himself vulnerable in a way that he would never again permit himself to record.[61] As far as he was concerned, this slip of the mask, five weeks after his twenty-fifth birthday, never happened. (These pages in the diary were lost until now.) The interlude behind him, Du Bois had little time for anything but academic work and worry about renewal of his fellowship. The answer from Baltimore came in late May 1893, after a desperate telegram. The Slater Fund trustees were "willing to renew" on the same terms as before. They awaited his note for $350.

The future secure again, he decided to take a large fourth-floor room in the Schöneberger Ufer, Berlin's fashionable canal neighborhood. Fairly spacious and comfortably furnished, these were ideal quarters in which to take the sweeps through literary and philosophical classics his perfection as gentleman scholar demanded. This was the period in which Du Bois committed to memory for a lifetime those salient passages he would recite to intimates or to captivated after-dinner guests. He delved more deeply than ever before into Goethe, Heine, and Johann Friedrich von Schiller. *William Tell* and *Don Carlos*, Schiller's great play establishing the use of blank verse in the German language, would have been familiar, as would the poet-dramatist's essay on the poetic imagination, "*Über naive und sentimentalische Dichtung*." A lengthy letter published in the September *Herald* charged Fiskites to master the culture of Europe and to immerse themselves in Goethe in order to speed "the rise of the Negro people."[62] Between Goethe and Du Bois there was a singular goodness of fit that made the experience of reading *Young Werther* and *Wilhelm Meister* one of unflagging exaltation; and that of communing with *Faust* an epiphany.

Du Bois felt a similar affinity for Hegel, from whose monumental *Phenomenology of Mind* he borrowed more or less intact notions of distinct, hierarchical racial attributes. And for all James's supposed pragmatic and empirical influences upon him, Du Bois found in the Hegelian

World-Spirit, dialectically actualizing itself through history, a profoundly appealing concept. "Lordship and Bondage," Hegel's lodestar essay, explicated a complex reciprocity of master and slave in which the identities of both could be fully realized only to the extent that the consciousness of one was mediated through that of the other. If the master understood dominance, it was the slave who truly understood the sovereign value of freedom. "Just as lordship showed its essential nature to be the reverse of what it wants to be," Du Bois read in Hegel, "so, too, bondage will, when completed, pass into the opposite of what it immediately is: being a consciousness repressed within itself, it will enter into itself, and change round into real and true independence."[63] Surely this was an idea Du Bois would eventually reformulate more poetically.

In early August at the beginning of the summer recess, he and "dear old Dollar" left for southern Germany, Switzerland, Austria, and Hungary. We learn a little more about John Dollar on this trip. In addition to being afraid of women, he had a positive hatred of Catholic priests and felt deep compassion for suffering humanity. He was also practical. It was Dollar's idea that they speak German in order to travel more cheaply. Although the ruse worked, he and Du Bois were somehow mistaken for French in the Roman Forum and stoned by angry Italian youngsters, an episode giving Du Bois an unforgettable glimpse of the jingoistic powder keg one day to be set off by the European system of alliances. After the funky charm of Naples, they headed north for Venice, then on to Europe's unrivaled metropolis of paradox—aristocratic, bourgeois Vienna. Dollar and Du Bois parted company there—"his engagements called him," Du Bois says simply.[64] Budapest offered another striking lesson in the havoc wrought by nationalisms. Hungarians were so intent upon thumbing their noses at Austrians that Du Bois had trouble finding officials who would admit to speaking German. More lessons came as he roamed the back roads of the Austro-Hungarian empire, always third class and frequently on foot. Few Americans had ever followed their Baedekers north to Slovakia and into the pines carpeting the High Tatras, as Du Bois did, a solitary brown scholar with knapsack and walking stick tacking along what many Europeans called the edges of civilization. Stanislaus Ritter von Estreicher, one of his Berlin colleagues, had almost dared Du Bois to visit him in Poland if he really wanted to see race problems.[65]

On he rode and walked, across lands where he saw a feudal agriculture strapped to the backs of peasants more ignorant, overworked, and fatalistic than any in the American South.[66] Seventeen years in the future, Booker

T. Washington would travel first class much the same route as Du Bois, but although the Tuskegee Institute principal and the university graduate reached similar conclusions after comparing the working poor of Europe and America, they put them to very different political and propaganda uses.[67] Du Bois entered the part of Poland still ruled from Vienna. By then, he had been routinely mistaken for a Gypsy and a Jew. Quoted the price of rooms in the Jewish section of a town by a carriage driver, he had assented readily, repeating "*Unter die[den] Juden*" (with the Jews). What he experienced in Poland of race hatred between Poles and Germans, with anti-Semitism evenly divided between both groups, was a truly depressing revelation. The lordly von Estreichers of Cracow were sensitive and enlightened when compared to the usual run of German masters among the Poles. They welcomed Du Bois to the former Polish capital as they would have any *grand seigneur*. They showed him a world of ancient customs, glacial change, much learning and gentilesse, but also a world rotten with religious and class hatreds. "It was an interesting visit and an old tale," Du Bois decided, finding the lot of the people at the bottom and of the religiously persecuted one of "tyranny in school work; insult in home and on the street." Von Estreicher would die in a concentration camp in 1940 for refusing to collaborate with the German occupiers.[68]

The final leg of his *Heimreise* took Du Bois through Breslau to Dresden and back to Berlin in late September, well in time to have a comprehensive outline of his doctoral thesis ready by the beginning of term. After the summer's experiences, he must have felt culturally equipped to compete no matter what the company. No longer could he "bear the thought of living alone again." He decided to risk the family-style setup of the Braun Pension, and he was soon smugly satisfied that he had done so—not only because of the "pleasant companionship and family life," but for the "opportunity to teach an American family what a 'nigger' is," he wrote, apparently of another prickly experience with his white compatriots.[69] The likes of Mr. and Mrs. Far West Professor would never disconcert him again.

WHEN THE German Democratic Republic renamed the University of Berlin in honor of its founder von Humboldt after World War II, it ordered carved above the columned entrance hall Marx's aphorism, "Until now philosophers have only explained the world, our task is to change it." More than sixty years earlier, as he strode with cane and gloves to lectures in its high-ceilinged halls, Du Bois increasingly came to embody this transforming conception of knowledge. The two professors of political economy, Schmoller and Wagner, had a profound impact on him in this direction. Not that old alumnus Marx's ideas were any less anathema at Berlin than at Harvard. Whereas Marx made the industrial proletariat the supreme agency of social change, Schmoller and Wagner were elitists who expected the cream of the Prussian bureaucracy, much of it trained by them, to guide the guardian state scientifically as it intervened between the citizen and the market place. Believing that capitalism was too serious a system to be managed solely by capitalists, they exhorted the state to ride herd on the great cartels; and with more than a suggestion of superior German lucidity, Wagner and especially Schmoller dismissed the self-correcting market laws of Manchester economics almost as finally as Marx had.[70] Their inspiration was Fichte's concept of an economy whose competing interests are kept in equilibrium by an intelligent state. Although this new German school of historical economics was rather a mixed bag, with large and small differences between Schmoller and Wagner, and colleagues at other German universities, its distinguishing premise was firm enough. Du Bois's seminar notes quoted Schmoller as saying "My school tries as far as possible to leave the *Sollen* [should be] for a later stage and study the *Geschehen* [what is actual] as other sciences have done."[71] It was another way of saying what James and Hart had said—that in history, large patterns emerge only after much sifting of the particulars.

If their claims to scientific methodology ring somehow both commonsensical and overblown today, this is partly because of the impact of Schmoller and Wagner in modernizing social science in their time. In stressing the primacy of observed phenomena over theory or ideal constructs, they were a force against the system-building dominant in the social sciences at the end of the nineteenth century, especially against the grandiose pretentions of the English engineer-turned-sociologist, Herbert Spencer, and his many enthusiastic disciples. Schmoller, whose subsequent disparaging of the value-free, "transcendentalist and purely formal ethic" of Weberian sociology would be notable, pounded home in his lectures that sociology was "as much a realistic science to me as economics."[72] Du Bois was by intellectual temperament profoundly susceptible to a belief in universals (and, in fact, to all manner of Hegelian excesses), and much restraint was provided by Schmoller's seminar in political economy and Wagner's lecture course in the same subject. Max Weber had not then clearly formulated his concepts of "ideal types" and objective rationality as a unique attempt to combine empirical sociological research with universals revealed through history.[73] Yet even a few lectures by Weber had impressed Du Bois by their universalist leanings. Had he fallen under the tutelage of Georg Simmel, the star of sociology at Berlin, Du Bois's approach to sociology might have been radically different. With Simmel, there was an analogous subordination of social behavior to comprehensive systems.

During the first two semesters at Berlin, what kept Du Bois busiest was research for his seminar thesis, "*Der Gross und Klein Betrieb des Ackerbaus, in den Sudstaaten der Vereinigten Staaten, 1840–90*," or "The Large and Small-scale System of Agriculture in the Southern United States, 1840–1890."[74] Although he was able to build on his work under Hart at Harvard, the bulk of the essay was based on new reading, as well as new thinking about history and economics from, so to speak, the bottom up. But Du Bois seems never to have explained why the comparative German-peasant dimension of the thesis failed to materialize. Schmoller expressed enough satisfaction that Du Bois had been able to inform the Slater Fund trustees (and condole the death of Hayes) that March of "a fair possibility" of being allowed to stand for his Ph.D. examination in economics once he had completed only three semesters in residence. A doctorate in economics from Berlin ("the most difficult of German degrees") would represent the capstone of western academic preparation. Not just for himself, then, but "for the sake of my race," he must try to obtain this degree, he wrote Gilman.[75] Renewal of his fellowship in May had seemed to seal the prospects for the German Ph.D. On top of the Schmoller seminar and one with Wagner in economics and history, he heaped on another in statistics under Professor Neitzen, as well as a lecture course in the Reformation under Professor Lenz during his third semester ending in mid-March 1894.

Calling all this "a deal of work" while writing his doctoral thesis, Du Bois managed, in addition to his fuller social life in the Braun Pension (and the affair with Amalie), to look in on the Socialists. Unable to win Reichstag approval of the military's seven-year budget, Chancellor Caprivi had risked national elections in June 1893 rather than attempting to govern through emergency powers as the tight, high-strung little circle around the kaiser had advised. The impressive Reichstag gains of the Social Democratic party (SPD) had surprised Du Bois more than most Germans. Because Germany's geography dictated vigilant preparation to fight a war on two fronts, his 1892 notebook ruminations had concluded that "a strong military monarchy [was] indispensable." Party government and democracy would be tantamount to "committing suicide," given the "almost total inexperience of her people today"—a significant notebook confession that would have delighted members of Mississippi's 1890 constitutional convention. But now, with Caprivi's conciliatory policies and the meteoric rise in Socialist voters from 1,427,000 in 1890 to almost 2 million, Du Bois was tempted to change his mind.[76] The ideological distinctions between Marx and the revisionist followers of Ferdinand Lassalle, August Bebel, and Karl Kautsky were "too complicated for a student like myself to understand," but he began attending SPD meetings in the working-class Pankow district, especially after his return from summer vacation.[77]

In the *Autobiography* he blamed his student status for hindering "that close personal acquaintanceship with [the] workers" that he needed in order to gain "complete understanding." At this stage in his political thinking, Du Bois's fascination with socialism was primarily exploratory, an ambivalent interest in a full-service ideology providing a comprehensive explanation, prediction, and solution for economic and social disorders. But for the present and for many years to come, he remained in the iron grip of an ideology of culture in which human progress was measured in terms of manners, the arts, great literature, and great ideals, a secular creed, the intellectual historian Lewis Perry has observed, which limited profoundly "how programs of reform were conceived" because of its relative indifference to material comforts and outright disdain for mass agitation. Just how far Du Bois had yet to go before his acquired elitism allowed him to empathize with the struggling workers is suggested by another revealing Berlin notebook entry, "The Socialism of German Socialists": too many of the Socialists belonged to "that anarchistic, semi-criminal proletariat which always, in all countries, attaches itself to the most radical party."[78] Still, he had taken a significant first step.

On December 6, 1893, the Slater Fund was sent news that the doctoral thesis was finished. Two days earlier, he had read part of it before Schmoller's seminar. As he had been given to understand by the dean of the philosophical faculty in March, he now needed only to submit his thesis to the Ministry of Education with a request to be examined at the close of the semester. Naturally assuming that the rest was a mere formality, he planned to spend his fourth and final semester abroad at either the University of Tübingen or the Ecole des Hautes Etudes des Sciences Politiques in Paris.[79] In a few weeks, he would realize the twenty-fifth-birthday-night vow to make a name in social science. On his twenty-sixth birthday, a Friday, he strolled Friedrichstrasse, savoring the contents of letters from three female admirers, then decided to drop in for a bit of reading in the seminar library. He took dinner in the Braun Pension. That night he spent with devoted Amalie, but before leaving his room about 7:30 he boasted in a confessional notebook: "I have finally proved to my entire satisfaction that my race forms but slight impediment between me and kindred souls. . . . I am here free from most of those iron bands that bound me at home. Therefore, I have gained for my life work new hope and zeal—the Negro people shall yet stand among the honored of the world."[80] In the mirror he saw a trim figure with bristling mustaches and a distinctive part—Herr Doktor W. E. Burghardt Du Bois of the august University of Berlin.

Du Bois's failure to win the German doctorate resulted from a combination of the adventitious and the sinister. Despite Schmoller's and Wagner's support and the dean's assurances, spirited objections from the senior professor of chemistry (later Du Bois erroneously blamed the professor of English) precluded Du Bois's exemption from the requirement of four completed semesters before a student was permitted to stand for the doctoral examination. As Du Bois explained to Gilman, this professor "threatened that if so great an exception was made in my case, he must bring forward ten similar cases from his laboratory."[81] Matters of precedent being as ferociously defended among professors as among lawyers, Dean Hirschfeld probably foresaw a half dozen more such objections, once the first had become a matter of record. Du Bois would have to spend a fourth semester at Berlin, which meant having to wait out the summer until the beginning of academic year 1894–95 to defend his thesis. If the Slater Fund agreed to one more renewal—and just for a half year—then he and the race would have their degree. "And here I am in doubt as to my course," a notebook entry reads, "a bit disappointed but"—the dogged will reasserts itself—"I will have a *Philosophiae Doctor* from Berlin." The puzzling minor chord in his notebook, that his thesis "does not suit me," he never let sound in his published writings.[82] Did Du Bois mean by that that the topic was either not broad enough or, more probably, lacked a European comparative dimension that he had not developed out of the Christmas study of the twenty village families? The disappearance of his German doctoral thesis makes the mystery unsolvable.

Wagner wrote a strong letter of support to the trustees, as did Schmoller, who pointed out that German universities required six semesters' work for the Ph.D, and that one semester was occasionally trimmed or, in Du Bois's case, even two ("because we were able to express so favorable an opinion"), but, due to the chemistry-professor complication, unfortunately not three. Du Bois's March 31 letter to Gilman, asking him "what is best under the circumstances," was uncharacteristically plaintive. In asking the fund for another extension, he didn't "wish to appear grasping on the one hand," yet, on the other, it was unthinkable to "relinquish a great opportunity without a struggle."[83] When Gilman's turndown came toward the end of April, its tone suggested that the "recent meeting" of Slater Fund trustees had been another of those pivotal gatherings at which leading white men, North and South, threshed out racial misgivings on African-American backs. Not only had they decided that it "was not best to renew your appointment," wrote Gilman, but, in the matter of fellowships to "advanced students," the trustees had voted "not to make any other at present." Gilman advised Du Bois to present himself for the Ph.D. at Harvard, adding, with a possible hint of their displeasure at Du Bois's recondite Berlin transcript, that, "particularly in respect of your course of study," some of the trustees "expressed, with great earnestness, the hope that . . . you will devote your talent and learning to the good of the colored race."[84] Was this Gilman's cryptic way of suggesting that Du Bois's program of study had become much too rarefied to suit the men who had the heavy responsibility of guiding Negro higher education into appropriate channels? The distinguished Johns Hopkins president seemed to be imparting the view—favored by grey colonels and portly divines—that Du Bois's case, by its superlative success abroad, merely proved the original unwisdom of Hayes's experiment in the higher education of Negroes. How useful to the education of a people one generation removed from slavery could a University of Berlin–minted teacher be, after all? What was left of John Slater's million henceforth went toward the training of primary school teachers and the construction of school buildings. Black Ph.D.s from Germany were not a priority in Booker T. Washington's America.

Du Bois grieved in his notebooks; consoling himself with favorite lines from *Faust*: "*Entbehren sollst du, sollst entbehren*" [Thou shalt forgo, shalt do without]."[85] Then he left for Paris. No clear picture of Amalie, the young Berliner with whom he spent many pleasurable evenings, emerges from anything he wrote. Was she blonde, plump, brunette and svelte, a bit common, or possessed of an inquiring mind? It's clear Du Bois used Amalie in the egocentric way that gentlemen of his time and class often did, because he spoke of her later as the Berlin shop girl with whom he "lived more or less regularly . . . but was ashamed."[86] Since he had just enough money left to last through Paris and London, it was out of the question to invite her along on his farewell tour of the south that spring.

Amalie fades from history, as Du Bois took the train for Magdeburg and Halberstadt in Saxony. He walked up the Brocken again, writing in his touched-by-destiny prose of fording streams and climbing mountains during his last day and night in Germany, "until in full darkness [he] came to an old inn." Ordering beer and *Kalbsbraten*, he dined alone. "This was my perfect farewell to a Germany which no longer exists."[87] As he took his leave, the Junkers and the great industrialists were making final preparations to bring down the reform ministry of Chancellor Caprivi. After October 1894, the tropism of German politics would move inexorably to the right, even as the voting strength of the Socialists continued to grow.

The Baedeker pages fly past from now on. Du Bois gamboled through France in May. "Saw Paris; wandered wide and deep and," he claimed, made his French "fairly understandable," an assertion gently qualified by French-speaking acquaintances. He saw Sarah Bernhardt in performance, applauded the cancan at the Moulin Rouge, and "haunted" the Louvre where he made elaborate notes on the collections. These notes reveal, unsurprisingly, an appreciation for art that was keener for its historical than for its aesthetic content, although two statues—the Praxiteles Venus and Winged Victory of Samothrace—sent his prose soaring.[88] A month later, he would have soaked up the impassioned sidewalk-café talk about the anarchist assassination of the president of the Third Republic, Sadi Carnot. That fall, Alfred Dreyfus, a young captain on duty with the army general staff, would be arrested and tried for treason. But Du Bois left France in late May for London to spend a few days with "dear old Dollar." Dollar's family maintained a prosperous veterinary surgical establishment in New Bond Street. He seems to have been one of those Victorians whose lives were too ordered even for quiet desperation. Methodically showing Du Bois a gentleman's London—Parliament, Westminster Abbey, St. Paul's, the National Gallery, the British Museum—Dollar fended off his visitor's every attempt to pay his own way, which was just as well because Du Bois had less than twenty dollars in his wallet. Their last hours together were spent discussing the architecture of Waterloo Station and casting a sociological eye on the disparate crowd heading for Southampton. Finally, as the boat train shuddered forward, they shook hands and Dollar reminded Du Bois of his advice about cabin selection. "Dollar, dear old boy, hadn't the slightest idea that I was going steerage," Du Bois chuckled in his notebook.[89] Perhaps not, but Dollar loaned him a small sum of money to make the passage pleasanter.

The return to America was vintage huddled masses. The smell of vomit from drunken fellow travelers woke and drove him out of a dockside shed into the early Southampton morning. At noon, unshaved and unbathed, he boarded the ship single file with eight hundred others. Descending with about 350 passengers to grim quarters deep below deck, he found a "picturesque and laughable crowd—young and old—lame and well—rags and fine clothes—Jew and gentile, Russians, English, Americans, Negroes, Poles, Germans, French, Greeks, Austrians. . . ." The old and slow *Chester* wallowed out of port like an unhappy hippopotamus, with the German scholar at the rails only just managing to keep his small breakfast down. Much better on day two, tapping about with cane and gloves, he began notebook studies of the *Chester's* population. He judged there were "about an even mixture of honest people and rascals," and, in finding the Jewish passengers "a half-veiled mystery," he revealed how ingrained and reinforced by WASP Harvard and Lutheran Prussia his New England cast of mind remained. Well acquainted with upper-class Jewish circles and averse to stereotypes "from principle," Du Bois nevertheless managed to sound like von Treitschke in deploring what he perceived as the absence among Jews of "that strong middle class which in every nation holds the brunt of culture." He supposed that the prevalence of "the low mean cheating *Pobel* [rabble]" was the result of a "curious history which being peculiar and unfortunate must have peculiar and unfortunate results."[90] Significantly, neither these observations nor the following extremely revealing one were later carried over into the published writings. Commenting on the African-Americans aboard, the posthumously edited *Autobiography* reads: "There are five Negroes aboard. We do not go together." In the original text, Du Bois had written: "There are two full-blooded Negroes aboard and (including myself) 3 half [crossed-out] mulattoes."[91]

This subtext of proud hybridization is so prevalent in Du Bois's sense of himself that the failure to notice it in the literature about him is as remarkable as the complex itself. Graduate student Du Bois had informed Harvard's trustees that his father was a quadroon, and had thought it equally useful to misrepresent Mary Silvina to them and the Slater Fund trustees ("my mother was a mulatto"), and to stress that he himself was "about one half or more Negro."[92] The vocabulary of Du Bois's generation resounded with the racialisms of Joseph-Arthur de Gobineau, Edouard Drumont, Francis Galton, Thomas Carlyle, and Bishop William Stubbs, with evolutionist buzzwords ranking "superior" and "inferior" races according to pseudo-anthropological findings. In syntactically tortuous observations made not many years after Du Bois's return, William James's brother, Henry, approached people off boats like the *Chester* with a deep, superior puzzlement that would become translated into the 1907 classic *The American Scene*. African-American college graduates were just as inclined to unthinking use of these buzzwords, as with Du Bois praising the full-blooded Negroes on the *Chester* for "their goodheartedness—their straightforwardness."[93] Moreover, it would have bespoken considerable humility, a quality Du Bois never intentionally displayed, for him not to have felt, with Fisk, Harvard, and Berlin imprinted on his haughty face, a certain class superiority to these ordinary men and women in steerage, whether Negro, Jew, Russian, or Greek. To the extent that he was parroting the received unwisdom of the day, he was himself still its victim—if one on the road to recovery. But was there not also a deeper culpability in these notebook reflections, a willfully arrogant, private, standing apart as a different breed from the great majority of the people of the race he believed it his destiny to uplift? If so, then it was to be anticipated that his racial militancy would be at once driven and circumscribed by a marrow-deep elitism for an as-yet-undetermined timespan.

Frédéric-Auguste Bartholdi's statue with Emma Lazarus's pedestal inscription welcomed Du Bois on a clear morning in mid-June 1894. For two years, he had grown more and more accustomed to meeting white "men and women as [he] had never met them before," and slowly, he found them becoming "not white folks, but folks." Resting his elbows on the ship's railing, he found himself remembering something a little French girl had said: "Oh yes the Statue of Liberty! With its back toward America, and its face toward France!" As the *Wanderjahre* of his Age of Miracles ended with the *Chester*'s hawsers being yoked to the pier, Du Bois wrote: "I dropped suddenly back into 'nigger'-hating America!"[94]

7.
Wilberforce
Book, Mentor, Marriage

ALMOST TWO years after returning to America, twenty-eight-year-old Professor Du Bois paused for breath and brought John Dollar up to date. Ticket fare home and two dollars had been the sum total of his wealth when he left the *Chester*, he wrote. As the train home had risen into the Berkshires, his own spirits had fallen at the prospect of two months or more in Great Barrington's well-intentioned curiosity, genuine pride, and inevitable jealousy. After dazzling them with travelogues at the Congregational and AME Zion churches, what was there to talk about with the black Burghardts or with GBHS pals who had become bank clerks and shoe salesmen? "It was too much of a disillusionment," he wrote his English listening post. With no money, Slater Fund debts, no positions available at any white college or university, and rural Tennessee authorities dismayed by a German-trained scholar's offer to teach public school, Du Bois was a perfect illustration of one of Booker T. Washington's jokes about the perils of runaway education. It was as though "the bottom of the universe was loose and might go down if, after all this learning, [he] stepped full feet upon it."[1]

The striking imagery was not quite apt, though; it was Du Bois, not the bottom of the universe, who had been in danger of dropping from sight. "I raise my hat to myself," the *Autobiography* boasted later; he had quickly steadied his shaken confidence, and sat down to write dozens of inquiries: to Howard, Hampton, Fisk, Tuskegee, Wilberforce—"so many letters that I scarcely remember where." "President Washington, Sir! May I ask if you have a vacancy in your institution next year?" one letter had inquired of the Tuskegee Institute principal on July 27, 1894. "The hot months rolled by and answers came slowly," he told Dollar. "It wasn't too much for a colored man with a Harvard A.M. to expect a bread and butter job—was it?"[2] Actually, the replies had come fairly quickly. Booker T. Washington's telegram arrived in Great Barrington on August 25: "Can give mathematics here if terms suit. Will you accept. Wire answer." By then, however, Du Bois had eagerly accepted the August 17 telegraphed offer of $800 a year to occupy the classics chair at Wilberforce University. He had felt honor-bound to decline a second generous $1,050 annual salary offer from Lincoln Institute in Missouri. "So late in hot August," Du Bois had departed Great Barrington for the oldest college for Negroes in the United States. The turning-point prose of the *Autobiography* shifts into paean: "Life was now begun and I was half happy. Up through the Berkshire Valley with its quiet beauty, then across New York I glided, wrapped in dreams. The lights of Buffalo bade me goodnight, and half asleep, I drifted across Ohio."[3]

The village of Wilberforce was about twenty miles southeast of Dayton and three dusty miles of buggy tracks from Xenia, the nearest incorporated town. Yellow Springs, seat of Antioch College, was ten miles due north—if anything in that part of western Ohio had been reachable directly. But this was rolling farmland where roads meandered through cornfields and forded rock-bedded streams under covered bridges. It was native country to Middle America's truest novelist, Sherwood Anderson, then an unfocused seventeen-year-old dreaming of adult life in Chicago. Wilberforce had come into being as the sylvan solution to the sins of slaveholding fathers. The place was originally called Tawawa Springs by the Native Americans, after the health-giving waters that drew rich planters to summer there in the early decades of the nineteenth century. The rambling, 350-room Tawawa Springs, with its arbored fountains and manicured grounds, was perhaps the most unusual resort hotel in America, however, because its clientele consisted of slave masters, their concubines, and their children.[4] The Quakers of the region deplored this monument to concupiscence with its langorous mores and rainbow population—the likes of which they might have expected to find on the banks of the Amazon, but certainly not a mere 160 miles south of antislavery Oberlin.

The savage Panic of 1837 and militant Ohio abolitionism gradually killed the great hotel, inducing a group of planters to buy the property for use as a school for their children from the other side of the blanket. In 1852, the white Methodists of Xenia acquired Tawawa Springs, renaming it after Britain's premier abolitionist, Bishop William Wilberforce, incorporating it as a university four years later. The African Methodist Episcopal denomination, the oldest religious sect in black America, bought the school in 1863, and twenty-four years later a wily black politician on his way to becoming an AME bishop introduced a bill in the Ohio legislature to create the "Combined Normal and Industrial Department at Wilberforce University"—guaranteeing, in one fell swoop, a rising annual appropriation from Ohio's taxpayers for one of the rare American universities under the authority of both church and state. The politician's bill also institutionalized racial segregation in the state's system of higher education.[5]

When President S. T. Mitchell fetched Du Bois from the waiting room of Xenia's railroad station on a late-summer afternoon in 1894, then, Wilberforce University had been the flagship institution of the AME Church since the school's purchase thirty-one years earlier by the sainted Bishop Daniel A. Payne for ten thousand dollars. A tiny, beige man of powerful intellect and austere principles who had reigned over fellow bishops and much of the AME denomination through sheer force of character, freeborn Daniel Payne had worn out his delicate frame through fund-raising in Europe and America. His death as presiding bishop the previous November had greatly unsettled the Wilberforce community, as another bishop, a man of flatter vision and values, who had lived until then in Payne's shadow, imposed his will. Du Bois told Dollar that he would never forget seeing the Wilberforce president's smile the first time—"it was the prettiest smile of any man I ever saw."[6] Pretty, but not genuine; an accomplished executioner's smile. President Mitchell clearly was not going to turn out to be cast from the mold of Erastus Cravath, Charles Eliot, or Daniel Payne.

Du Bois was encountering a new species, whose mid-twentieth-century perfection would be reached in novelist Ralph Ellison's saturnine Dr. Bledsoe in *Invisible Man*. Beholden to trustees concerned solely with racial good behavior, here grand inquisitors, there enlightened despots, these dynasts presided over Afro-America's other institutional pillar, the school (in its incarnations as institute, college, or university), with all the trappings of royalty but seldom royalty's true noblesse. For Du Bois, the effeminate, devious President Mitchell became "the most perfect realization of what the devil might be in the closing years of the 19th [century]." Behind the devil, though, there was Moloch himself—heavyset, one-legged Benjamin William Arnett, Sr., one-time member of the state legislature, church powerhouse, chairman of Wilberforce's trustee board, and soon to be chief advisor in all Negro matters to fellow Ohioan and twenty-fifth U.S. president, William McKinley.[7] The authority of President Mitchell was as nothing compared with the real power and influence of Bishop Arnett, who, now that the restraining influence of Daniel Payne was no more, intended to rule the university like a satrapy, monitoring and even controlling its curriculum, and periodically increasing its faculty with several of his five ambitious sons.

The first thing the seventeenth bishop of the AME Church had done was to fire William Scarborough, Wilberforce's most distinguished professor, from the chair of classics. Born in slavery to Georgia parents able to read and write, Scarborough had earned degrees in Greek and Latin from Atlanta University and Oberlin College. Only the third African-American admitted to membership in the American Philological Association, the classics professor's *First Lessons in Greek* (1881) was a standard textbook and his translation of Aristophanes' *Birds* (1886) critically lauded. But these were times in higher education when tenure was in most places still tenuous, and the courtly classicist quickly ran afoul of Bishop Arnett's nepotistic politics. "But I had assumed that I was to assist" Scarborough, an unsuspecting Du Bois stuttered upon discovering that he was instead the bishop's answer to faculty murmurings over the sacking of its most prestigious member.[8]

Into this Machiavellian situation Du Bois "landed with cane and gloves," innocent, arrogant, and dedicated to pedagogical standards that were no more useful to the bishop and president than the declensions found in Professor Scarborough's Greek textbook. He found the pastoral campus setting Edenic, but the culture of the community seemed to him not just parochial (that he had expected), but primitive and hysterically religious. People at Wilberforce flaunted their religion at every opportunity. Revival meetings could sweep the campus like wildfire, emptying classes for days and leaving students either too agitated or too exhausted for serious work for many days thereafter. Wandering into a religious gathering soon after arriving, the new faculty member heard a devout student say, " 'Professor Du Bois will lead us in prayer.' " Snapping back, " 'No, he won't,' " Du Bois believed he had only narrowly escaped the summary fate of his predecessor because of his bottomless capacity for work. That the new professor of Latin and Greek (and, as he discovered, English, German, and history) might be some sort of agnostic or a believer in impersonal forces would not have occurred to the bishop and his trustees. Their charitable conclusion that Du Bois (whose appointment had received publicity in the Negro press) was a sardonic, brainy eccentric easily worth twice his salary saved him.[9]

Ego and enthusiasm made for a zestful combination. Du Bois "wanted to help build a great university," readily taking on a schedule that worked him from daybreak chapel to final evening prayers. He tried to convey to his first-year Greek class something of the meaning and excitement of Sophocles' *Antigone*, and one student in particular, Charles Burroughs, responded brightly and recited well. This same Burroughs would serve Du Bois faithfully years later in connection with Du Bois's ambitious pageant, *The Star of Ethiopia*. The new professor suggested a new course in sociology, but President Mitchell and Bishop Arnett, not knowing what to make of it, firmly declined to sanction the experiment. He served on the student disciplinary committee. "My program for the day . . . looked almost as long as a week's program now," he recalled.[10] There is a rare, weary diary entry for this period:

> and my soul! but by this time I am weary—a struggle with Antigone's struggles by wise and spectacled youths, all fading away into dull headache and the bell for noon chapel. . . . The bit of day that comes between my last recitation and dinner is a source of great anxiety to me: I dislike to waste it and yet I can find little to fit in here except making my bed or taking a short walk. I eat dinner alone, before the crowd arrives and run a gauntlet of greetings back to my room. Then comes the longest hour of the day: in my tilted armchair, with the daily papers and a red apple I lose myself until the bell brings me back to Wilberforce.[11]

Lonely, hard work had paid off in the past, but not at Wilberforce. "Nothing stirred before [his] impatient pounding! Or if it stirred," Du Bois sighed of his efforts to quicken minds, "it soon slept again."[12]

During the first year at the University of Berlin, he had sketched the plot and written forty-seven pages of an uncannily prescient autobiographical novella, "A Fellow of Harvard." George Smith, who was "smart but a bit odd," briefly attends "X" College, declines a divinity-school scholarship, and, like the author, finally reaches Harvard. Studying in Europe on fellowship, Smith questions the meaning of life, becomes a committed Socialist, and, unable to finish his Harvard dissertation, accepts a teaching position in a southern Negro school "where his eccentricities get him in trouble with the blacks and his radicalism with the whites." Beleaguered, Smith finishes the dissertation, which is published as a "brilliant success."[13] Du Bois's prodigious capacity for work had enabled him to finish his twelve-chapter Harvard doctoral dissertation, "The Suppression of the African Slave Trade to the United States of America, 1638–1870," that first academic year. Like Smith's, it was destined for a brilliant success.

Much of the dissertation had already been worked up over a thirty-month period from late 1889 through most of 1891, but he had put it aside while working on southern land tenure under Schmoller and Wagner at Berlin. With the research done, Du Bois concentrated on shaping his argument and, "in some degree . . . transforming a dry historical treatise into readable prose," as he put it later.[14] Curiously, although the text of the monograph mailed to Harvard is typed in blue ribbon, the footnotes and their raised numerals are in Du Bois's best left-handed cursive, an indication of last-minute haste and probable difficulties with the typist. Albert Hart not only affixed his signature of approval to the dissertation on June 1, 1895, but he also recommended it for selection as the initiating monograph for Harvard Historical Studies, one of the earliest series of university-sponsored scholarly publications in the United States (after those at Johns Hopkins, University of Nebraska, and Brown).[15] It would be published in 1896 by the firm of Longman, Green & Company for Harvard (the university's press was yet to be incorporated).

The Suppression of the African Slave Trade was constructed on royal edicts, parliamentary and colonial proceedings, federal and state acts and statutes, census tabulations, court decisions, naval reports, bills of lading, and newspaper accounts. It was beyond reproach in its sweeping use of published materials and archival digging, an outstanding example of the new historiography of interpretation fused to fact that Hart demanded of his students. Document by damning document, Du Bois built his case for rife American participation in the internationally banned Atlantic trade until the cumulative evidence grew to be overwhelming that, after 1840, the Stars and Stripes in South Atlantic waters had become the pennant of slave cruisers, whose cargoes were immune from inspection. By 1850–1860, he argued, "nearly all the traffic found this flag its best protection." Looking at the North American slave population after the August 1619 arrival at Jamestown, Virginia, of "twenty negars" aboard a Dutch man 'o war, Du Bois concluded that its terrific increase to 700,000 in the 1790 census, 2 million in that of 1830, and finally to 3,953,760 thirty years afterward was due to importation from Africa, even after the 1808 ban.[16]

In the well-received 1891 paper ("The Enforcement of the Slave Trade Laws") before the American Historical Association, he had calculated the total number of Africans brought into North America during the long colonial period at 530,000. The number illegally sold in the United States after the 1808 federal banning of the Atlantic trade, Du Bois had estimated then at "not less than 250,000."[17] Certain, therefore, that the Cotton Kingdom's population growth was the consequence of "a demand for land and slaves greater than the country could supply," Du Bois reasoned in *Suppression* that there had been a fatal "bargain" between an indifferent and later corrupted North and a single-minded South resulting in a fifty-year nonenforcement of federal and state laws against further importation of Africans. His evidence disclosed for the first time the determined push during the 1850s of Deep South slaveholders to nullify the constitutional prohibition. It was not the practice in turn-of-the-century American scholarship to arraign the framers of the Constitution and to charge that the public morality of the new nation had been corrupted by clandestine commerce in the Atlantic slave trade. "It is neither profitable nor in accordance with the scientific truth to consider that whatever the constitutional fathers did was right," the young scholar lectured (with the venerable historian George Bancroft's orthodoxy clearly in mind), "or that slavery was a plague sent from God and fated to be eliminated in due time."[18]

At the grand moment in 1789 when slavery could have been destroyed (a Jamesian live option), the Founders had basely compromised. The "bargain" struck between the commercial North and the agrarian South over the closing of the Atlantic trade had left the Frankenstein monster breathing and the live wires from it inserted into Article I, Section 9, of the federal constitution, providing that: "The migration or importation of such persons as any of the States now existing shall think proper to admit, shall not be prohibited by Congress prior to the year one thousand eight hundred and eight"—thereby permitting the monster to grow too large nineteen years later to be destroyed short of a war. What Du Bois could not have known, however, was that, although many Americans in the two decades before the Civil War were becoming rich from transporting human cargo from Africa, the overwhelming majority of the slaves was not transported to the southern United States (excluding Louisiana) but to Cuba and Brazil.[19] It was an inevitable mistake that was not only logical but, in the final analysis, immaterial to the larger question of his argument's validity; it was the sort of mistake, nevertheless, that would generate strident academic correction. Seventy-eight years later, a sharp deflation of Atlantic slave trade numbers occurred when Professor Philip Curtin's exhaustive and now prevailing estimates became available. Instead of the 15 million to 50 million Africans historians had assumed to have been thrust into the wasting "middle passage" to North and South America, the new figures shrank to a fairly precise 9,566,100. Instead of Du Bois's illegal 250,000 imported after 1808, the authoritative Curtin figure was 54,000.[20]

What historians now knew (and Du Bois's contemporaries did not) was that the astonishing growth of the North American slave population came not from continuous and rising importation from Africa but from its own domestic birth curve and falling mortality rate—unlike the sugar economies of Cuba and Brazil in which high mortality of slaves was compensated for through high importation. Slaveholders in the American South not only mainly grew their own labor force, they encouraged living conditions that kept their investments alive, generally healthy, and augmenting in value.[21] In turn, the rising value of the domestic slave population caused most planters to oppose clandestine importation of slaves in order to protect the market values of their human investments. Du Bois would have hooted at such claims of market-driven humanitarianism, and indeed did so in *Suppression*. Once upon a time, he conceded, there may have been a softer, more "patriarchal serfdom" in Virginia and the Upper South before Eli Whitney ginned the Cotton Kingdom into fevered existence. But after 1820, the large slaveholders "found it cheaper to work a slave to death in a few years," he wrote, "and buy a new one, than to care for him in sickness and old age."[22]

Yet if the percentage of all the men, women, and children brought from Africa to the United States was barely 5 percent, or about 399,000, of the total number imported into the Western hemisphere in four centuries of the Atlantic slave trade, the substantial increase in the slave population had been driven by the white South's employing something like scientific use, abuse, and expansion of its labor force. The story of North American suppression of the Atlantic slave trade was more complex than Du Bois suspected, even though he proved much of his case for fifty years of national hypocrisy, nonfeasance, and collusion fueled by economics. And while it was true that the demographic consequences attributable solely to nonenforcement were not nearly as great as he believed, the real implications in *Suppression*—of vast profits coming not from the maritime slave trade but from the total slave-economy universe—should be understood as pathfinding. It would become characteristic of his scholarship that Du Bois's brilliant insights often transcended flawed specifics. The chapter in *Suppression* on Toussaint L'Ouverture and the Haitian revolution for the first time linked the American suppression of the Atlantic slave trade and Jefferson's fire-sale acquisition of Louisiana to that island's bloody insurrection and its defeat of the large expeditionary forces sent by Napoleon to reconquer it. The widespread alarm triggered by the Haitian overthrow of slavery had disposed colonial Americans to stop the flow of slaves into their new republic.[23]

Because the volume of information Du Bois poured into *Suppression* fell like rainfall over a continental divide, much of it draining off into nineteenth-century channels of thought and values while a good deal flowed forward into the new basin of twentieth-century social science, the book is split between two worlds. Its prose is inflected by period-piece adjectives qualifying public behavior as "vacillating," "immoral," or "discreditable," by loaded phraseology such as "the cupidity and carelessness of our ancestors." Kantian imperatives flash out, such as "the plain duty of a Revolution based on 'Liberty' to take steps toward the abolition of slavery."[24] As the unsigned reviewer in the *Atlantic Monthly* patronizingly pointed out, Du Bois was guilty of repeatedly moralizing about the wages of original sin. "Instead of calling the whole moral energy of the people into action, so as gradually to crush this potential evil," the Wilberforce professor lectured his readers, there was temporizing, cowardice, horse-trading, and complicity. In another twist of the blade, Du Bois doubted "if ever before such political mistakes as the slavery compromises of the Constitutional Convention had such serious results." *Suppression* ended with an admonition that the otherwise favorable reviewer (unsigned) in *The American Historical Review* regretted as more characteristic of "the advocate rather than the historian." "From this," Du Bois sternly declared, "we may conclude that it behooves nations as well as men to do things at the very moment when they ought to be done."[25]

Nearly sixty years after Longman, Green & Company published *Suppression*, Du Bois would write an "Apologia" to a new edition of his first book, published by the then Columbia University graduate student Eugene Genovese.[26] In many ways, it remains its most perceptive criticism. In the "Apologia," he regretted that he had failed to build on the excellent preparation under William James for understanding the social implications of Sigmund Freud. He reproached himself for missing the irrational and psychosexual energies behind what men and women said and did about the importation of slaves to North America. More Freud would have meant less of his own New England moral code in the reading of motives and expectation of principled public conduct. That virtually no other American historian or sociologist of his generation was exploring sexual and subconscious forces inherent in movements and institutions was but minimal comfort to the then eighty-six-year-old scholar-activist.[27] But though he would come to understand why he had failed to apply Freud to the rise and fall of the Atlantic slave trade, he was almost unable to forgive himself six decades afterward for missing Marx—still blaming Frank Taussig, a little unfairly, for being "absorbed in a reinterpretation of the Ricardoan 'Wages Fund.' " What *Suppression* had needed, Du Bois concluded, "was to add to my terribly conscientious search into the facts . . . the clear concepts of Marx on the class struggle for income and power, beneath which all considerations of right or morals were twisted or utterly crushed."[28]

Had his first book been written only a few years later, say, 1905 instead of 1895, the writings of Freud, Marx, and Max Weber might have impelled him to probe beneath the moral and political superstructure of the slave trade. Yet finally, here, too, he would concede that he asked too much of his late-nineteenth-century mind-set to have been "as wise in 1896 as I think I am in 1954." "Apologia" would end on the moderately forgiving note that, "at the beginning of my career, I made no more mistakes than apparently I did."[29] Yet if much of *Suppression* reduces social and political conduct to a matter of character (and Du Bois certainly believed in character), its numerous economic pronouncements have a distinctly modern, we might say proto-Marxist, ring. Despite the moralizing, at bottom Du Bois understood the source and force of slavery in the United States to lie in an indissoluble link between profits from unfree labor and the financing of modern capitalism. He had made that unmistakably clear in the 1891 AHA paper:

> If slave labor was an economic god, then the slave trade was its strong right arm; and with Southern planters recognizing this and Northern capital unfettered by a conscience it was almost like legislating against economic laws to attempt to abolish the slave trade by statutes. Northern greed joined to Southern credulity was a combination calculated to circumvent any law, human or divine.[30]

His chapter on the Cotton Kingdom opened with the engrossing sentence, "The history of slavery and the slave trade after 1820 must be read in the light of the industrial revolution through which the civilized world passed in the first half of the nineteenth century." Here was a jackpot observation that might well have taken control of the author; instead its startling brilliance faded before it could become a transforming paradigm—or even a fruitful tangent. As he would say with soft regret much later, he still "seemed to miss the clear conclusion that slavery was more a matter of income than morals."[31]

It is puzzling that Du Bois failed to carry his bedrock economic interpretation fully over into his first book, that, rather than apply himself to an audacious elaboration, he was content to make penetrating allusions. A late-Victorian intellectual temper, not yet capable of radically doubting the paramountcy of ideas in history, is a partial explanation only, as is the keen satisfaction Du Bois always derived from exposing hypocrisy in white people's hallowed institutions. One possibility is that he may have worked out the economic implications enough to suspect that they could wreak havoc upon *Suppression*'s main thesis—that of an interregional bargain sealed by profits from an illicit slave traffic. However much some northern interests may have benefited from the economics of slavery, it was, as Du Bois well understood, those other and larger economic profits, dependent upon protective tariffs and an advancing frontier of industry, free soil, and free labor, that increasingly governed the politics of North and West. It was during the 1840s and '50s, after all (the very decades that supposedly yielded maximum illegal profits), that the economic and political grounds for the Civil War were laid. A more neutral, impersonal rendering of motives and behavior—in keeping with a rigorous economic analysis (with a far-fuller exploration of countervailing trends)—could have left Du Bois wondering how to make his thesis apply to the final two decades before the Civil War. His interregional bargain might have looked more like a trumping of the South by the North. Finally, had he even been disposed to argue for an enveloping economic determinism, Du Bois would have sensed that by reducing morals exclusively to a function of profits he would be nullifying the major African-American strategy for improving race relations through leverage on the national conscience. *Suppression* was written, after all, at the very moment when economic forces were forging a new interregional deal at the expense of dark-skinned Americans whose last best defense was to invoke the nation's most exalted religious and civil ideals.

Had Du Bois done more research and spent a good deal more time reconceptualizing, he might have succeeded in mating economics to morals in a revised work of genius, rather than one simply written by a genius. As it stands, the economic analysis has been correctly if ungenerously dismissed by ahistorical critics as naive and not organically linked to the book.[32] *Suppression* may not have been the book Du Bois intended to write, but a fallback monograph after his German disappointment, and the sooner he had his doctorate, the sooner there would be life after Wilberforce. A pioneering, flawed work, it was, as his literary executor claimed, "the first full-length product of Afro-American scientific scholarship" and, as the *Nation* reviewer observed, one that "is an honor alike to its author, to the university whose approval it has received, and to American historical scholarship."[33] In his "Apologia" Du Bois knew it was unnecessary to remind readers that it was still a useful classic.

AS HE retrieved his dissertation from the hard-pressed typist to send to Hart, Du Bois probably anticipated the impending Wilberforce commencement exercises with annoyance. The bishop and his courtiers paraded the campus in high collars and cutaways, expecting and receiving obsequious attention while orations of marathon duration competed. The coming of the Episcopal priest Alexander Crummell, a commencement speaker and one of the most distinguished black men of the century, was the single bright spot in a week's ordeal. The Crummell encounter would leave a deep imprint on Du Bois, one that would become sharper and deeper in the few years remaining before the clergyman's death. Crummell's struggles as a pastor in New Haven (where Alexander Du Bois had lent him what support he could) and his remedial sojourn at Cambridge University were long behind the recently retired pastor of Washington's St. Luke's Episcopal, a black tabernacle of such refinement as to have attracted the occasional attendance of President Chester Arthur and banker William Corcoran.[34]

Crummell had assumed his duties in Washington in 1873, after nearly twenty years of mission labor in Liberia on behalf of the Episcopal Church. With another black expatriate, the tactless, brilliant West Indian Edward Wilmot Blyden, he had spearheaded the building of churches and schools to speed assimilation of Liberia's indigenous peoples: Kpelle, Bassah, Mano, and Kru who, like Native Americans, were being trampled and pushed aside by the Americo-Liberians—ex-slave settlers from Maryland and Virginia. Monrovia's new Liberia College was largely Crummell and Blyden's idea—their instrument for preparing the "ignorant, benighted, besotted and filthy" Americo-Liberians for the work of Christianity and civilization. Crummell's had been an active, controversial ministry, abruptly terminated by a coup d'état and the flight of his benefactor, Edward Roye, president of the republic.[35]

Crummell and Blyden, along with a handful of other well-trained men (and one or two women) such as Presbyterian minister Henry Highland Garnet, Episcopal bishop James Holly, AME bishop Henry McNeal Turner, and Martin Robinson Delany (one of the angriest and most resourceful), were forerunners of the Pan-Africanism and black nationalism that would expand early in the next century.[36] They formed an articulate chorus calling for the cream of Afro-America to be resettled in Haiti or South America or West Africa (or, as Garnet pleaded, if not Africa, wherever his people could become "great and powerful by colonization")—acrimonious partisanship prevented agreement—where by thrift and uplift "the intention of the Divine Mind towards Africa" could be fulfilled. Passions of color also divided them (Crummell and Garnet detested mulattoes), as did those of religion—Methodists had little use for Episcopalians and vice versa. But all were Victorian imperialists—"Afro-Saxons"—to whom native Africans were religiously and socially "primitive" and always sexually scandalous.[37] Blyden justified the European Scramble for Africa, rationalizing that it would teach "the natives to make the best use of their own country." And whatever their feelings about being outsiders in Anglo-Saxon civilization themselves (Bishop Turner hoped to see it destroyed, whereas the Sierra Leonean James Africanus Horton desired greater collaboration), as anguished *assimilés* they dreamed of replicating that civilization as the "highest and the best yet evolved in the history of the human race" on their own terms among "less developed" cousins.[38]

When Martin Delany, who burst racial stereotypes like tape across a finish line (he was Harvard's first black medical school student), turned up in Liberia near the end of 1859, Crummell had served as advisor and host under the palms at sleepy Cape Palmas. Delany and his "Niger Valley Exploring Party" pressed on to Nigeria, where in December they persuaded the *alake* of Abeokuta to sign a treaty permitting members of the "African race in America" to establish a colony. Delany concocted a catchy, arrogant slogan: "Africa for the African race, and black men to rule them."[39] Reading a providential augury into Delany's appearance, Crummell had hurried to the United States to raise money and preach the doctrine of manifest black destiny in Africa ("Ethiopianism" or "civilizationism," as his exacting biographer dubs it). Unhappily for him, his fund-raising tour coincided with the South's secession from the Union and the sudden and total indifference of American Negroes to emigrationism. Delany had then immediately abandoned his cotton-empire dream in Africa for a major's epaulettes in the Union Army (becoming Afro-America's highest ranking officer) and then an intrigue-filled career in postwar South Carolina politics, coming finally to settle and die in Wilberforce, Ohio, shortly before Du Bois took up his professorship.[40]

Although Crummell had soon returned to Liberia alone and with only enough funds to pay his own passage, he left behind two publications whose contents would be scattered widely by delayed fuse: *The Relations and Duties of Free Colored Men in America to Africa* (1861), and *The Future of Africa* (1862). Four years after his final return to America as St. Luke's pastor, Crummell had planted another explosive charge with "The Destined Superiority of the Negro," a take-heart sermon timed to inspire black America's leadership during the terrible post-Reconstruction era he saw approaching. The publication date, 1877, was significant—that very March the Republicans had frantically bartered just enough electoral votes in the bitterest, most corrupt election aftermath ever in order to hang on to the White House. In accordance with a deal in large part struck at Wormley House, the deluxe Washington hotel owned (ironically) by a black man, Rutherford Hayes's first act had been to call back most of the federal troops from the South while northern capitalists smacked their lips in anticipation of Congress's voting lavish subsidies for more transcontinental railroads. Henceforth, the white South would take care of its black people and the North would take care of most of the nation's business. *The Nation* had said starkly what President Hayes had no need to say publicly about the African-American: "Henceforth, the nation, as a nation, will have nothing more to do with him."[41]

Crummell's "The Destined Superiority of the Negro" would light up the coming bleakness with Plato, Hegel, Johann von Herder, and, with admiration bordering on imitation, François Guizot, the infamously smug prime minister–historian of France's July Monarchy (King Louis-Philippe's bourgeois regime overthrown in 1848). "The Almighty seizes upon superior nations and, by mingled chastisement and blessings, gradually leads them to greatness," Crummell prophesied.[42] This Old Testament premise he then linked to a Christian dialectic and a Social Darwinism of his own divining in which inexorable laws of God and nature wiped out weaker, non-Christian peoples like the Native Americans or the Pacific Islanders in order to advance ever-higher moral and material conditions—for Crummell, Anglo-Saxon civilization, in short. His "civilizationism" even led him to praise for a time the colonizing work of Africa's greatest despoiler, Leopold II, King of the Belgians, for its "noble imagination."[43]

Thus, the more history tested the Negro the more he emerged as chosen, as "taller, more erect, more intelligent, and more aspiring than any of his ancestors for more than two thousand years of a previous era." Count de Gobineau's racist classic, *Essai sur l'inégalité des races humaines*, sneered that Africans were imitative, artistic, "feminine" in intelligence. Crummell agreed; only he inverted these qualities on his own racial superiority scale, imitation being for him the stuff of racial greatness. In a notable turn of phrase describing the ancient Greeks and Romans as "cosmopolitan thieves," Crummell preached that imitation was even the authentic source of hardy, aggressive, "masculine" Anglo-Saxon greatness. Black imitation of the highest in white civilization foretold "that superiority and eminence which is our rightful heritage."[44] Yet this erudite Episcopalian priest was no more willing than Marx to leave history running entirely on autopilot. Vain, pedantic, autocratic, blessed with early advantages in education and career (owing much to aristocratic white New Yorkers), Crummell feared working-class white people and lacked confidence in the mass of black people.[45] He liked neither the social-contract theory of John Locke nor the individualism of Thomas Jefferson. It was the duty of educated, high-principled elites among all peoples—but especially among African peoples—to promote the work of Providence by preaching, teaching, and leading the common folk into abstinence, monogamy, cleanliness, and thrift.[46]

Although Crummell no longer espoused emigration to Africa these days, his catechism of Negro chosenness was as forceful as ever. The task now, he proclaimed and disseminated in a stream of pamphlets, was to build the moral fiber and institutions of the race in America, and he assigned to the recently freed women of the South a vital, transforming role in this endeavor. Among black men of his day, and men in general, the learned priest stood out boldly for solid education and full rights for women—"without them, no true nationality, patriotism, religion, cultivation, family life, or true social status" was possible.[47] If the reality of the crucial role he assigned them was quintessentially one of dutiful support in which men were made wiser and stronger in their supremacy as a result of them, Crummell's intentions were still enlightened for his times. In sermons such as "The Black Woman of the South, Her Neglects and Her Needs," he dwelt heavily upon the role of women in abating the lingering pathologies of slavery days through strong nuclear families—an emphasis that would contribute to the evolution of the school of Black Family scholarship, stretching from Du Bois to E. Franklin Frazier and Daniel Patrick Moynihan.[48]

Such was the Mosaic quality of the man who came to preach at Wilberforce in the spring of 1895. "Father" Crummell, as he was widely known, was now a stately seventy-six, his thinning hair and beard heavily salted, yet he still walked with the regal step of his princely West African forbears. What Crummell had to say impressed Du Bois as much because of the messenger as for the message. "Instinctively I bowed before this man, as one bows before the prophets of the world," he recalled almost a decade after the Wilberforce meeting.[49] St. Luke's emeritus favored a Platonic conception of social change that reduced economic realities to mere shadowy reflections on the wall of a cave. Not only did man not live by bread alone, the rapt faculty and students in Shorter Hall were told, but the problem of bread took care of itself once higher matters had been attended to. "The material aspect is only the surface aspect," Father Crummell explained. "There has rarely, if ever, been a strike, a labor riot, an industrial disturbance, an Agrarian outbreak, in all the history of man, but what has had an underlying, some absorbing moral problem which agitated the souls of men." Great ideas were the wheels of history; all else was false motion. "Man never passes beyond the boundary lines of dull content into the arena of strife or agitation, unless some deep moral conviction first circles his brain and fires his blood or tingles his imagination."[50]

"The Solution of Problems: The Duty and Destiny of Man," Crummell's commencement sermon, would have sounded deep metaphysical chords in Du Bois after study in Germany. In Crummell's sermon there were echoes of Herder's "law of humanity," reconciling the contending individual with the universal, and louder ones of Crummell and Du Bois's beloved Hegel, iterating that the "rational is the real and the real the rational." The heroism of moral struggle, involving abnegations that the small-minded found pitiable and whose triumphs would in time confound the skeptics, Du Bois had already embraced in favorite lines from *Faust*. Yet if history made sense—moral sense—Crummell stressed that it did so only when the noblest energies exerted themselves on its behalf. The priest intended for the masses to be guided by a patient, fearless, natural aristocracy of talent. The kernel of one of Du Bois's most intriguing and influential future ideas, that of the Talented Tenth leading the race—pulling it on to greatness—was all but tossed him by the old priest.[51]

Writing "Of Alexander Crummell" in *The Souls of Black Folk*, Du Bois would transform an opinionated old man into a racial cynosure, describing their Wilberforce meeting and its impact with poignancy. "Tall, frail, and black he stood, with simple dignity and an unmistakable air of good breeding," was Du Bois's immediate impression. They talked apart, "where the storming of the lusty young orators could not harm us." Their hours together introduced the junior scholar, whose models had thus far been Hosmer, James, and perhaps Schmoller, to a new and profoundly significant racial archetype. Aside from Grandfather Alexander, Crummell was the first living black man Du Bois found truly worthy of emulating—the first to whom he deferred with ready affection and intellectual affinity. Speaking to Crummell "politely, then curiously, then eagerly," the fatherless, self-created intellectual sensed in this campus visitor a gentle yet strong wholeness of mind and character whose development held enormous meaning for his own career.[52] "Some seer he seemed, that came not from the crimson Past or the gray To-come, but from the pulsing Now," Du Bois rhapsodized.

All his life Crummell had had to battle three temptations—hate, despair, and doubt, of which the worst was doubt, Du Bois said. "Of all the three temptations," the prodigy from Great Barrington declared with the force of personal experience, "this one struck the deepest. Hate? He had outgrown so childish a thing. Despair? He had steeled his right arm against it, and fought it with vigor and determination. But to doubt the worth of his life-work"—and here Du Bois surely was thinking of himself—"to doubt the destiny and capability of the race his soul loved because it was his"—this was soul-destroying doubt over which Crummell had triumphed magnificently.[53] In "Alexander Crummell" Du Bois offers a secular parable that mimics the Calvary—a moral and racial instruction in which the anointed messenger is tested, forsaken, rebuked, and allegorically sacrificed in order to redeem a people. However, the unmistakable New Testament imagery no longer represented deeply held religious convictions. By the time he reached Wilberforce, Du Bois's religious views were wholly decoupled from orthodox Christianity and from any notion of a personal deity. At best, he recognized a vague presence manifesting itself in laws slowly revealed through science—a force best expressed in Hegelianisms such as *Weltgeist* (world spirit) or *Dasein* (presence) and above all in private and without emotion. But although he had relinquished the Bible's theology, Du Bois would hold in reserve the language of the King James Version whenever, as with the import of Crummell, he strove to give an idea maximum emotional force.[54]

Recounting Crummell's determination to get a secondary school education, Du Bois would tell how the early New York abolitionist Beriah Green had braved community reproach in 1836 by bringing Crummell and his good friend Henry Garnet to the Oneida Institute in Whitesboro, New York. In all of North America, only Oneida, Gettysburg, Gilmore in Cincinnati, and Oberlin admitted African-Americans at that time. In fact, Crummell and Garnet, along with several others, had seen their New Canaan, New

Hampshire, schoolhouse yoked to oxen and dragged into a swamp by white farmers indignant that black boys were learning algebra and Latin.[55] Determined to serve his people in a Providence, Rhode Island, church, Crummell "worked and toiled, week by week, day by day, month by month. And yet month by month the congregation dwindled, week by week the hollow walls echoed more sharply, day by day the calls came fewer, and day by day the third temptation sat clearer and still more clearly within the Veil." Doubt came again. It was as if the nobler a prophet's commitment to the cause of his people, the more vulnerable to anguish and self-pity he could be in times of quotidian sloth and indifference. Writing on, filled with empathy for himself and Crummell, Du Bois re-created the awful moment when the priest heard "his own lips whispering, 'They do not care; they cannot know; they are dumb driven cattle,—why cast your pearls before swine?'—this, this seemed more than man could bear; and he closed the door, and sank upon the steps of the chancel, and cast his robe upon the floor and writhed."[56]

Then had come Crummell's joust with Bishop Benjamin T. Onderdonk of New York. Du Bois's detailed account of that meeting, which led to Crummell's being denied entry into the leading Episcopal seminary, was somewhat mistaken, but the picture of porcine bigotry was as truthful as it was exquisite: "Bishop Onderdonk lived at the head of six white steps,—corpulent, red-faced, and the author of several thrilling tracts on Apostolic Succession." Du Bois fancied he could "see that tableau: the frail black figure, nervously twitching his hat before the massive abdomen of Bishop Onderdonk; his threadbare coat thrown against the dark woodwork of the book-cases, where Fox's 'Lives of the Martyrs' nestled happily beside 'The Whole Duty of Man.' " In Du Bois's version of the encounter, his hero refuses Onderdonk's demeaning conditions of studying apart, retorting "slowly and heavily: 'I will never enter your diocese on such terms.' And saying this, he turned and passed into the Valley of the Shadow of Death."[57] Rather than succumb, Crummell wanders to England for more education. "Restless still, and unsatisfied, he turned towards Africa, and for long years, amid the spawn of the slave-smugglers sought a new heaven and a new earth." Never faltering, seldom complaining (Crummell's intimates often found him querulous, however), "he simply worked, inspiring the young, rebuking the old, helping the weak, guiding the strong."[58]

"The more I met Alexander Crummell," Du Bois continued, "the more I felt how much that world [behind the veil] was losing which knew so little of him." That the noble priest deeply penetrated the young scholar's armor is obvious. Unlike Alfred Du Bois, about whom the son now probably knew most of the unsavory truth, Crummell was an authentically patriarchal force—austere yet compassionate, admonitory yet trustworthy.[59] Despite the gulf of years and different training, Du Bois sensed that Crummell's demons, personal, professional, and racial, were very much like his own. The priest "did his work—he did it nobly and well," just as Du Bois had done, denying himself loves, friendships, and conventional satisfactions in order to pursue his calling to uplift a worthy people through knowledge. Crummell had "bent to all the gibes and prejudices, to all hatred and discrimination, with that rare courtesy which is the armor of pure souls."[60] The apostrophe with which Du Bois would wind up this essay is among the tenderest things he ever wrote. For once, there is a hint of genuine intimacy in the arresting prose. "And herein lies the tragedy of the age: not that men are poor,—all men know something of poverty; not that men are wicked,—who is good? not that men are ignorant,—what is Truth? Nay, but that men know so little of men." The final, filial words addressed to "the soul I loved" were meant for a saint: "I wonder where he is today? I wonder if in that dim world beyond, as he came gliding in, there rose . . . a dark and pierced Jew who knows the writhings of the earthly damned, saying, as he laid those heart-wrung talents down, 'Well done!' "[61]

CRUMMELL'S INFLUENCE on his new disciple would continue for decades, becoming almost too faint to detect only after Marx had taken such hold of Du Bois in the 1940s that the priest was even denied a place in the *Autobiography*'s index. To gauge that influence and its broader consequences, we have to steal a march on chronology before returning to celebrate Du Bois's twenty-eighth birthday in Wilberforce. Two years after the visit to the campus, Du Bois would play a major part in Crummell's new American Negro Academy. The date of the academy's start-up meeting, March 5, 1897, a Friday morning, was the 127th anniversary of the Boston Massacre in which the mulatto seaman Crispus Attucks had shed the first blood in the American Revolution. Sixteen other men attended the meeting convened by Crummell at Washington's Lincoln Memorial Church. That past December, five of them—Crummell, the young poet Paul Laurence Dunbar, Howard University philosopher Kelly Miller, Du Bois, and another—had met at the Washington home of John Wesley Cromwell, lawyer, newspaperman, and amateur historian, to plan this ambitious forum in an era when scholarly speculation among African-Americans was a luxury as rare as Mississippi snow.[62]

Booker T. Washington was invited to the March assembly, but this had been a formality and no one was surprised not to see him there. In fact, as the engine of the new organization, Crummell intended for the academy to welcome criticism of what was now known as the "Tuskegee Idea." When he had come to Wilberforce in May or early June of 1895, Crummell probably had no thought of openly challenging the rising race leadership of Tuskegee Institute's formidable principal, Booker Washington, a decision he finally, painfully, reached the following October. There was much in the Tuskegee vocational program he found praiseworthy, as is clear from his testimony before the U.S. House Committee on Education, in which he identified trade schools as the race's most pressing need.[63] But even as early as 1891, a certain tone and emphasis had increasingly begun to separate the priest and the educator. Washington, for example, had apparently taken to extolling the virtues of slavery as an early version of citizenship training. It had made Christians of pagans. "We went into slavery without a language; we came out speaking the proud Anglo-Saxon tongue," the educator was heard to rejoice on several occasions. "If in the providence of God the Negro got any good out of slavery, he got the habit of work," was another favorite bromide.[64]

Crummell's own considerable admiration for English had stopped far short of commending its inculcation through plantation slavery. He implied in several sermons that Washington's claims for the benefits of bondage were dubious. For Crummell, slavery had ruined both the African's honest paganism and his morals. As for work, the African in America had had 250 years of it "and everyone knew that it . . . never produced his civilization."[65] The Episcopal priest's ideas of education called for suiting instruction to aptitudes, building on work and learning without any presumption of limitations, and teaching courses in husbandry as well as hermeneutics, Latin as well as landscaping—rather than, as Washington was doing at Tuskegee, bending aptitudes to instruction. "The primal need of the Negro," Crummell once wrote to a journalist friend, "is absorption in civilization, in all its several lines, as a preparation for civil functions, and the use of political power. Just now he is the puppet and the tool of white demagogues and black sycophants."[66]

Du Bois would hurry from Philadelphia, where he now worked after escaping Wilberforce, to the 10:30 A.M. meeting in Washington of the American Negro Academy. He seconded Crummell's nomination for president with a filial ardor he would seldom confess again in public. There was "too little reverence" among the race for age and past achievement, the twenty-nine-year-old professor admonished, "and I say right here, there could be no greater a reverence paid by us to worth than by recognizing such a man as Dr. Crummell."[67] As Du Bois sat down to applause and an immediate unanimous vote for Crummell, the new president of the American Negro Academy rose to deliver in his measured voice an inaugural address whose title, "Civilization, The Primal Need of the Race," was a manifesto of high culture. Crummell told the body that a race was civilized only when it produced "letters, literature, science, philosophy, poetry, sculpture, architecture . . . all the arts." "No purblind philanthropy is to be allowed to make 'Industrial Training' a substitute for it."[68] After this swipe at Tuskegee, he went on to tell the academy members (everyone knew that he had in mind the dead Douglass who, many said, had been turned by age and a white wife into a radical assimilationist) that there were two great heresies: "That the colored people of this country should forget as soon as possible that they ARE colored people"; and "That colored men should give up all distinctive efforts, as colored men, in schools, churches, associations, and friendly societies."[69] If, in the mists of a far future, the priest did glimpse such harmony among peoples that caste and race (like feudal rank and privilege) would gradually pass out of history, for the indeterminate present racial chauvinism would be the sole guarantee of later racial integration—"assimilationist ends through separatist means," as Crummell biographer Wilson Moses explains. "If I forget that I am a black man [Crummell's wife, unlike Douglass's, was black], and you ignore the fact of race, and we both ostrich-like, stick our heads in the sand . . . what are you and I to do for our social nature?" No, they must never forget, Crummell concluded in Lincoln Memorial Church, that "we are a nation set apart in this country."[70]

But the words that were to dominate these self-conscious Negro leaders that March morning in 1897 were not those of Alexander Crummell, as arresting as they were, but those of W.E.B. Du Bois. Dunbar; Scarborough (now reemployed at Wilberforce); Miller; Francis Grimké, the Princeton-educated natural son of a South Carolina Grimké; William Henry Ferris, a young Yale prodigy; and the rest instantly sensed that high-flown Platonism was being recycled according to the latest findings in history and laws of sociology. Long and cruelly victimized by racism, Du Bois began, the Negro had himself been led to "deprecate and minimize race distinctions." Together with the great majority of all Americans, the Negro embraced the

Jeffersonian idea of democratic individualism, which had led to that impatient, antihistorical optimism later historians would call the doctrine of American exceptionalism—the faith, said Du Bois, that "while it may have been true in the past that closed race groups made history, that here in conglomerate America *nous avons changé tout cela*—we have changed all that." But "all that" had not changed. Implicitly drawing on Herder, Fichte, and Friedrich Schleiermacher's ideas of separate but equal contributions by the races and on Jacob Grimm's and von Treitschke's of irreducible somethings in the human family, Du Bois, in his precise, dry voice, intoned that there were differences—"subtle, delicate and elusive, though they may be—which have silently but definitely separated men into groups."[71]

Great confusion set in at this point, as the young professor wove back and forth between the subjects of English parliamentarianism and free trade, German excellence in science and philosophy, French and Italian fecundity in music, art, and literature, and the contributions of the "other race groups," hopelessly entangling nationality with race and institutions with cultural "traits."[72] Just exactly what race was Du Bois never did manage to say clearly, although he invoked the authorities Thomas Huxley and Friedrich Ratzel in support of his conviction that there were three primordial examples—white, Negro, and yellow; and eight "historic" ones—Teutons, Slavs, English of Great Britain and North America, "Romance nations," Negroes of Africa and America, Semites, Hindus, and Mongolians. Crummell's gratification must have been boundless when his new disciple paused to give memorable Hegelian expression to the key idea: "The history of the world is the history, not of individuals, but of groups, not of nations, but of races, and he who ignores or seeks to override the race idea in human history ignores and overrides the central thought of all history."[73]

Du Bois cast each "race" as a unique past, present, or prospective player in a millennial pageant, a drama he would unveil over and again in several forms and with numerous revisions. Some players, like the Japanese, were already beginning to act their part. Others, like the Negroes, must begin writing lines for the future. Those lines, of course, would be spoken first by the "advance guard of the Negro people—the eight million people of Negro blood in the United States of America," and, Du Bois had no need to add, with American Negro Academy members serving as drama coaches. But were not Negroes in America simply Americans who happened to be Negroes in melting-pot America? Inscribed on the very coins were the words "E Pluribus Unum" (out of many, one), reminding Irish, Italians, Germans, Jews, Slavs, Hispanics, Asians, and others in America that hyphens were un-American. Not only was there no terminology yet to describe cultural pluralism when Du Bois wrote "The Conservation of Races," but the idea for what urban writers like Randolph Bourne, Hutchins Hapgood, Horace Kallen, and Waldo Frank were to call "transnationalism" was almost universally regarded as heretical in 1897.[74]

The writings of James and Dewey would point the way for the "cultural radicals," the pluralists of the near future, but the boldest signpost was first erected by Du Bois when he asked rhetorically of the seventeen attentive men in the Washington church:

> [W]hat after all, am I? Am I an American or am I a Negro? Can I be both? Or is it my duty to cease to be a Negro as soon as possible and be an American? If I strive as a Negro, am I not perpetuating the very cleft that threatens and separates black and white America? Is not my only possible practical aim the subduction of all that is Negro in me to the American? Does my black blood place upon me any more obligation to assert my nationality than German, or Irish or Italian blood would?[75]

Frederick Douglass had gone to the grave pleading that, whenever and wherever practicable, African-Americans not form separate social and political organizations. In "our union is our weakness," he came to believe; "a nation within a nation is an anomaly. There can be but one American nation."[76] It was a debate that had raged for many years, even before the Civil War, among those Negroes whose livelihoods and northern residency had permitted it. The ringing answer offered by Du Bois before the academy invested ancient sentiment with fresh language, and balanced parochial pleading with sociological formulation. It apotheosized the concept of racial "twoness" and hugely contributed to the permanence of the concept in the collective mentality of a people. Beyond that, Du Bois secularized the deep belief widespread among African-Americans in heavenly deliverance from earthly troubles, declaring that salvation came through history to races in tune with the Zeitgeist:

> Here, it seems to me, is the reading of the riddle that puzzles so many of us. We are Americans, not only by birth and by citizenship, but by our political ideals, our language, our religion. Farther than that, our Americanism does not go. At that point, we are Negroes, members of a vast historic race that from the very dawn of creation has slept, but half awakening in the dark forests of its African fatherland. We are the first

> fruits of this new nation, the harbinger of that black tomorrow which is yet destined to soften the whiteness of the Teutonic today.[77]

Replaying themes first heard in the Harvard graduation speech on Jefferson Davis, Du Bois praised the nonacquisitiveness of African-Americans, their special sensibilities in music, humor, and imagination. He foresaw an indomitable march ahead for his people if they combined and pooled resources in strong "race organizations"—"our one haven of refuge is ourselves." But they needed clean havens, he said in closing. The late-Victorian Zeitgeist abhorred filth. The first and greatest step "toward the settlement of the present friction between the races," he said, echoing Crummell, "lies in the correction of the immorality, crime, and laziness among the Negroes themselves." Du Bois made it clear that he advocated not integration but parallel development, "side by side in peace and mutual happiness"; not social equality but "social equilibrium"—a goal that Booker Washington would have roundly applauded had he been there. Not only did he catalogue the races, Du Bois endowed each with special, if not unique, characteristics, ascribing essentially "soft" or "feminine" qualities to the African-American. Fundamentally different, races must above all safeguard their distinctiveness. This was a law of history, and if, "among the gaily-colored banners that deck the broad ramparts of civilization is to hang one uncompromising black," the German-trained scholar exhorted, "then it must be placed there by black heads . . . and hearts beating in one glad song of jubilee."[78]

Issued by the academy later that year as a fifteen-page pamphlet, "The Conservation of Races" was a magnificent assault weapon designed to lay down a deadly field of fire against racists in general and Negrophobes in particular. In the acclamation following delivery of the paper, however, the speaker and most of his auditors failed to realize that those who launched appeals of racial solidarity and racial purity were using a boomerang for a weapon. A surprising dissent did come from the diminutive divinity student William Ferris. He thought Du Bois had got the picture upside down. Men were great not because of the races they represented; races were great because they reflected the contributions of outstanding individuals.[79] Scarborough, too, wondered about the very peculiar situation of races coexisting yet never amalgamating, and one or two other members probably found the Hegelian nostrums a bit gassy. But when President Crummell glided to the lectern to pronounce Du Bois's paper "essentially a good one," debate subsided.[80]

Whatever type of ordnance it was, "The Conservation of Races" lobbed some of the most powerful projectiles of racial and cultural exclusivism onto the ideological landscape of the twentieth century; their repercussions as black nationalism, black Zionism, Pan-Africanism, black aestheticism, and isms yet to discharge in the next century, have caused regimes to shudder and crumble and very probably will shake future ones to their foundations.[81] And although Du Bois would later consider his academy paper to be a youthful effusion that was something of an embarrassment as he strode through the new century as slayer of racial doctrines, it would represent one highly significant skein of his complex intellectual makeup until the end of his days.[82] The raw racism that a future generation of Germans and other Europeans would espouse in the perverted names of Fichte, Hegel, Herder, de Gobineau, and Nietzsche was a stupendous irony that awaited not only Du Bois but large numbers of incredulous men and women whose intellectual maturity had come during the ebb tide of Victorianism.

THAT EVENING in February 1896 when Du Bois celebrated his twenty-eighth birthday, miserably, in his room in Shorter Hall, the distance from Wilberforce to Berlin seemed to be measured in terms of light-years rather than miles. "This queer world" had never puzzled him more than today, he told the diary. The campus had been engulfed by a paroxysm of religious fervor. Perhaps the frenzy served some purpose, he continued, but "yet do you know I've been a prisoner in my room for nearly a week, driven almost to distraction by wild screams and groans and shrieks that rise from the chapel below me . . . ?" He found himself in a state of near "mental imbecility."[83] Until the national attention that *The Suppression of the African Slave Trade* attracted at the beginning of 1897, his calvary at Wilberforce had been relieved only by Crummell, thoughts of marriage, two friendships, and the electricity discharged by Booker T. Washington's speech in Atlanta, Georgia.

What Washington had said at the opening of the Cotton States International Exposition on September 18, 1895, turned out to be one of the most consequential pronouncements in American history. Neither black people nor white people were ever quite the same again. His words had been telegraphed to every major newspaper in the country. Southern politicians and colonels had whooped and capered amid a savanna of ladies' handkerchiefs when he finished. Editor Clark Howell of the Atlanta *Constitution*, arbitral voice of the New South, rushed toward the speakers' platform to cry out, "That man's speech is the beginning of a moral revolution in America." Arriving in Atlanta a few days later, President Grover Cleveland had clasped the Tuskegee principal's hand firmly and spoken of "new hope" for Negroes.[84] Equally enthusiastic congratulations rained down on Washington from almost every prominent African-American, including a telegram from a young Wilberforce professor sent from Xenia on September 24: "Let me heartily congratulate you upon your phenomenal success at Atlanta—it was a word fitly spoken." Du Bois had followed it up with a letter to the New York *Age* saying that "here might be the basis of a real settlement between whites and blacks in the South, if the South opened to the Negroes the doors of economic opportunity and the Negroes cooperated with the white South in political sympathy."[85]

The full meaning of the Atlanta Exposition speech was yet to unfold, but, according to Louis Harlan, his careful biographer, Washington clearly intended the crux of his speech to be the mutuality of racial obligations in the Redeemed South. In exchange for black acceptance of restrictions on the franchise and no further demands for "social equality," the South's white rulers were to allow gradual progress in agriculture and business and to rein in the rednecks. His people in the South, Washington said at Atlanta, were thirsty men and women aboard a ship lost at sea, who should heed the voice crying, "Cast down your buckets where you are. . . . by making friends in every manly way of the people of all races by whom we are surrounded."[86] In return, the white people must cast down their buckets also "among these people who have, without strikes and labor wars, tilled your fields, cleared your forests, builded your railroads and cities." Raising his brown right hand, the educator illustrated a spellbinding image: "In all things that are purely social we can be as separate as the fingers, yet one as the hand in all things essential to mutual progress." Seldom in history and homiletics have a metaphor and simile accomplished so much as those in what was shortly called the "Atlanta Compromise" speech. As Du Bois understood Washington's words, the proposed bargain was one that he could fully approve.[87]

Meanwhile, there were friendships in the Wilberforce gulag. Second Lieutenant Charles Young and poet Paul Laurence Dunbar were as dissimilar physically and professionally as they were similar in terms of artistic temperament and interests. The tubercular young poet had operated an elevator in a downtown Dayton building to support himself and his mother until his first success at the beginning of 1893, *Oak and Ivy*, his first collection of poems. When he came over from Dayton for a reading sometime during Du Bois's second year, Dunbar's star was rising. *Majors and Minors* reached the public early in 1896. "Minors" referred to his Negro dialect poems, but his standard English "majors" (modeled after the Hoosier verse of James Whitcomb Riley) went unappreciated. He would be overwhelmed and finally disillusioned by the popularity of his dialect poetry. In *Harper's Weekly* the next year, William Dean Howells dubbed him "the only man of pure African blood and of American civilization to feel the negro life aesthetically and express it lyrically."[88] By contrast, Du Bois was amazed to see that Dunbar, whose work he had supposed to be that of a gifted white man, was a soft-spoken African-American.[89] Dunbar's even more popular *Lyrics of Lowly Life* came out in 1897. A friendship developed that would be renewed in the American Negro Academy and last until the poet's alcohol-wracked death nine years later.

Dunbar's physical opposite, thirty-one-year-old Charles Young was five feet eight inches of granite. A spit-and-polish officer with service in the army's hard-riding 9th Cavalry in Nebraska and recognized as an outstanding cartographer, Young was a study in remarkable willpower and self-control. A backwoods Kentuckian whose slave parents had brought him to southern Ohio after the Civil War, he had needed the full measure of such qualities in order to survive West Point as its ninth African-American appointee and third graduate. Young was trim, brown-skinned, low-keyed, gifted in languages and music, and was even grudgingly admired by an occasional white officer. He read widely, wrote clearly, and since 1894 had been on assignment with the War Department as a professor of tactics and military science at Wilberforce, where he also taught French and mathematics. Young lived near the campus with his mother, and Du Bois sometimes escaped from campus conniptions to enjoy a musical evening with them. "He and I both refused to attend the annual 'revivals' which interrupted school work every year at Christmas time," recalled Du Bois.[90] Christmas of '96, especially, the Youngs and Du Bois and several others would have something special to celebrate: Young was promoted to first lieutenant. Young's was the first genuine male friendship in Du Bois's life, one of a handful in which there was genuine affinity. Twenty years after leaving Wilberforce, he would lead a fight for Young's professional life that was one of the most cruel ever to engage him.

Friendship with the Youngs nearly turned out to be a boon in a rather curious encounter, as well. For some time now Albert Hart had contemplated Du Bois's predicament at Wilberforce with impatient dismay. Finally, at the end of 1895, he practically ordered his prize student to write Booker Washington about his plight. Du Bois did so early that January;

explaining that it was Hart's idea, he complained that he was not "wholly satisfied and am continually on the lookout for another position."[91] On April Fools' Day, Du Bois wrote again, presumably responding to an encouraging message. He felt that he "should like to work at Tuskegee if [he] could be of service" to Washington. He proposed the gradual buildup of a school of Negro history and social investigation. In any case, he was "willing and eager to entertain any proposition for giving service" to Tuskegee. The more he considered the prospect, the more it must have appealed to him, because five days later he invited the Tuskegee principal to be his personal guest when he visited the campus that June. Unfortunately, Du Bois added, he couldn't offer accommodations himself, but his friends the Youngs also wished Washington to be "their and my guest at their residence."[92] The sources are silent on what would have been their first face-to-face meeting—an indication that it probably never came to pass after all. Still, both men had taken their first steps toward one another, and Hart, one of Tuskegee Institute's influential northern boosters, was determined to steer them into a professional embrace.

It may have been the desolation of Du Bois's inner life at Wilberforce that drove him into a more personal embrace at this time. He was "quickly losing faith in the value of the way won. What business had I, anyhow, to teach Greek," he agonized, "when I had studied men?" He saw now that in going there he "had made a mistake."[93] Suddenly, he found himself in a row with Bishop Arnett that shook the campus. Du Bois had been drilling students for roles in *A Midsummer Night's Dream* with the gusto and fussiness of a great director. It was to be performed in a pastoral ravine dividing the "church side" from the "state side" of Wilberforce's two campuses, where the gentle waters of Tawawa Springs still ran. But the production was promptly abandoned when the bishop summarily appointed one of his incompetent sons professor of literature. Du Bois led faculty and students on strike. To their surprise, they won. Ben Arnett III stepped down, but Du Bois realized that the victory was a pyrrhic one.[94] William McKinley's favorite advisor on Negro affairs was not to be trifled with. Misery in work, the appearance of an attractive, caring woman, and a victory for academic standards in a lost war—these are familiar breeding grounds for dramatic, fateful personal decisions. And, after all, Du Bois had recently "carefully calculated" that he should marry before age thirty, and that his salary of eight hundred dollars should be sufficient for two—"if paid."[95]

Nina Gomer was one of three surviving children born to Charles Gomer, a Cedar Rapids, Iowa, hotel chef, and his deceased Alsatian wife.

She was not sophisticated, but she had excellent manners and was well spoken. She was Du Bois's student. Very likely, given her heritage and her lifelong fondness for the language and the country, she would have taken French from Charles Young. "A slip of a girl," *Darkwater* says of her, "beautifully dark-eyed and thorough and good as a German housewife." Adopting the Germanic usage of those days, Du Bois would often refer to her simply as "wife."[96] She had lustrous black hair, large, lovely, trusting eyes, and an hourglass figure. Her complexion was lighter than her future husband's but not so light as to appear white, although she could easily have been mistaken for a South American or even a southern Italian. She was popular with classmates, and she had a natural delicacy that other women tended to envy. Her friend Pearl Shorter "idolized Miss Nina Gomer" and thought she was "a sort of pattern" to be followed in her own life.[97] When Will (Nina would always call him that) came to the little prenuptial party held on the campus tennis court—the only male present—he charmed the celebrants by teaching them the game of gossip. Pearl Shorter was convinced that Nina and her fiancé were admirably matched. The next day, the happy bride-to-be took a train from Xenia for Cedar Rapids. Du Bois was to follow in a few days, with his year-end salary in hand. There was a heart-stopping moment's difficulty about the pay, when the university treasurer told him that salaries would be paid only after the AME Church's annual general conference. "Penniless and my bride . . . awaiting me in Iowa," Du Bois collared this worthy and, as the *Autobiography* delicately put it, "firmly persuaded him that until my salary due was paid, he was unlikely to see General Conference."[98]

Du Bois rushed to Cedar Rapids to be married on a Tuesday, May 12, 1896. In the blurred rush, he recalled a white cottage, the tall, heavy father and his young second wife, a "shy fat little sister," a kindly white minister, and the return trip the next day to two furnished rooms in the men's dormitory. A "gorgeous crimson couch cover" awaited the newlyweds, a mail-order purchase made by the groom from Carson-Pirie in Chicago. As Pearl Shorter remembered it, the bridal reception a day or so later was even something of a fashion show. She simply delighted "in each gown and hat she wore, and in the happiness of you both—Happy yesterdays!"[99] Three weeks later, a telegram came from the University of Pennsylvania promising release from Wilberforce: "Are ready to appoint you for one year at nine hundred dollars maximum payable monthly from date of service. If you wish appointment will write definitely."[100] The message bore the signature of C. C. Harrison, acting provost.

8.
From Philadelphia to Atlanta

IN THE *Autobiography*, Du Bois wrote of Professor Samuel McCune Lindsay of the University of Pennsylvania, the man responsible for his Philadelphia position, with generosity: "If Lindsay had been a smaller man and had been induced to follow the usual American pattern of treating Negroes, he would have asked me to assist him as his clerk in this study." Du Bois adds that he probably would have accepted the terms, whatever they were—anything to escape Wilberforce! Lindsay returned the admiration, writing in the introduction to *The Philadelphia Negro* that both Du Bois's training and his personal qualifications "proved to be far greater than our highest expectations."[1] But if the Wharton School professor seemed cut from the same cloth as Frank Hosmer, Du Bois never wrote generously about the treatment he received from the university itself. Its conduct toward him rankled increasingly as the years went by, so much so that he sometimes understated his nine-hundred-dollar salary by as much as a third.[2]

First, there was the matter of the unheard of title "assistant in sociology," without office or teaching responsibilities, except having once had to "pilot a pack of idiots through the Negro slums." "My name never actually got into the catalogue," Du Bois declared sourly in *Dusk of Dawn*, and claimed, somewhat contradictorily in the *Autobiography*, that it was "eventually omitted from the catalogue." "There must have been some opposition," he complained, because he believed the university's invitation had not been "particularly cordial."[3] But what really galled him, he insisted, was that after his study was finished and ready for the printer, it occurred to no one to offer at least a "temporary instructorship in the college or in the Wharton School." Then, as later, he knew an insult when he saw one. Certainly from today's perspective, Du Bois's slow burn was entirely understandable, but he had been slow to anger undoubtably because, as he admitted much later, the force of racial segregation in 1897 was such that an appointment simply "didn't occur to me."[4]

Two of his biographers have seen in Du Bois's delayed ire over the Pennsylvania affiliation further evidence of a racial prickliness that even the deftest solicitude occasionally failed to assuage. "These are bitter words," the Philadelphia sociologist E. Digby Baltzell tut-tutted in his introduction to the 1967 edition of *The Philadelphia Negro*, "and apparently . . . not quite true to the facts of the case." In its own defense, the university has underscored the special and temporary nature of the appointment, expressed profound puzzlement about any want of cordiality, and placed in evidence page 218 of its catalogue for 1897–98 announcing that the "special sociological investigation of the condition of the Negroes in Philadelphia in the Seventh Ward . . . under the direction of William E. Burkhartt [sic] Du Bois, Ph.D., will be concluded January 1, 1898." By then, however, Lindsay and the university had seen enough of the Seventh Ward manuscript to appreciate the author's extraordinary achievement, which probably explains why Du Bois had been there a year before the catalogue noticed him. Whatever the tricks of his memory, the October 1896 trustees' minutes seem to confirm Du Bois's suspicion of an intentional snub. In explaining the appointment, Acting Provost Charles Custis Harrison is recorded as stating that the former Wilberforce professor had not been "placed on the staff" and need not be listed in the catalogue. "Indeed," Harrison sniffed, "I would not have known where to place or what to call him."[5] Not only were Du Bois's feelings (if not his facts) essentially correct about the University of Pennsylvania, but almost surely, university authorities had initially seen him as an expendable black person brought there to do a predictable job.

A hidden agenda had brought Du Bois to Wilberforce, and another brought him to the University of Pennsylvania in the summer of 1896. But this time, he was much quicker to size it up. In the late 1890s, Philadelphia held the largest black community in the North. Because the city's corrupt political machine derived crucial support from African-Americans, the city's reforming elites hatched the scheme of documenting the alarming moral and social conditions among them in order to mount a more effective campaign to recapture city hall. The old Philadelphia of solemn Quakers and hardworking Germans going about their affairs while dark-skinned citizens gamely struggled and, in a fair measure, contributed to the general prosperity, was a thing of the pre–Civil War past. That soaring earnest of the good citizenship to which the city's African-Americans aspired, magnificent Mother Bethel, flagship worship place of the AME Church, stood a short block from the Seventh and Lombard address now home to the Du Boises. There had once been a time when race-proud, civic-minded black men like James Forten, worth a fabulous hundred thousand dollars from sailmaking; Robert Purvis, Sr., heir to an even larger textile fortune from his English-born father, Cyrus Bustill, owner of one of the city's most prosperous catering establishments; and Richard Allen, founder and first bishop of the "vastest and most remarkable product of American Negro civilization," the AME Church (as Du Bois would write), had been respectfully listened to by the controlling whites of the city.[6]

But Quaker humanitarianism had receded—first gradually, then in a seeming rout—before economic self-interest and population shifts. Abolitionist agitation, the Underground Railroad, and a rising number of plantation escapees became more than annoyances to the city's governing elites involved in cotton and textiles, and thus in growing solicitude for the South's Peculiar Institution. As the mills and foundaries pulled in more and more unskilled whites, Philadelphia's blacks found themselves whipsawed between elite displeasure and mudsill hatred. Race riots came as regularly as election campaigns, which were invariably won by the Democratic machine—1834, 1838, 1842, 1849. Helped by Quaker stalwarts, James Forten and Robert Purvis grew hoarse protesting the Scotch-Irish clamor for disfranchisement in 1837, but to no avail. By amendment to the state constitution the following year, voting became the exclusive privilege of white men. A few years later, Forten's finely educated sons found themselves barred from any career that gentlemen of means might have been expected to pursue.[7] When streetcars began to run in Philadelphia about 1850, they not only killed the coach business that black men had done so well in, but the newcomer Irish who had laid the tracks and bullied themselves into a monopoly as conductors were encouraged to demand that only white people should ride the new conveyances, although on some lines blacks might ride outside with the conductor. Professor Edward Turner, the white author of *The Negro in Pennsylvania*, winner of the American Historical Association's 1911 prize for scholarship, conceded, more bluntly even than Du Bois, that "the history of the relations between the negro and the white man in Pennsylvania is largely the history of increasing race prejudice."[8]

After the Civil War, a Republican machine replaced Philadelphia's Democratic model, and "as the Irishman had been the tool of the Democrats, so the Negro became the tool of the Republicans," Du Bois would write.[9] The new breed of finance capitalists and industrialists displayed even greater indifference to the city's physical character and social ills than the bankers and merchants of old. Railroads, steel, coal, and oil had taken the place of cotton for the city's financial mighty. Dignified Biddles, Drexels, and Cadwaladers receded before the likes of swashbuckling Jay Cooke, whose 1873 bankruptcy of the Northern Pacific Railroad sent a great shudder through the Gilded Age. Philadelphia expanded to fill up the county, spreading from the Delaware to the Schuylkill, leaving much of the historic heart of the city with its gridiron streets and redbrick federal facades to the genteel rich and the hard-pressed blacks. Although no longer the hub of the nation's banking or textile production, with its almost ninefold population increase from 120,000 in 1850 to 1,046,000 in 1890, Philadelphia was an industrial powerhouse, headquarters of the behemoth Pennsylvania Railroad, major producer of steel and ships, a piston in the racing industrial engine. The triumph of industrial capitalism was under way, even though its rationalization yet remained to be achieved in its several guises of genteel and technocratic reform and in the housebreaking of organized labor, launched with a vengeance after the bloody Pullman Strike of 1894.

Rapacity, conspicuous waste, and inequality were becoming as American as apple pie thanks to men—businessmen—whose predatory values were indicted as throwbacks to a feudal age, a view that would receive its canonical formulation in Thorstein Veblen's *Theory of the Leisure Class*, published in the same year as Du Bois's *The Philadelphia Negro*. There were some, like Edward Alsworth Ross, author of the influential book *Sin and Society*, who would soon warn with the pith and insight of a latter-day Galbraith that the Land of Opportunity was being stolen by the opportunists. As unchecked corporate wealth produced deep pockets of urban poverty everywhere, political machines fastened on the body politic like giant succubi, and Philadelphia's, by all accounts, was one of the worst. The year before the Du Boises moved to the city, fellow Harvard man Boies Penrose, 250 gourmandizing pounds of Machiavellian brilliance and personal licentiousness, had had to relinquish the Republican nomination for mayor after the opposition photographed him tumbling out of a house of prostitution at 3:00 A.M. Settling for the U.S. Senate two years later, Penrose would become the undisputed boss of the state and tireless opponent of reform for the next twenty years. Anticipating Lincoln Steffens's exposé in *The Shame of the Cities*, Du Bois would be quick to conclude that the government "of both city and State is unparalleled in the history of republican government for brazen dishonesty and bare-faced defiance of public opinion."[10] In Philadelphia, the plutocracy left the business of government to the machine, and the machine left business to business, an arrangement leaving the rich to get incomparably richer, the politicians answerable largely to themselves, and the working classes with the crumbs of patronage. "New Yorkers vote for Tammany Hall. The Philadelphians do not vote," Steffens would write; "they are disfranchised." But if the Philadelphia machine had become legendary for its orderly corruption by the mid-1890s, it was only one peculiarly outstanding example of what passed for municipal government in Boston, New York, Cleveland, St. Louis, Chicago, and other large cities.[11]

To stop the rot, to restore America to Puritan values and Jeffersonian traditions, to scale back Leviathan capital and empower Main Street and the town meeting again, a multifaceted, somewhat paradoxical reform movement arose in Philadelphia and throughout much of America in the 1890s, only to be partially coopted by the very forces it opposed. Historian Richard Hofstadter proposed the elegant thesis of a "status revolution" to explain who the Progressives were and why they had emerged. "The newly rich, the grandiosely or corruptly rich, the masters of the great corporations, were bypassing the men of the mugwump type," he contended—"the old gentry, the merchants of long standing, the small manufacturers, the established professional men, the civic leaders of an earlier era."[12] As the ground of deference gave way under their feet, as polyglot strangers from abroad ghettoized the cities and sold their votes to colorfully named traducers of the public trust, and robber barons plundered the ancestral legacy, the republic seemed to lose its moorings. Hofstadter pictured these Anglo-Saxon Protestant sons and daughters of parsons, lawyers, physicians, and small-town businessmen mounting a crusade to save America for small-town values and incomes even if it meant (as it did with Du Bois classmate Herbert Croly and his spiritual allies at the University of Wisconsin) using the Hamiltonian central government to accomplish Jeffersonian ends. Many were resentful, but even more were taken by surprise by the proliferation of the mega-rich. Anxious, resentful, or both, Hofstadter's Progressives trolled the utopian and Socialist classics—Henry George's *Progress and Poverty* (1879), Edward Bellamy's *Looking Backward*, (1888)—for ideas, wrote muckraking exposés of corporate perfidy in *McClure's* and *Cosmopolitan*, and captured, at least momentarily, city halls in New York, Detroit, Cleveland, Toledo, Pittsburgh, and even Jersey City.[13]

But historians have found themselves increasingly unhappy with Hofstadter's thesis of a revolution in status. In some cases, a careful nose count of the class and professional backgrounds of the reformers has shown that they were upper-class professionals fully in tune with the new business culture and untroubled by status anxiety; furthermore, much of the impetus for reform came from the much-reviled bankers and industrialists themselves—Carnegie, Russell Sage, and the Rockefellers, for example—who used the studies, exposés, religious zeal, chambers of commerce, and volunteerism of the distressed upper middle class for their own consolidating agendas. Machine politics could make doing business with a city expensive and inefficient.[14] In fact, insofar as it seems to have played a measurable part in reform, a great deal of the anxiety came from the builders of the new economic order—anxious not about their own status but about the growing disaffection of the lower classes. It was, for example, the apprehensions of the English capitalist Charles Booth and the nocturnal distress of the elder John Davison Rockefeller ("All the fortune I have made has not served to compensate for anxiety," the owner of virtually all of America's petroleum fretted. "Work by day and worry by night, week in and week out, month after month.") that produced ideas and money to fuel much of the reform movement. In his tremendously influential *Life and Labour of the People in London* (1889–1902), a monumental work of empirical sociology on which Du Bois was to base much of the structure and methodology of *The Philadelphia Negro*, Booth sifted, weighed, and graded the poor of East, Central, and South London with a chemist's cold precision, adding a dollop of behavioral psychology for good measure, into subclasses of income, work, and culture.

But looming over exhaustive research and inductive conclusions was Booth's anxiety that his message about preserving laissez-faire capitalism would be missed—a little socialism now in order to avoid too much later. "Thorough interference on the part of the State with the lives of a small fraction of the population," he winked at his upper-class readers, "would tend to make it possible, ultimately, to dispense with any Socialistic interference in the lives of all the rest."[15] Booth's researches and admonitions encouraged Charles Kingsley, Frederick Denison Maurice, and other sensitive young "Christian Socialists" from Oxford and Cambridge to establish Toynbee Hall in London's East End, the model for dozens of such settlement houses for workers in Great Britain and the United States. The board members who built Pittsburgh's new Kingsley House—three Carnegies, four Fricks, and five Mellons—also got the message.[16] Still, Rockefeller's Baptist conscience warned him that the rich were going to have to do much more to keep the poor happy with them. He couldn't stop "worrying about how it was all coming out."

In the end, Progressives seem to have been divided between those who were anxious about the future they could no longer afford, and those who worried about the future they already owned.[17] Hofstadter's indifference to the existence of the left and right wings of Progressive reform was misleading. The left-wing Progressives read in the crises of their times a mandate to embrace social reforms for the benefit of the exploited and the powerless (immigrants, workers, women, blacks). The right-wing Progressives saw these crises as symptomatic of beneficent technological and social consolidation and the coalescence of a positive new equilibrium. The divergent agendas of the two Progressive factions would become increasingly apparent over the next ten years or so, and their impact upon Du Bois would be highly significant.

AS THE Du Boises settled into their one-room apartment at 700 Lombard Street, William Jennings Bryan delivered his "Cross of Gold" speech before the Democratic convention in Chicago. The Republicans had just chosen Ohio's William McKinley to lead them at St. Louis, to the self-important satisfaction of Wilberforce's Bishop Arnett. From the window of their new apartment in the Seventh Ward, Du Bois and Nina saw and heard terrible sights and sounds of the extreme social misery that many of Bryan's supporters swore could be put right without destroying the capitalist system. Du Bois fully shared the widespread belief that the presidential contest of 1896 would be one of the most important in the history of the republic. Money redeemable in gold, high tariffs for home production, and self-regulating industries free of unions were at stake, the Republicans and *The New York Times* shouted. The world of trusts, banks, and industry was menaced by Bryan Democrats and Tom Watson Populists who wanted to drive gold out with silver, tax wealth, dismantle tariffs, nationalize transportation, create federal banks that accepted farmers' crops as collateral, and all manner of other madcap destruction of property and order. Although the Populists and Progressives overlapped, in the aggregate they came from different regions and class backgrounds. Populists were most numerous in the agrarian South and West and ranged downward from the middle-middle class. Progressives were northeasterners and midwesterners, were more citified, and had been recruited from the middle-middle upward.[18]

Du Bois wrote of having followed these developments with an intensity that made him begin to rethink the laissez-faire economics learned in Taussig's courses at Harvard. Those visits to Social Democratic gatherings in Berlin began to have an impact. Populism, he now started to believe, "was a third party movement of deep significance," and after McKinley's victory, financed by a then-fabulous election fund of almost $20 million, he began to see, too, that politics and economics were "but two aspects of a united body of action and effort."[19] It was a Populist insight that carried over into progressivism and an insight that would inform the large project of research and writing called for in his contract with the University of Pennsylvania and its affiliated welfare organization, the College Settlement Association (CSA).

Philadelphia's Seventh Ward was a progressive reformer's worst nightmare. Cut off from the Delaware River by the stubby Fifth Ward, it ran between Spruce and South streets, eighteen gridiron blocks due west from Seventh Street to the Schuylkill. About forty thousand African-Americans lived in the city, 9,675 of them in the Seventh Ward, of whom 5,174 were females. Philadelphia's ethnic groups tended to be spread throughout its wards, rather than to be densely packed in clearly demarcated German, Irish, Italian, Polish, or Jewish neighborhoods. It was fairly exceptional among other American cities in this respect.[20] But African-Americans, although also somewhat dispersed, lived mostly in four wards, with the seventh being home to 25 percent. Because so many lived there, because many of them were so poor, because many had recently arrived from the South, because they were responsible for so much crime, and because they stood out by color and culture so conspicuously in the eyes of their white neighbors, the area was the bane of respectable Philadelphia, its population the very embodiment of "the dangerous classes" troubling the sleep of the modernizing gentry.

Life was hard, noisy, and deadly for too many of the black people there. On Saturday nights the smoky, loud-music honky-tonks in Carver and Minister alleys and the miserable shotgun row houses squeezed together near the south end of Seventh up to South Street always disgorged maimed and murdered clients and dwellers before morning. Pennsylvania Hospital two blocks away on Pine Street was practically swamped by the grisly medical problems of black males in the grip of social pathologies. There was simply no evading the hard fact, as Du Bois quickly saw, that "from his earliest advent the Negro . . . has figured largely in the criminal annals of Philadelphia."[21] With eight of every ten males working at unskilled jobs, the Germans and Italians driving them out of catering and barbering, the Irish and other comparably unskilled newcomers fiercely maintaining a color bar in the craft and industrial unions, it was not surprising that many Seventh Ward blacks sought release in drugs and crime or savagely turned on each other out of rage and a sense of hopelessness.

Respectable Philadelphia habitually deplored these worsening conditions, and would have continued to do little about them, but for the fact that the Seventh Ward was also home to many of the city's most distinguished white families. When the better-government ladies had gone among their black neighbors in an effort to rally support for their 1895 slate of school-board reformers (enlisting the distinguished energies of Mrs. Fanny J. Coppin, Oberlin graduate and principal of the Friends Institute for Colored Youth), they ran into a stone wall of hostility. Reform had gone down to defeat greatly helped, Du Bois would explain, by Seventh Ward voters who preferred the corruption and patronage they knew to the high-toned platform of "women who did not apparently know there were any Negroes on earth until they wanted their votes."[22] It was then that Quaker Susan P. Wharton convened a strategy meeting in the ancestral town house at 910 Clinton Street near the heart of the Negro ghetto. Her Seventh Ward neighbor, retired sugar tycoon Dr. Charles Custis Harrison, presided. Harrison had recently taken up the post of acting provost of the University of Pennsylvania. Wharton urged a comprehensive study of the Negro population to be undertaken by the university in collaboration with the Philadelphia branch of the CSA, on whose executive committee she had served since its founding in 1890.[23]

Inspired by Booth's *Life and Labour* and pilgrimages to London's East End, the CSA had been founded by the crème de la crème of morally motivated America (Jane Addams, Ellen Gates Starr, Vida Scudder, Sophonisba Breckinridge, Stanton Coit, Charles Stover, and others) who rapidly established uplift houses in imitation of Toynbee Hall in the industrial North—Hiram House in Cleveland, South End in Boston, Kingsley in Pittsburgh, and, most famous of all, Hull House in Chicago.[24] The left wing of Progressive reform was alive and well in the settlement movement, although older and mostly male establishment types like Columbia University president and future New York reform mayor Seth Low, department-store magnate and Hampton Institute benefactor Robert C. Ogden, and even Wharton, represented more of the right wing's paternalism than the left wing's mobilizing fervor. Some eight hundred Smith, Vassar, Wellesley, and other suffragettes strong, and numbering men of influence among its cadre, the CSA was a feminist force to reckon with for civic leaders. For that reason alone, Provost Harrison would have given Wharton a hearing; and because she was a Wharton, he listened avidly to her proposal. She was sure that Ogden would support it, as would her family friend Talcott Williams of the Philadelphia *Press*. Miss Wharton thought she knew just the man to oversee the project: Samuel McCune Lindsay, assistant professor in the sociology department of the university's Wharton School and an active member of the CSA. Better still, her Smith College friend Miss Isabel Eaton, daughter of Union General John Eaton and candidate for the master's degree in sociology at Columbia, could do much of the field research.[25]

Harrison and Wharton, like many Progressives (especially older ones), were prey to eugenic nightmares about "native stock" and the better classes being swamped by fecund, dysgenic aliens. The conservative CSA gentry thought of poverty in epidemiological terms, as a virus to be quarantined—"a hopeless element in the social wreckage," as Lindsay had written in a report on municipal welfare, to be "prevented, if possible, from accumulating too rapidly or contaminating the closely allied product just outside the almshouse door."[26] Such was the virulence of this black plague that Lindsay urged that a promising young African-American scholar, a male, be given the direction of the Seventh Ward study, instead of one of Wharton's feminists. Not only was this dangerous work, but the deplorable findings would have greater credibility if they came from a researcher of the same race as his subjects. "I was the man to do it," said the nine-hundred-dollar-a-year assistant in sociology whose findings would determine the nature and duration of the quarantine that the city's notables intended to impose. Isabel Eaton, a specialist on sweatshops and domestic service, remained in the picture, nonetheless. She joined Du Bois in the fall of 1897, and would work closely with him while pursuing her parallel investigations among white employees.[27] Whatever Eaton's role, Du Bois was expected to take responsibility for diagnosing the exact nature of the virus among Philadelphia's African-Americans.

Harrison drew up Du Bois's charge: "We want to know precisely how this class of people live; what occupations they follow; from what occupations they are excluded; how many of their children go to school; and to ascertain every fact which will throw light on this social problem." But

Du Bois knew that his sponsors held a theory about the race to be studied. The city was "going to the dogs because of the crime and venality of its Negro citizens." "Something is wrong with a race that is responsible for so much crime," the theory ran, and "strong remedies are called for." Another junior academic (and a minority scholar at that), given the chance to impress rich and pedigreed sponsors for future assignments and fellowships, might have been conscientious about fleshing out the data but neutral or even collusive about their implications. To believe Du Bois, however, he "neither knew nor cared" about the agenda of the reformers. "The world was thinking wrong about race, because it did not know." He would teach it to think right. The task was "simple and clear-cut" for someone with his cutting-edge training in sociology. He proposed to "find out what was the matter with this area and why," and he would ask "little advice as to procedure."[28] It was an opportunity—a mandate, really—whose scientific and racial implications made the politics behind his appointment unimportant.

This pose of peerless wisdom and sublime self-assurance was overdrawn as usual. Du Bois knew what the ulterior aims of his sponsors were, and he knew that he had to care. As in his Jefferson Davis address at Harvard, in which adversary terms and symbols performed a seductive Apache dance, there would be several clashing premises in *The Philadelphia Negro*. Seeing himself as the custodian of privileged insights capable of transforming American race relations, Du Bois was determined to gain the widest and most respectful hearing possible. But to do this, he obviously must have calculated that it would be necessary to write what amounted almost to two books in one—one that would not be immediately denounced or ridiculed by the arbiters of mainstream knowledge, influence, and order for its transparent heterodoxy; and a second one that would, over time, deeply penetrate the social sciences and gradually improve race-relations policy through its not-immediately apparent interpretive radicalism. He set about, then, to write a study affirming and modifying, yet also significantly subverting, the received sociological wisdom of the day. He would give the CSA Progressives facts and judgments with which to support their moralizing and piecemeal reformism. And he would do so with a clear conscience, in large part because of his higher racial and social-science purposes, but also because his elitist temperament led him naturally into prim sententiousness about bottom-class manners and institutions. "The main results of the inquiry seem credible," he would write. "They agree, to a large extent, with general public opinion."[29] Like its author, *The Philadelphia Negro* was to enter the twentieth century frequently looking backward. But long stretches of the road were modern. "In other respects," Du Bois would signal, *The Philadelphia Negro* was based on interpretations "logically explicable or in accord with historical precedents." Behind the moralizing, and the stern admonitions to black people to behave like lending-library patrons, the book would speak calmly yet devastatingly of the history and logic of poverty and racism.[30]

Some have made the debatable claim that *The Philadelphia Negro* is the first study of its kind in America, but its pride of place as the first scientific urban study of African-Americans is as secure as the charge is misconceived that Du Bois's book is largely derivative. The groundbreaking *Hull House Maps and Papers*, appearing during his final year at Wilberforce, served as an invaluable model for his own study, while ongoing city surveys of low-income groups in New York, Boston, Washington, and Chicago, published regularly in the annual reports of the CSA and *The Congregationalist*, were additional guideposts. Finally, of course, he owed a large debt to *Life and Labour of the People in London*. What Booth called his "double method" of dividing his subjects by district "and again by trades, so as to show at once the manner of their life and work" decisively shaped Du Bois's Seventh Ward study. The six schedules in *The Philadelphia Negro*, covering families, individuals, homes, street activity, community institutions, and a special category dealing with individuals, were patterned on Booth's. *Hull House Maps and Papers* displayed a similar reliance on the methodology in *Life and Labour*.[31] The thoroughness with which Du Bois refined and applied what he borrowed, however, was characteristically remarkable.

Leaving Nina with the daily grocery list, which he prepared as carefully as one of his research schedules, Du Bois sallied forth on quick firm steps each morning, accoutered with cane and gloves, to spend an eight-hour day knocking on the doors of his new neighbors. Unassisted, indefatigable, he would sit for an average of twenty minutes patiently guiding often barely literate, suspicious adults through a series of questions on the six schedules while infants usually scampered and yawped under the kitchen table. More than a few times, he was challenged at the front door with the question, "Are we animals to be dissected and by an unknown Negro at that?" but only a dozen times was he flatly refused entry. Historian Herbert Aptheker has calculated that Du Bois spent some 835 hours interviewing approximately 2,500 households over the three-month period of field research beginning in early August 1896.[32] No representative sampling for Du Bois. As he tabulated some fifteen thousand household schedules, he had before him life histories of the entire black population of the Seventh Ward—nearly ten thousand men, women, and children.

Susan Wharton's friend, Isabel Eaton, had taken a tiny room in the Lombard Street settlement by then in order to collaborate on the study. Her specific interest was domestic service, an area of research in which her mentor, Professor Lucy Maynard Salmon of Vassar, had just produced a major monograph, *Domestic Service*. Although Du Bois would stress repeatedly that his great work of urban sociology was a solitary enterprise—that he alone conducted the interviews and made the tabulations—the fact that Eaton's signature follows several lengthy, informative footnotes in *The Philadelphia Negro* suggests her more than incidental input. She had firsthand knowledge of management-labor tensions around the issue of race, particularly at the Midvale Steel plant where the young efficiency expert Frederick W. Taylor's concepts clashed with the practices current elsewhere in Philadelphia of deferring to the racially exclusive demands of labor. Eaton was cut from the same cloth as Katherine Bement Davis, who ran the Lombard Street settlement house until 1897. Davis was known to vent her anger against slum tenements in the manner of a Carrie Nation destroying saloon counters. Both Eaton and Du Bois found a valuable friend in this future New York City commissioner of corrections.[33]

Eaton and Davis were members of the settlement movement's younger feminist vanguard, and as such were readily distinguishable from men like Harrison, Low, or department-store magnate John Wanamaker by their nonpaternalist concerns for the welfare of the disadvantaged. They were discovering that working-class males had no use whatsoever for well-intentioned centers run by upper-class-native females. They were still learning that immigrants had their own definite views about how to become Americans. And they were even beginning to grasp that solving the problems of urban African-Americans demanded the same white-knuckled patience and commitment to economic justice that they gave the European newcomers. Above all, unlike many of their solid-citizen male associates, they were sincerely trying to learn.[34] Few hard details of what was, for the times, a unique interracial collaboration exist, yet Eaton's presence and loyal support of Du Bois's conceptualization of the Seventh Ward project would be significant. Had Eaton—a social scientist in her own right and a gentlewoman of impeccable connections—not acquiesced in Du Bois's independent tack or had she opposed the fundamentally radical underpinnings of his evolving study, the storm clouds over 700 Lombard Street might well have drowned Du Bois's second book in controversy. Eaton's affinity for Du Bois would bring her to his side fourteen years later when the forces opposing Booker T. Washington rallied to establish an effective civil rights organization.

Nina offered him a different brand of support entirely. Their one room above a cafeteria was kept spotless and tastefully brightened by fresh flowers. There may have been an allegorical print on a wall, perhaps a lace antimacassar or two on the rather worn chairs. She was not expected to try to take part in her husband's intellectual life. "Her great gift," as Du Bois saw it, "was her singularly honest character, her passion for cleanliness and order and her loyalty." "Good and peaceful" Nina was a German professor's ideal mate. They believed they were deeply, mutually in love, and he relished the striking impression they made when strolling together on crisp autumn weekends; Du Bois boasted that "people used to stop and stare at her in the street." Years later, after little remained of the marriage save the husk of principled mutuality, he spoke guiltily of having made "their first home in the slums of Philadelphia."[35] During the day, "kids played intriguing games like 'cops and lady bums' " there, and when "pistols popped [at night], you didn't get up lest you find you couldn't"—circumstances Nina had never before encountered in her protected, parochial life.[36] Yet Du Bois's diary description of their social outings and playful private hours during the 1896 Christmas holidays suggests that Nina was joyfully unruffled at finding herself in a ghetto with the man she adored. On Christmas morning, Du Bois awoke, catching his "wife in her little gown secreting bundles in and around my socks." Laughing, he "kept as quiet" as he could. "Finally the whole day melted away in misty happiness."

Although this account, with its sexist condescension, grates today, there was nothing false or atypical about it in 1896 as a depiction of happy late-Victorian domesticity. These, and the twenty-odd months to follow in Atlanta, were probably the happiest of Nina's married life. Her only surviving letter from this honeymoon period was written in early September when she was waiting in Wilberforce until money arrived so she could join her "pet" in Philadelphia. "I'm feeling real good," she wrote in what may have been an indirect reference to her chronic health problems. "I think I'll be good and well when I come home to you."[37] Will and Nina had not yet begun to notice that they were different beyond incompatibility. Although Nina was obviously intelligent, she was as far from being an intellectual as one of the Great Barrington Burghardts. Will Du Bois was breadth and depth; she—or so it came to appear to most observers—was the flat, smooth surface of a plane. It was the union of a think tank and a millinery shop. Their lives together would be passed in different, incommensurable dimensions. Du Bois would tend to write about her with brevity and a tinge of condescension, and, as with intimate matters generally, would give the wrong year for their marriage when he wrote her obituary half a century later.[38]

From what Du Bois wrote in the *Autobiography* and confided much later to his daughter's first husband, Nina was a reluctant learner who never managed to overcome a feeling that sex was "fundamentally indecent." Persuading her otherwise was no "easy task for a normal and lusty young man," but in early February 1897, the month of his twenty-ninth birthday, they conceived a son, whose arrival, "suddenly, unexpectedly, miraculously," on October 2, 1897, Du Bois would celebrate ecstatically.[39] Nina's accouchement would take place in Great Barrington, where she was sent to stay with Uncle James and other Burghardt relatives, the little settlement-house room being clearly unsatisfactory. The demands of the Seventh Ward project were such that he would miss his son's birth. When he was finally able to tear himself away several weeks later, he confessed to not quite knowing how to respond to "this newborn wail from an unknown world"; but for Nina, his "girl-mother" now a "transfigured woman," the lustful lover experienced a powerfully deepened affection.[40]

His other child, *The Philadelphia Negro*, called him away from Great Barrington after a day or so. While Nina suckled her perfect Burghardt in the Berkshires, her husband drove himself to produce an equally perfect creation in Philadelphia. He had something of Herbert Spencer's confidence in both objective social science and in real-world application of its findings but without the British sociologist's mechanistic determinism. This faith was to be spelled out in two public speeches delivered while *The Philadelphia Negro* was well under way during 1897, the first at a CSA meeting in March and the second, fuller and more significantly, before the forty-fourth session of the American Academy of Political and Social Science on November 19 in Philadelphia. "The Study of the Negro Problems" before the academy was a replay of his precedent-breaking, well-received, and widely commented-upon American Historical Association presentation in 1891. Introduced by Provost Harrison, Du Bois began by complimenting the university's Seventh Ward undertaking, and went on to make the plea—the first ever before mainstream scholars—that the great research universities of Harvard, Columbia, and Johns Hopkins join with Pennsylvania to support, with money and resources, a comprehensive, long-term study of the "Negro question" at Tuskegee, Hampton, or Atlanta

University. "What more effective or suitable agency could be found," he asked (with himself obviously in mind for the role), "than to focus the scientific efforts of the great universities of the North and East, on an institution situated in the very heart of these social problems?"[41]

Du Bois pressed his audience with an advancement-of-mankind savvy that subsequent academic supplicants of foundation support have not greatly improved upon. "The American Negro deserves study for the great end of advancing the cause of science in general," the young phenomenon said, his normally dry voice registering the excitement of a self-anointed mandate:

> No such opportunity to watch and measure the history and development of a great race of men ever presented itself to the scholars of a modern nation. If they miss this opportunity—if they do the work in a slipshod, unsystematic manner—if they dally with the truth to humor the whims of the day, they do far more to hurt the good name of the American people; they hurt the cause of scientific truth the world over; they voluntarily decrease human knowledge of a universe of which we are ignorant enough, and they degrade the high end of truth-seeking in a day when they need more and more to dwell upon its sanctity.[42]

Applause followed, as well as spirited discussion of the academy paper by noted historian John Bach McMaster, Howard University physician Daniel Hale Williams, a future pioneer of heart surgery, and two ministers. But nothing else was forthcoming. It would not be the last time Du Bois would stand before a leading body of largely white influentials vainly appealing for a pittance of support for solid research into the conditions of his race. If men like Harrison and Lindsay (or Hart for that matter) felt any regret or guilt about the caste system that precluded hiring a brown-skinned Harvard man, the exceptional *Atlantic Monthly* commission for Du Bois along with the U.S. Bureau of Labor Statistics contract earlier that year may well have assuaged their consciences.

With the clock ticking on his Pennsylvania appointment (it expired January 1, 1898), Du Bois had responded to a February 16, 1897, letter from the head of the U.S. Bureau of Labor Statistics indicating the possibility of employment. The Bureau of Labor Statistics, then housed in the Department of the Interior, was headed by the eminent economist Carroll Davidson Wright, future president of Clark University, who served as first commissioner of labor from 1885 to 1905. Wright's comprehensive *Indus-*

trial Evolution of the United States had appeared in 1895 and he was finishing his prodigious *Outline of Practical Sociology*. Obviously abreast of the impressive job Du Bois was reported to be doing in Philadelphia, Wright wrote to inquire whether Du Bois would be interested in the bureau's plans to conduct investigations "relating to the economic progress of the colored people." In an almost enthusiastic reply to Wright on February 18, Du Bois told the labor commissioner that he had given the subject a great deal of thought and already had in mind some rather definite proposals that he would be pleased to discuss during a "half hour of leisure on the 3d, 4th, 5th or 6th of March," when he was due to be in Washington.[43] Six days later, Lindsay sent his acquaintance Wright a somewhat remote but encouraging endorsement of Du Bois. The Washington interview with Wright, which took place during the week of the American Negro Academy presentation of "The Conservation of Races," resulted in Du Bois's being hired temporarily to conduct studies of African-American social and economic conditions in the South.

There followed on May 5 and June 14 two closely reasoned letter proposals of the type that were to become the signature of Du Bois's scholarship. In the second, he announced his decision to locate and study a prototype township, "a small place of 1000–2000 Negro inhabitants, situated about midway between Petersburg [Virginia] and the North Carolina line; from this district a large part of the Negro immigration to Baltimore, Washington, Philadelphia, and New York sets out." The resulting paper, "The Negroes of Farmville, Virginia: A Social Study," would appear as the labor bureau's *Bulletin* 3, no. 14, in January 1898. "My idea," Du Bois would emphasize four years later before a congressional committee, "has always been that in order to really get at the South and carry out any theories we ought to have a very careful basis in fact."[44] Hard at work on *The Philadelphia Negro*, Du Bois managed to spend July and August in Farmville, the seat of stagnating Prince Edward County and the tobacco-trading center for six counties. The study was a small masterpiece of great range and depth, influencing the conclusions of the Seventh Ward monograph and serving as the standard for the Atlanta University Studies of which he was then planning to take charge. In that era of Spencerian sociology when theorizing took precedence over palpable knowledge, he plunged into the backwater community with gusto, determined to explore the place from the bottom up. He would boast of having "lived with the colored people, joined in their social life, and visited their homes."[45]

The people Du Bois had come to study were mainly men and women belonging to the second generation after slavery. Farmville's population had taken a century to grow from four thousand white and four thousand black people to a total of fourteen thousand, but the increase was due almost entirely to reproduction and in-migration of blacks. The town was the archetypal point of departure for the coming Great Black Migration. The schedules for the Virginia town—mortality, family structure, conjugal condition, sex, property holdings, businesses, employment, schooling, literacy—were the building blocks for Du Bois's novel, informed reflections on miscegenation, the impact of slavery on contemporary social behavior, Afro-America's evolving class structure, the complex character of the black family, and, above all, the ramifications of the industrial earthquake shaking up Farmvilles everywhere. Throughout "Farmville" he made comparisons to similar German, British, French, Hungarian, and Italian populations in order to demonstrate the generally corrosive impact of industry upon traditional cultures; but when it came to African-American morality Du Bois's measure was a rigid Calvinist ruler. Crummellian judgments abounded: "The moral tone of the Negroes has room for great betterment"; slum elements "receive recruits from the lazy, shiftless, and dissolute of the country around"; "When among any people a low inherited standard of sexual morals is coincident with an economic situation . . . promot[ing] abnormal migrations . . . then the inevitable result is prostitution and illegitimacy."[46]

Yet along with the moralizing came the first documented sociological insights into evolving Afro-America. Among the outstanding characteristics he recorded at the outset were "postponing marriage largely for economic reasons" and the outmigration of the young "to better its conditions." Du Bois predicted the disintegrative pressures on the race as it became urbanized. The black family, he insisted, was still recovering from the ravages of slavery. Its fragility would place African-Americans at high risk as they experienced the shocks of modernization. Initiative and enterprise were also tainted by the slavery experience. These people were too good for domestic service and were "coming to regard the work as a relic of slavery, and as degrading, and only enter it from sheer necessity." "The slum elements of Farmville are as yet small," he noted, "but they are destined to grow with the town." There was a positive side, nevertheless, to the collapse of primary institutions and the rise of self-inflicted indigence. They were the casualties of progress—"evils inseparable from a transition period, and they will remain until the industrial situation becomes satisfactory, migration becomes normal, and moral standards become settled." Du Bois's concluding observation about Farmville's social structure was seminal, although it would be consistently ignored by scholars for many years. Despite high crime rates, dysfunctional families, rudimentary education, and high levels of unemployment, he distinctly detected upward mobility and class formation in Farmville-America: "One thing, however, is clear, and that is the growing differentiation of classes among Negroes, even in small communities."[47]

There were to be four more Bureau of Labor Statistics studies, an 1899 study of five Black Belt counties in Georgia and one in Alabama, a second in 1901 of "The Negro Landholder of Georgia," a third expanding the previous one, and the 1906 chef d'oeuvre on the Negroes of Lowndes County, Alabama, which was destroyed.[48] But although Du Bois had probably hoped, at least originally, to win a civil service appointment in Washington through merit, he would remain only a sometime consultant. Meanwhile, it buoyed his spirits to hear that the editor of the *Atlantic Monthly* wanted a piece on current aspirations among black Americans. Another invitation had come to give a paper at the much-publicized General Conference of Negroes in July, sponsored by the Hampton Institute and meeting in Norfolk.[49] By now, favorable critical reception of *The Suppression of the African Slave Trade* had made him one of the most talked-about young scholars in the country. Nevertheless, as summer 1897 ended, he still needed a job and was about to become a new father.

In June, Hart pressed Booker T. Washington about hiring Du Bois, sending a follow-up letter on August 10 that betrayed puzzled impatience: "Have you no place for the best educated colored man available for college work?"[50] That was precisely the dilemma Washington confronted, and why his dealings with an influential Harvard professor and regular Tuskegee contributor had to be evasive. Among other letters to be answered at just that moment was trustee Henry Villard's of June 28. Owner of *The Nation* and New York *Evening Post*, former board chairman of the Northern Pacific Railroad, and president of the company reorganized as General Electric, Villard had been dismayed to receive a student's letter thanking him for scholarship aid and the opportunity to study such grown-up subjects as natural philosophy, ancient history, and civil government at Tuskegee. "You will remember," Villard admonished his favorite Negro educator, "that in a conversation with you when you were our guest, I expressed a strong depreciation of the attempts made at the Atlanta University to give young men and women of your race a regular university education such as is obtained at the highest institutions of learning in the

North."[51] A professorship for a man like Du Bois would have struck men like Villard as a subversion of the Tuskegee ideal. The job prospects for the "best educated colored man" (who was also among the best-educated Americans) were dim.

The summer before going to Farmville, Du Bois and Nina had received a visit at the CSA from the Yankee president of Atlanta University, Horace Bumstead. Another kindly, Congregationalist Quixote, Bumstead was guiding his beleaguered institution past the shoals of southern white hostility represented by Tom Watson and northern white fecklessness *à la* Henry Villard. Horace Bumstead was not a dynamic man but there was Sheffield steel behind the parson's collar. Atlanta University's academic standards were high, its curriculum having been modeled on the New England college, and its community life was racially integrated in a city whose phoenixlike rebirth symbolized the new separate-but-equal South. Sitting with the Du Boises that hot summer day, Bumstead warmed to the confident, quiet-spoken intellectual whose career from Fisk onward he had followed with satisfaction. At the June 1895 meeting of Bumstead's trustees, Boston philanthropist George C. Bradford had proposed an annual series of "systematic and thorough investigation[s] of the conditions of living among the Negro population of cities," patterned on the Hampton and Tuskegee conferences. Whereupon the aged professor of economics at Atlanta University had dropped dead. Hart then had told Bradford (who sought a second opinion from Harvard sociologist Edward Cummings), who in turn told Bumstead that Atlanta University had to get Du Bois for his faculty.[52] There was some dodging about religious faith, Bumstead recalled. Du Bois "seemed to be one of those persons who, when asked about their religion, reply that they 'have none to speak of.' " Despite this, the Atlanta University president decided that anyone living in the middle of a Negro slum with his new bride evidenced "genuine religion in that fact." They shook hands on a promise to leave the matter under active consideration. A year later, shortly after posting the *Atlantic Monthly* piece scheduled to appear in August 1897, Du Bois accepted the Atlanta University professorship at one thousand dollars per annum, effective July 9, with actual teaching not to begin until January 1898.[53]

"Strivings of the Negro People" was in a sense Du Bois's national debut. Until then, the literate public had known something of him largely through hearsay or quick mentions in press accounts of commencement exercises or learned society proceedings. When *Atlantic Monthly* subscribers read the August issue, few of them failed to recognize that the

African-American was beginning to find a new voice, and subscribers like Henry Villard certainly disliked what they were hearing. Almost two years were to elapse before Booker T. Washington hired his first (incompetent) ghostwriter and another two before white America would go gaga over Washington's racially reassuring *Up From Slavery*.[54] Meanwhile, the genteel white reading public encountered a troubling essay the likes of which had not been seen before—not even from Frederick Douglass's flaming pen. Forty-five years before there was a name for it, Du Bois produced an existentialist essay, one in which Herder seemed to nod at a yet undiscovered (for Du Bois) Freud. "Strivings of the Negro People" was startlingly personal. It abandoned the controlled prose of *The Suppression of the African Slave Trade* and *The Philadelphia Negro* (in progress) for the indignation of the English 12 writings and the lyricism of the student notebooks. "Between me and the other world there is ever an unasked question," he began, before giving the most unconventional answer yet to the "real question" on the minds of white people, "How does it feel to be a problem?" It was a "strange experience," he said, elegiacally recalling that first instance of searing rejection in the Berkshire "wee wooden schoolhouse" when he was "shut out from their world by a vast veil."[55] But rather than sulk and wither behind it, Du Bois boasted of the compensations of the veil, of holding "all beyond it in common contempt," and of living "above it in a region of blue sky and great wandering shadows"—bravura, meaning "I could beat my mates at examination-time, or beat them at a foot-race, or even beat their stringy heads." Solitary, destined, he would prevail through the sheer strength of his own character and the power of his mind.

Du Bois projected his own personal dilemma—the gift or curse of marginality—on to the group, thereby psychoanalytically defining for at least a century the supposedly unique tension beneath African-American racial identity. Whereas in "The Conservation of Races" there had been as many as eight races, he now numbered the Negro, "after the Egyptian and Indian, the Greek and Roman, the Teuton and Mongolian," as a "sort of seventh son, born with a veil and gifted with second-sight in this American world." "It is a peculiar sensation, this sense of always looking at one's self through the eyes of others," he wrote. "One ever feels his two-ness,—an American, a Negro; two souls, two thoughts, two unreconciled strivings; two warring ideals in one dark body, whose dogged strength alone keeps it from being torn asunder."[56] The word-pictures of the "history of this strife," of this "waste of double aims" and the racial logic implicit in it, were meant to wrench emotion and provoke thought from all of his audience, short of inveterate Negrophobes. He wove a deft allusion to a past wholly unknown to white readers: "The shadow of a mighty Negro past flits through the tale of Ethiopia the Shadowy and of Egypt the Sphinx." He invoked the superhuman strivings against a rigged American civilization, in which "the powers of single black men flash here and there like falling stars." He rehearsed the pathetic ingenuousness demonstrated by the self-improving citizenship of the deceived ex-slave: "So the decade flew away, the revolution of 1876 came, and left the half-free serf weary, wondering, but still inspired." Du Bois moved on to underscore the black American's belated perception that nothing tried, nothing aspired to, nothing achieved much mattered to the white world: "For the first time he sought to analyze himself, and not another." But the black American found himself virtually bereft of the resources to act upon the new wisdom, for "to be a poor man is hard, but to be a poor race in a land of dollars is the very bottom of hardships."[57]

Before and after the Civil War, black thinkers and doers had implored and denounced, embraced and renounced the American homeland, some of them managing to embrace and renounce it simultaneously. Du Bois's *Atlantic Monthly* jeremiads belonged to an old love-hate tradition that included hundreds of speeches by Richard Allen and Martin Delany, Frederick Douglass and Henry Turner, Robert Purvis and Alexander Crummell. That tradition had traveled two antagonistic yet somehow complementary paths of nationalism and integration, or cultural chauvinism and assimilation. One led to the old lion Douglass on his Cedar Hill estate above Washington, white second wife by his side, roaring, "Assimilation not isolation is our true policy and our natural destiny." The other path led to James Holly struggling in Haiti and Delany negotiating a chimerical cotton empire in the Niger Valley. In a jest that said everything about the dual track, Douglass once remarked that he thanked God for simply making him a man, "but Delany always thanks Him for making him a black man."[58] For Du Bois, the joke was on both. The breakthrough of "Strivings of the Negro People" was to offer a third path, a dialectical solution predicated as much upon the logic of antithesis as impelled by the predicament of its author's own marginality.

Double sighted, double conscious, the African-American must neither reject America nor vanish into it. This truly novel (Crummell-derived) concept of race in America Du Bois extolled in language of great staying power:

> In this merging he wishes neither of the older selves to be lost. He would not Africanize America, for America has too much to teach the world and Africa. He would not bleach his Negro soul in a flood of white Americanism, for he knows that Negro blood has a message for the world. He simply wishes to make it possible for a man to be both a Negro and an American, without being cursed and spit upon by his fellows, without losing the opportunity of self-development [without having the doors of opportunity closed roughly in his face].[59]

A further, final surprise for *Atlantic Monthly* readers of this supercharged essay was the author's reservations about the unnamed Booker Washington's educational and civil rights bargain at Atlanta. "The training of the schools we need today more than ever," Du Bois wrote in closing, "the training of deft hands, quick eyes and ears and the broader, deeper, higher culture of gifted minds." Then came the final taboo. "The power of the ballot we need in sheer self-defense. . . . Work, culture, liberty—all these we need, not singly but together, gained through the unifying ideal of Race."[60] When this warning flare reappeared six years later, retitled and slightly retouched as "Of Our Spiritual Strivings," it was as the opening salvo in *The Souls of Black Folk*.

Du Bois must have vacated the pestilential Seventh Ward in late summer of 1897 for more congenial quarters in which to lodge the family and press the writing of *The Philadelphia Negro*. *Gopsill's Philadelphia City Directory* for 1898 lists Du Bois, W. E. B., "physician" (meaning, of course, Dr. Du Bois), at 2325 St. Alban's Place. Burghardt Gomer, the miraculous infant, probably arrived with Nina from Great Barrington in late October. The two-story brick St. Alban's house was narrow and not large but grand in comparison with the Lombard Street room. It stood roughly in the middle of what was actually a charming alley that stretched between two cast iron fountains. Both parents doted on Burghardt, a large boy with spun-gold hair, large eyes, and his mother's mouth. Nina doted on him out of maternal love and pride; and Du Bois did so out of paternal devotion but also because of the significance he believed his son held for the future of the race and history. Musing above Burghardt's "little white bed," the father saw "the strength of [his] own arm stretched onward through the ages through the newer strength of his."[61]

The Philadelphia Negro was remarkable as an example of the new empiricism that was fundamentally transforming the social sciences at the beginning of the twentieth century. Although Du Bois's novel sociological insights would soon become conventional wisdom, as one of the last books of the nineteenth century and the first of the twentieth century, the Philadelphia study would be a breakthrough achievement, an important and virtually solitary departure from the hereditarian theorizing of the times. The armchair cerebrations of sociology's great nineteenth-century system builders—Auguste Comte, Karl Marx, and Herbert Spencer—would continue to inform, challenge, and inspire, but the watchword of the discipline was becoming *investigation*, followed by induction—facts before theory.[62] More than any other leading American sociologist during the decade after 1898, Du Bois undertook for a time the working out of an authentic objectivity in social science, "to put science into sociology through a study of the conditions and problems of [his] own group."[63] It was a methodology a student of Schmoller's was superbly equipped to advance just six years after the founding at the new University of Chicago of the first department of sociology in the United States.

Unlike Spencer's colossal *Social Statics*, whose tenth and final volume appeared in 1896, *The Philadelphia Negro* tended to understate its major premises, inserting them unobtrusively between data and analysis. Loyal to James's principles of psychology and Schmoller's inductive methodology, Du Bois's was among the first to break ranks with Spencerian sociology's analogizing of social processes to the laws of chemistry and genetics. "In the realm of social phenomena the law of survival is greatly modified by human choice, wish, whim and prejudice," Du Bois contended.[64] Significantly, the founder of what became known as the Chicago School of sociology, Albion W. Small, had also studied at Berlin with Schmoller. Despite a good deal of manifesto prose in Small's brand-new *American Journal of Sociology* about scientific "restraint," avoidance of "premature sociological opinion," and the like, the canon of empirically derived knowledge was as sinned against as it was obeyed. Small and Franklin Giddings, Columbia's founding sociology chairman, as well as Edward Ross at Wisconsin, were all given to extreme prejudices about immigrants, blacks, and women. For the arbitral Giddings, a primordial "consciousness of kind" forever determined relations between groups in society. Had the now lost "Sociology Hesitant" been published when it was completed sometime after 1900, Du Bois would have left an even more impressive record as a theoretical pacesetter. This bold essay challenged the giants of contemporary sociology and declared that the discipline's methodology was based on theoretical fallacies that ignored the ineradicable element of chance in human affairs. He, too, saw the "action of physical law in the actions of men," the young sociologist wrote, but, unlike Comte's ignoring of human will, Spencer's "verbal juggery," and Giddings's "gross abstractions," he saw "more than that." What Du Bois believed he saw were "rhythms and tendencies; coincidences and probabilities." Out of what William James would soon call a "blooming, buzzing confusion" Du Bois wrested two fundamental rhythms of social behavior—a "primary" and a "secondary." Primary rhythms were governed by physical laws (*viz.*, birth and death rates); secondary rhythms ("presenting nearly the same uniformity") were controlled by volition. "To confound the two sorts of human uniformity is fatal to clear thinking," Du Bois claimed as he served up a definition of his field: "sociology, then, is the science that seeks [to measure] the limits of Chance in human conduct." But even he may have had second thoughts on the threshold of professional acclaim about publishing what amounted to an arraignment of the leading lights of his discipline. Conceivably, Du Bois may have intended to retrieve "Sociology Hesitant" from a drawer for a more timely appearance, only to decide that what had once been cutting-edge lucidity was becoming conventional sociological wisdom.[65]

In *The Philadelphia Negro* and the later Atlanta University Studies, Du Bois strove to avoid apriority, to generalize cautiously only after questionnaires, census records, government archives, and cross-cultural data and the rest had been digested. "The problem lay before me," he explained. "Study it. I studied it personally and not just by proxy. I sent out no canvassers. I went myself. . . . I went through the Philadelphia libraries for data, gained access in many instances to private libraries of colored folk. . . . I mapped the district, classifying it by conditions." But there were a few instances of substantial help provided by others, as with Eaton's industrial data and the surveillance of Seventh Ward taverns by a class from the university. Anticipating the perspective commended by Max Weber, Du Bois bracketed the Philadelphia problem in a two-hundred-year time frame in order to give causal and evolutionary context to the contemporary Seventh Ward. Because sociology was history abstracted, it followed that "one cannot study the Negro in freedom and come to general conclusions about his destiny without knowing his history in slavery."[66] *The Philadelphia Negro* recounted the ascent through slavery and adversity by late-seventeenth-century Africans in the city until their progress was sharply checked, temporarily, by European migration in the mid-nineteenth; then through their rise and fall again later in the century—due, in part, to an influx of southern black folk. "Thus we see," Du Bois wrote, consciously evoking Roman history, "that twice . . . through the migration of barbarians a dark age has settled on [their] age of revival."[67]

Other ethnic groups have passed through cycles of socioeconomic adjustment and mobility, but what made them chronically and fundamentally different for the African-American, Du Bois observed cogently, was the interplay of race and economics. This comparative historical dimension in *The Philadelphia Negro* gave its interpretations exceptional force—as when detailing the rigged hand dealt African-Americans during the Industrial Revolution:

> Here was a mass of black workmen of whom very few were by previous training fitted to become the mechanics and artisans of a new industrial development; but here, too, were an increasing mass of foreigners and native Americans who were unusually well fitted to take part in the new industries; finally, most people were willing and many eager that Negroes should be kept as menial servants rather than develop into industrial factors. . . . Let them stagger downward.[68]

Readers were reminded repeatedly, sometimes in tones less than neutral, how the factor of race had played out over time differently for black people and white people: ". . . the difference is that the ancestors of the English and the Irish and the Italians were felt to be worth educating, helping and guiding because they were men and brothers."[69] Many of today's urban scholars insist on the concept of urban "arrival time" as a more objective explanation of the African-American's troubled adjustment as the last group to reach the industrial city, thereby diminishing the importance of the factor of racism.[70] Du Bois might have been intrigued, but he would undoubtedly have replied that such hypotheses erroneously substituted chronology for causality, reminding them that long before the post-industrial city arrived, "no differences of social condition allowed any Negro to escape from the group, although such escape was continually the rule among Irish, Germans, and other whites."[71]

The comparative approach had definite advantages though. Du Bois compared black Philadelphia death rates with those of Austrians, Hungarians, and Italians in Europe and concluded that the former, although high, were "not extraordinarily so." Returning to the same scene nearly eighty years later, however, the massive, numbers-crunching Philadelphia Social History Project of the University of Pennsylvania described the mortality rate among Philadelphia's black males as "fierce," and determined that half the African-American women with children in the 1880s were widows.[72] Similarly, when he took a multiethnic look at criminal behavior, Du Bois's social-science rigor sometimes faltered before his Victorian values. He counted a total of fifty-three prostitutes for the entire Seventh Ward, even though the *Inquirer* reported forty-eight being flushed on one night from a single alley two blocks from Lombard Street. On the one hand, taking comfort from comparisons, he found that "crime is rampant but not more so, if as much, as in Italy." The fundamental point was that Irish and Italians had been privileged in Philadelphia in a way African-Americans never had because "they were men and brothers."[73] On the other hand, Du Bois's tabulations of crime in black and white revealed the appalling fact that 22.5 percent of Philadelphia's robberies, burglaries, assaults, and homicides had been perpetrated by 4 percent of its people after 1889—up dramatically from a 14-percent rate before 1890. Italians were *hors de combat*.[74]

If sociologists were historians, Du Bois also thought of them as being analogous to archeologists, who dig until reaching the bedrock of organized human behavior. A curious and paradoxical consequence sprang from this conviction, however. On the one hand, Du Bois's volume carried the vivid narrative power that other urban studies would lack until Robert and Helen Lynd's enormously popular *Middletown* series more than thirty years in the future. *The Philadelphia Negro* was as "interesting as a novel, thanks to the skill with which the author has worked his material," the review in *City and State* would applaud. Du Bois wrote graphically of money and manners in "fourteen bawdy houses," of individual and institutional accomplishments of the "better classes," of stoic pertinacity and worn-out failure among the hardworking poor, of hovels in infamous Gillis's Alley worse than anything in the plantation South, and of an exceptional decision by the Pennsylvania Railroad to promote "one bright and persistent porter to a clerkship, which he has held for years."[75] But on the other hand, barely a single family among the 2,500 households meticulously interviewed was granted a voice in the monograph, except for a string of disembodied quotes in the chapter dealing with employment. No statements from pensive mothers, tired fathers, or children not yet dulled inform it. The history and sociology of their conditions interested Du Bois, not their individual, bruised-flesh lives. What the Philadelphia Negro thought about present and future Philadelphia he or she was not invited to say. It would be to inflict the fallacy of presentism, however, to fault Du Bois for his disinterest in teasing more of the personal out of his impressive field research. Almost twenty years would elapse before William I. Thomas and Florian Znaniecki produced their monumental *The Polish Peasant in Europe and America*, teeming with the voices of struggling men and women.[76] Still, it is hard not to regret the missed opportunity to hear the active voice of the people of the Seventh Ward.

Because Du Bois wrote in a manner generally designed to disclose rather than volubly to underscore his unorthodox sociological theories, most reviewers would laud the thorough scholarship of *The Philadelphia Negro* but overlook its radical subtext completely. Much of the monograph calculatedly lent itself to one-sided, unthreatening interpretations; and besides, Lindsay had taken care to send Du Bois's preliminary research plans to Booker Washington for reassurance.[77] Paternalist generalities abounded, such as: "the Negro is as a rule, willing, honest and good-natured, but he is also, as a rule, careless, unreliable and unsteady." Even when writing of the "aristocracy of the Negro population," the author noted "here and there . . ., too, some faint trace of careless moral training." Describing the people at the bottom of the Seventh Ward heap as a "class of criminals, prostitutes and loafers," he coined a memorably dismissive phrase—"the submerged tenth." The famous term "talented tenth" would come later, but the notion that elites (black as well as white) were the purifying, moving force in history was stated over and again—because a nation "can only be understood and finally judged by its upper class."[78]

Portions of chapter 28, "A Final Word," might have been written by Yale sociologist William Graham Sumner, whose antiwelfare nostrums were soon to make him a household name. His investigative forbearance taxed beyond measure by the level of crime in the Seventh Ward, Du Bois served notice of retribution: "Simply because the ancestors of the present white inhabitants of America went out of their way barbarously to mistreat and enslave the ancestors of the present black inhabitants, gives those blacks no right to ask that the civilization and morality of the land be seriously menaced for their benefit." If they were not yet up to "complete civilization" thirty years after slavery, African-Americans could still be expected to "make themselves fit members of the community within a reasonable length of time." And, "finally," on a note that was worthy of Booker Washington, "the Negroes must cultivate a spirit of calm, patient persistence in their attitude toward their fellow citizens."[79]

The unsigned reviews in *The Nation*, *The Literary Digest*, and *The Outlook* were typical of the establishmentarian response to *The Philadelphia Negro*, allowance made for the decision of the *American Journal of*

Sociology to ignore the monograph completely. "A very exhaustive study," *The Nation* decreed, commending it to readers for "the lesson taught by this investigation . . . of patience and sympathy toward the South, whose difficulties have been far greater than those of the North." Concurring, *The Literary Digest* decided that the book proved the southern business wisdom of Booker Washington, while *The Outlook* approvingly noted that Du Bois made no attempt "to bend the facts so as to plead for his race." In its comprehensive treatment, *The American Historical Review* rejoiced that the author was "perfectly frank, laying all necessary stress on the weakness of his people." Calling for more studies based on Du Bois's excellent model, the reviewer urged that they not fail to examine the "effects of the mixing of blood of very different races."[80]

Assessments of *The Philadelphia Negro* such as these were probably exactly what CSA backers like Wharton, Harrison, Lindsay, and Ogden had hoped for. With the book's publication in the fall of 1899, the good-government reformers had a full quiver of arrows to wield in the next electoral skirmish with the hated Republican machine and its Negro minions. In that sense, Du Bois had fulfilled his part of the bargain. He had even shared the limelight with Eaton by accepting her eighty-two-page "Special Report on Negro Domestic Service in the Seventh Ward" as the book's concluding section. Summarizing her tight analysis based on Du Bois's schedules, Eaton condemned most domestic labor as dull, dead-end, and racially circumscribed. Citing the new monograph on the subject by her radical feminist mentor, Lucy Salmon, she advocated profit sharing between employer and domestic as a remedy.[81] If the inclusion of Eaton's monograph was a concession to Wharton, and in any way displeased Du Bois, there is no indication of it in his correspondence. It was an unusually generous thing for him to have done, whatever the motives—respect and affection for Eaton, feminist solidarity, or University of Pennsylvania politics. Although her contribution was solid and useful, neither as a piece of research nor as literature does it complement Du Bois's majestic text. It would have been more appropriate relegated to the appendices.

But Du Bois had written equally for white and black readers who could read between the lines of Victorian cant and could reason beyond the problems of a single ward in a large American city—readers capable of "a fair basis of induction as to the present condition of the American Negro." It was the other *Philadelphia Negro* that Du Bois hoped would be appreciated by generations of scholars and would influence, as it has, works such as the monumental *Black Metropolis* of Horace Cayton and St. Clair Drake, the family studies of E. Franklin Frazier and Patrick Moynihan, and to serve as a model for the classic *An American Dilemma.*[82] Intent on reading into Du Bois the sanctioning of the Atlanta Compromise, *The Nation, The American Historical Review*, and most other review publications virtually ignored the novel triad of race-class-economics on which the Philadelphia study was erected. Race prejudice was not the cause of all that was disadvantaged, dysfunctional, and dismal in the history of the Negro, Du Bois readily conceded, but "on the other hand, it is a far more powerful social force than most Philadelphians realize." The racially disproportionate crime rate that he deplored owed much to feeble group morality, but crime was at bottom symptomatic of systemic ills. "The social environment of excuse, listless despair, careless indulgence and lack of inspiration to work is the growing force that turns black boys and girls into gamblers, prostitutes and rascals." Du Bois made it clear that the surrounding white community was responsible for these conditions—"How long can a city teach its black children that the road to success is to have a white face?"[83]

In a single, seminal statement, he collapsed the entire superstructure of the monograph—schedules, charts, books, and all—onto its foundation: "A glance at the tables shows how much more sensitive the lower classes of a population are to the great social changes than the rest of the group."[84] Reviewers who thought that *The Philadelphia Negro* blamed poverty, crime, and indolence on Philadelphia's Negroes had obviously skipped over chapter 16. Katherine Davis, who had left the Lombard Street house to write her doctoral dissertation at the University of Chicago by the time *The Philadelphia Negro* appeared, was one of the first reviewers to give it its economic due, writing that it "recognizes the economic side of the problem as that which presents at the same time the greatest importance and the greatest difficulties."[85] A careful reading of the same chapter 16, with its Puritan assault on sloth and ignorance, revealed that Du Bois reduced the complexities of the "Negro Problem"—the feeble family structure, cultural underdevelopment, poverty, disease, and crime—to their social and economic underpinnings. It was white racism that made the black experience different and increasingly dysfunctional, readers were told. Du Bois's prose soared on Progressive currents:

> Such discrimination is morally wrong, politically dangerous, industrially wasteful, and socially silly. It is the duty of the whites to stop it, and to do so primarily for their own sakes. Industrial freedom of opportunity has by long experience been proven to be generally best for all. Moreover the cost

> of crime and pauperism, the growth of slums, and the pernicious influences of idleness and lewdness, cost the public far more than would the hurt to the feelings of a carpenter to work beside a black man, or a shopgirl to start beside a darker mate. This does not contemplate the wholesale replacing of white workmen before Negroes out of sympathy or philanthropy; it does mean that talent should be rewarded, and aptness used in commerce and industry whether its owner be black or white.[86]

But if white leaders had their work cut out for them, so did their African-American counterparts. Opportunity meant responsibility, and Du Bois's research established that above the seemingly amorphous mass there existed a cohesive, responsible elite to offer guidance. Before it was identified and described in *The Philadelphia Negro*, the class structure of Afro-America was mostly unknown, utterly mysterious, and even widely assumed as nonexistent. Most white people supposed that the periodic appearance of exceptional or "representative" black people was due to providence, "mixed blood," or some mysterious current passing through a dark, undifferentiated mass. Otherwise, there were only good Negroes and bad ones.[87] Du Bois introduced white readers to four ubiquitous classes or "grades" of African-Americans (found equally in Philadelphia, Boston, or Farmville). First came the "aristocracy" (some 277 families numbering approximately 3,000 persons among Philadelphia's 40,000 African-Americans), described as "families of undoubted respectability, earning sufficient income to live well; not engaged in menial service of any kind." Next, there were families of the "respectable working class," or the "representative Negroes," with "steady remunerative work . . . [and] younger children in school." Grade three consisted of the working poor—"honest, although not always energetic or thrifty."[88] Finally, there was the "lowest class," Du Bois's "submerged tenth."

Two aspects of class analysis spelled out in *The Philadelphia Negro* were to govern Du Bois's thinking for many years ahead. First, that the advancement of the race was driven by a minuscule elite whose mainstream standards and goals must be deferred to by the majority. "In many respects it is right and proper to judge a people by its best classes," he insisted, "rather than by its worst classes or middle ranks." More than that, Du Bois predicted that this class was "itself an answer to the question of the ability of the Negro to assimilate American culture"—rather a different note of concern from that sounded in his *Atlantic Monthly* essay.[89] He acutely regretted, therefore, that the elites had faltered in their leadership role and "segregate[d] themselves from the mass." Second, Du Bois affirmed that the family structure, work ethic, and class behavior of African-Americans was still deeply embedded in the experience and culture of slavery. Although his research indicated that most black families were nuclear—headed by two parents—and that their instability was not markedly different, statistically, from that of Philadelphia's immigrant German, Italian, or Irish families during the 1890s (a finding reconfirmed later by the Philadelphia Social History Project), Du Bois unhesitatingly ascribed much of the blame for the deviant 25 percent to the "lax moral habits of the slave regime [which] still show themselves in a large amount of cohabitation without marriage." The seeds of the future social-pathology schools of urban and ethnic studies inhered in this interpretation.[90]

In chapter 16, "The Contact of the Races," Du Bois combined the practice of speaking for his subjects with quotations exposing routine white bigotry. They piled up page after page, with little comment from the author. "D—— 'Your work is very good,' they said to her, 'but if we hired you all our ladies would leave.' " "M—— is a good typesetter; he has not been allowed to join the union and has been refused work at eight different places in the city." " 'I wouldn't have a darky to clean out my store, much less to stand behind the counter,' answered one druggist." "H—— was a brickmason, but his employers finally refused to let him lay brick as his fellow workmen were all white; he is now a waiter."[91] When Du Bois finally wound up this catalogue of discrimination, the causal linkage of race and class to economics was unmistakable. Du Bois had ended by driving home his point, writing feelingly: "For thirty years and more Philadelphia has said to its black children: 'Honesty, efficiency and talent have little to do with your success; if you work hard, spend little and are good you may earn your bread and butter at those sorts of work which we frankly confess we despise; if you are dishonest and lazy, the State will furnish your bread free."[92]

Buttoning up his indignation once more, he brought his great, schizoid monograph to a close with two more chapters. With so many plaudits for all sorts of ulterior, superficial, and irrelevant reasons, Du Bois must have been gratified by *Yale Review*'s praise of *The Philadelphia Negro* as "a credit to American scholarship, and a distinct and valuable addition to the world's stock of knowledge concerning an important and obscure theme." That fitting tribute—to work that should have placed him among the most promising young sociologists in America—would be echoed in Albion Small's *American Journal of Sociology*, where Du Bois's remarkable Atlanta University Studies would soon receive a single, brief commendation.[93]

9.
SOCIAL SCIENCE, AMBITION, AND TUSKEGEE

THE DU BOISES celebrated Christmas of 1897 in their faculty apartment on the Atlanta University campus. Du Bois had decided that he, Nina, and the baby would take rooms in South Hall, the men's dormitory, rather than attempt to rent a house on the other side of town in the Auburn Avenue residential area where most black professional families lived. The treasurer and faculty dean, Myron Adams, a white New Englander, also lived in South Hall with his wife. The Adams baby, Margaret, had either just arrived, or soon would, to join Burghardt in raising the decibel level on the third floor. Another white New Englander, Miss Lizzie Pingree, the dormitory matron, lived across the hall from the Du Boises. Nina took to her immediately, initiating a friendship that would live on through letters and occasional visits long after she and Will had left Atlanta University and when Pingree was in retirement.

Bazolene Usher, an attractive and brilliant student who graduated second in the class of 1906, was one of the very few persons still alive in 1987 who remembered Nina Du Bois. As a first-year scholarship student from a small south-Georgia town, Usher devoted several hours each Saturday to odd domestic tasks in the Du Bois household. Lizzie Pingree regularly came to the apartment when Will was away, and Usher observed that the usually reticent Nina appeared to relax and become cheerful and quite talkative. As Usher put it more than three quarters of a century later, Nina, who "was just quiet and calm and had very little really to say," opened up with Pingree ("a fluffy kinda somebody") and their animated gossip sometimes distracted the serious student helper from the studies she found time to do there in 1902. "She didn't seem to me to have beyond a high school education," Usher mistakenly believed of Nina. "She was a beautiful woman . . . but very quiet and very few people knew her."[1]

In the winter of 1897–98, Nina was more alive than she would ever be again, except, possibly, for several charmed weeks in Paris in the late twenties. Cloistered parenting was scarcely possible with a baby like Burghardt, an intensely inquisitive boy, large for his age and determined to walk early. Will had to leave Burghardt's management to Nina much more than he wanted to, since the demands of class lectures, conferences, magazine deadlines, the final *Philadelphia Negro* chapters, and the ambitious new Atlanta University Studies left him only minutes each day to spend with the baby. Whether it was mainly because of such demands or by voluntary and mutual accord, Will increasingly ceded the domain of household finances to Nina as well. There were far fewer transactions like that of Christmas 1896 in Philadelphia: Herr Du Bois "sat down and figured carefully . . . finally evolv[ing] a surplus of $10.56, and t[elling] wife that [they] could spend five dollars apiece for the holidays."[2] Although she would never work outside the home, and so remained dependent on her husband's income, Nina's letters reveal that early on she became the better business brain of the family.

She probably did feel out of her depth intellectually in the small, earnest, and isolated university community of mostly third-generation abolitionists. Even so, she seems to have played the role of faculty wife commendably. Bessie Taylor (Page) was enchanted by Nina's unaffected grace at the first student reception soon after the couple's arrival—"such a dainty bride who made warm friends among us," she recalled. Whenever Nina appeared with a toddling Burghardt, a few students invariably joined them. He was "our baby," Taylor sighed, "how pretty we thought him."[3] Life was good for Nina. She looked after Burghardt and Will and furnished the South Hall apartment. Her first two years in Atlanta were rewardingly busy. There was one fact of life about which Nina absolutely refused to soft-pedal to anybody. She took an early and inveterate dislike to the Deep South with its raw racism, its nonexistent recreational facilities, and the lack of a single hospital or public high school to serve Atlanta's large African-American population. Nothing in provincial Iowa or backward Wilberforce had prepared her for the stinging apartheid in the capital of the so-called New South. Indeed, in the North, Nina's hair and color had generally shielded her from the hawk-eyed racial discernment exercised throughout the South.

For Du Bois, the twelve Atlanta years were the best and worst of times.

Serving up game prose in *Darkwater* and the *Autobiography*, he wrote of a time of "great spiritual upturning, of the making and unmaking of ideals, of hard work and hard play." He says that it was there that he "lost most of [his] mannerisms" and "grew more broadly human, made [his] closest and most holy friendships."[4] If Nina resented the South's racial climate viscerally, he suffered it philosophically in the belief that a few years of ground-breaking scholarship on his part would draw the generous attention of mainstream academe and philanthropy. When that happened, he would be able either to garner unprecedented resources at Atlanta or, better still, to move on to some independent and well-funded enterprise under his own direction in order to pursue the kind of research he had recently outlined before the American Academy of Political and Social Science. No miracles would be needed to make white scholars and benefactors appreciate his work, Du Bois believed. "The ultimate evil was stupidity," for which he had the ready cure in "knowledge based on scientific investigation," "carefully gathered scientific proof that neither color nor race determined the limits of a man's capacity or desert." To that end, then, he determined to isolate himself "in the ivory tower of race."[5]

An "ivory tower of race" was an apt description of Atlanta University, suggesting an isolation that was physical as well as intellectual. "AU's" three redbrick buildings stood angular and handsome on the highest of the hills cradling the ungainly new railroad city risen out of the ashes left in Sherman's wake. The school was connected to downtown Atlanta, two miles away, by a red-clay artery that sliced the base of the hill dead center and extended beyond the city limits to the undistinguished Chattahoochee River. The campus halves had been reconnected by a high and narrow iron bridge across which visits to the women in North Hall by men from South Hall were more carefully monitored than compulsory chapel attendance. The poet-songwriter and civil rights statesman James Weldon Johnson, class of '94, called Atlanta University "a spot fresh and beautiful, a rest for the eyes from what surrounded it, a green island in a dull, red sea." Like Fisk, Atlanta University had been established immediately after the Civil War by Congregationalist missionaries from the North. Its Yale-trained teachers made only the most unavoidable concessions to place, culture, and resources in order to conduct the school like an excellent New England liberal arts college. Matthew Arnold's precepts guided their pedagogy—the teaching of that "disinterested endeavor to learn and propagate the best that is known and thought in the world"—in Georgia.

The children of white fathers, or of parents whose fathers or grandfathers were white, came to the university from all over the South. Complexions in early morning chapel ranged from Anglo-Saxon alabaster to African bronze. So many of AU's students straddled the South's vigilant categories of black and white that a curious term, "no-nation," came into common use among them and many of the townspeople—denoting people who in time would face the wrenching choice of either falling back into Afro-America or exiting from it into troubled whiteness. When Du Bois took up his professorship, the school had been subjected for several years to an almost total boycott by white Atlanta, its faculty treated as pariahs and its students periodically intimidated. Whenever they stepped off the campus into West Mitchell Street, alumnus Johnson recalled, "they underwent as great a transition as would have resulted from being instantaneously shot from a Boston drawing room into the wilds of Borneo."[6] Through it all, President Horace Bumstead held fast to the classical curriculum imported from the North by Asa Ware of Yale, the founding president and his immediate predecessor, whose granite cenotaph stood like a small Gibraltar at the center of the campus. Yet he also improved upon what otherwise would have been a deadening compromise by adapting the vocational curriculum typical of Hampton and Tuskegee to the AU ethos. Ware had made the motto of Yale's class of 1863, "I Will Find a Way or Make One," the motto of Atlanta University, and Bumstead tried to put it into practice. At Atlanta, industrial training was reinforced by education in the liberal arts rather than undermined by them. So much so that, as Du Bois would write later, "even industrial training in the South was often in the hands of Atlanta graduates. Tuskegee had always been largely manned by graduates of Atlanta and some of the best school systems of the South were directed by persons trained at Atlanta University," and, he might have added, by himself.[7]

The unfolding reality, however, was that Du Bois's new affiliation was fatally out of step with the New South of insurgent rednecks and an increasing embarrassment to the children of northern abolitionists waxing rich and hypocritical from railroad debentures and textile holdings. The irony of this sixty-five-acre campus on the site of the Confederate ramparts that had slowed the Union Army's march—its white faculty taking common meals with the students (a few of whom were also white)—had finally proven too much for the Georgia legislature. Over the protests of Atticus Haygood, Atlanta's Methodist bishop, Slater Fund general agent, and AU trustee, the university had been deprived of its thirteen-year-old annual land-grant appropriation of eight thousand dollars in 1887, essentially for refusing to abandon race mixing in the dining hall. Five years later, the American Missionary Association withdrew its subsidy, consistent with a policy, it said, of encouraging the southern institutions that it had created to begin standing on their own feet. The creed of the nineties held that it was a dangerous conceit to expose black people to literature, history, philosophy, and "dead" languages, thereby "spoiling" them for the natural order of southern society in which their place was as voteless, industrious farmhands, primary schoolteachers, and occasional merchants. Demagogic Governor James K. Vardaman of Mississippi, "the White Chief," gave voice to the extreme southern version of that creed, bawling that the Negro was a "lazy, lying, lustful animal which no conceivable amount of training can transform into a tolerable citizen."[8]

While the white South prepared to gut higher education for African-Americans, Du Bois kept to Johnson's "green island in a dull, red sea." His contact with the surrounding white city "was limited to some necessary shopping. . . . [He] did not enter parks or museums, [but] assumed that when the public was invited to any place or function, either the white people were meant, or, if not, attendance of Negroes meant segregated parts or times."[9] There was more than enough teaching and writing to engage him on the hill. In addition to two advanced courses in "economics and history" and sociology, he taught a class in American citizenship and another in civil government in the high school run by the university. Enrollments were heavy in the high school classes, but he had a manageable fourteen students in economics and history, and twelve in his new sociology elective. Although he thought he was becoming "more broadly human," Professor Du Bois probably would have failed a student popularity contest during his first two or three years at Atlanta, especially among the youngest pupils. Bessie Taylor thought Professor Du Bois was a "silent unsociable kind of man" at first—and, later, she told him so. Jauntily wielding his walking stick about campus, he was oblivious to the fact that many of the high school students and even a few of the older ones backed away or reflexively flinched when he approached. "Some children came from the country," Bazolene Usher explained, "and were used to the white folks using canes" on them, a distressing observation corroborated by Clarence Bacote, Atlanta University's historian. Moreover, Du Bois quickly acquired a reputation for espying and reporting malefactors, especially those who violated the university's strict nonsmoking code.[10]

But it was his manner that astonished students most; he was a showman clearly aiming for effect. The impression upon Kathleen Adams, advantaged daughter of a local African-American businessman and one of

Du Bois's first sociology students, was still vivid in her mind in 1987. "He was a man of distinction; the way he walked, settled his shoulders, and his voice," she sighed. "You had to pay attention to him. When he entered the chapel, you looked at him, and you followed him until he got to his seat and sat down." Du Bois had stunned a chapel assembly during his first appearance by giving President Bumstead a terse "no" when asked to lead the morning prayer. For as long as the AU oral tradition endures, there will be amused accounts of Du Bois declining to lead chapel assemblies in their devotions, just as he had once done at Wilberforce. Those recollections must be qualified, however, by the intriguing fact that the heretic in their midst eventually offered occasional prayers of brevity and beauty in chapel, and at least once at commencement. "Give us grace, O God, to dare to do the deed which we know well cries out be done" was one such ecumenical appeal.[11] The figure he cut on the tennis court behind South Hall won high marks from female students, some of whom had begun calling him "Dube" behind his back. It was Bessie Taylor who told him twenty years afterward that she and her ogling classmates had suddenly realized that "you were young—you played tennis and in such a way that . . . [we] saw nothing of that formal dignity we knew indoors."[12] Will was lightly muscled, with fine buttocks and well-shaped calves that filled tennis whites appealingly.

The demeanor impressed, but, for many, there were allergic reactions to the upper-level courses. Adams says "it was just as quiet as a pin in his [class] room." Lectures in steepled old Stone Hall began precisely on the second, pocket watch on the lectern, and latecomers were barred without benefit of appeal. Classes ended just as punctually. Generally, Du Bois lectured the full period, but after gauging the level of alertness or sophistication, he sometimes fed the class questions to encourage participation. This was a high-risk technique, though, that could leave a student badly shaken by the professor's polite but mordant dismissal of an uninformed or unintelligent response.[13] Du Bois's appreciation of himself was a good deal less austere than his students'. He tried to be "natural and honest and frank, but it was bitter hard," he found, because most of the minds he was paid to mold were unready to understand how completely their destinies were in the hands of southern white people. "What would you say to a soft, brown face, aureoled in a thousand ripples of gray-black hair" blurting out in American history, " 'Do you trust white people?' " he asked himself on one occasion. "You do not and you know that you do not much as you want to." For the student's sake, nevertheless, and in service to some Ideal Truth above the truth of experience, Du Bois told her she "must trust them, that most white folks are honest, and all the while you are lying on every level, silent eye there knows you are lying . . . to the greater glory of God."[14]

As a rule, the brighter the student, the greater his or her admiration of Du Bois. Believing that the professor was an Episcopalian, Bazolene Usher's brother not only joined that church but became one of its first African-American priests in the South. Kathleen Adams and her best friend Alice Bell, another privileged Atlantan, sat spellbound in the high school history course as Du Bois "describe[d] places that were connected with what he was teaching." Brilliant Harry H. Pace from south Georgia, matinee-idol handsome and a venturesome future businessman, would be a Du Bois loyalist for the rest of his life. Round, brown Augustus Granville Dill, a peppery student from Ohio, who would earn a master's degree in sociology, worshipped him. Even though her best friend, Lizzie Coleman, failed Civic Government, Bessie Taylor remembered going daily "with such pride into this sacred class." She still considered that it had been a privilege to study with the demanding, brilliant young professor, as did Edward B. Thompson, who recalled Du Bois's "skill of trying to make you think . . . and he pulled on your intellectual powers with broad reading and open discussion." By the second semester of the second year, the college literary magazine, *The Scroll*, reported the following student research papers in economics and history and sociology: "Poverty"; "Rise of and Development of the Wages System in the South"; "The Credit System"; "Wages and Negroes"; "The Negro as Consumer"; "The Legal Position of the Negro"; "The Negro Merchant in Atlanta"; "The Well-to-Do in Atlanta"; and "The Negro Labor in Atlanta."[15]

These research papers were building blocks in the third Atlanta Conference of Negro Problems, the famous series of studies produced by Atlanta University, which were under Du Bois's direction after 1897. Du Bois put his talent into teaching, but his genius went into the studies. "Mortality Among Negroes in Cities" and "Social and Physical Condition of Negroes in Cities," the first and second in the Atlanta conference series, had appeared in 1896 and 1897, respectively, and reflected the biases of George Bradford, the white Boston businessman and university trustee—a Harvard graduate "who for several years has been making the study of the Negro the occupation of his leisure time." With Bumstead's help, Bradford recruited the secretarial and research skills of three of the university's most outstanding recent graduates and coming race notables, James W. Johnson, Boston lawyer Butler Wilson, and literature professor George A. Towns.

Questionnaires about general living conditions in nine cities were funneled to key Atlanta graduates Lucy Laney in Augusta, Dr. W. B. Matthews in Atlanta, and Lafayette M. Hershaw and Dr. W. Bruce Evans in Washington, professional men and women who would later rally to Du Bois's side in his struggles with Booker T. Washington.[16]

The idea for a series of annual research publications originated with the conferences on education, labor, and farming hosted each year since the early 1890s by Hampton and Tuskegee. Bradford's special contribution (influenced by Harvard sociologist Edward Cummings) was to recommend that the Atlanta University Studies adopt an urban agenda. Twelve percent of the country's seven million African-Americans (once overwhelmingly rural) had moved to the cities by 1890 (as compared with 16 percent of white people). At Tuskegee and Hampton, the one- and two-day conferences focused on the needs of the rural schoolhouse, the one-mule farmer, and the village blacksmith, paying little or no attention to the long-term significance of the demographics explored at the first Atlanta University conferences and in their publications. Bradford's stewardship rendered an important service to problems of the future, while Hampton and Tuskegee concentrated on inherited conditions that were already undergoing fundamental transformation. When he learned from Cummings of Du Bois's work on the Philadelphia project, Bradford knew he had found an ideal scholar to whom the baton of research could be passed. But if he expected Du Bois to endorse the interpretations thus far placed upon high mortality, disabling disease, stubborn illiteracy, crime, vagrancy, and unemployment among black urban dwellers, Bradford and his colleagues were in for a reeducation.

President Bumstead's inaugural introduction to the studies had set a tone of specious sociological neutrality and laissez-faire public policy. He wrote of his certainty that the "study of human life," which for purposes of "convenience" happened to center on the Negro, would have "practically the same result" if repeated "with any other race." As spelled out by the interracial Atlanta, Fisk, Berea, Lincoln, Spelman, and Howard University contributors to "Social and Physical Condition of Negroes in Cities," Bumstead's logic left the urban African-American to improve his lot through better morals and harder work. White Professor Eugene Harris of Fisk recognized that white people had an impact on the life chances of black people, but "in a very indirect and unimportant way." "Separate apartments in public conveniences, such as hotels, theatres, or railroad trains, social ostracism, exclusion from political preferment and the spoils of office, the suppression of his ballot, and the other discriminations which are made against the black man, have at least no immediate bearing on his health, vitality, or longevity," Harris wrote seriously. Without recorded dissent, the second Atlanta conference concluded that "the excessive mortality [of black people] cannot be attributed in any large degree to the unfavorable conditions of environment, but must be chiefly attributed to the ignorance of the masses of the people and their disregard of the laws of health and morality."[17]

If the first and second Atlanta University Studies seemed to bear out Hampton founder Armstrong's pronouncement that "the Kingdom of Heaven will come through sociology studied and applied wisely in a level-headed way," it was soon obvious that Du Bois was not the messiah the general had in mind. "Without thought or consultation," the new professor wrote that he "rather peremptorily changed the plans of the first two Atlanta Conferences." As he polished the last pages of *The Philadelphia Negro*, Du Bois dreamed of a laboratory in which the "concrete group of living beings artificially set off by themselves" would be studied broadly, intensely, incrementally, until, year by year "the vague mass of so-called Negro problems" lost its alien mystery and was reduced to the "laws of social living clearer, surer, and more definite."[18] He anticipated annual gatherings in late May in Atlanta featuring many of the best minds in the world. In the manner of University of Berlin students devouring their seminar bibliographies, the resultant Atlanta University Studies, generously funded by philanthropy, would systematically master all the possible topics in the field of race. It remained to be seen if, as he said, the major obstacle to this work was only "stupidity."

With only a small sum made available by Bradford, Du Bois fired off invitations to and requests for papers for the third Atlanta conference from his old Fisk classmate, Hugh Proctor, now pastor of Atlanta's exclusive First Congregational Church; Mrs. Helen Cook, president of the tony Women's League of Washington, D.C.; Lafayette M. Hershaw, destined to become one of Du Bois's most valuable collaborators; Miss Minnie Perry of the board of Atlanta's black orphanage; Alexander Crummell, living out his last months in Red Bank, New Jersey; and several others. Once again, however, Du Bois's memory improved somewhat on the facts pertaining to the editing of the third Atlanta report of 1898. Because he had arrived only four months earlier or, perhaps, because he decided to make a temporary, tactical concession to his predecessors' work, "Some Efforts of American Negroes for Their Own Social Betterment" was a rather conventional, disjointed piece—a statistical smorgasbord of cooperative enterprises, traditional businesses, insurance establishments, and property holdings by individuals and churches, combined with some routine observations about infant and adult death rates in southern cities. It was distinguished primarily by Crummell's essay burlesquing Booker Washington's salvation-through-industrial-education message and the editor's finger-wagging at the churches for not doing more to help consumers.[19]

By the following year, though, with the publication of the provocative "The Negro in Business," Du Bois's distinctive thinking began to shape the reports. The two-day conference on May 30 and 31, 1899, in Ware Memorial Chapel, was addressed by none other than Allen D. Candler, patriarch of the Coca-Cola clan and Bourbon governor of the state, who professed to know that there were as many "God-serving and God-loving" black Georgians as there were white. Getting down to business, Du Bois reminded the conferees that most "God-serving" African-Americans were "still serfs, bound to the soil or house servants," adding acidly, "the nation which robbed them of the fruits of their labor for two and a half centuries, finally set them adrift penniless." For all the boasting by some about the race's remarkable economic advancement since slavery, "The Negro in Business" was the first careful documentation of such claims. Putting the total number of African-American businessmen in the United States at five thousand, Du Bois broke them down by occupation—grocers, barbers, printers, hackmen, realtors, plumbers, and so on—and then put a magnifying glass to their activities in key cities. What emerged was a blueprint of the segregated black world's economic infrastructure.[20]

A handsome young professor at nearby Atlanta Baptist College for Men (the future Morehouse), John Hope, read three papers, one of which, "The Meaning of Business," presented a keen analysis of the "competition between the races in new fields" and the impending displacement of unskilled black labor caused by industrial development in the South. Hope sounded again the central theme of the conference—that the African-American community had to accumulate capital as rapidly as possible by creating its own markets. The resolutions of this fourth Atlanta University conference called for an upsurge in business activity and disciplined patronage of race "enterprises . . . even at some slight disadvantage"; resolution six in particular proposed "Negro Business Men's Leagues . . . in every town and hamlet," and a gradual federation "from these of state and national organizations." The empire-building Booker Washington paid Du Bois the compliment of appropriating the Negro Business League idea the following year.[21] The Atlanta professor's economic thinking in 1899 was no more radical than the Tuskegee principal's. Philosophically indistinguishable from the conventional American laissez-faire orthodoxy of personal and collective bootstrap improvement, "The Negro in Business" made its contribution in the area of data and organizational policy.

The reports of 1900 and 1901 on college and public school education seem impressive today mainly as time-bound feats, antiquarian atlases now of interest only to a small number of scholars. When he repeated "The College-Bred Negro" and "The Negro Common School" ten years later, in 1910 and 1911, respectively, Du Bois would greatly expand the information contained in them, although maintaining the same methodology and format: questionnaires sent to hundreds of college and common school students, letters from professors, teachers, and officials (private and public), curriculum requirements (texts used) and grade school attendance reports, per capita expenditures by state, tabulations of results. But once again, Du Bois was the first to compile and analyze what should have already been available to professionals and a concerned public. The college-bred Negro was to most white Americans a phenomenon even more curious than the revelation in *The Philadelphia Negro* of the existence of a Negro class structure. An illustration of this fact would come in February 1901 as Du Bois testified in Washington before the U.S. Industrial Commission. "Colored men?" an incredulous Commissioner Albert Clarke would interject when Du Bois mentioned African-American holders of bachelor's degrees.[22] The fifth Atlanta study (1900) digested responses ranging from purest Horatio Alger to bitterest fatalism from almost half the 2,600 living men and women graduates of postsecondary institutions. College education had been a success and would continue to be necessary for African-Americans, Du Bois concluded—just as necessary as industrial training. The lode of carefully tabulated facts, tracking for the first time three decades of gaping educational disparities between white and black children in the South, graphically justified the conclusion to "The Negro Common School": "*Race antagonism can only be stopped by intelligence. It is dangerous to wait, it is foolish to hesitate. Let the nation immediately give generous aid to Southern common school education.*"[23]

Du Bois's 1902 "Negro Artisan" study was one of his best in terms of methodology. From responses to comprehensive questionnaires sent to 1,300 skilled laborers in the South, he developed a wide-angle socioeconomic photograph of labor and race relations at the turn of the century. There were comparative data gathered by collaborating African-

American college graduates from thirty-two states, Canada, and Costa Rica, as well as analogous material from a large survey of black labor conducted earlier by the Chattanooga *Times*, a white newspaper. Wages, working conditions, skill levels, the extent of displacement by white people and the superannuation of certain crafts, and workplace race relations were tabulated and examined with the interspersed testimonials of the artisans themselves. Figures from organized labor revealed wholesale exclusion of African-Americans. Among 1.2 million union members nationally, Du Bois counted less than 40,000 nonwhites. Most were found among the organized workers in the Alabama, West Virginia, and Virginia coal mines, the New Orleans dock workers, and in the Louisiana timber camps.[24]

In both "The Negro Church" the following year and "The Negro American Family" five years later, impressive methodology was upstaged by historical sociology. Never before had the religious and family cultures and institutions of the African in America been linked to the preslavery past. The black African subsoil that had nurtured Egyptian religions, the spread of Obeah "sorcery" in West Africa after the collapse of strong kingdoms there, the power of the chieftaincy and the clan over the individual, the authority held by women in matrilineal family structures—all this Du Bois fascinatingly explored (making use of German ethnographer Friedrich Ratzel's writings) before tracking the African and his/her church and family into New World slavery. Hauled down from their auction blocks in Charleston, Baltimore, or Alexandria, Virginia, Africans in America transferred their obedience from the homeland chief to the new white master, Du Bois wrote, as they lost ties of family and clan and arrived chained and disoriented "on a plot of ground, with common rules and customs, common dwellings, and a certain communism in property." The power of the chief now became vested in an alien figure whose will to exploit, punish, and debauch was restrained primarily by self-interest. African-Americans had withstood three centuries of bondage in a state of denatured personality, family, and morality. A true disciple of Crummell, Du Bois rendered a condign verdict on slavery's debasement of black women, its corruption of black men, and its infection of every institution emerging from it—condign but not merciless. "At first sight it would seem that slavery completely destroyed every vestige of spontaneous social movement among the Negroes," his argument ran. "Home had deteriorated; political authority and economic initiative was in the hands of the masters, property as a social institution did not exist on the plantation."

Historians and sociologists assumed that "every vestige of internal development disappeared, leaving the slaves no means of expression for their common life," but Du Bois stopped short of making the southern plantation experience the equivalent of a lobotomy. "This is not strictly true." Africa had come to the rescue in the form of religious survivals in the Americas: the African priest lived on in the New World preacher. "It is this historic fact that the Negro Church of today bases itself upon the sole surviving social institution of the African fatherland that accounts for its extraordinary growth and vitality."[25] The surviving church was to play the dialectical role of resurrecting the family, in a nuclear, monogamous form, in African-American life. The new family institution would then speed the modernization of the church, which Du Bois somewhat cautiously implied was still much too parochial. With notable contributions on northern conditions from reformers Jane Addams and Mary White Ovington, "The Negro American Family" report concluded that the African-American was "farthest behind modern civilization in his sexual *mores*." Concupiscence engendered during slavery now preyed upon the African-American family in freedom, he contended, seriously inhibiting its adjustment to modern middle-class, Protestant norms. "More primitive, less civilized, in this respect, than his surroundings demand, . . . his family life less efficient for its onerous social duties, his womanhood less protected, his children more poorly trained," all this was "to be expected," sociologist Du Bois concluded, because "this is what slavery meant."[26]

With "The Negro Artisan" of 1902, "The Negro Church" of 1903, and especially "The Negro American Family" of 1908, Du Bois would push the Atlanta University Studies to the frontier of American social science research, virtually single-handedly and under the auspices of an institution whose revenues had become so skimpy that the average $5,000 cost of the conferences and publications (Du Bois's $1,200 salary included) gave President Bumstead and the trustees annual budgetary heartburn. Except for Carnegie manna to build its library in 1903, Atlanta University found itself generally bypassed by the philanthropic foundations. The predicament was puzzling, and seemed somehow the product of a conspiracy. William Garrison's youngest son, Francis Jackson Garrison of the prestigious Boston publishing house of Houghton Mifflin (still imbued with the old abolitionist values), wrote nephew Oswald Villard in May 1902 that this situation was outrageous. "I groan in spirit every time I read of a legacy or gift of $50,000 and $100,000 or $500,000 going to Harvard or Yale, or Columbia, or Chicago," when a fraction of those sums to a deserving Atlanta University could make a life-or-death difference.[27]

Whatever the reasons for the foundations' cold shoulder, the underfunded conferences achieved increasing celebrity. Lyman Abbott's influential *Outlook*, a consistent booster of Washington and his Tuskegee Idea, noticed Du Bois's labors as early as January 1898, praising the first social-betterment study as "a valuable sociological publication." Three years later, the London *Spectator* applauded the social-science work "being done with much intelligence, discrimination, and assiduity at the insistence and under the inspiration of Atlanta University." *Publications of the Southern History Association* echoed the *Spectator* four years later, calling Du Bois's work the "most admirable investigations into this vast ethnic problem." By then, even the *American Journal of Sociology* had called the Negro artisan monograph the "most exhaustive study thus far made of the economic aspects of the problem." Other endorsements followed, but, curiously, it was to be *The Outlook*'s second Atlanta notice in 1903 that topped them all, decreeing that "no student of the race problem, no person who would either think or speak upon it intelligently, can afford to be ignorant of the facts brought out in the Atlanta series." The *Chicago Tribune* sent the roving Clifford Raymond to interview Du Bois in his South Hall rooms in June of that year. Raymond's "Cultured Negro Model for Race" was a lyrical portrait of the young professor—"one of the most entertaining men I ever talked with." The professor's intelligence and culture Raymond attributed to mixed racial ancestry.[28]

In demand as commencement and learned-society speaker, national newspaper and magazine contributor, congressional commission witness, U.S. Department of Labor consultant and author ("The Negro Landholder of Georgia" [1901] and "The Negro Farmer" [1906]), Du Bois was becoming the second most sought-after spokesperson for his race after Booker Washington. Scholars and public figures began turning up for the May meetings or simply inviting themselves to the campus at their convenience. Washington, bearing honorary degrees from Harvard and Yale, spoke encouragingly to the 1902 assembly. Edwin R. A. Seligman, the wealthy, distinguished Columbia University economics professor, brought along a good number of the delegates to the 1903 annual meeting of the American Economic Association to meet Du Bois when their train halted for a few hours on Sunday, December 27.[29] Spellbinding Washington Gladden, the Billy Graham of the day, addressed the 1903 conference in his capacity as president of the American Missionary Association. Gladden departed so impressed by Du Bois and his work that he wondered in print whether the Tuskegee program deserved its monopoly. "All that Booker Washington is doing we may heartily rejoice in; but there are other things that must not be left undone," advised Gladden, paying Du Bois the compliment of being "perhaps the most cultivated man among American Negroes." Max Weber came to campus to participate in the conference on crime during his American visit in 1904. The great German sociologist had no recollection of Du Bois the Berlin student, but he wrote commending the Atlanta professor's researches and hoped to run a "short review of the recent publications about the race problem in America" in the *Archiv fur Sozialwissenschaft und Sozialpolitik*, which he did.[30] The year closed with a French version of a Du Bois essay appearing as "L'Ouvrier negre en Amérique" in the influential periodical *La Revue économique internationale*. The following year, William James dropped a note to Du Bois about the most recent study. "I wish the portraits might have been better printed, but it is splendid scientific work."[31]

WITH TWO large, critically acclaimed monographs published by age thirty-one, a major essay in Weber's arbitral *Archiv* at thirty-seven, his scholarship discussed in large-circulation newspapers and middlebrow periodicals, and his Stone Hall office becoming a stopping-off point for the famous, the influential, and the merely curious on southern learning safaris, Du Bois's professional achievements placed him in the vanguard of social-science scholarship in America. Atlanta seemed admirably positioned to become the great research center he had come from Philadelphia to make it. Foundation grants had not materialized so far, and he could have no inkling in the first few years of his eventual failure to win their full support; yet Du Bois had already begun to feel dissatisfied. Having made an international reputation as a social scientist and historian, the Atlanta University professor found himself becoming impatient that the world went along as before, unreconstructed in its rabid racism in the South and in its sublime cynicism in the North, and leaving his own material and professional prospects about as much unchanged.

It was the bitterest of revelations to a Calvinist and a Hegelian that scientific truth, repeatedly broadcast, was apparently impotent to ameliorate collective behavior. For all his professions of value-free and policy-neutral investigation, his rhetoric about isolated groups and human laboratories, Du Bois was temperamentally averse to moral relativism—there was always the *right* way to do a thing—and Hegelian Du Bois expected right ideas to become social forces within a reasonable time frame. He began to realize how intractable the here-and-now society beyond the conference walls of Ware Chapel was, even before he published the second Atlanta University Study in 1899. He had "overworked a theory—that the cause of the problem was the ignorance of people." He now saw that "the cure wasn't simply telling people the truth, it was inducing them to act on the truth."[32] It was not enough to determine truth scientifically; it had to be implemented politically. His mission to mobilize truth in order to alter behavior took on sudden urgency in the spring and summer of 1899.

In the autobiographical writings, Du Bois underscores a ghastly incident that shook him to his core during this period—the April lynching of Sam Hose. Hose was a farmer in Palmetto, a few miles outside Atlanta, who had shot and killed a white farmer after an argument over a debt. Justice was summary, ghoulish. After lynching and burning Hose to death, the white mob of two thousand men, women, and children had fought over pieces of his flesh for souvenirs. "Startled to his feet" by the lynching, Du Bois gathered up his cane and gloves and descended from South Hall into West Mitchell Street with a letter of introduction to the editor of the *Constitution*, Joel Chandler Harris. Another envelope contained his restrained letter on the lynching, intended for the editorial page. Until he was told, as he hurried downtown, Du Bois was unaware that Hose had been barbecued and that his blackened knuckles were on display in a white storeowner's window farther along Mitchell Street. Numbed by the horror, he retraced his steps to the university and, he recalled with soul-weary solemnity, "began to turn aside from my work."[33] From that moment forward, he recognized that "one could not be a calm, cool, and detached scientist while Negroes were lynched, murdered and starved." A few months later, he commented in the New York *Independent* on the terrible setbacks that had "followed faster and faster in the last ten years"—the bloody 1898 Wilmington, North Carolina, riot, the mob murder of a black postmaster, the epidemic of lynchings leading up to Hose. Fourteen years of preparation, research, and writing suddenly seemed mockingly irrelevant. "There was no such definite demand for scientific work of the sort that [he] was doing, as [he] had confidently assumed would be easily forthcoming."[34]

Brooding about his career, the butchering of Sam Hose, and the impotence of social science to improve society, Du Bois was suddenly struck broadside by a great personal tragedy. The death of Burghardt was an agony of such devastation that he would soon try to recast it in eschatological terms. In "Of the Passing of the First-Born," the apostrophe in *The Souls of Black Folk,* Du Bois would make Burghardt's life and death monumentally symbolic. Like another birth nearly two thousand years earlier, his son's coming foretold eventual deliverance of a people, symbolizing faith in some ultimate transcendence of the Veil by the African-American millions. Du Bois's lofty intent is manifest in his Adoration-of-the-Magi imagery: "A perfect life was his, all joy and love, with tears to make it brighter—sweet as a summer's day beside the Housatonic. The world loved him; the women kissed his curls, the men looked gravely into his wonderful eyes, and the children hovered and fluttered about him." He and Nina had felt vague unrest when they brought their child onto the "hot red soil of Georgia." "I saw the shadow of the Veil as it passed over my baby, I saw the cold city towering above the blood-red land," laments the father. Even so, Burghardt grew so "sturdy and masterful," "with his hair tinted with gold," that they were not far from "worshipping this revelation of the divine." Burghardt was his mother's reason for being. "Her own life builded and moulded itself upon the child." Du Bois permits himself one flash of bitter, understandable self-pity in a passage about his own obduracy in the face of racial prejudice. In the "dull land that stretches its sneering web about [him]," was not "all the world beyond these four little walls pitiless enough" that "[Death] must needs enter here?" Remorse then gives way to philosophical reflection. "Well sped, my boy, before their world had dubbed your ambition insolence, had held your ideals unattainable, and taught you to cringe and bow." Death within the Veil awaited the father, but surely through Burghardt "there shall yet dawn some mighty morning to lift the Veil and set the prisoned free."[35]

The elegiac prose of "The Passing of the First-Born" verges on bathos today. The plain facts are that Burghardt contracted nasopharyngeal diphtheria, grew progressively feverish, and died ten days later on May 24, 1899, a Wednesday, at sundown. He was two years and almost one month old. The night before, Du Bois had rushed out in a futile search for one of the two or three black physicians living on the other side of town. Although the elegy to Burghardt mentions Nina's grief ("in the chamber of death writhed the world's most piteous thing—a childless mother"), the supreme focus of the tragedy is Du Bois. "If one must have gone, why not [he]?" Burghardt's death is presented as Du Bois's calamity and, by extension, the race's, with Nina playing merely a supporting role. There is no doubt about the authenticity of Du Bois's pain, but it was Nina's emotional health that was permanently affected. As his wife, she understood why Will's work had brought them to a city practically devoid of doctors of their own race—a city where white physicians refused to treat even desperately sick black children. But as a mother, Nina would never forgive him.

Writing Nina's obituary a half century later, Du Bois would finally face the truth that, with their son's death, "in a sense my wife died too. Never after that was she quite the same in her attitude toward life and the world."[36] The nature of Will and Nina's early married life and the circumstances surrounding their son's death can be tentatively reconstructed even from a great distance in time. Burghardt's ten-day ordeal coincided with Du Bois's final arrangements for the May 30–31 conference on "The Negro in Business"—in effect, the first of the Atlanta conferences to which he put his stamp. The fact that he presided over these deliberations six days after burying his son in Great Barrington's Mahaiwe Cemetery, while a wrecked Nina remained behind in the Berkshires, testifies to the iron self-control and intellectual purpose typical of Du Bois. But it also suggests that his attention to Burghardt's symptoms was probably less than optimal, and that he accepted too readily a reassuring bad-cold diagnosis of the toxins slowly invading the boy's throat and intestines. "Of the Passing of the First-Born" leaves no doubt that medical help was inadequate (whether in fact it may not even have been available is less clear). The confession long afterward that Burghardt might have been saved "had we been persons of greater experience" further suggests his lack of focus until it was too late. The German immunologist Emil von Behring's diphtheria antitoxin was being experimentally tested on animals at that time. Another dozen years would pass, however, before its general administration to humans.[37] But Du Bois may well have known of its existence, and such knowledge would have festered in his and Nina's vague guilt.

The lynching of Sam Hose outside Atlanta in April, followed in May by their son's burial in Great Barrington, depressed both of them. Nina's aversion to the South turned into a visceral loathing. White people had turned to call them "niggers" as she and Will walked behind the horse-drawn cart carrying Burghardt's coffin to the Atlanta train station.[38] Even as praise for the fourth Atlanta University study arrived, Du Bois must have felt already that he had to find a position elsewhere. Atlanta was like a poisoned well, polluted with the remains of Sam Hose and reflecting the drawn image of Burghardt from its dark surface. The psychological punishment of the place was so severe at that time that Du Bois would claim years afterward that he had actually suffered a nervous breakdown. Before their son's death, Tuskegee had still seemed worth exploring. An offer there was much more problematic now, given Nina's state of mind, but it did afford the solace of escape from Atlanta, a larger salary, and the prospect of a well-endowed institution's full support of his researches. He and Washington had finally met face to face in Boston that March when President Bumstead had asked Du Bois to make a number of fund-raising speeches in New England on behalf of the university. Rather than have Du Bois's Boston appearance compete with his own $150,000 campaign, Washington had suggested to Bumstead that Du Bois appear with himself on the same platform along with Paul Laurence Dunbar.[39]

The Tuskegee principal gave a standard speech at the Hollis Street Theatre in Boston on the twenty-first, in which he decried the loss of civil rights in the South mainly because of the harm done to white civic virtue. "The Negro can afford to be wronged," Washington explained; "the white man cannot afford to wrong him without the proudest and bluest blood in your civilization being degraded." A few days away from his forty-third birthday, the principal was on the verge of physical and nervous exhaustion. At Tuskegee, he kept watch day and night over students, faculty, administrators, townspeople, and, above all, the endless stream of white people who came from North and South to probe and praise his fragile miracle in the Alabama Black Belt. But as his fame had grown, his opportunities and obligations, as the leader of the Negro people, were redoubled. He had lately spent as much time in Pullman cars, hurtling from one speaking engagement and power caucus to another throughout the United States, as in Tuskegee. Booker Washington's yellow complexion had grown even sallower, his gaze more opaque, and his often hoarse voice markedly lacking in crispness. The Hollis Street audience gave Du Bois and Dunbar the loudest applause that evening, and, as Du Bois recalled, Washington's friends "immediately raised a fund which sent him to Europe for three months rest."[40]

Upstaged or not, Washington returned to America well disposed toward the Atlanta professor. Another letter from Albert Hart pressing a Du Bois appointment (Hart called Du Bois "a striking refutation of some of the hardest things said about the negro race") was on his desk. Resigning from Atlanta University in the middle of the summer would have been thoroughly improper, but on July 12, Du Bois replied with encouragement to Washington's suggestion that he consider coming to Tuskegee in the academic year 1900–1901, writing that he would "decide during the winter as to whether I think a change best for all interests." Washington's offer must have been rather vague because Du Bois also asked to "hear . . .

more definitely as to the work you would expect and the salary." His social-science needs were almost laughably modest, after all, and the "dream was still splendid," he reflected long afterward. "If in a properly equipped institution I could have gathered four or five well-equipped young students, some tabulating machines and a small corps of travelling investigators, . . . at a cost of $10,000 to $25,000 a year," he was certain that he could perfect the scientific study of the American Negro.[41] Washington seemed to be edging toward a formal offer. As different as the two men were, their contrasting temperaments had actually tended to make them politely curious about each other. Washington had been generally complimentary of Du Bois, while Du Bois had publicly championed the cause of the Tuskegee educator on more than one occasion.

When the now-forgotten National Afro-American Council met in Chicago in late August 1899, there was trouble for Washington. The Afro-American Council was an outgrowth of an organization founded in 1887 by the brilliant T. Thomas Fortune, the lanky, alcoholic New York newspaperman who had given the teenaged Du Bois his first crack at journalism. The council did little, but the membership of its twenty-three state chapters embraced many of Afro-America's most prominent names. Enraged by his equivocation over the Sam Hose lynching and by his continual sightings of silver linings in every racial dark cloud, a militant minority noisily denounced Washington and his wife. AME minister Reverdy Cassius Ransom, whose gaunt appearance called to mind one of El Greco's martyrs, demanded the leader's expulsion from membership. Washington's supporters had been seized by apoplexy, and, in the ensuing hubbub, Du Bois stood out as one of Washington's loudest defenders, voting with the majority for a resolution excusing him from participation in organizational discussion "which might be radical in its utterances to the destruction of his usefulness in connection with many causes."[42]

In the aftermath of the Afro-American Council imbroglio, Washington's private secretary and principal lieutenant, the fastidious Emmett J. Scott, described by Washington's biographer as a "delicate-looking yellow man with a pince-nez," was delighted to inform his vacationing employer somewhat later that "Du Bois and others sustain you well in the Chicago *Record*." It was a curious role for Du Bois to play. Given his sympathy for the deceased Crummell's educational ideas and his own anger over Hose's mob murder, Du Bois ought to have shared some of the militants' doubts about Washington's leadership. Moreover, the affinity that later developed between himself and the slightly older, imperious Reverdy Ransom, one of

Wilberforce's most brilliant graduates, likely dated from the Chicago fracas. Still, Du Bois's behavior in Chicago was not entirely (or even mainly) a question of bald opportunism (he would have dismissed such a suspicion): for all Washington's silences, evasions, and panderings, Du Bois knew that the race leader occasionally departed from the pattern of accommodation that had served him so well. In Chicago the year before, with President McKinley and his cabinet on the speakers' platform, Washington had told the large Peace Jubilee audience that the patriotic sacrifice of his race in the just-concluded Spanish-American War deserved meaningful recognition, bluntly warning of the southern "cancer gnawing at the heart of the Republic, that shall one day prove as dangerous as an attack from an army without or within." Then there were Washington's open letters that year to Governor "Pitchfork Ben" Tillman of South Carolina and the Louisiana legislature vainly imploring both to impose the same franchise restrictions on white people as on black. Possibly, Du Bois had heard that one of the last white southern paternalists, Jabez Curry of the Slater Fund, had met with Washington at Tuskegee a few days before delivering a successful entreaty to the Louisiana lawmakers not to close the state's black public schools.[43]

Within four months of the Afro-American Council attack, Washington took what was for him another bold political step in Georgia against a franchise-restriction proposal pending before the legislature—the Hardwick Bill. As the state's powerful Bourbon forces mobilized to oppose the redneck radicalism behind the bill, he and Du Bois worked parallel lobbying and public-relations strategies. Henry Proctor, the friend from Fisk days and now a leading Atlanta minister, made his parsonage available to Du Bois and Washington during the crisis. "Many a time they came to my home, sometimes at night," Proctor recalled. On November 10, the influential Atlanta *Constitution* carried Washington's deferential interview in which he objected to the bill, although "dread[ing] the idea of seeming to intrude my views too often upon the public." Three weeks later, *The Independent* published Du Bois's anti-Hardwick piece along with the petition he and twenty-three prominent African-Americans in Georgia had submitted to the legislature. Du Bois could have given the *Constitution* interview and Washington written the *Independent* article. What both men and their allies found appalling was not the bill's deep reduction of the franchise but its unfairness in treating all classes of African-Americans alike—its Democratic "white" primary, grandfather clause (hereditary white voting rights), and fraudulent educational qualifications. "So far as the Hardwick Bill proposes to restrict the right of suffrage to all who, irrespective of race and color, are intelligent enough to vote properly," Du Bois's petition read, "we heartily endorse it."[44] In the end, the bill was seven years premature for Georgia, and the Du Bois–Washington collaboration had played some small part in its defeat.

Two weeks before coming up to Atlanta from Tuskegee to plot the Hardwick Bill strategy, Washington had finally sent Du Bois the definitive offer that Hart had been so long urging. It was generous: a salary of $1,400, a "comfortable and convenient house," offices, and the institute's printing office "wholly at your service." Explaining that he "would have made [him] this offer several years ago" had he not felt that Du Bois's hands would have been "tied with routine work," the head of the nation's most famous institution for the training of African-Americans was now ready to "make any reasonable changes" in his offer to woo Du Bois. When Du Bois claimed much later that, although the offer was "attractive . . . because at Atlanta [he] was only getting $1,200 a year," it bothered him that "he never could find out what he was to do" at Tuskegee, he was not being entirely candid. "What I would wish you to do," Washington stated without ambiguity, "is to make your home here and to conduct sociological studies that will prove helpful to our people, especially in the gulf states, including both the country districts, small towns, and cities."[45] Du Bois took the offer as a long-overdue confirmation of Washington's admiration and confidence. After all, his wonderfully evocative essay about Josie and the Fisk teaching days in rural Tennessee, "A Negro Schoolmaster in the New South," had appeared to raves in the January *Atlantic Monthly*. Three articles followed, one after the other, in the influential northern *Independent*, on African-American crime, the Afro-American Council meeting, and the Hardwick debate, which were all widely commented upon.[46] The first reviews of *The Philadelphia Negro* were appearing. By the close of 1899, he was an academic celebrity.

Ironically, it was at the very moment of seeming rapprochement between these two colossal egos that a mutual enmity insinuated itself. Du Bois misunderstood the deepest motives behind Washington's Tuskegee professorship offer, while the far more influential and famous Washington underestimated Du Bois's ability and willingness to repay deception. It seems reasonable to speculate that moving to Tuskegee would have had no other appeal to Nina, if at all, than that it was not Atlanta. Apologizing for his delay and indecision on February 17, Du Bois wrote to ask Washington if, after all, "would not [his] department be regarded by the public as a sort of superfluous addition not quite in consonance with the fundamental

Tuskegee idea?" To reassure himself, he accepted Washington's invitation to spend a day or two in mid-February 1900 on the Tuskegee campus. Washington showed him every courtesy and Du Bois supposed that he had made a favorable impression.[47]

The actual place must have impressed him. The campus rose, improbable and isolated, by a bend in the unpaved road just beyond its namesake village like a mirage MIT, which in architecture and scale it resembled more each year. Recent and current construction was everywhere, sustained by the skill and muscle power of students whose education came in pouring cement, carrying hods on scaffolds, wielding planes in the carpentry shop, or in brick kilns. Between 1895 and 1900, thirteen buildings bearing the names mostly of illustrious northern benefactors—Phelps, Parker, Slater-Armstrong, Huntington, Emery—sprang up. Seniors assembled demonstration houses in a flash onstage as part of their commencement valedictory exercises. President McKinley had come to sit on a platform of cotton bales during the winter of 1898 while the uniformed student body marched snappily in review.[48] Principal Washington was a worker of near miracles and all-black Tuskegee was an extraordinary experiment, but Du Bois was finally all but certain he should go elsewhere.

Elsewhere was Washington, D.C. Howard University, although a "poorly-run establishment," was a "strong possibility." But the truly exciting prospect, Du Bois wrote the principal immediately upon his return on February 17, 1900, was the assistant superintendency of colored schools of the District of Columbia. The new white public school superintendent, described by Du Bois as "rather eccentric," had pressed him to become a candidate for the post and would press the case in person when Du Bois came to the capital for the meeting of the American Negro Academy on March 5. If it appeared that he was willing to trade the profession of social scientist for that of school administrator, Du Bois probably thought—given his vast reserves of energy and Prussian discipline—that he could run the public schools of the District of Columbia and still crank out periodic monographs. The reality of the Washington position, of course, was that he would be a functionary—albeit a well-salaried, highly respected functionary—whose tenure was contingent upon discreet public pronouncements. In his excitement and Nina's state of mind, these are considerations to which he must have given little or no thought. Half a century later, he questioned his "fitness for such a job." Even though it paid twice his Atlanta salary, Du Bois claimed that he had only begun to "wonder if [he] should not accept" when "forces started moving in Washington" to take matters out of his hands.[49] But fifty years earlier he not only decided he wanted the position, he went after it aggressively.

Writing to Tuskegee, he broached his options in a manner calculated to flatter the powerful principal. Wasn't Washington the "most useful place of the three and could I not serve *both your cause and the general cause of the Negro* at the national capital better than elsewhere?" Then, on February 26, before the principal had had time to reply, Du Bois wrote again, appealing for his endorsement for the school superintendency. Messages had arrived, Du Bois said, urging him to become a candidate "before it was too late." No, he hadn't definitely decided against coming to Tuskegee, but his "present leaning, however, is toward Washington" and the chance to do "a great work." On March 1, three days later, he sent Reverend Hollis Burke Frissell, the white chaplain who had succeeded Armstrong as principal of Hampton, a similar message saying, if Frissell thought him "fitted for the place, may I ask you to send me as soon as convenient your testimonial, that I may forward it to Washington?"[50]

Nina probably leaned toward Washington even more than Will. It was only a matter of weeks before her newest pregnancy was confirmed, and the prospect of rearing another child in Atlanta must have distressed them both. Nina could imagine strolling with the new infant in Washington's unsegregated public parks and the zoo. Theaters were segregated, but public transportation and the restaurants at the train station were not. The public library, unlike Atlanta's Carnegie Library (shortly under construction), was open to the public, irrespective of color. From Du Bois's point of view, the national capital had almost everything: federal agencies and the Library of Congress with countless documents and books; Howard University, not yet the "capstone of Negro education" but clearly on the road to periodic excellence; and the stimulation of the American Negro Academy (of which he was now president). The sizable, educated African-American upper classes with their mulatto overlay were a visible, confident, and prosperous fact of civic life. An attractive city, Washington was like Athens to Sparta when compared to Atlanta. The D.C. assistant superintendency of schools was one of the most estimable and quietly influential positions available anywhere to an African-American, a plum. Anchored to the flagship M Street High School (the future Dunbar) with its classical curriculum, the city's segregated black public school system was said to provide one of the best educations in America.[51]

As of July 1, 1900, new congressional legislation called for a single superintendent (white) and two assistant superintendents (one for "colored" and one for "white" schools). Factional competition for the "colored" assistant superintendency was already frenetic. M Street High School principal Robert H. Terrell, Harvard magna cum laude and Howard Law School graduate, was an aspirant, and his formidable wife, national clubwoman Mary Church Terrell, Oberlin-educated and regal, meant her husband to have it. The restored Wilberforce classics scholar Scarborough was among the contenders, as were Winfield Scott Montgomery and Hugh M. Browne, Dartmouth alumnus and Princeton seminary man, respectively. The long-since-vanished letter of recommendation Booker Washington sent to Du Bois the first week in March must have been a strong one. Hollis Frissell's letter a few days later seemed equally enthusiastic. The Hampton principal regretted that Du Bois was tempted by school administration—Du Bois was the "only man that the colored race has thus far produced" who could turn out "excellent historical and sociological work"—but Frissell was ready and glad to do anything to "help [him] on."[52] Meanwhile, the information pipeline to Tuskegee was flowing full stream; John Wesley Ross, the white Democratic commissioner of D.C. schools, dutifully forwarded the names of all suggested candidates to Washington. Blow-by-blow accounts arrived in Tuskegee almost daily. Terrell was the "most popular." Du Bois was the "most acceptable from a scholarly standpoint." It was a fight "between Terrell and Du Bois against a minor field." Washington's name was mentioned, "and it is conceded that you could have it by a nod of assent."[53] Terrell was in the lead, causing those who disliked imperious Mrs. Terrell to flock to Du Bois—"or any outsider."

From Atlanta came disturbing information from the venerable William A. Pledger about Du Bois. Pledger, the self-made natural son of a Georgia planter, was Atlanta University–trained, a lawyer, and a newspaper editor whose service to the Republican party had brought him the distinction in his final years of titular state party chairman. Once a feisty civil rights militant, he was now a straddler, his editorials in the black Atlanta *Age* sometimes echoing Frederick Douglass but more often Booker Washington. "I am so sorry that you endorsed Du Bois," Pledger moaned. "He is not of your people. Your friends almost to a man are against him." He, too, claimed the people wanted either Terrell or Washington himself. Then, within a few days, from one of the capital's most prominent African-American physicians came a ringing endorsement of Du Bois.[54] Consorting with princes of finance and industry in New York, Boston, and Saratoga, able to make and break careers with a note or a nod, Booker Washington was much too important now to become a

Washington bureaucrat. He did not need or want Washington, D.C., but it now seemed that his backing of Du Bois could jeopardize his own influence in the capital. T. Thomas Fortune and another of Washington's most trusted lieutenants, D.C. insider, newspaperman, and government clerk Richard W. Thompson, pleaded with Washington to throw his support to Principal Terrell in order to keep the appointment from going to any District nonresident—above all to a certain William Hooper Councill, principal of the State Agricultural and Mechanical College for Negroes at Huntsville, Alabama, whose fawning over powerful whites made Booker Washington seem positively frosty by comparison. In Washington's eyes, the whole business had become unpredictable and distastefully amateurish. He really should "have consulted you before making any move," he admitted to Fortune, "then we could have all been working in the same direction."[55] It was a rare lapse in appearing to back Du Bois.

Washington corrected his course. Very likely, the advice from some of his key white northern backers confirmed what he already knew had to be done. On March 11, the Tuskegee principal sent Du Bois a curious letter from New York's Grand Union Hotel, where one of his periodic caucuses with rich white trustees had just concluded:

> Dear Dr. Du Bois:
>
> Please consider the contents of this letter strictly private. If you have not done so, I think it not best for you to use the letter of recommendation which I have sent you. I have just received a letter direct from one of the Commissioners in the District asking me to recommend someone for the vacancy there and I have recommended you as strongly as I could. Under the circumstances it would make your case stronger not to present the letter which I have given you for the reason that it would tend to put you in the position of seeking the position. It is pretty well settled, judging by the Commissioner's letter, that some one outside the District is going to be appointed.
>
> Yours truly,
> Booker T. Washington[56]

Du Bois might have heard rumors that Washington himself was a candidate for the assistant superintendency. He certainly knew that angry coalitions were fighting no-holds-barred against each other. But nothing had prepared him for the patent illogic of Washington's letter and the bad faith to be inferred from it. Instead of the strong written endorsement committing Washington to his candidacy, Du Bois was instructed to rely on verbal assurances that he was Washington's choice for the post. When he heard later that one of the African-American members of the District school board had wrangled a conference with President Theodore Roosevelt to warn of the " 'danger' of my appointment," Du Bois was absolutely convinced that what he now began to call the "Tuskegee Machine" had struck.[57]

10.
Clashing Temperaments

Du Bois's genius was obvious to Booker Washington. But Booker T. Washington had not walked out of slavery and a West Virginia coal mine thirty-six years and multiple personalities ago to find welcome in Theodore Roosevelt's White House and the foyers of the rich by mistaking merit for reality. Mistakes about people and policies could destroy everything he had built up. In a less fraught world, one configured to wider tolerances, Washington would have been more disposed to tolerate disagreement with himself; but his was the era of *Plessy v. Ferguson*, of the doctrine of separate but equal racial status—a doctrine enshrined by the highest court of the land one significant year after his own famous "separate as the five fingers" speech at the 1895 Atlanta and Cotton States Exposition. His public life, therefore, had been dictated by savvy calculation, accomplished deception, and perfect opacity—qualities either in short supply or wholly absent from Du Bois. Grappling for the key to his complex personality, Washington's masterful biographer, Louis Harlan, likened him to an onion whose peeled layers only exposed yet another layer until there were no more. Close associates called him the "Great Accommodator" and the "Wizard of Tuskegee."[1]

Whether or not he truly believed the bromides he dispensed far and wide and with indefatigable good humor, Washington never doubted their necessity. A leisurely perusal of *Black-Belt Diamonds*, the popular 1898 edition of his speeches, yielded such gems as that lynching "really indicates progress. There can be no progress without friction"; that slavery gave the African-American "the habit of work"; or that, if the oppressed

African-American "can be a medium of [southern whites'] rising into the atmosphere of generous brotherhood and self-forgetfulness, he will see in it a recompense for all that he has suffered." Washington's "darky" jokes were famous. At Harvard to receive an honorary master's, he let on as how he felt like a huckleberry in a bowl of milk. Negroes and mules had so much in common, he liked to say, that you were bound to find as many of one as the other in every Alabama Black Belt county. He would bring down the house with the anecdote about an old handy man who, when told to clean out the henhouse that was to serve as Tuskegee's first classroom, queried with astonishment, " 'What you mean, boss? You sholy ain't gwine clean out de hen-house in de *day*-time?' "[2]

Sometimes Booker Washington could go too far, seeming to demean his people in bread-and-butter situations that were no laughing matter to at least some genteel white Christians. Miss Martha Calhoun of Cambridge, Massachusetts, wrote him to say how appalled she had been by a December 1900 speech in which he had ludicrously depicted African-Americans bumbling themselves out of service-industry monopolies. She saw nothing in the story "to make an audience laugh. . . . It is not really because of improved methods that the white man has wrested this honorable and lucrative occupation [barbering] from his colored brother. It is because he is the *stronger* popular one, and in the majority." Washington knew this, but was serenely unruffled by such reproaches. As for the few mavericks among his own people who ventured to chastise him, he felt a puzzled contempt. Called "an apologist and a trimmer" by the influential Washington *Bee* in late 1899, he scratched his head and made a note to himself to buy the African-American newspaper. What was left, he would have asked them, now that the white South was ascendant, but the politics of compromise and the mien of ingratiation? It was and would remain an article of faith with him that the future prosperity of his race lay in the South "where the Negro is given a man's chance in the commercial world." What he had had to say at the 1898 anniversary of the founding of Hampton picturesquely summed up his philosophy:

> If today, we have fewer political conventions, we have more economic gatherings. If we have fewer political clubs, we have more building and loan associations. If we cherish fewer air-castles, we own more acres of land and more homes than has ever been true in the history of the Negro race. If we have fewer men in Congress, we have more merchants and more leaders in commerce.[3]

The founding in 1901 of the National Negro Business League under his presidency was meant to be the centerpiece of Washington's progress-through-prosperity agenda. The idea was Du Bois's, as was the wealth of data on which the organization was built, but the start-up energy, publicity, and resources came from Tuskegee. The unmistakable major premise of Washington's business gambit, in fact, was that through financial successes and by making themselves indispensable to the South's economic growth, eventually African-Americans would earn their way into full citizenship—regaining all and more of the rights and privileges they had provisionally surrendered. "The black man who spends ten thousand a year in freight charges can select his own seat in a railroad train," one of his "Black-Belt diamond" homilies gleamed, "else a Pullman palace car will be put on for him."[4] Washington believed this utterly. But he believed with equal fervency in the northern Midases supporting his bargain, for without the luster of their names—Carnegie, Eastman, Peabody, Baldwin, Rockefeller, Rogers, Schiff, Villard—and the manna from their cornucopia philanthropies, his leverage with southern white politicians and public officials would have been even less than it was. It is even possible that Booker Washington was their idea. Du Bois in *Dusk of Dawn*, years later, would scrutinize their motives with merciless accuracy. "This Northern group had clear objectives," he wrote:

> They were capitalists and employers and yet in most cases sons, relatives, or friends of the abolitionists. . . . These younger men believed that the Negro problem could not remain a matter of philanthropy. These Negroes were not to be encouraged as voters in the new democracy, nor were they to be left at the mercy of the reactionary South. They were good laborers and they might be better. . . . Properly guided they would restrain the unbridled demands of white labor, born of the Northern labor unions and now spreading to the South.[5]

For Booker Washington, the man who first personified these interests was the railroad magnate William H. Baldwin, Jr. If, as some have believed, Samuel Armstrong took the place of the father he never knew, then the intense Baldwin, with his steel-blue eyes and high forehead, was the kind overseer Booker had been too young to know in slavery. Former vice-president of the Southern Railroad Company, president of the Long Island Rail Road, workaholic Tuskegee trustee, Boston-bred Baldwin was seven years younger than Washington, yet he played from the beginning the role of grand vizier of Tuskegee. He had at first declined an invitation to sit on the board of trustees until a surprise visit afforded an inspection of the campus from chapel to kitchen. He had been so wrought up in the quarter hour before Washington delivered his Atlanta Compromise speech that he remained outside the pavilion pacing and waiting for the results. Chairing the board's executive committee, Baldwin took charge of the school's finances. So that Gilded Age grandees arriving by personal Pullman car might be minimally incommoded, Baldwin extended the tracks from the nearby whistle-stop at Chehaw to the campus. Nervous, impatient, intolerant of contrary opinions, and decisively convinced of African-American inferiority, Baldwin saw the solution to the South's race problem in salvation through work and rights after obedience. There had been too much pious nonsense about equality spouted by misguided Yankee idealists, his own ancestors included, he told the 1898 meeting of the American Social Science Association at Saratoga. "How false that theory was thirty long years of experience have proved. . . . Social recognition of the negro by the white is a simple impossibility, and entirely dismissed from the minds of the white, and by the intelligent negroes."[6]

Baldwin and his kind were determined to bring industrial progress and social harmony to the South. The profit motive drove them every bit as much as it did their European analogues scrambling across the African continent, many genuinely propelled by the tenets of a hardheaded Christianity that called for making amends for sins while turning a dollar. As Baldwin saw it, two forces posed the greatest threat to his enlightened work—the South's unreconstructed racists and the African-American intelligentsia. The latter especially made him furious, and he regularly communicated his contempt for such people to his friend at Tuskegee. Baldwin, himself a Harvard man, had a specific group in mind, the Negroes "who have been highly educated at Harvard College," he wrote in early February 1900, the same month in which Du Bois and Washington were discussing the Tuskegee and District of Columbia positions. Their problem was "purely an attempt on their part to be white people." The mere thought of Atlanta University's intellectual and social pretentions galled him. His views were shared by other Tuskegee trustees, especially by Philadelphia's Robert C. Ogden. Baldwin, Ogden, Frissell, and their kind would have regarded Du Bois's landing the D.C. position as the worst possible symbolism—a brainy, brown elitist heading what the government clerk Richard Thompson called "the greatest school system in the world controlled by colored people."[7] Baldwin may have arrived at the conclusion before

Washington did that installing Du Bois at Tuskegee was the best way to neutralize him. No doubt they made themselves heard soon after the Wizard checked into the Grand Union Hotel.

Washington's motives in dealing with the Atlanta professor as he did may have been more complex. On the one hand, powerfully connected individuals like Hart were not to be ignored, and the status of Tuskegee as a racial laboratory would certainly be enhanced by Du Bois's presence. On the other, Du Bois's conduct up to that point (especially after his performance during the Afro-American Council meeting) may have led Washington to think that Du Bois really could (as Du Bois had suggested when asking for a reference) "serve both [his] cause and the general cause of the Negro." In any case, it took the Wizard no time at all to get out of his quandary. On March 12, a day after Du Bois was told not to make use of the letter of endorsement for the assistant superintendency, commissioner John Ross wrote Washington, somewhat cryptically, that he would "take pleasure . . . in bringing your views to the attention of my associate Commissioners."[8] Whatever those views were (probably to select the assistant superintendent from the local candidates), they were not favorable to Du Bois's going to the District. That Du Bois was unhappy at Atlanta should have meant that he would be all the more ready to accept Tuskegee. To Washington's mind, he had merely assured the sociology professor of one estimable job by withholding his blessings from another, leaving all the parties—Baldwin, the Terrells, Pledger, and Du Bois himself—well disposed. The Atlanta professor's domestic situation—Burghardt's tragic death and Nina's trauma and pregnancy—would hardly have weighed in Washington's calculations, even if he had been aware of it. For Du Bois, however, the loss of the public school post was both professionally and personally wounding. The fact that he wanted it would have been, in his mind, sufficient reason for his elevation to it. Who could have been more qualified? When the District's board of education finally selected its new assistant superintendent, the pleasant, hesitant Winfield Montgomery, Du Bois would have decided that no more blatant proof of politics over merit was needed.

Condemned to more years of valorous research and teaching in his Masada above West Mitchell Street, he had been sharply confronted with what was in store for him and his family in the South just after returning from his first visit to Tuskegee that February. The experience had not been good for his peace of mind. United States' plans for participation in the Paris Exposition of 1900, which was to welcome in the new century, called for a "Negro Section" under the direction of Fisk classmate Thomas J.

Calloway, now an employee of the War Department and one of Du Bois's allies in the capital. Calloway had asked Du Bois to take charge of assembling exhibits primarily from Georgia but also from several other southern states. Boarding the train in Atlanta on the night of February 19 to attend the meeting of exposition commissioners in Savannah, Du Bois was flatly refused an overnight berth aboard the Cincinnati-Jacksonville express after arguing with the Pullman conductor, the train conductor, the flagman, and even the hapless car porter. Compelled to "sit up all night" in the crowded, filthy "colored" car hooked just behind the engine, he filed formal protest with the Southern Railway Company—"has the Railway given orders to its conductors to refuse Negroes sleeping car accommodations?"—sending a copy of the letter to Booker Washington.[9] The issue of Jim Crow public facilities infuriated Du Bois; many decades later he wrote about it in the language not of cool social science but of flesh and blood victimization. Passionately re-creating such an experience, he would ask readers of *The Autobiography*, "Did you ever see a 'jim-crow' waiting room?" Leading them from an unheated waiting room with a ticket sold by a snarling white agent after a long delay, Du Bois boards the dilapidated car "caked with dirt, the floor . . . gummy and the windows dirty" for a ride into segregation incomparably described:

> [An impertinent white newsboy] yells and swaggers and a continued stream of white men saunters back and forth from the smoker to buy and listen. The white train crew from the baggage cars uses the "jim-crow" to lounge in and perform their toilet. The conductor appropriates two seats for himself and his papers and yells gruffly for your tickets before the train has scarcely started. . . . It is difficult to get lunch or drinking water. Lunch rooms either "don't serve niggers" or serve them at some dirty and ill-attended hole in the wall. . . . If you have to change cars be wary of junctions which are usually without accommodation and filled with quarrelsome whites who hate a "darky dressed up." You are apt to have the company of a sheriff and a couple of meek or sullen black prisoners on part of your way and a couple of dirty colored section hands will pour in toward night and drive you to the smallest corner. "No," said a little lady in the corner (she looked like an ivory cameo and her dress flowed on her like a caress), "We don't travel much."[10]

What made racial discrimination so hard to bear for Du Bois was not only (or not even?) the enforced segregation but the utter, arrogant absence of all discrimination along class lines, as this vivid passage with its cringing cameo woman of breeding and beauty implied.

An angry Du Bois was ready and willing to enter into *cause célèbre* litigation. The battle to ride public transportation unsegregated had begun seventeen years before in Tennessee when one of Du Bois's most remarkable contemporaries had been hauled by a pack of bullying white men from a train with the conductor's flesh between her teeth. A tiny spitfire of a woman whose life was an uninterrupted civil rights crusade South and North, Ida B. Wells-Barnett dragged the Chesapeake & Ohio all the way to the state supreme court before losing in 1887 on the grounds that her "persistence was not in good faith." Nine years later, when the United States Supreme Court sided in effect with the state of Tennessee in *Plessy v. Ferguson*, African-Americans lost the battle for unsegregated public transportation and other facilities *within* the borders of a state. The interstate battle loomed ahead, and as Du Bois discussed his professional future with Washington, he also invited the principal's help, telling him that a high official of the Southern Railway in Atlanta conceded that separate but equal regulations "did not apply to interstate travel."[11] The Wizard's first reaction to a public and legal counterattack was encouraging.

He couldn't have known that five days after writing to Tuskegee about the Southern Railway matter, its former vice-president diplomatically yet firmly advised Washington how to proceed. On March 19 Baldwin informed his friend of a talk with some of the railroad presidents about segregated Pullman cars. "They feel that if the colored people should raise an issue it would cause nothing but bitterness." He assured Washington that "in such cases as that of Mr. Du Bois, or a possible interference with you," doing nothing "would help as much as anything to bring about a liberal interpretation of the Law." As in his responses to numerous other major and minor injustices along the color line, the tack taken by the Tuskegee principal in Du Bois's railroad-discrimination encounter ended, after much letter-writing, telephoning, and procrastination due to rumors of impending announcements of policy compromises by the railroads, ambiguously. Despite his forthright pledge of influence and financial assistance, the Wizard's backing of Du Bois would end four years later when Washington was imperiously rebuffed by the attorney for the Pullman Company. Du Bois was informed that the last best avenue had been tried. Washington saw no point then in financing a court battle and so it would be agreed not to bring suit against the offending railroad.[12]

The irresolution involving Jim Crow transportation lay ahead, but for a decisive temperament like Du Bois, the mandarin style of Booker Washington would have grated from the beginning. He would almost surely have entertained doubts about the Tuskegeean's good faith even as he went ahead with the agreement to organize a legal defense committee. Already smarting from the turn of events in the District of Columbia, Du Bois finally made up his mind about Tuskegee. Having given the matter long and earnest thought, he informed Washington on April 10, 1900, that he had "decided not to accept your very generous offer." His horizons were somewhat larger than the scope of Tuskegee, he felt. The only opening that would attract him "would be one . . . [that lay] nearer to the centres of culture and learning and thus gave me larger literary activity." Everything—instinct, personality, location, and politics—militated against his going to Tuskegee. It would never be an opportunity to further the enlightened interests of the race. Service at Tuskegee meant service to Booker Washington. Du Bois, however, had no intention yet of alienating the Wizard. There was too much riding on that powerful man's indulgence, if not his goodwill. Despite another disturbing example of bad faith a month after turning down the Tuskegee offer, Du Bois conducted himself with restraint verging on generosity. The loyalty he had displayed during the Afro-American Council fracas had been rewarded with the directorship of the council's Negro Business Bureau and the promise of a small budget to defray organizational and research expenses. After the work was completed and the request for reimbursement presented, however, Washington's man Fortune successfully moved that the executive committee annul the appropriation. Shortly thereafter, Washington asked Du Bois for his data categorizing and analyzing minority business activity, together with the all-important mailing list. Du Bois wrote back in mid-May that he would comply "in a week or two," and Booker T. Washington's National Negro Business League was born.[13]

Superficially, their relations remained cooperative and cordial. Du Bois would attend the annual two-day Tuskegee Conference in February 1901, writing a glowing summary of its achievements for *Harper's Weekly*; several more visits as Washington's guest were to follow. In March, an article on "The Negro in Business," ghostwritten for the Wizard in *Gunton's Magazine*, generously noted Du Bois's *The Philadelphia Negro* and the Atlanta University Studies. Du Bois even accepted an invitation to go on a well-publicized West Virginia fishing and camping trip with Washington, Fortune, two of the "wealthiest colored men in this country" (according to the newspaper *Colored American*), and several other notables of the race in late September of that year, canceling only at the last minute. Ironically, the management of the C.C.&S. railroad placed a private car at their disposal, even as Washington tried in vain to arrange a promised meeting about Du Bois's Southern Railway discrimination case with Robert Todd Lincoln, attorney for the Pullman Company and son of the assassinated president.[14]

All the while, Du Bois would keep a sharp eye on the D.C. assistant superintendency. He disguised his hurt at having been shabbily shunted aside, greatly underplaying it in his memoirs. In fact, he would pursue the position over the next six years. Maintaining a disengaged public stance, he covertly encouraged his Washington allies, who created considerable trouble for the vulnerable Montgomery. Attorney James Adlai Cobb, another astute, black Tuskegee agent in the capital and a future municipal court judge, reported regularly to the Wizard's secretary Emmett Scott about the endless board of education cabals, with Mrs. Terrell always in the thick of them (Mr. Terrell became a municipal court judge with Washington's blessing in 1901) and Du Bois waiting in the wings. In mid-August 1906, during intense scrimmaging for the colored superintendency (it had just been upgraded), the Du Bois forces would almost score a touchdown, "but it was too late," Cobb reported, "as Mrs. Terrell had done the work." The beleaguered Montgomery was given a year's reprieve. "The Du Bois turndown is rather interesting," an amused Cobb would add at the end of the month. "He seems determined to land in Washington if he can possibly do it."[15] The following year, however, Booker Washington's candidate, Harvard man Roscoe Conkling Bruce, able but imperious son of Mississippi's second African-American U.S. senator, would ascend from Tuskegee Institute to the District superintendency, killing Du Bois's hopes once and for all. By then, of course, civil estrangement between Du Bois and Washington would have led to civil war within the race.

BUT IN the summer of 1900 civility still prevailed, and in any case Du Bois was busy enough with other concerns. The fifth Atlanta University Studies conference behind him, he left Nina five months pregnant for New York City and Europe, sailing steerage in mid-June with several boxes of exhibits for the Paris Exposition Universelle. He was thirty-two now, still very much a Europhile, but a good deal more critical of the so-called White Man's Burden as he detected unmistakable signs of a fraying civilization. Ethiopian Emperor Menelik II's annihilation of a crack Italian army at Adwa in 1896 (the first significant military defeat in modern history of Europeans by Africans) he took to be a portent of prodigious significance. A military tribunal sitting throughout the month of August 1899 at Rennes had just found Captain Alfred Dreyfus guilty of treason a second time, although the identity of the real traitor and the conspiracy of the army general staff against the Jewish officer had been fully exposed. Implacably divided into Dreyfusards and anti-Dreyfusards, wallowing in anticlerical and anti-Semitic orgies, the French were said to be a disgrace to the white races. "Missionary work could be profitably performed in France as well as in the unexplored regions of Central Africa," Montana's attorney general declared. William James, deeply saddened by the behavior of the French, gave thanks that he "lived in a Republic."[16]

The letters written to Nina during his two months abroad have not survived, making it difficult to track his movements. Much later, his prose caught the spirit of a civilization serenely sunning itself at high noon. He was excited by this European punctuation in time whose immodest motto proclaimed the Exposition Universelle "*le bilan du siècle*"—the summation of the century. The splendid new Pont Alexandre III linked the exposition's 280 acres stretching along both banks of the Seine from the Eiffel Tower to the Place de la Concorde. Spectacular palaces erected to Arts and Letters, Agriculture, Civil Engineering, Education, Electricity, Housing, Hygiene, Mechanics, and Metallurgy competed with the arrogant national pavilions of Germany and Great Britain, and the vastly popular Russian one (containing a gigantic marble and jasper map of France with its cities marked by precious stones). France offered the flamboyantly baroque Grand Palais and its sister Petit Palais. "It was one of the finest, perhaps the very finest, of world expositions," Du Bois decided, "and it typified what the European world wanted to think of itself and its future."[17]

The building on the rue des Nations that housed the American Negro Exhibit, assembled by Thomas Calloway and Du Bois, was a plain white structure devoted to the "science of society." Because Du Bois had arrived well after the April opening of the exposition, some of the most interesting materials in the exhibit—books, models, patents, and so forth—had yet to be uncrated when the judges passed. However, what they saw among the five hundred photographs, captions, maps, and plans drawn from Atlanta University, Berea, Fisk, Howard, Hampton, and Tuskegee impressed them enough to award Du Bois, "Collaborator as Compiler of Georgia Negro Exhibit," a gold medal. If the world wanted to know what a disadvantaged people could do for itself, Du Bois proudly reported in *American Monthly*

Review of Reviews, there was "no more encouraging answer than that given by the American Negroes, who are here shown to be studying, examining, and thinking of their own progress and prospects."[18]

The Pan-African Congress meeting in London during the last week in July was another curious sign of disadvantaged peoples beginning to stir. Pan-Africanism came with the Zeitgeist, an inevitable, derivative idea, at once circumspect and revolutionary. It was another movement exploding into the twentieth century like a stick of dynamite—Pan-Hellenism, Pan-Germanism, Pan-Slavism—with the Irish, Afrikaners, Armenians, Serbians, and other historic "races" already lighting fuses for the new century. Its "civilizationist" forefathers—Africanus Horton, the Sierra Leonean philosopher; J. E. Casely-Hayford, the Gold Coast newspaper publisher; Blyden and Crummell, the Liberia expatriates; Delany and Turner, the sojourners—were Afro-Saxon gentlemen who acknowledged the tutelage of Africa by Europe as indispensable for many decades to run. None of them deplored the Scramble for Africa that the 1884 Berlin Conference had done so much to accelerate. None doubted that the gory sub-Saharan conquests of a King Leopold, a Cecil Rhodes, or a Henry Stanley were redeemed by noble ends—that, as Blyden wrote, European conquest "was ultimately for the good of that continent."[19] But their inherently revolutionary Pan-African idea was bound to take on a life of its own. The term itself, coined by Henry Sylvester Williams in a November 1899 letter to a London associate, was less than a year old when Du Bois first encountered it. Williams, a Trinidadian barrister trained in Canada, was thirty-one years old and recently established in London. One of the most visionary colored men of his generation, he was cultured, dedicated, and globe-wandering, but he would be practically forgotten when he died aged forty-two.

When Booker Washington met him during his 1899 summer visit to England, Williams was the moving force behind the two-year-old African Association, an organization of West Indian professionals whose constitution committed them to "encourage a feeling of unity and to facilitate friendly intercourse among Africans in general; to promote and protect the interests of all subjects claiming African descent, wholly or in part, in British colonies and other places." Tuskegee was preparing to send three of its graduates to Togoland early the following year to assist the German colonial administration and a quasi-private cartel in cotton cultivation and the setting up of vocational training centers for African boys. It was part of the Wizard's plan to have Tuskegee play a limited but well-publicized role in the continent's technical development as far north as Morocco and east to the Sudan. Williams's African Association intrigued the Wizard enough to make him attend one of its meetings and even to agree to sponsor a proposed Pan-African Congress in London the next year. He declined to be present himself. Washington felt about as much need for solidarity with Africans as did the explorer Stanley (who once explained to a like-minded Wizard that African-American emigration to Africa was impracticable), but Washington was sure that the more black people in America learned about European treatment of Africans, the more tolerable the conditions in the South would seem to them. It therefore pleased him to issue a public letter on July 15, 1899, begging and advising "as many of our people as can possibly do so," to attend the 1900 Pan-African Congress.[20] The success of Williams's novel effort in July 1900 was in no small degree due to the influence of Booker Washington.

The three days of meetings on July 23, 24, and 25 in Westminster Town Hall were historic. Joined by members of the Aborigines Protection Society, the Society of Friends, other observers, and spectators, thirty-three men and women representing people of African descent from throughout the world took their seats to be welcomed by the bishop of London. Among the six delegates from the United States were two women from Washington, D.C., Anna J. Cooper and Ada Harris. Cooper was an Oberlin graduate and only months away from succeeding Robert Terrell as principal of the famous M Street High School. She arrived anxious to read her conference paper, "The Negro in America," which flailed her country for its Christian shortcomings.[21] The honor of presiding over the congress had been bestowed upon another American, Bishop Alexander Walters of the AME Zion denomination, sometime president of the Afro-American Council and another figure whose independence and intelligence made the Wizard uneasy. Walters was a flexible conservative, a defender of Protestantism and profit who stood squarely for African-American voting rights. As late as 1910, the bishop was calling for his people to "furnish the Negro Cecil Rhodes to Liberia, the man who is to develop . . . a line of steamships between that country and ours."[22] Calloway, who had crossed the channel with Du Bois, found himself elected treasurer of the U.S. branch of the new Pan-African Organization. Du Bois was in the company of racial equals for a change: Benito Sylvain of Haiti, a Pan-African reincarnation of Talleyrand and former aide-de-camp to the Ethiopian emperor; Samuel Coleridge-Taylor of London, a musical prodigy; John Alcindor of Trinidad and London, an Edinburgh-trained physician and chief collaborator in Williams's African Association; and Henry "Box" Brown, aged hero of the

Underground Railroad, which had shipped him in a box out of slavery to freedom in Canada.[23]

The pitch in which the Westminster Town Hall proceedings was to be played had been pretty well fixed by Williams a few days earlier at Gough's Hotel in Dublin where the barrister chastised Great Britain for failing to uphold African rights, particularly in South Africa. The message to the world was a moderate, trusting appeal for an imperialism that lived up to its highest pieties. These were refined men and women who might have caused a character in a Kipling story to regret that they were not white—or not white enough. After the "magnificent repast" offered by the bishop of London at Fulham Palace on the second day, Alexander Walters's memoirs fairly burst with pride as Du Bois, Sylvain, Calloway, a certain Miss Jones, "and others moved about the palace grounds with an ease and elegance that was surprising; one would have thought they were 'to the manor born.' " In *The Times*'s coverage and during the delightful "at home" hosted by the Reform Club for the delegates, the unspoken satisfaction in observing such well-behaved, dark-skinned effigies of the White Man's Burden was implicit in the condescension.[24] Yet if there was nothing palpable in the Westminster papers and speeches for the Colonial Office to fret over, the congress itself was an unmistakable harbinger of distant restiveness.

Twenty-five years later, after Du Bois had come to personify the Pan-African movement, it was mistakenly assumed by scholars that he had dominated the 1900 deliberations, which is an exaggeration. Du Bois himself seems to have forgotten completely about Williams, not once mentioning his name in print until forty-seven years later.[25] A strange memory lapse; but perhaps he was so caught up in the forces Williams had set in motion that he soon convinced himself that he was as much the source of them as he was their premier interpreter and conductor. The ideological reality (as opposed to the historical truth) of the first Pan-African Congress was that Williams's lasting achievement came with the defining moment of "To the Nations of the World," Du Bois's speech delivered before the Westminster Town Hall audience in the closing session. "In the metropolis of the modern world, in this closing year of the nineteenth century" (the grave cadence and crisp diction prefigured momentous phrasings that would reappear slightly changed in *The Souls of Black Folk*), "there has been assembled a congress of men and women of African blood, to deliberate solemnly upon the present situation and outlook of the darker races of mankind." As he spoke now, the commercial sentiments of Booker Washington and Bishop Walters were absent:

> The problem of the twentieth century is the problem of the colour line, the question as to how far differences of race . . . are going to be made, hereafter, the basis of denying to over half the world the right of sharing to their utmost ability the opportunities and privileges of modern civilization. To be sure, the darker races are today the least advanced in culture according to European standards. This has not, however, always been the case in the past, and certainly the world's history, both ancient and modern, has given many instances of no despicable ability and capacity among the blackest races of men. In any case, the modern world must needs remember that in this age . . . the millions of black men in Africa, America, and the Islands of the Sea, not to speak of the brown and yellow myriads elsewhere, are bound to have great influence upon the world in the future, by reason of sheer numbers and physical contact. . . . If, by reason of carelessness, prejudice, greed and injustice, the black world is to be exploited and ravished and degraded, the results must be deplorable, if not fatal, not simply to them, but to the high ideals of justice, freedom, and culture which a thousand years of Christian civilization have held before Europe.[26]

For a few pregnant moments, rhetoric and platitudes yielded to prophecy. Yet, however edifying and prescient, the statement was not intended to signal some radical change in their thinking about Queen Victoria's legitimate overlordship. Du Bois's passage in "To the Nations of the World" in which he called "as soon as practicable [for] the rights of responsible self-government to the black colonies of Africa and the West Indies," was bold but not unprecedented and was not to be interpreted as a demand for independence from the British Empire. The independence of African peoples from European suzerainty seemed in 1900 a prospect incalculably far in the future, even to a clairvoyant Du Bois. Moreover, any clarion call for the demise of the British Empire would have been impolitic and severely reprimanded by the London hosts of these genteel Pan-Africanists.[27]

HEADING HOME as the last months of the nineteenth century ran down, Du Bois had the satisfaction of having fostered a new movement and fathered a second child. A very pregnant Nina was finishing her term in Great Barrington in the care of Uncle James and other Burghardts. Nina Yolande arrived sometime during Sunday, October 21, a large, lively baby girl, cafe-au-lait in color. Her parents were delighted; the new baby brought them closer together than they had been since Burghardt's death. The deep, concealed psychological wounds—his as well as hers—had a fair chance of beginning to heal. Looking back, it does seem that a certain amount of that healing occurred. The uncomplicated, affectionate letters that Nina wrote Will a bit later about diapers and toys and tantrums have the feel of reconnection about them but also of loneliness. She seemed to be coping with her research and lecture-circuit widowhood. What some women friends did begin to notice about her, though, was a heightened passion for cleanliness, her insistence on repeatedly scrubbing every item that Yolande wore or might come in contact with—especially the soles of the baby's shoes. Nina had always been meticulous, good as a German Frau, Will liked to say; but the care of Yolande was compulsive—a prophylactic regimen to assure to Yolande what in their inexperience she and Will had failed to give Burghardt. The neurotic basis of her behavior escaped Du Bois. He saw her repetitive conduct grow and shrugged it off as a mildly peculiar habit with little or no significance outside the affairs of the home. Individual behavior in any case was never to be his specialty; he excelled in analyzing the human condition, rather than human conditions.[28]

Friendships began to develop. Faculty families came around to admire Yolande. Invitations to teas and dinners were exchanged, although Nina begged off more often than Will would have liked, relying more and more heavily on Lizzie Pingree and one or two other women of somewhat flattened profiles in the community. The Bowens, Herndons, and Proctors cultivated them. They were closest to the Towns and Hope families. George Towns and John Hope were Du Bois's closest male friends in Atlanta. Towns had gone away to Harvard College for a second bachelor's after finishing Atlanta University in 1894, then returned there to become professor of pedagogy and English. His birthplace was the south Georgia town of Albany, but he had been transformed by his Atlanta and Harvard education into a classic Yankee type, erect, spare of words, self-reliant, honest, and punctilious. Towns was small and wore glasses. In appearance he was more suited to editing the *Crimson and Gray*, Atlanta's alumni magazine, and captaining the debating team than to coaching the football team, all of which he did with considerable success. Sixty years later, emeritus professor Towns would still take brisk early morning walks and repair his own roof. Almost as courtly as Du Bois, but without the sartorial flourishes, he shared with Du Bois not only their mutual admiration of Du Bois but also a deep belief in higher education for African-Americans.[29] Towns was already more alarmed about Booker Washington's philosophy than his older friend—and ready to shout out in public his delight over the editorial grenades that Harvard man Monroe Trotter began lobbing at the Tuskegee Machine late in 1901.

Over at Atlanta Baptist College for Men, just a few blocks from Atlanta University, John Hope taught classics, served as bookkeeper, and coached the future Morehouse College's first football teams. The same age as Du Bois, Hope became not only his most intimate male friend but one with whom Du Bois always dealt as an equal. Hope's wife, Lugenia, was a tall, attractive Chicagoan with a pioneering interest in the YWCA and social work; she would become as much a professional presence as her husband. Lugenia Burns Hope was not a talkative woman, and her horn-rimmed spectacles made her seem older and somewhat icy. She and Nina may not have made a good fit. John Hope was exceedingly handsome in a stern sort of way, with blue eyes and slightly wavy brown hair that he parted in the middle. He wore an easy confidence and had risen to the top of his class at Worcester Academy and Brown University, in tribute to which (for such was the notion of liberalism in those days) the white faculty and students had generally shut their eyes to the fact that he was a Negro. The Brown faculty had been so determined to save Hope from going out into the world as a Negro that on the eve of his graduation a small committee begged him to reconsider. He had been a founding editor of the Brown *Daily Herald*, whose advisory committee offered him a post on the Providence *Journal*, as a white man. Instead, after delivering the 1894 class oration the next day, he left campus and headed back to the South as a voluntary black man.[30]

Hope's life story was fabulous, so much so that it became the subject of a fine biography, *The Story of John Hope*, Ridgely Torrence's forgotten masterpiece. Fanny, his mother, was the slave mistress of an Augusta, Georgia, businessman, just as Alethea, her own mother, had been of an Augusta planter. Alethea was almost white herself, beautiful by Caucasian standards, accomplished, and farseeing enough to insist that Fanny be sent to a school for mulattoes in Charleston, South Carolina. James Hope, the Scots businessman who established the Augusta Manufacturing Company (one of the South's few textile mills), lost his head over Fanny, installed her in his town house, the center of Augusta cultural life, and then, with the Civil War about to erupt, took her and their children to New York City where the new firm of James Hope and Company, Dealers in Imported Wines and Liquors, was established at 125th Street and Third Avenue in the remote borough of Harlem. Years before, James had sold his share of the prestigious old firm of Acker, Merrall, and Condit, the family's New York business, to his brother, Thomas. No satisfactory explanation is offered as to why James decided to return with Fanny to Augusta, spending the war there in his elegant Ellis Street home. In 1867, he placed the property in her name. The following year, in June, John was born there.

There were other families like the Hopes in Augusta, as there were elsewhere in the Deep South, octoroon and quadroon mixtures on their way to often neurotic, either/or racial identities. Fifteen years after the Civil War, these men and women of the third race were being treated no differently from any other "niggers" (unless they escaped by "passing"), but until then, in many enclaves within the prostrate Confederacy, they sometimes lived privileged lives. "There was always a choice group," Hope told a riveted audience many years later, "a choice few who defeated circumstances. Then there was the group of people who independent of particular merit on their part, but because of circumstances, their relationships to their masters, received additional money or additional education and were to that extent ahead." Channing Tobias, a much younger product of similar Augusta heritage and destined for comparable professional-service renown with the national YMCA, explained that "it was possible for a Negro in the Augusta of John Hope's boyhood to aspire to the heights and to receive encouragement from white people in so doing."[31] Until James Hope's death in 1876, Fanny and her children shared fully in the reflected status and power of Augusta's most distinguished white citizen. Yet five years later, Fanny was nearly destitute, not a dollar of the monies left in trust having been paid out by Hope's three white executors, and only a slender annuity eventually forthcoming as a result of a suit filed on her behalf by Thomas Hope of New York.

As the family slipped behind the veil, John worked in Augusta's finest hotel (owned by a black man) and learned to take hard knocks, monetary and racial. Before reaching his teens, something happened across the Savannah River in the town of Hamburg, South Carolina, that served to fix his sense of racial identity unshakably. It was the sort of event that was becoming more and more frequent in the South, and having similar self-defining impact on great numbers of racially indeterminate young men and women. Hamburg was a center of black power in Reconstruction South Carolina, with a black justice of the peace among its elected officials, and an armed militia drilled to readiness by proud, black Union Army veteran "Doc" Adams. The state's Democrats determined to make a stand at Hamburg in the summer of 1876 in order to galvanize white voters and thereby deny the Republicans and their African-American supporters victory at the polls. The manufactured incident, during the militia's Fourth of July parade, led to a pitched battle that evening, with hundreds of armed white people crossing over from Augusta to join the attack on Adams's outgunned forces. At nightfall, after surrendering the armory from which they had battled the invaders and their artillery, a number of the black militiamen were slaughtered in cold blood and the town's stores and shops torched. Eight-year-old John Hope heard white men shouting, "This is the beginning of the redemption of South Carolina," and saw the red glow across the river. If there was to be a war of the races, Hope signed on early as a black man. "And remember," he was in the habit of remarking, "I heard the guns of the Hamburg Massacre."[32]

Coming to Atlanta in the fall of 1898 from Roger Williams University, a tiny black Baptist college in Nashville, Hope sensed that he was being groomed for the presidency of Atlanta Baptist Seminary, then headed by a white Canadian. Before moving to the state capital in 1879, Atlanta Baptist Seminary had been Augusta Institute. The Hopes enjoyed a special family connection to both academies. The founder of Augusta Institute, William Jefferson White, was another forceful racial question mark. White had dared to violate Georgia law by teaching African-American children their ABCs before the Civil War. Like James Hope, he fell in love with a woman of African ancestry. But Josephine Thomas was still owned by a master who refused to sell her. White solved the problem by marrying her and going to live in the home of Josephine's master as a black man. After the Civil War, he took up preaching, founded and edited the *Georgia Baptist*, for years the most widely read African-American newspaper in the South, and placed his lanky Anglo-Saxon frame, flashing blue eyes, and spellbinding vocals in the service of African-American uplift. An admiring Du Bois described him as "editor, educator, and leader, [who] held a hundred thousand people in the hollow of his hand."[33] Heading for the presidency of White's transplanted college, Hope had to be careful about what he said and did. As a rule, he managed to pair unobsequious diplomacy with staunch principles. When it came to the phenomenon of Booker Washington, however, his diplomacy was tested.

He said almost nothing in public, but with Du Bois and Towns he was frank about what was coming to be called the Tuskegee Machine and its philosophy. Hope was as alarmed as Towns by what he saw as the downhill course the Wizard's leadership was taking. Then, too, he had an advantage neither Towns nor Du Bois had. Hope had come to Atlanta from Nashville in 1895 to hear Washington deliver his great "cast down your buckets" speech at the Atlanta and Cotton States Exposition. A year later, during Roger Williams University's commemoration of George Washington's birthday, Hope's thoughts about the Atlanta Compromise had boiled over in a speech to faculty and students. "If we are not striving for equality," he cried, "in heaven's name for what are we living?" He said it was cowardly and dishonest for "our colored men to tell white people or colored people that we are not struggling for equality. . . . Yes, my friends, I want equality. Nothing less." And savoring its shock value, Hope had wound up: "I am going to say we demand *social* equality."[34] These feelings were so strong that he was ready to act upon them publicly, opposing the vast forces supporting Washington. On the other hand, it would have been in character, and in keeping with their friendship, for Hope to act as a moderating influence on Du Bois once the latter's own conflict with Washington deepened.

As Du Bois and his circle studied the balance sheet of the past five years, from 1895 to 1900, they found their apprehensions growing the more Booker Washington's feats of conciliation were extolled by others. Yet there was no gainsaying his influence in the highest places, his manifold services to his people, and, above all, the radiating influence of Tuskegee's good works. For the present, he was indispensable and untouchable. As for Washington himself, at first he good-naturedly discounted such fears and suspicions about his secular ministry as rank jealousy at worst and deplorable naivete at best. He was certain that he understood the real world and the real black and white people living in it. He saw with penetration through to the state of nature "red in tooth and claw" behind the nation's social and racial contract—behind the institutional, legal, and customary facade of the free market economy. Andrew Carnegie recognized in him a black version of his better self, and, when Washington was his guest at Skibo Castle in Scotland, delighted in "darky" stories and political homespun.[35] The Wizard of Tuskegee was much less sagacious when it came to the broader implications of the Industrial Revolution for the South.

The South was Washington's specialty, the region whose fabulous creation he was from earliest formation as Mrs. Viola Ruffner's Malden, West Virginia, houseboy to General Armstrong's "no ordinary darkey" student at Hampton.[36] If Du Bois's considerable and growing knowledge of the black South was, nevertheless, akin to a professional explorer's knowledge of Africa or the Amazon, Washington *was* the black South—the peasant South arrayed with honorary degrees. Half white himself (ignorant of his father's identity and of his own birth date, he liked to say that his existence at least was certain), he was a veritable tangle of the South's taboos, paradoxes, and feudal intimacies. Therefore, Washington was a southern black man who understood southern white men to the marrow. His views of Du Bois's much-discussed concept of African-American "two-ness" do not survive, but Washington could well have claimed to possess something like "three-ness"—the consciousness of being an American, a Negro, and, more perilously yet, an American Negro in the South.

The joke about Washington, that he never met a white man he didn't like, was precisely that—a joke. His gift (one Du Bois neither possessed nor wanted) was almost never to show his dislikes. The stakes were too high. If Ms. Calhoun of Cambridge and Mr. Washington *Bee* deplored his placatory pronouncements, it was because they had never experienced the white-sheeted fury engendered by a lack of obsequiousness. Less than a year after the Atlanta speech had made Washington a household name, the governor of Alabama had figuratively slapped him down in public. Apparently riled up by the proud manner in which the African-American customs collector of Wilmington, North Carolina, had delivered an otherwise Tuskegee-correct commencement address, Governor William C. Oates had torn up his prepared speech and given the Tuskegee assembly a red-faced dressing down. "I want to give you niggers a few words of plain talk and advice," he spluttered. "You might as well understand that this is a white man's country, as far as the South is concerned, and we are going to make you keep your place. Understand that." The Wizard rose, calling for prayer, and promptly terminated the proceedings. The etiquette of race relations was no less touch and go in the North. His boldest public moment, when he lectured white America on its civil rights obligations to black America at the 1898 Chicago Peace Jubilee, had practically been erased from the record when the Associated Press simply omitted his words. Washington complained to a white newspaper editor who had heard alarming accounts of it, that, "in a portion of my address which was not sent out," he had said nothing more radical than that "the Negro be given every opportunity in proportion as he makes himself worthy."[37]

Taught by such rebukes that there were no percentages in publicly advocating more than the right of African-Americans to live and work within the scheme ordained by the rich and powerful South and North, Washington increasingly moderated his moderation—the duties of the race rather than the rights it was denied were tirelessly, anecdotally emphasized. "When it gets down to hard pan," he told his northern mainstay T. Thomas Fortune, "it is hard to give an individual or race influence that it does not intrinsically possess." To his credit, whenever pinned down about fundamental rights, Washington, in statements usually cast in the negative and balanced on the faults of both races, declined to renounce outright the protections under the Fourteenth and Fifteenth Amendments of the Constitution. "I do not favor the Negro's giving up anything which is fundamental and which has been guaranteed to him by the Constitution," he stated on one notable occasion. "It is not best for him to relinquish his rights; nor would his doing so be best for the Southern white man." But it was quiet diplomacy and practical deeds that mattered. He came to expect the same approach from others, sincerely believing and publicly advising that what men and women said about racial injustice was more often than not unwise and, in any case, less important than what they did. The Wizard's white ghostwriter and future Chicago University sociologist Robert Park recalled that, after fifteen minutes or more ticking off firsthand instances of racial cruelty in the South, his new employer calmly interrupted to suggest that Park spend his time figuring out what to do about them.[38]

Although only a few influential white men and women within the Tuskegee inner circle knew of it at the time, historians have now unearthed the Wizard's impressive record of secret civil rights maneuverings. "Pitchfork Ben" Tillman, Tom Watson, James Vardaman, and the South's other redneck populists went to their graves never suspecting that much of the organized resistance to the extinction of the African-American as a civil being originated in the upstairs study of Tuskegee's principal. Having spoken directly to the Louisiana legislature about voting rights in 1898, he worked behind the scenes to raise legal fees from wealthy whites in an unsuccessful effort to test the constitutionality of Louisiana's grandfather clause in the courts. He played the same covert role three years later in his own state of Alabama, failing again with the legislature, but doggedly lobbying and funneling monies for a legal assault on the state's new disfranchisement clauses. He reached out to the antidisfranchisement forces in Maryland, where, for a change, they were strong enough to win. Court battles against Pullman car discrimination on the railroads in Tennessee, Georgia, and Virginia had his full if invisible backing—usually through the screen of the Afro-American Council. Lawyers fighting racial exclusion from juries in Alabama and Texas looked to him for a portion of their retainers. He savored a rare victory in a hard-fought, infamous case involving Alonzo Bailey, a dirt-poor Alabama farmer forcibly returned to his white employer's farm, having had the cheek to leave owing twenty dollars. The U.S. Supreme Court, grown somnolent in matters involving the rights of black people and laborers, finally roused itself to outlaw peonage (enslavement by contract), although the apparent technicalities were such that the court was unable to find a remedy for Mr. Bailey's specific predicament. Hardly surprising, then, that less than a month after seeking endorsement for the assistant superintendency in the District of Columbia, a furious Du Bois was writing Washington about hauling the Southern Railway before the Interstate Commerce Commission for its refusal to sell him a sleeping berth on account of race.[39]

Being leader of his race was more than a notion, Washington must often have thought, sighing, off the record, that in a two-year period he "spent at least four thousand dollars in cash, out of my own pocket . . . in advancing the rights of the black man." But if all the machination, manipulation, and dissembling had had no higher purpose than the mere physical survival of black people in the South, as well as the greater glory of Tuskegee Institute, Booker Washington's program would not have been so much tragic as pathetic. If he was the Machiavelli of the Black Belt, the Wizard of Tuskegee, like his Renaissance precursor, dreamed of noble ends even as he schemed ignobly. As his biographer discloses, Washington believed—and he had to believe it absolutely—that he personified the Faustian bargain into which his people had entered with the best elements of the white South and the wealthiest elements of the white North. The deal had been sealed at Atlanta in 1895: in exchange for docility in politics and discipline in work (and not even a whisper of social equality), African-Americans in the South were guaranteed due process in law, book learning for life's routines, and the opportunity to prosper economically, while the North, released from any moral, political, and constitutional duty to meddle, would provide money and personnel to make Henry Woodfin Grady's New South dream a reality.[40]

The deal was struck with the survivors of the old planter class and the allied new class of bankers, mill owners, railroad vice-presidents, mine owners, and furnishing merchants who had reclaimed the South from Reconstruction. Heterogeneous in background and disputatious in politics, they were variously called "Redeemers" or "Bourbons" or "Conservatives." Until the early 1890s, what had united them was a strategy (masterfully implemented by the likes of Mississippi senator Lucius Quintus Lamar and South Carolina governor Wade Hampton) of using poor black people to control poor white people and their rising cousins. By poll taxes, residency requirements, literacy laws, stuffed ballot boxes, and a host of discriminatory devices, the conservatives had tilted the electoral process heavily in their favor, disfranchising as many as a fourth of the white males who otherwise could have voted in many of the states of the former Confederacy. Twice as many if not more African-Americans were excluded in the same way—and by stronger measures ranging from economic reprisals to vigilante mayhem. Reliable estimates put the number of African-Americans in the South still voting by the early 1890s near 40 percent. Yet for many lower-class whites for whom the ballot had been an obstacle instead of a passport to advancement, this was far too many. For other whites determined to hold on to power or to challenge it, the rump African-American vote remained a temptation and, not infrequently, a trump card. "The greatest danger that threatens Democratic supremacy in the South," a leading white newspaper warned in 1883, "is that the 'out' faction always gravitates toward the Negro and secures his aid to rout the 'ins.' "[41] With the economic downturn beginning in the late 1880s, this situation had become volatile, with hardscrabble white people mobilizing behind Populist candidates and formerly quiescent black people awakening to their new balance-of-power opportunities. Overproduction had driven cotton from its 1870 high of twenty-nine cents a bale to five cents by 1890, threatening to drag Bourbon hegemony down with it. This had always been the white supremacist's nightmare, one inherent in southern politics so long as the African-American survived as a voter; and now loomed the even greater specter of a black and white coalition of empowered farmers.

It did not happen, and ten years after Booker Washington famously spoke in Atlanta, the nightmare and the specter were fast receding from the southern white consciousness. Where 130,344 African-Americans had been registered voters in Louisiana in 1896, 5,320 remained on the rolls four years later. After 1900, there were some 3,000 registered voters in Alabama out of a black male voting-age population of 181,471. Constitutional conventions in one southern state after another had, by 1910, "counted the Negro down and out," as one politician put it. Poor white people no longer needed to battle against Bourbon rule shored up by the Negro. The conservatives no longer needed dread biracial coalitions of taxing and regulating farmers. And so it became the task of the Wizard of Tuskegee to sanction what in any case he had absolutely no power to prevent—to sell it as a bargain, a compromise, an accommodation; to denounce and renounce the so-called Reconstruction experiment and hold out seductive prospects of a distant but realizable racial parity based on the unifying dollar rather than the divisive ballot. "Harmony will come in proportion as the black man gets something the white man wants," he preached. "Any movement for the elevation of the Southern Negro in order to be successful, must have to a certain extent the cooperation of the Southern whites. They control the government and own the property."[42]

But the fatal flaw in the bargain was that the conservatives who controlled the legislatures in the 1895 South were even then losing power or being forced to share more of it with the rising radicals. The courtly squires of antebellum days—the Haygoods, Currys, Hamptons, and Lamars (even Governor Oates who gave the Tuskegee dressing-down)— were in retreat across Dixie before the Vardamans, Aycocks, Heflins, and Tillmans. Conservative disfranchisement, historian Joel Williamson has written, had been "marked by a willingness to leave the best of the blacks enfranchised and, conversely, to disfranchise the worst of the whites." Vardaman of Mississippi, his lustrous brown hair flying, spoke plainly for the radicals: "I am just as opposed to Booker Washington as a voter, with all his Anglo-Saxon reenforcements, as I am to the coconut-headed, chocolate-colored, typical little coon, Andy Dotson, who blacks my shoes every evening."[43] As these men and their followers captured the statehouses, the margin of maneuver for African-Americans would dwindle almost to nothing, not only in the political sphere but also in practically every other arena.

But it was not at first the unraveling of the politics of accommodation that outraged Du Bois and the small number of mostly northern, urban, and college-educated men and women soon to be known as the Talented Tenth. Washington's stratagem had seemed plausible enough—at least for a time—as a political approach to race relations. But its cultural dimensions dismayed and finally alienated those African-Americans (like Du Bois, Towns, Hope, Trotter, Chicago social reformer Ida Wells-Barnett, and others) for whom higher education was not merely a passport to social and professional standing but the master key to collective empowerment as well. When the Great Accommodator derided Latin and philosophy and French on platforms across the country, Du Bois felt mocked in the very center of his considerable self-significance. "The proud fop with his beaver hat, kid gloves, and walking cane" was the bane, said Washington, of the practical black men of goodwill intent upon spreading the gospel of industrial education in the South. "I believe dis darkey am called to preach," the punch line of another of the Wizard's platform favorites, colorfully reinforced the stereotype of shiftless Negroes ever ready to dodge useful labor.[44] Increasingly, it seemed to Du Bois, darky jokes were giving way to jokes about high-falutin' city types. Du Bois and his peers might agree with

Washington that a dollar in hand was worth far more to most of their people than a box seat at the opera, but they bridled when the Wizard suggested that higher degrees were a cover for distinguished indolence.

Interestingly, the Wizard gave Hampton students their 1898 commencement marching orders just as Du Bois returned to Fisk for the first time in ten years on a similar mission. Echoing Washington, he told Fiskites that African-Americans must grow into "a source of strength and power instead of a menace and a burden to the nation." "Captains of industry" were desperately needed. Du Bois stressed repeatedly on that day that a great variety of educations and occupations had to be fostered. But if all honest labor was essential, his "Careers Open to College-Bred Negroes" made it clear that Fisk men and women were not meant to be Pullman porters. "Even the higher branches of house-service . . . and the great field of skilled labor" were to be left to the skilled graduates of our "great industrial schools," he advised. They must understand that Fisk was special, that they were destined to go forth to sound the trumpet awakening their "dark historic race." With old classmate Proctor on the dais, Du Bois recalled his exaltation ten commencement mornings past. Winding up on an elitist note that Washington would never have played at Hampton or Tuskegee, he commanded, "Remember next that you are gentlemen and ladies, trained in the liberal arts and subjects in that vast kingdom of culture that has lighted the world from its infancy and guided it through bigotry and falsehood and sin."[45] Du Bois's concept of a saving elite took another step toward completion that morning.

In the role of educator, then, Washington was becoming too much for Du Bois to bear. Conflict hung over both men like heavily seeded clouds, although the year 1901 seemed to be passing with a fair prospect of no cloudburst until *Up From Slavery* appeared. The March edition of the *Atlantic Monthly* carried Du Bois's scholarly, historical evaluation of the work of the Freedmen's Bureau. In June, another piece of Black Belt scholarship, "The Negro As He Really Is," appeared in *World's Work*. That same month saw his very favorable *Harper's Weekly* article on the accomplishments of the Tuskegee conferences, further indication of social scientist Du Bois seemingly too busy for the passions and distractions of partisanship.[46] Meanwhile, *Up From Slavery*, ghostwritten by Max Bennett Thrasher, a white Vermont newspaperman and released by Doubleday, Page and Company in late February, was a stupendous success. "Negro" was rendered in upper case (almost unprecedented for a major publishing house). The story was vintage American: faith in God and hard, hard work overcoming bleakest adversity. The cast of edifying characters included an unlettered, devoted mother, aristocratic and kindly white families, the white matron who admitted him to Hampton after a parlor-sweeping examination, father-figure General Armstrong and his "gospel of the tooth-brush," the visionary ex-slave, Lewis Adams, who negotiated Tuskegee's existence, Washington's self-sacrificing wives, and good friend Andrew Carnegie.

William Dean Howells, called by some the dean of American letters, was enthusiastic in his long *North American Review* praise of author Washington, noting somewhat critically only that the Tuskegee principal evinced "rather more tolerance for the rich than the New Testament expresses." Du Bois's old professor, Barrett Wendell, trumpeted the autobiography's "manly distinctness," and the U.S. commissioner of education judged it "one of the great books of the year." Industrialist George Eastman's rave review reached Tuskegee in the form of a check and a message: "I cannot dispose of five thousand dollars to any better advantage than to send it to you for your institute."[47] Then came a review of the book in the July 16 issue of *Dial* unlike any other. "It is as though Nature must needs make men a little narrow to give them force," Du Bois began tersely. Neither originality nor sophistication had propelled Washington to the leadership of his race. Industrial education was already a full-blown doctrine before Washington became an educator. Racial accommodation had been advocated and practiced long before he was anointed the Great Accommodator. This leader's singularity lay elsewhere, in Washington's astute reading of his age, his native understanding of his region, and in the "unlimited energy and perfect faith he put into this programme"—his changing of "a by-path into a Veritable Way of Life." Conceding the "honest purpose which is accomplishing something," Du Bois fair-mindedly recalled the stubborn, instinctive opposition to Washington's work among those anchored to the older abolitionist faith and others suspicious of southern white people. Who but Washington had ever before possessed the "tact and power" to command "not simply the applause of those who believe in his theories, but also the respect of those who do not[?]" The danger of all this, however, was that the success of Washington's ideas threatened to overwhelm perspective and proportion. The nub of the concern was that Washington had "learned so thoroughly the speech and thought of triumphant commercialism . . . that he pictures as the height of absurdity a black boy studying a French grammar in the midst of weeds and dirt. One wonders," Du Bois asked with rhetorical mischief, "how Socrates or St. Francis of Assisi would receive this!"[48]

The real task that Du Bois set himself in the *Dial* review was twofold: first, to demystify Washington by placing his leadership in the context of the sociology of politics; and, second, to identify and explicate for mainstream America the existence within Afro-America of a loyal opposition to Washington. The means by which groups select their champions was one of the "nicest problems of social growth," Professor Du Bois disclosed. For "beleaguered" or "imprisoned groups" the structure of survival could take three main forms—revolt and revenge, accommodation to the major group, or self-development. Washington's was simply one of the possible leadership paradigms. Toussaint L'Ouverture, Richard Allen, Nat Turner, Blanche Bruce, and Frederick Douglass represented other leadership models. African-American leadership selection was peculiarly vulnerable to distortion and cooptation by the majority group. Coming "with a clear simple programme at the psychological moment," the Wizard was a phenomenon of a time when the nation was a little ashamed of having "bestowed so much sentiment on Negroes and was concentrating on dollars." Du Bois spelled out the who and why of the opposition, which must have come as unwelcome news to most white readers. This opposition was committed to self-determination, a "large and important group represented by Dunbar, Tanner, Chesnutt, Miller, and the Grimkés." These men and women believed "in the higher education of Fisk and Atlanta Universities; they believe in self-assertion and ambition; and they believe in the right of suffrage for blacks on the same terms with whites." This "important group" was not at all large, and its members were little known, but, in announcing what they stood for, Du Bois had fired the opening salvo in the war between the Tuskegee Machine and the Talented Tenth.

11.
THE SOULS OF BLACK FOLK

ALMOST ONE year to the day after publication of his review of *Up From Slavery*, in mid-July 1902, Du Bois received an unusually sympathetic letter from Booker T. Washington. *The Outlook* had just carried Du Bois's editorial on southern public school conditions, a piece the Tuskegee principal apparently thought much of, and he went on to praise the "hard work" behind the Atlanta University investigations. Washington's communiqué was also a much-delayed reply to Du Bois's note that March explaining that a northern lecture tour had kept him from attending the annual Tuskegee conference. In that note Du Bois had seemed to hint at a tactical understanding between them. Washington had to grant, he wrote, that he, Du Bois, had "sought in every way to minimize the breach between colleges and industrial schools and [had] tried in all possible ways to cooperate with Tuskegee in its work." Unfortunately, Tuskegee had not entirely reciprocated, Du Bois thought. "You may feel that you are not very much encouraged in your efforts," Washington's July letter purred, but he wanted the professor to know that his labors were appreciated.[1] Superficially fine in sentiment, the Wizard's letter also served to remind Du Bois of how isolated and impotent he really was. After he had turned down the Tuskegee professorship in April 1900, ever-more-powerful forces—forces profoundly unsympathetic to his aspirations—were reshaping the higher education of African-Americans.

In the white South, these forces spoke derisively of the very notion of higher education for black people; some of them barely conceded even the utility of the three R's. In the North, the new creed found more euphemistic expression, such as that issuing from the 1896 conference on "the higher education of the colored people" at Saratoga, New York, in early September. Reporting to philanthropist and Hampton Institute trustee George Foster Peabody (cousin of the Peabody Fund founder) on this watershed conclave, Baptist H. L. Wayland of Philadelphia was delighted by the new thinking. Booker Washington had spoken at Saratoga "admirably" about the need for practical education and for getting away from the liberal arts and Latin. A few sentimentalists like General T. J. Morgan and Rhode Island's Episcopal Bishop William MacVickar still pushed for Greek and Latin and refused "to take counsel with common sense," regretted Wayland, but they were now clearly in the minority. As an officer of the Baptist Home Mission Society, Wayland himself had argued at Saratoga a duty "to give them [the colored people] what we conscientiously think best, and it is our right to do so since we pay for it ourselves." If schools like Atlanta and Fisk continued with dead languages, then the Baptists would simply withdraw funding from their students "and give it to the support of Baptist young men at Hampton and Tuskegee."[2]

When Du Bois received Washington's compliments about his piece in *The Outlook*, the work of the new educational creed was already being mightily advanced by two new foundations. Supplementing and soon absorbing the work of the Peabody and Slater funds were the Southern Education Board (SEB), founded in 1901, and the prodigiously endowed General Education Board (GEB), established early the following year. A partial roster of the officers and trustees of the new SEB was a roll call of the arbiters of the Industrial North and the New South: Robert C. Ogden, director of New York's new Wanamaker's department store; William H. Baldwin, Jr., of railroads North and South; George Foster Peabody of Wall Street and Episcopalian benignity; Charles D. McIver, president of the Southern Educational Association; North Carolinian Walter Hines Page of Doubleday, Page and Company, publishers, and future ambassador to the Court of Saint James; Daniel Gilman of Johns Hopkins University; and Jabez Curry, Edgar Gardner Murphy, and Charles William Dabney, three distinguished southern educators and moderates. In terms of budget, the SEB was a relatively modest enterprise operating on an annual subsidy of less than sixty thousand dollars from the GEB. Its role was primarily one of scrutiny, advice, propaganda, and lobbying for public funding of education, not direct disbursement of funds to institutions. Eleven of the SEB's officers sat continually on the board of the GEB, influencing policy in all matters pertaining to African-Americans.[3]

Jabez Curry, whose spare frame bore saber slashes from Confederate cavalry campaigns, recorded in his diary the historic New York dinner at which the junior Rockefeller pledged one million dollars of his father's money to start the GEB. The setting that evening could hardly have been more propitious for interregional understanding—an oak-paneled study with the fire in the great hearth reflecting in generous brandy snifters. "Meeting harmonious and every vote unanimous," Curry noted. "We sat until after midnight."[4] There were to be many such evenings and many more millions—a head-spinning $52 million bestowed by John D. Rockefeller, Sr., between June 1905 and July 1909. Reverend Frederick Taylor Gates, spiritual counselor to the Baptist Rockefellers, had warned the cadaverous patriarch that, unless some institutional means of disbursing them were devised, the obscene piling up of millions would bring ruin upon the family. A legion of muckrakers had already declared open season on the God-fearing founder of Standard Oil and his robber-baron fraternity. Gates's solution to Rockefeller social and spiritual disquietude was in what he called "scientific giving" (a variation of Carnegie's principle of "scientific philanthropy"), primarily through the GEB.[5]

The impact of the board was unprecedented as it substituted for a nonexistent federal department of education. Its cautious decisions at 61 Broadway (an easy stroll to Rockefeller headquarters at 26 Broadway) were paramount in matters of endowment, capital construction, professional schools, fields of specialization, and fellowships for scholars. Twenty-eight years after its founding, the GEB would have distributed $176,984,000 to historically white colleges and universities and $21,999,349 to those serving African-Americans (although less than $1 million would be allocated to the latter until after World War I).[6] Something of a visionary with a morbid fear of germs and a greater faith in science than in the dogmas of his Baptist denomination, the compelling Gates chose a former New York postal clerk to run the Leviathan GEB. Wallace Buttrick was forty-nine, a large man with a slim theological education, affable and cautious, and thoroughly ignorant of the South and of black people everywhere. Soon after taking up the executive secretaryship, a troubled Buttrick confided that, while the dictates of "absolute justice" should reserve a proportionate share of GEB largesse to African-Americans, the philanthropy would risk destruction if it demanded "too much from the white people of the South."[7]

That was exactly how the GEB's first chairmen, Baldwin and Ogden, saw the matter. Looking back after sixty years, Raymond B. Fosdick, the last chairman, would admit that Baldwin's conviction that African-Americans "could not be educated much beyond the three R's" was slightly surprising in a Bostonian of abolitionist pedigree. Fosdick could explain it only by underscoring the "vast revolution of ideas and social habits [that] has swept over the decades since."[8] Baldwin and Ogden were determined to let nothing impede the regional reconciliation and southern modernization that their kind of educational policy and capital investment was intended to foster. Their supreme faith in the path they were exhorting others to follow led them to impute wicked and dangerous motives to those who insisted on traveling another route. George Foster Peabody, now retired to Abenia, his Lake George estate, usually urged more kindly dealings with the misguided; but, in the final analysis, he invariably leant his considerable influence to the promotion of the Ogden-Baldwin monopoly in African-American education. Although Washington was not invited to deliberate with them when the new foundations were conceived, Baldwin duly informed the Tuskegeean of his appointment as a salaried field agent of the SEB.[9] Poker-faced, devious, honored by Harvard, Yale, and Amherst, graced with a special relationship to Presidents McKinley and Roosevelt, and supreme gatekeeper of rewards, Washington was now assigned the part of disciplinarian of truant African-Americans.

Yet even in their era of Anglo-Saxon election, Billy Baldwin and Bob Ogden had critics among their own ranks, men and women like Boston Brahmin Francis Garrison, Manhattan journalist-entrepreneur John Edgar Milholland, and New York reformer Mary Ovington who pleaded that deeply disadvantaged people needed more, not less, education and employment and that enlightened northern interests must hold fast to the distinction between principled collaboration with the white South and frantic appeasement of it. These Old Believers, as they might have been labeled, saw the influence of Baldwin and Ogden as eventually ruinous to the cause of the African-American and, ironically, eventually fatal to Booker Washington. "You cannot educate men, even in manual skill," William Garrison, Jr., warned the Wizard, "and fit them to occupy the menial position that a caste community (like the South) decrees." Milholland, one of the country's most successful businessmen and a staunch defender of civil liberties, issued similar warnings.[10]

In fairness to Baldwin, Ogden, and the younger Peabody, whose considerable Yankee energies and a portion of whose fortunes went into the cause of racial conciliation, what they were attempting was inherently thankless and unknowingly flawed in theory. In their vision of a racially placid South with a two-tiered, complementary work force, black people as well as white would prosper gradually, capital would flow into the region and handsome profits would flow out of it, and, at some distant point, civil rights and political democracy would be restored. To the extent that Baldwin, Ogden, and the others genuinely embraced that vision, they were extravagantly sanguine. They insisted on ignoring the raw scramble for resources in the region, the irresistible temptations for politicians to exploit class and race, and thus they were bewildered when confronted with that crimson factor of which northern philanthropists lived in awful dread and could never fully comprehend—the South's peculiar, underdeveloped mentality of violence and irrationality. The occasional insight—such as Ogden's that the South "is not yet through with the effort to reenslave the Negro"—never counterbalanced the belief that public criticism of southern white extremism would only make matters much worse. Moreover, from SEB headquarters in Montgomery, Alabama, the young, easily depressed executive secretary, Episcopal clergyman Edgar Gardner Murphy, would keep up a steady tattoo of alarums about powder kegs, tinder boxes, uncontrollable passions, and other quotidian southern dangers. "It is useless—utterly useless—to challenge it," he cautioned in report after report.[11]

If their postabolitionist assumptions about the South conveniently rationalized its inequality and repression, Baldwin, Ogden, and Peabody would have shrilly protested the inference of bad faith. Like the revered Rockefeller Senior, they, too, rejoiced to find in the precepts of Carnegie's "Gospel of Wealth" article the justification for business and social behavior that was second nature anyhow. Intense individualism was good and produced great wealth, but enormous wealth, Carnegie had warned, carried with it the awesome duty of administering wealth "for the common good . . . through the hands of the few."[12] Above all, therefore, Ogden, Baldwin, and their collaborators labored to bring prosperity to the South in order to bring prosperity to themselves—which is not to say that the Ogdens and Baldwins schemed to turn a profit directly from their good works. Rather, they subscribed to a secular brand of Calvinism that anticipated compensation in ways large, indirect, and delayed as signals from a pleased Providence of their election. In making the South a place where commerce and industry flourished, they were contributing to the greater prosperity of the American commonwealth—and thus, inevitably, to the value of their own myriad, interlocked investments. There had been a few temptations for immediate gain at the outset, but they had been resisted. On becoming one of General Armstrong's earliest trustees, Ogden had toyed briefly with a late-1870s scheme to supply Wanamaker's of Philadelphia with calico shirts produced by cheap black laborers trained and supervised by Hampton student teachers. "The fact speaks for itself," Ogden's enthusiastic expert at Hampton had advised. Northern manufacturers could be underbid by the skill the students provided. "In fact," Ogden's man ventured, "you could be able to work in more student labour than you would imagine, for . . . they seem to be even more quick to learn than the average outside hand."[13]

Baldwin and Ogden never ceased to enjoin black people in the South to fill menial positions and to farm land they would seldom own so that white people could monopolize the industrial and urban sectors. They spoke of the migration of black people from the countryside to the South's new cities and towns as the greatest of calamities, a phenomenon bound to imperil "racial harmony" and good business. The pulse of the New South was urban, nonpaternalistic, industrial, stimulated by the Atlantas, Birminghams, Charlottes, Durhams, and Spartanburgs, and other Piedmont factory and textile towns—expanding centers where low-income white and black people rubbed each other raw in public spaces and voting booths.[14] Mass migration of African-Americans to the cities and towns of the South meant continual political turbulence and the nourishment of demagogues pledged to save the region from "nigger rule." Bad as conditions were, pragmatic northern philanthropists like Baldwin, Ogden, Peabody, and others saw worse coming: the erection of an ironclad system of legal and physical apartheid, the coming of Jim Crow with its quadruple public bathrooms, special trains and tramways, separate restaurants and hotels, double waiting rooms, color-coded drinking fountains—an absurd array of artificial distinctions prohibitive to cost-effective business.[15]

By 1902, Ogden's stake in the New South was unique. If the ebullient Peabody exemplified the northern businessman who devoted large amounts of time to philanthropy in the South, Ogden's business *was* philanthropy. Baldwin remained the man of affairs deeply involved in southern good works, but Ogden became northern philanthropy's special emissary, devoting a good portion of his tax-free annual salary of a hundred thousand dollars to the region. Others sent money; Ogden sent himself. In 1900, he became president of the Conference for Education in the South, a two-year-old conclave at Capon Springs, West Virginia, using the Lake Mohonk meetings as its model and taking place under the guidance of Edgar Gardner Murphy. "In the Negro is the opportunity of the South," alter ego Baldwin declared at the second Capon Springs meeting—a statement that could have served as the motto for what became widely known as the "Ogden Movement."[16] Ogden now applied to his movement the business and public-relations abilities that had pushed Wanamaker's to the front rank of American department stores. The first "Ogden Special" sped out of New York City the third week in April 1901, to be followed every April for the next eight years by a special Pullman caravan rolling through the South to the conference meeting sites, halting a few hours at principal white and black colleges and universities to disgorge the Anglo-Saxon Protestant power elite of the United States.

White college presidents all but threw themselves across the tracks to stop the Ogden Special. "The Davidson [College] campus is less than one hundred yards from the station," Dr. Henry Louis Smith telegraphed Ogden, pleading for a visit. "The rapid disappearance of sectionalism," President Abercrombie of the University of Alabama swore, was "in large measure due to your labor."[17] At Hampton Institute, Rockefellers, Doubledays, Macys, Phelps-Stokeses, Villards, Plimptons, Pages, and other families rested a day or more in the campus's guest house, watched the cadets drill, and thrilled to the student choir's spirituals. "Hope you can arrange program and remain at Tuskegee until 12:45 or 1 o'clock," Washington telegraphed as the fourth special approached, for so keen was the competition that not even his campus was guaranteed a place in the itinerary—though this time Ogden penciled across the bottom, "Will stay another hour." The popularity of these excursions into the exotic South was enormous. The junior Rockefeller continued to hope that he and Mrs. Rockefeller "might enjoy a repetition of the pleasure which I derived" on the first sortie in 1901.[18] It was, he added, "the most instructive experience of my life." Ogden had successfully floated the plan for the SEB amid the plush and copious provisions of that first caravan, receiving assurances of Rockefeller support. Not even the crash of the 1905 Special near Greenville, South Carolina, from which Mrs. Henry Farnam emerged with a broken nose and Jabez Curry minus his Bible (Ogden covered all damages), dampened enthusiasm. An indignant Ogden did contemplate disbanding the Specials after southern white criticism began likening them, as one New Jersey clergyman wrote him, to "driving a coach and six to give charity and . . . misleading the Negroes." The delicate Murphy persuaded him not to do so, however.[19]

For Ogden, much more than for Baldwin, the successful policy was one that was micromanaged. As he said to Murphy, speaking of the Negro problem: "We cannot meet the views of our colored friends and must be content to be greatly misunderstood." Were Dr. William Crum to withdraw his name before the Senate took up his confirmation as Charleston customs collector, Ogden told the Great Accommodator, it would be seen as "a stroke of wise and triumphant policy." He approved Tuskegee trustee Henry C. Davis's second thoughts about the principal's presence in New York at the Union League dinner in Edgar Murphy's honor. Courtesy demanded that alumnus Washington be invited to attend Hampton's anniversary unveiling of busts honoring white donors, but Ogden advised Principal Frissell that he thought it would "be in line of delicacy for [Washington] to decline." When Washington finally complained loudly about being shut out of SEB deliberations, Baldwin decided not to forward the principal's letter to Ogden "because it would seem like a criticism."[20]

Since Ogden's feelings about African-American liberal arts schools, especially Atlanta University, verged on pure hatred, the Special steamed through Georgia without the pilgrims bothering to visit the Atlanta University campus. "Your fellow-travellers were so strongly—not to say bitterly—prejudiced against it," Francis Garrison angrily noted in a letter to Oswald Villard after his nephew's return from the 1902 excursion. "When the Ogden party visited Atlanta last year, they deliberately ignored the University." Ogden's animus was reinforced by associates like Murphy who warned that visiting black liberal arts colleges was tantamount to waving Union battle flags before Confederate infantry. "It would be a serious mistake to go to Talladega [College], at all, at this time," the clergyman would write before the 1904 Special left New York. With Tom Heflin, Alabama's star Negrophobe, fulminating that election year, "battle lines [were] now slowly forming," Murphy bleated.[21]

With so much at stake, the men behind the SEB and the GEB displayed considerable skill in spotting potential troublemakers. "The control was to be drastic," Du Bois claimed in *Dusk of Dawn*. "The Negro intelligentsia was to be suppressed and hammered into conformity. The process involved some cruelty and disappointment, but that was inevitable."[22] Cosmopolitans like Du Bois, espousing higher learning for African-Americans, embodied all the deracination and uppityness bred by the cities. The foundation notables and their peers increasingly looked upon him with his haughty self-assurance and compellingly written findings and opinions as an intolerable sport. As suspicion turned into hostility, the formidable suasion of the SEB and the unprecedented resources of the GEB were applied to marginalize a thirty-five-year-old academic whose only defenses were a brain, a pen, and audacity.

IN THE Bookerite scheme of things, Du Bois was a minor irritant with the capacity for major damage, unless he were coopted or neutralized. Frissell's vague proposal early in 1900 for a scholarly journal at Hampton had died shortly after Du Bois insisted on being the sole judge of its editorial policy. Much later, Du Bois wondered if more diplomacy on his part might not have won him a free editorial hand, but, upon further reflection, he doubted it—"any magazine launched at that time would have been seriously curtailed in its freedom of speech."[23] Then, a little more than a month after Washington sent him a "personal and confidential" promise to help defray the legal expenses connected with his railroad segregation case before the ICC ("provided I can hand it to you personally"), an invitation to an early January 1903 interracial conference in New York came from Wallace Buttrick. The conference was badly set up, with Buttrick and several others who were expected to attend making only perfunctory appearances, although Baldwin, who presided, seemed genuinely pleased, convinced that the meeting was a promising step toward the establishing of a permanent organization. In fact, the Mount Olivet Church meeting did eventually lead to something more—the National Urban League—but in Du Bois's version, *he* was the central issue, and the late-afternoon Conference on the Negro in New York City was mainly a smokescreen. He found himself in Baldwin's cordial care, whisked from the West Fifty-third Street church to a sumptuous dinner with Ruth Standish Baldwin on their Long Island estate. "Both he and his wife insisted that my place was at Tuskegee," that the school needed the Atlanta professor's training and intelligence. The Baldwins were accomplished persuaders, a combination of steel and velvet (a Smith College alumna, Ruth Baldwin thrived on causes, becoming the National Urban League's first president); Du Bois very likely returned to Manhattan aboard the GEB chairman's railroad pledged to reopen the Tuskegee option.[24]

Two meetings with the Wizard are supposed to have taken place in New York, presumably at the end of 1902 and early the following year. Du Bois's description of them was satirically and dramatically triumphant, but it fails to square with the facts. He wrote as though he and Washington were complete strangers. "He did not know me, and I think he was suspicious," wrote Du Bois. "On the other hand, I was quick, fast-speaking and voluble. I found at the end of the first interview that I had done practically all the talking. . . . In fact, Mr. Washington had said as near nothing as possible." On his guard during their second encounter, Du Bois claimed that he held his tongue, with the result that the two of them sat together in almost complete silence. Had the New York interviews occurred before 1901, Du Bois's re-creation would be credible, but giveaway references to Buttrick and the GEB fix the time frame as post 1902, and by then there had been much letter writing, several public encounters, and at least two visits (February 1900 and 1901) to the Tuskegee campus.[25] Of greater significance, there had been the painfully fishy business of the D.C. assistant superintendency.

Either these two fateful meetings occurred much earlier than Du Bois remembered (before the evening at the Baldwins and before the creation of the two education boards), in which case they lose some of their sinister power in the retelling, or, more plausibly, they are imaginative rearrangements of actual fragments, composite truths, throwing into stark relief the hostility faced by Du Bois and his circle in Booker T. Washington's America. Du Bois's representation is one of mental and moral estrangement that was almost molecular—an oil-and-water antinomy making misunderstanding and conflict inevitable. But if Du Boisian license cast Washington as the straight man in their epic rough-and-tumble routine, the Columbia University oral history, almost sixty years later, may have been as accurate as a GEB ledger: "Oh, Washington was a politician. He was a man who believed that we should get what we could get. It wasn't a matter of ideals or anything of that sort. . . . He had no faith in white people, not the slightest, and he was most popular among them, because if he was talking with a white man he sat there and found out what the white man wanted him to say, and then as soon as possible, he said it." That had never been Du Bois's approach to what African-Americans invariably called the other race. Invited to lecture on Atlanta University to the annual and exclusive education conference at Bar Harbor, Maine, in late August 1903, he politely turned aside the Tuskegee counsels of lexicographer Charles Merriam, financier Jacob Schiff, pharmaceuticals heir William Jay Schieffelin, and several others. *Outlook* editor Lyman Abbott was impressed by Du Bois's advocacy of higher education for African-Americans, he told Du Bois at Bar Harbor, but Abbott pleaded with him to rethink racial priorities: "Industrial intelligence is of the first importance."[26]

By then, Du Bois had made up his mind to measure his beliefs against those of Washington. The full implications of what he was about to do, however, may not have been entirely clear. One should believe his repeated insistence that he never wanted to descend from his tower of contemplation and research to lead a protest movement, that he was "no natural leader of men," as well as his admission that, at that time, he was still not "in absolute opposition to the things that Mr. Washington was advocating." He was still keeping a safe distance from the handful of men and women like Harvard classmate Monroe Trotter, successful Chicago attorney and statehouse legislator Edward H. Morris, itinerant philosopher and Yale and Harvard graduate William Ferris, and antilynching crusader and settlement house pioneer Ida Wells-Barnett who mounted platforms to denounce the Atlanta Compromise at every opportunity. Du Bois was far from ready to cry out, as Morris did, that Washington was "largely responsible for the lynching in this country," or even to charge him with willful promotion of the doctrine of black racial inferiority, as Ferris did in early 1903 before the District of Columbia's distinguished Bethel Literary and Historical Association.[27] Du Bois must have also clearly understood that to attack Washington was to mistake shadow for substance, to fall into a trap of internecine battling instead of laying the ground for all-out war on the real enemy—the white people who ordained that an entire race should remain indefinitely subordinate.

The problem with this view was that the Great Accommodator repeatedly thrust himself between the cross hairs of Du Bois's true targets. The Atlanta professor wanted not so much to throw down the gauntlet to the Wizard's leadership as to protest what he perceived as the latter's heavy-handedness in dealing with even the most tentative dissent from the Tuskegee ideology. "Things had come to such a pass," Du Bois insisted many years afterward, "that when any Negro complained or advocated a course of action, he was silenced with the remark that Mr. Washington did not agree with this." As Du Bois saw his people descending rapidly into the caste status of subhumans in the South and into a marginalized mass in the North, the embrace of the Great Accommodator and of his miscreant self-help nostrums increased. Behind the ninety-nine lynchings of 1901, behind what one of his younger disciples would call "The Nadir"—tidal years of African-American disfranchisement and victimization—Du Bois saw a metaphysic of oppression that was both cause and effect. Forty-six years after Judge Roger Brooke Taney's *Dred Scott* opinion that African-Americans were "so far inferior that they had no rights the white man was bound to respect," Du Bois agonized that the humanity of an entire race was again a serious national question.[28]

It was, then, the ethos, science, and propaganda of racial dehumanization as much as Bookerite compromises that unsettled and finally drove

Du Bois into the ranks of so-called civil rights radicals. It was grim enough that his people were being lynched in the South and ghettoized in the North, but there now loomed the even more horrendous prospect that such brutalities could cease to be deplored (however formally or hypocritically) as un-American and become, in the regime of the emergent ideology, officially sanctioned instruments of racial subjugation. With rare exception, noted anthropologists located Negroes somewhere on the frontier between the great apes and hominids. Biologists found their average brain weight less than Caucasians'—considerably less than English-speaking Protestants. Psychologists identified a primal sexuality and irrationality in Negroes that were invariably supposed to erupt in situations of intimacy or stress. Physicians predicted their extinction from disease and depravity, while criminologists and eugenicists warned of the menace of Negro brutality and fecundity. The national white consensus emerging at the turn of the century was that African-Americans were inferior human beings whose predicament was three parts their own making and two parts the consequence of misguided white philanthropy. Not long before serving Booker Washington dinner in the White House, a characteristically blunt Theodore Roosevelt had given a nutshell opinion: "A perfectly stupid race can never rise to a very high plane; the negro, for instance, has been kept down as much by lack of intellectual development as by anything else."

The Mystery Solved: The Negro a Beast was one of the notable book titles of 1900, followed two years later by Thomas Dixon's bestseller, *The Leopard's Spots*, a building block for D. W. Griffith's film *The Birth of a Nation*. One historian of the South claims that the raving romantic Dixon "probably did more to shape the lives of modern Americans than have some Presidents." Du Bois had entered this debate head on with a forthright review in *Dial* of *The American Negro* by William Hannibal Thomas, an eccentric mulatto whose book denouncing his own people had been published in 1901 by Macmillan. It was too unfair, Du Bois wrote, that, just as "a new race literature of a promise has appeared, and a race consciousness such as the modern world has never before seen among black folk," major publishing houses in the United States were giving over their presses to pseudo-scientific and Gothic-romance libels. Whether he felt rage or deep sadness when three years later his old Harvard geology professor's magnum opus appeared, Du Bois left unrecorded. Shaler's *The Neighbor: The Natural History of Human Contacts* was no best-seller, but its amalgam of anthropology, science, and history commended it to serious readers. It asserted that, even under the best conditions, African-Americans would remain civilization's wards.[29] In such a national climate, the inclination among white people to discriminate between well-educated African-Americans and those still marked by slavery was becoming rare.

Du Bois, who, as a student in Germany, had found great appeal in theories that ranked races and invested them with specific attributes, now began fully to grasp their inconvenient implications. The Harvard man who had dismissed the Lodge Bill as unnecessary and betrayed vicarious sympathy for the ruling classes veered in the direction of social and economic democracy, although aristocratic prejudices continued to tug at him. He resolved to write of the genius, humanity, and enviable destiny of his race with such passion, eloquence, and penetration that claims of African-American inferiority would be sent reeling, never to recover full legitimacy and vitality, despite their enormous resiliency.

THE SOULS OF BLACK FOLK, brought out by the Chicago firm of A. C. McClurg and Company on April 18, 1903, redefined the terms of a three-hundred-year interaction between black and white people and influenced the cultural and political psychology of peoples of African descent throughout the western hemisphere, as well as on the continent of Africa. It was one of those events epochally dividing history into a before and an after. Like fireworks going off in a cemetery, its fourteen essays were sound and light enlivening the inert and the despairing. It was an electrifying manifesto, mobilizing a people for bitter, prolonged struggle to win a place in history. Ironically, even its author was among the tens of thousands whose conceptions of themselves were to be forever altered by the book. James Weldon Johnson, a judge of great perspicacity in such matters, said the book's impact was "greater upon and within the Negro race than any other single book published in this country since *Uncle Tom's Cabin*." With comparable perspicacity but less satisfaction, Henry James wondered how things could have run to ground so badly that Du Bois's "was the only 'Southern' book of any distinction published in many a year." Max Weber set about arranging for a German translation, writing Du Bois from Heidelberg that he would be pleased to do the introduction to his "splendid book."[30]

In a rather offhand passage in *Dusk of Dawn* about the genesis of the collection, Du Bois explained that the McClurg company had pressed him during 1902 to write several essays for immediate release as a book. Demurring "because books of essays almost always fall so flat," he finally agreed to gather "a number of my fugitive pieces." As his literary executor, Herbert

Aptheker, has noted, Du Bois's account of the origins of *The Souls of Black Folk* is "excessively modest." Nine of the fourteen essays had seen life previously in major publications of the day—*Atlantic Monthly, Dial, World's Work*—as well as the more specialized *Annals of the American Academy of Political and Social Science* and *New World*, a religious quarterly. But they were to be cut, polished, and mounted with a jeweler's precision for the McClurg collection. A good deal of new material was added in some cases, and themes heightened by new endings. The lyrical sociology of "Of the Black Belt" and "Of the Quest of the Golden Fleece" was decanted from "The Negro As He Really Is," which had appeared in the June 1901 *World's Work*. The polemical centerpiece, "Of Mr. Booker T. Washington and Others," was a deft reworking and expansion of the review of *Up From Slavery* in *Dial*. The five new essays ranged from confessional to fictional; all were intensely literary, and the best of them—"Of the Wings of Atalanta," "Of the Sorrow Songs," and, debatably, "Of Alexander Crummell"—of surpassing emotional power and beauty, while "Of the Passing of the First-Born" and "Of the Coming of John" ran to bathos and crimson. Yet what is weak or less successful in *The Souls of Black Folk* is but relative demerit in an ensemble of transcendent intellectual passion and numinous prose.[31]

Until *The Souls of Black Folk*, the souls of black folk had relied mostly on the sorrow songs—spirituals—to find expression. Du Bois would carry throughout the volume the device of pairing Negro spirituals with European verse—by Browning, Byron, Swinburne, Symons, Tennyson—as epigraphs for each essay. He twinned them in this manner in order to advance the then-unprecedented notion of the creative parity and complementarity of white folk and black folk alike. Du Bois meant the cultural symbolism of these double epigraphs to be profoundly subversive of the cultural hierarchy of his time. Three years into yet another century of seemingly unassailable European supremacy, *Souls* countered with the voices of the dark submerged and unheard—those voices heard by him for the first time in the Tennessee backcountry. Until his readers appreciated the message of the songs sung in bondage by black people, Du Bois was saying, the words written in freedom by white people would remain hollow and counterfeit.

The "Forethought" to *The Souls of Black Folk* has something of the function of a tuning fork, keeping the collection's marvelous prose vibrations in low, perfect pitch. The tone is calmly portentous, as the author settles the reader into his tale of "the strange meaning of being black here at the dawning of the Twentieth Century." Elucidating that meaning, Du Bois pens again the incomparable phrase that leaps from the page into indelible memory: "This meaning is not without interest to you, Gentle Reader; for the problem of the Twentieth Century is the problem of the color-line."[32] "It is hard for us, across the vast expanse of years"—St. Clair Drake, intellectual disciple of Du Bois and author himself of an American classic, would exhort a civil rights era audience—"to appreciate the significance of these words or the courage it took to fling them forth."[33] Du Bois possessed such courage in abundance. He also possessed passion in equal measure—passion mediated by the written word. The shaping empire of intellect reigned over both. From the first page of *The Souls of Black Folk*, Du Bois's mind, courage, and passion interact to create a splendid diapason. It is as though the small hurts and large insults of his own life—the visiting-card incident, the Harvard Glee Club rejection, the dreadful day in Lübeck, the demeaning University of Pennsylvania title—have fused with those of the Sam Hoses and Ida B. Wellses and ten millions more to merge Du Bois, for a noetic moment in history, uniquely with the souls of all black people.

Souls opens with "Of Our Spiritual Strivings." It had been titled "Strivings of the Negro People" in the August 1897 *Atlantic Monthly* version, but its reincarnation here came with more élan and pathos. Du Bois capped it with an epigraph of English poetry and bars from the spiritual "Nobody Knows the Trouble I've Seen." The troubles he and his people had seen, almost from the day the first Africans were brought ashore from a Dutch ship in Jamestown harbor, Du Bois memorably posed as a question in the opening page of the essay. "Between me and the other world there is ever an unasked question: unasked by some through feelings of delicacy; by others through the difficulty of rightly framing it." Posed in whatever form, that question was, finally, "How does it feel to be a problem?" Du Bois announced that he would address that problem from a new, unusual angle. "Leaving, then, the white world, I have stepped within the Veil, raising it that you may view faintly its deeper recesses—the meaning of its religion, the passion of its human sorrow, and the struggle of its greater souls." It was, as Du Bois said, "a tale twice told," but it was being told, and told by him, for the first time in print.

Adopting a mythic, threnodic prose sometimes evocative of the Old Testament, Du Bois illustrated this "strange experience" of being defined as a problem through the traumatic, Great Barrington visiting-card incident. In that "wee wooden schoolhouse" the bright, carefree young boy suddenly discovers that he is forever different from his white peers—"shut out from their world by a vast veil." As in Genesis, wherein innocence in Eden is followed by wisdom, exile, and pain, *Souls* mimics the language of that sweeping record of suffering, wandering, and spiritual triumph. Du Bois contrasts his own persevering adolescence—a David meeting and besting the odds ("But they should not keep these prizes, I said")—with the destroyed lives of so many of the sons of Ham and Job: other black youth "shrunk into tasteless sycophancy, or into silent hatred of the pale world," crying out, "Why did God make me an outcast and a stranger in mine own house?" It was the rare David whose spirit was not compressed and stunted by the "walls strait and stubborn" of race hatred. Between these walls, the "sons of night" had plodded on in resignation, "or beat unavailing palms against the stone."[34]

Du Bois compressed a quarter century of black history into two long, flowing paragraphs in "Of Our Spiritual Strivings," the kind of feat that was to become his signature. Suddenly, personal testimony and lamentation give way to vast tableaux of Sphinxes and African grandeur, then the descent into slavery follows where racial memory was kept vivid by the black preacher until Jubilee Day commenced the heady time of Reconstruction. Faith in the ballot was the first talisman of the freedmen. After the ballot came the "new vision . . . of 'book-learning.' " Blocked and scorned again, it was hoped that the wages of obedient toil and sweat could purchase security and respect. With what results, asked Du Bois? "The bright ideals of the past—physical freedom, political power, the training of brains and the training of hands—all these have waxed and waned, until even the last grows dim and overcast." They had been forced by serial disappointments to reevaluate what they could become, yet the bedrock of black people's work, culture, and liberty must remain the ballot. "The power of the ballot we need in sheer self-defense."[35] Clearly, here, he chose to overestimate the immediate practical value of votes for southern black sharecroppers and day laborers, many of whose ballots would be either controlled or excluded by white planters.

But something more was needed—the race must learn the lesson of the Veil by cultivating the moral and creative energies that lay hidden in the conditions of its very alienation. Scorned and exploited throughout its history in the land of opportunity, his people had gradually undergone a halving of identity, acquired a unique angle of vision, and become habituated to a psychic subordination that handicapped it in the past but could be turned to strengths in its future. This, the primordial condition or dilemma of Du Bois's race, had never been so nakedly exposed before, not even by Crummell. The African-American "ever feels his two-ness—an American, a Negro; two souls, two thoughts, two unreconciled strivings," Du Bois wrote, echoing almost surely his beloved Goethe's words in *Faust* and even possibly those of Ralph Waldo Emerson in "The Transcendentalist." "Two warring ideals in one dark body, whose dogged strength alone keeps it from being torn asunder," he continued, repeating word for word the ardent prose of his *Atlantic Monthly* essay. "The history of the American Negro is the history of this strife—this longing to attain self-conscious manhood, to merge his double self into a better and truer self." Others brooding over the outcast status of their people ultimately wished it away in visions of future racial harmony or heavenly rewards, or, like Douglass, put their faith in full assimilation. A few—Garnet, Delany, Holly—had chosen the path of cultural separatism and expatriation. Debate about what African-Americans were and what they should become had been like a zero-sum game, shuttlecocking between the Integrated Society and the Black Zion. The genius of *The Souls of Black Folk* was that it transcended this dialectic in the most obvious way—by affirming it in a permanent tension. Henceforth, the destiny of the race could be conceived as leading neither to assimilation nor separatism but to proud, enduring hyphenation.

It was a revolutionary conception. It was not just revolutionary; the concept of the divided self was profoundly mystical, for Du Bois invested this double consciousness with a capacity to see incomparably farther and deeper. The African-American—seventh son after the Egyptian and Indian, the Greek and Roman, the Teuton and Mongolian—possessed the gift of "second-sight in this American world," an intuitive faculty (prelogical, in a sense) enabling him/her to see and say things about American society that possessed heightened moral validity. Because he dwelt equally in the mind and heart of his oppressor as in his own beset psyche, the African-American embraced a vision of the commonweal at its best. But the gift was also double-edged—always potentially enervating—because the African-American only saw him/herself reflected from a white surface, "a world which yields him no true self-consciousness, but only lets him see himself through the revelation of the other world." If it was true that large numbers (perhaps even a majority) of the race had never thought of themselves as having such a convoluted, refractive existence, Du Bois's foray into group psychology was certainly valid for those African-Americans (like himself) whose cultural backgrounds predisposed them to hold fast to the values of the dominant class of the dominant society. In all probability, Sam Hose had had a simpler self-concept, one uninfluenced by Hegel and more fixed by a common identity based on color and raw oppression. It is not certain what he would have made of Du Bois's confident prescription—"This, then, is the end of his striving: to be a co-worker in the kingdom of culture." Even as Du Bois assumed the role as its premier advocate, a definite tension (not quite a contradiction) existed, therefore, in the Du Boisian affirmation of the race's soul.

Had Du Bois left double consciousness in this epiphenomenal limbo—as a sort of non-ego or psychic negative pole ("measuring one's soul by the tape of a world that looks on in amused contempt and pity")—the partial legacy of *Souls* would have been one of perpetual, devastated psychic passivity. But Du Bois intended the divided self to be a phenomenon that was spiritually and socially evolving—one that would define itself through struggle and attain "self-conscious manhood" through "strife." The German influences are unmistakable with their suggestion of materializing spirit and dialectical struggle, the whole surging process coming to concretion in *das Volk*—a mighty nation with a unique soul. It is as though the voices of Schopenhauer and Sojourner Truth were blended. The divided self was destined to cohere and to merge, yet, in Du Bois's special vision, "neither of the older selves [shall] be lost." Du Bois deeply believed that, in time, the Negro self would comprehend its true essence and the American self would become, in turn, more robust. What was apparent contradiction, he resolved in the following cogent formula:

> He would not Africanize America, for America has too much to teach the world and Africa. He would not bleach his Negro soul in a flood of white Americanism, for he knows that Negro blood has a message for the world. He simply wishes to make it possible for a man to be both a Negro and an American, without being cursed and spit upon by his fellows, without having the doors of Opportunity closed roughly in his face.[36]

The divided self was, of course, not original with Du Bois. The construct was central to the fiction of Goethe and Chesnutt, two of his favorite writers. Emerson, another favorite, had used the term "double consciousness" in "The Transcendentalist," the 1843 published lecture in which he even characterized the dilemma as one in which the "two lives, of the understanding and of the soul, . . . really show very little relation to each other." But in *Souls* the divided self would not remain flawed, compromised, unstable, or tragic. It would become in time and struggle stronger for being doubled, not undermined—the sum of its parts, not the dividend. Du Bois's concept of racial twoness at the beginning of the twentieth century was profoundly radical. With millions of Europeans arriving from religious and cultural backgrounds strikingly dissimilar to earlier immigrant infusions, Anglo-Saxon Protestant guardians of the established culture recoiled in horror at the idea that there should be alternative versions of what it meant to become an American. Du Bois was a decade ahead of the generation of mainstream younger artists and writers who would express their disenchantment with the Anglo-Saxon cultural paradigm by celebrating immigrants and workers, mounting scandal-raising art shows, launching iconoclastic little magazines, and clamoring for social revolution.[37]

It would be exquisitely fitting if there were some indication that Santayana had catechized Du Bois in that upper room at Harvard about the doom of those who fail to learn from the past; but no such evidence exists. Such admonition was perhaps unnecessary. Those who were gifted with double vision were able to see dilemmas far in the future. "Of the Dawn of Freedom" begins with Du Bois's lines from the Pan-African Congress address about the problem of the twentieth century being the problem of the color line—"the relation of the darker to the lighter races of men in Asia and Africa, in America and the islands of the sea."[38] This problem is the leitmotif of the book, a problem Du Bois examined from the perspective of institutions and ideals, and from that of the educated, the ignorant, the rural hard-pressed, and the urban beleaguered. Based on "The Freedmen's Bureau" in the March 1901 *Atlantic Monthly*, "Of the Dawn of Freedom" was the strongest academic piece in the collection and decades ahead of its time. Scholars then writing of the period condemned the Freedmen's Bureau as an unwise and maladministered experiment in racial uplift in the South. The general public blamed it for engendering harmful, unrealistic expectations of forty acres and a mule among the ex-slaves, as well as for foisting on the South Yankee schoolmarms with their radical teachings, those "horsefaced" secular nuns W. J. Cash would ridicule savagely in *The Mind of the South*. Du Bois argued that the bureau was a revolutionary departure for the nation, an organization whose achievements on balance were impressive and lasting. "For a sum of fifteen million dollars . . . and the dole of benevolent societies, this Bureau set going a system of free labor," he wrote, "established a beginning of peasant proprietorship, secured the recognition of black freedmen before courts of law, and founded the free common school in the South."

The lost possibility of a permanent Freedmen's Bureau might have precluded the wasting problems now racking the South, but Du Bois conceded that such ongoing federal activism was "unthinkable in 1870"—too alien to the political culture of a nation committed to individual initiative and limited government. What is remarkable about "Of the Dawn of Freedom" was the political conservatism still present in Du Bois. Had the South behaved charitably toward the newly emancipated peasants instead of lashing them back into slavery with Black Codes, not only would Reconstruction have been unnecessary but, Du Bois believed, "restricted Negro suffrage" in the South would have been a solution that "every sensible man, black and white, would easily have chosen."[39] Booker Washington could not have said it better.

"Of the Sons of Master and Man," the ninth essay, derived from a 1901 article in the *Annals of the American Academy of Political and Social Science*, might have been taken from a speech by Baldwin or Ogden at a Capon Springs education conference. The focus of the essay was the history and sociology of racial adjustment in the South—the exigent need for "study frank and fair, and not falsified and colored by our wishes and fears." Like the Freedmen's Bureau study, this piece reflected the earlier antidemocratic mindset of an evolving Du Bois. It saw the old, quasi-feudal South being swamped by new classes thrown up by industrial exploitation, with southern gentlemen being pushed aside by Snopeses. Whereas before, the profit motive had been restrained by hierarchy and paternalism, democracy and competition unleashed it in full savagery. Power, Du Bois wrote, "has passed to . . . the sons of poor whites fired with a new thirst for wealth and power, thrifty and avaricious Yankees, and unscrupulous immigrants."[40] In its formulation of southern change in which the fate of both white and black labor was reduced to the "cold question of dollars and dividends," "Of the Sons of Master and Man" suggested something of the later, arbitral interpretations of the historian C. Vann Woodward. Woodward, in *The Origins of the New South*, saw racial segregation as a late development imposed by the South's "new men," mostly sprung from the rednecks. Alluding to that noblesse oblige which he still believed characteristic of dynastic social structures, Du Bois lamented the abrupt decline of the planters in language that may have been embarrassing in later years. Freely acknowledging "that a partially undeveloped people should be ruled by the best of their stronger and better neighbors," he firmly stated that, "if the representatives of the best white Southern public opinion were the ruling and guiding powers in the South today, the conditions indicated would be fairly well fulfilled."[41]

For all his talk of scientific objectivity, some of Du Bois's best scholarship began with intuition, but in this essay authoritarian elitism clouded his usual prescience. Like the perceptive Woodward, later, it did not occur to Du Bois to ask himself if the New South might not be so new in terms of its dominant class structure. Subsequent scholarship would show that a surprisingly large number of race-baiting, rabble-rousing leaders of the period were sons and cousins of the planters and colonels of old. Along with its jarring references to Jewish merchants in the South ("the Jew is the heir of the slave-baron," Jews are "shrewd and unscrupulous foreigners"), "Of the Sons of Master and Man" had a good deal of the regressive Du Bois in it, as well as the evolving civil rights radical. Here was a striking example of that "provincial and narrow thinking" one of his future collaborators noted about Du Bois's early ideas about class and politics.[42]

The two essays "Of the Black Belt" and "Of the Quest of the Golden Fleece," numbers seven and eight in the collection, were adaptations of a long *World's Work* article lacking somewhat in tightness of prose. But, taken with "Of the Meaning of Progress," the elegy to Josie's pastoral time warp, they succeeded in reconstructing a culture and its institutions—the rural South—that were as mysterious to most early twentieth-century readers as Livingstone's Africa. Not since Frederick Law Olmsted crisscrossed the region before the Civil War, graphically recounting its inefficient productivity, its isolation and ignorance, the sparse luxury even among its seigneurs, and the ubiquity of stunted human and natural potential, had there been such a cogent blend of detailed observation and generalization. Du Bois made certain that the sociological novelty of these essays was evident, stating in "Of the Quest of the Golden Fleece" that readers could "only learn by intimate contact with the masses, and not by wholesale arguments covering millions separate in time and space." Roaming forlorn counties and peering into crowded cabins, describing people in misery and misery in people, the visual prowess of the writing drew Du Bois's readers deeper and deeper into "their daily lives and longings . . . their homely joys and sorrows . . . their real shortcomings and the meaning of their crimes!" "The keynote of the Black Belt is debt," Du Bois wrote simply. "The county is rich, yet the people are poor." "The single great advantage of the Negro peasant is that he may spend most of his life outside his hovel, in the open fields," he noted. A short train ride brought Du Bois to the region's largest town. Albany, Georgia, in the heart of the Black Belt, "six days in the week . . . looks decidedly too small for itself, and takes frequent and prolonged naps. But on Saturday suddenly the whole county disgorges itself upon the place, and a perfect flood of black peasantry pours through the place." Riding back to Nashville on the Jim Crow car, he pondered the meaning of his meanderings: "all this life and love and strife and failure—is it the twilight of nightfall or the flush of some faint-dawning day?"[43]

More yet of the subsisting world of slavery was revealed in his original essay, "Of the Sorrow Songs." Du Bois confessed that he knew little of music but "something of men." What he wrote has for the most part stood the test of scholarship, primarily, no doubt, because academic appreciation of the spirituals was for a long time indebted to his pioneering excursion into the sociology of this music—the "great service . . . in his unforgettable chapter," which the learned humanist Alain Locke would extol in his own essay on the spirituals. The once-heated debate about the origins of the spirituals—African or Puritan hymns—might have been briefer had the perceptive analysis of Du Bois's essay been more widely accepted. Distributing his ten master songs along a developmental continuum from Africa to white America, he identified four stages: African music; Afro-American music (slave music); a new form—"a blending of . . . Negro and Caucasian"; and, finally, mainstream music "distinctively influenced by the slave songs." The sorrow songs were, paradoxically, songs of hope, Du Bois explained, expressive of "a deep faith in the ultimate justice of things."

A few lines more and the reader is no longer following a discussion of folk music, for Du Bois used the meaning of the sorrow songs to make a transition to the subject of racial destiny. Sounding a chord he would replay again with more vibrato in his later books *The Negro*, *Darkwater*, and *The Gift of Black Folk*, he scoffed at European presumptions of racial superiority as the "arrogance of peoples irreverent toward Time and ignorant of the deeds of men." A thousand years ago, there were solid grounds for dismissing the possibility "of the blond races ever leading civilization." Arriving before the *Mayflower*, the African in America had sung his sorrow in the key of the Zeitgeist, Du Bois proclaimed. "Around us the history of the land has centered for thrice a hundred years." Not only have they fought for and built this country, the final essay in *The Souls of Black Folk* claims for black folk the perfection "through our song, our toil, our cheer, and our warning" of the real meaning of Justice, Mercy, and Truth among a "headstrong, careless people."[44] The shade of Crummell and the argument of "The Conservation of the Races" filled the closing paragraphs.

Contrary to what Du Bois later claimed, the initial conflict with Washington had been professional and then bitterly personal before it became ideological. Ideological estrangement and the fundamental and enduring rift it created among African-Americans was more in the nature of a consequence rather than a cause. The Du Bois–Washington controversy began with differences in emphases, suspicions and insinuations, and, above all, with doctrinal shaping and hardening in the force fields of two antithetical egos. As Du Bois certainly understood, *The Souls of Black Folk* not only "settled pretty definitely any further question of [his] going to Tuskegee as an employee," but it also forced him to embrace fully both the logic and the politics of opposition to the philosophy behind Tuskegee. Arranged as the third essay, "Of Mr. Booker T. Washington and Others" made *Souls* a contemporary bombshell. Readers of *Dial* were familiar with the essentials of the argument, as articulated in the measured 1901 review of *Up From Slavery*, but, in its expanded, honed form, this was virtually a new piece altogether.[45]

Epigraph lines from Byron—"From birth to death enslaved; in deed, unmanned!"—set the essay's ironic tone. There was a much fuller account of the evolution of African-American leadership, initially centered on the free people of the North. Du Bois mentions "Forten and Purvis of Philadelphia, Shad of Wilmington," and "Du Bois of New Haven," his grandfather. The Civil War and its aftermath produced a combined leadership class of older free spokespersons and the newly manumitted, but, until the ascendancy of Washington, according to Du Bois, all had been selected "by the silent suffrage of their fellows, had sought to lead their own people alone, and were usually, save Douglass, little known outside their race." Unlike these, the Wizard was the celebrity born of a single event, the instantaneous wonder of an afternoon's deed more acclaimed by the other race than by his own. He was leader "not of one race but of two"; the most outstanding southern leader since Jefferson Davis, which only naive readers would have mistaken for a compliment. Vocational education and racial conciliation were recipes for advancement antedating Booker Washington, Du Bois stressed, citing the experiments of the AMA and the politics of black North Carolinian J. C. Price. What the Wizard had done, however, was to link vocationalism and accommodationism, to "put enthusiasm, unlimited energy, and perfect faith into this program, and changed it from a by-path into a veritable Way of Life." "Thus, by national opinion, the Negroes began to recognize" the Wizard's primacy. Very soon, "the voice of criticism was hushed."[46]

The Wizard's creed was an old one of submission combined with an almost religious materialism. It was one, Du Bois warned, that "practically accepts the alleged inferiority of the Negro races" as part of a bargain of timid, circumscribed advancement. And its triumph was extraordinary: "In the history of nearly all other races and peoples the doctrine preached has been that manly self-respect is worth more than lands and houses . . . , that a people who surrender voluntarily such respect, or cease striving for it, are not worth civilizing." Washington would have his people renounce three means of empowerment: political power, civil rights, and higher education. History, Du Bois asserted, offers no example of possible progress through such concessions. If the African-American masses had fallen down on the job in terms of work ethic and morality, white America must not be allowed to dodge its part of the blame for "the relentless color-prejudice [that] is more often a cause than a result of the Negro's degradation."[47]

Du Bois readily conceded that the men and women in his own camp applauded Washington's emphasis on thrift, practical education, and property. They recognized the South's special economic and demographic complexities. As realists, they knew that "the free right to vote, to enjoy civic rights, and to be educated will [not] come in a moment." But they were ready to declare war on all those who justified the South's degradation of the Negro as well as those who claimed that "the prime cause of the Negro's failure to rise more quickly is his wrong education in the past." Finally, Washington's attempt to silence those whom he could not command compounded the misunderstandings and the sharp divergences. Other views must be heard, Du Bois commanded. He and others had "no right to sit silently by while the inevitable seeds are sown for a harvest of disaster to our children, black and white."[48] "Of Mr. Booker T. Washington and Others" was the manifesto of the Talented Tenth, a turn of phrase to be found, however, only once in the collection—in the sixth essay, "Of the Training of Black Men." The precise meaning and significance of this pivotal term was outlined that same year in another collection of essays compiled by a now unidentifiable white editor, *The Negro Problem: A Series of Articles by Representative American Negroes of Today*, where Du Bois wrote, "The Negro race, like all races, is going to be saved by its exceptional men." In that seminal essay, "The Talented Tenth," Du Bois posed a rhetorical question in order to give a definitive answer to the role of class dynamic in racial progress: "Was there ever a nation on God's fair earth civilized from the bottom upward? Never; it is, ever was, and ever will be from the top downward that culture filters."[49]

The fifth *Souls of Black Folk* entry, "Of the Wings of Atalanta," offered readers a deeper insight into the politics and social beliefs of the leaders for whom Du Bois spoke. Their names would become more familiar once the Du Bois–Washington controversy really got under way. He identified a few of them—John Hope; Archibald and Francis Grimké; Kelly Miller; John Wesley Edward Bowen of Gammon Theological Seminary in Atlanta; Bishop Benjamin Tucker Tanner of the AME Church; Paul Laurence Dunbar; and novelist Charles Waddell Chesnutt of Cleveland. Among the women he failed to mention, who would soon enter the ranks, were Ida Wells-Barnett; Josephine St. Pierre Ruffin, still the uncompromising integrationist; Mary Terrell; Lugenia Hope; and a young high school teacher Jessie Redmon Fauset. Strong-willed and often hair-splitting, the camp was never ideologically in sync, especially when it came to gaining the cooperation of key players like Monroe Trotter and Wells-Barnett, both of whom would cause Du Bois almost as much heartburn as they did Washington. Dunbar, Du Bois's friend from Wilberforce days, had personal and medical troubles that prevented anything more than the use of his name in the service of the cause. The short, natty mathematician and philosopher Miller, then perhaps Howard's most distinguished faculty member, would show an enraging propensity for standing simultaneously with both sides in the controversy.[50]

These men and women were defined by the specifics of their class background and, to a somewhat lesser degree, the region in which they made their living. Born between 1855 and 1875, most were urban northerners (whether originally from elsewhere or not), descended from relative affluence or privilege, college-educated, and engaged in the professions. Doctors, lawyers, undertakers, preachers, and teachers, with a smattering of businessmen, civil servants, and journalists, they were known as "quality folk," "representative Negroes," people whose parents had made a successful go of it in slavery times and had family silver to go with their genteel manners. Numerically, they were not significant in a population of more than nine million—perhaps several hundred hard-core families in the North and several dozens in the South. Nor did the majority of those who matched the Talented Tenth profile consider themselves part of the movement Du Bois and his handful were spearheading. Most of them were intimidated by the Tuskegee Machine's power to make and break careers. Amherst and Harvard graduate William H. Lewis and Harvard man Roscoe Conkling Bruce were among the more prominent who fell prey. Even the Grimkés sometimes waffled. But there were also those like Harry Thacker Burleigh, the gifted, conservatory-trained composer, or Hugh Browne, the Princeton-educated Philadelphia high school principal, for whom Washington's program simply made more common sense than any other.[51] Those whom the profile of family, education, profession, region, and urban dwelling fit were not necessarily members of the Talented Tenth, therefore; but those who were members fit the profile. A far more accurate characterization would have been the Talented Hundredth.

A good deal of their growing opposition to Booker Washington was visceral, simply a matter of who they were and who he was. Few of them doubted that by virtue of breeding and accomplishment they merited equal social treatment with their white peers. The suggestion that they should soft-pedal their personal abilities and civic prerogatives, patiently waiting for the lot of the black masses to improve, was extremely distasteful to them. Even when they commended parts of the Tuskegee program, in their well-appointed parlors and high-toned churches, they spoke with condescension. Although the National Negro Business League idea interested and engaged numbers of them, at bottom they dismissed the Wizard's conjurings as fatalistic hoodoo for southern peasant consumption and sophisticated Uncle Tomism for ruling whites. In the last paragraph of "Washington and Others," Du Bois clearly voiced their elitist, cosmopolitan tones of mockery. "So far as Mr. Washington preaches Thrift, Patience, and Industrial Training for the masses," they were ready, said Du Bois, to "hold up his hands and strive with him, rejoicing in his honors and glorifying in the strength of this Joshua called of God and of man to lead the headless host."[52] But in "Of the Wings of Atalanta" Du Bois went on to speak to and for the deepest concerns of his class, protesting Washington's turning the black world upside down so that the starring roles went to peasant farmers, skilled mechanics, and domestics, forcing the Talented Tenth offstage. The models venerated in the past had read a number of inspirational books beyond the Bible; many were widely traveled; some had even thought deeply; and most had pretended, at least, to think nobly. Yet how often and effectively had they been mocked by the Wizard onstage and in Park Avenue mansions. "Into their places are pushing the farmers and gardeners, the well-paid porters and artisans, the businessmen—all those with property and money."[53]

The true spelling of this progress, Du Bois might have written, was Mammon, the commercialization of ideas and institutions by white and black people who knew only how to fix prices but nothing about values. The feelings of the men and women to whom Du Bois appealed were akin to those of genteel white Protestants witnessing with mounting resentment and alarm the new American social order that was suddenly, bumptiously emerging at the turn of the century. If the concept of status anxiety had validity, then the Talented Tenth experienced it as farmers, preachers, peddlers, grocers, and hairdressers formed up behind the Wizard for a march into prosperity. Refinement of person, concern for the quality of success, dignity before expediency—these were attributes as much at a discount in the Tuskegee ideology as in that of Republican boss Mark Hanna or financier J. Pierpont Morgan. "In an age of unusual economic development," the Wizard was bound to be hailed as a sage, Du Bois granted, his "gospel of Work and Money" completely overshadowing "the higher aims of life."[54] The prospect was too dismal to accept as inevitable, nevertheless, and Du Bois hoped in the next breath for a more balanced outcome.

In that regard, he wrote next of Atalanta (Atlanta), hub of the spreading, corroding compromises that have made "material prosperity . . . the touchstone of all success." But "the hundred hills of Atlanta are not all crowned with factories," he reminded readers. There was hope for both the white South and the black South through its colleges and universities, vital enclaves from which "a few white men and a few black men of broad culture, catholic tolerance, and trained ability" would annually infiltrate the region's "social unrest and commercial selfishness." Du Bois celebrated the idea behind Atlanta University, Fisk, and Howard. Whatever the naivete and errors of their Yankee founders, "they were right when they sought to found a new educational system upon the University: where, forsooth, shall we ground knowledge save on the broadest and deepest knowledge?"[55] Higher education was the grounding of the Talented Tenth, the certification of their worth, and, as such, it was a privilege of their class that was nonnegotiable in the final analysis.

IF DU BOIS sincerely feared, as he suggested in "The After-Thought," that his book might fall "still-born into the world wilderness," reassurance came quickly. *The Souls of Black Folk* went into its third printing in June of its first year. By October 1903, McClurg's was selling about two hundred copies weekly of a second edition and remitting royalties to Du Bois at the rate of fifteen cents per copy. Five years after publication, 9,595 books had been sold. For a controversial work about African-Americans by an African-American, such sales were exceptional, and, by any measure, the book enjoyed an impressive run. The London firm of Constable published a British edition in the spring of 1905 and Max Weber's expectation that there would soon be a German translation was still very much alive.[56] Despite the success of the Tuskegee Machine in preventing the book from being noticed in a large segment of the African-American press, the powerful AME *Christian Recorder* of Philadelphia lauded *Souls* as possessing "penetration of thought and a glow of eloquence that is almost unexampled in the literature on the Negro question." In Cincinnati, the black *Ohio Enterprise*, edited by Wendell Phillips Dabney, a rascally eccentric who would become Du Bois's lifelong friend, issued a command in upper case: "SHOULD BE READ AND STUDIED BY EVERY PERSON, WHITE AND BLACK." Trotter's Boston *Guardian* concurred, as did the Detroit *Informer* and Cleveland *Gazette*.[57]

Ida B. Wells-Barnett wrote from Chicago that quite a debate had taken place over the book at a literary gathering during which the formidable white Unitarian minister, Celia Parker Woolley, announced her intention to devote her life to "help black folks with their problems." J. Douglas Wetmore, James Weldon Johnson's Atlanta University roommate and the model for the protagonist of Johnson's novel *The Autobiography of an Ex-Colored Man*, felt "compelled to write and thank [Du Bois] in the name of the Race." Not since Frederick Douglass had their people heard such a voice, Wetmore wanted him to know. A moved Francis Grimké hurried to his writing desk to tell Du Bois, "More than ever do I feel that God has raised you up at this juncture in our history, as a race, to speak to the intelligence of the country on our behalf." From the Talented Tenth of the mother continent came congratulations on Du Bois's "great work" from barrister, publisher, and recent author of *Gold Coast Native Institutions*, J. E. Casely-Hayford. The leading intellectual and politician of British West Africa, Casely-Hayford believed "this century would be likely to see the race problem solved" with more books like Du Bois's.[58]

A Cornell University English major, who had written previously seeking advice about her summer school studies, was enraptured. Jessie Fauset, a third-year student from one of Philadelphia's oldest African-American families who was headed for election to Phi Beta Kappa in an institution that had graduated a mere handful of women, thanked Du Bois "as though it has been a personal favor." She was "glad, glad" he wrote it. "We have needed someone to voice the intricacies of the blind maze of thought and action along which the modern educated colored man or woman struggles." Fauset ended on a personal note (as she would many times in the future): "It hurt you to write that book, didn't it?" for she knew so well that "the man of firm sensibilities has to suffer exquisitely, just simply because his feelings are so fine."[59] Here was an admirer with whom Du Bois decided he should become much better acquainted.

Like the Bookerite press, most southern white newspapers pretended not to notice *The Souls of Black Folk*. Those that did claimed, like the *Tennessee Christian Advocate*, not to know what to make of the book or the author. The Nashville *American*, however, was sure of one thing: "This book is indeed dangerous for the negro to read." The reviewer for the Houston *Chronicle* unmasked the author's terrible design and demanded the authorities indict Du Bois for "inciting rape." Southern coverage of his book was about what Du Bois would have expected, but the wide attention paid to it outside the South was sometimes just as obtuse or mean-spirited. To admit that its arguments were persuasive, that its eloquence was moving, was to risk destabilizing the entente cordiale between the North and the South, an admission that could lead to fundamental reexamination of the dogmas and policies underpinning the racial status quo. The editors of *The New York Times* took no chances. They chose a white southerner whose anonymous review conceded that *Souls* was interesting and even deserving of praise here and there. The book's fatal flaw, nonetheless, was that its author was a sophisticated northerner with only a superficial understanding of southern black people and of the history of the South. Du Bois's hidden personal agenda, the *Times* reviewer disclosed, was simply to be able to "smoke a cigar and drink a cup of tea with the white man in the South." Mrs. Elia W. Peattie harbored the same suspicion in her lengthy *Chicago Tribune* review. Having discharged her obligation to the status quo, however, Peattie allowed her professional conscience to speak about "this passionate book, incomplete and sometimes self-conscious though it is," a book compelling "profound respect. It is a real, not an imitation book."[60] Joseph Pulitzer's New York *World* agreed with Mrs. Peattie about the caliber of the writing and the searing honesty of the author.

But neither *Collier's Weekly* nor *The Outlook* faltered in their duty to uphold *Plessy v. Ferguson* and the Atlanta Compromise. *Collier's*, the muckraking weekly par excellence, dismissed concerns about the black man's soul. "With sufficient food, drink and warmth, the negro is happy, come what may." When an offended Du Bois upbraided *Collier's* editor, Richard L. Jones, for the magazine's racial stereotyping, the latter feigned hurt puzzlement, claiming "not to know just what particular article or statement has appeared in our paper to cause this offense." More serious in its concerns, *The Outlook* of May 23, 1903, reviewed *Souls* along with Washington's *The Future of the American Negro*, didactically rehearsing the latter's program of solid, slow, practical advancement and warning of the dangers of Du Bois's impatience and impertinence. The Atlanta professor was "half ashamed of being a negro, and he gives expression to his own bitterness of soul in the cry which he puts into the mouth of his race." The black person must learn not to "think about yourself. Do not think about your woes and wrongs. Meditate not on the 'souls of black folk,' but on 'the future of the American negro,' " it counseled.[61]

With so much calculated, critical misunderstanding, Du Bois needed to know that there were white men and women among what he called the "better classes" who were giving *Souls* a fair reading. Sending brother Henry a copy that June of the volume by "a mulatto ex-student of mine," William James complimented Du Bois that year on writing a "decidedly moving book." Robert Hunter, the well-known social worker, future author of *Socialists at Work*, and a thinker Du Bois admired, compared *Souls* to *Uncle Tom's Cabin*, while Washington Gladden was positively rhapsodic. Called the "father of the Social Gospel," and currently president of the AMA, Gladden deplored *The Outlook*'s disapproving review. "I want you all to read it," he thundered from his Sunday pulpit in Columbus, Ohio. "It will give you, I think, a deeper insight into the real human elements of the race problem than anything that has yet been written." The sometimes grumpy Albert Hart loved it. Fourteen years later, he was still insisting that his finest Ph.D. student's collection was "the only literature published by a Harvard graduate in forty years."[62]

Over the next few years, as *Souls* went through additional printings, it retained its capacity to move readers of different racial, religious, and social backgrounds. From New York's squalid Lower East Side, D. Tabak, a new American, would share with Du Bois his epiphany after a chance discovery of *Souls* "upon a book shelf in a corner of Delancy [sic] Street." The young Russian immigrant wrote of being "overpowered by a peculiar pain that was so much akin to bliss." Tabak's words fairly tumbled off the page as he confessed that he was "ashamed of being white," of now envying the "despised and abused." He found it unbearable to be a citizen of a country in which 10 percent of the population was persecuted and "denied all rights a thousand times more cruel than we Jews are in Russia."[63] In closing, Tabak thanked Du Bois for the greatly heightened sense of humanity and "sympathy to all nature's children" he had derived from *The Souls of Black Folk*.

When Professor W. D. Hooper of the University of Georgia, an old-stock American at the opposite end of the social scale from the Russian Jew, got around to reading the book in the fall of 1909 he would write immediately to tell Du Bois how profoundly moved he was—"but even the pure

English was very refreshing in this day of slovenliness." Hooper was ashamed that the South had fallen from the control of its "best people." The problem was "the problem of the lower class whites," against whom, Hooper sighed, he and his kind were "utterly powerless." Having long grieved about the treatment of Du Bois's people, the professor was racked with despair that he could find no way to alleviate the situation. But upon reflection, he decided that in a small way he had been able to contribute. He begged his fellow academic to know that his own "skirts are at least clean. I have never wittingly wronged one of your race in any way." Hooper added that he had raised his son to respect black men and women. Appreciative of the moral tumult Hooper must have experienced in bringing himself to write, Du Bois would reply that he had been touched by the letter, which he had read "again and again with increasing sympathy." But with Du Bois sympathy was seldom confused with absolution. "Comrade," he admonished, "you and I can never be satisfied with sitting down before a great human problem and saying nothing can be done. We must do something. That is the reason we are here on Earth."[64]

Challenging letters like the one Du Bois received from Caroline H. Pemberton were rare. This lucid northern white woman shared her thoughts very soon after McClurg and Company released *Souls*. After praising his eloquence and insights, she gently chided Du Bois for failing to see that race hatred was a camouflage for class warfare. He did "not seem to be aware that the white laborers of the North are facing the same alternative of starvation—or submission and unceasing, unrecompensed toil." Another serious failing, she thought, was Du Bois's embrace of the culture and civilization of the white man. "What he boasts of as 'civilization' is a hideous mockery."[65] Pemberton's letter seems to have played a part in quickening Du Bois's appreciation of the possibility of solidarity across racial lines among black and white workers. The theme of class conflict was shortly to be heard, if faintly, in an article or two and an occasional speech.

Meanwhile the New York *Evening Post* and *The Nation* (both owned by Oswald Garrison Villard) had broken ranks with the pro–Booker Washington press. The unsigned review running in both publications had all the earmarks of Villard, until then counted among the Wizard's firmest supporters. Unlike Baldwin or Ogden, Villard permitted himself to doubt that the Tuskegee program was a panacea. A race whose leaders' education was largely limited to masonry and accounting Villard saw as a race unfitted for the modern world. Did it really make sense to renounce civil rights in the present on the assumption that they would be hauled up some day by cast-down buckets? Here was a "profoundly interesting and affecting book," infused with intellectual passion and unquestionable knowledge of the character and ideas of black people, said the *Evening Post* reviewer. Perhaps its criticism of Washington went too far; yet, upon reflection, the reviewer conceded that Du Bois's charges deserved "the carefullest consideration."[66]

The liberal and influential *Independent*, while also troubled by the presentation of Washington, decided that *Souls* was "the best and most logical expression of the clear facts of race hatred yet made by any student of the negro question."[67] This was a review with which Du Bois found himself in complete agreement. He knew that the triumph of *Souls* lay in its luminous presentation of the minds of thinking black folks. For the first time in the brutal, mocked, patronized, and embattled history of Negro life on the North American continent, there was now a revelation of the race's social, economic, and psychological realities and prospects of such lyricism, lucidity, and humanity as to leave its mark on a white America guilty of evasion, obfuscation, and hypocrisy.

12.
GOING OVER NIAGARA

Du Bois and Washington

BOOKER T. WASHINGTON lived in a two-story redbrick house separated from the Tuskegee campus by a narrow road. It was a large house, a comfortable one, T-shaped under a sharply sloping roof, with a deep, colonnaded porch bordered by gleaming white balustrades. He called it The Oaks. It stood almost directly opposite the newly erected Carnegie Library, also a two-story brick structure, which had been built with such economy by Tuskegee students that the donor's modest $20,000 gift had proved exactly sufficient to the task. The current mistress of The Oaks was the former Margaret James Murray, the third Mrs. Booker T. Washington, as handsome as she had been during Du Bois's undergraduate years at Fisk, but considerably fuller in figure and, after careful Fisk grooming, a polished queen bee bearing no trace of her humble origins. What was discussed between Dr. and Mrs. Washington and their distinguished dinner guest on the evening of July 6, 1903, as white-jacketed students served choice cuts of poultry and meat, is unrecorded. Du Bois had come to Tuskegee without Nina and baby Yolande to lecture in the institute's summer session and to maintain correct relations with its master. A letter from Washington to his director of the summer school, Harvard-educated Roscoe Conkling Bruce, suggests that Du Bois was being well compensated for his services.[1]

An appropriate topic of dinner conversation would have been a review of the plans drawn up by Du Bois at Washington's suggestion for a major conference bringing together leaders of the principal factions of the race. Confidentially canvassing some of these leaders, among them Kelly Miller,

Du Bois had written enthusiastically in early February of this unprecedented "chance for a heart to heart talk with Mr. Washington," enclosing a typically bold and comprehensive ten-point working agenda covering such things as education, voting, civil rights litigation, a legal defense fund, and a national publication. The Wizard's interest in a conference flagged immediately. Since then, Washington had said no more about it; probably nothing was said about it at dinner. What seems most remarkable in retrospect is that the Washingtons and Du Bois were able to dine together barely four months after the publication of *The Souls of Black Folk*. Despite the welling controversy surrounding Du Bois's book, the Tuskegee principal felt secure enough to welcome a severe critic into his home. After all, while national newspapers and journals of opinion were full of reactions to *Souls*, Tuskegee's endowment, thanks to a single night of fund-raising at Madison Square Garden, was overflowing.

Perhaps Washington had blanched inwardly that April night in the Garden when ex-President Grover Cleveland spoke of "a grievous amount of ignorance . . . laziness and thriftlessness" among nine million African-Americans; perhaps he had felt some distress when Edgar Gardner Murphy of the SEB characterized them as "a rotting body . . . polluting the atmosphere we breathe"; and Washington may even have grieved when Lyman Abbott rose to praise the superiority of the white race. Had a meteor collapsed the roof of the Garden that night, much of the nation's leadership community of finance, philanthropy, and higher education would have been buried beneath the rubble. In serried rows of self-satisfied paternalism sat the Baldwins, the Ogdens, the Peabodys, the Carnegies, Mrs. Collis P. Huntington, Jacob Schiff, William Schieffelin, Oswald Villard, Nicholas Murray Butler, and a great many more. On April 24, ten days after the fund-raiser, and not quite three weeks after McClurg released *Souls*, Andrew Carnegie handed over $600,000 in U.S. Steel bonds to the Tuskegee endowment fund, $150,000 of which was to be set aside for the personal use of the Wizard and his family.[2] With an endowment placing Tuskegee in the ranks of the country's richest educational institutions, the principal must have found it as easy to be gracious at dinner with Du Bois as to pronounce a homily on dental hygiene before his student body.

There was undoubtedly another factor at play. The invitation to dine at The Oaks came less than a week after the Wizard's forces had humiliatingly routed Monroe Trotter and other opponents at the annual meeting of the Afro-American Council at Louisville, Kentucky. Smarting from the clean sweep by Bookerites the previous year, the Trotter faction came to Louisville with a quiver full of anti-Washington resolutions, determined to disrupt the final session, if necessary. Trotter had excoriated Du Bois for remaining neutral at the 1902 meeting in Minnesota, claiming that Du Bois was "like all the others who are trying to get into the bandwagon of the Tuskegeean." Du Bois had decided to stay away from Louisville, where Trotter was procedurally outmaneuvered by a temporarily sober Thomas Fortune (now the organization's president and faithful servant of Tuskegee), drowned out by the huzzahs greeting the arrival of the Wizard, and finally silenced with threats of physical expulsion.[3]

Every Saturday since November 1901, Trotter and George Forbes, his coeditor and a librarian at the Boston Public Library, had published the Boston *Guardian*, what Trotter called a "clean, manly, and newsy race paper," regularly giving Washington and his allies a well-edited raking over the coals. The *Guardian* was exactly like its editor, indiscreet, brilliant, and merciless in the pursuit of perceived racial fraud. Fortune's *Age* gagged that the newspaper was "putrescent." Sometimes, it was simply outrageous, as in this 1902 description of Booker Washington addressing a public meeting in Boston:

> His features were harsh in the extreme. His vast leonine jaws into which vast mastiff-like rows of teeth were set clinched together like a vice. His forehead shot up to a great cone; his chin was massive and square; his eyes were dull and absolutely characterless, and with a glance would leave you uneasy and restless during the night if you had failed to report to the police such a man around before you went to bed.[4]

Cautious, apprehensive, Du Bois found himself drawn, nevertheless, by the old school tie to Monroe Trotter and Geraldine ("Deenie") Pindell Trotter, still beautiful and full of fire. The three shared Harvard and Boston and a belief in social equality, and, by extension, a gnawing disgust with Booker Washington's cruel parodying of their values. But Trotter's biting ridicule of the Wizard struck Du Bois as extreme and self-defeating. As the last course was served at The Oaks that Monday evening, the unwisdom of aligning himself openly with a noisome faction against the master politician at the other end of the dinner table may well have been on Du Bois's mind.

Within the month, however, Trotter returned to the offensive, and when he did the scandal he created soon brought the Du Bois–Washington controversy to flashpoint. Learning that Washington had accepted an invitation to address the Boston chapter of the National Negro Business

League at the Columbus Avenue AME Zion Church on the evening of July 30, Trotter and Forbes orchestrated the disruption of the meeting. For nearly a decade, the Tuskegee principal's public appearances had attracted the widest attention. Leading citizens of both races—politicians and preachers, traction magnates and university presidents—turned out to hear him and to ponder the broad implications of his social philosophy. On a stiflingly hot night, therefore, some two thousand Bostonians packed the black church on Columbus Avenue.

When William Lewis of Amherst and Harvard football renown rose in the packed and overheated church to introduce Thomas Fortune—widely viewed as the brains of the Tuskegee Machine, especially when in good health—there was hissing and the scraping of feet. Since the beginning of 1903, Lewis had been a fervent Bookerite. Five years earlier, his radical feelings had been so strong that, when the Wizard risked a rough-and-tumble session with college students at Young's Hotel in Boston, Lewis had bluntly told the Tuskegeean to confine his creed of accommodation to the South. The Wizard had dangled a racial first under Lewis's nose—assistant U.S. attorney for the state of Massachusetts. Neither Lewis's new federal distinction nor singer-composer Harry Burleigh's voice were able to contain the disaffection spreading among the capacity interracial audience. At least a score of Trotter's followers sprang into action, shouting, filling the aisles, and moving toward the dais. After police arrived to enforce calm, a fit of violent sneezing gripped Fortune when he tried again to speak. Someone had sprinkled cayenne pepper on the rostrum during the confusion. When Lewis rose again, it was as though an earthquake struck the tabernacle on Columbus Avenue the moment he presented Booker Washington.

Fistfights broke out. Trotter's sister was alleged to have stabbed patrolman "Pat" Malley with her hatpin. Many women swatted adversaries with hats and purses, while others fainted in the terrific heat of the night. Trotter jumped up and down on a pew, bellowing awkward questions at the Wizard, until he was overwhelmed by the din and the police. The Wizard's daughter, Portia, then a student at nearby Bradford Academy, was there that night. She hated Trotter and his newspaper for announcing to the world that she had washed out of Wellesley, and felt she might have struck out at him had her seat not been so far away. Immobile and expressionless, Dr. Washington surveyed the pandemonium from the platform. Trying to make sense of what was happening, a stunned white reporter wrote that many were shouting such things as "We don't like you" and "Your views and aims are not what we sympathize with or think best for our race." The scrimmaging finally stopped, and when the savior of his people was able to speak, it was clear that he had nothing new to say. The morning after the Columbus Avenue church assembly, newspapers across the nation carried reports of riotous clashes, bodily ejections, one knifing, and the arrest of Monroe and Maude Trotter and two others.[5] To horrified northern philanthropists and alarmed southern segregationists, as well as to Washington's vast numbers of African-American admirers, the Boston "Riot" was as unexpected as an earthquake.

If the Wizard had failed to find the words to restore his authority that hot July night, his Tuskegee Machine clanked immediately into high gear in order to achieve that goal. Washington, Fortune, and Scott knew that white philanthropy would not bankroll a leader whose northern itinerary was strewn with broken church furniture, jailed Ivy League graduates, and screaming headlines. If the impact of *The Souls of Black Folk* on civil rights was like that of *Uncle Tom's Cabin* on slavery, then Trotter's Boston "Riot" had its civil rights analogue in John Brown's raid on Harper's Ferry. A tiny band of men and one woman had caused the Wizard the greatest embarrassment of his career to date. The faithful Scott assured his employer that he knew the identity of the real culprits behind Trotter—"men who have more brains, if no more character, then [sic] he: Archibald H. Grimké, . . . Clement G. Morgan, George W. Forbes, W. H. Ferris, all college men, and J[ohn] W. A. Shaw . . . down at the heels." The Wizard's personal communiqué to President Roosevelt in mid-September had the feel of being written with sweaty palms. He was "sorry that the matter has caused [Roosevelt] any concern"; reports were "very much exaggerated"; his attackers were "artificial" men, "graduates of New England colleges." But the president should know that "rank and file" colored people loved and supported both of them.[6] Prosecution of the jailed Trotter was set in motion. Assistant U.S. Attorney William Lewis testified at the trial that his former Harvard friend had entered into a conspiracy to disturb the peace, and Trotter's maximum sentence of thirty days in jail would be sustained on appeal. Meanwhile, Forbes, the quiet librarian, was threatened with dismissal from the Boston Public Library and eventually intimidated into signing over his stock in the *Guardian* to Lewis. Three rival black Boston newspapers rose and collapsed in rapid succession, each covertly financed by the Tuskegee Machine. That September, a libel suit to break the *Guardian* was filed by a young African-American senior at Yale, William Pickens, a poor, quick-witted Arkansas man whose college expenses were probably partially defrayed by the Wizard. Pickens's prizewinning speech in the 1903 Yale oratorical contest questioned the capacity of Haitians for self-government, and Trotter's newspaper had called Pickens "a little black freak student at Yale," a man devoid of "self-respect." New York lawyer Wilford H. Smith, the Wizard's personal attorney, leapt to take charge of Pickens's indignation.[7]

Meanwhile, Du Bois had reached Boston from Tuskegee several days after the riot, without any "inkling or suspicion in any way of the matter," as he assured the aghast George Foster Peabody months later. Indeed, although he placed much of the blame for the imbroglio on the manner in which Lewis had chaired the meeting, Du Bois had firmly deplored the conduct of Trotter, in whose house he was a guest. As he followed developments, Du Bois saw that he was going to have to choose, that he couldn't "occupy middle ground and try to appease the *Guardian* on the one hand and the Hampton-Tuskegee idea on the other." A blunter formulation of his dilemma at that stage would have been that it was far less a choice of ideas than of evading an irresistible juggernaut. He could feel the tenseness, the plotting, the "strength and implacability of the Tuskegee Machine." Even so, he joined his faculty colleague George Towns in sending Trotter letters of sympathy in early October, on the eve of the editor's unsuccessful appeal of his thirty-day sentence. Both Atlanta professors wrote that Trotter and his followers were being persecuted for exercising the right of free speech, Du Bois charging that they were victims of "petty persecution and dishonest attack." Towns's letter, however, even went so far as to excuse the riotous behavior. Trotter and Forbes were "too radical to suit me," Du Bois wrote an influential Talented Tenth associate, "but they are self sacrificing," and the attack on Pickens's Yale speech was honest. Meanwhile, as Trotter angrily paced his cell, the shellshocked Forbes complied with Pickens's demand that a full apology be printed in the *Guardian*.[8]

Nursing his wounds in Europe, the Wizard was much put out by clippings from the *Guardian* and several articles from the Boston *Transcript*, which reached him in Paris. Under the byline "Fair Play," Kelly Miller, a man whose consistent moderation annoyed both Trotterites and Bookerites, had ventured to observe that "few thoughtful colored men espouse what passes as Mr. Washington's policy," although Miller insisted that he opposed the immoderation of the Trotterites. Rattled, and mindful of Ogden's distress at the turn events were taking, Washington finally launched a personal attack on the man he had done so much to convert. He thought Ogden ought to know, he wrote immediately after returning from Europe, that he had "evidence which is indisputable showing that Du Bois is very largely behind the mean and underhanded attacks that have been made upon me during the last six months." In fact, Washington had no such proof, yet he repeated these charges to Frissell of Hampton in early November, even while he was discussing strategy about the Pullman Company discrimination case by telephone with Du Bois. As that long-pursued matter sank into a permanent limbo, Washington and Du Bois's enmity rapidly came into the open. Ogden, now almost apoplectic, had seen enough of this Talented Tenth insurgency. He told Washington he was "beginning to think that the toleration of such men as Towns and Du Bois" would prove fatal to Atlanta University. Du Bois was not even "intellectually honest," and President Bumstead himself was probably implicated in the Boston Riot, Ogden added.[9]

Baldwin and the troubled George Foster Peabody had lodged a formal protest over Towns's sympathy letter after it had been promptly published in the *Guardian*, while reliable sources signaled to Horace Bumstead that the institution's chances of ever receiving money from Carnegie and Rockefeller benefactions were nonexistent. By the end of the year, Atlanta University's president and trustees were nervous wrecks. Towns's letter "was so objectionable and the situation in which it involved the University was so serious," the distraught Bumstead informed Du Bois, as to require action by the executive committee of the trustees. Bumstead could not bring himself to believe the numerous rumors that Du Bois had any "connection with the conspiracy of which Mr. Trotter was convicted." Formal apologies to the Wizard (magnanimously accepted) were voted by the trustee board, and Towns received a blistering reprimand from Bumstead.[10] Even though Du Bois had never justified the riot as Towns had, in his eyes the reaction of his university in groveling before Booker Washington verged on surrender of academic freedom. Aroused and thoroughly disgusted, he took it upon himself to answer Peabody's concerns in a lengthy letter precisely accounting for his movements during the weeks in question. Even the shaken Bumstead found it splendid, regretting only the final paragraph, which, when read aloud, had elicited "an outburst of dissent" from half the trustees. It was in that final paragraph that Du Bois had taken another fateful step on the field of battle. "As between [Trotter] and Mr. Washington," the author of *The Souls of Black Folk* declared, "I unhesitatingly believe Mr. Trotter to be far nearer the right." Du Bois wished only for more restraint and better judgment on the part of Trotter in order "to save to our cause his sincerity and unpurchasable soul in these days when every energy is being used to put black men back into slavery and when Mr. Washington is leading the way backward." In tones of gravest regret over Du Bois's "unfrank and vague words," Peabody advised Du Bois that he was "in too important a relation to your race to indulge them."[11]

A FEW weeks before the Atlanta University commotion, Du Bois had been wondering what to make of an October 28 letter from Tuskegee. After completely ignoring the project for months, the Wizard had written to solicit Du Bois's approval of the plans and invitation list for a January 1904 conference of key African-American leaders to be held in New York City. Du Bois was urged to recommend changes or additional names. On November 8, a more detailed communiqué arrived from Tuskegee, reiterating the pressing need to "agree upon certain fundamental principles and to see in what way we understand or misunderstand each other." It might have been an encouraging overture, but the Wizard's heavy-handedness was too apparent. The list of proposed conferees was filled either with converts or Bookerite beneficiaries. "The more I think of it, the more I feel convinced," Washington would insist whenever Du Bois suggested names, that this or that person decidedly had to be added to or deleted from the list. Too many men from the North would be a mistake, of course, because "the bulk of our people are in the South." His own suggestions were entirely reasonable, Washington insisted, and he advised Du Bois to make "a special effort to drop out of consideration all personal feelings." By mid-November, Du Bois had become thoroughly disgusted and Tuskegee was worried. Did he have more suggestions? Could he be counted on to attend? a worried Washington telegraphed Du Bois. The undated reply from Atlanta was frosty. Du Bois did not think it would "be profitable . . . to give further advice which will not be followed. The conference is yours and you will naturally constitute it as you choose." After seeing the final list, he would decide then "whether [his] own presence is worth while."[12]

Du Bois was turning the tables on Washington, and Washington sensed that if he failed to coopt or neutralize this score of articulate, mutinous, mostly northern college graduates, he would sooner rather than later become merely one among several leaders. The power to make and unmake careers (even those of white men desirous of presidential favor), his near monopoly over the philanthropic monies assigned to his people, his stewardship of their civil liberties and of their broad agenda for advancement—all would collapse into relative insignificance if he failed to discipline the upstart celebrity Du Bois and his admirers. "There are about fifteen colored people who practically control the public sentiment of the

Alfred Du Bois, W.E.B. Du Bois's father, in Union army uniform. *(University of Massachusetts at Amherst)*

Mary Silvina Burghardt Du Bois, W.E.B. Du Bois's mother, soon after Willie's birth. *(University of Massachusetts at Amherst)*

W.E.B. Du Bois at age four or five. *(University of Massachusetts at Amherst)*

Alexander Du Bois, W.E.B. Du Bois's grandfather. *(University of Massachusetts at Amherst)*

The first and last pages of W.E.B. Du Bois's letter to his mother when the fifteen-year-old boy visited his Du Bois grandfather for the first time. *(University of Massachusetts at Amherst)*

New Bedford July 21, 1883.

Dear Mam,

I arrived here safely friday after noon. It was just noon when I got to Hartford. After eating my lunch & buying my ticket I went up to the capitol which is but a little ways to the depot. The grounds are laid out beautifully [illegible] building is magnificent. It consists of a main part and two wings. The main part is surmounted by a tower & dome, which, by the way, is gilded, & upon this is a bronze statue. As you go in the main entrance the

anything to him. Grandma says by and bye he'll talk more. I like it very much here & am having a nice time. Last night grandma & I took a walk up street & visited some of her friends. I have been walking out this after noon. We are going on a picnic to Onset point next week & down to Martha's Vineyard & to hear the Miss Davis the elocutionist &c. I have not been to Mr. Freedom's yet but will go next week. Tell Jennie not to forget the counter. Tell Grace I would like to slap her once. I suppose you are very lonesome. I felt a little home sick this after noon. Write soon, with love to all, good by

Your son,

W E D Bois.

The Fisk University graduating class of 1888 (Du Bois seated at left). *(University of Massachusetts at Amherst)*

Erastus Milo Cravath, the president of Fisk University when Du Bois was a student. *(Special Collections, Fisk University)*

Frank Hosmer, Du Bois's principal at Great Barrington High School. *(University of Massachusetts at Amherst)*

Professor Frederick A. Chase, Du Bois's science teacher at Fisk University. *(Special Collections, Fisk University)*

William James in Keene Valley, New York, in the 1890s. James was a defender of the remnant Adirondack wilderness from the depredations of lumbermen. *(Houghton Library, Harvard University)*

Geraldine Pendell Trotter, wife of Monroe Trotter, who befriended Du Bois at Harvard. *(Moorland Spingarn Research Center, Howard University)*

Harvard graduation, 1890. The six class day speakers; Du Bois is at the far right. *(University of Massachusetts at Amherst)*

Carter G. Woodson, Howard University Professor and Harvard Ph.D., who founded the Association for the Study of Negro Life and History and the *Journal of Negro History*. Woodson was the originator of Negro History Week. *(University of Massachusetts at Amherst)*

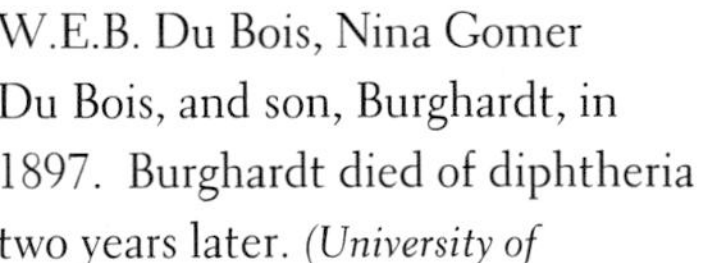

W.E.B. Du Bois, Nina Gomer Du Bois, and son, Burghardt, in 1897. Burghardt died of diphtheria two years later. *(University of Massachusetts at Amherst)*

Du Bois at the Paris Exposition Universelle in the spring of 1900. *(University of Massachusetts at Amherst)*

Group photograph of some of the members at the first meeting of the Niagara Movement, 1905. Norris F. Herndon is the boy in sailor suit, Clement Morgan is in the front row, second from left, and Du Bois is in center. *(University of Massachusetts at Amherst)*

Du Bois with, left to right: J.R. Clifford, L.M. Hershaw, and F.H.M. Murray, probably at the 1906 Niagara Meeting at Harper's Ferry. *(University of Massachusetts at Amherst)*

Segregated dining at Tuskegee; visitors from the "Ogden Express" are served by students. *(Library of Congress)*

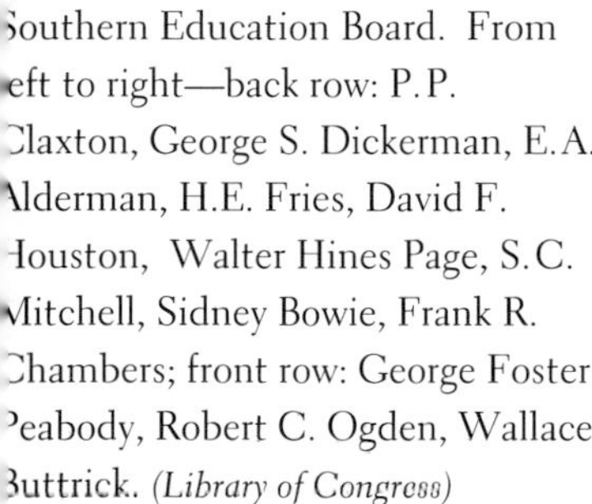

Southern Education Board. From left to right—back row: P.P. Claxton, George S. Dickerman, E.A. Alderman, H.E. Fries, David F. Houston, Walter Hines Page, S.C. Mitchell, Sidney Bowie, Frank R. Chambers; front row: George Foster Peabody, Robert C. Ogden, Wallace Buttrick. *(Library of Congress)*

Robert C. Ogden is on the left and Andrew Carnegie on the right. Booker T. Washington is in the middle. Du Bois never accepted their educational agenda for black America. Tuskegee Institute. *(Library of Congress)*

Booker T. Washington in his office at Tuskegee with Emmett J. Scott, circa 1902. *(Library of Congress)*

Archibald Grimké, at about the time of the "parting of the ways" battle between Booker T. Washington and Du Bois in New York City, 1904; Grimké refused to grant Du Bois his undivided support. *(Moorland Spingarn Research Center, Howard University)*

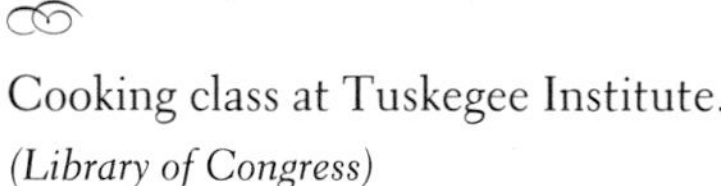

Cooking class at Tuskegee Institute. *(Library of Congress)*

"An Authors' Evening, 1915." Left to right—seated: Will Irwin, Edwin Markham, Lincoln Steffens, Arturo Giovannitti, Percy MacKaye, Du Bois; standing: Mrs. Flora Gaitliss, Ellis G. Jones, Elizabeth Freeman, William Hard, Mrs. Paula Jakoti, Mr. and Mrs. Frederick Howe. *(NAACP Collection, Library of Congress)*

The Silent Parade of the NAACP protesting East St. Louis riot and lynching in 1917. Du Bois and other officers marched at head of parade. *(Library of Congress)*

Du Bois in Amenia, New York, 1916.
(Photo Courtesy of Sondra Wilson)

Joel E. Spingarn, sketched for the cover of *The Crisis*. *(Library of Congress)*

1906 Harper's Ferry meeting of the Niagara Movement. Du Bois seated at center, F. H. M. Murray seated second from left, Morgan second from right. *(University of Massachusetts at Amherst)*

Du Bois and the Atlanta University faculty, circa 1909. His daughter, Yolanda, is seated second from right, front row. Nina Du Bois is standing back row, center. George Towns standing, far right. *(University of Massachusetts at Amherst)*

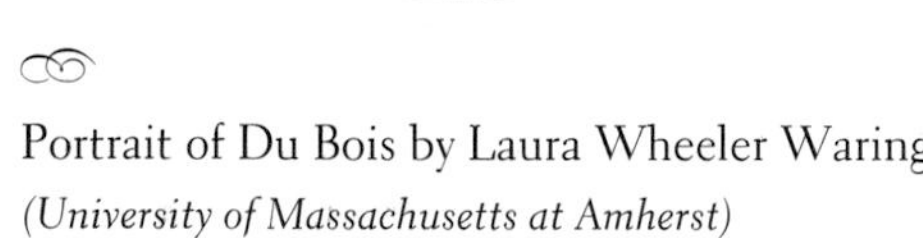

Portrait of Du Bois by Laura Wheeler Waring. *(University of Massachusetts at Amherst)*

Newly admitted women members at the 1907 meeting of the Niagara Movement in Boston. Du Bois is with Harvard classmate Clement G. Morgan. Half of the delegates were women. *(University of Massachusetts at Amherst)*

Mary White Ovington, a Du Bois loyalist and a founder of the NAACP. *(University of Massachusetts at Amherst)*

Jessie Fauset, literary editor of *The Crisis* and intimate friend of Du Bois. *(Moorland Spingarn Research Center, Howard University)*

Ida B. Wells, the anti-lynching crusader. *(University of Chicago Library, Department of Special Collections)*

John and Lugenia Hope with their children on the porch of the president's house at Morehouse College. *(University of Illinois at Chicago, Department of Special Collections)*

Oswald Garrison Villard, a founder of the NAACP and Du Bois combatant. *(University of Massachusetts at Amherst)*

Du Bois at his desk in *The Crisis* office, circa 1915. *(Schomburg Center for Research in Black Culture, New York Public Library)*

Du Bois in *The Crisis* office. *(Schomburg Center for Research in Black Culture)*

The cover of *The Crisis* with the unidentified woman, which caused controversy among the board members of the NAACP. *(Moorland Spingarn Research Center, Howard University)*

The Waco lynching, 1916. *(Library of Congress)*

African-American officers, graduates of Camp Des Moines, with the American Expeditionary Forces. *(Moorland Spingarn Research Center, Howard University)*

Publishers conference to support the "war effort," Washington, D.C., 1918. Emmett Scott is in front row, third from left; Robert Russo Moton is in center; Du Bois is second figure to the right of Moton; Joel E. Spingarn is in major's uniform, next to Du Bois. *(University of Massachusetts at Amherst)*

Major Charles Young in dress uniform. *(Library of Congress)*

A session of the Pan-African Congress, Paris, February 19–22, 1919. Du Bois is seated in the foreground. *(Moorland Spingarn Research Center, Howard University)*

Major Walter H. Loving, left, the Military Intelligence Branch's African-American agent, with Roscoe Conkling Simmons, Booker T. Washington's nephew by marriage. *(Marcus Garvey Papers, Courtesy Robert Hill)*

Negro race," the Wizard had told Baldwin in a letter dated October 26, 1903, explaining the need for the New York conference. Having "thought it over pretty carefully for some time," the conference was the most effective way of bringing things back under control. "What do you think of the plan?" Baldwin had not been sure. With the SEB's spineless Murphy warning that he had "never seen so much sentiment against the Negro," Baldwin, Ogden, and Buttrick seem to have decided against the New York conference because of probable southern white opposition. Faced with Baldwin's veto and abject humiliation before his own followers as well as the dissenters, Washington's biographer Louis Harlan thinks the Wizard finally lost his temper. "I think I owe you an apology for the manner in which I spoke to Mr. Baldwin over the telephone concerning the conference," said a letter hurried off to Buttrick in early November. His leadership was at stake, Washington explained. Buttrick, Baldwin, and Ogden would simply have to accept his judgment that "we have already gone as far as decency permits in our attempt to avoid stirring up southern feeling."[13]

The conference was now definitely on, set for January 6–8, 1904, in the meeting rooms at Carnegie Hall, with Baldwin, Ogden, Buttrick, and other arbitral whites pledged to attend briefly. Baldwin stood the Wizard to an extra thousand dollars expense money "until February." Du Bois, however, still refused to commit himself. Without his participation the Carnegie Hall conference would lose much of its raison d'être. But Washington gambled that Du Bois could not afford to be saddled with the blame for an aborted meeting. A test of nerves ensued in a game of epistolary poker, with Du Bois resisting the latest names proposed by Washington and raising several new ones himself, and vice versa, and both men threatening to refuse to play another hand. He wished "we could invite them, but [Washington] hesitate[d] because of the fear of making the conference too large." As for Francis Grimké's brother, Archibald, a distinguished Boston attorney and President Cleveland's former consul to the Dominican Republic, Tuskegee objected that "we have already invited one prominent Democrat." Furthermore, Boston must not have "an undue representation." William Lewis could represent Boston adequately, and possibly Clement Morgan, Du Bois's old classmate. Trotter and Forbes were anathema to the Wizard. On the other hand, for appearance's sake, he not only pleaded with Edward H. Morris, the feisty Chicago attorney who had denounced him as a racial sellout, to come to New York, but offered to pay his way.[14]

Less than two weeks before the conference, Du Bois sent an important confidential memorandum to his allies. Although Washington was kept guessing until the last minute, its contents left no doubt that Du Bois intended to be present at Carnegie Hall, but he and they had to be ready for devious parliamentary gambits and deceptive reasonableness. Those who stood with him had to come with the bottom-line resolve to fight for full, candid criticism of the Wizard on suffrage, officeholding, civil rights, and college and industrial training according to ability. The number of participants had risen from twenty to a final twenty-eight, with Du Bois able to count solidly on no more than four (Clement Morgan, Edward Morris, Frederick L. McGhee, a Minnesota attorney, and, as an eleventh-hour Tuskegee concession, Archibald Grimké). Another four or five, perhaps, belonged to the Miller camp of straddlers. Come prepared to "keep a good temper and insist on free speech," Du Bois warned. They should not allow cloture, and if the proceedings became too underhanded, they had to be ready to protest "even to the extent of leaving the meeting." Those who had incriminating documents—"every speech or letter or record of Washington"—should bring them so that the Wizard can "face his record in print." "The main issue of this meeting," Du Bois pointed out, "is *Washington*, refuse to be side-tracked."[15] All anti–Booker Washington men were to assemble in New York on the eve of the conference, Tuesday night, where Du Bois would meet and brief them further. He had been stood the price of his round-trip ticket by the Wizard.

Du Bois's suspicions of a cabal more powerful than his own were confirmed the first day. As he remembered it five decades later, he and Booker Washington had ridden together uptown on the Madison Avenue trolley to Carnegie's Georgian mansion on Riverside Drive before the conference opened at ten o'clock that morning. As they stood together at the back of the car, Washington, "who very seldom said anything," turned to Du Bois and asked, "Have you read Carnegie's book [*The Gospel of Wealth*]?" Du Bois said he had never thought it worthwhile to do so. "You ought to read it," the Wizard gravely advised. "He likes it." Du Bois pondered these words as they walked to Carnegie's, where, after retiring to the philanthropist's bedchamber for a brief discussion, the Wizard rejoined Du Bois in the anteroom, saying importantly "Mr. Carnegie is coming to address us."[16] Carnegie's money having paid for the conference, it was both courtesy and politics for the tiny personification of the Age of Steel to appear before this gathering of black leaders whose total assets, had they been tabulated that afternoon, probably would not have amounted to the cost of one of his smaller libraries. The fifty-odd black and white men who finally assembled at Carnegie Hall listened respectfully as the great benefactor praised Booker Washington and stressed the unerring wisdom of the Great Accommodator's policies, signalling in accents of stern Scots practicality the chaos certain to engulf those who challenged or deserted. The patronizing Lyman Abbott followed with more praise and warnings. Since no written record was made of the conference, exactly what was said is speculative. But the intentions of Ogden, Baldwin, Peabody, Villard, and William Hayes Ward, editor of the *Independent*, were obvious. Having delivered their message of compliance, the whites hurried off to boardrooms and banks with fulsome injunctions that the blacks should deliberate in the freest and most honest manner. "Even if all they said had been true," Du Bois thought, "it was a wrong note to strike in a conference of conciliation."[17]

In the plain speaking that took place on Thursday and Friday, tempers and suspicions occasionally flared around the meeting room, as when a Bookerite charged that the letter Clement Morgan was writing to his wife was a secret transcript of the deliberations. But as the hours wore on, a tone of compromise prevailed. Washington superbly played Solon for the occasion, adopting a pose of such reasonableness that Du Bois lost the undivided support of Archibald Grimké, while the ever-undecided Miller began to lean toward the Wizard. In the closing speeches both men delivered, the Wizard's practiced mixture of earthy humor and group psychology served him better than Du Bois's dry intellectual appeal to principles. There were newspaper reports of a statement by Washington, apparently not for public dissemination, that he favored "absolute civil, political, and public equality," and that he generously applauded the principle of higher education for the elite. For their part, the Du Boisians were said to have conceded that the great majority of African-Americans should remain in the South, and that the education of the masses should be confined to industrial training. Both factions agreed to support lawsuits to protect and expand access to public accommodations and the ballot box (Baldwin had offered to finance them); specifically, a test case was to be initiated against the Pullman Company's Jim Crow policies in Tennessee. By unanimous vote, the conferees created a "Committee of Safety with twelve members," a sort of executive body of national leadership, charged with harmonizing, guiding, and communicating race policy and tactics. Washington and Du Bois were charged to organize the Committee of Twelve, along with Hugh Browne, now principal of a Pennsylvania teacher-training college for African-Americans and a man Du Bois mistakenly believed to be critical of the Tuskegee Machine.[18]

Du Bois must have left Carnegie Hall with a far clearer sense of his own limitations within a group setting as well as of the inevitability of conflict with Tuskegee. And when the time came that he could no longer delay a declaration of war, he saw himself being maneuvered into facing Booker Washington and his numerous troops on the field of battle with barely even a squad to command. Morris of Chicago was the exception, returning to the charge after Carnegie Hall, denouncing the Wizard in even hotter language as a fraud and a tool in the hands of white racists. Courtly Archibald Grimké, however, was typical of those who went about praising Washington's Carnegie Hall address as "unanswerable." Du Bois heard that Grimké no longer doubted that the Wizard was "working for the best interests of the Negro." The uninvited Trotter was undeceived, of course, but the shrill predictableness of his editorials undermined their influence. The Wizard himself was cautiously pleased with the results of the conference, reporting to Baldwin that his opponents were "either silenced or won over to see the error of their way." Du Bois was still a major annoyance, and the Wizard advised his ally Robert Russa Moton of Hampton against inviting the Atlanta professor to campus for a private meeting. He suspected Du Bois was simply looking for more ammunition to fire against the Tuskegee Machine.[19]

Meanwhile, Du Bois found himself locked into a troika with two members primed to exploit whatever cooperation he undertook. The understanding at Carnegie Hall had been that he, Washington, and Browne were to meet in New York in February or March to plan the membership and structure of the Committee of Twelve. Without much faith that it would be adopted, he drafted a four-page proposal in late February that would have transformed the Committee of Twelve into a genuinely national body with a broad base in the African-American leadership community. His Committee of Safety would have numbered approximately 120, nationally recruited from all factions and regions, and comprised of six subdivisions: public action; legal redress; social reform; information and defense; economic cooperation; and organization and finance. The twelve original members would function as an executive committee, meeting quarterly. There was more for Browne and the Wizard to mull over: a "Committee of Correspondence" branching throughout the nation even as far as the smallest towns in which there were black communities; its major task would be the drumming up of a $12,000 annual "relief fund" for lawsuits, propaganda, and staffing.[20] Here lay the roots of the National Association for the Advancement of Colored People, still years away, and also next year's Niagara Movement. At that point in time, the plan was probably too grandiose to be practical, but it had undeniable visionary value for those African-Americans with influence who were dedicated to civil rights.

His proposal drew a response that Du Bois must have anticipated. Booker Washington praised its long-range desirability, then followed up with a characteristic demurral. "The more I think of it," the more he thought it best to wait a year or so to see how the twelve-member body panned out. Imagine trying to deal with large numbers of colored people all at once, he commented to Hugh Browne by letter a few days later. As Du Bois suspected they would, the Wizard and Browne excluded him from preparations for the Committee of Twelve planning meeting, shifting the venue from New York to St. Louis, then finally back to New York for July 6. Du Bois had already decided that the Wizard's gambit was to "have me at his mercy by simply having his men out vote me," as he told the waffling Archibald Grimké and Kelly Miller.[21] He was not yet quite ready to resign, but "The Parting of the Ways" salvo from the April issue of *World Today* made his exit from the Committee of Twelve a mere formality.

Refusing to "kiss the hands that smite us," Du Bois's article disparaged the Tuskegee program and served up a biting parody of the Wizard's wisdom: "The trimmings of life, smatterings of Latin and music and such stuff—let us wait till we are rich. Then as to voting, what is the good of it after all? Politics does not pay as well as the grocery business, and breeds trouble." For their children's sake let black men and women fight for full citizenship, Du Bois countered, "and if they fail, die trying." With even more fervor, he prepared an address to the graduating class of Washington, D.C.'s elite M Street High School that June (not delivered for some reason) in which he flayed the lies "sprung from the father of lies." They must know that "there are men who are afraid that they will know too much, wield too much power and aspire to too great position; that therefore they are seeking to cut down the opportunities of education." Kelly Miller wrung his hands over "The Parting of the Ways," as well as the evidence of equally bad faith on the part of the Wizard, asking, "Is it war to the knife, and knife to the hilt?" Du Bois would provide a definitive answer soon after the Committee of Twelve was set up in New York. Nina telegraphed from Atlanta that he was ill, which was true, but he was more fed up than sick.[22] But the Wizard was also fed up. This time, the boss in Booker Washington controlled his behavior. Whatever had been said by way of conciliation at the January Carnegie Hall conclave was a dying letter, if not yet completely dead. There had been a vintage Lincoln's Birthday Address at Madison Square Garden, in mid-February, with Washington yet again extolling the educational superiority of Hampton-Tuskegee. "For my race one of its dangers," he bellowed into the great arena, "is that it may grow impatient and feel that it can get upon its feet by artificial and superficial efforts rather than by slower but surer progress . . . of industrial, mental, moral and social development."[23]

"He is whipped oftenest who is whipped easiest," advised Charles ("Charlie") William Anderson, chief accountant for the New York State Racing Commission, and one of the Wizard's craftiest recruits. Charlie Anderson was northern-born, light-skinned, bluff, tough, and self-made. His heavyweight political talents were soon to be rewarded through the Wizard with a plum appointment from Teddy Roosevelt as collector of internal revenue for the Second District in New York City. By the time of the July meeting, Washington hardly needed Charlie Anderson to tell him to be himself and take charge. He whipped the New York meeting into line, getting himself elected chairman, the devious Browne secretary, and the credulous Grimké treasurer of a Bookerite-packed Committee of Twelve for the Advancement of the Interests of the Negro Race. Du Bois and Miller were included for the sake of form. But the bald manipulation actually proved too much for Grimké after a few days' reflection. Submitting his resignation, he complained to Du Bois, "There was nothing for men like ourselves to do in such a Committee." In late July, a circular sent by Hugh Browne dropped the importance of higher education acknowledged at Carnegie Hall, as well as the "paramount importance" of the ballot. Instead, there was to be a conference of white men from the South and North, together with an equivalent group of southern and northern black men, to "consider race conditions." When the final program of the Twelve was released a few weeks later, even a mild addendum on voting had vanished. Finally, due to the delays and evasions of everyone but himself ("I would say that I have done everything I could to get such a suit started"), the Wizard despaired of ever being in a position to challenge the segregation policies of the Pullman Company in court. Du Bois received the Wizard's rather lame explanation that "Mr. Baldwin wanted us to wait until he could have the opportunity to have a conference with Robert T. Lincoln himself"—the same Lincoln who had icily rebuffed earlier approaches. After much delay, Washington claimed he had urged his associates in Nashville to proceed, "but there is a failure to act so far."[24]

Resigning from the Committee of Twelve a month after the July 1904

New York meeting, Du Bois went off to swim in different waters. Looking back, he sighed that the Committee of Twelve scheme initially had "seemed to me of some value, but of no lasting importance and having little to do with the larger questions and issues." The committee would flow on through 1907 and part of 1908, its course dominated by Tuskegee, but with Miller and Grimké (having rescinded his resignation) swimming vainly upstream. "I have actually found people who seemed to suppose that you and Trotter were working together," Hart wrote his favorite student in disbelief. But in fact that was precisely what Du Bois had in mind. There was no turning back now for Du Bois, no more socially correct sojourns at Tuskegee, no further charades of compromise and cooperation. As Miller (who continued to profess not to understand Du Bois's reasoning) had lamented, "It was war to the knife, and knife to the hilt." *The Souls of Black Folk* had examined the ideas of Washington and found the best of them to be flawed, but with "The Parting of the Ways" and his withdrawal from the Twelve, Du Bois began to impugn the man behind the message. He was discovering a truth that Washington had known his entire, calculating life—that the force of an idea, at least in the short term, is only as good as the politics of the people advancing it. He thought he finally understood Booker Washington completely, grasped his remorseless opportunism: " 'Now what is your racket? What are you out for?' " And as he reflected, Du Bois came to appreciate how puzzling his own behavior was to Washington. "You see, he couldn't quite think of me as a man with purely scholastic ambitions," Du Bois mused many years later. "There must be something else. He was a terribly suspicious man."[25] To get at the Wizard's ideas, Du Bois now saw that he would have to cripple the man.

In a scolding letter to Grimké and Miller, accusing them of being caught up in an intellectual exercise that merely amused the men in the Tuskegee Machine, Du Bois draped himself in the mantle of a solitary, cocky David:

> I count it a clear misfortune to the Negro race when two clear-headed and honest men like you can see their way to put themselves under the dictation of a man with the record of Mr. Washington. I am sorry, very sorry to see it. Yet it will not alter my determination one jot or tittle. I refuse to wear Mr. Washington's livery or put on his collar. I have worked this long without having my work countersigned by Booker Washington or laid out by Robert Ogden, and I think I'll peg along to the end in the same way.[26]

If he was to bring down the most powerful black symbol in American society, Du Bois now knew he would have to construct a formidable symbolism of his own, both captivating and candid. The politics of ideas boiled down to strategies of public relations and propaganda, especially for the party whose resources of money and numbers were inferior. Millions of Americans thought they knew what Booker Washington's beliefs were. It was time for Du Bois to broadcast his own—eloquently, succinctly. Like so much else that he wrote, the "Credo" was meant to serve a dual purpose: manifesto to a few thousand influential whites outlining the social and civil rights ideals Du Bois and his few supporters embodied; and catechism for great numbers of ordinary men and women of his race whose beleaguered pride was faltering. His mood must have been especially reflective as he wrote this powerful piece at his South Hall desk, with the October 2 anniversary of Burghardt's death just a few days away.

The nine-paragraph "Credo" was published by editor William Ward (sympathetic to Tuskegee but, like Villard, not uncritical) in the edition of the *Independent* for October 6, 1904. Du Bois sprinkled it with pieties about peace and beauty and goodness—patience, even—and appeared to profess a belief in God and spoke of green pastures beside still waters, for he especially needed to persuade a white public schooled in the black world by *Up From Slavery* that he was not a rash and godless intellectual, but a committed exponent of Judeo-Christian harmony and justice. "Credo" was a majestic incantation whose surface and subliminal meanings were easily misread. White readers of a sanctimonious or myopic bent were profoundly gratified by the expression of religious sentiments, as were the overwhelming majority of his own people. Perceptive readers, on the other hand, heard, in a staccato modeled on Zola's *J'accuse*, distinct sounds of white supremacy crumbling. A good many black people heard the thunder of avenging racial parity. They would hang the "Credo" on their living room walls after Du Bois included it in *Darkwater* sixteen years later, just as their grandchildren would mount "I Have a Dream" on theirs.

He believed in God, he began, "in God who made of one blood all races that dwell on earth." He believed that "all men, black and brown and white, are brothers, varying through Time and Opportunity, in form and gift and features, but differing in no essential particular, and alike in soul and in the possibility of infinite development." "Especially do I believe in the Negro Race," "Credo" sang in the key of destiny, "in the beauty of its genius, the sweetness of its soul and its strength in that meekness which shall yet inherit this turbulent earth." Sweetness and meekness but also and equally "pride of race." He believed in "lineage and self . . . so deep as to scorn injustice to other selves; in pride of lineage so great as to despise no man's father; in pride of race so chivalrous as neither to offer bastardy to the weak nor beg wedlock of the strong. Knowing that men may be brothers in Christ, even they be not brothers-in-law." The seventh paragraph disclosed the immediate agenda: "I believe in Liberty for all men; the space to stretch their arms and souls; the right to breathe and the right to vote, the freedom to choose their friends, enjoy the sunshine and ride on the railroads, uncursed by color; thinking, dreaming, working as they will in a kingdom of God and love."[27] "God has gifted you," rejoiced the Reverend Francis Grimké, whose views of the Wizard were less patient than his brother's. "Credo" was what was "need[ed] today more than anything else." "It makes me ache with anger at one's own impotence," sighed Mary Ovington in a letter written to Du Bois early on in their lifelong friendship. "Credo" would be widely reprinted in the African-American press and made available on cardboard rectangles slightly larger than playing-card size by a Memphis printing establishment.[28]

Despite the biblical allusions in "Credo," however, Du Bois was far from successful when it came to reassuring conventional white liberals that he might not be willing to overturn their society in order to advance the condition of black people. Twelve days after its appearance, he surprised the genteel delegates to the American Missionary Association conclave in Des Moines, Iowa, by declaring from the podium, in language widely reported in the press as "menacingly" socialist, that the race problem "was but the sign of growing class privilege and caste distinction in America, and not, as some fondly imagine, the cause of it." He seemed to be giving voice to Caroline Pemberton, who had qualified her admiration for *The Souls of Black Folk* by regretting its failure to stress the primacy of class to race; but it was the first flash of a recurring insight, rather than the beginning of a philosophical revision. His letter to a prominent socialist and welfare specialist, who had been intrigued by news reports that Du Bois had advocated class warfare, is an excellent measure of his thinking then. While he would "scarcely describe [him]self as a socialist," he explained to Isaac Max Rubinow of Washington, D.C., still he had much sympathy with the movement and had "many socialistic beliefs."[29] The absorbing problem of the hour, he believed, was the abject racial discrimination against black people in America—and the collusion with oppression that Booker T. Washington called compromise.

. . .

IN THE January 1905 issue of the new African-American magazine *Voice of the Negro,* Du Bois wrote an article titled "Debit and Credit, The American Negro in the Year of Grace Nineteen Hundred and Four." *Voice of the Negro* was an aggressive, year-old monthly skillfully edited by a young Virginia Union University graduate named Jesse Max Barber. The reaction to "Debit and Credit" caught Du Bois off guard. Taking a hip shot at the Wizard, he had made the shocking allegation that the Tuskegee Machine had spent three thousand dollars during the previous year in bribes to the press. Du Bois suddenly found himself caught in a blistering crossfire from Tuskegee admirers. The *Independent's* William Ward politely but firmly demanded proof of the newspaper "hush money" story, warning Du Bois that it was "unpleasant to find one whom we so heartily respect as you should be losing the sympathy of the colored people, as if you had been guilty of a slander." Only those who already belonged to the "Syndicate" disbelieved his charge, Du Bois assured Ward, but washing "our dirty linen in public" was unwise and so Du Bois had promised that, unless forced to do otherwise by later developments, he would "say nothing further in print on the subject." Oswald Villard had not been put off so easily, complaining that to level "so grave a charge" against the Wizard was to libel the work of the most influential men and women in America. "Kindly let us have the facts for publication in the *Evening Post,*" he commanded. Although Du Bois had been certain that he was right, urgent letters to Trotter asking for "every scrap of evidence you have . . . by return mail" prove that evidence had unscientifically followed hypothesis in this instance.[30]

Having behaved impetuously, Du Bois very nearly compounded his embarrassment by assailing Villard for daring to doubt him. "You do not realize the fight for sheer existence that the American Negro is today waging," he had retorted in the first draft of his letter. "You do not realize the underground and persistent series of attacks being made on him. I am sorry to see you disposed to dismiss the plaint of some of us who are fighting in the open for justice." Fortunately, he decided against sending an indignant reply, settling instead for a short, courteous refusal of the *Evening Post's* offer, assuring Villard of his readiness "to furnish for your personal information the nature of the proof." Meanwhile President Bumstead had implored his stellar faculty member to consider more carefully the ramification of his accusations. Even if they could be "morally certain" that Booker Washington had bought much of the black press and influenced federal appointments based on loyalty to Tuskegee, Bumstead thought it would be "almost impossible to prove to the satisfaction of skeptics." And was it worth the cost? Villard had become much more sympathetic to Atlanta University lately, partly thanks to Du Bois's writings. The worried president had suggested bearing in mind that the wealthy publisher was "in a position to render us much help, personally, through his paper and by his relation to the men of the General Education Board and the Slater Fund Trust."[31]

Finally, on March 24, 1905, Villard received from Du Bois a lengthy document with numerous subparagraphs and exhibits intended to prove the *Voice of the Negro* charges. He had made a strong, circumstantial case (strong but not overwhelming), but Villard decided that "frankly . . . it will take a great deal more than the evidence you have presented to shake my faith in Mr. Washington's purity of purpose." The mere fact that that "very dangerous, and almost irresponsible young man," Trotter (Villard had known him well at Harvard), had supplied Du Bois with evidence was almost *prima facie* grounds for dismissing the charges. At that, Villard's reaction had been better than most—he had at least conceded that the conduct of Emmett Scott's Tuskegee literary bureau had been "extremely injudicious," even as he maintained that Du Bois had utterly failed to substantiate the Wizard's "use of political patronage." Du Bois could not have known that Villard's uncle, Francis Garrison, upon returning Du Bois's letter and exhibits to his nephew, had casually mentioned that his wife speculated that the Wizard drew "on his personal income ($7,500) from the Carnegie gift for this press business." "Debit and Credit" had touched a nerve, and Du Bois's reply to the powerful publisher's excusing the Wizard and blaming Scott was tantamount to a rebuke. "Such actions are not 'injudicious,' Mr. Villard; they are wrong."[32] Always ready to lecture others, and unkindly disposed to receiving one—especially one from an African-American gentleman—Oswald Villard would not soon forget Du Bois's presumptuousness.

So by early summer of 1905, Du Bois and a handful of others had seen themselves as much like the figure of Shakespeare's Cassius, lesser beings darting between the legs of a giant tyrant. The situation was intolerable to Frederick McGhee and Charles E. Bentley. McGhee had been born a slave in Monroe County, Mississippi. The respected and influential Bentley was freeborn, in Cincinnati, and was now the leading African-American physician in Chicago, where he had played a key role in founding Provident Hospital, the first hospital in the country owned and operated by African-Americans. Du Bois called McGhee "brilliant" and was impressed by the tall, sharp-featured Mississippian's "intense and eloquent speech." Somehow McGhee had managed to graduate in 1885 from what became Northwestern University Law School, then set up practice in St. Paul, Minnesota, to become one of the city's most successful criminal lawyers. At forty-four, McGhee, like Bentley, was somewhat older than the Niagarite average of forty; he was also a staunch Catholic and a Democrat with a large interracial clientele.[33] An early member of the Afro-American Council, he had praised the Wizard's policies at first, but had become disgusted by the logrolling politics of the 1903 and 1904 meetings of the council. They must do something, he told Du Bois. Bentley agreed. Du Bois suggested that they convene a meeting of like-minded men in Buffalo, New York. He wrote to book a bloc of rooms in one of the city's medium-sized hotels, then set about drafting a statement of intentions. Drafted and circulated by Du Bois in early June, the call stated two forthright purposes: "organized determination and aggressive action on the part of men who believe in Negro freedom and growth"; and opposition to "present methods of strangling honest criticism." Those signing represented the vanguard of the Talented Tenth—educators, lawyers, publishers, physicians, ministers, and several businessmen secure enough in their professions and principles to risk Booker Washington's retribution. Du Bois described them as "educated, determined, and unpurchasable"—fifty-odd men he had hoped but doubted he could find who "had not bowed the knee to Baal."[34]

The twenty-nine men and one teenage boy who arrived throughout the day to join Du Bois at the comfortable old Erie Beach Hotel in Ontario, on July 10, knew they were about to make history. It was the "beginning of a new epoch," Du Bois proclaimed. The "Call" which brought them to the Canadian side of Niagara Falls that Monday in 1905 had been signed by fifty-nine men of distinction in the District of Columbia and sixteen states from Rhode Island to South Carolina and as far west as Kansas. (The issue of membership for women was to be decided affirmatively the following year but only after Trotter's opposition had been overcome.) Fort Erie, on the Canadian side of Niagara Falls, had never seen thirty black people together in the town before. However, from time to time African-Americans visiting the Falls crossed over, and Fort Erie townspeople were inclined by tradition and commerce to show them hospitality. Three days of roast beef dinners served to a filled dining room at Burnett's Restaurant down the road from the hotel put the manager and his family in an especially warm mood. Du Bois's tense mood of the first day was also much better by then. Race prejudice on the part of the Buffalo hotel establishment had forced the conference organizer to rush to Fort Erie on the evening of the ninth to arrange alternate accommodations. Du Bois remembered his extreme agitation: "If sufficient men had not come to pay the hotel, I should certainly have been in bankruptcy and perhaps jail." In view of the expense, distance, professional risk, and eleventh-hour confusion, the quorum of twenty-nine men from every region of the country except the Far West was a distinct coup for Du Bois and Trotter. Led by Trotter and old Harvard classmate Morgan, seven of what were to become known thereafter as Niagarites came from New England. There were eight from the Midwest, including Charles Bentley, W. L. McGhee, and Harry Clay Smith, editor of the Cleveland *Gazette*. Six came from the South, four from the Middle Atlantic states and from the District of Columbia.[35]

There was irony in the fact that the first collective attempt by African-Americans to demand full citizenship rights in the twentieth century (without even indirect support of influential whites) had been forced to spring to life on Canadian soil. There was also an incidental advantage to the locale that almost certainly escaped Du Bois at the time: the spy sent by Booker Washington to report on the Niagarites looked for them in the wrong place. Boston attorney Clifford Plummer, enjoying his underwritten sortie, reported to Tuskegee from Buffalo that he had stationed himself there "from Wednesday morning until Friday" and that "none of the men named in the report were [sic] present except Du Bois."[36] Plummer was much more successful in discharging his instructions to prevent any news coverage of the meeting. Except for the report in the Boston *Transcript*, his visit to the Buffalo offices of the Associated Press resulted in an almost total blackout in the white press. For its part, the Tuskegee Machine enforced the African-American press's widespread silence. Outside of the Niagarite circle comprised of the *Bee*, the *Guardian*, the *Gazette*, and a few others, the historic meeting went unnoticed. The highly restricted coverage by race newspapers lent credibility to Du Bois's shocking claim that the Wizard had spent three thousand dollars during 1904 in bribes to the press.

The new arrivals at the rambling Erie Beach Hotel were all the more intriguing due to their impressive livery and comportment. They exuded an air of self-assurance and professional success, Du Bois with cane and handlebar mustache; Trotter displaying the nervous energy of Teddy Roosevelt, whom he resembled from a distance; Edwin Jourdain with the grace and elegant tailoring befitting his ancient, wealthy New Bedford, Massachusetts, lineage; William H. Hart, professor of law at Howard University, who, by demeanor and color, was an illegitimate copy of his aristocratic, slaveholding Eufala, Alabama, father. Something of their self-conscious purpose and the impression they must have made upon Niagara during those four days of ideal July weather was captured in a photo of many of the Fort Erie group members, which was later misidentified as dating from 1906. The falls cascade on a mock background as three rows of men in white Panama hats and Stetsons (Norris, the boy in the sailor suit, was the son of Georgia Niagarite Alonzo Herndon) stare straight ahead—although a debonair Du Bois, obviously pleased with himself, looks off to his right from the second row.[37]

Of the thirty who failed to come to the Canadian side of the Falls, about half were likely kept away by genuine conflicts in schedule, or by financial or family problems, rather than by eleventh-hour caution. Such was the case of Georgians John Hope and George Towns, as well as young Monroe Work, an incredibly hardworking instructor at the industrial college in Savannah who held the University of Chicago's first degree in sociology awarded to an African-American. That inveterate Tuskegee-hater from Chicago, Edward Morris, and the brilliant young AME minister Richard R. Wright, Jr., were absent for similar reasons. Ten Massachusetts men signed the call. Of the five who stayed away, two, Reverdy Ransom and Charles Burleigh Purvis, were newcomers to the state who were unlikely to have had manufactured alibis. Ransom, tall, handsome, theatrical, and already recognized as the AME Church's most charismatic preacher, would steal the show from Du Bois at the next Niagara Movement meeting at Harper's Ferry, West Virginia. Purvis, a graduate of Oberlin and Western Reserve University Medical School, was an authentic aristocrat whose South Carolina–born father had attended Amherst and raised African-American troops for the Union Army. Charles Purvis himself had been an officer in the Army Medical Corps during the Civil War, the first occupant of the Thaddeus Stevens Chair at Howard University Medical College, and the first physician on the scene to attend President Garfield after he was mortally shot by Charles Guiteau, a disgruntled civil servant. Two newspaper publishers notorious for their independence, New York's John Edward Bruce ("Bruce Grit") and Cincinnati's Wendell Dabney, would have had to borrow even to buy the reduced tickets being offered by the railroads in connection with the Elks Convention in Buffalo at the same time.[38]

Archibald Grimké and Kelly Miller were omitted from the invitation list. To the extreme annoyance of Du Bois, they were still trying to make something more of the Committee of Twelve than a Bookerite sounding board. Grimké and Miller had even presumed to lecture Du Bois about what seemed to them his arbitrary withdrawal from the Twelve, an impertinence that Du Bois took with steely grace. Theirs was an attitude that might have chilled his Talented Tenth conclave, Du Bois decided. "Because you both belonged to Mr. Washington's committee," he wrote them after the meeting, their presence at Niagara would have been "inconsistent"—an exclusionary attitude the Wizard would have fully understood. There was glee in Tuskegee over a reported rupture between the two men and Du Bois, with the Wizard writing Scott from his Massachusetts summer home of a detailed conversation with Grimké about Du Bois's "insult": "He seems more than anxious now to line up with us."[39] As for Miller, said the Wizard, he remained as mushy as always.

What brought the Niagara men together were negative attitudes ranging from unease to enmity toward the Wizard, but even Du Bois cannot have taken for granted that they would come to common agreement about a positive agenda. Lafayette Hershaw and Freeman Henry M. Murray were Du Bois loyalists, men who would place their professional lives at his service repeatedly and selflessly in the future. Hershaw, a sad-eyed man with a fuzzy little mustache, was an 1886 Atlanta University graduate. He had been principal of a segregated Atlanta secondary school before moving to Washington in the early 1890s to take up a clerical position in the department of the interior. Suspicions of un-Tuskegeean activities had fallen upon Hershaw in 1903, and he had nearly been sacked from his federal position. Murray, an older Niagarite originally from Cleveland, Ohio, one of two self-educated men in this group of college graduates, managed the Washington printing company that he and his brothers owned.[40] On the grounds of the hotel and over meals in Burnett's Restaurant, Hershaw and Murray pushed the Du Bois line. Twenty-seven-year-old Max Barber, the youngest Niagarite at Fort Erie, admired Du Bois with an acolyte's devotion, and Booker Washington would soon make him pay dearly for it. Barber had naively accepted Washington's suggestion that Emmett Scott serve as associate editor of the *Voice of the Negro*, along with the distinguished Methodist clergyman and professor, John Bowen of Atlanta, the second African-American after Du Bois to earn a doctorate. Dismissing Scott's objections and Bowen's qualms, Barber not only opened his magazine to Du Bois, he would make it the unofficial organ of the Niagara Movement until he was forced to leave Atlanta in 1906. From then on, he would be blocked by the Wizard in every attempt to make a new start until, finally, Barber abandoned journalism and turned to dentistry.[41]

Even in this group, some shared Archibald Grimké's aversion to

Trotter as a loose cannon. Clement Morgan, whose oratorical skills had contributed to his success as a lawyer, came to Niagara Falls ready to cooperate with his volatile Boston friend, but he had learned from experience to be wary of Trotter's stubbornness. On this occasion, though, the firm hand of Du Bois and the exhilarating conviction that they were making racial history had a pacifying effect on the radical. Trotter and Du Bois were then on better terms than before or after, the *Guardian* editor having been of critical help in the "Debit and Credit" crisis. "My wife says you are a brick, all you need is a red head," Trotter had good-naturedly ribbed Du Bois at the time.[42] The elegant Edwin Jourdain, at forty-nine one of the oldest men at the Erie Beach Hotel, had admired both Du Bois and Trotter from his Boston University Law School days in the early 1890s. His grand old family home was popularly known as the New Bedford annex of the Boston radicals. Reverend Byron Gunner, also a wary Trotter admirer, was noted for a temper almost as terrible as his. Gunner was a combative Alabamian, educated at Talladega College, and pastor of a Congregationalist church in Providence, Rhode Island, that could have been described as another radical annex. A clear sense of the other Niagarites is elusive, although it seems reasonable to assume, from what little is known of them, that the Howard-educated, Howard University law professors Henry Lewis Bailey, William Hart, and William Henry Richards held views somewhat to the right of Du Bois's.[43] All were members of the capital's very proper Bethel Literary Association, a larger, somewhat less-exclusive institution modeled after the prestigious but faltering American Negro Academy.

There may have been a few others at Fort Erie like Alonzo F. Herndon, whose public career marked him as an astute businessman rather than an activist moved by the radical ideas of the day. A Georgian born into slavery, with the color and features of a white man, Herndon was about to parlay a tidy sum—earned from his chain of gleaming barbershops catering to white Atlantans—into the Atlanta Life Insurance Company. Within a few years, he would become one of the wealthier men in America, irrespective of race, his beautifully proportioned, columned mansion a mise-en-scène for the grand balls the dreamy, gay Norris would host after his parents' death. Atlanta gossips attributed Mr. Herndon's presence among the Niagarites to Mrs. Herndon's influence. Adrienne Herndon—whose life was cut short by a rare disease just as the great mansion was finished in 1910—was a Giselle-like beauty with raven hair and ivory skin who taught French at Atlanta University, where a lively friendship with Du Bois had blossomed. While

Nina preferred the confines of the South Hall apartment where little Yolande's needs and Lizzie Pingree's gossip engrossed her, Will and Adrienne frequently attended the closed campus community's social affairs together. Whether or not there was ever more than friendship with Du Bois, it was widely noticed that she delighted in his urbanity.[44] In Adrienne Herndon's large, dark eyes, Booker Washington was a perfect boor.

Well after the final roast beef dinner on Thursday, the men at Niagara sat haggling and amending at the Erie Beach Hotel. The structure they imposed on the movement reflected the organizational schema Du Bois had proposed to Washington for the Committee of Twelve. They decided on an executive committee comprised of the chairmen of each Niagara state chapter (to be organized immediately). The Press and Public Opinion Committee, with Du Bois and Trotter as members, along with the Committee on Finance, was the most important of the ten special committees created. Annual membership dues of five dollars were assessed. Du Bois was elected general secretary and attorney George Jackson of Cincinnati general treasurer. Working harmoniously with Trotter, Du Bois drafted the document defining and excoriating the wrongs inflicted because of race. Fifty-seven years earlier, Elizabeth Cady Stanton, Lucretia Mott, and Frederick Douglass had come to Seneca Falls, New York, less than a hundred miles away on Lake Ontario, to demand equal rights for women and had drafted the uncompromising "Declaration of Sentiments." Man had endeavored in every way he could, Stanton and Mott charged, "to destroy [woman's] confidence in her own powers, to lessen her self-respect, and to make her willing to lead a dependent and abject life." No further indication exists other than the similarity of language that either Du Bois or Trotter (a reluctant feminist in any case) consciously looked back to that other small gathering of civil rights pioneers for their model. Nevertheless, the Niagara "Declaration of Principles" appeared to owe much to a distaff lineage. "We refuse to allow the impression to remain that the Negro American assents to inferiority," Du Bois and Trotter declared, that he "is submissive under oppression and apologetic before insults. Through helplessness we may submit, but the voice of protest of ten million Americans must never cease to assail the ears of their fellows, so long as America is unjust."[45]

In its final form, the "Declaration of Principles" crackled with indignation and brimmed with imperatives—the language beneath each upper case heading uncompromising yet disciplined, defiant yet devoid of hyperbole. The declaration under "EMPLOYERS AND LABOR UNIONS" bore Du Bois's unmistakable imprint. It struck an economic note then rarely heard among African-American leaders and only infrequently sounded by the thirty-nine-year-old Du Bois himself:

> We hold up for public execration the conduct of two opposite classes of men: The practice among employers of importing ignorant Negro American laborers in emergencies, and then affording them neither protection nor permanent employment; and the practice of labor unions in proscribing and boycotting and oppressing thousands of their fellow-toilers, simply because they are black. These methods have accentuated and will accentuate the war of labor and capital, and they are disgraceful to both sides.

Those words were drawn from his bombshell Des Moines address to the American Missionary Association. Labor relations were important, but "PROTEST" was at the heart of Niagara, and what protest would mean from then on, until the reign of Booker Washington ended, Du Bois and Trotter passionately expounded:

> The Negro race in America stolen, ravished and degraded, struggling up through difficulties and oppression, needs sympathy and receives criticism; needs help and is given hindrance, needs protection and is given mob-violence, needs justice and is given charity, needs leadership and is given cowardice and apology, needs bread and is given a stone. This nation will never stand justified before God until these things are changed.

As they boldly redrew guidelines for the future of the African in America, some of the Niagarites reminded their fellows of the vast debt ("HELP") owed to white Americans of Christian and humanitarian principles—"our fellow men from the abolitionist down to those who today still stand for equal opportunity and who have given and still give of their wealth and of their poverty for our advancement." With the voting of the "Constitution and By-Laws of the Niagara Movement," a document inspired by Du Bois's rejected Committee of Twelve proposal, the first Niagara meeting closed with thanks voted to general secretary Du Bois and others. The new civil rights organization would be incorporated in late January 1906.[46]

BOOKER WASHINGTON'S case would have been better served if his machine had been less efficient in opposing the Niagara Movement. The flow of money, the deluge of cautionary letters, and the Wizard's own public dismissal of the "Declaration of Principles" as so much idle talk (when he spoke in September 1905 before the annual meeting of the National Negro Business League), began to strike some of his white supporters as excessive. At first, Du Bois heard only a "furor of the most disconcerting criticism" and a series of savage personal attacks; but a slow shift of alliances was under way that would put the Wizard increasingly on the defensive. The canny educator instantly would have sensed the earth beginning to move under his feet as he read Francis Garrison's long, frank letter of September 25, 1905, about Niagara and other matters. "On the whole," he concluded, Du Bois's platform "seemed to [him] a very able and forceful presentation, and one to which [he] could heartily subscribe." Furthermore, Garrison had not at all liked the Wizard's explanation of the recent Wanamaker affair—another dinner brouhaha, this one at Saratoga Springs with male and female members of that socially prominent white family. The Wizard denied lending his arm to Miss Wanamaker upon entering the dining room, complaining to the editor of the Montgomery, Alabama, *Advertiser* that it was just about impossible to avoid socializing with white people when in the North. "I must say that in tone and substance it seemed to me unworthy of you," Garrison sniffed, "and calculated to delight equally your white detractors at the South and your colored critics and opponents at the North."[47]

Ever since Baldwin's disabling brain tumor toward the end of 1904, things had begun to go slightly out of kilter for the Wizard. When the Long Island Rail Road president died suddenly the following January, the Wizard's sense of loss was akin to experiencing the death of an older brother. In one of his last letters to Baldwin—a long and uncharacteristically personal one written in May 1904—the Wizard had unburdened himself. The Ogden Special, packed with happy philanthropists, had remained at Hampton Institute two full days while its passengers basked in an ether of humble deference and spirituals. It had then come to Tuskegee for four perfunctory hours. Invidious comparisons had been drawn by journalists on board the special, to the detriment of the Wizard's fiefdom. "It is wholly untrue that our students refuse to sing or dislike to sing plantation songs," he protested to Baldwin, or that Tuskegee's students were "not as wide-awake and alert as the Hampton students." The problem was, as he reminded Baldwin again, that, since not even a distinguished educator like himself was permitted aboard the special because of race, misconceptions arose easily.

Washington had reason to feel cruelly mocked. Had he been able to read Edgar Murphy's doomsday letter to Ogden in March 1904, Washington's dogged faith in accommodation might have wavered for a terrible hour or so. "Poor fellow!" Murphy sighed, "I am glad he does not see—and cannot see—the situation as it is."[48] There were, however, situations Washington could see only too clearly. Another of his white dinner companions was currently a source of considerable political embarrassment to him. Despite the favorable publicity surrounding Teddy Roosevelt's refusal to withdraw Dr. Crum's name for Senate confirmation to the port of Charleston, Du Bois and his Talented Tenth crowd noisily noticed that the president had appointed fewer African-Americans to federal positions than had any of his precedessors. After the 1904 elections, the Wizard had been able to win hardly any appointments at all. The president's conduct toward the white South began to signal that the Republican party took Booker Washington and the black vote for granted.[49]

As Du Bois's battle with Washington intensified, he searched desperately for a publication to advance the ideology and program of the Talented Tenth among the general African-American public. Thus far, the opposition's stranglehold on newspapers and magazines was patent proof that freedom of the press belonged to those who owned one. Besides the nationally read New York *Age*, Indianapolis *Freeman*, and numerous other city newspapers trumpeting the Hampton-Tuskegee line, there was the well-edited *Southern Workman*, a monthly published at Hampton, and the homespun "To My People," the Wizard's regular bulletin from Tuskegee, fairly saturating the African-American reading market. As early as June 1903, Du Bois had sounded out the critically acclaimed African-American novelist Charles Chesnutt on the subject of founding a "national Negro journal."[50] Most Negro publications were little more than "mediums for hair straightening advertisements and the personal laudations of 'self-made men,' " replied Chesnutt. A reputable publication was needed, but he wondered about the "question of support."

Du Bois wondered too, but in March of the following year he took action. He formed a partnership first with Edward L. Simon, and then with Harry Pace, both recent Atlanta University graduates, and together they bought the Memphis printing plant of W. J. Yerby at 163 Beale Street for a total investment of $2,734.74. The three men risked their savings to come up with the funds necessary to buy and reequip the press, but Simon and Pace, who obviously admired their former professor a great deal, risked their livelihoods. Simon resigned his teaching post at Lemoyne College in

Memphis to run the press on a monthly salary of sixty dollars, and Pace a few months later left his instructorship at a small Georgia institute to become business manager. Having invested his own money in the plant, which by December 1904 had earned more than thirteen hundred dollars from printing contracts, Du Bois had some reason to expect encouragement from philanthropic whites. "The present is a very critical time for the American Negro," he told prospective backers. "Certain ideals, racial and cultural, must be brought home to the rank and file."[51]

Financier Jacob Schiff, on whom he pinned high hopes, had replied cordially in early April 1905. Schiff "well remember[ed] our meeting in Bar Harbor" in summer 1903. Du Bois's proposal was "interesting" and had his "sympathy." Before deciding whether he ought to part with ten thousand dollars, however, the Wall Street financier asked for permission to show Du Bois's letter to men "whose opinion in such a matter I consider of much value." In granting him permission, Du Bois was certain that the much-valued opinion Schiff would seek resided at Tuskegee. Before Schiff's reply came, Du Bois wrote another Bar Harbor acquaintance, the dictionary publisher George Merriam, about his plans for a magazine and expressed the hope that his publication could avoid being "knocked promptly on the head" by the Wizard. Finally, in January 1906, Schiff turned Du Bois down; Washington almost certainly had thought poorly of the proposal.[52] Still hopeful, Du Bois approached Isaac N. Seligman, a progressive financier, asking unsuccessfully for half the amount he had requested of Schiff. "I have begun to publish," he told Seligman. "I have already begun and I am sending samples." But when it came down to a choice between Du Bois and Washington, not even Isaac Seligman contemplated breaking ranks with his fellow capitalists. Meanwhile, old traveling companion John Dollar sent an admiring, chatty letter. Du Bois had hinted broadly to Dollar about a loan of two hundred (whether in pounds or dollars was ambiguous) if Dollar were "rolling in wealth (as no doubt you are)." The money would be as safe as the Bank of England's, Du Bois bantered, because he and two "modest" partners "planned [for the publication] to become the periodical of the century." Dollar missed "dear old Burghardt," and the "glorious Italian sun" they had shared, and expressed amazement that his American friend kept up his spirits "after all you have gone through," but Dollar appears not to have sent money.[53]

The Moon Illustrated Weekly made its debut on December 2, 1905. It was the first illustrated weekly in Afro-America, with illustrations that look as though they might have been drawn by the editor. The Guardian Real

Estate Company ("Lots for Sale to Good Colored People Only"), Union Painless Dentists ("Welcomes Colored Patients"), the Leland Pressing Club ("all work guaranteed"), Atlanta Mutual Insurance Association (A. F. Herndon, president), and about a half dozen other Memphis and Atlanta businesses were to be mainstay advertisers. It seemed more than reasonable to editor Du Bois to suppose that of the fifty thousand black people in Memphis and sixty thousand in Atlanta, *The Moon*'s other distribution point, many would sign up for a five-cent publication (averaging less than ten pages) intended to stimulate "wide self-knowledge within the race." Only four of a run of thirty-four issues have survived, and the first issues for December 1905 are among the missing (publication ceased either in July or early August 1906).[54]

Du Bois grouped *The Moon*'s materials under resonant captions such as "Along the Color Line," "Whirl of the World," "Tidings of the Darker Millions," and "The Man in the Moon." With Du Bois selecting or writing most of its copy, weekly subject matter included both domestic (paving roads in Fort Smith, Arkansas; an Oswald Villard high school address in Washington, D.C.; a race riot in Springfield, Ohio; the novelist Lew Wallace's alleged African ancestry; Alabama disfranchisement) and international (commercial, political, or racial developments in Barbados, Liberia, and Zululand) events. *The Moon* for March 2 was dedicated to the memory of Paul Laurence Dunbar, Du Bois's friend from Wilberforce days who had died of consumption in early February—"a writer of true and catholic feeling and inspiration." Each issue reprinted a broad range of editorials on civil rights and labor topics drawn from newspapers throughout the North and South. There was news of the new Constitution League organized principally by New York businessman John Milholland; of the opposition of Massachusetts African-Americans to a state appropriation for the segregated 1907 Jamestown Exposition tercentenary; of the Negrophobe ravings of Mississippi's Vardaman; of disfranchisement in Alabama and Georgia; as well as of much that held local or professional appeal.[55]

Just three months after Du Bois, Simon, and Pace founded their weekly, one of the now-missing issues must have reported (as had Barber's *Voice of the Negro*) on a Deep South gathering that would have been barely conceivable a few years earlier, the first annual meeting that February of the Georgia Equal Rights Convention. Two hundred African-American delegates from the state's eleven congressional districts assembled at Macon under the guidance of William J. White, that racially indeterminate civil rights firebrand from Augusta; John Hope; Max Barber; Bishop Henry M. Turner, the voice of black emigration; Du Bois; and eight others. The delegates were respectful of Washington's accomplishments, but they applauded and approved the adoption of an address by Du Bois that was tantamount to a militant manifesto in the heart of Georgia. "We do not desire association with any who do not wish our company," he proclaimed from the rostrum, "but we do expect in a Christian, civilized land, to live under a system of law and order, to be secure in life and limb and property, to travel in comfort and decency and to receive a just equivalent for our money." Furthermore, although "some of us are not yet fit for the ballot," Du Bois swore that most were, that none of the Jim Crow laws could withstand scrutiny, and that he and the two hundred men at Macon would insist on full civil rights for their people.[56]

How many readers *The Moon* attracted can only be guessed at, but they almost surely numbered in the hundreds rather than the thousands. Yet *The Moon* turned the heat up higher and higher on the Wizard. The piece "Then and Now," in May 1906, presented a dismal balance sheet. Noting that the *Age* had drawn a parallel between hard times the race experienced under the leadership of Frederick Douglass and those of the present, Du Bois was at his trenchant best in demolishing Fortune's casuistry. Under Douglass there had been the Klan, race riots, the end of Reconstruction, ballot fraud, adverse court decisions, and the first separate passenger-train laws. Hardly a triumphant legacy, it was true, but what had come with the ascendancy of the Wizard? asked Du Bois: Separate passenger trains in nine states, disfranchisement in six states, annual lynchings by the hundred. Finally, public opinion in the North had virtually ceded civil rights to the white South. Could readers imagine Frederick Douglass or John Mercer Langston, another towering leader of the period after Reconstruction, telling African-Americans "not to worry over 'Jim Crow' cars but to proceed to buy up railways?" Or that ballot fraud "was an encouragement to industry?" "But granted all these heavy calamities are not wholly or even mainly due to the leadership of the last quarter century," Du Bois conceded as he moved in for the kill, "can Mr. Fortune say of Mr. Washington what he so justly says of Mr. Douglass?" Had Booker Washington "stood before this bewildered, crushed and outraged race as 'a champion always great, eloquent and dignified'?"[57] Du Bois assumed that merely to pose these questions obliged a categorical negative.

"We need faith," *The Moon* for June 23, 1906, exhorted. "Particularly is this true among the thinking classes." The thinking classes were promised a major reconsecration of faith when the Niagara Movement held its next meeting. Du Bois and his associates selected a time and place for that meeting that resounded with significance in the history of black peoples' struggles: Harper's Ferry, West Virginia, on August 15–18—a meeting fitly celebrating "the 100th anniversary of John Brown's birth, and the 50th jubilee of the battle of Osawatomie. Rates for board will not exceed $1 per day." The month before, Trotter's stiff opposition to the admission of women to the movement (and specifically to the admission of one of the Grimké wives) had been overridden. Du Bois had forced the issue by organizing on his own authority a Massachusetts Niagara Women's Auxiliary, putting Clement Morgan's wife in charge. Trotter still disapproved of official admission of women to the movement but would come to Harper's Ferry resigned to the ratification of Du Bois's proposal, and in a mood remarkably free of his usual cantankerousness.[58]

THE SECOND meeting of the Niagara Movement opened on August 15, 1906, at the time of year when the Blue Ridge Mountains are at their greenest. Calvin Chase's *Bee* reported trains arriving from Washington all day Wednesday (over the same railroad tracks that had brought federal reinforcements to defeat the demonic John Brown), bringing delegates and visitors "until the ample dormitories of Storer College were filled."[59] Harper's Ferry was an occasion for reconsecration of Talented Tenth ideals. The delegates and sympathizers came on foot and by horse-drawn carriage from the station in the seasonably warm town below to the spacious, shaded campus of Storer College, another AMA institution for the uplift of ex-slaves, men in high, starched collars and women in hats that looked like mushrooms or flying saucers. Women were not allowed into the meetings, an explosive issue that would be resolved at Harper's Ferry in their favor for the next Niagara conclave. One of them, handsome Mary Ovington, came as a reporter for the New York *Evening Post*. She had admired Du Bois from afar for the better part of a year before finally meeting him during a roving visit to the South in spring 1904 (she had not guessed, nor had Du Bois, that her Radcliffe years coincided with his at Harvard). Since then, she had conferred by letter with him whenever a thought about the Negro came into her head, placing her considerable energies and influence at her hero's service. It was she who had first suggested that he invite her to the meeting. Trotter brought a piece of John Brown's Springfield, Massachusetts, house to present to the movement. Byron Gunner of Rhode Island, Professor Hart and Lafayette Hershaw of the District of Columbia, Dr. O. M. Waller of

New York, Lewis Douglass, Frederick's son who had survived his Civil War regiment's famous assault on Fort Wagner, and many others came to rekindle the fires of Fort Erie.[60]

As the people listened to reports on the scourge of Jim Crow, Du Bois worried about the comprehensive, eloquent statement he was expected to have ready for the closing session on Sunday. Writing it out in his left-handed scrawl, he dashed about in vain looking for a typewriter. Somehow his own portable had failed to follow him from Atlanta. At the same time, he presided over sessions and conferred in committee and with individuals about urgent Niagara business. Meanwhile, the speeches continued: Freeman Murray's call to order; followed by Miss Eva Herrod's solo and college president Henry T. MacDonald's welcome; and the main address by J. R. Clifford, secretary of the West Virginia branch of the Niagara Movement. Thursday night—"Niagara Night"—Trotter and Max Barber spoke before Miss Mary Clifford recited the stirring "Credo." Early Friday after the women's meeting, the men and women of the Niagara Movement marched barefoot on dewy grass with candles cupped against the morning breeze in silent procession down the steep road from their hilltop residence halls to pay homage to Brown's memory in the old arsenal. They made the silent march in obedience to Du Bois's flair for drama. That afternoon they heard his praise of Brown's rage and rectitude, after which they sang again "The Battle Hymn of the Republic"—"but never with such enthusiasm as this afternoon," Ovington wrote in the *Evening Post*. But it was left to Reverdy Ransom to electrify the significance of place and moment when they reassembled on the hilltop in Anthony Hall. "God sent John Brown to Harper's Ferry," the tall, long-maned preacher told them, "to become a traitor to the government in order that he might be true to the slave."[61] Ransom's address was as lengthy as it was cathartic, going straight to the heart of the Niagara Movement, his voice booming from the auditorium's rafters:

> Today, two classes of Negroes, confronted by a united opposition, are standing at the parting of the ways. The one counsels patient submission to our present humiliations and degradations; it deprecates political action and preaches the doctrine of industrial development and the acquisition of property. . . . The other class believes that it should not submit to being humiliated, degraded, and remanded to an inferior place. It believes in money and property, but it does not believe in bartering its manhood for the sake of gain.[62]

Nothing was to match the applause given to Ransom's oratory until Hershaw read Du Bois's cadenced and compelling "Address to the Country" on the last night of the conference. The men and women at Harper's Ferry were exalted by Du Bois's five-point resolution demanding quality education, enforcement of the Fourteenth Amendment provision for reduction in the congressional representation of states where black people had been eliminated from the ballot, and justice and jobs for black people and laboring people ("here at last I approached," he would write in the *Autobiography*, "the fundamental matter of the exploitation of the worker, regardless of race and color"). His typist had finally rendered the handwritten text legible, and, as Hershaw recited it dramatically, the language lifted the Niagarites. "We will not be satisfied to take one jot or tittle less than our manhood rights," Du Bois had written:

> We claim for ourselves every single right that belongs to a freeborn American, political, civil and social; and until we get these rights we will never cease to protest and to assail the ears of America. The battle we wage is not for ourselves alone but for all true Americans. It is a fight for ideals, lest this, our common fatherland, false to its founding, become in truth the land of the thief and the home of the Slave—a by-word and a hissing among the nations for its sounding pretensions and pitiful accomplishments.

"The Address to the Country" ended with the irrefutably reasonable demand, "Cannot the nation that has absorbed ten million foreigners into its political life without catastrophe absorb ten million Negro Americans into that same political life at less cost than their unjust and illegal exclusion will involve?"[63]

LITTLE MORE than an hour away by train from Harper's Ferry, Theodore Roosevelt studied an alarming report that would lead to a fateful decision as Du Bois led his votive procession to John Brown's fort. The president's popularity at that moment with African-Americans was enormous. Had he not broken bread in the White House with the Great Accommodator? Had he not stood fast when the white South fulminated against Senate confirmation of William Crum as Collector of the Port of Charleston? He had even shut the post office in Indianola, Mississippi, after the competent Minnie M. Cox had been terrorized by local whites into resigning as postmistress. The fact that Roosevelt had badly needed the support of southern African-

American delegates to the 1904 GOP national convention in order to fend off a nomination challenge engineered by party boss Mark Hanna accounted for much of his unconventional behavior. Elected in his own right in 1904, the brilliant, impetuous president immediately began to distance himself from his many African-American admirers (of whom Du Bois was never one). In his Lincoln Day address in February 1905, he appealed for white racial purity. On swings through the South in April and October, Roosevelt stressed his mother's southern birth, lectured Tuskegee undergraduates about the dangers of falling into crime, and derided African-Americans as a "backward race."[64] Yet until November 1905, he was still the most popular president for African-Americans since Abraham Lincoln.

In a dust-swept river town on the Texas border with Mexico, ten minutes of rifle fire would cause the president to make a decision that would destroy much of his popularity with black people. The Brownsville Raid, in which black infantry soldiers were alleged to have shot up the town, killing a white bartender and wounding a police lieutenant, happened around midnight on Monday, August 13. From the hour the white battalion commander, Major Charles W. Penrose, had marched his three companies, B, C, and D, smartly down Elizabeth Street into the fort from the train station, the behavior of Brownsville's ruling white minority and some six thousand Mexicans had been hostile. When the raid occurred, the Niagara delegates and visitors were still a day and a few hours away from taking trains for Harper's Ferry. All that they knew at the time from news accounts was that charges had been lodged against virtually all the men of the First Battalion of the 25th Infantry Regiment (Colored), recently transferred to sun-baked Fort Brown at the mouth of the Rio Grande. The 25th Infantry was one of the four congressionally authorized military units whose men, and occasionally a few of whose officers, were African-Americans. It was a crack regiment, hardened by combat with the Great Plains Sioux, jungle rot in Cuba, firefights with Filipino guerrillas, and four years of garrison duty in Nebraska.[65]

The matter receded to newspaper back pages and then disappeared. The army investigated. The White House kept its counsel. Congressional elections approached in November with Republican control of the House hanging in the balance. African-American votes were significant to the GOP in Maryland, New York, Missouri, Ohio, New Jersey, and Kansas. A few days before the elections, Teddy Roosevelt signed an unprecedented order and, temporarily withholding it from the public, steamed away to Panama aboard the presidential yacht to see America's new canal. After a preliminary and inexpert investigation and without benefit of courts martial, what Roosevelt had done was to order the discharge en masse of 167 of the First Battalion's 170 soldiers without honor and with forfeiture of pension, among them men with twenty-five years service, six of them Medal of Honor winners. The world press would shortly carry the grinning image of a muscular, khaki-clad president at the controls of a behemoth canal dredge, a fitting posture for a chief executive who had significantly expanded the writ of the Monroe Doctrine the previous year. Roosevelt had steamed out of Washington after once again trashing the courage of black fighting men just as he had done immediately after the Spanish-American War. Ironically, it had been the men of the 25th who had reinforced the Rough Riders at a desperate moment in the famous charge up San Juan Hill.[66]

Roosevelt had informed the Wizard of his intentions at the White House on October 30, in strictest confidence. Appalled by the "great blunder," Washington had begged Roosevelt to reconsider. Almost simultaneously, John Milholland of the new, interracial Constitution League telephoned Mary Terrell from New York on the morning of the third, a Saturday, telling her she must bustle off to find Secretary of War Taft at home. The elephantine secretary of war took the extraordinary step of telegraphing Roosevelt that he was suspending the dismissal order until his return. But all of them—Washington, Terrell, and Taft—ran up against the president's rock-solid opposition. "You cannot have any information to give me privately, to which I could pay heed, my dear Mr. Washington," Roosevelt had already written his old dinner companion. On November 7, the day after the elections in which the Republicans retained control of the House, Roosevelt's discharge of the men of the 25th Infantry's First Battalion was made public. Had the news come earlier, said Richard Thompson in his syndicated column in the black press, "there would have been a disastrous slump in the colored Republican vote." Roosevelt's son-in-law, brand-new representative Nicholas Longworth, acknowledged a debt to African-American voters for his narrow victory. But if the announcement's timing was cynical, the administration's proof of the men's guilt was a tissue of circumstance and conjecture, amounting, said the *World*, to "lynch law." Even *The New York Times* gagged: "Not a particle of evidence is given in the 112 pages" proving the guilt of a single enlisted man. The new Constitution League's investigators returned from Texas with hard evidence of the regiment's innocence.[67]

For African-Americans, Brownsville was the nadir. From pulpits across the land imprecations were hurled at the president and the Wizard. "Once enshrined in our hearts as Moses," cried Reverend Adam Clayton Powell, Sr., of Harlem's Abyssinian Baptist Church, Roosevelt was "now enshrouded in our scorn as Judas." If Roosevelt refused to change his mind, a member of the Tuskegee Machine wrote Emmett Scott, "his name will be anathema with the Negroes from now on," leaving unsaid the obloquy in store for all that Tuskegee stood for. Leonine senator Joseph Bensen Foraker of Ohio (ally of the recently deceased Hanna) demanded a full, open investigation, and Taft fretted that the Brownsville incident might put the ambitious senator into the White House. The Wizard sadly warned Taft that he had "never in all my experience with the race experienced a time when the entire people have the feeling that they now have in regard to the Administration." Hurried appointments of Boston's William Lewis and four or five other African-Americans to largely honorific federal posts made little difference. "Neither Mr. Washington nor the colored people . . . can risk the hazard to be moved as mere pawns on this chess board of the President," Fortune editorialized in the *Age*, virtually ending his close collaboration with the Tuskegee Machine. The Cleveland *Gazette* offered a much blunter warning: "Politics will yet KILL the great Tuskegee school. *Mark our prediction!*"[68]

Summer and fall of 1906 were to be a watershed for African-Americans, the weeks following the Harper's Ferry conference bringing almost unrelieved turmoil. In late August 1906, Du Bois was in Lowndes County, Alabama, fulfilling a research commission for the U.S. Bureau of the Census, when news of the Atlanta race riot reached him. Before midnight on September 22, ten thousand white people (most of them under twenty) had beaten every black person they found on the streets of the city. The post office, train station, and white-owned businesses had been pillaged whenever the marauding mob, ferreting out its prey like a huge bloodhound, sniffed terrified black employees in hiding. At Five Points, Atlanta's busy intersection where electric trolleys coming from all parts of the city rumbled through, the mob plucked out dark-skinned passengers like cotton balls for ginning, finally bringing the transit system to a dead stop before midnight. "In some portions of the streets," the *Constitution* reported, "the sidewalks ran red with the blood of dead and dying negroes." Sôme African-Americans fought back before heavy rainfall and the militia finally scattered their assailants shortly before dawn. John Hope's wife recalled a white mob's abrupt halt and about-face when it thought better of invading a notoriously tough black ghetto near the Morehouse campus.

The attack by county police and other rioters on Brownsville in far southeast Atlanta, a prosperous black community of neat homes and two institutions of learning, resulted in the deaths of two white county policemen and the serious wounding of two others. "Atlanta," the august Memphis *Commercial Appeal* decreed, "brought shame to the South."[69] From Roosevelt's White House there was only silence.

The immediate cause of the terrible Atlanta riot of 1906 had been the newspaper drumfire of alleged assaults upon white women by black men. The underlying cause was to be found in the politics of class conflict among the white people. As cities of the New South like Atlanta filled with poor whites and blacks, the planters and politicians in rural counties mobilized the "wool hat boys" to brake the power of the urban colossi. Bloodsucking railroads, flint-hearted banks, merciless factories, the loss of white men's jobs to black men, sin, corruption, and race mixing—the rural diatribe against the cities was shrill and long. It had almost as much resonance in the cities; in Wilmington, North Carolina, in November 1898, nimble upper-class white people had made common cause with frenzied rednecks to purge the city with fire and blood of Negro rule. It was now the turn of Atlanta, the capital of the New South, where black men and women were accused of setting terrible examples for their country cousins by throwing off three hundred years of servility. Black people were denounced because they threatened to become a labor reserve against white workers, because they were learning to bargain their ballots with the sons of the Bourbons for public schools and sewage systems, while poor white people, with only skin color in their favor, struggled to keep from becoming proletarianized. As Du Bois wrote in a moving essay in *The World Today*, the explosion had occurred inevitably after "two years of vituperation and traduction of the Negro race by the most prominent candidates for governorship, together with a bad police system."[70] There was bitter justice in the fact that the Atlanta Compromise of 1895 would end in the Atlanta riot of 1906. In the Gresham's law of New South race relations, the "good nigger," loyal and undemanding, would cease to exist almost overnight, supplanted by the "bad nigger," criminal and sexually barbarous.

Hoke Smith, former interior secretary in Grover Cleveland's cabinet, and Clark Howell, natty *Constitution* editor and stalwart of the Wizard's Atlanta Compromise (both upper class, moderate, and well connected to business), went to great extremes to capture redneck votes for the Georgia governorship. Smith, a Democrat supported by the Atlanta *Journal*, at first posed as something of a Populist, advocating regulation of railroad rates and avoiding the issue of the Negro. Howell, Democrat and undisguised friend of order and wealth, attacked Smith as a bogus friend of the little man who had furthered the careers of well-connected African-Americans while serving as secretary of the interior. Unnerved, Smith switched from lambasting railroads to bashing Negroes as the price for Georgia Populist Tom Watson's crucial support. Take the black people out of politics, finally, decisively, Watson demanded of Smith—"nothing can be done as long as the South is forever frightened into political paralysis by the cry of 'negro domination.' " "What does Civilization owe to the negro? Nothing! *Nothing!* NOTHING!" he shrieked in *Tom Watson's Magazine*. Having uncorked the red genie of race and class conflict, Howell tried in vain to put it back, declaring that the African-American was already a dead letter in politics, so there was no need to disfranchise him by law. Smith won the Democratic primary that August, and pledged to shut the ballot box to Georgia's African-Americans by constitutional referendum. Exactly one month and one day later, after tens of thousands of rural white people had streamed into Atlanta to hear the Democratic candidate for president, Bryan the Great Commoner, Atlanta exploded.[71] The Bookerite press would insinuate that Du Bois had gone there to hide out until calm was restored while a courageous Wizard had hurried from New York to help his people. Neither report was correct. Washington stayed put for several more days, issuing deeply pained, even-handed condemnations of black rapists and white rioters. Du Bois rushed to the city by train to sit on the steps of South Hall to protect Nina and Yolande with a shotgun. An exact tally of the dead was never known, though it must have approached two dozen black people and five or six white. "The Atlanta riot was if anything worse than reports," Du Bois wrote Ovington a few days after reaching the city.

"On the way," Du Bois related of his rush from rural Alabama, "I wrote the 'Litany of [sic] Atlanta.' " One sees him in the segregated passenger car, perhaps a smelly one filled with women, children, and farmhands, his temples throbbing as he wrote slowly and with fierce deliberation line after phosphorescent line. Three weeks later he would tell Ovington that he knew "A Litany at Atlanta" was "a bit hysterical," which it appropriately was—both a bit hysterical and a bit heretical. Its publication in the October 11 *Independent* was like a thunderstorm. "*Hear us, good Lord!* Listen to us, Thy children: our faces dark with doubt are made a mockery in Thy Sanctuary." But the God Du Bois apostrophizes is neither innocent nor omnipotent. "*Have mercy upon us, miserable sinners!* And yet, whose is the deeper guilt? . . . *Thou knowest, good God!* Is this Thy

Justice, O Father, that guile be easier than innocence and the innocent be crucified for the guilt of the untouched guilty?" With impassioned hubris Du Bois verged on blasphemy. "Is not the God of the Fathers dead? Have not seers seen in Heaven's halls Thine hearsed and lifeless form stark amidst the black and rolling smoke of sin, where all along bow bitter forms of endless dead?" But God was not dead, Du Bois decided, rather He has left the neighborhood, "flown afar, up hills of endless light, through blazing corridors of suns, where worlds do swing of good and gentle men."[72]

Then, abruptly, Du Bois turned melodramatically to the phoenix of the New South: "A city lay in travail, God our Lord, and from her loins sprang twin Murder and Black Hate. Red was the midnight; clang, crack, and cry of death and fury filled the air and trembled underneath the stars where church spires pointed silently to Thee. And all this was to sate the greed of greedy men who hide behind the veil of vengeance!" The riot, he as much as says, is the spawn of the unholy bargain of 1895. "Behold this maimed black man, who toiled and sweated to save a bit from the pittance paid him. They told him: *Work and Rise!* He worked. Did this man sin? Nay, but someone told how someone said another did—one whom he had never seen nor known. Yet for that man's crime this man lieth maimed and murdered, his wife naked to shame, his children to poverty and evil. *Hear us, O heavenly Father!*" "A Litany at Atlanta" rose to a coruscating pitch of remonstrance, all but commanding the Deity to make sense of black suffering and to relieve it: "Bewildered we are passion-tossed, mad with the madness of a mobbed and mocked and murdered people; straining at the armposts of Thy throne, we raise our shackled hands and charge Thee, God, by the bones of our stolen fathers, by the tears of our dead mothers, by the very blood of Thy crucified Christ: What meaneth this? Tell us the plan; give us the sign! *Keep not Thou silent, O God!*" But as he hurried from the old abolitionist Calhoun School in Lowndes County to the racial ceasefire in Atlanta, the last excruciating lines of "Litany" implied that Du Bois had no near-term expectation of divine signs and plans. "*Hear us, good Lord!* In night, O God of a godless land! Amen! In silence, O Silent God. Selah!"[73]

Du Bois's controlled fury would not be present at the awkwardly intense conference of white and black civil leaders called by Mayor James Woodward on Sunday. In all probability, he had not yet reached the city. Alonzo Herndon, Bishop Turner, and Reverend Proctor were among the eight African-Americans whose aggrieved, dignified bearing shamed the leading white people present into almost evangelical contrition. Charles T. Hopkins, standing at the pinnacle of power, called for contributions to bury the slaughtered and repair property damage, crying out, "If we let this dependent race be butchered before our eyes, we cannot face God in the Judgment Day." Pledges were exchanged, promises of police reform made, and within days the citizens group that would eventually become the Commission on Interracial Cooperation (CIC) was formed. Booker Washington actually thought the aftermath of the Atlanta riot offered grounds for renewed optimism about southern race relations. Du Bois understood that the compact Washington had struck no longer held because the parties on the other side no longer needed it. The Bourbon South, the South redeemed by conservative planters and colonels, had become, with the swiftness of the Mississippi at flood tide, the New South of urban industries, textile towns, railroads, the crop-lien system, competing labor, convict lease, and professional Negrophobes. The tornado of southern populism abating rapidly after 1896 had left the patriarchal politics of racial collaboration, practiced so skillfully by South Carolina's Wade Hampton and Mississippi's Lucius Lamar, splintered and pulped like uprooted trees. Yet it was still *plus ça change*, the more things remained the same. The conservative planters and colonels were not so much submerged in "new men" or pushed aside by Snopeses as reincarnated in the "radical" younger generation that had appropriated the language of the Populists, the racism of the rednecks, and the economic agenda of Yankee capitalists.[74] This was partly what Edgar Gardner Murphy had meant when he said he pitied Washington for not being able to see the racial situation as it truly was.

What the Wizard could see clearly, though, was the erosion of his power. At the July 1907 meeting of the Afro-American Council in Baltimore, once little more than an echo chamber for the Wizard, the members voted to censure President Roosevelt. In Cleveland, the president's favorite for mayor went down to defeat partly because of the African-American vote. While Washington complained to intimates that he had to keep his "lips closed," Du Bois made excellent use of the opportunity to advance his leadership influence.[75] He had a new monthly now, *The Horizon: A Journal of the Color Line*, debuting in January 1907 and published in Washington (and later Alexandria, Virginia) on the presses of Du Boisian loyalists Freeman Murray and his brother F. Morris Murray, with Hershaw as editor. *The Moon* had long since run through its final phase, extinguished in July or August of 1906. The partners had blamed each other for the weekly's failure, Simon feeling particularly bitter about Du Bois's attitude. The plant had been mortgaged for five hundred dollars,

Pace had worked without ever drawing a salary, and Simon snappishly informed Du Bois that something could be salvaged and debts repaid if only Du Bois would be "quiet"—"you may get a great deal more out of this business than you think."[76]

Better edited and more widely circulated than the Memphis publication, *The Horizon* was to have consistently more bite. The magazine was to be Du Bois's dress rehearsal for a career in propaganda journalism. Its words were like darts, sharper than *The Moon's* barbs had been, and the targets were larger. Du Bois noted derisively that the pious Edgar Gardner Murphy, who had lately taken to calling for repeal of the Fifteenth Amendment as a solution to worsening race relations, was equally exercised about the increasing "evil Negro leadership," which was guilty of stirring up "grievances and fostering hate." *The Horizon* attempted to cover the global world behind the veil, such as developments in Africa and Asia, as well as peonage in Alabama and lynching generally. The editor drew attention to persecution of Galician Jews and thundered against imperialism everywhere—denouncing the diabolic Congo policies of Leopold of the Belgians and calling the "Rape of Cuba and the Conquest of the Philippines" the blackest deeds in American history since the Seminole Wars.[77] In the second issue the editor now declared his faith in socialism more firmly than ever before. Mary Ovington never lost an opportunity to influence him in that direction, and his own reading of works like Jane Addams's *Democracy and Social Ethics*, Jack London's *People of the Abyss*, Robert Hunter's *Poverty*, and John Spargo's *Socialism*, as well as Ida Tarbell, Upton Sinclair, Lincoln Steffens, and other muckrakers had caused him to become more receptive. He was a "socialist-of-the-path." Black peoples' natural allies were not "the rich but the poor, not the great but the masses, not the employers, but the employees." Du Bois spoke obvious truths that were, nevertheless, far from obvious to most African-Americans (and not even to himself a few years previously), who still felt an almost religious loyalty to the Republican party. He didn't believe in the total abolition of private property, but he was certain that America was "approaching a time when railroads, coal mines, and many factories can and ought be run by the public for the public." In socialism lay "the one great hope of the Negro American."[78]

But socialism would have had little more than casual appeal for most of his readers. It was in "The Lash," a May 1907 editorial in which Du Bois presented a devastating psychological profile of the Wizard's minister of information for the North—Thomas Fortune—that Talented Tenth readers found potent ammunition. Fortune, once a great talent of moral force, had succumbed to the Wizard's lash of money and power. Du Bois recalled the avuncular encouragement Fortune had given to his own beginner's efforts as a journalist. "No matter how far the writer has fallen and grovelled in the dust," Du Bois wrote that he would forever be grateful. The great newspaperman had become increasingly "bitter, wild and strained." "Drink, women, and debt" assailed him. Then came the "Arch-Tempter"—Booker T. Washington—whispering that he had "a commission from the Gods-that-be to buy your soul." And so, Fortune was lost to the cause of civil rights. But Du Bois entreated readers to examine their own consciences to decide where the ultimate fault lay. "Who refused to hold up his hands? Who refused his wiser youthful leadership? Who withheld the money and bread and clothes due him and his suffering family? We did." Du Bois displayed no such tenderness for Teddy Roosevelt. Brownsville was a burning issue, and the editor served up hot coals. "If the truth must be told," Du Bois told readers, "Theodore Roosevelt does not like black folk. He has no faith in them. I do not think he really ever knew a colored man intimately as a friend." Stoking the coals, he asked rhetorically, "What after all have we to thank Roosevelt for?" Three things—"for asking a man to dine with him, for supporting another man, quite worthy of the position, as Collector of the Port of Charleston, and for saying, publicly, that the door of opportunity ought to be held open to colored men?" But Du Bois then noted acidly, "The door once declared open, Mr. Roosevelt by his word and deed since has slammed most emphatically in the black man's face."[79]

Du Bois's platform presence was improving, and he sensed that his message was beginning to draw sympathizers from around the edges of the powerful Tuskegee Machine. He reproached himself for not being able to "slap people on the shoulder, and I forgot their names." But he was determined somehow "to get these people together"—these Niagarites. Rallying most of them in a large audience of some eight hundred (the largest number ever) in Boston for the third annual meeting at the end of August 1907, he read once again another "Address to the Country." Flaying Roosevelt for "swaggering roughshod over the helpless black regiment whose bravery made him famous," he stirred the audience in Faneuil Hall. "We are not discouraged," he declared in that dry voice often more moving to his listeners than the standard, full-throated oratory typical of such occasions. "Help us brothers, for the victory which lingers, must and shall prevail." The Bookerite Indianapolis *Freeman* dismissed the Boston meeting as a "final shriek of despair," but it was a shriek that many had heard. The Niagara Movement's treasury had less than four hundred dollars in it, and many members were under mounting pressure from the Tuskegee Machine, but there were now thirty-four state chapters (although only one in the Deep South—Atlanta), more than ten thousand pamphlets, tracts, and the mobilization of African-American opinion to help defeat a passenger-segregation amendment to a federal railroad-rates bill.[80]

Modest success brought problems, though. Du Bois had decided to hold the third Niagara meeting in Boston only after forcing Trotter and Morgan to a truce in a dispute of such bitterness that movement unity had been taxed. There was ample wrong on both sides—Trotter was hypersensitive, Morgan was vain; Trotter opposed the state governor's reelection; Morgan supported it and high-handedly eliminated the Trotters from planning meetings for a Niagara money-raising social in Cambridge. Governor Curtis Guild was anathema to Trotter because of his approval of state funds for the segregated tercentenary exposition at Jamestown, Virginia. Far worse, Morgan had campaigned for Guild's successful reelection in return for GOP backing for a seat in the legislature. During several days' sojourn with the Trotters in mid-June, Du Bois was driven almost to distraction as he mediated between the Trotters and the Morgans. No sooner had new terms been agreed to by one side than the other side rejected them. Deenie Trotter huffily announced she was quitting the movement after Du Bois refused to cave in to her husband's twenty-two-page ultimatum. Trotter objected to his former colleague George Forbes's soldierly help and Morgan's large planning role in the third Niagara meeting. A "very difficult man to get along with whenever he differs from your opinion," Du Bois wrote Mary Ovington resignedly. His own leadership role was pretty exasperating, Du Bois added, "because it does not really belong to me . . . nevertheless I am going to try and do my duty."[81] Finally, thoroughly disgusted, Du Bois banged together an uneasy truce and then sailed for Europe. The Trotter rift, however, never mended, and the successful Boston meeting that August was really the beginning of the end of Niagara.

By July 1908, Du Bois was calling in *The Horizon* and elsewhere for a black exodus from the Republican party. For the great majority of the race, he knew that to urge desertion from the party of Lincoln was an almost incomprehensible heresy. On the other hand, now that Roosevelt had made a circuit through the South pandering to white supremacy and Taft had come out unabashedly for lily-white Republicanism, he thought it just barely possible that a significant number of his people might vote Democratic to show their contempt for the GOP's contempt of them. "It is high noon, brethren," he challenged in Trotter's *Guardian*—"the clock has struck twelve. What are we going to do? I have made up my mind. You can do as you please—you are free, sane and twenty-one. If between the two parties who stand on identically the same platform you can prefer the party who perpetuated Brownsville, well and good! But I shall vote for Bryan."[82] As he rallied to the lesser of two political evils, he saw the credibility of the Tuskegee Machine being put to the test as never before. Economic progress in exchange for political impotence was the touchstone of Booker Washington's creed, a vision of better times coming slow but sure as toil and savings earned relief from misery and respect from white folk. Beyond the fine buildings and manicured grounds of the Tuskegee campus, however, signs of black progress and white benignity had become rare ten years after the Atlanta Compromise. The price of cotton had been falling once again since 1903 from an already abysmal low, and with it constraints on white violence in the South. A plague of "whitecappings" (mob violence) infested southwestern Mississippi as poor white people lashed out against all signs of black success and tried to drive out black storekeepers, businessmen, and landowning farmers.

Few race leaders had embraced the Gospel of Tuskegee more fervently than Isaiah Montgomery, lone African-American delegate to the disfranchising 1890 Mississippi constitutional convention and founder of all-black Mound Bayou township. But in the fall of 1904, even the simple faith of Montgomery seemed to waver as he wrote desperately to the Wizard of terrible goings-on. At West Point, Reverend C. A. Buchanan, owner of "the best appointed printing establishment of any colored man in the state," and his genteel daughter were ordered by white people to sell his business and leave town. Thomas Henry, who ran a "neat little grocery and kept a buggy," was told to sell it and walk. Mr. Meacham, owner of a pool hall, was ordered to liquidate and report for manual labor in overalls. Montgomery's long, bleak letter evoked from the normally imperturbable Wizard the admission that such "conditions certainly do seem all but unbearable." So unbearable, indeed, that Governor Vardaman—white supremacy incarnate—had finally moved to suppress the lawlessness through the use of Pinkerton informers when it flared up again in 1906.[83]

The Atlanta riot spoke grim volumes about the extent to which the Bookerite bargain had become a fatal trap. Brownsville tore the veil of trust to shreds. At Jane Addams's Hull House in Chicago in 1907, Du Bois had played seer with uncanny perfection, warning that the "Door of Opportunity" was swinging shut and that times were coming "even here in the Twentieth Century when if an Abraham Lincoln should arise in the United States and if he should be a Jew in race or a Japanese in color, or a Negro in descent . . . his soul would be pressed and shut out of the republic of the civilized." When the fourth, and second to last, annual Niagara Movement meeting convened in Oberlin, Ohio, in August 1908, Du Bois brought tidings of doom. "Once we were told: Be worthy and fit and the ways are open," delegates heard him declare. "Today the avenues of advancement in the army, navy and civil service, and even in business and professional life, are continually closed to black applicants of proven fitness, simply on the bald excuse of race and color."[84] Du Bois and the Niagarites had tried to do their best to present an alternative to the Tuskegee Machine and to become an effective force against racial discrimination, but in terms of actual accomplishment they had largely preached to the converted. The real task lay perilously ahead.

13.
ATLANTA
Scholar Behind the Veil

HALFWAY THROUGH his thirty-seventh year, as the Niagara Movement was starting up, Du Bois remained outwardly motivated and organized in his professional activities, doing work that would have taxed a committee of scholars. Even so, his leadership role in the battle with Booker T. Washington not only increasingly distracted him, the impact of that burgeoning contest on funds for his own research and the financial health of Atlanta University became more stifling month by month. "I kept on writing and publishing [but] not with as much concentration of effort as I ought to have had," he recalled, adding, however, with wry understatement that he had still done so "with some effectiveness." Articles and essays flowed from his pen, a major biography was under way, and, while tending to the esprit de corps of his Niagarites, Du Bois continued to organize and edit for publication the annual conferences for which he was now nationally and becoming internationally known. The secret of his remarkable activity lay in the work routine he developed at some point between his Berlin days and the early Atlanta years. The regimen was formulated on lengths of graph paper on which each day of the week was segmented into precisely timed tasks that began after breakfast and ended, invariably, at nine in the evening. Bed by ten always, he would acquire a habit of saying later when asked to explain his excellent health in old age. As the years passed, the work charts would grow longer, scroll-like, covering whole desk tops and segmenting entire months in their rectilinear discipline—so much history, philosophy, or sociology read before eleven; so many pages of a monograph or novel written after lunch; essays and book reviews polished off before dictating institutional correspondence by dinnertime; so many letters to friends composed after dinner, and a work of fiction read until bedtime.[1]

Admired by visitors, Du Bois remained isolated and ignored by the white people of the city that his extraordinary labors were putting on the map of social science. Becoming a tale of two cities, the capital of the New South was a place in which black and white people possessed angry and embarrassed memories of a fast-receding epoch of more informal and comparatively flexible racial separation. Nothing symbolized the arbitrary and outcast status more humiliatingly than the total ban enforced by Atlanta's white people on the Talented Tenth's admission to the city's new public library, an ornate, well-stocked building that was the largest of its kind in the South. Du Bois railed against an exclusion that must, of all exclusions, have been hard to bear. What right had the City of Atlanta to take money "raised from the taxes of black and white" for the use of one race only, he demanded in a "Petition of Negroes to Use the Carnegie Library." Fortunate in having a handful of stimulating academic colleagues, traveling much in the North, and able to measure himself during the annual conferences against some of the nation's finest minds and major influences, Du Bois kept fully abreast of the contemporary intellectual ferment. But astute observers perceived something of his almost always tightly, proudly disguised suffering in purgatory. And sometimes Du Bois frankly confessed it. He had "often thought of what you told me about the gulf fixed between you and the white people of Atlanta," a northern white acquaintance wrote him. Then, too, as Columbia University's outstanding professor of economics, Edwin Seligman, himself Jewish, wrote, "A Litany at Atlanta" was really a public avowal of "the horror of it all" and the "tragedy for men like you—a tragedy all the greater because of the seeming impasse."[2] Atlanta was surely the major component in that arresting metaphor in *Dusk of Dawn* summing up a phase of his life, a life crucified on a vast wheel of time, whereon he "flew round and round with the Zeitgeist, waving my pen and lifting faint voices to explain, expound, and exhort."[3]

He could whirl with the Zeitgeist, but Nina was pretty much stuck. Walking the two-mile stretch to downtown Atlanta because she, like so many of her middle-class peers, refused to patronize the segregated transit system, Nina never knew when a shopping errand (often delayed until unavoidable) would end in an incident. It galled her to have to wait until every white customer had been served before a drawling department-store clerk deigned to recognize her. Along her route, there was not a single water fountain or park bench lawfully permitted to Negroes. Her Will could sublimate much of his outrage at Atlanta's racial grossness in letters to editors, *Atlantic Monthly* essays, and sociological studies. Nina was shy, intellectually average, and, like most women of her era and class, corseted by mores and conventions that prevented much of action, adventure, and variety. She was becoming a shadowy, silent figure seen less and less in public with or without her husband, a devoted—excessively devoted—mother to spunky, chubby, large-boned Yolande. If Lugenia Hope—an unusual woman able to combine her domestic and maternal duties as a distinguished professional's wife and mother with her own social-work involvement in slum improvement—ever offered discreet mentoring, Nina was emotionally poorly equipped (and probably never encouraged by Du Bois) to respond. The Atlanta riot had, in fact, actually been something of a mixed blessing because Will eventually decided that she should take Yolande to Great Barrington for the school year.[4]

The surviving letters from the early Atlanta years (and they are not numerous) reveal almost nothing of her inner feelings, her emotional needs during the period. In one letter (one of the earliest), Nina tells Will about baby Yolande searching for him in his study and saying, when told where he was, " 'why I know he's gone away and it's useless to look for him.' " "Useless to look for him" may have been Nina speaking through Yolande, for she added wistfully, "We are very lonely evenings here alone." Even when Will was home, he may not have been there for her. They had drifted apart to such a degree that Bazolene Usher noticed how often "Dr. Du Bois was cranky" and how little he and Mrs. Du Bois seemed to interact. Psychological cause and effect are seldom obvious, and from this distance in time they are murky in the extreme. Whether Burghardt's death wedged between them or whether they allowed it to push them apart because there was so little holding them together in the first place, each felt increasingly alienated from the other. Nina concentrated fussily and determinedly on their daughter, watching over her constantly, niggardly apportioning Yolande's playtime with the few children approved for contact, and having her clothing washed over and over. She behaved as though the hated city were only waiting to strike Yolande down and take her away like Burghardt. The absence of available public parks, the considerable distance to the other side of the city where a few more eligible children resided, and the proximity of slums like Buttermilk Bottom, crammed with unsavory adults and dirty children, nourished maternal fixation and unhealthy protectiveness, as did her own psychosomatic ups and downs. By the time Will finally made it possible to escape Atlanta, Nina had become prey to chronic ailments of a nonspecific character. "I am feeling some better today," her last surviving letter from this period ends. "I hope it will last."[5]

The best of husbands and fathers would have been sorely challenged by Du Bois's research and writing schedule, but, as Du Bois himself confessed, he was no model husband or father under any circumstances. He loved Yolande, and that love would be constant until she died. Seldom finding time to spend with her, he tried to express his affections periodically by letter. One Sunday in March 1907, after dictating letters into the gramophone in the South Hall apartment, it occurred to him there was just space enough on the record to address one to Yolande in Great Barrington. He wondered what she was doing, supposed she must be in bed at that moment, and told her that he missed her. Yet in this rare, early letter, Du Bois showed how almost inevitably he connected thoughts of his daughter to the real substance of his life. "But most of all," he said in closing, "I think papa misses you when he comes in and has nobody to interrupt his work. He'd be very glad to have you interrupt his work a little while now."[6] Wife and daughter were increasingly subordinated to the intellectual care and feeding of the African-American people. And even if he had been totally immune to the domestic insensibilities of most Edwardian males, which he was not, Du Bois would have sincerely believed that his unique insights and training amounted to a covenant with his people to serve them and, if possible, save them from a future as blighted as their past had been sorrowful. Zeitgeist prevailed over hearth.

The 1905 Atlanta University Studies Conference convened at the end of May as usual. The tenth in the series, it resulted in what was probably the most comprehensive bibliography on the African-American then available. But "Select Bibliography of the Negro American" was not Du Bois's main objective, and he was rather harsh on himself for having compiled what he decided was "a very imperfect" document. What was really significant about this tenth conference, he emphasized, was that it commenced a reformulation of all that had gone before. Each of the studies conducted thus far was to be repeated with greater amplitude and depth in ten-year cycles so as to provide social science with a firmer grasp of what was invariable, contingent, and evolving in the racial group whose unmatched authority Du Bois had become. The loyal Hershaw was among the participants, as well as the wife of Niagarite Butler Wilson of Boston, Mary Evans, who was as much a racial militant and public activist as her husband. But the drawing power of the conferences was now such that

Frances Kellor, the white New York social reformer, fresh from organizing the Inter-Municipal Committee on Household Research, accepted Du Bois's invitation to Atlanta. Writing Du Bois that she and her associates had been scandalized by the working and lodging conditions of black females, Kellor hurried to Atlanta to become better informed.[7] In 1906, she and Ruth Baldwin (even more active since the death of husband William) would establish the influential National League for the Protection of Colored Women.

Mary Ovington's arrival on campus was especially gratifying. By then, she and Du Bois had developed an unbuttoned intimacy in their correspondence, she the admiring novice, he the uncharacteristically chatty preceptor. When Ovington wrote how she had ached over his "Credo," Du Bois shared with her a secret psychic aspect of civil rights leadership, the elation that came to him from living deeply and defiantly in an evil world—"after all, there are wonderful compensations in all this thing." One compensation was the money Ovington began to remit for the Atlanta Studies, small but badly needed amounts she raised from such good-works patrons as V. Everit Macy, William Schieffelin, and Jacob Schiff. "Have I then been entertaining a millionaire unawares—a mere millionaire?" a grateful Du Bois teased.[8] Initially, he had been merely intrigued by her, and appreciative of her fan letters and modest financial contributions to Atlanta University, but gradually his respect for Ovington's solid social work credentials evoked his admiration. Ovington had come home from a 1900 study tour of London's East End slums shaken to the core, writing angrily in an unpublished autobiographical fragment of the brutal social conditions thrown up by capitalism—of "the life so far from the beauty and health of the life" that she had always known. Determinedly, she set out to change those conditions, plunging into the work of Greenwich House, New York's first neighborhood improvement association. She turned to socialism (a well-mannered and rather patient variety of it) and soon to the plight of African-American working women in New York. "I want to get a model tenement built in one of the crowded Negro quarters," she explained to Du Bois, adding that she was determined to get some of the Phipps settlement house money for that purpose, which she did.[9]

Meanwhile, she was reading everything on the subject of African-American urban conditions. Her talks with settlement house doyenne Mary Kingsbury Simkhovitch led her to Columbia's Franz Boas and the new anthropology stressing nurture over nature. She sought out the wise African-American pastor, William Henry Brooks, in his "little study" in St.

Mark's Episcopal Church in Brooklyn, and learned more about the needs of her new interest. Philanthropist Henry Phipps eventually declined to finance an entire settlement-house facility, but he gave Ovington enough to build The Tuskegee, a model tenement. Her articles in influential publications like *The Outlook* had already afforded her a level of respect that many veteran reformers never attained. A few years after her first visit to Atlanta, Du Bois was recommending her writings on urban black economic conditions as indispensable: "She knows more about it than anyone I know."[10] Much of what Ovington knew about African-American urban conditions had come, after all, from bibliographies and general advice that he had readily provided her. Yet Ovington found that what she had to say about the potential of black city-dwellers and the woeful inadequacy of industrial education as a panacea quickly became unpopular. *McClure's* rejected her article on tenement conditions as too upbeat. She claimed to have found a surprising degree of domestic pride and cleanliness among poor African-American families in New York. Their children as a rule were "better trained than most of our city poor," Ovington added. The essay eventually appeared in the *Colored American* magazine. Oswald Villard's New York *Evening Post* and William Ward's neoabolitionist *Independent* took her pieces, but the rest of the press disapproved of them. "Du Bois had broken into the *Atlantic Monthly* by the sheer force of his genius," she sighed later, "but no one could follow him." In fact, Du Bois had found by then that he could no longer follow himself.[11]

Ovington neither looked nor behaved like the stereotyped social reformer. She was tall, blonde, and handsome, with ice-blue eyes and an hourglass figure, the perfect product of old upper-crust Brooklyn society. Du Bois's Harvard friend, Bob Lovett, who had known her when she was at Radcliffe, described Ovington as "austerely beautiful." There had been dalliances when she was in her early twenties, and a more than casual relationship with the dashing John Milholland ("as sincere, enthusiastic, lovable a friend as the Negro ever had") perhaps was about to begin. Ex-newspaperman Milholland was a manufacturer of pneumatic message cylinders and founder of the Constitution League, something of a forerunner of the American Civil Liberties Union. Large, ruddy, handsome, and of Irish descent, he had become increasingly disillusioned after 1900 with the Republican party's abandonment of the African-American. Drawn to Booker T. Washington at first, he had been introduced by the Tuskegeean to Du Bois. They had liked each other instantly, which was unusual for Du Bois. Milholland and Ovington met for the first time in January 1905 when she introduced him to settlement house and tenement reform activities. Milholland was deeply religious and married, which made Ovington's entrance into his life a small earthquake. After comparing his and Ovington's diary entries for 1905, Ovington's biographer believes they rendezvoused in the Adirondacks for three weeks in July, where they became lovers.[12]

But the first and steadfast passion in the life of this forty-year-old woman was bettering the life of the poor and the abused. She had a special talent for empathizing with gifted individuals whose abilities were discounted or misunderstood by powerful white men, a perspective owing much to gender and disenchantment of class. She came to understand the workings of Du Bois's hair-trigger temperament and so was able a number of times to repair the damage it caused in situations where compromise and consensus were essential. Du Bois had practically commanded Ovington's attendance at the 1905 conference, writing that he "should like you to be here at Baccalaureate, May 28 and to stay until Commencement, June 1." She had once chaired a dinner in New York for Booker Washington, heard him speak and found him too much the Pollyanna. Du Bois, on the other hand, had excited her to a pitch of admiration through his writings and letters—"it was impossible to read him and not be moved." Twenty years later, she was still impressed by Du Bois's genius, its superb racial blending of French clarity and Dutch doggedness, as she speculated, but above all of its "African 'passion.' " Du Bois was unusually frank with Ovington about race matters from the beginning of their friendship. She would come about as close as any white person ever would to being a confidante and advisor. A year after her coming to Atlanta, he would write to her of his "extreme contempt and dislike" for Fred Moore, the Bookerite publisher of the New York *Age*, of his certainty that the officers of the Association for the Protection of Negro Women were "largely crazy," of his esteem for William Bulkley, the New York high school principal, and of the well-intentioned mediocrity of another prominent African-American.[13]

Ovington came to Atlanta at Du Bois's decree, therefore, dutifully and joyously—as well as to write about the South for Villard's *Evening Post*. They met at long last in the Atlanta University dining hall, where she took her seat beside Du Bois at dinner, marveling at his head "like Shakespeare's done in bronze." He talked nonsense throughout the meal just to show her, as he remarked in an aside to other faculty at table, that he was not "weeping all the time." Du Bois's response to Ovington that evening would be repeated many times in the future—a teasing levity tinged, in her case, with innocent flirtation. They would often behave as though they were or wished to become lovers, but, despite Du Bois's considerable and tested appeal to intelligent women, they almost certainly never were. A role Ovington would find herself reluctantly having to assume in numerous crucial situations was that of stern schoolmistress to the sulking star pupil Du Bois. But that evening in the Atlanta University refectory, the auguries were bright. Her "cup of happiness" at meeting him "was full," notwithstanding the hostile environment of the city.

Atlanta's color line was drawn "more rigorously . . . with more gusto, than in less commercial southern cities," Ovington noted; and she noted further what was to her the delicious irony that the city had "to endure the knowledge that its most distinguished citizen was black."[14] Describing the segregated cage in which Du Bois was forced to live, she dwelt on the cruel paradox of admiring northern and European visitors stopping at hotels "into whose lobby he [Du Bois] might not step. They saw a caste system as if a Brahmin had laid out the city. And to acquire wisdom, they went up the hill to see this colored 'untouchable.'" Ovington may not actually have noticed the expression during their first meeting (a feature that became more pronounced a few years later), but it was unlikely to have been entirely absent at the time—that "cruel look in Du Bois's sensitive, poet's face" that lurked somewhere about the mouth—"a half sneer, a scorn." She met Nina, the Herndons, the Hopes, the Townses, and heard from the very light-skinned Mrs. Towns of her husband's recent arrest for race mixing as he and she rode together in their automobile into the city. Apartheid notwithstanding, the gallant Max Barber collected Ovington from the campus for a bold sightseeing ride into Atlanta with Ovington riding up front. "He was evidently a dare-devil," she decided.[15]

Du Bois had managed an even more considerable coup in corralling Professor Walter Willcox of Cornell and the U.S. Census Bureau. He and Willcox had worked together closely, if not always harmoniously, on a number of projects since the beginning of 1902, when Willcox had invited Du Bois to recommend topics pertaining to "Negro conditions" for the December 1904 annual meeting of the American Economic Association. Du Bois had objected to some of Willcox's findings ("trying to spin a solution of the Negro problem out of the inside of your office"), especially to his 1904 monograph, bristling with data and heavy on dogma, *Negroes in the United States*. For Du Bois, race prejudice was a sufficient explanation of black peoples' socioeconomic shortcomings, whereas Willcox claimed to be "an agnostic on the subject." Du Bois had agreed to affix his name to the special American Economic Association's report to be presented to the 1904 convention, "The Economic Position of the American Negro," only with great reluctance after he and Willcox had sparred about percentages of African-Americans engaged in farming and the number of families supported by income from domestic service.[16]

Another participant in the 1905 conference was the Hull House official and University of Chicago teaching-staff member Sophonisba P. Breckinridge, descended from the leading family of Kentucky, consumed by her mission to uplift and consternated that there might not be time enough to fulfill it. Such was her social standing and reform reputation that Ovington (hardly a parvenue herself) was almost beside herself with delight at finding Breckinridge at the conference—"such a glorious radical was a complete surprise." Breckinridge was fresh from winning her doctorate from the University of Chicago, the first ever awarded to a woman in the field of political science. She and close Hull House companion Julia Lathrop were driving forces in the Institute of Social Science, which they would eventually transform into the University of Chicago's unique Graduate School of Social Work Education, the preeminent influence in social-work training in America. Breckinridge must have had a good deal to say at the conference. No doubt she found much nonsense being aired that had to be instantly set right. Later, in an admiring note to Du Bois, she hoped he didn't think her "plain speaking at the University did more harm than good." The dating of another message is uncertain, but it cannot have been too long after the tenth conference that Breckinridge wrote from Atlanta's Piedmont Hotel asking urgently to see Du Bois again. He must telephone her "in the morning if there is any way by which I can see you. Perhaps you would come to see me here," a suggestion that might have had humiliating, even tragic, consequences had Du Bois been so unwise as to act upon it. She would "gladly go to [his] office." She had "no special messages" but her visit "would have lost so greatly in its value" to leave without "at least a word with you."[17] Whatever she had in mind, Breckinridge's enthusiasm for Du Bois and his work was certainly remarkable in comparison to that of many other distinguished visitors to Atlanta for its insouciance about southern mores.

With the considerable success of the tenth and eleventh Atlanta University conferences of 1905 and 1906, Du Bois began to hope that the period of philanthropic cold-shouldering was really over. At the eleventh conference, on "The Health and Physique of the Negro-American," Franz Boas, the nation's outstanding anthropologist, had delivered a paper on the cultural basis of racial behavior. For Du Bois, Boas's visit had an impact of lasting importance. Du Bois already held a visceral faith in the historic significance of Africa; Boas supplied intellectual reinforcement at a critical point. The Columbia professor's commencement address and their conversations together afforded the Atlanta professor the most informed revelations then available about the primordial role of sub-Saharan cultures in promoting the development of ancient civilizations.[18] The procession through Atlanta University of scholars, social reformers, religious leaders, university administrators, and public officials became more impressive each spring. Du Bois was not boasting but merely stating an acknowledged truth when he told the members of Boston's Twentieth Century Club that his "small and poor southern college" was the single American institution of learning that was making "systematic and conscientious study of the American Negro." "The object of this research is primarily scientific," the standard preface to his studies asserted—advocacy had no place in it—"a careful search for truth conducted as thoroughly, broadly, and honestly as the material resources and mental equipment at command will allow."[19] The "mental equipment" had proven itself fully up to the task. It was the material resources that Du Bois was starved for and frequently teased by.

Nor could he help saying and writing things—repeatedly and with what seemed perverse arrogance—that only poisoned further the well of white beneficence. Organizing and keeping on track the large egos in the Niagara Movement had taught him something of patience and reciprocity. Nevertheless, compromise was cousin to cowardice for Du Bois, a moral holiday that might have to be taken in unusual circumstances but never for long, and never with pleasure. In fact, he was profoundly averse to compromise on anything that mattered intellectually or racially. The more crucial the idea or cause (and Du Bois saw most ideas and causes that way), the more intransigent he tended to become. He held in polite contempt those who thought, like Booker Washington, that silence or a deal was frequently the optimal means to gain an advantage. If he seldom avoided conflicts others considered eminently avoidable, it was not usually because of egotism, self-righteousness or folly. His was a response that all readers of his day familiar by heart with the lines of Kipling's *If* should have understood, had not so many African-Americans been forced to unlearn public courage. Du Bois saw his approach as being racially manly while all others about him were losing or trading their principles and dignity. Caustic criticism from a dais or prose sweeping over adversaries like electric storms were Du Boisian answers to stereotyped expectations. "He insists upon making them either angry or miserable," Ovington noted of most white reactions to Du Bois.[20]

It certainly imperiled the Atlanta University Studies to attack the boosters of vocational education from the same Hampton Institute platform where the president of the United States had just finished praising them. On June 30, 1906, in the citadel of "head and hand" learning, Du Bois delivered to the institute's summer school the widely published address, "The Hampton Idea." His "Hampton Idea" that Saturday evening stunned into stone silence its audience of scrubbed and prim black educators and avuncular white dignitaries. With Theodore Roosevelt's emphatic words of duty and subordination still ringing in the air, Du Bois inveighed against the "Great Fear" that elevated the duties of Negroes above their rights and commanded, "above all, [they] watch and ward against the first appearance of arrogance or self-assertion or consciousness of great power." He had come frankly to express dissent as strongly as he was able from the "educational heresy" of Hampton. The race was at the crossroads with respect to higher education, he continued in the utterly still auditorium. Carefully selected men and women of "power, of thought, of trained and cultivated taste" were indispensable to the forward march. For others, the practical training of the best quality was equally essential.

But Du Bois was assailing more than Hampton's curriculum of cabinet-making, plastering, masonry, steam fitting, and the obsolescent rest. It was the animating spirit of its curriculum that was the travesty—the "manner and tone that would make Socrates an idiot and Jesus Christ a crank." As black people squirmed and white people reddened, Du Bois illustrated his meaning by taking on Roosevelt. Hampton was "an institution where the President of the United States can with applause tell young men not to hitch their wagons to a star but to hitch them to mules." He knew that the "great duty before you and me and our people today is to earn a living," but he also believed that Hampton's understanding of this doctrine was "so fundamentally false as to call for a word of warning." Whatever truth was contained in the Hampton idea was ineradicably corrupted. When he thought of future generations of young people nurtured by Hampton graduates, he was truly alarmed, for they would know only the handicapping of intellectual ambition, the inculcation of civic timidity, and the rationalization of second-best as the best possible for them. Hollis Frissell, a majordomo for the GEB, must have regretted the invitation to Du Bois that summer as one of the larger mistakes of his principalship. Two world wars would be fought before Du Bois received another invitation to

Hampton.[21] Against such offenses to the memory of General Armstrong and the work of the philanthropic trusts, occasional good behavior on his part counted for very little.

BETWEEN 1898 and 1904, the U.S. Department of Labor had promptly published four ground-breaking Du Bois studies of the rural South. In 1906, the department reissued the 1904 "Negro Farmer," a model of its kind, with extensive analytical tables derived from the twelfth census. Du Bois's standing with Willcox and the new commissioner of labor, Charles P. Neill, was seemingly unassailable at the time, and he had persuaded the department to fund a sharecropping study of Lowndes County, Alabama, for the bargain price of $2,000, $750 of it going for his salary. Securing the collaboration of Monroe Work and Richard R. Wright, among the most scrupulous of younger sociologists, and about a dozen other investigators, Du Bois drove his team relentlessly throughout summer and fall of 1906, paying them a daily wage of $1.50. He would be caught there in rural Alabama when the Atlanta riot broke, living among black farmers in the county, supervising from the old Calhoun missionary school a network of paid investigators, brazening his ambitious project past clenched-jawed and finally violent white landowners. Hard-pressed Atlanta University officials agreed, with grave misgivings, to advance Du Bois several hundred dollars until labor department accountants got round to reviewing and reimbursing his expenditures.[22]

By early November, shuttling back and forth between Atlanta and the Calhoun School headquarters, Du Bois reported to Neill that about 25,000 of Lowndes County's 31,000 black farmers had been interviewed and tabulated even though two of his men "were shot at and run out of one corner of the county." Neill had approved the special release of two white agents from the Bureau of Labor that October after Du Bois spelled out the daring scope and depth of his study. He intended to uncover every mechanism behind landownership and labor control in the county from 1850 to the present, with the two white agents conducting "confidential talks" with white men about politics and sexual morality, in order to uncover the dynamics behind the statistics. The two white agents, identified as Foster and Clark, did their work expertly. Records of justices of the peace and other county officials were combed, every law pertaining to landholding in Lowndes and throughout the state since 1830 was scrutinized (with labor department lawyers in Washington assisting). Du Bois was still euphoric in the *Autobiography* when he recalled what had been accomplished by the end of 1906. The schedules were tabulated and chronological maps made of the division of the land: "I considered the distribution of labor; the relation of landlord and tenant; the political organization and the family life and the distribution of the population. The report was finished by hand with no copy, and rushed to Washington."

He must have been somewhat surprised when commissioner Neill informed him almost immediately that there were problems with the Lowndes County study—technical problems, he wrote, in a letter that also alluded to an aborted conference with Du Bois in Washington due to a scheduling mixup. "Were your schedules perfect, their tabulations would be comparatively easy," Neill lectured Du Bois, but they were going to need inspection and editing. Departmental policy strictly required that only schedules "that are perfectly plain and capable of but one meaning" could be accepted. Technical problems and scheduling of meetings in Washington to thrash them out grew more complicated with each exchange of letters until it became obvious that publication of the Lowndes County sharecropping study by the U. S. Department of Labor hung in the balance. Determined to save his work, Du Bois rechecked, revised, and disputed the alleged problems with such dogged perseverance that by mid-March 1907 Neill conceded Du Bois's "rulings on the greater number of points." But not all, and after camping in Washington for three weeks of additional revisions in April, Du Bois saw Neill disappear behind a portentously named W. W. Hanger, acting commissioner, who finally declared on August 30 that "it would be extremely unwise to make any use whatever of the material which was gathered in this form."[23]

Convinced that the integrity of his scholarship was at risk, almost certainly discounting the looming signals from Washington of race-relations politics embroiling his study, Du Bois simply refused to take no for an answer. A cat-and-mouse game with Neill ensued, Du Bois periodically springing unannounced into the commissioner's office ("I called on you Monday . . . but you were not in the office, nor could I find you all day"); meantime, the Lowndes data underwent more surgery, with a desperate Du Bois uncharacteristically apologizing for errors that the department now deemed incorrigible. A thousand-dollar check for the balance owed for the study finally arrived in June 1908, but in early November of that year Du Bois was asking Neill plaintively, "Can you give me any idea as to when you are going to be able to take up the investigation of Lowndes County?" Finally they told him, as he later recalled, that his manuscript "touched on political matters." He was convinced now, finally, that the study had been given a runaround just as the magazine publisher Samuel McClure had done in 1899 when Du Bois had been paid for an investigative article on social conditions in Georgia that was never published. Du Bois might entreat, but he was incapable of groveling. He asked for the return of his controversial manuscript. "They told me," he exploded incredulously, that "it had been destroyed!"[24]

The last act in the labor-department tragedy was still five years or more in the future when Du Bois embarked on another scholarship venture, in early 1904, whose course would prove as treacherous and its denouement even more outrageous. Just before leaving for Boston where he would praise Atlanta University before the prestigious Twentieth Century Club, there was jolting news. Since the previous November, he had been turning over in his mind the intriguing biography he was to write of Frederick Douglass for the Philadelphia firm of George W. Jacobs & Company. He was not an exponent of what might be called Douglass's radical assimilationism, yet Du Bois still greatly admired the leader whose statesmanship he had paid tribute to in an 1895 memorial service at Wilberforce. Now came a letter from Jacobs & Company editor Ellis Paxson Oberholtzer on January 25, 1904, begging Du Bois to choose another subject for the *American Crisis* series. Oberholtzer explained that his earlier invitation to Booker Washington had gone unanswered, and he had therefore felt free to approach Du Bois. But now, out of the blue, Washington's acceptance had just arrived. Oberholtzer's delicate suggestion to the Wizard to consider another subject from a later period ("one that calls for less historical learning") had been rebuffed. "Can you suggest any other name?" the genuinely embarrassed editor (on the brink of sending the contract) asked Du Bois.[25]

Whether by design or chance, Du Bois's nemesis denied the world a provocative biography by a major twentieth-century African-American of the nineteenth century's major African-American. But what is equally regrettable, Du Bois was to be denied his second choice. What Du Bois would have said about Nat Turner, the slave whose 1831 insurrection in Virginia rocked the South, might have been something of an event in historiography as well as biography. Du Bois enthusiastically described to Oberholtzer the flesh-and-blood paradigm he proposed to make of Nat Turner: "Around him would center the slave trade, foreign and internal." He proposed to trace slave insurrections from Toussaint L'Ouverture to John Brown, recapturing the beginnings of abolitionism, the activities of free Negroes in the North, the antebellum plantation economy, "which was changing critically in the thirties, and the general subjective Negro point of view of the system of slavery." As he promised Oberholtzer, "no single man before or since 1850 had a greater influence on Southern life and feeling than Nat Turner." Clearly Du Bois intended to focus for a time the attention of intelligent white readers and historians on much that was unfamiliar and on much that he would reinterpret in an unfamiliar mode. This may have been a great deal more than the editor bargained for. He was "a little ignorant about the life of Nat Turner," Oberholtzer replied. He deliberated awhile, consulted the arbitral historian John McMaster, and, regretting that no one known to him knew of Turner and his significance, counterproposed a biography of John Brown.[26]

It would take Du Bois five years filled with teaching, lecture tours, scholarly writings and popular essays, editing two periodicals, and the captaincy of the Niagara Movement to finish *John Brown*. He intended the research to be thorough, though not exhaustive; he contacted one of Brown's last surviving contemporaries and pressed Freeman Murray's brother, Daniel Alexander, special assistant at the Library of Congress (whose contribution to the Negro pavilion at the 1900 Paris Exposition had been crucial), for materials. Along the way, he underwent a tonsillectomy, and somewhat later suffered the "loss of nearly a month . . . of working time," as he wrote Oberholtzer in October 1908, due to Yolande's appendectomy. There was also an exchange of letters with Oswald Villard, at work on a Brown biography of his own, the significance of which would become clear only after George W. Jacobs & Company released Du Bois's in the fall of 1909. Replying to Villard's now-lost inquiry about the biography, Du Bois stressed frankly that he was writing an interpretation and was "not trying to go very largely to the sources." Most of the source material was contained in the work of Franklin B. Sanborn and one or two others, Du Bois thought, but he supposed that Villard already knew this. In any case, Du Bois said he'd be "very glad" to assist Villard further if he could. About mid-December 1908, the complete manuscript for the book went off to the publisher.[27]

Like the novel Du Bois was writing whenever he could steal time, *John Brown* was an uneven product. Because he tried to accomplish so much during these Atlanta years, the quality of some things was bound to be flawed. Portions of the *John Brown* biography justified its author's belief that it was "one of the best books that [he] ever wrote," but many others belie the judgment. Quotations run on for pages—typical of biographies of the period, but still excessive. Chapter 7, "The Swamp of the Swan," recapitulates events from chapter 6 ("The Call of Kansas"), passing them under a magnifying glass rather than enhancing what has already been said about John Brown's national debut with a broadsword at Osawatomie; and by page 175 the chapter's padding began to show badly. Chapter 9, "The Black Phalanx," covered the history of Afro-America from 1830 to 1840 admirably, showcasing the author's interpretive prowess and command of detail in a narrative as engrossing as it was decoupled from the protagonist. Du Bois poured into it the unknown history of African-American protest before the Civil War, the appearance of black journalism beginning in the 1820s, the Negro Convention Movement in the 1830s, and the appeal of emigrationism in the 1850s. At the very end of this chapter, which reads like a composite of brilliant papers prepared for historical conferences, John Brown's reappearance seemed almost a clumsy tack-on, saying both too much and too little: "Of all this development," Du Bois wrote, coming back to his protagonist, this saint of gore "knew far more than most white men and it was based on this great knowledge that his great faith was based."[28]

Du Bois draped his Old Testament hero in Old Testament prose, an excellent technique at its best, as when the reader meets the "belated Covenanter" for the first time: "John Brown was a stalwart, rough-hewn man, mightily yet tenderly carven. To his making went the stern justice of a Cromwellian 'Ironside,' the freedom-loving fire of a Welsh Celt, and the thrift of a Dutch housewife." The image throughout of rough-hewn granite glowing from a fire at its core was surely on the mark, even if Du Bois's prose occasionally turned as purple as the Harper's Ferry elocution of Reverdy Ransom, by which it was almost certainly colored. Du Bois suspected that his book contained mistakes, and he was certainly too much the trained scholar—and too much the representative of the race, besides—to be unconcerned. But, as he told Villard, his primary concern was not with facts but interpretation. In this respect, *John Brown* was a milestone, revealing Du Bois's increasing willingness to commingle advocacy with scholarship, to envelop history and social science in judgment and prophecy. For all the well-phrased chronicling of *John Brown*, the biography was much more an allegory than a critical study. He endeavored passionately to convey the meaning of the life of the wrathful, violent abolitionist to the twentieth century. "Has John Brown no message—no legacy, then?" the author asked rhetorically in the closing pages. "He has and it is this great word: the cost of liberty is less than the price of repression." Du Bois had said as much in *The Suppression of the African Slave Trade*, but there the strictures had been far more restrained by scholarship, whereas in *John*

Brown the relationship was reversed. "The price of repressing the world's darker races," he continued, "is shown in a moral retrogression and an economic waste unparalleled since the age of the African slave-trade."[29]

Du Bois's handling of revolutionary violence, the paramount question of force and bloodshed in order to "bring peace and good will," reflected an Edwardian aversion to the justification of means by ends. Du Bois cast John Brown's homicidal swath through Kansas and bloody apotheosis at Harper's Ferry, therefore, as exceptional deeds in the service of truths that none could challenge—the morality of the "Hebrew religion," the principles of the French Revolution, the sanguinary watering of the Jeffersonian tree of liberty. Brown's violence prefigured the terrible yet purifying national fratricide. It was an avenging odyssey, to be celebrated in song and sanctified by the blood of millions of men marching to Manassas and the Wilderness. When the second edition of *John Brown* appeared in 1962, Du Bois's new preface and his insertion of new textual matter would reflect the Marxism of his later years—especially his rethinking of revolutionary violence—but his John Brown of 1909, like the Lord God Jehovah, was a lightning flash of Good striking Evil rather than a violent revolutionary. "Revolution is not a test of capacity," Du Bois wrote solemnly in 1909; "it is always a loss and a lowering of ideals." Although a discussion of how and why Du Bois's views underwent profound change in the second edition belong elsewhere, mention must be made here of these lines he would insert later: "But if it is a true revolution," he would write, "it repays all the losses and results in the uplift of the human race."[30]

Sales were disappointing. Jacobs & Company was not especially aggressive in marketing the biography, and reviews were less glowing than those for *The Philadelphia Negro* or *The Souls of Black Folk*. Within a few months of Du Bois's *John Brown*, Oswald Villard's huge, long-awaited, and definitive *John Brown: A Biography* appeared. Professor William E. Dodd of the University of Chicago, a distinguished historian and biographer and future ambassador to Germany, sternly corrected the shortcomings of the first *John Brown* in the *American Historical Review*, regretting its "hero-worship," "sensational" prose, and "somewhat inaccurate story." Dodd found "much that commends the book," but he was unenthusiastic about Du Bois's rendering of the life as "simply the work of God in human hands, as the first battle of the righteous North against the wicked South." Two major assertions in *John Brown*, which struck Dodd as fanciful, came to be recognized as accurate when American historiography caught up with Du Bois: the role of fugitive slaves in the two Seminole Wars and the connection between Haiti's Toussaint L'Ouverture and the Louisiana Purchase. The appreciation of the biography in the *Independent* was all that its author could have wished, a review that took the book on Du Bois's own terms. The facts were not new, it said, but "the viewpoint—that of a champion of the negro race—is notable, and the argument made for justice to that race is forcible and moving."[31]

The savaging of the biography in *The Nation* must have damaged its sales. And there is no question about the damage it did to Du Bois's ego and to the collaboration just then beginning between himself and Villard in connection with what would shortly emerge as the National Association for the Advancement of Colored People. The long, unsigned *Nation* review ran on October 28, 1909 (republished in the New York *Post* that same week), rendering Du Bois apoplectic. It was instantly obvious that Villard, owner of *The Nation* and the *Post* and author of the forthcoming Brown biography, had written it. With admirable self-restraint, Du Bois conceded a number of errors in his letter to the editor of *The Nation*: Brown's Mayflower descent; the slave birth of one of Brown's men and the Canadian citizenship of another; an incorrect middle name for another; mistaken attribution of Negro blood to yet another; an inaccurate date for Brown's sojourn in Iowa. (The 1973 Aptheker edition of *John Brown* would discern more "slips on dates" that would have pleased Villard.) As for the question of sources raised in the *Nation* review, Du Bois asserted that he remained satisfied with his choice of Sanborn, Hinton, Redpath, Anderson, and several other contemporaries of Brown. Finally, it struck him as puzzling that, beyond the lambasting of factual errors, nothing was said about the point of view of his biography, which Du Bois had emphatically identified in his preface as the main theme—"the little known but vastly important inner development of the Negro American" as seen through Brown's career.[32]

Errors conceded and disagreements noted, Du Bois concluded that "courtesy calls for the insertion of the enclosed letter in your columns." Not only did Paul Elmer Moore, *The Nation*'s editor, refuse to publish the letter, he gave Du Bois a tutorial in historiography, condescendingly advising him that "it would be of no service to you to print your reply." The problem, Moore explained (undoubtedly prompted by Villard), was that Du Bois failed to understand "what is really source material and what is not." Large collections of original materials had become available since Hinton, Redpath, and Sanborn, none of which had been used for his *John Brown*. The editor struck a final blow for good measure, writing that "the reviewer could have said more about your factual inaccuracies." Temples throbbing,

Du Bois shot back, aiming to smoke out the invisible Villard. He and the rich, imperious publisher had been three years apart at Harvard, both of them excelling in their graduate work under Hart. The Atlanta professor might not be a "judge of original historical material," but he "certainly should not think of seating [him]self at the feet of Mr. Villard for instruction either in History or English." Books have mistakes in them, "but savagely to emphasize these so as to give an impression of total falsity is a contemptible thing to do." He would not be patronized. He demanded the courtesy that gentlemen extend to one another. "Whether . . . or not [it] will 'help' me or not is my business and the public's and not yours," Du Bois roared.[33] And besides, the author of the contemptible review was also the author of a rival biography.

Moore closed the debate on a pained note of superiority, and an amazed letter from Villard followed, professing "deep interest" in Du Bois and his "usefulness in the community," as well as the merits of *The Souls of Black Folk*. Surely his desire to promote Du Bois to an important position with the "new National Negro Board" certified goodwill, Villard averred. Really, he had been done an injustice. As for the fate of his own biography, "I confess myself to be quite indifferent," Villard sniffed. In time, Du Bois and Villard would develop a grudging mutual respect, but for Du Bois such respect would be driven by labor in a common cause and the discipline of intellect. Rancor would always exist between them just below the surface. "To a white philanthropist like Villard," Du Bois said long afterward, "a Negro was quite naturally expected to be humble and thankful or certainly not assertive and aggressive." Finally, if Villard's critically acclaimed and brisk-selling *John Brown* seemed unmarred by error, it, too, was stitched together with lengthy quotations and full to the brim with moralizing. It contained no direct reference to Du Bois's book, but there was a skewering comment in the preface about erroneous comparisons of Brown to "Hebrew prophets or to a Cromwellian Roundhead."[34] Like Du Bois's Brown, Villard's was the high-minded agent of destiny. Slavery "was bound to be overthrown because, in the long run, truth and righteousness prevail." Villard took greater pains than Du Bois, however, to wrap John Brown in the mantle of grandfather William Lloyd Garrison's tradition of nonviolence. It was Brown's "wonderful readiness to die with joy and in peace," not the example of his righteous wrath—Brown on the scaffold, not Brown at Harper's Ferry—that was transcendent and enduring. Du Bois would never know of a letter in which Hart not only chided Villard for his "rather severe" review of Du Bois's biography but recalled that "not so many years ago . . . you envisaged the whole controversy very much as Du Bois does now."[35]

The origin and reception of his John Brown biography was typical of the fate of much of his output during the Atlanta years. Over and again he would have to recast ambitious plans to fit frail budgets, take the leavings of research projects he should have been asked to design or direct, and persevere against heartbreaking odds in order to complete seminal work to which major white foundations, universities, or learned journals gave only cursory notice, when they noticed at all, or, like the Department of Labor and Villard, tasked his efforts from ulterior motives. The silences and dismissals greeting his pleas for research funds must have etched that "cruel look" Ovington saw on Du Bois's sensitive face. Willcox had sought his expertise in preparing the American Economic Association paper, but it never occurred to Willcox to plead Du Bois's case to the Carnegie Institution when a 1902 "race mixture" investigation was being proposed.[36] The year following publication of *The Souls of Black Folk*, Edgar Gardner Murphy's book of eight essays, *The Present South*, arguing that the African-American masses were falling away from civilization, was lauded as the ultimate wisdom in *The Outlook*, *The New York Times*, and the New York *Tribune*. Secretary of State John Hay wrote the neurasthenic Murphy that he had "read nothing referring to the vital question it discusses at all comparable with your book in vigor, fairness, and lucidity." Baldwin and the venerable Carl Schurz agreed, and George F. Peabody bought a thousand copies of *The Present South* for free distribution.[37]

The same year in which he delivered the "Hampton Idea" speech, Du Bois was strikingly portrayed in *The Future in America*, a widely discussed book by H. G. Wells, the latest European visitor in the tradition of Tocqueville and Lord Bryce. After a leisurely luncheon in Boston with Booker Washington, Wells had decided that the slow-talking Tuskegee principal possessed the "scope and range of a statesman," while Du Bois ("perhaps as English as you or I") was said to betray the anguish of the cultured mulatto. The author of *The Souls of Black Folk* concealed "his passionate resentment all too thinly," Wells believed. "He batters himself into rhetoric against these walls. He will not repudiate the clear right of the black man to every educational facility, to equal citizenship, or equal respect."[38] Men like Robert Ogden and Teddy Roosevelt had no need of a book by a roving Englishman to recognize Du Bois for what he was—a dangerous racial malcontent. And although he never actually dissembled, there were a few occasions when Du Bois decided it was expedient to reign in his acidulous temper and try to court influential white people. At Bar Harbor in July 1905, he appears to have done his courtly best to be especially winsome. Edward T. Ware, Atlanta University's friendly new president and a white northerner, ribbed him about Mrs. Schieffelin's eager anticipation of Du Bois's morning lecture to the ladies' swimming club. "You see, I told her you were a fine swimmer and looked particularly well in tights." Ware spoofed on to suggest that Du Bois give his lecture in the swimming pool "illustrating [it] by various dives."[39] A graceful swimmer, Du Bois still could not help making waves. In almost every instance, the experiment in conciliation fizzled or soured, and merely reinforced his profound pessimism concerning the goodwill of most whites.

There was one goodwill experiment in which he invested much patience. In his dealings with the important white journalist Ray Stannard Baker, he practiced consummate diplomacy, repeatedly stifling the urge to deliver a rebuke to the uninformed midwesterner about the race problem. Baker came to Atlanta at the beginning of 1907 on a circuit to major cities in order to write a series of magazine pieces on race in America. These pieces would be published the next year as the influential book *Following the Color Line* (a title almost certainly suggested by Du Bois). Two years younger than Du Bois, Baker was quick, congenial, and, Du Bois thought, malleable, a widely known investigative reporter whose articles in the large-circulation *American Magazine* about the Atlanta riot could be invaluable. From Baker's first note sent from the Piedmont Hotel, it was obvious to Du Bois that Baker knew nothing about African-Americans, North or South. Ovington, who knew him well and tried to educate him for the southern trip, agreed with a friend's estimate that Baker was "a young person whose mother didn't know he was out."[40] Du Bois responded with unusual cordiality to Baker's proposal for a give-and-take about southern race relations in the study of Reverend C. B. Wilmer, the city's leading white moderate. Du Bois and Wilmer might debate such subjects, Baker suggested, as "what does the white man mean when he speaks of justice and what does the Negro mean?" Baker thought the three-hour colloquium with Wilmer and Du Bois went so well that he asked their permission to rework it for publication in *American Magazine*.[41]

Meanwhile, he put himself to school at Du Bois's lectern, reading a few recommended books, asking questions, submitting copy for criticism. Du Bois purred that, "on the whole," he liked Baker's first article on the riot. In that article, Baker's description of Brownsville, the neighborhood devastated by white vigilantes, gave the lie to sensational newspaper accounts written in the heat of the riot. Baker found "a large settlement of negroes practically every one of whom owned his own home, some of the houses being as attractive without and as well furnished within as the ordinary homes of middle class white people." The *American Magazine* piece on Atlanta had drama and tragedy, portraying both races as victims of dark, irrational forces. "Of course I think that you exaggerate somewhat the influence of crime upon the race problem," Du Bois had added as an instructive afterthought. Back in New York, Baker was anxious to have Du Bois "look over the endorsed proof of my next article." Meanwhile, editing of the Wilmer–Du Bois dialogue was coming along, he mentioned. This time, though, the tutor had sharper reservations: Baker was letting hysteria about rape, bestiality, and black criminality get out of hand. "The reasons for white people leaving the Black Belt are social and economic and not criminal," Du Bois wrote. If there was widespread fear of blacks by whites, "it is the fear the oppressor has of the oppressed." But Baker had had all the lessons he needed; a few "modifications . . . somewhat along the lines" of Du Bois's suggestions, he noted, and the articles on the South were finished. He advised Du Bois that he had found that white people in the South "really felt" afraid—"the fear of Negro crime is indeed a very potent influence down there, especially among the women." Baker mentioned only in passing the editorial comments arriving from Tuskegee. Patient to the end, Du Bois hoped that at least he had shown how wrong Baker had been to think that it was possible for African-Americans to have economic and spiritual freedom without "defense of the ballot."[42] As the journalist was about to head north to study the race problem, Du Bois offered to supply introductions to prominent leaders there.

The articles Du Bois offered to write for *American Magazine* were rejected, nor did the Wilmer–Du Bois dialogue ever appear in its pages. As his access to Baker was indirect, buffered by editorial assistants, Du Bois could at least console himself that *Following the Color Line* was better than it would have been had he not done his best to educate Baker. He had gotten the inexperienced author to endorse the "barest sort of justice for Black Men." Baker, too, had walked a tightrope between what Du Bois taught him and what he felt it would have been impolitic, if not fatal to his book's success, to write. Ovington's experience with magazine publishers had served as a warning to him.[43] As if the effort of gathering facts about the lives of black people in America had wearied him, Baker concluded his book with what sounded like a sigh—the less said about the problem of the color line the better, he advised. White America generally preferred to believe that African-Americans were either backward as a group—and therefore beyond ready remediation—or, like the examples in Booker Washington's speeches, striding up from slavery, and therefore in little need of political and legal redress. Not even a perceptive progressive like Baker was willing to run the risks to his career that forceful drawing out of the civil rights implications in *Following the Color Line* would surely have entailed.

For Du Bois, the moral grounding of intellectual and civic activity was derived from the social and political conditions of life behind the veil. All else was persiflage, evasion, hypocrisy, and conspiracy. Teamed together with the Wizard as late as 1907 in a jointly authored book about southern conditions, the difference between his and Washington's racial ideology, as well as the texture of expression, was never more striking. *The Negro in the South: His Economic Progress in Relation to His Moral and Religious Development* received wide and favorable comment but left suspicions about Du Bois unchanged. Increasingly, he made much of the genteel white public uncomfortable. Although their texts were bound together between the same covers, the two leaders seemed in accord on nothing more than the book's title. Washington delivered vintage homilies such as that there was no "human law that can prevail against" a race living high ideals, nor any that could affect "the Negro in relation to his singing, his peace, and his self-control." Du Bois, as usual, affirmed truths unpopular in the white South: disfranchisement was supposed to lead to "more careful attention to the Negro's moral and economic advancement. It has on the contrary stripped them [sic] naked to their enemies."[44]

By 1907, Du Bois's incorrigible candor was having a lethal impact on Atlanta University. The new young president, Edmund Ware, Yale-educated son of founding president Asa Ware, felt the chill wind from 61 Broadway blowing across his hilltop campus within weeks after assuming office. Du Bois liked Ware and applauded his enthusiasm but seems to have thought him somewhat high-strung. Ware's increasingly troubled demeanor was certainly understandable, however. Requesting fifteen thousand dollars over a three-year term in order to build a slender endowment in late 1907, the young president was informed by Wallace Buttrick that the GEB was "perplexed by the fact that there are so many colleges for colored people in the one city of Atlanta." Ware wrote back immediately that he was afraid Atlanta University was in disfavor with the omnipotent philanthropy. The silence greeting his letter caused him to beg Buttrick in early February 1908 to write him "very frankly on the subject and tell me in what respects we incur their disapproval." There was no disapproval, Buttrick replied. He hoped an opportunity would come someday "to help uphold your hands in the noble work you are doing with the colored people."[45] President Ware would still be waiting for Buttrick's opportunity three years later.

While the new president fretted, the worn-down former president continued his game quest for dollars for the school. At the beginning of May 1907, Horace Bumstead's New England reserve gave way momentarily as he excitedly wrote Du Bois a run-on letter about a chance Manhattan encounter with Robert W. De Forest of the new Russell Sage Foundation. He felt that there was a strong possibility of a five-thousand-dollar annual appropriation for the conference studies. De Forest told Bumstead that "he knew all about Atlanta University, and its work commanded his respect, and he seemed much interested in all I told him about the Conference and looked over with care the leaflet that I handed him which you wrote several years ago." Du Bois prepared a lengthy résumé of the conference studies along with an itemized budget projection, which he sent off by return mail to Bumstead for delivery to the Russell Sage Foundation. It would probably take a miracle to pry a few thousand dollars out of Russell Sage, he predicted in a note to William James, thanking his favorite professor for encouraging words about the last conference study. "I wish we could do better. However, it is something to be doing something."[46] There is no record of either Du Bois or Bumstead ever receiving a reply from the philanthropy.

The year before Bumstead's talk with De Forest, Du Bois had himself approached Andrew Carnegie, in late May 1906, expressing the hope that the steel colossus would "remember [him] as being presented to you and Mr. Carl Schurz at Carnegie Hall some years ago." Appreciating that Carnegie must be "overwhelmed with communications of this sort," Du Bois drafted a letter of model conciseness that told Carnegie everything he needed to know in order to invite further inquiry.[47] No record of a reply from Carnegie exists, but shortly after his direct appeal to Tuskegee's principal benefactor, Du Bois thought he saw another opportunity to win Carnegie funds. In response to remarks quoted in *The Independent* by its president, Du Bois sent the vastly rich Carnegie Institution of Washington, D.C., an unsolicited research proposal comprehending virtually all the possible future agendas for the study of Africans in the Americas and of American race relations. Du Bois proposed to accomplish a catholic research enterprise at Atlanta University for the asking price of $7,500 annually ($2,000 at a minimum). He would build on historical studies of Africa, the Atlantic slave trade, of institutions and customs of U.S. slavery, education, economics, and politics after manumission; move on to comparative studies of slavery in the western hemisphere, peoples in Africa, manners and mores broadly; then to anthropological and ethnographic studies of racial types, racial intermixtures, and ethnic and cultural variations on the African continent; ending with sociological studies intended to consolidate, classify, and derive "scientific" generalizations. Fearing that the gentlemen at the Carnegie Institution would blunder, Du Bois warned them, "If we miss this opportunity either by willful neglect or by unsystematic and slip-shod work, we not only will fail to furnish philanthropists with a body of truth on which they can depend in present and future work, but we shall hurt the cause of scientific research in all lines and decrease human knowledge in a universe of which we know all too little."[48]

This time, Du Bois got an oblique and demeaning reply. He was still waiting to hear from Carnegie or his philanthropy when he opened a letter from Mississippi planter and amateur sociologist Alfred Holt Stone, the first of several from Stone during June 1906. The Mississippian, who controlled the lives of hundreds of black tenants on Dunleith, his extensive Delta plantation, was brilliant, charming, gregarious, and intellectually duplicitous. The contents of his letters underscored, as little else could have, the absurdity of Du Bois's position in the world of mainstream scholarship. Here was Stone, the gentleman amateur and standard bearer of the South's planter oligarchy, writing to Du Bois in full confidence that his own petition to do the sort of work Du Bois himself had proposed time and again would be approved by the Carnegie Institution. Stone was proposing a broad study of the American race problem, one that he promised would be "frank, without being offensive to either race."[49] He desired Du Bois's counsel, even collaboration.

The author of *The Philadelphia Negro* and eleven interdisciplinary monographs on Afro-America marveled "that to [Stone's] direction, Mr. Carnegie and others entrusted a fund for certain studies among Negroes." Stone's lectures in the North on the problematic future of African-Americans (he expected them to die out) were well known, as well as his almost catastrophic experiment in substituting southern Italians for black sharecroppers on his sprawling plantation. The Italian surrogates had proven "too handy with the knife," Du Bois chuckled. "Why they selected him and neglected an established center like Atlanta University," Du Bois tongue-in-cheekedly wrote thirty-odd years later, "I cannot imagine." He could have speculated that the Carnegie Institution's motives reflected the strong contemporary endorsement of the trend to wildly speculative or dismally "scientific" books on the African-American by self-taught Anglo-Saxon experts such as Viscount James Bryce, Maurice Evans, Robert W. Shufeldt, Harry Johnston, and, above all, Prudential Life Insurance Company chief physician Frederick Hoffman, whose 1896 *Race Traits and Tendencies of the American Negro* was the source book on the subject. Within a short time, another of Du Bois's attempts to secure research funds from the Carnegie Institution would be politely turned down by the august John Franklin Jameson, a founder of the American Historical Association and future manuscripts chief at the Library of Congress. In January 1907, Jameson replied that he had read "with pleasure" *The Suppression of the African Slave Trade*, but regretted that there was no "opportunity for doing the sort of work you mention in this department of the Carnegie Institution."[50]

By the time Jameson replied, Du Bois had negotiated his collaboration with Stone. The twelfth Atlanta conference plans called for the study of the African-American in politics, a potentially explosive subject; but prospects for funding were so dismal that the university's agonizing trustees were considering an adjournment. Seeing a way to funds, Du Bois offered to help Stone by substituting a study of African-American economic conditions if the Carnegie Institution would underwrite the topic as the twelfth conference study. Writing from Dunleith plantation on January 1, 1907, Stone thought Du Bois's request for a thousand dollars "entirely justified by the work we have in view." On the nineteenth, Du Bois sent Stone an understanding that the Carnegie Institution would pay Atlanta University one thousand dollars in four payments. The twelfth Atlanta Study, "Economic Cooperation among Negro Americans," a wide-ranging historical overview and inventory of contemporary commercial and business activity, was the result.[51] But before the second Carnegie installment reached him, Du Bois discovered that he had been cynically used by Stone as part of a maneuver that proved too injurious to African-Americans even for Booker Washington. The Wizard had also been deceived by the planter's aristocratic affableness, until he read the articles soon to be gathered in book form as the widely read *Studies in the American Race Problem* (1908).

White blood alone made black intelligence possible, Stone argued. Were it not for stern and steady Caucasian controls, Negro atavism and savagery would run amok. When the Wizard advised the Carnegie Institution that Stone was an inappropriate recipient of funds to investigate race relations, however, he was told that no less an authority than Du Bois had certified Stone's fitness. At almost that same moment, a furious Du Bois was writing Stone to protest the deviousness behind his articles. In personal conversation and letters, Stone was "perfectly fair," Du Bois conceded. But in Stone's writings, he never had "a good word for the Negro, you never give any excuses for his condition, you simply attack him—not, to be sure, as some people attack him, but, nevertheless, in a way which really does a great deal more harm." Unfazed, the planter thanked Du Bois for his "frank criticism" which was "something very difficult to secure." Six weeks later Stone sent him a testimonial about the great value of the Atlanta University Studies on Carnegie Institution stationery.[52] He and Stone would tangle again soon, and rather famously, but in the meantime Du Bois, stoic and indefatigable, turned his energies to his Lowndes County study, the twelfth conference, *John Brown*, articles, speaking engagements, and a host of other projects.

At Bumstead's urging, Du Bois had spent January and February of 1907 speaking to northern audiences about Atlanta University. It was not the sort of work Du Bois enjoyed, although he seems to have done it better than he cared to admit. But since it was seldom his practice to speak extemporaneously in the fashion of a Ransom or a Wright, the obligation to compose different speeches—suited to the oak-and-leather settings of exclusive white men's clubs, the charged atmosphere of many black churches, and of public meeting halls filled with well-meaning white people—taxed his energies considerably. The itinerary assigned to Du Bois by the retired president had kept him in motion with a Carnegie Hall speech arranged by Felix Adler's Society for Ethical Culture ("very insistent that you should not attack Booker Washington"), another at the Episcopal Church of the Ascension, and a string of others in the New York area. In a note from Bumstead during this period he regretted not having known sooner "of your desire not to speak more than once on Sunday. I would have spared you."[53]

Du Bois rarely spared himself, though. Less than a week later, he was in Illinois to deliver "Sociology and Industry in Southern Education" before the Social Study Clubs of the University of Chicago, featuring a lucid blend of common sense and history. "It seems to most southerners, white and black," he told the audience, "as though the situation in which they find themselves today is absolutely unique, that never before had two diverse races ever met in the world's history." Without the education that would give to race relations a comparative perspective—a broad knowledge of culture contacts in other places and times—the South's people were doomed to a brutal and futile racial impasse, he warned. The day before the lecture at the university, he spoke on Abraham Lincoln to a capacity Hull House audience assembled by Jane Addams. It would be surprising if Ida Wells-Barnett and her husband, Ferdinand, editor of the strongly anti-Tuskegee newspaper *The Conservator*, had not come to hear Du Bois. The Barnetts had risked a great deal in defending *The Souls of Black Folk* among white and black Chicagoans when it first appeared.[54] In any case, Du Bois had learned by then to expect the aggressive Ida Wells-Barnett to volunteer all the advice she could. These speeches, along with the vintage Du Bois essay "The Value of Agitation," were printed in full in Max Barber's doughty *Voice of the Negro*, alive in Chicago but not well.[55]

Du Bois's pen might have yielded more during this period; but since the appearance in *Collier's* of his prophecy that Japan's 1904 defeat of czarist Russia signified the beginning of the end of "white supremacy," he had been unsuccessful in placing pieces in the major monthlies. As he warned an English friend who hoped to place an article or two of his, it was "very difficult to get anything favorable to the Negro into many of the American journals just now." *Collier's* was unreceptive to his idea of a series to be called "Along the Color Line," and Bliss Perry at the *Atlantic Monthly* returned an entry as regrettably "too technical and difficult for the average magazine reader to comprehend easily." Walter Hines Page of Doubleday (blistered by Du Bois for publishing Thomas Dixon's racist novels) declined the honor of a collection of essays titled "Sociology of the Negro American." Du Bois also gathered information about atrocities committed by American forces in the Philippines from the Anti-Imperialist League, apparently intending to write a critical piece on America's new membership in the club of empire.[56]

Unexpectedly, Doubleday Page & Company invited him to do a book of his choosing in March 1907. Du Bois leapt at the suggestion, requesting an advance to do a large study of the West Indies and Africa. That very week he had written the well-traveled Milholland about "an English lady who visited this institution" and offered to underwrite a four-week vacation abroad. Frances Elizabeth Hoggan of London's New Hospital for Women was one of Great Britain's leading physicians, coauthor (with her physician husband) of numerous medical-journal articles, and she was soon to sail to South Africa, at age sixty-five, to study health conditions there. Hoggan had been as impressed by Du Bois as Mary Ovington and Sophonisba Breckinridge. "You seemed a little uncertain about your trip to England," she wrote sympathetically, "invigorating and refreshing as I am sure you felt it would be." She not only insisted that he get away, Hoggan sent Du Bois fifty pounds in late March 1907 with a promise that another fifty would be deposited to a London account for his use. He wanted the trip to England "more than I can say," Du Bois replied. "A check on London would be quite satisfactory." Doubleday Page & Company declined Du Bois's ambitious book idea, but Milholland replied quickly with a Lake District itinerary and a list of important persons to meet. William James wrote that he was sending Henry ("who lives at Rye, two hours from London on the coast") a note in case Du Bois found time to pay a call.[57]

Du Bois's four-week reprieve from scholarship and civil rights came between unhappy revisions in June of the Lowndes County tabulations and the well-attended Boston Niagara meeting at the end of August. His ship on the Allen Line weighed anchor from Montreal on June 20. Ten leisurely days later, he cycled out of Glasgow toward a week's tour of the Lake District. The bicycle, which he also took to France, seems to have been of an excellent make, and Du Bois expended considerable correspondence after returning to the States trying to undo a curious mixup in which the bicycle of a Miss Moreland of Saskatchewan, Canada, was mistakenly shipped instead of his from England.[58] There was much taking of tea with distinguished Britons, although a good number of those on Milholland's list were on vacation themselves. Too far from London to propose "any brief or convenient form of visit," Henry James hoped he might still find Du Bois at his hotel when he reached the capital after August 22. As James feared, a meeting at which two of the most perceptive observers of American society might have compared notes never took place.[59] Had they survived, his dutiful letters to Nina in Great Barrington with Yolande would help fill in the large blanks of this first sojourn abroad since the full summer of 1900.

The emotional lift from the upper-middle-class European salons in which Du Bois dined and conversed as an outstanding personality unstigmatized by color went a long way toward drawing the poison from wounds he tried never to let show in America. In Europe, his confident bearing and reserve marked him as a gentleman, as a person whose prepossession elevated him above the common run of subjects and citizens of any country. Yet, as he pedaled, gaitered, through soft summer countrysides, stopping at inns and cafés, his thoughts occasionally turned to the ceaseless struggle for personal and collective respect in his native land and the contrasting graciousness of his European hosts and of the ordinary people casually encountered along the way. He let himself dream a bit in this summer Europe "of past beauty and present culture, fit as I fondly dreamed to realize a democracy in which [he] and [his] people could find a welcome place."[60] He returned home to sentinel duty along the color line (and a skirmish with Monroe Trotter at the Niagara meeting) in a much better frame of mind.

He needed to be. Racial tensions in America were rising sharply, and Alfred Holt Stone was among those inciting them. The explosive exodus of African-Americans from the South known as the Great Migration was less than a decade away, but the early beginnings of the massive relocation to the urban North had already caused great concern among social reformers and much resentment among low-income northern whites. About 185,000 African-Americans had streamed into Chicago, Cleveland, Philadelphia, Pittsburgh, and New York since 1890, 30,000 more than all those who had come in the previous twenty years. Like Richard R. Wright, the able AME bishop who had moved to Chicago from Augusta, Georgia, in 1899, many of the vanguard migrants were so highly motivated and educated that their coming came to be called "the migration of the talented tenth."[61] But even though they came before lynching and the boll weevil would push and the northern labor recruiter pull them out of the South after 1916, they were largely as unprepared for the pace, anomie, and exploitation ahead as many of the Italians, Poles, and Hungarians pouring into these same cities; but, unlike the incoming ethnics, their skin color would mark them for special abuse. Paul Laurence Dunbar's 1902 novella, *The Sport of the Gods*, foresaw the splintering of families and descent into moral license and crime awaiting large numbers of these migrants. The likes of Florence Kellor, Jane Addams, Susan Wharton, and Mary Ovington had bustled forward to help manage the disorder. Alfred Stone, however, spoke for those who saw in the disorder the exigency of stern and bloody correction.

At the 1907 meeting of the American Sociological Society in Madison, Wisconsin, that December, Stone read his paper "Is Race Friction in the United States Growing and Inevitable?" Du Bois, a member of the society since 1905, had agreed to respond along with Willcox and three other scholars. If there had ever been any doubt about the Mississippi planter's views, Madison resolved the question. Race friction resulted from what Stone called a "natural contrariety, repugnancy of qualities." It emerged from "pressure" the white man feels "almost instinctively in the presence of a mass of people of a different race." Quoting from "The Future of the Negro Race in America," Du Bois's wide-ranging, thoughtful essay in the January 1904 British magazine *East and the West*, Stone gleefully underscored Du Bois's contention that civil rights meant "the abolition of the color line." In stark opposition to such sentiments, Stone coolly proposed that the very vitality of American democracy was directly dependent upon a "concomitant intolerance toward men of another race or color." More candid than many of the distinguished professors who preferred measured statements and tentative conclusions, Stone's crimson peroration nevertheless spoke to most of them in their hearts: "The superiority of race cannot be preserved without pride of blood and an uncompromising attitude toward the lower races."[62] Either white supremacy must maintain itself through the logic of force or, said Stone, it would be swallowed up in a mongrelization on the pattern of Latin America.

If it occurred to Du Bois that the ideas of his own "Conservation of Races" had returned to haunt him in a demented form, he must have felt relieved that Stone appeared not to know this early essay. Unable to pay his way to the Madison meeting, Du Bois's rejoinder had to wait for publication in the May 1908 volume of the *American Journal of Sociology* (his paper was said to have arrived too late to be read). "A Reply to Stone" was unusually restrained, even complimentary in places, but it dismissed the planter's argument as regressive, countering his apocalyptic pessimism with optimistic historicism. Although his own racial beliefs had once been perilously close to the planter's (were ambivalent still), Du Bois was careful to avoid reference to "instinct," "folkways," "pride of blood," "consciousness of kind," and other popular sociological concepts in opposing Stone. Instead, he proclaimed that the Zeitgeist was operating through economics. "A new standard of national efficiency is coming," he maintained. "And that efficiency is marked by the way in which a great modern advanced nation can be neighborly to the rest of the world." Nowhere did he admit as much, but to a large extent Stone's argument must have prompted Du Bois to stress economic explanations of collective behavior. His former collaborator's Darwinian rhetoric was of no "particular importance, except when it encourages those Philistines who really believe that Anglo-Saxons owe their preeminence in some lines to lynching, lying, and slavery, and the studied insult of their helpless neighbors. God save us from such social philosophy!" he exclaimed in closing.[63]

But the Zeitgeist was to prove far more recalcitrant than anticipated. Du Bois's appealing turn of phrase (intended to correct Stone's dire prediction) that "the world is beginning to work for the world," reflected the confidence he and many other racial liberals placed in economic and scientific progress. But it was a seriously flawed hypothesis. The grim truth was that the march of science and industry tended to exacerbate race relations in the North as well as the South, rather than to improve them—

at least in the short term. With industrialization came competition under capitalism, classes struggling to maintain status, and races being manipulated against one another. Patriarchy and noblesse oblige were as untenable in Birmingham, Alabama, or Charlotte, North Carolina, as they had become in the Chicago stockyards or the textile mills of Paterson, New Jersey. For all his field research and pioneering, however, it would not be Du Bois but Robert Park, Booker Washington's former ghostwriter who was well along the road to becoming recognized as the University of Chicago's leading sociologist, who would come closest to a valid formulation of twentieth-century racial adjustment. In Park's race-relations cycle, contact between different races generated sharp competition, followed by a period of accommodation, leading, eventually, to assimilation. In "The Future of the Negro in America," Du Bois had identified perpetual serfdom, extinction, outmigration, and full citizenship as the four possible destinies of his people, with full citizenship as the almost certain long-term fate.[64] Yet Park's was the kind of Hegelian elaboration that might well have occurred to Du Bois, had he not found himself handicapped by professional disabilities surrounding the race he so devoutly wished to study objectively.

In the climate of national victimizing, Du Bois began to feel like the legendary Canute bidding the waves to obey his commands. It was impossible to ignore the dismal implications of American democracy and racism, for it was cruelly apparent that a sense of full citizenship came to many white newcomers the instant they learned to call others, whose forebears had come long before, "nigger." To some extent, Du Bois might suffer the quickly learned racism of the humble from abroad, but when high-born Massachusetts men—for example, a Harvard overseer, and an Adams at that—published articles in *Century Magazine* that were "ill-considered and wrong but [also] distinctly sensational in the worst sense," he rushed to repair the damage trowel in hand. "I trust that before publishing further matter on the race problem, you will study it," he upbraided the supremely distinguished historian-businessman Charles Francis Adams, Jr., great-grandson of John Adams and son of the Civil War ambassador to the Court of Saint James. "To this end I am sending you some literature."[65] Adams replied that he took his instruction from no lesser authorities than Booker Washington and Alfred Stone.

Du Bois's experience with the Sons of the American Revolution in summer 1908 abraded his ego in its innermost core. Following to the letter the procedures forwarded by the Massachusetts chapter of the Sons, he had painstakingly accumulated evidence from muster rolls and tax registries of his eighteenth-century ancestor's participation in the War of Independence. Family pride—from a man who felt so ambivalent about much of his family history—was an expression of self-confirmation, an exorcising of Alfred's taint through official recognition of Tom Burghardt's few days of military service and of his own legitimate, unbroken descent from the Great Barrington warrior. Told that his credentials for admission had been approved by the Massachusetts chapter of the Sons of the American Revolution, Du Bois savored what was to him another crucial step in the plausible construction of a gentrified self, one superior to all but the most exceptional man or woman, white or black. Then came the communiqué from the Massachusetts chapter that the general secretary of the national Sons of the American Revolution in Washington demanded proof of "marriage of the ancestor 'Tom' Burghardt and record of birth of the son." Failing that, SAR headquarters would be compelled to rescind the actions of the Massachusetts chapter, which it promptly did, as Du Bois could provide no such evidence.[66] That rejection seared his soul, although the decision of the national headquarters may have been technically correct. It seemed to be the cruellest of affronts in a cruel, affronting world.

THE AUGUST 1908 Niagara gathering in Oberlin, Ohio, was poorly attended. Du Bois himself reached Oberlin on the mend from an early August tonsillectomy performed in Chicago's Provident Hospital. Ovington missed it because of her father's poor health and had been "very unhappy," especially as Du Bois had agreed to let her speak for twenty minutes on behalf of the Socialist party. She wrote Du Bois not to flag an instant "with the effort to win the rights of manhood for every Negro in the country." It was a warm letter, reminiscing about the "memorable time" at Harper's Ferry and striking a Socialist note about Republicans and Democrats. "There is a workingman's party in the country," Ovington reminded Du Bois. "How can the Negro belong with any other?"[67] There was no Fred McGhee at Oberlin either. The Minnesota criminal lawyer, who had been among the first to take on the Wizard, had withdrawn from active participation in the movement after the Boston meeting. Driving himself brutally in his work (he would be dead in four years), McGhee felt he had to choose between his practice and Niagara. "Yet something worth the doing has been done," he was pleased to say as he took his leave of the executive committee. The worldly wise Charles Chesnutt seemed never quite to be able to arrange his summer schedule to permit attendance at a Niagara meeting, and that of 1908 also took place without him. In August 1903,

Chesnutt had written one of the wisest, longest, and most eloquent appraisals of the Wizard's racial philosophy ever to be read by the master of The Oaks. The Cleveland author and insurance executive was certain that Washington's "institution, your system of education, whatever it may be, is too apt to dwarf everything else and become the sole remedy for social and political evils which have a much wider basis." Organized, public opposition to Washington was not to Chesnutt's taste, however. Whether another gifted novelist, the Baptist preacher Sutton Griggs, came to Oberlin is unclear, but Du Bois was pleased to make known that the Tennesseean was "interested" in the movement.[68]

Maintaining interest in the movement had become as challenging for Du Bois as winning a foundation research grant. The Tuskegee Machine had done all it could to stifle and intimidate through patronage, philanthropy, and the press. Max Barber's star-crossed career served as a daunting object lesson to prudent breadwinners. William Lewis, once a promising militant, was the new U.S. assistant attorney for the six New England states, a heady object lesson to the ambitious. Contributions from Episcopalian and Baptist plutocrats were remitted to Hampton and Tuskegee as dutifully as Sunday collection-plate tithings. The Niagara Movement was not listed among approved charities. But, in the final analysis, defeat came as the Niagarites met the enemy and discovered the enemy to be themselves. The movement was not large enough to accommodate two moving forces—Du Bois and Trotter. The Morgan-Trotter truce had disintegrated immediately after the 1907 Boston meeting, and the Wizard's agents moved to exploit the feuding. Hosting a sumptuous banquet in one of Boston's finest hotels to honor Du Bois, William Lewis invited Morgan, Forbes, Grimké, Ferris, and others for whom the *Guardian* had only criticism or ridicule, omitting an enraged Trotter from the guest list. Reporting to Tuskegee, Lewis chortled, "the pins are all down but one." In retaliation, Trotter demanded that Morgan be removed as secretary of the Massachusetts chapter and that all state secretaries be elected locally rather than appointed by the general secretary. Du Bois made matters worse when he succumbed to understandable impatience and finally peremptorily backed Morgan. At least that was the heartsick Ovington's view. She heard the snickering of the Bookerites and almost admonished her hero to be more understanding. It was such a pity, she wrote Du Bois, because Morgan was really insufferably conceited, while Trotter, of whom she had once been wary, she "had grown increasingly to admire."[69]

A midwinter meeting of the Niagara Executive Committee in Cleveland (with Du Bois and Trotter absent) accomplished little more than the drafting of a pious circular to the membership pleading for conciliation. Instead, there was animus and drift. In early April 1908, Trotter effectively abandoned the Niagara Movement by presiding over the founding of the Negro American Political League, not only a rival organization but, according to Trotter's publicity about it, one that included an unconsulted Du Bois and Fred McGhee, as well as other Niagarites. The Negro American Political League would have numerous incarnations after 1908—National Independent Political League, National Independent Political Rights League, and, finally, National Equal Rights League (NERL), but it remained, above all, an extension of Trotter's eccentric honesty and phenomenal energy, and of the *Guardian*.[70] Their loss was fatal to Niagara. The general secretary continued to put up a game front, as in an oddly plain letter earlier that year to a prospective member: "I am glad you like the Niagara men. They are a fine set of fellows if we can only keep them together and keep them working." But by summer 1909, the number of Niagara members writing to Du Bois of "never look[ing] forward to anything with as much joy as meeting that body of manly men," as attorney J. R. Clifford did, was fast dwindling. And Clifford himself would miss the August 1909 meeting at Sea Isle City, New Jersey. The movement, Du Bois sighed, "began to suffer internal strain from the dynamic personality of Trotter and my own inexperience with organizations."[71] Trotter's obduracy and Du Bois's calm self-certitude had factionalized the Niagara Movement to such a degree that the members found that in coming together they only exposed and exacerbated their divisions.

Du Bois's situation at Atlanta University underwent a much-needed superficial improvement in early July 1908 when President Ware finally made available a room in the basement of Stone Hall to serve as an office. A few weeks later Du Bois was even able to expand his office space when a Miss Hancock agreed to give up her recitation room. This stroke of good fortune came about through an eleventh-hour grant of a thousand dollars from the Slater Fund to cover conference-studies expenses. A dollop of Slater money had made possible the most recent Atlanta University Study, *The Negro American Family*, completed that May and on its way to the printer.[72] This 1908 conference brought Jane Addams to Atlanta, a presence Du Bois immensely valued, finding scarce funds to pay her expenses from Chicago. Insisting that Addams accept the hospitality of the university rather than stay with white friends in the city, he explained that otherwise Addams might find all manner of mysterious mishaps suddenly obstructing her way to the campus. *The Negro American Family* contained Addams's settlement-house insights into ethnic family life in the urban North, as well as Ovington's comprehensive survey, "The Negro Family in New York." In "The Economics of the Family," Du Bois's students had produced detailed drawings of eight African-American homesteads in Georgia ranging from low-income to affluent. Urban manners, diet, dress, and education in urban alley homes and spacious residences in stable neighborhoods were meticulously described.[73]

As a frame of frozen sociological time, *The Negro American Family* was of major importance. But coming nine years after *The Philadelphia Negro*, it was jarringly regressive in language, if not erroneous in its conclusions that sexual mores were the Negroes' overriding problem, making their family life "less efficient for its onerous social duties." The economic factors behind weak primary institutions still remained enveloped in Victorian values, as had been the case in *The Philadelphia Negro*. The fragile nuclear family with its handicapped father and thin culture were legacies of slavery, Du Bois posited, grating the modern ear with the conclusion, "This does not mean that [the African-American] is more criminal in this respect than his neighbors. Probably he is not. It does mean that he is more primitive."[74] He persisted in emphasizing the legacy of slavery to such an extent that he often tended to understress the modern reasons for that legacy's continuing to impede. Yet he remained inconsistent, trying, with increasing success, to distance himself from the prevailing racial or cultural hypotheses that excluded or minimized economic exploitation. In May 1907, he had already written excitedly of the fatal analytical flaws Washington economist Max Rubinow exposed in census chief Willcox's racial explanations for the disparity in white and black mortality rates. Du Bois quoted Russian-born Rubinow as explaining that "we have here not a dying of black folk but a slaughter of the poor."[75] Du Bois would begin to internalize such insights.

With the last-minute Slater Fund grant that July, he would successfully undertake the 1909 *Efforts for Social Betterment among Negro Americans*, also valuable, especially for its data on African-American women's self-help organizations. Fortunately, although there was less money to carry on, there was more talent available due to the return the previous year of Augustus Dill from Harvard, where he had taken a second bachelor's degree. Dill, class of 1906, was one of Du Bois's ablest students. His graduate work in sociology was so exemplary that Atlanta University bestowed one of its rare master's degrees on him in 1908, at the end of his first year back on campus. The word *bonze* best described Dill, a rotund little man with a perfectly round brown head. Fastidious and a predestined bachelor, he would find his greatest enthusiasms in life with service to Du Bois, his demanding mentor. From 1908 until Du Bois's departure in 1910, Dill collaborated on each Atlanta University Study. Thereafter, he directed them until the last one in 1914, and then left to join Du Bois in New York at the new National Association for the Advancement of Colored People.[76]

With thirteen studies in as many years by 1908—uneven in quality but useful, and several still recognized as archetypes—Du Bois now saw that his work in Atlanta was even further from winning significant, sustained foundation support than it had been when he produced the 1898 *Efforts of American Negroes for Their Own Social Betterment*. His researches were still living hand to mouth, dependent on extraordinary interventions by influential sympathizers like Seligman at Columbia or token sums funneled through respected racists like Stone. Even so, this loose change barely kept the recipient's vital signs from becoming increasingly feeble. "The Finance Committee have made up their minds that we have got to curtail still more until Atlanta University has prospect of a larger annual income," Ware notified his prize faculty member after the 1908 conference on the family. Despite the words of Harvard's Eliot, quoted in the university's 1909 brochure, encouraging the public to realize that "the colored race in our land must have its own representation in all departments of professional life," such sentiments were alien to the dominant philanthropic thinking. "Eventual withdrawal from Atlanta University seemed wise," Du Bois had about decided. He was sure that Ware had been told that "under certain circumstances increased contributions from the General Education Board and other sources might be expected," and it was clear that he was one of those "circumstances."[77]

But it was not quite time to leave, and he threw himself into two projects that might still turn things around. In early April 1909, he wrote to Edward Blyden in Sierra Leone and a score of other authorities concerning his scheme for an "Encyclopedia Africana," a multivolume study "covering the chief points in the history and condition of the Negro race." From Blyden, the doyen of black nationalism, he requested names of several outstanding white men to serve on the encyclopedia's international advisory board, stressing, nevertheless, that "the real work I want done by Negroes." His plan was "still in embryo," but within a few weeks Du Bois was generating an extensive correspondence about the project. His stationery announced that the first of five projected volumes would appear in

1913, the "Jubilee of Emancipation in America and the Tercentenary of the Landing of the Negro." Seeking Eliot's inclusion, he informed the Harvard president that August that some sixty distinguished authorities in numerous fields had agreed to serve on the editorial board. Eliot declined, but Harvard was already well represented by Hart, James, and Hugo Munsterberg. The English ethnographers Harry Johnston and Flinders Petrie, Professor Giuseppe Sergi of Italy, and scholars from Germany, France, and Belgium joined Columbia's Franz Boas and Clark University president Granville Stanley Hall on the encyclopedia's letterhead. Du Bois's unhappiness with Kelly Miller and Archibald Grimké had abated sufficiently for him to persuade these old Committee of Twelve adversaries to serve on the board along with African-American notables John Hope, Benjamin Brawley, Bishop Scarborough, Henry Ossawa Tanner, Sutton Griggs, Anna Jones, George Edmund Haynes, Richard Greener, and a half dozen others.[78] The Gold Coast barrister and newspaperman Casely-Hayford also agreed to serve.

Du Bois had assured Blyden that the encyclopedia project could be "put through," but he was again mistaken about the enlightened disposition of influential and potent whites. Wallace Buttrick's four-year-old statement that the GEB head wished "it were within my power to cooperate with you in ways more practical" was still as meaningless as ever.[79] Du Bois's vision of an "Encyclopedia Africana" dimmed, but, a quarter century later, he would resurrect it as the "Encyclopedia of the Negro," and almost succeed in endowing it with resources adequate to its large purpose. Eighty years later, he would find the resources for the *Encyclopedia Africana* in Nkrumah's Ghana. By then, of course, his own physical and intellectual resources would be nearing their epochal term.

At first, it had seemed to be easier to implement his plans for an enlarged *Horizon*. Since the monthly magazine's debut in January 1907, Du Bois had written on a vast array of subjects in *The Horizon*'s "Over-Look" column—socialism, peonage, books, and voting; Roosevelt, Taft, Bryan, and Stone; Darwinism, race relations, the struggles of Jews, Ray Stannard Baker's investigations, Africa, and particularly Niagara. His collaborators had their columns, as well: Hershaw's "Out-Look" and Murray's "In-Look." Du Bois's influential "Over-Look" was invariably better written and more hard-hitting, as with the controversial "Negro Vote" piece for August 1908: "Standing then in the presence of the Republican and Democratic parties we have to ask ourselves: not, which party stands for our principles—neither does." It was a matter of trading votes for favors: "Because two-thirds of the Democrats (that is, the Northern Democracy) have long deserved our support, and would do more to deserve it if the solid Negro vote did not put them in slavery to the Solid South."[80] This was an argument groping toward the balance-of-power dictum that would eventually rule African-American political strategy to a large degree.

Another significant "Over-Look" piece, of remarkable eloquence even for Du Bois, was devoted to Ida Dean Bailey, a Niagara colleague's deceased wife. It reflected the author's brand of heroic feminism, praising this dedicated, terminally ill woman's service as joint-secretary of the women of the Niagara Movement, her ability to be "companion and co-worker of men . . . [and] leader and confidante of women." Du Bois offered Ida Bailey as a model: "She was born to play a part on a world stage—no narrow pent-up niche of life for her, but great sweeping vistas and glorious vision of eternal success." Unfortunately, there were more contemptible white men than exemplary women to write about. *The Horizon* noted that Lyman Abbott weeped in *The Outlook* for justice toward the Filipinos and that his "heart just aches for Russia," but the American race problem passed again without comment. The Negro pavilion at the Jamestown Exhibition was three quarters of a mile from the midway, "away from everybody and everything." "The Peabody fund of $1,000,000 left for education in the South has been given to a Tennessee institution which bars black Southerners. Mr. Peabody is still dead."[81]

The pocket-sized, twenty-eight-page *Horizon* appeared regularly, had a larger and more stable circulation than *The Moon*, and was printed on better paper. The early issues carried some of the poetic and literary effusions on Africa, women, and racism that Du Bois would republish in *Darkwater*. "The Song of the Smoke," "The Burden of Black Women," and "A Day in Africa" were passionate, moving pieces of Victoriana. Some, like the molten "My Country 'Tis of Thee" in the November 1907 issue, seemed to curl the pages:

My country tis of thee,
Late land of slavery,
Of thee I sing.
Land where my father's pride
Slept where my mother died,
From every mountain side
Let freedom ring![82]

But despite the vigor of prose and principles, the magazine sputtered along, with Du Bois and his fellow publisher-editors working without salary and putting several hundred dollars of their own money into the venture. As with *Moon* collaborators Simon and Pace, Du Bois had his hands full keeping Murray and Hershaw on speaking terms. At one point (July 1908) friction was so great that Murray sulked and refused to hand over the list of subscribers to Hershaw. The exasperated Hershaw told Du Bois he was "convinced that it is useless for Murray and myself to attempt further to collaborate in the business affairs of the *Horizon*." The lurching of the magazine from printing presses in Washington to Alexandria, Virginia, and then back to Washington in 1909 played havoc with the business, as Du Bois's March 29, 1909, apology to subscriber A. B. Humphrey at the Republican Club in New York indicated. Returning Humphrey's dollar, Du Bois explained, "The men are perfectly honest but they seem quite unable to keep accounts."[83]

While his partners feuded, Du Bois negotiated with Milholland and Barber, now associated with the Constitution League (expensively quartered across from "the classic pile," said Milholland of the Forty-second Street Library) to merge the league's proposed new magazine with *The Horizon*. Du Bois was fond of Milholland and seemed amused by the generous, tough Irishman's occasional affectation of aristocratic manners. The goals of Niagara and the league were fully compatible and the financial resources of wealthy manufacturer Milholland impressive. Once again, a fair-sailing document in precise Du Bois prose circulated from Atlanta. Out of the merger a *New Horizon*, published in New York, with Du Bois as editor-in-chief and Barber as managing editor, was supposed to come. There would be an interracial board, and $25,000 in start-up capital raised with Milholland's help. But once again, ambition and resources went separate ways. Murray broke his arm, causing a delay in production. Finally, in November 1909, an eight-by-eleven-inch *Horizon: A Journal of the Color Line* (reduced to twelve pages) appeared. It was not the large, well-funded magazine Du Bois's circular had promised, but another labor-intensive coup of the three editors who were somehow still working together. The promised *New Horizon* had been abandoned, however, its aborted merger with Milholland's league unexplained.

Still, Du Bois told Hershaw he thought "the first number of the *Horizon* was excellent."[84] It was certainly defiant. "THIS IS A RADICAL PAPER," Du Bois announced. "It stands for progress and advance. It advocates Negro equality and human equality; it stands for Universal suffrage, including votes for women." There was a brief account of the fifth annual meeting of the Niagara Movement. It was vintage Du Bois: "On us rests to no little degree the burden of the cause of individual Freedom, Human Brotherhood, and Universal Peace in a day when America is forgetting her promise and destiny. Let us work on and never despair because pigmy voices are loudly praising ill-gotten wealth, big guns and human degradation. They but represent back eddies in the tide of Time. The causes of God cannot be lost."[85] In the December issue, under the ironic title "Constructive Work," a merciless caricature of the Wizard's achievements appeared. If the magazine's future was in doubt, subscribers to the January 1910 edition would never have guessed it reading Du Bois's upbeat "The Balance": "We have progressed. The chains are still clanking, the coward and the traitor are still at large, the poor and guilty and unfortunate are still with us. Our enemies smile. So do we. We have progressed." *The Horizon* would vanish at the end of the year, but the effort of keeping it alive would prove to be of incalculable value when Du Bois turned to the challenge of launching his next magazine.[86]

Without money, both scholarship and advocacy faltered. The university's trustees doubted the conferences could be kept going much longer. For want of enough subscribers, *The Horizon* was certain to follow *The Moon* into extinction, taking along with it hundreds of the partners' scarce dollars. Money worries were threatening to keep Du Bois from reading a paper on Reconstruction at the December 1909 meeting of the American Historical Association, an appearance Du Bois regarded as a personal honor and a racial challenge. Explaining his withdrawal from the panel to Hart, he confessed that he couldn't "afford the expense of coming North." Hart's former student's financial straits were a detail easily remedied, however, and, thanks to Hart, within the week Du Bois was able to confirm his participation in the American Historical Association session in New York. Another star of Hart's graduate seminar, Oswald Villard, declined to participate as a commentator for Du Bois's paper. He would merely risk exposing his own "monumental ignorance" of the topic, Villard explained, but he also warned that Du Bois "was rather unsafe on the question."[87]

The AHA paper contained the germ of Du Bois's massive, revisionist book, *Black Reconstruction*, then twenty-five years off. Coming at the end of the first decade of the twentieth century, "Reconstruction and Its Benefits" was a reinterpretation incompatible with the contemporary historiography, advancing facts and arguing positions diverging so radically from what the gentlemen listening to Du Bois knew that it could find no meaningful place in their tradition of inquiry. To suggest that there had been benefits to Reconstruction was equivalent to descrying benefits in the aftermath of plague. Only a few feet away from the lectern on which Du Bois arranged his speech sat Columbia University's William Archibald Dunning, high priest of the regnant dogma in Reconstruction writing—the Dunning School, whose successive generations of historians deplored the decade of federal intervention in the South as a "tragic era" of Negro misrule. That some African-American politicians had been corrupt, that many of the former slaves were easily misled and exploited, Du Bois conceded with specifics. "Granted then that the Negroes were to some extent venal but to a much larger extent ignorant and deceived," the real issue, Du Bois told his fellow historians, was whether or not "they show[ed] any signs of a disposition to learn better things?" It was the failure of the federal government to create and sustain an effective Freedmen's Bureau, "established for ten, twenty or forty years with careful distribution of land and capital and a system of education for the children" that allowed the perpetuation of slavery in other forms. In the midst of all these difficulties, "The Negro governments in the South accomplished much of positive good," he concluded on a note never before sounded among professional historians. The collaboration of white Democrats and black politicians "of the better elements" late in Reconstruction to exorcise scandal and recapture public confidence in Louisiana, South Carolina, and Mississippi had been buried underneath post–Civil War scholarship until Du Bois exhumed it for his New York audience. "We may recognize three things which Negro rule gave to the South," he concluded: "1. Democratic government. 2. Free public schools. 3. New social legislation."[88]

Finding Reconstruction historiography standing on its head, Du Bois could have said that he had left it upright. Hart wrote how "very proud" he was of his student's impressive "ability to handle complicated materials." "Reconstruction and Its Benefits" had elicited much comment, he crowed to Du Bois a few days after the AHA meeting, adding that "Professor Dunning also had spoken . . . of the paper in high terms."[89] The July 1910 volume of the *American Historical Review* published the paper, after which virtually nothing more was ever said among white professional historians about its heterodox interpretation. Scholarship concerning the politics of race now served the urgent goal of regional reconciliation in which the African-American's place was one of unquestioningly merited subordination. For these reasons, Du Bois's cogently reasoned paper virtually failed to have any impact upon the mainstream scholarship of the day.

The impact on Du Bois, however, was considerable. A curious thing happened to "Reconstruction and Its Benefits" on the way to publication—one more tap of the coffin nail, as Du Bois saw it. Returning the proofs for the article to the *American Historical Review*, he asked editor J. Franklin Jameson, "as a matter of courtesy," to be allowed to capitalize the word Negro. If on no other issue than this one, Du Bois and Washington were in total agreement; each of them consistently urged the adoption of upper-case treatment by mainstream publications. Du Bois's *Suppression* and *Philadelphia Negro* monographs had been among the first to have the noun placed in capitals, and Washington's success in getting Doubleday, Page and Company to capitalize the word in *Up From Slavery* represented a significant breakthrough. It was not a concession Jameson felt he could make. Du Bois insisted, crisply dismissing the argument that "mere uniformity in office practice is sufficient excuse for inflicting upon a contributor . . . that which he regards as a personal insult." Jameson's long, agitated reply of June 22, 1910, either missed the larger point raised by Du Bois or (more likely) intentionally obfuscated it with a profession of personal innocence in all matters of racial prejudice. He was, he wrote, "astonished" that he, the "grandson of an old Abolitionist, brought up to know no difference between black and white," could be charged with insulting a professional colleague, and so on. Negro—Spanish for black—had nothing to do with nationality, with American or German or Hindu, any more than "white man, brown man, or red man," which were mere characterizations of physical traits. "The question was simply one of typography," Jameson assured Du Bois; but in any case, nothing could be done about it in the *American Historical Review*.[90]

In future disputes over the capitalization of Negro Du Bois would be more combative. This time he let his article appear under Jameson's rules but not without a final sharp correction about the "authority of that usage" in Europe, Great Britain, and increasingly this country. He regretted deeply that Jameson had ranged himself "with the least authoritative and more insulting usage."[91] The *American Historical Review* skirmish was just one more incident bringing home to Du Bois the fact that his solution of the race problem through scholarship was no more likely than the Wizard's civil rights nostrums of industry and good behavior to break the shackles of cultural, political, and economic retardation.

14.
NAACP
The Beginning

GENTLEMEN," ATLANTA University's famous professor of economics and history wrote on July 5, 1910, "having accepted the position of Director of Publicity and Research in the National Association for the Advancement of Colored People, I hereby place in your hands my resignation." Expressing regret immediately, President Ware hoped that somehow Du Bois could continue directing the annual studies and that Augustus Dill, Du Bois's selfless factotum, might remain behind to make that possible. Twenty-seven days later, the trustees accepted the resignation and voted official appreciation for the "great ability and devotion" with which Du Bois had served the university, noting with particular emphasis (and significantly in light of the general impression he gave of aloofness) that the "charm of his personality and his prevailing good cheer have added much to the enjoyment of life in the school family." Dean Myron Adams, whose family had shared the same floor with the Du Boises from earliest days, wrote that his New York–bound colleague would be much missed.[1]

Du Bois was leaving in such a hurry, however, that there seems to have been little or no time for ceremonial farewells. Nina and Yolande were staying behind, the trustees' executive committee having graciously complied with his request that they be allowed to retain their South Hall apartment during the coming academic year. Frankly owning up to the vagaries of the NAACP offer, William English Walling, one of the new association's organizers, had written Du Bois in early June, "if I were an old and intimate friend of yours, I should certainly urge you to take the risk."[2] The risk was just the sort of live option William James would have applauded, a chance to create a new language and chart a new course for racial assertiveness.

The organization Du Bois was leaving Atlanta to serve was still undergoing birth trauma. Since its beginning the year before, as the Conference on the Status of the Negro, the evolving NAACP had tacked between two divergent conceptions of itself: the first, as primarily a white organization dedicated to African-American uplift through well-financed suasion; the second, as an interracial phalanx challenging the mainstream public to accept ever-greater civil and social rights for the nation's historic minority. Those who wanted Du Bois on board in a commanding role favored the latter course, but Mary Ovington said that most of their energies had gone into "trying to keep the conservatives from capturing us and get[ting] money from the radicals to do a minimum of constructive work." The widely held perception that what became the NAACP was started by African-Americans is understandable but only symbolically true. For that very reason, Du Bois deliberately inflated the contributions of African-Americans when he chronicled the events of the 1909 National Negro Conference. But Ovington and the millionaire Socialist Walling, rather than Du Bois and Trotter, were the sparks of the association; and Charles Edward Russell and Oswald Villard were the engines.[3] Kept away from New York by classes and limited funds, Du Bois was able to exercise no more than a secondary influence during the association's first months. On the other hand, without Du Bois's imperial personality and his books, articles, and lectures on race relations, the handful of influential whites who broke ranks with the prevailing creed that nothing could be done for black Americans would have been even smaller. He and that handful of whites found themselves working together in a single organization in 1910 primarily in response to the northern version of the Atlanta riot.

The riot that devastated Springfield, Illinois, on the night of August 14, 1908, signaled that the race problem was no longer regional—a raw and bloody drama played out behind a magnolia curtain—but national. The alleged rape of the white wife of a street railwayman by a well-spoken young black man was the immediate cause of the riot, but its tremendous explosive power had to do with economics and demographics. Springfield's population was only 10 percent African-American, but the numbers were growing, and many of the new arrivals were hardworking and even prosperous. A large percentage of the white newcomers came from the upper South to work in the mines and rail transportation. When the Springfield sheriff arranged to have George Richardson spirited out of town to save his life, the angry crowd of street railwaymen that had gathered around the jail was goaded into violence by a large, crude woman crying out, "What the hell are you fellas afraid of? . . . Women want protection!" Boardinghouse keeper Kate Howard's bawling challenge (the press called her "Joan of Arc of the mob") led to more than eighty injuries, six fatal shootings, two lynchings, more than $200,000 in damage, and the flight of some two thousand African-Americans before the National Guard restored order. In the centennial year of his birth and in the town where the Great Emancipator lay entombed, a white mob of thousands swept like locusts through black neighborhoods, howling "Lincoln freed you, we'll show you where you belong!"[4] Nor had the ordeal ended, for now that their lives were safe, Springfield's African-American storekeepers found that their businesses were endangered by the near-total boycott of the white inhabitants.

There was shock outside the South, and much smug comment within it. In Illinois, however, there was equivocation as farmers and miners poured into the town to join the mob, many of them heard shouting, "Curse the day that Lincoln freed the niggers!" "It was not the fact of the whites' hatred toward the negroes," the *Illinois State Journal* suggested, "but of the negroes' own misconduct, general inferiority or unfitness for free institutions that were at fault." The governor was heard to wonder if an elderly black businessman had not invited his own lynching by trying to defend himself.[5] Invidious rationalizations such as these held fearful significance for the nation, said the peripatetic Walling, who raced to the city with his Russian wife, Anna Strunsky, just as the violence was subsiding. Two years earlier, the handsome twenty-nine-year-old Walling had dashed to St. Petersburg after news of "Bloody Sunday," the massacre of peasants and workers before the Winter Palace, reached him in Paris. His mother's people had been Kentucky slaveholders, but the aristocratic Walling was a passionate reformer who had left the University of Chicago to become an Illinois factory inspector, a resident of New York's University Settlement, a disciple of the magnetic social reformer Robert Hunter, and a member of the American Socialist party.[6]

"Race War in the North," Walling's article in the September 3 edition of the *Independent*, threw down the gauntlet to those who cared about civil liberties and fair treatment. It was published less than twenty-four hours after the adjournment of the fourth annual Niagara Movement meeting in Oberlin, Ohio. If the Springfield riot had occurred thirty years ago, the North would have been outraged, Walling wrote. Instead, " 'mitigating circumstances' " were offered up everywhere. The real cause of the riot was "race hatred," but "we at once discovered that Springfield had no shame," he lamented; but then neither did the nation. The issue was clear, the moment historic: "Either the spirit of the abolitionists, of Lincoln and of Lovejoy, must be revived and we must come to treat the negro on a plane of absolute political and social equality, or Vardaman and Tillman will soon have transferred the race war to the North." His final words about the widening persecution of African-Americans had taken the form of an anguished question: "Yet who realizes the seriousness of the situation, and what large and powerful body of citizens is ready to come to their aid?"[7] Race relations now constituted the American dilemma.

Mary Ovington had become obsessed with Walling's call to conscience. She had decided instantly to commit herself to creating that large and powerful body, writing Walling from her tenement in the San Juan Hill section of Manhattan that he must count on her. Walling was already counting on his close friend in the Liberal Club, Charles Russell, the Socialist reformer, investigative journalist, and muckraker novelist, to help him put together an organization of "fairminded whites and intelligent blacks." One Saturday in May 1908 at New York's Republican Club, Russell had listened to a judge, a minister, and a public official discourse on the race problem, and then Du Bois spoke and "eclipsed the rest." Twenty-five years later, Russell would remember that luncheon speech in minute detail. "In the logical and coherent arrangement of his matter, in apt illustration, in research and knowledge, in the polished and carefully chosen cameos of his language, in the faultless fluency of his utterance—unequalled." Henceforth Russell would be a Du Bois stalwart. But it was Ovington who supplied the start-up spark after meeting Walling at the close of his lecture on Russian politics at Cooper Union. Negroes were treated even worse than Jews in Russia, Walling had said, but as yet he had done little to put a stop to it. Pressed by her in the weeks that followed, he finally called a meeting in his New York apartment on West Thirty-ninth Street during the first week in 1909. Ovington was there, along with social worker Dr. Henry Moskowitz, but Russell was detained elsewhere. It was the seminal trio, "a descendant of an old-time abolitionist, the second a Jew, and the third a Southerner," Ovington recalled.[8]

Once he got going, Walling was a powerhouse, bringing into the group the cream of progressive reform—Ray Baker, Lillian Wald, Rabbi Stephen Wise, Reverend John Haynes Holmes, Oswald Villard, and several others. A manifesto or "call" was drafted, with Walling doing most of the writing; something dramatic yet not too radical was needed. Both Ovington and Holmes probably suggested Villard as the ideal final draftsman in light of his social distinction and newspaper ownership. The publisher of the *Evening Post* and *The Nation* "received our suggestion with enthusiasm," Ovington remembered, and set himself immediately to the task.[9] The idea was to have a call approved, signed, and released to the public on February 12, 1909, Lincoln's birthday. As the group grew too large for Walling's apartment and began meeting at the Liberal Club on East Nineteenth Street, it was Walling who drove it forward, enthusiastically backing Ovington's recommendation that their "Committee on the Status of the Negro" include two prominent African-American clergymen: Bishop Alexander Walters, an organizer of the 1900 Pan-African Conference, and Ovington's friend Reverend William Brooks. By the third or fourth meeting sometime in March, Dr. William L. Bulkley, the only public school principal of his race in New York City, had joined the core membership group of fifteen, which by then also included Du Bois's *Philadelphia Negro* collaborator Isabel Eaton. It was at this Liberal Club meeting that the decision was taken to launch a biracial campaign to defend African-American rights and to hold a public conference in the spring of that year.[10] Meanwhile, release of Villard's call, with Du Bois's signature eleventh among sixty-nine, had begun to generate considerable comment and even alarm in some quarters.

Although Villard was an egocentric man of limited personal warmth, he, like Du Bois, tended to express himself in writing with passion and generosity. His appeal was no exception. Reeling off the mounting outrages against the race of Africans in America, North as well as South, he infused his prose with righteous wrath. The nation today would dismay Lincoln. The Great Emancipator would find justice in some states enforced, if enforced at all, by judges "elected by one element in a community to pass upon the liberties and lives of another":

> He would see the black men and women, for whose freedom a hundred thousand of soldiers gave their lives, set apart in trains, in which they pay first-class fares for third-class service, in railway stations and in places of entertainment, while State after State declines to do its elementary duty in preparing the negro through education for the best exercise of citizenship.[11]

Silence in the face of such outrages meant tacit approval. "This government cannot exist half slave and half free any better today than it could in 1861," warned Villard. The call summoned concerned men and women, white and black, to New York's Charity Organization Society on Monday morning, May 31, 1909, for the first meeting of what had now become the National Negro Conference. Booker Washington's name was not among the conferees. Although thoroughly disillusioned with the architect of the Tuskegee program after hearing him bellow platitudes in Carnegie Hall "like a hoarse bullfrog" and at the Lincoln dinner that year, Villard extended an invitation that he was sure Washington would decline. Washington did, replying with a slight hint of sarcasm, perhaps, that his presence might "tend to make the conference go in a direction which it would not like to go." His spies would be on the job, though. The indispensable New York agent, Charles Anderson, had already promised to do everything he could "to discredit this affair."[12]

The high-ceilinged auditorium in the Charity Organization Society building not far from Astor Place was filled on the morning of May 31, its distinguished audience keenly aware of the history about to be made. William Ward, editor of the *Independent*, gave the ringing keynote address. His newspaper, along with Villard's, had been one of the rare white clarions of racial fair play. It was imperative to draw battle lines, Ward told the capacity audience, time to proclaim to the nation the "absolute divergence of view between the ruling majority in the South . . . and ourselves." The three hundred or so men and women listening to the newspaperman ranged from experienced social uplifters, affluent dabblers in reform, descendants of abolitionists, public-minded academics, and suffragettes, to a few labor organizers. Women comprised almost a third of those attending, their perfumes and lotions combining with the acrid body odors released as the warm day advanced. Although overt discord between white women and black men had greatly abated since the bitter days immediately after the Civil War, when Frederick Douglass had colluded in sacrificing female suffrage for the half loaf of ballots for black men, the tension still existed, below the surface.[13] The presence of Fanny Garrison Villard, Inez Milholland Boissevain, Isabel Eaton, and other women backers of female suffrage was an encouraging augury. "The curiosity of the spectators was toward the darker and less known portion of the audience," Du Bois noted. African-Americans were a distinct numerical minority in the hall, dark faces here and there interrupting the rows of white—yet their presence was all the more remarkable because their numbers that morning were not negligible and some of their best minds were represented, including Monroe Trotter and Mary Terrell, Archibald Grimké and Ida Wells-Barnett, Kelly Miller, Bishop Walters, and William Scarborough from Wilberforce.[14]

Ward's voice rose as he reaffirmed equal justice "done to man as man, and particularly to the Negro, without regard to race, color or previous condition of servitude," a principle long since abrogated in the South and now receding pell-mell in the North. Four learned white people stepped to the podium: Columbia University anthropologist Livingston Farrand; Cornell University neurologist Burt Wilder; Columbia political economist Edwin Seligman; and, closing the charged morning session, philosopher John Dewey, whose instrumentalist verdict on racism was that it deprived society of "social capital." The rights denied to an entire people because of color deeply troubled these progressive savants, but the theme of the National Negro Conference in general and the morning's speeches in particular concerned the basic humanity of black people—their mental and biological parity with white people. Professor Wilder, after presenting an array of charts, photographs, and measurements relevant to the "alleged prefrontal deficiency in the Negro brain," thought it reassuring to tell the audience that "many white brains have lateral or ventral depression of the prefrontal lobe." Professor Seligman focused the proceedings on what he took to be legitimate southern white social and political dilemmas. He hypothesized that the African-Americans in the hall "would feel about the whole subject as they [southerners] do" if they were to put themselves objectively into the predicament of white southerners.[15]

With heartening evidence of biological and mental equivalency in the air, both races headed for lunch together at the Union Square Hotel close by, so as to get to know each other. Interracial meals even in large northern centers were rare and never risk-free. The previous year, a well-attended dinner at Peck's Restaurant on Fulton Street, sponsored by the progressive Cosmopolitan Club, was compromised by leering white newsmen. The following morning the New York press, the *Times* included, had salaciously reported the conduct of Ovington and other white women and black male guests in fancy dress.[16] To Ovington's immense relief, lunch in Union Square went smoothly. When the conference reassembled that afternoon in the vaulted auditorium of the Cooper Union for the Advancement of Science and Art, Celia Woolley spoke. She was the Unitarian minister who had pledged herself to black uplift, partly in response to *The Souls of Black Folk*. This redoubtable suffragette and founder of Chicago's Frederick Douglass Center informed the audience that the black man could better afford to lose his vote "than the white man can afford to deprive him of it." Du Bois's thoughts as he sat on the dais reading facial expressions in the audience—Susan Wharton from his *Philadelphia Negro* period was there, along with Sophonisba Breckinridge, Florence Kelley, Ray Baker, and many more familiar allies in the struggle—can be guessed with fair accuracy. But for the present, he would abide by the etiquette of black gratitude for white solicitousness, writing animatedly in the June issue of *Survey* that the two-day conclave had found the Negro to be fully human and the opposing argument to be "utterly without scientific basis."[17]

When it was his turn to speak, Du Bois served up a fair amount of history and economics. His text that afternoon was entitled "Politics and Industry," and he began by taking the Cooper Union audience through "three waves" of black disfranchisement, starting with the first after 1700, in order to show the inevitable connection between cheap labor and racial policy. He did not say so directly, but the impression was unmistakable that he felt proof of Negro intelligence was a matter of secondary importance. He did assert that, in their well-intentioned concern with the deplorable housing, employment, health, and morals of black people, white progressives mistook effects for causes. Black people had lost their own self-respect and become almost a different species in the eyes of many whites (of Farrand and Wilder?) not because they were forced to live in squalid conditions but because they were no longer citizens—civil persons—in the South, because they were degraded by a "new slavery" that could never be abolished until they had the ballot. His clipped tones filled the hall of almost fifteen hundred listeners as he declaimed that the voteless Negro was a provocation, "an invitation to oppression" serving always "to distract attention from real issues and to ride fools and rascals into political power."[18] Until the African-American regained the ballot, his own economic advancement would remain illusory and his value as an ally to white labor and mainstream parties negligible. Economic power would come once political power had been regained, not, as the Tuskegee creed maintained, through abstention from politics and accumulation of wealth through patient, humble industry.

When Walling spoke later that evening, he amplified Du Bois's analysis with considerable brilliance, unmasking the antilabor and undemocratic linkages being forged between southern and northern oligarchies. In much of what was said in speeches as well as in freewheeling discussions, Du Bois, Walling, and several others seemed on the verge of proposing an alliance between African-Americans and organized labor. Du Bois's tightly reasoned "Economic Aspects of Race Prejudice," running at that moment in the *Editorial Review*, strongly implied such a strategy. But both he and Walling knew, as did Ovington, that the black and white working classes were decades away from being ready to collaborate, that the mutual hostility of their leaders would prevent any meaningful overtures. Active in the American Federation of Labor, Walling had no illusions about the economic and racial conservatism of the skilled-labor organization being built by the iron-willed immigrant Samuel Gompers. Gompers would be inaccurately reported as saying in St. Louis the following year that African-Americans should be expelled from the labor movement, but his telegram to Du Bois in which he denied the statement would merely show how plausible the mistaken report was, for the Jewish labor president also said he doubted that blacks were capable of understanding the labor movement.[19] The linking of the two movements, then, would remain for long a minor chord in the official theme music of civil rights. Moreover, even to speculate about such a linkage struck Villard and the other conservatives as dangerous.

The scientific evidence of human equality (the official theme of the conference) and the ideal of interracial labor solidarity variously moved the conference participants, but access to the ballot box for black people, and collective action designed to bring that about, emerged as the main business of the men and women at Cooper Union. The black men and women who had bantered and deferred so nicely over lunches at the Union Square Hotel seemed to the white participants suddenly to have abandoned their concern for consensus on the second day. Du Bois caught the mood that Tuesday in his *Survey* account of the conference. "The scientific calm" vanished, he wrote. "The black mass moved forward and stretched out their hands to take charge. It was their problem. They must name the condition."[20] Was the transformation of unskilled black labor into skilled workers of "first importance," as Reverdy Ransom amended; of "great importance," as the resolutions committee proposed; or, of "vital importance" as Bishop Walters successfully amended? How could there be "too much racial agitation"? Trotter and Wells-Barnett demanded to know, after a white participant had seemed to say as much. Wells-Barnett spoke passionately, without any hint of diplomacy, for those who favored the boldest declarations. She must have been the woman Du Bois described as leaping to her feet when someone proposed inviting Booker Washington to serve on a prospective committee, and crying "in passionate, almost tearful earnestness—an earnestness born of bitter experience—'They are betraying us again—these white friends of ours.' "[21] President Taft should be censured without qualification, Trotter claimed, in view of his announced intention to appoint to federal office only those African-Americans whom the South regarded as trustworthy. Speaking on behalf of his National Independent Political League of Boston, and joined by Max Barber and others—but especially by J. Milton Waldron, founder of the National Negro American Political League of the District of Columbia—Trotter doggedly raised objections and proposed amendments until the proceedings were gaveled to their close.[22]

Earlier in the evening, Walling had fumbled badly as chairperson of the resolutions committee, and Villard had stepped into the breach to pound out the final resolutions that were to be voted on by the full conference. Villard's resolutions were received like live bait tossed to piranhas, mangled, chewed, and regurgitated, until the call for the question decided their fates. The National Committee for the Advancement of the Negro came into being on June 1 after interminable wrangling over semantics and points of order lasting until midnight. The African-American participants were little men "always with a nasty spirit," bent on talking "incessantly," Villard would complain to his uncle, Francis Garrison; their conduct was so atrocious, in fact, that the owner of the *Evening Post* found Du Bois's behavior by contrast "most useful." Wells-Barnett was incensed by the turn the proceedings took in the last exhausted minutes before midnight. Presiding officer Russell recognized Du Bois as chair of the committee to nominate the interim governing body—the Committee of Forty. Du Bois read the names quickly, and in the whorl of ensuing motions, Russell declared the nominating committee's recommendations approved and gaveled the National Negro Conference to a close. In a philosophical mood afterward, Villard decided that "these poor people who have been tricked so often by white men" ought not to be blamed for being so fractious, yet the experience had been "none the less trying." The unflappable Russell "saved us from being blown up," Ovington wrote afterward. Trying times were far from over, though. Du Bois sounded positively euphoric in *Survey*, but he knew better; he was writing for both public consumption and for the benefit of institutional solidarity.

> So the conference adjourned. Its net result was the vision of future cooperation, not simply as in the past, between giver and beggar—the older ideal of charity—but a new alliance between experienced social workers and reformers in touch on the one hand with scientific philanthropy and on the other with the great struggling mass of laborers of all kinds, whose condition and needs know no color line.[23]

The thousand or so men and women streaming out of Cooper Union into the night of June 21 had voted a reprimand of the president of the United States, demanded strict enforcement of civil rights under the Fourteenth and Fifteenth Amendments, appealed for African-American access to the ballot on the same terms as other citizens under the Fifteenth Amendment (female suffrage was not addressed), and called for equal educational opportunities for all Americans in all the states.[24] But agreement on these significant matters was temporarily diminished by the commotion over organizational structure. It was the resolution calling for a Committee of Forty on permanent organization—the resolution Villard had drafted with particular care—that set off explosions. Ida Wells-Barnett was not on the list for the Committee of Forty, nor were Monroe Trotter and Milton Waldron. They walked out into Cooper Square in the early dawn stunned and angry. In her fury, Wells-Barnett broadcast the charge that Du Bois and Ovington were responsible for her omission from the Committee of Forty, a charge still circulating today. Ovington, Wells-Barnett claimed, was jealous of her accomplishments and Du Bois resented her frank independence.

In a vivid autobiographical account, Wells-Barnett claimed that, surrounded by a knot of dismayed white people in the near empty hall, Du Bois, race radical, confirmed feminist, and sole African-American member of the nominating committee for the Forty, lamely apologized for crossing out her name. He had thought, said she, that her place should go to Chicagoan Woolley. According to Wells-Barnett, Du Bois also told her that by deleting her name, he had been able to place the loyal Niagarite male, Dr. Charles E. Bentley, another Chicagoan, among the Forty. Du Bois and several others supposedly now pleaded with Wells-Barnett for permission to reinstate her. "Of course, I did a foolish thing," she wrote of her refusal and rustling departure, eyes glistening. "My anger at having been treated in such a fashion outweighed my judgment. . . ."[25]

Although he did present the final list of names for the Forty that evening, Du Bois's role on the committee was decidedly subordinate to that of Villard, who had, as Walling wrote ruefully to Du Bois (who had immediately returned to Atlanta), arbitrarily added and deleted names during the week following the conference. Moreover, as Ovington remembered that night, whatever her feelings about Wells-Barnett, she repeatedly applauded Charles Russell's "quite illegal" decision to add Wells-Barnett to the Committee of Forty after the tiny crusader had cornered him, bursting with indignation as the conference adjourned. Insofar as Du Bois was concerned, failure to include Wells-Barnett on the original list of Forty was probably motivated far less by personal animus than by well-intentioned (though possibly sexist and perhaps mistaken) calculations as to the most positive public effect of the final, "balanced" roster—calculations influenced by chairperson Villard's dogmatic opinions. On the other hand, Wells-Barnett was a woman of unrestrained outspokenness who seldom acknowledged the gender etiquette of her day when fighting for a cause. She may have presumed a good deal on Du Bois's large ego. In any event, the affront to Wells-Barnett was exceedingly costly because it figured in her decision, after some hesitation, to withdraw from the work of the NAACP.[26]

Villard, the real force behind the Committee of Forty, was accustomed to moving in the world as one whose anointed course was manifest and impervious to correction. His was the imperiousness of an eleven-year-old who in 1883 had traveled to Montana country with deferring dignitaries from Washington and Europe to watch Henry Villard, his father and president of the German-financed Northern Pacific, hammer home a golden spike linking the northern route across the continent. The son heard as well the high calling of Garrisonian reform from his maternal forbears. It was said by many who endured his peremptory competence that Oswald's legacy was "compounded of New England abolitionism, the German Revolution of 1848, and Northern Pacific Railroad shares." Since 1902, he had helped raise $150,000 for the Tuskegee endowment fund. He was founder and current chairman of the Men's League for Women's Suffrage. Uncle Francis, youngest son of the great William Garrison, told him he was the "natural successor to the custodianship" of the family's abolitionist tradition. If the idea for a national Negro committee originated with Walling and Ovington, Villard presumed that its success depended on him—"the people who have it in charge are well-meaning but they are inexperienced and impractical," he wrote Uncle Francis.[27]

The Committee of Forty would determine the ideological mold of the new civil rights organization, choose its board of directors, and hire its staff; and Villard made it clear that he intended to be the ringmaster of the Forty. He was certain that no civil rights organization could be credible if led by radicals, which meant excluding African-Americans like Trotter and Wells-Barnett from leadership positions and minimizing the damage that could be done by Du Bois. Although Booker Washington had been rightly excluded from their proceedings, Villard spoke for his mother, Fanny Villard, Uncle Francis, family friend and former Massachusetts attorney general Albert E. Pillsbury, Edwin Seligman, and others on the National Negro Committee when he insisted that the preeminent race leader must not be publicly disavowed. Villard had promised the Wizard: "It is not to be a Washington movement, or a Du Bois movement." In order not to shut the door on accommodation with those friendly to Tuskegee, Trotter, Waldron, and Wells-Barnett, all bitter detractors of the Wizard, were excluded from the Committee of Forty. But the donnybrook at Cooper Union had shown Villard that "the whole colored crowd was bitterly anti-Washington."[28] Little wonder that Wells-Barnett declared later that Washington had seemed to sit astride them during the Cooper Union proceedings.

Du Bois returned to Atlanta knowing that he was going to have to make the most important decision of his professional life. Many of the men and women at the Cooper Union meeting expected him to play a major role in marshaling a new civil rights coalition. As much as Villard and other well-meaning white friends of civil rights wanted to spare Booker Washington's reputation and to continue paying lip service to his program of compromise, Du Bois understood with cool clarity that the success of this new organization necessitated the deflation of the Great Accommodator's national standing and ultimately the destruction of his machine. Manners, modesty, and good politics precluded any such averral by the parties, but observant spectators appreciated the degree to which American race relations had now become personified. Down in Tuskegee where he thought he had become, "for all intents and purposes, a Negro," sociologist Robert Park put such thoughts on paper. "These two men have divided the white and dark world between them," he wrote. "Du Bois has defined the situation as one of radical and irreconcilable opposition. Washington is cooperative despite divergences and differences, not, however, minimizing the conflict of interest where it exists." Du Bois would have agreed with Park about irreconcilable opposition.

This two-day conference marked the end of the era of accommodation, the twilight of Baldwin, Ogden, and Washington, Du Bois wrote. "The answer long forced on the American world has been: Let them alone; do not agitate; do not let loose dangerous forces and passions," he thundered in *Survey*. Now the passions were loose. The problem of the twentieth century was about to be attacked, vigorously and collectively. And on his shoulders and those of the Talented Tenth, which he had largely nurtured, the race's destiny would fall. It was, he wrote long after the experiment had run its course, "the opportunity to enter the lists in a desperate fight aimed straight at the real difficulty: the question as to how far educated Negro opinion in the United States was going to have the right and opportunity to guide the Negro group."[29]

Du Bois began to hear of machinations intended to confine the policy decisions to a coterie of distinguished white men. Service with the national committee was to be voluntary and unsalaried. All personnel decisions were the exclusive province of the committee chairman, Oswald Villard, and, as Walling complained to Du Bois, Villard soon showed himself unreceptive to having more than a few African-Americans on the Committee of Forty. Even worse, Walling confided further that Villard had committed a "stupendous error" (according to Milholland) in removing six or seven African-American names after three or four new ones had been added. Having already successfully proposed enlarging the Committee of Forty to fifty, Walling was determined to force a showdown over this issue. (Villard and his uncle dismissed the idea as preposterous; they would have preferred a Committee of Twelve.) Du Bois, Wells-Barnett, Bentley, Mary Terrell, Hershaw, Richard R. Wright, Bishop Walters, Scarborough, and the educator Leslie Pinckney Hill of Virginia were already in place. Walling and Ovington steadily pushed the numbers of African-Americans higher, adding Waldron, Grimké, the Philadelphia physician William A. Sinclair, and Reverend William Brooks of New York to the Forty (but Kelly Miller never made the cut).[30]

Villard's great wealth and influence, as well as his devotion to the cause, were lost on none of the organizers, but, for Walling, Ovington, and Milholland, Du Bois was indispensable both as an organizer and a symbol, a view shared by Brooks, Bulkley, Grimké, Hershaw, Sinclair, and most of the other African-Americans on the Committee of Forty. But Villard's influence in the National Negro Committee continued to grow, especially after he became acting chairman of the Committee of Forty after Walling, claiming ill health (in reality, a bruising breach of promise suit was in the offing), lay down the chairmanship at the end of the first meeting on November 8, 1909, a gathering at the Liberal Club that Atlanta-bound Du Bois was unable to attend.[31] There has never been a suggestion that Villard's unsigned review in *The Nation* of Du Bois's *John Brown*, which ran ten days before the meeting at the Liberal Club, was directly connected to policy clashes within the National Negro Committee. A man of Villard's patrician self-righteousness quite likely never paused to consider the impact that his trashing of a rival's biography might have upon the incipient NAACP. All along, he had found fellow Harvard man Du Bois astonishingly lacking in deference and too inclined to extreme views in the area of social equality (Villard's Georgia-born wife insisted that her husband invite neither black people nor Jews to their home). Both took pains to write well in order to acquire wide influence, and both presumed that their large ideas mirrored the destinies of many lesser folk. "There was much I liked in Villard himself," Du Bois said, but this railroad tycoon's son "naturally expected [African-Americans] to be humble and thankful or certainly not assertive and aggressive."[32] Villard, on the other hand, believed that Du Bois's famed intellect and even his character were not quite authentic when measured against the highest white standards which he, Villard, embodied—as the grossly deficient *John Brown* proved. Du Bois was enraged by the harsh review at the worst possible moment, and the resulting fracas between the two impaired the work of the committee.

By the first months of 1910, the impressive momentum of the 1909 National Negro Conference was almost entirely lost. Increasingly distracted by medical and personal concerns, Walling had flagged, while Pillsbury, as well as many Committee of Forty members like Milholland, Wald, or Wise, were compelled to divide their energies among several professional and reform activities. But the committee's real problems—for example, its miserable success in raising even part of the ten thousand dollars Villard thought minimally necessary—had less to do with book reviews or individual demands than with Tuskegee.[33] Too astute to oppose this new National Committee for the Advancement of the Negro openly, and probably not yet sure of the threat it posed, the Wizard pulled levers from offstage, instructing his New York people—Fred R. Moore and Thomas Fortune at the *Age* and Charles Anderson—to redouble their surveillance efforts. White House chats and numerous letters also urged "true friends of President Taft not . . . to be deceived concerning the present state of mind of the colored people of the country," as Washington reminded Judge James Cobb, one of his influential satellites in the federal capital. Dismayed and pained by white collusion in black mischief, George F. Peabody and Robert Ogden frostily withheld their blessings. Except for the predictable *Evening Post*, *Nation*, and *Independent*, mainstream coverage of the conference was negligible. The New York *Sun* sent a reporter, but published instead an interview with the Wizard.[34]

Faced with tantrums from Walling and the group's general churlishness (which his own conduct had done much to provoke), Villard exhorted, jollied, and once or twice threatened to resign until the stalwarts on the

Committee of Forty managed grudgingly to pull together. At the Liberal Club on February 14, and in special session a few days later, Villard pressed his colleagues into action. A firm mid-May date was set for the second annual conference, and Villard introduced Frances Blascoer, an attractive no-nonsense white woman with experience in settlement-house work, whose position as salaried executive secretary to the National Committee for the Advancement of the Negro was ratified. Again, Du Bois was absent, in Atlanta.[35] Next came the composition of a Preliminary Committee on Permanent Organization, chaired by Villard. Du Bois, Milholland, and Seligman (all of whom were absent) along with Walling and Russell were voted members. The first meeting of this crucial committee was fixed for Wednesday, March 30. One of Blascoer's first duties was to record the reaction to a detailed plan for the organization's permanent form submitted by the still-absent Du Bois. "Prof. Du Bois sent a fine scheme for organization," she wrote an unidentified correspondent, and Villard, who read the proposal to the group, agreed with Ovington and the majority that it should guide the deliberations of the new preliminary committee. Blascoer found Villard, whose mother paid Blascoer's salary, to be "a pretty fine fellow, even if he hasn't Walling's damnably acute intelligence."[36]

The February meetings had pretty much decided the name of the organization as the National Committee for the Advancement of the Negro (Villard was adamant about "advancement" figuring in the title), plans for incorporation were discussed, and the problematic motion by Milholland that the committee merge with his Constitution League had been dodged by referring it to the Preliminary Committee on Permanent Organization. There was unmistakable progress. In Boston, Du Bois had delivered a public address in late March and sent a letter to the *Transcript* impugning the Wizard's fatal monopoly of power, "for the last eight years. . . . the sole referee for all political action concerning 10,000,000 Americans." Only those African-Americans who agreed with the Wizard's policy of "giving up of agitation and acquiescence in semi-serfdom" have been advanced by the Tuskegee Machine, Du Bois thundered.[37] In his Boston address and then in the May *Horizon,* Du Bois was at his most merciless in his denunciation of the Tuskegee forces, pressing the attack in terms of economic exploitation and working-class solidarity. The Niagara Movement was the future. "The vested interests who so largely support Mr. Washington's program . . . are to a large extent, men who wish to raise in the South a body of black laboring men who can be used as clubs to keep white laborers from demanding too much."

At this critical juncture Villard threw down the gauntlet to Washington and tendered an olive branch to Du Bois, writing the editorial in the April 1 edition of the *Evening Post*, "Mr. Washington in Politics." Du Bois noted the strategic compliment Villard paid him of virtually paraphrasing *in extenso* the Boston *Transcript* letter, as well as "Of Mr. Booker T. Washington and Others," Du Bois's devastating essay in *The Souls of Black Folk*. Villard told *Evening Post* readers that there was a cleavage now beyond repair in Afro-America, a breach the nation must now make the effort to understand. "Eternal vigilance is the price of liberty for the negro as for the white man," he proclaimed, "and Du Bois is merely living up to the highest traditions of American life when he fights for the rights of his own people to a voice in their government." Booker Washington, on the other hand, had a perfect right to subordinate "everything else to the uplifting of the negro industrially and economically . . . and so he reaches the ears and softens the hearts of thousands who would not listen to a word from Dr. Du Bois."[38]

A few weeks later, Lillian Wald secured a small donation from Jacob Schiff, a major defection from Bookerite financiers. Money had begun to flow in, and Horace Bumstead, Susan Wharton, Clarence Darrow, Franz Boas, Albert Hart, Mary Terrell, Reverdy Ransom, and a growing cast of boosters publicized the goals of the committee and its forthcoming conference set for May 12. Secretary Blascoer, who had written her friend at the end of March that dealing with Walling, Wells-Barnett, and especially with the very Russian Mrs. Walling had plunged her into a "blue funk" and caused her to tear her hair, now breathed easier. Wells-Barnett had "finally calmed down, and has practically accepted an invitation to come on again, and speak—we pay her expenses."[39] In choosing Blascoer, Villard had put the national committee in the competent hands of someone wholly in accord with his businesslike approach who could be expected to defer to him. He recognized that Du Bois's pen and his Niagara loyalists were invaluable. But it was certainly not his wish to install Du Bois—in his eyes an icily proud and uncontrollable extremist—in New York with a salaried title and an organizational mandate to make war on the hosts of bigotry. Attendance at Executive Committee meetings, the forwarding of reports and memoranda, publication of articles on behalf of the Association and its causes would be service enough. For Du Bois, the new organization was the chance of a lifetime. "When in the past overtures have been made to me to leave the work in Atlanta and go at a higher salary, to Hampton, to Tuskegee, to Public Schools in Washington and elsewhere," Du Bois told

Horizon readers, invariably, he had decided his "duty lay in Atlanta." But here was a "pioneer organization, an experiment, but an attempt to do bravely and courageously a work that must be done."[40]

Assessing his situation, Du Bois had good reason to appreciate the high price of courage. Across the country, African-American men and women of modest means and major ambitions were being compelled to look into themselves, weighing principles against careers, in order to make fateful decisions about whether to risk falling in with his small band of underfinanced, politically insignificant college-bred adventurers or to pledge allegiance to the mighty Tuskegee empire. Du Bois himself expressed surprise at the degree to which the controversy with Booker Washington had become "more personal and bitter than [he] had ever dreamed and which necessarily dragged in the University." Although nothing was said explicitly, Du Bois knew that the president and trustees were suffering extreme discomfort in the Wizard's tightening vise. And if he reasonably blamed his opposition for the polarizing of loyalties in Afro-America, Du Bois's own conduct was as much a factor in causing neutrality to be censured as rank evasion and pragmatism to be arraigned as virtual treason. His warm friendship with Hope nearly foundered on the shoals of the controversy earlier that year when Hope revealed that, "through the kindness of Mr. Booker Washington," he had secured a conditional offer of ten thousand dollars from Andrew Carnegie. One early January evening at Towns's home, Du Bois and a small group of Niagarite men had roasted the Atlanta Baptist College president about being a turncoat, what Hope himself described as "not a scorching, just a comfortable warm brown." Yet, later mulling over what had been said (especially by Du Bois), Hope was prompted to write his good friend a nineteen-page letter from Providence, Rhode Island. It was a remarkable document, a mixture of contrition and self-exoneration. Although sometimes misunderstood by the public, the college president said that never before had he defended himself, preferring to let his actions speak for him. But Du Bois "was the one man to whom I thought I might owe an explanation."

The power of Du Bois to exact loyalty based on principle and of the Wizard to compel choices based on reality was seldom more vividly illustrated: why did he owe Du Bois an explanation? Hope continued. "Because I have followed him; believed in him; tried even, where he was not understood, to interpret him and show that he is right; because I have been loyal to him and his propaganda—not blatantly so, but, I think, really loyal; and because, in spite of appearances, I am just as truly as ever a disciple of the teachings of Du Bois regarding Negro freedom."[41] Hope pleaded for understanding, imploring, "no matter whether you doubt the wisdom of or resent my action, are we friends?" Yet Hope also made it clear that his decisions must be governed by a college "that needed the assistance and ought to be helped rather than hampered by its president." He should not have to feel himself caught between "a *tyranny* of views," after all. How well Hope understood Du Bois is shown by the close of his apology: "The opposing views of other men do not so much concern you in your thinking because you have hardly needed them in your equation. That is genius. I am a plodder." Friendship yes, but not full absolution, Du Bois admonished Hope. "One thing alone you must not, however, forget. Washington stands for Negro submission and slavery."[42] The Devil would surely take his pound of flesh. Hope put in writing thoughts that Atlanta's Ware had entertained. For a good many years to come, the fate of African-American higher education would require the patience and conciliation of plodders. Geniuses need not apply.

As the reformers, academics, settlement workers, Niagarites, Constitution Leaguers, suffragettes, and the rest filed into the Charity Organization Society building once again on the afternoon of May 12, 1910, the status of African-Americans in politics and public service, already grim, was becoming ever more dismal. Whereas Theodore Roosevelt had made a show of a handful of black federal appointments, William Howard Taft slowed the trickle to a few drops, insisting that he could not alienate the white South, as his predecessor had done, by uncongenial black appointments. With their power to influence federal patronage sputtering badly, the doctors, lawyers, preachers, teachers, and undertakers aboard the Tuskegee Machine now began to check their road maps. Judge Robert Terrell, whose independent-minded wife served on the Committee of Forty, would shortly warn the Wizard of widespread disaffection among their forces. Whether in Ohio or Michigan, Terrell found "all of them and their friends bitter in their expressions and their attitude against the national administration." Robert Russa Moton ("Major" Moton, the head of cadets at Hampton), who would succeed the Wizard as principal of Tuskegee, issued the same warning.[43] And while the professional classes were being battered, the people Booker Washington had pledged to empower in his famous Atlanta address—the black peasantry of the South—had become mudsill.

Charisma, as Max Weber would famously postulate, imparted momentum to institutions, which then created the basis for effective bureaucracy. For Walling, Ovington, Russell, Milholland, and the critical mass of

African-Americans in the National Committee, charisma meant W. E. Burghardt Du Bois. Until they offered a place and a wage to "a colored leader of nationwide prominence, Dr. Du Bois," Walling argued, they could do little to further the cause of civil and social rights.[44] Race politics, the horrific plight of black tenant farmers, the lynching of ninety-two African-Americans a year, and the partisans of Du Bois within the organization finally caused Villard to change course when the second annual conference opened. The theme of the conference had after all been largely set by Du Bois. The first conference had focused on the humanity of African-Americans; this one concentrated on "Disenfranchisement and Its Effects upon the Negro." Finally meeting face to face again, Villard and Du Bois shook hands publicly (they "shook hands across the chasm," Ovington said) and collaborated in clockwork concert during three days of high-pressure sessions on May 12, 13, and 14.[45] But enmity as crystalline as their egos would govern their dealings with each other over the decades to come.

On Saturday evening the second National Negro Conference adopted the report of the Preliminary Committee on Organization. This was a tribute to Du Bois's carefully drawn plans sent up earlier from Atlanta, plans bearing the unmistakable imprint of the lordly, competent Villard as well. What was to become the nation's oldest civil rights organization now officially sprang into being as the National Association for the Advancement of Colored People (NAACP) in the great hall of the Charity Organization Society. "Colored" was chosen instead of Afro-American or Negro in order to proclaim the association's intention to promote the interests of dark-skinned people everywhere, Du Bois said, and his wishes in the matter were probably decisive.[46] Contrary to general belief later, neither the Constitution League nor the Niagara Movement was formally affiliated with the new association, the issue of the former's relationship having been held over for future action in order not to foreclose conciliation with Tuskegee.[47] Although altered somewhat when the 1911 constitution was approved, the basic shape of the NAACP emerged from the 1910 conference.

A national Committee of One Hundred was created; as well as a thirty-person executive committee, with its members to be elected from the national committee. Fifteen members of the executive committee were to reside in New York, and fifteen elsewhere. Membership called for payment of two-dollar annual dues, with life memberships purchasable for five hundred dollars, two hundred dollars for donors. As president of the

NAACP, the members chose Moorfield Storey, a cornerstone of the Boston establishment, past president of the American Bar Association and, as a young lawyer, personal secretary to the venerable abolitionist Senator Charles Sumner. Judicious, principled, possessing enormous, if waning, influence in national circles of power, the white-maned Brahmin was the perfect choice to head an organization for which no black person, however distinguished, could be considered in 1910. Storey, who had not been able to attend the conference, was notified after the fact. The new officers of the association were Walling as chairperson, Milholland as treasurer, and Villard as assistant or "disbursing" treasurer.[48]

But there was still no place for Du Bois until the executive committee convened on Saturday morning, May 14, presided over by Russell. Titles were debated and approved, salaried positions created, and duties (Blascoer's in particular) redefined. Emphasis shifted from Villard's membership rallies and fund-raising to investigation and propaganda, the sort of work Walling and Ovington knew Du Bois would accomplish with distinction. The situation was still fluid, nevertheless. "With some hesitation I was asked to join the organization," Du Bois recalled. "The secretary then in charge was alarmed about her own job and suspicious of my designs." The incorrigibly frank Blascoer announced that she was not going to work for an organization that subordinated her duties to research and publication activities. She made her views known to Villard's mother; and, after the executive committee meeting on May 25, when the position of salaried "director of publicity and research" was finally voted, she let Du Bois have a piece of her mind. The NAACP should first be put on a sound financial footing before plunging into the "immense amount of work" involved in publicity, she wrote him. Du Bois intimated that he thought that part of Blascoer's problem was an aversion to working with a black man. "In some most incomprehensible manner," she snapped back, he had twisted her objections into "a refusal on my part to work with you . . . because of your color."[49] Blascoer left the NAACP shortly thereafter to work with black schoolchildren in New York and wrote an important book about the experience. She was unlikely to have been prejudiced in the way Du Bois thought, but the *malentendu* prefigured Du Bois's relations with the association's whites.

Meantime, while Blascoer stewed, Du Bois's $2,500 salary as the prospective director of publicity and research was nowhere in sight. As late as June 20, treasurer Milholland would "regret to say that things are not moving along the line" as fast as he had hoped. Income from the sales of printed conference speeches, a few large donations like those of Mrs. W. H. Forbes of Massachusetts and Jacob Schiff (most gratified by the second annual conference resolution condemning the czar's expulsion of Kievan Jews), and pledges from members of the Committee of One Hundred had put only a few hundred dollars in the treasury. Milholland proposed an alternative to Du Bois: office space in the Philadelphia branch of his Constitution League if Villard continued to drag his feet. Finally, in his upbeat letter of June 8, formally offering Du Bois the position, Walling was certain that when the "wealthy people of New York and Boston" returned from summer vacations in Europe, Du Bois's salary would be secure. "I have no doubt you realize, that we are offering you work and an opportunity," Walling hardly needed to point out, "rather than a financially promising, or steady position."[50] Du Bois replied that he would run "any reasonable risk" to commit himself to work of "paramount and critical importance." And besides, with the Tuskegee Machine roaring at the university's gates, his usefulness in Atlanta was greatly compromised.

The impertinent criticism by Du Bois and Milholland of the Tuskegeean's public statements during his trip to England that fall had deeply rankled Tuskegee. Washington had confidentially blamed what he called the gang of "absolute failures" surrounding his rival. The Wizard was certain that rich, busy white folk up North would never have thought such things had it not been for that writing machine Du Bois and his Niagara Movement. "I think it is too bad," Washington bristled in a letter to the Atlanta *Constitution*'s Clark Howell at the end of November, "that an institution like Atlanta University has permitted Dr. Du Bois to go on from year to year stirring up racial strife in the heart of the South." The next time Schiff or some other wealthy northerner asked the Tuskegee principal's advice about disbursal of monies to southern schools, the odds against a significant grant to Atlanta University were sure to grow even longer.[51] Fortunately for Atlanta University, Du Bois had departed for New York four months before the Wizard's angry letter to Howell. He was lucky to have a job to go to, and the association, as Ovington said, was finally really in business. "These days were the climacteric of my pilgrimage," Du Bois noted of his leave taking, with more fustian than usual. "Stepping, therefore, in 1910 out of my ivory tower of statistics and investigation, I sought with bare hands to lift the earth and put it in the path in which I ought to go."[52]

15.
Rise of *The Crisis*, Decline of the Wizard

THE MOVE from Atlanta to New York, from the classroom in ivy-covered Stone Hall to an editorial desk in Villard's *Evening Post* building at 20 Vesey Street, Du Bois always regarded as the fork in his career leading from science to propaganda. The problem of the twentieth century impelled him from mobilizing racial data to becoming the prime mobilizer of a race. It was the great sacrifice forced upon him by a world vastly more atavistic beneath its surface culture and modernity than he had dreamt possible as a young scholar. At age forty-two, a series of ugly incidents and unfair developments had pushed and pulled him, he explained repeatedly, to forsake the tower for the platform, monographs for editorial columns: Sam Hose's severed knuckles on display in a Mitchell Street grocery; the Ogden express figuratively rushing past Atlanta University on its way to Tuskegee; Carnegie Institution funds for a Mississippi planter while the Atlanta Studies went begging; Teddy Roosevelt dishonoring a battalion of decorated soldiers—and, no matter what the legerdemain or outrage, always there was the imperturbable Booker T. Washington ready with a disingenuous explanation. Yet, if, as he rightly said, "this fact of racial distinction based on color was the greatest thing in my life and absolutely determined it," the shift from science to propaganda—however disjunctive professionally—was also supremely suited to Du Bois's temperament and talent.[1] As a very young man, and then many years later, he confessed to wanting to be a novelist, and he would, of course, write a number of works of fiction, as well as some poetry. This Apollonian social scientist was also a born Dionysian prophet, left-handed, deeply intuitive, creative, and mystical. If Du Bois's new career represented a sacrifice, it was also a gift.

He arrived at Vesey Street determined to try out an idea that some members of the executive committee thought was impractical to the point of folly—a national monthly magazine. The name for it, "Crisis," came either from Ovington or Walling one early August afternoon as the three sat planning the magazine's life in suite 610 of Villard's new Viennese Secessionist building with its elaborately detailed, copper mansard roof. James Russell Lowell's poem "The Present Crisis" was the inspiration. The skeptical Albert Pillsbury warned Du Bois from Boston, "periodicals are as numerous and as pestilential nowadays as flies were in Egypt, and most of them meet with the very same reception."[2] A militant civil rights journal, edited by an African-American primarily for African-Americans, appeared no more likely to find a sufficient number of subscribers than would a block of preferred Standard Oil securities in the new Harlem. *The Moon* had died in its earliest phases and *The Horizon*, after much clamor about the Milholland merger, was fast receding. "From a talk with Murray, I gather we are about at the end of the row," Hershaw had sighed in early April, although the magazine would run for another three months during 1910. Du Bois's editorial success rate thus far fully justified Pillsbury's prognosis. Nor did the NAACP possess funds for a publication; as Villard told Du Bois his first morning on the job, " 'I don't know who is going to pay your salary; I have no money.' " From the would-be editor's point of view, nevertheless, the office space provided by Villard and his provisional support of the enterprise were more critical at that stage than the money. *The Crisis: A Record of the Darker Races*, edited by W. E. Burghardt Du Bois, "with the cooperation of Oswald Garrison Villard," conveyed cachet and implied gold-plated publishing experience.[3] Most likely, Villard backed Du Bois's *Crisis* scheme because he intended to be as much a force behind it as he had been behind the National Negro Committee. If so, this was, of course, a monumental miscalculation on his part.

"On November 1st there will appear the first number of a new monthly called *The Crisis*," Du Bois's prospectus announced in mid-September. Five thousand subscribers were needed in order to insure its success. "For this reason the subscription is put at the nominal price of One Dollar." His publication was to fulfill several functions: "First and foremost," as a newspaper recording "very important happening and movement in the world which bears on the great problem of interracial relations and especially those which affect the Negro-American"; second, as a comprehensive review "of opinion and literature" pertinent to the race problem; third, as a forum for "a few terse" articles; finally, the editorial page, mainly though not exclusively animated by Du Bois, standing "for the rights of men, irrespective of color or race, for the highest ideals of American democracy." Along with Villard and Russell, the prospectus boasted the impressive credentials of contributing editors Kelly Miller, "an author and critic," Max Barber, "formerly editor of the *Voice of the Negro,*" William Stanley Braithwaite, a poet and writer of "international reputation" (Braithwaite, an African-American, was poetry editor of the Boston *Transcript*), and Mary Dunlop Maclean, "a staff writer on the New York *Times*"—an editorial board made up of two white men and one white woman, and three black men. A special meeting of the executive committee, on September 6, had approved Du Bois's magazine as "the organ of the National Association for the Advancement of Colored People," with the proviso that the editor submit to all the committee members the copy for the first number.[4] Having to supply copy far enough ahead of the publication deadline was the least of the editor's worries, since he wrote nearly all of it himself.

To a "young English woman," as he referred to Mary Maclean, Du Bois owed "more than I can say" for technical help and long hours. Maclean had been born and raised in the Bahamas. Ovington, who was a competent judge of the profession, called her one of the best women journalists of the day. Somehow Maclean continued to write full-time for the Sunday edition of the *Times* while serving as tireless managing editor of *The Crisis*. She had been stirred by the first National Negro Conference and had gone to Russell to volunteer her talents. Her colleagues came to call her "Miss Sunbeam" because she brought such unflagging buoyancy to the work in Vesey Street. Du Bois owed a great deal as well to the firm of Robert N. Wood ("we print for the *Vogue* Magazine and refer by permission to Mr. Condé Nast"—spelled "Nash" in the first issue) for breakneck delivery at a price reduced by the cost of an ad in *The Crisis*. Wood was an African-American printer well-connected to Tammany Hall.[5] *The Crisis* went on sale at the beginning of November 1910 at ten cents a copy, a sixteen-page volume ten inches high, backed by a one-year, fifty-dollar-a-month line of credit voted by the NAACP executive committee.

The culmination of Du Bois's brand of militant journalism, *The Crisis* actually traced its lineage from Frederick Douglass's *North Star* and William Garrison's *Liberator* back to the first newspaper in North America published by persons of African descent, Samuel Eli Cornish and John

Russwurm's *Freedom's Journal.* Garrison's iron rectitude and Douglass's unbending dignity can be said to have infused *The Crisis,* but part of its inspiration came from the polemical voice of Fortune of the *Globe* and *Freeman,* in Du Bois's Great Barrington youth a model of intrepid civil rights activism but now a fallen angel in the kingdom of Tuskegee.[6] On the cover of the inaugural issue was the smudged figure of a black child of undetermined gender, probably drawn by Du Bois, holding a hoop in the right hand and a stick in the other. Madame E. Toussaint's Conservatory of Art and Music ("The Foremost Female Artist of the Race") purchased a full page on the reverse side of the cover, a lifeline ad for the magazine, as was real estate broker Philip A. Payton's full-page ad for "New York's Pioneer Negro Real Estate Agents," the company that had driven a wedge into white Harlem. L. C. Smith & Bros. Typewriters of Syracuse, New York, took another full page for some reason. The Henry Phipps Model Tenements for Colored Families bought half a page. Marshall's Hotel on West Fifty-third Street, "The Leading Colored Restaurant in America," placed a quarter-page ad, and so did the Nyanza Pharmacy, "the only colored Drug Store in New York City."[7]

The agenda and tone of *The Crisis* were set by Du Bois's introductory editorial stating its firm intention to set forth "those facts and arguments which show the danger of race prejudice." Its name came from the fact that the editor "today believes that this is a critical time in the history of the advancement of men." No clique or party would sway the magazine, Du Bois continued, and "personal rancor of all sorts" would be avoided (a promise often unkept). The format of the first *Crisis* would be more or less constant in succeeding issues over the next four years: "Along the Color Line," with its subsections on topics such as politics, education, social uplift, organizations and meetings, science, and art; "Opinion," a canvass of the press and representative correspondence; "Editorial," with subsections; a large section varying each month from coverage of NAACP business to essays on various topics; "The Burden," for coverage of civil, economic, political, and literal atrocities against African-Americans; and "What to Read." "Talks About Women" and "Men of the Month" were added in December 1910 and May 1911, respectively.[8]

The November *Crisis* invited readers to contemplate two racial infamies—one a lynching by a mob, the other a presidential hanging. Du Bois's editorial on the lynching of two swarthy Italians (recently naturalized) in Florida dripped with irony. "The inalienable right of every free American citizen to be lynched without tiresome investigation and penalties is one which families of the lately deceased doubtless deeply appreciate." In "Athens and Brownville," Moorfield Storey recounted the 1904 rampage in Athens, Ohio, by fifty or more soldiers of the 14th Battery of U.S. Artillery who had sprayed bullets into Main Street as they marched on the city jail to liberate a comrade. Although a militiaman was killed and two or more civilians wounded, manipulation of the evidence by the War Department's representative, who denounced the prosecution, resulted in the sentencing of a single soldier to a year in prison and the fining of another. "Here the facts were clear," the distinguished constitutional authority noted, "but the guilty men were white." Both incidents had occurred during Roosevelt's watch. "Why did he not apply the same rule in both cases?"[9]

In "Along the Color Line," readers of the first *Crisis* learned of the election in South Carolina of Governor Coleman Blease on a platform endorsing prohibition and opposing Negro education; of the founding of an organization to promote the Democratic party, the United Colored Democracy of New York State; of President Taft's nomination of the distinguished Tennessee African-American lawyer-politician James C. Napier to the post of register of the United States Treasury; of "about $400,000 from the Dolger bequest" to Tuskegee; and of a French anthropologist's report of "powerful Negro empires of great size and some culture exist[ing] in the Sudan before the white races entered Africa." There was detailed news of the founding of the NAACP at the second annual conference on the Negro, along with horror stories under "The Burden" about the association's intervention in the Pink Franklin and Steve Greene peonage cases.[10]

Pink Franklin, an illiterate South Carolina tenant farmer, was the nation's current object lesson in peonage. He had been speedily tried and sentenced to death for killing a white sheriff who had crashed into his house at night to arrest him for leaving his landlord's farm. After the state supreme court decreed that it saw nothing amiss in the trial and sentence (that no lynching had occurred was proof enough of due process), Milholland's Constitution League persuaded former U.S. attorney general Charles J. Bonaparte to prepare Franklin's case for the Supreme Court. Meanwhile, Villard's *Evening Post* and Hayes's *Independent* transformed Pink Franklin's case into a cause célèbre during the spring of 1910. Two weeks after the second annual National Negro Conference, Villard wrote Uncle Francis of the "terrible blow" delivered by the U.S. Supreme Court. Dodging the peonage question at the heart of the case, it had upheld the South Carolina decision.[11] Ten weeks later, as Villard, Ogden, and

Washington worked behind the scenes to have Franklin's death sentence commuted to life imprisonment, Steve Greene, an illiterate tenant farmer, staggered out of Chicago's railroad terminal with bullets from his white Arkansas landlord's pistol still imbedded in his neck, arm, and leg. Greene was another black man whose gall in refusing slave wages had ended in the killing of a white man. Extradited to Arkansas, where a Crittenden County lynch committee awaited him at the depot, Greene was saved when Wells-Barnett's Negro Fellowship League secured a writ of habeas corpus, offered a hundred-dollar reward to any Illinois sheriff intercepting Greene and his Arkansas deputies, and then rallied a defense committee. Steve Greene finally reached safety in Canada.[12] Curiously, Du Bois's coverage of the dramatic events behind Greene's removal from the clutches of his Arkansas warders omitted any mention of Wells-Barnett and her Negro Fellowship League.

The "Opinion" column assembled representative views on important questions of the day from prominent African-American leaders, many of whom, of course, saw eye-to-eye with the editor. "What to Read," which would evolve from a laundry list of recommended titles to annotations and concise reviews, alerted subscribers to the existence of more than a dozen magazine articles (four dealing with India and three with Africa) and thirteen books, four of them on Africa, one of them in French, and one, *Three Lives*, by Gertrude Stein. In light of the earthquake that his editorial writings on racial integration would set off thirteen years later, Du Bois's pronouncements in the first issue deserve attention. "Some people," the editor alleged, without specifying names or race, in Chicago, Philadelphia, Columbus, Ohio, and a number of other northern cities, were promoting separate public schools for African-American children. This was wrong, and must not be. "Separate them by color and they grow up without learning the tremendous truth that it is impossible to judge the mind of a man by the color of his face. Is there any truth that America needs to learn more?"[13]

The Crisis was to be more like a rocket than Pillsbury's Egyptian flies. It came "at the psychological moment," a triumphant Du Bois exclaimed, "and its success was phenomenal." With the first issue of a thousand selling out completely (a George Wesley Blount of Hampton, Virginia, was the first subscriber), he doubled the number of pages in the December *Crisis* and increased the printing to 2,500. This issue carried "Talks About Women," a segment written by Mrs. John Milholland, which broadcast Du Bois's commitment to women's causes and contributed to a boost in sales. It also included Franz Boas's second annual conference paper, a highly significant demolition of the pseudo-science surrounding racial differences. Booker Washington would have expected to be noticed, and he was not disappointed. The items column of the first *Crisis* contained a straight-faced comment on the Wizard's recent European tour. "On landing in America, Mr. Washington announced that the Negroes in the United States were better off than the poor classes in Europe."[14] A cheerful book on the subject, *The Man Farthest Down*, would issue from the Tuskegee ghostwriters' factory the following year.

That so little ink was expended on Du Bois's adversary in the first issues was probably because Du Bois's petition denouncing the Wizard, "An Appeal to England and Europe," was still gathering signatures in the United States. While in London, the Tuskegee principal had assured the distinguished members of the Anti-Slavery and Aborigines Protection Society that the American race problem was virtually solved. Milholland, also in London at the time, had contacted Du Bois immediately, urging him to puncture Washington's hot-air balloon. A long letter from Milholland had appeared in the September 6 London *Standard* dismissing such statements as "really a farcical declaration were the background not so ghastly tragic." Ask W.E.B. Du Bois about the American race problem, Milholland of the Constitution League challenged, "this brilliant graduate of Harvard University, this student of Heidelberg [sic] and member of the International Law Association, the recognized authority on sociology . . . [who] is compelled to travel on a 'Jim Crow' car from Atlanta to Washington." Before the Wizard left the British Isles, Du Bois's rebuttal in the name of the NAACP, and signed by twenty-three leading African-American men from Barber through Grimké and Trotter to Bishop Walters, was being circulated by Milholland. On December 1, 1910, with the first number of *The Crisis* still eliciting widespread comment, "An Appeal to England and Europe," with nine additional signatories, was published in the New York *Sun*, which, like most of the "white" press, had ignored the founding conference of the NAACP.[15]

They were compelled to point out "that Mr. Washington's large financial responsibilities have made him dependent on the rich charitable public," Du Bois explained to interested Britons. "He has for years been compelled to tell, not the whole truth, but that part of it which certain powerful interests in America wish to appear as the whole truth." The truth according to Du Bois was radically different. "Our people were emancipated in a whirl of passion, and then left naked to the mercies of their enraged and impoverished ex-masters." The history lesson that followed in "An Appeal to England and Europe" was a marvel of compression, outlining the "systematic attempt to curtail education," the mob violence aroused when "property in better quarters" was bought, the universality of "lower wages for equal work," the cardinal disgrace to black women in the South "without protection in law and custom," and, finally, "worse than all this," the systematic miscarriage of justice in the courts—topics dealt like cards snapped from a deck. Here was a Talented Tenth manifesto that had, if not world impact, an impact in the world. In this three-page leaflet, Du Bois crystallized the divisions between so-called radical and conservative African-Americans. Washington's performance in Europe was "like a blow in the face," he charged. "It is one thing to be optimistic, self-forgetful and forgiving, but it is quite a different thing, consciously or unconsciously, to misrepresent the truth."[16]

"Is a toothache a good thing?" Du Bois had asked in his first editorial. It was in any case "supremely useful" in warning of decay, dyspepsia, and death. No issue of *The Crisis* ever failed to expose its quota of useful toothaches—such as Du Bois's May 1912 criticism of the black church. The institution had saved the race in slavery. "One must bow with respect" before it. Yet all was not well with the church. Its upper ranks were "choked with pretentious ill-trained men and in far too many cases with men dishonest or otherwise immoral." Dishonesty was compounded by parochialism, the depressing fact that the church was "still inveighing against dancing and theatregoing, was still blaming educated people for objecting to silly and empty sermons." Perhaps not since the similar reproaches of Martin Delany before the Civil War had a prominent African-American publicly lambasted the race's one institution that above all others united millions of men and women of all classes and regions. Did the memory of "Pops" Miller, the grim foe of Terpsichore who meddled into innocence at Fisk, play a subconscious part in Du Bois's editorial spleen, long years afterward?

Other shortcomings within the veil were exposed with Du Bois's characteristic asperity. Wilberforce University, where the editor's old Negro Academy colleague Scarborough was now serving out an earnest if routine presidency, was said to be falling almost hopelessly behind the trends in higher education. The "New Wilberforce"—the adjacent institution being supported by state funds—was an object lesson on how to avoid the lack of vision and paltry funding of the original Wilberforce. While Scarborough's and the Wilberforce alumni's wounded protests were being taken seriously by a deeply concerned Villard, Du Bois raced on to his next target—the formidable black press. Down in Washington, irascible Calvin Chase's *Bee* had mocked *The Crisis* and its editor as the catspaws of arrogant, powerful whites. Lobbing the grenade back, Du Bois sneered at the anti-intellectualism and plain bad grammar not only of the *Bee* but of much of the Negro press, challenging it to report on events other than weddings and murders if it wanted to be taken seriously by his magazine. Villard and the other white officers were certain that the association would be engulfed in a firestorm as hostile editorials flamed up across the country. The *Bee* sneered at "Harvardized English." The less-heated Richmond *Planet* advised readers to ignore the "professional bookworm" Du Bois. A gloating *Age* observed that Du Bois had seriously damaged his own cause. Moorfield Storey decided that the director of publicity and research must be deranged, a brilliant mind undoubtedly warped, Storey wrote Villard, by being "treated as inferior by many men whom he knows to be his inferiors."[17] At the annual spring conference in 1914, the NAACP membership would vote a placatory resolution praising the Negro press and hold its breath. *The Crisis* published the resolution but declined to extend the olive branch itself.

Just as Du Bois said, the success was phenomenal. The January 1911 *Crisis* (with a fighting-spirit editorial by Jane Addams) sold 3,000, February 4,000, March 6,000. This last carried Mary Maclean's astonishing Afrocentric essay on the black sources of Egyptian civilization. The publisher of Villard's *John Brown*, Doubleday, Doran & Company, bought a half page in the December 1910 number, as did the publisher of *The Souls of Black Folk*. By March 1911, most of the major African-American colleges and universities would join the growing list of advertisers—Atlanta, Fisk, Howard, Shaw, Virginia Union—even Wilberforce. Hampton and Tuskegee were not among them, however. With the addition of "Earning a Living" in June 1911, the magazine launched a popular section on Talented Tenth firsts—inventors, surgeons, psychiatrists, architects, and other models worthy of professional emulation. With the 1911 anniversary number, the amateur cover sketches gave way to the handiwork of professional Washington, D.C., photographer George Scurlock, who specialized in poised Talented Tenth women, and to fine drawings by New York artist Louise Latimer.[18] Circulation would reach 22,500 in April 1912. The editor's year-end financial statement submitted to the NAACP treasurer would report total sales from November 1910 to November 1912 of 350,000 copies, generating an income of $17,374.51, with a balance of $242.48 after deducting $17,132.03

for personnel, printing, shipping, and other costs. Du Bois calculated that the magazine's future would be secure once circulation reached 50,000.[19] For a two-dollar membership in the association or ten cents an issue, the editor of *The Crisis* gave readers exceptional value.

But what made Du Bois's magazine unique was Du Bois himself. Although he had long ago abandoned belief in a personal deity for a meld of Kant and Hegel, Du Bois's gospel of race and politics was infused with a mystical fervor that bordered on the religious. He catechized readers with the pursuit of Democracy, Justice, and Progress (almost always in uppercase), achievable only by following a straight path. Pulsating prose in service to synoptic visions was not to everyone's taste, to be sure, and that fighting African-American newspaperman known as "Bruce Grit" (John Bruce) spoke for many who found *The Crisis* "too stiff in manner and liv[ing] too much in the upper ether." But as the oratorio of praise welled higher, minor chords of dissatisfaction (except among confirmed Bookerites) went largely unheard. Marie Brown, who married and, according to John Hope, civilized the famous sociologist E. Franklin Frazier, still spoke of the magazine in her widowhood as having been "just like the Bible to me" as an adolescent. Which was how literary critic J. Saunders Redding remembered its reception in his parents' Delaware home, where *The Crisis* "was strictly inviolate until my father himself had unwrapped and read it—often . . . aloud." At Livingstone College in Salisbury, North Carolina, undergraduate student J. E. Aggrey, on the way to becoming one of West Africa's most influential educators, sent a worshipful letter in July 1913 begging Du Bois to take him on as a summer intern at *The Crisis* (though this appears not to have occurred).[20]

Just as men and women of all races were deeply moved by the passion and prophecy of *The Souls of Black Folk*, readers of the magazine were often forced to face prejudices they would have finessed, but for Du Bois's edifying wrath and vision of deliverance. Votes for women was a case in point. For many African-American men of the leadership class, the issue of votes for women was complicated by unhappy memories of their nineteenth-century collaboration, and by alienation from the current suffragist leadership of women like Anna Howard Shaw, president of the National American Woman Suffrage Association (NAWSA). " 'Do not touch the Negro problem. It will offend the South,' " Du Bois quoted her as saying in the October 1911 *Crisis*. Despite what he hoped was a more enlightened position of women such as the imperious Alva Belmont and Fanny Villard, he feared that "the war cry is rapidly becoming 'Votes for White Women

Only.' " As a leading authority on women's rights, Nancy F. Cott, states, "the suffrage movement since the late nineteenth century had caved in to the racism of the surrounding society, sacrificing democratic principle of the dignity of black people if it seemed advantageous to white women's obtaining the vote."[21] The women of NAWSA and the more radical ones who were about to form Heterodoxy and the Congressional Union, the founts of mass feminist demonstrations, also had their own bitter memory of black men who, at the time of the Fifteenth Amendment, had caved in to the sexism of the surrounding society in order to win universal manhood suffrage. Du Bois cared passionately about women's rights and determined to make "Suffering Suffragettes" wince under the plain speaking in *The Crisis*. He forced the issue of African-American female membership in NAWSA. Mrs. Shaw lamely protested that, "if they do not belong to us," it was simply because African-American women had "not organized and have not made application for membership." When, in 1911, suffragist Martha Gruening had unsuccessfully sought to introduce on behalf of the NAACP a resolution calling on the organization to express "sympathy with black men and women who are fighting the same battle," corresponding secretary Mary Ware Donnet wrote Du Bois that the Louisville conference had "not deemed advisable to include the resolution . . . among those to be presented to the convention."[22]

Hammering away at such duplicity of white suffragette officialdom, *The Crisis* set itself to educating the sizable number of readers who, from motives ranging from spite to genuine conservatism, displayed little or no enthusiasm for female suffrage. The extreme fragility of African-American men's earning power made for fragile male self-esteem in face of the reality that, in all but the most fortunate families, women were compelled to work outside the home at an earlier age and in far greater percentages than were white women. The editor dropped the "Talks About Women" section that he had allowed white women to monopolize, replacing it in October 1911 with a "Women's Club" column—(Afrocentered and written by Mrs. Addie Hunton), to be followed by a much-discussed September 1912 "Woman's Suffrage Symposium" featuring Fanny Villard, Adela Hunt Logan, Mary Terrell, and Martha Gruening. Framing the debate in dogmatic racial terms, Mary Terrell's piece, "The Justice of Woman Suffrage," found it "difficult to believe that any individual in the United States with one drop of African blood in his veins can oppose woman suffrage." Answering the covert thoughts of many other black men, Du Bois granted that there was "not the slightest reason for supposing that white American women . . . are going to be any more intelligent, liberal, or humane toward the black, the poor and unfortunate than white men are." Even so, equivocation on the issue was unthinkable:

> Every argument for Negro suffrage is an argument for women's suffrage; every argument for woman suffrage is an argument for Negro suffrage; both are great moments in democracy. There should be on the part of Negroes absolutely no hesitation whenever and wherever responsible human beings are without voice in their government. The man of Negro blood who hesitates to do them justice is false to his race, his ideals and his country.

Du Bois's outraged reaction to some five thousand mostly white women being jeered, jostled, and singed by cigarettes in the nation's capital as they marched down Pennsylvania Avenue, "Hail Columbia!," roared out of the April 1913 issue of the magazine. "Again the glorious traditions of Anglo-Saxon manhood have been upheld!" While police grappled ineffectively with the mob, while cavalry rushed from Fort Myer to restore order in the capital, and ambulances sped dozens of suffragists to emergency wards, the women pressed on, "trudging stoutly" through their gauntlet. Louts leaped upon automobile running boards, snatching "flags from the elderly women" and attempting "to pull the girls from their floats," Du Bois continued dramatically. What black man would want to emulate these "Leaders of Civilization," he sneered, these "magnificently vindicated white men," whose message to the other half of humanity was: "Beat them back, keep them down; flatter them, call them 'visions of loveliness' and tell them that the place for woman is in the home, even if she hasn't got a home"? "Hail Columbia, Happy Land!"[23]

Editorial policy on organized labor and socialism were more complicated. Du Bois would often attack both, infuriated by a gap between ideals and reality. "*The Crisis* believes in organized labor," he insisted in July 1912. In theory, the fate of the great mass of black men and women depended on the continued progress of organized labor. The reality in the United States, however, was first the gradual and then the accelerated expulsion and exclusion of African-Americans from the unions. Du Bois's criticism of organized labor paralleled that of the Socialist leaders Eugene Debs and Daniel De Leon, namely, that in building up an aristocracy of labor in collusion with capital, Gompers and his associates in the AFL were trading short-term gain for the long-term economic impotence of the mass of workers. "Organized Labor" appeared in the July 1912 *Crisis*, more than three months after the spectacular victory of the Lawrence, Massachusetts, textile workers over their employers. "Big Bill" Haywood's Industrial Workers of the World ("Wobblies"), the radical union of unions open to all trades and all races, had channeled the anger of the ethnic work force in Lawrence into organized, triumphal resistance. Yet even though thousands of African-Americans flocked to the Wobblies (especially Philadelphia longshoremen and southern lumber workers), Du Bois said he remained unimpressed. Possibly, he was less pessimistic at the time, but when he summed up the significance of the IWW in the *Autobiography*, he claimed never to have sung the songs of Joe Hill, "and the terrible strike at Lawrence, Massachusetts, did not stir me, because I knew that factory strikers like these would not let a Negro work beside them, or live in the same town."[24]

As far as Du Bois was concerned, then, exceptions to the labor color bar were superficial and transitory. The strategy of white labor was to "beat or starve the Negro out of his job if you can by keeping him out of the union; or, if you must admit him, do the same thing inside the union lines," he charged in "Organized Labor." Hence, the ideal of interracial solidarity became a dangerous illusion in the face of monopolizing white labor. Labor's "mission is divine" when it fights for humanity, but when it became "a clique of Americans, Irish or German monopolists," Du Bois thundered, then blacks would inevitably see the "union white man as their enemy." If white workers went on strike, then black workers should cross the picket lines to claim their jobs, for the white workers deserved "themselves the starvation which they plan for their darker and poorer fellows." Thus spoke the editor for whom the imperatives of race far outweighed those of economics and class—a reading of the social order that he would gradually revise but never reverse. In the late 1930s, he would recognize this zero-sum battle cry as "my provincial racialism"—a visceral reaction to a dilemma rather than a long-term solution to the manipulation of labor by capital.[25]

Likewise, Du Bois applauded the rhetoric of the Socialists and blasted their politics. They had "rung truest on the race question in their theoretical statements," he wrote, and his membership in New York Local Number 1 of the Socialist party attested to their appeal—as well as to Ovington's influence upon him at this time. He was drawn to the Socialist party's presidential candidate, a Hoosier of French Protestant descent, whose command of language and undogmatic espousal of socialism he found temperamentally and intellectually attractive. Without the Wilhelmine mustache and goatee, Debs even bore a slight physical resemblance to an older Du Bois. Du Bois admired Debs's refusal to address segregated audiences in the South during his presidential campaigns, writing in *The Crisis* that "if it lay in our power to make him President of the United States we would do so."[26] Du Bois had voted for Debs in 1904, but the 1912 presidential election was so crucial to the declining fortunes of African-Americans that he was convinced that support of the Socialists was futile. Moreover, he found Socialist party policy on African-Americans all the more culpable because of its hypocrisy. Although officially abhorring racism, as long ago as 1903 Debs had articulated the party's position that it could not "make separate appeals to all races. . . . There is no 'Negro problem' apart from the general labor problem"—a proposition that Du Bois regarded as pure sophistry. The truth was, when it came to African-Americans, the party's racial policy was captive of its right wing, led by the Wisconsin Negrophobe and future congressman Victor Berger. Berger sounded like Alfred Stone when he talked about African-Americans. Their "free contact with the white race has led to further degeneration," he argued. Du Bois saw that the divine mission of socialism, like the labor movement, had bogged down in color conflict. The Socialists "teach, agitate and proselyte, while among ten million Negro Americans they have scarcely a single worker and are afraid to encourage such workers." The magnificent Debs had been wrong, the editor would thunder in the *New Review* after the 1912 elections; "The Negro problem, then, is the great test of the American Socialist."[27]

The Negro problem was also the great test of Negro leadership in 1912. Taft's four years in the White House had been an unmitigated disaster. What Du Bois called the "Taft Doctrine," contained in the president's statement that the African-American "ought to come and is coming more and more under the guardianship of the South," had virtually nullified what remained of Republican party interest in civil rights. For the first time in postwar history the 1912 GOP platform was silent on the Fourteenth and Fifteenth Amendments. With an unprecedented four national parties contending for the presidency, the editor saw again, as in 1908, the strong possibility of an arrangement with the Democrats. With the approach of national elections in the fall, the importance of *The Crisis* in molding opinion was broadcast by ads placed by the Republican, Democratic, and Progressive parties. "They have done this out of no love for this magazine," Du Bois was proud to point out, "but because they needed the publicity which this magazine alone could give and because they knew that our news columns and editorial pages were not for sale." The reelection of Taft was unthinkable, *The Crisis* roared. "In spite of the fact that over 200 Negroes have been publicly murdered without trial during his administration, the utmost those 10,000,000 black men have elicited from his lips is a hesitating statement that he is sorry—and helpless." Declaring that such a man had "no business to be President of the United States," the editor explored the Progressive party candidacy of Teddy Roosevelt for a few exciting weeks during the summer of 1912. Brownsville could never be forgiven, but Roosevelt's Bull Moose agenda was irresistible to many of the people around Du Bois. He shared the excitement of Jane Addams, Henry Moskowitz, Joel Spingarn, Lillian Wald, and Frances Kellor at the vision of an America working an eight-hour day, a six-day week, without child labor, and with accident, old age, and unemployment insurance, and female suffrage. Here was the opening that had not come in 1908 for a "broad platform of votes for Negroes and industrial democracy," the editor hoped. Addams, Moskowitz, and Spingarn went forth from Vesey Street with the plank drafted by Du Bois for adoption at the Bull Moose convention that August:

> The Progressive party recognizes that distinctions of race or class in political life have no place in a democracy. Especially does the party realize that a group of 10,000,000 people who have in a generation changed from a slave to a free labor system, reestablished family life, accumulated $1,000,000,000 [in] property, including 20,000,000 acres of land, and reduced their illiteracy from 80 to 30 per cent, deserve and must have justice, opportunity and a voice in their own government. The party, therefore, demands for the American of Negro descent the repeal of unfair discriminatory laws and the right to vote on the same terms on which other citizens vote.[28]

The Progressive convention in Chicago gathered the hosts of reform—social workers, consumer advocates, muckraking journalists, suffragists, economists, professors, the aroused middle class of small-town America—in a crusade of evangelical fervor, pealing out stanzas of "Onward Christian Soldiers" and "The Battle Hymn of the Republic." But African-Americans were excluded from the chorus. At the end of the day, Roosevelt, who was busily courting southern lily-white delegates, approved the denial of convention seats to most of the African-American delegates, and instructed the platform committee to ignore the Du Bois plank introduced by Spingarn. The candidate "would have none of it," Du Bois learned. "He told Mr. Spingarn frankly that he should be 'careful of that man Du Bois' who was in Roosevelt's opinion a dangerous person." Addams, who gave a nomination speech for Roosevelt, said she had been deeply disturbed by the candidate's obduracy, although in her memoirs she made no mention of the Du Bois plank, confessing instead that the plank fortifying the Panama Canal "was really harder for me to accept than any other one."[29] The "New Nationalism" had no place for New Negroes.

This time, however, there seemed to be an equally attractive alternative in Woodrow Wilson's "New Freedom"—an America where the "curse of bigness" would give way to open competition and Jeffersonian virtue. Wilson, the Virginia son of a Presbyterian parson, possessed a sense of destiny at once cerebral and mystical, like Du Bois's. As professor of political economy and jurisprudence at Bryn Mawr, Wesleyan, and Princeton, Wilson had given oracular speeches and authored essays and books that had brought him a national celebrity dreamt of but seldom achieved by academics. As president of Princeton, he had transformed a second-rate college (almost despite itself and with a stubborn zeal foreshadowing the League of Nations controversy) into a great national university. Elected reform governor of New Jersey in 1910 and now a presidential candidate, Wilson hinted that, under his inspired leadership, the Democratic party and the African-American could find a *modus vivendi*. His advisors anticipated that, with the popular Roosevelt appealing to the South, the Democrats would need every spare vote in order to defeat the Republicans. African-Americans like Monroe Trotter, Bishop Walters, Max Barber, Byron Gunner, Milton Waldron, and a handful of other significant race leaders approached Wilson. As reported in the African-American press and *The Crisis*, Waldron's audience was almost too good to be true. Waldron claimed to have been promised that federal patronage would be distributed irrespective of color, that a Democratic Congress would be moderate in race matters, and that Wilson would veto legislation hostile to African-Americans. Another interview with Wilson in July, at Sea Girt, New Jersey, reported similar commitments from the candidate. Villard was able to assure Du Bois that his own conference with Wilson in Trenton had yielded the encouraging vow to be "President of all the people."[30] Du Bois was made distinctly uneasy when Wilson expressed astonishment at these published reports, and he grew even more distressed after Wilson refused, on press secretary William McAdoo's advice, to approve a clarifying statement Du Bois and Villard sent him in order to publish in *The Crisis*. Still, the editor remained hopeful.

It was left to Walters to seal the bargain. As Du Bois remembered the chain of events, he and Walters spelled out to Wilson the benefits to be had from a sizable shift of African-Americans from the Republican party and an unequivocal *Crisis* endorsement. Walters delivered the message. There was every likelihood that the competition of three major parties—Democrat, Republican, and Progressive—would result in a narrow margin for the victor. Fifty thousand African-American votes deciding the election was a prospect quickly inducing the Democratic candidate to send the AME Zion bishop a written pledge. It was Wilson's "earnest wish to see justice done in every matter, and not mere grudging justice, but justice executed with liberality and cordial good feeling."[31] For the editor, the Walters letter was decisive. Wilson, like Debs, was a kindred spirit—as a visionary academic, even more so. If this Virginian had presided over the sole Ivy League institution refusing to admit African-American students (it had summarily rejected Paul Robeson's brilliant brother, William), Du Bois rationalized that "a man, however, is not wholly responsible for his birth place or his college." The editor doubted that the Democrat "admires Negroes" and suspected that Wilson's ideal "would be a world inhabited by flaxen haired wax dolls with or without brains." Still, Thomas Woodrow Wilson was a gentleman, a scholar, and a man who commanded others to reach for their better selves. His personality "gives us hope," Du Bois psychologized in a compelling August endorsement of the Democratic nominee. "He will not advance the cause of oligarchy in the South, he will not seek further means of 'Jim Crow' insult, he will not dismiss black men wholesale from office, and he will remember that the Negro in the United States has a right to be heard and considered."[32] The measurable part that *The Crisis* played in some one hundred thousand African-Americans voting for a Democratic president from the South remains conjectural, but Du Bois's endorsement clearly represented a monumental gamble. The first southerner since Zachary Taylor and the first Democrat since Grover Cleveland entered the White House.

THE DISTINCTIVE tone of *The Crisis* was one of grievance enobled and pride stiffened; a good number of editorials would have failed to satisfy Barrett Wendell's minimalist composition criteria. The editor was in the business of arousing and edifying his audience, of reshaping a race's image of itself, and of serving a resounding notice to white people of a New Negro in the making. "I am by birth and law a free black American citizen," was his New Year's greeting for 1913. Du Bois commanded his people to follow his battered but unbowed example:

> Boldly and without flinching, I will face the hard fact that in this, my fatherland, I must expect insult and discrimination from persons who call themselves philanthropists and Christian gentlemen. I do not wish to meet this despicable attitude by blows; sometimes I cannot even protest with words; but may God forget me and mine if in time or eternity I ever weakly admit to myself or to the world that wrong is not wrong, that insult is not insult, or that color discrimination is anything but an inhuman and damnable shame.[33]

Booker Washington might deserve much credit for Pink Franklin's reprieve, announced in the February 1911 *Crisis*, and even more for the U.S. Supreme Court's flawed but significant opinion a month earlier, in *Bailey v. Alabama*, that peonage was unconstitutional. Yet somehow his achievements now caused far less wonderment than in years past. Men and women with proud family lineages, those trained in liberal arts colleges, newcomers learning to survive in northern cities, and even many in the South secure enough to have perspective, reveled in the impatience of the NAACP's director of research and publicity. Who would freely choose accommodation, compromise, and cast-down buckets if they could vicariously soar with Du Bois and say boldly to the Man things only whispered previously? On the death in 1913 of Robert Ogden, Du Bois pained white philanthropy by writing unforgivingly that "a self-helping Negro was beyond Mr. Ogden's conception. Mr. Ogden looked upon the Negro as an incomplete man. He was willing to help him and he thought he wanted the Negro to help himself. But he did not."[34]

Taboos fell like tenpins in *The Crisis*, even the deadly delicate one of intermarriage. When Clarence Darrow had called for nullification of laws banning marriage between the races at the second annual conference, Villard fretted for several days about adverse public reaction. The renunciation of social equality was the granite rock upon which the Tuskegee creed stood. In much of the North as in all parts of the Bourbon South the conviction prevailed that intimate contact between the races—eating together, being entertained together, voting together—would lead to miscegenation as inexorably as the pull of gravity increased in proportion to mass. "Social Equality" was the lead *Crisis* editorial in September 1911. A prominent African-American physician had practically sworn before a white audience in Denver that his race fully accepted its subordinate social status. Of course we want full social equality, Du Bois snarled, and all who were too cowardly to say so ought to have the decency to "preserve a dignified silence." Intermarriage was a question "colored people seldom discuss," Du Bois commented further in a February 1913 editorial. With "very few" exceptions, he expected white and black people in the United States to marry within their race. The legal right to amalgamate, however, was as legitimate as any group's preference for bonding with one's own kind. Thus, the rights of exceptional cases must be defended not only as a matter of principle but for the sake of exploited women. The Bourbon South "would rather uproot the foundations of decent society than to call the consorts of their brothers, sons and fathers their legal wives." Writing with a bluntness almost as shocking to many of his African-American readers as it was to his white audiences, the editor railed against social practices reducing "colored women in the eyes of the law to the position of dogs. Low as the white girl falls, she can compel her seducer to marry her. . . . Note these arguments, my brothers and sisters, and watch your State legislatures."[35]

If lynching was not taboo as a topic, the victim was usually portrayed in the mainstream press as someone owing the lynch mob an apology for its sadism. How often had Booker Washington not regretted the harm done by lynching to the morals of the perpetrators? Many racially enlightened northerners were convinced, as Du Bois had found Ray Baker to be, that the deplorable practice was rooted in understandable southern white alarm over the African-American's alleged reversion to barbarism. That had been old Nathaniel Shaler's argument in the book he wrote shortly before his death. "Triumph," Du Bois's ironically titled editorial, might have been called "Let the Eagle Scream," the phrase repeated throughout the text. Its subject was a lynching barbecue of a deranged black man in Coatesville, Pennsylvania, that year. No apologies to lynch mobs were extended. The driving force behind lynching had nothing to do with black barbarism but everything to do with white supremacy. "Again the burden of upholding the best tradition of Anglo-Saxon civilization has fallen on the sturdy shoulders of the American republic," he mockingly opened this September 1911 piece, going on to detail the Sunday procession by car and on foot from Philadelphia and Chester County of thousands of whites pouring out of churches and converging on the butchered victim's smoking pyre.

"Men and women poked the ashes and a shout of glee would signalize the finding of a blackened tooth or mere portions of unrecognizable bones." According to Du Bois, the victim had been a crazed drunkard who committed an unpremeditated homicide. "The point is he was black. Blackness must be punished. Blackness is the crime of crimes. . . . It is therefore necessary, as every white scoundrel in the nation knows, to let slip no opportunity of punishing this crime of crimes. Of course, if possible, the pretext should be great and overwhelming—some awful stunning crime, made even more horrible by the reporters' imagination. Failing this, mere murder, arson, barn burning or impudence may do." America knew her true heroes, he bored in. "Again, let the eagle scream!" The editorial ended with a defiant paragraph anticipating the wildly acclaimed poem "If We Must Die," written almost a decade later by the Jamaican radical Claude McKay: "But let every black American gird up his loins. The great day is coming. We have crawled and pleaded for justice and we have been cheerfully spit upon and murdered and burned. We will not endure it forever. If we must die, in God's name let us perish like men and not like bales of hay."[36]

IF BOOKER WASHINGTON'S duties and travels kept him from reading each issue of Du Bois's monthly, the fastidious Emmett Scott unfailingly digested whatever his employer needed to know, especially the alarming circulation figures. Writing in July 1911 to Fred Moore, the new owner of what had been Fortune's newspaper, Washington pressured him to increase the *Age*'s circulation in order to compete with Du Bois. When the Wizard began finding large ads for the magazine and the NAACP in black barbershops about the country, he became alarmed. The positive response within the leadership community to the "Appeal to England and Europe" had been truly distressing to him. After Villard fobbed off his injured protests about the mailing of the appeal in NAACP envelopes as an inadvertence, Washington decided to unleash his troops. An editorial in the Washington *Bee* (now in the Tuskegee fold) unmasked Du Bois's plot for the "pulling down of Dr. Washington from the high pedestal he occupies." The editor's allies were called "a few human jokes who are but impecunious camp-followers." Innuendo and outright falsehoods abounded. The old story fabricated by the Tuskegee Machine that Du Bois had cravenly stayed away from Atlanta until it was safe to return during the 1906 riot was recirculated. Moore's *Age*, again making use of the lethal if unstable Fortune, began a series of quasi-libelous articles about the editor, with Fortune clucking about routing the opposition once "we get done with Dr. Du Bois." Key lieutenants of the Machine received their marching orders. The Wizard admonished them that the NAACP was nothing more than a cover for Villard and Milholland "to run and control the destinies of the Negro race through Du Bois."[37]

Individuals who wavered from the faith were warned. Mary Terrell, who had signed Villard's call and then had served on the Committee of Forty, particularly incensed the men of Tuskegee, especially Charles Anderson, who found Judge Terrell's inability to control his wife shameful. Washington had once flattered Mary Terrell (who was fluent in German) by arranging a private introduction at the Waldorf Astoria to the kaiser's visiting brother, Prince Henry of Prussia. Cultivation of this articulate, influential club woman was followed by an expenses-paid visit to commencement exercises at Tuskegee, where Terrell had marveled at seeing cows milked on stage, construction materials assembled, houses built and painted, "and so on down the line." But now, as she signed NAACP appeals and even made public speeches in its behalf, the Wizard wanted her silenced. In a letter to her husband he explained, none too subtly, that her conduct "naturally makes it harder for your friends to help you when the time comes."[38] Because his life testified to the power and success that the white world could, when it chose, bestow on one able black man, Washington genuinely doubted that his compounding troubles could be due to the initiative of another able black man. Ego and experience told him that the editor of *The Crisis* must be a deputized agent of white mischief, like himself an accomplished actor who regularly improvised his script but who never forgot the part the audience expected to see him play. That Du Bois, although dependent upon white patronage, was as much director as actor, that he was the dynamo charging a new energy field in American race relations, was inconceivable to him.

Misconception and panic, then, led Washington to depart from the caution he usually exercised when dealing with influential white people and to attack the progressives supporting the NAACP—Ovington, Walling, Villard, Milholland, and others. Charley Anderson was informed of a scheme under way in the District of Columbia to jeopardize the government contracts held by Milholland's International Pneumatic Tube Company. The Bookerite press, especially the *Age* and *Bee*, began a drumroll denunciation of Villard, causing the publisher-editor, who had once dismissed Du Bois's newspaper-manipulation charges, to complain to Moton about "villainous" attacks.[39] Washington and Anderson's plans for embarrassing the guests at the January 1911 banquet sponsored by the Cosmopolitan Society of America were cause for thigh-slapping glee. Despite its imposing name, the Cosmopolitan Club consisted of only a small group of reformers first gathered together in 1906 by Ovington in her Brooklyn family home to promote interracial social contacts between the well-bred civic-minded. The Wizard had hoped for a repeat of the lurid press accounts of the club's

1908 banquet. On his orders, similar press treatment was manufactured for the 1911 banquet at the Cafe Boulevard, although Anderson reported with disappointment that this time the *Times*, *Sun*, and *Herald* inexplicably failed to mention the affair. But the *World* served up "proper sensational headlines" and the front-page account in the New York *Press*, "Three Races Mix at Banquet for Man's Brotherhood," fully satisfied the master of The Oaks, whose masterminding of the Cosmopolitan Club scandals was exposed many years later by his biographer Louis Harlan's detective work. New York straphangers read in the January 26 edition of the *Press* that "white women, evidently of the cultured and wealthier classes, fashionably attired in low-cut gowns, leaned over the tables to chat confidently with negro men of the true African type."[40] Whatever the *Press* meant by true African types, Du Bois, in tuxedo and one of the evening's speakers, was among the banquet's maligned.

Warming for the kill, a few days later the Wizard sent orders to the *Age*—"Burn Walling up." During late February and early March, the city newspapers covered the sensational breach-of-promise suit brought against Walling by Miss Anna Bertha Grunspan, a Parisian seamstress of Russian-Jewish heritage. Offering the letters exchanged between them in evidence, the dark-haired, well-tailored Miss Grunspan testified that Walling had courted her in Paris and taken her to Russia with the promise to bring her brother back with them; then, upon reaching Paris, Grunspan claimed that the wealthy Socialist had proposed marriage in the presence of her family, giving her a diamond ring to seal the pledge. The plaintiff became hysterical in the courtroom and her mother attempted to assault Walling and his wife when the defendant's lawyer called for testimony from a witness who claimed to have information about Grunspan's unsavory conduct. The newspapers reported the imbroglio in graphic detail. Professing shock that numerous African-American hostesses had innocently welcomed the NAACP official to their homes, the March 23 edition of the *Age* expressed the hope that "no colored man or woman will in the future disgrace our race by inviting Mr. Walling in their home or ask him to speak at any public meeting."[41]

But Booker T. Washington's own public disgrace began four nights earlier in the San Juan Hill district of Manhattan. The Great Accommodator had only just arrived in the city, fresh from a speaking engagement in Michigan, in order to speak that Sunday at two churches, and had checked into the upscale Hotel Manhattan. That night, he walked alone to 11½ West Sixty-third Street and rang the doorbell of an apartment there.

Receiving no answer, he walked back and forth on the sidewalk in front of the building for almost an hour before reentering, apparently to try to locate on the dimly lit register the name of the person he was seeking. It was an altogether strange outing for Tuskegee's principal. San Juan Hill was still the preserve of working-class Irish, although African-Americans, pushing above Fifty-third Street from the notorious Tenderloin district, had begun to cluster in its tenements since the 1890s. The address to which Washington had come was, as proper folk of that era were wont to say, decidedly demimondaine. It lay, according to his biographer, just outside a notorious red-light district but which Du Bois, who was living nearby, described as a "neighborhood of high class prostitutes." A vaudeville theater stood directly across the street.

Exactly what happened next remained unclear in the tangle of conflicting testimony and rumor spanning an eight-month period from the March arraignment of Henry Albert Ulrich to his trial and acquittal in November 1911 for assault. Two facts were clear: that Washington needed sixteen stitches to his scalp on the night of March 19 to close a terrible gash; and, second, that Ulrich, a burly German-American carpenter, physically attacked the great race leader because he was convinced that an illicit arrangement had been proposed to a woman he knew intimately. (Seemingly incredible testimony was given by Mrs. Ulrich that, when she sashayed with her leashed Pomeranian past the pacing educator, he had greeted her with " 'Hello, sweetheart,' " and looked her "right in the face."[42]) A sharp tussle had occurred in the hallway of the apartment building, spilling out on to the sidewalk with Ulrich allegedly slashing Washington repeatedly with a bystander's cane. Unable to defend himself against the much larger, younger man, the completely rattled educator finally stumbled into the arms of a patrolman. At the station house, Ulrich's account at first resulted in charges of attempted burglary against the bloodied, tattered African-American. The situation was transformed in a flash, however, when Washington, regaining control of himself, finally located patent proof of his identity in his wallet. Ulrich was charged with felonious assault and clapped in a cell pending payment of $1,500 bail.[43]

In the days immediately afterward, a procession of worthies (the likes of which had not assembled since the last Ogden Special) filed through the lobby of the Hotel Manhattan to condole and console Booker Washington. Seth Low, chairman of the Tuskegee Institute board of trustees, headed the parade of distinguished sympathizers, which included Carnegie, Schiff, Schieffelin, and Paul M. Warburg. Until news of the grizzly Triangle

Shirtwaist Company fire, which claimed the lives of 146 women sweatshop workers, pushed the case onto the back pages, newspapers enjoyed a field day with the Wizard's memorable night. President Taft publicly proclaimed his confidence in Washington's character; Carnegie stated that his trust remained rock solid; Peabody refused to entertain a moment's doubt as to the veracity of his great friend; Paul D. Cravath, New York's leading attorney, son of Fisk's first president, Erastus Cravath, and chairman of the Fisk University trustees, placed his formidable services at Washington's disposal; ex-President Roosevelt privately sympathized but said nothing about confidence; and Villard accepted his friend Low's account of the fracas and ran it in the *Post* without comment.[44]

Washington's case against his assailant was strengthened after Anderson and Wilford Smith, the Wizard's African-American attorney, exposed Ulrich as a bigamist whose New Jersey wife had sued him for desertion and nonsupport, and revealed that the alleged Mrs. Ulrich was one Laura Page Alvarez, mother of a young daughter and still married to Mr. Alvarez. But when the white auditor of Tuskegee's books categorically denied, as the Wizard had initially maintained, that he had ever expected to meet his employer at 11½ West Sixty-third Street (the address was unknown to him), and when Scott's letter to the Hotel Manhattan directing Washington to the San Juan Hill address was said to have been destroyed, many folk, black and white, were troubled and puzzled. Despite their recent disputes, Villard was deeply concerned for Washington's reputation, writing to Uncle Francis that the very foundation of the Tuskegee edifice was imperilled. "If he should not be able to substantiate his story in court it would be a terrible thing," Villard trembled, "and I have been sick at heart over it because there are all sorts of stories . . . that he really went to the place to meet a white woman, etc."[45]

The editor of *The Crisis* had heard the same stories, and he was positive they were true. Du Bois's exact New York address during this period is unknown, but it must have been close by Marshall's Hotel (where he frequently took meals), the famous African-American establishment memorably recaptured by James Weldon Johnson in *Black Manhattan*. Marshall's, two large, overfurnished brownstones at 127–129 West Fifty-third Street, was the caravansary of bohemia, in which aspiring and thriving actors and musicians, striving and established writers and intellectuals, as well as handsome men and women of dubious distinction and designs, commingled in interracial ease, many of them well past dawn. Du Bois gleaned most of the facts about the sensational Washington affair shortly after the story broke, and very likely in Marshall's dining room. Washington had gone on at least one previous occasion to the apartment building where he and Ulrich tangled, guided there to sample one of the ladies of leisure by his bosom friend and chief New York agent, Charles Anderson. The Wizard's costly mistake, Du Bois thought, had been to visit the address alone and probably not entirely sober. "Most great men have had an occasional moral lapse," he confided to a fellow African-American scholar more than thirty-five years later. "The only surprising thing is that [Booker T. Washington] had only one to come to the surface."[46] By then, Du Bois's own private history of extramarital pursuits may have disposed him to sympathize with his long-dead adversary.

Most of the Talented Tenth greeted news of the night of March 19 with snickers and hoots among themselves. But, although the Wizard's embarrassment was too delicious not to savor, even his most inveterate enemies generally had better political and race-relations instincts than to exploit his misfortune publicly. The humiliation of Washington could have meant the crumbling of a valuable asset to his people—Tuskegee Institute. And besides, the sooner the odor of illicit interracial sex dissipated, the better for everybody. Du Bois confined *The Crisis* to culling the white and black press for coverage of the assault. Trotter's *Guardian* aimed at restraint, too, although somewhat less convincingly, having told readers it had "no desire to take any advantage of his present troubles. We want to fight men when standing up." The white South also generally preferred to strike a pose similar to Washington's African-American enemies, taking its cue from the Richmond *Times-Dispatch*. In the past, the Wizard's supposed infractions of race-relations etiquette had occurred in the course of professional business involving the family of the president of the United States and that of the head of a department-store chain. Considered to be morally innocent, he had been fair game for noisy Jim Crow abuse. This time, however, the Great Accommodator's moral innocence was uncertain to say the least. If they now failed to give him the benefit of the doubt, then the South's white leaders would be destroying their most useful creation. As another Virginia newspaper, the Lynchburg *News*, editorialized, "Anything likely to seriously impair Booker Washington's usefulness as a conservative influence among negroes . . . would furnish cause for genuine and profound regret."[47]

Yet if they were willing to spare the man and to finesse the issue of character, Du Bois and his allies were determined to gain what advantage they could for the NAACP. The third annual conference was to be held in Boston that May. There was general nervousness about the momentum of the new organization. Trotter and his circle were still smarting from real and imaginary slights in connection with the centennial observance of the birth of Charles Sumner in Boston that past January. In his usual take-charge way, Du Bois had simply reserved Faneuil Hall for the Sumner celebration without bothering to consult Trotter, who, as president of the New England Suffrage League, had already laid elaborate plans. Silken stroking of Trotter by Storey, Pillsbury, Francis Garrison, and other Brahmins had saved the Sumner centennial from being the occasion of bitter internecine competition; Du Bois and others agreed in the end to come to Boston as guests of the New England Suffrage League.[48] There was more concern about money than Trotter in planning the third annual conference, however—which really meant that Storey, Garrison, Pillsbury, and Bumstead of the organizing committee were deeply apprehensive about Washington's attitude. After Villard placed his sympathy telephone call on March 19 to the recovering leader, fund-raising for the annual conference turned out to be remarkably successful. Villard had agreed with the Tuskegeean that misunderstandings rather than objectives divided them, that the time for a truce had arrived.[49]

Du Bois expected Washington to recover much of his prestige. He knew that the Tuskegee Machine was badly damaged but far from broken. But he interpreted the Tuskegeean's request for a truce as a sign of desperation. With some reluctance, then, Du Bois went along with Villard's proposal to invite Washington to issue a public endorsement of the NAACP to be read at the conference. Even Trotter held his fire for the moment. Meanwhile, shaken officers of the Bookerite realm urged their sovereign to take Villard up on his offer. Moton argued for its advantages; Anderson warned that it would be "unwise" not to accept; and William Lewis, on his way to the first subcabinet post ever held by a black American, cabled the working text to Tuskegee. On March 30, 1911, Washington issued a statement of virtual concession in the form of a telegram to Villard. "The time has come," it stated, "when all interested in the welfare of the Negro people should lay aside personal differences and personal bickerings, and keep in mind only rendering the service which will best protect and promote the race in all its larger interests. . . . I am sure that all of my friends everywhere will happily cooperate with you in the directions that I have mentioned." In return, Washington expected the NAACP conference to vote to send two delegates to the annual meeting of the National Negro Business League and to issue an encouraging statement about his current troubles. In the driver's seat now, the delegates at the Boston meeting finally voted a resolution devoid of warmth and supportive of the injured leader only in the most superficial sense: "Resolved, that we put on record our profound regret at the recent assault on Dr. Booker T. Washington in New York City, in which the Association finds renewed evidence of race discrimination and increased necessity for the awakening of the public conscience."[50] Du Bois, Walling, Ovington, Morgan—all thought that was about as generous a statement as the Wizard deserved.

But even the appearance of a truce was short-lived. President Storey, treasurer Villard, and executive committee members like Butler Wilson hoped for lowering of voices, whether or not actual cooperation between the association and the Machine ever developed. This was no time for African-Americans to be divided; "they should present a solid front to the enemy," Villard urged in a friendly letter to Moton. But it was precisely because Du Bois had concluded that they had no such common purpose—or should not—that his editorial in the June *Crisis* was intended to have the impact of a mortar projectile. Harmonious cooperation with the Tuskegee Machine was the last thing Du Bois could have wanted. Was it not even philosophically impossible? he asked himself. Far more than personalities and specific events were at play.[51] Insisting that the magazine would state "openly the opinion of its editor," then, Du Bois's June editorial, "Starvation and Prejudice," gave the association's president and treasurer, among others, heartburn. Not content simply to reject Washington's defense of his remarks in England, Du Bois smashed the Great Accommodator to the core in his conclusion:

> Awful as race prejudice, lawlessness and ignorance are, we can fight them if we frankly face them and dare name them and tell the truth; but if we continually dodge and cloud the issue, and say the half truth because the whole stings and shames; if we do this, we invite catastrophe. Let us then in all charity but unflinching firmness set our faces against all statesmanship that looks in such directions.[52]

If he left his adversary's character unassailed, Du Bois clearly intended to wound him as a leader, to do all that he could to prevent both the man and the Machine from ever regaining their former power. Much, much later, the editor confided to Charles H. Thompson of Howard University's School of Education (the same acquaintance in whom he had confided about the Ulrich scandal) that he attributed Washington's death "to some extent to this affair."[53] The scandal and the editorial marked a watershed in the civil rights advocacy of African-Americans.

16.
CONNECTIONS AT HOME AND ABROAD

NINA YOLANDE Du Bois's role as an effaced and dutiful wife was not entirely of her own choosing. She possessed average intelligence rather poorly served by mediocre schooling. She was a caring, though perhaps not warm, woman, and certainly a loyal and resourceful one. She was unsure of herself both among strangers and in the cosmopolitan world in which her husband increasingly spent his time. Still waters run deep, yet by no stretch of feminist empathy could it be claimed truthfully that Nina's depths yielded rich treasure. Even so, there was probably a period after the death of Burghardt when her talents and fragile self-confidence could still have been nurtured by her husband: a time when, instead of becoming intimidated by scholarship and causes, she might have learned to be comfortable with them. Nina knew that Will cared for her and their daughter, and was as good as most men of his generation about observing the special occasions of domestic life. She knew also that Will saw marriage among prominent African-Americans as an institution to be maintained, no matter what the emotional cost, in order to negate white stereotypes about the black family.

Perhaps she could have put her finger on some moment when the cord of intimacy had finally snapped and she and her famous husband had learned to conceal from each other their feelings of estrangement during those increasingly rare times when they were together. But it is more likely that they grew apart more gradually than Will's representation of it (many years later, after the invisible Nina was dead) would have us believe. Her letters to him give the impression that Nina tried over and again to reach out to him, to engage Du Bois somehow and make him recognize her as a person in her own right, rather than as an abstraction and a significant, though uninteresting, extension of himself. She made a bad job of it, usually. Although there were poignant exceptions, the general run of her letters was one of narcotic banality, relieved only by crises of health—her own and daughter Yolande's. The "Dear Will" salutations, followed by itemized accounts of her week, were like heavy dough falling to a kitchen floor, thuds breaking the powers of concentration in Vesey Street. "Dear Will, I went to town yesterday and bought thirty-four dollars worth of sheets, pillow slips, towels and two bedspreads." "Dear Will, I have had to spend quite a bit for Yolande's medicines and for things to eat for her, and I'm afraid I'll run short before the first of the month." "Dear Will," Miss Pingree and Mr. Dill were in good health, and "we had a beautiful day yesterday for Easter." "Dear Will," the family doctor thinks Yolande has a sprained foot that "she kept on using . . . until the joints have become inflamed." Nina also worried about Will's health, and thought that he went "too long without eating very much and then eat[ing] too much."[1]

Sometimes she made a valiant effort to cross over into her spouse's orbit of concerns; she wrote that "we read and enjoyed" the fiery "Souls of White Folk" appearing in the *Independent* on August 18, 1910. A few weeks later, she called his attention to a laudatory newspaper editorial about him—"I suppose you've seen it." Nina expressed mild distress that there wasn't anyone "so far directing the work here that should be done for the opening of school," an inconceivable state of affairs if Will had been on campus. She was sure that the Howard University debating team had "stolen" its victory over Atlanta. When Stephen Wise, the reform rabbi, leading American Zionist, and founding member of the Committee of Forty, visited the campus with his wife and spoke to the student body, Nina did her best to capture the proud occasion. Rabbi Wise had discussed the stirrings in race relations of which Will was an indispensable part. He spoke of their personal friendship and of "your worth to the negro," she wrote. "But here is the disappointing part of the visit," she complained, reverting to the usual concerns: somehow she and Miss Pingree had missed the arrival of the Wises' cab, although they had waited at the indicated spot for an hour. Worse still, Yolande "was not well as usual so was lying down she had a headache so both Dr. and Mrs. Wise peeped in the bedroom at Yolande."[2]

Busy hurling his editorial thunderbolts and carrying the new gospel of civil rights far and wide beyond New York, Will let his correspondence with

Nina lag. "I presume you will write to us some time," she admonished mildly after weeks of silence. He failed to do better, however. Since leaving them behind in August 1910, he found himself tired, distracted, on the road, or constantly engaged. Throughout late summer and into fall of 1911, Du Bois had worked what seemed a miracle in bringing *The Crisis* to life. He did manage to steal a few days from the magazine to see in the New Year with Nina and Yolande in Atlanta; but he was gone almost before his daughter realized he had been there. "Poor Yolande awoke about midnight after you left and cried because she didn't see you before you left," Nina wrote. The family physician diagnosed a "lack of lime in her system" when Yolande again fell ill immediately after Will's departure. In fact, the illness was another in a pattern of maladies for which medical explanations were usually inadequate. Her child's confused mind may have told her that she somehow caused her father's sudden leavings. When he dashed to New York at Walling's invitation to join the NAACP, Nina wrote Will that Yolande had written him a letter, "and then for some reason she decided she wouldn't send it."[3] In the years ahead, his daughter would repeatedly try to capture his love and attention by becoming sick or refusing to do what was expected of her.

The family's extended separation, then, was as much emotional as it was geographical. Nina surrendered the keys to the South Hall apartment in late May 1911 and left with Yolande, eventually to join Will in New York; yet more and more he would manage to spend large blocks of time away from them. The pace the editor had set himself left little time for family. His first report to the NAACP directors on the activities of the Department of Publicity and Research listed ninety-nine speeches delivered to fifty-three mainly white and forty-six mainly black audiences—a total of 35,000 people—during the period ending December 1911. Then, as he and Mary Maclean rushed the December 1911 *Crisis* to press, he had somehow found time to prepare "The Rural South," a major paper on peonage, disfranchisement, and the spreading socioeconomic decay of the South for the annual meeting of the American Economic Association.[4] There was no immediate reunion in New York. Household goods had been shipped instead from Atlanta to New Haven, Connecticut, where George W. Crawford, a young Niagarite and Yale man from the South then embarking on an outstanding career in law and real estate, apparently arranged for Nina and Yolande to stay until permanent living accommodations could be found. Will sailed for England in early June 1911 to address the Lyceum Club, the British Sociological Society, and to participate in what he believed was an epochal interracial congress in London. The house-hunting during the late summer fell to Nina.

"I'm glad you had a pleasant voyage," she wrote him in London, as she canvassed the few affordable neighborhoods in New Haven and New York City open to respectable African-American families. There was so little available and most of it was undesirable. Even if they could raise the five-hundred-dollar down payment, she didn't at all care for "those new houses Mr. Crawford spoke to us about." They had almost no front yards and the streets were too narrow.[5] A rash of municipal ordinances and restrictive covenants from Atlanta and Louisville, Kentucky, to Baltimore and Providence, Rhode Island, was suddenly making the housing situation for families like the Du Boises much worse. The new codes and policies were drafted in response to the migration from farm to town to city of poor and generally unskilled African-Americans, unassimilated newcomers who, like many of their "strange" eastern and southern European counterparts, were regarded with aversion (often bordering on hysteria) by much of Protestant white America. In *The Sport of the Gods*, one of the first works of fiction dealing with urban life, Du Bois's Ohio intimate, the poet Dunbar, had authentically described this raucous, black migrating mass turning older, livable black communities into bursting slums. Talented Tenth families who had lived and prospered for a generation now pushed against the envelope of their ghettoes, trying to buy into healthier, less-crowded living spaces occupied exclusively by white Americans. The right to buy decent housing would be at the center of one of the NAACP's first major court battles—the Louisville case of *Buchanan v. Warley*—one of its first paper victories before the U.S. Supreme Court in 1917. But in the real world of real estate hypocrisy, not even the editor of *The Crisis* could do better than the dogged Nina. The general manager of a model suburban community, the Russell Sage Foundation Homes Company (the foundation itself had been established to promote the welfare of African-Americans, Native Americans, and other needy groups), would regret to inform Du Bois in November 1912 that, after much deliberation, it had been decided that "it would be a doubtful plan for you to settle in a community . . . of white people."[6] The Du Boises finally rented a small, neat house in the Bronx at 3059 Villa Avenue.

Nina's worries tended to range from household needs to her daughter's health, from cooking to covenants. Will took notice, expressed concern, offered advice, and forwarded money. But his own preoccupations in the summer of 1911 were far more lofty. They lifted him far above the plane of the quotidian and the narrow. So compelling was the mission drawing him to the United Kingdom, he thought, that members of the Niagara Movement were sent a last-minute circular canceling his plans for another annual meeting. Du Bois advised them to join the NAACP, which most did, thereby definitively disbanding the first institutional insurrection against Booker Washington.[7] For almost two years, the British wing of the Ethical Culture movement, principally guided by the boundlessly dedicated Gustave Spiller, had planned for an ambitious ecumenical conclave, an unprecedented Universal Races Congress embracing all the peoples of the planet. Kiplingesque sentiments about parliaments of man in the federation of the world clearly inspired the European and Eurocentric planners—an intellectual aristocracy genuinely desirous of making the globe safe for imperialism with a human face.

Du Bois had been urged to attend by Milholland, one of the initiators of the Universal Races Congress (offering to pay his way), and to leave early in order to undo the harm caused by the Wizard during his trip to Great Britain the year before. In addition to speaking before the Anti-Slavery and Aborigines Protection Society, the editor was to enlighten the ladies of the highly influential Lyceum Club concerning the true state of American race relations. But the long arm of Tuskegee stirred up such commotion that Du Bois had tried to withdraw, until the steadfastness of club president Dr. Ettie Sayer made him, as he wrote, "feel like a deserter from the forefront of battle." Milholland had also rattled the members of the Anti-Slavery Society by telling its distinguished secretary, Travers Buxton, that the object of Du Bois's visit "was definitely to oppose Mr. Washington's view." Both organizations were reassured. The upshot was that the editor delivered a gracious Monday-evening dinner speech on June 26, attended, Du Bois was pleased to recall forty years afterward, by the ranee of Sarawak, "a bishop and two countesses, several knights and ladies with Maurice Hewlett and Sir Harry Johnston."[8] Truly alarmed now, Booker Washington ordered Robert Moton to attend the Races Congress and to do all he could to counter Du Bois. But after spending time with Du Bois and Milholland and learning the gist of Du Bois's "purely impersonal—and very dignified" address, Moton reported back to his incredulous protector that there was no cause for alarm.[9] Moton had even seconded the editor's statements when he followed him immediately to the podium of the congress.

For Du Bois, however, the internationalizing of varsity combat with the Tuskegee Machine was a secondary matter. For the remainder of his life, he was incapable of discussing the Universal Races Congress without recourse to superlatives, always insisting that "it would have marked an epoch in the racial history of the world if it had not been for the World War." Photographically preserved for *Crisis* subscribers, Du Bois stands erect, well tailored in the center of a good gathering of the congress's savants and divines in front of the arched gateway to the University of London, his incised goatee and upturned mustaches accentuating the fine nose and perfect oval head. A thousand delegates representing "fifty races" had assembled that Wednesday morning, July 26, in Fishmongers' Hall for the Right Honorable Lord Weardale's presidential welcome. Later many of them listened as Du Bois recast Kipling's "Recessional" to fit this "great and inspiring occasion." Elected cosecretary of the American delegation with Ethical Culture founder Felix Adler, he greeted the first working session in the great hall of the University of London with "A Hymn to the Peoples," seven iambic stanzas considerably more distinguished for their elevated sentiments than for the purity of verse.

Truce of God! And primal meeting of the Sons of Man,
Foreshadowing the union of the World!
From all the ends of the earth we come!
. . . .
We be blood-guilty! Lo, our hands be red!
Not one may blame the other in this sin!
But here—here in the white Silence of the Dawn,
Before the Womb of Time,
With bowed hearts all flame and shame,
We face the birth-pangs of a world:
. . . .
Save us, World-Spirit, from our lesser selves!
Grant us that war and hatred cease,
Reveal our souls in every race and hue!
Help us, O Human God, in this Thy Truce
To make Humanity divine![10]

He came before the congress twice again, once to deliver a scheduled address in which he made a figurative bow to Tuskegee's philosophy of uplift through enterprise while underscoring that "intellectual emancipation should proceed hand in hand with economic independence"; and again to substitute at one of the main sessions for the renowned gentleman ethnographer Sir Harry Johnston, stricken with tropical fever from his sub-

Saharan sojournings. Du Bois claimed that his speech "gained wide reading." His conviction seems curiously naive that "a few world congresses like this," assembling every four years, would have changed history, but Du Bois held to the religion of ideas no matter how passionately he came to embrace a program of action. Despite the faith-shaking memory of Sam Hose's knuckles and the Atlanta litany, he still wanted the Hegelian Real to fulfill the Hegelian Rational. Felix von Luschan, a towering name in biology, came from Berlin to postulate the "monogenetic origin of humanity"—the emergence of all the races, white, yellow, red, and black, from the same stock. Professor N. R. D'Alfonso of Italy expatiated on the universality of "psychological possibilities"; history and culture, not innate differences, said he, accounted for the great variety of human behaviors. From Brazil came Dr. Jean-Baptiste De Lacerda, who praised, with qualification, the large service rendered historically by the mixed races of his country. From South Africa came Booker T. Washington's alter ego, the Bantu educator J. Tengo Jabavu, who argued persuasively for the indigenous African languages and traditions of his land. Felix Adler was convinced that the greater the interaction of dissimilar peoples the greater the understanding of the "weak points in each."[11] Essentially the same point was made to the delegates by West Africa's Dr. Mojola Agbebi.

"When fifty races look each other in the eye, face to face, there arises a new conception of humanity and its problems," the editor rhapsodized in *The Crisis*. His old faith in the transforming potency of the social sciences came flooding back. Religious dogmas, all the delegates seemed to agree implicitly, had no legitimacy or place in matters of serious social reform. The parasitic by-product of imperial competition—finance capital—was devastatingly exposed and denounced by the English economist John A. Hobson. In a similar vein, the elegant Muhammad Bey Sourbour underscored the reality of imperial exploitation by advocating for Egyptians some part "in the making and execution of laws." The status of women in the world was systematically reviewed, and the imperative moral and social justification for their liberation was applauded. If Du Bois regretted that the global implications of the "labor question" and the time frame for the independence of India and Egypt had not been addressed, he felt exhilarated, nevertheless, that so many of the planet's great problems had been earmarked for systematic investigation.[12]

But there was another reason for his euphoria. The Universal Races Congress appealed to Du Bois's elitism and flattered his self-conceit. If the Talented Tenth could deliver Afro-America from ignorance and persecution, then surely this multiracial parliament of the world's illustrious had the potential to do the same for mankind. "The personnel of the Congress was marvelous." "The two Egyptian Beys were evidently negroid, the Portuguese was without a doubt a mulatto, and the Persian was dark enough to have trouble in the South." A Japanese parliamentarian, another from the Cape Colony (its only black member), a Sioux from the United States, the Liberian secretary of state, Mrs. Annie Besant of the mystical Theosophical Society, who gave a fiery critique of the British Empire, and the novelist and Zionist Israel Zangwill, who was a highly interested spectator, especially caught Du Bois's attention. The anarchist Russian prince, Pyotr Kropotkin, attended most of the sessions. (When Kropotkin was told that Du Bois was a radical and Washington a conservative, he exclaimed that he couldn't imagine what a black person had to conserve.)[13] Observing her friend's elation during these days in London, Mary Ovington was impressed by how at ease and buoyant Du Bois was as he strolled in the countess of Warwick's topiary gardens in evening dress, the beautiful young daughter of General Legitime, Haiti's president, on his arm, a wisp from his Benson and Hedges cigarette curling above them. Ovington thought the sylphlike Mademoiselle Legitime was stunning: "As she walked across the perfect English lawn . . . she might have been a young queen honoring England with her visit."

On another gossamer night—the last night of the congress—Ovington turned from Milholland to see her friend descending the ballroom steps with another woman of remarkable beauty and culture. Totally absorbed in each other, the two glided beneath the brilliant chandeliers onto the polished floor and into the glittering gathering. "They were talking earnestly, of course of the race problem," and Ovington "thought her the loveliest person there, except perhaps the darker daughter of the Haitian president." Neither she nor Du Bois ever identified the woman of the occasion. His significance to this cosmopolitan femme fatale or to the French-educated Mademoiselle Legitime, for that matter, is also unknown, but their company made an impression upon Du Bois that was agreeably lasting. Ovington was absolutely positive that the lady of the ballroom was the model for the protagonist of *The Dark Princess*, Du Bois's second novel, written seventeen years afterward.[14] This Races Congress and its social setting were heady brew for a lonely, sensitive genius, few of whose days ever passed without the stultifying intrusion of racism into his private desires and professional achievements. In the summer of 1911, Du Bois addressed respectful and illustrious Europeans, embraced the hope that understanding between different peoples could be advanced by a rainbow convention of intellectuals, and took a pleasant furlough from skirmishes along the color line.

Little wonder, then, that he was almost as beguiled by the swan song of the European world order as were the German professors and knighted Englishmen present at the congress. Pax Britannica and free trade were transforming the globe, linking the farthest outposts with the centers of civilization and commerce. "World peace, world organization, conference and conciliation, the gradual breaking down of trade barriers, the spread of civilization to backward peoples, the emancipation of suppressed groups like the American Negro—seem[ed?] to me the natural, the inevitable path of world progress." But he would come down to hard earth soon enough. Du Bois's powers of perception invariably tamed his European susceptibilities. Three summers in the future, he would write one of the twentieth century's most powerful analyses of Europe's planetary spread into chaos. Then, he would see in retrospect that the *Panther* incident, occurring some three weeks before the Races Congress convened, had been "the forewarning of coming doom." On the pretext of protecting German interests from the encroaching French in Morocco, a German gunboat had sailed into the port of Agadir, creating what diplomats called the Second Moroccan Crisis. But as Du Bois sailed for New York, he described his mood as thoroughly sanguine. "I fancied at the time that I knew my Europe pretty well," he boasted, "but familiarity with the dangers of the European scene had bred contempt of disaster."[15] Plans for a second Races Congress in Paris were to be aborted by an assassin's bullet in the Bosnian capital of Sarajevo.

Du Bois came home to the heating up of quadrennial presidential politics and would soon ask his readers to gamble on Woodrow Wilson. He came home also to what was for him a major literary event, the publication that October of his first novel, *The Quest of the Silver Fleece*. By the winter of 1911, only a few months away from his forty-third birthday, Du Bois was so well known and admired among growing numbers of African-Americans that clubs bearing his name had sprung up. The Du Bois Club in Detroit was already nine years old, and another had been started more recently at Cornell University. Most members of the Du Bois clubs, like much of the general public, would have been surprised to learn that the austere editor who wrote empirical studies of the race, championed Latin and philosophy in the college curriculum, and disdained the evangelism of the black church was really "a poet and a dreamer." Yet that description, from a letter by a reader of manuscripts to Du Bois's publisher, was accurate and revealing. The soaring expectations for the Races Congress and the themes in *The Quest of the Silver Fleece* had their source in that part of Du Bois's fecund intelligence governed by imagination, intuition, and sentiment. The landscape of black America was and would continue to be littered with the emotional wreckage of men and women whose escapist dreams had enveloped their shattered intellects and, on the other hand, of those whose remorseless intellects had poisoned their dreams. With Du Bois, however, the tension between the creative and the logical was generally (but with notable exceptions) constructive, reciprocally enhancing. Fanny Hale Gardiner, McClurg's reader of Du Bois's manuscript, finally decided, after seeing two versions, that, despite its defects in "style and language" and "much less interesting" second half, *The Quest of the Silver Fleece* deserved to be published because it was a remarkable social novel by a "poet" and "dreamer," cogently exposing the "unscrupulousness and heartlessness" of those who lived by calculation.[16]

Du Bois himself called *The Quest* "an economic study of some merit." His later emphasis upon its economic underpinnings sought to excuse many of the first-novel flaws that Gardiner had sympathetically enumerated for McClurg editor Francis Fisher Browne. Yet it would have been entirely out of character for Du Bois not to have had large hopes for *The Quest*, not to have wanted it to be seen as more than an economic treatise embellished by dialogue. In one form or another—when not doing research, giving speeches, organizing the Niagara Movement, or publishing two magazines—he had worked on the novel over a period spanning more than five years. With a cocksureness inspired by the success of *The Souls of Black Folk*, he appears to have promised to whip off a novel for Francis Browne in time for the 1904 fall list. An early April letter from Browne complained that Du Bois's failure to do so "will leave us in pretty bad shape." By winter 1905, a first draft of "Scorn" had been sent to the McClurg editors, who frankly confessed to Du Bois that they failed "to get the central thought of the story; the plot does not seem to advance and fulfill itself in a logical sequence."[17] Once the manuscript for *John Brown* was accepted by the Jacobs publishing company, however, Du Bois reshaped and completed his novel.

By April 1910, Du Bois's manuscript was on Gardiner's desk, where it was given a qualified approval, but with a caveat that David Graham Phillips, the muckraking journalist and current bestselling novelist, had published *Golden Fleece* in 1903. Du Bois's final, slightly amended title was faithful to the economic *idée maîtresse* of the work, an idea that had become stronger as he reworked the numerous plots in his large narrative. As his literary executor, Herbert Aptheker, has noted, novels exploring market forces were the rage of the day: Frank Norris's wheat novels (*The Octopus*, 1901, and *The Pit*, 1903); James Allen's on hemp (*The Reign of Law, A Tale of the Kentucky Hemp Fields*, 1900); and Upton Sinclair's meat-packing exposé (*The Jungle*, 1906).[18] And there was another type of commodity novel that was equally popular—white supremacist fiction, of which *The Leopard's Spots: A Romance of the White Man's Burden* (1902) and *The Clansman* (1905), by Thomas Dixon, Jr., were outstanding contemporary examples. The few reviews of *The Quest* were kind, but sales were extremely modest. The author's Boston friend, William Braithwaite, praised it in *The Crisis*, astutely comparing it with *The Pit*. The *Nation* reviewer gasped over the machinations, miscegenation, and misery, asking "can these things be true?" The unsigned review in the *Independent* was more impressed by the author than by the novel, wondering "What will not Professor Du Bois write next?" Perhaps the fact was sufficiently well known that reviewers of *The Quest* felt no need to mention that Du Bois had joined the ranks of possibly the country's most exclusive twentieth-century profession—the African-American novelist. After the publication in 1902 of Dunbar's *The Sport of the Gods*, followed three years later by Chesnutt's *The Colonel's Dream*, and the appearance in 1908 of *Pointing the Way*, the last novel by the fiery, now practically forgotten Baptist preacher Sutton Griggs, nothing else had been published until *The Quest*.[19]

Based loosely on the classical myth from which the novel derived its title, the plot weaves together black and white lives in the rural South, Washington, D.C., and New York. There are cynical, complicated bargains between northern finance and southern politics, while black characters of varying hues, class backgrounds, and principles struggle simply to survive. At the heart of the novel is Zora, the beautiful, untamed black girl, the "heathen hoyden," pure and intrinsically innocent though sexually exploited by local white men. She lives in the deepest depths of the swamp with her mother, the aged, amoral witch Elspeth (emblematic both of Medea and the pagan African past). There Zora inveigles handsome Bles Alwyn (Jason), model student of Yankee schoolmarms, to clear, plough, and plant seed in soil that "was virgin and black, thickly covered over with a tangle of bushes," and from which (conjured by Elspeth) springs forth a golden green field of plants. "Never before was such a magnificent beginning, a full month of other cotton."[20]

While the cotton ripens, the lovers attend the school run by Miss Sarah Smith and her northern white helpers. Zora wonders why they should do so, questioning what the white people can possibly teach her that she hasn't already learned from the swamp and her native wit. Bles, the New Negro (who steps out of "Of the Coming of John," a cameo part in *The Souls of Black Folk*), explains that the white people "know things that give them power and wealth and make them rule." Zora's reply echoes the argument Du Bois had first advanced in the essay "Conservation of the Races," an argument that recurred in books like *The Negro* and *The Gift of Black Folk* and many of his shorter writings—the splendid, even superior, characteristics of black folk. " 'No, no. They don't really rule; they just thinks they rule. They just got things—heavy, dead things. We black folks is got the spirit. We'se lighter and cunninger; we fly right through them; we go and come again just as we wants to. Black folks is wonderful.' " But Bles, like Du Bois in his writings and speeches, tells Zora that the feral energies and intuitive culture of the swamp must be tamed: " 'Even if white folks don't know everything they know different things from us, and we ought to know what they know.' "[21] Zora and Bles learn together happily at first in Miss Smith's school.

Verisimilitude and symbolism commingle here; Sarah Smith's school was based on the Calhoun School, where Du Bois had directed research for his 1906 land tenantry study, later destroyed by the U.S. Department of Labor. This rural version of an urban settlement house was the product of a remarkable educational venture by two northern white women of granite courage, Mabel Dillingham and Charlotte Thornton, who had founded the Calhoun School in 1892 in Lowndes County, a retreat to which Du Bois had beckoned Ovington to join him while completing the ill-fated Lowndes County study, describing it as "floods of sunshine, frost in the morning air; good company, with some exceptions, and an excuse of most interesting work." Miss Smith's establishment, uncorrupted by servile schemes, represents the uplift ideal in all its radiance. "In her imagination the significance of these half dozen gleaming buildings perched aloft seemed portentous—big with the destiny not simply of a county and a State, but of a race—a nation—a world."[22]

But the money promised her school by a multimillionaire widow in the North has strings attached to it. A "Negro education steering committee" composed of northern notables rolls out of Jersey City aboard a special train for fictional Toomsville to study Sarah Smith's academy. Du Bois's caricature of the General Education Board and the Ogdenites is rather wicked: Temple Bocombe, the sociologist, confident, after a week's reading about the race problem, that he "understand[s] it thoroughly"; the Rev. Dr. Boldish of "St. Faith's rich parish"; Mr. Easterly, "who thought this a good business opportunity"; the Vanderpools (Mr. Vanderpool "induced . . . to come by stories of shooting"); all accompanied by "the necessary spice of young womanhood." John Taylor, the northern businessman who grows richer by the day, is the catalyst of the Negro steering committee, and Du Bois has him promise, " 'We'll see that on such committee you Southerners get what you want—control of Negro education.' "[23]

The novel weaves between fable and realism, the pastoral and the picaresque; sometimes effectively, sometimes jarringly. As appealing as the author makes Zora, her behavior often disconcerts the reader not so much because it is erratic or capricious, but because it is too violative of the logic of psychological development. The same Zora who clings to her deep suspicion of the elaborate learning and rigid institutions of Sarah Smith's world has the equivalent of a postgraduate semester in Washington and New York as the maid of the rich, cynical Mrs. Vanderpool. She takes to reading *The Washington Post* and gossiping "with old Herodotus across the earth to the black and blameless Ethiopians," then listening "to Demosthenes and walk[ing] the Appian Way with Cornelia—while New York streamed beneath her window."[24] *Deus ex machina* forces toss Du Bois's African-American characters about like flotsam on a roiling sea; these mysterious and prerational forces belong to some earlier phase of evolution, uninfluenced by those forces generated by the impersonal workings of industrial capitalism.

The author gives frequent expression to his maverick socialism, as when Zora steals the Cresswell's mule so she and Bles can plough and plant for two days, or when, after a white teacher reproaches Zora for the theft of her pin, she hisses: " 'But you don't need it; you've got four other prettier ones—I counted.' 'That makes no difference.' 'Yes it does—folks ain't got no right to things they don't need.' " Near the novel's end the exchange between Zora and a poor white mother echoed the lost possibilities of agrarian populism at its finest: watching haggard white mill hands and downtrodden black sharecroppers milling in a town square, the white woman sighs, " 'Durned if I don't think these white slaves and black slaves had ought ter git together.' 'I think so, too,' Zora agreed."[25] But the theme of socialism in *The Quest* is randomly presented and undeveloped, like Du Bois's own real-life advocacy of the political philosophy during this time.

Capitalist greed, by contrast, is amply described in the novel. The moth-eaten Cresswell family owns the great plantation with its " 'signs of taste and wealth. But it was built on a moan,' cried Miss Smith to herself."[26] An aging land baron, Colonel Cresswell embodies the gentry of the Old South whose economic rapacity is tempered by patriarchal conscience and status anxiety. The colonel's son, syphilitic and heartless Harry, rushes pell-mell into the new order of Wall Street, Montgomery, and Atlanta, marrying Mary Taylor, a Bryn Mawr graduate and teacher at Sarah Smith's school, thereby uniting the new-generation white people of both regions. When Zora brings the bales of fabulous silver fleece from the swamp into town for sale, the Cresswells claim it against fabricated debts. The fleece, woven into a wedding gown, will caress the delicate frame of Harry's bride. The fleece is the second bitter loss to civilization for Zora. Bles had found her love unworthy after learning of the white men in her past from ambivalent liberal Mary Taylor. Meanwhile, Taylors and Cresswells, Smiths and Vanderpools, and other cardboard characters representing the new alliance of gold and cotton grow rich at the expense of tradition, decency, and democracy. The scenes in "The Cotton Corner," Du Bois's chapter on the market combine, struck many readers knowledgeable about market transactions as vividly modern and realistic. Rattled almost to the point of putting a bullet through his brain because every Cresswell cent is at stake, Harry watches John Taylor at the telegraph machine in a Montgomery hotel suite:

> The ticker whirred, "8?—9—9½—10." Then it stopped dead. "Exchange closed," said Taylor. "We've cornered the market all right—cornered it—d'ye hear, Cresswell? We got over half the crop and we can send prices to the North Star—you—why, I figure it you Creswells are worth at least seven hundred and fifty thousand above liabilities this minute," and John Taylor leaned back and lighted a big black cigar. "I've made a million or so myself," he added reflectively. Cresswell leaned back in his chair, his face had gone white again, and he spoke slowly to still the tremor in his voice. "I've gambled—for money—and—women—but—" "But not on cotton, hey? Well, I don't know about cards and such; but they can't beat cotton." "And say, John Taylor, you're my friend." Cresswell stretched his hand across the desk, and as he bent forward the pistol crashed to the floor.[27]

The Quest is a sprawling novel—biracial, biregional, and bisexual in the sense that characters of both genders play prominent parts. As Arnold Rampersad, its keenest academic critic, concludes, *The Quest* is typical of the "conflict between realism and romance common in so much serious writing at the turn of the century."[28] And it is to his women that Du Bois assigns the dominant, interesting parts. His men, on the other hand, are relatively uncomplex, if not mechanical, whether clever and ignoble like white John Taylor and Harry Cresswell, respectively, or noble like Bles Alwyn and sleazy like Tom Teerswell, a black political hack in the nation's capital, the setting for the second part of the novel. Women possess vision, intelligence, and the capacity to act—Zora, the protagonist, above all, and the cynical, delicious Caroline Wynn, the well-connected Washington schoolteacher and accomplished hostess "sprung from at least three generations of respectable mulattoes." Whether Caroline Wynn was a composite personality or based on an acquaintance of Du Bois's (perhaps the novel's dedicatee "To One Whose Name May Not Be Written"?), she and her Washington circle may also have been suggested by another Harvard man's social novel. Henry Adams's *Democracy* (1880) comes to mind, with its intellectual and disenchanted heroine, Madeleine Lee. Handsome, possessed of an "almost unconscious mental aggressiveness," and well-educated, Caroline Wynn believes her life has been thwarted because she is doubly cursed as a woman and a black person. Recognizing Bles's great good heart and his ability to stir others by his moral indignation, Caroline introduces him (along with Du Bois's white readers) to Washington's pigmentocracy, its secret city of handsome, cultured, tragic African-Americans now hidden in the deep shadows cast by the afterglow of Reconstruction, a "world-in-world with its accusing silence, its emphatic self-sufficiency." But Bles—"the Fool—and the Man"—proves incorruptible in the face of a unique opportunity for wealth and power through political skulduggery. With sadness but without reluctance, Caroline Wynn of the Talented Tenth accepts the marriage offer of Stillings, a backstairs creature on his way to white rewards and clearly modeled on the Wizard. "Bles, almost thou persuadest me—to be a fool. Now go," says Miss Wynn as she shows the addled hero to her parlor door with a farewell kiss.[29]

The Quest reflected the force and sincerity of Du Bois's feminism, his credo that the degree of society's enlightenment and of the empowerment of disadvantaged classes and races was ultimately to be measured by its willingness to emancipate women—and, above all, black women. What he would later affirm with pistol-shot accuracy was found on virtually every page of the novel: that the race question was "at bottom simply a matter of the ownership of women; white men want the right to own and use all women, colored and white, and they resent any intrusion of colored men into this domain." When Kelly Miller argued against votes for women on the grounds that women need to be protected, Du Bois heatedly dismissed the statement "as sheer rot" and the same sort of thing "that we hear about 'darker races' and 'lower classes.' " Probably with his own mother in mind, Du Bois had begun his earliest piece of published fiction, a novelette in the Fisk *Herald*, with the sentence, "It's hard to be a woman, but a black one—!"[30] The main character in that three-part *Herald* novelette, "Tom Brown at Fisk," had been a woman, too, Ella Boyd, a summer schoolteacher, like Du Bois, in the Tennessee backcountry. In *The Quest*, Mary Silvina, Ella Boyd, Du Bois himself, and the unforgettable Josie seem to merge into the luminous Zora, symbol of the childhood of the race, corruption in slavery, white-world skills and black-world intuitive wisdom and humanity, and of the truly developed woman. Echoing Crummell and reverberating in future African-American fiction and scholarship is the conviction that the race will be saved by its Zoras, by the black woman charting the course to culture, dignity, family, and work.[31]

Not only is his main character female, but for the first time in African-American fiction Du Bois created a heroine who is dark-skinned, unpedigreed, and sympathetic. Seeking what she repeatedly calls "The Way," Zora's intuition (for Du Bois, the trump card of "racial" faculties) slowly yet surely guides her through the swamp of civilization (Washington and New York) and back to the South with money in hand for Sarah Smith's school. In her dwelling, where all is harmony, Zora displays her small treasure of books—the symbolic building blocks of her new wisdom: Plato's *Republic*, representing Du Bois's conviction that the good society must be led by the broadly educated; Tennyson's *Poems*, underscoring Du Bois's belief, in opposition to Plato, in the value of poetic vision in the republic; Spencer's *First Principles*, a salute to logic and system-building applied to society; Gorky's *Comrades* and Balzac's novels, literature imbued with a social and moral perspective; and an encyclopedia of agriculture, Du Bois's balancing concession to the vocational idea informing Hampton and Tuskegee. *The Quest* ends with Zora in Bles's arms—both committed to a program of agrarian self-sufficiency based on learning, cooperative labor, and a politics of dignity and pragmatism. Du Bois places the last words of the novel in Zora's mouth—" 'Will you—marry me, Bles?' "[32]

IF NINA DU BOIS ever committed to paper any thoughts about her husband's first novel, they have not survived. The unidentified person to whom he dedicated *The Quest* is almost certainly a woman, and it is absolutely certain that Nina is not that person. None of the characters seems likely to have been modeled on Nina, and her absence from *The Quest* seems to suggest her diminishing presence in Will's emotional life. A theoretical feminist whose advocacy could erupt with the force of a volcano (as in "The Burden of Black Women" in the November 1907 *Horizon*, or in "The Damnation of Women" in the 1921 collection of essays, *Darkwater*), Du Bois proved to be consistently patriarchal in his role as husband and father. The all-too-commonplace truth is that he increasingly acted as a well-intentioned tyrant at best and a bullying hypocrite at worst. Over the next two years, when he found time to pay some attention to Nina and Yolande he saw them as symbols—as Wife and Daughter, special enough, to be sure, because they were *his* wife and daughter, and therefore the paradigmatic wife and daughter of the Talented Tenth. If his expectations of Nina were narrow, they remained exacting. She had the duty not to hinder his own private and public involvements and to follow his prescriptions for their daughter's intellectual development. His expectations of Yolande were as exalted as they were unrealistic.

Daughter Yolande was to be sacrificed time and again to the cruelest of double standards. On the one hand, her life, like her mother's, was controlled by the head of the family—a man whose faith in his own wisdom was serene and always unequivocal; but, whereas other late-Victorian husbands and fathers were determined to shelter their womenfolk from overexposure to education and public life, Du Bois's marching orders commanded Yolande to become superlatively educated and emancipated. Her birthday fell in the same month McClurg published *The Quest*. She was only eleven, but the time had come for her to recognize her father's high expectations. In Du Bois's vision, Yolande was to mature into a wise and moral Zora endowed with the cosmopolitanism of a Caroline Wynn. But there was surely something more—the sublimation of a father's loss of a son through a daughter. What the golden-haired Burghardt could have done, spunky Yolande would do as well—and with less risk, because, although it was hard to be a black woman, it was not usually fatal to be an intelligent, enterprising one, as often was the case with black men. Du Bois had consoled himself on his son's death with a "Well sped, my boy, before the world has dubbed your ambition insolence, has held your ideals unattainable, and taught you to cringe and bow."[33] Yolande would attain her goals and she would not cringe. He told her that repeatedly—in letters, at the dinner table, and during those increasingly rare bedtime sessions that she relished for the closeness between them.

Du Bois prodded and exhorted Yolande to meet the challenge of the world. Nina obediently repeated the catechism. Even so, as the months of school terms passed, he felt that Yolande was slipping. He observed with concern and annoyance her tendency to overeat and become flabby ("nibbling and tasting all day"). She lacked motivation, discipline, and needed outdoor exercise "and training in games." The worst of it was Yolande's command of the language. It had been "rather our pride a few years back." Of late, however, it had become "very slovenly and 'American,' " he wrote to the headmaster of the English school in which he contemplated enrolling her. In summer 1914, Du Bois convinced Nina that their thirteen-year-old daughter should attend Bedales School in Hampshire, one of England's first experimental country boarding schools, in order to prepare for college. Bedales developed mind and character through freedom of expression, group discussion, and pupil self-government. It was the first public (i.e., private) school in the United Kingdom to dare coeducation. As his letter of instructions to Bedales headmaster John Haden Badley stipulated, although Du Bois did not "look for brilliance or genius," he wanted Yolande "trained for efficient work and not simply for breeding."[34]

On September 24, 1914, seven weeks after the outbreak of the European war, Du Bois wrote a personal letter to William Jennings Bryan, now Woodrow Wilson's Secretary of State, requesting expedition of Nina's and Yolande's passport applications. The matter was urgent, he explained to Bryan, as his wife and daughter were booked to sail within days for the United Kingdom. Ramsay MacDonald, leader of the Labour party and one of Du Bois's many important Races Congress contacts, had been only too happy to recommend Yolande to Bedales, where two of his sons were also enrolled. Dr. Frances Hoggan, the old friend who had financed Du Bois's summer trip to England in 1907, stood ready to help Nina find lodgings in London after Yolande had settled in at Bedales. The organizer of the Races Congress, Gustav Spiller, could be counted upon to encourage his wife to draw Nina into her large, sophisticated social circle. A similar welcome awaited her from the West Indian family of John Alcindor; an organizer of the 1900 Pan-African Congress, Alcindor had a thriving surgical practice in the borough of Paddington. From teenage worries about an "awfully rickety" swing in the front yard (the topic of her last letter to her father before leaving for England), Yolande was transported to a foreign land and into vicissitudes she had never imagined. She and Nina descended the gangplank of the *St. Paul* on October 6, 1914, to be met by a deputy U.S. consul at Liverpool.[35]

Predictable letters filled with advice and instructions came from 70 Fifth Avenue, the new address of *The Crisis*. On October 29, Du Bois poured his thoughts into five full paragraphs, anxious that Yolande comprehend fully the grand implications of her new life. She had turned fourteen on Wednesday of the previous week. The letter was classic. He had waited for his "Dear Little Daughter" to settle in. He knew she missed the familiar, that all was "new and unusual." Probably she was lonely and a little afraid. Above all, she must remember her "great opportunity."

> You are in one of the world's best schools, in one of the world's greatest modern empires. . . . You are there by no desert or merit of yours, but only by lucky chance. Deserve it then. Study, do your work. Be honest, frank and fearless and get some grasp of the real values of life. . . . Remember that most folk laugh at anything unusual whether it is beautiful, fine or not. You, however must not laugh at yourself. You must know that brown is as pretty as white or prettier and crinkly hair as straight even though it is harder to comb. . . . Don't shrink from new experiences and custom. Take the cold bath bravely. Enter into the spirit of your big bedroom. Enjoy what is and not pine for what is not. Read some good, heavy, serious books just for discipline: Take yourself in hand and master yourself. Make yourself do unpleasant things, so as to gain the upper hand of your soul. Above all remember: your father loves you and believes in you and expects you to be a wonderful woman. I shall write each week and expect a weekly letter from you. Lovingly yours, Papa.[36]

Less than two weeks later, Yolande received a second editorial. Her father was pleased that she was liking Bedales. He promised her a watch and riding lessons, if he could stand the expense. "But most and foremost—lessons, lessons, lessons! Learn, learn, learn!" She must read English, French, and German history in order to "see the reasons of this war." Finally, he enclosed the latest *Crisis* "because it is about our people—your people and mine, whom we must love and of whom we must be proud." Yolande should "show it to the girls and never be ashamed of your folk." There was a barrage of such letters throughout 1915.[37]

Meanwhile, Nina husbanded her pounds sterling ("not complaining, I'm simply telling you how I've spent the money"), kept track of Yolande (reporting that her combs and brushes had been stolen and that her feet and hands were swelling), and suffered in a London suburb from the miserable English weather. The best lodging she could find was a boarding house in High Barnet, a part of London beyond the Underground, where she had to share a drab room with another woman. Nina's mood became as grey and heavy as London's winter cloud-cover. Coal for the little stove was in short supply and she suffered constantly from the penetrating damp. She was going to have to buy heavier clothing; there was no sign of her furs. They must be "at the bottom of the ocean," she sighed to Will in early February 1915. All the English people she met knew, despite the news blackout, that U-boats were taking a heavy toll of shipping in the Atlantic. Yolande's Christmas visit had been especially hard. They had had to double up in the poorly heated room and "Ouchie" (Yolande's Bedales nickname, explained by her tender extremities) consumed enormous amounts of scarce, expensive meat and vegetables. "I'm sorry to have to trouble you about money matters again but I must" became a refrain in Nina's letters home.[38]

She felt she had to have her own room despite the weekly cost of a few shillings more. Although the private room was much better heated, Nina's physical condition deteriorated. "I can't get on on the average English meals"—she ate them but couldn't "digest them." She assured Will that she was doing her best "to get my stomach straightened out, am living mostly on eggs and milk, oil, etc." Frances Hoggan had prescribed this diet, but as the weeks passed there was only a slight improvement in Nina's condition. She was spending most of her days resting. Her eyes troubled her a great deal in early March 1915, but the tone of her letters over the period of a year suggests that boredom and cold were the worst of it. "Dear Will, There isn't anything new happening with us," she sighed on March 5, 1916. "We have been having some snow and cold in London but on the whole it has not been a cold winter, still one is always more or less cold here." Will received detailed accounts of board and dietary expenditures, but he must appreciate that the "change of food and climate and the living in general reduced my strength considerable [sic] . . . as I had none too much to start with." In that same letter she thanked Will for sending the latest *Crisis* and for taking the time "to tell me about your own speech" at the NAACP meeting. She was genuinely grateful because she realized how monumental his concerns were, how unyielding his self-imposed regime. One of Will's earliest letters, a chatty one about Augustus Dill, Monroe Trotter, Woodrow Wilson, and "our ups and downs in the Association," had been dictated with an apology: "You will have to pardon this machine-made letter. My left hand is so tired that I have not been using it for a few days."[39]

Gradually, she grew stronger and began to get about. She enjoyed Dr. Hoggan's club and Mrs. Spiller's at-home, but they, the Coleridge-Taylors, and others who took an interest in her well-being lived in central London, a long, expensive double-decker ride (forty pence) from High Barnet—a trip too long and too taxing on her delicate health to make often. And besides, she added, "London is one dirty city." She was lonely. Aida Young, the wife of Major Charles Young, Will's old friend from Wilberforce, was not expected to pass through London from Liberia until late May. The U-boats prevented the regular arrival of her *Independent*. Her furs, although fortunately insured by Will through Wanamaker's, were definitely lost at sea. Zeppelins were beginning to bomb the city. Racial prejudice prevented a change of address. The places that "were comfortable and reasonable in price won't accommodate colored people [and] other places are very expensive or very dirty."[40] Then, finally, toward the end of March 1915, just before Yolande's Easter vacation, Nina found a large, comfortable room at 13 Chepstow Place in Bayswater for ten shillings and sixpence weekly. When Yolande came down from Bedales, Nina held her breath. Mrs. Turner, the very proper Bayswater landlady, enforced strict rules of conduct. Yolande's manners had been disagreeable, altogether insolent during the Christmas vacation, Nina reported. "I was always wondering what she would say and do next."[41]

A taller, thinner Yolande arrived in Chepstow Place as hard as ever to satisfy, and at about the same time the back issues of the *Independent* came in a bundle. Dr. Hoggan called on them, recommended a specialist for Yolande's blistered feet (the English climate was the culprit), and brought Nina news that she had full privileges in the Emerson Club. They spent time in Kensington Park, which was within walking distance of their boarding house, saw *Peg O My Heart* ("a pretty light play [but] Yolande enjoyed Peg very much"), took in Madame Tussaud's wax museum, and visited the Spillers. She wrote Will that Bedales said Yolande was "as good as gold." Nina said she was frankly suspicious—the report "reads . . . almost too good." Bedales was a fine place and she was certainly no expert in these matters, but Nina didn't think "they require as much of the pupils here as they do in the schools at home." The head matron sent word that Yolande appeared to be unhappy. Maybe she wasn't *that* unhappy because Yolande "had a way of not expressing herself," Nina reminded Will, but it certainly was true that, except for one Belgian student, "Ouchie" didn't "take to the girls and of course she hates the boys." Yolande was cagey, disinclined to show her true feelings. She refused to say "right out one way or the other," so Nina had to declare that she "really could not form any opinion" about Yolande's adjustment at the school.[42] Their daughter not only wanted nothing to do with the war (she refused to read anything about it), Nina was afraid Yolande was uninterested in almost everything—sports, hobbies, studies, people her age, travel, reading.

Nina didn't want to worry Will, especially as he had written that he was about to take a brief vacation in Jamaica. She had been so relieved that he was trying to pace himself after finishing his new book, *The Negro*, the strain of the NAACP's fierce campaign against *The Birth of a Nation*, and his preparations for the Washington, D.C., mounting that fall of *The Star of Ethiopia*, his pageant with a cast of hundreds. "You've had such a full life for the last few years," Nina was sure he needed to relax. Actually he was "feeling in pretty good shape," Will reassured her from his new home at 248 West Sixty-fourth Street, "but at the same time" he agreed that he "ought to take a good rest so as to be ready for next year's work which is going to be hard with the pageant and other things." Yes, she was "so sorry to trouble" him when he was "so busy trying to make the work go and meet expenses there in the office." Yet how could they continue to afford Bedales? Prices were rising steeply now, shortages were becoming acute. Yolande's fees per term came to thirty-five pounds; her vacation expenses were large; the boarding house was almost two pounds weekly, everything included; and the specialists Dr. Hoggan referred them to were bound to be expensive. Nina calculated a global sum approaching 360 pounds a year—1,800 dollars. Will's annual pay was 2,500 dollars. "Dr. Hoggan doesn't realize that your salary isn't enough to meet such demands," she wrote despairingly.[43]

As he left for Jamaica, Will sent a check for sixty pounds, astonishing Nina with his promise to send sixty pounds every other month—nearly 1,800 dollars, which, somehow, he did. The Jamaica trip was something of an event, with a garden reception hosted by Sir Sydney Olivier, the royal governor, and press coverage of Du Bois's well-attended address. He extended a receiving-line handshake to a short, very dark-skinned man of remarkable intensity, one Marcus Mosiah Garvey, who later left his calling card at Du Bois's stopping place.[44] On this island, the editor's reserve gave way almost to ecstasy as he described a jewel "thrown on the face of the sea with gash and shadow and veil." For the first time in his life, he told *Crisis* readers, "I lived beyond the color line." It was as though God had decided to implement the resolutions of the Universal Races Congress in "a most amazing land." People of color ran the society—the mayor of Kingston, "smart, dark constables in gleaming white hats," department store and postal clerks with "a curl or tint . . . that proclaimed the most ancient of blood." Ecstatic but not blinded, Du Bois saw that the ultimate political and economic power was wielded by the white people and witnessed the "tragedy of a poverty almost incomprehensible" that shackled the "great mass of hard working black laborers." Nevertheless, Jamaica was "the most marvelous paradox," even after three hundred years in which the "white world has reaped its millions." It represented "the gift of racial peace, the utter overturning of the barbaric war of color."[45]

Jamaica amazed Will. Sixty pounds every second month amazed Nina, prompting two unanswered inquiries that June.[46] Mysteriously relieved of money concerns, she put a brave face to other worries. The war intruded. Outside the Medieval Flemish city of Ypres, the Allied and German forces sustained colossal losses throughout April and May 1915. When the generals ordered a pause in the slaughter, 250,000 British and French soldiers were dead from bullets, shrapnel, and poison gas (used by the Germans for the first time in warfare). The controlled British press concealed the casualties, but families in mourning were ubiquitous and there was much talk of ghastly numbers in clubs and pubs. The sinking of the British ocean liner *Lusitania* in early May 1915, resulting in 1,198 civilian fatalities (128 of them American citizens), horrified the American and British public. Nina shared the feelings of outrage—so much, in fact, that she refused her German neighbor's invitation to walk in Regent's Park the morning after the sinking. "I thought it most too much," she tutted to Will. She made the best of an alien, unsafe world. Zepellins were unloading more tonnage on London now, Bedales teachers were reporting for military duty, and food and fuel were much dearer. Even in the midst of the hazards, she wrote that she was "really just beginning to appreciate London" now that she was no longer "half frozen or starved." There were visits to the Coleridge-Taylor and the Ira Aldridge families. Aida Young finally came from Liberia, somewhat ill and the worse for wear, but full of news about the war and determined to cross the Channel as soon as possible to enroll her two children in a Paris lycée. "Afraid to cross the Channel now," Nina declined Aida's invitation. Charles Young had sailed directly for New York and Nina advised Will not to breathe a word about the former U.S. military attaché's poor health. "Should you by chance write to Major Young don't write anything very personal for it seems their mail is all tampered with," she disclosed darkly.[47]

Although life was much fuller and more agreeable, Nina remained deeply troubled about Yolande. She clearly misread Headmaster Badley's progress reports (they were less positive than she thought), but she sensed that her tight-lipped daughter's emotions were in commotion. Nina wondered if the cause was racial, and intimated that the daughter of W. E. Burghardt Du Bois had not yet come to terms with her own identity. "I know of course she feels strange," Nina confided, "and I presume, though she wouldn't acknowledge it, that she's beginning to feel she's colored." She hastened to concede that Yolande was "better off here than she would be in America," yet both of them lived an odd existence among the English. "I have had people stare at me until I'm sure there is something wrong with me."[48] But it was less the rude racial customs of many Britons that bothered Nina than her daughter's alternately withdrawn and surly response and mounting insouciance about her education. Nina now felt that the Bedales philosophy of progressive education was wrong for Yolande. If not "rather firmly guided," she would be "like many other colored girls I know, especially colored girls whose way has been rather easy." In a remarkably perceptive letter of May 16, 1915, about Yolande's deficiencies, Nina also poignantly evaluated herself, if only subconsciously, as one of those women of color who "suddenly find out that they don't know anything and therefore can't do anything. Then the whole world becomes a bore to them and they hate themselves for having wasted their opportunities."[49]

Du Bois either genuinely missed the troubling implications of his wife's reports or was too busy fully to appreciate them. Yolande had repeatedly tried to fix her father's attention. Child psychologists today might argue that the overeating, the vague maladies, and the periodic disciplinary crises stemmed largely from her need for attention. Through her mother she had asked him to renew her subscription to *St. Nicholas Magazine* in February 1915 and reminded him about the promise of the watch. The watch came, but it is unclear whether Du Bois got around to the subscription. "Dear Papa," a note from Bedales bleated, "I haven't had a letter from you for years." Even though Nina had told him that their daughter "won't read the war news or stories," Yolande, hoping to draw a reply, asked, "Do you think America'll join the war, don't you think she ought to? I do." Soon she wrote that the war had come to Bedales. A Zeppelin passed over Bedales and dropped bombs not far away. One Sunday Yolande felt so unfairly treated by her dormitory matrons, she poured out her feelings to her father: "P.S. I wish I'd never seen England or Miss Ruth."[50]

Often when he attempted a fatherly letter, Du Bois was unsure of his tone and phrasing. In a lengthy, typewritten description of Niagara Falls that he had sent her four years earlier, pronouns were changed and one or two signature forms tried out before the final WEBD. But this time, in a July 15 letter, he found his most human, intimate voice, telling Yolande about his personal vulnerabilities. The world was unfair. Learning to get along without the things you wanted most was part of growing up, he advised. Then came an uncharacteristic personal revelation:

> I remember when I was a little boy that there was one boy who lived near me who was almost my only playmate. When, therefore, he got obstreperous and cut at my fingers with a hatchet and was otherwise naughty, I had to give him up. Oh! It was an awful time! I felt absolutely alone in the world and then I began to see how I could arrange to play with myself and I have been doing that largely ever since.[51]

Yolande wrote back that she was trying cricket. She didn't like it; the boys bowled too hard. He must have wanted to continue the correspondence, but his work in connection with *The Crisis* and the association kept him busy writing and constantly traveling—fifty lectures in fourteen states in 1915, thirty-seven in eight states the following year. The NAACP was becoming truly national now, with branches set up across the country and plans for more in the Deep South. Mary Maclean's unexpected death in July 1912 had affected Du Bois profoundly (she may be "The Princess of the Hither Isles," an enigmatic, moving prose poem in the October 1913 *Crisis*), but the staff and magazine continued to grow (the average monthly circulation reached thirty thousand in 1915).[52] There were only insignificant parts available to Nina and Yolande in the drama starring W.E.B. Du Bois.

During this time, in fact, the editor had transformed himself into a stage director. Robert Wood, the African-American printer well connected to Tammany Hall, had arranged for Du Bois's appointment to the New York Emancipation Exposition Committee. The great success in 1913 of what came to be called *The Star of Ethiopia*, presented in the 12th Regiment armory as part of New York's commemoration of the fiftieth anniversary of the Emancipation Proclamation, had thrilled him. "The Pageant is the thing. This is what the people want and long for," he exulted after some fourteen thousand men and women of both races had filed through the armory that October. By early 1915, Du Bois was determined to "teach on the one hand the colored people themselves the meaning of their history . . . and on the other to reveal the Negro to the white world." The bishops of the AME church would invite the editor to mount *The Star of Ethiopia* in Philadelphia's Convention Hall during the denomination's hundredth-anniversary general conference in May 1916. The Philadelphia production "in its smoothness and finish was technically the best," Du Bois said years afterward, but the earlier Washington, D.C., premiere in autumn 1915 was also such a success that, as he exuberantly told *Crisis* readers, he "walked home and knew the joys of God."[53] There would be a final Hollywood Bowl presentation in 1925.

Refining and enlarging the original 1911 draft (probably completed after the Races Congress), he transformed *The Star of Ethiopia* into a three-hour extravaganza in six episodes, featuring a thousand creamy-complexioned young women and tawny, well-built men, and flocks of schoolchildren marching through history. The anticipated costs of the Washington production ran to three thousand dollars, a sum well beyond the NAACP's discretionary budget, but Du Bois somehow raised and risked five hundred of his own dollars. At the last moment, "a wonderful gift of one young woman" brought in another fifteen hundred dollars. The pageant was supported by enthusiastic citizens' committees and organizations (President Wilson's daughter Margaret lent her name to the Washington pageant committee). Except for two selections from Verdi's *Aida*, Du Bois chose music composed by black men: Bob Cole, Rosamond Johnson, Coleridge-Taylor, and Charles Young, his accomplished army friend, who contributed a prelude and four additional pieces. Du Bois described the act of creation in a tumult of *Crisis* prose: "It sweeps you on and you hang trembling to its skirts. Nothing can stop it. It is. It will. Wonderfully, irresistibly the dream comes true." Eight searchlights sliced the Indian summer night and six thousand Washingtonians watched from bleachers in the American League ballpark as trumpets blared and the stentorian voice of a herald proclaimed from the steps of a papier-mâché Egyptian temple the six gifts of "the Eldest and Strongest of the Races of men whose faces be Black. Hear ye, hear ye!" Misses Adella Parks, Eleanor Curtis, and Mrs. Gregory Fraser, representing Sheba, Ethiopia, and Meroe, respectively (as well as the flower of Talented Tenth pulchritude), were serially replaced center stage by a pharaoh, Mali's fourteenth-century Islamic ruler Mansa Mūsā, Columbus's pilot Alonzo; moaning slaves in chains; Spanish lancers; Toussaint L'Ouverture; Sojourner Truth; Frederick Douglass; and, to the accompaniment of rolling drums, the Massachusetts regiment of Colonel Robert Gould Shaw; followed by children, the professions, and the working class. Iron and fire, the herald intoned, was Africa's first gift to mankind, then came Egypt's civilization, followed by Faith in Righteousness, then Humility, and the gift of "Struggle Toward Freedom" and finally "the Gift of Freedom for the workers"—all this in "a great cloud of music that hovered over them and enveloped them."[54]

Local newspapers applauded the edifying message and ambitious scale of the pageant and congratulations poured into *The Crisis* over a three-year period from leading citizens in New York, Washington, and Philadelphia. The *Bee* described the pageant as "electrical, spiritual." "All the Grimkés were enthusiastic," Archibald wrote Du Bois. Another Washingtonian whose opinion Du Bois valued enough to request it in writing, Dr. H. B. Humphrey, a white official of the U.S. Department of Agriculture, found the pageant full of "interest and delightful surprises." Perhaps it was "a bit too slow between parts to support the interest of the average American . . . used to things mov[ing] before the eye with Kaleidoscopic regularity," Humphrey wrote; nevertheless, it was certainly a force for breaking down prejudice. Humphrey's opinion is revealing, in light of the fascinating fact that *The Star of Ethiopia* was the most patent, expansive use yet made by Du Bois of an ideology of black supremacy in order to confound one of white supremacy. In its fabulous dramaturgy, he worked out the basics of an Afrocentric aesthetics and historiography—the sweeping interpretive claims he was just then inserting into the scholarship on which the forthcoming books *The Negro* and *The Gift of Black Folk* were based. Clearly anticipating the message of his pageant in *The Crisis*, Du Bois wrote that the Negro "is essentially dramatic. His greatest gift to the world has been and will be the gift of art, of appreciation and realization of beauty."[55] If European philosophers from Hegel to de Gobineau (and soon the American sociologist Robert Park) had been saying much the same things for a century, in *The Star of Ethiopia* Du Bois presented those attributes as the source of mankind's greatest achievements.

The 242-page book *The Negro*, published simultaneously in the United States and Great Britain in May 1915, was stippled with similar double-edged generalizations, broad characterizations of African peoples that would have been seen as invidious if propounded by a European scholar. In what was the first general history yet written in English on the subject, Du Bois casually informed readers that "in disposition the Negro is among the most lovable of men," that there could be "no doubt of the Negro's deep and delicate sense of beauty in form, color, and sound," or that Haiti's peasantry is "the happiest and most contented peasantry in the world."[56] Yet, as the editor of the popular Home University Library series and Alfred Harcourt at Henry Holt and Company immediately recognized,

Du Bois's original 75,000-word manuscript was a pioneering synthesis of the latest scholarship brilliantly beamed through a revisionist lens. The author ranged from the dawn of civilization to the turn of the twentieth century and over three continents. *The Negro* was a large building block in an Afrocentric historiography that has achieved credibility through the writings of scholars such as Basil Davidson, Martin Bernal, and Cheikh Anta Diop. Although several mainstream reviews were conventionally racist (such as one by a future associate editor of *The Encyclopaedia of Social Sciences*), most praised Du Bois's sixth book as a major contribution, although many barely concealed their inadequate grasp of the subject.[57]

Greatly indebted to Boas, von Luschan, Alexander F. Chamberlain, Robert H. Lowie, Jacques Loeb, and other social and physical scientists (all extensively quoted), the pages of *The Negro* were littered with the fallacious concepts exploded by Du Bois—estimates of black African technological backwardness in the Neolithic Age, Aryan and Hamitic foundations of ancient civilizations, color-based presumptions of inferiority prior to the Industrial Revolution in northern Europe, absence of high culture and complex political structures in precolonial Africa, and so on. Du Bois presented slavery in the American South as integral to modern capitalism, but an institution that worked badly and mirrored "the modern factory system in its worst conceivable form." His interpretation of Reconstruction remained radically at variance with the prevailing Dunning dogma. His prediction of Pan-African unity and the global solidarity of darker peoples would have a deep impact upon nonwhite elites in the United States, the Caribbean, and West Africa. "A belief in humanity means a belief in colored men," Du Bois proclaimed at the close of *The Negro*, much as the herald of his pageant had. "The future world will, in all reasonable probability, be what colored men make it."[58]

Near the end of October 1915, Nina received a typed, single-spaced, three-page account of the pageant's reception in the capital. "The people of Washington were very good indeed, but skeptical," Du Bois said; "they just could not believe that the thing could be done, especially in so short a time." Nina had worried about the unpunctual Charles Burroughs, the drama director (one of Will's Wilberforce students), but Will wrote that Burroughs, though late as usual, had done "splendid work." The wet weather had held off almost miraculously. The only mishap had had to do with Will's own injudiciousness on the night before the opening. Despite nagging stomach trouble, he had gone with Dill and a few others to a party and eaten crab salad and ice cream. "It nearly knocked out the pageant although the public did not know it."[59] He closed with a query about the Zeppelins. Maybe Nina would prefer living in a smaller town. But, on second thought, he supposed a new town "would be lonesome after your many acquaintances." The next news Nina had from him would be about his trip to Florida and Georgia in February 1916. In Atlanta he had seen Miss Pingree ("and talked and talked and talked"), Proctor, and the Hopes, and had spoken in both the Morehouse (the new name for Atlanta Baptist) College and Atlanta University chapels. There had been some sharp exchanges with Ware and the trustees in 1912 about transferring the Atlanta University Studies to New York and Du Bois would make a final grab for them through the Slater Fund that November. After publication of the excellent *Negro American Artisan* in 1912, Du Bois had pulled Dill away in September of the following year to become business manager of *The Crisis*. The last of the conference reports, *Morals and Manners among Negro Americans*, appeared in 1914.[60]

Whatever the tensions caused by the Atlanta Studies issue, all was conviviality during Du Bois's visit, with "everybody ask[ing] about you and Yolande," and a Saturday evening lecture and faculty reception. After his lecture, Will wrote that he went over to the Townses with some of the teachers and danced until midnight. From Atlanta, he sped to Boston to attend the Spingarn Medal ceremony in honor of Charles Young, who gave an excellent address. He, Young, and twenty others returned together to New York for a dinner to send Young off to command his cavalry regiment in the punitive expedition against Pancho Villa.[61] While in Atlanta, though, Du Bois had seen a woman with whom both he and Nina had been friendly. As people remember her, she was not beautiful in any conventional sense, but Louie Davis Shivery was a handsome woman with panache. She was college-trained, exceedingly intelligent, taught English in the segregated public school system, and was given to wearing outlandish clothes. She and her dentist husband, George, lived in discord in a tidy corner house on Chestnut, a narrow street at the foot of the Atlanta University campus. Dr. Shivery was a brute whose mistreatment of his wife was common knowledge in the neighborhood. There were many nights when the daughter of one faculty family on Chestnut Street overheard her parents consoling the tormented wife. George Shivery's demands, it seems, "were more than she could tolerate," Josephine Harreld Love says, "so it wasn't, you know, exactly an idyllic marriage." That was exactly what Will had written Nina that February—that Louie Shivery "has a hard time. Her husband gets drunk and beats her now and then for exercise."[62] Will's concern for Louie Shivery's welfare, which led to their much-gossiped about relationship of many years, may well have crossed the line dividing compassion from adultery at this time.

Nina's knowledge of Will's various affairs is elusive. She would have had to have been deliberately undiscerning not to have had any suspicions, because by then Will had carried on more than a few such relationships. Mildred Bryant's name would have meant nothing to her then. Will must have met this mischievous, fast-talking piano teacher in Louisville, Kentucky, on an NAACP speaking circuit during 1913 or 1914. "Another favor to ask (don't you feel like shaking me and calling me a bother? Well, please put such thoughts away!)," Bryant chirped in a March 1916 letter about a public school position in Washington, D.C.[63] Although he sent a reference immediately, Bryant would soon move on to Chicago, where the frayed little places that she rented or later owned on the South Side would warm a visiting Du Bois on many nights over the next thirty-odd years. But Nina would have known Jessie Fauset well. The Philadelphia-born Cornell graduate was the epitome of what shallow folk regarded as the highest Talented Tenth virtues—cosmopolitan, comely, and café au lait. Her effusive 1903 letter about *The Souls of Black Folk* had led to her becoming Du Bois's protégée, then collaborator, and soon lover. Fauset had taught since 1906 at Washington's academically demanding M Street (later Dunbar) High School.

Her ambition, which Du Bois sincerely encouraged, was to write the Great African-American Novel, something she called "There Is Confusion" even then. In March 1912, she had begun writing the "What to Read" section in *The Crisis*. In December and January, the twenty-seven-year-old French teacher had almost seemed to monopolize the magazine with "Emmy," a fat, serialized, illustrated story about prejudice, "passing" for white, and star-crossed romance. An opportunity to write, while pursuing advanced work in French, came in June 1914 with a fellowship to study in Paris. Du Bois sent a tureen of steamed lobsters to the S. S. *Cedric* as it weighed anchor from New York, with a note in his nearly illegible left-handed script. When Du Bois wanted to, Fauset gushed aboard ship, he could be "so unspeakably kind and nice." She had delayed opening fifteen other letters (some from relatives) and two telegrams in order to read his first, "and reread it and tucked it under my pillow my one sea-sickish night and thought literally 'on' it many times."[64]

Whatever her qualms about Will's relationships, Nina's pressing concern remained Yolande, whose roller-coaster performance at Bedales had finally stuck fast by spring of 1916. Headmaster Badley gravely informed the Du Boises in early April of his sad conclusion that "either the girl is not by temperament and natural bent able to respond to the influences around her here, or that we have quite failed to find the means of reaching what may be yet undeveloped in her." It was time to come home, Nina announced in a letter barely concealing her relief. "I think we better, taking all things into consideration." They would sail on the *St. Louis* on August 5, she said. Yolande's reaction was unexpected and traumatic. It was her father who had forced her into this alien environment and had caused her to disgrace herself, even though she had done her best. Subconsciously, she must have wanted to blame him; but since W. E. Burghardt Du Bois was infallible, she could not bring herself to dare it; instead, she let her anger and impertinence overflow, arguing that she had the right to try to do better and make him proud of her. She collected her classmates' signatures on a letter that amounted to a petition. Molly Scott was so upset that she wrote directly to "Dear Dr. Du Bois," pleading on Yolande's behalf for another year. She'd rather do "*anything* in all the world than leave Bedales," Yolande insisted. "I know I've worked hard at lessons this term and I can't do more and I can't help it if I'm stupid." Why had he made her come there if she had to leave now "just when I am a senior and getting to [be] old enough to be something like a vice-boss . . . ?"[65]

Nina and Yolande sailed into New York harbor in mid-August of 1916. Will met them and escorted them to Sea Isle City, New Jersey, where he settled them into Ocean House. Then he left for his summer vacation in Maine.[66]

17.

Crises at *The Crisis*

It was still audacious in 1913 to write, as William Ferris did, that "Mr. Washington is now a waning influence in the country amongst the colored people," that Du Bois's star was "in the ascendancy," and that *The Souls of Black Folk* was the "political bible of the Negro race." With a bachelor's degree from Yale (1891) and a master's from Harvard (1900), the thirty-nine-year-old Ferris had been one of the first recruits to the Niagara Movement, although his usual state of financial duress as free-lance journalist and lecturer seems to have kept him from attending the annual meetings. Recently, he had been treated to a dose of Du Bois's most solvent candor, via a reproving note in which Du Bois said Ferris was "lazy and will not keep clean," which precluded companionship with "people of your intellectual level." Admiration for the *Crisis* editor remained unshaken, nevertheless, and if personal hygiene continued to make Ferris an infrequent guest at the interracial Civic Club, Du Bois held his nose long enough to praise *The African Abroad or His Evolution in Western Civilization*, Ferris's 1913, two-volume tour de force, as "keen and even brilliant in parts." A disjointed display of nineteenth-century learning, in which history fulfilled the Hegelian world spirit, the Anglo-Saxon race was the "advance guard of civilization," and the "Negrosaxon" was endowed with uplifting "spiritual and emotional qualities," the book was also a panegyric to Du Bois, whom Ferris called "the political messiah of the race."[1]

Nevertheless, in the official mind of white America Booker T. Washington still reigned, and a great many African-Americans, North and South, would also have questioned Ferris's judgment. True, Washington's intimates saw a rapid decline from the remarkable vigor he had exhibited in the days before the Tenderloin incident. His physicians either could not or would not identify precisely what was causing his nervous system's progressive collapse. Increasingly, Emmett Scott carried the load. Under Woodrow Wilson, the Tuskegee principal no longer held anything like the political influence he had appeared to exert during Roosevelt's two terms. His two most powerful agents, Charles Anderson and William Lewis, had been forced to resign their plum federal appointments. Yet he was still a considerable force among his own people, and, as far as most influential white people were concerned, he was the only reliable one. When Ruth Baldwin, William's widow, helped create the National Urban League in 1910, the Wizard and his allies were able to extend their influence to an African-American organization well-funded enough to rival the NAACP. Men like George F. Peabody remained almost blindly trusting in Washington and sick at heart about Du Bois's loud agitation and defiance. He knew of no people "whose splendid attitudes throughout hundreds of years so fully confirms the virtue and ultimate value of non-resistance," Peabody wrote Du Bois, chastising him for his attacks "on individuals who are leaders of the movement." Washington himself seemed to be evolving with the times, speaking out more about egregious racial discrimination, encouraging (by letter and telegram) resistance to residential segregation, lending his name to a successfully organized public protest against a bill in the Senate to bar immigration of Africans to the United States, and even going as far as to write an article in the November 1912 *Century Magazine* deploring labor exploitation of convicts, lynching, disfranchisement, inequalities in education, and the rank injustice of substandard separate transportation facilities. Although he opposed outright censorship, he joined the chorus condemning the vicious propaganda of D. W. Griffith's *The Birth of a Nation.*[2]

But Washington was trying awkwardly and too late to accommodate deep and broad developments that enhanced Du Bois's leadership with each passing year. Segregation in the South after 1890 dulled minds and reduced tens of thousands to torpor, as was its economic and political design, yet the new version of white supremacy continued to encounter real resistance. Jim Crow, with its posted signs and arbitrary customs, could demoralize and intimidate through a thousand daily indignities. It could destroy livelihoods and entire neighborhoods periodically, as in Wilmington in 1898 and Atlanta in 1906, but the permanent leveling of the small merchant and professional classes of the cities and towns—classes that Du Bois's Atlanta University Studies showed were managing to prosper despite cruel and bulky obstacles—would have been counterproductive for the white South itself. The generation of African-Americans born after slavery was in its mid-forties and the next, like Yolande, was entering its teens. They were already reading *The Crisis*, and many would soon come under the influence of local branches of the NAACP. And there was steady movement out of the South as thousands voted with their feet against Jim Crow and went to make a living in the East and Midwest. These were motivated men and women, many skilled and schooled, who filled the ranks of the older, established African-American urban communities where Washington's agrarian and vocational program had an appeal now every bit as faint as the white South's memory of the bargain struck at Atlanta in 1895.[3]

Ironically, the Wizard himself had named the phenomenon that now undermined his power and appeal in a book published under his signature in 1900, *The New Negro for a New Century*, but Du Bois had unveiled the soul of that Negro. The latter's star was rising, if not yet as brilliantly as Ferris claimed. Overwhelmingly, the Talented Tenth thought and spoke Du Bois. Its civil rights organizations, colleges, clubs, and Greek letter and professional societies were increasingly imbued with and guided by his ideals and goals. When he declared long afterward in *Dusk of Dawn* that his "stinging hammer blows made Negroes aware of themselves . . . so much so that today common slogans among the Negro people are taken bodily from the words of my mouth," he was referring to the triumph of the trend that Ferris had ballyhooed. To believe Du Bois, however, although he was willing to inaugurate and give authoritative direction to the trend, he had no desire to lead a civil rights organization. Just as he protested that his Niagara Movement role had distracted him from scholarship and taxed his personality, he insisted that he wanted only to be left alone to run *The Crisis*. He was not a " 'mixer' and there is no use in my trying to be a popular leader," he wrote old Boston friend Butler Wilson. He had not "and never had a desire to lead the NAACP."[4]

Du Bois said this repeatedly. He saw himself as an intellectual turned propagandist, not as the general officer of an organization. On the other hand, there would be more than a few crises within the association that would convince him of the racial or moral necessity to assume command of institutional tasks that he would otherwise have wished to renounce. It was not in his nature, after all, to doubt his capacity. What controlled his every decision was the form and the reality within the NAACP of interracial deference, of active participation by the African-American officers. As he wrote later, "ordinarily the white members of the committee formed of

Negroes and whites" dominated that committee. On the other hand, "if the Negroes attempt to dominate and conduct the committee, the whites become dissatisfied and gradually withdraw." This was an *idée fixe*, a chronic Du Boisian sensibility of such tenderness that even the doting, keenly empathetic Mary Ovington sometimes failed to gauge it accurately. Yet she also understood why she failed to, once confessing to Oswald Villard that she found herself "still occasionally forgetting that the Negroes weren't poor people for whom I must kindly do something. . . . They were men with most forceful opinions of their own."[5] Any perception of the slightest racially tinged condescension or arbitrariness caused her friend to react instantaneously, vigorously, and not infrequently with an acerbity that even his partisans thought overblown or plain petty.

Du Boisian displeasure was almost never like an explosion; it was a shard of ice down the back. Time and again, Villard, Florence Kelley, Joel Spingarn, and other well-meaning officers would depart from the boardroom in a redfaced hurry, discommoded and furious. This behavior was strategic; Du Bois understood that the best defense is usually an offensive one, and that the harder and oftener hit they were, the more likely rich and powerful white people were to learn to couple genuine consideration with formal civility. Obedient to this preemptive tactic, Du Bois conducted himself in public like a wary lion, concealing uncertainty and sensitivity behind a proud tread and a readiness to spring at the first shadow in his path. The effect was one of intriguing unapproachability at its best. At its worst, it seemed boorishly arrogant, and on rare occasions he was called to account. Passing John Milholland's daughter, Inez, on Fifth Avenue near the public library one afternoon, Du Bois had looked straight ahead, not even touching the brim of his hat. When the fiery young suffragist charged into his office to demand an explanation—"You didn't speak to me!"—a stunned Du Bois fumbled for an explanation. "I didn't know whether she would dare to speak to me. . . . It wasn't up to me," he protested.

But there was more to it than that. An attentive reading of "The Souls of White Folk," written for the *Independent* in the summer of 1910, reveals a profound hardening of Du Bois's expectations of white people. A coruscating essay, it was a dark coda to *The Souls of Black Folk*. Culture made races different, and some races were demonstrably more advanced than others, Du Bois granted, but he railed against what he took to be the unique racial perversion foisted on mankind by Western civilization during the nineteenth century: "Those in whose minds the paleness of their bodily skins is fraught with tremendous and eternal significance." Yet in the sweep of time, the achievements of white folk were as recent as yesterday, he reminded readers. What tragicomic arrogance, he fumed, is the presumption that "whiteness alone is candy to the world child." At every turn, whether stated outright or revealed in facial expressions, Du Bois read the thought, "My poor un-white thing! Weep not nor rage." Interracial hypocrisy was the lot even of reformers, because, like the great majority of white souls, they tended to see only the color of a man's or woman's ability:

> So long, then, as humble black folk, voluble with thanks receive barrels of old clothes from lordly and generous whites, there is much mental and moral satisfaction. But when the black man begins to dispute the white man's title to certain alleged bequests of the Father's in wage and position, authority and training; and when his attitude toward charity is sullen anger rather than humble jollity; when he insists on his human right to swagger and swear and waste—then the spell is suddenly broken and the philanthropist is apt to be ready to believe that Negroes are impudent [and that] the South is right. . . .[6]

Du Bois took this mindset from Atlanta University to Vesey Street. "Boldly and without flinching," he threw down the gauntlet to those false collaborators "who call themselves philanthropists, and Christians and gentlemen," in "A Philosophy for 1913" in the January *Crisis*.

The Crisis was to remain a paradox from its inception—a self-financing publication whose freewheeling, militant editor was expected to advance policies of an organization guided by the careful decisions of a board of directors. With Du Bois formally answerable to the NAACP board, on which he sat as one of the thirty directors, paradox was compounded by anomaly. It was as though the first and last links in the NAACP chain of command connected to form a circle.[7] A good portion of the trouble derived from the fact that the association was in its infancy, its tactics of protest still inchoate, and its bureaucratic structures still evolving. With its incorporation in May 1911 and its adoption of Albert Pillsbury's constitution the following month, the NAACP's founding executive committee yielded to a thirty-member board of directors presided over by a president (Storey), two or more vice-presidents (Milholland and Bishop Walters), and a chairman (Villard). The salaried secretary, whose decision-making power within the association would eventually rival the chairman's, was for the time being a subordinate employee (the frustrated Frances

Blascoer). Although the full powers of office were not spelled out at the first board meeting in February 1912 (a second constitution and new bylaws would be drafted and approved in July 1914), Villard, the dedicated, imperious board chairman, naturally expected to be deferred to by his colleagues, most of whom were in fact content to do so. Ovington, for instance, seemed at first to be a model of compliancy—"a most ladylike, refined and cultivated person," the chairman wrote Uncle Francis. Moreover, she continued to be busy with labor conditions and settlement-house activities that had provided the grist for *Half a Man*, her perceptive study of the social and economic conditions of New York's African-Americans. As for salaried officers, they were expected to implement the will of the board (as communicated through the orders of the chairman) with a minimum of dissent. Press lord Villard intended to run the NAACP with the same hierarchical vigor that had been successfully applied to the new version of *The Nation*, which he predicted would be a "broad, fine paper with O.G.V. as absolute dictator of the policy."[8]

The first of many major disputes involving conflict over authority came to a head early in 1913. It was inevitable that, in the start-up competition for the association's modest resources, issues would become personalized and personalities would become inflated into issues. Du Bois's participation, however, put the inevitable into overdrive. He and Villard were kindred egos whose interplay was complicated by racial presumptions and haunted by John Brown's ghost. Collaboration could never have been other than conditional, edgy, and flammable, but Du Bois saw his role in the association as so indispensable and symbolic that virtually any interference was judged to be either racist or perverse. With a fair measure of grace, he suffered Villard's displeasure over the writing of *The Negro* on the NAACP's time. But when he was informed in the spring of 1913 that, in the interests of balanced reporting, *The Crisis* should regularly publish a list of crimes committed by African-Americans, Du Bois's forbearance ended, and he bluntly refused. "I count myself not as your subordinate," he wrote Villard, "but as a fellow officer." Called to settle the dispute, the board sided with Du Bois against Villard, probably, in part, to scotch any suggestion of undue white influence on policy, but also because, above all, as Walling reminded Villard and another board member the following year, they must "attach an extreme value to [Du Bois's] services to the Association and the cause." The board's rebuff was more than Villard could tolerate. No organization could be run effectively from three centers of authority—his own,

Du Bois's, and the board's. On April 2, 1913, a stern note reached the editor's desk: "Will you kindly make sure that my name does not appear as Contributing Editor of *The Crisis* from this time forth."[9]

Meanwhile, trouble was brewing from another quarter. At first, Du Bois ignored the intrusions of the new, salaried secretary, May Childs Nerney, a young, hot-tempered, former librarian recruited by Ovington, who brought both prodigious energy and abrasive conduct to her multiple tasks of fund-raising, publicity, branch development, and legal affairs. Blascoer, her predecessor, had wilted under the strain of her work. After resigning in March 1911, she continued for a time as a field officer, a shadowy figure whose salary Storey assumed as much for charity's sake as from real benefit to the association. Taking up her duties in May 1912, Nerney was far tougher than Blascoer, fully prepared to deal forcefully with the egos in Vesey Street—Villard, Ovington, Walters, and, most recently, former Columbia Professor Joel Elias Spingarn—in which company Du Bois ranked first among equals. From his bastion in Publicity and Research, the editor observed her brusque arrival and commended her program to build up the branches, advertise the association, and, selectively but vigorously, sue those guilty of discrimination. He found her outspokenness refreshing, and very likely enjoyed her occasional sarcasm about the elderly Storey and the elegant Spingarn. She was, he told an associate, "of excellent spirit and indefatigable energy."[10]

But he was wary. For Nerney, the association's mission demanded full cooperation from *The Crisis*; even its subordination, if need be. For Du Bois, the relationship between the NAACP and *The Crisis* was governed by the otherwise repellent doctrine of separate but equal; and the subordination of the former to the latter, if need be. The mind that once confessed to its midnight diary that it would raise a race or die trying was an unfamiliar type to the former white employee of the state library in Albany, New York. Nerney could not be expected to concede that the lucid yet mystical editor with the goatee held a monopoly over the ideals and aspirations of assertive African-Americans. For the emergent class of urban-bred professionals, Du Bois *was* the NAACP, and, as Walling sighed, it was simply necessary "to make the most sweeping concessions in order to give him free play to exercise all his abilities and energy and enthusiasm." Missing the significance of Walling's dictum, Nerney immediately pushed a reorganization program and began to complain to the board that Du Bois put the business of his department before that of the NAACP, citing the repeated failure of *The Crisis* to carry enough news about the association or to prepare and print pamphlets containing general or current information. Furthermore, she soon ran afoul of Dill, now serving as Du Bois's devoted but apparently not very competent secretary. A great hubbub was raised over a direct order of Nerney's about some minor matter that Dill had adamantly and with bare courtesy refused to obey. Complaining that Dill was insolent and uncooperative, Nerney insisted on his dismissal. When Dill stayed, Nerney tendered her own resignation in February 1913, but Villard persuaded her to reconsider and gave her a new office.[11]

In the spring of 1913, Villard had persuaded the board to create two committees in order to increase the association's efficiency. The first, charged with devising systems and economies, was composed of the dutiful Ovington; the very social Charles Studin, who was a politically ambitious attorney practicing law with Joel Spingarn's ebullient brother, Arthur; the wealthy Chicago businessman and uneasy NAACP treasurer, Walter Sachs; and Francis Batchelder, the accountant brother of Ovington's secretary. The second committee was supposed to advise *The Crisis*. Ovington, Joel Spingarn, and Reverend William Brooks assumed the responsibility for encouraging Du Bois to become more responsive to the organizational needs of the association. But neither the NAACP nor *The Crisis* was susceptible to correction by committee. The board continued to toss in a sea of policy conflict, even debating what to call the organization—either "New Abolition Movement" or "Garrison-Douglass Association."[12] New Yorkers Milholland, Walling, and Russell attended board meetings irregularly and gradually lapsed into passivity.

Tensions in the New York headquarters caused or exacerbated tensions in the association's affiliates. In Chicago, Ida Wells-Barnett once and for all withdrew from association affairs after Villard tactlessly convened a meeting of the local branch without informing her. In Washington, the second-largest branch was in raucous disarray as Archibald Grimké and other dissidents tried to oust Milton Waldron, the local president, for soft-pedaling criticism of Woodrow Wilson's federal segregation policies, allegedly in order to gain political office. Vice-President Walters, whose self-esteem was every bit as healthy as the chairman's, finally resigned his office in November after Villard publicly drew a connection between Walters's appointment as minister to Liberia and his reluctance to attack Wilson's segregationist policies. Grimké took his place. In Boston, a sulky Monroe Trotter obstructed the work of the local branch, partly because of Du Bois's barely concealed disregard. The January 1914 *Crisis* had somehow not found it newsworthy that a Trotter-led delegation from the

National Equal Rights League had made national headlines by being granted an audience with President Wilson to protest federal segregationist policies. Storey sent a formal complaint to Spingarn's *Crisis* committee, which Du Bois answered by claiming (unconvincingly) that the magazine's copy had already been set.[13]

Du Bois continued on his own course, taking an extended promotional circuit throughout the Southwest into California and Oregon during summer 1913. "Twenty-eight talks to audiences aggregating 18,000 human souls," he rhapsodized in *The Crisis*, and he claimed to be "overwhelmed almost to silence" by all that he had seen, heard, and felt. Censorious *Crisis* editorials rained down on the black church, black colleges, and black newspapers, as well as the sympathetic *Survey Graphic* for declining to publish one of his essays. He continued to be polite toward Nerney, though now he quietly complained that she had a "violent temper and [was] depressingly suspicious of motives." Nerney herself slowly came to appreciate the complexities of her position, writing to Grimké, whom she had begun cultivating as an ally against Du Bois, "really this job requires more tact and patience than I possess."[14] Although she still found Du Bois's arrogance troubling, Nerney also wrote that she was "beginning to understand better everyday Mr. Du Bois's attitude" as Villard behaved even more high-handedly than the editor. She was about ready to fall in line with a plan to strip the chairman of his powers. Her plan, however, called for replacing Villard not with Du Bois but with Vice-President Grimké. The last board meeting of the year, in late November 1913, was a climax of frustrations. The more Du Bois and Villard grew to detest each other, the more their movements became like two boxers elaborately squaring off for a murderous pounding.

Du Bois had prepared for the bout, meeting beforehand with Ovington and the Spingarn brothers to win their support for his own three-point plan to restructure the association. *Crisis* circulation figures were on a hard rise, in part due to the 18,000 "human souls" Du Bois claimed to have addressed in thirty states during the year. By early 1914, still increasing, *The Crisis* would reach 33,000 subscribers. Because the editor's salary and travel expenses were charged to the NAACP, Villard maintained that a thriving *Crisis* was largely the result of its connection with the association, while Du Bois dismissed this as an accountant's quibble. Under the first of his three points, then, the association and the magazine would sever their ties completely. Du Bois proposed to make *The Crisis* his own instrument just as Villard was about to make the revitalized *Nation* his. If the board refused, then the editor recommended (in his second point) making Ovington chairwoman, hiring a young African-American as executive secretary, and placing himself under salaried contract to the NAACP as the editor of *The Crisis*. Such a contract, presumably, would impose few editorial restrictions.

The third alternative, which Du Bois claimed he least preferred, would merge the office of secretary with that of director of publicity and research. With the likely departure of Villard, to be replaced either by Ovington or Joel Spingarn, this arrangement would give him effective control of the association, a goal he now secretly harbored. That prospect "nearly made a wreck of me and almost caused a riot in my family," Nerney gasped to Grimké. For Villard, the stark choice was the NAACP or Du Bois. Things had come to such a pass, he informed the board, that he could "no longer conscientiously remain as Chairman of the Board, without having the function of that position more clearly defined."[15] Dill had "directly refused to obey official instructions" and the public was being misled into believing that an entirely out-of-control magazine spoke for the multiple goals and programs of a national organization. The situation was intolerable, Villard continued; Du Bois's title ought to be changed to editor of *The Crisis* and the magazine and staff severed from the association. The chairman's proposal would save the NAACP more than three thousand dollars in *Crisis* salaries and expenditures, and, as intended, it called Du Bois's bluff on the issue of running the magazine by himself.

The board stretched to keep both men in its embrace, principally relying on Ovington and Joel Spingarn to encourage tact in Du Bois and magnanimity from Villard. A certain affinity of temperament drew Du Bois and Spingarn together, a New England kinship of patrician combativeness and superior culture. Gracious and generous toward their few intimates, both men projected a frosty elegance in public and professional settings. Fluent in languages, a master teacher and internationally read author, disciple of Italian philosopher Benedetto Croce, and founder himself of the American school of New Criticism in literature, Spingarn, like the editor of *The Crisis*, was contemptuous of compromise. When Nicholas Butler, Columbia's headstrong, autocratic president, dismissed without due process a prominent professor accused of an extramarital affair in 1911, threatening what little remained of faculty rights, Spingarn had spoken out, resigned in protest, and in the serenity of Troutbeck, his Hudson River estate, composed "Heloise sans Abelard," a famously mocking poem about the travesty.

O passionate Heloise,
I too have lived under the ban,
With seven hundred professors,
And not a single man.[16]

While Du Bois weighed the counsel of someone he considered to be his intellectual near-equal, Villard pondered the full implications of Ovington's letter about his own resignation as chairman. "To you it means just Dr. Du Bois and Mr. Dill," she warned, "but to me it means a confession to the world that we cannot work with colored people unless they are our subordinates." Did he really wish to set an example by which "everyone who believes in segregation will become a little more firmly convinced that he is right?"[17] By giving neither man complete satisfaction, the board hoped to make room for their monumental egos. Villard had the satisfaction of seeing Du Bois's bid for the secretaryship, along with other alternatives in his three-point plan, rejected. Du Bois was consoled by the vote to defer any further enhancement of the powers of the chairman and by Dill's retention. On balance, however, the editor emerged in a slightly stronger position vis-à-vis his chief critic, which had the effect of transforming the intolerable into the humiliating, from Villard's point of view. With Nerney indicating her lack of support, Ovington ever faithful to his adversary, and Walling alarmed that Du Bois might resign, Villard decided to step down, rightly suspecting that he was about to be stripped of authority. The threatened November resignation became a fact at the end of the year. Joel Spingarn, whose boardroom manners were more pleasing all around, became chairman while Villard, explaining to Ovington that, "quite aside from the question of Dr. Du Bois," his other affairs had begun to suffer, assumed the post of treasurer. Shortly thereafter, and much to Villard's relief, the association moved to 70 Fifth Avenue, where the editor arranged for more expensive space ($108 per month, twice the cost of the Vesey Street office) than the unconsulted new chairman had anticipated. Villard would remain unshakably convinced that *The Crisis* was "never going to do the service or have the influence it ought to until it had another editor."[18]

The new *Crisis* quarters at 70 Fifth Avenue hummed. The building, a tall white one owned by Ginn and Company, publishers, was larger than Villard's, equipped with more elevators, and, Du Bois wrote John Hope, more "light and air. Do drop in." Behind a large, heavy, dark wooden desk, an immaculate, waistcoated Du Bois read copy and correspondence into a Dictaphone whose wax cylinders he regularly shaved and recycled. The self-important Dill put his talents, Harvard-honed in sociology, to accounts and editorial work (replacing Frank M. Turner, the tall, sharp-featured circulation manager whom the magazine had had to share with the NAACP); and Albon L. Holsey, the round-faced, cross-looking little advertising manager, demonstrated the high-level dedication that the editor expected of him. There was now space for a large safe as well as a new, electric multigraph machine that saved up to fifty dollars monthly in printing costs. Various secretarial duties were discharged by Misses Allison, Jarvis, and Sousa, all of whom looked more southern European than the attractive, presumably competent, African-Americans they were. The total staff rose to eight not long after the move from Vesey Street, leading Nerney to begin referring to Du Bois's "personal machine." It was all wrong, she wrote Grimké. "People were employed because of personal devotion to him, and retained for that reason."[19] To Du Bois, Nerney's concerns—although well-meaning—seemed as misguided as Villard's.

But putting distance between the editor of *The Crisis* and the master of *The Nation* left fundamental problems unresolved. The root cause of the NAACP's troubles was its split personality, its institutional uncertainty as to what its primary mission should be. Because progressive white people had founded it, the organization was inclined to proceed in its litigation, lobbying, and propaganda efforts in a phased and deliberate manner, mindful of the racial prejudices and stereotypes harbored by the majority of Americans, and of what they themselves often perceived as the unfortunate yet understandable reasons behind such prejudices and stereotypes. More than half the association's annual budget of about $11,000 came from eighteen white philanthropists, men and women who believed that, in order to fight racism, it made sense to deemphasize race, and to whom, therefore, much of the thunder and lightning in *The Crisis* seemed dangerously inflammatory. Jane Addams, Albert Pillsbury, Florence Kelley, and the tentative Reverend John Holmes, among others, were inclined to agree that Du Bois failed to hold the scales of justice between the races "absolutely even by scoring colored wrongdoers precisely as he scores white offenders." To Villard, it sometimes seemed that Du Bois invariably took the side of the colored man against the white man "and never stops to ask what the facts are on the other side."[20]

And running deeper than questions of policy and strategy was the bedrock of psychology. Villard spoke for what might have been called the Fourteenth and Fifteenth Amendment reformers, the privileged white people who championed the constitutional rights of black people but were distinctly unsympathetic to aspirations of "social equality." At its crudest, most visceral, social equality meant interracial sex, whether blessed by marriage vows or not—explicitly, black men possessing white women. In its sublimated form, social equality meant impertinent demeanor or expression, intrusion into "white" social space, and the obliteration of all the "natural" and necessary economic and professional hierarchies based on skin color. Du Bois was absolutely convinced that one of his essays had been rejected by the usually friendly *Survey* editor Paul U. Kellogg because of a paragraph unequivocally calling on the African-American to "demand his social rights: His right to be treated as a gentleman, when he acts like one, to marry any sane, grown person who wants to marry him, and to meet and eat with his friends without being accused of undue assumption or unworthy ambition." As late as 1920, Florence Kelley, bustling and bristling, would threaten resignation from the board unless the NAACP dissociated itself from a *Crisis* editorial in which Du Bois had explained that social equality was "just as much a human right as political or economic equality."[21]

Thus, with the Old Testament prose of *The Souls of Black Folk* and the jeremiads and Carlylian effulgences of *Crisis* editorials, Du Bois sought to transform his people's leadership class through inspiration, agitation, and even imprecation. "The jeremiads were needed to redeem a people," he wrote in one *Crisis* editorial. Forty years later, the anti-imperialist philosopher Frantz Fanon would almost certainly have Du Bois in mind when he exhorted the nonwhites of the world to unite and risk losing nothing but the chains of their minds. Writing of its cleansing power in *The Wretched of the Earth*, this Afro-French psychiatrist from Martinique, whose ideas would fuel revolutions from Algeria to Cuba, proclaimed that violence liberated the oppressed "from his inferiority complex and from his despair and inaction; it makes him fearless and restores his self-respect." For Du Bois, physical violence—assassinations, conspiracies, barricades—was repugnant in principle and counterproductive in practice. But the violence of ideas, the insurgency of attitudes, the rupture of deference, and the constitutional assault upon oppressive institutions were the essential preconditions of black racial liberation. It was self-evident to him that had not *The Crisis* "been in a sense a personal organ and the expression of myself," it would never have attained its popularity and effectiveness.[22]

When it was not hurling thunderbolts, *The Crisis* dripped acid, issue after issue. Mordant observations and gratuitous asides filled its pages. Writing about his summer 1913 promotional trip to the "Great Northwest" and the warm reception among Seattle's minority community, the editor remarked that it took "extraordinary training, gift and opportunity to make the average white man anything but an overbearing hog, but the most ordinary Negro is an instinctive gentleman." The August issue covering the western trip carried a full-page photograph of the editor standing with a well-dressed group of citizens, captioned "Colored Los Angeles Greets *The Crisis*," once again enraging Villard, who pointed out to the board that the NAACP had been, as usual, ignored. Theodore Roosevelt's invidious essay in *The Outlook*, "Brazil and the Negro," Du Bois deemed barely worthy of rebuttal. Unable to avoid noticing Brazil's large African and racially mixed population at the end of his spring 1914 visit, the globetrotting former president commended the absence of a color bar there—which Du Bois applauded—but he went on to claim that in the United States the best men believe " 'in treating each man of whatever color absolutely on his worth as a man, allowing him full opportunity to achieve the success warranted by his ability and integrity' "—which Du Bois heatedly denied. Roosevelt compounded mendacity with insult by observing that Brazilians regarded the "Negro element" in their blood as a slight weakening. All this was nonsense, the editor fumed, quoting *in extenso* Brazilian authorities; but to expect Roosevelt to write about race relations "without twistings and equivocation is to expect the millennium."[23]

Did the editor really "imagine that it is the slightest help to our purpose to denounce Mr. Roosevelt's statement as a 'falsehood'?" a distinguished white sympathizer cautioned about such provocation. The sarcastic *Crisis* reply was that the African-American "has nothing but 'friends' and may the good God deliver him from most of them, for they are like to lynch his soul." " 'Don't antagonize, don't be bitter; say the conciliatory thing; make friends and do not repel them; insist on and emphasize the cheerful and good and dwell as little as possible on wrong and evil' "—this was the counsel of those who expected every African-American to sound like Booker T. Washington. "But Mr. Dole's feet [the white sympathizer] never walked the ways we tread. He does not know—he cannot conceive this darker world of insult, repression, hunger, and murder," Du Bois wrote with almost personal poignancy. "He and Charles William Eliot and Woodrow Wilson and millions of others have given no encouragement to lynching except by silence! *Except by silence*! EXCEPT BY SILENCE!"[24] From Calhoun, Georgia, came a subscription check and Jessie E. Guernsey's grateful letter. Miss Guernsey allowed her name to be published in the letters column, fearlessly declaring that what improvements there had been in relations between the races had been due not to patience and compromise but to "the constantly increasing number of able, educated, cultivated men and women of the race who . . . bring a new demand for recognition and give the question of social justice new prominence and new meaning." E. C. Williams, principal of the District of Columbia's M Street Public High School, found Du Bois's well-phrased pugnacity admirable. It improved with age, Williams wrote, "and it alone justifies the existence of the NAACP," a view that most African-Americans shared.[25]

For the association's white conservatives, as well as for a few old Niagarites like Archibald Grimké and Butler Wilson, this galloping tendency to regard Du Bois as the personification of the movement was the height of poor judgment. When all-white Johns Hopkins University rejected the application of a qualified African-American high school graduate, Du Bois passed over the dean's barely plausible explanations to blast the university's hypocrisy—another occasion for Villard to protest *The Crisis* going off "half cocked on this as it had so many other things." The collapse of a dogged vocational experiment of his friend Will Benson, the handsome dreamer from Kowaliga, Alabama, brought an impassioned May 1915 editorial indicting flabby white philanthropists for taking their cues from a silent, hostile Booker Washington. Villard, who was marginally involved in Kowaliga, was furious again. Fine white men who let Benson have "too free a reign" were being defamed for trying to uplift a needy people. "Simply incredible. It is treason to the race," he fumed to Joel Spingarn.[26]

Even Ovington winced occasionally over her hero's editorials, finally taking a deep breath to advise from the family building at 246 Fulton Street that she had begun to feel "there was something the matter with *The Crisis* from the viewpoint of its white readers." With the greatest delicacy, she wrote that she did wonder if, in his own way, Du Bois was not sometimes as abrasive as Villard. Must he really offend white readers "by saying that they are reactionary heathen" and constantly make them feel that they were insulting him "when they have no insult in their heart?" Ovington closed by asking if the association were not a "work for colored and white people to do together," or was it instead "a work of revolution for the colored people only? . . . Should we preach race consciousness just as the socialist preaches class consciousness . . . ?" From a well-earned, active retirement, Horace Bumstead also felt compelled to give his erstwhile subordinate a "scolding." For some months past, the former Atlanta University president had been "disturbed" over the conduct of *The Crisis*. He was finding "it hard to defend [Du Bois] with friends who come to me with complaints." There had been an attack on the Episcopal Church, a savage personal attack on the editor of *The Congregationalist*, and, most troubling of all, Du Bois had ignored Trotter's "unexcelled" plain speaking to President Wilson. "Is there something demoralizing in an editor's chair," the old abolitionist asked the scholar who had made Atlanta University world famous. Lamely explaining again that a deadline and subsequent editorial slip had kept Trotter out of the magazine, Du Bois replied that it still seemed to him that Episcopalians were "a little ahead" when it came to sin.[27]

Like the Jacobin followers of Danton during the French Revolution, civil rights–conscious African-Americans expected audacity above all from Du Bois, his magazine, and his organization. By 1919, when the contributions of more than 62,000 members, the great majority of them black, would make up most of its $44,000 operating budget, Du Bois's vision of the civil rights struggle in America as the driving wedge in the global empowerment of darker peoples would find greater resonance in the association's program. To this end, organizational requirements, matters of budget and agenda, the sensitivities of fellow officers, additional personnel to build branches, and even scarce resources needed to haul malefactors before the courts, were secondary. Villard and his kind, Du Bois knew, could never fully understand that if black people in America did not build their own regiments and raise up their own colonels and generals, then both the plan of battle and the terms of the armistice would be compromised. He would see the contest with Villard in Zeitgeistian terms in the *Autobiography*, writing that it might be understood "as a matter of the actions and thoughts of certain men, or as a development of larger social forces beyond personal control." He supposed the latter aspect "is the truer."[28]

Meanwhile, the struggle over the organizational direction raged throughout 1914 and 1915. April 1914 was especially rancorous. In his new post as treasurer, Villard now insisted that all departments, including that of the director of publicity and research, submit their books for line-item scrutiny. It was the only way, he insisted, that economies and lines of authority essential to the association's effectiveness could be enforced. At the strained board meeting on April 7, Du Bois icily demurred when Joel Spingarn invited comments on the proposed restructuring of the association. Simply unacceptable, he declared, brushing aside the treasurer's spluttering objections and forcing the matter to the table. It was obvious to all that a test of wills was at hand. "Vexed" at Spingarn for failing to call the editor on what he decried as the "outrageous assault" on his dignity, Villard raged that Du Bois "show[ed] himself in his true colors. What a pity that he was never house-broken." One more such contretemps, Villard continued, and he would "be through." Du Bois was telling Ovington the same thing in a long letter two days later. They had come to a parting of the ways. Probably it was better "to fight the matter out now" on the issue of whether the NAACP was to stand on its "original radical platform or is to go that way of conservative compromise which turned the Ogden movement, the Southern Education Board and the General Education Board so completely from their original purpose." This new reorganization plan aimed to put him and *The Crisis* "under the immediate charge" of Villard; it barred "all real initiative"; and its adoption would be tantamount "to a vote or lack of confidence and [he] should immediately resign [his] position." "No other executive officer is thus humiliated," he maintained, ignoring the fact that he was the only executive officer who wore two hats. He knew what Villard was up to. "He opposed my coming to the position in the first place."[29]

Du Bois clearly intended to get rid of his nemesis. For his part, Villard made it plain that what had eluded him as the board's chief officer he was now determined to enforce through vouchers and audits. Minutes of board meetings during this period reflect Du Bois's dogged determination to have his way, to save the association, as he believed, by wrenching it from the groove into which Villard had forced it. "Each member of the Board is urged to be present and to express his opinion on this very important matter," read a late-March notice about a new Du Bois scheme to reduce the treasurer's duties to fund-raising, transfer chairman Spingarn's powers to a new executive committee, and make *The Crisis* the exclusive province of its editor. Du Bois had what must have been an especially candid talk that March with Spingarn to win his support. The following day, he received a diplomatic reassurance that Spingarn's "criticism was not offered in the spirit of fault-finding but (as friend's criticism should always be) was given for no other purpose than that of helping."[30] Hoping to defuse the explosive overhaul proposal, Spingarn, Ovington, Brooks, Milholland, Sinclair, and others succeeded in deferring action at three roiling April meetings until a special subcommittee headed by Studin could propose new bylaws at a meeting in June or July. But while Spingarn went to Louisville, Kentucky, to organize the local branch's protest of the city's recent residential segregation ordinance, civil war erupted in the association.

The plan to vest the board's powers in a new executive committee had originated with Nerney. Like Du Bois, she sensed growing conservative tendencies in the astonishing new recommendation by the committee impaneled to award the association's new Spingarn Medal to Hampton Institute administrator Robert Russa Moton. The forceful secretary helped scotch the bestowal of the medal on the coming leader of the Bookerites. The first Spingarn Medal would go instead to Dartmouth alumnus Ernest Everett Just, a young cytologist and Howard University professor. But Nerney's reorganization plan would have put Spingarn, herself, and Grimké on the new executive committee. After the board dawdled, Du Bois aggressively reintroduced her plan as his own with himself in a starring role. If protecting his monopoly over *The Crisis* meant that he must take over the running of the NAACP, Du Bois was finally prepared to do so. To Nerney and Grimké, he seemed clearly bent on usurping the association. Even the funds for the legal campaign against the grandfather clause in Oklahoma and the spread of residential segregation were diverted to *The Crisis*. His department of publicity and research went "gaily on expanding merrily while the NAACP is forced to retrench and retrench," Nerney charged with only slight exaggeration.[31]

Despite the alleged budget constraints, 1915 was to be a banner year for the NAACP's embryonic legal department. Although he elected not to appear before the Supreme Court himself, Storey's brief on the unconstitutionality of the Oklahoma grandfather clause was accepted as an *amicus curiae* (friend of the court) argument in *Guinn v. United States*. Oklahoma's preferential registration of white voters was unanimously struck down, with Chief Justice Edward D. White, ex-Confederate and Bourbon Redeemer, writing the first opinion to nullify a state law under the Fifteenth Amendment in forty-five years. Still, Villard became more acerbic and Nerney continued to storm and threaten, provoking an annoyed Du Bois's accusation that, although the secretary hadn't "an ounce of conscious prejudice, . . . her every step is unconsciously along the color line."[32] It was, in the end, a question of two incommensurable perspectives. Fifteen years later, Villard would entitle a book about his visit to the Soviet Union *Russia from a Car Window*. A book about his civil rights perspective might have been called *Race Relations from the Boardroom*. Ovington above all tried to help him understand. She knew that they could "never agree about Du Bois," she told Villard during one of her numerous unsuccessful attempts to make him see the world through the eyes of a black man. "He does do dangerous things. He strikes out at people with a harshness and directness that appalls me," she admitted, "but the blow is often deserved and it is never below the belt."[33] Du Bois's perspective was that of his beleaguered people who were deprived of the ballot and lynched in the South, shut out of labor unions and socially ostracized in the North, taxed to pay for public education systems that excluded them. It was one in which the virtues of patience and objectivity seemed as dubiously beneficial to him as to Native Americans on reservations or Zulu farmers in South Africa.

The anxiously awaited July 1914 meeting of the board resulted in sharper varsity combat between the editor and the treasurer, with victory going to the editor. Although the new bylaws, investing the chairman with full executive authority and the treasurer with audit powers over all the association's departments, were approved, Du Bois demanded a vote effectively nullifying them. Under Du Bois's proposal, full powers would be vested in a new executive committee, each of its four members—chairman, treasurer, editor, and secretary—equal in power: "The Executive Committee shall meet as often as necessary and shall have general supervision over the work of the . . . Association and all the departments thereof"—and it was obvious that, under this plan, board meetings would decrease and executive meetings would increase. Spingarn was left to run the association; Du Bois reigned at *The Crisis*. Florence Kelley joined Villard in outraged objection, but the majority, having just reasserted dominion over *The Crisis*, blinked and reversed itself, giving Du Bois exactly what he wanted—impunity to run his department through an executive quartet in which no member had more power than the others. At long last, correct principles and respectful authority seemed to mesh, Du Bois wanted to believe—"two branches of the same work, one with a white head and one with a colored; working in harmony and sympathy for one end."[34] Everything about Joel Spingarn presaged actual collaboration. From the moment Du Bois had seconded Spingarn's nomination to the board, the two intellectuals had grown closer personally and in organizational understanding. The editor saw himself finally being left alone to fight racism from the pages of *The Crisis* while the new chairman, seconded by an admiring Ovington, kept Villard and Nerney in check, on the one hand, and did all he could, on the other, to put association resources behind the editor.

FREQUENTLY CHARACTERIZING their mission as the "New Abolitionism" (there had been a notable public tiff with Villard when Spingarn claimed that William Lloyd Garrison would never have advocated meekness), Spingarn spoke Du Bois's language. Shortly after joining the board, Spingarn had begun tireless, annual travels north, south, and west across the country, first as chair of the branches committee then as board chair, in order to explain the NAACP and drum up support among white people as well as black. He had little of the gregariousness of his younger brother Arthur. With his gleaming black hair, long, dark face, and intense eyes that drew men and women into his discourse, Spingarn propagated the faith on black and white college campuses, in churches of every denomination, men's and women's clubs of high and low social standing—everywhere and among anyone to whom the new abolitionism (immediate winning of civil rights for African-Americans) brought confidence and commitment. Ovington had always understood that, in order to build mass support, the NAACP had to be seen as a crusading force increasingly guided by African-Americans themselves. If Villard ever grasped this, he was temperamentally incapable of conveying any urgent commitment to such a goal. Joel Spingarn understood, believed, and had the requisite fire and flair. With his ascent to the chairmanship, the Bookerite tendencies in the association decidedly waned. He had told a group of African-Americans shortly after joining the board that he was "tired, too, of the philanthropy of rich white men toward your race." He wanted black people to "fight your own battles with your own leaders and your own money."[35]

There were times when Villard was almost as uneasy about the former professor's ideas as about the editor's. Had Spingarn's civil rights radicalism been matched by economic radicalism, Villard would probably have bailed out the NAACP altogether, and Du Bois's evolving socialism very likely would have speeded up. But when it came to property rights, income distribution, and government regulation of business, Joel Spingarn was much more cautious than his hero Teddy Roosevelt. His biographer, B. Joyce Ross, called him an "economic liberal"—that is, not very liberal at all. His words, she wrote, were to be "more provocative than his actions throughout his career in the NAACP."[36] The words of this humanist, whose austere elegance and lofty eloquence evoked the image of some scholar prince of the Renaissance wandered into the twentieth century, stirred Du Bois deeply. "I do not think that any other white man ever touched me emotionally so closely," was Du Bois's astonishing verdict on their courtly, contentious friendship. He added that he was "both fascinated and antagonized by some of his quick and positive judgments." Their affinity was as intense as the misunderstandings between them were analytically merciless. For almost three years, however, Du Bois and Spingarn worked together almost without friction. The similarity in temperament and civil rights optic was strikingly evident during their trip together to Memphis in 1914 to protest the exclusion of African-American delegates to a national conference of charitable organizations. Instead of quietly buttonholing key officers or submitting petitions to the appropriate committees, Spingarn and Du Bois hired a local hall and placed a full-page statement in the Memphis *Commercial Appeal*—"All Those Who Love Truth and Dare Hear It Are Cordially Invited."[37]

The Crisis gave generous coverage to Spingarn's speaking tours. "NAACP Notes" for March 1915 reported, "This tour, like the one a year ago, resulted in the widest publicity in the white as well as the colored press." The chairman's progress from Chicago to Topeka had been a triumph. After a hard-hitting speech at Chicago's Lincoln Center, Spingarn was warned by wealthy young Roger N. Baldwin (Villard's private school classmate and nephew of William) that he would not be allowed to address the City Club of St. Louis unless he tamed his withering references to Booker Washington. Informing the future head of the American Civil Liberties Union that he would rather withdraw than limit his freedom of speech, Spingarn (tailed by Baldwin) proceeded to give a somewhat modulated speech to the St. Louis club. A fascinating sidelight on the racial preconceptions of the times turns up in his letter to Amy Einstein, his artistic, southern-born wife, after the St. Louis City Club talk: a local reporter had wanted to know "insolently (or perhaps merely in ignorance) whether I was a Negro."[38]

Spingarn's magnetism pulled in a wide variety of people. Students in Fisk University's Cravath Memorial Chapel were stirred, and they, in turn, deeply stirred Spingarn. Reporting to Amy of that April 1912 epiphany, Joel said that he had risen to tell them "to be strong and wise and good, not for their sakes but for my country's, which could not fulfill my vision of its ideal beauty and justice unless they were wise and good and strong." He wrote Amy of his utter agony at having to abide by the etiquette of Jim Crow on a sleeper heading for Memphis in which it had been necessary to talk separately to a noted white southern educator, James Hardy Dillard ("almost ashamed of some of the half-measures he himself is obliged to support") and a distinguished African-American professor at Howard University, "unless I wanted to embarrass Dillard and his work." Lunch in Atlanta with Du Bois's best friend, John Hope, left him with the ethnocentric thought that the Morehouse president was a man "absolutely indistinguishable in looks, culture, instinct, or temperament from an educated white man, and a very fine one at that."[39]

As he moved among black people, perhaps because of his own people's historic troubles, Spingarn's observations were generally distinguished by nuance, depth, minimal preconception, and broad understanding. "I have seen the negro do almost everything," he wrote Amy from the South in 1912—"perform a surgical operation, fill teeth, print 300,000 copies of a pamphlet in his own printing plant, work in the factories of the white man, teach and learn, and (at the other end of life) sink to the level of yielding to the white man's pleasure, and you will want to hear these things when I get back to town, but not now." Spingarn, the supremely assimilated Austrian Jew, also keenly observed other Jews in his travels, writing Amy from Kansas City in a somewhat superior tone about the well-known lawyer and civic reformer Jacob Billikopf, of Russian origins. Related by marriage to one of New York's most influential Jewish families, future NAACP board member Billikopf, "despite every alien touch of speech and feature, has won for himself a real place in the civic life of a whole city."[40]

Later, in a reflective mood, Du Bois spoke of his friend as one of those "vivid, enthusiastic but clear-thinking idealists which from age to age the Jewish race has given the world." Yet Joel Spingarn presented himself to the world, and to the association, as an upper-class unhyphenated American, of formidable humanist culture, and only then, and incidentally, as a Jew. Insofar as he allowed his motives for devotion to the NAACP to be fathomed, he explained them in terms of a sense of justice and a void stemming from his splendid exit from academe. His consternation upon reading of the barbarous treatment of the Arkansas farmer Steve Greene, extradited from Chicago, had indeed impelled him to volunteer his services to Villard, Ovington, and Du Bois. The fact that he was Jewish was, nonetheless, certainly not irrelevant. In the valuable collection of essays edited by Charles Herbert Stember, *Jews in the Mind of America* (1966), one contributor's observation that, "as history has shown only too often, any serious strain in a society may become a threat to Jews," suggests the motive behind Spingarn's motives.[41] The "race problem" in Spingarn's America—its lynchings, disfranchisings, economic exclusions, educational deprivations, and social stigmas—remained overwhelmingly a "Negro" problem, but, as it spread from the South in a period of great influx from eastern Europe and of deepening industrial unrest, antagonism against African-Americans would inevitably spawn a contagion infecting even those Jews with deep roots in the republic.

Spingarn's presence in the NAACP coincided roughly with the arrival of Jewish philanthropy in Afro-America, with Jacob Schiff's Tuskegee beneficence, Sears, Roebuck and Company president Julius Rosenwald's funding of a good part of the South's black public school buildings, and

Benjamin Altman and Dorothy Straus's support of the National Urban League. The tradition of giving was ancient in the Jewish community, commanded by scripture and strengthened by adversities in times and places near and remote. One of the nation's leading constitutional lawyers, Louis Marshall, a founder of the American Jewish Committee and president of New York's Temple Emanu-El, had warned the men and women of his circle that they would cut a "sorry figure" indeed by not denouncing racial discrimination against black people in America as they lifted their voices against pogroms in Russia. Moreover, on the authority of the founder of modern Zionism himself, a vague affinity between Jews and transplanted Africans was said to exist. A character in *Altneuland*, Theodor Herzl's 1903 novel, proclaimed, "The depths of that problem in all their horror, only a Jew can fathom. I mean the Negro problem."[42]

Second-nature generosity received further incentive through status-enhancing collaboration with Carnegie and Rockefeller benefactions. Great Jewish fortunes began supplementing the older, Protestant charities by the close of the first decade of the century, encouraged by Gentile veterans of "Negro uplift" grateful for their millions and who hinted at future quid pro quo in boardrooms and clubhouses. Almost from the moment of its creation, increasing Jewish interest in the NAACP had come with the ceremonial or actual involvement among others of Henry Moskowitz, Lillian Wald, Edwin Seligman, Jacob Mack, and Rabbi Stephen Wise. Voted at the 1910 National Negro Conference, the so-called Russian Resolution condemning the government-sponsored pogrom and renewed expulsion of Jews from Kiev had been applauded and was undoubtedly a factor in Jacob Schiff's annual donations through Du Bois during the association's early years. Genuine compassion combined with sage self-interest, therefore, to prompt many Uptown Jews to begin monitoring the evolving social welfare and civil rights status of African-Americans.[43]

Anti-Semitism was not something Spingarn was inclined to discuss publicly. Even within his circle, anti-Semitism was talked about obliquely and guardedly, although it had been festering and spreading in America since the late 1800s. Yet alert and influential Jews were uneasy. Clubs in which their membership had once been accepted, like New York's prestigious Union League (with Jews among its founders), now excluded them. University trusteeships were closing to them, even at Columbia where, as long ago as the 1780s, the learned Rabbi Sheareth Israel had sat among the college's benefactors.[44] Still, notwithstanding the paranoid style in populism, prejudice against Jews had remained diffuse in America until the onset of the twentieth century. Jewish faith in the American creed of merit and mobility remained unshaken. The Uptown Jews deemed their robust commercial establishments, powerful financial institutions, and majestic reform temples, as well as their splendid contributions to science, law, and the humanities, to be sturdy rungs to the commanding heights of national status and influence. Interviewed in the same city where five years later he would dramatically reverse himself on Zionism, Louis Brandeis summed up the attitude of these assimilationists in 1910, telling a reporter from Boston's *Jewish Advocate*, "Habits of living or of thought which tend to keep alive difference of origin or classify men according to their beliefs are inconsistent with the American ideal of brotherhood, and are disloyal."[45]

There was something of paradox, and of dilemma, then, in their quest for high standing among the Gentile rich and powerful, because what Spingarn and his class really desired was eventually to win recognition *as Jews* by leading superlative public lives no different in appearance, customs, and values from those of wealthy Protestant, and largely Republican, Americans. Schiff's "confidential" note to Villard when department-store millionaire and civic benefactor Benjamin Altman died in the fall of 1914 captured the paradox perfectly. Could not Villard have the *Evening Post* present this life as a fine object lesson to the million or so Jewish people in New York, suggested Schiff, since no newspaper had mentioned that Altman "has lived and died as a Jew. When a Jew does any wrong haste is only too frequently made to emphasize the fact that it was a Jew who has done it," the great banker reminded Villard. "Everybody knows that he was a Jew," the blunt publisher replied, managing in the same breath both to affirm and dismiss the significance of Altman's Jewishness. "To draw attention to the fact would . . . rather diminish than increase the moral effect of that knowledge."[46]

In the recent past, Spingarn and his class had seen the new virulence as largely centered in the lower classes and aimed mainly at the hundreds of thousands of inrushing poor from Russia, Poland, and the Balkans, who were almost as exotic and vexatious to them as to the Anglo-Saxon Protestant families whose social respect had been so successfully cultivated. But now the so-called Uptown Jews—the Altmans, Guggenheims, Lehmans, Schiffs, Seligmans, Sulzbergers, and other wealthy Ashkenazic families whose ancestors had come to the United States during the long German migration from 1830 to 1880—began to see the 1.5 million Jewish newcomers streaming through Ellis Island after 1896 as the source of growing misunderstanding and hostility. Conditions were ripe for a scapegoating that could well make the genteel discrimination of the last few decades seem benign and trivial. That many influential Jews began to feel ambivalent and vaguely unsure was scarcely surprising in a time when a successful Atlanta Jewish businessman of upstanding Confederate pedigree, Leo Frank, could be convicted in 1913 of raping little Mary Phagan, a white employee, on the testimony of a black janitor. An American Dreyfus Affair in the making, the case was cut short two years later when a redneck mob, riled up by the fallen Populist leader Tom Watson, lynched Leo Frank in the Marietta, Georgia, town square a few days after the governor commuted his death sentence.[47] After 1900 (with all the influx portended for Spingarn and Samuel Gompers), three out of every four Jewish immigrants to America came from the Russian pale. As they streamed past Emma Lazarus's inscription beckoning the huddled masses, Jewish commentators in Lower East Side union halls as well as Uptown mansions drew closer parallels between these immigrants and black people—peoples of two diasporas. Abraham Cahan, the editor of the Socialist *Jewish Daily Forward*, would find an exact one in the East St. Louis race riot of 1917 and the Kishinev pogrom of 1903.[48] Increasingly after 1910, philanthropy and civil rights in Afro-America attracted sustained Jewish participation.

Joel Spingarn kept up his scholarly interests, producing anthologies and works of criticism. He played a major part in founding the publishing house of Harcourt, Brace in 1914. But until he left for military service after America entered the Great War, what most often and urgently took him away from Troutbeck, his fine country estate in Dutchess County, New York, was service to the NAACP. Arthur, his less-glamorous brother, had already begun to replace Storey as the association's chief legal advisor. As the influence of the Spingarns grew, Du Bois's interaction with them became more crucial to the evolution of the NAACP than ever before. The July reorganization vote having gone his way, he thought the lines of authority between the NAACP and *The Crisis* were more or less permanently disentangled. The splitting of the association's authority among Spingarn, Villard, Nerney, and himself was deemed by Du Bois as much superior to any unitary and hierarchical arrangement. The overall financial health and circulation figures of his magazine were robust. While the new legal department slowly prepared its briefs for cases that could be resolved only one case at a time and after long intervals, his magazine gave monthly encouragement to the race and monthly heartburn to hypocrites and racists. *The Crisis* had nearly forty thousand monthly readers, and Du Bois remitted half of the one-dollar annual subscription to the association's treasury, potent mitigation of Villard's reproaches. Another of the immensely popular, special children's numbers was scheduled for October 1914, and the following month's issue would carry "World War and the Color Line," one of the most perceptive editorials Du Bois ever wrote.[49]

Du Bois had supposed the chairman understood that shortsighted economies would merely stifle the magazine's growth. Indeed, the extra rental expenditure at 70 Fifth Avenue was actually "an illusion," if all the cost benefits were computed. Du Bois considered his own two-thousand-dollar yearly salary, together with the underwriting of the office space, as not one cent less than his due. Tending to the souls of black folk was not a business of budgets but an apostolic concern in which he knew himself to be an anointed healer. Yet there was Spingarn's September 1914 memorandum stating that the chairman had "always felt that *The Crisis* was rather extravagant in this matter." Had he misjudged the new chairman, after all? *The Crisis* was still evolving. "It can be one of the great journals of the world," Du Bois told Spingarn. It was all very simple, and Spingarn ought to see that: what he was working for was "to make the NAACP *possible*. Today it is *not* possible." But when he wrote this late-October plea, Du Bois and Spingarn had already clashed over the latter's public insistence that the editor give more time to association matters and that the magazine do a more conscientious job of broadcasting them. Du Bois would have liked to, but the labor of assembling *The Crisis* was intense and unforgiving, frequently keeping him away not only from the routine business of the NAACP but from urgent policy decisions as well. Deadlines could stall contact with the outside world. Butler Wilson, down from Boston for a board meeting, was once curtly turned away from the magazine's offices by a secretary. Apologizing after a fashion, Du Bois explained that his staff had been instructed to protect him "against agents and casual inquiries."[50] Then there were numerous speaking engagements drawing him away, and think pieces in other publications.

Although in sympathy with the editor's special requirements, the chairman lost his patience in late 1914. The association's revenues were dropping because of a general economic downturn in the country. Spingarn expected all departments to accept retrenchment. His long October 24 letter to Du Bois (one of the most remarkable in the latter's enormous correspondence) combined psychoanalysis with schoolmasterly admonition. Not until Yolande's piercing Bedales cry from the heart a year later was

Du Bois so bluntly spoken to. The letter begs extended quotation. He would be frank, Spingarn warned—"so frank that I may wound your feelings deeply, but at this critical juncture I cannot waive a friend's right to the frankest criticism." Never for a moment had he doubted Du Bois's honesty:

> I do think, however, that like Roosevelt and other men I know and admire, you have an extraordinary unwillingness to acknowledge that you have made a mistake, even in trifles, and if accused of one, your mind will find or even invent reasons and quibbles of any kind to prove that you were never mistaken. The rent of *The Crisis* office is a case in point. . . .
>
> This, however, is only a trifle. . . . Surrounding you always, I may say frankly, I have found an atmosphere of antagonism. It is not merely Mr. Villard and Miss Nerney and the Board generally; it is in the whole colored world, and even some of your most intimate friends feel toward you a mingled affection and resentment. I realized from the outset that this was in part due to a devotion to principle, and the sacrifice that such devotion must always entail. . . . I realized too (it was your boast) that you could never accept even the appearance of "inferiority" or "subserviency" without treason to the race ideals for which you fight, although in this matter it may be weakness rather than manliness to protest too much. On the other hand, I found on the part of others, even those who sympathized with your ideas as much as I did, a conviction that the ideals which they shared with you had nothing to do with the cause of their disagreement with your actions and your methods. . . . They have come to feel that you prefer to have your own way rather than accept another way even when no sacrifice of principle is involved. They have come to feel that you are in fact ready to erect a personal difference into a question of principle. . . .
>
> Whenever I have come to talk over such matters with you, . . . I found that I could not act toward you as I would toward other co-operators in a great cause. You had to be approached with care and diplomacy, and made to do things by wheedling and questioning, as children are induced to do them. . . .
>
> Now I shall not hide from you the fact that many people whose devotion to this cause is as deep as yours or mine feel that the time has come to put an end to this tragic trifling. They are at last willing, indeed anxious, to "create a scene." They think you are the chief if not the only source of the disorder and lack of unity in our organization.[51]

Mary Ovington had told Du Bois just a few weeks earlier, when he sought her advice, that key board members had finally decided to "get rid of him." Nerney, she was certain, no longer wanted him "associated with us." Despite Ovington's warning, he had clearly failed to gauge the danger his single-minded policies and imperious demeanor had created. By forcing the board to validate his authority at the expense of Villard, Nerney, Spingarn, Grimké, and others, in July, after which he did very little to nurture and maintain it, Du Bois had virtually guaranteed a gradual rapprochement and counterattack by unhappy association officers. He had decided it was simply not worth skirmishing day after day with Nerney, even though he saw that the consequence of yielding was, "slowly but surely," to be "elbowed out of all real connection with the general work." Villard's disgust and mistrust were notorious, but Du Bois had not seen that even men like Butler Wilson and that paragon of the Talented Tenth, Francis Louis Cardozo, Jr., of the Baltimore NAACP branch, had come to agree with Grimké that *The Crisis* was leaching the life out of the NAACP. To the hard-driving editor, who was bent on molding the mind of Afro-America, the mission had seemed well in hand, however, even though there was a significant financial indebtedness after August due to continued expansion.[52]

Although offended by Spingarn's letter, Du Bois was above all stunned. The letter he wrote on October 28, one week before a dramatic Wednesday meeting of the board, appears to have been his longest ever. (Du Bois's letters were remarkable for consistent economy of expression.) If he did not bare his soul, he wrote with rare intensity. He admitted that some of Spingarn's criticism was fair. Yet some, he was sure, "is not." But the spirit of the letter was "right and that, after all, is the chief thing." Before addressing the main charges, though, Du Bois gave his version of the office-rent dispute, arguing that the efficiencies gained by spending more for rent were not extravagances but an economy. Laying that issue to rest, he moved on to the gravamen of Spingarn's letter. His temperament *was* "a difficult one to endure." Sounding an uncommon confessional note, he conceded that, given his "peculiar education and experiences, it would be miraculous if I came through normal and unwarped. . . . But for heaven's sake let me do the work. Do not hamper and bind and criticize in little matters." He was not obstinate, governed by "personal likes and dislikes." Throughout his life, however, his fine plans had been obstructed and spoiled, seldom permitting him to do the best work of which he was capable. *The Crisis* was a moment in a life—his and the African-American's. It was Du Bois's turn to lecture now:

> We can piddle on, we can beat time, we can do a few small obvious things: but the great blow—the freeing of ten million—and of other millions whom they pull down—that means power and organization on a tremendous scale. The men who will fight in these ranks must be educated and *The Crisis* can train them: not simply in its words, but in its manner, its pictures, its conception of life, its subsidiary enterprises. With a circulation of a hundred thousand we shall have begun work. Then the real machinery of the NAACP can be perfected. Is this a plan of disorganization, of hindrance, of lack of cooperation?

What astonished him, Du Bois went on, was Spingarn's charge that his activities were "tragic trifling." Given the problems he had had to face, did Spingarn "honestly think that [he] would have made fewer mistakes?"[53]

Reviewing the dispute with Villard over reporting African-American crime in *The Crisis*, the sharp exchange between Nerney and Dill during his absence, and the repeated second-guessing and overriding of his best judgments by Nerney ("because none of my type ever spoke to her or her friends with authority"), Du Bois invited his friend to step behind the veil in order to see the authentic character of their joint enterprise. This collaboration across racial lines was unprecedented. "No organization like ours ever succeeded in America: either it became a group of white philanthropists 'helping' the Negro like the Anti-Slavery Societies; or it became a group of colored folk freezing out their white co-workers by insolence and distrust." Spingarn did not even begin to realize "the pathos of an organization like ours," that "the real rift in the lute" was the insolence and distrust of the color line. He often listened to the chairman "quite speechless when you urge easily cooperation and understanding. You do not realize this because there is no shadow of the thing in your soul," because Spingarn, like Ovington, was not " 'American.' " In the real American world, there was a single, stark reality, Du Bois contended: white authority over black was as inimical to organizational success as black authority over white. ("I have seen the experiment [unsuccessfully] made a dozen times.")[54] What this said about the integrationist goals of the NAACP (and implicitly about his own criticisms of Booker Washington) Du Bois ignored.

In forcing the association to redeem itself, Du Bois explained, he had sought to make it possible for white and black people to work *separately* together in order to work well *together* separately—"two branches of the same work, one with a white head [Spingarn] and one with a colored [himself]." But at this point in the letter, he seemed to become entrapped in self-contradiction, partly explained by the hurry of composition, but primarily by those unresolved elements of racial chauvinism and racial egalitarianism in his civil rights philosophy. Admitting that his separate-but-equal solution for the association had not worked well—that the "connecting and unifying power between the two branches had not been found"—he suggested that this unifying power "must eventually be one man." Yet if Du Bois believed himself to be that one man (and almost certainly he did), then what of the bedrock racial incompatibility among civil rights professionals that had caused him to overturn the powers of the board in the first place? Whatever the contradictions and misunderstandings ("any unprejudiced judge would have at least acknowledged the reasonableness of my stand"), he demanded that the board "give the man of ability and integrity the right to make mistakes if the final result is big enough to justify his effort."[55] Failing that, he ended crisply, no "scene" would be needed to terminate his services.

At the Wednesday meeting of the board, on November 4, 1914, Du Bois and Spingarn savaged each other, while an appalled Ovington (partisan to Du Bois) tried in vain to mediate. The magazine must be answerable to himself, Spingarn announced. If its circulation was growing, so were its debts to the printer and to office-supply firms. The editor voyaged about the country on the association's budget in order to talk about himself and his magazine. The time Du Bois spent on NAACP business was insufficient, as Nerney had long complained. Du Bois coldly retorted that he could not be dictated to. Instead, he would assume full responsibility for *Crisis* debts, accept general guidance from a three-man committee appointed by the board with his concurrence, and relinquish his NAACP salary. It was a declaration of a clean break with the NAACP. Spingarn snapped that Du Bois was "childish and difficult," and in the heat of the meeting went on to charge that the NAACP's problems centered around "a single individual"—an "insubordinate" officer. A flabbergasted Ovington surprised herself by crying out that she could "get on with Du Bois if others couldn't." Grimké, who had come up from Washington, joined by Cardozo from the Baltimore branch, sailed into Du Bois for his obduracy, eloquently backing Spingarn's demands with a motion to abolish the July executive committee.[56]

"You think I idolize him—and perhaps I do," Ovington wrote Spingarn three days afterward. "To me, the rest of us on the Board are able journeymen doing one day's work to be forgotten tomorrow. But Du Bois is the master builder, whose work will speak to men as long as there is an oppressed race on the earth." Du Bois's sentiments exactly. The furious editor wrote to new board member George Crawford in New Haven that Spingarn had behaved exactly like Villard. Without prior discussion, the chairman "suddenly demanded complete and supreme power over the affairs of the Association, including *The Crisis.*" Du Bois and Spingarn lobbied for their cause with the intensity of ward heelers, neither willing any longer to give the other a hearing. Du Bois's temperament was hardly the "fragile and delicate thing" idolaters (Spingarn used the word) like Ovington claimed. Du Bois was tough, and he played the race card to get his way. Spingarn absolutely failed to see the logic of Du Bois's contention that the NAACP couldn't "fetter him in any way because it is important that a colored man should have the opportunity to acquire authority." Furthermore, Spingarn argued that because of his "tactless temperament" and inability to "mix," Du Bois's unpopularity among African-Americans was "extraordinarily wide and deep." Much of the unpopularity stemmed from jealousy, to be sure, but the plain fact, nevertheless, was that the board had to protect Du Bois from himself—in order to save him for the mission. Talk to Grimké, Cardozo, and Sinclair, Spingarn urged doubters. "They resent spending their hard-earned money in order merely to furnish Dr. Du Bois with a halo and a luxurious setting for *The Crisis.*" Du Bois's position with us must be "impregnable; he must not be a source of controversy but part and parcel of all our work and all our plans. He must not be coddled as a thing apart, a constant disproof of our hopes that white men and black men can work together."[57] Finally, Spingarn claimed to be fully ready for an African-American head of the NAACP ("a likely and appropriate thing to do"), but he hardly supposed that Du Bois was temperamentally fitted for the office.

That Spingarn, like Villard, could diminish *The Crisis* as merely "a good illustrated magazine" proved, Du Bois believed and underscored, that only vision could make an organization—never vice versa. For the sake of a large vision, he would not have any of his "power and discretion taken away." He and Spingarn might find a way to work together, but he would never be "reduced to the position of Mr. Spingarn's assistant instead of being a responsible officer, responsible directly to the Board." The struggle within the NAACP was both personal and symbolic—epic, he told Crawford, summoning the New Haven ally to the December board meeting. "Of course, the old thing that we always fear is tending to happen in the

Association. It is tending to become a white man's organization working for the colored people in which no colored people have any real power." In the white world, ability, temperament, determination were assets—"the rule of effective work"—but, as his racial experience of nearly half a century cruelly reconfirmed, "the colored man gets no such chance. He is seldom given authority or freedom; when he gets these things he gets them accidentally," as with the creation of *The Crisis*. "Even when his ability is patent," wise and cautious white people deem it "inexpedient to trust him." Everything "tends to this break along the color line."[58] For Du Bois, the encouraging fact that there were small yet growing numbers of white people free of prejudice and unequivocally enlisted in the crusade against Jim Crow was reason not for celebration but for rededicated militancy, and he governed his office manners accordingly.

There was little need for the editor's posturing, said Grimké at the tempestuous December 1 board meeting, delivering an impassioned criticism of the editor's motion virtually exempting himself from Spingarn's control. Even Ovington shared Spingarn's apprehensions about Du Bois assuming the magazine's debts. A bankrupt *Crisis* would have a devastating impact upon the movement. The smooth Paul Kennaday, a white board member who acted as secretary, succeeded in tempering the deliberations by presenting a series of compromise draft motions, some based on Du Bois's arguments and some on Spingarn's. The final result was the disbandment of the executive committee established under the July order. The chairman recovered full control as the association's executive officer with authority over the heads of all departments between meetings of the board. All but four of the twenty members present—Ovington, Crawford, Kennaday, and Verina Morton-Jones, one of the few female African-American physicians—sided against Du Bois. For Villard, the editor's defeat was made even more gratifying because of the six-month financial retrenchment program Villard was asked to put together. Within two months, the treasurer's economies would generate an interest-bearing "nest egg" for the first time.[59] But Du Bois's rebuff was actually more apparent than real. He himself had adroitly reversed gears and joined in recommending abolition of the executive committee in return for the incorporation of the magazine, the establishment of a special *Crisis* fund under his control, and the creation of a *Crisis* committee consisting of the chairman and two other board members (one of whom, it was understood, would be Ovington). "The Director of Publications and Research" (he had his title slightly changed), the voted motion read, "with the advice and consent of the *Crisis* Committee shall have power to administer the *Crisis* Fund and formulate the policy of *The Crisis*."[60] The more or less permanent structure of the NAACP, and Du Bois's position in it, had finally coalesced.

Motions were voted and committees formed, yet very little remained settled for long in the early NAACP. Exactly one year after the December 1914 board meeting that restructured the organization, Du Bois and his supporters were once again repulsing attacks by Spingarn, Villard, and others. Du Bois's commitment of time to the Washington production of the *Star of Ethiopia* pageant was under attack. The cover of the November 1915 *Crisis* displaying a beautiful, very light skinned woman, whose bare shoulder and sultry gaze glowed seductively at readers from the chiaroscuro of her stylish chapeau, scandalized the Boston branch, along with Villard who called it "simply shocking." But what outraged practically the entire board was this anniversary issue's "We Come of Age," a lengthy, self-satisfied piece about the magazine's success. The relationship between the association and *The Crisis* was straightforward. Very simply, Du Bois explained, the NAACP was the "legal owner of *The Crisis* and *The Crisis* is its official organ." But as astonished board members read with consternation, Du Bois informed the public that the NAACP had "never expended a single cent for the publication of *The Crisis*." In fact, rent, utilities for the magazine's quarters, as well as salaries of Du Bois's staff were billed to the association's budget. The editor's salary from the NAACP had risen to $3,000—$750 more than Nerney's. According to the editor, however, the story of large successes was due entirely to himself, his devoted staff, and "volunteer workers like Mary White Ovington, Maud Cuney Hare, Martha Gruening and others." On January 1, the magazine would be entirely on its own, the board learned, with the editor's salary transferred from the NAACP budget to a special *Crisis* fund. By April 1, 1915, Du Bois predicted "the great goal of FIFTY THOUSAND subscribers and purchasers." "The only comment I have to make," a despairing Villard told Spingarn, who was now deeply distraught about Du Bois's one-man show, "is that the National Association will never do its duty by itself until it removes a man of Dr. Du Bois's spirit from all connection with it."[61]

If the chairman recognized that dispensing with the editor's services was out of the question, he thought that a majority of the board would surely support a recommendation by the three-person *Crisis* committee ordering Du Bois to confine his activities to *The Crisis*, unless the board gave explicit permission for an exception. Once again, the editor turned from female suffrage, lynching, Haitian sovereignty, and discrimination in education to present a ringing ultimatum to the board. The December 1914 compromise had been unfair, he now declared in December 1915, explaining that he had accepted it merely to avoid "further bickering and to appease all parties." Since then, however, the "supervisory" authority of the chairman had stealthily become more intrusive, threatening to stand between the editor and the board. That could not be. He could not be confined to his office, forgoing speaking engagements, theatrical productions, book contracts, and writing commissions. "This Association knew who I was before it appointed me; it knew my ideas and personality." He had not come to the NAACP "as a clerk." He came as an executive "with power and direction." As board members took their seats around the long table on Monday afternoon, December 13, each of them knew that the director of publications and research had his resignation in his pocket, "to be accepted at the earliest possible convenience of the Board." Once again, the squirming board, faced with an inescapable choice, abandoned the chairman for the editor, voting that it would be "inexpedient" to issue commands to Du Bois. Spingarn exploded, submitting his resignation as chairman. Villard joined him, provoking Nerney to write that he had done so "nine hundred and ninety nine times."[62]

The stage seemed finally set, then, for an association remade in Du Bois's image. Either Milholland or Ovington would become chairperson, while the Department of Publications and Research would function independently, smiting white iniquity and galvanizing the oppressed. Taking advantage of what appears to have been a momentary softening, Du Bois invited Grimké to join him in recommending a new chairperson. The choices were limited, he explained. Spingarn's replacement would have to live in New York (which eliminated Grimké), would have to have independent means, and, above all, would have to work with Nerney. Who else could such a person be but Ovington? "Men simply do not understand her and are quite unable to cope with her." Less than a month after this December 23 letter, Nerney decided she had had enough and surprised Du Bois and the board by resigning. Until then, she had been "racking [her] brains" to come up with a successor to Spingarn, identifying Jessie Fauset and Theodore M. Gregory, a Howard University assistant professor, as possible candidates. Her last official recommendation was that an able, diplomatic African-American succeed her and that a "competent organizer or field agent with the sole responsibility for organizing branches" be hired. As the executive secretary prepared to leave and the chairman began to regret his temper tantrum, Du Bois proposed an ingenious solution to the association's troubles. He would become executive secretary while retaining his post at *The Crisis*. Nerney found herself toying with the idea. She confessed to a disconcerted Spingarn (still acting as chairman) that she was "one of those who regard his [ability] as infinitely superior to my own."[63] If Du Bois weren't black and she weren't a woman they would both have had an easier time, she sighed.

The prospect of an NAACP dominated by Du Bois galvanized the opposition. Joseph Prince Loud, a Boston Brahmin, along with Butler Wilson, simultaneously pushed Archibald Grimké for chairman while pleading with Spingarn to reconsider. "My friend, you must not quit us now," Wilson wrote Spingarn. Meanwhile, the search for Nerney's replacement proceeded. Whether Du Bois suggested John Hope first or urged his candidacy after Spingarn mentioned him as a possibility, a quick consensus on the Morehouse president emerged among key board members. It is also likely that Spingarn, already reconsidering his resignation, favored Hope in order to keep Du Bois out of the secretaryship. Hope would also be an effective answer to any charges of too much white input in the association. Alerting his friend to the offer coming his way, the sardonic editor wrote that Nerney "complained and fussed and worked herself into such hysteria that everybody was glad to have her go."[64] Hope gave the offer serious consideration, but well before his definitive refusal in late October, the association's mix of egos and agendas had been stirred several times over by new crises. Spingarn and Villard had been flattered back on to the board. Du Bois was preoccupied with his magazine. A major interracial conference of radicals and conservatives had been held on Spingarn's estate in Amenia, New York. Writing Spingarn that his offer was "one of the most attractive offers that can come to a colored man at this time," Hope stayed at Morehouse and Royal F. Nash, a white social worker, succeeded Nerney.[65] But Du Bois's concern about the African-American presence in the NAACP was significantly alleviated when James Weldon Johnson was hired as branch organizer that December.

The turbulence during these two years—1915 and 1916—left most of the NAACP's institutional problems unresolved, yet it did establish that the editor of *The Crisis* was indispensable and that, when disputes arose and policy was recast, the NAACP would have to accommodate itself to its brilliant, battling, contumacious director of publications and research.

18.
THE PERPETUAL DILEMMA

BOOKER T. WASHINGTON'S obituary in the December 1915 *Crisis* was neither too long nor too short. Villard had feared that Du Bois would make it disgracefully brief, something like " 'B. T. Washington, the well-known educator, died at Tuskegee last week'—his usual style," he predicted to Spingarn. The Great Accommodator's end had been an anticlimax, the final punctuation mark to a career long in decline. Stricken in New York, he had overridden the advice of the physicians at St. Luke's Hospital and boarded the Pullman for Tuskegee. An incurable disease bearing the earmarks of syphilis had reached its terminal phase. His body ruined by kidney failure and high blood pressure, Washington was quoted by the press as saying "I was born in the South, I have lived and labored in the South, and I expect to die and be buried in the South." His wishes were fulfilled when, two days after his death on November 4, a vast crowd of mourners accompanied his remains to a small plot of ground next to the institute's chapel. Near the grave would rise, eight years later, a bronze monument nearly ten feet tall. It depicted a heroic Booker T. Washington lifting a veil symbolizing ignorance from a crouching figure, an emancipated slave, although detractors among the Talented Tenth would insist that the veil was actually being lowered.[1]

Du Bois's farewell to his nemesis was both stately and judgmental. Washington's death marked "an epoch in the history of America." He was the "greatest Negro leader since Frederick Douglass, and the most distinguished man, white or black," to emerge from the South since the Civil War. There was much to thank him for, Du Bois noted—Tuskegee, the ideal of interracial cooperation in the South, the encouragement of thrift and business among African-Americans, the acquisition of land. "Stern justice" commanded, however, that "we must lay on the soul of this man a heavy responsibility for the consummation of Negro disfranchisement, the decline of the Negro college and public school and the firmer establishment of color caste in this land." But what was done was done. "This is no fit time for recrimination or complaint. Gravely and with bowed head let us receive what this great figure gave of good, silently rejecting all else."[2] Villard probably thought it a good thing, after all, that the obituary was no longer than it was. The personal combat with Washington was over, but the competition by the two belief-systems for minds and hearts engendered by that combat now entered another phase, one in which all points of reference, every undertaking (economic, educational, political), and even the most casual relationships, were to be subordinated to the Manichean social and civil values of what succeeding generations of African-Americans called the Du Bois–Washington controversy. And as intensely personal and egocentrically articulated as it had been, the controversy was really not about Du Bois and Washington in an ultimate sense, and would have emerged inevitably in one form or another. Essentially, the Talented Tenth and the Tuskegee Machine were responses by two African-American leadership groups to white supremacy as it existed in two regions of the United States. In that sense, Washington's impoverished, agrarian South, with its monocrop economy and biracial demographics, was no fit arena for the high-minded cultural and exigent civil agenda of the people for whom Du Bois spoke. Conversely, the lowest-common-denominator realities and patient abnegation embraced by Washington was no program for racial advancement in the urban, industrial, multiethnic North. Du Bois and Washington, in speaking for two dissimilar socioeconomic orders, were really speaking past each other rather than to the same set of racial problems and solutions; but Du Bois, for all his Victorian sensibilities and elitism, had the advantage of speaking to the future, while Washington, business-oriented and folksy, spoke, nevertheless, for the early industrial past.

Washington's death, as Du Bois rightly gauged, coincided with the beginning of a new epoch in African-American history and in American race relations. Robert Russa Moton was about to assume the helm at Tuskegee, and the editor promised him the "sympathy and good will of his many friends both black and white." Sympathy and goodwill would still be intact in July 1916 when *The Crisis* published its editor's "Open Letter to Robert Russa Moton." Disturbing news reports that Moton had begun to parrot the bromides of his predecessor about segregated transportation were dismissed for the moment. Moton's well-wishers hoped for and expected patent proof that Tuskegee believed "in the right to vote," Du Bois stressed, "that it does not believe in Jim-Crow cars, that it recognizes the work of the Negro colleges, and that it agrees with Charles Sumner that 'Equality of rights is the first of rights.' "[3] Reconciliation between radical and conservative forces in Afro-America was overdue, and even seemed feasible now that the affable, better-educated Moton was leader of the Bookerites. The Amenia Conference, which was to bring the several civil rights elements together that summer, would have been an unrealistic project otherwise.

There was a new epoch in world history, as well. Most Americans believed that the country could stay out of the war in Europe. President Wilson promised to keep the United States neutral. Pacifism was a considerable force in Congress and in the cabinet, with Secretary of State Bryan as deeply opposed to involvement as Ovington and Villard were at NAACP headquarters. Neither an isolationist nor a philosophical pacifist, Du Bois was far less committed to the belief that the American fire wall could withstand the conflagration in Europe. His student class at the University of Berlin was fast approaching fifty, not too old to fight but old enough not to have to. Many of them, he knew, were in field grey officers' tunics on the eastern front or in the trenches in France. From England, Nina wrote that the male teachers at Bedales were leaving for the front. Du Bois experienced the civil war among Europeans, then, with a trenchancy many Americans could not have shared. His admiration for European nations—for the kaiser's Germany, Edward VII's empire, Clemenceau's France—was both deeply held and yet conditional, an ambivalence conveyed by "Of the Children of Peace," a vivid reflection in the children's number of *The Crisis* for October 1914 on his Berlin student days as spectator to martial pageantry: "The King bowed to the Emperor and the Emperor bowed to the King, and there rose a great cry of pride and joy and battle from the people. With that cry I seemed suddenly to awake. I somehow saw *through*; (you know sometimes how you seem to see, but are blind until something happens and you really see?)." He felt both sadness and satisfaction at the carnage. "Civilization has met its Waterloo," he solemnly declared in *The Crisis* after the sinking of the *Lusitania*. "Brothers, the war has shown us the cruelty of the civilization of the West. History has taught us the futility of the civilization of the East."[4]

"The African Roots of the War," appearing in the May issue of the *Atlantic Monthly*, was one of the analytical triumphs of the early twentieth century. Du Bois poured into it his mature ideas about capitalism, class, and race, anticipating by two years Lenin's *Imperialism, The Highest Stage of Capitalism*. The essay opened with a novel proposition—that, "in a very real sense," Africa was the prime cause of the World War. Using a quotation from Pliny as his text—"*Semper novi quid ex Africa*" ("Africa is always producing something new")—Du Bois passed in kaleidoscopic review the ravages of African history from earliest times to the European Renaissance, Stanley's two-year charge from the source of the Congo River to its mouth in 1879, the partition five years later of the continent at the Berlin Conference, and the miasma of Christianity and commerce suffocating indigenous cultures and kingdoms. European hegemony based on technological superiority had produced the "color line," which became "in the world's thought synonymous with inferiority. . . . Africa was another name for bestiality and barbarism." The color line paid huge dividends, and Du Bois described the "lying treaties, rivers of rum, murder, assassination, rape and torture" excused in the name of racial superiority with his staple power and imagery. The Scramble for Africa, in which England was speediest, humiliated the French, encouraged the Belgians, belatedly aroused the Germans, and irrationally involved the Italians. "The African Roots of the War" enumerated the flashpoints that might have ignited an earlier European firestorm: "France and England at Fashoda, Italy at Adua, Italy and Turkey in Tripoli, England and Portugal at Delagoa Bay, England, Germany, and the Dutch in South Africa, France and Spain in Morocco, Germany and France in Agadir, and the world at Algeciras."[5]

The creation by finance capital of mutually exclusive economic spheres lay behind the accelerating crises. But what of the progressive forces ostensibly opposing and retarding exploitation—parliamentary democracy, socialist parties, trade unions? Borrowing insights from John Hobson's 1902 book, *Imperialism*, source text for much of the twentieth century's neo-Marxism, Du Bois disclosed one of the great paradoxes of triumphant democracy: "The white workingman has been asked to share the spoil of exploiting 'chinks and niggers.' " It was no longer merchants, bankers, and industrialists monopolizing the spoliation of the planet, "it is the nation, a new democratic nation composed of united capital and labor." Even though labor's percentage of the gross was still minimal, its "equity is recognized." This was the real secret, he contended, of that "desperate struggle for Africa which began with Stanley in 1877 and is now culminating." The gravamen of his analysis anticipated the thesis Lenin was soon to propound to explain the failure of capitalism to succumb to the consequences of overproduction and class conflict. The white working class had been appeased by state welfare concessions, on the one hand, and, on the other, cowed by capital with threats of "competition by colored labor." "By threatening to send English capital to China and Mexico, by threatening to hire Negro laborers in America, as well as by old-age pensions and accident insurance, we gain industrial peace at home at the mightier cost of war abroad." But the globalizing economic exploitation only delayed the unavoidable holocaust of spreading European fratricide. In time, the planet's majority colored population would be able to take advantage of European disunity, "and the War of the Color Line will outdo in savage inhumanity any war this world has yet seen," Du Bois prophesied. That racial Götterdämmerung could be avoided only if "European civilization" extended the "democratic ideal to the yellow, brown, and black peoples."[6]

When John Hope finished reading "The African Roots of the War" aloud to his dinner guests on campus, one of them remarked that Du Bois was a great man because of his exceptional advantages. Hope wrote his friend that he had replied, "You are able because you are honest." That the editor was the ablest public personality in black America would have been contested only by diehard Bookerites. Babies were named after him, social organizations founded in his honor, civil rights risks taken because of his exhortations. From Kentucky came a request from the Garrett Distributing Company to name a brand of cigar after him and place his photograph "on our box labels and cigar brands." Du Bois replied that he was agreeable, "if the cigar is not too bad." The daughter of one avid *Crisis* reader reported that her expiring father's last wish had been to read the December 1915 issue, but that he had died the day before it arrived. "So we placed it in his coffin," wrote Dorothy Pohle of her parent's devotion to the magazine.[7] Du Bois paid the Pohle family the high compliment of a year's free subscription. A young Jamaican who had met Du Bois briefly during his visit to the island the previous year could imagine no more auspicious circumstance, immediately upon arriving in New York, than to seek out the editor at 70 Fifth Avenue in order to invite him to chair "my first public lecture to be delivered at St. Mark's Hall, 57 W. 38th Street." A secretary's polite note of regret, April 29, 1916, informed Marcus Garvey that the editor would be "out of town." When, during Du Bois's serious illness at the end of the year, a prominent African-American wrote that his loss would have been "a racial calamity," William Henry Crogman spoke for the great majority of black people.[8]

Du Bois's influence among northern whites outside the NAACP orbit was solidifying, although it would never live up to his own expectations of what it should be. But there was a growing number of tributes, as when, one glacial November evening in 1915, nine hundred Manchester, New Hampshire, townspeople turned out to hear "The World Problem of the Color Line," a stimulating lecture containing the nub of Du Bois's *Atlantic Monthly* roots-of-war essay. There was a gratifying letter from Walter Lippmann in January 1916, stating that, as a result of their recent conversation, the *New Republic* would capitalize Negro from then on.[9] What little growing influence he had among the mainstream public, Du Bois used to the fullest during spring and summer of 1915 to fight against the screening of *The Birth of a Nation*. The film, then titled *The Clansman*, had premiered at Clune's Auditorium in Los Angeles on February 8, 1915. The alert West Coast branch of the NAACP wired New York that D. W. Griffith's adaptation of Thomas Dixon's popular novel and melodrama had yielded a vicious, powerful work of racial propaganda for the white South. The film's producers and the NAACP raced to corral supporters, with Dixon garnering memorable endorsement by his old Johns Hopkins classmate, Woodrow Wilson, after a screening in the East Room of the White House on February 18. The president exclaimed that *The Birth of a Nation* (the new title) was "like writing history with lightning," adding that it was "all so terribly true."[10] The chief justice of the Supreme Court, Edward White (a former Klansman), and a number of congressmen were similarly moved after viewing the film a few days later. George F. Peabody found Griffith's portrayal of the prostrate South—misruled by simian black legislators and the flower of its womanhood menaced by rape—worthy of endorsement. Hailed by three branches of the federal government, populated by "68,000 People, 3,000 Horses," and "8 Months in the Making," the film came to New York's Liberty Theater on Forty-second Street in early March.[11]

The full membership of the National Board of Censorship of Motion Pictures (then in New York) was aghast. "The proprietors of the film fought madly but the Censors met, viewed the film and immediately withdrew their sanction," a breathless Du Bois told his readers. Then came a few insignificant modifications submitted by the producers and "this remarkable Board of Censors met a third time," the editor sneered, "and passed the film over the protests of a minority of nine persons," including its chairman.[12] Because *The Birth of a Nation* was such potent propaganda, its opponents were ready to go to almost any lengths to stop it. The film's detractors may have blundered in paying the film too much public attention, but the medium was brand new in 1915 and its racist message, they feared, would prove inexpungible. Du Bois readily conceded that there were "a number of marvelously good war pictures" in the first half. But then came the second part, "with the Negro represented either as an ignorant fool, a vicious rapist, a venal or unscrupulous politician or a faithful but doddering idiot." The "main incident" in *The Birth of a Nation*, Du Bois explained to his 35,000 readers, was the charge that Thaddeus Stevens, "the great abolition statesman, was induced to give the Negroes the right to vote and secretly rejoice in Lincoln's death because of his infatuation for a mulatto mistress."[13] This was such dynamite at the time—when lynching was epidemic, segregated residential ordinances proliferating, and hostility to migrating African-Americans rampant in the North—that even Joel Spingarn defended censorship. After seeing *The Birth of a Nation* in Lafayette, Indiana, a white patron would shoot a teenage African-American boy to death. In Houston, audiences shrieked "lynch him!" during a scene in which a white actor in blackface pursued Lillian Gish. In St. Louis, real-estate interests would distribute leaflets in front of the cinema calling for residential segregation ordinances. Du Bois noted in *Dusk of Dawn* that the "number of mob murders so increased that nearly one hundred Negroes were lynched during 1915 and a score of whites, a larger number than had occurred for more than a decade."[14] "We are aware now and then that it is dangerous to limit expression," the editor argued in the heat of battle, "and yet without some limitations civilization could not endure." It was a "miserable dilemma," and he found his censorship views opposed by the Milhollands as well as Booker Washington.

The paradox was that *The Birth of a Nation* and the NAACP helped make each other. Du Bois was quick to appreciate that the fight against the film "probably succeeded in advertising it even beyond its admittedly notable merits."[15] But the fight also mobilized thousands of black and white men and women in large cities across the country (outside the Deep South) who had been unaware of the existence of the association or indifferent to it. Singing marchers, well-dressed picketers, drums of printers' ink, and court injunctions accompanied the film in its circuit of openings. The association succeeded in blocking its showing in Pasadena, California, and Wilmington, Delaware. In Chicago, Republican Mayor "Big Bill" Thompson, anticipating a close primary race and attentive to Julius Rosenwald, appointed Reverend Archibald Carey, AME bishop and NAACP stalwart, to the board of censors. The city board promptly banned the film—temporarily. In New York City, after the National Board of Censorship defeat, the fight was carried on at the mimeograph machine and on the picket line. The calumny at the heart of the film mobilized the National Urban League, the *New Republic*, Jewish and Protestant religious leaders, and the flower of reform (Addams, Wald, Wise, Villard) to march in lockstep with the NAACP to city hall. The Tuskegee Machine also rallied, although Charley Anderson and Fred Moore stole a march on the NAACP-led delegation to reach Mayor John Purroy Mitchel first. The five hundred men and women who crammed into the mayor's antechamber along with Du Bois, Ovington, Villard, and Spingarn made a spirited appeal. Mayor Mitchel temporized, several deletions were ordered, courts deliberated requests for injunctions, and by the end of March New Yorkers waited in long lines to buy tickets.[16]

The NAACP's fight against *The Birth of a Nation* would last for years, recharging in the early 1930s when the film was rereleased with a sound track. The initial contest closed with Du Bois, Ovington, and Spingarn heading for Boston where Trotter's National Equal Rights League and the Bookerites (working independently of each other) led by William Lewis had generated a public furor. The failing Wizard had earlier wired the Boston *Transcript* that if the film couldn't be stopped, "it ought to be modified or changed materially." (His reaction to Hollis Frissell's decision to show the film to Hampton students is unknown.)[17] Mayor James M. Curley's compromise before the April 10 opening was to order deletion of scenes depicting slavering South Carolina black legislators, an interracial wedding, and an attempted rape. Griffith, who had come to the public meeting with the mayor to make a game defense, offered his hand to Storey, who icily refused it. Ovington and Butler Wilson's wife were enraptured by the gesture—a distinguished white gentleman publicly cutting another white gentleman over a black controversy. Trotter and his followers charged the segregated movie house on the tenth, clashing with the police, and throwing eggs at the screen when a handful (minus the jailed Trotter) were finally admitted. Thousands gathered at Faneuil Hall eight days later, joined by the United Irish League (representing another maligned, subject people), marching from there up Beacon Street to the statehouse singing "Nearer My God to Thee."[18] A mass rally on the Common was held that same Sunday afternoon, with Du Bois placing the occasion in racial context.

With the governor ordering the film banned and the Massachusetts legislature poised to enact the Sullivan Censorship Law, Woodrow Wilson and George Peabody corrected their earlier enthusiasms. As Du Bois left for a rest in Jamaica, *The Crisis* milked the Chicago and Boston successes for all they were worth, typically failing to detail the crucial role played by

Trotter and the NERL. He did not propose "to burden *The Crisis* simply with names, and particularly names of small organizations," the editor sniffed to an unhappy Boston letter-writer.[19] While Griffith's film went on to gross unprecedented millions (Louis B. Mayer's ground-floor investment would transform fledgling Metro-Goldwyn-Mayer into the giant of the industry), Du Bois and Ovington explored an offer from Carl Laemmle of Universal Pictures to make a film called *Lincoln's Dream*, provided that the NAACP could contribute ten thousand dollars to the cost.[20] Ovington thought she could raise the money, and Albert Hart approved an outline scenario, but Du Bois quickly lost interest. Others in the association toyed with promoting *Rachel*, a play by Angelina Grimké, Archibald's gifted daughter, as a worthy (and infinitely cheaper) foil to *The Birth of a Nation*. There was no interest at 70 Fifth Avenue in Du Bois's pageant. Part of the reason for disinterest in *The Star of Ethiopia* may have been the feeling that it would make a static and prohibitively costly film. Villard and soon Joel Spingarn tended to be highly critical at this time of Du Bois's outside interests, including the pageant. Yet *The Star of Ethiopia*, which played to large crowds over several nights in Washington and Philadelphia, was to be the most thoughtful, ambitious theatrical response to Dixon and Griffith's racist epic. There was also irony in the eventual loss of $140,000 by Julius Rosenwald and the able business types affiliated with the Tuskegee Machine who attempted to bring *The Birth of a Race* to the screen, a project conceived by Emmett Scott and filmed atrociously by The Selig Polyscope Company.[21]

FIVE WEEKS before the Los Angeles premiere of *The Birth of a Nation*, the January *Crisis* had carried belated news of a White House debate that had astonished the country, and which had everything to do with the national deterioration in race relations. Accompanied by officers of his National Independent Political League (another variation of the NERL), Trotter had returned to Washington in November 1914 for a second interview with Woodrow Wilson. A year earlier, press secretary Joseph P. Tumulty had arranged a thirty-five-minute audience during which Trotter, Wells-Barnett, Murray, Gunner, and Sinclair had presented the president with a petition signed by twenty thousand persons in thirty-six states protesting racial segregation.[22] This November 1913 colloquium had gone extremely well for the White House, with the usually remote Wilson charming the delegation with affable assurances of concern. In the interim, however, as each month's *Crisis* revealed, the plight of black people had grown steadily worse. Armed with an executive order, cabinet officers Albert Burleson, William McAdoo, and Josephus Daniels, southerners all, had proceeded to purify federal workspaces of African-American civil servants shortly after Wilson's inauguration. In the well of the House and Senate, southern lawmakers raged against the presence of nineteen thousand African-Americans on the federal payroll, called for the segregation of African-Americans in public parks, facilities, and transportation in the District of Columbia, the elimination of commissions for nonwhites in the armed services, and for the exclusion from the United States of all immigrants of African descent. Cafeterias in the post office, treasury, and navy departments were placed off-limits at all times to nonwhites; lavatories to accommodate both sexes twice sprang up like kudzu. Photographs were suddenly required by the Civil Service Commission on all applications. Of thirty-one honorific, federal patronage positions held by African-Americans in 1913, eight would remain three years later.[23]

Shortly before the first Trotter delegation had headed for Washington, Du Bois published "Another Open Letter to Woodrow Wilson" in the September 1913 *Crisis*. As it had turned out, the president had not needed black votes to win the 1912 election; two million more Americans had voted for him than for the second-place Roosevelt. But an honorable man must keep his word, Du Bois protested. It was no exaggeration to say, sir, that "every enemy of the Negro race is greatly encouraged; that every man who dreams of making the Negro race a group of menials and pariahs is alert and hopeful. . . . Vardaman, Tillman, Hoke Smith, Cole Blease and Burleson are evidently assuming that their theory of the place and destiny of the Negro race is the theory of your administration. . . . *The Crisis* still clings to the conviction that a vote for Woodrow Wilson was NOT a vote for Cole Blease or Hoke Smith."[24] Villard, as credulous as Du Bois, had had his civil rights illusions shattered when his plans for a National Race Commission, a fifteen-person, "scientific, nonpartisan" fact-finding body, were scuttled. "I see no way out," his friend the president had confessed over lunch morosely in early October 1913. "It will take a very big man to solve this thing."[25] From Abenia, his Saratoga Springs estate, the usually sanguine Peabody, observing the abandonment of the African-American by his friend Wilson, solemnly warned his fellow paternalists, "If the friends of the Negro do not now stand up for him it will be most difficult to make opportunities in the future to do it effectively." The radicals were gaining, and Peabody startled Hampton's Dr. Pangloss by writing Hollis Frissell that "if I were a Negro I should have no use for Hampton or any other place that did not in a quiet, dignified way express its opinion" of the president's attitude.[26]

When an out-of-patience Monroe Trotter and the NIPL delegates entered the White House a second time, on November 12, 1914, Woodrow Wilson was in the worst possible mental state over the death of his wife. Just three days earlier he had written a friend that he wanted "to run away, to escape something."[27] There was no escape from Trotter. The founder of the NIPL bluntly stated that he and his associates had returned to protest the continuing segregation in the federal bureaucracy. Wilson gravely explained that "segregation was caused by friction between the colored and white clerks, and not done to injure or humiliate the colored clerks, but to avoid friction." Trotter interrupted to say that African-Americans were not wards of the government. The problem of federal segregation had been drastically accelerated "soon after your inauguration." The president snapped, "Your manner offends me." "How?" Trotter wanted to know. "You are the only American citizen that has ever come into this office who has talked to me with a background of passion that was evident." Trotter respectfully assured Wilson that he "misinterpreted earnestness for passion." Voices were raised; they began to interrupt each other. When Trotter broke in to tell Wilson, "Two years ago you were regarded as a second Abraham Lincoln," the agitated Virginia Democrat ordered that there be no further personal references. But the Bostonian barreled on to say that those leaders who had supported Wilson's election were being denounced in the churches "as traitors to our race." (The Bookerite *Age* reminded readers that Du Bois, Trotter, and Waldron had helped make possible the Democratic administration.) A furious exchange and the verbal expulsion of the NIPL delegation followed, with the president telling his press secretary afterward that he had lost his temper "and played the fool." Whether or not, as Trotter believed, Wilson had recovered his composure and smiled as the group left his office, Tumulty was struck dumb when Trotter held a press conference in the White House, reenacting the debate through verbatim quotes.[28]

In an era when it was deemed a prodigious favor for a distinguished black leader to be granted an audience with the president of the United States, Trotter's impertinence was almost beyond belief. Julius Rosenwald and Albert Pillsbury deplored his "rude" behavior, as did Moton, who sent Wilson a letter from Hampton regretting the "very unfortunate incident of Mr. Trotter." It was hardly necessary to observe that Booker Washington (sinking fast at St. Luke's) would never have been guilty of such conduct, even though he had publicly pronounced himself deeply troubled by the administration's policies. Much of the white press shared the sense of consternation that prevailed in the White House and in the South. Leading national newspapers and journals of opinion, however, repeated the judgments of the New York *World* and the *New Republic*, which found Wilson's "complaint of the 'intolerable burden' of his own office" inappropriate to people "who come to the President with real grievances due to the President's own inaction in a moral crisis."[29] Notwithstanding the NAACP's public meetings, letter-writing campaign, lobbying on Capitol Hill, *Crisis* editorials, the well-publicized official *Letter to President Wilson* in August 1913, and Nerney's carefully documented pamphlet, *Segregation in Government Departments*, in December, Trotter's White House debate exposed the president's hypocrisy as nothing before had succeeded in doing.[30]

Du Bois was unequivocally supportive of Trotter's position in this instance. It made amends, to some extent, for his bad-faith response to Trotter's November 1913 White House audience, which he had failed to notice until the February issue of *The Crisis*. Now he awarded his difficult friend a full editorial in the December 1914 issue, followed by the complete text of the November exchange in January, along with a full survey of press reactions. Du Bois generously praised Trotter for voicing "the feelings of nine-tenths of the thinking Negroes of this country." As for Woodrow Wilson, Du Bois indicted him as being "by birth and education unfitted for largeness of view or depth of feeling" on the race question.[31] The magazine's generosity toward Trotter was temporary, however. Later that year, when covering the NIPL's vanguard role in opposing *The Birth of a Nation*, Du Bois reverted to muted or elliptical response. To critics like Storey and Villard, Grimké and Wells-Barnett, this was the sort of egocentric, stubborn behavior they had learned to expect periodically from the nation's most distinguished African-American intellectual and civil libertarian. That memorable line from Joel Spingarn's letter of October 24, 1914—"your mind will find or even invent reasons or quibbles of any kind to prove that you were never mistaken"—expressed their feelings precisely.[32] Ego and obduracy were integral to Du Bois's makeup, certainly—he was touched with a sense of infallibility. But when these characteristics worked to the advantage of collective effort, another name for them was vision.

Seeing his people's predicament as that of an undermanned fire brigade facing an inferno, the editor came to regard uncoordinated and freelance undertakings within the race as nothing less than reprehensible.

"Organization is sacrifice," he catechized readers in the April 1915 *Crisis*. "It is sacrifice of opinions, of time, of work and of money, but it is, after all, the cheapest way of buying the most priceless of gifts—freedom and efficiency."[33] It was not a question of power hunger, and only moderate impatience with dissent, but passion in pursuit of a common objective. As his renown and influence grew among the educated, surpassing that of Booker Washington, as the membership of the NAACP climbed above ten thousand, as the readership of *The Crisis* passed the thirty thousand mark, and as the Tuskegee Machine crumbled and the well-funded Urban League began to confine itself to business networking and research, Du Bois saw a unique opportunity to expand and consolidate civil rights forces.[34] When he deplored the dismissal of Charley Anderson from his Internal Revenue Service post in the spring of 1914, the editor's gesture was both a genuine tribute to Anderson's superior professionalism and a sign of welcome to Bookerites scurrying from Wilson's scythe. Some, like Roscoe Bruce, who had landed the D.C. school superintendency once coveted by Du Bois, signed on. In Trotter's case, Du Bois could not help feeling that the common objective was handicapped by an eccentric independence backed by little more than a newspaper and a few hundred people in Boston, Chicago, and Washington. Several of the NAACP officers privately reproached the NIPL for refusing to share access to the White House. Still, whatever the momentary notoriety of others, Du Bois's own leadership position now towered above all. Ferris's celebration of Du Bois's ascendancy may have been somewhat premature in 1913; by 1916 that ascendancy was a fact.

He still had detractors, and they were numerous. Editors Fred Moore and Calvin Chase could always amuse their readers by poking fun at Du Bois's alleged hauteur. *Crisis* editorials remained anathema in faculty lounges at Hampton and Tuskegee. His friend Major Charles Young alerted him in January 1916 to a rumor that the Justice Department's new Bureau of Investigation was looking into gossip about Du Bois's personal life. The editor realized that Nina's absence in England had "led to endless table talk and conjecture as to things that people have not seen," but, in thanking Young for his vigilance, he told Young that he was quite unconcerned.[35] Trotter and Grimké continued to attack Du Bois's public character, and were soon joined by Neval H. Thomas, a District of Columbia adversary who by comparison would make Trotter seem positively meek. For Villard, dyspepsia and Du Bois were usually inseparable. The editor's readiness to take on the General Education Board and the Southern Education Board in

1915, just as the Rockefeller interests were fixing the parameters of privately funded higher education in black America for the next fifteen years, was deemed to be an infuriating impertinence by the "philanthropoids." Peabody's advice to his philanthropic friends—that they try placing themselves in Du Bois's shoes as a gifted, scorned black intellectual—failed utterly to persuade them.[36] Unsympathetic white students of race relations attempting to explain Du Bois began to characterize him as a "marginal man," a typology that had a propensity to degenerate into a modern version of the tragic mulatto.[37] But in Du Bois's case, marginality, for all its deracination, tension, and reinvention, meant the very opposite of impotence and tragedy. His offended ego and rage at personal and collective injustice swept increasing numbers of African-Americans as well as whites into its force field. Du Bois's marginality was of the conquering variety that ultimately compelled the prevailing hierarchies of values and power to take it into account and even to seek an accommodation with it.

The Crisis spoke to a widening range of issues with impassioned authority, reaching a circulation of 45,000 by April 1916. Sometimes readers needed strong stomachs. "The Lynching Industry," a tabulation by year of the 2,732 African-Americans lynched between 1885 and 1914, supplemented by names, dates, and states of those murdered during the twelve months of 1914, was a statistical horror story. "All this goes to show how peculiarly fitted the United States is for moral leadership of the world," Du Bois scoffed.[38] The group lynching of six black men in Lee County, Georgia, the following year, was depicted in full-page ghoulishness in the April 1916 *Crisis*. "The Waco Horror," reported in June and July, broke new ground in lynch journalism. Walling and several others were shocked by the choice of cover for the June issue—the ghastly, burnt-cork husk of Jesse Washington suspended by chain from a tree. Du Bois poured into the special July supplement the bloodstained detail of an undercover investigation. Studin and Arthur Spingarn warned the board that the magazine still contained libelous statements, even after the several deletions that Du Bois had consented to make.[39] *The Crisis* carried lengthy, verbatim statements by lynching-party participants, and Du Bois editorialized with his usual withering irony. The young victim was a mentally impaired field hand who, after raping and killing his white employer's wife in the kitchen, returned to hoe cotton placidly beside the husband, son, and daughter. Jailed for safekeeping in Dallas and then tried in Waco, he was set upon and dragged from the courthouse by most of the white men, women, and children of the town. Hitched to a car and dragged till the chain broke, Jesse Washington's ears were severed, his body doused with kerosene, pieces carved from it, and, in final Gothic glee, the shouting, cavorting townspeople hoisted him to a tree on the courthouse lawn and finished incinerating him. Woodrow Wilson was still to redeem his promise to denounce lynching.

When *The Crisis* looked beyond Lee County and Waco, prospects were somewhat more encouraging. The issue for June 1916 related the discrimination suffered by Dr. Anna M. Comfort, the nation's oldest living female physician, when she had been a student at New York's Bellevue Medical School in the 1860s. Du Bois rarely missed an opportunity to illustrate the connection between the battle for the liberation of women and the civil rights of his own people and others. Returning to the theme in the September issue, he presaged after the war "the advent of many things—notably the greater emancipation of European women, the downfall of monarchies, the gradual but certain dissolution of caste and the advance of true Socialism." Another outcome of the war, he thought, would be the national liberation of Poland. He had decided by 1916 that Germany would lose the war—that it should lose the war. For all its faults, Great Britain stood for the right principles of parliamentarianism, liberalism, and colonial responsibility—"as the best administrator of colored peoples"—although by the war's end he would write of a "great dull doubt in my mind—a feeling of world apprehension." In the global mayhem of the present, it was the German empire that deserved condign censure. "Compared with Germany," England was an "Angel of light." The record of the Second Reich was the "most barbarous of any civilized people." Like many other Americans educated in Germany, Du Bois's reaction to Germany's war conduct sprang from emotions deeper than patriotism. Thorstein Veblen blamed the war on the romantic, unscientific character of that nation's schools of philosophy. In *German Philosophy and Politics*, John Dewey arraigned *The Critique of Pure Reason* as the root of German militarism. It was as if they and Du Bois were driven to abjure and recant the intellectual affections of their youth out of bitter, heartfelt disenchantment. He had "deep cause to love the German people," Du Bois reminded readers. Twenty years ago, they had made it possible for him to "believe in the essential humanity of white folk when he was near to denying it." All the more reason, then, to denounce them for trampling world morality and order under the heel of Hindenburg and the Prussian general staff. The beloved Germany of Beethoven and Goethe had been betrayed by that of Nietzsche and von Treitschke.[40]

On the other hand, Du Bois carefully checked any creeping Anglophilia. He championed Irish liberation, writing of the old enmity in America between African-Americans and the Irish, "All this is past." Editorializing about the 1916 Easter Rebellion, he mused that it may have been foolish, "but would to God some of us had sense enough to be fools!" A month later, apotheosizing Sir Roger Casement, the Irish patriot hanged by the British, Du Bois cited Casement's exposés of atrocities in the Congo, South America, and Turkey. Of British justice in this case, Du Bois wrote, "Someone has blundered."[41] In defending the Irish, did the editor intend to forsake "culture, refinement, service and love"? a distressed young woman asked. Du Bois gave a debater's answer that fell short of actually embracing assassination, sedition, and war. "Terrible as it may be," he lectured, "the awful fact faces the colored races in this world. That no human group has ever achieved freedom without being compelled to murder thousands of members of other groups who were determined that they should be slaves." He hoped for the young woman's sake it would not be necessary. "War is Hell," he ended, "but there are things worse than Hell, as every Negro knows."[42]

One thing worse than hell was the grinding down year after year of black people in the Deep South. The conservative leadership represented by Moton called on the race to stay put, while police in Georgia were being armed with rifles to stop folk from leaving the towns. The October 1916 *Crisis* cheered the outmigration, predicted its geometric increase, and placed it in the broad context of global industrialization enabling Jews from Russia and peasants from Austria to escape oppression and find economic opportunity.[43] In a witheringly frank letter to Professor Paul Hanus, the current president of the American Association for the Advancement of Science, the ostensible topic was Hampton ("deliberately educating a servile class"), but Du Bois's larger concern was social and economic adaptability. The fact of the matter was, he wrote Hanus, "if the Negro race survives in America and in modern civilization it will be because it assimilates that civilization and develops leaders of large intelligent calibre."[44] Du Bois saw early on that the great migration would be a powerful agency in that assimilation.

On to and out of the pages of *The Crisis* walked persons of great significance and many whose prominence was fleeting. Beautiful babies, debutantes, families on the steps of spacious homes, successful businesspersons, high school valedictorians, a white northern university or college's first African-American graduate (but not from Princeton or Vassar, Du Bois regularly reminded readers), annual conventions of professional organizations and Greek letter societies, and more.[45] The issue for May 1916 contained a brief announcement utterly belying the capital significance of its subject. It reported that Marcus Garvey had arrived in New York from the West Indies and would be giving a series of lectures "in an effort to raise funds for the establishment of an industrial and educational institution for Negroes in Jamaica." Garvey's prospects went unappreciated, but the deaths of William Ward and Josiah Royce were noted with poignancy in November 1916, as were those of Inez Milholland Boissevain and the African-American YMCA official William A. Hunton, whose able son Alphaeus would join Du Bois in devoted West African exile forty-three years later.[46]

The stellar career of Charles Young was tracked almost monthly: his return from attaché duty in Liberia, in January 1916, to assume a command in occupied Haiti; a striking photo of the major in dress uniform and sword in March as the second Spingarn Medalist and current squadron commander in the 10th U.S. Cavalry. In May, Major Young was with U.S. expeditionary forces in Mexico ("foolish venture"); in October (one of the "Men of the Month"), the new lieutenant colonel's children were reported to have left Belgium safely to continue schooling in the United States. The editor's good friend, as an outstanding West Point graduate and the most combat-experienced officer of his rank, would be eligible in the near future for command of a brigade. Young had served as a captain in the Philippines, seeing action in such hot spots as Samar and Blanca Aurora. A stint in military intelligence in Washington had followed, then exemplary duty in the chaotic Liberian backcountry where he was ambushed and wounded while organizing the country's frontier forces. "His service in the Army has been highly creditable to his race from any standpoint," General Leonard Wood, former chief of staff of the army, wrote his Troutbeck neighbor Spingarn upon Young's return from Liberia, a letter Spingarn passed along to his friend.[47] In the increasingly likely event that the United States entered the European war, Du Bois counted on General Young to lead the Talented Tenth into battle.

Dusk of Dawn credited Joel Spingarn with the idea for the Amenia Conference, but it would not have been possible without Du Bois's enthusiasm. With a sense of history shifting gears, he would write that Amenia "marked the end of an era and the beginning."[48] The NAACP had intended to hold its 1916 annual meeting on February 12, Lincoln's birthday. When Emmett Scott and the Bookerites announced that their memorial service for Booker Washington would be held on that day, however, Du Bois and Spingarn, seeing a unique opportunity to bring the factions together later that year, persuaded the association to postpone its affair. Du Bois joined the chairman in a plan for a conference of all factions "in the peace and quiet of Amenia."[49] Although "under the auspices of the NAACP," the assembly was carefully characterized as an independent affair. The two hundred or so invitations for August 24 through 26 were issued in Spingarn's name as master of Troutbeck in Dutchess County, New York. The invitees, both white and black, came from across the civil rights spectrum—from Monroe Trotter through Kelly Miller to Emmett Scott. Du Bois was pleased to make a show of objectivity and to assume a secondary role in the actual proceedings. When his opinion was sought about one guest in particular—"the editor of a certain paper" who had had "an exceedingly good time at any expense"—Du Bois noted that "Mr. Spingarn was pleased to see that I agreed with him in this." The nuts and bolts of organizing the Amenia Conference largely fell to Roy Nash, an affable young man about whose competence there were mounting concerns as he was inclined to sit in his office writing memos inviting suggestions for something to do; but Nash did an excellent job procuring and shipping the array of tents, cots, mattress covers, blankets, and towels needed for the conference. The lot went off from New York on August 15, with a note to Spingarn about providing straw "for filling the mattresses up there."[50]

Despite appearances, Du Bois was the moving force behind Amenia, and Nash had dutifully traveled and returned earlier that same day to confer with him at Sea Isle City, New Jersey, about the final details of the conference program. Leaving the running of *The Crisis* to Fauset and Dill, the editor was recovering from an attack of kidney stones that would necessitate surgery at the end of the year, but his powers of concentration were unimpaired. Nina and Yolande may have been with him, although there is no mention of them in correspondence from this period. The editor received Nash with a range of "suggestions" that was actually a schematic design for the conference. He had already divided Spingarn's invitation list into Niagarites, Washingtonians, and others. John Hope might preside over a session on higher education. Chesnutt, the novelist and insurance executive, could conduct the education and industry discussions. Bookerite James Napier, dismissed by Wilson as register of the treasury, and now president of the National Negro Business League, could lead a roundtable on industrial opportunity. Lucy Laney, founder of an influential elementary school in Augusta, Georgia, and Judge Robert Terrell, a rare survivor of the federal purge, were suggested as moderators of what Du Bois called "practical path" roundtables. Nash reported to Spingarn that Du Bois had insisted that James Weldon Johnson's address ought come on the final afternoon, rather than the first day, "for fear that the line Johnson wants to follow will simply crystallize the Conference into two hard groups."[51] Johnson was suspected of being too pro-Tuskegee. Nash was also carefully lectured on the significance of seventy-year-old John R. Lynch's attendance. "Du Bois says that by all odds he is the most distinguished colored man there, barring none." A fine relic of Reconstruction, the tall, sharp-featured former speaker of the Mississippi House of Representatives had gaveled the 1884 Republican National Convention to order and been a U.S. army major in the Cuban occupation. Lynch should speak on the last afternoon, Du Bois suggested, and the "so diffident" Moton ("Major" Moton, as his peers called him) "might perhaps feel that we were making him bear more than his fair share" if asked to chair the first afternoon.[52]

The cast had continued to shift until the last days before the conference, with the white invitees eventually deciding that the proceedings would be better served by their absence. Milholland went to California, Ovington to Seal Harbor, Maine. George Peabody, Florence Kelley, and Ray Baker sent regrets, and Samuel Gompers's unavailability was anticipated.[53] Among the African-Americans who did not attend were Trotter and Moton. The founder of the NIPL had decided to stay away just three days before the conference was to begin. The new Tuskegee principal's final decision may have been influenced by "An Open Letter to Robert Russa Moton" that July, an exceptionally restrained editorial for Du Bois, but a stern, somewhat patronizing warning to Moton, nevertheless, to watch his accommodationist inclinations. Du Bois's personal letter to Moton in mid-July, intended to smooth their differences, may only have made matters worse.[54] But in the absence of the Wizard's successor, Emmett Scott, Fred Moore, and William Lewis came to represent their cause. The independent-minded Kelly Miller shared a tent with AME bishop Levi J. Coppin. Ill health kept Charley Anderson, Roscoe Bruce, and Francis Cardozo from attending.[55] Carter Godwin Woodson, a recent African-American history Ph.D. from Harvard, sent regrets. Woodson had just begun editing his *Journal of Negro History* that January, publicized in *The Crisis* with Du Bois's reproach that thus far it "has *only 1000 subscribers*." Archibald Grimké stayed away, but Francis shared tent number four with Charles Chesnutt and J. Rosamond Johnson, the brother of James. Tent number one housed Mary Terrell, Lucy Laney, Nannie Burroughs, the founder of National Training School for Women and Girls in the District of

Columbia, and Mary Burnett Talbert, the current president of the National Association of Colored Women.[56]

No sooner did Du Bois set eyes on Troutbeck for the first time than he rhapsodized that he "knew it was mine. It was just a long southerly extension of my own Berkshire Hills."[57] Joel and Amy Spingarn's manor house with its Tudor facing and steeply inclined roof was about two miles from the town. A stream pierced the rolling, wooded grounds, widening as it flowed through a broad clearing where eleven tents to shelter about fifty men and women conferees were set up. The immensely pleased Du Bois doubted "if ever before so small a conference of American Negroes had so many colored men of distinction" who represented practically "all phases of Negro thought." The opening morning of the conference, Thursday, he described as "misty with a northern chill in the air and a dampness all about."[58] There were pockets of tension and some posturing; old grievances lurked just below the surface civilities. But by Saturday afternoon, the impeccable hospitality of the Spingarns, the arrival of messages from Theodore Roosevelt, William Taft, Charles Evans Hughes, and Woodrow Wilson, flattering visits from Governor Charles A. Whitman, Congressman William S. Bennett, "a university president, an army officer," and other prominent white people, and the perfect weather and catered meals all conspired to camaraderie and confidence. Attorney Inez Boissevain's visit delighted the connoisseur in Du Bois. John Milholland's tall, brunette daughter (who had given him a dressing down for not speaking) was "in the glory of her young womanhood," he sighed, but she would die within the year, tumbling exhausted from a suffragist platform in California.[59] There was tennis, which Du Bois played well, and croquet, which the women played without bonnets. A delighted Chesnutt attributed the success of the three days to Spingarn and the collegial Nash. With a "few more men like you in the United States, the solution of race problems would be a matter of a very short time," he graciously exaggerated in his note to the master of Troutbeck.[60]

Instead of keeping to their original plan of secrecy, the conferees voted to make public what Du Bois characterized as "a virtual unanimity of opinion in regard to certain principles." "All forms of education" were desirable; the race's "highest development" was impossible without "complete political freedom"; antiquated subjects of controversy and "ancient suspicions and factional alignments" must be banished. They had now "learned to understand and respect" the "peculiar difficulties" that southern race leaders faced in promoting racial advancement; and all endorsed the view that the leaders ought to hold annual meetings "for private and informal discussions under conditions similar to those" at Amenia. "Probably on account of our meeting, the Negro race was more united and more ready to meet the problems of the world," Du Bois would proclaim later.[61] In reality, the Amenia Conference would prove to have been remarkable mainly because it had taken place. It marked a definite shift in the balance of power within black America, a reflection of the increasingly industrial, northern, and national character of the American Dilemma. It affirmed the NAACP's primacy as advocate of the rights and protections under the Constitution of Americans of African descent, but it accomplished much less in the way of converting veteran Bookerites to the activist goals of the NAACP. If the conservatives hoped for more understanding and respect from Du Bois, they were sharply disabused by the *Crisis* editorial, "Hampton," in November 1917, in which education at the institute was dismissed as "a wellnigh fatal loss of time."[62] Trotterites remained as suspicious as ever of Du Bois and the association's monopolizing tendencies. The legacy from Troutbeck was far less one of genuine understanding and real unity than of cosmetic harmony and pragmatic tolerance among the various factions now more than ever pressed by forces of implacable racism abroad in the land. There would not be another Amenia Conference until 1933.

At some point, Du Bois, in tent number eight, revealed to the conference his long-term prognosis about the struggle for rights "in the face of so deep-seated and unreasonable human force as American race prejudice." Du Bois's remarks were as grim as they were far-sighted. No direct frontal attack, "however courageous and high of principle, can be of the slightest avail," he foresaw. Several more generations would suffer under disfranchisement and separate and unequal schools. "Only through this valley of human nature" could the goal of true equality be reached. But if the goal was distant, the team was now being assembled in order to pursue it. His estimate of what had been accomplished recalled his euphoria at the 1911 Races Congress. Like those London ballrooms, Du Bois found Troutbeck a fitting place from which to launch a new era in race relations. How appropriate, then, "that so fateful a thing should have taken place in the midst of so much quiet and beauty, in a place of poets and fishermen, of dreamers and farmers."[63] In addition to fixing a truce among African-American leaders, Amenia repaired and deepened the bond between the editor and the chairman. It would lead to a surprising willingness to undertake a course of action that would seem to others at odds with

Du Bois's convictions. The easy grace of squire Spingarn in his well-endowed demesne, his notable neighbors and establishment entrée, the family library with sunlight streaming through leaded glass panes on to oak bookcases, the well-stocked wine cellar—all this affected Alexander Du Bois's grandson, a racial radical but far from a social leveler.

Woodrow Wilson and Charles Hughes had sent their greetings to Amenia, but Du Bois called down a plague on both presidential candidates that year. "Between these two great parties," the October *Crisis* announced, "as parties there is little to choose." Hughes and the GOP (now supported by Roosevelt) were the "natural enemy of the humble working people who compose the mass of Negroes." Wilson's record in the White House fairly taxed the editor's civility. The signal exception, Du Bois wrote, was the nomination of Louis Brandeis ("a modern man") to the Supreme Court, able, principled, sympathetic to labor, and knowing the meaning of " 'despised and rejected of men.' " An October 17 "personal" letter from Tumulty, the president's secretary, informing the editor that Woodrow Wilson wished him to know that he had "tried to live up to them [pledges to African-Americans], though in some cases his endeavors have been defeated," must have seemed a pathetic rationalization.[64] Not only was Wilson's New Freedom a disaster for Americans of African descent, Du Bois had repeatedly inveighed against its policies in Latin America and the Caribbean. A U.S. expeditionary force had toppled Mexican President Victoriano Huerta from power in 1914 and General "Black Jack" Pershing had invaded the country in March 1916 after Pancho Villa, provoked by the American government's preference for his rival, murderously struck Columbus, a border town in New Mexico. A war with Mexico only awaited Wilson's reelection, but if America blundered "into murder and shame," Du Bois warned, "it will not be war. It will be a crime." U.S. Marines, already busy policing Dominican Republicans and Nicaraguans, had occupied Haiti in summer 1915, provoking howls from *The Crisis*—"SHAME ON AMERICA!" Ten million African-Americans were told to write the White House to demand an interracial presidential commission to bring a quick, honorable end to American violation of the republic's sovereignty. "Hayti can, and will, work out her destiny," Du Bois asserted, "and is more civilized today than Texas."[65]

Because four more years of Wilson's New Freedom would mean "ascendancy only by the help of the Solid South," *The Crisis* proposed an electoral strategy suggested by Inez Boissevain—"a Negro Party on the lines of the recently formed Woman's Party." The White House was a

Hobson's choice (indecisive, Du Bois momentarily favored Hughes), but African-Americans could find leverage in congressional elections, crossing party lines to vote Republican, Democrat, or Socialist, or even fielding their own candidates. He knew, of course, that the inveterate Republicanism of the great majority of African-Americans and the absence of choice in the white-primary South made his desperate electoral scheme a distant hypothetical in a rainbow coalition of the future. The November 1916 editorial betrayed its editor's deepening frustration—black people should vote for the Socialist presidential candidate, Allan Benson, or stay home.[66] The irony that Woodrow Wilson had gone to bed unsure whether he would still be president the next day bitterly mocked Du Bois's political advice. In 1912, Wilson had become president without needing the hundred thousand black votes he had thought it essential to bargain for. Four years later, when his victory in California by four thousand votes decided the election, his racial policies had made another pledge to Bishop Walters out of the question. The solid South held a lock on a Democratic White House. Big business made the Republicans equally unresponsive, and there was no way out through the labor movement and socialism for the African-American.

That fall, a seeming anomaly, deplored by Marcus Garvey during his brief visit to 70 Fifth Avenue, was addressed. Not only were the officers of the association white, except for Du Bois, but Garvey was surprised to find that, to his color-sensitive eyes, the African-American staff was as white as the officers, except for Dill and one or two others.[67] Nerney's recommendation that an African-American be retained to organize branches had been much too long deferred. After Amenia, a consensus had emerged that James Weldon Johnson would make the best candidate for field organizer. Songwriter, diplomat, novelist, poet, Johnson was a suave, self-created success on an heroic scale. "Fifty Years," his stately poem commemorating the Emancipation Proclamation, had been exuberantly praised in *The New York Times* and by Roosevelt, Washington, Chesnutt, and Du Bois when it appeared at the beginning of 1913. The dealings between Booker Washington and the trim, cosmopolitan Johnson were well known, however. Johnson had been treasurer of Charley Anderson's Colored Republican Club and, with his brother, Rosamond, had written Roosevelt's 1904 campaign song, "You're All Right, Teddy," for which James was rewarded with postings as U.S. consul general to Venezuela and Nicaragua.[68] In 1912, Consul Johnson had strapped a forty-five to his belt and superintended the defense of Nicaragua's main port city, Corinto, against attack until the arrival of U.S. Marines ended a rebellion against a pro-American president. The Wilson State Department had declined to approve his promised assignment to France, and the sputtering Tuskegee Machine could do no better than make him editor of the *Age* in late 1914. He and Du Bois had been tentmates at Amenia, where the editor's apprehensions about Johnson's Tuskegee connections had been so well assuaged that the two of them speculated about forming a "secret organization" to energize the civil rights elements represented at the conference.[69] Johnson's gracious informality and infinite tact had impressed both Du Bois and Spingarn.

The ex–foreign service officer was impressed by the association's growing power and augmenting treasury. With John Hope's final decision in late October not to seek the position offered by Spingarn, the board approached Johnson immediately. Ovington seems to have remained suspicious about his Bookerite background, but Du Bois and Spingarn may have felt that this made Johnson's recruitment all the more valuable. "Your letter appeals to me very strongly," Johnson replied as soon as the chairman's offer reached him.[70] The editor followed Spingarn's letter with his own pitch that, after initial misgivings, he was convinced that "contact with human beings will be an incentive rather than a drawback to your literary work" (which Johnson would have known). Du Bois reminded him of the secret organization "that you and I talked of sometime ago. . . . We might be able to tie a durable knot to insure the permanency of the main organization" with Johnson as field organizer."[71] Johnson accepted the offer in November 1916, and over the next two years he spearheaded a phenomenally successful membership drive.

As though his people's misery were a misfortune to be borne personally, Du Bois became seriously ill in early December 1916. "I went down into the valley of the shadow of death," he later wrote.[72] An anxious Nina, awaiting news in their Bronx home, received word from Will's secretary that her husband would undergo surgery on Friday the fifteenth, 10:30 A.M. at St. Luke's Hospital. It was his first major illness since those Fisk days when the college community had hung on every bulletin. Joel Spingarn had full confidence in St. Luke's medical staff, but he still insisted on having his personal physician present in the operating room, "as much for my own peace of mind as for yours," he told Du Bois. Because of the long-term damage to the left kidney, the patient's doctors determined that the organ would have to be removed in a second operation. Du Bois sent Dr. Frances Hoggan a clinical account of the ordeal under the knife and his six-week recovery, as well as an apology for failure to remit his overdue debt. Spingarn received a similar letter and a similar request for the deferral of another loan. His painful incapacitation was such that Dill, Ovington, and Spingarn were asked to write the editorials for December and January.[73]

The illness hushed detractors and heightened the fervency of his admirers. The editor played to his public with all the flair of an accomplished publicist. Job of Fisk, Harvard, and Berlin bore his affliction in Old Testament accents. "Above the Hill where St. John's Divine Cathedral raises its bald and mighty arch, hang the Curtains of Pain," the February editorial intoned. "There is moaning here and writhing and now and then a cry, and yet less, infinitely less, than one expects." There was "no Race; there is no Age; there is but one language"—that of sympathy. "I am glad I am here."[74] Mary Terrell's sympathy note was unusual for its jocular tone. She wrote that, although she had long known that Du Bois modeled himself on her, she had not expected him to imitate her own kidney troubles of two years past. From his Park Avenue parsonage, John Holmes trembled to think "what it would have meant to the members of your race, to say nothing of the cause of liberty in general," had Du Bois succumbed. Mrs. Sadie Conyers, a Brunswick, Georgia, acquaintance wrote to say how thankful she was "that there has been and is a Du Bois." William Crogman of Atlanta rejoiced that St. Luke's had spared them "a racial calamity." Wendell Dabney's Cincinatti social club sent a bottle of sherry to be consumed once the curtains of pain were raised. Spingarn received an encouraging note on January 20: "I am up and walking around and feeling quite well." The patient was discharged on January 22. A week later, he wrote Carrie Clifford that he was "glad to learn how important I am."[75] His recovery was rapid and complete.

WHEN WOODROW WILSON took America into the Great War on April 2, 1917, Du Bois welcomed the decision. "The Battle of Europe," the mystical, apocalyptic editorial the previous September, revealed the Du Boisian vision of a radically transformed world order after the guns fell silent. "Well, civilization has met its Waterloo," he wrote in the aftermath of the *Lusitania*. "The civilization by which America insists on measuring us and to which we must conform our natural tastes and inclinations is the daughter of that European civilization which is now rushing furiously to its doom." "What good can come out of it all?" A return to ancient ideals, was Du Bois's answer. "Old standards of beauty beckon us again, not the blue-eyed, white-skinned types which are set before us in school and literature but rich, brown and black men and women with glowing dark eyes and crinkling hair." The sooner the rotten edifice of racism and class exploitation crumbled, the sooner the world would be bathed in a "golden hue that harks back to the heritage of Africa and the tropics."[76] But it was the red hue from the Urals rather than a golden glow from the sub-Sahara that occasioned general, if temporary, rejoicing among progressives—the news that March of Aleksandr Kerensky's overthrow of the czar and proclamation of a republic. Du Bois believed that the moment was more propitious than ever before for American Socialists to embrace the principles of interracialism.

It was as one of the fifteen members of the executive committee of the Intercollegiate Socialist Society that Du Bois made another eloquent, carefully honed appeal to the American left soon after the November election. He told the conference that the greatest crime of socialism "was the conspiracy of silence" that surrounded the Negro problem in the United States. "Revolution is discussed," he lectured, "but it is the successful revolution of white folk." Black people in America had suffered as much as Russian and Polish peasants and had struggled for generations, sometimes violently. He went on to skewer those pacifists among them for whom war was a horrible thing; "but yesterday, when war was confined to the Belgian Congo, to the headwaters of the Amazon, to South Africa and parts of India and the South Seas it was not war, it was simply . . . carrying civilization on to the natives."[77] Warming to his theme, he indicted the response of white labor to the steady northward migration of black workers. Five years earlier, in a forceful *New Review* essay, he had warned organized labor that its exclusionary charters had convinced the American Negro that his greatest enemy was not the employer who robs him "but his white fellow workingmen. . . . White Northern laborers find killing Negroes a safe, lucrative employment which commends them to the American Federation of Labor." The emancipation of black labor, he pleaded, was fundamental to the success of "forward-looking and radical" forces.[78]

He was so far recovered from surgery in March that he traveled south to speaking engagements in Atlanta, Augusta, Chattanooga, and Charleston, South Carolina—six states in all. One purpose of the trip was to gather information on the rising outmigration of black people. It was evident to keen African-American observers like Carter Woodson, editor of the *Journal of Negro History*, and George Edmund Haynes, special assistant in the U.S. Department of Labor, as well as to many of the white progressives, that the South, the Nation, and the Negro would be changed by this exodus, but whether it was a good thing or, as Woodson concluded, a phenomenon in which "the maltreatment of Negroes will be nationalized," was a matter of intense discussion. While Du Bois had been recuperating there had been two major conferences on the controversial subject in January. At Tuskegee, Moton had presided over a conclave of conservatives whose Bookerite resolutions deplored the migration as unjustified and extremely unwise. In New York, the white estate lawyer and Quaker activist L. Hollingsworth Wood had presided over a meeting of National Urban League and NAACP officials that became so tempestuous that Spingarn despaired for the spirit of Amenia. Butler Wilson insisted on a motion urging African-Americans to evacuate the South until it "shall accord them their political rights."[79] Du Bois's trip would yield some of the earliest firsthand information available concerning the migration's causation and numbers.

Atlanta—the affluent white part of it—was setting the regional pace for suburban development. Du Bois was offended by Druid Hill, the new, forested enclave of the Coca-Cola rich expanding along "mile on mile of nine-inch water mains and sewers . . . wrung [by] city taxes out of poor blacks and whites." In the heart of Atlanta, there were neighborhoods where children grew sick and died "because there is no city water" (he must have been thinking of Burghardt) and five thousand black children "sit in the streets, for there are no seats in the schools." But there was praise for Atlanta University and John Hope's Morehouse College, then in its fiftieth year, which boasted "carefully selected male students" and "the best athletic record of the colored country."[80] In Augusta, he visited Lucy Laney's remarkable, struggling academy, where Mary McLeod Bethune had taught at the beginning of her remarkable career. It did not offer its students much of an academic experience, with "dishwashing substituted for English," but it had heart.[81]

Charleston captivated, evoking images combining deliquescence and vitality—"subtle flavor of Old World things, a little hush in the whirl of American doing." It was Africa and Anglo-Saxon decay, where "white aristocrats . . . perched like solemn owls about the Dead Sea of the 'Battery.' " "Colored Charleston" generally delighted Du Bois. He paid diplomatic calls to all the churches, "in rhythm on a great blue day." A "slim black woman whirled and screamed" in one church. In another, the preacher "beat upon his audience with skillful repetitions, which alone meant little, but his hearers surged and bowed." In St. Mark's Episcopal, the fifty-two-year-old godbox of the city's endogamous mulatto upper crust, Du Bois sensed the presence of the famous slave insurgents, Cato of the

Stono rebellion and Denmark Vesey. In *The Crisis*, he railed against Charleston's peculiar violation of separate equality—the monopoly held by white teachers in the black public school system. Charleston's African-Americans should put a stop to it, Du Bois commanded. Tell the white people that such an arrangement was as incongruous as having "Turks teaching Armenians."[82]

He returned from the South with impressions and notes for a major essay on migration, but before he drafted the piece, he came to terms with a lengthy February 26 letter from Joel Spingarn about the creation of a training camp for African-American officers. It was the dilemma of the moment, Spingarn's officer-training camp, a project the chairman had originated three months before the declaration of war and virtually without consulting the board. General Wood, his Dutchess County neighbor, had mentioned that the War Department might approve an officers' camp if Spingarn could recruit a respectable number of eligible African-American candidates.[83] Dismissing the pacifist and integrationist qualms of fellow board members, Spingarn had written pamphlets and taken to the lecture circuit to rally support for a segregated military facility to be located in Des Moines, Iowa—about as remote from the centers of African-American life as could have been conceived. For the chairman, patriotism ranked with civil rights as an unmitigated good. Villard's unwavering support of neutrality struck Spingarn as irresponsible. He had even less patience with Ovington's pacifism. The Socialist party's vote to oppose the war in a special convention in St. Louis only days after Congress had approved the president's request struck him as a folly verging on treason. The Socialists Russell and Walling fully shared Spingarn's consternation and would quit the party, as would the theorist John Spargo, a Du Bois favorite, Upton Sinclair, and J. G. Phelps Stokes, an extremely wealthy parlor Socialist and Tuskegee supporter. Once again, the editor would decide to break with Debs, Ovington, and the party that he continued to claim represented his political and social ideals.

When Spingarn began turning up on college campuses, the African-American newspapers became increasingly hostile to his mission. Villard and Ovington had contended that his personal crusade would inevitably drag the NAACP into a controversy neither the board nor the membership had formally debated, but their objections were grandly, disdainfully waved aside. "There is only one thing you can do at this juncture," the chairman of the NAACP wrote in "Educated Colored Men of the United States," his widely circulated open letter, "and that is to get the training that will fit you to be officers, however and wherever this training may be obtained." At Howard University, George E. Brice, an articulate, energetic student, stirred by the appeal, wrote Spingarn that a speech to his fellow students would greatly advance the cause. After an exchange of telegrams, and word of the Howard president's approval, the chairman came to the campus on March 20. Dashing to other colleges, Spingarn spoke to impressionable young men about the unique opportunities available for service to country and race. Nash, the uncertain executive secretary, was in Washington lobbying for the camp on Capitol Hill and reporting regularly by letter and telegram to the chairman on his progress.[84]

"I shall not feel hurt at any position you may take," Spingarn had written Du Bois on February 20, just as the black press began to hiss. His friend must appreciate that there was "no other motive than to help black men no less than white men." Speaking not only for the Talented Tenth but for perhaps a majority of African-Americans, the Chicago *Defender* and Baltimore *Afro-American* made it clear that this campaign was not the best means of helping black men. Even though it was beyond contemplation that black officers could ever command white troops, they argued that training alongside them, whether or not the races ate and slept apart, was the *sine qua non* of a genuinely minted commission. The "colored" camp in the hinterlands risked being a substandard undertaking, if not an outright fraud corroborating the claims of Major Robert Shufeldt and other white "authorities" that military command was beyond the psychological and intellectual capacities of the race.[85] Du Bois must have wrestled with himself, for his writings had long ago indicated that Du Bois the racial integrationist could coexist with Du Bois the racial separatist. There was the chauvinist "Conservation of the Races" versus the uncompromising integrationism of the Niagara "Address to the Country." There was the skeptic who inveighed against those who "speak of human brotherhood as though it were the possibility of an already dawning tomorrow." There was the integrationist who demanded to know why "cannot the nation that has absorbed ten million foreigners . . . absorb ten million Negro Americans . . . ?"[86]

By late March, he had allowed Spingarn to convince him that the segregated camp in Iowa would advance the race. Harry Smith, militant publisher of the Cleveland *Gazette*, member of the NAACP's Committee of One Hundred, and a friend, told Du Bois that the camp was a major miscalculation. He argued by letter with Charles Young, now commanding cavalry at Fort Huachuca, Arizona, who agonized over the matter with him. "Dr. Spingarn is right in practice, you see," Young wrote, "as you are right in theory. We are going to need leaders for the Colored regiments." Du Bois's protégé, George Crawford, strongly dissented, writing Spingarn that it was not, after all, "foolishly theoretical, but it is sometimes better to endure temporary disadvantages than to yield a principle." Richard R. Wright and the affluent, aristocratic public servant George Cook were typical members of the minority advocating the camp.[87] They believed themselves not to be abjuring the principle of integration, but to be laying firm ground for its future achievement by accepting a demeaning expediency. Hope may have been similarly inclined, although correspondence is silent on the matter.

In supporting Camp Des Moines, Du Bois tried to accommodate both his chauvinism and his integrationism. By fighting for a democracy in which too few Europeans and white Americans truly believed, the Africans of the diaspora would quicken the collapse of European global hegemony and the emergence of peoples of color. In a less romantic spirit, and more in keeping with the class instincts of his Talented Tenth, Du Bois envisaged black soldiers fighting and dying across Flanders fields, led by Des Moines officers, as the high price of full citizenship in America—civil rights through carnage. Yet it remained uncertain until the last minute whether African-Americans would be excluded from the military conscription legislation emerging from Congress. Conceivably, white America, controlled by Wilson's Democrats, might go to war without allowing black Americans the privilege of dying alongside it—as they had in every war since the founding of the republic. In the racial and political climate of the moment, then, Du Bois, whose own father had worn the uniform, convinced himself that, given the opposition even to black enlisted men, the commissioning of black officers in whatever circumstances was imperative. He might well have eventually supported the segregated-camp proposal anyway, but Spingarn's influence accelerated the decision. Gritting his teeth, he accepted the absurd logic of having to fight "even to be segregated."[88]

Once decided, he plunged into the debate with typically fiery conviction. "We continually submit to segregated schools, 'Jim Crow' cars, and isolation because it would be suicide to go uneducated, stay at home, and live in the 'tenderloin,' " he wrote in his April 1917 editorial berating the "many hasty editors" attacking Spingarn and the camp. It was a "perpetual dilemma," he conceded. But he had made the sole possible choice, as his readers must, "between the insult of a separate camp and the irreparable injury of strengthening the present custom of putting no black men in positions of authority." Then, like officers in training, the editor's argument advanced in quickstep:

Our choice is as clear as noonday.
Give us the camp.
Let not 200, but 2,000, volunteer.
We did not make the damnable dilemma.
Our enemies made that.
We must make the choice else we play into their very claws.
It is a case of camp or no officers.
Give us the officers.
Give us the camp.[89]

Two months later, in "Officers," Du Bois flayed Smith's *Gazette* for suggesting that he had been pressured into his defense of the camp. But most readers knew that the editor really had Trotter in mind. Incredulous at Du Bois's support of Spingarn, the mugwump of civil rights had bluntly stated that Du Bois was "a rank quitter of the fight for our rights." Now was the moment when African-American leaders should dig in and demand, not conciliate without even asking for concessions, he pleaded. Trotter pronounced a searing verdict on Du Bois. He had "at last finally weakened, compromised, deserted the fight, betrayed the cause of his race." Dismissing such charges as muddle-headed, Du Bois was able to report a last-minute development in the June editorial: "We have won! The camp is granted; we shall have 1,000 Negro officers in the United States Army! Write us for information."[90] What had begun as a repugnant expediency became a shining triumph.

Opposition to Camp Des Moines continued among many of the old Niagarites, and Archibald Grimké remained skeptical of Du Bois's increasing enthusiasm for the war. Another node of opposition was *The Messenger* magazine, a politically robust and culturally iconoclastic monthly just founded by Asa Randolph and Chandler Owen, two young African-Americans who had recently joined the Socialist party, from which Du Bois was now again distancing himself. "Our aim," Randolph and Owen boomed in the first *Messenger*, "is to appeal to reason, to lift our pens above the cringing demagogy of the times and above the cheap, peanut politics of the old, reactionary Negro leadership"—by which they meant, among others, Du Bois.[91] But few African-Americans yet paid attention to *The Messenger*, and Du Bois's *Crisis* helped most of them to change their minds about Camp Des Moines—at least to give the argument the benefit of their doubts. His critics had expected him, understandably, to choose for himself the role of magisterial flagellant, to inveigh against racist policies imposed in a war for democracy, to heap imprecation on the powers of bigotry, even if it led to *The Crisis* being suppressed under the new Espionage Act of June 1917. Yet, strangely, his very powers as propagandist appear to have pushed him in the other direction, as if to preclude the possibility that his renown might be exploited in order to stigmatize African-Americans as whining, divisive, unpatriotic. With German-Americans about to vanish as a visible and vocal ethnic group and with pacifists prime candidates for lynching, the radical Du Bois pivoted about to agree with Frederick Douglass's officer son and Lieutenant Colonel Young—"When the storm is past, we can take up the idealism of the cause."[92]

Worrisome developments rapidly ensued, however. Charles Young's command of a squadron of 10th Cavalry troops in Mexico had been the stuff of legend. In sharp encounters costing the regiment the lives of twenty-two men, Young, still a major, was ordered to lead his men in an advance, pressing Pancho Villa's forces hard, and in two notable firefights, at Aguascalientes (where American troops attacked for the first time under protective machine gun fire) and at Santa Cruz de Villegas (where his bugle charge dispersed six hundred *federales* about to obliterate an American squadron), Young earned from his white superior, Colonel William C. Brown, the commendation "excellent in all categories." That July, Black Jack Pershing himself presided over Young's examination in the field, leading to his promotion to lieutenant colonel. "He was strong, fit, and only 49 years of age," Du Bois cheered, "and in the accelerated promotion of war-time would have been a general in the army by 1918."[93]

The first clouds over Young's career gathered on March 31, the week before the declaration of war. To the crucial question number 20 on his efficiency report about general fitness to command, two of the examining officers at Fort Huachuca remarked that Young was "a very intelligent colored officer, hampered with characteristic racial trait of losing his head in sudden emergencies." Simultaneously, a white Mississippian, Lieutenant Albert B. Dockery, wrote his senator that his aversion to service under Lieutenant Colonel Young had reached a possibly homicidal point. Senator John Sharp Williams promptly communicated the lieutenant's misery to the president of the United States. At that moment, the army general staff was pressing the secretary of war for the creation of a small, rudimentarily equipped, single black division. Charles Young would have been the obvious choice to command such a division, an eventuality that powerful elements within Congress and the army intended to prevent.[94]

In the same month in which his editorial exulted, "We have won! The camp is granted," Du Bois received a long, anguished letter from Letterman General Hospital, San Francisco, where Young had been ordered to undergo extensive medical tests by General Tasker H. Bliss, the chief of staff. Was the lieutenant colonel's health so impaired by Bright's disease ("chronic nephritis") that continued active duty would be "a menace to the Army and to his own life," as the final medical hearing on July 7, 1917, determined? His medical records (which include an examination by Young's personal civilian physician) indicate that elevated blood pressure and albuminuria had been detected in 1910. It seems clear that Young did have high blood pressure and that he managed to conceal the fact from several examining boards. On the other hand, except for a single recurrence in 1913 of blackwater fever contracted in Liberia, he was never absent from duty and his overall performance was considered to be "excellent." Medical officers had surprised their cavalry and infantry colleagues by opposing their examining board's May 7 recommendation of Young as "entirely fit for promotion" to full colonel. Woodrow Wilson was so well informed about the matter that he was able to assure Senator Williams, who wanted action on Lieutenant Dockery's case, that Young "is not in perfectly good health" and that a final disposition of his case would occur within "the next two or three weeks."[95]

"No one in the regiment, either officer or man, believes me sick and no one save the doctors here at this hospital," Young wrote Du Bois from San Francisco on June 20. One of his nurses had said his case seemed a joke, he continued. It was a joke—at the expense of the country. "Without an ache or pain, here I sit twirling my thumbs . . . when I should this minute be at Des Moines helping to beat those colored officers into shape," he told Du Bois. "It was a miserable ruse," Du Bois protested.[96] As a member of the *New Republic*'s editorial board, he alerted Lippmann, hoping to enlist the magazine's support. The move to eliminate Young generated a cyclone in the African-American press and a monsoon of letters and telegrams to the White House. Despite the detailed report to the army surgeon general on July 24, that Young suffered from advanced nephritis and "marked hypertrophy of the heart," Secretary Baker appears to have decided initially on a waiver of the regulations. In the interim, he instructed the general staff to hold Young's case "in suspense."[97] Villard, still under the illusion that Wilson was willing to redeem something of his pledge to African-Americans, had interceded with Baker and his young assistant, Francis P. Keppel, extracting from Keppel a promise to alert him before any final adverse actions were taken.

Baker was inclined to protect this unique symbol of minority excellence for the good of the race's wartime morale. But the former reform mayor of Cleveland reckoned without the obduracy of the military bureaucracy. On July 27, army chief of staff Bliss informed him that, in the opinion of the adjutant general, it would be impossible "to promote any officers junior to Colonel Young as long as the proceedings of the examining board are not acted upon." Three days later, the White House ordered Young promoted to full colonel and retired from the active list. William Garrison's grandson was annoyed with his Washington contacts. "You gave me your word," he upbraided Keppel. He was certain that there had been "a miscarriage of justice; at least Young is the huskiest retired officer I have ever seen."[98] Young refused to go quietly as expected, however. To prove his stamina, he rode horseback from his National Guard command in Chillicothe, Ohio, to Washington, cheered on by the black press. The White House managed to avoid noticing the feat. At Du Bois's urging, Young was offered the position of executive secretary of the NAACP, after Nash resigned to assume an army commission and command of a black unit. Young expressed interest, but typically imposed the condition that he could serve only if unity and loyalty to the government took precedence over civil rights.[99] He soon took a seat on the board.

19.
"THE WOUNDED WORLD"

"To say that Negroes of the United States were disheartened at the retirement of Colonel Young is to put it mildly," Du Bois wrote; "but there was more trouble."[1] Some 700,000 African-Americans registered on July 5, 1917, the first day of enrollment under the new Selective Service Act. As tens of thousands of these recruits reported to camps for training in Georgia, Kansas, and Texas, *The Crisis* was vigilant. It needed to be. While the work of assembling Camp Des Moines sputtered along, the War Department decreed that no nonwhite officers above the rank of captain would be commissioned. Nor did the generals intend to see many snappy, Talented Tenth graduates of Fisk, Howard, and Atlanta taking the salutes of their men. For good measure, they dismayed Du Bois and Spingarn by decreeing that some 250 of the African-American officers would be selected from the ranks of regular army privates and NCOs, men who were well trained but often barely literate and accustomed to taking orders from white superiors.[2]

Meanwhile, the War Department packed existing and planned units comprised of African-Americans with white officers. Reports reached Du Bois of disgraceful conditions, harrassment by white military policemen, white NCOs who spat "nigger" and "coon" at every opportunity, camps lacking USO facilities available to African-American enlisted men, and the case of a major general at Fort Riley, Kansas, Charles C. Ballou, who confined the men of his all-black 92nd Division to camp for insisting on admission to a movie theater in the town. "No matter how legally correct" they had been, barked the general, "the greater wrong" was to do "*anything*, no matter how *legally* correct, that will provoke race animosity." General Ballou was generally believed to have meant well. The same could not be said of those overseeing the black soldiers stationed near Houston. Then came the rapid, one-two punch of racism that enraged Du Bois almost to the point of abandoning his tack of patient patriotism, and which badly jarred the White House and the War Department. "In the very hour of our exaltation," as the editor put it with his customary flair for drama, "the whirlwind struck us again"—first in East St. Louis, Illinois, then in Houston, Texas.[3]

Du Bois had sought to examine the commencing mass migration of southern black people in "The Migration of Negroes," a taut, analytical piece ticking off what today would be called the "push" and "pull" of economic, demographic, and social factors driving "about 250,000" northward in little more than a year. From his "own travel and observation," he sensed the epic consequences that would result from this relocation. Some 2,400 African-Americans had been pushed and pulled to East St. Louis, Illinois, the "Pittsburgh of the West," since the beginning of 1916. They arrived in the midst of a heated election and an industrial war—ripe conditions for a cataclysm. The outcome of voting in Illinois was critical to Woodrow Wilson's reelection, and, as Du Bois had foreseen, the rising numbers of African-Americans in the state would affect that outcome. If there was no hard proof of the Democrats' charges that the state GOP had imported black voters from the South in order to capture southern Illinois, there was little doubt as to their validity in the minds of hard-pressed white workers in East St. Louis, the great majority of them, like the black people, newly arrived from other parts. These white workers hated to see the Republicans take the state, and hated even more to see Republican William Rodenberg returned to the U.S. House of Representatives. His Democratic opponent had railed against Rodenberg's "Black Belt," the African-American shantytown abutting the railroad tracks and industrial plants, a group of dwellings little different from the grim, unsanitary hovels of the white immigrants. Dr. Leroy Bundy, prosperous dentist and flamboyant organizer, personified black Republicanism to the city's white people and its new, bumbling Democratic mayor, Fred Mollman.[4]

But it was the threat to white jobs from black newcomers that finally provoked two days of the worst urban violence yet experienced in the peacetime history of America. East St. Louis was home to the Armour and Swift meat-packing houses and to the Aluminum Ore Company and the Missouri Malleable Iron Company. Organized labor was reeling from its defeat by the Aluminum Ore Company. The company paid its nonunion workers a better wage than the average for East St. Louis; but working conditions were brutal, and the number of African-Americans hired to replace white workers had risen from 280 in November to 410 in December. By February 1917 there were 470 working at the plant—all but a handful in jobs at the lowest rungs of production. Fighting back desperately against the successful demolition of its union, the AFL tried to reorganize with the support of unskilled white labor. The union exaggerated trends that the Slavic and southern European workers already feared were irreversibly under way. Armour, Swift, and Morris, the large meat-packing companies, hardly bothered to hire black workers because union organizing had gone nowhere in the packing houses. Should the need arise, however, the precedent set by Aluminum Ore was certain to be copied. White skilled labor told its unskilled brothers that it could either strike with the union or step aside to make room for more black newcomers arriving on the Illinois Central.[5]

On May 29 and 30, the tinder of politics and jobs ignited, then rapidly flamed out with little damage done because of the presence of the National Guard. One month later, on the night of July 1, however, the conflagration came, after a car filled with plainclothes police was fired upon by African-Americans who probably mistook it for returning drive-by shooters. The city exploded the next morning. More than six thousand men, women, and children were made homeless and many fled the city in the first hours or would return under the protection of the National Guard to root for their few belongings before departing forever. Two policemen died and two square blocks of black shanties went up in flames. All day long on the third, white people roamed the downtown area, exchanging souvenirs from the rampage, ghoulishly touring the morgues, and cheering whenever an increase in the black body count was announced. Mangled black corpses ("horribly mutilated floaters") bobbed to the surface of the Mississippi. By July 5, almost $400,000 worth of property had been destroyed and thirty-nine black and eight white people were dead. The final tally was grim enough—Du Bois would insist until the end on 125 fatalities—but the first reports he received counted several hundred dead, with untold numbers of bodies yet to be disgorged by Cahokia Creek and the Mississippi.[6] And whether it was $373,605 or, as initial reports calculated, $1.4 to $3 million in houses and businesses lost, the ghastly reality remained that this northern city of 59,000 had been the site of the first American pogrom.

With the board's full backing, Du Bois left for East St. Louis on Sunday, July 8, with Martha Gruening, the aggressive white social worker who served as field agent and *Crisis* staffer. From offices provided by the Knights of Pythias, an African-American mutual-aid society, he and Gruening issued orders to a staff of five hired workers and twenty-five volunteers during their seven working days there. They were a formidable duo, with Du Bois canvassing the African-American community with something of the lightning speed and thoroughness of his Philadelphia days, and Gruening doing skillful detective work in the white community. Mayor Mollman squirmed through an exacting session with Du Bois, and city and state officials found themselves interrogated with a civil intensity distinctly not to their liking, as they sought to assign blame for the riot on a conspiracy headed by Dr. Bundy, the African-American dentist. The NAACP board members convening to hear the editor's report were grimly impressed by what he and his assistant had uncovered. Given the national implications of the terrible riot and the intrepid fact-finding by its agents, only William Walling expressed surprise when Du Bois relieved *The Crisis* of sharing in the East St. Louis expenses and presented the full $350 bill to the NAACP along with a motion (eventually approved) to deduct the sum from its recently established Antilynching Fund.[7]

While he and Gruening amassed information (eighty-two white and twenty-three black people were indicted on August 14) in order to draft their public report, Du Bois prompted Jessie Fauset to send the letter "A Negro on East St. Louis" to the *Survey*. She sounded like the editor at his pontifical sternest: "We are perfectly well aware that the outlook for us is not encouraging. . . . We, the American Negroes are the acid test for occidental civilization. If we perish, we perish. But when we fall, we shall fall like Samson, dragging inevitably with us the pillars of a nation's democracy." Fauset's letter sought to put a bold face upon the numb discouragement of a people. Although there was widespread handwringing in northern newspapers, followed by crocodile editorials throughout the South, black Americans began, as never before, to fear that they were an endangered species. On the left, as Du Bois would write in "The Problem of Problems," organized labor found "killing Negroes a safe, lucrative employment."[8] At a Carnegie Hall meeting organized to applaud the revolution in Russia, Gompers excused the white workers of East St. Louis, although Du Bois was pleased to note that Theodore Roosevelt had rebuked the AFL head from the platform. On the right, the New Freedom implemented much of the Progressive agenda, but consistently ignored African-Americans when it was not proscribing them. A delegation of prominent citizens from Baltimore was turned away from the White House without a hearing. James Weldon Johnson managed to see Tumulty, who testified that reading accounts of the riot had sickened him physically, but his lofty superior remained silent.[9]

It was Villard who suggested another means of getting through to Woodrow Wilson—a silent parade of thousands in Manhattan. The preliminary planning of the demonstration fell to Johnson (Nash was on leave) until Du Bois arrived from East St. Louis on the eighteenth. Ten days later, Saturday morning, July 28, between eight and ten thousand well-dressed African-American men, women, and children marched down Fifth Avenue. It seems inconceivable today that this was the first time a procession such as this had ever been seen in New York City. The women and children were dressed in white. The men wore dark suits. They marched silently, except for the steady roll of muffled drums carried by several men at the head. Du Bois strode in the second rank behind the drummers, walking stick in his left hand and suit coat unbuttoned to the summer heat. Banners demanded: MR. PRESIDENT, WHY NOT MAKE AMERICA SAFE FOR DEMOCRACY?—A child's sign read MOTHER, DO LYNCHERS GO TO HEAVEN? Behind the Stars and Stripes floated the giant streamer, YOUR HANDS ARE FULL OF BLOOD.[10] The Silent Parade, captured in a widely reprinted photograph, was the second impressive sign (after the picketing of Griffith's film) that there existed an aggressive national civil rights organization representing black people.

Du Bois and Gruening's "The Massacre of East St. Louis" in the September *Crisis* pushed circulation almost to the long-coveted fifty-thousand mark. The January 1916 issue had narrowly escaped destruction from a fire at the printer's. This issue threatened a conflagration. The feature essay was prefaced by the editorial "Awake America," with the prophet Jeremiah and the avenger John Brown lending inspiration. "The New Freedom cannot survive if it means Waco, Memphis and East St. Louis," Du Bois warned. Lynching must stop. Race and gender disfranchisement must stop. Jim Crow cars must go. Racism in trade unions, civil service, public schools, and public accommodations must end. Justice must be done in the courts and ability recognized in the workplace—the litany lost nothing in power for being familiar. "Awake! Put on thy strength, America—put on thy beautiful robes," Du Bois intoned in biblical accents intended to mask shaken confidence. "Russia has abolished the ghetto—shall we restore it? India is overthrowing caste—shall we upbuild it? China is establishing democracy—shall we strengthen our Southern oligarchy?" His closing sentence would be repeated in thousands of churches and homes, becoming both slogan and catechism for African-Americans: "No land that loves to lynch 'niggers' can lead the hosts of Almighty God."[11]

When readers turned to "The Massacre of East St. Louis" they faced twenty-four pages of investigative journalism that re-created the riot through photographs and victim interviews. These verbatim testimonies and black and white images of mayhem and arson combined to convey an experience just short of actually being in the ravaged city, missing only the stench of fire and death. Du Bois and Gruening applied themselves to fleshing out the socioeconomics of the riot: the desperate conditions driving African-Americans from the South; the widespread disaffection among already brutalized white workers; manipulation by capital of both races in order to break the unions; and the understandable collusion of black workers with management in reaction to organized labor's racism. It was clear that East St. Louis hardened Du Bois's animus for organized labor in general and Gompers's AFL in particular. Socialist though he continued to proclaim himself, he must have hooted at *The Messenger* when Randolph and Owen wrote that it was the stifling of class solidarity by capital rather than the force of racism that was behind East St. Louis.[12] Seeing the riot mainly in racial terms rather than as a brutal manifestation of the capitalist divide-and-conquer maneuver, Du Bois would later succumb to the temptation to romanticize the facts. When "The Massacre of East St. Louis" was reprinted three years later, in a drastically revised form, as "Of Work and Wealth," it contained a famous paragraph describing a confrontation that never occurred:

> The Negroes fought. They grappled with the mob like beasts at bay. They drove them back from the thickest cluster of their homes and piled the white dead on the street, but the cunning mob caught the black men between the factories and their homes, where they knew they were armed only with their dinner pails. Firemen, policemen, and militiamen stood with hanging hands or even joined eagerly with the mob.[13]

The editor must have considered the propaganda value of this passage to outweigh by far the sacrifice of historical accuracy. It captured the kind of desperate, ennobling resistance to oppression he had admired in the Irish conspirators behind the Easter Rebellion.

Houston struck as the month drew to a close. On the night of August

23, more than one hundred soldiers from the 3rd Battalion of the decorated 24th Infantry marched from Camp Logan into Houston, Sergeant Vida Henry and Corporal Charles W. Baltimore of the military police in the lead. That morning, Corporal Baltimore had been beaten, shot at, and then arrested by a city policeman for inquiring about another battalion member, who had been clapped into jail for trying to stop the beating of a black woman by a policeman. Both men had been released to their white captain later in the day. After weeks of insults, assaults, Jim Crow trolleys and cinemas, the African-American regulars of the 24th Infantry, used to the kinder racial mores of Manila, California, and Wyoming, cut through downtown Houston like a scythe.[14] Moving in assault formation on the nearest police station, they shot dead sixteen whites (including five policemen) and wounded eleven others in two hours. Two black citizens were killed. Four members of the 3rd Battalion died, one, Sergeant Henry, by his own hand. Here was fulfillment of white America's deepest fear—bloody black retribution, the other element besides sex at dead center of the historic psychosis about race.

Houston was awkward for Du Bois. As he wrote of it, the editor was brokenhearted. It was hard, he said, "for one of Negro blood to write of Houston. Is not the ink within the very wells crimsoned with the blood of black martyrs? Do they not cry unavenged, saying—Always WE pay; always WE die; always whether right or wrong."[15] Whatever feelings of elation he may have harbored about retribution for East St. Louis, they were more than counterbalanced by fear of what white backlash from Houston could do to the larger cause of civil rights. The officers' camp and black troops in combat units were at stake, not to mention the prospect of more East St. Louises exploding in reaction to the reaction. "This, at least, remember you who jump to judgment," Du Bois implored, "Houston was not an ordinary outburst." That was certainly evident, and what he meant to say was that only extraordinary provocation could have caused this highly decorated unit to run berserk. "Contrary to all military precedent the Negro provost guard had been disarmed and was at the mercy of citizen police." As Martha Gruening (this time on her own) uncovered the facts that would go into a compelling exposé, as Sam Houston's son accepted the NAACP's retainer to defend the soldiers, the army rushed the first sixty-three through secret courts-martial, hanging the first batch without right of appeal in December. Newton Baker persuaded Woodrow Wilson to reduce the total number of soldiers hanged from twenty-four to nineteen, despite the demands of southern senators for even more object lessons. Sixty-seven others were given sentences ranging from a few years to life. Much later, citing Pershing's earlier praise of the 24th Infantry, the editor wrote bitterly of the summary punishment meted out to those who had "volunteered to a man to clean up the yellow fever camps when others hesitated" in Cuba. Ultimately, there seemed no other recourse but to fall back upon a biblical caution—"if those guiltless of their black brothers' blood shot the punishing shot, there would be no dead men in that regiment."[16]

Emmett Scott, shadow figure behind the Wizard, was the African-American chosen by the Wilson administration to advise the secretary of war on "Negro affairs" and to oversee the training and morale of troops. Scott was the classic subordinate type—fastidious, resourceful, and non-threatening. As Young went into excruciating retirement in Ohio, Scott, disappointed and surprised at not being chosen to succeed Washington, took up his consolation prize in an office in the Department of Interior. Scott's note of December 1, letting Du Bois know that he had "personally presented to Secretary Baker the last issue of *The Crisis* with your editorial referring to him," was an encouraging sign that the spirit of Amenia still lived. Baker's conduct thus far had been fairer than one would have expected from a member of Wilson's cabinet, the editor had written. But a few days later, Du Bois sensed that skulduggery was afoot. Villard had learned of the chief of staff's confidential plan to assign at least 70 percent of the African-American draftees to labor service and stevedore units, preventing the great majority from bearing arms and seeing action under fire. Except for a limited number of corporals, all officers and noncommissioned officers in the labor units (Pershing suggested renaming them Service of Supply, "SOS") would be white. "I can't think this is true," Du Bois wrote Baker. The secretary's reply of December 13 was one long exercise in obfuscation. When Scott followed up Baker's letter with a tortured evasion of the army's racial policy for the labor units, Du Bois replied that other sources had confirmed the army's plans. "It is shameful," he snapped. "What can be done about it?" The special assistant for Negro Affairs fell silent, at least for the moment. Meanwhile, there were equally dispiriting reports from Camp Des Moines confirming what young career sergeant George Schuyler had found after his assignment as an instructor there—that "none of the prescribed courses of study given at other (white) camps were given to the colored candidates."[17]

After all the controversy and suspicions about standards, Camp Des Moines graduated its first class of officers on October 15, an extra month having been tacked on to their ninety-day training period. Until the end, the actual commissioning of any of the 1,250 men had remained doubtful. His credibility on the line as never before, Du Bois insisted on seeing Baker "for his [Baker's] soul's good" (as he jested to Archibald Grimké) at the end of September. As he recalled the exchange at the War Department, the secretary asserted stonily that the army was not "trying by this war to settle the Negro problems." "True," Du Bois retorted, "but you are trying to settle as much of it as interferes with winning the war." With 106 captains, 329 first lieutenants, and 204 second lieutenants having joined their units in October, the editor unsuccessfully urged the War Department to create a second camp for African-American officer candidates.[18]

Now that the right had been won to die discriminated against in the war for world democracy, Du Bois momentarily stood back from the fray to write another synoptic piece akin to "The African Roots of the War." Once again, he said what no other public figure, irrespective of race, thought or wanted to say—that the future of Africa was one of the most important questions "to be answered after this war." He presumed that several centuries of exploitation had made it psychologically implausible for Europeans to be other than indifferent or silent about the fate of Africa—and "of something between 150,000,000 and 200,000,000 human beings?" Yet, Africa ("The Negro's Fatherland," as the essay in the November *Survey* was titled) was playing a role exactly analogous to that of Africa in America. "Negro troops have saved France," he wrote, with the First Battle of the Marne in mind. "They have conquered German Africa. They and their American Negro brothers are helping to save Belgium."[19] If the franchise and the erosion of Jim Crow were dividends that African-Americans would reasonably expect in return for their services, then a "great free central African state" was a reasonable form of compensation for what Du Bois called "the terrible world history between 1441 and 1861," roughly the span of the Atlantic slave trade. "Surely after Belgium has suffered almost as much from Germany as Africa has suffered from her," Du Bois proposed, going well beyond the resolutions of the first Pan-African Congress of 1900, "she ought be willing to give up the Congo to this end; and it would be right that England should refrain from taking German East Africa as well as refrain from handing it back."[20] Like the League of Nations envisaged by the visionary racialist in the White House, Du Bois's postwar Africa ignored nationalism and economics. That the author of "The African Roots of the War" did so in this essay was not only because Du Bois the Victorian idealist—for all his cogent economics—still tended to dominate Du Bois the Socialist, but also because Du Bois often believed that he must disregard the logic of his own economic analyses for the sake of his racial and social aspirations.

JANUARY AND February 1918 brought Du Bois two memorable rewards. The NAACP minutes for January 14 show that he was absent when the board took formal notice of *The Crisis* finally going over the fifty thousand mark—53,750 sold in December. January was a very good month indeed for the editor. Perennially strapped for cash and forced to borrow regularly from affluent admirers, he was granted a $3,600 annual salary by the board. Field secretary Johnson, whose work toward organizing various branches had been immensely successful, moved up to $3,000, and both he and Du Bois were gratified to have their recommendation of young Atlanta University graduate Walter Francis White accepted as NAACP assistant secretary.[21] In fact there was a host of major personnel changes in January, but Du Bois's speaking engagements kept him from most of the board meetings well into March. At the January 7 meeting, Joel Spingarn's leave of absence as chairman had been accepted. Appealing to Theodore Roosevelt, sundry congressmen, Emmett Scott, and contacts within the army, during the previous year the forty-three-year-old Spingarn had spent fretful months seeking a waiver of the age regulation for officers, until he was finally admitted to officer training at the beginning of May. Obtaining the rank of infantry major after a superb response to the rigors of training, he had been about to embark for France with his battalion from Hoboken, New Jersey, when he was struck by a crippling attack of ulcers. Then, in December, Troutbeck had burnt to the ground just as he was recovering from surgery. Undaunted, Major Spingarn was now on his way to Military Intelligence in Washington.[22]

But not before Du Bois prevailed upon him to nominate Ovington as his replacement, in order, he wrote tactfully, to avoid "the usual unpleasant candidate"—Villard. At the same meeting, Lillian Wald and Florence Kelley had suggested a permanent replacement for Nash. The polished and effective Johnson would have seemed an ideal successor, but Ovington continued to believe that he lacked sufficient fire, and Wald and Kelley would have had reservations about putting an African-American in such a position of authority. Villard's candidate, his old classmate and fellow pacifist, Roger Baldwin, was opposed on account of his friendship and his pacifism.[23] And so, again, another white social worker, John R. Shillady, took over the daily running of the NAACP. Keeping Villard at bay was always paramount, of course, and the editor took for granted that Ovington's accession to the chair would mean an ever freer rein on *The Crisis*. But the January issue carrying Du Bois's brief editorial, "Thirteen," had been slipped past the magazine's editorial committee. In scorching language, it condemned the Wilson administration for hanging thirteen of the Houston soldiers without even the formality of appeal. We raise our clenched fists, the editor cried, "against the hundreds of thousands of white murderers, rapists, and scoundrels who have oppressed, killed, ruined, robbed, and debased their black fellow men and fellow women, and yet, today, walk scot-free, unwhipped of justice, uncondemned by millions of their white fellow citizens, and unrebuked by the President of the United States."[24] Despite her strong support for Du Bois's independence, Ovington called Du Bois to account as strenuously as Villard and Spingarn ever had.

Reprimanded by one friend, Du Bois was celebrated by another. Joel Spingarn was well enough that he was able to take charge of what would become an annual major celebratory occasion—a Du Bois birthday. Spingarn's recuperation was mentioned with gladness in *The Crisis*, "For who can replace the few white friends who are willing to work WITH us and not merely FOR US," the editor challenged. Du Bois would turn fifty that February, and his friend intended to orchestrate a testimonial dinner in Manhattan that would surpass Amenia in terms of the luster of its guest list. Jessie Fauset and Georgia Douglas Johnson, the Washington poet, were unable to participate, but the latter contributed "Sonnet to Dr. W.E.B. Du Bois"—"Grandly isolate as the God of day,/Blazing an orbit through the dark and gloom/Of misty morning, fair and far you loom. . . ." Herbert Croly and research scientist Simon Flexner also sent regrets, as did William Bulkley, Horace Bumstead, Albert Hart, and Ray Stannard Baker. Hart's regrets included lavish praise for his old student, and Du Bois expressed pleasure in the tribute, but added that Hart's *American Year Book* "always says surprisingly little about the Negro in America and elsewhere." From Great Barrington came warm salutations from Frank Hosmer, to whom he owed, "more than to any single person, the fact that I got started toward the higher training in my youth." Sophonisba Breckinridge wished him well with a simple, "You have of course known for many years of my admiration and gratitude." Detained in Atlanta, John Hope wrote praising his friend as a man dedicated to serving "other people rather than yourself." Bessie Taylor Page, a former Atlanta University student, was not on Spingarn's list, but, after reading about the birthday banquet, she sent her professor a remarkable chronicle of his tenure at the university and the apt tribute: "It is a wonderful opportunity to be Dr. Du Bois."[25]

Bessie Page's words were uncannily echoed in Du Bois's after-dinner text, "The Shadow of Years," an autobiographical survey of his life. The tuxedo was perfectly cut and the brilliance of the chandeliers accented his bronze complexion. The distinguished and the merely important listened as the short, balding intellectual spoke of the golden river and the shadow of two great hills. "The most disquieting sign of my mounting years," he said, was a certain garrulity about himself, "quite foreign to my young days." It was his evening, and his garrulity was splendidly self-indulgent. He acknowledged Nina, sitting somewhat careworn and closed but deeply proud of her Will, as he led the full room at a gallop from the Berkshires to *The Crisis*. "*The Crisis* succeeded, and here I am on my fiftieth birthday." A pause for dramatic effect, and he finished. "Last year, I looked death in the face and found its lineaments not unkind. But it was not my time."[26] In the admiring fellowship of that Saturday night, February 23, 1918, Du Bois surveyed the struggle of his life from its summit, a high peak from which he alone peered down and hurled thunderbolts. If there were others scaling those heights who would soon deploy competing banners aloft, for the present they remained insignificant specks on the face of the mountain. Bessie Page was exactly right, being Dr. Du Bois was a "wonderful opportunity."

The wonderful opportunity of being Du Bois was fully impressed upon the White House, the American Federation of Labor, and the General Education Board that spring. They were virtually written off in *The Crisis*. His "The Black Man and the Unions" was the acrid fruit of East St. Louis and would fix Du Bois's antiunion hostility for years to come. He had reached this personal decision "reluctantly and in the past have written and spoken little of the closed door of opportunity," but it was now absolutely clear that, under the leadership of the AFL, there was "absolutely no hope of justice for an American of Negro descent."[27] The GEB, an old *bête noire*, came in for a drubbing that would become the primer of Talented Tenth educators as they retreated and regrouped before the juggernaut benefactions financed by the Rockefellers. Their worst fears had begun to materialize as the interlocked philanthropies of the GEB mounted a concerted campaign to dismantle liberal arts instruction in African-American colleges. Long and anxiously awaited, the 724-page definitive report of the U.S. Bureau of Education and the Phelps-Stokes Fund on African-American higher education appeared at the close of 1917. The death of Hollis Frissell in October of that year had already evoked one of Du Bois's most condign verdicts yet about the vocational education that

Armstrong, Baldwin, and Ogden had foisted on Afro-America. Frissell's death coincided with the approaching fiftieth anniversary of Hampton's founding. An imprudent white administrator had invited Du Bois's considered views of the institute as part of a commemorative edition. In his "Dear Miss Davis" letter in the November *Crisis*, Du Bois had written that little that Hampton had done or possibly would do commended itself to the Talented Tenth. "We have seldom voiced this opposition," he admitted in concluding his lengthy indictment, "and I voice it now only at your invitation."[28]

The author of the GEB-inspired report, Thomas Jesse Jones, was a transplanted Welshman and former Hampton Institute professor who had become one of the "Negro experts" consulted by the large foundations to the almost total exclusion of Du Bois and his circle. Even if his two-volume *Negro Education: A Study of the Private and Higher Schools for Colored People in the United States* was not as irresponsible, inaccurate, or negative as Du Bois asserted in a blistering review in the February *Crisis*, there is little doubt that the report's overall impact was to lower the peaks in African-American college and professional training and intensify its isolation from the academic mainstream for more than a decade.[29] The men behind Jones's report—the mandarins of the foundations—had been increasingly dismayed and finally exasperated by the persistent unwillingness of many black educators and students to embrace the system of higher education that the GEB and its affiliates deemed appropriate to the economic and social needs of the New South. Time after time, the foundation mandarins had believed that the Hampton-Tuskegee model of industrial education had been broadly and lastingly implanted, only to discover that scores of so-called universities and even tiny academies throughout the black South were still attempting to emulate the standard curriculum of the better white colleges and universities.

Not only had such courses somehow survived the scrutiny of white trustees, the adamant assurances of black presidents and principals, the formal excision from catalogues, and even the systematic discrimination by the great foundations against uncontrite miscreants such as Atlanta, Fisk, Lincoln, and Talladega, but there was considerable evidence that liberal arts and physical science (literature and languages, history and philosophy, physics and biology) were on the rebound. The former president of Tulane University, Dr. James Dillard, a kindly Virginian elevated to the directorship of both the Anna T. Jeanes and the John F. Slater funds, had been flabbergasted by what he had found in 1915 at the Ben Hill County

Training School deep in rural Georgia. The enterprising African-American principal had divided his academy into four departments offering Greek, German, psychology, ethics, moral philosophy, economics, and evidences of Christianity. Nor was Ben Hill County Training School an anomaly. The GEB's Jackson Davis (he would someday prove to be one of Du Bois's most valuable supporters) blamed the problem of creeping higher education on the failure of administrators and faculty to resist "the popular demand of colored people for pretentious and high sounding courses."[30] Instead of wanting instruction in cooking, carpentry, tailoring, laundering, and animal care—skills mandated by the GEB—too many African-American students and their instructors repeatedly betrayed an incorrigible propensity for college subjects that could lead to careers in teaching, law, medicine, preaching, and business.

Du Bois was even more aware than the Dillards and the Joneses of the skimpy resources and inflated courses existing in scores of such colleges. The mandarins at the GEB could pretend to ignore *The College-Bred Negro* and *The Negro Common School* (repeated in 1910 and 1911, respectively), but the inescapable fact remained that Du Bois's monographs were the first, and, until the Jones study, the most comprehensive on the subject. The curriculum at the Ben Hill School or that in place at Fort Valley High and Industrial School (another Georgia institution) would not have astonished the well-traveled editor. The crucial difference between the GEB officials and Du Bois, however, was that the former saw such schools as educational follies fully justifying the foundation's policy of wholesale elimination from African-American higher education of valid, grown-up arts and science courses. For Du Bois, the proliferation of bogus colleges and anemic academies provided evidence of a people's edifying desire to escape the dead end of being hewers of wood and drawers of water. But the real problem, he believed, was not that there were too many bad African-American schools but that the emergence of a few excellent ones had been systematically impeded by white philanthropy. Du Bois saw the sabotaging of the strongest institutions as the underlying purpose of Jones's report.

As Jones documented with abundant data, there were too many black institutions whose collegiate and university standards were inferior—"only 33 of the 653 private and State schools for colored people are teaching any subjects of college grade." In many of the strongest schools, the curriculum, heavy with Greek, Latin, and philosophy, remained essentially as the first wave of earnest Yankee preceptors had left it at the end of the nineteenth century. Jones had in mind situations such as the one at Fisk, where fierce resistance to reform of the curriculum had come to Du Bois's attention through a frantic letter from the daughter of his old professor of Greek. "All over the South pressure has been brought to bear in favor of industrial and vocational training," Mary Spence wrote. She added, barely able to credit what she had heard, that Talladega "does not require either Latin or Greek for the B.A. degree."[31] She and her allies intended to "lay down our lives for the cause." Du Bois realized that such antiquarianism (repeatedly illustrated in Jones's report) did the cause of higher education a disservice. Greek and Latin alone were not the measure of the modern educated man and woman. Moreover, as he had repeatedly written during his jousting with the Wizard, it was a tragic error to frame the issue as a choice between either the Hampton-Tuskegee model or the Fisk-Atlanta model. Knowing that the "ordinary reader unacquainted with the tremendous ramifications of the Negro problem" would welcome the report with "unstinted praise," Du Bois bluntly stated the charge: *Negro Education* was intended "to make the higher training of Negroes practically difficult, if not impossible." It was not what the report stated, but the *tone* of its argument and its ulterior purpose. Jones's report invoked the aphorisms of Booker T. Washington in the opening pages—"It has been necessary to demonstrate to the white man in the South that education does not 'spoil' the Negro, as it has been so often predicted that it would."[32]

Du Bois fumed that it was not "merely a silly desire to study 'Greek,' " as Jones had repeatedly intimated, that lay behind the preference for liberal arts at Atlanta, Fisk, Howard, and Lincoln. Rather, it was the Talented Tenth goal of developing "a class of thoroughly educated men according to modern standards." To do so, he argued, "these Negro colleges must be planned as far as possible according to the standards of white colleges." There must be no misunderstanding of the ulterior goals behind the Jones document. *Negro Education* was a master plan to bring about the restriction and replacement of "academic and higher education among Negroes . . . by a larger insistence on manual training, industrial education, and agricultural training; *secondly*," he lectured, "the private schools in the South must 'cooperate' with the Southern whites; and *third*, there should be more thoroughgoing unity of purpose among education boards and foundations working among Negroes."[33] Du Bois knew what few other Americans, black or white, knew (in part, because John Hope had been present at the critical moment): that the outline of Jones's "scientific" document had been largely drafted in late November 1915 at a meeting in

New York attended by foundation officials for the purpose of gaining consensus and direction in the wake of Booker Washington's death.

Chaired by Frissell, the conference began promptly at 10:00 A.M. at 61 Broadway. Among the eleven white men attending were Abraham Flexner, author of the revolutionary report (1910) on medical and scientific education in America (Flexner had recently ascended to a GEB secretaryship); Eban Charles Sage, distinguished Baptist preacher and one of the GEB's most influential secretaries; James Dillard (arriving late); Jackson Davis, one of the GEB's most indefatigable "circuit riders"; Wycliffe Rose, soon to head the Rockefeller Foundation's new International Education Board; and Jones.[34] Moton, still at Hampton, and Hope from Morehouse were also present. Four items comprised the agenda, but the first and fourth were paramount: GEB cooperation with public school authorities in the South "in developing state school systems for Negroes adequate in extent and adjusted in content to local needs"; and the ascertaining of "sound policy" appropriate as to the "number, scope, support and development of higher academic institutions for Negroes." But for its grave and enduring consequences, the session that morning at the GEB was, as Du Bois would later learn, hilarious. On the subject of adequate preparation of public school teachers, the principled but diplomatic Hope observed that if African-American salaries continued to slide, fewer qualified men and women would enter the profession. The Morehouse president touched upon the bedrock issue of the racially discriminatory allocation of public education funds in the South. Frissell, however, wondered if that were really a problem: "I am always saying to our students at Hampton that any man that goes out, if he has industrial training and goes into the country with the amount of land that there is, and knows about farming, that he can combine teaching and farming in such a way as to really make a living, even with a small salary."[35]

Jones, the future author of the two-volume report, was enthusiastic about the concept of a teaching cadre that would be virtually self-financing through farming. "Our ideals as yet, in many of these schools, are the literary ideals," he explained. Farming would be pedagogically invaluable. "Well, that is very questionable, Doctor," interposed the dogged Hope. "If a man is really going to do the teaching that you want him to do, he won't have much time for farming." All heads turned to Major Moton for an opinion. "You are right and wrong, sir," Moton said firmly. "That is my opinion." Moton, a large man, smiled disarmingly. He went on about a man named Johns ("I was thinking, since you have been talking, of Johns") who had a family and wanted to teach, but whose salary with the Pittsburgh insurance company paid him seventy-five dollars monthly, plus commissions. "We could not move him at all," Moton explained. "His family is staring him in the face, and it will take two thousand dollars to equip a farm to do any farming. . . . That is the difficulty, sir." Frissell was annoyed by the turn things were taking. Hope pushed the discussion toward an unwelcome conclusion by voicing the growing suspicion among African-Americans that the GEB intended to sanction "actually a different kind of education for Negroes." Flexner broke in to say that a different kind of education was exactly what was appropriate. "They do not give the colored teachers the same examinations they give the white teachers," Hope countered, "and the question is arising whether there is to be a public school education for white children in the South, and another for education for colored children in the South, and I was just wondering," he concluded, closing in on the essence of the meeting, "I was just wondering whether this 'adequate in extent and adequate in content' had any reference to that at all."[36]

It was time for the more philosophical observations of Rose and Flexner. Indeed it had, Flexner replied emphatically. "It seems to me, Dr. Frissell," Flexner purred, "it is very important to distinguish between what it is worthwhile doing for no better reason than that the white schools are and have been doing it, and what all schools, both white and colored, had better be doing." "A costly mistake had been made," said he, in granting women the same educational opportunities as men. What society had to settle for now were "secondary schools and colleges for women organized precisely the way the colleges for men and secondary schools for boys were organized, with the result that we have got a very widespread and deep seated dissatisfaction for both." It would have been enormously better for women, Flexner explained, to have worked out "an education for white girls that really met their needs."[37] As the educators adjourned for lunch, it was painfully apparent to Hope—just as it would be to Du Bois when he reviewed Jones's *Negro Education* almost three years later—that African-Americans were not to have the benefit of "mistakes" made in the case of white women.

To assail the work of the GEB, the Phelps-Stokes Fund, and the U.S. Bureau of Education was audacious. But to predict the undermining of European dominion over darker races and the radical redrawing of the color line in the United States invited a federal indictment. Refusing to be intimidated at first, Du Bois wrote in *The Crisis* for June 1918 that "soon or late" would come an independent China, self-government for Egypt and India, and "an Africa for the Africans and not merely for business exploitation. Out of this war will rise, too, an American Negro, with a right to vote and a right to work and a right to live without insult." The circulation of the magazine was approaching eighty thousand, and those elements in the federal government preoccupied with sedition and subversion took particular notice. There had already been a clumsy effort at intimidation in June 1917 when federal agents called at *The Crisis* to make inquiries about "two German girls" rumored to work for the editor.[38] Military Intelligence and the Justice Department had already assembled dossiers on the "questionable activities" of NAACP personnel and the inflammatory editorial line of its monthly organ. Even Spingarn found his military career threatened because of his involvement in the segregated officer-training camp. Given to dramatic oratorical gestures, the chairman had sometimes indulged in reverse psychology, agreeing with young Talented Tenth critics that America had given them little to fight for, in order to gain their confidence. Literal-minded to the point of absurdity, Military Intelligence and Bureau of Investigation officers had begun to keep careful record of Spingarn's seditious statements.

Spingarn regarded suspicions about the depth of his patriotism as an intolerable affront, and quite probably motivated in part by anti-Semitism. He responded by going on the offensive at the end of April, having himself placed in the Military Intelligence Branch (MIB) of the army. Simultaneously, he complained of pacifist dawdling at the NAACP; in a memorandum to legal advisor Studin he charged that the government would tolerate "no carping and bitter utterances likely to foment disaffection and destroy the morale of our people for the winning of the war."[39] As Emmett Scott pressed his case with Newton Baker, Major Spingarn proposed the creation of an intelligence unit to encourage and monitor African-American participation in the war—a subsection of MI-4 (counter-espionage) for special work on "Negro subversion." The colonel in command of Military Intelligence (bearing the studio-cast name of Marlborough Churchill) was favorably disposed at first. Fully informed of the dossiers being compiled in the Justice Department, the post office, and Military Intelligence that could lead to suppression of *The Crisis*, Spingarn urged Scott to suggest that the U.S. Committee on Public Information (the "Creel Committee," for its chairman, George E. Creel) arrange a Washington conference of black editors. Spingarn sent letters to the White House pleading for the president to express concern for improved race relations.

With Moorfield Storey's guidance and Missouri representative L. C. Dyer's pledge to introduce it, he worked furiously on the states' rights complexities of a bill to make lynching a federal crime.[40]

But as he prepared to take up his assignment with Military Intelligence, Spingarn made a decision that would come deadly close to wrecking the career of the friend whose fifty years of intellect and courage he had recently caused to be celebrated. That decision had all the marks of invincible rectitude. Any pausing to consider opposing views was deemed misguided, if not indicative of a character flaw. For that very reason, when Joel Spingarn brought Du Bois to the capital on June 4 to urge him to consider a captaincy in Military Intelligence, his proposal derived from a mentality that inflated self-justification into a science. As Joel reconstructed the exchange between them for the benefit of Amy ("don't breathe a word of this to a human soul"), he had given Du Bois "the shock of his life by offering him a commission." In the quarters he had rented near 1330 F Street, NW, the office of Military Intelligence ("my new work is to be Jim-Crowed"), where Spingarn had already begun recruiting African-American agents, he described in glowing terms the work they would do together to win the war for democracy in Europe and for civil rights in America. Given the major's growing influence in Washington and the captain's established influence upon African-American opinion, theirs would be an effective operation designed to speak to the people for the government and to the government on behalf of the people. "It will mean a great deal, not only for him and his, but for the whole country," Amy read. Spingarn's elation was contagious. He had given Colonel Churchill "a big vision of things to be accomplished" and Du Bois seemed to come round, remarking after the "shock," Joel told Amy, that Spingarn ought be in the State Department rather than the War Department.[41]

But there was no time for delay; Spingarn needed a quick answer. It is now clear that Du Bois gave an affirmative answer before leaving Spingarn's office, although it must have been understood that ratification by the NAACP board would be indispensable. Without waiting for the formalities, Spingarn assured Colonel Churchill and others in the Justice Department that he had the editor's promise to "change the tone" of *The Crisis* to make it "an organ of patriotic propaganda hereafter." In fact, passage of the Sedition Act that May, containing draconian penalties for speaking, writing, or publishing "disloyal, profane, scurrilous, or abusive language," had already led the editor and the board to agree that Studin should have formal responsibility for reviewing the magazine's copy. A visit by an agent from the American Protective League (a citizens' organization) to a much-rattled Dill that June further confirmed the need for extreme caution. Spingarn's assurance, then, to intelligence officials of Du Bois's alleged agreement could be interpreted as a response to federal law.[42] Not only did going to jail hold no attraction, Du Bois was as much a patriot, according to his own lights, as any citizen.

The commission option, like the camp, should have caused Du Bois at least a few days of introspection. He would have anticipated serious opposition from the board on the part of Villard and Grimké, not to mention savage recriminations from Trotter and his allies. But his quick response to Spingarn's offer was in many ways a replay of the D.C. assistant superintendency, not fully thought through, a radical departure from activities that had defined him for others, and an exercise in personal conceit. To a parochial mind, or one more organizationally attuned, the perils of service in Military Intelligence would have been unmistakable, but to Du Bois, for whom parochial concerns and institutional constraints were always poorly tolerated, the captaincy was another challenge to be turned to magnificent personal and group advantage in defiance of the odds. Spingarn's tug on him was not one of intellectual affinity alone but also in the nature of a debt to a friend, a friend whose purse was available for loans, whose personal physician stood by in sickness, and whose influence enhanced a friend's achievements. Du Bois reached his decision before conferring with the NAACP board or inviting the counsel of solid friends like Ovington, Hope, or Crawford. In two full pages of single-spaced type, he declared himself conscious of "no inconsistency with or change of attitude" from his long-held conduct and opinions. "A remarkable opportunity for far-reaching work" in military service beckoned, he wrote Colonel Churchill. By the end of June, he was as intoxicated as Spingarn, whose letters to Amy boasted of success in effecting "an almost epoch-making alliance of all the factions—if the thing goes through. It means that twelve millions are unanimously mobilized in support of the country, and the sleeping volcano may not become dangerous after all."[43]

Spingarn's "epoch-making alliance" referred to the Washington conference of forty-one prominent African-Americans, thirty-one of whom were publishers and editors, arranged by Scott during June 19, 20, and 21, 1918. Trotter smelled a sellout and boycotted it (holding his own Washington meeting with Wells-Barnett and others a week later). In addition to most of the Amenia participants, the Scott conference was attended by Moton, Grimké, Calvin Chase, Mary Terrell, and Robert S. Abbott of the powerful

Chicago *Defender*. George Creel, as near to a minister of propaganda as anything the nation had seen before, failed to persuade the president to address the meeting. Speaking with Trotter in mind, Wilson told Creel that in previous encounters with him, prominent African-Americans had "gone away dissatisfied. I have never had the opportunity to do what I promised them I would seek an opportunity to do," he added, just as he was dodging yet another such opportunity. Newton Baker, navy assistant secretary Franklin Delano Roosevelt, Creel, Scott, and Spingarn gave rousing speeches, and Du Bois drafted the conference's carefully balanced resolutions affirming that the African-American was "not disposed to catalogue, in this tremendous crisis, all his complaints and disabilities." The African-American asked, instead, for "that minimum of consideration which will enable him to be an efficient fighter for victory."[44] None of the forty-one participants knew then that four days earlier, Du Bois had reported for his army physical examination. Both his age and his failure to pass the examination were overlooked on Baker's instructions, and Du Bois had proceeded to Scott's meeting assured of a captain's commission (Spingarn had even suggested the probability that it might be upped to major). As he looked back on this extraordinary chapter of his life, Du Bois claimed that he had been spellbound by Spingarn, that "due to his influence" he had come "nearer to feeling myself a real and full American than ever before or since."[45]

Real Americans are frequently past masters at making deals, and evidence points to the fact that Du Bois struck a deal, through Spingarn, with the War Department to use the enormous influence of his magazine toward rallying African-Americans behind the war in return for the heady opportunities he and Spingarn persuaded themselves their military commissions would yield. Personal vanity and civil rights aspirations were inextricably enmeshed, and the strategy adopted by Du Bois to win over the public was intended to preempt, disconcert, and even cow critics of the captaincy offer before there could be any widespread, reasoned discussion. The deal implied cold calculation and make-or-break audacity, and it was unworthy of Du Bois not because what he proceeded to write could not have been honorably defended on its own terms but because what he wrote was in large part written in order to consummate the bargain. "Close Ranks," his editorial for July 1918, was the first installment payment on that bargain. When he recapitulated the chronology of writing "Close Ranks" for the head of the Cleveland branch of the NAACP, the editor would claim that it was not "until June 15th that the tentative offer of the captaincy was made" and that this famously controversial editorial had been written on June 6 in time for the printer's June 10 deadline. But as Du Bois knew, the offer of the commission had actually been proffered by Spingarn on June 4. June 15 was the date of the physical examination, and, in any case, as with the earlier neglect of Trotter, the *Crisis* printing deadline tended to be inflexible only when it suited the editor. Little wonder, then, that he would claim more than twenty years later that he had difficulty "in thinking clearly" when trying to "reconstruct in memory my thought . . . during the World War."[46] Nor is it surprising that the *Autobiography* omits any mention of the Military Intelligence venture.

Whatever the conflictive origins of "Close Ranks," readers were transfixed by its prose. "This is the crisis of the world," Du Bois intoned. "For all the long years to come men will point to the year 1918 as the great Day of Decision . . ."

> We of the colored race have no ordinary interest in the outcome. That which the German power represents today spells death to the aspirations of Negroes and all the darker races for equality, freedom and democracy. Let us not hesitate. Let us, while this war lasts, forget our special grievances and close our ranks shoulder to shoulder with our white fellow citizens and the allied nations that are fighting for democracy. We make no ordinary sacrifice, but we make it gladly and willingly with our eyes lifted to the hills.[47]

If Trotter, stunned and disgusted, found nothing more to say than that "Close Ranks" was a mistake, it evoked bitter reproach from Harry Smith, Archibald Grimké, and much of the African-American press. Du Bois wrote, almost as if flinching from the reaction, that "the words were hardly out of my mouth when strong criticism was rained upon it." Niagarite Byron Gunner wrote Du Bois pleading that "now, 'while the war lasts,' is the most opportune time for us to push and keep our 'special grievances' to the fore." Crawford grasped both sides of the issue; he agreed that Du Bois's work with Military Intelligence "would be a magnificent thing for the race," but he worried about the fate of *The Crisis*. "The learned Dr. Du Bois has seldom packed more error into a single sentence," the New York correspondent for the Pittsburgh *Courier* wrote—words less harsh than those of the editor of the New York *News,* who declared that Du Bois's actions amounted to "crass moral cowardice." Randolph and Owen at *The Messenger* ("The Only Radical Negro Magazine in America") alternated between ridicule and regret in their response to the *Crisis* editorial line. Many of those who might have favored acceptance of the commission were incensed at the racial insult of a mere captaincy.[48]

As *The Crisis* reached its subscribers, Du Bois's July 2 circular letter to the board announced that, with the blessings of Spingarn and Ovington, he was disposed to accept a commission in Military Intelligence but only if the NAACP agreed to two conditions—to his retaining control of the magazine and to his officer's pay being supplemented in order to maintain "my present income." At the meeting that same day, board members Ovington, Spingarn, Cook, Waller, and Young supported the editor's request, but they were adamantly opposed by the majority ("the pacifists," as Du Bois called them). Grimké, backed by the sharp-tongued Neval Thomas, informed the board that he would lead the Washington branch out of the association unless the editor severed his connection with the magazine upon assuming military rank. As far as Thomas was concerned, Du Bois had "reversed his whole life, and is no more good to us." Joseph Loud of the Boston branch was equally opposed, while Villard, Kelley, and others against his retention of the magazine looked upon Du Bois's behavior as shameful.[49] There seemed to be no reason why James Weldon Johnson could not run *The Crisis* except that the editor objected to it.

The Crisis continued to defend the new tack in August and September. "This is Our Country: We have worked for it, we have suffered for it, we have fought for it; we have made its music, we have tinged its ideals, its poetry, its religion, its dreams," the editor lectured in "A Philosophy in Time of War," a rhetorical excess that read more like the script for *The Star of Ethiopia* than an editorial. "We are the Ancient of Days, the First of the Races and the Oldest of Men. Before Time was, we are," he huffed and puffed. "Patience, then, without compromise." In "Our Special Grievances," readers were assured that his July editorial had been circulated and approved by "prominent members and officers of the Board," that nothing in it was "in the slightest degree inconsistent" with the battle for the "full manhood rights of the American Negro," and that the editorial echoed the resolution unanimously adopted by the editors "of all the leading Negro publications in America"—at the very moment when most of the editors were condemning him. Much had already been accomplished, he insisted; equal rights under the draft; nearly a thousand officers trained at Camp Des Moines; Scott as special assistant in the War Department; higher wages and better employment; the overthrow of segregation ordinances (unspecified); and, at long last (and due to Spingarn's desperate plea after more than eighty lynchings had occurred that year), a public statement from Woodrow Wilson in late July denouncing mob violence.[50]

But, in the week following the explosion within the board, Du Bois began to take the full measure of his Washington alliance, writing to Spingarn about the "incredible stupidity" of the opposition, the undreamed of "upheaval," and the "mistaken feeling among colored people that I should not take this work"; but he did wonder now "how far it is my duty to fly in the face of this opinion." Then, too, there was the serious financial risk, if the board forced him to choose between his editorial salary and a captain's pay. If he were younger, of course, it would never occur to him to hesitate, he said. Furious with the association, threatening to leave it altogether, and even going so far as to tell Studin that he would broadcast that "the organization is dangerously unpatriotic and anti-American," the badly unnerved Spingarn practically begged Du Bois not to cave in and leave him to run his department alone. Spingarn could not believe that his friend would falter. "The opportunity to do such work as this will never come again," he argued, "and it would be madness . . . to let the opportunity slip by."[51] As for the monetary risk, Major Spingarn observed that there were ready ways of handling that. But Captain, or perhaps Major Du Bois had already begun to retreat.

On July 12, the same day he wrote to Spingarn, Du Bois had finally sought Hope's advice in a letter that was also designed to suggest the offer of a Morehouse professorship after military service. Hope's reply, a masterpiece of good sense, granted the supreme value of patriotism but argued that African-Americans must be "patriots *efficiently*." He wondered whether Du Bois's most useful service lay in becoming "a secret service man pure and simple?"[52] Put that way, of course, the answer was inescapable. Spingarn soon learned from both Studin and Shillady that Du Bois's agonizing dilemma over salary was largely concocted. Although the board was firm in its insistence that either Grimké or Johnson (who soon asked to be taken out of consideration) should take over *The Crisis*, both the attorney and the executive secretary insisted that there had never been any reservation about maintaining Du Bois's gross income at its present level while he served his country. Even more remarkable was Studin's and Shillady's revelation that the editor had not made "an effective presentation of his case at the Board meeting" and that he had gone away on vacation with only a vague promise to return around the first of August. Studin was inclined to doubt that Du Bois "really wants the commission now in view of the storm that has been raised." Ovington had thought so, too, for she wrote Du Bois that he was "probably glad" about the board's decision.[53]

"Fortunately the matter never came to an issue," Du Bois claimed in the section of *Dusk of Dawn* dealing with the captaincy. He wrote blandly of the denouement. "Reaction and suspicion against Spingarn arose in the War Department." The editor was finally left "to work in *The Crisis* which was probably by far the best result."[54] But the reality was that Du Bois had found himself in the unusual and perturbing position of having to play a passive role until events decided for him. On the one hand, he now saw his alliance with Spingarn as potentially disastrous. Yet, on the other, he felt bound both by his word and the still-strong appeal of the great national work they might yet accomplish in Military Intelligence—to the consternation of their black and white critics. In the whipsaw of options, Du Bois decided to escape to the Maine backcountry, leaving Spingarn to cobble together the bureau in Washington and to forward the paperwork approving his epaulettes.

In Washington, however, resistance to Spingarn's plan had become formidable. Southern white officers in the MIB not only considered themselves experts on "Negro Subversion" by virtue of birth, but, as captains James L. Bruff and Harry A. Taylor's confidential memoranda to Colonel Churchill indicated, Du Bois's presence among them would be tantamount to the fox guarding the chicken coop. They noted that *The Crisis* was "extremely radical and antagonistic in tone," and was a major force in creating African-American unrest. As adverse information about Du Bois was being accumulated, a similar report about Spingarn arrived at MIB from its New York office. Major Nicholas Biddle cited a "recent report" that Spingarn had told the men of Harlem's 369th Infantry Regiment they had "no reason" to fight, that they were "discriminated against." Biddle thought it wise to remind Churchill that Spingarn "of course, as you know, is of Jewish race, and has often experienced the results of race prejudice."[55]

Under attack by Negrophobic southern officers and possibly anti-Semitic northern officers, Du Bois and Spingarn received the coup de grace from Major Walter H. Loving, one of a half dozen African-Americans working for the MIB. Loving's title came from service in the Philippines Constabulary, where he had directed the Manila Band until an early retirement. His intelligence activities among his own race were indefatigable. He seemed to be everywhere, comforting the mother of one of the hanged Houston soldiers, persuading her to "have a quiet funeral" for her son, seldom missing a church-basement rally of Garveyites or a Harlem street-corner oration by Asa Randolph or the black nationalist Hubert Harrison, or paying quiet courtesy calls to Talented Tenth leaders. On March 5, 1918, after an interview with Grimké, Loving reported to the MIB that he had made a friend "of one whom we have thought was an enemy of the government." Nine days later, Loving noted with satisfaction the more moderate tone of Kelly Miller's speeches and writings "since my first interview with him."[56] Chicago *Defender* publisher Robert Abbott was reported to have been similarly impressed after a visit.

Even after making allowance for his tendency to take credit for good weather, Loving's reports were remarkable for the subtlety of their analysis and their ultimate racial integrity, qualities which go far to explain his later friendship with Du Bois, a friendship that was to last until Loving's execution by the Japanese a few days before the Allied liberation of Manila in 1945.[57] On July 22, 1918, Loving delivered to Major Biddle a lengthy, engrossing report, "Conditions among Negroes in the United States," which was forwarded to Colonel Churchill immediately. "Close Ranks" was "in reality a boomerang," Loving explained. Du Bois was a man of "high intellectual attainments who has never been popular with his people because of his exclusive tendencies." The captaincy controversy convinced large numbers of African-Americans that *The Crisis* had "abandoned its stand on the race question." Loving concluded that the best service Du Bois could perform now was to continue at his magazine. The captaincy controversy would gradually die out, "whereas his appointment to a commission in the Army would give the radicals a continued thread for discussion and opportunity to implicate the government in the affair." Eight days later, Churchill informed Spingarn that, although his "hard work" was appreciated, the MIB would leave African-Americans to Bruff and Taylor of the Military Morale Section and would concentrate on the "morale of negro troops." In a private letter written on August 24, Churchill regretted the rejection of the program and expressed the hope that Spingarn could appreciate "how difficult for me was the situation which made it necessary for me to withdraw my unqualified support."[58] But by then, new orders had terminated Major Joel Spingarn's assignment to the MIB and sent him to the front. Churchill had informed Du Bois of rejection of his application for a commission in the MIB at the end of July. The War Department had had the benefit of their excellent services without being saddled with either NAACP man.

. . .

WOODROW WILSON sailed for Europe aboard the *George Washington* on December 4, 1918. The European civil war had ground to a close on November 11, after the deaths of 21 million civilians and combatants, in an armistice presumptively based on the American president's Fourteen Points. Four days later, Du Bois followed aboard the *Orizaba*, the official boat for the press. He, Moton, the newspaperman Lester Walton, and Moton's secretary Nathan Hunt were the only African-Americans, and they shared a cabin with bath. Walton was credentialed as a correspondent for the *Age* and Moton was on a government fact-finding mission (with Thomas Jesse Jones serving as chaperone) to investigate the treatment of African-American troops. Scott had had a hand in getting Du Bois on board as a member of the fifty-two-person press delegation, although the editor's own dramatic account of having buttonholed George Creel at dockside is certainly not to be discounted. Already aboard were Abraham Cahan of the *Jewish Daily Forward*; Ralph Pulitzer and Herbert B. Swope of the *World*; David Lawrence of the *Evening Post*; Arthur M. Evans of the *Chicago Tribune*; and Samuel S. McClure of the McClure Newspaper Syndicate.[59] Du Bois was on a mission for the NAACP to serve as special representative to the Peace Conference. The "primary" objective, however, was stipulated to be the "securing of material for the Negro history" of the war, for which $2,000 had been appropriated and $1,500 already advanced by Ovington. In Du Bois's account of the events leading up to this fateful voyage, the charge had fallen "out of a clear sky" when the board unexpectedly asked him to assumed these two responsibilities.[60]

But Du Bois owed his presence aboard the *Orizaba* mainly to Du Bois. The board's ratification in October 1918 of his proposal to convene a Pan-African Congress in Paris was certainly more than a formality, even though there was every indication that the State Department would deny passports to any Americans wishing to attend and the French government would refuse to act as host. But the board's interest in a Pan-African Congress was decidedly secondary, if not minimal, over and against the possibility of representation at Versailles and of a firsthand, comprehensive study of the treatment of black soldiers. Du Bois's ambitious "Memorandum on the Future of Africa," portions of which he had read at the Armistice Day meeting of the board, resulted in a resolution to send twenty-five "representative Negroes" to discuss with President Wilson the future of Africa at the peace conference. In a letter to Wilson concerning the peace, Du Bois implied that his accredited presence as an observer at Versailles would gratify peoples of African descent worldwide. By the time the State Department deigned to respond to the memorandum, inviting him to meet with the acting secretary in January, Du Bois was in Paris. "Only quick and adroit work on my part" and that of friends avoided the charade of official consideration awaiting him in Washington. But the Pan-African Congress still existed largely in his fecund mind.

What the NAACP board did not know, however, was that the much-described preparation for a collaborative project to research a three-volume history of the war also existed largely in Du Bois's mind. He would eventually give his planned book about the war the evocative title, "The Wounded World." As originally conceived, it served the dual purpose of satisfying his desire to write a sweeping historical narrative and the association's objective of presenting an assessment of black troop conditions in Europe. But the "Wounded World" project had been badly wounded only days after its October vote of approval, when Du Bois, Johnson, and Scott had dined together on Sunday, November 3, to discuss a common peacetime African-American agenda. Plans to commemorate the tercentenary of 1619 (the arrival of African-Americans in North America) were entirely satisfactory to Scott, as was the promotion of consumers' cooperatives through the National Negro Business League, but when they turned to the history of the war, collaboration faltered. Scott revealed that he was already considering publishers' proposals. The tone of Du Bois's memorandum to Scott five days afterward scarcely seemed appropriate to massaging a collaboration. The NAACP war history would be the "complete and definitive work, done with scientific accuracy and literary skill, and based on an exhaustive collection of facts and documents"—what was Scott's decision?[61] In light of the definitive November 10 reply by the War Department's special assistant, Du Bois's subsequent memorandum to the board that, in accordance with its vote, he had "arranged to cooperate with Emmett Scott on a History of the Negro in the Great War" was puzzling. Scott had said no, adding that his plans "need [not] interfere with your program." Collaboration with the always-cantankerous Carter Woodson at the Washington-based Association for the Study of Negro Life and History was equally doomed.[62]

That the NAACP board would only learn of these difficulties officially in April 1919, after the editor's return from abroad, raises the intriguing possibility that the Paris mission held an ulterior importance for Du Bois. Confessing that he had been "disposed to report to the board that any attempt to compile a history was inadvisable," he had decided, instead, to sail for France (leaving disclosure of difficulties with the historical collaboration until later). A sheet of stationery from Washington's Willard Hotel, bearing no date but obviously penned shortly before Joel Spingarn left for France in September 1918, contained a startling speculation. "Du Bois has never recovered from the blow to his popularity among his own people," he told Amy, but the board was "hoping that the Pan-African Congress may help somewhat to resuscitate him."[63] Du Bois bore a major responsibility for the fate of some 200,000 African-American doughboys shipped overseas. Most of them had ended up in Pershing's "SOS" units where they fought the war with strong backs and shovels, and where they had been generally treated like subhumans by southern white officers and NCOs.[64] Forty-two thousand black men had marched to the guns, though. In the last hours of the wasting Meuse-Argonne offensive, a regiment of the all-black 92nd Division had been thrown into the inferno for five days, and then withdrawn in disgrace. Du Bois saw its alleged shame as a personal affront. The battlefield performance of the four infantry regiments comprising the rump 93rd Division (devoid of artillery, transportation, quartermaster, or engineers) had been spectacular, yet reports reaching the NAACP of the army high command's determination to put the men "in their place" after service in French uniforms with French divisions was further cause for Du Bois to defend those who had closed ranks.

Whether or not Spingarn's interpretation was overdrawn, Du Bois may well have concluded that it was advisable, book or no book, to hurry to France whatever the pretext. Otherwise, like his nemesis Washington, he, too, risked discredit from a bargain that the other party had found it convenient not to honor. Behind the thunderous prose of this period a false note of commencing doubt is just audible. A riveting dithyramb, his armistice editorial in the December *Crisis* trembled with archaic passion, yet it seemed a measure or two over the line separating honest exhilaration from melodrama: "The nightmare is over. The world awakes. The long, horrible years of dreadful night are passed. Behold the sun! We have dreamed. Frightfully have we dreamed unimagined, unforgettable things—all lashed with blood and tears. Bound and damned we writhed and could not stir. . . . And now suddenly we are awake! It is done. We are sane. We are alive." Yet the grim, urgent question was to what extent those who were awake and alive now truly believed that their sacrifice had made sense. And did Du Bois, romantic but also skeptical and prescient, truly believe his own edifying words? The doubt festering behind the game prose was not yet doubt that he had been wrong ethically to call for the closing of ranks in the war but pragmatic doubt that he should have commended it so unequivocally (or given the appearance of doing so) in a situation in which no possibility of intrinsic right could exist.

Somewhat shaken, then, his certitude remained intact at its core that, in terms of the broad picture, there was no real distinction to be drawn between what was important to him and what was of value to those he claimed to speak for—both a strength and a besetting flaw. In that sense, Du Bois and Woodrow Wilson were kindred intellects, both bearers of ecumenical schemes that were visionary for the times. Leaders of hosts they believed they had created, both ex-college professors assumed that the multitudes could be converted to an idea through cogent, principled explanation. Aboard the *George Washington*, the president conducted a memorable seminar in the grand salon to explicate his Fourteen Points and League of Nations idea to the attending scholars, technocrats, and government servants.[65] Aboard the *Orizaba*, the editor, in interviews, didactically outlined his thirteen points promoting a "vast state in central Africa," in which "the actual government should use both colored and white officials and later natives should be worked in." "I went to Paris," he explained in *The Crisis*, "because today the destinies of mankind center there. Make no mistake as to this, my readers."[66] Du Bois's flight to Paris in the winter of 1918–19, whatever the tangle of motives, would achieve historic and enduring symbolism. These were days of almost delirious innocence and expectations, it must be remembered, with the American President touring European capitals like a messiah. Until the Council of Ten got down to business at the Hotel Crillon in Paris (quickly reduced to the Big Three after Italy bolted in a huff over Balkan real estate), millions of ordinary men and women joyously awaited the affirmation of their national aspirations, the drafting of just and open covenants, and the securing of world peace through international treaties upheld by a world body. Point Five of Wilson's Fourteen Points might have been drafted by Du Bois himself: "An absolutely impartial adjustment of all colonial claims, based on the principle that the interests of the population must have equal weight with the equitable claims of the government."

One hundred thousand readers followed his and the world's destinies in a stream of superbly narrated, often confessional, letters filling *The Crisis*. Monday morning, December 9, he docked at the military port of Brest, and marveled at the speed with which black SOS stevedores unloaded the *Orizaba*'s cargo. A sixteen-hour train ride brought him into the Gare Montparnasse, the scene of incredible confusion ("the worst I ever conceived of in well-ordered France")—"no one to collect tickets, no porters, no cabs and a surging crowd."[67] Leaving Moton and Walton at the station, Du Bois forged into the city with Hunt to find a hotel. Securing a hotel together in the Rue Richelieu near the Bibliothèque Nationale, Du Bois looked up Moton, with whom he had gotten on well, to ask Washington's successor to use his influence to expedite his application for a military pass to visit the African-American troop units. Then he hurried off to make arrangements to see Walter Lippmann, one of President Wilson's principal confidants.[68] Du Bois was counting on the fifth of Wilson's Fourteen Points to serve as the basis for his appeal on behalf of Africa to the world leaders assembled at Versailles. Opposition in Europe and America to the application of the Wilsonian charter to yellow, brown, and black peoples was, as the editor fully understood, formidable. "Reconstruction and Africa," another *Crisis* letter, inveighed against the "civilized" who claimed to fear regression and barbarism. "The truth is," he wrote plainly, "white men are merely juggling with words—or worse—when they declare that the withdrawal of Europeans from Africa will plunge that continent into chaos. What Europe, and indeed only a small group in Europe, wants in Africa is not a field for . . . civilization, but . . . exploitation." And here Du Bois posited a civilizing role in Africa for American-Africans that was intended (presumptuously, patronizingly, in the tradition of Crummellian Ethiopianism) both to counter European naysayers and to invest twelve struggling millions with an empowering cultural and political mystique. "The African movement means to us what the Zionist movement means to the Jews," Du Bois proclaimed, as Garvey would, "the centralization of the race effort and the recognition of a racial fount. To help bear the burden of Africa does not mean any lessening of effort in our own problem at home. . . . Amelioration of the lot of Africa tends to ameliorate the condition of colored peoples throughout the world."[69]

If there had ever been any doubt as to why he had come to Paris, if he himself had departed with mixed motives, now that Du Bois breathed French air, abused the language with verve (his French would never be more than passable), and found himself recognized in significant circles, the scab of racist America fell away. John Hope was there, ensconced at 12 rue d'Aguesseau in the aristocratic Faubourg St. Honoré, on YMCA business. They shared in each other's exhilaration.[70] Not long before sailing, he had dined in Cambridge with William James and been deeply grateful for that pleasure. That November, he had finally met Theodore Roosevelt in person for the first time, and, notwithstanding the former president's deplorable racial politics, Du Bois had introduced him to a Carnegie Hall meeting with pride and *Schadenfreude*. It was Roosevelt's last public address before dying. Yet, as Du Bois said over and again, he was convinced that "most Americans did not wish my personal acquaintance or contact with me except in purely business relations, and that many of them would repay any approach on my part with deliberate insult, while most of them would be at least embarrassed."[71] Europe restored his faith in humanity, whites included. "My God! For what am I thankful for this night?" he exclaimed soon after arriving. "For nothing. For nothing but the most commonplace of commonplaces: a table of gentlewomen and gentlemen—soft-spoken, sweet-tempered, full of human sympathy, who made me, a stranger, one of them." His African-American readers would have finished the short account with glistening eyes, as the editor recounted laughing and bantering without "the *Thing*—the hateful, murderous, dirty *Thing* which in America we call 'Nigger-hatred.' " "Paris, Paris by purple facade of the Opera, the crowd on the Boulevard des Italiens and the great swing of the Champs-Elysées."[72] For a few charged weeks he lived beyond the accursed veil.

"Vive la France!" in the March issue was another dithyramb, inspired by the ceremony in the Trocadero organized by the Colonial League to honor black, brown, and yellow men who had fought for the republic. " 'Mine eyes have seen' and they were filled with tears," Du Bois gushed. A black man in dress uniform, Bekhane Diop, his chest already beribboned, had been kissed by a general as the Legion of Honor was draped across him. "The great audience arose, roared and cried again when the crimson badge was pinned on an Arab who stood next to the Negro's left and the Annamite who stood to his right."[73] The general who kissed and knighted these nonwhite chevaliers that Sunday night, December 29, was none other than Louis Archinard, the architect, after Savorgnan de Brazza, of the French empire, an icon of the expansionists and protector of the dashing young navy and infantry officers who had won glory for *la patrie* overseas after the disastrous Franco-Prussian War of 1870. Had Marcus Garvey witnessed the spectacle in the Trocadero, he would hardly have been elated to see black men honored by their colonial masters for service that had prolonged their own subordination and exploitation. That Du Bois, author of "The African Roots of the War" and impresario of Pan-Africanism, saw no irony, paradox, and certainly no pathos, in Bekhane Diop's elevation, was a measure of the eccentric Eurocentrism and radicalism-from-above that still resided in the marrow of the author of *The Souls of Black Folk*. Perhaps European imperialism was ultimately reprehensible to Du Bois less for its inequities than because, at its Anglo-Saxon worst, it was founded on skin color. Thus, one result of the war, "of seemingly secondary, but really of prime importance," he told readers, was that "the American Negro should speak French" and Spanish, the languages of nations that Du Bois chose to deceive himself into believing discriminated on the basis of culture rather than color.[74]

The euphoria expressed in the *Crisis* letters belied the desperate predicament of the Pan-African Congress plans. The American secret service expected nothing to come of Du Bois's almost manic visits to politicians, journalists, distinguished academics, aides-de-camp to statesmen, and, finally, one or two highly placed members of Woodrow Wilson's court. In the three weeks of scurrying about ("with the American Secret Service at my heels"), Du Bois had failed to obtain approval for the congress. David Lloyd George, the British prime minister, was inaccessible and uninterested, and the French government informed American Secretary of State Robert Lansing of Du Bois's scheme to discuss African self-determination and of its decision to prohibit it.[75] Suddenly, there was a breakthrough. "Had it not been for one circumstance," Du Bois wrote dramatically, "it would have utterly failed; and that circumstance was that black Africa had the right to send from Senegal a member to the French Parliament."[76] Blaise Diagne was one of seven black members of the Chamber of Deputies and high commissioner for the Republic with special authority for French West Africa, a title so exalted that he outranked all of France's white servants in the colonies. Diagne was France's ideal African *évolué*, another of those colonials for whom the opening words in French elementary school primers—"*Nos peres, les Gaulois*" ("Our Fathers, the Gauls")—defined for a lifetime a conception of self.

In the hour of its greatest need, when German gunners had been close enough to site their artillery on the Eiffel Tower, Diagne raised 680,000 African soldiers for France in one year, and another 240,000 for labor duty. Like Du Bois, Diagne had wagered on greater rights for his people in return for fighting and dying in war. If Diagne would profess to be satisfied in the years ahead, however, it was not because France would have kept its pledge to the Africans of Senegal, but because Senegal's African deputy would be so well rewarded.[77] He was also Georges Clemenceau's trusted factotum. Through Diagne came news that the French government would permit Du Bois to hold his conference. Although as a young deputy Clemenceau had scoffed when the so-called M'Koko treaties, the building blocks of France's new empire, were ratified (with X's for signatures) by the Senate, he was in no way inclined to promote the independence of Africans or Asians in 1919. The cynical "Tiger" may have wanted to tweak the nose of the self-righteous Wilson by enabling one of the president's black American critics to obtain publicity in the United States by upholding Wilsonian principles in Paris. Some slight propaganda advantage in final discussions about the distribution of former German colonies might come, Clemenceau must have supposed, from Diagne's guarantee that the Pan-African Congress would extol France's *mission civilisatrice* overseas. Finally, the Pan-African Congress would afford France's favorite African statesman, Diagne, along with his fellow black deputies, an impressive, anodyne opportunity to posture for a few days just off center-stage.

Du Bois's memorandum to Diagne spelling out the composition and purpose of the conclave was dated January 1, three days after the high commissioner had presided over the Trocadero ceremony. Although it makes no mention of a vast, autonomous state in Central Africa and concedes the former German colonies to the "oversight of the League of Nations," item 4(d) called for "development of autonomous government along lines of native custom, with the object of inaugurating gradually an Africa for the Africans."[78] Clemenceau had originally stipulated February 12, 13, and 14 as the three days authorized for the congress, but the first planning session, which met during the first or second week in January, must have found that time frame unrealistic. The appearance on the scene of the enthusiastic and well-connected suffragist, Madame Calman-Lévy, widow of the prominent publisher, greatly facilitated the efforts of Du Bois and an American female companion whose devotion and efficiency in Paris proved indispensable. Thanks to "this quiet, charming woman," their planning and lobbying took place in one of the capital's prominent salons. Du Bois's American companion was Ida Alexander Gibbs Hunt, Oberlin-educated daughter of an extremely successful, Philadelphia-born businessman who had received an appointment as U.S. Consul to Madagascar in 1897 from McKinley. Ida Gibbs was a talented student of languages and literature, politically informed, handsome, and may have served as a model for Carolyn Wynn in *Quest of the Silver Fleece*. In 1904, after years of teaching in Washington's exclusive M Street High School, she had married William Henry Hunt, whose career as an African-American foreign service officer had begun, like her father's, in Madagascar but who would enjoy a twenty-year span as U.S. consul general in St. Etienne,

France. She and her husband were Du Bois loyalists and she would serve as assistant secretary to the Pan-African Congress.[79]

Relatively assured about prospects for the congress, Du Bois now concentrated on the other half of his NAACP mandate, the military fact-finding mission. The exact date of his departure from Paris to visit the 92nd Division in the Marbache sector is uncertain, but it must have been shortly after Major General F. P. Schoonmaker's January 1 alert to the division's intelligence officers that "a man by the name of Du Bois" would be touring the area. His presence was to be "immediately reported in secret enclosure to Assistant Chief of Staff, G-2."[80] The Army High Command had good reason to surveil the editor because the morale of the all-black 92nd was pitifully low and physical conditions at the camp bordered on the outrageous, even after round-the-clock improvements just prior to Moton's December inspection visit. Hope, who had already spent considerable time among the African-American fighting and SOS units throughout France, was a veritable fount of analysis and anecdote. Moton and his party, with Du Bois sitting in, had been given a full briefing by Hope the night before leaving for the camps. He had described the almost total lack of recreational facilities for the troops and the dearth of African-American YMCA officers, which the quietly furious college president had done his best to remedy.

The army command may have been somewhat anxious about Du Bois, but it was not prepared to court him. After leaving the 368th Infantry Regiment near Mayenne, he was sent a remarkably detailed letter by a sergeant contrasting his and Moton's visits. "You were watched as if you were a German spy. It grieved us all when we learned about it." Du Bois had met with tight-lipped brusqueness by white army personnel at every point. At Domfront, their uncivil behavior was so obviously hostile that the mayor of the village was distressed. "The mayor apologized gravely; if he had known of my coming, he would have received me formally at the Hotel de Ville—me whom most of my fellow-countrymen receive at naught but back doors, save with apology." Instead, they sang the *Marseillaise* together in the mayor's living room. Certainly they needed reminding, readers of the Easter *Crisis*, that African-American soldiers had helped save the world—"a little less in the United States than elsewhere, where the actual fighting took place and others could see our valor." Leaving Toul on the Moselle River in the "deepening dark of early afternoon," Du Bois heard the sound of private Tim Brimm's bugle as he came to the garrison town of Maron. Private Brimm stood by the town pump as the sun set, blowing tunes that

Du Bois recognized from the streets of Harlem. "Wild and sweet and wooing leapt the strains upon the air." Stepping out of his chauffered auto, Du Bois found a joyful welcome in the midst of troops from Washington, Philadelphia, Alabama, and Mississippi. He had arrived in the sector assigned to the 92nd, whose division headquarters at Marbache was farther along the arc of the Moselle and below the fortress city of Metz.[81]

"The Ninety-second Division went through hell," Du Bois found. It had been the single black division to receive its full complement of men and support units, but the army had distributed its units among some seven encampments until the division was united and shipped to France in September 1918. Many of its officers and men had been total strangers until then. Training in the use of artillery and machine guns had been largely ignored at Fort Dix on grounds that mastery of such weapons was beyond the mental faculties of the men. Within weeks after disembarkation at Brest, the division's African-American officers were battered by a hailstorm of arbitrary transfers and courts-martial. Their number dropped from 82 to 58 percent, and new regulations that September gave 50 percent of the captaincies (the ceiling rank for African-Americans) to white officers.[82] Du Bois was never able to determine whether General Ballou, the division's commander, was an inveterate racist or simply incompetent—or both. In the case of Robert Bullard, commander of the American 2nd Army, and Ballou's superior, Du Bois documented both that general's racism and his competency.[83] When the guns fell silent on November 11, the men of the 92nd had been strictly confined to the muck and mire of their encampments as an alleged precaution against the rape of French women, and more than thirty of the remaining African-American officers were court-martialed for the Meuse-Argonne fiasco.

If Du Bois concluded that "American white officers fought more valiantly against Negroes than they did against the Germans," it was understandable hyperbole. There was no question in his mind about the high command's designs. The 92nd was to be vilified. "Everywhere an opportunity presented itself I talked with white officers," Du Bois recalled. "In almost every instance they [African-American soldiers] were referred to as cowards, rapists, or other remarks made relative to their work which were absolutely untrue, and which were intended to cause a bad impression." The civil, racial, and sexual symbolism of the black officer flew in the face of hegemony and tradition. All the more so as the American officer corps of the time was disproportionately recruited from white southerners. Among the trove of documents Du Bois uncovered during his sorties from

Paris to the black units, one specimen in particular from the headquarters of the 372nd Infantry Regiment requesting "Replacement of Colored Officers by White Officers" best summarized the prevailing mentality: "The racial distinctions which are recognized in civilian life naturally continue to be recognized in the military life and present a formidable barrier to the existence of that feeling of comradeship which is essential to mutual confidence and *esprit de corps*."[84]

An endangered species, black officers were vanishing by the week, and by the time Du Bois crisscrossed the silent war front from the Marne to the Vosges, they were almost totally gone from the three National Guard New York 15th, the "Harlem Hellfighters" (called up as the 369th Infantry Regiment), one of the first fighting units to reach France, had been stripped of all but one or two African-American officers after giving a good account of itself in the Second Battle of the Marne—"except the bandmaster and the chaplain," wrote Du Bois in the first draft of his history.[85] Du Bois took no comfort in the fact that the 369th's bandmaster, Lieutenant James Reese, was the musician who introduced jazz to Europe. The "famous 8th Illinois," as the editor saluted it (federalized as the 370th), had sailed with only African-Americans leading it. The commander, cocky Colonel Franklin A. Dennison, had marched his men back to Newport News, Virginia, where they were given unsegregated quarters aboard ship. Dennison, the last remaining officer of field rank, was eventually mysteriously repatriated, but most of the other African-American officers survived under the bitterly resented leadership of their new white colonel.[86] Brigaded with the French 59th Division, the 370th had swept up Mont Dessinges in September 1918 and then into the charnel house at Grand Lup.

The materials Du Bois gathered would be published as "Documents of the War" in *The Crisis* for May 1919. Postmaster Burleson's shock would result in a one-day delay before the government decided against suppressing the issue. "The following documents have come into the hands of the editor. He had absolute proof of their authenticity," Du Bois would crow. The secret communiqué from the French Military Mission stationed with the American army was a bombshell. Until its suppression by the appropriate French ministries, the infamous "Secret Information Concerning Black American Troops," had been circulated, at the request of the American high command, to French military units as well as to prefects and subprefects of the *départements*. French attitudes toward people of color were a menace to the American social order, readers of *The Crisis* learned along with much of the rest of the country. "As this danger does not exist for the French race, the French public has become accustomed to treating the Negro with familiarity and indulgence." The document announced that this must end, as such indulgence and familiarity were matters of "grievous concern to the Americans. They consider them an affront to their national policy. They are afraid that contact with the French will inspire in black Americans aspirations which to them [the whites] appear intolerable."[87]

There would be much more. An inflammatory letter to a U.S. senator from the white chief of staff of the 92nd denigrated the men and officers, alleged "about thirty cases of rape," and described the lamentable engagement in the Meuse-Argonne after September 26 as one in which "they failed in all their missions, laid down and sneaked to the rear, until they were withdrawn."[88] Du Bois found, as Moton had, that there had been five convictions for attempted rape and one execution for rape (photographed by the division's white photographer, who two hours later skipped a Croix de Guerre ceremony for two black officers). As for the controversial disgrace of the 368th Infantry Regiment (for which the entire 92nd division had been stigmatized), the complicated story that ultimately emerged would largely confirm Du Bois's charge that a disaster had been engineered to prove a calumny. Already demoralized by its white officers ("dumping ground for white officers," an NCO informant told Du Bois), the regiment was ordered over the top without maps, grenade launchers, heavy-duty wirecutters, or signal flares. Its artillery had been loaned to another division. One white battalion commander remained in the rear during the entire five-day engagement. Another, a New York lawyer, ordered his machine gunners to retreat. General Pershing's original orders had been to use the 92nd as a reserve and to fill the space between the French 37th Division on its left and the American 77th Division. In the preliminary draft for "The Wounded World," Du Bois would sum up the perfidy of the army high command in four terse sentences: "First, was the effort to get rid of Negro officers; second, the effort to discredit Negro soldiers; third, the effort to spread race prejudice in France; and fourth, the effort to keep Negroes out of the Regular Army."[89]

The wonder was that there were four African-American units that had performed outstandingly—the 369th, 370th, 371st, and 372nd of the never-completed 93rd Division. These were the infantry regiments that Pershing had rushed to fight alongside the French. In addition to the American high command's promise to lend a number of units to the French while the American Expeditionary Army was being assembled, the racial friction in towns near the camps of these units had led Scott to urge their relocation. Two months after Houston, the men of the 369th had come within minutes of shooting up Spartanburg, South Carolina, after Private Noble Sissle's cap had been slapped off in a hotel lobby. The former New York National Guard regiment, the sole unit permitted to fly its state flag, arrived in Brest in December 1917, among the first American fighting units in France. Desperate for manpower, the French high command pounced on the unit. Its uniforms, weapons, and order of march became French. The 369th had spent 191 days under continuous fire, the longest stretch of any American unit. Sergeant Henry Johnson and Private Needham Roberts had won the first Croix de Guerre awarded to Americans, after capturing a German patrol. The regiment's combat performance at Château-Thierry, Belleau Wood, and Cantigny earned it the singular honor of leading the advance of the French army into German-occupied territory after the Armistice.[90] They would be absent along with the other African-American units when the great allied victory parade streamed down the Champs-Elysée in late summer. The 372nd, composed of National Guard battalions from Ohio, Massachusetts, Maryland, Tennessee, and the District of Columbia, had managed to hold on to many of its officers, while the 371st (a regiment composed of South Carolina draftees) had never seen a black officer.[91]

Since Robert Moton had scrupulously avoided investigating the full depth and extent of racial discrimination against African-American military personnel, Du Bois concluded that his mission had been a fraud, a harsh judgment he would share with his readers in the famous May issue. Moton knew the appalling neglect and the intentional hardships visited on the troops by government officials and a collusive YMCA. In Brest, 40,000 men awaited transportation home with only one African-American YMCA officer to handle their needs. "Sometimes, even when there were no signs, services to colored soldiers would be refused," Addie Hunton and Kathryn Johnson, two women serving overseas with the "Y," revealed. They reported incidents of soldiers wounded in the Argonne offensive who had languished three days before they received "attention of either a doctor or a nurse." The catalogue of insult and cruelty was a long one. "What did Dr. Moton do?" Du Bois asked of the Tuskegee principal. "He rushed around as fast as possible. He took with him and had at his elbow every moment that evil genius of the Negro race, Thomas Jesse Jones, a white man. Dr. Moton took no time to investigate or inquire. He made a few speeches, of which one is reported by a hearer as follows." The text of the Moton address before an assembly of African-American officers was ceremonious and cagey in the best tradition of the Wizard.[92] Two months later, in "Our Success and Failure," Emmett Scott's turn would come. "For four long months story after story and document after document poured into the editor's hands substantiating the above charges" about the policies of the High Command, said Du Bois in announcing the results of his trip to the front. How was it, he demanded to know, that the single most informed black official, the person strategically placed in the executive branch of government, had been able to accomplish so little to protect the rights of 200,000 of the "best blood of our young manhood?" They had been "crucified, insulted, degraded and maltreated, while their fathers, mothers, sisters and brothers had no adequate knowledge of the real truth."

The editor conceded that Scott alone could not have improved racial policies that had behind them the full force of tradition, party politics, and institutional prerogative. But it was not "simply a question of what Mr. Scott personally could or could not accomplish—God knows we are all of us helpless enough in this bitter fight." Du Bois thundered that Scott's conduct raised "the vaster question of the right of concealing fatal knowledge. . . . If Mr. Scott did not know, why did he not find out? If he did know, what did he do about it?"[93] The attack on Scott would unleash a furious controversy in the black press, with significant segments of the NAACP membership siding with Booker T. Washington's former secretary against what was seen as the editor's pitiless, unfair reproach. While the debate raged, Scott's well-written, informative, cautious *Official History of the American Negro in the World War* appeared, with a preface by Newton Baker and endorsements from Theodore Roosevelt and General Pershing.[94]

On Wednesday afternoon, February 19, Blaise Diagne delivered the opening address to the three-day Pan-African Congress at the Grand Hotel in the boulevard des Capucines. It was a paean to French colonialism and to the privileges subject peoples slowly evolving under its tutelage were said to enjoy. As president of the congress the distinguished Senegalese Frenchman expressed the hope that the ideal of racial unity "would inspire all of African descent throughout the entire world." The Pan-African Congress was more "pan" than African, with only a handful of the fifty-eight delegates from sixteen nations, protectorates, and colonial entities able to claim any firsthand knowledge of the continent. Like the secretary of the congress himself, Du Bois, none of the sixteen delegates from the United States had yet visited sub-Saharan Africa. The next-largest delegation consisted of thirteen persons from the French West Indies. Seven were from

Haiti, and an equal number, like the chairman of the foreign affairs committee of the Chamber of Deputies, were from France. Algeria, the Belgian-ruled Congo, the Spanish and Portuguese colonies, Ethiopia, and Egypt provided one delegate each. A single delegate was listed as representing the entirety of British Africa, Lloyd George's government obviously having had no interest in seeing its subjects participate in such a proceeding. The "colored" ex-mayor of Battersea, London, was the sole exception to a British ban on passports issued to attend the congress. Even the secretary of the venerable Aborigines Protection Society was refused.[95] That the Pan-African Congress numbered almost sixty persons was largely due to Madame Calman-Lévy's salon and to the ingenious publicity campaign and coordination efforts devised by Du Bois and the tireless Ida Hunt at the Hotel de Malte in the rue Richelieu. The Hotel de Malte served as a center of attraction for a surprisingly large number of African-Americans in the French capital, most of whom were recruited to serve as delegates. African-Americans who had applied to the State Department for passports to attend the congress had been immediately refused.[96]

As he and Hunt pressed their cause, Du Bois was seized by the same visionary enthusiasm that he had experienced in London nineteen years before. He imagined the immediate creation of a far more effective Pan-African Movement capable of maintaining "a central headquarters with experts, clerks and helpers" (instead of a single room in a small hotel) while the deliberations of the Versailles Peace ran their course. Paris was the cockpit of Europe, the refuge of the "little groups who want to be nations," said Du Bois, "like the Letts and Finns, the Armenians and Jugo-Slavs, Irish and Ukrainians. Not only groups, but races have come—Jews, Indians, Arabs and All-Asia." His readers must realize that "the destinies of mankind for a hundred years to come" were being settled in a small room of the Hotel Crillon by four "unobtrusive gentlemen who glance out speculatively now and then to Cleopatra's Needle on the Place de la Concorde." If "unobtrusive" and "speculative" were increasingly inappropriate descriptions of the Council of Four (Woodrow Wilson, Lloyd George, Clemenceau, and, for the moment, Orlando of Italy), Du Bois was entirely right regarding its impact on millions of destinies. He had come to defend the destiny of a great number of millions—"to help represent the Negro world in Africa and America and the Islands of the Sea." And he had done so for $750, the cost of the Pan-African Congress, he said. He had done what he had to do and done it well, yet, in the immediate, heady aftermath of the Paris conclave, he speculated grandly that if the Negroes of the world had provided the money and personnel, "they could have settled the future of Africa at a cost of less than $10,000."[97]

Then, upon reflection, Du Bois decided that the results of the first (really the second) Pan-African Congress "were small. But it had some influence."[98] The three days of speeches at the Grand Hotel exude a time-bound quaintness now. Monsieur Van Overgergh of the Belgian Peace Commission spoke of promising reforms that were under way in the Congo, and the Portuguese former minister of foreign affairs, Freire d'Andrade, cited progress in Africa's oldest European empire. The Francophone Africans were predictably rhapsodic about progress under the Third Republic. If the Liberian delegate had less to point to, he too was confident of the future advancement of his country and of Africans worldwide. The Americans sounded the full keyboard—from Charles Russell's celebration of the end of world racism and the historic significance of the congress through William Walling's appeal to the U.S. Congress that its body reflect the diversity of races in the manner of the French Chamber of Deputies, to George Jackson's personal expression of shame for the discrimination his people suffered in their own land. Addie W. Hunton eloquently reminded the overwhelmingly male assembly of the global role women would play to secure democracy. Hunton's words were amplified in the final session when Madame Jules Siegried, president of the French National Association for the Rights of Women, brought greetings from her organization. Du Bois quoted her as saying that no one could appreciate better than women "the struggle for broader rights and liberties."[99] John Hope and Joel Spingarn in his officers' uniform were in the audience but did not speak from the platform. Villard, who was also in Europe at the time, ignored these Pan-African activities completely.

Diagne gaveled the meeting to a close on Friday evening, the twenty-first. The resolutions of the Pan-African Congress were to be presented to the Peace Conference for action. They called for direct League of Nations supervision of the former German colonies. In the days following the Pan-African Congress, Du Bois was finally able to meet with members of the Wilson inner circle. Walter Lippmann, one of the president's most valued advisors at Versailles, had written him just before the proceedings adjourned to say that he was "very much interested" in the congress. He invited Du Bois to send along "whatever reports you may have on the work"—which Du Bois promptly did. Joel Spingarn used his influence in order to arrange for Du Bois to meet George Louis Beer, the chief American advisor on colonial matters at the Peace Conference. Du Bois would claim a few years afterward that the idea for the Versailles administration of colonial territories—the Mandates Commission—had sprung from this interview. If so, however, the system of mandates was alien to the concept originally envisaged by him and most of the congress delegates, for it really only amounted to a fiction by which the United Kingdom and France were given the German territories as de facto colonies.[100] The resolution calling for the drafting of a code of law "for the international protection of the natives of Africa" was another idea implemented largely on paper. The fine pen of congress secretary Du Bois was evident in this as in most of the other resolutions. Another Pan-African Congress was proposed for 1920, as well as the creation of an international quarterly to be called *Black Review* and published in several languages.[101]

Publicity for the congress delighted Du Bois, a payoff for the cordial attention he had uncharacteristically paid to white journalists aboard the *Orizaba*. The New York *Evening Globe* gave the event considerable play on February 22, breathlessly describing the opening session with black people "seated at long green tables . . . in the trim uniform of American Army officers, other American colored men in frock coats or business suits, polished French Negroes who hold public office, Senegalese who sit in the French Chamber of Deputies . . ." Two days later, a dispatch in the New York *Herald* advised readers that there was "nothing unreasonable in the programme." The correspondent for the *Chicago Tribune* realistically noted that the memorandum Du Bois had drafted for Wilson's contemplation was "quite Utopian, and has less than a Chinaman's chance of getting anywhere at the Peace Conference, but it is nevertheless interesting."[102] The French press was considerably more solicitous, tracking Du Bois's appearances before the League of the Rights of Man (the powerful civil liberties organization that had defended Dreyfus) to his audience with dignitaries having some connection to the peace conference.

The attention paid by the Paris press and the courtesies extended by Clemenceau and distinguished organizations made it unavoidable for Colonel Edward M. House, Wilson's unusually urbane alter ego from Texas, to meet with Du Bois. The colonel was fascinated by the congress, proved extremely helpful in arranging other appointments for Du Bois, but kept his counsel about the fate of the Pan-African Congress resolutions. Interestingly (and mischieveously), House confided to Du Bois that upon seeing Moton he had urged the latter to stay in Paris in order to "appear in person before the Peace Conference" to represent the Negro world. Moton, however, had chosen to return to Tuskegee, standing up Lloyd George.[103]

(House neglected to extend the same courtesy to Du Bois, though.) For the first time since the Berlin Conference on West Africa and the "scramble" unleashed by it, the principles of self-determination and the fundamental rights and liberties to which subject African peoples were entitled had been articulated by accomplished men and women who purported to speak for Du Bois's darker millions. While their immediate and practical consequences would be negligible, a powerful idea to bind up the wounds of the world had been launched in Paris.

Du Bois returned to the United States and his magazine (edited in his absence by Fauset) on April 1, 1919, just in time to write his second-most-famous editorial—one that would go a long way toward redeeming the perceived imprudence of "Close Ranks." "Returning Soldiers" appeared in the May issue, which Postmaster Burleson had wanted to suppress and which would sell 106,000 copies:

> We are returning from war! *The Crisis* and tens of thousands of blackmen were drafted into a great struggle. For bleeding France and what she means and has meant and will mean to us and humanity and against the threat of German race arrogance. . . .
>
> This is the country to which we Soldiers of Democracy return. This is the fatherland for which we fought! But it is *our* fatherland. It was right for us to fight again. The faults of *our* country are *our* faults. Under similar circumstances, we would fight again. But by the God of heaven, we are cowards and jackasses if now that the war is over, we do not marshal every ounce of our brain and brawn to fight a sterner, longer, more unbending battle against the forces of hell in our own land.
>
> We return.
> We return from fighting.
> We return fighting.
>
> Make way for Democracy! We saved it in France, and by the Great Jehovah, we will save it in the United States of America, or know the reason why.[104]

Yet "the problem of the twentieth century," as Du Bois himself had presciently told the delegates to the 1900 Pan-African Congress in London, "is the problem of the color line." And race would remain the basis for denying "to over half of the world the right of sharing to their utmost ability the opportunities and privileges of modern civilization." Moorfield Storey saw clearly that racial backlash was the reason why democracy was in danger of being swept aside. Anticipating the heightened sense of pride that tens of thousands of them would feel when the war ended, he knew that "Negroes will come back feeling like men and not disposed to accept the treatment to which they have been subjected."[105] The tribal and institutional power of those "forces of hell in our own land," editorially challenged by Du Bois, were starkly manifested in the lynching of seventy-eight African-Americans during 1918 and in the boasts of white newspapers in the South about the bloody fate in store for any black man daring to come back from the war expecting to be treated like a white man. Less than six weeks after he returned to his desk at *The Crisis*, the Saturday-night murder of a black civilian by a white sailor in Charleston, South Carolina, marked the first incident in what became a tidal wave of homicides, arson, mayhem, and organized racial combat sweeping up from the Deep South and Longview, Texas, into Washington, D.C., across the country to Chicago, and, dipping down to Knoxville, Tennessee, rolling on finally over Omaha, Nebraska.

In the outburst of editorials during this "Red Summer" of 1919, the *Whip*, a militant black Chicago weekly, put the national atrocity in best perspective: "[The rioters] really fear that the Negro is breaking his shell and beginning to bask in the sunlight of real manhood." Unmistakably, a new manhood—and, as Du Bois above all underscored, a new womanhood—was asserting itself. The "New Negro" was virtually an overnight discovery. "We would be less than men, then," *The Crisis* insisted, "if our experience in the war had not left us quickened and fired, rubbing our eyes and asking in clearer and clearer accents 'Where do we come in?' "[106] Yet even Du Bois found his editorial antennae twisting wildly from the extraordinary national unrest and violence in the wake of the Great War. Race riots on a national scale, the flight out of the South of hundreds of thousands of African-Americans, the explosion of labor strikes from coast to coast shutting down shipyards, coal mines, steel works, and even the Boston police force, and the panic among the propertied classes inspired by the Bolshevik revolution in Russia—each of these developments, individually and in combination, made race relations far worse than they already were. Sixteen years after the publication of *The Souls of Black Folk*, the virtual exclusion of his people from meaningful citizenship in American society gave few signs, if any at all, of diminishing. "One ever feels his two-ness—an American, a Negro," Du Bois had written there, proclaiming another great twentieth-century truth.[107] He was stunned and deeply saddened by this upsurge of racial hostility, but it was not in Du Bois's nature to be either intimidated or demoralized. There could be no turning back now from the fight for full civil rights he and some thirty others had begun on the Canadian side of Niagara Falls in the summer of 1905. "Brothers we are on the Great Deep," he wrote in *The Crisis* as the barbaric summer ended. "We have cast off on the vast voyage which will lead to Freedom or Death."[108]

NOTES

1. Postlude to the Future

1. Details of March On Washington: "200 Thousand March for Civil Rights," *New York Times*, Aug. 29, 1963, p. 1; "Throng Gets Quick Start," Washington *Evening Star*, Aug. 28, 1963, p. 1; Thomas Gentile, *March on Washington: August 28, 1963* (Washington, D.C.: New Day Publications, 1983), pp. 228, 237–40. ". . . jobs and freedom.": Randolph quoted: Gentile, *March*, p. 225; see also Paula F. Pfeffer, A. *Philip Randolph, Pioneer of the Civil Rights Movement* (Baton Rouge: Louisiana State University Press, 1990), esp. ch. 6, p. 262.

2. For evolution of John Lewis's speech and discussion of March participants: John Booker, "March Officials Avert Breakdown," *Amsterdam News*, Aug. 31, 1963, p. 1; Taylor Branch, *Parting the Waters: America in the King Years, 1954–63* (New York: Simon and Schuster, 1988), pp. 879–80; Gentile, *March*, pp. 176–81, 206; David J. Garrow, *Bearing the Cross: Martin Luther King, Jr., and the Southern Christian Leadership Conference* (New York: William Morrow, 1986), pp. 281–83; David L. Lewis, *King: A Biography* (Urbana and Chicago: University of Illinois Press, 1978), pp. 224–25. Young: Nancy J. Weiss, *Whitney M. Young, Jr., and the Struggle for Civil Rights* (Princeton, N.J.: Princeton University Press, 1989), p. 109.

3. ". . . today in this cause.": Wilkins quoted: Gentile, *March*, p. 209; Branch, *Parting the Waters*, p. 878. ". . . hovered in our midst.": Rachel Davis Du Bois, *All This and Something More: Pioneering in International Education* (Bryn Mawr, Pa.: Dorrance & Co., 1984), p. 211. ". . . enter the promised land.": Aronson quoted: Gerald Horne, *Black and Red: W.E.B. Du Bois and the Afro-American Response to the Cold War* (Albany: State University of New York Press, 1986), p. 356.

4. ". . . 'What old man?' ": Killens quoted: *W.E.B. Du Bois, An ABC of Color: Selections Chosen by the Author from Over a Half Century of His Writings, with an Introduction by John Oliver Killens* (New York: International Publishers, 1971), 2nd printing, p. 9.

5. ". . . and call me inferior.": Percival Prattis quoted: Kay Pankey, "Introduction," *W.E.B. Du Bois, An ABC of Color* (Berlin: Seven Seas Publishers, 1963), pp. 9–14 (p. 12). For enumerations of Du Bois's published writings and summary appreciations of his achievements, the following sources may be consulted: "Du Bois, William Edward Burghardt," in Rayford Logan and Michael R. Winston, eds., *Dictionary of American Negro Biography* (*DANB*) (New York: W. W. Norton & Co., 1982), pp. 193–99; "Du Bois, W(illiam) E(dward) B(urghardt)," *The New Encyclopaedia Britannica* (Chicago, 15th ed., 1989), 4:

241–42; Herbert Aptheker, ed., *Annotated Bibliography of the Published Writings of W.E.B. Du Bois* (Millwood, N.Y.: Kraus-Thomson, 1973) and *The Complete Published Works of W.E.B. Du Bois* (Millwood, N.Y.: Kraus-Thomson, 1973–1985), 35 vols.; also, Paul Partington, *W.E.B. Du Bois: A Bibliography of His Published Writings—Supplement* (Whittier, Calif.: pub. by Paul Partington, 1984); and Partington and Robert W. McDonnell, *The Definitive Bibliography About Works Dealing with W.E.B. Du Bois* (Whittier, Calif.: pub. by Paul Partington, 1989)—this edition claims to correct all errors allegedly made by the Herbert Aptheker bibliography; William L. Andrews, ed., *Critical Essays on W.E.B. Du Bois* (Boston: G. K. Hall & Co., 1985); John Henrik Clarke, Esther Jackson, and J. A. O'Dell, eds., *Black Titan: W.E.B. Du Bois* (Boston: Beacon Press, 1970); Julius Lester, ed., *The Seventh Son: The Thought and Writings of W.E.B. Du Bois* (New York: Vintage Books, 1971), 2 vols, 1, esp. "Introduction"; Rayford W. Logan, ed., *W.E.B. Du Bois: A Profile* (New York: Hill & Wang, 1971), Logan introduction; Henry Lee Moon, ed., *The Emerging Thought of W.E.B. Du Bois: Essays and Editorials from the Crisis with an Introduction, Commentaries and a Personal Memoir* (New York: Simon and Schuster, 1972); Nathan Huggins, ed., *W.E.B. Du Bois, Writings* (New York: The Library of America, 1986), especially "Chronology" and "Notes on the Texts"; Meyer Weinberg, ed., *W.E.B. Du Bois: A Reader* (New York: Harper & Row, 1970).

6. Of the seven most useful English-language studies of Du Bois: Two were written more than thirty years ago—Francis Broderick, *W.E.B. Du Bois: Negro Leader in Time of Crisis* (Stanford, Calif.: Stanford University Press, 1959), and Elliott Rudwick, *W.E.B. Du Bois: Propagandist of the Negro Protest* (New York: Atheneum, 1968; orig. pub. 1960). Professor Broderick's limited access to the Du Bois papers (revoked at the behest of the second wife, Mrs. Shirley Graham-Du Bois) was confined primarily to the period before 1910. Professor Rudwick's access to the Du Bois papers (then in the keeping of Dr. Herbert Aptheker) was even more restricted—he was compelled to rely on Broderick's notes. The tone of the Broderick and Rudwick biographies is frequently acerbic, particularly when they are discussing their subject's racial sensibilities and communist sympathies. In the main, however, they display rigorous analysis and strive for objectivity. Professor Arnold Rampersad's *The Art and Imagination of W.E.B. Du Bois* (New York: Schocken Books, 1990; orig. pub. 1976) is the most insightful study to date. It is exceedingly well written and thoroughly researched (skillful use is made of the Harvard student years materials). Rampersad's appreciation of the egoistic, complex, principled Du Boisian personality is a model of sophistication. His Du Bois is, as the title suggests, a literary figure, although the civil rights activist is adequately treated. The Du Bois Papers now housed at the University of Massachusetts at Amherst were, however, not available to Rampersad.

Professor Manning Marable's *W.E.B. Du Bois: Black Radical Democrat* (Boston: Twayne, 1986) makes use of the Microfilming Corporation of America microfilmed edition of the University of Massachusetts collection (89 reels). Manning's is a comprehensive, well-written and well-argued treatment of Du Bois's career as agitator and political philosopher. Manning underplays elitism and inconsistency in Du Bois, and sees his subject as a "radical democrat" from the earliest days who moved virtually without deviation to the left. Jack B. Moore's *W.E.B. Du Bois* (Boston: Twayne, 1981) is a superb introduction to Du Bois as a thinker and activist.

Shirley Graham-Du Bois, *His Day Is Marching On: A Memoir of W.E.B. Du Bois* (Philadelphia and New York: J. B. Lippincott Co., 1971) is as indispensable for its intimate details of his and her private and public lives (especially their sojourns in the former USSR and the Republic in China) as it is unsatisfactory due to subjectivity and factual inaccuracies. Professor Gerald Horne's *Black and Red*, although not a full-fledged biography, is so exhaustively researched as to have significantly influenced Du Bois scholarship. At times, however, Horne's cogent, formidably documented monograph tends to become a lawyer's brief for the defense at the expense of full discovery of the evidence. ". . . death was practically requested.": Du Bois quoted: Du Bois, *The Autobiography: A Soliloquy on Viewing My Life from the Last Decade of Its First Century* (New York: International Publishers Co., 1968), p. 414.

7. Shirley Graham-Du Bois biographical sources: Graham-Du Bois, *His Day Is Marching On*; "Shirley Graham-Du Bois: Recorded Interview with Jim and Camille Hatch-Billops, 5/28/75," Hatch-Billops Collection; Kathy A. Perkins, "Shirley Graham: A Real Milestone for Theatre," [Unpublished] Essay Submitted to NEH Summer Faculty Seminar, Howard University, Aug. 7, 1984; "Shirley Graham-Du Bois," FOIPA No. 308,499, released Dec. 2, 1992/U.S. Department of Justice.

8. Composite details of Du Bois state funeral: William Branch, "Ghana Gives State Burial to Dr. Du Bois," *Amsterdam News*, Sept. 7, 1963, pp. 1, 25; Lester, *Seventh Son*, pp. 149–50; "Father Du Bois Laid to Rest," *Ghana Evening News*, Aug. 30, 1963, p. 6; "State Burial for the Great Man," *Ghanaian Times*, August 29, 1963, p. 1; "A Phenomenon," *Ghanaian Times*, August 30, 1963, pp. 1–2; "His Death Was One Last Grand Protest," *Afro-American*, Sept. 14, 1963, p. 16; "Du Bois Is Buried," *Daily Graphic* (Ghana), Aug. 30, 1963, p. 7; "W.E.B. Du Bois Dies in Ghana; Negro Leader and Author, 96," *New York Times*, Aug. 28, 1963, p. 23, *Guardian*, Sept. 5, 1963, p. 3.

9. "Arrangements for the Burial of W.E.B. Du Bois, Aug. 23, 1963": (Personal) 2 pp. The Papers of W.E.B. Du Bois/Archives and Manuscripts. University Library, University of Massachusetts at Amherst. Also "Ghana Gives State Burial," *Amsterdam News*, p. 25.

10. State linguist quoted: "We Mourn Du Bois, A Great Son of Africa," *Evening News*, Aug. 30, 1963, p. 1; "Ghana Gives State Burial," *Amsterdam News*, pp. 1, 25; "Last Grand Protest," *Afro-American*, p. 16; "State Burial for Great Man," *Ghanaian Times*, p. 1.

11. "State Burial," *Amsterdam News*, p. 25.

12. Du Bois Papers/U. Mass. Kwame Nkrumah, *Ghana: The Autobiography of Kwame Nkrumah* (Edinburgh: Thomas Nelson and Sons, Ltd., 1959).

13. Consult the following for the early history of the West African slave trade: James David Apter, *Ghana in Transition* (Princeton, N.J.: Princeton University Press, 1972, 2d rev. ed.; orig. pub. 1955), pp. 1–32; James Pope-Hennessy, *Sins of the Fathers; A Study of the Atlantic Slave Traders, 1441–1807* (New York: Alfred A. Knopf, 1968), pp. 2–12, 60–61; James A. Rawley, *The Transatlantic Slave Trade, A History* (New York: W. W. Norton & Co., 1981), p. 23; Edward Reynolds, *Stand the Storm: A History of the Atlantic Slave Trade* (London and New York: Allison & Busby, 1985), ch. 2.

A spirited debate continues among scholars as to both the numbers of persons transported from Africa and the centrality of the transatlantic slave trade in the Industrial Revolution of northern Europe and North America. Until recently, the large numbers given by earlier students (*viz.*, Davidson, James, Williams) have been considerably reduced: Basil Davidson, *Black Mother, Africa: The Years of Trial* (London: Galloway, 1961), p. 68, estimates 50 million; C.L.R. James, *Black Jacobins: Toussaint L'Ouverture and the San Domingo Revolution* (New York: Vintage Books, 1963; orig. pub. 1938); Eric Williams, *Capitalism and Slavery* (New York: Capricorn Books, 1966; orig. pub. 1944). The consensus on the figure of roughly nine million computed by Philip Curtin has begun somewhat to fray, as newer data pushes the numbers gradually upward, although still far from approaching the forty to fifty million previously asserted. Rawley, *Transatlantic Slave Trade*, pp. 328–29, adjusts Curtin's figures to about eleven million. Prominent among scholars arguing for reduced volume and reduced economic significance of the slave trade are: Roger Antsey, "The Volume and Profitability of the British Slave Trade, 1761–1807," in Stanley Engerman and Eugene Genovese, eds., *Race and Slavery in the Western*

Hemisphere: Quantitative Studies (Princeton, N.J.: Princeton University Press, 1974); Philip Curtin, *The Atlantic Slave Trade: A Census* (Madison: University of Wisconsin Press, 1969); David Eltis, *Economic Growth and the Ending of the Transatlantic Slave Trade* (New York: Oxford University Press, 1987), esp. tables on pp. 243–54; Engerman, "The Slave Trade and British Capital Formation in the Eighteenth Century: A Comment on the Williams Thesis," *Economic History Review*, 2d series, 13 (1960): 430–43; David Brion Davis, *Slavery and Human Progress* (New York: Oxford University Press, 1984), p. 73. Some representatives of the school of larger numbers and greater economic significance of slavery in jump-starting capitalism are: Jay Coughtry, *The Notorious Triangle: Rhode Island and the Slave Trade, 1700–1807* (Philadelphia: Temple University Press, 1981); William Darity, Jr., "The Numbers Game and the Profitability of the British Trade in Slaves," *Journal of Economic History*, 45 (1985): 693–703; and J. E. Inikori, "Measuring the Atlantic Slave Trade: An Assessment of Curtin and Antsey," *Journal of African History*, 17 (1976a): 197–223.

I am indebted to Professors Wendell P. Holbrook of Rutgers University (Newark), Edward Reynolds of the University of California at San Diego, and Ronald Bailey of Northeastern University for general enlightenment and bibliography. I profited enormously from Bailey's excellent monograph, "Africa, the Slave Trade, and the Rise of Industrial Capitalism in Europe and the United States: A Historiographic Review," *American History: A Bibliographic Review*, 2 (1986): 1–91.

14. ". . . to the home of his ancestors.": "A Phenomenon," *Ghanaian Times*, Aug. 30, 1963, p. 1.

15. ". . . what colored men make it.": Du Bois quoted: Du Bois, *The Negro* (Millwood, N.Y.: Kraus-Thomson, 1975; orig. pub. 1915), p. 242. ". . . new slavery to old masters overseas.": Du Bois quoted: Du Bois, "Message to the First All-African People's Conference, Accra, Ghana, December 9, 1958," in Graham-Du Bois, *His Day* (Appendix 1), p. 373; "The Africans and the Colonialist Tactic," Aptheker, ed., *Writings by W.E.B. Du Bois in Periodicals Edited by Others* (Millwood, N.Y.: Kraus-Thomson, 1982, vol. 4 (1945–1961), p. 291. See Horne, *Black and Red*, pp. 342–43.

16. ". . . better than I could have done.": Du Bois quoted: "Du Bois Is Buried," *Daily Graphic*, p. 7.

17. Early Du Bois–Nkrumah association: Du Bois, *Autobiography*, pp. 399–401; Kwame Nkrumah, *Ghana: The Autobiography of Kwame Nkrumah*, pp. 52–53; James R. Hooker, *Black Revolutionary: George Padmore's Path from Communism to Pan-Africanism* (New York: Praeger, 1967), pp. 92–98. ". . . May he rest in peace.": Nkrumah quoted: "We Mourn Du Bois," *Ghanaian Times*, p. 1; Branch, *Parting the Waters*, pp. 882–83; Gentile, *March*, p. 240; Lewis, *King*, pp. 227–29.

18. Ulbricht and Choe En-lai quotes: "World Leaders' Tributes," *Ghanaian Times*, Aug. 30, 1963, p. 1; other tributes, *G. Times*, Sept. 2, p. 1; Sept. 3, p. 1; Nikita Khrushchev to Shirley Graham-Du Bois, Aug. 30, 1963, Du Bois Papers/U. Mass.; "Last Grand Protest," *Afro-American*, p. 16. Akan farewell: "Du Bois Is Not Dead," *Evening News*, Aug. 31, 1960.

2. *Mary Silvina's Great Barrington*

1. Alfred Du Bois and Mary Silvina Burghardt were married by the Reverend Amos Lawrence in Housatonic, on February 5, 1867. Both gave their ages as thirty-four. *Registry of the Town of Great Barrington, 1867, Marriages* (Great Barrington Town Hall), p. 43. "Married," *Berkshire Courier*, Feb. 7, 1867, p. 2. Du Bois birth certificate: "Certificate of

Births from the Records of Births in the Town of Great Barrington, Massachusetts, USA." Pronunciation of surname: W.E.B. Du Bois to Chicago Sunday Evening Club, Jan. 20, 1939; and Du Bois to S.R.S. Spencer, Jr., Dec. 3, 1946—Du Bois Papers/U.Mass.

2. *The Souls of Black Folk* (Millwood, N.Y.: Kraus-Thomson, 1973; reprint of 1953 ed., orig. pub. by A. C. McClurg & Co., Chicago), pp. 2–4. Great Barrington history and lore: Charles J. Taylor, *History of Great Barrington* (Great Barrington, Mass.: Published by Town of Great Barrington, 1928), 2 parts, Pt. I (1676–1882), Pt. II (1882–1922), pp. 10, 12–22; Rollin Hillyer Cooke, ed., *Historic Homes and Institutions and Genealogical and Personal Memoirs of Berkshire County, Massachusetts* (New York: Lewis Publishing Co., 1906), 2 vols., I, 56–57. Discussions and correspondence about Great Barrington history and leading citizens with Mrs. Lila Parrish, Great Barrington chapter president of the Daughters of the American Revolution, were most helpful in illuminating fine points of and controversies in local history.

3. Taylor, *History*, pp. 21, 43.

4. On Tom Burghardt: James T. Burghardt to W.E.B. Du Bois, Dec. 16, 1907—Du Bois Papers/U. Mass.; Du Bois, *Autobiography*, p. 62, and *Dusk of Dawn* (Millwood, N.Y.: Kraus-Thomson, 1975; orig. pub. 1940), p. 111; "The Life of W.E.B. Du Bois," speech in seven drafts, delivered in June 1953—Du Bois Papers/ U. Mass.; Du Bois, *Darkwater: Voices from Within the Veil* (Millwood, N.Y.: Kraus-Thomson, 1975; orig. pub. 1920), p. 5; *Autobiography*, p. 62; Matt Bigg, "The Family History of W.E.B. Burghardt Du Bois," An American Studies Dissertation, 3 Oct. 1988/U. Mass at Amherst, pp. 10–11.

5. Burghardt family history: Reel 89, Du Bois Papers/U. Mass., contains Burghardt family materials Du Bois assembled over time from various Massachusetts sources; "The Black Burghardts: A Family Tree": prepared by the Anthropology Department of the Univ. of Mass. at Amherst; *Darkwater*, p. 10; *Autobiography*, p. 62; "A Pageant in Seven Decades," in Herbert Aptheker, ed., *Pamphlets and Leaflets by W.E.B. Du Bois* (Millwood, N.Y.: Kraus-Thomson, 1986), pp. 244–74; Bigg, "Family Hist. of Du Bois," pp. 10–13; Taylor, *Great Barrington*, pp. 266, 271.

6. "Freeman, Elizabeth [Mumbet, Mum Bett]": *Dictionary of American Negro Biography* (DANB), p. 244; Gerard Chapman, "Mum Bett's Heroism," *Berkshire Eagle*, Feb. 24, 1987.

7. "Do bana coba" and various versions: *Dusk*, p. 114 (and p. 111); *Autobiography*, p. 62; *Darkwater*, p. 5. Possible provenance of the African ancestor's song: I am much indebted to Mrs. Denise M. Williams of Cape May, New Jersey, a collateral descendant of Du Bois's, for details about the Burghardts and for generously giving access to materials generated by her own research into the African song; Ian Hancock (University of Texas at Austin) to Denise Williams, 19 Mar. 1989/Williams personal correspondence: "Right off I must say that I don't recognize the language, although its syllable structure is clearly African. . . . If the traders were Dutch, it would make sense to look at languages spoken in those parts of West Africa where the Dutch were taking slaves—the Gambia area and the Gold Coast." Sulayman S. Nyang, African Studies & Research Program, Howard University, to Denise Williams Jan. 22, 1990/Williams personal correspondence: "There is a remote possibility, however, that the song is originally a Wolof song from Senegambia. . . . If the song is a creolized version of a Wolof song, it should go like this:

Duga na chi pah, gene ma, gene ma./ Duga na chipah, gene ma, gene ma./ bena njuli, njuli. Translation: I have fallen into a pit, get me out. Get me out!/ I have fallen into a pit, get me out. Get me out!/ One circumcised boy, one circumcised boy, one circumcised boy."

A strange song, it would seem, for a female ancestor to sing. I have not been able to solve this mystery.

8. ". . . better than I can explain?": *Dusk*, p. 116.

9. On Joyner: *Autobiography*, p. 91 ("Joyner . . . was a Democrat and we suspected him of low origins and questionable designs"); Taylor, *History*, p. 391. On Radical Reconstruction and African-Americans: Du Bois, *Black Reconstruction in America, 1860–1880* (New York: Atheneum, 1992; orig. pub. 1936), chs. 10, 11, 12; Richard L. Hume, "Negro Delegates to the State Constitutional Conventions of 1867–69," pp. 129–53, and Thomas C. Holt, "Negro State Legislators in South Carolina during Reconstruction," pp. 223–46, in Howard Rabinowitz, ed., *Southern Black Leaders of the Reconstruction Era* (Urbana and London: University of Illinois Press, 1982); Eric Foner, *Reconstruction: America's Unfinished Revolution, 1863–1877* (New York: Harper & Row, 1988), esp. chs. 6 and 7; John Hope Franklin, *From Slavery to Freedom: A History of Negro Americans* (New York: Alfred A. Knopf, 1980. 5th ed.), esp. ch. 14.

10. Western Massachusetts before and during the Gilded Age: Van Wyck Brooks, *The Flowering of New England, 1815–1865* (New York: E. P. Dutton & Co., 1936), esp. ch. 20 ("West of Boston"); Donna Drew, *A History of Monument Mills in Housatonic, Massachusetts* (Great Barrington, Mass.: Attic Revivals Press, 1984), esp. pp. 6–7; Christopher Clark, *The Roots of Rural Capitalism: Western Massachusetts, 1780–1860* (Ithaca, N.Y.: Cornell University Press, 1990), pp. 135–51. On the national social and economic upheaval of the late nineteenth century, two quite different books (analytically and in terms of perspective) are Robert H. Wiebe, *The Search for Order, 1877–1920* (New York: Hill and Wang, 1985; orig. pub. 1967), ch. 2, and Nell Irvin Painter, *Standing at Armageddon: The United States, 1877–1919* (New York: W. W. Norton & Co., 1987), ch. 1.

11. Taylor, *History*, p. 497; ". . . large openings at the sides.": "Special Town Meeting," *Berkshire Courier*, June 4, 1884, p. 5. Leavitt's barn and Horace Greeley: Taylor, History, p. 425.

12. Features of the town: Taylor, *History*, pp. 410, 426; *Dusk*, p. 13. On William Cullen Bryant: Cooke, *Historic Homes*, pp. 56–57.

13. Drew, *Monument Mills*, pp. 5–6; Taylor, *History*, pp. 379, 390.

14. *Autobiography*, p. 83. Sampling of Burghardt family property transactions: *Registry of Deeds, Great Barrington*, vol. 122, p. 163; vol. 125, p. 195; vol. 135, p. 123; vol. 142, p. 67. Bigg, "Family History," pp. 12–13. Economic pressures: *Darkwater*, pp. 9–11; *Autobiography*, pp. 63, 82. For more general treatment of socioeconomic changes affecting northern African-Americans in the late nineteenth century, see Robert Austin Warner, *New Haven Negroes: A Social History* (New York: Arno Press and the New York Times, 1969; orig pub. 1940), esp. pp. 11–29. Taylor, *History*, p. 380.

15. ". . . in high esteem . . .": *Autobiography*, p. 63. ". . . and yet not absolutely drawn": *Dusk*, p. 10. On African-American political participation in northern communities, see Du Bois, *The Philadelphia Negro* (Millwood, N.Y.: Kraus-Thomson, 1973; orig. pub. 1899), esp. ch. 16; *Autobiography*, p. 83; Theodore Hershberg, ed., *Philadelphia: Work, Space, Family, and Group Experience in the Nineteenth Century, Essays toward an Interdisciplinary History of the City* (New York: Oxford University Press, 1981), esp. ch. 14 ("A Tale of Three Cities"); Warner, *New Haven Negroes*, pp. 185–206.

16. Clark, *Roots of Rural Capitalism*, p. 151. *Registry of Deeds*, vol. 135, p. 123; vol. 142, p. 67.

17. *Autobiography*, p. 64; "Du Bois, William E. B.," Interview conducted by William T. Ingersoll, May 1960, no. 517/Columbia University Oral History Project/Oral History Research Office, Columbia U., pp. 5–6. "No occupation": 7th Federal Census, 1850, M-432, Reel 306 (Massachusetts, Berkshire County), p. 173; 8th Federal Census, 1860, M-653, Reel 488 (Mass., Berkshire County), p. 347; 9th Federal Census, 1870, M-593, Reel 601 (Mass., Berkshire County), p. 311.

18. ". . . idiomatic New England tongue . . .": *Dusk*, pp. 115, 12.

19. Taylor, *History*, p. 453; Cooke, *Historic Homes*, pp. 241–42.

20. Du Bois quoted: *Dusk*, p. 91; *Autobiography*, p. 61; *Darkwater*, p. 5.

21. Du Bois quoted: *Darkwater*, p. 5; *Autobiography*, pp. 62, 63.

22. ". . . a mighty family . . .": *Autobiography*, p. 62. ". . . house of my grandfather Othello!": *ibid.*, p. 64. "Mother was dark shining bronze . . .": *ibid.*, p. 64.

23. ". . . small and beautiful of face . . .": *Autobiography*, p. 71. On Alexander Du Bois: *ibid.*, pp. 65–68; *Darkwater*, pp. 7–9; *Dusk*, pp. 105–9. Du Bois's details of his grandfather's movements vary considerably. I have attempted to reconstruct a more accurate record of Alexander Du Bois's early years using a variety of sources, including the suggestive information provided by Du Bois himself through Shirley Graham-Du Bois, *His Day Is Marching On*, pp. 197–208. In this connection, the professional assistance of Roger D. Joslyn, fellow of the American Society of Genealogists, New Windsor, N.Y., has been of inestimable value. Among sources utilized were: Bigg, "Family History," pp. 14–24; Joseph Carvalho III, *Black Families in Hampden County, Massachusetts, 1650–1855* (New England Historic Genealogical Society and Institute for Massachusetts Studies, Westfield State College, 1984), pp. 48–49; Warner, *New Haven Negroes*, p. 87; *Patten's New Haven Directory for the Year 1840, to which are Appended some Useful and Interesting Notices* (New Haven: Published by James M. Patten, Jr., 1840), p. 37; *Vital Records of New Haven, 1649–1850* (Hartford: The Connecticut Society of the Order of the Founders and Patriots of America, 1976), 2 parts, Pt. I ("Marriages), p. 496: "New Haven, May 4, 1823, the subscriber as minister of the United Society in this city married Alexander Dubois to Sally [Sarah] M[arsh] Lewis. Samuel Merwin." Pt. II ("Deaths"): 30 May 1831, p. 656 ("Du Bois, 15mos—Hydrochephaluz, Colored"); 22 March 1839, p. 739 ("Daugr of A. Dubois, 15 mos, convulsions, colored"); 27 Dec. 1841, p. 772 ("daughter of Alexander Dubois, 16 mos, hydrocephalus, colored"); Alexander Du Bois resident in New Haven: 6th Federal Census, 1840, M-704, Reel 27 (Connecticut, New Haven District No. 6), p. 63.

24. Entries throughout June and July 1861, "Dairy of Alexander Du Bois, 1856 and 1861/Du Bois Papers [Reel 89]/U. Mass.; *Autobiography*, pp. 67–71—"It may be that he [Alexander] had left Alfred in Haiti, when he left in 1830 . . . ," p. 70. Roger D. Joslyn to David Levering Lewis, 27 Oct., 6 Dec. 1989/Personal correspondence of David Levering Lewis. "Chart of Du Bois Family," compiled by Roger D. Joslyn, C.G., F.A.S.G., Dec. 1989. Bigg "Family History," pp. 18–22. Graham-Du Bois, *His Day*, pp. 199–20. Alfred Du Bois is listed at various residences in Albany, N.Y.: *Directory of the City of Albany, New York* (for 1858, 1859, 1861, 1862). 8th Federal Census, 1860, Ward 3, Albany, Albany County, N.Y. County Copy No. 89-10438. Albany County Hall of Records. No date or page given—Alfred Du Bois, age 28, "B[lack]," "barber," with place of birth given as "Rinodent"(?) The third copy of the 1860 census (N.Y., Albany County, M-653, Reel 719, p. 447) was forwarded to the National Archives, Washington, D.C. That copy mistakenly gives Alfred Du Bois's age as eighteen. A check of the original record retained for Albany County, however, lists Alfred Dubois as twenty-eight. "B[lack]." Hanna [sic], "B[lack]." At same residence, is said to be Cathrina [sic] Dillman, white, and described as "servant," twenty-one years of age. "Alfred . . . seemed a splendid vision . . .": *Darkwater*, p. 7.

25. "indolent, kind, unreliable": *Darkwater*, p. 7; *Dusk*, p. 109. The following account by Du Bois late in life is incompatible with other accounts he gave, is speculative, and expresses much wish fulfillment: "Then he sent for my mother, but her family wouldn't let her go. She'd never been out of Great Barrington, so she didn't go, and that broke the family, so that I never saw my father. He died, probably very soon after that, and I was brought up with my mother's family." Interview/Columbia OHP, p. 5. Compare this reminiscence with Du Bois's subsequent conjecture: "The family objected to her leaving

and expressed more and more doubt to father. The result was in the end that mother never went and my father never came back to Great Barrington. If he wrote, the letters were not delivered. I never saw him, and know not where or when he died.": *Autobiography*, pp. 72–73.

26. *Darkwater*, p. 7; *Dusk*, p. 109; *Autobiography*, p. 72. Photo of Alfred Du Bois in Union Army uniform, in Du Bois Papers/U. Mass. "Alfred never actually did much of anything.": *Dusk*, p. 108. ". . . to come to New Milford": *Darkwater*, p. 10. ". . . know not where or when he died.": *Autobiography*, p. 73.

27. Alexander Du Bois, resident in New Bedford, Massachusetts, after 1872, died 7 December 1887, survived by his wife, Annie M. F[reeman] Du Bois. One Alanson Borden was administrator of Alexander's estate, against which several claims of indebtedness were made. More than a year after Alexander's death, Annie sought relief from the probate court in order to obtain money from the estate. "Petition of Annie M. Du Bois to the Probate Court of Bristol County, Commonwealth of Massachusetts, February 15, 1889," Probate File 4744, Bristol County, Mass. This document lists Alexander Du Bois's "next of kin the person whose name, residence and relationship to the deceased are as follows, *viz.*: Augusta N. Du Bois, wife of James Davis of New Bedford, Mass.—daughter. *Alfred Du Bois—Meriden, Conn. Son* [my italics]. Henrietta D. Bates, wife of H.W. B. S. Bates of Cumberland, Maryland—Daughter." This information was provided by and attested to by Annie, dated December 23, 1887. See *Massachusetts Vital Records*. Microfilm (The New England Historic Genealogical Society, Boston, Massachusetts), 382:149. No trace of Alfred Du Bois in Meriden could be found: Joslyn to Lewis, 6 Dec. 1989: "I checked death, estate, census, and cemetery records and city directories, but the only Du Bois I found in Meriden was Joseph, listed in the 1844 and 1890 city directories." Erie Railroad battle: see Maury Klein, *The Life and Legend of Jay Gould* (Baltimore and London: The Johns Hopkins University Press, 1986), p. 84.

28. "Gay and carefree": *Dusk*, p. 108. Joslyn to Lewis, 10 Nov. 1989, and Albany city directory for 1865 listing "Hannah, washerwoman, 9 Hunter's alley."

29. Alfred Du Bois volunteered for military service in 1864. He listed his birthplace as Connecticut, age as thirty, and profession as barber. He enlisted from Amenia, N.Y., on Jan. 23 and was mustered into his unit at Poughkeepsie, N.Y., on February 23, 1864. He served in the 20th U. S. Colored Troops as an infantryman. His unit served in Tennessee and Louisiana. He entered military hospital in New Orleans suffering from dysentery and diarrhea. After recovery, Alfred served as an orderly until he was ordered to return to his unit, at which time, Jan. 1865, he went AWOL. He was officially declared as "deserter" on Feb. 7, 1865. Record Group 94. Records of the Adjutant General's Office. Colored Medical Records, Volunteers, Mexican and Civil War, 1846–64, 20th USCT. Box 3568/National Archives of the United States; also RG 94/Military Service records. Charles F. Cooney, formerly of the National Archives, was extremely helpful in locating these service records.

30. Marriage registry for 1867 at Great Barrington Town Hall: *Dusk*, p. 109.

31. ". . . impression of infinite patience . . .": *Autobiography*, p. 64; *Dusk*, p. 11.

32. Interview/Columbia OHP, p. 18.

33. ". . . only one illigitimate [sic] child . . .": *Dusk*, p. 111. "Romance": *ibid.*, p. 11; *Autobiography*, p. 65. Although Adelbert was once reported as saying (in 1900) that he was born in 1861, the evidence is persuasive that 1862 is the correct date: 9th Federal Census, 1870, M-593, Reel 601 (Mass. Berkshire County), p. 311; 12th Federal Census, 1900, T-623, Reel 675 (Mass., Middlesex County), li. 39. Living in Cambridge, Mass., in 1900, Adelbert's birth date is noted as Oct. 1861; place of birth is given as Connecticut. He was then a "coachman," married to Ida (no maiden name recorded), and two children are in residence.

34. 8th Federal Census, 1860, M-653, Reel 488 (Massachusetts, Berkshire County), p. 347; 1865 Interim Census (Mass., Berkshire County), no page. In 1850, Mary Silvinia is undoubtedly the nineteen-year-old black female employed as a servant in the household of Benjamin F. Durant, a white Great Barrington merchant. If so, her age does not correspond to that she gave (thirty-four) in the marriage registry—she would have been two years older: 7th Federal Census, 1850, M-432, Reel 306 (Mass., Berkshire County), p. 174.

35. 9th Federal Census, M-593, Reel 601 (Mass., Berkshire County), p. 295. In 1942, Adelbert discussed Burghardt family history with John S. Brown, a relative and emissary of W.E.B. Du Bois, revealing that his own father was Charles Craigg (?), not John Burghardt: John S. Brown to W.E.B. Du Bois, Jan. 25, 1942/Du Bois Papers, U. Mass.

36. *Dusk*, p. 12.

3. *Berkshire Prodigy*

1. ". . . but, thank God! no 'Anglo-Saxon,' . . .": *Darkwater*, p. 9. Facts about Old Jeff: Roz La Fontana, "The Long Search," *Berkshire Courier*, July 15, 1971, pp. 6, 7, 13; *Autobiography*, p. 72. Du Bois's birthplace at 51 Church Street was demolished circa 1900.

2. Mary Silvina's marriage: Du Bois gives various accounts of the marriage and reasons why Alfred left Great Barrington; they tend to blame his mother's relatives. "Du Bois Interview" (William T. Ingersoll, May 1960/Columbia OHP), p. 3; *Dusk*, pp. 108–9; *Autobiography*, p. 72: "He recoiled from grandfather Burghardt's home where Mary and her baby were expected eventually to live." It is interesting to note, however, that in the lengthy memoir which he read on the occasion of his seventieth birthday celebration at Atlanta University, Du Bois rendered this judgment on the Burghardts: "My family were pleasant and miscellaneous: the father was dead before I can remember; the mother brown and quietly persistent: the aunts and one uncle a bit censorious but not difficult to get on with; and then an endless vista of approving cousins.": "A Pageant in Seven Decades: 1868–1938," in Herbert Aptheker, ed., *Pamphlets and Leaflets by W.E.B. Du Bois* (Millwood, N.Y.: Kraus-Thomson, 1986), p. 244.

3. ". . . sank into depression.": *Autobiography*, p. 73. Allison Davis, Sr., late professor of social anthropology and psychology at the University of Chicago, and an African-American acquaintance of Du Bois's, has presented a seminal interpretation of Du Bois's rationalizing of his single-parent upbringing: "Such fantasies, which protected Du Bois's ego by denying the realities of his fatherlessness and his dark skin, served him well as a child. Fantasies of a handsome cavalier father protected his ego from the reality—the pain of having been deserted and left dependent upon charity.": Davis, *Leadership, Love & Aggression* (San Diego: Harcourt Brace Jovanovich, 1983), p. 111; see also pp. 13–15.

4. Adelbert's relationship to Du Bois: "silent" *Autobiography*, p. 73; ". . . thought they were after him": Adelbert, quoted in John S. Brown to W.E.B. Du Bois, Jan. 25, 1942/Du Bois Papers/U. Mass; W.E.B. Du Bois to Thomas S. Jones, Department of Welfare, N.Y.C., Jan. 20; W.E.B. Du Bois to John S. Brown, Jan. 20, 1942/Du Bois Papers/U. Mass. Adelbert stated that Alfred Du Bois moved to Copake, N.Y., and established a lucrative barbershop trade ("the whites idolized him"); however, no trace of Alfred is revealed in the 9th Federal Census, 1870, or in the *Gazeteer and Business Directory for Columbia County for 1871–2*; Roger D. Joslyn, F.A.S.G., to David Levering Lewis, 27 Oct. 1989/Lewis personal correspondence.

5. "Uncle Tello" and "very happy.": *Darkwater*, p. 9. ". . . My family were pleasant and miscellaneous.": "Pageant of Seven Decades," p. 244. On new home and school: *Autobiography*, p. 74.

6. Railroad Street: *Autobiography*, pp. 74, 81; *Darkwater*, p. 9; *Dusk*, p. 12; Interview/Columbia OHP, p. 5; also author's discussions with Mrs. Lila Parrish of Great Barrington.

7. Du Bois variously says Mary Silvina's left arm or left leg was impaired: *Autobiography*, p. 74; Interview/Columbia OHP, p. 5.

8. ". . . I just grew up that way.": Interview/Columbia OHP, pp. 4, 5; but see Davis, *Leadership*, p. 116.

9. ". . . a little bit, but not very much": *Autobiography*, p. 81; Interview/Columbia OHP, p. 4 ". . . I just didn't do it, . . .": *ibid*., p. 4.

10. The Russell family: *Autobiography*, p. 79. ". . . poorer than the well-to-do whites.": *ibid*., p. 75. ". . . no real discrimination . . .": *ibid*., p. 75. ". . . poor, drunken and sloven.": *ibid*., p. 75.

11. "annexed the rich . . .": *Darkwater*, pp. 10–11. On baseball: *Autobiography*, p. 85. "nigger": *ibid*., p. 82; Interview/Columbia OHP, p. 5.

12. "Mother . . . insisted . . .": Interview/Columbia OHP, p. 7.

13. ". . . to justify myself.": *ibid*., p. 5. ". . . sort of overseeing custody . . .": *Autobiography*, p. 73. "luxury . . . never dreamed was so rare": *Autobiography*, p. 74; Russian-language edition: *Vospominaniya* (Moscow: Izdatelstvo Innostranoii Literaturi, 1962).

14. The Cass house and "walking very straight . . .": *Autobiography*, pp. 81, 95; Interview/Columbia OHP p. 5.

15. ". . . stern and inflexible": *Autobiography*, p. 76. "Trounced": *Darkwater*, p. 11; *Autobiography*, p. 91. Du Bois had perfect elementary school attendance: "Report of Attendance for 1876–7, Roll of Honor," p. 10. (Copy of document was graciously provided by Ms. Lois Larken, school secretary for Searles Middle School, Great Barrington, Oct. 13, 1989.)

16. Playground sociology: *Autobiography*, pp. 75, 77, 82, 91; *Darkwater*, p. 11.

17. ". . . shut out . . . by a vast veil.": *Souls of Black Folks* (*SOBF*), p. 2.

18. On uncertain dating of visiting-cards trauma: Giving no date, Du Bois expressed umbrage as intensely as if the wound was still fresh to his Columbia interlocuter: "To be left out was inexplicable," Interview/Columbia OHP, p. 15; in *SOBF* (p. 2) and *Darkwater* (pp. 11–12) it seems to have occurred while Du Bois was in elementary school (and most probably did). In the *Autobiography* (pp. 83, 85, 95) the cards incident appears to take place in high school. A curious document deposited in the Harvard University Archives (Jan. 1986) dates the visiting-cards rebuff as happening in the spring of 1878; the author of this monograph states that he interviewed Du Bois twice and that Du Bois read the manuscript and even "suggested revisions.": Benjamin F. Rogers (typescript), "Different from the Others: An Autobiographical Study of William Edward Burghardt Du Bois, written in 1940"/Harvard University (Pusey Library), HU 92 40 751. ". . . otherwise she was negligible.": *Autobiography*, p. 85. ". . . began to feel the pressure . . .": *ibid*., p. 83.

19. ". . . days of secret tears.": *Darkwater*, p. 11. ". . . brown skin a misfortune . . .": *ibid*., p. 11. Judge Dewey: *Autobiography*, pp. 91, 183. "pale companions . . .": *Darkwater*, p. 12.

20. Frank Hosmer: Obituary, *New York Times*, May 29, 1918, p. 13; *Autobiography*, p. 101. "soldiers of light and love": Jacqueline Jones, *Soldiers of Light and Love: Northern Teachers of Georgia Blacks, 1865–1873* (Chapel Hill: University of North Carolina Press, 1980), p. 9; a more approving monograph is Robert C. Morris, *Reading 'Riting, and Reconstruction: The Education of Freedmen in the South, 1861–1870* (Chicago: University of Chicago Press, 1976), pp. 182–83.

21. Aspiring to college (". . . ancient tongues"): *Autobiography*, p. 101; W.E.B. Du Bois to Frank Hosmer, Feb. 16, 1918/Du Bois Papers/ U. Mass.: "I am sure that I owe to

you, more than to any single person, the fact that I got started toward the higher training in my youth."; ". . . suggested . . . take the college preparatory course.": *Dusk*, p. 15.

22. On books and the Russells: *Autobiography*, p. 86; *Dusk*, p. 16.

23. "Long Search," *Berkshire Courier*, July 15, 1971. "Report of Attendance for 1876–7, Roll of Honor," p. 10. (I am grateful to Ms. Lois Larken, secretary of Searles Middle School, Great Barrington, for sending this document on Oct. 13, 1989/David Levering Lewis personal correspondence.) Only other black student: *Dusk*, p. 20. "grimly determined . . .": *Darkwater*, p. 11; *Autobiography*, p. 84.

24. George Beebee, Mary Dewey: *Autobiography*, p. 84.

25. Courses and theatricals at GBHS: *Great Barrington High School Catalogue, 1882–1883*, Du Bois Papers/U. Mass.; "Annual Report of the School Committee of the Town of Great Barrington, for the Year 1883–1884" (courtesy of Ms. Lois Larken to David Levering Lewis, Oct. 13, 1989/David Levering Lewis personal correspondence); *Autobiography*, pp. 80, 85, 92.

26. Macaulay's *History of England*: *Autobiography*, p. 87: "distinct . . . without distinction.": Lytton Strachey, *Portraits in Miniature and Other Essays* (London: Chatto & Windus, 1931), pp. 173, 179; Charles Firth, *A Commentary on Macaulay's History of Ireland* (New York: Barnes & Noble, 1964), p. 34—"But his inclination is to use a swelling phrase when a plainer and more natural one would often be preferable."

27. *Globe*: *Autobiography*, p. 95; On Fortune: Emma Lou Thornbrough, "The National Afro-American League, 1887–1908," *Journal of Southern History*, 27 (Nov. 1961): 494–512; Thornbrough, "T. Thomas Fortune: Militant Editor in the Age of Accommodation," in John Hope Franklin and August Meier, eds., *Black Leaders of the Twentieth Century* (Urbana and Chicago: University of Illinois Press, 1982), pp. 19–37; and (E.L.T. *Thomas Fortune: Militant Journalist* (Chicago: University of Chicago Press, 1972), esp. 44; "Fortune, T[imothy] Thomas," *DANB*, pp. 236–38; August Meier, *Negro Thought in America: 1880–1915: Racial Ideologies in the Age of Booker T. Washington* (Ann Arbor: University of Michigan Press, 1991; orig. pub. 1963), pp. 30–32, 70–74.

28. Du Bois's admiration of Fortune: Du Bois, "Editorial," *Fisk Herald* (Nov. 1887): 9–10; "The Lash," *The Horizon*, I (May 1907): 3–10 [reprinted in Aptheker, ed., *Selections from The Horizon*, p. 16]; "W.E.B. Discusses the Negro Press," New York *Age*, Nov. 4, 1935, p.3.

29. Herbert Aptheker, ed., *Newspaper Columns by W.E.B. Du Bois. Compiled and Edited by Herbert Aptheker* (Millwood, N.Y.: Kraus-Thomson, 1986), 2 vols., I, pp. 1–23. ". . . contrabands . . .": *Autobiography*, pp. 83, 93. ". . . glimpses of the colored world.": *Dusk*, p. 23.

30. Aptheker, ed., *Newspaper Columns*, pp. 1, 4, 5, 10.

31. Quotes from Du Bois and newspaper articles: *Globe*, May 5 [p. 2]; *Globe*, April 14 [p. 1]; *Globe*, May 26 [p. 3]; *Globe*, Sept. 29, 1883 [p. 7], Aptheker, ed., in *Newspaper Columns*, I.

32. *Dusk*, p. 109; *Autobiography*, p. 97. 10th Federal Census, 1880, T-9, Reel 525 (Mass. Bristol County), p. 12.

33. "Dear Mam": W.E.B. Du Bois to Mary Silvina Du Bois, July 21, 1883, Du Bois Papers/U. Mass.; also Aptheker, ed., *The Correspondence of W.E.B. Du Bois* (Amherst: University of Massachusetts Press, 1973), 3 vols., I, pp. 4–5; *Dusk*, p. 20.

34. "British Emancipation Day," *Providence Journal*, Aug. 2, 1883; *Autobiography*, p. 99; *Dusk*, p. 20.

35. "Dear Mam" letter, July 21, 1883. ". . . I never forgot that toast.": *Autobiography*, p. 98; Shirley Graham-Du Bois, *His Day Is Marching On*, p. 199.

36. Graham-Du Bois, *His Day*, pp. 197–208; Reel 89, Du Bois Papers/U. Mass.

contains extensive documentation gleaned from the New Haven and New Bedford vital records by Du Bois of his Du Bois family history.

37. *Autobiography*, p. 66. *Vital Records of New Haven, 1649–1850*, 2 parts, I, p. 496. (On May 4, 1823, Alexander Du Bois married Sarah Marsh Lewis.)

38. Diplomacy and black migration during Boyer presidency: Rayford W. Logan, *The Diplomatic Relations of the United States with Haiti, 1776–1891* (Chapel Hill: University of North Carolina Press, 1941), pp. 189–217; Alfred N. Hunt, *Haiti's Influence on Antebellum America: Slumbering Volcano in the Caribbean* (Baton Rouge: Louisiana State University Press, 1988), pp. 161–174; Robert Debs Heinl and Nancy Gordon Heinl, *Written in Blood: The Story of the Haitian People, 1492–1971* (Boston: Houghton Mifflin, 1978), p. 179; Immanuel Geiss, *The Pan-African Movement: A History of Pan-Africanism in America, Europe and Africa* (New York: Africana Publishing Co., 1974), pp. 86–92; John Edward Baur, "The Mulatto Machiavelli," *Journal of Negro History*, 32 (1947): 307–53, esp. pp. 324, 326.

39. ". . . under Haitian beneficence.": Logan, *Diplomatic Relations*, p. 217; Geiss, *Pan-African Movement*, p. 92.

40. Alexander Du Bois in Haiti and New Haven: *Autobiography*, pp. 66–67; *Vital Records of New Haven*, I, p. 571 (Alexander Du Bois married Emily Jacklyn of Milford, Connecticut, on 19 July 1835.); Robert Warner, *New Haven Negroes*, pp. 86–87; Wilson Jeremiah Moses, *Alexander Crummell: A Study of Civilization and Discontent* (New York: Oxford University Press, 1989), pp. 30–37.

41. "Alexander Crummell," *DANB*, pp. 145–47; Moses, *Crummell*, pp. 16–20. Alexander Du Bois, "Account of Contributions for the Benefit of Alexander Crummell, 1840–41," Du Bois Papers/U. Mass.; *SOBF* ("Of Alexander Crummell").

42. 7th Federal Census, 1850, M-432, Reel 319 (Mass. Hampden County), p. 43; Joseph Carvalho III, *Black Families in Hampden County, Massachusetts, 1650–1855* pp. 48–49; *Autobiography*, p. 68; Alexander Du Bois, "Diary," entries during 1856, Du Bois Papers/U. Mass.

43. "James Theodore Holly": *DANB*, pp. 319–20; Carter Godwin Woodson, *The History of the Negro Church* (Washington, D.C.: Associated Publishers, 1921, 1945), pp. 158–59; Hunt, *Haiti's Influence*, p.174. Floyd J. Miller, *The Search for Black Nationality, Black Emigration and Colonization, 1787–1863* (Urbana: University of Illinois Press, 1975), pp. 107–110, 162–63; P. J. Staudenraus, *The African Colonization Movement, 1816–1865* (New York: Columbia University Press, 1961), p. 85; James M. McPherson, *The Negro's Civil War: How American Negroes Felt and Acted during the War for the Union* (Urbana and London: University of Illinois Press, 1982; orig. pub. 1965), pp. 76–97.

44. Douglass quoted: Miller, *Search for Black Nationality*, p. 240. On emigrationist thinking: see Benjamin Quarles, *Black Abolitionists* (New York: Oxford University Press, 1969), pp. 216–31; Heinl and Heinl, *Written in Blood*: "Led by a black Episcopal priest, James Theodore Holly, a group of American blacks numbering nearly 2,000 emigrated in May 1861 from New Haven to Haiti where Geffrard settled them on the old Habitation Drouillard east of Croix des Bouquets," p. 215. "Jackasses, Negroes, mud . . .": May 9, June 1, June 3, and undated 1861 entry, Alexander Du Bois, "Diary," Du Bois Papers/U. Mass.

45. François-Élie Du Bois, a relative of Alexander's: Heinl and Heinl, *Written in Blood*, p. 216. Hunt, *Haiti's Influence*, p. 166; *Autobiography*, p. 70.

46. Bigg, "Family History," p. 17. *The Name and Family of Du Bois* (Media Research Department, Washington, D.C.). ". . . he was a man!": *Autobiography*, p. 71.

47. ". . . Sons of Men": May 19, 1861, entry "Diary," Du Bois Papers/U. Mass., p. 18.

48. On influence of *Springfield Republican*: Samuel Eliot Morison and Henry Steele Commager, *The Growth of the American Republic* (New York: Oxford University Press,

1962), 2 vols., II, p. 112. Du Bois, "The Housatonic Festival," *Springfield Republican*, Sept. 26, 1884. "From Our Special Correspondent": Paul Partington's *Springfield Republican* researches have led him to believe that there were probably four (rather than the two listed by Aptheker), in Partington, "The Mistakes of Herbert Aptheker as Contained in the Book, Annotated Bibliography of the Published Writings of W.E.B. Du Bois" [typescript courtesy of Paul Partington], p. 1; *Autobiography*, p. 89. First Congregational Church—fire, rebuilding: Howard J. Conn, *The First Congregational Church of Great Barrington, 1743–1943* (Great Barrington: *Berkshire Courier*, 1943), pp. 6–12 [and Mary Silvinia's affiliation, p. 107]; *Autobiography*, p. 89. ". . . handsomest church in the county . . .": *Globe*, Sept. 29, 1883, in *Newspaper Columns*, p. 7; Lila Parrish, *A History of Searles Castle in Great Barrington, Massachusetts* (Great Barrington: Attic Revival Press, 1985), p. 9. Willie at Sunday School: *Autobiography*, p. 89. "'*He alethia eleutherosi humas*'": *Autobiography*, p. 89. "both popular and a little dreaded . . .": *ibid.*, p. 89. Of his own religious development, Du Bois writes, summing up, ""My religious development has been slow and uncertain. I grew up in a liberal Congregational Sunday School and listened once a week to a sermon on doing good as a reasonable duty. Theology played a minor part and our teachers had to face some searching questions.": *Autobiography*, p. 285. Dewey on outmoded Articles of Faith: Conn, *First Congregation*, p. 39. Justin Dewey and grape juice: Conn, *ibid.*, pp. 39–40.

49. ". . . provoked repeated applause.": *Berkshire Courier*, July 2, 1884; *Autobiography*, pp. 99–100.

50. "gatling gun" mind: Brooks, *Flowering of New England*, II, p. 3. "Our work is not done.": James M. McPherson, *The Abolitionist Legacy: From Reconstruction to the NAACP* (Princeton, N.J.: Princeton University Press, 1975), p. 13; ". . . labor, the creator of wealth . . . ," Vernon L. Parrington's summary of Wendell Phillips's socialism: *Main Currents in American Thought: The Beginnings of Cultural Realism in America, 1860–1920*, vol. 3 (Norman: University of Oklahoma Press, 1878, orig. pub. 1930), pp. 144–45.

51. ". . . a wider conception": *Dusk*, p. 20. "It would be a great calamity . . .": Blaine letter reproduced in *Berkshire Courier*, July 23, 1884, p. 1. Parrington, *Main Currents*, III, p. 51; McPherson, *Abolitionist Legacy*, pp. 15, 38–39. Brooks, *Flowering of New England*, I, p. 528.

52. College "settled in . . . own mind": *Autobiography*, p. 101; *Dusk*, p. 20.

53. ". . . plump, brown girl . . .": *Autobiography*, p. 108.

54. "The Damnation of Women": *Darkwater*, pp. 163–64.

55. "Deaths Registered in the Town of Great Barrington for the year 1885," *Mass. Vital Records*, 364.35 (23 Mar. 1885). ". . . choking gladness . . .": *Autobiography*, p. 102; *Darkwater*, p. 12. Julius Lester, ed., *Seventh Son*, p. 7: "Her death, however, did not affect him greatly at the time, and in a practical sense it freed him from the worry of who would care for her when he went away to college."

Davis, *Leadership*, p. 116: "He felt sorry for his mother, he nursed her, and he expressed concern and solicitude for her. But these are not love. In fact, they might have been defensive expressions of guilt from resenting her for having disgraced him."

Rampersad, *Art and Imagination*, p. 4: "There can be little doubt that Du Bois's remarkable regard for all women, especially black women, had its roots in his deep regard for his mother." This assessment, in Rampersad's otherwise perceptive biography, is clearly too credulous. A similar appreciation is offered by Nellie McKay, "W.E.B. Du Bois: The Black Women in His Writings—Selected Fictional and Autobiographical Portraits," in William L. Andrews, ed., *Critical Essays on W.E.B. Du Bois* (Boston: G. K. Hall & Co., 1985), pp. 230–52, esp. p. 234.

56. J. Carlisle Dennis, "A Globe Agent's Distinction," *Globe*, July 12, 1884, p. 1, *ibid.*, p. 15.

57. "fabulous wage": Interview/Columbia OHP, p. 34; *Autobiography*, p. 104. Taylor, *History*, pp. 479–80. See Lila S. Parrish, *A History of Searles Castle*, esp. 9–12. "Searles had the glamour . . ." and "with the contractors . . .": *Autobiography*, p. 104; Parrish monograph contains detailed biographical material about Searles and his intimates, *ibid.*, esp. pp. 24–25.

58. Du Bois, "The Famous $100,000 Leavitt Barn Burned," *Springfield Republican*, July 8, 1885. Lawrence A. Cremin, *American Education: The Metropolitan Experience, 1876–1980* (New York: Harper & Row, 1988), p. 379; Frederick Rudolph, *The American College and University: A History* (Athens and London: University of Georgia Press, 1990; orig. pub. 1962), pp. 290–95. Four Congregational churches: Interview/Columbia OHP, p. 34; *Autobiography*, p. 103.

59. "the South of slavery . . .": *Autobiography*, p. 105. Hampton Quartet: Interview/Columbia OHP, p. 18; *Autobiography*, p. 106. "glad to go to Fisk.": *ibid.*, p. 106. "age of miracles": *Darkwater*, p. 14.

4. The Age of Miracles: Fisk and Josie's World

1. An end to "spiritual isolation . . .": *Autobiography*, p. 106.

2. James D. Anderson, *The Education of Blacks in the South, 1860–1935* (Chapel Hill: University of North Carolina Press, 1988), p. 6: "W.E.B. Du Bois was on the mark when he said: 'Public education for all at public expense was, in the South, a Negro idea.' "; Jacqueline Jones, *Soldiers of Light and Love*, pp. 135–37; also Robert Morris, *Reading, 'Riting and Reconstruction*, pp. 192–93; and Henry Allen Bullock, *A History of Negro Education in the South: From 1619 to the Present* (New York: Praeger, 1967), pp. 22, 54. ". . . wonderful days . . .": Booker T. Washington, quoted in Joe M. Richardson, *A History of Fisk University, 1865–1946* (Tuscaloosa: University of Alabama Press, 1980), p. 7; and Richardson, *Christian Reconstruction: The American Missionary Association and Southern Blacks, 1861–1890* (Athens: University of Georgia Press, 1986), p. 42.

3. Ogden's improvements: Richardson, *Fisk*, pp. 13, 14. "the best normal school": Horace Mann Bond, *The Education of the Negro in the American Social Order* (New York: Octagon Books, 1966; orig. pub. 1934), p. 131.

4. The Jubilee Singers: Mark Twain, quoted in Richardson, *Fisk*, pp. 29–33; L. M. Collins, *One Hundred Years of Fisk University Presidents* (Nashville: Hemphill's Creative Printing, 1989), pp. 1–2; *Autobiography*, p. 123.

5. Jubilee Singers and the growing campus: Collins, *One Hundred Years*, pp. 2–14; John Hope Franklin, *From Slavery to Freedom*, pp. 272–73; Richardson, *Christian Reconstruction*, p. 134, judges that Atlanta University was academically the outstanding AMA college.

6. Assessing the caliber of these schools, Jones, *Soldiers of Light and Love*, states, p. 135, that Atlanta University "offered courses of study inferior to those at good New England colleges but superior to western or southern schools at the same level." Expressing strong misgivings about the literary skew of the AMA colleges, Carter Godwin Woodson, *The Miseducation of the Negro* (New York: AMS Press, 1977; orig. pub. 1933), pp. 1, 12, 136, concluded, "The race needs workers, not leaders." Richardson, *Fisk*, pp. 44–60; Collins, *One Hundred Years*, pp. 3–10; Henry Hugh Proctor, *Between Black and White, Autobiographical Sketches* (Boston: The Pilgrims Press, 1925), p. 34.

7. Building Fisk: *Autobiography*, p. 112; Richardson, *Fisk*, pp. 15–21, and *Christian Reconstruction*, p. 61.

8. Southern white hostility: Bond, *Education of the Negro*, p. 96; Louis Harlan, *Separate and Unequal: Public School Campaigns and Racism in the Southern Seaboard States* (Chapel Hill: University of North Carolina Press, 1958), pp. 19, 17.

9. ". . . if equal, give him the same.": quoted in Richardson, *Fisk*, pp. 20–21, and 61. "In general, the ex-slaves were unable to reconcile the planters to the idea of black education," says Anderson, *Education of Blacks*, p. 22 and 92.

10. Du Bois arrives at Fisk: *Autobiography*, pp. 103, 107, 112; *Dusk*, p. 31. "know what the Greek language meant": *Dusk*, p. 30; Proctor, *Between Black and White*, p. 32; Collins, *One Hundred Years*, pp. 3–4.

11. See Woodson, *Miseducation*, p. xiv, "The large majority of this class, then, must go through life denouncing white people because they are trying to run away from the blacks and decrying the blacks because they are not white." And see Henry Allen Bullock, *History of Negro Education*, p. 8; and William H. Ferris, *The African Abroad or His Evolution in Western Civilization* (New Haven: The Tuttle, Morehouse & Taylor Press, 1913), 2 vols., I, p. 205.

12. Civil rights and segregation: Richard Bardolph, ed., *The Civil Rights Record: Black Americans and the Law, 1849–1970* (New York: Crowell, 1970), pp. 82–83; John W. Cell, *The Highest Stage of White Supremacy: The Origins of Segregation in South Africa and the American South* (New York and London: Cambridge University Press, 1982), ch. 5; Richard Kluger, *Simple Justice: The History of Brown v. Board of Education* (New York: Vintage Books, 1977; orig. pub. 1975), esp. pp. 51–69; Joel Williamson, *The Crucible of Race: Black-White Relations in the American South since Emancipation* (New York: Oxford University Press, 1984), pp. 90–101.

13. ". . . exciting and eternal ties.": *Autobiography*, p. 107; *Dusk*, p. 30.

14. Margaret Murray Washington: Louis Harlan, *Booker T. Washington: The Making of a Black Leader, 1856–1901* (New York: Oxford University Press, 1972), pp. 179–82. "coarse-looking Sherrod . . .": *Autobiography*, p. 111.

15. Social background of Fisk students: *Autobiography*, pp. 108, 111; Interview/ Columbia OHP, p. 38.

16. "Lots and lots of mulattoes . . ." *ibid.*, p. 39; *Autobiography*, pp. 108, 109; Proctor, *Between Black and White*, pp. 29–30. "Such airs, and colored men at that . . .": *Autobiography*, p. 107.

17. "Who Are We?": *Fisk Herald*, 7 (Oct. 1889): 11–12; see Howard N. Rabinowitz, *Race Relations in the Urban South, 1865–1890* (Urbana and London: University of Illinois Press, 1980; orig. pub. 1978), pp. 334–35; see, also, Willard B. Gatewood, *Aristocrats of Color: The Black Elite, 1880–1920* (Bloomington: Indiana University Press, 1990), pp. 265, 266; J. Morgan Kousser, *The Shaping of Southern Politics, Suffrage Restrictions and the Establishment of the One-Party South, 1880–1910* (New Haven: Yale University Press, 1974), pp. 71, 76, 107.

18. "Coming out of New England . . .": Proctor, *Between Black and White*, p. 29. ". . . physical difference between men and women": *Autobiography*, p. 280.

19. ". . . praised the food.": G. M. McClellan to W.E.B. Du Bois, Feb. 21, 1918, Du Bois Papers/ U. Mass.

20. ". . . two of the most beautiful beings . . .": *Darkwater*, p. 13; *Autobiography*, pp. 107, 108; Interview/Columbia OHP, p. 38. ". . . oh, a perfectly lovely girl.": *ibid.*, p. 38.

21. Margaret Murray: *Autobiography*, p. 113; ". . . miraculous . . . to a boy of seventeen . . .": *Darkwater*, p. 14.

22. Du Bois was 5′ 5½″: "Life Extension Institute Survey of the Physical Condition,

Family and Personal History, and Activities of Mr. William E. B. Du Bois, July 1925," Du Bois Papers/U. Mass.; in an interview conducted by me with Rayford W. Logan, one of Du Bois's closest associates, Logan stressed the discrepancy between the actual height of Du Bois and the commanding impression he invariably made—Logan Interview, Oct. 1974; taped interview deposited with Schomburg Center for Research in Black Culture, N.Y. "Don't you do that again!": *Autobiography*, p. 109.

23. ". . . whole school hung on the bulletins": *Autobiography*, p. 109; Interview/ Columbia OHP, p. 40.

24. "Pops" Miller controversy: *Dusk*, p. 33; *Autobiography*, p. 110; Interview/ Columbia OHP, p. 62.

25. No "respect for Paul since": *Dusk*, p. 33; *Autobiography*, p. 110; Arna Bontemps erroneously concluded that *The Logic of Christian Evidences* was published in 1895: Arna Bontemps to Shirley Graham, Dec. 3, 1954; W.E.B. Du Bois to Arna Bontemps, Dec. 10, 1954, Du Bois Papers/U. Mass.; Rampersad, *Du Bois*, p. 74.

26. "forty conversions": *Autobiography*, p. 110; W.E.B. Du Bois to Reverend Evarts Scudder, Feb. 3, 1886, Du Bois Papers/U. Mass.; and Aptheker, ed., *Correspondence of W.E.B. Du Bois*, I, p. 5.

27. "Its theory had presented no particular difficulties . . .": *Dusk*, p. 33; Du Bois, *Prayers for Dark People* (Amherst: University of Massachusetts Press, 1980), ed. H. Aptheker, p. viii.

28. Views about God: *Darkwater*, pp. 3, 105, 123; W.E.B. Du Bois to E. Peña Moreno, Nov. 15, 1948, Du Bois Papers/U. Mass.; also Aptheker, *Correspondence*, III, p. 223.

29. ". . . they are all my people . . .": Du Bois to Scudder, Feb. 3, 1886, Du Bois Papers/U. Mass. ". . . captain of [his] soul . . .": *Darkwater*, p. 14. ". . . leadership of men like myself . . .": *Autobiography*, p. 112. A similar public declaration is found in, Du Bois, "Oration" [untitled, undated], cited by Broderick, *Du Bois*, p. 8 (note 13), but not found by me in the Du Bois collections consulted.

30. Racial etiquette in the South: *Dusk*, p. 30; *Darkwater*, p. 14; *Autobiography*, p. 121. G. W. Cable quoted, in Morison and Commager, *Growth of the American Republic*, II, p. 90; W.E.B. Du Bois to George Washington Cable, Feb. 23, 1890, Du Bois/U. Mass.; and Aptheker, *Correspondence*, I, p. 7.

31. Tennessee backcountry: *Fisk Herald*, 4 (Oct. 1886); 6–7, Fisk University Library. The Du Bois Papers/U. Mass. [reel 89] contain the contract with School No. 5, Wilson County, 1886, awarding Du Bois twenty-eight dollars monthly for his services.

32. ". . . touched the very shadow of slavery.": *Autobiography*, p. 114.

33. On the road to Alexandria: Lowell Afton Bogle, *Watertown History* (Watertown Public Library: Typescript 1973. Revised 1984); David Levering Lewis retraced Du Bois's route during January 1990; *SOBF*, p. 61.

34. ". . . awful shadow of the Veil.": *SOBF*, p. 63. Mrs. Dowell, "strong, bustling, and energetic . . .": *ibid.*, p. 62; *Autobiography*, p. 115.

35. Teaching in the backcountry: *Autobiography*, pp. 117, 118; *SOBF*, p. 65. "How I Taught School," *Fisk Herald*, 4 (Dec. 1886): 9–10.

36. ". . . transient glimpses of the dawn . . .": *loc. cit.*, p. 10; "wouldn't take $200 . . .": *loc. cit.*, p. 10.

37. "I would visit Mun Eddings . . .": *SOBF*, p. 65.

38. ". . . reckless bravado.": *SOBF*, p. 68. "pythian madness . . .": *Autobiography*, p. 120.

39. " 'White folks would get it all' ": *ibid.*, p. 118. " 'We've had a heap of trouble . . .' ": *SOBF*, pp. 69–73.

40. My impressions of Alexandria, Tennessee, in 1990, based on a one-day visit.

41. ". . . literally raped . . .": *Autobiography*, p. 280.

42. Du Bois's sense of racial identity: Rayford W. Logan, ed., *W.E.B. Du Bois: A Profile*, p. ix. In a 1961 recorded interview, Du Bois stated that, at Fisk, he learned to go to bed early and to accept "quite willingly to be a Negro and work with the Negro group": "W.E.B. Du Bois/A Recorded Autobiography" (interviewed by Moses Asch), Folkways Records (FH 5511, 1961); side 1; also Houston D. Baker, Jr., "The Black Man of Culture; W.E.B. Du Bois and the *Souls of Black Folk*," in William L. Andrews, ed., *Critical Essays on W.E.B. Du Bois*, esp. p. 132. On creolism in the United States: Carl Degler, *Neither Black nor White: Slavery and Race Relations in Brazil and the United States* (New York: Macmillan, 1971), pp. 213–32; Caroline Bond-Day, *Some Negro-White Families in the United States* (Westport, CT: Negro Universities Press, 1970; orig. pub. 1932), p. 34, plate 50, describes Du Bois as "apparently a third generation cross, has light brown skin color with frizzy black hair." Edward B. Reuter, *Race Mixture* (New York, McGraw-Hill, 1969; orig. pub. 1931); W. Lloyd Warner, Buford Junker, Walter A. Davis, *Color and Human Nature: Negro Personality Development in a Northern City* (Washington, D.C.: American Council on Education, 1941), pp. 130, 161, esp. ch. 4 ("Volunteer Negroes and Other Passable People"); Joel Williamson, *New People: Miscegenation and Mulattoes in the United States* (New York: The Free Press, 1980).

43. More on vagaries of color: Degler, *Neither Black nor White*, ch. 5, esp. pp. 239–43; Williamson, *New People*, pp. 1–102. See also Winthrop Jordan, *White Over Black: American Attitudes toward the Negro, 1550–1812* (Chapel Hill: University of North Carolina Press, 1968), pp. 167–78. For excellent analyses of the elaborations of racialist ideology as a means of social control of poor black and white people, see Leon Higginbotham, *In the Matter of Color: Race and the American Legal Process* (New York: Oxford University Press, 1978), pp. 19–37; Edmund S. Morgan, *American Slavery, American Freedom: The Ordeal of Colored Virginia* (New York: W. W. Norton, 1975), ch. 16; and also Hortense Powdermaker, *After Freedom: A Cultural Study on the Deep South* (New York: Viking Press, 1939), esp. ch. 9 ("The Color Line"), pp. 175–96.

44. Frazier, assessing Du Bois's racial psychology, wrote that Du Bois retained his New England "mulatto characteristics," and that "during his short sojourn in the South as an undergraduate . . . he never was thoroughly assimilated into Negro life.": E. Franklin Frazier, "The Du Bois Program in the Present Crisis," *Race, Devoted to Social, Political and Economic Equality*, 1935–36 [reprinted by Negro Universities Press, 1970]: 11–13, p.11. Allison Davis, *Leadership, Love and Aggression*, pp. 119–20, advances similar conclusions. "W.E.B. Du Bois/A Recorded Autobiography" (interviewed by Moses Asch), Folkways Records (FH 5511, 1961).

45. "talented tenth": "The New Negro," mentioned by Du Bois in "A Pageant in Seven Decades," *Pamphlets and Leaflets*, p. 247.

46. "An Open Letter to the Southern People," in Aptheker, ed., *Against Racism: Unpublished Essays, Papers, Addresses, 1887–1961 by W.E.B. Du Bois* (Amherst: University of Massachusetts Press, 1985), pp. 1–4.

47. ". . . sophomoric effusions.": *Fisk Herald*, 3 (Nov. 1885): 4; 3 (July 1886): p. 5.

48. "Editorial Toothpick," *Fisk Herald*, 3 (Nov. 1887): 9–10. See Paul Partington, *W.E.B. Du Bois: A Bibliography of His Published Writings*, p. 1 (for *Fisk Herald* issues contributed to by Du Bois); Aptheker, ed., *Annotated Bibliography*, pp. 5–7 (for *Fisk Herald* issues contributed to by Du Bois). ". . . impassioned orator": *Dusk*, p. 31—at least on one occasion, however, Du Bois says that he became so animated during a debate that "I forgot my lines" ("A Pageant in Seven Decades," p. 247); "Student Papers, Fisk University c. 1888," Du Bois Papers/U. Mass. [Reel 89].

49. ". . . but a quarter of a century removed . . .": "Editorial," *Fisk Herald*, 5 (Feb. 1888): 8–9, in Aptheker, *Annotated Bibliography*, p. 7. *Autobiography*, p. 123.

50. Aptheker, *Annotated Bibliography*, pp. 6–7; Partington, *Bibliography*, p. 1. "At last we have a historian": "Editorial," *Fisk Herald*, 5 (Jan. 1888): 8. For the life and works of Williams, see John Hope Franklin, *George Washington Williams: A Biography* (Chicago: University of Chicago Press, 1985). "[Fortune] Editorial," *Fisk Herald*, 5 (Nov. 1887): 8–9.

51. "the Age of Women is surely dawning.": "Editorial," *Fisk Herald*, 5 (Dec. 1887): 8–9. "Tom Brown at Fisk," *Fisk Herald*, 5 (Nov.–Dec., 1887—Feb., 1888); also "Tom Brown at Fisk in Three Chapters," Aptheker, ed., *Creative Writing by W.E.B. Du Bois: A Pageant, Poems, Short Stories, and Playlets* (White Plains, N.Y.: Kraus-Thomson, 1985), pp. 56–62; Rampersad, *Du Bois*, p. 21.

52. Carlyle at Fisk: "Editorial Toothpick," *Fisk Herald*, 5 (Mar. 1888): 8–9; For Carlyle's influence on Du Bois, see, esp., Rampersad, *Du Bois*, p. 66; interestingly, Alexander Crummell took issue with Carlyle's "great man" paradigm and was generally dismissive of the English thinker—Wilson Jeremiah Moses, *Alexander Crummell: A Study of Civilization and Discontent*, pp. 94–95, 187–88.

Thomas Carlyle, *On Heroes and Hero-Worship and the Heroic in History* (New York: Wiley and Putnam, 1846); and Fritz R. Stern, ed., *Varieties in History: From Voltaire to the Present* (London: Macmillan, 1970, 2d ed.), pp. 90–107, for Carlyle; also, James Wetfall Thompson, *A History of Historical Writing* (New York: Macmillan, 1942), pp. 301–304; the indispensable biography is now, Fred Kaplan, *Thomas Carlyle: A Biography* (Berkeley and London: University of California Press, 1983).

53. ". . . words of encouragement . . .": "Editorial," *Fisk Herald*, 5 (Feb. 1888): 8–9. ". . . surpasses in superciliousness . . .": "Editorial Toothpick," *Fisk Herald*, 5 (Nov. 1887): 9–10.

54. Maria Benson and Du Bois: Maria Benson to classmates, Sept. 23, 1890, Du Bois Papers/U. Mass. W.E.B. Du Bois to "Dear Classmates," 19 Nov. 1890, p. 12, in Hugh Smyth Papers, Fol. 9(a)/Schomburg Center for Research in Black Culture, N.Y.; also Du Bois Papers/U. Mass. Du Bois informs his classmates that his "*penchant* for hurting other peoples' feelings is a little on the wane—for which I'm sure you're all thanking God.": pp. 12–13.

55. After training at Fisk and Yale Divinity School, Proctor pastored the First Congregational Church of Atlanta, Georgia, for much of the early twentieth century (1894–1920). An able, principled community and civil rights leader (his role in the aftermath of the 1906 Atlanta riot was crucial), Proctor maintained a close personal association with both Du Bois and Booker T. Washington. After leaving Atlanta in 1920, he pastored a church in Brooklyn, N.Y.: "Proctor Henry Hugh (1868–1933)," *DANB*, pp. 505–6; Proctor, *Between Black and White*; *Autobiography*, p. 109.

56. ". . . little understood each other . . .": Circular letter to Fisk classmates, Nov. 19, 1890, p. 13. Stern advice to classmates: ". . . let me give you a remedy: one all-absorbing life work. This is the very ultimatum of pleasure": *ibid.*, p. 11.

57. Fisk professors' evaluations of Du Bois: contained in "Du Bois, William Edward Burghardt, A.B. 1890": The Class Folders, Nathan Marsh Pusey Library/Harvard University.

58. "Nellie": "Program for the Celebration of My Twenty-fifth Birthday," Du Bois Papers/U. Mass. [Reel 87]; also Aptheker, ed., *Against Racism*, pp. 27–29. "Bismarck . . . my hero": *Dusk*, p. 32; *Autobiography*, p. 126; and Nathan I. Huggins, "W.E.B. Du Bois and Heroes," *Amerikaststudien, American Studies* (*AMST*), 34 (1989): 167–74.

59. For Bismarck and imperialism, the literature is vast. Useful overviews are contained in Prosser Gifford and William Roger Louis, eds., *Britain and Germany in Africa:*

Imperial Rivalry and Colonial Rule (New Haven: Yale University Press, 1968); William L. Langer, *European Alliances and Alignments, 1871–1890* (New York: Knopf, 1931), pp. 281–321; Ruth First, *South West Africa* (Baltimore, MD.: Penguin Books, 1963), pp. 69–83; G. N. Sanderson, *England, Europe and the Upper Nile, 1882–1899* (Edinburgh: Edinburgh University Press, 1965), pp. 25–54. Fisk a "good college" *Autobiography*, p. 123. Marx translated: G.D.H. Cole, A *History of Socialism: Marxism and Anarchism, 1850–1890* (London: Macmillan, 1961) 5 vols., II, p. 268. "blithely European and imperialist . . .": *Autobiography*, p. 126.

60. "Anglo-Saxon Influence.": *Autobiography*, p. 126. See also Wilson J. Moses, *The Golden Age of Black Nationalism, 1850–1925* (New York: Oxford University Press, 1978): of such turn-of-the-century leaders of Afro-America as Blyden, Holly, Garnet, Daniel A. Payne, Henry M. Turner, and Alexander Crummell, Moses writes perceptively, "Their dream of a renascent Africa, like their dream of a reconstructed black America, always implied making blacks more like whites."—p. 23; see also Hollis Lynch, "The Attitude of Edward W. Blyden to European Imperialism in Africa," *Journal of the Historical Society of Nigeria*, 3 (Dec. 1965): 249–59.

5. *The Age of Miracles: "At but not of Harvard"*

1. Du Bois's enthusiasms and exhortations, quoted: W.E.B. Du Bois circular letter to Fisk classmates, Nov. 19, 1890, 12pp., in Hugh Smythe Papers/Schomburg Center, NYC; also in Du Bois Papers/U. Mass.

2. Grateful Outsider: *Dusk*, pp. 34–36. *Autobiography*, p. 135. The Philosophical Club: *ibid.*, p. 143.

3. ". . . unhappiness or resentment.": conceded in *Dusk*, p. 36; but resentment is denied in *Autobiography*, pp. 136, 143.

4. "Of course, [he] wanted friends . . .": Du Bois, "A Negro Student at Harvard at the End of the Nineteenth Century," *Massachusetts Review* (Spring 1960): 439–54, p. 441. For an informatively skeptical reading of Du Bois's version of his Harvard years, see Allison Davis, *Leadership, Love and Aggression*, pp. 121–22.

5. White classmates and "teachers better known": *Autobiography*, pp. 133, 139. Augustus Noble Hand, *Who's Who in America, 1926–1927* (Chicago: Marquis, 1926), p. 887; and Robert Herrick, *Who's Who, 1914–1915*, p. 1096.

6. For in-group, out-group ethos of late nineteenth-century Harvard, see Du Bois, "A Negro Student at Harvard"; John McCormick, *George Santayana: A Biography* (New York: Random House, 1988), pp. 37–38; Robert Morss Lovett, *The Autobiography of Robert Morss Lovett* (New York: Viking, 1948), pp. 33–34; David W. Levy, *Herbert Croly of the New Republic: The Life and Thought of an American Progressive* (Princeton, N.J.: Princeton University Press, 1985), pp. 53–54; Helen Lefkowitz Horowitz, *Campus Life: Undergraduate Cultures from the End of the Eighteenth Century to the Present* (New York: Alfred A. Knopf, 1987), pp. 76–77; Marcia Graham Synnott, *The Half-Opened Door: Discrimination and Admission at Harvard, Yale and Princeton, 1900–1970* (Westport, Conn.: Greenwood Press, 1979), pp. xvii–xviii, 17, 49, 81; Caldwell Titicomb, "The Black Presence at Harvard: An Overview," in Werner Sollors, Caldwell Titicomb, and Thomas A. Underwood, eds., *Blacks at Harvard: A Documentary History of African-Americans at Harvard and Radcliffe* (New York and London: New York University Press, 1993), pp. 1–7.

7. Eliot's Harvard: Lawrence A. Cremin, *American Education: The Metropolitan Experience, 1783–1876* (New York: Harper & Row, 1988), p. 379; Synnott, *Half-Opened*

Door, p. 4; Frederick Rudolph, *The American College and University*, ch. 14; Samuel Eliot Morison, ed., *The Development of Harvard University. Since the Inauguration of President Eliot, 1869–1929* (Cambridge, Mass.: Harvard University Press, 1930), pp. lxviii–lxx; Synnott, *Half-Opened Door*, pp. 47–48. ". . . with their poverty . . . ambition and purity.": Morison, *Dev. of Harvard*, p. lxx. "Greener, Richard T[heodore] (1844–1922)," *DANB*, pp. 267–8.

8. *Autobiography*, p. 124.

9. W.E.B. Du Bois to the secretary, Harvard University, Oct. 29, 1887, in "Du Bois, William Edward Burghardt A.B. 1890," The Class Folders, Pusey Library/Harvard University. Frank Hosmer to the secretary, April 9, 1888, The Class Folders. James J. Burghardt, Parents' or Guardians' Certificate, Mar. 1888, The Class Folders; Du Bois circular letter to Fisk classmates, Nov. 19, 1890, p. 1, Fol. 9(a), Hugh Smythe Papers/Schomburg Ctr.

10. Summer work: *Autobiography*, p. 127.

11. *Autobiography*, p. 128; *Dusk*, pp. 33–34. *Darkwater*, pp. 111–13.

12. ". . . a rather disillusioning experience.": *Autobiography*, p. 127.

13. "could not or would not learn": *Dusk*, p. 34; *Autobiography*, p. 127.

14. ". . . seemed the most available advance agent": Du Bois circular letter to Fisk classmates, Nov. 19, 1890, pp. 2–3.

15. Ten dollars poorer: *ibid.*, p. 4; *Autobiography*, p. 130. Tuition problems: Du Bois circular letter, p. 4.

16. Ownership of 20 Flagg Street: Charles M. Sullivan, executive director, Cambridge Historical Commission, to David Levering Lewis, October 20, 1989/Lewis Correspondence; Du Bois circular letter, Nov. 19, 1890, p. 1.

17. "tightest place" of his life.: Du Bois circular letter, Nov. 19, 1890, pp. 4–5. Emory J. West, "Harvard's First Black Graduates: 1865–1890," *Harvard Bulletin*, 74 (May 1972): 24–28, p. 27. On size of 1890 class: *Harvard University Annual Report 1886–1890*, p. 34, courtesy of Mike Raines, curatorial assistant, Harvard University Archives, to David Levering Lewis, March 23, 1990/Lewis correspondence.

18. ". . . poorest and the richest . . . equally welcome . . .": Morison, *Harvard*, p. lxix; Rudolph, *American College*, pp. 291–94; Cremin, *American Education*, p. 379. Ignorant of Hasty Pudding Club: Du Bois, "A Negro Student at Harvard," p. 439.

19. Attitudes of Lovett, Hapgood, Villard: Lovett, *Autobiography*, p. 34; Norman Hapgood, *The Changing Years: Reminiscences of Norman Hapgood* (New York: Farrar & Rinehart, 1930), p. 46; Hutchins Hapgood, *A Victorian in the Modern World* (New York: Harcourt, Brace, 1930), p. 66; Oswald Garrison Villard, *Fighting Years: Memoirs of a Liberal Editor* (New York: Harcourt, Brace, 1939), p. 80.

20. Harvard's sympathetic critics: Du Bois, *Autobiography*, p. 142; Levy, *Croly*, p. 53; Paul Conkin, *Puritans and Pragmatists. Eight American Thinkers* (Bloomington: Indiana University Press, 1968), p. 409; Henry Adams, *The Education of Henry Adams: An Autobiography* [1918], in *The Library of Henry Adams* (New York: Library of America, 1983), pp. 769–77; Tom Bottomore and Robert Nisbet, eds., *A History of Sociological Analysis* (New York: Basic Books, 1978), p. 316.

21. Shaler: Lovett, *Autobiography*, p. 38. Wendell: H. Hapgood, *A Victorian*, pp. 67–68. Santayana, *Persons and Places: The Background of My Life* (Cambridge, Mass.: MIT Press, 1986; orig. pub. 1944), p. 405. *Autobiography*, pp. 143–44; *Dusk*, p. 38.

22. "Stinker" Taussig: Levy, *Croly*, p. 44; *Dusk*, p. 40; *Autobiography*, p. 141.

23. Sociology: Cremin, *American Education*, pp. 394–97; Bottomore and Nisbet, *History of Sociological Analysis*, pp. 294–97, 312–14.

24. Social concerns—"like sitting in a club window . . .": Villard quoted—D. Joy Humes, *Oswald Harrison Villard, Liberal of the 1920s* (Syracuse, N.Y.: Syracuse Univer-

sity Press, 1960), p. 9. John Frazier Wall, *Andrew Carnegie* (New York: Oxford University Press, 1970), pp. 197–98. *Autobiography*, p. 133. "What the white world was doing, . . .": *Dusk*, p. 27.

25. Lovett, *Autobiography*, p. 32; Andrew S. Berkey and James P. Shelton, eds., *The Historians' History of the United States* (New York: G. P. Putnam's Sons, 1966), pp. 623–30. On Hart: "He was methodical. He was dry as dust, so far as that's concerned.": Du Bois Interview/Columbia OHP, p. 90.

26. Philosophy at Harvard: Bruce Kuklick, *The Rise of American Philosophy: Cambridge, Massachusetts, 1860–1930* (New Haven: Yale University Press, 1977), esp. ch. 7 and pp. 238–40.

27. *Ibid.*, pp. 238–39.

28. James's ideas: *Ibid.*, pp. 55–63, 162; Ralph Barton Perry, *The Thought and Character of William James: As Revealed in Unpublished Correspondence and Notes, together with his Published Writings* (Boston: Little, Brown, 1935), 2 vols., II, esp. pp. 263–65; Conkin, *Puritans and Pragmatists*, pp. 278–95; R.W.B. Lewis, *The Jameses: A Family Narrative* (New York: Farrar, Straus and Giroux, 1991), ch. 16; Bruce Kuklick, ed., *William James, The Varieties of Religious Experience, Pragmatism, A Pluralistic Universe, The Meaning of Truth, Some Problems of Philosophy, Essays* (New York: The Library of America, 1987); Gerald E. Myers, *William James: His Life and Thought* (New Haven: Yale University Press, 1986), p. 278—"Above all, James wanted to establish kinship of belief to emotion, recalling Hume and anticipating Russell, he insisted that belief is a *sui generis* feeling, something with a distinct felt quality and which cannot be analyzed introspectively" (see also pp. 57 and 83); compare Myers's statement to that of James as quoted by Perry, II, p. 263: "Man spontaneously *believes* and spontaneously *acts*. But as acts and beliefs multiply, they grow inconsistent. To escape *bellum omnium contra omnes*, reasonable principles, fit for all to agree upon, must be sought." ". . . decided by our will.": James, *The Will to Believe*, pp. 22–23; Paul Henle, "William James," in Max H. Fisch, ed., *Classic American Philosophers* (New York: Appleton-Century-Crofts, Inc., 1951), pp. 115–27.

29. Royce " 'Funny-looking man . . .' ": *Autobiography*, p. 143; Kuklick, *American Philosophy*, pp. 140–42. " . . . we are the notes.": quote from Otto F. Kraushaar, "Josiah Royce," in Fisch, *Philosophers*, p. 192. Several scholars have suggested a plausible Du Bois influence upon Royce, as reflected in Royce's 1908 collection of essays, *Race Questions: Provincialisms, and Other American Problems*. On this speculation, see Joseph P. De Marco, *The Social Thought of W.E.B. Du Bois* (New York: University Presses of America, 1983), pp. 38–41; and Du Bois quotes approvingly from Royce's *Race Questions and Other American Problems* (1908), in "Josiah Royce," *The Crisis*, 13 (Nov. 1916): 10–11. Royce's proof of the existence of a supreme reality, Du Bois found a "new original argument which I cannot shake.": Nancy Muller Milligan, "W.E.B. Du Bois' American Pragmatism," *Journal of American Culture*, 8 (Summer 1985): 31–37, p. 31.

30. ". . . fresh as a new born babe": Perry, *James*, p. 43. Santayana quoted: Kuklick, *American Philosophy*, p. 143, and Royce on epistemology, p. 152.

31. Santayana's social and intellectual formation and tenure at Harvard are cogently described in McCormick, *Santayana*; Eliot on Santayana: *ibid*. p. 97; Palmer on Santayana: Morison, *Dev. of Harvard*, p. 15. "curious Latin beauty . . .": H. Hapgood, A *Victorian*, p. 76; McCormick, *Santayana*, p. 55; Eastman on Santayana: quoted in Ronald Steel, *Walter Lippmann and the American Century* (New York: Vintage Books, 1981), p. 19.

32. Santayana and Du Bois: *Autobiography*, p. 143; Interview/Columbia OHP, p. 71; Conkin, *Puritans and Pragmatists*, p. 423.

33. Santayana's students: McCormick, *Santayana*, p. 99; see also Leonard Harris,

ed., *The Philosophy of Alain Locke: Harlem Renaissance and Beyond* (Philadelphia: Temple University Press, 1989), p. 11.

34. ". . . burned no midnight oil": *Dusk*, p. 38. "Rising at 7:15 and breakfast. . . .": circular letter to Fisk classmates, Nov. 19, 1890, p. 9; *Autobiography*, p. 134.

35. "Waterloo at Harvard.": *Autobiography* pp. 143, 144. "upon regular forensic paper . . .": "Did the United States Government Act Wisely in Conferring the right of suffrage upon Negroes?" Dec. 3, 1888, Du Bois Papers/U. Mass. [Reel 87].

36. *Ibid.*; ". . . into one sentence, . . .": *ibid.*; Autobiography, p. 144.

37. Helen Keller: Du Bois, "Helen Keller," in Aptheker, ed., *Writings by W.E.B. Du Bois in Non-Periodical Literature edited by Others* (Millwood, N.Y.: Kraus-Thomson, 1982), p. 164; also Van Wyck Brooks, *Helen Keller: Sketches for a Portrait* (New York: E. P. Dutton, 1956), p. 138; and Nathan Huggins, ed., *W.E.B. Du Bois, Writings* (New York: The Library of America, 1986), "Chronology," p. 1285. James's "underdog" cultivation and "lame ducks . . .": Santayana, *Persons and Places*, I, p. 241; Morison, *Dev. of Harvard*, p. 5. Du Bois and James: Lewis, *Jameses*, p. 144; George Cotkin, *William James, Public Philosopher* (Baltimore and London: Johns Hopkins University Press, 1990), p. 32.

38. Metaphysical and Philosophical Clubs: *Dusk*, p. 38; William James to W.E.B. Du Bois, Feb. 9, 1891, Du Bois Papers/U. Mass.—"Dear Mr. Du Bois, Won't you come to a philosophical supper on Saturday, Feb. 14th, at half past seven o'clock?" (see also Aptheker, Correspondence, I, p. 10.); *Dusk*, p. 38; Interview/Columbia OHP, p. 91; *Autobiography*, p. 143: "I was repeatedly a guest in the home of William James; he was my friend and guide to clear thinking; I was a member of the Philosophical Club and talked with Josiah Royce and George Palmer." See also Kuklick, *Philosophy*, pp. 48, 63; and David Levering Lewis, "John Fiske: A Transitional Figure in American Social Darwinism," submitted for the Master of Arts degree in History, Columbia University, 1958.

39. James to Santayana: McCormick, *Santayana*, p. 56: "You don't really want to go in for philosophy, do you?" James's advice to Du Bois: *Autobiography*, p. 148; and, see, Broderick, *Du Bois*, p. 16.

40. "glad to receive a serious student . . .": *Autobiography*, p. 141. "tender-minded": Lewis, *Jameses*, p. 551. "systematic reading in that line . . .": Perry, *James*, p. 48.

41. Perry, *James*, p. 226.

42. James on intuition, beliefs, action: Lewis, *Jameses*, p. 510; Conkin, *Puritans and Pragmatists*, p. 295; Kuklick, *Philosophy*, p. 310; Cotkin, *James*, pp. 1–2. ". . . and something elsifications.": James quoted—Cotkin, *James*, p. 55. ". . . he got nowhere.": Santayana, *Persons and Places*, p. 401; Lewis Perry, *Intellectual Life in America: A History* (Chicago and London: University of Chicago Press, 1984), pp. 297–99.

43. Philosophy 4 lecture notes: "Philosophy IV Notebook, 2nd Half-Year," Du Bois Papers/U. Mass. [Reel 87]; and Perry, *Intellectual Life*, pp. 263–65.

44. ". . . Science of Ethics possible . . .": W.E.B. Du Bois '90, Phil. 4, Du Bois Papers, Fol. 9(a)/Hugh Smythe Papers/Schomburg Ctr.

45. "The Renaissance of Ethics": Du Bois, "The Renaissance of Ethics: A Critical Comparison of Scholastic and Modern Ethics," Ser. I, Box No. III, Fol. 53, James Weldon Johnson Memorial Collection/Beinecke Library/Yale University, 52 pp. James's comments: *ibid.*, pp. 2, 13.

46. "Good! first rate!": *ibid.*, p. 16. Here Du Bois was virtually paraphrasing James.

47. James's marginalia: "all becomes obscure here," p. 37; "All this conclusion becoming very hazy. What is the criterion of truth in our search, etc.?" p. 40. ". . . underneath the everlasting Ought.": *ibid.*, p. 52.

48. ". . . 'under the sword of the future.' ": Du Bois, "Philosophy IV Notebook,"

Du Bois Papers/U. Mass. *Autobiography*, p. 143. Marx, Engels and "The Renaissance of Ethics": G.D.H. Cole, *Marxism and Anarchism*, pp. 305–6, is particularly suggestive—"But it was not 'materialistic' in the older sense of the term, in which matter and mind were contrasted as two different substances, but a materialism in which this dualism was got rid of, and mind, as distinct from the 'idea,' was regarded as part of nature, and as governed by nature's laws." This dialectic was, of course, not, as Edmund Wilson famously caricatured it in *To the Finland Station*, an escalator requiring nothing from those riding it into history. The active interpenetration of mind and matter *caused* the escalator to move. Du Bois's philosophical temperament: While Du Bois applauded the following Jamesian injunction, his intellectual proclivities were not wholly congenial to it—"But now, since we are all such absolutists by emotion, what in our quality of students of philosophy ought we to do about it? Or shall we treat it as a weakness of our nature from which we must free ourselves, if we can? I sincerely believe that the latter course is the only one we can follow as reflective men." (From James's "The Will to Believe," 1897, in David A. Hollinger and Charles Capper, eds., *The American Intellectual Tradition, vol. 2, 1865 to the Present* [New York: Oxford University Press, 1989], p. 85.)

49. James's dissent and influence: "independent thought . . . and vigorous [sic] expressed."—"To me, that is impossible . . ." "Renaissance," p. 52. ". . . realist pragmatism": Du Bois, "Negro Student at Harvard," *Mass. Review*, p. 440; *Autobiography*, p. 148.

50. Jamesian influences: Du Bois, *SOBF*, pp. 3–4. (For an interesting comment on the contrasting influences of James and Wendell, see, Steel, *Lippmann*, pp. 16–17) James's principal writings about mind and consciousness and about politics and society—*The Varieties of Religious Experience* (1902); *Pragmatism* (1907); *A Pluralistic Universe* (1909)—are found in The Library of America, *William James* (New York: 1984), edited by Bruce Kuklick. James's *Principles of Psychology* (1890); *The Will to Believe* (1897); and *Essays on Radical Empiricism* (1912) ought be consulted. The standard introduction remains Ralph Barton Perry, *Thought and Character of William James*; Bruce Kuklick, *The Rise of American Philosophy: Cambridge, Massachusetts, 1860–1930*, is indispensable. Perry should be supplemented by R.W.B. Lewis's splendid *The Jameses, A Family Narrative*; Fisch, *Classic American Philosophers*, is excellent. For intriguing speculations about the philosophical influence on Du Bois's concept of the divided consciousness—his "two selves" construct—see, Rampersad, *Du Bois*, pp. 73–74; Werner Sollors, *Beyond Ethnicity: Consent and Descent in American Culture* (New York: Oxford University Press, 1986), p. 249; Eric J. Sundquist, *To Wake the Nations: Race in the Making of American Literature* (Cambridge and London: The Belknap Press of Harvard University, 1993), esp. pp. 571–72, which makes the broadest and most elaborate claims for James's impact; and Dickson D. Bruce, Jr., "W.E.B. Du Bois and the Idea of Double Consciousness," *American Literature*, 64 (June 1992): 299–309, p. 304. What is somewhat unsatisfactory about the premises and evidence in the foregoing monographs is their readiness to infer connections between ideas largely because of similarity, possibility of contact, or plausible nexus, in the absence of sufficient documentary evidence available from the subject's life.

51. ". . . lack of exact data . . ." on Alfred: *Autobiography*, p. 149. Boylston Prizes: "Pageant in Seven Decades," p. 249.

52. "Morgan, Clement G[arnett] (1859–1929)," *DANB*, p. 452; "A pleasant, unassuming person . . .": *Autobiography*, p. 140; Jonathan Cedarbaum, "Clement Garnett Morgan: Vita," *Harvard Magazine* (May–June 1992): 36.

53. Boylston Prize: *Autobiography*, p. 139.

54. Rejection: *Dusk*, p. 35; *Autobiography*, pp. 134, 139. Robert Morss Lovett: *ibid.*, p. 288. ". . . one aspect of eloquence.": Robert Morss Lovett, "Du Bois," *Phylon*, *The*

Atlanta University Review of Race and Culture, 2 (3rd quarter, 1941): 214–17. Interracial encounters usually fizzled.: Allison Davis, *Leadership*, p. 118.

55. On Trotter at Harvard: Stephen R. Fox, *The Guardian of Boston: William Monroe Trotter* (New York: Atheneum, 1970), pp. 14–19. Parrington, quoted in Richard Hofstadter, *The Progressive Historians, Turner, Beard, Parrington* (Chicago: University of Chicago Press, 1979; orig. pub. 1968), p. 364. ". . . at Sachs [School for Boys].": Steel, *Lippmann*, p. 12.

56. Racism in the 1890s and beyond: The bibliography on this topic is vast. The following titles are merely indicative—John W. Cell, *The Highest Stage of White Supremacy: The Origins of Segregation in South Africa and the American South*, chs. 5–6; Thomas Gossett, *Race: The History of an Idea in America* (Dallas, Tex.: Southern Methodist University Press, 1963), pp. 105–21, 207–26, 346–76; James M. McPherson, *The Abolitionist Legacy*, pp. 38–39; Alexander Saxton, *The Rise and Fall of the White Republic: Class Politics and Mass Culture in Nineteenth-Century America* (New York: Verso, 1990), pp. 313–16; David Southern, *Malignant Heritage: Yankee Progressives and the Negro Question, 1901–1914* (Chicago: Loyola University Press, 1968), ch. 3; C. Vann Woodward, *Origins of the New South* (Baton Rouge: Louisiana State University Press, 1951), pp. 320–60, and *The Strange Career of Jim Crow* (New York: Oxford University Press, 1966), pp. 89–97; Joel Williamson, *The Crucible of Race*, pp. 111–20.

57. ". . . rather to negative than to positive conclusions . . .": Albert Hart, *The Southern South* (New York: D. Appleton and Co., 1910), p. 99. " 'How does it feel to be a problem?' ": *SOBF*, p. 2. ". . . building a Nation.": W.E.B. Du Bois to George Washington Cable, Feb. 23, 1890, Du Bois Papers/U. Mass.; and Aptheker, *Correspondence*, I, 7.

58. Matthews Scholarship: *Dusk*, p. 37; circular letter, Nov. 19, 1890, pp. 8–9. "grind.": *Autobiography*, p. 139.

59. A string of a's: Record of Class of 1890, UAIII 15 75. 10, p. 314 ("Record of W.E.B. Du Bois"), Pusey Library/Harvard University.

60. Class orators: *Autobiography*, p. 140; Cedarbaum, "Morgan," p. 36; West, "Harvard's First Black Graduates," pp. 26–27.

61. "Jefferson Davis": *Autobiography*, p. 147; "Jefferson Davis as a Representative of Civilization," Aptheker, ed., *Against Racism: Unpublished Essays, Papers, Addresses, 1887–1961*, pp. 14–16.

62. ". . . Ethiopia of the Outstretched Arm.": Aptheker, ed., *Against Racism*, p. 16.

63. Praise of Du Bois: *Autobiography*, p. 147; *Nation*, July 3, 1890; *Kate Field's Washington*, Oct. 8, 1890, in "Harvard University Years," Du Bois Papers/U. Mass.; Aptheker, *Correspondence*, I, pp. 8–9. Racialist conceptions: Moses, *Golden Age of Black Nationalism*, pp. 168–69.

64. "Suppression . . .": Du Bois circular letter, Nov. 19, 1890, p. 8. The actual dissertation pertained, of course, to the suppression of the Atlantic slave trade. W.E.B. Du Bois to the dean of Harvard College [n.d.], Class Folders, Pusey Library/Harvard University. ". . . A's and even A-plus.": *Autobiography*, p. 148; Record of Class of 1890 ("Record of W.E.B. Du Bois," Pusey Library/Harvard).

65. Hart and Shaler: Hart, *Southern South*, pp. 99–105; Nathaniel Shaler, *The Neighbor: The Natural History of Human Contacts* (Boston and New York: Houghton Mifflin, 1904), pp. 148–49.

66. References received from A. B. Hart (Du Bois, W.E.B., Litt. 1928), The Records of the Harmon Foundation, Library of Congress. "distinct ability": Hart, Du Bois, Class Folders. ". . . special favorable consideration . . .": *ibid.*; Bradley Thayer profile, in Morison, p. 481.

67. *Autobiography*, p. 149; Du Bois circular letter, Nov. 19, 1890, pp. 7–8; "had a good time there.": *ibid.*, p. 8.

68. Activities in Boston's African-American community: *Dusk*, p. 36; *Autobiography*, pp. 135, 136; Rudwick, *W.E.B. Du Bois*, p. 24, believes that well-bred black Bostonians found Du Bois somewhat disagreeable and "had little patience for his Negro nationalism since they believed fervently in integration within American society." However, it seems most unlikely that Du Bois would have been thought of as a black nationalist at that time or that he would have expressed anti-integrationist ideas. On the other hand, the statement by Mrs. Maude Trotter Stewart, in her interview with Rudwick (p. 319, note 20), that black Bostonians found Du Bois "conceited" certainly rings true.

69. Boston's African-American high society: Ray Stannard Baker, *Following the Color Line* (New York: Doubleday, Page & Co., 1908), pp. 121–23; John Daniels, *In Freedom's Birthplace* (New York: Arno Press, 1969; orig. pub. 1914), pp. 95–96, 188–209. Gatewood, *Aristocrats of Color*, pp. 109–13; Stephan Thernstrom, *The Other Bostonians: Poverty and Progress in the American Metropolis, 1880–1970* (Cambridge: Harvard University Press, 1973), esp. pp. 189–197; Adelaide Cromwell Hill, "The Negro Upper Class in Boston" (Ph.D. Radcliffe College, 1952).

70. "Ruffin, George L[ewis] (1834–1886)," "Ruffin, Josephine St. Pierre (1842–1924)," *DANB*, pp. 535–36. Gatewood, *Aristocrats of Color*, pp. 111–12, 239–40; "Which race?": *Autobiography*, p. 137. On the putative mixed racial heritage of Robert Browning: Du Bois, *Dusk*, p. 27.

71. Daniels, *Freedom's Birthplace*, p. 210; Charles H. Wesley, *The History of the National Association of Women's Clubs: A Legacy of Service* (Washington, D.C.: National Association of Colored Women's Clubs, 1984), pp. 14, 35.

72. *Courant*: *Autobiography*, p. 137.

73. ". . . universal love-making": Du Bois circular letter, Nov. 19, 1890, p. 12. Fox, *Guardian of Boston*, pp. 22–23.

74. "tall, imperious brunette, . . .": *Autobiography*, p. 138; Maud Cuney Hare, *Norris Wright Cuney: A Tribune of the People* (New York: The Crisis Publishing Co., 1913), pp. 1, 16; "Cuney, Norris Wright (1846–1896)," "Cuney-Hare, Maud (1874–1936)," *DANB*, pp. 151–52.

75. Fox, *Guardian of Boston*, pp. 18–19. Trotter's father: *ibid.*, pp. 10–14; "Trotter, James Monroe (1842–1892)," "Trotter, [William] Monroe (1872–1934)," *DANB*, pp. 602–5. ". . . and they liked him. . . .": Du Bois, "William Monroe Trotter," *The Crisis*, 41 (May 1934): 134; in Aptheker, ed., *Selections from The Crisis*, II, 752–54, p. 752.

76. "Grimké, Archibald H[enry] (1849–1930)," "Grimké, Francis James (1850–1937)," *DANB*, pp. 271–75; August Meier, *Negro Thought in America, 1800–1915*, pp. 223–24.

77. "Price, Joseph Charles (1854–1893)," *DANB*, pp. 503–4; Meier, *Negro Thought*, pp. 80–82.

78. *Autobiography*, p. 138.

79. ". . . wanted the color of my group to be visible": *Dusk*, p. 102.

80. ". . . planned a new world.": *Autobiography*, p. 136.

81. *The Birds*: *ibid.*, p. 137; "Pageant in Seven Decades," p. 249. "to the Negroes of Boston.": Du Bois, "Does Education Pay?" in Aptheker, ed., *Periodicals Edited by Others*, I, p. 2.

82. "five-foot shelf of books.": Cremin, *American Education*, p. 385. ". . . being a carpenter is to be a man.": Du Bois, "Does Education Pay?" p. 7.

83. ". . . his life all planned before him": *Autobiography*, p. 145. James—Philosophical Club: Aptheker, *Non-Periodical Literature*, p. 164; *Du Bois* (Library of

America), p. 1285; William James to W.E.B. Du Bois, Feb. 9, 1891, Du Bois Papers/U. Mass.

84. "Report of W.E.B. Du Bois," Bromfield Rogers Memorial Fellow, 1890–91, The Class Folder/Pusey Library/Harvard. Blue books: A.B. Hart Student Papers U.S. History, 1887–1899, HUG 4448.65/; Student Papers U.S. Government, 1884–1914 HUG 4448.65/Pusey Library/Harvard.

85. "The Free Coinage Controversy" in "Student Papers Harvard University 1888–91," Du Bois Papers/U. Mass.; *Autobiography*, pp. 142–43.

86. Haymarket—Homestead—Coeur d'Alene: Paul Avrich, *The Haymarket Tragedy* (Princeton: Princeton University Press, 1984), pp. 138–39; Nell Painter, *Standing at Armageddon: The United States, 1877–1919*, esp. ch. 4, pp. 110–40; David Montgomery, *The Fall of the House of Labor: The Workplace, the State, and American Labor Activism, 1865–1925* (New York: Cambridge University Press, 1987), esp. ch. 5, pp. 214–56; Melvyn Dubofsky, "The Origins of Western Working-Class Radicalism, 1890–1905," in Daniel J. Leab, ed., *The Labor History Reader* (Urbana and Chicago: University of Illinois Press, 1985), pp. 230–53.

87. On populism: Lawrence Goodwyn, *The Populist Movement: A Short History of the Agrarian Revolt in America* (New York: Oxford University Press, 1978), esp. ch. 4, pp. 97–124; Woodward, *Origins of the New South*, esp. pp. 253–63; Richard Hofstadter, *Age of Reform: Bryan to F.D.R.* (New York: Vintage Books, 1955), pp. 60–109; Painter, *Armageddon*, pp. 98–103.

88. Wage theory: Du Bois, "A Constructive Critique of Wage-Theory: An Essay on the Present State of Economic Theory in Regard to Wages by XYZ," entered for the Toppan Prize, 1891, Records of Class 1890, HU 89.385.30 VT, Pusey Library/Harvard University, p. 158, and pp. 124–25; also Du Bois, "Value" (5 Dec. 1890), in Aptheker, ed., *Against Racism*, p. 17.

89. On turn-of-century economic theories: Martin J. Sklar, *The Corporate Reconstruction of American Capitalism: The Market, the Law and Politics* (New York: Cambridge University Press, 1988), pp. 1–80. Du Bois's knowledge of Marxist economics: Du Bois, "Constructive Critique of Wage-Theory," pp. 54–57.

90. Deep-seated elitism and the race problem: *Autobiography*, pp. 142–43.

91. Aristocratic proclivities: "Contributions to the Negro Problems," in Aptheker, ed., *Against Racism*, pp. 21–22; Moses, *Golden Age*, pp. 134, 138—Moses, p. 138, astutely observes, "What Du Bois found most appealing about socialism was neither its opposition to private ownership, nor its leveling tendencies, but rather its war on the values of upstart bourgeois culture." See also Meier, *Negro Thought*, esp. p. 196; and Paul Richards, "W.E.B. Du Bois and American Social History: The Evolution of a Marxist," *Radical America. Special Issue on Radical Historiography*, 4 (Nov. 1970): 37–65, esp. p. 41.

92. ". . . dry as dust . . .": Interview/Columbia OHP, p. 90. Hart's seminar method: Berkey and Shelton, *Historians' History*, pp. 623–30; and James McPherson, *Abolitionist Legacy*, pp. 337–38.

93. Hart's ideas: Hart, *Southern South*, p. 134; Berky and Shelton, *Historians' History*, p. 624.

94. Hart on Negro inferiority: Hart, *Southern South*, pp. 101, 137. Reference from A. B. Hart (Du Bois, W.E.B. Litt.), Records of the Harmon Foundation/Library of Congress.

95. "vast economic mistake": Du Bois, "Harvard and the South: A Commencement Pact, 1891," "Student Papers, Harvard University 1888–91," p. 1: Du Bois Papers/U. Mass. [Reel 87]. For economic interpretations of the postbellum South bearing favor-

ably on Du Bois's argument, see John Cell, *Highest Stage of White Supremacy*, pp. 156–61, Barrington Moore, Jr., *Social Origins of Dictatorship and Democracy: Lord and Peasant in the Making of the Modern World* (London: Allen Lane and the Penguin Press, 1967), esp. pp. 120–27; Eugene Genovese, *Political Economy of Slavery: Studies in the Economy and Society of the Slave South* (New York: Pantheon Books, 1965), pp. 4–16; Jonathan Wiener, *Social Origins of the New South, Alabama, 1860–1885* (Baton Rouge: Louisiana State University Press, 1978), pp. 84–85.

96. ". . . one at the spelling book.": "Harvard and the New South," pp. 15–16.

97. Mistake of historians: On influx of African slaves, see summations of arguments in Ronald W. Bailey, "Africa, the Slave Trade, and the Rise of Industrial Capitalism in Europe and the United States," *American History: A Bibliographic Review*, 2 (1986): 2–23; Peter Duignan and L. H. Gann, eds., *The United States and Africa: A History*, pp. 8–25; J. E. Inkori, ed., *Forced Migration: The Impact of the Export Slave Trade on African Societies*.

98. ". . . its strong right arm.": Du Bois, "The Enforcement of the Slave Trade Laws," in Aptheker, ed., *Periodical Literature, 1891–1909*, I, p. 27.

99. ". . . in the matter of race distinctions."—quoted: (Aptheker, "Introduction") Du Bois, *The Suppression of the African Slave Trade to the United States, 1638–1870* (Millwood, N.Y.: Kraus-Thomson, 1973; orig. pub. 1896), p. 10.

100. English 12: *Autobiography*, pp. 143, 145; Interview/Columbia OHP, p. 83; "Report of W.E.B. Du Bois, Bromfield Rogers Memorial Fellow, 1890–91," The Class Folders, Pusey Library/Harvard University. "explosive and confused.": Santayana, *Persons and Places*, p. 405.

101. ". . . in order to say it well.": *Dusk*, p. 39; also "Something About Me" (3 Oct. 1890), "Student Papers at Harvard University—English 12 (1890–91)," The Class Folders, Pusey Library/Harvard University; also in Aptheker, *Against Racism*, p. 17.

102. Essays and comments: "Autumn Leaves" (5 Oct. 1890), "Historical Conference" (14 Feb. 1891), "Frightened" (16 Mar. 1891), "The American Girl" (10 April 1891), "Dekalb County" (16 April 1891), in "Student Papers," The Class Folders, Pusey Library/Harvard University; and (minus "Frightened," "Historical Conference," and "Dekalb County") in Aptheker, *Against Racism*, pp. 17–20. For Howells's reference, Henry Steele Commager, *The American Mind: An Interpretation of American Thought and Character since the 1880s* (New Haven: Yale University Press, 1950), pp. 58–59.

103. Slater Fund: *Dusk*, p. 43; W.E.B. Du Bois to Rutherford B. Hayes, Nov. 4, 1890, in Louis D. Rubin, ed., *Teach the Freeman: The Correspondence of Rutherford B. Hayes and the Slater Fund for Negro Education* (Baton Rouge: Louisiana State University Press, 1959), 2 vols., II, p. 159; also in Aptheker, *Correspondence*, I, p. 10; "A Pageant in Seven Decades," pp. 249–50.

6. Lehrjahre

1. Slater and Peabody funds: John Hope Franklin, *From Slavery to Freedom: A History of Negro Americans*, pp. 269–70; Joe M. Richardson, *A History of Fisk University, 1865–1946*, pp. 60–61; Horace Mann Bond, *The Education of the Negro in the American Social Order*, pp. 131–33; and Hugh C. Bailey, *Edgar Gardner Murphy: Gentle Progressive* (Coral Gables, Fla.: University of Miami Press, 1968), esp. p. 53.

2. ". . . with mighty little change.": On southern white educational attitudes and politics, see Louis R. Harlan, *Separate and Unequal: Public School Campaigns and Racism in the Southern Seaboard States*, pp. 9–19 (quote, p. 104); James D. Anderson, *The Education of Blacks in the South, 1860–1935*, esp. pp. 36, 92; Robert A. Margo, *Race and*

Schooling in the South, 1880–1950: An Economic History (Chicago and London: University of Chicago Press, 1990), pp. 19–33; and Bond, *Education*, pp. 92–122.

3. Bailey, *Murphy*, p. 140; Harlan, *Separate and Unequal*, pp. 10–13. On Christian noblesse and mammon: Anderson, *Education of Blacks*, ch. 3, pp. 79–109; Harlan, *Separate and Unequal*, pp. 10–13; Margo, *Race and Schooling*, p. 33; Paul M. Gaston, *The New South Creed: A Study in Southern Mythmaking* (New York: Alfred A. Knopf, 1970), pp. 10–52.

4. Harrison's message—quoted: Rayford W. Logan, *The Betrayal of the Negro, from Rutherford B. Hayes to Woodrow Wilson* (New York: Collier Books, 1965; orig. pub. 1954), p. 65. On Blair Bill: *ibid*., pp. 67–74; Harlan, *Separate and Unequal*, pp. 6–7; Woodward, *Origins of the New South*, pp. 63–64.

5. Lodge's Force Bill—quoted: Logan, *Betrayal*, pp. 77–81.

6. Du Bois on Lodge Bill—quoted: August Meier, *Negro Thought in America, 1880–1915: Racial Ideologies in the Age of Booker T. Washington*, p. 192. The Mississippi Plan: Logan, *Betrayal*, pp. 74–75; Richard Kluger, *Simple Justice: The History of Brown v. Board of Education and Black Americans' Struggle for Equality*, pp. 67–68; Meier, *Negro Thought*, pp. 38–39.

7. ". . . lay my case before you.": Du Bois to Rutherford B. Hayes, Nov. 4, 1890, Du Bois Papers/U. Mass.; also in Louis D. Rubin, ed., *Teach the Freeman: The Correspondence of Rutherford B. Hayes and the Slater Fund for Negro Education, 1888–1893*, II, p. 159; and Aptheker, ed., *Correspondence of W.E.B. Du Bois*, I, pp. 10–12. Du Bois to Hayes, April 19, 1891, Du Bois Papers/U. Mass.

8. On the Mohonk Conferences: *First Mohonk Conference on the Negro Question, Held at Lake Mohonk, Ulster County, New York, June 4, 5, 6, 1890. Reported and Edited by Isabel C. Barrows* (New York: Negro Universities Press, 1969; orig. pub. 1890–91), p. 8; Bailey, *Murphy*, pp. 142–43.

9. Hayes at Mohonk, quoted: *First Mohonk Conference*, pp. 9–10. On Mohonk: Larry E. Burgess, *Mohonk, Its People and Spirit: A History of One Hundred Years of Growth and Service* (New Paltz, N.Y.: Mohonk Mountain House, 1980).

10. Botume quoted: *First Mohonk Conference*, p. 22. Mohonk critics (Cable and Washington) quoted: B. T. Washington to G. W. Cable, April 7, 1890, in Louis R. Harlan and Raymond W. Smock, eds., *The Booker T. Washington Papers* (Urbana and London: University of Illinois Press, 1972–84), 13 vols., III, pp. 45–46. Cable published *The Negro Question* in 1890, in which he defended the civil rights of African-Americans and demanded equal education for both races in the South; Cable's *The Silent South* was published in 1885. See, Philip Butcher, "George Washington Cable and Negro Education," *The Journal of Negro History*, 34 (Apr. 1949): 119–34, pp. 123–24.

11. Scarborough and Abbott, quoted: William T. Scarborough to B. T. Washington, April 17, 1890, and Lyman Abbott quoted in a letter from T. Thomas Fortune to B. T. Washington, July 23, 1890, *Booker T. Washington Papers*, 3, p. 70.

12. Mohonk participants (Tourgee, MacVickar, Harris, Gates, White, Howard, Armstrong) quoted: *First Mohonk*, pp. 13, 24, 54, 99, 118–20, *et passim*.; and *Second Mohonk Conference on the Negro Question, Ulster County, New York, June 3, 4, 5, 1891. Reported and Edited by Isabel C. Barrows* (New York: Negro Universities Press, 1969), p. 57. I have conflated the first and second conferences for convenience. On Armstrong's educational and racial views, see Henry Allen Bullock, *A History of Negro Education in the South: From 1619 to the Present*, pp. 76–77.

13. Racial hard-liners at Mohonk (White, Abbott, Allen), quoted: *First Mohonk*, pp. 117–18; *Second Mohonk*, pp. 67–68, 71.

14. Rise of industrial education: Cremin, *American Education*, pp. 181–85; Meier,

Negro Thought, pp. 85–89; Edmund L. Drago, *Initiative, Paternalism, and Race Relations: Charleston's Avery Normal Institute* (Athens and London: The University of Georgia Press, 1990), pp. 82–84.

15. ". . . division of labor applied to races.": Anderson, *Education of Blacks*, p. 28, and see pp. 33–43. Among the best summary analyses and histories of the relationship of white philanthropy to African-American education is Michael R. Winston, "Through the Back Door: Academic Racism and the Negro Scholar in Historical Perspective," *Daedalus: Journal of the American Academy of Arts and Sciences* (Summer 1971): 678–719. Winston's assertion, p. 683, is excellent: "The debate between advocates of industrial education and advocates of college education for Negroes is meaningless when viewed strictly in educational terms. The real conflict was about the status of Negroes in American life."

16. Armstrong's Hampton: Mrs. M. F. Armstrong and Helen W. Ludlow, *Hampton and Its Students by Two of Its Teachers with Fifty Cabin and Plantation Songs* (Chicago: Afro-American Press, 1969; orig. pub. 1874); Harlan, *Booker T. Washington: The Making of a Black Leader, 1856–1901*, pp. 48, 57–58. Armstrong, quoted: *First Mohonk Conference*, pp. 13–14.

17. Education "of heart and hand": Bond, *Education of the Negro*, pp. 122–25; Bullock, *Negro Education*, pp. 76–77.

18. Hayes to Du Bois: *Dusk*, p. 44; Aptheker, ed., *Correspondence*, I, p. 13. Rudin, *Teach the Freeman*, II, esp. pp. 154, 162, 167, 191. ". . . otherwise have been given attention.": *Dusk*, p. 44.

19. Slater Fund references (Curry and Shaler): Rudin, *Teach the Freeman*, II, pp. 189–90. Taussig, Peabody, Dunbar quoted: Du Bois, *Testimonials* (Wilberforce, Ohio: Wilberforce University Printer, 1895?), pp. v–vi; and (Peabody) Aptheker, *Correspondence*, I, p. 12. Shaler: Williamson, *Crucible of Race*, p. 120.

20. Du Bois to Rutherford B. Hayes, May 25, 1891, Du Bois Papers/U. Mass.; also Aptheker, ed., *Correspondence*, I, pp. 13–14; and Rudin, *Teach the Freeman*, II, pp. 204–5.

21. ". . . intelligence of characterful leaders.": Quoted: Rudin, *Teach the Freeman*, II, p. 192; Du Bois to Rutherford B. Hayes, April 3, 1892, Du Bois Papers/U. Mass.; also Aptheker, ed., *Correspondence*, I, pp. 245–47.

22. Du Bois to Hayes, April 3, 1892; *Dusk*, p. 45; Charles R. Williams, ed., *Diary and Letters of Rutherford B. Hayes* (Columbus, Ohio: Heer Publishing Co., 1926), 5 vols., V, pp. 74–76.

23. *Autobiography*, p. 157.

24. " 'I must be dreaming!' ": *ibid.*, p. 156.

25. ". . . well-ordered mud-puddle": *ibid.*, p. 158; Du Bois, "Holland" [n.d.], in "Sketches, 1889–1896," Du Bois Papers/U. Mass. [Reel 87].

26. "in the solemn arched aisles.": *Autobiography*, p. 160; *Dusk*, pp. 45–46. I have reconstructed what a meticulous Du Bois would in all probability have seen from histories and travel guides of the period.

27. The Du Bois Papers/U. Mass., contain a 1907 note, under the heading "Memorabilia from Germany," offering condolences on the death of Johannes Marbach, Doctor of Theology and Philosophy.

28. ". . . a slave to America.": W.E.B. Du Bois to the Congregational Sunday School, Sept. 29, 1892, Du Bois Papers/U. Mass.; Aptheker, *Correspondence*, I, pp. 19–20.

29. Du Bois in Eisenach: *Autobiography*, p. 156. ". . . more human.": *ibid.*, p. 160.

30. He "drew back.": *ibid.*, p. 160. ". . . genuine pleasure and satisfaction.": Du Bois, "The Problem of Amusement," in Aptheker, ed., *Periodical Literature, 1891–1909*, I, p. 39.

31. ". . . had work to do.": *Dusk*, p. 46. On Far West visitors and Dora: *Autobiography*,

pp. 160, 162; *Dusk*, p. 46; and Davis, *Leadership, Love and Aggression*, pp. 124–25—Davis is surely mistaken in dismissing the Dora dalliance.

32. More about Dora: *Autobiography*, p. 161; Shirley Graham-Du Bois, *His Day Is Marching On*, p. 100; W.E.B. Du Bois to President D. C. Gilman, Oct. 28, 1892, Du Bois Papers/U. Mass.; also Aptheker, ed., *Correspondence*, I, pp. 20–21; "Celebration of My Twenty-fifth Birthday," Du Bois Papers/U. Mass.; also in Aptheker, *Against Racism*, pp. 26–29, esp. 29.

33. University of Berlin and Fichte, Schmoller, and Wagner: James J. Sheehan, *German History, 1770–1866* (Oxford: Clarendon Press, 1989), pp. 377–79; Frederick Copleston, S.J., *A History of Philosophy* (Garden City, N.Y.: Doubleday & Co., 1965), 7 vols, VI, pp. 54–55; Wolfgang J. Mommsen and Jurgen Osterhammel, eds., *Max Weber and His Contemporaries* (London: Allen and Unwin, 1987), pp. 63–64.

34. University of Berlin—Hegel, Marx, Weber: *Autobiography*, p. 162; Reinhard Bendix, *Max Weber: An Intellectual Portrait* (Garden City, N.Y.: Doubleday & Co., 1960), p. 26; Sheehan, *German History*, p. 568.

35. "a most ornamented young man": Du Bois, "Harvard in Berlin" [1892], Du Bois Papers/U. Mass., p. 4; also in Aptheker, *Against Racism*, pp. 29–32. Du Bois to President Gilman, Oct. 28, 1892, Du Bois Papers/U. Mass.; also Aptheker, ed., *Correspondence*, I, p. 21; "Pageant in Seven Decades," p. 251.

36. Courses and lodging: "Harvard in Berlin," p. 4; Du Bois to Gilman, Oct. 28, 1892.

37. Berlin student culture and Hapgood: *Autobiography*, p. 165; Hutchins Hapgood, *A Victorian in the Modern World*, p. 344.

38. Du Bois in Berlin: *Autobiography*, p. 169; W.E.B. Du Bois to the Educational Committee . . . of the Slater Fund, March 10, 1893, Du Bois Papers/U. Mass.; also Aptheker, ed., *Correspondence*, I, pp. 23–25; "Harvard in Berlin."

39. . . . veil or security blanket . . . : The psychodynamic of nineteenth-century black racial chauvinism is instructively explored in Rodney Carlisle, *The Roots of Black Nationalism* (Port Washington, N.Y.: Kennikat Press, 1975), esp. pp. 77–81; Moses, *Golden Age*, p. 25; and Moses, "The Poetics of Ethiopianism: W.E.B. Du Bois and Literary Black Nationalism," *American Literature*, 47 (Nov. 1975): 411–26, pp. 411–12.

40. . . . Amalie, two or three others.: W.E.B. Du Bois to himself, Feb. 23, 1894, in Du Bois Papers/U. Mass. [Reel 87], 6pp; "Celebration of My Twenty-fifth Birthday," Du Bois Papers/U. Mass.; also in Aptheker, *Against Racism*, p. 28

41. ". . . habit of travelling alone.": *Autobiography*, p. 169.

42. ". . . piteous look of despair.": Untitled piece, undated [1892–94], Du Bois Papers/U. Mass. This odd composition would seem to be, at least in part, a subconscious evocation of a trauma in Mary Silvina's life.

43. "They look and part forever.": "Plot for a Story," Du Bois Papers/U. Mass. [Reel 87]; also in Aptheker, *Against Racism*, pp. 25–26.

44. ". . . happiest days of my life.": Du Bois recounts his twenty-fifth birthday in the diary entry for the "Celebration of My Twenty-fifth Birthday," in Du Bois Papers/U. Mass.; and *Autobiography*, pp. 170–71; also in Aptheker, *Against Racism*, pp. 27–29.

45. ". . . and is life all?": as cited *supra*.

46. ". . . life-ruin of Amalie . . .": "Twenty-fifth Birthday" [*Against Racism*], p. 29; *Autobiography*, p. 280.

47. Strum and Drang: "Twenty-fifth Birthday"; Copleston, *History of Philosophy*, VI, p. 168. Davis, *Leadership*, p. 127.

48. ". . . I remember these facts.": Alfred Eisenstaedt to W.E.B. Du Bois, Mar. 26, 1942, and W.E.B. Du Bois to Alfred Eisenstaedt, Mar. 31, 1942, Du Bois Papers/U. Mass.

49. Eisenstaedt to Du Bois, Mar. 26, 1942, Du Bois Papers/U. Mass.

50. ". . . thrilled at the sight . . .": *Autobiography*, p. 169; Interview/Columbia OHP, p. 113.

51. Von Treitschke quoted: *Autobiography*, p. 165; Heinrich von Treitschke, *History of Germany in the Nineteenth Century, Edited with an Introduction by Gordon A. Craig* (Chicago: University of Chicago Press, 1975), p. xiv.

52. . . . a culture in search of a nation.: Ernest John Knapton and Thomas Kingston Derry, *Europe, 1815 to the Present* (New York: Charles Scribner's Sons, 1966), pp. 306–7; Geoffrey Barraclough, *The Origins of Modern Germany* (Oxford: Basil Blackwell, 1966), ch. 14, pp. 406–66. . . . fustian civil service: *ibid.*, pp. 304–5.

53. ". . . half military stride.": Du Bois, "The Present Condition of German Politics," Student Papers, Du Bois Papers/U. Mass. ". . . state founded on obedience.": *ibid.*

54. Caprivi's ministry: Barraclough, *Modern Germany*, pp. 428–29; Knapton and Derry, *Europe*, pp. 324–25; Agatha Ramm, *Germany 1789–1919* (London: Mathuen & Co., 1967), pp. 381–88.

55. ". . . complete Guards officer.": quoted in Alan Palmer, *The Kaiser: Warlord of the Second Reich* (New York: Charles Scribner's Sons, 1978), p. 22.

56. Travel and research with Dollar: *Autobiography*, p. 172; "Pageant in Seven Decades," in *Against Racism*, p. 251. Du Bois to President Gilman, Oct. 28, 1892, Du Bois Papers/U. Mass.; also Aptheker, ed., *Correspondence*, I, p. 21. ". . . everything to make us comfortable.": *Autobiography*, p. 172.

57. ". . . no visible results": *ibid.*, p. 173.

58. ". . . Galleries of Modern Europe": "The Art and Art Galleries of Modern Europe," in *Against Racism*, pp. 33–43. W.E.B. Du Bois to the Educational Committee . . . Slater Fund, Mar. 10, 1893, Du Bois Papers/U. Mass.; also Aptheker, ed., *Correspondence*, I, pp. 23–25.

59. More travel, alone: Aptheker, ed., *Correspondence*, I, p. 24; "Spring Vacation," Du Bois Papers/U. Mass. [Reel 87]. ". . . girl who met and loved me . . .": *ibid.*

60. ". . . new life of toil and gladness.": Du Bois, "A Spring Wandering," March 24, 1893 (material recently deposited by Herbert Aptheker on student years in Germany), Du Bois Papers/Box 343, Ser. No. 23, Fol. 19h/U. Mass.

61. . . . never again permit himself to record.: *ibid.*

62. "willing to renew": D. C. Gilman to W.E.B. Du Bois, May 5, 1893, Du Bois Papers/U. Mass.; also Aptheker, ed., *Correspondence*, I, p. 25. ". . . rise of the Negro people.": Du Bois, "Letter," Fisk *Herald*, Sept. 1893: 5–7, p. 6.

63. ". . . true independence.": G.W.F. Hegel, *The Phenomenology of Mind* (New York: Harper and Row, 1967, orig. trans. 1910, orig. pub. 1807), pp. 234–37; still one of the most accessible expositions of Hegel is Frederick Copleston, *A History of Philosophy*, vol. 7, *Fichte to Hegel*, esp. pp. 222–23; the broad and continuing influence of this particular discussion of ownership and bondage is discussed in David Brion Davis, *The Problem of Slavery in the Age of Revolution, 1770–1832* (Ithaca, N.Y.: Cornell University Press, 1975), pp. 557–64; Irene L. Gendzier, *Frantz Fanon: A Critical Study* (New York: Pantheon Books, 1973), pp. 22–23; Sundquist, *Wake the Nations*, pp. 40–2; the richly suggestive essay by Werner Sollors should be consulted: "Of Mules and Mares in a Land of Difference: or Quadripeds All?" *American Quarterly*, 42 (1990): 182; also, Bruce, "Double Consciousness," pp. 301–02.

64. More travel with Dollar: "Spring Vacation," Du Bois Papers/U. Mass. [Reel 87]; *Autobiography*, p. 173. "his engagements called him": *ibid.*, p. 174.

65. . . . to see race problems.: *ibid.*, p. 174; W.E.B. Du Bois to the . . . Trustees of the John F. Slater Fund, Dec. 6, 1893, Du Bois Papers/U. Mass.; also Aptheker, ed., *Correspondence*, I, p. 26.

66. . . . in the American South: *Autobiography*, p. 174.

67. . . . political and propaganda uses: Washington's foreign travels were the basis for his ghost-written book *The Man Farthest Down: A Record of Observations and Studies in Europe* (Garden City, N.Y.: Doubleday, Page and Co., 1912), as an argument for the relative advantages of African-Americans living in the South.

68. From Vienna to Cracow: *Autobiography*, pp. 173, 175; "Pageant in Seven Decades," p. 251.

69. ". . . what a 'nigger' is": "Spring Vacation," Du Bois Papers/U. Mass.

70. Economic ideas of Schmoller and Wagner: Mommsen and Osterhammel, *Max Weber*, pp. 59–70; *Autobiography*, p. 167; and Francis L. Broderick, "German Influence on the Scholarship of W.E.B. Du Bois," *Phylon*, 19 (1958): 367–71, p. 368.

71. ". . . the *Geschehen* . . ." quoted: Broderick, "German Influence," p. 369; Copleston, *History of Philosophy*, VI, p. 97.

72. ". . . realistic science . . ."—Schmoller quoted: Mommsen and Osterhammel, *Max Weber*, p. 68; Broderick, "German Influence," pp. 369–70. The best introduction in English to the thought of Schmoller is by Pauline Relylea, "Gustav von Schmoller (1828–1917)," in Bernadette E. Schmidt, ed., *Some Historians of Modern Europe* (Port Washington: Kennikat Press, 1966; orig. pub. 1942), esp. pp. 415–21.

73. . . . universals revealed through history.: Mommsen and Osterhammel, *Max Weber*, p. 34; Robert Gildea, *Barricades and Borders, Europe 1800–1914. The Short Oxford History of the Modern World* (Oxford: Oxford University Press, 1987), pp. 387–89.

74. ". . . Agriculture in the Southern United States": Du Bois to the Honorable Trustees, Mar. 1893, Du Bois Papers/U. Mass.; also Aptheker, *Correspondence*, I, p. 23.

75. "for the sake of my race": Aptheker, ed., *Correspondence*, I, p. 24.

76. Du Bois, "Present Condition of German Politics," Student Papers, Du Bois Papers/U. Mass. Socialism, Caprivi, and Du Bois: Barraclough, *Modern Germany*, pp. 430–32.

77. SPD meetings: *Autobiography*, p. 168; Knapton and Derry, *Europe*, p. 311.

78. disdain for mass agitation: Lewis Perry, *Intellectual Life in America: A History* (Chicago and London: University of Chicago Press, 1989), pp. 267, 271–72. Perry writes suggestively of an aspect of Du Bois's conservatism that Du Bois asserted that "the proper goal of a black leader was 'to be a co-worker in the kingdom of culture.' To Du Bois this goal meant fostering the traits and talents of the Negro, not in opposition to, but in conformity with, the greater ideals of the American Republic." ". . . semi-criminal proletariat . . .": "Present Condition of German Politics," Du Bois Papers/U. Mass.

79. Sciences Politiques in Paris: Du Bois to Slater Fund Trustees, Mar. 10, 1893, and Mar. 29, 1894, Du Bois Papers/U. Mass.; also Aptheker, ed., *Correspondence*, I, pp. 22–27.

80. ". . . stand among the honored of the world.": Du Bois to Du Bois, Feb. 23, 1894, Du Bois Papers/U. Mass.

81. ". . . ten similar cases . . .": Du Bois to President Gilman, Mar. 29, 1894; references from Gustav Schmoller, Mar. 31, 1894, and Adolph Wagner, Mar. 28, 1894, Du Bois Papers/U. Mass.; also Aptheker, ed., *Correspondence*, I, pp. 27–28.

82. ". . . does not suit me": Du Bois to Du Bois, Feb. 23, 1894.

83. ". . . without a struggle.": W.E.B. Du Bois to President Gilman, Mar. 31, 1894, Du Bois Papers/U. Mass.; also Aptheker, ed., *Correspondence*, I, p. 29.

84. D. C. Gilman to W.E.B. Du Bois, Apr. 13, 1894, Du Bois Papers/U. Mass.; also Aptheker, ed., *Correspondence*, I, p. 29.

85. "*Entbehren sollst du* . . .": *Autobiography*, p. 212.

86. ". . . but was ashamed.": *ibid.*, p. 280.

87. ". . . Germany which no longer exists.": *ibid.*, p. 176.

88. Paris: *Autobiography*, p. 176; Interview/Columbia OHP, p. 124; "Art and Art Galleries of Modern Europe," *Against Racism*, p. 39. Rayford Logan, fluent in French himself, gave Du Bois only a passing grade in the language: Logan interview (taped) with David Levering Lewis, Oct. 1974 [deposited in the Schomburg Center for Research in Black Culture, N.Y.C.].

89. "Dollar" [fragment June 2, 1894], Du Bois Papers/U. Mass. [Reel 87]. Dollar, Thomas Aitken & Sons, Veterinary Surgeons, 56 New Bond Street (W), in *The Post Office London Directory for 1910* (London, 1910), p. 493. ". . . I was going steerage.": *Autobiography*, p. 177.

90. Aboard the *Chester*: *Autobiography*, p. 179; "Dollar," Du Bois Papers/U. Mass.

91. ". . . We do not go together.": *Autobiography*, p. 179; "The Negro," [June 1894], Du Bois Papers/U. Mass. [Reel 87]. I am grateful to Gila Bercovitch and staff members of the Library of America for bringing this matter of Aptheker's textual revisions to my attention on June 10, 1987.

92. ". . . about one half or more Negro.": W.E.B. Du Bois to the Honorable Board of Trustees of the John F. Slater Fund [May 1892], Du Bois Papers/U. Mass.; also Aptheker, ed., *Correspondence*, I, p. 15; Davis, *Leadership*, p. 111, is the exception in paying attention to the color factor in Du Bois's psychology. Interestingly, Davis suggests that Du Bois was extremely sensitive that his complexion was somewhat dark.

93. On contemporary racial vocabulary: A classic case of racialist preconceptions adopted by an African-American is William H. Ferris, *The African Abroad or His Evolution in Western Civilization*, pp. 34, 286, 429; Henry James, *The American Scene* (New York: Scribner's Sons, 1946; orig. pub. 1907), pp. 119–20, 131–32; also, for cogent review of such attitudes, Moses, *Golden Age*, esp. pp. 18–23; and Moses, *Alexander Crummell: A Study of Civilization and Discontent*, pp. 6–8. On "superior" and "inferior" races: Reginald Horsman, *Race and Manifest Destiny: The Origins of American Racial Anglo-Saxonism* (Cambridge: Harvard University Press, 1981), pp. 178–211; Gossett, *Race: The History of an Idea*, pp. 109, 205–26; Stephen J. Gould, *The Mismeasure of Man* (New York: Norton, 1981); John Higham, *Strangers in the Land: Patterns of American Nativism, 1860–1925* (New Brunswick, N.J.: Rutgers University Press, 1988; orig. pub. 1955), p. 66. ". . . their straightforwardness.": "The Negro," Du Bois Papers/U. Mass.

94. ". . . not white folks, but folks.": *Darkwater*, p. 16. ". . . face toward France!": *Autobiography*, p. 182. ". . . 'nigger'-hating America!": *Darkwater*, p. 16.

7. *Wilberforce*

1. ". . . stepped full feet upon it.": Letter to John Dollar, dated by Du Bois 1892–95, and captioned, "The Passing of Wilberforce," Du Bois Papers/University of Massachusetts at Amherst; Du Bois, *Autobiography*, p. 184.

2. ". . . a bread and butter job—was it?": "The Passing of Wilberforce"; *Autobiography*, p. 184.

3. B. T. Washington's telegram, quoted: B. T. Washington to W.E.B. Du Bois, Aug. 25, 1894, Du Bois Papers/U. Mass.; also Aptheker, ed., *Correspondence*, I, p. 38. Wilberforce offer: S. T. Mitchell to W.E.B. Du Bois, Aug. 17, 1894, Du Bois Papers/U. Mass.; also Aptheker, ed., *Correspondence*, I, p. 38. Lincoln offer: *Autobiography*, p. 185; and *Dusk of Dawn*, p. 49. ". . . I drifted across Ohio.": *Autobiography*, p. 185.

4. Background of Wilberforce University: Horace Talbert, *The Sons of Allen: Together with a Sketch of the Rise and Progress of Wilberforce University* (Xenia, Ohio: The Aldine

Press, 1906), pp. 264–67; Frederick A. McGinnes, A *History and an Interpretation of Wilberforce University* (Wilberforce, 1941), pp. 29–43.

5. Origins of Wilberforce: W.E.B. Du Bois, "Wilberforce," *The Crisis*, 20 (August 1920): 176–78; also Aptheker, ed., *Writings in Periodicals Edited by W.E.B. Du Bois: Selections from The Crisis* (Millwood, N.Y.: Kraus-Thomson, 1983), 2 vols., I, 268–71.

6. Bishop Payne: "Payne, Daniel A. (1811–1893)," *DANB*, pp. 484–85. ". . . prettiest smile . . . I ever saw.": Du Bois to John Dollar, 1892–95, Du Bois Papers/U. Mass.

7. ". . . closing years of the 19th [century].": Letter to John Dollar, dated by Du Bois 1892–95. Bishop Arnett: "Arnett, Benjamin William (1838–1906)," *DANB*, pp. 17–18; Meier, *Negro Thought in America*, p. 57.

8. On Scarborough: "Scarborough, William Sanders (1852–1926)," *DANB*, pp. 545–46; Meier, *Negro Thought*, p. 213. Machinations at Wilberforce: *Autobiography*, p. 186.

9. Prayer incident: *Dusk*, p. 19; *Autobiography*, p. 186; "A Pageant in Seven Decades," in Aptheker, *Pamphlets and Leaflets*, p. 252.

10. Laboring at Wilberforce: *Autobiography*, pp. 186–87.

11. ". . . brings me back to Wilberforce.": Du Bois, "Wilberforce University" [ca. 1896], Du Bois Papers/U. Mass.

12. ". . . it soon slept again.": *Autobiography*, p. 187.

13. "brilliant success.": Du Bois, "A Fellow of Harvard" [1892], Du Bois Papers/U. Mass.

14. ". . . historical treatise into readable prose": *Dusk*, p. 269.

15. *Suppression*: The original dissertation clearly suggests eleventh-hour typing problems—"The Suppression of the African Slave Trade in the United States of America, 1638–1871." A Thesis for the Degree of Philosophiae Doctor et Magister Artum at Harvard University by W. E. Burghardt Du Bois, 2 vols., Pusey Library/Harvard University. Harvard Historical Studies was not, as has sometimes been stated, the first such series; see "Introduction" by Herbert Aptheker, ed., *The Suppression of the African Slave Trade to the United States of America, 1638–1870* (Millwood, N.Y.: Kraus-Thomson, 1973), p. 11.

16. Du Bois's explanation for increasing slave population: *Suppression*, pp. 142–43.

17. "not less than 250,000.": Du Bois, "The Enforcement of the Slave Trade Laws," *Annual Report of the American Historical Association for the Year 1891* (Washington, D.C.: Govt. Printing Office, 1892): 163–74; also Aptheker, ed., *Writings in Periodical Literature*, I, p. 27; see comments on Du Bois in James A. Rawley, *The Transatlantic Slave Trade: A History*, p. 323.

18. ". . . eliminated in due time.": Aptheker, ed., *Suppression*, pp. 197–98, and pp. 169, 171, 173, and 154.

19. Du Bois on the "bargain": Aptheker, ed., *Suppression*, p. 190. Cuba and Brazil: on market patterns for slaves—see A. Norman Klein, "Introduction," *The Suppression of the African Slave Trade* (New York: Schocken Books, 1969), pp. xx–xxii; Rawley, *Transatlantic Slave Trade*, pp. 323–29; Herbert S. Klein, *African Slavery in Latin America and the Caribbean* (New York: Oxford University Press, 1986), pp. 140, 150.

20. Curtin figure of 54,000: Philip D. Curtin, *The Atlantic Slave Trade: A Census*, p. 75. Literature on the numbers controversy is cited *supra*, chapter 1, note 14, *in extenso*: *viz.*—David Brion Davis, *Slavery and Human Progress*; Stanley Engerman and Eugene Genovese, eds., *Race and Slavery in the Western Hemisphere: Quantitative Studies*; Ronald W. Bailey, "Africa, the Slave Trade, and the Rise of Industrial Capitalism in Europe and the United States: a Historiographical Review," *American History*, II (1986): 1–91; J. E. Inikori, "Measuring the Atlantic Slave Trade: an Assessment of Curtin and Antsey," *Journal of African History*, 17 (1976a): 197–223; etc.

21. Compensation through high importation: Richard S. Dunn, *Sugar and Slaves: The Rise of the Planter Class in the English West Indies, 1624–1713* (Chapel Hill: University of North Carolina Press, 1972), esp. pp. 224–26, 312, 324; Franklin W. Knight, *Slave Society in Cuba during the Nineteenth Century* (Madison: University of Wisconsin Press, 1970), p. 32; Joseph C. Miller, *Way of Death: Merchant Capitalism and the Angolan Slave Trade, 1730–1830* (Madison: University of Wisconsin Press, 1988), esp. pp. 757–92. Haiti is the oustanding example of deaths compensated by imports: see C. L. R. James, *The Black Jacobins: Toussaint L'Ouverture and the San Domingo Revolution*, esp. pp. 27–61.

22. ". . . in sickness and old age.": Aptheker, ed., *Suppression*, p. 154.

23. On Haiti and U.S. slave importation: *ibid.*, pp. 70–74; and A. N. Klein's "Introduction" to the 1969 Schocken edition of *Suppression*, pp. xxi–xxiii.

24. ". . . abolition of slavery.": Aptheker, ed., *Suppression*, p. 198.

25. ". . . when they ought to be done.": *ibid.*, p. 197, and pp. 198, 199.

26. Genovese's edition of *Suppression*: Du Bois, "Apologia," *Suppression of the African Slave Trade . . .* (New York: Social Science Press, 1954) [reproduced in the Aptheker 1973 Kraus-Thomson edition, pp. 327–29.]

27. In "Apologia," p. 327, Du Bois states that he "had received at Harvard excellent preparation for understanding Freud under the tutelage of William James, Josiah Royce and George Santayana. At this time psychological measurements were beginning at Harvard with Munsterberg; but the work of Freud and his companions and their epoch-making contribution to science was not generally known when I was writing this book, and I did not realize the psychological reasons behind the trends of human action which the African slave trade involved."

28. ". . . twisted or utterly crushed.": *ibid.*, p. 329.

29. ". . . more mistakes than apparently I did.": *ibid.*, p. 329.

30. ". . . law, human or divine.": Du Bois, "The Enforcement of the Slave Trade Laws," AHA *Annual Report for 1891*; also Aptheker, ed., *Periodical Literature*, I, p. 27.

31. ". . . of income than morals.": "Apologia," p. 329.

32. Economics not organically linked to book: A. N. Klein's "Introduction" to 1969 edition of *Suppression*, p. xxii, criticizes Du Bois for a "ruthless consistency with his original premises . . . which prevented him from perceiving developing relationships in those very economic conditions he had concluded were most important." On the other hand, Bailey's "Africa, the Slave Trade," p. 8, underscores the seminal if undeveloped economic insights in *Suppression*, especially its discussion of the economic impact to Britain of the *asiento*. Philip Foner, in his "Introduction" to the 1970 Dover Publications, New York, edition of *Suppression*, p. vii, has only positive things to say about pioneering scholarship which still "remains a model of historical research and writing."

33. ". . . honor . . . to American historical scholarship.": *The Nation*, 63 (Dec. 31, 1896): 498–500.

34. Alexander Crummell: "Crummell, Alexander (1819–1898)," *DANB*, pp. 145–47; see Wilson J. Moses, *Alexander Crummell: A Study of Civilization and Discontent*, the excellent and definitive biography; also Gregory U. Rigsby, *Alexander Crummell in Nineteenth-Century Pan-African Thought* (New York: Greenwood Press, 1987); Meier, *Negro Thought*, pp. 42–44. President Chester Arthur: Moses, *Alexander Crummell*, p. 200.

35. Crummell and colleagues in Liberia: see Hollis R. Lynch, *Blyden, Pan-Negro Patriot, 1832–1892* (New York: Oxford University Press, 1971), pp. 73–74; Floyd J. Miller, ed., "Introduction," in Martin R. Delany, *Blake, or the Huts of Africa* (Boston: Beacon Press, 1970; orig. pub. 1861–62); Moses, *Crummell*, pp. 145–47; Moses, *Golden Age*, pp. 119–36; Rigsby, *Crummell*, pp. 119–36. Flight of President Roye: Moses, *Crummell*, pp. 193–94.

36. Forerunners of black nationalism: by way of introduction, see Rodney Carlisle, *The Roots of Black Nationalism*, pp. 77–85; Lynch, *Blyden*; Moses, *Golden Age*; Immanuel Geiss, *The Pan-African Movement: A History of Pan-Africanism in America, Europe and Africa*, ch. 9, esp. pp. 163–74 *et passim*; Floyd J. Miller, *The Search for Black Identity: Black Emigration and Colonization, 1787–1863* (Urbana: University of Illinois Press, 1975), pp. 171, 191, *et passim*; and Miller, ed., "Introduction," in Delany, *Blake, or the Huts of Africa*, pp. xiii–xvi; Edwin S. Redkey, ed., "Introduction," in *Respect Black: The Writings and Speeches of Henry McNeal Turner* (New York: Arno Press, 1971); Sterling Stuckey, *The Ideological Origins of Black Nationalism* (Boston: Beacon Press, 1972); Earl E. Thorpe, *The Mind of the Negro: An Intellectual History of Afro-Americans* (Westport, Conn.: Negro Universities Press, 1961); Victor Ullman, *Martin R. Delany, The Beginnings of Black Nationalism* (Boston: Beacon Press, 1971).

37. . . . sexually scandalous: Miller, "Introduction," *Blake*, p. xiv; Moses, *Golden Age*, pp. 23, 32, 214; Carlisle, *Black Nationalism*, p. 77; Lynch, *Blyden*, p. 17; Geiss, *Pan-Africanism*, pp. 150–51; Moses, *Crummell*, pp. 124–28; Benjamin Quarles, *Black Abolitionists*, pp. 199–222.

38. "less developed" cousins.: Moses, *Golden Age*, pp. 42, 214; William H. Ferris, *The African Abroad*, I, pp. 429–43, *et passim*; Meier, *Negro Thought*, pp. 42–43.

39. Delany in Africa: Miller, "Introduction," p. xv; Moses, *Crummell*, pp. 128–29. "Delany, Martin R[obinson], (1812–1885)," *DANB*, pp. 169–72. "Africa for the African Race . . .": Miller, "Introduction," p. xv; Moses, *Golden Age*, p. 36.

40. Delany's postwar career: Miller, "Introduction," pp. xvi–xix; James McPherson, *The Negro's Civil War: How American Negroes Felt and Acted during the War for the Union*, pp. 173, 239; Eric Foner, *Reconstruction: America's Unfinished Revolution, 1863–1877*, pp. 543, 546–47; Thomas Holt, *Black Over White, Negro Political Leadership in South Carolina during Reconstruction* (Urbana: University of Illinois Press, 1977), pp. 75, 223; Joel Williamson, *After Slavery, The Negro in South Carolina during Reconstruction, 1861–1877* (New York: W. W. Norton and Co., 1965), pp. 114, 353–54.

41. End of Reconstruction: *ibid.*, p. 581; Kenneth Stampp, *The Era of Reconstruction, 1865–1877* (New York: Vintage Books, 1965), pp. 205–11; Howard N. Rabinowitz, *Race Relations in the Urban South, 1865–1890* (Urbana, Chicago, London: University of Illinois Press, 1980), esp. ch. 13. ". . . nothing more to do with him."—quoted: Foner, *Reconstruction*, p. 582.

42. Plato, Hegel, Herder, Guizot: Moses, *Crummell*, pp. 214–15; Moses, *Golden Age*, p. 77; Rigsby, *Crummell*, p. 34; Guizot's three-volume *Histoire de la Civilisation en Europe* (1828) enjoyed an immense vogue in this country because of its liberal, bourgeois teleology—see Charles A. and Mary Beard, *The American Spirit: A Study of the Idea of Civilization in the United States*, vol. 4 (*The Rise of American Civilization*) (New York: Macmillan, 1948), pp. 90–93. ". . . gradually leads them to greatness": Moses, *Golden Age*, p. 77.

43. "noble imagination."—quoted: Moses, *Crummell*, p. 251. Blyden's similar views: Lynch, "The Attitude of Edward W. Blyden to European Imperialism in Africa," *Journal of the Historical Society of Nigeria*, 3 (Dec. 1969): 249–59, p. 254.

44. ". . . which is our rightful heritage."—quoted: Moses, *Crummell*, p. 235; Moses, *Golden Age*, pp. 25, 78.

45. Crummell's autocratic tendencies: Moses, *Golden Age*, pp. 78–79; Moses, *Crummell*, pp. 188–89, 294; Rigsby, *Crummell*, pp. 39–40.

46. Monogamy, cleanliness, and thrift: Moses, *Crummell*, pp. 218, 299; Rigsby, *Crummell*, p. 116; Meier, *Negro Thought*, p. 43.

47. ". . . true social status" was possible.: Crummell, "The Black Woman of the

South, Her Neglects and Her Needs" [1885 pamphlet], p. 14; Crummell states here, quoting the French historian Jules Michelet, p. 9, that " 'the Negress, of all others, is the most loving, the most generating; and this, not only because of her youthful blood, but we must also admit, for the richness of her heart.' " See also Moses, *Crummell*, p. 299. Compare Douglass's advanced ideas about women's rights, in Waldo Martin's perceptive *The Mind of Frederick Douglass* (Chapel Hill: University of North Carolina Press, 1984), pp. 6, 136–37; even Douglass insisted on a proper Victorian demarcation of women's functions between the public and domestic spheres, and believed, Martin asserts, p. 142, that "to make the family work, it was imperative that the wife-mother be warm, loving, intuitional, and the protector of manners and morals." See also William S. McFeeley, *Frederick Douglass* (New York: W. W. Norton, 1991), esp. pp. 266–67, on the pragmatic politics of Douglass's feminism.

48. On the Crummellian lineage of the Black Family paradigm: see W.E.B. Du Bois, *The Negro American Family, with a Foreword by Daniel Patrick Moynihan and Introduction by James E. Conyers* [Atlanta University Studies] (Cambridge, Mass.: M.I.T. Press, 1970; orig. pub. 1909); E. Franklin Frazier, *The Negro Family in the United States* (Chicago: The University of Chicago Press, 1963, rev. and abridged; orig. pub. 1939), Foreword by Nathan Glazer (see pp. x–xi); Moses, *Crummell*, pp. 218, 299.

49. ". . . one bows before the prophets . . . : Du Bois, *Souls of Black Folk*, p. 216; Manning Marable, *W.E.B. Du Bois: Black Radical Democrat* (Boston: Twayne Publishers, 1986), pp. 32–34.

50. ". . . tingles his imagination.": Moses, *Crummell*, pp. 246–476.

51. Crummell's concept of leadership and Du Bois: Moses, *Crummell*, pp. 240–41; Rigsby, *Crummell*, pp. 39, 40. Lines from *Faust*: *Autobiography*, p. 212.

52. Crummell and Du Bois: *SOBF*, p. 216.

53. Du Bois thinking of his own doubts: *SOBF*, pp. 221, 215.

54. Du Bois and religious terminology: see W.E.B. Du Bois, *Prayers for Dark People, edited with an Introduction by Herbert Aptheker* (Amherst: University of Massachusetts Press, 1980).

55. Crummell and Garnet at Oneida: "Garnet, Henry Highland (1815–1882)," *DANB*, pp. 252–53; Earl Ofari, *Let Your Motto Be Resistance: The Life and Thought of Henry Highland Garnet* (Boston: Beacon Press, 1972), pp. 6–7; Quarles, *Black Abolitionists*, pp. 90–91, 112–13.

56. *SOBF*, p. 222.

57. On Crummell and Onderdonk: Moses, *Crummell*, pp. 26–28; and Rigsby, *Crummell*, pp. 27–28. ". . . the Shadow of Death.": *SOBF*, p. 224, and pp. 222, 223.

58. ". . . guiding the strong.": *SOBF*, p. 226.

59. . . . compassionate, trustworthy yet admonitory: *SOBF*, p. 226; Moses, "Founding of the American Negro Academy: Idealism, Materialism and Hero Worship" (unpublished paper, courtesy the author, delivered at the Age of Booker T. Washington Conference, The University of Maryland at College Park, May 2, 1990): 1–12, pp. 6, 11. Marable, *Du Bois*, p. 34, observes, "It is curious, therefore, that many researchers of Du Bois have not examined the important relationship between Crummell's ideology and the emerging social thought of Du Bois. It is no exaggeration to suggest that Crummell became Du Bois's 'spiritual father,' the personification of the young scholar's image of what all Afro-American intellectuals should be."

60. ". . . the armor of pure souls.": *SOBF*, p. 226.

61. ". . . 'Well done!' ": *ibid.*, p. 227.

62. . . . rare as Mississippi snow.: on founding the American Negro Academy, see Alfred A. Moss, Jr., *The American Negro Academy: Voice of the Talented Tenth* (Baton Rouge: Louisiana State University Press, 1981), pp. 38–39. Moss, p. 11, estimates that, at

the time of the Academy's establishing, educated African-Americans comprised no more than 3 percent of the total black population.

63. Crummell on vocational education: Moses, *Crummell*, p. 249.

64. Bromides quoted: Washington, *Black Belt Diamonds, Gems from the Speeches, Addresses, and Talks to the Students, Selected and Arranged by Victoria Earle Matthews. Introduced by T. Thomas Fortune* (New York: Negro Universities Press, 1969; orig. pub. 1898), esp. pp. 9, 14, *et passim*; Moses, *Crummell*, p. 249.

65. ". . . never produced his civilization.": Moses, *Crummell*, p. 249.

66. On Crummell's opposition to B. T. Washington's educational ideas: Moses, *Crummell*, pp. 249–51, 252; Moss, *Negro Academy*, p. 258; also Bullock, *Negro Education*, p. 82. ". . . white demagogues and black sycophants.": see Crummell to John E. Bruce, Oct. 30, 1896, in Moses, *Crummell*, p. 258.

67. ". . . such a man as Dr. Crummell.": Du Bois, quoted: Moses, "Founding the American Negro Academy," p. 2 (footnote 2).

68. Crummell again on industrial training—quoted: Harlan, ed., *B. T. Washington Papers*, IV, p. 321 (footnote 1); Moss, *Negro Academy*, p. 39.

69. ". . . associations, and friendly societies.": quoted: Meier, *Negro Thought*, p. 43.

70. "assimilationist ends . . .": Moses, *Golden Age*, p. 30; Moses, *Crummell*, p. 138; Marable, *Du Bois*, p. 33; Williamson, *Crucible of Race*, has an especially cogent appreciation of the racial dialectic propounded by Du Bois, ch. 13, p. 411—"It is only by getting out that they [African-Americans] can get in." ". . . set apart in this country."—quoted: Moses, "Founding of the American Negro Academy," p. 10.

71. ". . . we have changed all that.": Du Bois, "The Conservation of Races," in *Pamphlets and Leaflets*, pp. 2–3. The historical literature on the concept of American "exceptionalism" is enormous. A still-useful introduction to the subject is Bernard Strensher, *Consensus, Conflict, and American Historians* (Bloomington: University of Indiana Press, 1975). On Germanic racialist sources for Du Bois's ideas in "Conservation": Moses, *Golden Age*, pp. 21, 49; Rampersad, *Du Bois*, p. 74; Copleston, *History of Philosophy*, VII, pp. 183–93.

72. . . . cultural "traits.": "Conservation of Races," *Pamphlets and Leaflets*, pp. 2, 3. On Du Bois's conceptual confusion in which race and nationality, culture and genotype are interchangeably and imprecisely employed: Moses, *Golden Age*, p. 135, calls Du Bois's essay "disgracefully inconsistent." Also, Moses, " 'The Conservation of Races' and the American Negro Academy"; Williamson, *Crucible*, pp. 397–403, *et passim*, has a spirited analysis of Du Bois's racialist ideas; Anthony Appiah, "The Uncompleted Argument: Du Bois and the Illusion of Race," in Henry Louis Gates, Jr., ed., *"Race," Writing and Difference* (Chicago: The University of Chicago Press, 1986), pp. 21–37, who finds Du Bois's attempt to transform racialism into a weapon for African-American advancement fatally flawed, makes the illuminating observation, p. 25, that "we find it in feminism also—on the one hand, a simple claim to equality, a denial of substantial difference; on the other, a claim to a special message, revealing the feminine Other not as the helpmeet of sexism, but as the New Woman." See also Thomas C. Holt, "The Political Uses of Alienation: W.E.B. Du Bois on Politics, Race and Culture, 1903–1940," *American Quarterly*, 42 (June 1990): 301–23, which states, p. 302, that "Conservation" posits "the social-biological reality of racial differences for social progress, a theme to which Du Bois would frequently return." But see Houston A. Baker, Jr., "Caliban's Triple Play," in Gates, *"Race,"* pp. 381–95, who believes that racialism can serve a positive purpose. Marable, *Du Bois*, gives a softer reading to the troublesome implication of "Conservation," arguing, p. 36, that the lecture "was not a plea for parochial racial chauvinism, but an appeal for the preservation of the Negro's cultural integrity and identity. Du Bois's entire speech was rooted in the

conception of race as an 'ethical' rather than biological category; each 'race' possessed specific aesthetic and moral gifts." Rampersad, *Du Bois*, gives a more literal reading to the racialism of "Conservation," p. 61—"Du Bois flatly declared his belief in racial theory and the 'hard limits of natural law.' " An excellent introduction to the racialist ideas of German philosophers is Sander L. Gilman, *On Blackness without Blacks: Essays on the Image of the Black in Germany* (Boston: G. K. Hall and Co., 1982), esp. pp. 93–118.

73. ". . . central thought of all history.": "Conservation," p. 2.

74. "advance guard of the Negro people . . .": "Conservation," p. 4. Pluralism as heterodoxy: On early twentieth-century concepts of ethnicity, see Edward Abraham, *The Lyrical Left: Randolph Bourne, Alfred Stieglitz and the Origin of Cultural Radicalism in America* (Charlottesville: University of Virginia Press, 1988), esp. pp. 15–19, 67–68; Christopher Lasch, *The New Radicalism in America: [1889–1963] The Intellectual as a Social Type* (New York: Alfred A. Knopf, 1965), esp. pp. xi, 74–77, and ch. 4 ("Mabel Dodge Luhan: Sex as Politics"), indispensable for the antiparochial and antihegemonic social role of the new class of intellectuals in America; also, Lasch notes, p. 77, that *The Outlook* and *The Independent* were the household journals of the Bourne family—two publications featuring some of Du Bois's most significant early writing on race and society; also Tom Lutz, *American Nervousness, 1903: An Anecdotal History* (Ithaca, N.Y.: Cornell University Press, 1991), for an intriguing explanation of changing cultural attitudes at century's turn; and Stanley Coben, *Rebellion Against Victorianism: The Impetus for Cultural Change in 1920s America* (New York and London: Oxford University Press, 1991), makes the cogent point, p. 27, that Victorianism in America "was basically the culture of an ethnic and religious group: a confederation of Protestants of British-American descent." For an introduction to the enormous bibliography on American cultural and ethnic pluralism, see Milton M. Gordon, *Assimilation in American Life: The Role of Race, Religion, and National Origins* (New York: Oxford University Press, 1964), esp. pp. 81–101; Thomas Archdeacon, *Becoming American: An Ethnic History* (New York: The Free Press, 1983); Roger Daniels, *Asian Americans: Chinese and Japanese in the United States since 1850* (Seattle and London: University of Washington Press, 1988); Nathan Glazer and Patrick Moynihan, *Beyond the Melting Pot: New York City* (rev. 1970); Andrew Greeley, *Ethnicity in the United States: A Preliminary Reconnaissance* (New York: John Wiley & Sons, 1974); Oscar Handlin, *The Uprooted: The Epic Story of the Great Migrations that Made the American People* (New York. Grosset & Dunlap, 1951); John Higham, *Strangers in the Land: Patterns of American Nativism, 1860–1925* (New Brunswick and London: Rutgers University Press, 1988; orig. pub. 1955); John Higham, ed., *Ethnic Leadership in America* (Baltimore and London: The Johns Hopkins University Press, 1978); Horace M. Kallen, *Culture and Democracy in the United States* (New York: Boni and Liveright, 1924); and Kallen, "Democracy versus the Melting Pot: A Study of American Nationality," *Nation*, (Feb. 18, 1915): 190–94; Ronald Takaki, *Strangers from Another Shore: A History of Asian Americans* (New York: Penguin, 1990); Stephen Thernstrom, ed., *Harvard Encyclopedia of American Ethnic Groups*.

75. ". . . German, or Irish or Italian blood would?": "Conservation," *Pamphlets and Leaflets*, p. 5. For analogous perceptions among Greenwich Village intellectuals, see Abrahams, *Lyrical Left*, p. 6.

76. ". . . but one American nation.": Douglass, quoted: Meier, *Negro Thought*, p. 77. Martin, *Mind of Douglass*, p. 98.

77. ". . . the Teutonic today.": "Conservation," *Pamphlets and Leaflets*, p. 5.

78. Du Bois's statement on parallel development, morality, etc.: *ibid.*, pp. 6, 7. ". . . one glad song of jubilee.": *ibid.*, p. 4.

79. Dissenters from "Conservation": Ferris, in Moses, *Crummell*, p. 265; and Scarborough, *ibid.*, p. 265.

80. "essentially a good one": *ibid.*, p. 265.

81. Impact of Pan-Africanism: Geiss, *Pan-Africanism*, pp. xxx; James P. Hooker, *Black Revolutionary: George Padmore's Path from Communism to Pan-Africanism* (New York: Praeger, 1967), pp. 39–41, 92–98; Peter Duignan and L. H. Gann, *The United States and Africa: A History* (Cambridge: Cambridge University Press, 1984), ch. 19, esp. pp. 251–68; John Henrik Clarke, ed., *Marcus Garvey and the Vision of Africa* (New York: Vintage Books, 1974), pp. 388–401; Jabez Ayodele Langley, "Marcus Garvey and African Nationalism," reprinted in Clarke, *Garvey*, pp. 402–13; Geiss, *Pan-Africanism*; Robert A. Hill, Jr., ed., *The Marcus Garvey and the Universal Negro Improvement Association Papers* (Berkeley: University of California Press, 1983–1990), 7 vols.; Sylvia M. Jacobs, *The African Nexus: Black American Perspectives on the European Partition of Africa, 1880–1920* (Westport, Conn.: Greenwood Press, 1981); J. A. Langley, *Pan-Africanism and Nationalism in West Africa, 1900–1945* (Oxford: Clarendon Press, 1973), Hollis R. Lynch, *Black American Radicals and the Liberation of Africa: The Council on African Affairs, 1937–1955* (Ithaca, N.Y.: Cornell University Press, 1978); Tony Martin, *Race First: The Ideological and Organizational Struggles of Marcus Garvey and the Universal Negro Improvement Association* (Westport, Conn.: Greenwood Press, 1976); Edwin Redkey, "The Flowering of Black Nationalism: Henry McNeal Turner and Marcus Garvey," reprinted in Clarke, *Garvey*, pp. 388–401; George Shepperson, "Notes on Negro American Influences on the Emergence of Afrcian Nationalism," *Journal of African History*, 1 (1960): 299; Janet G. Vaillant, *Black, French, and African: A Life of Leopold Sedar Senghor* (Cambridge and London: Harvard University Press, 1990), pp. 133–35; Williamson, *Crucible of Race*, p. 411.

82. Burden of "Conservation": see Williamson, *Crucible*, p. 397, which appropriately describes Du Bois's racialist ideas as "Volksgeistian Conservatism." See also Meier, *Negro Thought*, p. 194; and Rudwick, *Du Bois*, pp. 275–80.

83. . . . near "mental imbecility.": Du Bois, "Wilberforce University," Du Bois Papers/U. Mass. [Reel 87].

84. . . ."new hope" for Negroes—Cleveland, quoted: Harlan, *B. T. Washington*, I, p. 224. Reactions by Howell and others: *ibid.*, p. 220, pp. 220–24.

85. ". . . a word fitly spoken.": Du Bois to B. T. Washington, Sept. 24, 1895, in Aptheker, ed., *Correspondence*, I, p. 39; Harlan, *B. T. Washington Papers*, IV, p. 26. ". . . white South in political sympathy.": *Autobiography*, p. 209.

86. ". . . by whom we are surrounded.": Harlan, *B. T. Washington*, I, p. 218.

87. On Du Bois and the Atlanta Compromise: I subscribe fully to the elitist and good-faith interpretations of Marable, *Du Bois*, p. 44; and Rampersad, *Du Bois*, pp. 63–64; also Meier, *Negro Thought*, p. 196.

88. ". . . and express it lyrically.": Howell's review, *Harper's Weekly* (June 27, 1896), quoted in "Dunbar, Paul Laurence (1872–1906)," *DANB*, pp. 200–203, p. 201; and Jean Wagner, *Black Poets of the United States: From Paul Laurence Dunbar to Langston Hughes* (Urbana: University of Illinois Press, 1973), pp. 108–9. Sterling Brown, *Negro Poetry and Drama and the Negro in Fiction* (New York: Atheneum: 1969), pp. 32–36.

89. Dunbar an African-American: *Autobiography*, p. 187.

90. ". . . every year at Christmas time.": *Autobiography*, p. 187. "Young, Charles (1864–1922)," *DANB*, pp. 677–79. Biographical material on Young is contained in Florette Henri, *Black Migration*, pp. 278–84, 289; Bernard C. Nalty, *Struggle for the Fight: A History of Black Americans in the Military* (New York: The Free Press, 1986), esp. pp. 60–61, 66, 98–99.

91. ". . . on the lookout for another position.": W.E.B. Du Bois to B. T. Washington, Jan. 3, 1896, in Harlan, *B. T. Washington Papers*, IV, p. 114.

92. ". . . my guest at their residence.": W.E.B. Du Bois to B. T. Washington, April 6, 1896, in Harlan, *B. T. Washington Papers*, IV, p. 158.

93. ". . . had made a mistake.": *Darkwater*, p. 19.

94. Pyrrhic victory: *ibid.*, p. 189.

95. . . . sufficient for two—"if paid.": *ibid.*, p. 188.

96. On Nina Gomer: *Autobiography*, pp. 187–88; S. J. Brown to W.E.B. Du Bois, June 24, 1949, Du Bois Papers/U. Mass., an attorney in Des Moines, Iowa, contains information on the Gomer family; W.E.B. Du Bois, "I Bury My Wife," *Negro Digest*, 8 (July–Oct. 1950): 37–39. ". . . as good as a German housewife.": *Darkwater*, p. 19. . . . simply as "wife.": *ibid.*, p. 195.

97. "a sort of pattern": Pearl Shorter Smith to W.E.B. Du Bois, Feb. 26, 1918, Du Bois Papers/U. Mass.

98. ". . . to see General Conference.": *Autobiography*, p. 188.

99. Date of marriage: W.E.B. Du Bois to Bureau of Vital Statistics, Cedar Rapids, Iowa, June 22, 1949, and June 24, 1949, Du Bois Papers/U. Mass. ". . . Happy yesterdays!": Pearl Shorter Smith to W.E.B. Du Bois, Feb. 26, 1918.

100. ". . . will write definitely.": C. C. Harrison to W.E.B. Du Bois, Du Bois Papers/ U. Mass.; also Aptheker, ed., *Correspondence*, I, p. 40.

8. *From Philadelphia to Atlanta*

1. ". . . our highest expectations.": Samuel McCune Lindsay, "Introduction," in W.E.B. Du Bois, *The Philadelphia Negro: A Social Study. New Introduction by Herbert Aptheker* (Millwood, N.Y.: Kraus-Thomson, 1973; orig. pub. 1899), p. xi; Du Bois, *The Autobiography: A Soliloquy on Viewing My Life from the Last Decade of Its First Century*, p. 194.

2. Du Bois, *Dusk of Dawn*, p. 57; "A Pageant in Seven Decades: 1868–1938," in Aptheker, *Pamphlets and Leaflets*, p. 252.

3. "particularly cordial.": Du Bois, *Autobiography*, p. 194. Other Du Bois comments on Pennsylvania appointment: *ibid.*, pp. 154, 197.

4. "didn't occur to me.": Du Bois, interviewed by William T. Ingersoll, May, June 1960, Columbia University/Oral History Project, p. 135.

5. ". . . the facts of the case.": E. Digby Baltzell, "Introduction," in W.E.B. Du Bois, *The Philadelphia Negro* (New York: Schocken Books, 1967), p. xix. ". . . or what to call him.": Charles Custis Harrison, quoted from the minutes of the Trustees of the University of Pennsylvania (Oct. 5, 1896), in a letter from J. Y. Burke, secretary of the board, to S. M. Lindsay, Feb. 11, 1897. Matter contained in Folder, "Du Bois, Walter [sic] Edward Burghardt"/Archives of the University of Pennsylvania. Harrison is further quoted by Burke as saying that Du Bois's appointment "was not considered one which placed him on the staff and was therefore not reported to the Edition of the Catalogue."

6. African-American civic participation: Du Bois, *Phila. Negro*, pp. 17–24; Allen Ballard, *One More Day's Journey: The Making of Black Philadelphia* (Philadelphia: Ishi Publications Institute for the Study of Human Issues, 1984, 1987), pp. 76–78; Willard B. Gatewood, *Aristocrats of Color, The Black Elite, 1880–1920*, pp. 96–103; Theodore Hershberg, "Free Blacks in Antebellum Philadelphia: A Study of Ex-Slaves, Freeborn, and Socioeconomic Decline," in Hershberg, *Philadelphia: Work, Space, Family, and Group Experience in the Nineteenth Century, Essays Toward an Interdisciplinary History of the*

City (New York: Oxford University Press, 1981), pp. 17–25; Edward Raymond Turner, *The Negro in Pennsylvania, 1639–1861* (New York: Arno Press and the New York Times, 1969; orig. pub. 1911), pp. 113–14, 146–48.

7. Disempowerment of Philadelphia's African-Americans: Du Bois, *Phila. Negro*, p. 30; Ballard, *Day's Journey*, p. 83; Turner, *Negro in Pennsylvania*, pp. 148–49.

8. ". . . increasing race prejudice.": Turner, *Negro in Pennsylvania*, p. 143.

9. ". . . the tool of the Republicans.": *Phila. Negro*, p. 373.

10. On Machine politics in Philadelphia and elsewhere: E. Digby Baltzell, *Puritan Boston and Quaker Philadelphia: Two Protestant Ethics and the Spirit of Class Authority and Leadership* (New York: The Free Press, 1979), pp. 329, 372–76; Sam Bass Warner, Jr., *The Private City: Philadelphia in Three Periods of Its Growth* (Philadelphia: University of Pennsylvania Press, 1968), pp. 83–86; Roger Lane, *Roots of Violence in Black Philadelphia, 1860–1900* (Cambridge, Mass.: Harvard University Press, 1986), p. 13; also Samuel Eliot Morison and Henry Steele Commager, *The Growth of the American Republic*, II, pp. 243–314, 444. On Boies Penrose: Baltzell, *Boston and Philadelphia*, pp. 406–9; Lane, *Roots of Violence*, p. 125. ". . . defiance of public opinion.": *Phila. Negro*, p. 372.

11. On reform of city governments: John Whiteclay Chamber II, *The Tyranny of Change: America in the Progressive Era, 1890–1920* (New York: St. Martin's Press, 1992, 2d ed.); Samuel R. Hays, "The Politics of Reform in Municipal Government in the Progressive Era," *Pacific Northwest Quarterly*, 55 (Oct. 1964): 157–69; Richard Hofstadter, ed., *The Progressive Movement, 1900–1915* (New York: Simon and Schuster, Inc., 1963); Lincoln Steffens on Tammany and Philadelphia, quoted in Baltzell, *Boston and Philadelphia*, p. 378; Robert H. Wiebe, *The Search for Order, 1877–1920* (New York: Hill and Wang, 1967), pp. 301–302; Samuel P. Hays, "The Politics of Reform in Municipal Government in the Progressive Era": 157–69; and Richard L. McCormick, "The Discovery that Business Corrupts Politics: A Reappraisal of the Origins of Progressivism," *American Historical Review*, 86 (Apr. 1981): 247–74.

12. ". . . leaders of an earlier era.": Robert M. Crunden, *Ministers of Reform: The Progressive Achievement in American Civilization, 1889–1920* (New York: Basic Books, 1982), p. 164; Richard Hofstadter, *The Age of Reform: From Bryan to F.D.R.*, p. 137.

13. More on Progressive reform: Chambers, *The Tyranny of Change*, pp. 50–51; Morison and Commager, *American Republic*, pp. 321–23, 363; Wiebe, *Search for Order*, pp. 72–75.

14. Status revolution revised: Paul W. Glad, "Progressivism and the Business Culture of the 1920's," *Journal of American History*, 53 (June 1966): 75–89, esp. pp. 80, 88; Gabriel Kolko, *The Triumph of Conservatism: A Reinterpretation of American History, 1900–1916* (New York: The Free Press, 1963), pp. 2–3, 285, 303; Gerald N. Grob and George Athan Billias, eds., *Interpretations of American History: Patterns and Perspectives*. Vol. II: *Since 1877* (New York and London: The Free Press, 1987, 5th ed.), ch. 6 ("The Progressive Movement"); Jack Tager, "Progressivism, Conservatism, and the Theory of the Status Revolution," *Mid-America*, 48 (July 1966): 162–75; David P. Thelen, "Social Tensions and the Origins of Progressivism," *Journal of American History*, 56 (Sept. 1969): 323–47.

15. ". . . lives of all the rest.": Charles Booth, *Life and Labour of the People in London* (New York: Augustus M. Kelley Publications, 1969; orig. pub. 1889–91) 4 vols., p. 166; for context, see Gertrude Himmelfarb, *The Idea of Poverty: England in the Early Industrial Age* (New York: Alfred A. Knopf, 1984), p. 10.

16. Settlement houses in the U.S.: Allen F. Davis, *American Heroine: The Life and Legend of Jane Addams* (New York: Oxford University Press, 1973), pp. 53–60; Rivka Shpak Lissak, *Pluralism & Progressivism: Hull House and the New Immigrants, 1890–1919* (Chicago: University of Chicago Press, 1989), pp. 14–20; John F. McClymer, *War and*

Welfare: Social Emergency in America, 1890–1925 (Westport, Conn.: Greenwood Press, 1980), pp. 20–22.

17. Cooptation of Progressivism: Alan Trachtenberg, *The Incorporation of America: Culture & Society in the Gilded Age* (New York: Hill & Wang, 1982), p. 7; Glad, "Progressivism and Business Culture," pp. 79–80; Kolko, *Triumph of Conservatism*, p. 8; Tager, "Progressivism, Conservatism . . . Status Revolution," pp. 166, 175. ". . . how it was all coming out."—Rockefeller, quoted: McClymer, *War and Welfare*, p. 4.

18. Turning point, 1896 election: Hofstadter, *Age of Reform*, p. 109; Chambers, *Tyranny of Change*, p. 43; Morison and Commager, *Growth of the American Republic*, II, pp. 359–62; Nell I. Painter, *Standing at Armageddon, The United States, 1877–1919*, pp. 135–39.

19. ". . . body of action and effort.": *Dusk*, p. 54; *Autobiography*, p. 208.

20. Philadelphia's ethnic distribution: *Phila. Negro*, pp. 58–59; Alan Burnstein, "Immigrants and Residential Mobility: The Irish and Germans in Philadelphia, 1850–1880," written for the Philadelphia Social History Project (PSHP); Allen F. Davis and Mark Haller, eds., *The People of Philadelphia: A History of Ethnic Groups and Lower Class Life, 1870–1940* (Philadelphia: Temple University Press, 1973), esp. pp 203–30.

21. Social conditions in Ward 7: Frank F. Furstenberg, Jr., John Modell, and Theodore Hershberg, "The Origins of the Female-Headed Black Family: The Destructive Impact of the Urban Experience," in Hershberg, *Philadelphia*, and Alan Burstein, Eugene P. Eriksen, and William L. Young, "A Tale of Three Cities: Blacks, Immigrants, and Opportunity in Philadelphia, 1850–1880, 1930–1970," in Hershberg, *Philadelphia*, chs. 13 and 14; Lane, *Roots of Violence*, pp. 3, 20. ". . . criminal annals of Philadelphia.": *Phila. Negro*, p. 235.

22. ". . . until they wanted their votes.": *Phila. Negro*, p. 384; *ibid.* (Aptheker), p. 11.

23. Wharton and the CSA: *ibid.* (Aptheker), p. 8; *ibid.* (Baltzell), p. xvii.

24. CSA: *ibid.* (Baltzell), p. xvii; and McClymer, *War and Welfare*, pp. 3, 15, 20, 22, 30; Lissak, *Pluralism and Progressivism*, pp. 7, 20–21.

25. Wharton's influence and associates: Aptheker, "Introduction," in Du Bois, *Phila. Negro*, pp. 7–15; Mary Jo Deegan, "W.E.B. Du Bois and the Women of Hull House, 1895–1899," *The American Sociologist*, 19 (Winter 1988): 301–11, pp. 303–5, 309; Baltzell, "Introduction," *Phila. Negro*, p. xviii; Crunden, *Ministers of Reform*, pp. 65–66; Fred H. Matthews, *Quest for American Sociology: Robert H. Park and the Chicago School* (Montreal and London: McGill-Queens University Press, 1977), pp. 93–94.

26. ". . . outside the almshouse door."—Lindsay, quoted: Aptheker, "Introduction," *Phila. Negro*, pp. 7–15; Deegan, "W.E.B. Du Bois and the Women of Hull House," pp. 303–5, 309; Baltzell, "Introduction," *Phila. Negro*, p. xvii; Crunden, *Ministers of Reform*, pp. 65–66; Matthews, *Quest for American Sociology*, pp. 93–94.

27. Isabel Eaton and Du Bois: Deegan, "W.E.B. Du Bois and the Women of Hull House," pp. 304, 307; in *Dusk*, p. 56, Du Bois claims that Philadelphia's reformers "wanted to prove this [black civic culpability] by figures and I was the man to do it." See Aptheker, "Introduction," *Phila. Negro*, p. 14.

28. Harrison's charge: C. C. Harrison to W.E.B. Du Bois, Aug. 15, 1896, Du Bois Papers/U. Mass.; Aptheker, ed., *The Correspondence of W.E.B. Du Bois*, I, p. 40. Du Bois's conception of his charge: *Dusk*, p. 38; *Autobiography*, p. 199. ". . . advice as to procedure.": *Autobiography*, p. 199.

29. ". . . with general public opinion.": *Phila. Negro*, p. 4.

30. ". . . in accord with historical precedents.": *Phila. Negro*, p. 4. . . . logic of poverty and racism: Paul Richards, "W.E.B. Du Bois and American Social History: The

Evolution of a Marxist," *Radical America*, 4 (Nov. 1970): 37–65, pp. 40–41; Aptheker, "Introduction," *Phila. Negro*, pp. 22–23.

31. Varying assessments of monograph's significance: The consistently severe Broderick, *Du Bois*, p. 43, concedes of Du Bois's achievement in *The Philadelphia Negro* that, "Even Columbia and Chicago, the great centers of academic sociology, were only a few years ahead of Du Bois in making empirical enquiries the basis of their sociology." Dan S. Green and Edwin D. Driver, eds., *W.E.B. Du Bois on Sociology and the Black Community* (Chicago: University of Chicago Press, 1978), p. 39, laud Du Bois as rightly deserving "a place among the giants of sociology for his work during the years 1896–1910, when sociology was being established as an economic discipline." Ernest Kaiser's "Introduction" to *The Atlanta University Publications* (New York: Arno Press, 1968), p. iii, makes the claim that *The Philadelphia Negro* is "the first scientific sociological study in the United States." Lane, *Roots of Violence*, renders the more appropriate judgment, p. 148, that the monograph is "arguably the best piece of sociology written by an American in the nineteenth century." Rudwick, "Du Bois As Sociologist," p. 33 *et passim*, observes that Du Bois's "generalizations about social problems later became standard in sociology. But when *The Philadelphia Negro* was written, they contrasted strongly with the racist assumptions held by most sociologists and by the general public." This view is fully shared by Werner J. Lange, "W.E.B. Du Bois and the First Scientific Study of Afro-America," *Phylon*, 44 (1983): 135–46, who makes the further compelling observation, p. 137, that, without Du Bois's published research, the scientific exploration of black America might "have been postponed for over two decades." Dan S. Green and Edwin D. Driver, "W.E.B. Du Bois: A Case Study in the Sociology of Sociological Negation," *Phylon*, 37, no. 4 (1976): 308–33, p. 309: "It is one of the earliest, if not the earliest, empirical monograph published in United States Sociology." *Life and Labour* as model: Aptheker, "Intro.," *Phila. Negro*, pp. 6–7, 16; Francis L. Broderick, "German Influences on the Scholarship of W.E.B. Du Bois," *Phylon*, 19 (1958): 367–71, p. 369; and Elliott Rudwick, "W.E.B. Du Bois as Sociologist," in James E. Blackwell and Morris Janowitz, eds., *Black Sociologists: Historical and Contemporary Perspectives* (Chicago: University of Chicago Press, 1974), pp. 25–55, esp. p. 49.

32. "Are we animals . . . ?": *Phila. Negro*, p. 170. Seventh Ward field research: Aptheker, "Intro.," p. 16.

33. Influences on Eaton: (Salmon and Davis), Aptheker, "Intro.," pp. 18, 29.

34. Progressive women and immigrants: *ibid.*, p. 14; Lissak, *Pluralism and Progressivism*, pp. 7, 20–21; McClymer, *War and Welfare*, pp. 37, 110; Roy Lubove, *The Professional Altruist: The Emergence of Social Work as a Career, 1880–1930* (Cambridge, Mass.: Harvard University Press, 1965), pp. 14, 140–44; Sheila M. Rothman, *Woman's Proper Place. A History of Changing Ideas and Practices: 1870 to the Present* (New York: Basic Books, 1978), pp. 111, 118–19.

35. ". . . passion for cleanliness . . .": Du Bois, "I Bury My Wife," *Negro Digest*, 8 (July–Oct. 1950): 37. ". . . people used to stop and stare . . . ": *ibid.*, p. 37. ". . . the slums of Philadelphia."—Du Bois, quoted: Shirley Graham-Du Bois, *His Day Is Marching On: A Memoir of W.E.B. Du Bois*, p. 126.

36. *Autobiography*, p. 195.

37. Christmas morning 1896: *Autobiography*, pp. 196–97. ". . . come home to you.": Nina Gomer Du Bois to W.E.B. Du Bois, Sept. 4, 1896, Du Bois Papers/U. Mass.

38. Wrong marriage date: "I Bury My Wife," p. 37—Du Bois gives his age at the time of marriage as twenty-seven; he was twenty-eight.

39. ". . . fundamentally indecent.": *Autobiography*, p. 57; also W.E.B. Du Bois to Countee Cullen, Feb. 11, 1928, Countee Cullen Papers/Amistad Research Center/Tulane University. Birth of a son: "I Bury My Wife," p. 39; *Autobiography*, p. 281.

40. ". . . transfigured woman.": Du Bois, *SOBF*, p. 208.

41. ". . . these social problems.": *Autobiography*, p. 201; "The Study of the Negro Problems," *Annals of the American Academy of Political and Social Science*, 11 (Jan. 1898): 1–23; also Aptheker, ed., *Writings by W.E.B. Du Bois in Periodicals Edited by Others*, I, 40–56, p. 52; see also Aptheker, "Intro.," p. 17 (footnote 20).

42. ". . . dwell upon its sanctity.": *Autobiography*, p. 200.

43. ". . . economic progress of the colored people.": W.E.B. Du Bois to Carroll D. Wright, Esq., Feb. 18, 1897, Bureau of Labor Statistics/R.G. 257/Nat. Archives; Wright's Feb. 16, 1897, letter has not been recovered; Samuel McCune Lindsay to Carroll D. Wright, Feb. 24, 1897, Bureau of Labor Statistics/Record Group (R.G.) 257/Nat. Archives. ". . . 3d, 4th, 5th or 6th of March.": W.E.B. Du Bois to Carroll D. Wright, Esq., Feb. 18, 1897 [holograph], Bureau of Labor Statistics, Records Relating to Chief, Job Applications, 1885–1901, R.G. 257/National Archives; *Autobiography*, p. 202; W.E.B. Du Bois (Enclosures), Feb. 17, 1897, Bureau of Labor Statistics/RG 257/Nat. Archives.

44. Research scheme for Bureau enterprise: W.E.B. Du Bois to Carroll D. Wright, Esq., May 5, 1897, Du Bois Papers/U. Mass.; also in Aptheker, *Correspondence*, I, pp. 41–43; W.E.B. Du Bois to Carroll D. Wright, Esq., June 14, 1897, Bureau of Labor Statistics, R.G. 257/Nat. Archives. ". . . careful basis in fact.": Du Bois, "Testimony before Industrial Comission," U.S. Industrial Commission/*Reports on Immigration. Including Testimony, with Review and Digest, and Special Reports* . . . (Washington, D.C.: Government Printing Office, 1901), pp. 159–75; also in, Aptheker, ed., *Contributions by W.E.B. Du Bois in Government Publications and Proceedings* (Millwood, N.Y.: Kraus-Thomson, 1980), p. 67.

45. ". . . visited their homes.": Du Bois, "The Negroes of Farmville, Virginia: A Social Study," *Bulletin of the Department of Labor*, 14 (Jan. 1898): 1–44; also in Aptheker, ed., *Govt. Publications and Proceedings*, pp. 12–13.

46. ". . . prostitution and illegitimacy.": Du Boisian moralizing: "Negroes of Farmville, Va.," p. 17, and pp. 28, 29, 30.

47. ". . . from sheer necessity.": *ibid.*, p. 27. ". . . grow with the town.": *ibid.*, p. 29. ". . . standards become settled.": *ibid.*, p. 17. ". . . even in small communities.": *ibid.*, p. 44.

48. Four Bureau of Labor studies: "The Negroes in the Black Belt: Some Social Sketches" [1899]; "The Negro Landholder of Georgia" [1901]; "The Negro Farmer" [1906]; all are reproduced in Aptheker, ed., *Govt. Pubs.* "The Negroes of Lowndes County, Alabama," is the research monograph that was destroyed by bureau officials—see *Autobiography*, pp. 226–27.

49. Du Bois, "The Problem of Amusement," published in *The Southern Workman*, 26 (Sept. 1897): 181–84, after its delivery at the General Conference of Negroes, July 1897, Hampton Institute; also in Aptheker, *Periodical Literature*, I, pp. 32–39; also see Aptheker, *Annotated Bibliography of the Published Writings of W.E.B. Du Bois*, p. 9.

50. ". . . available for college work?": A. B. Hart to B. T. Washington, June 14, 1897; and A. B. Hart to B. T. Washington, Aug. 10, 1897, in Harlan, ed., *B. T. Washington Papers*, IV, pp. 299, 320.

51. ". . . institutions of learning in the North.": Henry Villard to B. T. Washington, July 5, 1897, *ibid.*, pp. 311–12.

52. Bumstead's Atlanta University offer: *Autobiography*, p. 209; Clarence Bacote, *The Story of Atlanta University: A Century of Service, 1865–1965* (Princeton, N.J.: Princeton University Press, 1969), pp. 131, 133; *The Atlanta University Publications* (New York: Arno Press, 1968), preface by Ernest Kaiser, esp. p. iii.

53. Atlanta University commitment: Bacote, *Story of Atlanta University*, p. 131; *Autobiography*, p. 210.

54. *Up From Slavery*: Harlan, ed., *B. T. Washington Papers*, I. *The Autobiographical Writings* (Urbana: University of Illinois Press, 1972), pp. xv–xvii.

55. ". . . by a vast veil.": "Strivings of the Negro People," *Atlantic Monthly*, 80 (Aug. 1897): 194–98, p. 194; as reproduced in *SOBF*, pp. 1–2, Du Bois's alterations of the text were negligible. In the single instance where a change was made in materials quoted here, the new material has been added between brackets.

56. ". . . from being torn asunder.": *ibid.*, p. 194; in *SOBF*, p. 3.

57. ". . . bottom of hardships.": *ibid.*, p. 196; in *SOBF*, p. 8.

58. Douglass on assimilation: Waldo Martin, *The Mind of Frederick Douglass*, p. 219. ". . . making him a black man."—Douglass, quoted: Moses, *Alexander Crummell*, p. 120.

59. "[. . . roughly in his face].": "Strivings of the Negro People," p. 195; in *SOBF*, p. 4.

60. ". . . unifying ideal of Race.": *ibid.*, p. 197; in *SOBF*, p. 11.

61. Description of St. Alban's Place location is based on my visit to the neighborhood sometime in 1989. ". . . newer strength of his.": "Strivings of the Negro People," p. 211.

62. On sociological system building: see Baltzell, "Intro.," p. xxiv; Tom Bottomore and Robert Nisbet, eds., *A History of Sociological Analysis* (New York: Basic Books, 1978), pp. 55, 119, 173, *et passim*; and Hermann Schwendinger and Julia R. Schwendinger, *The Sociologists of the Chair: A Radical Analysis of the Formative Years of North American Sociology* (New York: Basic Books, 1974), pp. xxvi–xxvii; and 141–42, 165, 315–16, 386.

63. ". . . problems of [his] own group.": *Dusk*, p. 51; Broderick, "German Influences on Scholarship of Du Bois," pp. 369–70; also Broderick, "The Academic Training of W.E.B. Du Bois," *Journal of Negro Education*, 27 (Winter 1958): 10–16; Rudwick, "Du Bois As Sociologist," in Blackwell and Janowitz, *Black Sociologists*, p. 25.

64. ". . . wish, whim and prejudice.": *Phila. Negro*, p. 98; Broderick, "German Influences," p. 370.

65. On Small, Giddings, and Ross: Bottomore and Nisbet, *History of Sociological Analysis*, pp. 292–94, 301–2; Pettigrew, *Sociology of Race Relations*, pp. xxi, 2–3. Forrest G. Wood, *The Arrogance of Faith: Christianity and Race in America from the Colonial Era to the Twentieth Century* (Boston: Northeastern University Press, 1990), esp. pp. 371–75; Du Bois, "Sociology Hesitant," unpublished essay summarized with quotations in Francis L. Broderick, W.E.B. Du Bois Research Material [notes taken from William E. B. Du Bois's letters and documents in his personal library by Broderick in preparation for his biography of Du Bois], Box 3, M6 197/Schomburg Research Center/NYPL; see the useful comments of Green and Driver, "Du Bois: A Case Study in the Sociology of Sociological Negation." ". . . blooming, buzzing confusion . . .": James, "The Thing and Its Relations" (1905), in *Essays in Radical Empiricism* (Cambridge: Harvard University Press, 1978), p. 46.

66. ". . . classifying it by conditions.": *Autobiography*, p. 198. Note interesting observation about Max Weber and structure of *Philadelphia Negro*: Mary Jo Deegan, p. 306. ". . . his history in slavery.": Du Bois, "The Study of the Negro Problems," *Annals of the American Academy of Political and Social Science* (Philadelphia), 11 (Jan. 1898): 1–23; in Aptheker, ed., *Writings in Periodical Literature*, I, 40–52, p. 46.

67. ". . . age of revival.": *Phila. Negro*, p. 11.

68. ". . . stagger downward.": *ibid.*, p. 387.

69. ". . . they were men and brothers.": *ibid.*

70. Race and urban adjustment: see Hershberg, *Philadelphia*, pp. 113, 482, for comparison of Irish and African-American industrial experience in Philadelphia; and, for analogous multiethnic experience, John Bodnar, Roger Simon, Michael P. Weber, *Lives of*

Their Own: Blacks, Italians, and Poles in Pittsburgh, 1900–1960 (Urbana and London: University of Illinois Press, 1982), esp. ch. 2 ("Backgrounds and Great Expectations").

71. ". . . Irish, Germans, and other whites.": *Phila. Negro*, p. 11. Du Bois conceded more than many students of labor have about the comparable skills of African-Americans versus those of white labor. Hershberg, p. 113, for example, asserts that Irish immigrants arrived with skills no better suited to Philadelphia's industries than African-Americans. Nevertheless, *Phila. Negro*, p. 126, Du Bois stressed racism as the final barrier to black labor irrespective of skills—"Here was a mass of black workmen of whom *very few were by previous training fitted* to become the mechanics and artisans of a new industrial development; here, too, were an increasing mass of foreigners and native Americans who were *universally well fitted* to take part in the new industries; finally, most people were willing and many eager that Negroes should be kept as menial servants rather than develop into industrial factors." [Italics added] Philip S. Foner argues that organized labor systematically eliminated and excluded black labor throughout the country, even, and especially where, as in much of the urban South, a significant pool of skilled and semiskilled black workers were to be in extractive industries, railroads, and building trades—Foner, *History of the Labor Movement in the United States: The Policies and Practices of the American Federation of Labor, 1900–1909* (New York: International Publishers, 1964), 6 vols., III, p. 238.

72. African-American mortality rates: *Phila. Negro*, p. 150; Furstenberg, Modell, and Hershberg, "Origins of the Female-Headed Black Family" [PSHP Archives/U. Pa.], p. 11; also Lane, *Roots of Violence*, pp. 3–4.

73. ". . . men and brothers.": *Phila. Negro*, pp. 387, 241, 311, and ch. 13 ("The Negro Criminal") *passim*; Lane, *Roots of Violence*, p. 148, charges that Du Bois "shrank from the dismal implications of his own findings, with the result that his frequent references to crime, drink, gambling, and prostitution are collectively the weakest parts of the book."

74. *Phila. Negro*, p. 249; Lane, *Roots of Violence*, pp. 4, 149.

75. ". . . held for years.": *Phila. Negro*, p. 344. (Review by C. R. Woodruff), *City and State*, Jan. 4, 1900. Robert S. Lynd and Helen Merrell Lynd, *Middletown: A Study in American Culture* (New York: Harcourt, Brace & World, 1956; orig. pub. 1929).

76. William I. Thomas and Florian Znaniecki's *The Polish Peasant in Europe and America, Monograph of an Immigrant Group* (Chicago: University of Chicago Press, 1918), 2 vols.

77. Samuel McCune Lindsay to B. T. Washington, Nov. 28, 1896, *Washington Papers*, IV, p. 240.

78. Paternalist generalities: *Phila. Negro*, pp. 97, 318, 311. ". . . judged by its upper class.": *ibid.*, p. 7.

79. On William Graham Sumner: Thomas Pettigrew, p. xxi; Bottomore and Nisbet, *History of Sociological Analysis*, pp. 294–97; Richard Hofstadter, *Social Darwinism in American Thought* (Boston: Beacon Press, 1992; orig. pub. 1944), ch 3; Robert C. Bannister, ed., *On Liberty, Society, and Politics: The Essential Essays of William Graham Sumner* (Indianapolis, IN: Liberty Fund, Inc., 1992), esp. essay no. 22 ("The Absurd Effort to Make the World Over" [1894]). ". . . menaced for their benefit.": *Phila. Negro*, p. 389. ". . . their fellow citizens.": *ibid.*, p. 393.

80. ". . . very different races.": *American Historical Review*, 7 (Jan. 1901): 164; *Literary Digest*, 19 (Dec. 16, 1899): 732; *Nation*, 69 (Oct. 26, 1899): 310; *Outlook*, 63 (1899): 647–48. Rudwick, "Notes on a Forgotten Black Sociologist: W.E.B. Du Bois and the Sociological Profession," *The American Sociologist*, 4 (Nov. 1969): 303–6; and John H. Bracey, Jr., August Meier, and Elliott Rudwick, eds., *The Black Sociologists* (Belmont, Calif.: Wadsworth Publishing Co., 1971), p. 4.

81. *Phila. Negro*, pp. 501, 503.

82. *An American Dilemma*: Gunnar Myrdal, *An American Dilemma* (New York and Toronto: McGraw-Hill, 1964; orig. pub. 1944), 2 vols., II, p. 1132—"We cannot close this description of what a study of a Negro community should be without calling attention to the study which best meets our requirements, a study which is now all but forgotten. We refer to W.E.B. Du Bois, *The Philadelphia Negro*, published in 1899." The Du Boisian influence: See E. Franklin Frazier, *The Negro Family in the United States* (Chicago: University of Chicago Press, 1963; orig. pub. 1939), pp. xi, 11–15; and Frazier, *The Negro in the United States* (New York: Macmillan, 1957; orig. pub. 1949), p. 334; St. Clair Drake and Horace R. Cayton, *Black Metropolis: A Study of Negro Life in a Northern City* (New York: Harper & Row, 1962; orig. pub. 1945), 2 vols., II, pp. 787–88; Broderick, "The Academic Training of W.E.B. Du Bois," pp. 33–34, is useful on Du Bois's impact on Cayton and Drake; as is Baltzell, "Intro.," pp. xxv–xxvi; some insights on Myrdal's appreciation of Du Bois are found in David Southern, *Myrdal and Black-White Relations: The Use and Abuse of An American Dilemma, 1944–1969* (Baton Rouge: Louisiana State University Press, 1987), pp. 21, 90–91; the nexus to Frazier is well done in Anthony Platt, *E. Franklin Frazier Reconsidered* (New Brunswick, N.J.: Rutgers University Press, 1991), pp. 23–26, 132–33; on Moynihan's *The Negro Family: The Case for National Action*, see the invaluable Lee Rainwater and William L. Yancey, *The Moynihan Report and the Politics of Controversy* (Cambridge, Mass.: M.I.T. Press, 1967), which reproduces the "Moynihan Report," pp. 30–124.

83. ". . . have a white face?": *Phila. Negro*, p. 351.

84. ". . . the rest of the group.": *ibid.*, p. 49.

85. ". . . the greatest difficulties.": *ibid.*, p. 30.

86. ". . . its owner be black or white.": *ibid.*, p. 395.

87. . . . good Negroes and bad ones.: *ibid.*, p. 315; Gatewood, *Black Aristocrats*, p. 7, observes that "the idea of a black aristocracy, a black Four Hundred, or an 'old upper class' was so alien to most whites that it regularly encountered ridicule and scorn."

88. ". . . always energetic or thrifty.": *Phila. Negro*, pp. 311, 315.

89. *Ibid.*, p. 318.

90. ". . . cohabitation without marriage.": *ibid.*, p. 67. Refer to note 82 for titles relevant to Du Boisian origins of the social pathology school of ethnic studies.

91. ". . . he is now a waiter.": *Phila. Negro*, p. 341.

92. ". . . furnish your bread free.": *ibid.*, p. 352.

93. Brief commendations: *Yale Review*, 10 (May 1900): 110–11; *American Journal of Sociology* (May 1903): 112; for comment on Small's racial attitudes, see, Elliot Rudwick, "W.E.B. Du Bois as Sociologist," in Blackwell and Janowitz, eds., *Black Sociologists*, pp. 25–55, 51—although Rudwick states that no mention was made of Du Bois's work until publication in the May 1908 issue, vol. 3, of the *American Journal of Sociology*, pp. 834–38, of Du Bois's response to Albert Holt Stone's paper, "Is Race Friction Between Blacks and Whites in the United States Growing?" (read before the 1908 meeting of the American Sociological Association), he was mistaken.

9. *Social Science, Ambition, and Tuskegee*

1. ". . . few people knew her.": Bazolene Usher, taped interview, June 25, 1987/D. L. Lewis; Kathleen Adams, taped interview, Nov. 12, 1987 D. L. Lewis; also Clarence Bacote, *The Story of Atlanta University: A Century of Service, 1865–1965*, p. 128.

2. ". . . five dollars apiece for the holidays.": Du Bois, *The Autobiography: A Soliloquy on Viewing My Life from the Last Decade of Its First Century*, p. 195.

3. Bessie Taylor Page to W.E.B. Du Bois, Mar. 4, 1918, Du Bois Papers/U. Mass.

4. ". . . most holy friendships.": *Autobiography*, p. 213; *Darkwater: Voices from Within the Veil*, p. 20.

5. ". . . ivory tower of race.": *Autobiography*, p. 208 and pp. 197, 228.

6. ". . . in a dull, red sea.": James Weldon Johnson, *Along This Way: The Autobiography of James Weldon Johnson* (New York: Penguin Books, 1990; orig. pub. 1933), p. 65. The term "no-nation": Adams interview/D. L. Lewis. ". . . wilds of Borneo.": Johnson, *Along This Way*, p. 65.

7. AU motto: Bacote, *Atlanta University*, p. 22. On subordination of industrial training at AU: see August Meier, *Negro Thought in America, 1800–1915: Radical Ideologies in the Age of Booker T. Washington*, p. 91. ". . . persons trained at Atlanta University.": Du Bois, *Dusk*, p. 69. Many Tuskegee instructors were trained at Atlanta University and many others were graduates of Fisk, Howard, and Harvard, Oberlin, Dartmouth, and other northern schools (see Harlan, *Booker T. Washington*, I, *The Making of a Black Leader, 1856–1901*, and II, *The Wizard of Tuskegee, 1901–1915*; I, p. 140; and II, ch. 7 ("Tuskegee's People"); George A. Towns, "Phylon Profile, XVI: Horace Bumstead, Atlanta University President (1888–1907)," *Phylon*, 9, no. 2 (1948): 109–14.

8. On funding for AU: Bacote, *Atlanta University*, pp. 12–22. ". . . into a tolerable citizen."—Vardaman quoted: Albert D. Kirwan, *Revolt of the Rednecks, Mississippi Politics: 1876–1925* (Gloucester, Mass.: Peter Smith, 1964), p. 146; see also William F. Holmes, *The White Chief: James Kimble Vardaman* (Baton Rouge: Louisiana State University Press, 1970), pp. 88, 432, for disclosure of ambiguities in Vardaman's rabid racism; Towns, "Horace Bumstead," p. 111.

9. ". . . segregated parts or times.": *Autobiography*, p. 234.

10. Campus impressions of Du Bois: Usher interview/D. L. Lewis; Bessie Taylor Page to W.E.B. Du Bois, Mar. 4, 1918, Du Bois Papers/U. Mass.; Bacote, *Atlanta University*, p. 132, says that Du Bois "was held in awe by students because of his cane and gloves . . . and because of the austere manner in which he spoke. Furthermore, he was unpopular in the beginning because of his heavy outside assignments and exacting standards in the class room." A colorful group of interviews provides an excellent *aperçu* in Dorothy Cowser Yancey, "William Edward Burghardt Du Bois's Atlanta Years: The Human Side—A Study Based upon Oral Sources," *Journal of Negro History*, 63 (Jan. 1978): 59–67, esp. p. 60. Classes taught by Du Bois along with grade rosters for second semester 1897 are in Du Bois Papers/U. Mass.

11. ". . . cries out to be done": Du Bois, *Prayers for Dark People*, p. 21. Bessie Taylor Page to W.E.B. Du Bois, Mar. 4, 1918, recalls that when President Bumstead asked Du Bois to address the student assembly "on your first morning in the Assembly Room to the students, you said very promptly 'No' and kept your seat while saying it. We were disappointed." Adams interview/D. L. Lewis; Edward R. Thompson, quoted—Yancey, "Du Bois's Atlanta Years," p. 61.

12. "Dube": Yancey, "Du Bois's Atlanta Years," p. 60. ". . . dignity we knew indoors.": Bessie Taylor Page to W.E.B. Du Bois, Mar. 4, 1918.

13. Du Bois's classroom: Adams interview/D. L. Lewis; Yancey, "Du Bois's Atlanta Years," pp. 60–61.

14. ". . . greater glory of God.": *Darkwater*, p. 82.

15. Student praise: Bessie Taylor Page to W.E.B. Du Bois, Mar. 4, 1918; Adams interview/D. L. Lewis; Thompson quoted—Yancey, "Du Bois's Atlanta Years," p. 61; "Dill, Augustus Granville (1881–1956)" *DANB*, pp. 177–78. "The Negro Labor in Atlanta": Bacote, *Atlanta University*, pp. 132–33, contains the student research assignments listed in the Atlanta University *Scroll* for February 1899.

16. Origins of AU Studies: Horace Bumstead, "Introduction," in the first study, *Mortality Among Negroes in Cities: Proceedings of the Conference for Investigation of City Problems, held at Atlanta University, May 26–27, 1896. No. 1* (Atlanta: Atlanta University Press, 1896), pp. 3–4. Synopses of each of the Atlanta University Studies are found in Herbert Aptheker, ed., *Annotated Bibliography of the Published Writings of W.E.B. Du Bois*, pp. 524–36. Numbers 1, 2, 4, 8, 9, 11, 13, 14, 15, 16, 17, and 18 are reproduced in their entirety, with a preface by Ernest Kaiser, in *The Atlanta University Publications* (New York: Arno Press, 1968). Unless indicated, all references henceforth are to the Arno Press edition.

17. More on origins of AU Studies: see Harlan, *B. T. Washington*, I, p. 200. Bradford's role: see Du Bois Interview/Columbia OHP, pp. 135, 137. ". . . laws of health and morality.": *Social and Physical Condition of Negroes in Cities: Report of an Investigation under the Direction of Atlanta University, held on May 25–26, 1897. No. 2*, p. 3; Harris quoted—*ibid.*, p. 20.

18. Armstrong: Samuel Chapman Armstrong to Robert C. Ogden, July 6, 1892, Box 6, in Robert C. Ogden Papers/Library of Congress. ". . . surer, and more definite.": *Dusk*, pp. 63–64.

19. *Some Efforts of American Negroes for Their Own Social Betterment: Report of an Investigation under the Direction of Atlanta University; Together with the Proceedings of the Third Conference for the Study of the Negro Problems, held at Atlanta University, May 25–26, 1898*, pp. 37, 90, *et passim*. Elliott Rudwick, "W.E.B. Du Bois As Sociologist," p. 45, finds little nexus between assertions and conclusions in this third report.

20. *The Negro in Business: Report of a Social Study made under the Direction of Atlanta University; Together with the Proceedings of the Fourth Conference for the Study of the Negro Problems, held at Atlanta University, May 30–31, 1899*; Governor Allan D. Candler quoted—*ibid.*, pp. 53–54; Du Bois quoted—*ibid.*, p. 5.

21. Du Bois's business-league idea: see "Resolutions of Conference," in *The Negro in Business*, p. 50; also Aptheker, *Annotated Bibliography*, p. 527; and Harlan, *B. T. Washington*, I, p. 266. John Hope, "The Meaning of Business," *The Negro in Business*, pp. 56–57.

22. Du Bois, "Testimony before U.S. Industrial Commission," *Report on Immigration, Including Testimony . . .*, p. 83. *The College-Bred Negro American: Report of a Social Study Made by Atlanta University under the Patronage of the Trustees of the John F. Slater Fund; with the Proceedings of the 15th Annual Conference for the Study of the Negro Problems, held at Atlanta University on May 24, 1910*, p. 83—the 1910 college-bred study is an expansion of the fifth AU Study of 1900. The Arno Press edition does not contain the fifth (1900) study. See Aptheker, *Annotated Bibliography*, pp. 527.

23. ". . . *common school education.*": quoted in *ibid.*, p. 528. The fifth and fifteenth studies should be consulted in conjunction with the sixth and sixteenth, *The Common School and the Negro American: Report of a Social Study Made by Atlanta University under the Patronage of the Trustees of the John F. Slater Fund, with Proceedings of the 16th Annual Conference for the Study of the Negro Problems, held at Atlanta University on May 30, 1911* [*a reprise of the 1901 common school study*].

24. *The Negro Artisan: Report of a Social Study Made under the Direction of Atlanta University; Together with the Proceedings of the Seventh Conference for the Study of Negro Problems, held at Atlanta University, on May 27, 1902* (*repeated in 1912 as report no. 17*), pp. 158, 188. Rudwick, "Du Bois As Sociologist," p. 47, ranks both artisan studies as the best of the Atlanta University Studies. It should be noted that Du Bois's endeavor to refine his labor data for incorporation in a paper to be presented to the American Economic Association resulted in a curt reply from the head of the American Federation of Labor: Samuel Gompers to W.E.B. Du Bois, Jan. 5, 1903, Du Bois Papers/

U. Mass.—"let me say further, that I have more important work to attend to than to correct 'copy' for your paper."

The debate as to which party bears greater culpability for the exclusion of African-Americans from the labor movement—organized labor or industrialists—is a standoff. For two contrasting interpretations, see the synoptic view presented by David Montgomery, *The Fall of the House of Labor: The Workplace, the State, and American Labor Activism, 1865–1925*, esp. pp. 82–86, in which capital is seen at its divide-and-conquer worst, as it separates, splits, and subordinates black, yellow, and brown newcomers from white workers as the former enter the industrial centers from the "periphery"; Philip Foner, by contrast, in *Organized Labor and the Black Worker, 1619–1981* (New York: International Publishers, 1982), esp. 70–81—"Gompers," Foner believes (p. 75), "for all his eloquent pleas for unity of all workers regardless of race, color, or national origin, was basically a bigot."

25. ". . . extraordinary growth and vitality.": *The Negro Church: Report of a Social Study Made under the Direction of Atlanta University; Together with Proceedings of the Eighth Conference for the Study of Negro Problems, held at Atlanta University, May 26, 1903*; Du Bois quoted—*ibid.*, pp. 5, 3–4. *The Negro American Family: Report of a Social Study Made Principally by the College Classes of 1909 and 1910 of Atlanta University, under the Patronage of the Trustees of the John F. Slater Fund; Together with the Proceedings of the 13th Annual Conference for the Study of the Negro Problems, held at Atlanta University, May 26, 1908*, p. 13.

26. ". . . what slavery meant.": *The Negro American Family*, p. 37; *The Negro Church*, pp. 86, 88.

27. Budgeting the AU Studies: *Autobiography*, p. 252; Bacote, *Atlanta University*, p. 138. Puzzling philanthropy: Carnegie did give Atlanta University $25,000 for a library in 1905—*ibid.*, p. 201; Harlan, *B. T. Washington*, II, p. 135; Rockefeller beneficence other than to Tuskegee was directed to the Atlanta Baptist Female Seminary, renamed in 1884 Spelman College, for Mrs. John D. Rockefeller, and recipient of funds for the institution's first brick building (Rockefeller Hall)—Florence Matilda Read, *The Story of Spelman College* (Atlanta, 1961), pp. 82, 93; see, too, Henry Allen Bullock, *A History of Negro Education in the South: From 1619 to the Present*, pp. 77, 89. Francis Jackson Garrison to Oswald Garrison Villard, May 12, 1902, in *B. T. Washington Papers*, VI, p. 548.

28. AU Studies lauded (*Spectator, Journal of Sociology, Outlook*, etc.): appended to *The Health and Physique of the Negro-American. Report of a Social Study Made under the Direction of Atlanta University; Together with the Proceedings of the Eleventh Conference for the Study of the Negro Problems, held at Atlanta University, on May 29, 1906*, pp. 111–12. Clifford Raymond, "Cultured Negro Model for Race," Chicago *Tribune*, June 18, 1903, p. 1, in Du Bois Papers/U. Mass.; also Aptheker, *Annotated Bibliography*, p. 18.

29. Edwin R. A. Seligman to W.E.B. Du Bois, Dec. 22, 1903, Du Bois Papers/U. Mass. Emmett Scott to W.E.B. Du Bois, June 12, 1902, Du Bois Papers/U. Mass.—"Mr. Washington has gone North for the summer. He very thoroughly enjoyed his visit to Atlanta and the opportunity provided to speak before your Conference."

30. On Gladden and Du Bois: see Ronald G. White, Jr., and C. Howard Hopkins, *The Social Gospel: Religion and Reform in a Changing America* (Philadelphia: Temple University Press, 1976), ch. 10 ("The Souls of Black Folk"), pp. 103–113, p. 107. [I wish to thank Professor Maceo C. Dailey of Spelman College for bringing this reference to my attention on Sept. 5, 1990.] *Sozialwissenschaft und Sozialpolitik*: Max Weber to W.E.B. Du Bois, Mar. 30, 1905, Du Bois Papers/U. Mass.; and Aptheker, ed., *Correspondence*, I, p. 106; and see Aptheker, "Introduction," in *SOBF*, p. 35; "Die Negerfrage in den Vereinigten Staaten," *Archiv fur Sozialwissenschaft und Sozialpolitik*, 22 (Jan. 1906): 31–79, in Aptheker, ed., *Writings in Periodical Literature, 1891–1901*, I, pp. 277–312.

31. *Dusk*, p. 84. William James to W.E.B. Du Bois, May 23, 1907, Du Bois Papers/ U. Mass.; also Aptheker, *Correspondence*, I, p. 133. "Methods and Results of Ten Years' Study of the American Negro," May 30, 1905, in Du Bois Papers/U. Mass., includes list of conference participants. "L'Ouvrier negre en Amérique," *La Revue économique internationale*, 4 (Nov. 1906): 298–348, in Aptheker, *Annotated Bibliography*, p. 25.

32. ". . . act on the truth.": Du Bois Interview/Columbia OHP, pp. 146–47.

33. ". . . turn aside from my work.": *ibid.*, p. 148; *Autobiography*, p. 222; *Dusk*, p. 67; "A Pageant in Seven Decades," p. 254.

34. ". . . easily forthcoming.": *Autobiography*, p. 222. Du Bois, "Two Negro Conventions," *Independent*, 51 (Sept. 7, 1899): 2425–27; also Aptheker, ed., *Periodical Literature*, pp. 60–63, p. 60.

35. ". . . set the prisoned free.": *SOBF*, pp, 213, 211, 209.

36. ". . . toward life and the world.": Du Bois, "I Bury My Wife," p. 39. Henry F. May's judgment that Du Bois embraced the "culture of the most conservative custodians, and [that] the way he talked about it was soon rejected" should be noted: Henry F. May, *The End of Innocence. A Study of the First Years of Our Time, 1912–1917* (New York: Alfred A. Knopf, 1959), p. 87.

37. Du Bois, "I Bury My Wife," p. 39. Fielding H. Garrison, *An Introduction to the History of Medicine* (Philadelphia: W. Saunders & Co., 1966), 4th ed., p. 683.

38. *SOBF*, p. 212.

39. . . . a nervous breakdown.: Du Bois's averral is obtained from his medical history in the Life Extension Institute, Inc., report, Oct. 6, 1933, forwarded to Louis T. Wright, Du Bois's personal physician, Du Bois Papers/U. Mass. Harlan, ed., *B. T. Washington Papers*, I, p. 119; also *ibid.*, V, pp. 54–58.

40. Boston speech—quoted: Harlan, ed., *B. T. Washington Papers*, V, p. 55. Washington on the Hose lynching: *ibid.*, V, pp. 90–91—"I would like to speak at length upon these Georgia occurrences and others of a like nature . . . but in view of my position and hopes in the interest of the Tuskegee Institute and the education of our people, I feel constrained to keep silent." ". . . three months rest.": *Autobiography*, p. 372.

41. Albert B. Hart to B. T. Washington, June 5, 1899 [p. 127], in Harlan, ed., *B. T. Washington Papers*, V. Du Bois and Tuskegee negotiations: "A Pageant in Seven Decades," p. 255. W.E.B. Du Bois to B. T. Washington, July 12, 1899 [p. 152].

42. ". . . with many causes."—Du Bois quoted: Harlan, *B. T. Washington*, I, p. 175; Du Bois, "Two Negro Conventions," reproduced in *Literature*, I, p. 62; Meier, *Negro Thought in America*, pp. 129–30. Emma Lou Thornborough, "The National Afro-American League, 1887–1908," *Journal of Southern History*, 27 (Nov. 1961): 494–512, pp. 503–4.

43. Emmett Scott, described—in Harlan, *B. T. Washington*, I, p. 260. "Ransom, Reverdy Cassius (1861–1959)" *DANB*, pp. 512–14. On Du Bois at Chicago meeting: Emmett Scott to B. T. Washington, Aug. 23, 1899, in Harlan, ed., *B. T. Washington Papers*, V, p. 181. Washington's ambiguous civil rights behavior: Harlan, *B. T. Washington*, I, p. 291; B. T. Washington, *Black-Belt Diamonds*, pp. 6–8; Meier, *Negro Thought*, pp. 108–16.

44. Du Bois and Washington collaborating: Henry Hugh Proctor, *Between Black and White*, p. 102; Harlan, *B. T. Washington*, I, p. 292; Rudwick, *Du Bois*, p. 54. ". . . we heartily endorse it.": Du Bois, "The Suffrage Fight in Georgia," *Independent*, Nov. 30, 1899; also in Aptheker, ed., *Periodical Literature*, I, p. 65.

45. ". . . small towns, and cities.": B. T. Washington to W.E.B. Du Bois, Oct. 26, 1899, in Harlan, ed., *B. T. Washington Papers*, V, p. 245; Du Bois Interview/Columbia OHP, p. 157.

46. Three articles: "The Negro and Crime," May 18, 1899; "Two Negro Conventions," Sept. 7, 1899; "The Suffrage Fight in Georgia," Nov. 30, 1899—all in *Independent*; also Aptheker, *Annotated Bibliography*, pp. 11–12. W.E.B. Du Bois to Hollis B. Frissell, Jan. 18, 1899 [holograph], in Hollis B. Frissell Papers/Hampton University Archives. Du Bois, "A Negro Schoolmaster in the New South," *Atlantic Monthly*, 83 (Jan. 1899): 99–104.

47. W.E.B. Du Bois to B. T. Washington, Feb. 17, 1900 [p. 444]; and W.E.B. Du Bois to B. T. Washington, Feb. 26, 1900 [p. 450]—in *B. T. Washington Papers*, V, p. 444.

48. Descriptions of Tuskegee on show: Harlan, *B. T. Washington*, I, p. 286; Mary Church Terrell, *A Colored Woman in a White World* (Washington, D.C.: National Association of Colored Women's Clubs, 1968), pp. 191–92; commenting on Tuskegee's vaunted display of cows being rapidly milked on stage, Bond, *Education of the Negro*, p. 10, wryly noted, "It is hardly necessary to remember that there is no 'Negro way' of milking a cow: there is a right way and a wrong way." L. Albert Scipio II, *Pre-War Days at Tuskegee: Historical Essay on Tuskegee Institute (1881–1943)* (Silver Spring, Md.: Roman Publications, 1987) is an excellent source for early Tuskegee, replete with period photographs and maps.

49. Du Bois to Booker T. Washington, Feb. 17, 1900, in Harlan, ed., *B. T. Washington Papers*, V, p. 443. ". . . forces started moving in Washington": *Autobiography*, p. 252.

50. W.E.B. Du Bois to Booker T. Washington, Feb. 17 [p. 444], and Feb. 26 [p. 450], 1900 [my italics], in *B. T. Washington Papers*, V. ". . . forward it to Washington?": W.E.B. Du Bois to Hollis B. Frissell [holograph], Mar. 1, 1900, Hollis B. Frissell Papers/Hampton University Archives.

51. Du Bois, "Petition of Negroes to Use the Carnegie Library," 1902/1903, in Du Bois Papers/U. Mass. On Washington, D.C., and its public school system: Gatewood, *Aristocrats of Color*, pp. 256–62; Constance McLaughlin Green, *The Secret City*, p. 210; David L. Lewis, *District of Columbia: A Bicentennial History* (New York: W. W. Norton & Co., 1976), pp. 71–74, 105–10.

52. ". . . help [him] on.": Hollis B. Frissell to W.E.B. Du Bois, Mar. 10, 1900, in H. B. Frissell Papers/Hampton University Archives; *Autobiography*, p. 243. "Terrell, Robert Herberton (1857–1925)," *DANB*, pp. 585–86; "Terrell, Mary Church (1863–1954)," *DANB*, pp. 583–85.

53. ". . . by a nod of assent.": Richard W. Thompson to B. T. Washington, Mar. 14 [p. 463], and Mar. 27 [pp. 473–74], 1900; Timothy Thomas Fortune to B. T. Washington, Mar. 12 [pp. 459–60], and Mar. 16 [p. 465], 1900; John Wesley Ross to B. T. Washington, Mar. 6 [p. 452], and Mar. 12 [p. 459], 1900—all in Harlan, ed., *B. T. Washington Papers*, V.

54. ". . . to a man are against him.": William A. Pledger to B. T. Washington, Mar. 16, 1900, in Harlan, ed., *B. T. Washington Papers*, V, p. 466; "Pledger, William A[nderson] (1851?–1904)": *DANB*, pp. 496–97. John R. Francis to B. T. Washington, Mar. 22, 1900, in Harlan, ed., *B. T. Washington Papers*, V, p. 466 (note 1).

55. William H. Councill, a rival: "Councill, William Hooper (1849–1909)" *DANB*, p. 138; see Meier, *Negro Thought*, p. 209, who states that "few careers so vividly illustrate the transition from agitation and politics to sycophancy, economics, and self-help as do Councill's." Harlan's observations are equally instructive, in Harlan, *B. T. Washington*, I, pp. 168–70. A note of alarm is unmistakable in the Bookerite correspondence about Councill at this time—Timothy Thomas Fortune to B. T. Washington, Mar. 12 [pp. 459–60], 1900; B. T. Washington to Timothy Thomas Fortune, Mar. 14 [pp. 460–61], 1900; Timothy Thomas Fortune to B. T. Washington, Mar. 16 [p. 465], 1900—all in *B. T. Washington Papers*, V. ". . . working in the same direction.": B. T. Washington to Timothy Thomas Fortune, Mar. 18, 1900, in *ibid*, p. 467.

56. ". . . Yours truly . . .": B. T. Washington to W.E.B. Du Bois, Mar. 11, 1900, Du Bois Papers/U. Mass.; also Aptheker, ed., *Correspondence*, I, p. 44.

57. The "Tuskegee Machine.": *Autobiography*, p. 252.

10. Clashing Temperaments

1. "Wizard of Tuskegee.": For details of Washington's intellectual formation and arrival on the national scene, see the superlative biography by Louis R. Harlan, *Booker T. Washington, I, The Making of a Black Leader, 1856–1901, II, The Wizard of Tuskegee, 1901–1915*, I, chs. 2–3; and August Meier, *Negro Thought in America, 1880–1915: Racial Ideologies in the Age of Booker T. Washington*, pp. 100–18.

2. Washington, *Black-Belt Diamonds, Gems from the Speeches, Addresses, and Talks to Students*: (on lynching), p. 72; (on slavery), p. 10; (on suffering), p. 5. "Darky" jokes: (Harvard) Harlan, *B. T. Washington*, I, p. 236; (Negroes and mules) *ibid.*, I, p. 47. ". . . hen-house in de *day*-time?": Harlan, *B. T. Washington*, I, p. 124.

3. Washington reproved: Martha Calhoun to B. T. Washington, Dec. 18, 1900, in Harlan, ed., *The B. T. Washington Papers*, 13 vols., V, p. 629; "Booker T. Washington. What the Negroes Think of Him," Washington *Bee*, Dec. 2, 1899. Faith in white South: Washington, *Black-Belt Diamonds*, p. 10. ". . . more leaders in commerce."—Washington quoted: *ibid.*, I, pp. 28–29.

4. National Negro Business League: refer to chapter 9, note 21 *supra* and chapter 10, note 13 *infra*. ". . . put on for him.": *ibid.*, p. 28.

5. ". . . spreading to the South.": Du Bois, *Dusk of Dawn*, p. 74.

6. Baldwin's personality and public activities: see Harlan, *B. T. Washington*, I, pp. 215–16, 319–20; and *ibid.*, II, pp. 135–36 *et passim*; also biographical note 2, in Harlan, ed., *B. T. Washington Papers*, III, pp. 529–30. ". . . by the intelligent negroes."—Baldwin quoted: "Problems of Negro Education," Springfield *Republican*, Aug. 25, 1898.

7. ". . . educated at Harvard College": William H. Baldwin, Jr., to Henry C. Davis, Feb. 21, 1900, Harlan, ed., *B. T. Washington Papers*, V, p. 445. ". . . controlled by colored people.": Robert W. Thompson to B. T. Washington, Mar. 27, 1900, in *ibid.*, V, p. 376.

8. ". . . general cause of the Negro.": W.E.B. Du Bois to B. T. Washington, Feb. 17, 1900, Harlan, ed., *B. T. Washington Papers*, V, p. 444. ". . . my associate Commissioners.": John Wesley Ross to B. T. Washington, Mar. 12, 1900, in *ibid.*, V, p. 459.

9. Paris Exposition: Du Bois, "The American Negro at Paris," in Aptheker, ed., *Writings in Periodical Literature*, 3 vols., I, pp. 86–88. ". . . refuse Negroes sleeping car accommodations?": W.E.B. Du Bois to S. H. Hardwick [assistant general passenger agent], Mar. 15, 1900, Du Bois Papers/U. Mass.; also in Aptheker, ed., *The Correspondence of W.E.B. Du Bois [Selected]*, 3 vols., I, pp. 45–46; W.E.B. Du Bois to B. T. Washington, Mar. 16, 1900, in Harlan, ed., *B. T. Washington Papers*, V, p. 464.

10. " 'We don't travel much.' ": *Autobiography*, p. 235.

11. Ida B. Wells's suit: related in Alfred A. M. Duster, ed., *Ida B. Wells-Barnett—Crusade for Justice: The Autobiography of Ida B. Wells* (Chicago and London: University of Chicago Press, 1970), pp. 18–20; see "Barnett, Ida Bell (1862–1931)" *DANB*, pp. 30–31. Wizard's legal assistance: complicated story, Harlan, *B. T. Washington*, II, pp. 247–49. ". . . interstate travel.": W.E.B. Du Bois to B. T. Washington, Mar. 16, 1900, in *B. T. Washington Papers*, V, p. 464.

12. ". . . liberal interpretation of the Law.": William H. Baldwin, Jr., to B. T. Washington, Mar. 19, 1900, in Harlan, ed., *B. T. Washington Papers*, V, p. 468. Harlan notes (*B. T. Washington*, II, p. 248) that Washington ignored Baldwin's advice and continued to

support Du Bois's plan to sue the railroad. The vigor of Washington's support, however, may have struck Du Bois as increasingly ambiguous—even suspect—as it unfolded in letters and telephone exchanges about attorneys' fees and the obduracy of the railroad's lawyer, Robert Todd Lincoln. On April 7, 1901, Du Bois wrote to ask Washington's advice about consulting a District of Columbia law firm (in Harlan, ed., *B. T. Washington Papers,* VI, p. 91). On November 22, 1902 (*ibid.*, VI, p. 590), Du Bois wrote again to inform Washington that he had organized a defense committee and asked Washington, "Are you still disposed to stand part of the expenses and if so what part?" On November 28, 1902 (*ibid.*, VI, pp. 597–98), Washington replied that he could not be associated with Du Bois's committee, but that he would assume an unspecified portion of the legal fees, "provided I can hand it to you personally." Du Bois's suit was finally abandoned.

13. Du Bois declines "very generous offer.": W.E.B. Du Bois to B. T. Washington, Apr. 10, 1900, Du Bois Papers/U. Mass.; also *B. T. Washington Papers,* V, p. 480. National Negro Business League: W.E.B. Du Bois to B. T. Washington, Apr. 10, 1900, in *B. T. Washington Papers,* V, p. 480; Harlan, *B. T. Washington,* I, pp. 266–67; and see Du Bois, *The Negro in Business. Report of the Social Study Made under the Direction of Atlanta University; Together with the Proceedings of the Fourth Conference for the Study of the Negro Problems, held at Atlanta University, May 30–31, 1899* ("Resolutions of Conference"), p. 50.

14. Tuskegee Conference: W.E.B. Du Bois to B. T. Washington, Feb. 11, 1901, in Harlan, ed., *B. T. Washington Papers,* VI, p. 33; Du Bois, "Results of the Ten Tuskegee Conferences," *Harper's Weekly,* 45 (June 22, 1910): 641—in Harlan, ed., *Periodical Literature,* I, pp. 90–91; B. T. Washington, "The Negro in Business," *Gunton's Magazine,* 20 (Mar. 1901): 209–19 [reproduced in Harlan, ed., *B. T. Washington Papers,* VI, pp. 76–88, esp. p. 80]. Strained cordiality: W.E.B. Du Bois to B. T. Washington, July 3, 1901, accepting invitation to go camping in West Virginia, in Harlan, ed., *B. T. Washington Papers,* VI, p. 165; "Camp in West Va.," *Colored American,* Sept. 14, 1901, news story lists campers and the fact that the C. C. & S. Railroad has placed a private Pullman at Washington's disposal. Du Bois was unable to join the party—in *ibid.*, VI, p. 209. Robert Todd Lincoln's rebuff: Harlan, *B. T. Washington,* II, p. 248.

15. The assistant superintendency scramble: James A. Cobb to Emmett Scott, July 12, Aug. 17, Sept. 3, Sept. 13, and Sept. 29, 1906—all in Charles H. Thompson Papers. Cobb letter of Sept. 3, 1906, is particularly suggestive: "The school question is warmer than ever, Du Bois is turning heaven and earth to be appointed superintendent. . . . The friends of Du Bois are trying to cut him [Montgomery] and place Du Bois in his place. Mrs. Terrell came home Saturday night and hasn't slept any since." [Also reproduced in Harlan, ed., *B. T. Washington Papers,* IX, p. 68.] ". . . possibly do it.": Emmett Scott to James A. Cobb, Aug. 21, 1906, in Charles H. Thompson Papers (Unprocessed), Moorland-Spingarn Research Center/Howard University; and, in particular, "[Editorial] Mr. Roscoe Conkling Bruce," Washington *Bee,* May 18, 1912, p. 4—"If Mr. Bruce should drop out from his position today, Dr. Du Bois would be among the first seeking to insure the good-will of the white trustees in order to get the place now held by Mr. Bruce; he has made several unsuccessful attempts in the past." I am highly appreciative of Mrs. Esme Bhan who called this valuable unprocessed collection to my attention, and to Mr. Carroll Miller, emeritus dean in the school of education at Howard University, whose knowledge of this collection is unexcelled.

16. Du Bois abroad: Du Bois, "The American Negro at Paris," *Periodical Literature,* p. 86. Italy's defeat as harbinger: Du Bois, *Africa—Its Place in Modern History* (Millwood, N.Y.: Kraus-Thomson, 1977; orig. pub. 1930), pp. 63–64; *Dusk of Dawn,* p. 52; David Levering Lewis, *The Race to Fashoda: European Colonialism and African Resistance in the*

Scramble for Africa (New York: Weidenfeld and Nicolson, 1987), ch. 5, esp. pp. 120–21. "lived in a Republic."—James quoted: David Levering Lewis, *Prisoners of Honor: The Dreyfus Affair* (New York: William Morrow & Co., 1973), p. 299.

17. Exposition Universelle: Du Bois, *ibid.*, pp. 2–3; Du Bois, "The American Negro at Paris," p. 86; Jacques Chastenet, *Histoire de la Troisieme Republique* (Paris: Librairie Hachette, 1952–63), 7 vols., III, *La Republique Triomphante, 1893–1906*, pp. 181–86; Lewis, *Prisoners of Honor*, pp. 305–6. ". . . itself and its future: W.E.B. Du Bois, *The World and Africa* (Millwood, N.Y.: Kraus-Thomson, 1976; orig. pub. 1947), p. 2.

18. ". . . studying . . . prospects.": Du Bois, "Negroes at Paris," pp. 88–89; Du Bois, *World and Africa*, p. 2.

19. Victorian Pan-Africanism: see Owen Charles Mathurin, *Henry Sylvester Williams and the Origins of the Pan-African Movement, 1869–1911* (Westport, Conn.: Greenwood Press, 1976), esp. p. 43; Rodney Carlisle, *The Roots of Black Nationalism*, pp. 85, 116; Immanuel Geiss, *The Pan-African Movement: A History of Pan-Africanism in America, Europe and Africa*, pp. 5–6, ch. 9; Wilson J. Moses, *The Golden Age of Black Nationalism, 1850–1925*, pp. 7, 11. ". . . good of that continent."—Blyden, quoted: Hollis R. Lynch, "The Attitude of Edward W. Blyden to European Imperialism in Africa," *Journal of the Historical Society of Nigeria*, 3 (Dec. 1965): 249–59, p. 254.

20. Washington on the Pan-African Congress: B. T. Washington, "To the Editor," Indianapolis *Freeman*, Aug. 12, 1899, p. 1 [in Harlan, ed., *B. T. Washington Papers*, V, pp. 154–57, p. 156]; Clarence G. Contee, *Henry Sylvester Williams and the Origins of Organizational Pan-Africanism: 1897–1902* (Washington, D.C.: Department of History, Howard University, 1973), p. 11. Wizard's motives: B. T. Washington, "To the Editor," Washington *Colored American*, Aug. 19, 1899, p. 6, stated that he saw "no way out of our present condition in the South by returning to Africa. Aside from other almost insurmountable obstacles, there is no place in Africa for us to go where our own condition would be improved. All Europe, especially England, France, and Germany, have been running a mad race during the last twenty years, to see which could gobble up the greater part of Africa, and there is practically nothing left." [Reproduced in *B. T. Washington Papers*, V, 164–66, p. 164.]; Harlan, *B. T. Washington*, I, p. 242.

21. U.S. delegates to congress: Du Bois, "Report of the Pan-African Conference, July 23, 24, 25, 1900 [typescript]," in Du Bois Papers/U. Mass.; Contee, *Williams*, p. 13; Mathurin, *Williams*, pp. 65–69; Alexander Walters, *My Life and Work* (New York: Fleming H. Revell Co., 1917), pp. 253–55; "Walters, Alexander (1858–1917)," *DANB*, pp. 630–31; "Cooper, Anna Julia (1858–1964)" *DANB*, pp. 128–29; and Louise Daniel Hutchinson, *Anna J. Cooper: A Voice from the South* (1981), p. 112.

22. Relations between Washington and Walters: Harlan, *B. T. Washington*, II, p. 40; and Meier, *Negro Thought*, pp. 130, 180–81. ". . . between that country and ours.": Walters, *My Life and Work*, p. 173.

23. Pan-African peers: Walters, *My Life and Work*, pp. 255–61; and see Contee, *Williams*, pp. 7–10; Jeffrey P. Green, "West Indian Doctors in London: John Alcindor (1873–1924) and James Jackson Brown (1882–1953)," *Journal of Caribbean History*, 20 (1985–6): 49–77, pp. 56–57; and Mathurin, *Williams*, p. 74.

24. Manners and message of Pan-Africanists: see *ibid.*, Mathurin, *Williams*, pp. 55, 71; Contee, *Williams*, p. 11; Walters, *My Life and Work*, p. 261; Du Bois, "Report of the Pan-African Conference, July 23, 24, 25, 1900."

25. Du Bois on Sylvester Williams: Du Bois, *The World and Africa*, p. 2, omitted any mention of the 1900 conference; Mathurin, *Williams*, pp. 74–75, notes that Du Bois first mentioned Williams in a 1945 "Winds of Change" article in the Chicago *Defender*; curiously, in that article, "Revival of Pan-Africanism," Sept. 29, 1945, Du Bois twice

referred to Sylvester Williams not by name but only as a "West Indian barrister." [Reproduced in Aptheker, ed., *Newspaper Columns by W.E.B. Du Bois* (White Plains, N.Y.: Kraus-Thomson, 1986), 2 vols., II, p. 656.]

26. ". . . held before Europe.": "To the Nations of the World," in *Report of the Pan-African Conference*, reproduced in Aptheker, ed., *Writings in Non-Periodical Literature* (Millwood, N.Y.: Kraus-Thomson, 1982), pp. 11–12, p. 11.

27. Mathurin, *Williams*, p. 71; Contee, *Williams*, pp. 7, 11.

28. Nina Du Bois's behavior: Mildred Johnson, taped interview, May 1977/David Levering Lewis/Schomburg Center for Research in Black Culture; Usher interview/D. L. L.; Du Bois Williams, taped interview, July 1987/D.L.L.

29. For George A. Towns, consult James Weldon Johnson, *Along This Way: The Autobiography of James Weldon Johnson*, pp. 103, 137, 239; Bacote, *Atlanta University*, p. 130; Ridgely Torrence, *The Story of John Hope* (New York: Arno Press, 1969; orig. pub. 1948), p. 134; and my own adolescent recollections of George Towns, a neighbor.

30. On John and Lugenia Hope: *Autobiography*, p. 287; *Dusk*, pp. 315, 318; "Hope, John (1868–1936)" *DANB*, pp. 321–25; Jacqueline Anne Rouse, *Lugenia Burns Hope: Black Southern Reformer* (Athens and London: University of Georgia Press, 1989); Torrence, *Story of John Hope*, esp. pp. 104–5.

31. Hopes during the Civil War: Torrence, *Story of John Hope*, pp. 29–33. Creoles in the South: In addition to Torrence, several useful monographs on this complex subject are, Carolyn Bond Day, *A Study of Negro-White Families in the United States*; Gatewood, *Aristocrats of Color*, pp. 80–89; Rodolphe Desdunes, *Our People and Our History* (Baton Rouge: Louisiana State University Press, 1973; orig. pub. 1911, as *Nos hommes et notre histoire*); Joel Williamson, *New People: Miscegenation and Mulattoes in the United States*; notes 23 and 24 in chapter 4, *supra*, should be reviewed. ". . . were to that extent ahead."—Hope, quoted: Torrence, *Story of John Hope*, p. 54. ". . . white people in so doing."—Channing Tobias, quoted: *ibid.*, p. 59.

32. Significance of Hamburg: Eric Foner, *Reconstruction: America's Unfinished Revolution, 1863–1877*, pp. 570–71; Joel Williamson, *After Slavery: The Negro in South Carolina during Reconstruction, 1861–1877* (New York: W. W. Norton and Co., 1965, 1975), p. 270. ". . . Hamburg Massacre."—Hope, quoted: Torrence, *Story of John Hope*, p. 50, and pp. 48–50.

33. On William Jefferson White: Torrence, *Story of John Hope*, pp. 54–55; Meier, *Negro Thought*, pp. 221–2. ". . . hollow of his hand."—Du Bois, quoted: Torrence, *Story of John Hope*, p. 55.

34. ". . . we demand *social* equality."—Hope, quoted: Torrence, *Story of John Hope*, pp. 114–15.

35. Washington's *Realpolitik*: Harlan, *B. T. Washington*, I, p. 254, observes that the Wizard "became a minority group boss"; and pp. 256–58 and chap. 13 ("The Tuskegee Machine") *passim.*; also Meier, *Negro Thought*, pp. 248–55. Carnegie and Washington: Harlan, *B. T. Washington*, II, pp. 290, 133–37; Joseph Frazier Wall, *Andrew Carnegie* (New York: Oxford University Press, 1970), pp. 972–73.

36. "no ordinary darkey"—Armstrong quoted: Harlan, *B. T. Washington*, I, p. 152.

37. "Understand that."—Governor Oates, quoted: *ibid.*, I, p. 231. *SOBF*, p. 3. ". . . makes himself worthy."—Washington, quoted: Harlan, *B. T. Washington*, I, pp. 124–25.

38. All-purpose wisdom: advice to Park—Fred Matthews, *Quest for an American Sociology*, p. 80.; Meier, *Negro Thought*, p. 109.

39. Wizard's covert civil rights: W.E.B. Du Bois to B. T. Washington, Mar. 16, 1900,

Du Bois Papers/U. Mass.; Aptheker, *Correspondence*, I, p. 45; and Harlan, ed., *B. T. Washington Papers*, V, p. 464; (Alonzo Bailey) Harlan, *B. T. Washington*, I, p. 259; Meier, *Negro Thought*, p. 113; (Tennessee, Georgia, Virginia rail segregation) *ibid.*, p. 111; Harlan, *B. T. Washington*, I, pp. 296–99.

40. Faustian bargain—Washington, quoted: Meier, *Negro Thought*, p. 111; Harlan, *B. T. Washington*, I, pp. 220–23; Anderson, *The Education of Blacks in the South, 1860–1935*, esp. p. 92; Williamson, *Crucible of Race*, pp. 71–72; Rayford W. Logan, *The Betrayal of the Negro: From Rutherford B. Hayes to Woodrow Wilson*, pp. 283–85, esp. p. 285, in which Logan rightly "wonders whether the disfranchising constitutions adopted during the following ten years by Louisiana, North Carolina, Virginia, Alabama and Georgia fitted into the solution."

41. ". . . rout the 'ins.' ": quoted in J. Morgan Kousser, *The Shaping of Southern Politics, Suffrage Restriction and the Establishment of the One-Party South, 1880–1910* (New Haven: Yale University Press, 1974), p. 18; John Cell, *The Highest Stage of White Supremacy*, pp. 178–79, 184–87; C. Vann Woodward, *Origins of the New South*, pp. 209–218.

42. Potential black-white coalition: Kousser, *Southern Politics*, pp. 18, 147; Cell, *Highest Stage*, pp. 178–79, 184–87; Frederickson, *White Supremacy*, ch. 6; Woodward, *Origins*, p. 256. Black disfranchisement: Franklin, *From Slavery to Freedom*, p. 265. ". . . They . . . own the property."—Washington quoted: Hawkins, *Booker T. Washington and His Critics*, p. 12.

43. ". . . disfranchise the worst . . . whites.": Joel Williamson, *Crucible of Race*, p. 231. ". . . my shoes every evening."—Vardaman quoted: Franklin, *From Slavery to Freedom*, p. 266; and William F. Holmes, *The White Chief: James Kimble Vardaman*, p. 99.

44. Future in the South: Washington, *Black-Belt Diamonds*, p. 10. ". . . darkey am called to preach."—Washington, quoted: Hugh Hawkins, *Washington and His Critics*, pp. 15–16.

45. ". . . falsehood and sin.": Du Bois, "Career Open to College-Bred Negroes," in *Non-Periodical Literature*, 1–10, p. 10, and pp. 5–6; Washington, "A Draft of an Address at Hampton Institute," in Harlan, ed., *B. T. Washington Papers*, IV, pp. 406–8.

46. Du Bois, "The Freedmen's Bureau," *Atlantic Monthly*, 87 (Mar. 1901): 354–65; and "Results of the Ten Tuskegee Conferences," *Harper's Weekly*, 45 (June 22, 1901): 641 (reproduced in *Periodical Literature*, I, 90–91).

47. *Up From Slavery:* Harlan, ed., *B. T. Washington Papers*, I, pp. xxviii, 207, 307–8. ". . . five thousand . . . for your institute.": in *ibid.*, I, p. xxx; (W. T. Harris, Barrett Wendell), in *ibid.*, I, pp. xxix, xxxii.

48. ". . . Assisi would receive this!": Du Bois, "The Evolution of Negro Leadership," *Dial*, 31 (July 16, 1901): 53–55 [reproduced in Aptheker, ed., *Book Reviews by W.E.B. Du Bois* (Millwood, N.Y.: KTO Press. A U.S. Division of Kraus-Thomson Organization Ltd., 1977), pp. 3–5]; also in Harlan, ed., *B. T. Washington Papers*, VI, 175–78, (*Book Rev.*) p. 5.

11. The Souls of Black Folk

1. ". . . cooperate with Tuskegee in its work.": W.E.B. Du Bois to B. T. Washington, Mar. 4, 1902, in Louis R. Harlan, ed., *The Booker T. Washington Papers*, 13 vols., VI, p. 413. ". . . encouraged in your efforts.": B. T. Washington to W.E.B. Du Bois, July 15, 1902, Du Bois Papers/U. Mass.; also in Aptheker, ed., *The* [*Selected*] *Correspondence of W.E.B. Du Bois*, 3 vols., I, p. 46.

2. “. . . young men at Hampton and Tuskegee.” H. L. Wayland to Robert C. Ogden, Sept. 10, 1896, Box 6, Robert C. Ogden Papers/Library of Congress.

3. SEB and GEB organized: *The General Education Board. An Account of Its Activities: 1902–1914* (New York: The General Education Board, 1930), pp. 3–10; see Raymond B. Fosdick, *Adventure in Giving: The Story of the General Education Board, A Foundation Established by John D. Rockefeller* (New York: Harper & Row, 1962), pp. 8–14; Hugh C. Bailey, *Edgar Gardner Murphy: Gentle Progressive*, pp. 33–34, 142–43, 146; Louis R. Harlan, *Separate and Unequal: Public School Campaigns and Racism in the Southern Seaboard States, 1901–1915*, pp. 75–87; John Anderson, *The Education of Blacks in the South, 1860–1935*, pp. 83–87; Henry Allen Bullock, A *History of Negro Education in the South: From 1619 to the Present*, pp. 106–7; Horace Mann Bond, *The Education of the Negro in the American Social Order*, p. 138.

4. “. . . until after midnight.”—Curry quoted: Fosdick, *Adventure in Giving*, p. 8; and see Bailey, *Murphy*, p. 151.

5. Gates's influence: Fosdick, *Adventure in Giving*, pp. 13–14; and Gerald Jonas, *The Circuit Riders: Rockefeller Money and the Rise of Modern Science* (New York: W. W. Norton & Co., 1989), pp. 22–25. Muckraking: a concise account is Louis Filler's *Crusaders for American Liberalism* (Yellow Springs, Ohio: The Antioch Press, 1964; orig. pub. 1939), chs. 5 and 10; as well as the staples, Kathleen Brady, *Ida Tarbell: Portrait of a Muckraker* (New York: Seaview/Putnam, 1984), ch. 7. GEB endowment: *General Education Board . . . 1902–1914*, p. 16. “Scientific philanthropy”—a concept: see Jonas, *The Circuit Riders*, esp. p. 21; also Joseph Frazier Wall, *Andrew Carnegie*, p. 806.

6. GEB disbursements: Fosdick, *Adventure in Giving*, p. 1—the GEB's last grants were made in 1960. Between 1902 and 1960 appropriations from income totaled, according to Fosdick, $136,491,002.05, and from principal funds $187,703,918.78, for a total appropriation of $325 million. By the end of fiscal 1930, total appropriations to “white” academic institutions amounted to $176,984,883 and to “black” institutions $21,999,349; see also *Annual Report, 1930–1931*, p. 15. According to *General Education Board . . . 1902–1914*, p. 17, as of June 1914, a toal of $699,781.13 had been disbursed to Negro schools and colleges.

7. On Gates: *ibid.*, pp. 13–14; a curious letter from Wallace Buttrick to Robert C. Ogden, Dec. 27, 1905, Box 9, Robert C. Ogden Papers/L.C., describes Gates as a man of strange behavior. “. . . white people of the South.”—Buttrick, quoted: Harlan, *Separate and Unequal*, p. 94; also, Buttrick, discussed in Fosdick, *Adventure in Giving*, p. 11.

8. “. . . the decades since.”: Fosdick, *Adventure in Giving*, p. 11.

9. Washington's unhappy SEB exclusion: William Henry Baldwin, Jr., to B. T. Washington, Nov. 9, 1901, in Harlan, ed., *B. T. Washington Papers*, VI, p. 311; also Louis R. Harlan, *Booker T. Washington: The Wizard of Tuskegee, 1901–1915*, II, pp. 187–90.

10. Washington admonished: John Elmer Milholland to B. T. Washington, Feb. 12, 1903, VII [pp. 72–73]; William Lloyd Garrison, Jr., to B. T. Washington, Mar. 3, 1904, III [pp. 456–58]; Francis Jackson Garrison to Oswald Garrison Villard, Mar. 12, 1902, VI [pp. 458–59]—all in Harlan, ed., *B. T. Washington Papers.*

11. On northern philanthropists and the South: Anderson, *Education of Blacks in the South*, pp. 87–92; and John H. Stanfield, *Philanthropy and Jim Crow in American Social Science* (Westport, Conn.: Greenwood Press, 1985), pp. 6–9. Northern philanthropists were exceedingly gullible in their embrace of the New South—see Paul G. Gaston, *The New South Creed: A Study in Southern Mythmaking* (New York: Alfred A. Knopf, 1970), pp. 7, 221; also, for the reality of the myth, see Don H. Doyle, *New Men, New Cities, New South: Atlanta, Nashville, Charleston, Mobile, 1860–1910* (Chapel Hill: University of North Carolina Press, 1990), esp. pp. 90–96, 262–65. Mentality of violence: On the other hand,

the philanthropists were even more alarmist about regional violence—see Harlan, *Separate and Unequal*, p. 94; and Bailey, *Murphy*, pp. 116–17. Ogden's southern insight: Robert Custis Ogden to Dr. James E. Russell, Mar. 27, 1906, Box 9, Ogden Papers/L.C. ". . . useless—to challenge it."—Murphy quoted: Edgar Gardner Murphy to B. T. Washington, Jan. 31, 1903, Harlan, ed., *B. T. Washington Papers*, VII, p. 17; Harlan, *Separate and Unequal*, p. 94.

On historical and cultural impediments to modernity: see Wilbur J. Cash's classic, *The Mind of the South* (London: Thames and Hudson, 1971; orig. pub. 1941); Daniel Joseph Singal, *The War Within: From Victorian to Modernist Thought in the South, 1919 to 1945* (Chapel Hill: The University of North Carolina Press, 1982), esp. pp. 11–33; Morton Sosna's excellent, and politically more incisive, *In Search of the Silent South: Southern Liberals and the Race Issue* (New York: Columbia University Press, 1977), pp. 4–25; and Joel Williamson, *The Crucible of Race: Black-White Relations in the South since Emancipation*, ch. 6 ("In Violence Veritas"), an illumination of the sources of white racial rage as well as of the racialist eccentricities of the author's own analysis.

12. ". . . the hands of the few.": Wall, *Carnegie*, p. 807.

13. ". . . the average outside hand.": Charles E. Whiting to Samuel Chapman Armstrong, Dec. 28, 1878, and Jan. 21, 1879, Box 6, Ogden Papers/L.C.

14. Southern urban tensions: Robert C. Ogden to Mrs. Arthur Gilman, May 12, 1903, Box 7, Ogden Papers/L.C.—". . . the aim of the whole institution [Hampton] is to create labor leaders and common school teachers. One great problem is to attach the Negro to the soil and prevent his exodus from the country to the city." Baldwin was of the opinion that the African-American "will willingly fill the more menial positions, do the heavy work, at less wages," leaving the "more expert labor" to whites—quoted in Harlan, *Separate and Unequal*, p. 78. On the urban South and segregation: Cell, *The Highest Stage of White Supremacy*, pp. 131–70; Doyle, *New Men, New Cities, New South*, pp. 11–13; Howard Rabinowitz, *Race Relations in the Urban South, 1865–1890*, pp. 18–30; C. Vann Woodward, *The Strange Career of Jim Crow*, pp. 89–97.

15. Legal segregation: Cell, *The Highest Stage*, pp. 131–70; George M. Frederickson, *White Supremacy*, ch. 6; Rabinowitz, *Race Relations*, pp. 152–96; Woodward, *Jim Crow*, p. 97.

16. "Ogden Movement.": Bailey, *Murphy*, pp. 142–43; Bullock, *Negro Education*, pp. 93, 77–90; Lawrence Cremin, *American Education: The Metropolitan Experience, 1876–1980*, p. 218; Harlan, *B. T. Washington*, II, p. 43.

17. The Ogden Special: Henry Louis Smith to Robert C. Ogden, telegram, Apr. 7, 1905, Box 8; John W. Abercrombie to Robert C. Ogden, telegram, Dec. 25, 1905, Box 9—in Ogden Papers/L.C.

18. Aboard the Ogden Special: J. D. Rockefeller, Jr., quoted in Fosdick, *Adventure in Giving*, p. 5; J. D. Rockefeller, Jr., to Robert C. Ogden, Mar. 29, 1906, Box 9, Ogden Papers/L.C.; also Bailey, *Murphy*, p. 151; Booker T. Washington to Robert C. Ogden, telegram, Mar. 5, 1904, Box 7, Ogden Papers/L.C.

19. Ogden Special wrecked: Bailey, *Murphy*, p. 168; see Fol. May 28–31, 1905, Box 9, Ogden Papers/L.C., for correspondence relating to the wreck. ". . . misleading the Negroes.": Rev. Rollin A. Sawyer, D.D., to Robert C. Ogden, Feb. 13, 1906; Robert C. Ogden to Rollin A. Sawyer, Feb. 14, 1906, Box 9, Ogden Papers/L.C.; Bailey, *Murphy*, pp. 168–69.

20. ". . . content to be greatly misunderstood."—Ogden, quoted: Bailey, *Murphy*, p. 150; Robert C. Ogden to B. T. Washington, Feb. 25, 1903, Harlan, ed., *B. T. Washington Papers*, VII, p. 162, on presidential appointee Crum; Henry C. Davis to B. T. Washington, Mar. 7, 1900, *ibid.*, VII, p. 453—"I shall not be surprised if your reply to my

invitation is that your judgment is that you had better not be there." ". . . seem like a criticism.": William H. Baldwin to B. T. Washington, Aug. 11, 1902 (p. 500); and B. T. Washington to Robert C. Ogden, Aug. 6, 1902 (p. 500), Harlan, ed., *B. T. Washington Papers*, VI.

21. ". . . deliberately ignored the University.": Francis Jackson Garrison to Oswald Garrison Villard, May 12, 1902, in Harlan, ed., *B. T. Washington Papers*, VI, p. 457. "Battle lines now slowly forming.": Edgar Gardner Murphy to Robert C. Ogden, Apr. 8, 1904, Box 7, Ogden Papers/L.C.

22. ". . . but that was inevitable.": *Dusk of Dawn*, p. 74.

23. ". . . its freedom of speech.": *Autobiography*, p. 242.

24. Du Bois on the Baldwins: Du Bois Interview/Columbia Oral History Project (OHP), p. 159; Wallace Buttrick to W.E.B. Du Bois, Dec. 31, 1902, Du Bois Papers/U. Mass.; *Autobiography*, p. 243; *Dusk*, p. 78; "First Meeting of Persons Interested in the Welfare of the Negroes of New York City (1903)," in Herbert Aptheker, ed., *Against Racism: Unpublished Essays, Papers, Addresses, 1887–1961: W.E.B. Du Bois* (Amherst: The University of Massachusetts Press, 1985), pp. 72–74; and Nancy Weiss, *The National Urban League, 1910–1940* (New York: Oxford University Press, 1974), pp. 21–23; W. H. Baldwin, Jr., to B. T. Washington, Jan. 23, 1903, Harlan, ed., *B. T. Washington*, VII, p. 9; profile of Ruth Standish Baldwin, *ibid.*, VII, p. 10.

25. Du Bois's version of meeting Washington: *Autobiography*, p. 243; *Dusk*, p. 78; and see Aptheker, "Introduction," in *The Souls of Black Folk*, p. 6. In contrast to Du Bois's dramatic version of his meeting Washington, see his friendly correspondence with Washington during this period—W.E.B. Du Bois to B. T. Washington, Feb. 26, 1900—"I want to thank you again for your hospitality during my stay at Tuskegee"—Harlan, ed., *B. T. Washington Papers*, V, p. 450; W.E.B. Du Bois to B. T. Washington, Feb. 11, 1901, *ibid.*, VI, p. 33; W.E.B. Du Bois to B. T. Washington, July 3, 1901, *ibid.*, VI, p. 165.

26. ". . . he said it.": Du Bois Interview/Columbia OHP, p. 150. ". . . of the first importance.": Lyman Abbott to W.E.B. Du Bois, Sept. 8, 1903, Du Bois Papers/U. Mass.; *Autobiography*, pp. 244, 224.

27. ". . . things that Mr. Washington was advocating.": *Autobiography*, pp. 242, 254. The anti-Bookerites: "[Ferris] Attacked Booker Washington," Washington *Post*, Feb. 3, 1903, p. 10; "Interview [Edward H. Morris]," Chicago *Inter-Ocean*, July 28, 1903, p. 2; and Harlan, *B. T. Washington*, II, pp. 32–62, 76–78; August Meier, *Negro Thought in America, 1880–1915*, pp. 207–47.

28. ". . . Washington did not agree . . .": *Autobiography*, p. 241. *Dred Scott v. Sanford*—quoted: Richard Kluger, *Simple Justice: The History of Brown v. Board of Education . . .*, p. 39.

29. "A perfectly stupid race . . ."—Roosevelt, quoted: Rayford W. Logan, *The Betrayal of the Negro*, p. 270. . . . civilization's wards: see Thomas Cripps, *Slow Fade to Black: The Negro in American Film, 1900–1942* (New York: Oxford University Press, 1977), pp. 41–52; Logan, *Betrayal*, pp. 165–74; Florette Henri, *Black Migration: Movement North, 1900–1920*, ch. 7 ("Counterattack: Racist Thought"); Thomas Gossett, *Race: The History of an Idea*, ch. 7, Stephen J. Gould, *The Mismeasure of Man*, pp. 73–112.

30. Henry James, *The American Scene* (New York: Scribner's Sons, 1946; orig. pub. 1907); pp. 119–20, 131–32; James Weldon Johnson, *Along This Way*, p. 203. ". . . splendid book.": Max Weber to W.E.B. Du Bois, Mar. 30, 1905, Du Bois Papers/U. Mass.; also Aptheker, *Correspondence*, I, 106–7, p. 106.

31. Previously published essays: see Aptheker, "Introduction," *SOBF*, pp. 10–11—"Strivings of the Negro People," *Atlantic Monthly*, 80 (Aug. 1897): 194–98 ["Of Our Spiritual Strivings"]; "Of the Dawn of Freedom," *ibid.*, 87 (Mar. 1901): 354–65 ["The

Freedmen's Bureau"]; "The Evolution of Negro Leadership," *Dial*, 31 (July 16, 1901): 53–55 ["Of Mr. Booker T. Washington and Others"]; "A Negro Schoolmaster in the New South," *Atlantic Monthly*, 82 (Jan. 1899): 99–104 ["Of the Meaning of Progress"]; "Of the Training of Black Men," *ibid.*, 90 (Sept. 1902): 289–97 [Identical]. The essays for *The Souls of Black Folk*, according to information obtained from a contemporary newspaper interview, were typed for submission to McClurg's on Du Bois's new upright by his Atlanta University secretary, Inez Canty, sometime during the summer of 1902. Ms. Canty's cousin, Ms. Maurice Thomas, recalls being "fascinated by the machine Inez was typing on" as her cousin sat on the family front porch at 419 21st Street in the Rose Hill section of Columbus, Georgia—Bill Winn, "Du Bois Helped Reshape the American Mind," Columbis *Ledger-Enquirer*, Mar. 27, 1988, pp. F1, F4 (p. F1).

32. Negro spirituals: see the excellent discussion of Du Bois's epigraphs in John Edgar Wideman, "Introduction," *SOBF* (New York: The Library of America, 1992), pp. xiv–xv; also in Jack B. Moore, *W.E.B. Du Bois*, pp. 67, 71. See, Eric J. Sundquist, *To Wake the Nations: Race in the Making of American Culture*, pp. 458–59, who argues elaborately "for the centrality of the sorrow songs." ". . . problem of the color-line.": *SOBF*, p. vi.

33. ". . . to fling them forth.": St. Clair Drake, "Dr. W.E.B. Du Bois: A Life Lived Experimentally and Self-Documented," *Contributions in Black Studies*, 8 (1986–1987): 111–134, p. 122.

34. ". . . palms against the stone.": *SOBF*, p. 3, and p. 2.

35. ". . . in sheer self-defense.": *ibid.*, p. 11, and pp. 7, 10.

36. ". . . roughly in his face.": *ibid.*, p. 4, and p. 3. Review the discussion of the plausible sources of Du Bois's concept of the divided self in chapter 6, endnote 63. The essay by Thomas C. Holt, "The Political Uses of Alienation: W.E.B. Du Bois on Politics, Race, and Culture, 1903–1940," 42 (June 1990): 301–23 is illuminating; also, Dickson D. Bruce, Jr., "Du Bois and the Idea of Double Consciousness"; Bruce reminds us that George Eliot wrote a story titled "The Lifted Veil," and that John Greenleaf Whittier also employed the term "double consciousness." Again, Sundquist, *Wake the Nations*, is essential.

37. Critics of the Anglo-Saxon paradigm: see Edward Abraham, *The Lyrical Left: Randolph Bourne, Alfred Stieglitz and the Origins of Cultural Radicalism in America*; Christopher Lasch, *The New Radicalism in America: The Intellectual as a Social Type*; Stanley Coben, *Rebellion Against Victorianism: The Impetus for Cultural Change in 1920s America*; Van Wyck Brooks, *The Confident Years, 1885–1915* (New York: E. P. Dutton, 1952); Arthur Frank Wertheim, *The New York Little Renaissance: Iconoclasm, Modernism, and Nationalism in American Culture* (New York: New York University Press, 1976), esp. ch. 1.; refer to chapter 7, note 74. For some recent criticisms of Du Bois's concept of racial merging (ranging from emotional to penetrating), see Gerard Early, ed., *Lure and Loathing: Essays on Race, Identity and the Ambivalence of Assimilation* (New York: Allen Lane The Penguin Press, 1993), esp. the essays by Nikki Giovanni, C. Eric Lincoln, and Stanley Crouch.

". . . little relation to each other": Emerson, "The Transcendentalist," in Brooks Atkinson, ed., *The Selected Writings of Ralph Waldo Emerson* (New York: Modern Library, 1940), p. 100; Charles W. Chesnutt, *The House Behind the Cedars* (1900); and, for a critical appreciation of the theme of racial duality, see Judith Berzon, *Neither White Nor Black: The Mulatto Character in Fiction* (New York: New York University Press, 1978), p. 103.

38. ". . . the islands of the sea.": *SOBF*, p. 13.

39. ". . . easily have chosen.": *ibid.*, p. 38, and pp. 35, 39.

40. ". . . Yankees, and unscrupulous immigrants.": *SOBF*, p. 169—in the 1953 edition of *SOBF* "immigrants" was changed to "foreigners" [see "Introduction," p. 40, and p. 164].

41. Origins of the New South: Cell, *Highest Stage*, pp. 156–57; Frederickson, *White Supremacy*, ch. 5; J. Morgan Kousser, *Shaping of Southern Politics*, pp. 3–5; Pierre L. Van den Berghe, *Race, Racism, A Comparative Perspective* (London: John Wiley & Sons, 1967), for pioneering examination of race relations in the "competitive model" society, pp. 26–30. In the Woodward tradition, is Albert D. Kirwan, *Revolt of the Rednecks, Mississippi Politics: 1976–1925* (Gloucester, Mass.: Peter Smith, 1964), esp. pp. 146–47. ". . . fairly well fulfilled.": *SOBF*, pp. 176–77.

42. ". . . provincial and narrow thinking": Irene Diggs, "Introduction," to *Dusk of Dawn* (New Brunswick, N.J.: Transaction Books, 1984), p. viii; Moore, *Du Bois*, p. 71; *SOBF*, p. 169, and pp. 170, 177.

43. ". . . some faint-dawning day?": *SOBF*, p. 74, and pp. 114, 140, 137.

44. ". . . his unforgettable chapter": Alain Locke, "The Negro Spirituals," in *The New Negro* (New York: Atheneum, 1992; orig. pub. 1925), p. 200—more than twenty years after *SOBF*, Locke would confess, pp. 199–200, that it "still requires vision and courage to proclaim [the spirituals'] ultimate value and possibilities." See also Eileen Southern, *The Music of Black Americans: A History* (New York: W. W. Norton, 1971), pp. 96–98, 145–47, 249–51. On the once-heated debate about origins: see the excellent recapitulation and analysis in Lawrence Levine, *Black Culture and Black Consciousness: Afro-American Folk Thought from Slavery to Freedom*, pp. 19–30—speaking of the Eurocentric exponents, Levine, p. 20, notes that "they proved without question the existence of significant relationships between white and black religious song. But their work was weakened inevitably by their ethnocentric assumption that similarities alone settled the argument over origins." ". . . influenced by the slave songs.": *SOBF*, p. 256, and 353. ". . . ultimate justice of things.": *ibid.*, p. 261. ". . . ignorant of the deeds of men.": *ibid.*, p. 262. ". . . headstrong, careless people.": *ibid.*, p. 263.

45. ". . . any further question of . . . Tuskegee . . .": *SOBF*, p. 81. *Up From Slavery*, review: Du Bois, "The Evolution of Negro Leadership," *Dial*, 31 (July 16, 1901): 53–55.

46. ". . . criticism was hushed.": *SOBF*, p. 50, and p. 42. Moore, *Du Bois*, p. 72, notes the irony of the Byron epigraph in the Washington essay, as well as Du Bois's implicit contempt of Washington in calling him as great a man as Jefferson Davis.

47. ". . . the Negro's degradation.": *SOBF*, p. 53, and p. 51.

48. ". . . our children, black and white.": *ibid.*, p. 56, and pp. 57, 54.

49. ". . . saved by its exceptional men.": Aptheker, *Non-Periodical Literature*, pp. 17–29, p. 17. Sole mention of term in *SOBF*, p. 105. ". . . from the top downward . . . culture . . .": Du Bois, "The Talented Tenth," in *The Negro Problem: A Series of Articles by Representative American Negroes of Today* (New York: James Pott & Co., 1903), pp. 33–75 (reproduced in Aptheker, *Non-Periodical Literature*, pp. 17–29), p. 20.

50. Biographical and ideological information on the following: "Miller, Kelly (1863–1939)" *Dictionary of American Negro Biography* (*DANB*), pp. 434–39; Miller, *Race Adjustment: Essays on the Negro in America* (New York and Washington: Neale Publishing Co., 1908) also Harlan, *B. T. Washington*, II, pp. 64, 65, 72, *et passim.*; August Meier, "The Racial and Educational Philosophy of Kelly Miller, 1895–1915," *Journal of Negro Education* (Spring 1960): 121–27. "Trotter, William Monroe" *DANB*, pp. 603–5; Stephen R. Fox, *The Guardian of Boston: William Monroe Trotter* (New York: Atheneum, 1970). "Wells-Barnett, Ida Bell (1862–1931)" *DANB*, pp. 30–31; Alfreda Duster, *Crusade for Justice—Ida B. Wells*.

"Fauset, Jessie Redmon (1885?–1961)" *DANB*, pp. 219–20; David Levering Lewis, *When Harlem Was in Vogue* (New York: Oxford University Press, 1989; orig. pub. 1980), pp. 121–25; Carolyn Wedin Sylvander, "Jessie Redmon Fauset: Black American Writer: Her Relationships, Biographical and Literary, with Black and White Writers, 1910–1935,"

(Univ. of Wisconsin Ph.D. diss., 1976). "Chesnutt, Charles Waddell (1858–1932)" *DANB*, pp. 103–7; Sylvia Lyons Render, ed., *The Short Fiction of Charles W. Chesnutt* (Twayne, 1980). "Bowen, John Wesley Edward (1855–1933)," *DANB*, pp. 52–53; Meier, *Negro Thought*, pp. 211–12.

51. Talented Tenth numbers: A total of only 2,132 African-Americans was attending college and university in 1917. Ten years later, the number would have increased to 13,580, with between 200 and 300 matriculating in "white" institutions. By 1930, according to Carter G. Woodson, *The Negro Professional Man and the Community* (Washington, D.C.: Association for the Study of Negro Life and History, 1934), pp. 30–31, there were 1,748 African-American physicians, 1,230 lawyers, and 2,131 academic administrators, with some hundreds of bankers, businessmen, engineers, architects, and scientists. The size of the Talented Tenth, therefore, was infinitesimal in a total African-American population of ten million. For an early attempt to isolate, define, and analyze upper-class status in a major urban center, see August Meier and David L. Lewis, "History of the Negro Upper Class in Atlanta, Georgia, 1890–1958," *Journal of Negro Education*, 28 (Spring 1959): 130–39; see the comprehensive, but more narrative than analytical, monograph by Willard B. Gatewood, *Aristocrats of Color: The Black Elite, 1880–1920*; also an eccentric but valuable class *aperçu* of marriage and milieux is the photographic essay by Gerri Majors with Doris Saunders, *Black Society* (Chicago: Johnson Publishing Company, 1976).

52. ". . . lead the headless host.": *SOBF*, p. 59.

53. ". . . those with property . . .": *ibid.*, p. 80.

54. ". . . higher aims of life.": *ibid.*, p. 50.

55. ". . . touchstone of all success.": *ibid.*, p. 78. ". . . and deepest knowledge?": *ibid.*, p. 83.

56. Aptheker, "Introduction," *SOBF*, p. 25; Royalty Statement, May 1, 1903; Royalty Statement, Jan. 1, 1905—both in Du Bois Papers/U. Mass.

57. Aptheker, "Introduction," *SOBF*, p. 16.

58. J. E. Casely-Hayford to W.E.B. Du Bois, June 8, 1904, Du Bois Papers/U. Mass.; Francis Grimké to W.E.B. Du Bois, Oct. 16, 1903, Du Bois Papers/U. Mass.; J. Douglas Wetmore to W.E.B. Du Bois, Oct. 20, 1903, Du Bois Papers/U. Mass.; also Aptheker, *Correspondence*, I, p. 60; Ida B. Wells-Barnett to W.E.B. Du Bois, Mar. 30, 1903, Du Bois Papers/U. Mass.; *Correspondence*, I, pp. 55–56.

59. ". . . his feelings are so fine.": Jessie Fauset to W.E.B. Du Bois, Feb. 16, 1905, Du Bois Papers/U. Mass.; also Aptheker, *Correspondence*, I, pp. 94–95.

60. ". . . not an imitation book.": Elia W. Peattie, Chicago *Tribune*, May 22, 1903; p. 20; N.Y. *Times*, Apr. 25, 1903, pp. 19–20; Houston *Chronicle*, Aug. 15, 1903, p. 18; *Christian Advocate*, July 16, 1903, p. 16; Nashville *American*, Sept. 26, 1903, p. 17—all in Aptheker, "Introduction," *SOBF*.

61. ". . . happy, come what may.": *Collier's Weekly*, Aug. 29, 1903, p. 6. ". . . cause this offense.": Richard L. Jones to W.E.B. Du Bois, Jan. 18, 1904, Du Bois Papers/U. Mass. ". . . 'the future of the American negro.' ": "Two Typical Leaders," *Outlook*, 74 (May 25, 1903): 214–16, Du Bois Papers/U. Mass.; also reproduced in Harlan, ed., *B. T. Washington Papers*, VII, pp. 149–54, p. 153.

62. ". . . decidedly moving book.": William James to Henry James, June 6, 1903, in Henry James, ed., *The Letters of William James* (Boston: Little, Brown, 1926), 2 vols., II, p. 196. ". . . anything that has yet been written."—Gladden, quoted: Ronald C. White, Jr., and C. Howard Hopkins, *The Social Gospel: Religion and Reform in a Changing America*, p. 106. ". . . Harvard graduate in forty years.": Albert Bushnell Hart, *Books and Reading* (New York City), Oct. 1917, p. 66; in Aptheker, "Introduction," *SOBF* (Millwood, N.Y.: Kraus-Thomson Organization, 1973; orig. pub. 1903), p. 31 (note 25).

63. ". . . we Jews are in Russia.": D. Tabak to W.E.B. Du Bois [n.d.], Du Bois Papers/U. Mass.

64. ". . . here on Earth.": W.E.B. Du Bois to W. D. Hooper, Sept. 11, 1909; and W. D. Hooper to W.E.B. Du Bois, Sept. 2, 1909—both in Du Bois Papers/U. Mass. The context of Hooper's gesture was that the memory of the Bassett affair was still vivid in the South. In 1903 one of the South's leading historians, John Spencer Bassett, of Trinity College (later Duke University), founder of the *South Atlantic Quarterly*, was forced to resign his professorship and relocate in the North. Bassett's offense was that he had written an essay in the *South Atlantic Quarterly* deploring the racist excesses of certain white journalists and, in the same piece, ventured the opinion that the greatest man to be produced in the South since Robert E. Lee was Booker T. Washington. On this controversy, see Sosna, *In Search of the Silent South*, p. 14; and, for a fuller treatment of the ramifications, Williamson, *Crucible*, pp. 261–71.

65. ". . . a hideous mockery.": Caroline H. Pemberton to W.E.B. Du Bois, Dec. 12, 1903, Du Bois Papers/U. Mass.

66. ". . . the carefullest consideration.": N.Y. *Evening Post*, June 12, 1903.

67. ". . . any student of the negro question.": *The Independent*, May 28, 1903; *Dial*, May 1, 1903.

12. Going Over Niagara

1. The Oaks: Louis R. Harlan, *Booker T. Washington: The Making of a Black Leader, 1856–1901*, I, pp. 180–87; L. Albert Scipio II, *Pre-War Days at Tuskegee: Historical Essay on Tuskegee Institute (1887–1943)*, pp. 98–99, 126–27. On Du Bois's Tuskegee arrangements: see Charles H. Thompson, "Negro Criticism Begins to Mount," Charles H. Thompson Papers [unprocessed collection], Moorland-Spingarn Res. Ctr./Howard University, p. 2; and B. T. Washington to Roscoe Conkling Bruce, Apr. 21, 1903, in Louis R. Harlan, ed., *The Booker T. Washington Papers*, 13 vols, VII, p. 119.

2. Du Bois's conference plans: W.E.B. Du Bois to Kelly Miller, Feb. 25, 1903, Du Bois Papers/U. Mass. (also in Herbert Aptheker, ed., *The [Selected] Correspondence of W.E.B. Du Bois*, 3 vols., I, p. 53). Washington's dinner invitation: B. T. Washington to W.E.B. Du Bois, July 6, 1903, Harlan, ed., *B.T. Washington Papers*, VII, p. 194. Garden speech: "Extracts from An Address in New York City," Harlan, ed., *B. T. Washington Papers*, VII, pp. 113–19, note 1, pp. 118–19; Harlan, *Booker T. Washington: The Wizard of Tuskegee, 1901–1915*, II, pp. 134–35; a significant negative reaction in letter from Francis Jackson Garrison to B. T. Washington, Apr. 24, 1903, *B. T. Washington Papers*, VII, p. 130. Carnegie gift: Harlan, *B. T. Washington*, II, pp. 135–36. Washington surrendered Carnegie's $150,000 gift to Tuskegee, interest from this sum went to replace the salary formerly paid by the institute.

3. Afro-American Council meeting: Harlan, *B. T. Washington*, II, pp. 40–43. ". . . the bandwagon of the Tuskegeean."—Trotter, quoted: *ibid.*, p. 40.

4. . . . raking over the coals: Stephen R. Fox, *The Guardian of Boston: William Monroe Trotter*, p. 32; Du Bois, *The Autobiography of W.E.B. Du Bois: A Soliloquy on Viewing My Life from the Last Decade of Its First Century*, p. 238. Fortune's *Age* gagged: Fox, *Guardian of Boston*, p. 31. ". . . before you went to bed."—Trotter, quoted: *ibid.*, p. 39.

5. Boston "riot": "An Account of the Boston Riot," Boston *Globe*, July 31, 1903, pp. 1, 3 (Harlan, ed., *B. T. Washington Papers*, VII, pp. 229–40; Fox, *Guardian of Boston*, pp. 50–51; Harlan, *B. T. Washington*, II, pp. 44–46; Ruth Ann Stewart, *The Life of Portia*

Washington Pittman, The Daughter of Booker T. Washington (Garden City, N.Y.: Doubleday & Co., 1977), pp. 50–51. "Lewis, William H[enry] (1868–1949)" *Dictionary of American Negro Biography (DANB)*, pp. 396–97.

6. "rank and file" colored people . . . : B. T. Washington to Theodore Roosevelt, Sept. 15, 1903, *B. T. Washington Papers*, VII, pp. 284–85. "An Account of the Boston Riot," *ibid.*, VII, p. 241.

7. . . . devoid of "self-respect."—Trotter, quoted: Harlan, ed., *B. T. Washington*, II, p. 54; and W.E.B. Du Bois to G. W. Andrews, [n.d.], Du Bois Papers/U. Mass.

8. Defense of Trotter: *Autobiography*, p. 247; W.E.B. Du Bois to G. W. Andrews, *supra*; W.E.B. Du Bois to George Foster Peabody, Dec. 28, 1903, Du Bois Papers/U. Mass. (also Aptheker, *Correspondence*, I, pp. 67–69). Forbes apologizes: Harlan, *B. T. Washington*, II, p. 55.

9. ". . . Mr. Washington's policy.": Kelly Miller to Emmett Scott, Sept. 24, 1903, in Harlan, ed., *B. T. Washington Papers*, VII, p. 292; Samuel Edward Courtney to B. T. Washington, Oct. 18, 1903, *ibid.*, VII, pp. 295–96; B. T. Washington to Hollis Burke Frissell, Nov. 3, 1903, *ibid.*, pp. 325–26—"[p. 325] I often find myself among other colored people, becoming rather tried with Kelly Miller. The trouble is no one ever knows where to find him; he tries to keep in favor with all parties." ". . . during the last six months.": B. T. Washington to Robert Custis Ogden, Oct. 20, 1903, *ibid.*, VII, p. 298; B. T. Washington to Hollis Burke Frissell, Nov. 3, 1903, in Harlan, ed., *B. T. Washington Papers*, VII, pp. 325–26; Harlan, *B. T. Washington*, II, p. 50. The Pullman Company: B. T. Washington to W.E.B. Du Bois, Dec. 14, 1903, *B. T. Washington Papers*, VII, p. 369. "intellectually honest"—Ogden quoted: Harlan, ed., *B. T. Washington*, II, p. 51; and Fox, *Guardian of Boston*, p. 50.

10. Warned about Carnegie, Rockefeller funding: Harlan, *B. T. Washington*, II, p. 51. ". . . Mr. Trotter was convicted.": Horace Bumstead to W.E.B. Du Bois, Dec. 5, 1903, *ibid.* Bumstead reprimand: Horace Bumstead to W.E.B. Du Bois, Dec. 5, 1903, Du Bois Papers/U. Mass.; Horace Bumstead to B. T. Washington, Dec. 5, 1903, in Harlan, ed., *B. T. Washington Papers*, VII, p. 360; B. T. Washington to Horace Bumstead, Dec. 15, 1903, *ibid.*, VII, p. 370.

11. "an outburst of dissent": Horace Bumstead to W.E.B. Du Bois, Jan. 26, 1904, Du Bois Papers/U. Mass. (also Aptheker, ed., *Correspondence*, I, pp. 69–70). ". . . leading the way backward.": W.E.B. Du Bois to George Foster Peabody, Dec. 28, 1903, Du Bois Papers/U. Mass. (also Aptheker, ed., *Correspondence*, I, pp. 67–9). ". . . race to indulge them.": George Foster Peabody to W.E.B. Du Bois, Jan. 9, 1904, Du Bois Papers/U. Mass.; (also Aptheker, *Correspondence*, I, p. 69).

12. Proposing the Conference: B. T. Washington to W.E.B. Du Bois, Oct. 28, 1903, Du Bois Papers/U. Mass. (also *B. T. Washington Papers*, VII, p. 315). ". . . drop . . . all personal feelings.": B. T. Washington to W.E.B. Du Bois, Nov. 8, 1903, Du Bois Papers/U. Mass. (also Aptheker, ed., *Correspondence*, I, pp. 53–3; also in Harlan, ed., *B. T. Washington Papers*, VII, pp. 339–40). ". . . presence is worth while.": B. T. Washington to W.E.B. Du Bois, Dec. 4[?], 1903, Du Bois Papers/U. Mass.; W.E.B. Du Bois to B. T. Washington [n.d.], Du Bois Papers/U. Mass. (also Aptheker, ed., *Correspondence*, I, p. 54).

13. "What do you think of the plan?": B. T. Washington to William Henry Baldwin, Jr., Oct. 26, 1903, Du Bois Papers/U. Mass. (also Harlan, ed., *B. T. Washington Papers*, VII, pp. 311–12). Washington apologizes: Harlan, *B. T. Washington*, II, p. 69. ". . . stirring up southern feeling."—Washington, quoted: *ibid.*, p. 69.

14. Haggling over the list: B. T. Washington to W.E.B. Du Bois, Nov. 8, Dec. 4, 1903, Du Bois Papers/U. Mass. (also Harlan, ed., *B. T. Washington Papers*, VII, pp. 339–40; Harlan, *B. T. Washington*, II, p. 67. A barrage of Du Bois letters pertaining to

Carnegie Hall Conference plans—to Archibald Grimké, Clement Morgan, Fred McGhee, Edward Morris—during November-December 1903. B. T. Washington to William Henry Baldwin, Jr., Dec. 30, 1903, in Harlan, ed., *B. T. Washington Papers*, VII, p. 382—"If needed, can you let me have one thousand dollars to use in connection with New York conference expenses until February. Answer."

15. Number of conferees: Harlan, *B. T. Washington*, II, p. 65; B. T. Washington to W.E.B. Du Bois, telegram, Dec. 29, 1903, Du Bois Papers/U. Mass.—"necessary all business arrangements connecting New York conference be closed. Be kind enough to telegraph today my expense whether you plan to be present." B. T. Washington to W.E.B. Du Bois, Jan. 1, 1904, Du Bois Papers/U. Mass.—sends Du Bois money for New York trip. ". . . refuse to be side-tracked.": W.E.B. Du Bois, "memoranda on the Washington Meeting (confidential)," Du Bois Papers/U. Mass.

16. "Mr. Carnegie is coming to address us.": Du Bois Interview/Columbia OHP, p. 151; Harlan, *B. T. Washington*, II, p. 134.

17. ". . . wrong note . . . conciliation.": *Autobiography*, p. 247; *Dusk of Dawn*, p. 81. Two useful assessments of the Carnegie Hall conference are Harlan, *B. T. Washington*, II, pp. 70–71; and Elliott Rudwick, *W.E.B. Du Bois: Propagandist of the Negro Protest*, pp. 80–82.

18. Conference divisions and Committee of Twelve: see Harlan, *B. T. Washington*, II, pp. 71–73; August Meier, *Negro Thought in America, 1880–1915: Racial Ideologies in the Age of Booker T. Washington*, pp. 177–78; Rudwick, *Du Bois*, p. 83.

19. On Morris of Chicago: Cyrus Field Adams to B. T. Washington, Jan. [18?], 1904, in Harlan, ed., *B. T. Washington Papers*, VII, pp. 397–98, p. 398. ". . . error of their way.": B. T. Washington to William Henry Baldwin, Jr., Jan 22, 1904, *ibid.*, VII, pp. 409–11, p. 411. B. T. Washington to Robert Russa Moton, Jan. 22, 1904, *B. T. Washington Papers*, VII, p. 407.

20. Du Bois's expanded committee: W.E.B. Du Bois, "Outline for the Committee of Safety," Feb. 20, 1904, Du Bois Papers/U. Mass.; B. T. Washington to W.E.B. Du Bois, Feb. 25, 1904, in Harlan, ed., *B. T. Washington Papers*, VII, pp. 451–52; also Rudwick, *Du Bois*, p. 83.

21. Wizard's reaction: B. T. Washington to W.E.B. Du Bois, Feb. 25, 1904, in Harlan, ed., *B. T. Washington Papers*, VII, pp. 451–52; B. T. Washington to Hugh Mason Browne, Mar. 4, 1904, *ibid.*, VII, p. 459. ". . . having his men out vote me": W.E.B. Du Bois to Archibald Grimké and Kelly Miller, Mar. 21, 1905, Collection 39, Box 4, Archibald Grimké Papers/Moorland-Spingarn Res. Ctr./Howard University.

22. Committee of Twelve machinations: Kelly Miller to W.E.B. Du Bois, July 8, 1904, Du Bois Papers/U. Mass.; Harlan, *B. T. Washington*, II, p. 80. ". . . knife to the hilt?": Kelly Miller to W.E.B. Du Bois, Apr. 23, 1904, Du Bois Papers/U. Mass.; Du Bois, "The Parting of the Ways," *World Today*, 7 (Apr. 1904): 521–23 (also in Aptheker, ed., *Writings by W.E.B. Du Bois in Periodicals Edited by Others, Periodical Literature*, 3 vols., I, pp. 200–2, p. 200); Du Bois, "The Joy of Living," *Periodical Literature*, I, pp. 16–222, p. 218.

23. ". . . moral and social development.": B. T. Washington, "Negro Education Not a Failure," (Lincoln Birthday Address), in Harlan, ed., *B. T. Washington Papers*, VII, pp. 429–40 (quote) p. 439.

24. "Anderson, Charles William (1866–1938)" *DANB*, pp. 14–15; see also Gilbert Osofsky, *Harlem: The Making of a Ghetto: Negro New York, 1890–1930* (New York: Harper & Row, 1963), pp. 161–64. Disillusionment with committee: Archibald Grimké to W.E.B. Du Bois, Aug. 13, 1904, Du Bois Papers/U. Mass.; Harlan, *B. T. Washington*, II, p. 80. Final Committee of 24 program: Hugh M. Browne and W.E.B. Du Bois, "Circular Letter," July 28, 1904, Du Bois Papers/U. Mass.; see also Rudwick, *Du Bois*, p. 84. ". . . failure to

act so far.": B. T. Washington to W.E.B. Du Bois, Feb. 27, 1904, in Harlan, ed., *B. T. Washington Papers*, VII, p. 453.

25. ". . . larger question and issues.": *Autobiography*, p. 247. ". . . were working together.": Albert Bushnell Hart to W.E.B. Du Bois, Apr. 24, 1905, Du Bois Papers/U. Mass. ". . . knife to the hilt.": Kelly Miller to W.E.B. Du Bois, Mar. 15, 1905, Du Bois Papers/U. Mass.—"It appears that the movement was of your own suggestion. You served on the inner committee of three which selected the Twelve, and, as you assured us, it was your full intention to attend the St. Louis meeting." ". . . a terribly suspicious man.": Du Bois/Columbia OHP, p. 159.

26. ". . . end in the same way.": W.E.B. Du Bois to Archibald Grimké and Kelly Miller, Mar. 21, 1905, Collection 39, Box 4, Archibald Grimké Papers/Moorland-Spingarn Res. Ctr./H.U.

27. ". . . kingdom of God and love.": Du Bois, "Credo," *Independent*, 5 (Oct. 6, 1904): 787 (also Aptheker, *Periodical Literature*, I, pp. 229–30), p. 229; also *Darkwater: Voices from Within the Veil*, pp. 3–4.

28. Francis J. Grimké to W.E.B. Du Bois, Jan. 7, 1905, Du Bois Papers/U. Mass. (also Aptheker, ed., *Correspondence*, I, pp. 91–92, p. 91); Mary White Ovington to W.E.B. Du Bois, Du Bois Papers/U. Mass. (also Aptheker, ed., *Correspondence*, I, pp. 81–82).

29. "many socialistic beliefs.": W.E.B. Du Bois to I. M. Rubinow, Nov. 17, 1904; and I. M. Rubinow to W.E.B. Du Bois, Nov. 10, 1904, Du Bois Papers/U. Mass. (also Aptheker, *Correspondence*, I, pp. 81–82).

30. ". . . say nothing further in print . . .": W.E.B. Du Bois to William Hayes Ward, Mar. 10, 1905; William Hayes Ward to W.E.B. Du Bois, Feb. 18, 1905, Du Bois Papers/U. Mass. (also Aptheker, *Correspondence*, I, p. 96). Du Bois, "Debit and Credit, The American Negro in the Year of Grace Nineteen Hundred and Four," *Voice of the Negro*, II (Jan. 1905): 677. ". . . let us have the facts . . .": Oswald Garrison Villard to W.E.B. Du Bois, Feb. 7, 1905, Du Bois Papers/U. Mass. (also Aptheker, *Correspondence*, I, p. 97). ". . . by return mail": W.E.B. Du Bois to William Monroe Trotter, Mar. 15, 1905, Du Bois Papers/U. Mass. (also Aptheker, *Correspondence*, I, pp. 97–98).

31. ". . . the nature of the proof.": W.E.B. Du Bois to Oswald Garrison Villard, Mar. 9, 1905, Du Bois Papers/U. Mass. (Aptheker, ed., *Correspondence*, I, p. 97). ". . . and the Slater Fund Trust.": Horace Bumstead to W.E.B. Du Bois, Jan. 24, 1905, Du Bois Papers/U. Mass.

32. ". . . purity of purpose.": W.E.B. Du Bois to Oswald Garrison Villard, Mar. 24, 1905, Du Bois Papers/U. Mass. (Aptheker, ed., *Correspondence*, I, pp. 98–102; also Oswald Garrison Villard Papers, Houghton Library/Harvard); Oswald Garrison Villard to W.E.B. Du Bois, Apr. 18, 1905, Du Bois Papers/U. Mass. (also Aptheker, ed., *Correspondence*, I, pp. 102–3; and Oswald Garrison Villard Papers, Houghton Library/Harvard University). ". . . Carnegie gift for this press business.": Francis Jackson Garrison to Oswald Garrison Villard, Apr. 9, 1905, in Harlan, ed., *B. T. Washington Papers*, VIII, pp. 251–52. ". . . they are wrong.": W.E.B. Du Bois to Oswald Garrison Villard, Apr. 20, 1905, Du Bois Papers/U. Mass. (also Aptheker, *Correspondence*, I, pp. 103–4; and Villard Papers, Houghton Library/Harvard University).

33. Niagarite forerunners—McGhee and Bentley: "McGhee, Frederick L[amar] (1861–1912)" *DANB*, pp. 415–16; an extremely valuable source is the monograph prepared for the Special Studies Department of the College of Holy Cross, and submitted May 14, 1980, under Professor Randall Burkett's direction, by Patrick H. Carroll, "The 1905 Niagara Movement Attendants: An Interpretative Analysis of Their Lives and Ideologies," [copy in Moorland-Spingarn Res. Ctr./H.U.] pp. 82–87; for Charles E. Bentley, *ibid.*, pp. 78–81.

34. ". . . strangling honest criticism.": *Dusk*, pp. 88–89; (unsigned, Du Bois), "The

Significance of the Niagara Movement," *The Voice of the Negro*, 2 (Sept, 1905): 600–4; also Du Bois, "The Niagara Movement," *ibid.*: 619–22. ". . . bowed the knee to Baal.": W.E.B. Du Bois to Archibald Grimké and Kelly Miller, Aug. 13, 1905, Archibald Grimké Papers, Collection 39, Box 4, Moorland-Spingarn Res. Ctr./H.U.

35. ". . . beginning of a new epoch": "The Significance of the Niagara Movement," *Voice of the Negro*, 2 (Sept. 1905), p. 600; Du Bois, "The Niagara Movement" (Private and Confidential), in Aptheker, ed., *Pamphlets and Leaflets*, pp. 53–54. Fort Erie: Michael Clarkson, "Niagara Was a Mecca for Blacks Seeking Freedom," *St. Catherine's Standard*, June 8, 1989, p. 1, Du Bois Papers/U. Mass.; Fox, *Guardian of Boston*, p. 103. ". . . bankruptcy and perhaps jail.": *Autobiography*, p. 249; *Dusk*, p. 88. Niagara delegates: see Carroll, "Niagara Movement Attendants," p. 6; Fox, *Guardian of Boston*, p. 90.

36. ". . . present except Du Bois.": Harlan, *B. T. Washington*, II, p. 87.

37. "Hart, William Henry Harrison (1857–1934)," *DANB*, pp. 294–95; and Carroll, "Niagara Movement Attendants," p. 51. Niagara group photograph: "The Significance of Niagara," p. 601; *Autobiography*, p. 192—the photo is from the 1905 meeting, not, as indicated by editor Aptheker, 1906.

38. Niagara absentees—Morris, Purvis, Ransom, Work, Wright: see Carroll, "Niagara Movement Attendants"; *DANB* entries; Du Bois, "The Niagara Movement" (Circular), in Aptheker, ed., *Pamphlets*, pp. 53–54.

39. Du Bois on Grimké and Miller: W.E.B. Du Bois to Archibald Grimké and Kelly Miller, Aug. 13, 1905, Du Bois Papers/U. Mass. (also Collection 39, Box 4, Grimké Papers/ Moorland-Spingarn Res. Ctr./H.U.); and Kelly Miller to W.E.B. Du Bois, Mar. 15, 1905, in Du Bois Papers/U. Mass. ". . . to line up with us.": Booker T. Washington to Emmett Jay Scott, Aug. 7, 1905, in Harlan, ed., *B. T. Washington Papers*, VIII, p. 337.

40. For Hershaw and Murray: see Carroll, "Niagara Movement Attendants," pp. 54–56 and 61–62.

41. "Barber, J[esse] Max (1878–1949)" *DANB*, pp. 27–28; Harlan, *B. T. Washington*, II, pp. 104–5; Meier, *Negro Thought*, pp. 180, 182, 185.

42. ". . . is a red head.": William Monroe Trotter to W.E.B. Du Bois, Mar. 26, 1905, Du Bois Papers/U. Mass.; Fox, *Guardian of Boston*, pp. 101–3.

43. On Edwin Jourdain: Carroll, "Niagara Movement Attendants," pp. 29–32. On Byron Gunner: *ibid.*, pp. 33–34. Views of Bailey, Hart, Richards: *ibid.*, pp. 50–51, 59.

44. Kathleen Adams taped interview/David Levering Lewis, pp. 14–15. This portrait is based, to some extent, on the author's recollection of family and Atlanta lore, and is as reliable as such evidence ever is.

45. Committees and officers: "Constitution and By-Laws of the Niagara Movement as Adopted July 12 and 13, at Buffalo, N.Y.," *Pamphlets*, pp. 59–62; Fox, *Guardian of Boston*, p. 90. ". . . so long as America is unjust": "Declaration of Principles," Du Bois Papers/U. Mass. (Aptheker, *Pamphlets*, pp. 55–58), pp. 56–57; "Declaration of Sentiments," in Thomas A. Bailey, with Stephen M. Dobbs, *Voices of America: The Nation's Story in Slogans, Sayings, and Song* (New York and London: The Free Press, 1976), p. 89; see, also, Ellen Carol Du Bois, *Feminism and Suffrage: The Emergence of an Independent Women's Movement in America, 1848–1869* (Ithaca and London: Cornell University Press, 1978), pp. 22–24.

46. ". . . until these things are changed.": this and other quotes from "Declaration of Principles," pp. 55–58; *Autobiography*, p. 249. Incorporated in late January 1906: *Autobiography*, p. 249; "Declaration of Principles," pp. 55–58; "Constitution and By-Laws," pp. 59–62.

47. *Autobiography*, p. 249. ". . . opponents at the North.": Francis Jackson Garrison to B. T. Washington, Sept. 25, 1905, in Harlan, ed., *B. T. Washington Papers*, VIII, pp.

371–72, p. 372; B. T. Washington to the editor of the Montgomery *Advertiser*, Aug. 20, 1905, *ibid.*, VIII, pp. 343–44.

48. Mounting troubles: see B. T. Washington to James Sullivan Clarkson, June 14, 1904, in Harlan, ed., *B. T. Washington Papers*, VII, p. 531: "I have been having a tough wrestle with the President over matters in Louisiana. . . . It would be very disastrous, in my opinion, to have it go out from Chicago that the Lily Whites had triumphed in Louisiana and had the confidence of the President." Ogden Special at Hampton—Washington, quoted: Harlan, *B. T. Washington*, II, p. 168; B. T. Washington to William H. Baldwin, Jr., May 19, 1904, in Harlan, ed., *B. T. Washington Papers*, VII, pp. 505–8, p. 507. ". . . the situation as it is.": Edgar Gardner Murphy to Robert Custis Ogden, Mar. 8, 1904, Box 7, Ogden Papers/Library of Congress.

49. Roosevelt on the South: see concerned letter from Charles William Anderson to Emmett Jay Scott, Feb. 3, 1906, in Harlan, ed., *B. T. Washington Papers*, VIII, pp. 516–17: "I hope this continued dropping of our men will not go much further. Remember, we have lost three good places in the consular service alone. . . . These, together with the loss of the naval officer at New Orleans, the Postmaster at Athens, Georgia, and the office held by Postmaster Vick in North Carolina, and the Collectorship of the Port of Wilmington, North Carolina, and the receivership of public Moneys in Alabama." An early reaction to Bookerite patronage concerns is almost humorously revealed in the letter from Theodore Roosevelt to B. T. Washington, Feb. 6, 1903, *ibid.*, VIII, p. 36: "That is excellent; and you have put epigrammatically just what I am doing—that is, though I have rather reduced the *quantity* I have done my best to raise the *quality* of negro appointments." Also see Harlan, *B. T. Washington*, II, pp. 318–20; and Lewis L. Gould, *The Presidency of Theodore Roosevelt* (Lawrence: University of Kansas Press, 1991), p. 238.

50. Wizard's press influence: Harlan, *B. T. Washington*, II, pp. 58–61. "national Negro journal.": Charles W. Chesnutt to W.E.B. Du Bois, Jun. 17, 1903, Du Bois Papers/U. Mass. (Aptheker, ed., *Correspondence*, I, pp. 56–57).

51. On Simon and Pace: Aptheker, *Against Racism*, pp. 79–80; Paul Partington, "The Moon Illustrated Weekly—The Precursor to the Crisis," *Journal of Negro History*, 48 (July 1963): 206–16, p. 210. ". . . the rank and file.": Du Bois, "A Proposed Negro Journal" (Apr. 1905) (in Aptheker, *Against Racism*, pp. 77–81, p. 71).

52. ". . . I consider of much value.": Joseph Schiff to W.E.B. Du Bois, Apr. 9, 1905, Du Bois Papers/U. Mass. (Aptheker, ed., *Correspondence*, I, p. 109). ". . . promptly on the head.": W.E.B. Du Bois to George S. Merriam, May 9, 1905, Du Bois Papers/U. Mass.; W.E.B. Du Bois to Jacob Schiff, Apr. 4, 1905, Du Bois Papers/U. Mass. (Aptheker, *Correspondence*, I, pp. 108–9); and Partington, "The Moon Illustrated," p. 209. Schiff declines: *Dusk*, p. 82.

53. ". . . all you have gone through": John Dollar to W.E.B. Du Bois, Jan. 31, 1905; W.E.B. Du Bois to John Dollar [n.d. 1905], Du Bois Papers/U. Mass.; W.E.B. Du Bois to Isaac N. Seligman [n.d.] 1906, *ibid.*

54. *The Moon*: see Aptheker, *Annotated Bibliography*, pp. 108–9; Partington, "Preface," *The Moon Illustrated Weekly: Black America's First Weekly Magazine* (Thornton, Colo.: C. & M. Press, 1986); Du Bois, "A Proposed Negro Journal," p. 77.

55. *Moon* captions: Du Bois had unsuccessfully proposed these headings as the basis for investigative pieces on the color line in early 1904 to the editor of *Collier's Weekly*—W.E.B. Du Bois to Richard Lloyd Jones, Jan. 30, 1904, Du Bois Papers/U. Mass. (Aptheker, ed., *Correspondence*, I, p. 73). Issues for Mar. 2; Mar. 12; Mar. 17; June 23, 1906, in Partington, *The Moon Illustrated*. ". . . of catholic feeling and inspiration.": "Their Voices," *Moon*, Mar. 2, 1906, pp. 4–5, 10.

56. Equal Rights Convention: Du Bois, "Address of the First Annual meeting of the

Georgia Equal Rights Convention," *Voice of the Negro*, 3 (Mar. 1906): 175–77 (reproduced in Aptheker, ed., *Periodical Literature*, I, pp. 322–25); see also Meier, *Negro Thought*, p. 176.

57. ". . . 'eloquent and dignified?' ": Du Bois, "Then and Now," from the typescript of an entire page of a missing May 1906 issue of *The Moon* (reproduced in Partington, *Moon Illustrated*, no page number).

58. Trotter, Morgan, Du Bois and women's auxiliary: Du Bois, "A Brief Resume of the Massachusetts Trouble" [1907], Du Bois Papers/U. Mass.; Fox, *Guardian of Boston*, pp. 101–3; Du Bois, "The Man in the Moon," *The Moon*, Jun. 23, 1906, p. 12.

59. ". . . Storer College were filled.": "The Niagara Movement," Washington *Bee*, Aug. 25, 1906, p. 1.

60. Niagarites at Harper's Ferry: *ibid.*, p. 1; Mary White Ovington, "The Spirit of John Brown," N.Y. *Evening Post*, Aug. 20, 1906, p. 7; Fox, *Guardian of Boston*, pp. 101–3. Mary White Ovington: see Mary White Ovington, *The Walls Came Tumbling Down* (New York: Harcourt, Brace and Co., 1947), esp. pp. 53–59, 101; The Du Bois–Ovington relationship is richly explored by Professor Carolyn Wedin of the University of Wisconsin at Whitewater in her soon-to-published Ovington biography. Professor Wedin graciously allowed me to read "Volunteer Transplant; Social Researcher to Activist, 1904–1908," chapter four of her monograph, after its existence was called to my attention by Mrs. Esme Bhan of the Moorland-Spingarn Res. Ctr. Wedin quotes Ovington, in one letter pertaining to Harper's Ferry, as asking, "Would you like me there as a reporter for the N. Y. *Evening Post* if it should work out that I could go?" [p. 43] The following letters track the early Du Bois–Ovington friendship—Mary White Ovington to W.E.B. Du Bois, Jan. 25; Mar. 25; June 27; Sept. 2, 1905; and Feb. 5, 1906, Du Bois Papers/U. Mass. (also the lengthy letter for May 20, 1906, reproduced in Aptheker, ed., *Correspondence*, I, pp. 118–21).

61. "Niagara Night": "Niagara Meeting Program." ". . . true to the slave."—Ransom, quoted: *Bee*, Aug. 25, 1906, p. 1; "Niagara Meeting Program, Aug. 15–19, 1906," Du Bois Papers/U. Mass.; Ovington, *Evening Post*, Aug. 20, 1906, p. 1.

62. ". . . for the sake of gain.": *Bee*, Aug. 25, 1906, pp. 1, 4.

63. ". . . regardless of race and color": *Autobiography*, p. 251; "Address to the Country," p. 64. ". . . illegal exclusion will involve?": Du Bois, "Address to the Country," Du Bois Papers/U. Mass. (reproduced in Aptheker, ed., *Pamphlets*, pp. 63–65, p. 63, and p. 65; *Bee*, Aug. 25, 1906, p. 4.

64. T.R.'s pro-Negro politics: Gould, *Roosevelt*, pp. 118–31; Bailey, *Murphy*, p. 116; Harlan, *B. T. Washington*, II, pp. 5, 7, 12. Cox and Crum: Holmes, *Vardaman*, pp. 100–1; Gould, *Roosevelt*, p. 118; Williamson, *Crucible of Race*, pp. 351–52. "backward race."—Roosevelt, quoted: Bailey, *Murphy*, pp. 117–19, p. 117; Gould, *Roosevelt*, p. 238.

65. Brownsville incident: still somewhat murky, although recent scholarship has tended strongly toward the exculpation of the soldiers—see Bernard C. Nalty, *Strength for the Fight: A History of Black Americans in the Military* (New York and London: The Free Press, 1986), pp. 90–97; and John D. Weaver, *The Brownsville Raid* (New York: W. W. Norton & Co., 1970), esp. pp. 107–8. Summation of the events of Brownsville: The white battalion commander, Major Charles W. Penrose, ordered his men confined to barracks on the night of the shooting, after a leading white citizen alleged that his wife had been assaulted by a soldier. The townspeople claimed to have seen at least twenty soldiers marching through the town that night—spent regulation cartridges supposedly scooped up from Brownsville's streets were offered as evidence. On the other hand, Companies C and D mustered immediately upon the call to arms, and B Company almost as quickly. An inspection of weapons conducted by officers failed to find that any had been recently fired. Three investigations, one by a U.S. Senate committee, and two by the army, failed to identify a

single soldier on the streets of the town on the night in question. Although the army charged and many white and black Americans sincerely believed that there was a "conspiracy of silence," every man of the First Battalion of the 25th Infantry Regiment went to his grave swearing innocence.

66. Logan, *Betrayal of the Negro: From Rutherford B. Hayes to Woodrow Wilson*, p. 350; Weaver, *Brownsville*, pp. 105–7; and Emma Lou Thornbrough, "The Brownsville Episode and the Negro Vote," *Mississippi Valley Historical Review*, 44 (Dec. 1957): 469–93, p. 470.

67. Brownsville and the Wizard: Harlan, *B. T. Washington*, II, p. 310. November election and reactions: N.Y. *Times*, cited in Weaver, *Brownsville*, pp. 107–8; Harlan, *B. T. Washington*, II, p. 321. Taft on Brownsville: Weaver, *Brownsville*, p. 105–6. ". . . I could pay heed . . ."—Roosevelt, quoted: Thornbrough, "Brownsville," p. 474; Gould, *Roosevelt*, pp. 237–40; Weaver, *Brownsville*, p. 98. Election results: ". . . slump in the colored . . . vote.": quote—Thornbrough, "Brownsville," p. 472, and pp. 470–71.

68. Powell and Scott informant, quoted: Thornbrough, "Brownsville," pp. 473, 472. Wizard warns Taft: quote—Weaver, *Brownsville*, p. 98. Fortune's *Age*, quoted—Harlan, *B. T. Washington*, II, p. 320; and Weaver, *Brownsville*, p. 98. ". . . *Mark our prediction!*": Cleveland *Gazette*, quote—Weaver, *Brownsville*, p. 275.

69. According to his biographer, Robert E. Park wrote in his diary that Du Bois had hidden in a country farmhouse during the Atlanta riot: Winfred Raushenbush, *Robert E. Park: Biography of a Sociologist* (Durham, N.C.: Duke University Press, 1979), p. 471. Details of the riot: taken from Atlanta *Constitution* ("Atlanta Is Swept by Raging Mob," Sept. 23, 1906, p. 1; "Negroes Attack Inman Park," Sept. 23, 1906, p. 3; "State Troops Quiet Atlanta," Sept. 24, 1906, p. 1; "Peace in Atlanta Till Night Brought Blood in Suburbs," Sept. 25, 1906, p. 1); Ray Stannard Baker, *The Atlanta Riot* (Issued by the Afro American Council, 1907); and Baker, *Following the Color Line: American Negro Citizenship in the Progressive Era* (New York: Harper Torchbooks, 1964; orig. pub. 1908), esp. pp. 9–20; Charles Crowe's indispensable "Racial Massacre in Atlanta, Sep. 22, 1906," *Journal of Negro History*, 54 (Apr. 1969): 150–75; and Williamson, *Crucible of Race*, pp. 215–23, a detailed account, but characteristically problematic in its interpretation. See also Jacqueline Anne Rouse, *Lugenia Burns Hope: Black Southern Reformer* (Athens and London: University of Georgia Press, 1989), pp. 41–43. Myth and fact about Du Bois and riot: *Dusk*, p. 84; Du Bois, *John Brown* (Millwood, N.Y.: Kraus-Thomson, 1973; orig. pub. 1909), p. 14, states in his preface that he possessed a pistol permit and always kept a shotgun while living in the South; and see Aptheker, ed., "Introduction," *Contributions by W.E.B. Du Bois in Government Publications and Proceedings*, p. 1; Harlan, *B. T. Washington*, II, p. 300. ". . . worse than reports.": W.E.B. Du Bois to Mary White Ovington, Sept. 28, 1906, Ser. 1, Box 1, Mary White Ovington Collection, Walter Reuther Library/Wayne State University. ". . . blood of . . . dying negroes.": *Constitution*, Sept. 23, 1906, p. 1. ". . . shame to the South."—*Commercial Appeal* quoted: "Editorials of Southern Press," Atlanta *Constitution*, Sept. 26, 1906, p. 6.

70. Urban riots in the South: Don H. Doyle, *New Men, New Cities, New South, Atlanta, Nashville, Charleston, Mobile, 1860–1910*, pp. 11–13; Williamson, *Crucible*, esp. ch. 6, "In Violence Veritas"; and Woodward, *Origins of the New South*, pp. 135–37. ". . . bad police system.": Du Bois, "From the Point of View of the Negroes," *World Today*, 11 (Nov. 1906): 1173–75 (reproduced in Aptheker, ed., *Periodical Literature*, I, pp. 339–42 (quote) p. 340.

71. Politics of the riot—Watson, quoted: C. Vann Woodward, *Tom Watson: Agrarian Rebel* (New York: Oxford University Press, 1976; orig. pub. 1938), pp. 378–79; and Dewey W. Grantham, Jr., *Hoke Smith and the Politics of the New South* (Baton Rouge: Louisiana

State University Press, 1958), p. 134; see also Charles Crowe, "Racial Violence and Social Reform—Origins of the Atlanta Riot of 1906," *Journal of Negro History*, 53 (July 1968): 234–56.

72. ". . . I wrote the 'Litany of [sic] Atlanta.' ": *Dusk*, p. 86. "a bit hysterical": W.E.B. Du Bois to Mary White Ovington, Oct. 6, 1906, ser. 1, Box 1, Ovington Collection, Reuther Library/WSU. ". . . good and gentle men.": Du Bois, "A Litany at Atlanta," in *Darkwater*, pp. 25–86, p. 26.

73. ". . . Silent God. Selah!": "Litany," *Darkwater*, p. 28.

74. CIC origins: there is an illuminating typescript made at the time of the first interracial meeting after the Atlanta riot by the southern liberal, Dr. C. B. Wilmer, "Atlanta Riot," Box 65, Fol. 1, Commission on Interracial Cooperation Files, Woodruff Library/ Atlanta University; also "To Meet to Stop Riots," *Constitution*, Sept. 25, 1906, p. 1; and Morton Sosna, *In Search of the Silent South, Southern Liberals and the Race Issue*, pp. 23–25; Williamson, *Crucible*, p. 485. *Plus ça change*: see Jonathan Wiener, *Social Origins of the New South, Alabama, 1860–1885*, pp. 33, 84—in a perceptive, if overly hypothetical, interpretation of contending forces, Wiener argues, p. 104, "Thus the rise of the agrarian radical movement in the eighties did not unite the two branches of the ruling class against a mutual enemy. Instead, the planters used the agrarian rednecks to further weaken their merchant rivals in the black belt." Grantham, *Hoke Smith*, p. 131, asserts of the political upheaval of the late 1890s and 1900s that it resulted from the "clash of the two major factions in the Democratic party, but the very existence of the struggle revealed underlying grievances and social disorders that demanded attention." Woodward, *The Strange Career of Jim Crow* (New York: Oxford University Press, 1966, 2nd rev. ed.), sees the urban violence as the backwash from the 1890s turbulence—(p. 82) "The bitter violence and blood-letting recrimination of the campaign between the white conservatives and white radicals in the 'nineties had opened wounds that could not be healed by ordinary political nostrums and free silver slogans. The only formula powerful enough to accomplish that was the magical formula of white supremacy."

75. ". . . lips closed": B. T. Washington to Charles William Anderson, Nov. 7, 1906, in Harlan, ed., *B. T. Washington Papers*, IX, p. 119. Thornbrough, "Brownsville Episode," pp. 482, 481.

76. *Horizon*: see, Aptheker, "Introduction," *Selections from the Horizon* (White Plains, N.Y.: Kraus-Thomson, 1985), p. viii; and *Annotated Bibliography*, pp. 109–10. ". . . more . . . than you think.": E. L. Simon to W.E.B. Du Bois, Jan. 16, 1907, Du Bois Papers/U. Mass.

77. ". . . fostering hate.": Du Bois, "Periodicals," *Horizon*, I (Mar. 1907): 3–10 (in *Selections from the Horizon*, pp. 8–11 [p. 9]). ". . . Conquest of the Philippines": Du Bois, "The Negro Voter," *The Horizon: A Journal of the Color Line*, 4 (July 1908): 1–8 (reproduced in Aptheker, *Horizon*, pp. 61–64, p. 63); Du Bois, "Austria," *ibid.*, I (Feb. 1907), (in *Selections from the Horizon*, pp. 5–7, p. 7).

78. ". . . hope of the Negro American.": Du Bois, "Socialist of the Path"; and "Negro and Socialism," *ibid.*, 1 (Feb. 1907): 3–4, 6–10 (in *Selections from the Horizon*, pp. 5–7, both quotes p. 6); under the caption, "Magazines," the February *Horizon* recommends the books on socialism that Du Bois has been reading.

79. ". . . in the black man's face.": Du Bois, "Roosevelt," *ibid.*, 1 (Jan. 1907): 2–10 (in *Selections from the Horizon*, pp. 3–4 [p. 3]); also "Hearken, Theodore Roosevelt," *ibid.*, 1 (Feb. 1907): 3–4, 6–10 (*Horizon Selections*, pp. 9–10); see also Du Bois, "The President and the Soldiers," *Voice of the Negro*, 3 (Dec. 1906): 552–53 (reproduced in *Periodical Literature*, I, pp. 343–45).

80. ". . . get these people together": Du Bois Interview/Columbia OHP, p. 152.

". . . must and shall prevail.": "Third Annual Meeting of the Niagara Movement, Aug. 26–29, 1907, at Parker Memorial Hall, Boston" (Aptheker, *Pamphlets*, pp. 74–76 (p. 76); also in Du Bois, "The Overlook," *Horizon*, 2 (Sept. 1907): 3–6, 8–10 (reproduced in *Selections from the Horizon*, pp. 26–29, p. 27). ". . . final shriek of despair"—Indianapolis *Freeman*, quoted: Wedin, Ovington MS—ch. 4, "Volunteer Transplant," p. 109.

Niagara accomplishments: see Fox, *Guardian of Boston*, p. 101—the movement claimed to have contributed to the defeat of a Jim Crow amendment to the Hepburn railroad rates bill.

81. Placating Trotter: Du Bois, "A Brief Resume of the Massachusetts Trouble in the Niagara Movement," Du Bois Papers/U. Mass.; Fox, *Guardian of Boston*, pp. 104–5. Ovington cautioned Du Bois against impatience and his bias for the Morgan clique. She found Morgan "exceedingly vain"—Wedin, "Volunteer Transplant," p. 110. ". . . and do my duty.": W.E.B. Du Bois to Mary White Ovington, Oct. 14, 1907, Ser. 1, Box 1, Ovington Collection/Reuther Library/WSU.

82. ". . . vote for Bryan."—Du Bois in *Guardian*, quoted: Thornbrough, "Brownsville Episode," p. 490; Du Bois, "Taft," *Horizon*, 3 (Apr. 1908): 1–8 (reproduced in *Selections from the Horizon*, pp. 53–54); Du Bois, "The Negro Vote," *ibid.*, 4 (Sept. 1908): 1–9, (reproduced *supra*, pp. 70–71).

83. Whitecapping's: Holmes, *The White Chief: Vardaman*, pp. 134–42.

". . . all but unbearable.": B. T. Washington to Isaiah T. Montgomery, Sept. 16, 1904; Isaiah T. Montgomery to B. T. Washington, Sept. 6, 1904, in Harlan, ed., *B. T. Washington Papers*, VIII, p. 69, and "Montgomery, Isaiah T[homas] (1841–1924)" *DANB*, pps. 445–46.

84. ". . . republic of the civilized.": Du Bois, "Abraham Lincoln," *Voice of the Negro*, 4 (June 1907): 242–47 (reproduced in *Periodical Literature*, I, pp. 373–80, p. 376). '. . . excuse of race and color.": Du Bois, "Niagara Movement," *Horizon*, 4 (Sept. 1908): 1–9 (reproduced in *Selections from the Horizon*, pp. 69–70).

13. *Atlanta: Scholar Behind the Veil*

1. ". . . with some effectiveness": Du Bois, *Autobiography*, p. 259. . . . nine in the evening.: "W.E.B. Du Bois/A Recorded Autobiography" (interviewed by Moses Asch), Folkways Records (FH 5511, 1961). Du Bois's work routine: Detailed calendars of reading and writing activity are found in Box 260, Corr-Personal 1900–1936, Fols. 4863, 4870, Du Bois Papers/U. Mass.

2. "Petition of Negroes to Use the Carnegie Library," 1902/03, Du Bois Papers/U. Mass. ". . . the white people of Atlanta.": Julius Dreher to W.E.B. Du Bois, Sept. 9, 1904, Du Bois Papers/U. Mass. ". . . the seeming impasse." E.R.A. Seligman to W.E.B. Du Bois, Oct. 28, 1906, Du Bois Papers/U. Mass.; also Aptheker, ed., *Correspondence*, I, p. 123; *Autobiography*, p. 227.

3. ". . . explain, expound, and exhort": Du Bois, *Dusk of Dawn*, p. 4.

4. Yolande to Great Barrington: *Library of America Du Bois*, p. 1290. Rouse, *Lugenia Burns Hope*, pp. 37, 65–70, *et passim*. Due in part to Du Bois's interest in her social concerns, he involved Lugenia Hope in a 1899 or 1900 conference on "The Welfare of the Negro Child," which led immediately to her organizing with several other women a committee to establish free kindergartens in Atlanta. Nina Du Bois was not among the group. Rouse, *Hope*, p. 28.

5. ". . . evenings here alone.": Nina Du Bois to W.E.B. Du Bois, Jan. 5, 1902, Du Bois Papers/U. Mass. "Dr. Du Bois was cranky": Usher Interview/D. L. Lewis. ". . . I hope it will last.": Nina Du Bois to W.E.B. Du Bois, Sept. 25, 1910 [?], Du Bois Papers/U. Mass.

6. No model husband: Du Bois, "I Bury My Wife," *Negro Digest*, 8 (July-Oct. 1950): 37—"I was not, on the whole, what one would describe as a good husband." ". . . a little while now.": W.E.B. Du Bois to Yolande Du Bois, Mar. 13, 1907, Du Bois Papers/U. Mass.

7. W.E.B. Du Bois to Mary White Ovington, Apr. 3, 1905, Ovington Collection/Reuther Library/WSU. On Mary Evans Wilson: "Wilson, Butler R[oland]" (1860–1939), *DANB*, pp. 662–63. A *Select Bibliography of the Negro American: A Compilation Made under the Direction of Atlanta University; Together with the Proceedings of the Tenth Conference for the Study of the Negro Problems, held at Atlanta University, on May 30, 1905* (Atlanta: Atlanta University Press, 1905); see also *Atlanta University Publications* (New York: Arno Press, 1968), p. vi.; in Aptheker, ed., *Annotated Bibliography*, pp. 531–32; and Du Bois, "My Evolving Program for Negro Freedom," in Rayford Logan, ed., *What the Negro Wants* (Chapel Hill: University of North Carolina Press, 1944), p. 47. Kellor at 1905 conference—quoted in: Nancy Weiss, *National Urban League*, p. 17.

8. ". . . compensations in all this thing.": Du Bois to Mary White Ovington, Nov. 8, 1904. The stream of Ovington letters to Du Bois, before their meeting in Atlanta, runs most significantly from June 10, 1904 to Jan. 9, 1905—of particular interest are those from Ovington dated, June 16; Oct. 7; Oct. 27; Nov. 4; Nov. 10, 1904; and Jan. 9, 1905, Ovington Collection/WSU. Funds funneled through Ovington: information contained in Carolyn Wedin, "Ovington MS—ch. 4," p. 5. ". . . a mere millionaire?": W.E.B. Du Bois to Mary White Ovington, Nov. 8, 1904, Ovington Collection/Reuther Library/WSU; also Aptheker, ed., *Correspondence*, I, p. 78.

9. Ovington's evolving socialism: Wedin, "Ovington MS—ch. 4," pp. 1–6; ". . . the life so far from". . . . known.: Unpublished Autobiographical Material, Box 1, Ser. 1/Ovington Collection. Phipps money for Ovington's settlement house: Ovington to W.E.B. Du Bois, Jan. 25, 1905, Du Bois Papers/U. Mass.; Ovington, *The Walls Came Tumbling Down*, p. 34.

10. Ovington—Boas—Simkhovitch—Brooks: Mary Simkhovitch to Mary White Ovington, Nov. 25, 1904, Ovington Collection/Reuther Library/WSU; Wedin, "Ovington," p. 2. Ovington, "Beginnings of the NAACP: Reminiscences," *The Crisis*, 32 (June 1926): 76–77, p. 76. ". . . than anyone I know.": W.E.B. Du Bois to George Edmund Haynes, Feb. 26, 1909, Du Bois Papers/U. Mass.

11. ". . . our city poor."—Ovington quoted: Wedin, p. 27. ". . . no one could follow him.": Ovington, "Beginnings of the NAACP," p. 76.

12. Milholland biography: see *Who's Who in America 1914–1915* (Chicago: Marquis, 1914), p. 1619. Harlan, *Booker T. Washington*, II, pp. 311–12, 367–69, 374–75; Du Bois, *Autobiography*, p. 262. Ovington's affair with Milholland: Wedin, "Ovington," pp. 61–62.

13. Impression of the Wizard: Fol. 38, n.d., pp. 31–38, Box 11, Ovington Collection/Reuther Library/WSU. ". . . African 'passion.' ": Ovington, *Portraits in Color* (New York: Viking Press, 1972; orig. pub. 1927), p. 79. ". . . well-intentioned mediocrity of another.": W.E.B. Du Bois to Mary White Ovington, June 7; Oct. 30, 1906, Ovington Collection/Reuther Library/WSU.

14. Ovington on meeting Du Bois: Ovington, *Walls Came Tumbling Down*, p. 54. Ovington and Du Bois were extremely close for many years, although she gradually grew to admire James Weldon Johnson more than Du Bois in some respects. The Du Bois–Ovington correspondence was sometimes playful, sometimes intense, occasionally scolding—"I very much want you to be at Atlanta University, Tuesday, May 30. I should like you to be here at Baccalaureate, May 28 and to stay until Commencement, June 1."—Ovington Collection/Reuther Library/WSU. Ovington, *Portraits in Color*, pp. 82–83; Ovington, "Beginnings of the NAACP," p. 76. ". . . most distinguished citizen was black.": Ovington, *Portraits in Color*, p. 82.

15. ". . . this colored 'untouchable.' ": Ovington, *Portraits in Color*, p. 83. ". . . a half sneer, a scorn.": *ibid.*, p. 86. ". . . evidently a dare-devil.": Ovington, *Walls Came Tumbling Down*, p. 59.

16. American Economic Association meeting: Walter F. Willcox to W.E.B. Du Bois, Jan. 8, 1902, Dec. 6, 1904, Du Bois Papers/U. Mass.; cf. Du Bois, "The Economic Future of the Negro," *Publications of the American Economic Association*, 7 (Feb. 1906, 3d series): 219–42; also in Aptheker, ed., *Periodical Literature*, I, 346–57; and Aptheker, *Annotated Bibliography*, p. 24. ". . . agnostic on the subject.": Walter F. Willcox to W.E.B. Du Bois, Mar. 13, 1904; Du Bois to Walter F. Willcox, Mar. 29, 1904, Du Bois Papers/U. Mass.; also Aptheker, ed., *Correspondence*, I, pp. 74–75. "The Economic Position of the American Negro." Walter F. Willcox to W.E.B. Du Bois, Jan. 8, 1902; Nov. 5, 1904; Du Bois to Walter F. Willcox, Nov. 7, 1904; Walter F. Willcox to W.E.B. Du Bois, Nov. 17, 1904, Du Bois Papers/U. Mass.

17. ". . . a complete surprise.": Mary White Ovington to W.E.B. Du Bois, June 27, 1905, Du Bois Papers/U. Mass. On Breckinridge's social work influence, see Roy Lubove, *The Professional Altruist: The Emergence of Social Work as a Career, 1880–1930* (Cambridge: Harvard University Press, 1965), pp. 140–44; Fred H. Matthews, *Quest for an American Sociology: Robert H. Park and the Chicago School*, p. 94. ". . . more harm than good.": Sophonisba Breckinridge to W.E.B. Du Bois [n.d.] 1905, Du Bois Papers/U. Mass. ". . . a word with you.": Sophonisba Breckinridge to W.E.B. Du Bois [n.d.], Du Bois Papers/U. Mass.

18. Boas on African civilizations: Immanuel Geiss, *Pan African Movement: A History of Pan Africanism in America, Europe and Africa*, p. 114; see also Aptheker, *Annotated Bibliography*, p. 531; also Du Bois, *The Negro* (Millwood, N.Y.: Kraus-Thomson, 1915), pp. 114–15, cites *in extenso* Boas's commencement address at Atlanta University on May 31, 1906, as Atlanta University Leaflet, No. 19 (Atlanta: Atlanta University Press, 1906).

19. ". . . conscientious study of the American Negro.": Du Bois, "Caste and Class in the United States," Boston *Post*, Feb. 12, 1904, in Aptheker, *Periodical Literature*, I, 196–97, p. 16. ". . . equipment at command will allow.": *Dusk*, p. 64.

20. ". . . either angry or miserable.": Ovington, *Portraits in Color*, p. 78.

21. Du Bois at Hampton: Aptheker, *Annotated Bibliography*, p. 25; Thomas Jesse Jones, speaking for Frissell, wrote Du Bois of the institution's satisfaction that Du Bois would "be present with us and we are anxious to hear from you as often as possible," June 18, 1906, Du Bois Papers/U. Mass. Du Bois, "The Hampton Idea," *The Voice of the Negro*, 3 (Sept. 1906): 631–36, pp. 634, 632. The Hampton curriculum: Content or courses was secondary at Hampton before World War One to inculcation of what General Arnmstrong believed was the appropriate attitude of industry and patient citizenship, as evidenced by the pamphlet, "Work with the Hands in Hampton Institute" [n.d.], Fol. Hampton Institute, Box 19, Ogden Papers/LC—"Didactic and dogmatic work has little to do with the formation of character which is our point," it quotes Armstrong as saying. The four-year course consisted of auto mechanics, carpentry, blacksmithing, bricklaying, plastering, cabinetmaking, machine work, painting, printing, steamfitting, plumbing, tailoring, wheelwrighting. James D. Anderson, *The Education of Blacks in the South, 1860–1935*, pp. 46–66, describes the Hampton curriculum as clustered into three areas—(1) elementary academic program; (2) manual labor systems; and (3) strict social discipline routine—none of which comprehended serious academic or even advanced technical instruction.

22. Lowndes County investigation: Du Bois, *Autobiography*, p. 226–27; see Du Bois–Charles P. Neill correspondence running from June 27, 1905 to Oct. 17, 1906, Du Bois Papers/U. Mass.; Aptheker, ed., *Government Publications and Proceedings*, p. 1; Du Bois, "The Negro Farmer," *ibid.*, pp. 231–95.

23. ". . . one corner of the county.": W.E.B. Du Bois to Charles P. Neill, Nov. 2, 1906, Du Bois Papers/U. Mass. . . . sexual morality, etc.: W.E.B. Du Bois to Charles P. Neill, Oct. 1, 1906, Du Bois/U. Mass.

Negotiations around the Lowndes data: see exchange of Du Bois–Neill (Labor Bureau) letters, Feb. 28, 1907, through Nov. 9, 1908, Du Bois Papers/U. Mass., esp. Neill/Du Bois, Feb. 28, 1907; Neill/Du Bois, Mar. 19, 1907; Du Bois/Neill, Oct. 8, 1907. ". . . gathered in this form.": G.W.W. Hanger to W.E.B. Du Bois, Aug. 30, 1907, Du Bois Papers/U. Mass.

24. Du Bois presses for publication: W.E.B. Du Bois to Charles P. Neill, Nov. 7, 1908; W.E.B. Du Bois to Charles P. Neill, Oct. 8, 1907, Du Bois Papers/U. Mass. "touched on political matters.": Du Bois, *Autobiography*, p. 227. ". . . had been destroyed!": *ibid.*, p. 227.

25. Du Bois Wilberforce tribute: "Douglass as a Statesman," reproduced in *Periodical Literature*, I, p. 28–30; W.E.B. Du Bois to Ellis Paxson Oberholtzer, Nov. 18, 1903, Du Bois Papers/U. Mass.; also Aptheker, *Correspondence*, I, p. 62. ". . . suggest any other name?": Ellis P. Oberholtzer to W.E.B. Du Bois, Jan. 25, 1904, Du Bois Papers/U. Mass.; also Aptheker, ed., *Correspondence*, I, p. 63–64, p. 63.

26. ". . . Negro point of view . . . of slavery.": see Aptheker, "Introduction," *John Brown* (Millwood, N.Y.: Kraus-Thomson, 1973; orig. pub. 1909), p. 7. Oberholtzer proposes John Brown: Ellis P. Oberholtzer to W.E.B. Du Bois, Feb. 3, 1904; Feb. 16, 1904, Du Bois Papers/U. Mass.; also Aptheker, ed., *Correspondence*, I, p. 64–65. ". . . greater influence . . . Nat Turner": W.E.B. Du Bois to Ellis P. Oberholtzer [n.d. 1904], Du Bois Papers/U. Mass.; also Aptheker, ed., *Correspondence*, I, p. 64–65.

27. Yolande's appendectomy: W.E.B. Du Bois to Ellis P. Oberholtzer, Oct. 10, 1908, Du Bois Papers/U. Mass. *John Brown* manuscript completed: Aptheker, "Introduction," *John Brown*, p. 10; George W. Jacobs to W.E.B. Du Bois, Dec. 15, 1908, Du Bois Papers/U. Mass.

28. ". . . great faith was based.": Du Bois, *John Brown*, p. 247.

29. ". . . age of the African slave-trade.": *ibid.*, p. 383.

30. Revolutionary violence: *ibid.*, pp. 143–44. ". . . uplift of the human race.": *ibid.*, pp. 395–96, paragraph added by Du Bois when the biography was reissued by International Publishers in 1962.

31. ". . . against the wicked South."—Dodd, quoted: Aptheker, "Introduction," *John Brown*, p. 17. ". . . forcible and moving."—*Independent*, quoted: *ibid.*, p. 18.

32. *The Nation*: cited in Aptheker, "Introduction," *ibid.*, pp. 18–19; W.E.B. Du Bois to *The Nation*, Nov. 6, 1909, Du Bois Papers/U. Mass.; Paul Elmer Moore to W.E.B. Du Bois, Nov. 12, 1909; W.E.B. Du Bois to Paul Elmer Moore, Nov. 15, 1909; also Aptheker, *Correspondence*, I, pp. 154–57; and Aptheker, "Introduction," *John Brown*, p. 23. . . . seen through Brown's career.: Du Bois, *John Brown*, p. 7.

33. ". . . more about your factual inaccuracies.": Paul Elmer Moore to W.E.B. Du Bois, Nov. 12, 1909, Du Bois Papers/U. Mass.; also Aptheker, *Correspondence*, I, 155–57, p. 156. ". . . instruction either in History or English": W.E.B. Du Bois to Paul Elmer Moore, Nov. 15, 1909, *loc. cit.* ". . . my business . . . and not yours.": W.E.B. Du Bois to Paul Elmer Moore, Nov. 15, 1909, Du Bois Papers/U. Mass.; also Aptheker, *Correspondence*, I, 157.

34. ". . . quite indifferent": Oswald Garrison Villard to W.E.B. Du Bois, Nov. 26, 1909, Du Bois Papers/U. Mass.; also Aptheker, *Correspondence*, I, 158–59; Paul Elmer Moore to W.E.B. Du Bois, Nov. 20, 1909, Du Bois Papers/U. Mass.; also Aptheker, *ibid.*, p. 158. ". . . not assertive and aggressive.": Du Bois, *Autobiography*, p. 256. ". . . a Cromwellian Roundhead.": Villard, *John Brown: A Biography* (Garden City, New York: Doubleday, Doran & Co., 1929; orig. pub. 1910), p. viii.

35. ". . . truth and righteousness prevail.": Villard, *John Brown*, p. 589. ". . . with joy and in peace.": *ibid.*, p. 589. ". . . very much as Du Bois does now.": Albert Bushnell Hart to Oswald Garrison Villard, Jan. 15, 1910, Oswald Garrison Villard Papers/Houghton Library/Harvard.

36. "race mixture" investigation.: Walter F. Willcox to W.E.B. Du Bois, Apr. 8, 1902, Du Bois Papers/U. Mass.

37. *The Present South*: see Hugh Bailey, *Edgar Gardner Murphy: Gentle Progressive*, pp. 128–29.

38. Wells on Booker T. Washington: ". . . or equal respect.": H. G. Wells, *The Future in America* (New York: Arno Press, 1974; orig. pub. 1906), p. 197.

39. "illustrating [it] by various dives.": Edward T. Ware to W.E.B. Du Bois, June 3, 1905, Du Bois Papers/U. Mass.

40. ". . . didn't know he was out."—Ovington, quoted: Wedin, "Ovington Ms," p. 80. Ray Stannard Baker to W.E.B. Du Bois, Jan. 30, 1907—"What does the white man mean when he speaks of justice and what does the Negro mean? Are the two conceptions of justice . . . far apart?" Ray Stannard Baker, *The Atlanta Riot*, republished by permission, from the *American Magazine*, 1907 (The Phillips Publishing Co., 1907); Baker, *Following the Color Line: American Negro Citizenship in the Progressive Era* (New York: Harper Torchbooks, 1964; orig. pub. 1908). In the Du Bois Papers there is a penciled and undated holograph (*circa* Jan. 1904) draft of a letter Du Bois sent to Richard L. Jones, editor of *Collier's Weekly*, proposing, "Would it not be an interesting experiment to start in *Collier's* a column—or half a column—called 'Along the Color Line' or the 'Voice of the Darker Millions' and put there from week to week or month to month notes and documents on the darker races in America, Africa, Asia, etc., from their standpoint and the standpoint of the serious student and observer, the spirit of it being rather informing and interpretive than controversial?"

41. ". . . what does the Negro mean?": Ray Stannard Baker to W.E.B. Du Bois, Jan. 30, 1907, Du Bois Papers/U. Mass. *American Magazine*: Ray Stannard Baker to W.E.B. Du Bois, Mar. 29, 1907, Du Bois Papers/U. Mass.

42. ". . . middle class white people.": Baker, *The Atlanta Riot*, p. 8. ". . . crime upon the race problem.": W.E.B. Du Bois to Ray Stannard Baker, Apr. 3, 1907, Du Bois Papers/U. Mass.; Ray Stannard Baker to W.E.B. Du Bois, May 2, 1907, Du Bois Papers/U. Mass. ". . . especially among the women.": Ray Stannard Baker to W.E.B. Du Bois, May 10, 1907, Du Bois Papers/U. Mass.; see Harlan, *B. T. Washington*, II, 306. "defense of the ballot.": W.E.B. Du Bois to Ray Stannard Baker, May 20, 1907, Du Bois Papers/U. Mass.

43. Wilmer–Du Bois colloquy: Ray Stannard Baker to W.E.B. Du Bois, Dec. 2, 1908, Du Bois Papers/U. Mass. ". . . justice for Black Men."—Du Bois quoted: Harlan, *B. T. Washington*, II, p. 308. Baker's tightrope: see *ibid.*, 308. Ovington and publishers: Wedin, "Ovington," p. 28; also *ibid.*, p. 101, Wedin writes that Ovington was astonished that Baker's attitude about race-problem solutions changed so little; "she was probably disappointed that she had had so little impact." See Robert C. Bannister, Jr., *Ray Stannard Baker: The Mind and Thought of a Progressive* (New Haven: Yale University Press, 1966), esp. pp. 128–30.

44. ". . . and his self-control.": Washington, "The Economic Development of the Negro Race in Slavery," in Booker T. Washington and W.E.B. Du Bois, *The Negro in the South* (New York: Carol Publishing Group, 1970; orig. pub. 1907). ". . . naked to their enemies.": Du Bois, "The Economic Revolution in the South," in *ibid.*, p. 112.

45. ". . . in the one city of Atlanta.": Wallace Buttrick to Edward T. Ware, Nov. 6, 1907, GEB, Box 49, Series 1, Fol. 443/Rockefeller Archives/Pocantico, N.Y. ". . . with the colored people.": Wallace Buttrick to Edward T. Ware, Feb. 6, 1908; Edward T. Ware to

Wallace Buttrick, Feb. 3, 1908, Records of the General, Box 48, Series 1, Fol. 443/ Rockefeller Archives/Pocantico, N.Y.

46. ". . . you wrote several years ago.": Horace Bumstead to W.E.B. Du Bois, May 3, 1907, Du Bois Papers/U. Mass. ". . . to be doing something.": W.E.B. Du Bois to William James, May 27, 1907. William James to W.E.B. Du Bois, May 23, 1907, Du Bois Papers/ U. Mass.; also Aptheker, *Correspondence*, I, 133–34.

47. Andrew Carnegie: W.E.B. Du Bois to Andrew Carnegie, May 22, 1906, Du Bois Papers/U. Mass.; also Aptheker, *Correspondence*, I, 121–122.

48. ". . . we know all too little.": W.E.B. Du Bois to the Carnegie Institution [n.d.], Du Bois Papers/U. Mass.; Du Bois, "My Evolving Program for Negro Freedom," in Logan, *What the Negro Wants*, p. 47.

49. ". . . offensive to either race.": Alfred H. Stone to W.E.B. Du Bois, June 23, 1906, Du Bois Papers/U. Mass.

50. ". . . handy with the knife.": Du Bois, *Autobiography*, p. 225. ". . . I cannot imagine.": Du Bois, *Dusk of Dawn*, p. 84. Racist monographs: see the excellent discussions in Florette Henri, *Black Migration: Movement North, 1900–1920*, pp. 208–36; and Thomas F. Gossett, *Race: The History of an Idea in America*, ch. 7. Stone: Alfred H. Stone to W.E.B. Du Bois, June 23, 1906; Jan. 1, 1907, Du Bois Papers/U. Mass. ". . . the Carnegie Institution.": J. Franklin Jameson to W.E.B. Du Bois, Jan. 14, 1907, Office File, Box 80, J. Franklin Jameson Papers/Library of Congress.

51. ". . . the work we have in view.": Alfred H. Stone to W.E.B. Du Bois, Jan. 1, 1907, Du Bois Papers/U. Mass. "Economic Cooperation among Negro Americans": *Economic Cooperation among Negro Americans. Report of a Social Study Made by Atlanta University, under the Patronage of the Carnegie Institution of Washington, D.C., Together with the Proceedings of the Twelfth Conference of the Study of the Negro Problems, held at Atlanta University, on Tuesday, May the 28th, 1907*; also Aptheker, *Annotated Bibliography*, p. 532.

52. Booker Washington criticizes Stone: Harlan, *B. T. Washington*, II, 259. Stone unfazed: Alfred H. Stone to W.E.B. Du Bois, Apr. 23, 1907; June 28, 1907, Du Bois Papers/U. Mass.

53. Bumstead's Du Bois itinerary: Horace Bumstead to W.E.B. Du Bois, April 6, 1907, Du Bois Papers/U. Mass.; see also Aptheker, *Annotated Bibliography*, p. 27. ". . . would have spared you.": Horace Bumstead to W.E.B. Du Bois, Feb. 7, 1907, Du Bois Papers/U. Mass.

54. ". . . two diverse races . . .": Du Bois, "Sociology and Industry in Southern Education," *Voice of the Negro*, 4 (May 1907): 170–75, in *Periodical Literature*, I, 366–72, p. 369. The Barnetts: Alfreda M. Duster, ed., *Crusade for Justice: The Autobiography of Ida B. Wells*, pp. 280–81.

55. "The Value of Agitation," *Voice of the Negro*, 4 (Mar. 1907): 109–10, in Aptheker, *Annotated Bibliography*, p. 27.

56. . . . end of "white supremacy": Du Bois, "The Color Line Belts the World," *Collier's*, 28 (Oct. 20, 1906): 20, in Aptheker, *Annotated Bibliography*, p. 26. ". . . American journals just now.": W.E.B. Du Bois to Frances Hoggan, Oct. 30, 1907, Du Bois Papers/U. Mass. Frances Hoggan to W.E.B. Du Bois, Mar. 24; Apr. 21; June 24; July 16, 1907, Du Bois Papers/U. Mass. Bliss Perry, *Atlantic Monthly*, to W.E.B. Du Bois, Dec. 20, 1904, Du Bois Papers/U. Mass. Richard L. Jones, *Collier's Weekly*, to W.E.B. Du Bois, Jan. 18, 1904; Walter Hines Page to W.E.B. Du Bois, Nov. 27, 1905, Du Bois Papers/U. Mass. Philippine occupation: Erving Winslow, Secretary of the Anti-Imperialist League, to W.E.B. Du Bois, Oct. 25, 1907, Du Bois Papers/U. Mass.

57. Lanier of Doubleday to W.E.B. Du Bois, Mar. 26, 1907; W.E.B. Du Bois to Henry Lanier, Apr. 9, 1907, Du Bois Papers/U. Mass. . . . four-week vacation abroad.:

W.E.B. Du Bois to John Milholland, May 2, 1907, Du Bois Papers/U. Mass. ". . . would be quite satisfactory.": W.E.B. Du Bois to Frances Hoggan, Mar. 26, 1907; Frances Hoggan to W.E.B. Du Bois, Mar. 24, 1907, Du Bois Papers/U. Mass. James to Du Bois: June 23, 1907, Du Bois Papers/U. Mass.

58. Du Bois abroad: Du Bois, *Dusk of Dawn*, p. 222; W.E.B. Du Bois to Frances Hoggan, May 27, 1907, Du Bois Papers/U. Mass. Bicycle mixup: Allen Line of Royal Maitland Steamship to W.E.B. Du Bois, Nov. 6, 1907, Du Bois Papers/U. Mass.

59. Henry James to W.E.B. Du Bois, Aug. 9, 1907, Du Bois Papers/U. Mass.; also Aptheker, ed., *Correspondence*, I, 134.

60. ". . . find a welcome place.": Du Bois, *Dusk of Dawn*, p. 223.

61. ". . . migration of the talented tenth.": James R. Grossman, *Land of Hope: Chicago, Black Southerners, and the Great Migration*, p. 32.

62. ". . . people of a different race.": Stone, "Race Friction," *loc. cit.*, p. 18. In addition to Du Bois and Willcox, the other respondents to Stone were professors Weatherby of the University of Indiana and Aldrich of Tulane, and Dr. Chancellor of Washington, D.C.—C.W.A. Verditz, Secretary, American Sociological Society, to W.E.B. Du Bois, Oct. 4, 1907, Du Bois Papers/U. Mass. ". . . abolition of the color line.": Stone, "Is Race Friction Between Black and White in the United States Growing and Inevitable?" *American Journal of Sociology*, 13 (May 1908): 435–69, in Thomas F. Pettigrew, ed., *The Sociology of Race Relations: Reflection and Reform* (New York: The Free Press, 1980), p. 18; Du Bois, "The Future of the Negro Race in America," *East and the West*, 2 (Jan. 1904): 4–19, in Aptheker, *Annotated Bibliography*, p. 19. ". . . the lower races."—Stone quoted: *Periodical Literature*, I, 390, note 3.

63. ". . . rest of the world.": Du Bois, "Race Friction Between Black and White," *American Journal of Sociology*, 13 (May 1908): 834–38, in *Periodical Literature*, I, 386–90, p. 389; also Pettigrew, *Sociology of Race Relations*, p. 32. ". . . from such a social philosophy!": Du Bois, "Race Friction," p. 390; also Pettigrew, *Sociology of Race Relations*, p. 32.

64. ". . . world . . . for the world.": Du Bois, "Race Friction," *Periodical Literature*, I, 389. Park's race-relations cycle: see Bottomore and Nisbet, eds., *A History of Sociological Analysis*, pp. 464–68; Fred H. Matthews, *Quest for an American Sociology: Robert H. Park and the Chicago School*, p. 132; Pettigrew, *Sociology of Race Relations*, pp. 606–23. Du Bois, "The Future of the Negro in America," *East and the West*, in Aptheker, *Annotated Bibliography*, p. 19.

65. ". . . sending you some literature.": W.E.B. Du Bois to Charles Francis Adams, Nov. 23, 1908; Charles Francis Adams to W.E.B. Du Bois, Nov. 28, 1908, Du Bois Papers/U. Mass.—"I infer that your purpose is to administer me a rebuke. . . . I do not know any direction in which to go for safer guides than to Mr. Washington and Mr. Stone. But perhaps you can instruct me better."

66. SAR rejection: George G. Bradford to W.E.B. Du Bois, Dec. 20, 1907; June 5, 1908, Du Bois Papers/U. Mass.; David Levering Lewis to the executive director, Sons of the American Revolution, Aug. 21, 1991; Everett H. Sanneman, Jr., M.D., genealogist general, The National Society of the Sons of the American Revolution, to David Levering Lewis, Sept. 4, 1991—"The policy of the National Society of the Sons of the American Revolution has never excluded anyone because of race, color or creed. The qualifications for membership include two factors: (1) Demonstration of Revolutionary War service either in the military or as a patriot, and (2) Documentation of birth, marriage, and death dates of the applicant's lineage." I remain skeptical.

67. Tonsillectomy: George E. Schambaugh, M.D., to W.E.B. Du Bois, n.d., 1908, Du Bois Papers/U. Mass. ". . . belong with any other?": Mary White Ovington to W.E.B. Du Bois, Aug. 29, 1908; Apr. 24, 1908. Du Bois Papers/U. Mass.

68. ". . . something . . . has been done.": Fred McGhee to W.E.B. Du Bois, Dec. 27, 1907, Du Bois Papers/U. Mass. ". . . a much wider basis.": Charles W. Chesnutt to Booker T. Washington, Aug. 11, 1903, in Harlan, ed., *B. T. Washington Papers*, VII, 262–67, p. 265. . . . "interested" in the movement.: W.E.B. Du Bois to E. G. Routzahn, Mar. 27, 1908, Du Bois Papers/U. Mass.

69. ". . . all down but one.": Wedin, "Ovington," p. 108. ". . . increasingly to admire."—Ovington, quoted: Fox, *Guardian of Boston*, p. 107; Wedin, "Ovington," p. 110. W.E.B. Du Bois to Mary White Ovington, Oct. 14, 1907, Box 1, Series 1, Ovington Collection/Reuther Library/WSU.

70. Trotter's league: Fox, *Guardian of Boston*, p. 140.

71. Trotter abandons Niagara: Fox, *Guardian of Boston*, p. 110. ". . . keep them working."—Du Bois quoted: *ibid.*, pp. 112–13. ". . . inexperience with organizations.": Du Bois, *Dusk of Dawn*, p. 95. J. R. Clifford to Dear Secretary and Comrades, Aug. 16, 1909, Du Bois Papers/U. Mass.

72. *The Negro American Family: Report of a Social Study Made Principally by the College Classes of 1909 and 1910 of Atlanta University, under the Patronage of the Trustees of the John F. Slater Fund; Together with the Proceedings of the Thirteenth Annual Conference for the Study of the Negro Problems, held at Atlanta University, May 26, 1908* (Atlanta: Atlanta University Press, 1908); Aptheker, *Annotated Bibliography*, pp. 532–33. Slater Fund support: Edward T. Ware to W.E.B. Du Bois, July 15, 1908; July 29, 1908, Du Bois Papers/U. Mass.

73. "The Economics of the Family": Ovington, "The Negro Family in New York"; Addams, "Conclusions"—*ibid.* Jane Addams to W.E.B. Du Bois, Oct. 25, 1907; W.E.B. Du Bois to Jane Addams, May 18, 1980; May 19, 1908; May 20, 1908, Du Bois Papers/U. Mass.

74. ". . . he is more primitive.": Du Bois, *Negro American Family*, p. 37.

75. ". . . a slaughter of the poor.": Du Bois, "Dying," *The Horizon*, 1 (May 1907): 3–10, in Aptheker, ed., *Selections from the Horizon*, 17–18, p. 17.

76. "Dill, Augustus Granville (1881–1956)," *DANB*, pp. 177–78. *Efforts for Social Betterment among Negro Americans: Report of a Social Study Made by Atlanta University under the patronage of the Trustees of the John F. Slater Fund; Together with the Proceedings of the Fourteenth Annual Conference for the Study of the Negro Problems, held at Atlanta University on May 24, 1909* (Atlanta: Atlanta University Press, 1909). This study includes "The Social Betterment of the Russian Peasant," by I. M. Rubinow; Aptheker, *Annotated Bibliography*, pp. 533–34.

77. ". . . prospect of a larger annual income.": Edward T. Ware to W.E.B. Du Bois, July 10, 1908, Du Bois Papers/U. Mass. . . . one of those "circumstances.": Du Bois, *Autobiography*, p. 253. Eliot: Atlanta University Brochure (1909), in Du Bois Papers/U. Mass.

78. Planning the *Encyclopedia*: Letterhead stationery listing members of the board of advisors for the *Encyclopedia Africana*, in Du Bois Papers/U. Mass. W.E.B. Du Bois to Edward Wilmot Blyden, Apr. 5, 1909, Du Bois Papers/U. Mass., also Aptheker, *Correspondence*, I, 146.

79. ". . . in ways more practical": Wallace Buttrick to W.E.B. Du Bois, Apr. 3, 1905, Du Bois Papers/U. Mass.

80. Enlarged *Horizon*: Aptheker, *Annotated Bibliography*, p. 109; Aptheker, *Selections from the Horizon*, p. viii. ". . . slavery to the Solid South.": Du Bois, "Negro Vote," *The Horizon*, 4 (Aug. 1908): 1–8, in Aptheker, ed., *Selections from the Horizon*, p. 66.

81. ". . . vision of eternal success.": Du Bois, "Ida Dean Bailey," *Horizon*, 3 (Mar. 1908): 1, 2–8, in Aptheker, ed., *Selections from the Horizon*, p. 48. ". . . Mr. Peabody is still dead.": Du Bois, "Notes," *The Horizon*, 1 (Mar. 1907): 3–10, in *ibid.*, p. 11.

82. ". . . Let freedom ring!": Du Bois, "My Country 'Tis of Thee," *The Horizon*, 2 (Nov. 1907): 5–6, in Aptheker, ed., *Creative Writings by W.E.B. Du Bois: A Pageant, Poems, Short Stories, and Playlets* (White Plains, N.Y.: Kraus-Thomson, 1985), p. 15; this edition includes "The Song of the Smoke," "The Burden of Black Women," and "A Day in Africa."

83. Financing *The Horizon*: Aptheker, ed., "Introduction," *Selections from the Horizon*, p. viii. ". . . the business affairs of the *Horizon*.": L. M. Hershaw to W.E.B. Du Bois, July 4, 1908, Du Bois Papers/U. Mass. ". . . unable to keep accounts.": W.E.B. Du Bois to Mr. A. B. Humphrey, Mar. 29, 1909, Du Bois Papers/U. Mass.

84. "Guarantors of *The Horizon*," Mar. 10, 1909, Fol. Du Bois, W.E.B., Box 95-2, Joel E. Spingarn Papers/Moorland-Spingarn Res. Ctr./Howard University; John Milholland to W.E.B. Du Bois, Mar. 4, 1909, Du Bois Papers/U. Mass. *The New Horizon*: Du Bois Circular Letter, Mar. 11, 1909, Du Bois Papers/U. Mass.; Du Bois, "The New Horizon," *The Horizon*, 4 (Nov.–Dec. 1908): 11–14, in Aptheker, ed., *Selections from the Horizon*, p. 79. ". . . *Horizon* was excellent.": W.E.B. Du Bois to L. M. Hershaw, Dec. 1, 1909, Du Bois Papers/U. Mass.

85. ". . . votes for women.": Du Bois, "Our Policy," *The Horizon*, 5 (Nov. 1909): 1–2, 8–9, in Aptheker, ed., *Selections from the Horizon*, p. 80. ". . . God cannot be lost.": Du Bois, "Niagara Movement," *The Horizon*, 5 (Nov. 1909): 1–2, 8–9, in *ibid.*, p. 84.

86. Du Bois, "Constructive Work," *The Horizon*, 5 (Dec. 1909): 2, in Aptheker, *Creative Writings*, p. 73. Aptheker, "Introduction," *ibid.*, p. viii. ". . . We have progressed.": Du Bois, "The Balance," *The Horizon*, 5 (Jan. 1910): 1–4, 7, in Aptheker, ed., *Selections from the Horizon*, p. 95.

87. ". . . afford the expense of coming North.": W.E.B. Du Bois to Albert Bushnell Hart, Dec. 17, 1909; Dec. 17, 1909, Du Bois Papers/U. Mass. ". . . unsafe on the question.": Oswald Garrison Villard to Albert Bushnell Hart, Dec. 6, 1909; Albert Bushnell Hart to Oswald Garrison Villard, Dec. 4, 1909, Oswald Garrison Villard Papers/Houghton Library/Harvard.

88. . . . "tragic era" of Negro misrule.: Albert Bushnell Hart to Oswald Garrison Villard, Dec. 4, 1909, expressed the distinctly unpopular view that his "own candid opinion is that Reconstruction did [*a great*/crossed out] many good things for which it has never been properly credited." For summations of early Reconstruction historiography, see David Levering Lewis, "Introduction," in W.E.B. Du Bois, *Black Reconstruction in America, 1860–1880* (New York: Atheneum, 1992; orig. pub. 1935), pp. vii–xvii; Howard N. Rabinowitz, "Introduction: The Changing Image of Black Reconstructionists," in Rabinowitz, ed., *Southern Black Leaders of the Reconstruction Era* (Urbana and London: University of Illinois Press, 1982), pp. xi–xxiv; Eric Foner, "Epilogue: The River Has Its Bend," in Foner, *Reconstruction: America's Unfinished Revolution, 1863–1877*, pp. 602–12; Howard K. Beale, "On Rewriting Reconstruction," *American Historical Review*, 45 (July 1940): 802–27; Eric Foner, "Reconstruction Revisited," *Reviews in American History*, 10 (Dec. 1982): 82–100; and Du Bois, "The Propaganda of History," *The Library of America Du Bois*, pp. 1026–47. "Reconstruction and Its Benefits"—quoted: *Periodical Literature*, II, pp. 9, 16. ". . . New social legislation.": Du Bois, "Reconstruction and Its Benefits," *American Historical Review*, 15 (July 1910): 781–99, in *Periodical Literature*, II, p. 18.

89. ". . . the paper in high terms.": Albert Bushnell Hart to W.E.B. Du Bois, Jan. 2, 1910, Du Bois Papers/U. Mass.

90. ". . . a matter of courtesy . . .": W.E.B. Du Bois to J. Franklin Jameson, June 2, 1910; J. Franklin Jameson to W.E.B. Du Bois, June 10, 1910, Du Bois Papers/U. Mass.; also Aptheker, *Correspondence*, I, p. 171. Booker Washington and "Negro": Harlan, *B. T. Washington Papers*, I, 207, and X, 614. ". . . regards as a personal insult.": W.E.B. Du Bois

to J. Franklin Jameson, June 13, 1910, Du Bois Papers/U. Mass.; also Aptheker, *Correspondence*, I, 172. ". . . simply one of typography": J. Franklin Jameson to W.E.B. Du Bois, June 22, 1910, Office File, Box 80, J. Franklin Jameson Papers/Library of Congress.

91. ". . . more insulting usage.": W.E.B. Du Bois to J. Franklin Jameson, July 5, 1910, Du Bois Papers/U. Mass.

14. NAACP: The Beginning

1. "Gentlemen . . . my resignation.": W.E.B. Du Bois to the president and trustees of Atlanta University, July 5, 1910, W. E. Matthews Collection/Atlanta University Archives/Woodruff Library. Du Bois resigns: Myron W. Adams to W.E.B. Du Bois, July 25, 1910, Du Bois Papers/U. Mass.; "Minutes of the Resignation of Dr. Du Bois," Aug. [n.d.] 1910, Du Bois Papers/U. Mass.; Edward T. Ware to W.E.B. Du Bois, Aug. 1, 1910, Du Bois Papers/U. Mass.

2. Nina and Yolande in Atlanta: W.E.B. Du Bois to Edward T. Ware, Aug. 1, 1910; Edward T. Ware to W.E.B. Du Bois, July 22, 1910, Du Bois Papers/U. Mass. ". . . take the risk.": William English Walling to W.E.B. Du Bois, June 8, 1910, Du Bois Papers/U. Mass.

3. NAACP progenitors: see, Du Bois, *The Autobiography*, pp. 254–76; Du Bois, "National Committee on the Negro," *Survey*, 22 (June 12, 1909): 407–9, in Aptheker, ed., *Periodical Literature*, I, pp. 399–402; Ovington, "Beginnings of the NAACP," pp. 76–77; John Haynes Holmes, *I Speak for Myself: The Autobiography of John Haynes Holmes* (New York: Harper and Row, 1959); Mary White Ovington, *The Walls Came Tumbling Down* (New York: Harcourt, Brace and World, 1947), pp. 103–5; Charles Edward Russell, *Bare Hands and Stone Walls: Some Recollections of a Side-Line Reformer* (New York: Charles Scribner's Sons, 1933), p. 225; Oswald Garrison Villard, *Fighting Years: Memoirs of a Liberal Editor* (New York: Harcourt, Brace and Co., 1939), pp. 193–94. ". . . a minimum of constructive work.": Mary White Ovington, "Beginnings of the NAACP, Reminiscences," *The Crisis*, 32 (June 1926): 77. General works of value, and articles and monographs dealing with the NAACP, are Charles Flint Kellogg, *NAACP: A History of the National Association for the Advancement of Colored People* (Baltimore: The Johns Hopkins University Press, 1967), I, 1909–1920, to date the best monograph on the subject, of which only volume one was finished before Kellogg's demise; Langston Hughes, *Fight for Freedom: The Story of the NAACP* (New York: W.W. Norton and Co., 1962); Warren D. St. James, *The National Association for the Advancement of Colored People: A Case Study in Pressure Groups* (New York: Exposition Press, 1958); Elliott Rudwick and August Meier, "The Rise of the Black Secretariat in the NAACP, 1909–35," in Meier and Rudwick, eds., *Along the Color Line: Explorations in the Black Experience* (Urbana and London: University of Illinois Press, 1976), pp. 94–127, esp. pp. 94–95; the papers of the NAACP are deposited with the Library of Congress. For an excellent recent overview of the progressive origins of the NAACP, see August Meier and John H. Bracey, Jr., "The NAACP as a Reform Movement, 1900–1965: 'To Reach the Conscience of America,'" *Journal of Southern History*, 49 (Feb. 1993): 3–30, esp. pp. 3–9.

4. Springfield's racial demographics: Walling, "Race War in the North," pp. 529–30; Kellogg, *NAACP*, pp. 10–11. ". . . Women want protection!"—quoted: "Frenzied Mob Sweeps City, Wreaking Bloody Vengeance for Negro's Heinous Crime," *The Illinois State Journal*, Aug. 15, 1908, p. 1. ". . . where you belong!"—quoted: William English Walling, "The Race War in the North," *The Independent*, 65 (Sept. 3, 1908): 529–34, p. 529; and "Frenzied Mob Sweeps City," *The Illinois State Journal*, Aug. 15, 1908, p. 1.

5. ". . . freed the niggers!"—quoted: "Frenzied Mob," p. 1. White reactions: Walling, "Race War," pp. 530–31.

6. Walling's biography: see Mary White Ovington, "William English Walling," *The Crisis*, 43 (Nov. 1936): 335; "Walling, William English," obituary, *New York Times*, Sept. 13, 1936, p. 11.

7. Fourth Niagara meeting: "Fourth Annual Meeting—Oberlin, Ohio, Aug. 31 to September 2, 1908," in Aptheker, ed., *Pamphlets and Leaflets by W.E.B. Du Bois*, p. 78. ". . . to come to their aid?": Walling, "Race War," p. 534. ". . . Springfield had no shame.": *ibid.*, p. 531.

8. Ovington contacts Walling: Kellogg, *NAACP*, p. 11. ". . . intelligent blacks.": Russell, *Bare Hands and Stone Walls*, p. 224. ". . . fluency of his utterance—unequalled.": *ibid.*, p. 219. ". . . the third a Southerner": Ovington, "William English Walling," *The Crisis*, 43 (Nov. 1936): 335; Ovington, *How the National Association for the Advancement of Colored People Began* (New York: Published by the NAACP, 1914), p. 1.

9. Walling organizes the progressives: Kellogg, *NAACP*, pp. 29–32; Russell, *Bare Hands*, p. 225; Ovington, *Walls Came Tumbling Down*, p. 103. ". . . our suggestion with enthusiasm.": Ovington, *How the NAACP Began*, p. 2.

10. "Minutes of the National Negro Conference (1909)," Monday, Nov. 8, at the Liberal Club, 4:30 P.M., Du Bois Papers/U. Mass. Ovington, *How the NAACP Began*, p. 2; Kellogg, *NAACP*, pp. 12, 15.

11. ". . . exercise of citizenship.": Villard, "The Call," Appendix A, in Kellogg, *NAACP*, p. 298.

12. ". . . it would not like to go."—Washington, quoted: Kellogg, *NAACP*, p. 19; Oswald Garrison Villard to William Lloyd Garrison, Feb 24, 1909, Oswald Garrison Villard Papers/Houghton Library/Harvard. ". . . discredit this affair."—Anderson quoted: Harlan, *B. T. Washington*, II, 361.

13. ". . . in the South . . . and ourselves."—Ward quoted: *Proceedings of the National Negro Conference, 1909* (New York: Arno Press, 1969), pp. 9–10; Ovington, *Walls Came Tumbling Down*, pp. 104–5; Du Bois, *Autobiography*, p. 254; Du Bois, "National Committee on the Negro," in Aptheker, ed., *Periodical Literature*: 399–400. Civil rights and women's rights: Kellogg, *NAACP*, pp. 25, 26; Nancy F. Cott, *The Grounding of Modern Feminism* (New Haven: Yale University Press, 1987), p. 68—"Despite links between early women's rights and anti-slavery reformers, the suffrage movement since the late nineteenth century had caved into the racism of the surrounding society, sacrificing democratic principle and the dignity of black people if it seemed advantageous to white women's obtaining the vote."

14. African-Americans at the conference: Du Bois, "National Committee on the Negro," p. 400; Du Bois, *Autobiography*, p. 254; *Proceedings*, 13–19; Ovington, *Walls*, pp. 106–7.

15. ". . . previous condition of servitude."—Ward, quoted: *Proceedings*, p. 10. Kellogg, *NAACP*, pp. 20–21. ". . . social capital."—Dewey quoted: *ibid.*, p. 73. ". . . depression of the prefrontal lobe."—Wilder, quoted: *ibid.*, p. 40. ". . . subject as they [southerners] do . . ."—Seligman, quoted: *Proceedings*, p. 70.

16. Cosmopolitan Club dinner: Carolyn Wedin, "Ovington MS—ch. 4," pp. 117–18; Harlan, *B. T. Washington*, II, pp. 376–77; Ovington, *Walls Came Tumbling Down*, pp. 104–5.

17. ". . . deprive him of it."—Walling, quoted: *Proceedings*, p. 75; Alfreda M. Duster, ed., *Crusader for Justice: The Autobiography of Ida B. Wells*, p. 287. ". . . utterly without scientific basis.": Du Bois, "National Committee of the Negro," Aptheker, ed., *Periodical Literature*, I, p. 400.

18. ". . . rascals into political power.": Du Bois, "Politics and Industry," *Proceedings*, p. 87.

19. On interracial labor solidarity: see B. Joyce Ross, *J. E. Spingarn and the Rise of the NAACP, 1911–1939* (New York: Atheneum, 1972), pp. 18–19; Kellogg, *NAACP*, p. 35; Du Bois, "The Economic Aspects of Race Prejudice," *The Editorial Review*, 2 (May 1910): 488–93, in Aptheker, ed., *Periodical Literature*, II, 1–5. Gompers on labor solidarity: Du Bois, "Fair Play for the Negro," letter to New York *Evening Post*, Nov. 25, 1910, p. 8, in *Periodical Literature*, II, 35.

20. ". . . name the condition.": Du Bois, "National Committee," p. 401.

21. Villard presiding: see Kellogg, *NAACP*, p. 21; Broderick, *Du Bois*, p. 21; *Proceedings*, pp. 203–4. ". . . most useful."—Villard quoted: Kellogg, *NAACP*, p. 22. ". . . white friends of ours."—quoted: Du Bois, "National Committee," p. 401, also in Francis L. Broderick, *W.E.B. Du Bois: Negro Leader in a Time of Crisis*, p. 91—Broderick speculates that the unidentified woman at the conference must have been Wells.

22. Amendments and resolutions: Stephen R. Fox, *Guardian of Boston: William Monroe Trotter*, pp. 127–28; "Resolutions," *Proceedings*, pp. 223–24.

23. ". . . none the less trying.": Oswald Garrison Villard, June 4, 1909, Oswald Garrison Villard Papers/Houghton/Harvard. ". . . from being blown up.": Ovington, "Beginnings of the NAACP," p. 77. ". . . know no color line.": Du Bois, "National Committee," p. 402.

24. "Resolutions," *Proceedings*, pp. 223–24; also in Appendix C, Kellogg, *NAACP*, pp. 302–3.

25. Interpretations by Du Bois, Ovington, Wells: Du Bois, *Autobiography*, p. 254; Kellogg, p. 22; Wells, *Autobiography*, pp. 325–26; Ovington, *Walls*, p. 106. ". . . outweighed my judgment.": Wells, *Autobiography*, p. 326.

26. Wells-Barnett and the NAACP: Ovington, "Beginnings of the NAACP," p. 77; Du Bois, *Autobiography*, p. 254. Villard's "balanced" roster: Kellogg, *NAACP*, pp. 19, 22; William English Walling to W.E.B. Du Bois, June 8, 1909, Du Bois Papers/U. Mass.; also Aptheker, *Correspondence*, I, pp. 147–49—"I did not attend the sub-committee because I had complete confidence that none of those present would make any important changes in the list of thirty names which Mr. Villard had so carefully drawn up. You had agreed with me that perhaps several colored members should be *added*. Mr. Milholland had the same feeling of confidence, as did several others who had seen the list. Here is what happened: Only three or four new colored names were added to the Committee, as I had urged; but I was no less than shocked to find that where three or four had been added, six or seven had been taken off."

27. ". . . film of his brain.": Oswald Garrison Villard, *Fighting Years: Memoirs of a Liberal Editor*, p. 46. ". . . Northern Pacific Railroad shares.": Quote and Villard profile: see D. Joy Humes, *Oswald Garrison Villard, Liberal of the 1920s* (New York: Syracuse University Press, 1960), esp. pp. 1–9; Kellogg, *NAACP*, pp. 12, 26; Meier, *Negro Thought in America*, pp. 181–83. ". . . are inexperienced and impractical": Oswald Garrison Villard to Francis Jackson Garrison, May 4, 1909, Oswald Garrison Villard Papers/Houghton Library/Harvard.

28. ". . . or a Du Bois movement.": Harlan, *B. T. Washington*, II, 360; Kellogg, *NAACP*, p. 19. ". . . bitterly anti-Washington.": Oswald Garrison Villard to Francis Jackson Garrison, June 4, 1909, Oswald Garrison Villard Papers/Houghton/Harvard.

29. "irreconciliable opposition.": Park quoted—Winifried Raushenbush, *Robert E. Park*, p. 75 and p. 49. ". . . guide the Negro group.": Du Bois, *Autobiography*, p. 254.

30. Additions to Committee of Forty: "The Committee of Forty," Appendix B, in Kellogg, *NAACP*, pp. 300–1; Du Bois, "Prospect for the Enlargement of the Committee of Forty to Fifty," Du Bois Papers/U. Mass.; William English Walling to W.E.B. Du Bois, June 8, 1909, Du Bois Papers/U. Mass.; also Aptheker, ed., *Correspondence*, I, 147–50.

31. November 1909 meeting: "Minutes of the National Negro Conference," Liberal Club, Nov. 8, 1909, Box A-8, Group I, Series I/NAACP Board Minutes/Library of Congress.

32. ". . . assertive and aggressive.": Du Bois, *Autobiography*, p. 256; Villard himself was a consistent, if not always sensitive, partisan of Jewish causes—see Humes, *Villard*, p. 96.

33. Loss of momentum and money: Kellogg, *NAACP*, p. 49.

34. Bookerite machinations: Kellogg, *NAACP*, p. 45; George Foster Peabody to W.E.B. Du Bois, Sept. 1, 1911—"I am really very sorry to have your letter fully confirm my feeling that you expected to win strength for the cause you have at heart, which you think the better way by fighting, and by definitely encouraging the idea of attacks upon the individuals who are leaders of the movement with which you so lack sympathy. . . . I know of no people whose splendid attitude throughout hundreds of years so fully confirm the virtue and ultimate value of non-resistance as the great and intensely interesting negro race." ". . . state of mind of the colored people . . .": Booker T. Washington to James A. Cobb, Apr. 1, 1910, Harlan, ed., *B. T. Washington Papers*, X, pp. 306–8; Harlan, *B. T. Washington*, II, p. 364.

35. . . . absent in Atlanta.: Kellogg, *NAACP*, p. 45. Frances Blascoer to "Dear Lady," Mar. 26, 1910, Du Bois Papers/U. Mass.

36. Preliminary committee: Kellogg, *NAACP*, p. 38; Special Meeting, National Negro Committee, Mar. 30, 1910/Box A-8, Group 1, Series A/NAACP Board Minutes/ Library of Congress. ". . . damnably acute intelligence.": Blascoer to "Dear Lady," Mar. 26, 1910, Du Bois Papers/U. Mass.

37. Boosters of the Committee: Blascoer to "Dear Lady," Mar. 26, 1910, Du Bois Papers/U. Mass.; Kellogg, *NAACP*, pp. 37–38. ". . . acquiescence in semi-serfdom"—Du Bois, quoted: "The Outlook," *Horizon*, 5 (May 1910), in *Selections from The Horizon*, p. 112; also "Editorial," N.Y. *Evening Post*, Apr. 1, 1910, in Harlan, ed., *B. T. Washington Papers*, X, 309–10.

38. ". . . from demanding too much.": "In-Look," *Horizon*, 5 (May 1910), in Aptheker, ed., *Selections from The Horizon*, 112. ". . . a word from Dr. Du Bois."—Villard, quoted: Harlan, ed., *B. T. Washington Papers*, X, 311.

39. ". . . pay her expenses.": Blascoer to "Dear Lady," Mar. 26, 1910, Du Bois Papers/ U. Mass.

40. Villard's objective approach: Kellogg, *NAACP*, p. 42. ". . . must be done.": Du Bois, "Atlanta University," *Horizon*, 6 (July 1910), in Aptheker, ed., *Selections from The Horizon*, 122.

41. ". . . dragged in the University.": Du Bois, *Autobiography*, p. 223. ". . . regarding Negro freedom.": John Hope to W.E.B. Du Bois, Jan. 17, 1910, Du Bois Papers/U. Mass.; also Aptheker, ed., *Correspondence*, II, 165–67.

42. ". . . I am a plodder.": John Hope to W.E.B. Du Bois, Jan. 17, 1910. ". . . Negro submission and slavery": W.E.B. Du Bois to John Hope, Jan. 22, 1910, Du Bois Papers/ U. Mass.; also Aptheker, ed., *Correspondence*, I, p. 167.

43. Terrell and Moton warnings: Robert Heberton Terrell to Booker T. Washington, Aug. 10, 1910, in Harlan, ed., *B. T. Washington Papers*, X, pp. 365–66 (p. 365); Moton, in Kellogg, *NAACP*, p. 42.

44. ". . . a colored leader . . . Dr. Du Bois"—Walling quoted: Kellogg, *NAACP*, p. 44.

45. "Disfranchisement and Its Effects upon the Negro," The National Negro Committee, Du Bois Papers/U. Mass. "shook hands across the chasm"—Ovington quoted: Kellogg, *NAACP*, p. 34.

46. Choice of "colored": Du Bois, "Gandhi and the American Negroes," *Gandhi Marg*, 1 (July 1957): 1–4, in Aptheker, *Annotated Bibliography*, p. 100.

47. Constitution League and NAACP: Du Bois, *Autobiography*, p. 254; Meier, *Negro Thought*, p. 182.

48. Association's new officers: Kellogg, *NAACP*, pp. 43, 44.

49. ". . . suspicious of my designs.": Du Bois, *Autobiography*, p. 254; *Dusk*, p. 225. "director of publicity and research": Blascoer to W.E.B. Du Bois, June 15, 1910, Du Bois Papers/U. Mass.". . . because of your color.": Frances Blascoer to W.E.B. Du Bois, June 15, 1910, Du Bois Papers/U. Mass.

50. ". . . promising, or steady position.": William English Walling to W.E.B. Du Bois, June 8, 1910, Du Bois Papers, Du Bois Papers/U. Mass.; also Aptheker, ed., *Correspondence*, I, 169–70.

51. "absolute failures": Harlan, ed., *B. T. Washington Papers*, p. 483; Harlan, *B. T. Washington*, II, p. 364. Wizard's displeasure: Booker T. Washington to Clark Howell, Nov. 23, 1910, in Harlan, ed., *B. T. Washington Papers*, X, pp. 483–84, (p. 484); also Booker T. Washington to Jacob Schiff, Sept. 18, 1909, *ibid.*—"My dear Mr. Schiff: Referring to the use of the Three Thousand Dollars ($3,000) to the credit of the Southern Education Fund, I would make the following suggestions."

52. ". . . in which I ought to go.": Du Bois, *Dusk*, p. 271.

15. *Rise of* The Crisis, *Decline of the Wizard*

1. ". . . color . . . absolutely determined it.": Du Bois, *Dusk of Dawn*, p. 136.

2. "The Present Crisis": Charles Flint Kellogg, *NAACP: A History of the National Association for the Advancement of Colored People*, I, p. 51; Du Bois, "The Second Birthday," *The Crisis*, 5 (Nov. 1912): 27–28, also in Herbert Aptheker, ed., *Selections from The Crisis* (Millbank, N.Y.: Kraus-Thomson, 1983), 2 vols., I, 42–43; Du Bois, *Dusk*, p. 225. ". . . the very same reception.": Albert E. Pillsbury to W.E.B. Du Bois, July 26, 1910, Du Bois Papers/U. Mass.; Du Bois, *The Autobiography: A Soliloquy on Viewing My Life from the Last Decade of Its First Century*, p. 259.

3. *The Horizon*: L. M. Hershaw to W.E.B. Du Bois, Apr. 9, 1910, Box 5, Fol. *Horizon*, W.E.B. Du Bois Collection/Fisk University Library. "' . . . I have no money.' "—Villard quoted: Du Bois, *Dusk*, p. 225. ". . . the cooperation of Oswald Garrison Villard.": The Cover Page, *The Crisis*, 1 (Nov. 1910).

4. ". . . the nominal price of One Dollar.": Du Bois, "Prospectus," in Aptheker, ed., *Pamphlets and Leaflets by W.E.B. Du Bois* (White Plains, N.Y.: Kraus-Thomson, 1986). The editorial board: Du Bois, "Prospectus," in *ibid.*, p. 94. *The Crisis* appears: Kellogg, *NAACP*, p. 52; Special Meeting of Executive Committee, Sept. 6th, 1910, Box A-8 (Group 1, Series A), 1909–12, NAACP Board Minutes/NAACP Papers/Library of Congress.

5. ". . . more than I can say . . ." Du Bois, "The Second Birthday," *The Crisis*, in Aptheker, ed., *Selections from The Crisis*, I, p. 43; Du Bois, *Dusk*, p. 226. "Miss Sunbeam" Mary White Ovington, "Mary Dunlop Maclean," *The Crisis*, 4 (Aug. 1912): 184–85. "Nash": Advertisement, *The Crisis*, 1, no. 2 (Dec. 1910): 4; Du Bois, "Editorial," *The Crisis*, 1, no. 1 (Nov. 1910): 10–11; *Autobiography*, p. 292; Kellogg, *NAACP*, p. 52.

6. Lineage of *The Crisis*: Aptheker, ed., *Documentary History of the Negro People in the United States* (New York: The Citadel Press, 1951), 5 vols., I, pp. 82–86, 108–11, 413–16, *et passim*. Frederick G. Detweiler, *Negro Press in the United States* (Chicago: University of Chicago Press, 1922), pp. 32–52. Martin Duberman, ed., *The Antislavery Vanguard: New Essays on the Abolitionists* (Princeton, N. J.: Princeton University Press, 1965), pp. 103–4;

John Hope Franklin, *From Slavery to Freedom*, pp. 172–73, 186–89; Aileen S. Kraditor, *Means and Ends in American Abolitionism: Garrison and His Critics on Strategy and Tactics, 1834–1850* (New York: Pantheon Books, 1969), pp. 86–87; Sterling Stuckey, *The Ideological Origins of Black Nationalism* (Boston: Beacon Press, 1972), contains the full text of David Wakler's *Appeal*; Emma Lou Thornbrough, *T. Thomas Fortune: Militant Journalist*, p. 44; Wilson J. Moses, *The Golden Age of Black Nationalism, 1850–1925*, pp. 83–101; Benjamin Quarles, *Black Abolitionists* (New York: Oxford University Press, 1969), pp. 85–89.

7. ". . . colored Drug Store . . .": Advertisements, *The Crisis*, 1 (Nov. 1910): 16–17.

8. ". . . rancor of all sorts . . .": Du Bois, "Editorial," *The Crisis* 1 (Nov. 1910): 10–11, p. 10. "Men of the Month": "Talks About Women," *The Crisis*, 1 (Dec. 1910): 28; "Men of the Month," *The Crisis*, 2 (May 1911): 10–11; to follow the magazine's evolution from January 1911, see Aptheker, ed., *Selections from The Crisis*.

9. ". . . doubtless deeply appreciate.": Du Bois, "Editorial," *The Crisis* 1 (Nov. 1910): ". . . the same rule in both cases?": Moorfield Storey, "Athens and Brownsville," *ibid.*, p. 13.

10. ". . . white races entered Africa.": Du Bois, "Along the Color Line," *ibid.*, pp. 3–5. Steve Greene peonage case: Du Bois, "The Burden," *ibid.*, p. 14.

11. Pink Franklin Case: Kellogg, *NAACP*, p. 59; Richard Kluger, *Simple Justice: The History of Brown v. Board of Education*, p. 101; for general treatment of peonage, see Pete Daniel, *The Shadow of Slavery: Peonage in the South, 1901–1969* (Urbana and London: University of Illinois Press, 1972), pp. 68–69.

12. . . . safety in Canada: Ross, *Spingarn*, pp. 19–21; Kellogg, *NAACP*, pp. 59–62.

13. ". . . America needs to learn more?": Du Bois, "Segregation," *ibid.*, p. 10. Du Bois, "What To Read," *The Crisis* 1 (Dec. 1910): see Aptheker, ed., *Annotated Bibliography*, p. 124.

14. ". . . its success was phenomenal.": Du Bois, *The Autobiography*, p. 259; *Dusk of Dawn*, p. 226. Subscriptions: "Document, Dec. 1912" (Department of Publicity and Research), Du Bois Papers/U. Mass.; Du Bois, *Dusk of Dawn*, p. 226; "Photo of First Subscriber," *The Crisis*, 5 (Nov. 1912); and "The Second Birthday," *ibid.*, pp. 27–28; also in Aptheker, ed., *Selections from The Crisis*, pp. 42–43. ". . . poor classes in Europe.": Du Bois, "Along the Color Line," *The Crisis* 1 (Nov. 1910): p. 5; (see Harlan, *B. T. Washington*, II, p. 293 for genesis of *The Man Farthest Down*). Franz Boas, "The Real Race Problem?" *The Crisis*, 2 (Dec. 1910): 22–25; Mrs. John E. Milholland, "Talks About Women," *ibid.*, p. 28.

15. "An Appeal to England and Europe": John Milholland, "Letter," Sept. 6, 1910, in Du Bois Papers/U. Mass.; "Interview with W.E.B. Du Bois" [n.d.], Charles H. Thompson Papers (unprocessed collection)/Moorland-Spingarn Res. Ctr./Howard; and Du Bois, "An Appeal to England," in Aptheker, *Pamphlets and Leaflets*, pp. 95–98.

16. . . . miscarriage of justice in the courts: "Appeal," in Aptheker, ed., *Pamphlets and Leaflets*, p. 97. ". . . misrepresent the truth.": Du Bois, *ibid.*, p. 97; Du Bois, *Dusk*, p. 229; and, Kellogg, *NAACP*, p. 77.

17. Black institutions assailed (". . . empty sermons."): Du Bois, "The Negro Church," *The Crisis*, 4 (May 1912): 24–25; Du Bois, *Autobiography*, p. 110; Du Bois, "The New Wilberforce," *The Crisis*, 8 (Aug. 1914): 191–94; Kellogg, *NAACP*, p. 99; Rudwick, *Du Bois*, p. 168. ". . . his inferiors."—Storey, quoted: Elliott M. Rudwick, *W.E.B. Du Bois: Propagandist of the Negro Protest*, pp. 171, 168; Kellogg, *NAACP*, p. 99.

18. See "Magazines Edited by W.E.B. Du Bois," in Aptheker, *Annotated Bibliography*, pp. 130–33.

19. Circulation figures: Du Bois, "The Second Birthday," *The Crisis*, 5 (Nov. 1912): 27–28; "Document," Dec. 1912, Du Bois Papers/U. Mass. Mary Maclean, "African Civilization," *The Crisis*, 1 (Mar. 1911): 23–25.

20. ". . . too much in the upper ether.": John E. Bruce to Alain Leroy Locke, Apr. 14, 1913, Box Brop-Burk, Alain Leroy Locke Collection/Moorland-Spingarn Res. Ctr./Howard University. Marie Brown Frazier—quoted: Anthony M. Platt, *E. Franklin Frazier Reconsidered* (New Brunswick, N.J.: Rutgers University Press, 1991), p. 60. J. Saunders Redding—quoted: David Levering Lewis, *When Harlem Was in Vogue*, p. 7. *Crisis* fans: J. E. Kwegyir Aggrey to W.E.B. Du Bois, July 1, 1913, Du Bois Papers/U. Mass.; also Aptheker, ed., *Selected Correspondence of W.E.B. Du Bois*, I, 182–84.

21. ". . . White Women Only.' ": Du Bois, "Forward Backward," *The Crisis*, 2 (Oct. 1911): 243–44, p. 243. ". . . women's obtaining the vote.": Nancy F. Cott, *The Grounding of Modern Feminism*, p. 68; and Paula Giddings, *When and Where I Enter: The Impact of Black Women on Race and Sex in America* (New York: William Morrow and Co., 1984), pp. 162–63.

22. ". . . do not belong to us . . .": Irene Diggs, "Du Bois and Women: A Short Story of Black Women," *A Current Bibliography on African Affairs*, 7 (Summer 1974): 260–379, p. 284; Kellogg, *NAACP*, p. 207. ". . . presented to the convention."—Donnet, quoted: Diggs, "Du Bois and Women," p. 284.

23. . . . greater percentages than were white women.: Giddings, *When and Where I Enter*, pp. 156–60, 162–63; and Cynthia Neverdon-Morton, *Afro-American Women of the South and the Advancement of the Race, 1895–1925* (Knoxville: The University of Tennessee Press, 1989), p. 68. ". . . can oppose woman suffrage."—Du Bois, quoted: "A Women's Suffrage Symposium," *The Crisis*, 4 (Sept. 1912): 243; Du Bois, "Votes for Women," *ibid.*, p. 234. ". . . his ideals and his country.": Du Bois, "Woman Suffrage," *The Crisis*, 9 (Apr. 1915): 285. ". . . Happy Land!": Du Bois, "Hail Columbia!" *The Crisis*, 5 (April 1913): 289–90; and Aptheker, *Crisis Selections*, I, pp. 55–56.

24. Labor and African-Americans: see Du Bois, "Organized Labor," *The Crisis*, 4 (July 1912): 131; *ibid.*, p. 204; Manning Marable, *W.E.B. Du Bois: Black Radical Democrat*, pp. 87–88. ". . . live in the same town.": Du Bois, *Autobiography*, p. 305; Sterling D. Spero and Abram Harris, *The Black Worker. The Negro and the Labor Movement* (New York: Columbia University Press, 1931), pp. 192–204. The actual success in organizing African-Americans by the IWW is significantly qualified by the most careful student of the subject. Disputing the claim made by Sterling D. Spero and Abram Harris, *The Black Worker*, of 100,000 membership cards issued to African-Americans, Philip Foner states that "it is likely that the Wobblies never succeeded in recruiting a very large Negro membership": Foner, "The IWW and the Black Worker," *Journal of Negro History*, 55 (Jan. 1970): 45–64, p. 50. It is also significant that the IWW, like the Socialists, understood the racial problem to be a subordinate aspect of the primary labor problem.

25. ". . . inside the union lines": Du Bois, "Organized Labor," p. 131. ". . . their darker and poorer fellows.": *ibid.*, p. 131. ". . . my provincial racialism": Du Bois, *In Battle for Peace* (Millwood, N.Y.: Kraus-Thomson, 1976), p. 180.

26. "rung truest on the race question . . .": Du Bois, *Dusk*, p. 235; Rudwick, *Du Bois*, p. 251. ". . . we would do so.": Du Bois, "Politics," *The Crisis*, 4 (Aug. 1912): 180–81, p. 181.

27. ". . . further degeneration."—Berger, quoted: Nick Salvatore, *Eugene V. Debs: Citizen and Socialist* (Urbana and Chicago: University of Illinois Press, 1982), p. 226. ". . . apart from the general labor problem."—Debs, quoted: *ibid.*, pp. 266, 228; Spero and Harris, *The Black Worker*, p. 405. ". . . afraid to encourage such workers.": Du Bois, "Forward Backward," *The Crisis*, 2 (Oct. 1911): 243–44, p. 244. ". . . test of the American Socialist.": Du Bois, "Socialism and the Negro Problem," *New Review*, 1 (Feb. 1, 1913): 138–41; Paul Richards, "W.E.B. Du Bois and American Social History: The Evolution of a Marxist," *Radical America*, 4 (Nov. 1970): 37–65.

28. ". . . editorial pages were not for sale.": Du Bois, "The Last Word in Politics," *The Crisis*, 5 (Nov. 1912): 29. ". . . sorry—and helpless.": Du Bois, "Politics," *The Crisis*, 4 (Aug. 1912): 129–30. ". . . votes for Negroes and industrial democracy.": Du Bois, "A Pageant in Seven Decades: 1868–1938," in *Pamphlets and Leaflets*, p. 263; Ross, *Spingarn*, pp. 18–19. ". . . on which other citizens vote.": Du Bois, "A Pageant in Seven Decades: 1868–1938," in *Pamphlets and Leaflets*, p. 263.

29. The Progressive party convention: Ross, *Spingarn*, pp. 18–19; Kellogg, *NAACP*, p. 155. ". . . a dangerous person."—Roosevelt quoted: Du Bois, "A Pageant in Seven Decades," p. 263; Du Bois, "The Last Word in Politics," p. 29. ". . . than any other one.": Jane Addams, *Forty Years at Hull House: Being "Twenty Years at Hull House" and "The Second Twenty Years at Hull House"* (New York: Macmillan, 1935), p. 37; Kellogg, *NAACP*, p. 155.

30. Wilson's profile: see John Morton Blum, *Woodrow Wilson and the Politics of Morality* (Boston: Little Brown, 1956), esp. pp. 18–31; Jan Willem Schulte Nordholt, *Woodrow Wilson: A Life for World Peace* (Berkeley: University of California Press, 1991), pp. 23–65; Sigmund Freud and William C. Bullitt, *Thomas Woodrow Wilson: A Psychological Study* (Boston: Houghton Mifflin Company, 1967), pp. 50–63. "President of all the people.": Humes, *Villard*, p. 80; Stephen Fox, *Guardian of Boston*, p. 167; Kellogg, *NAACP*, pp. 157–58; Meier, *Negro Thought*, p. 187. Arthur S. Link, "The Negro as a Factor in the Campaign of 1912," *Journal of Negro History*, 32 (Jan. 1947): 81–99.

31. ". . . and cordial good feeling."—Wilson quoted: Woodrow Wilson to Alexander Walters, Oct. 16, 1912, Du Bois Papers/U. Mass.; Alexander Walters, *My Life and Work*, p. 195; Du Bois, "A Pageant in Seven Decades," p. 263; Humes, *Villard*, p. 80; Kellogg, *NAACP*, p. 157.

32. On William Robeson: Martin Bauml Duberman, *Paul Robeson* (New York: Alfred A. Knopf, 1988), p. 28. ". . . or his college.": Du Bois, "Politics," p. 181. ". . . gives us hope.": Du Bois, "The Election," *The Crisis*, 5 (Dec. 1912): 75. ". . . heard and considered.": Du Bois, "Politics," *The Crisis*, 4 (Aug. 1912): 181.

33. ". . . damnable shame.": Du Bois, "A Philosophy for 1913," *The Crisis*, 5 (Jan. 1913): 127.

34. *Bailey v. Alabama*: Du Bois, "Pink Franklin's Reprieve," *The Crisis*, 1 (Feb. 1911): 15; Harlan, *B. T. Washington*, II, 249–50; Daniel, *Shadow of Slavery*, p. 79. ". . . But he did not.": Du Bois, "A Well Wisher," *The Crisis*, 7 (Apr. 1914): 274–75, p. 275; Kellogg, *NAACP*, p. 98.

35. ". . . preserve a dignified silence.": Du Bois, "Social Equality," *The Crisis*, 2 (Sept. 1911): 195–97. ". . . watch your State legislatures.": Du Bois, "Intermarriage," *The Crisis*, 5 (Feb. 1913): 180–81, p. 181.

36. ". . . portions of unrecognizable bones.": Du Bois, "Triumph," *The Crisis*, 2 (Sept. 1911): 195. ". . . not like bales of hay.": *ibid*.

37. Wizard alarmed by *The Crisis*: Harlan, *B. T. Washington*, II, p. 365. ". . . impecunious camp-followers.": *ibid*., p. 371. ". . . through Du Bois."—Washington quoted: *ibid*., p. 376.

38. Anderson, quoted: Wedin, "Ovington MS—ch. 4," pp. 68–69. ". . . on down the line.": Mary Church Terrell, *A Colored Woman in a White World* (Washington, D.C.: National Association of Colored Women's Clubs, 1968), p. 192. ". . . when the time comes.": Booker T. Washington to Robert Heberton Terrell, Apr. 27, 1910, Harlan, ed., *B. T. Washington Papers*, X, p. 323; Harlan, *B. T. Washington*, II, p. 366.

39. Milholland's Pneumatic Tube Co.: Wedin, "Ovington MS—ch. 4," p. 65. ". . . villainous" attacks.: Oswald Garrison Villard to Robert Russa Moton, Apr. 5, 1911, Harlan, ed., *B. T. Washington Papers*, XI, p. 83.

40. ". . . true African type.": N.Y. *Press*, in Harlan, *B. T. Washington*, II, pp. 377–78.

41. "Burn Walling up.": Washington quoted: Kellogg, *NAACP*, p. 80. ". . . at any public meeting."—*Age*, quoted: Kellogg, *NAACP*, p. 80; "Warsaw Girl on Witness Stand Makes Charges Against Mr. Walling," N.Y. *Herald*, Feb. 21, 1911; "Love Notes Amuse Wife in Suit Against Mr. Walling," N. Y. *Herald*, Feb. 24, 1911.

42. The Tenderloin: see Herbert Asbury, *The Gangs of New York: An Informal History of the Underworld* (New York: Paragon House, 1990; orig. pub. 1927), pp. 177, 336; and Lewis, *When Harlem Was in Vogue*, p. 27. ". . . high class prostitutes.": "Interview with W.E.B. Du Bois," Thompson Collection (unprocessed)/Moorland-Spingarn Res. Ctr. ". . . right in the face.": Harlan, *B. T. Washington*, II, p. 380.

43. Ulrich and Washington: "Booker T. Washington Is Confused Regarding Encounter," N. Y. *Herald*, Mar. 22, 1911, p. 1, in Harlan, ed., *B. T. Washington Papers*, XI, 16–17; Harlan, *B. T. Washington*, II, pp. 380–81.

44. Washington's consolers: Theodore Roosevelt to Booker T. Washington, Mar. 28, 1911, in Harlan, *B. T. Washington Papers*, XI, p. 50 (also Taft [p. 10]; Low [p. 28–29]); Harlan, *B. T. Washington*, II, pp. 380–81, 383–84.

45. ". . . meet a white woman, etc."—Villard, quoted: Harlan, *B. T. Washington*, II, p. 884.

46. Marshall's: see Mary White Ovington, *Half a Man: The Status of the Negro in New York* (New York: Hill and Wang, 1969; orig. pub. 1911), pp. 21–22; James Weldon Johnson, *Black Manhattan* (New York: Da Capo Press, 1991; orig. pub. 1930), pp. 118–20; Lewis, *Vogue*, pp. 28–29. Rumor and circumstantial evidence that Washington had a drinking problem is plentiful, and the following observation upon meeting Washington by Thomas Jesse Jones, the white Hampton instructor and future "Negro expert," is revealing: "I went down to the car and said I wanted to see Mr. Washington. He was out in the open pullman. Mr. Scott came and stood by him. In general, whenever he was going to talk to anybody about anything that was important, his secretary was there. Mr. Scott could tell him in the next day just what had happened." Jones, quoted by Linda O. McMurry, *Recorder of the Black Experience: A Biography of Monroe Nathan Work* (Baton Rouge: Louisiana State University Press, 1985), p. 51. A self-appointed, white citizens' Committee of Fourteen attempted to close Marshall's in 1912 because of the "persons of the Caucasian race who frequent the place." Du Bois rallied Henry Moskowitz, Isaac Seligman, and others in the hotel's defense, as the following correspondence reveals: Frederick H. Whitin, general secretary of the Committee of Fourteen, to W.E.B. Du Bois, Oct. 11; Oct. 15, 1912; W.E.B. Du Bois to the Committee of Fourteen, Oct. 10, 14, 18, 29, 1912, Du Bois Papers/ U. Mass. ". . . come to the surface.": "Interview with W.E.B. Du Bois," Thompson Collection.

47. ". . . men when standing up."—*Guardian*, quoted: Harlan, *B. T. Washington*, II, p. 385; Du Bois, "An Assault on Mr. Washington," *The Crisis*, 2 (May 1911): 33. ". . . genuine and profound regret.": "Editorial," Lynchburg *News*, Mar. 23, 1911, in Harlan, ed., *B. T. Washington Papers*, XI, pp. 34–35 (p. 34); Harlan, ed., *B. T. Washington*, II, p. 386.

48. The Sumner celebration: Kellogg, *NAACP*, pp. 54–55.

49. Truce time: *ibid.*, p. 80.

50. ". . . the directions that I have mentioned.": Booker T. Washington to Oswald Garrison Villard, Mar. 30, 1911, in Harlan, ed., *B. T. Washington Papers*, XI, pp. 54–55; Charles William Anderson to Booker T. Washington, Mar. 29, 1911, *ibid.*, pp. 52–53; William Henry Lewis to Booker T. Washington, Mar. 29, 1911, *ibid.*, p. 55; Robert Russa Moton to Booker T. Washington, Mar. 29, 1911, *ibid.*, p. 53. ". . . the public conscience."—NAACP resolution, quoted: in Harlan, ed., *B. T. Washington Papers*, XI, p. 69; Kellogg, *NAACP*, p. 82.

51. ". . . solid front to the enemy": Oswald Garrison Villard to Robert Russa Moton, Apr. 5, 1911, in Harlan, ed., *B. T. Washington Papers*, XI, p. 83; Kellogg, *NAACP*, p. 82.

52. ". . . in such directions.": Du Bois, "Starvation and Prejudice," *The Crisis*, 2 (June 1911): 62–64, p. 64; Kellogg, *NAACP*, p. 83.

53. ". . . to some extent to this affair.": "Interview with W.E.B. Du Bois," Thompson Collection (unprocessed).

16. Connections at Home and Abroad

1. ". . . then eat[ing] too much.": Nina Gomer Du Bois to W.E.B. Du Bois, Nov. 10, 1910; Jan. 9, 1911 [?]; Tuesday 1911; Apr. 17, 1911 [?]; May 7, 1911, in Du Bois Papers/ U. Mass.

2. ". . . I suppose you've seen it.": Nina Gomer Du Bois to W.E.B. Du Bois, Nov. 13, 1910, Du Bois Papers/U. Mass. ". . . for the opening of school.": Nina Gomer Du Bois to W.E.B. Du Bois, Aug. 28, 1910, Du Bois Papers/U. Mass. ". . . in the bedroom at Yolande.": Nina Gomer Du Bois to W.E.B. Du Bois, Tuesday 1911, Du Bois Papers/ U. Mass.

3. ". . . write to us some time.": Nina Gomer Du Bois to W.E.B. Du Bois, Apr. 17, 1911[?]. ". . . lime in her system.": Nina Gomer Du Bois to W.E.B. Du Bois, Jan. 9, 1911[?]. ". . . she wouldn't send it.": Nina Gomer Du Bois to W.E.B. Du Bois, Aug. 28, 1910.

4. A busy Du Bois: Du Bois, "The Rural South," *Publications of the American Statistical Association*, 13 (Mar. 1912): 80–84; "Progress Report, Department of Publicity and Research, 1911," Du Bois Papers/U. Mass.

5. ". . . I'm glad you had a pleasant voyage.": Nina Gomer Du Bois to W.E.B. Du Bois, June 21, 1911. ". . . Mr. Crawford spoke to us about.": Nina Gomer Du Bois to W.E.B. Du Bois, June 21, 1911, Du Bois Papers/U. Mass.

6. Early residential segregation: John Hope Franklin, *From Slavery to Freedom: A History of Negro Americans*, p. 311; Richard Kluger, *Simple Justice: The History of Brown v. Board of Education*, p. 109; John Higham, *Strangers in the Land: Patterns of American Nativism, 1860–1925*, pp. 87–105.

On migration north and its tensions: by way of an only preliminary bibliography, see Du Bois, *The Philadelphia Negro*, esp. chap. 16, pp. 322–53; John Bodnar, Roger Simon, and Michael P. Weber, *Lives of Their Own: Blacks, Italians, and Poles in Pittsburgh, 1900–1960*, pp. 188–192; St. Clair Drake and Horace R. Cayton, *Black Metropolis: A Study of Negro Life in a Northern City*, I, pp. 17–18, 61–64; James R. Grossman, *Land of Hope: Chicago, Black Southerners, and the Great Migration*, pp. 127–46; Gilbert Osofsky, *Harlem: The Making of a Ghetto, Negro New York, 1890–1930*, pp. 35–46. Move to the Bronx: see The Library of America *Du Bois*, p. 1291. ". . . community . . . of white people.": John M. Demarest, general manager, Sage Foundation Homes Co., to W.E.B. Du Bois, Nov. 2, 1912, Du Bois Papers/U. Mass.

7. Disbanding Niagara: "Circular Statement from W.E.B. Du Bois, 1911," Du Bois Papers/U. Mass.

8. Milholland on the Wizard and the conference: Du Bois, *Dusk of Dawn*, p. 230; Mary White Ovington, *The Walls Came Tumbling Down*, p. 131; and an early planning letter from Du Bois to Mary Church Terrell, Jan. 30, 1911, Box 1, Fol. 24, Mary Church Terrell Papers/Moorland-Spingarn Res. Ctr./Howard. ". . . deserter from the forefront of battle.": W.E.B. Du Bois to Dr. Ettie Sayer [n. d.] 1911; Dr. Ettie Sayer to W.E.B. Du Bois, Feb. 21, 1911, Du Bois Papers/U. Mass. ". . . oppose Mr. Washington's view.": Travers

Buxton to W.E.B. Du Bois, Mar. 21, 1911, Du Bois Papers/U. Mass. ". . . and Sir Harry Johnston.": Du Bois, *Autobiography*, p. 263.

9. ". . . very dignified"—address . . . : Robert Russa Moton to Booker T. Washington, July 23, 1911, in Louis R. Harlan, ed., *Booker T. Washington Papers*, XI, p. 273; Elliott M. Rudwick, *W.E.B. Du Bois: Propagandist of the Negro Protest*, p. 144; Charles Flint Kellogg, *NAACP: A History of the National Association for the Advancement of Colored People*, p. 84;

10. ". . . not been for the World War.": Du Bois, *Dusk*, p. 231. ". . . To make humanity divine!": Du Bois, "A Hymn to the Peoples," in Aptheker, ed., *Creative Writings of W.E.B. Du Bois*, pp. 22–23 (p. 22); Du Bois, *Autobiography*, p. 263; see Du Bois, "The Races Congress," *The Crisis*, 2 (Sept. 1911): 200–9—also contains a two-page wide-angle-lens photo of the conference delegates—reproduced (*sans* photo) in Aptheker, ed., *Selections from The Crisis*, I, pp. 18–29.

11. ". . . gained wide reading.": Du Bois, *Dusk of Dawn*, p. 231; Du Bois, "Races Congress," *Selections from the Crisis*, I, p. 25. ". . . a few world congresses like this . . .": Du Bois, *ibid.*, p. 27; Arnold Rampersad, *The Art and Imagination of W.E.B. Du Bois*, pp. 156–57. ". . . weak points in each.": Du Bois, "Race Congress," *Selections from the Crisis*, pp. 23–24.

12. ". . . new conception of humanity and its problems": Du Bois, "Races Congress," in Aptheker, ed., *Selections from The Crisis*, p. 26. ". . . making and execution of laws.": *ibid.*, p. 22. The planet's problems: *ibid.*, p. 27.

13. ". . . personnel . . . was marvelous.": Du Bois, "Races Congress," in Aptheker, ed., *Selections from The Crisis*, I, p. 20. Kropotkin quoted: Louis Filler, *Crusaders for American Liberalism* (New York: Harcourt, 1939), p. 276.

14. *The Dark Princess*: (Ovington's surmise, mentioned in Aptheker, "Introduction" to *The Dark Princess: A Romance* (Millwood, N.Y.: Kraus-Thomson, 1974; orig. pub. 1928), p. 8. ". . . darker daughter of the Haitian president."—Ovington, quoted: *ibid.*, p. 8.

15. ". . . inevitable path of world progress.": Du Bois, *Dusk*, p. 232. ". . . bred contempt of disaster.": *ibid.*, p. 231.

16. Du Bois clubs: Detriot, Aug. 18, 1902; Hollie Queen, Cornell University, to W.E.B. Du Bois, Feb. 15, 1908, Du Bois Papers/U. Mass. "poet" and "dreamer": Fanny Hale Gardiner, "The Golden Fleece," Du Bois Papers/U. Mass.; Aptheker, "Introduction," *The Quest of the Silver Fleece* (Millwood, N.Y.: Kraus-Thomson, 1974; orig. pub. 1911), p. 9.

17. ". . . an economic study of some merit.": Du Bois, *Dusk*, p. 269. ". . . leave us in pretty bad shape.": F. G. Browne to W.E.B. Du Bois, Apr. 6, 1904, Du Bois Papers/U. Mass. ". . . in a logical sequence.": F. G. Browne to W.E.B. Du Bois [undated, 1904?, holograph fragment], Du Bois Papers/U. Mass.

18. Title change: Gardiner, "The Golden Fleece," Du Bois Papers/U. Mass. Novels of the period: see Aptheker's useful remarks in "Introduction," *Quest*, p. 5.

19. ". . . Professor Du Bois write next?"—*Independent* reviewer, quoted: Aptheker, "Introduction," *Quest*, p. 15. African-American novels before *Quest*: see Arthur P. Davis, *From the Dark Tower: Afro-American Writers, 1900 to 1960* (Washington, D.C.: Howard University Press, 1974), pp. 1–9; Lewis, *Vogue*, p. 89; Lewis, "The Politics of Art: The New Negro, 1920–1935," *Prospects*, 3 (1977): 237–61; Rampersad, *Du Bois*, p. 116.

20. Zora . . . "heathen hoyden": Du Bois, *Quest*, p. 44. Rampersad's *Du Bois* is especially suggestive as an aid to interpretation of this novel. ". . . full month of other cotton.": Du Bois, *Quest*, pp. 125–26.

21. ". . . wealth and make them rule."—Zora: Du Bois, *Quest*, p. 46. "'. . . Black folks is wonderful.'"—Zora: *ibid.*, p. 46. "'. . . to know what they know.'": *ibid.*, p. 46.

22. ". . . a nation—a world.": *ibid.*, p. 22.

23. ". . . spice of young womanhood.": *ibid.*, p. 163. ". . . control of Negro education.": *ibid.*, p. 161.

24. ". . . streamed beneath her window.": *ibid.*, p. 251.

25. ". . . to things they don't need."—Zora: *ibid.*, p. 79, also p. 94. ". . . 'I think so, too' . . ."—Zora: *ibid.*, p. 395.

26. " '. . . built on a moan,' . . .' "—Miss Smith: *ibid.*, p. 141.

27. ". . . pistol crashed to the floor.": *ibid.*, p. 199.

28. ". . . at the turn of the century.": Rampersad, *Du Bois*, p. 127.

29. ". . . three generations of . . . mulattoes.": Du Bois, *Quest*, p. 253. Henry Adams, *Democracy: An American Novel* (1880), in the *Library of America Henry Adams*. ". . . emphatic self-sufficiency.": *Quest*., p. 304. Caroline Wynn's kiss: *ibid*., p. 325.

30. ". . . colored men into this domain.": Irene Diggs, "Du Bois and Women: A Short History of Black Women, 1910–1934," *Current Bibliography on African Affairs*, 7 (Summer 1974): 260–379, p. 260. ". . . sheer rot" . . . "and 'lower classes.' ": Du Bois, "Woman Suffrage," *The Crisis*, 11 (Nov. 1915): 29–30, in *Selections from The Crisis*, I, pp. 111–12 (p. 111). ". . . woman, but a black one—!": Du Bois, "Tom Brown at Fisk in Three Chapters," Fisk *Herald*, 5 (Dec. 1887): 5–7; 5 (Jan. 1888): 6–7; 5 (Mar. 1888): 5–7, in *Creative Writings*, pp. 56–62 (p. 56).

31. . . . saved by its Zoras: see Du Bois, "The Burden of Black Women," *The Horizon*, 2 (Nov. 1907): 3–5, in Aptheker, *Creative Writings*, pp. 12–14.

32. Dark-skinned female protagonist: Aptheker, "Introduction," Du Bois, *Quest*, pp. 14–15; Rampersad, *Du Bois*, p. 132. " 'Will you—marry me, Bles?' ": Du Bois, *Quest*, p. 434.

33. ". . . to cringe and bow.": Du Bois, *The Souls of Black Folk*, p. 213.

34. ". . . very slovenly and 'American.' ": W.E.B. Du Bois to J. H. Badley, Sept. 25, 1914, Du Bois Papers/U. Mass. ". . . and not simply for breeding.": *ibid*.

35. Arrangements: W.E.B. Du Bois to Secretary of State William Jennings Bryan, Sept. 24, 1914; Acting Secretary of State Robert Lansing to W.E.B. Du Bois, Sept. 26, 1914; W.E.B. Du Bois to Ramsay MacDonald, Jan. 10, 1914; Ramsay MacDonald to W.E.B. Du Bois, Feb. 6, 1914, Du Bois Papers/U. Mass.; Du Bois–MacDonald letters also in Aptheker, ed., *Correspondence*, I, pp. 187–88. Welcoming Britons: Alcindor, Hoggan, Spillers: Nina Gomer Du Bois to W.E.B. Du Bois, Jan. 27, 1915, Du Bois Papers/U. Mass.; and see, Jeffrey P. Green, "John Alcindor (1873–1924): A Migrant's Biography," *Immigrants and Minorties*, 6 (July 1987): 174–89. Arrival at Liverpool: American consul at Liverpool to W.E.B. Du Bois, Oct. 6, 1914, Du Bois Papers/U. Mass.

36. NAACP's new address: Kellogg, *NAACP*, p. 97. ". . . Lovingly yours, Papa.": W.E.B. Du Bois to Yolande Du Bois, Oct. 29, 1914, Du Bois Papers/U. Mass.; and Aptheker, ed., *Correspondence*, I, pp. 207–8.

37. Barrage of letters: W.E.B. Du Bois to Yolande Du Bois, Nov. 10, 1914–several such letters during fall and spring—to July 15, 1915.

38. ". . . not complaining . . . I've spent the money.": Nina Gomer Du Bois to W.E.B. Du Bois, Jan. 27, 1915, Du Bois Papers/U. Mass. Money matters: Nina Gomer Du Bois to W.E.B. Du Bois, Mar. 10, 1915; Mar. 20, 1915; Mar. 28, 1915, Du Bois Papers/U. Mass.

39. Nina's troubles: Nina Gomer Du Bois to W.E.B. Du Bois, Mar. 5, 1916; Feb. 4, 1915, Du Bois Papers/U. Mass. ". . . none too much to start with.": Nina Gomer Du Bois to W.E.B. Du Bois, Mar. 4, 1915, Du Bois Papers/U. Mass. ". . . about your own speech": Nina Gomer Du Bois to W.E.B. Du Bois, Mar. 4, 1915, Du Bois Papers/U. Mass. ". . . using it for a few days.": W.E.B. Du Bois to Nina Gomer Du Bois, Nov. 30, 1914, Du Bois Papers/U. Mass.

40. Nina's social life: Nina Gomer Du Bois to W.E.B. Du Bois, Jan. 27, 1915; Feb. 4, 1915; Feb. 10, 1915, Du Bois Papers/U. Mass. Aida Young and U-boats and zeppelins: Nina Gomer Du Bois to W.E.B. Du Bois, June 6, 1915; May 30, 1915; June 30, 1915; [n.d.] 1915; Feb. 4, 1915, Du Bois Papers/U. Mass. ". . . very expensive or very dirty.": Nina Gomer Du Bois to W.E.B. Du Bois, Mar. 4, 1915/U. Mass.

41. Nina moves: Nina Gomer Du Bois to W.E.B. Du Bois, Mar. 20, 1915, Du Bois Papers/U. Mass. ". . . say and do next.": Nina Gomer Du Bois to W.E.B. Du Bois, Apr. 4, 1915, Du Bois Papers/U. Mass.

42. ". . . really could not form any opinion": Nina Gomer Du Bois to W.E.B. Du Bois, Mar. 28, 1915; Apr. 4, 1915, Du Bois Papers/U. Mass.

43. ". . . such a full life . . .": Nina Gomer Du Bois to W.E.B. Du Bois, Mar. 20, 1915, Du Bois Papers/U. Mass. ". . . the pageant and other things.": W.E.B. Du Bois to Nina Gomer Du Bois, Apr. 2, 1915, Du Bois Papers/U. Mass. ". . . enough to meet such demands.": Nina Gomer Du Bois to W.E.B. Du Bois, Mar. 10, 1915; June 27, 1915—"your salary of $2500"—Du Bois Papers/U. Mass.

44. Meeting Marcus Garvey: Marcus Garvey to W.E.B. Du Bois, Apr. 30, 1915, Du Bois Papers/U. Mass.; and Robert A. Hill, ed., *The Marcus Garvey and Universal Negro Improvement Association Papers*, 10 vols. (Berkeley: University of California Press, 1983–), I, p. 120—a handwritten message on Universal Negro Improvement and Conservation Association stationery says, "Mr. Marcus Garvey presents his compliments to Dr. E. B. Du Bois and begs to tender to him, on behalf of the Universal Negro Improvement Association, a hearty welcome to Jamaica, and trusts that he has enjoyed the brief stay in the sunny isle."

45. ". . . barbaric war of color.": Du Bois, "An Amazing Island," in Aptheker, ed., *Selections from The Crisis*, I, pp. 100–1 (p. 100).

46. Nina Gomer Du Bois to W.E.B. Du Bois, June 6, 1915 ("You haven't told me yet how you are managing the expenses of our being over here and your trip, etc."); June 27, 1915, Du Bois Papers/U. Mass. The mystery of Du Bois's supplementary income is largely explained by fees received (and kept) for lectures and speeches in connection with the NAACP, payments and royalties from writings, and loans. During this period, Du Bois owed Frances Hoggan $485.05, due Dec. 14, 1914, and Mary White Ovington $250, both bearing 5 percent interest—W.E.B. Du Bois to Mary White Ovington, Aug. 5, 1913; W.E.B. Du Bois to Frances Hoggan, Dec. 14, 1912, Du Bois Papers/U. Mass.

47. *Lusitania:* Nina Gomer Du Bois to W.E.B. Du Bois, May 8, 1915, Du Bois Papers/U. Mass. ". . . half frozen or starved.": Nina Gomer Du Bois to W.E.B. Du Bois, *ibid.* ". . . their mail is all tampered with.": Nina Gomer Du Bois to W.E.B. Du Bois, June 20, 1915, Du Bois Papers/U. Mass.

48. ". . . something wrong with me.": Nina Gomer Du Bois to W.E.B. Du Bois, May 2, 1915, Du Bois Papers/U. Mass. ". . . beginning to feel she's colored.": *ibid.*; and "Bedales School Report for Autumn Term 1914"; and for autumn term 1915, Du Bois Papers/U. Mass.

49. ". . . wasted their opportunities.": Nina Gomer Du Bois to W.E.B. Du Bois, May 16, 1915, Du Bois Papers/U. Mass.

50. Yolande's letters: [n.d.] 1915; [n.d.] 1915; Feb. 4, 1915, Du Bois Papers/U. Mass. ". . . seen England or Miss Ruth.": Yolande Du Bois to W.E.B. Du Bois, Sunday 1915, Du Bois Papers/U. Mass.

51. Yolande's Niagara letter: W.E.B. Du Bois to Yolande Du Bois, exact date unknown, 1911?; Yolande Du Bois to W.E.B. Du Bois, Aug. 5, 1916, Du Bois Papers/U. Mass. ". . . largely ever since.": W.E.B. Du Bois to Yolande Du Bois, July 15, 1915, Du Bois Papers/U. Mass.

52. Lectures and travels: Du Bois, "I Go A-Talking," *The Crisis*, 6 (July 1913): 130–32; Du Bois, "Colored California," *The Crisis*, 6 (Aug. 1913): 192–95—both reproduced in Aptheker, ed., *Selections from The Crisis*, I, pp. 58–61 and 62–63, respectively. *Crisis* staff and circulation: "Report of the Department of Publications and Research, from November 1914 to October 1915," Du Bois Papers/U. Mass.; "Men of the Month" [on Dill], *The Crisis*, 6 (Sept. 1913): 222–23; Du Bois, "The Princess of the Hither Isles," *The Crisis*, 6 (Oct. 1913): 22–31; also Du Bois, *Darkwater: Voices from Within the Veil* (Millwood, N.Y.: Kraus-Thomson, 1975; orig. pub. 1921), pp. 75–80; see obituary by Mary White Ovington, "Mary Dunlop Maclean," *The Crisis*, 4 (Aug. 1912): 184–85.

53. ". . . the Negro to the white world.": Du Bois, "The Drama Among Black Folk," *The Crisis*, 12 (Aug. 1916): 169–73; also in Aptheker, ed., *Selections from The Crisis*, I, pp. 121–23 (p. 122); see also Du Bois, "The People of Peoples and Their Gifts to Men," *The Crisis*, 6 (Nov. 1913): 339–41; also reproduced by Aptheker, ed., *Creative Writings*, pp. 1–5; Du Bois, *Dusk of Dawn*, p. 272. ". . . knew the joys of God.": Du Bois, "The Star of Ethiopia," *The Crisis*, 11 (Dec. 1915): 91–93; also Aptheker, *Selections from The Crisis*, I, pp. 114–15 (p. 115).

54. Pageant donations: see Du Bois, "A Pageant" (a four-page leaflet printed in [Nov. ?] 1911), in Aptheker, *Annotated Bibliography*, p. 543; Du Bois, "Drama Among Black Folk," p. 122. ". . . the dream comes true.": Du Bois, "The Star of Ethiopia," p. 115; Du Bois, *Dusk of Dawn*, p. 273. ". . . Hear ye, hear ye!": Du Bois, "Drama Among Black Folk," p. 121: "The Great Pageant," Washington *Bee*, Oct. 23, 1915, p. 1. ". . . and enveloped them.": Du Bois, "The People of Peoples and Their Gifts to Men," p. 4; Du Bois, *Dusk*, p. 273.

55. "electrical, spiritual.": "The Great Pageant," *Bee*. ". . . Grimkés were enthusiastic.": Archibald Grimké to W.E.B. Du Bois, Nov. 6, 1915, Du Bois Papers/U. Mass. . . . breaking down prejudice.: H. B. Humphrey to W.E.B. Du Bois, Nov. 14, 1915; W.E.B. Du Bois to H. B. Humphrey, Nov. 11, 1915, Du Bois Papers/U. Mass. ". . . and realization of beauty.": Du Bois, "Drama Among Black Folk," p. 121.

56. ". . . most contented peasantry . . .": Du Bois, *The Negro* (Millwood, N.Y.: Kraus-Thomson, 1975; orig. pub. 1915), p. 178.

57. See excerpted reviews: Aptheker, "Introduction," *The Negro*, pp. 20–23. Afrocentric influence of *The Negro*: Alfred Harcourt to W.E.B. Du Bois, Aug. 10, 1914, Du Bois Papers/U. Mass; see Aptheker, "Introduction," *The Negro*, pp. 7–8, 17; the following influential works are within the tradition promoted by Du Bois—Basil Davidson, *A History of West Africa, 1000–1800* (London: Longman, 1977, new and rev. ed.); Davidson, *Black Mother; Africa: The Years of Trial* (London: Victor Gollancz, 1961); Davidson, *Old Africa Rediscovered* (London: Victor Gollancz, 1959); Martin Bernal, *Black Athena: The Afroasiatic Roots of Classical Civilization* (New Brunswick, N.J.: Rutgers University Press, 1987, 1991), 2 vols., I, pp. 436–38; Cheikh Anta Diop, *Antériorité des civilisations negres: mythe ou vérité historique* (Paris: Présence Africaine, 1967); and Diop, *Civilization or Barbarism: An Authentic Anthropology* (New York: Lawrence Hill Books, 1986), esp. pp. 25–108; Frank M. Snowden, Jr., *Before Color Prejudice: The Ancient View of Africa* (Cambridge: Harvard University Press, 1983), p. 63.

58. ". . . its worst conceivable form.": Du Bois, *The Negro*, p. 191. ". . . what colored men make it.": *ibid.*, p. 242.

59. ". . . splendid work.": Nina Gomer Du Bois to W.E.B. Du Bois, Mar. 20, 1915, Du Bois Papers/U. Mass. ". . . public did not know it.": W.E.B. Du Bois to Nina Gomer Du Bois, Oct. 21, 1915, Du Bois Papers/U. Mass.

60. ". . . talked and talked and talked": W.E.B. Du Bois to Nina Gomer Du Bois, Feb.

25, 1916, Du Bois Papers/U. Mass. Attempt to relocate AU Studies: W.E.B. Du Bois to John Hardy Dillard, Slater Fund, Nov. 10, 1916; John Hardy Dillard to W.E.B. Du Bois, Nov. 14, 1916; W.E.B. Du Bois to Edward T. Ware, June 11, 1916; Edward T. Ware to W.E.B. Du Bois, June 11, 1912; Atlanta University Trustees to W.E.B. Du Bois, July 20, 1912, Du Bois Papers/U. Mass. Du Bois, ed., *Morals and Manners among Negro Americans: Report of a Social Study Made by Atlanta University under the Patronage of the Trustees of the John F. Slater Fund; with the Proceedings of the 18th Annual Conference for the Study of the Negro Problems, held at Atlanta University, on May 26, 1913* (Atlanta: Atlanta University Press, 1913).

61. Young's farewell: W.E.B. Du Bois to Nina Gomer Du Bois, Feb. 25, 1916, Du Bois Papers/U. Mass.

62. ". . . now and then for exercise.": Josephine Harreld Love Interview/D. L. Lewis/ Oct. 28, 1988.

63. ". . . please put such thoughts away!": Mildred Bryant [Jones] to W.E.B. Du Bois, Mar. 21, 1916; W.E.B. Du Bois to Mildred Bryant [Jones], Mar. 28, 1916, Du Bois Papers/ U. Mass.

64. Fauset and Du Bois: Jessie Redmon Fauset to W.E.B. Du Bois, Dec. 26, 1903, Du Bois Papers/U. Mass.; the intimate character of this relationship is based on numerous on-and-off-the-record interviews conducted by the author, as well as of a careful reading of the correspondence—*viz.*, Arthur P. Davis Interview/D. L. Lewis/Mar. 1977; Rayford W. Logan Interview/D. L. Lewis/Oct. 1974; Mae Miller Sullivan Interview/D. L. Lewis/Apr. 1977. "There Is Confusion": Jessie Redmon Fauset to W.E.B. Du Bois, June 24, 1914, Du Bois Papers/U. Mass. "Emmy": Jessie Fauset, "Emmy," *The Crisis*, 5 (Dec. 1912–Jan. 1913): 79–87; 34–42. ". . . 'on' it many times.": Jessie Fauset to W.E.B. Du Bois, June 24, 1914; W.E.B. Du Bois to Jessie Fauset, July 11, 1914, Du Bois Papers/U. Mass.; "Fauset, Jessie [Redmon] (1885?–1961)" *DANB*, pp. 219–20; Lewis, *Vogue*, esp. pp. 121–25; Carolyn Wedin Sylvander, "Jessie Redmon Fauset: Black American Writer: Her Relationships, Biographical and Literary, with Black and White Writers, 1910–1935" has written the definitive Fauset study, unfortunately bowderlized in its published form as *Jessie Fauset: Black American Writer* (Troy, N.Y.: Whitson Pub. Co., 1981).

65. "... yet undeveloped in her.": J. H. Badley to Nina Gomer Du Bois, Apr. 6, 1916, Du Bois Papers/U. Mass. ". . . all things into consideration.": Nina Gomer Du Bois to W.E.B. Du Bois, May 28, 1916, July 21, 1916, Du Bois Papers/U. Mass. ". . . something like a vice-boss . . . ?": Yolande Du Bois to W.E.B. Du Bois [n.d.] 1911; Molly Scott to W.E.B. Du Bois, July 8, 1916, Du Bois Papers/U. Mass.

66. Maine vacation: W.E.B. Du Bois to Nina Gomer Du Bois, Aug. 22, 1916, Du Bois Papers/U. Mass.

17. *Crises at* The Crisis

1. ". . . political bible of the Negro race.": William H. Ferris, *The African Abroad or His Evolution in Western Civilization* (New Haven, Conn.: The Tuttle, Morehouse & Taylor Press, 1913), 2 vols., I, p. 276. ". . . intellectual level.": W.E.B. Du Bois to William H. Ferris, Mar. 23, 1912, in Du Bois Papers/U. Mass.; Charles H. Wesley Interview/D. L. Lewis, Apr. 1917—expressed similar sentiments to this author; "Ferris, William H[enry] (1874–1941)" *DANB*, pp. 221–22. ". . . brilliant in parts.": Du Bois, "What To Read," The Crisis, 7 (Jan. 1914): p. 147.". . . political messiah of the race."—Ferris, quoted: Ferris, *The African Abroad*, I., p. 276, and pp. 245–46, 296–311, *et passim*.

2. Wizard's declining influence: see Harlan, *B. T. Washington*, II, 405–37;

August Meier, *Negro Thought in America, 1880–1915*, pp. 256–78; Florette Henri, *Black Migration: Movement North, 1900–1920*, pp. 237–48; Nancy J. Weiss, *The National Urban League, 1910–1940*, pp. 61–64. ". . . leaders of the movement.": George Foster Peabody to W.E.B. Du Bois, Sept. 1, 1911, Du Bois Papers/U. Mass. Wizard on *Birth of a Nation*: Louis R. Harlan, *Booker T. Washington*, II, pp. 431 and 417–22.

3. Resistance to segregation: see George M. Frederickson, *White Supremacy: A Comparative Study in American and South African History*, pp. 234–38; and see the valuable introductory comments in Neil R. McMillen, *Dark Journey: Black Mississippians in the Age of Jim Crow* (Urbana and Chicago: University of Illinois Press, 1989), pp. 6–32; the still valuable if hyperpsychological study by John Dollard, *Caste and Class in a Southern Town* (Garden City, N.Y.: Doubleday, 1957; orig. pub. 1937), esp. pp. 97–133; and, indispensably, C. Vann Woodward's *The Strange Career of Jim Crow*, also Abram Harris, *The Negro as Capitalist: A Study of Banking and Business among American Negroes* (Philadelphia: The American Academy of Political and Social Science, 1936), esp. pp. 177–84; and William F. Holmes, *The White Chief: James Kimble Vardaman*, pp. 132–42, an insightful discussion of Negrophobe Vardaman's abandonment of a pledge to distribute public education funds according to the amount of taxes paid by white and black people and his vigorous suppression of white attacks on black merchants and prosperous farmers ("whitecapping").

4. "taken bodily from the words of my mouth": Du Bois, *Dusk of Dawn*, p. 303. B. T. Washington, *The New Negro for a New Century* (Chicago: American Publishing House, 1900). ". . . desire to lead the NAACP": W.E.B. Du Bois to Butler Wilson, Jan. 12, 1916, Du Bois Papers/U. Mass.

5. ". . . dissatisfied and gradually withdraw.": Du Bois, *Dusk of Dawn*, p. 227. ". . . forceful opinions of their own.": Mary White Ovington to Oswald Garrison Villard, June 2, 1909, Villard Papers, Box 120, Fol. 1, Oswald Garrison Villard/Houghton Library/Harvard.

6. ". . . It wasn't up to me": Du Bois, "Interview," Columbia Oral History Project, p. 164. ". . . tremendous and eternal significance.": Du Bois, "The Souls of White Folk," *The Independent*, 69 (Aug. 18, 1910): 339–42, in Aptheker, ed., *Writings by W.E.B. Du Bois in Periodicals Edited by Others* (*Periodical Literature*), II, pp. 25–29 (p. 25). ". . . the South is right . . .": *ibid.*, p. 26.

7. Du Bois, "A Philosophy for 1913," *The Crisis*, 5 (Jan. 1913): 127, in Aptheker, ed., *Selections from The Crisis*, I, pp. 47–48 (p. 47); Meier and Rudwick, *Along the Color Line*, pp. 94, 99. Du Bois's dual position: Charles Flint Kellogg, *NAACP: A History of the National Association for the Advancement of Colored People*, p. 91; August Meier and Elliott Rudwick, *Along the Color Line: Explorations in the Black Experience*, p. 94.

8. Cohesion and conflict: Kellogg, *NAACP*, pp. 93–98. ". . . refined and cultivated person."—Villard, quoted: *ibid.*, p. 94; Ovington, *Half a Man: The Status of the Negro in New York*. ". . . dictator of the policy.": Kellogg, *NAACP*, p. 98.

9. ". . . but as a fellow officer.": W.E.B. Du Bois to Oswald Garrison Villard, Mar. 18, 1913, Du Bois Papers/U. Mass.; Kellogg, *NAACP*, p. 94. ". . . an extreme value . . . to the . . . cause.": William English Walling to Joel E. Spingarn, Nov. 14, 1914, Box 12, Fol. WA-WI1, Joel E. Spingarn Papers/NYPL. ". . . from this time forth.": Oswald Garrison Villard to W.E.B. Du Bois, Apr. 2, 1913, Du Bois Papers/U. Mass.

10. ". . . indefatigable energy."—Du Bois, quoted: Kellogg, *NAACP*, p. 98 and 94; Meier and Rudwick, *Color Line*, pp. 95–97.

11. ". . . energy and enthusiasm.": William English Walling to Joel E. Spingarn, Nov. 14, 1914, Spingarn Papers/NYPL. Nerney's Du Bois problem: Kellogg, *NAACP*, pp. 94, 101; Meier and Rudwick, *Color Line*, p. 99; W.E.B. Du Bois to Joel E. Spingarn, Oct. 28,

1914, Du Bois Papers/U. Mass., in Aptheker, ed., *The Correspondence of W.E.B. Du Bois*, I, pp. 203–7 (p. 205).

12. "Garrison-Douglass Association.": "Minutes of the Board of Directors," Dec. 11, 1916, NAACP Papers/LC; Kellogg, *NAACP*, p. 90; B. Joyce Ross, *J. E. Spingarn and the Rise of the NAACP, 1911–1939*, p. 28.

13. D.C. branch of the NAACP: Fox, *Guardian of Boston*, p. 172; several letters from Nerney relating to D.C. branch disputes—May Childs Nerney to Joel E. Spingarn, July 2, 1913; July 7, 1913; July 31, 1913, Box M-R, Joel E. Spingarn Papers/Moorland-Spingarn Res. Ctr./Howard; Meier and Rudwick, *Color Line*, p. 97; Kellogg, *NAACP*, p. 97. Storey complains about Du Bois: Moorfield Storey to Joel E. Spingarn, Jan. 15, 1914, Box 11, Fol. Storey, Moorfield/Joel E. Spingarn Papers/NYPL; William Monroe Trotter to Joel E. Spingarn, Jan. 28, 1914, Box S-Z, Joel E. Spingarn Papers/Moorland-Spingarn Res. Ctr./ Howard University; Kellogg, *NAACP*, p. 97; Fox, *The Guardian of Boston*, p. 178. Vice-President Walters: "Minutes of the Board of Directors," Nov. 6, 1913, Du Bois Papers/U. Mass.; Kellogg, *NAACP*, p. 97.

14. ". . . overwhelmed almost to silence . . .": Du Bois, "I Go A-Talking," *The Crisis*, 6 (July 1913): 130–32, Aptheker, ed., in *Selections from The Crisis*, I, pp. 58–61 (p. 58); Du Bois, "Colored California," *The Crisis*, 6 (Aug. 1913): 192–95, in Aptheker, ed., *Selections from The Crisis*, I, 62–63. Controversial editorials: Paul Kellogg, *Survey Graphic*, to W.E.B. Du Bois, Jan. 23, 1914, Du Bois Collection/Moorland-Spingarn Res. Ctr.; W. S. Scarborough to Joel E. Spingarn, Sept. 8, 1914, Box S-Z, Joel E. Spingarn Papers/NYPL; Du Bois, "The Negro Church," *The Crisis*, 4 (May 1912): 24–25, in Aptheker, ed., *Selections from The Crisis*, I, pp. 34–35; Du Bois, "Editorial," *The Crisis*, 7 (Mar. 1914): 239–40; Du Bois, "The New Wilberforce," *The Crisis*, 8 (Aug. 1914): 191–94; Du Bois, "Education," *The Crisis*, 10 (July 1915): 132–33, in *Selections from The Crisis*, I, pp. 103–5. ". . . suspicious of motives."—Du Bois quoted: Kellogg, *NAACP*, p. 97. ". . . patience than I possess."—Nerney, quoted: Meier and Rudwick, *Color Line*, p. 98.

15. ". . . better everyday Mr. Du Bois's attitude"—Nerney, quoted: Meier and Rudwick, *Color Line*, p. 99. Growth of *The Crisis*: Du Bois, "Report of the Crisis to the Meeting of the Board of Directors," Apr. 7, 1914, Du Bois Papers/U. Mass.; Du Bois, "I Go A-Talking," in Aptheker, ed., *Selections from The Crisis*, p. 58. ". . . a riot in my family"—Nerney, quoted: Emma Etuk, "Crusader for Justice: Archibald Henry Grimké, 1849–1930" (Ph.D. diss.: History Department, Howard University, Dec. 1991), p. 215; Meier and Rudwick, *Color Line*, p. 101. ". . . more clearly defined.": Oswald Garrison Villard to the board of directors, Nov. 19, 1913, Box 120, Oswald Garrison Villard Papers/Houghton/ Harvard University.

16. "And not a single man.": Joel E. Spingarn to H. L. Mencken [n.d.], H. L. Mencken Collection, Manuscript Discussion/NYPL; for discussion of Spingarn's place in American letters, see Alfred Kazin, *On Native Grounds, An Interpretation of Modern American Prose Literature* (New York: Reynal and Hitchcock, 1942), pp. 173–74; also Thomas Bender, *New York Intellect: A History of Intellectual Life in New York City, from 1750 to the Beginnings of Our Own Time* (Baltimore: The Johns Hopkins University Press, 1988), p. 285; the definitive biography is by B. Joyce Ross, *J. E. Spingarn and the Rise of the NAACP*, esp. pp. 5–8.

17. ". . . convinced that he is right?": Mary White Ovington to Oswald Garrison Villard, Nov. 25, 1913, Box 120, Fol. 1, Oswald Garrison Villard Papers/Houghton/ Harvard; Meier and Rudwick, *Color Line*, p. 98.

18. Villard's resignation, NAACP's relocation: Oswald Garrison Villard to Mary White Ovington, Nov. 21, 1913, Box 12, Fol. 1, Oswald Garrison Villard Papers/ Houghton/Harvard; Kellogg, *NAACP*, pp. 97–98; Joel E. Spingarn to W.E.B. Du Bois,

Oct. 22, 1914, Du Bois Papers/U. Mass.; and see interesting exchange pertaining to the association's new lease—G. A. Plimpton to Joel E. Spingarn, Jan. 30, 1914, Box M-R, Joel E. Spingarn Papers/NYPL. ". . . another editor.": Oswald Garrison Villard to Joel E. Spingarn, July 21, 1914, Box 12, Fol. 1, Oswald Garrison Villard Papers/Houghton/Harvard.

19. ". . . Do drop in.": W.E.B. Du Bois to John Hope, Jan. 10, 1914, Du Bois Papers/U. Mass. New *Crisis* offices and staff: Joel E. Spingarn to W.E.B. Du Bois, Oct. 24, 1914, Du Bois Papers/U. Mass., in Aptheker, ed., *Correspondence*, I, pp. 200–2 (p. 201); Du Bois, "We Come of Age," *The Crisis*, 2 (Nov. 1915): 25–28, in Aptheker, ed., *Selections from The Crisis*, I, pp. 107–10; (photograph of *Crisis* staff), *The Crisis*, 5 (Nov. 1912). ". . . retained for that reason."—Nerney quoted: Etuk, "Archibald Grimke," p. 216.

20. The early NAACP budget: Kellogg, *NAACP*, p. 107. ". . . facts are on the other side.": Oswald Garrison Villard to Joel E. Spingarn, July 21, 1915, Box 12, Fol. 1, Joel E. Spingarn Papers/NYPL. According to Thomas Lee Philpott, *The Slum and the Ghetto, Neighborhood Deterioration and Middle-Class Reform, Chicago, 1880–1930* (New York: Oxford University Press, 1978), pp. 299–300, both Jane Addams and Florence Kelley continued to find Du Bois's social ideas disturbing.

21. ". . . or unworthy ambition."—Du Bois, quoted: Elliott Rudwick, *W.E.B. Du Bois; Propagandist of the Negro Protest*, p. 166; W.E.B. Du Bois to Joel E. Spingarn, Oct. 28, 1914, Du Bois Papers/U. Mass., in Aptheker, ed., *Correspondence*, I, p. 206. ". . . political or economic equality.": Philpott, *The Slum and the Ghetto*, p. 300.

22. ". . . restores his self-respect.": Frantz Fanon, *The Wretched of the Earth* (New York: Grove Press, 1963), pp. 35–106; *Black Skin, White Masks* (New York: Grove Weidenfeld, 1991); Hussein Abdilahi Bulhan, *Frantz Fanon and the Psychology of Oppression* (New York: Plenum Press, 1985); Irene L. Gendzier, *Frantz Fanon: A Critical Study*, esp. pp. 200–204. . . . popularity and effectiveness.: Du Bois, *The Autobiography: A Soliloquy on Viewing My Life from the Last Decade of Its First Century*, p. 261.

23. ". . . an instinctive gentleman.": Du Bois, "The Great Northwest," *The Crisis*, 6 (Sept. 1913): 237–40, in Aptheker, ed., *Selections from The Crisis*, I, pp. 67–68, (p. 68). ". . . to expect the millennium.": Du Bois, "Brazil and the Negro," *The Crisis*, 7 (Apr. 1914): 286–87, p. 287. Du Bois, "Colored California," 6 (Aug. 1913): 192–95; Rudwick, *Du Bois*, p. 167.

24. ". . . EXCEPT BY SILENCE!": Du Bois, "The Philosophy of Mr. Dole," *The Crisis*, 8 (May 1914): 24–26, in *Selections from The Crisis*, I, pp. 74–77 (p. 76); also Du Bois, "A Question of Policy," *The Crisis*, 8 (May 1914): 23.

25. ". . . new prominence and new meaning."—Jessie Guernsey, quoted: *ibid.*, p. 95. ". . . justifies the existence of the NAACP."—Williams quoted: Du Bois, "Letters," *The Crisis*, 9 (Jan. 1915): 94–96, p. 94.

26. ". . . half cocked on this . . .": Oswald Garrison Villard to Joel E. Spingarn, July 21, 1914, Box 12, Fol. 1, Joel E. Spingarn Papers/NYPL. ". . . treason to the race.": Oswald Garrison Villard to Joel E. Spingarn, July 21, 1915, Box 12, Fol. 1, Joel E. Spingarn Papers/NYPL. The Benson vocational and entrepreneurial experiment in Kowaliga, Alabama, was something of a mini-Tuskegee Institute. Benson, a vivacious, driven African-American planter, was one of Du Bois's few close friends. Villard and several northern philanthropists supported Kowaliga. Booker T. Washington, however, appears to have been hostile to the experiment—see Du Bois, "Editorial," *The Crisis*, 10 (May 1915): 27–33; Du Bois, "The Late W. E. Benson," *The Crisis*, 11 (Dec. 1915): 79–80; Du Bois, *Dusk*, pp. 74–75.

27. ". . . Should we preach race consciousness . . . ?": Mary White Ovington to W.E.B. Du Bois, Apr. 11, 1914, Du Bois Papers/U. Mass., in Aptheker, ed., *Correspon-*

dence, I, pp. 191–93 (p. 192). . . . when it came to sin.: W.E.B. Du Bois to Horace Bumstead, Jan. 7, 1914; Horace Bumstead to W.E.B. Du Bois, Jan. 2, 1914, Du Bois Papers/U. Mass.

28. ". . . is the truer.": Du Bois, *Autobiography*, p. 255; Kellogg, *NAACP*, p. 107.

29. . . . would "be through.": Oswald Garrison Villard to Joel E. Spingarn, Apr. 9, 1914, Box 12, Fol. 1, Joel E. Spingarn Papers/NYPL; "Minutes of the Board of Directors," Apr. 17, 1914, NAACP Papers/LC; Oswald Garrison Villard to Joel E. Spingarn, Apr. 16, 1914, Box S-Z, Fol. Villard, Oswald Garrison/Joel E. Spingarn Papers/Moorland-Spingarn Res. Ctr./Howard. ". . . from their original purpose.": W.E.B. Du Bois to Mary White Ovington, Apr. 9, 1914, Du Bois Papers/U. Mass., in Aptheker, ed., *Correspondence*, I, pp. 188–91. ". . . in the first place.": ibid., pp. 188–91.

30. ". . . present . . . on this very important matter.": "A Notice to the Board of Directors," Mar. 28, 1914; "Minutes of the Board of Directors," Apr. 17, 1914, NAACP Papers/LC; Kellogg, *NAACP*, pp. 99–103. ". . . purpose than that of helping.": Joel E. Spingarn to W.E.B. Du Bois, Mar. 11, 1914, Du Bois Papers/U. Mass.

31. Spingarn Medal: "Minutes of the Board of Directors," Oct. 7, 1913, NAACP Papers/LC; see "Just, Ernest Everett (1883–1941)" *DANB*, pp. 372–75; and Kenneth R. Manning, *Black Apollo of Science: The Life of Ernest Everett Just* (New York: Oxford University Press, 1983), pp. 52–56. Nerney's plan: Meier and Rudwick, *Color Line*, p. 101. ". . . forced to retrench and retrench."—Nerney quoted: Etuk, "Crusader for Justice," p. 216.

32. *Guinn v. United States*: Kellogg, *NAACP*, pp. 205–6; Richard Kluger, *Simple Justice: The History of Brown v. Board of Education*, pp. 102–4. ". . . unconsciously along the color line.": W.E.B. Du Bois to J. E. Spingarn, Oct. 28, 1914, Joel E. Spingarn Papers/ Beinecke Library/Yale University; Meier and Rudwick, *Color Line*, p. 99.

33. Villard, *Russia From a Car Window* (New York: The Nation, 1929). ". . . never below the belt.": Mary White Ovington to Oswald Garrison Villard, Aug. 10, 1915, Box 120, Fol. 1, Oswald Garrison Villard Papers/Houghton/Harvard.

34. "Minutes of the Board of Directors," July 7, 1914, NAACP Papers/LC; Kellogg, *NAACP*, p. 99; Meier and Rudwick, *Color Line*, p. 101. ". . . and sympathy for one end.": W.E.B. Du Bois to Joel E. Spingarn, Oct. 28, 1914, Du Bois Papers/U. Mass., in Aptheker, ed., *Correspondence*, I, 203–7, p. 207.

35. Spingarn's 'New Abolitionism': Ross, *Spingarn*, p. 66. ". . . and your own money."—Spingarn quoted: *ibid.*, p. 68.

36. ". . . more provocative than his actions . . .": *ibid.*, p. 29, and p. 68.

37. ". . . quick and positive judgments. . . .": Du Bois, *Dusk of Dawn*, p. 255. ". . . Are Cordially Invited.": *ibid.*, p. 27.

38. ". . . as well as the colored press.": "NAACP Notes," *The Crisis*, 9 (Mar. 1915): 249. Spingarn and Roger Baldwin: Joel E. Spingarn to Amy E. Spingarn, Jan. 12, 1913, Box 1, Joel and Amy Spingarn Collection/Schomburg Res. Ctr./NYPL; Ross, *Spingarn*, p. 31. ". . . whether I was a Negro.": Joel E. Spingarn to Amy E. Spingarn, Jan. 20, 1914, Box 1, Joel and Amy Spingarn Collection/Schomburg Center for Research in Black Culture/NYPL—Joel Spingarn's complexion was swarthy.

39. ". . . good and strong.": Joel E. Spingarn to Amy E. Spingarn, Jan. 17, 1914, Box 1, Fol. 1, *ibid.* ". . . Dillard and his work.": Joel E. Spingarn to Amy E. Spingarn, May 8, 1914, Box 1, Fol. 1, Schomburg. ". . . a very fine one at that.": Joel E. Spingarn to Amy E. Spingarn, Dec. 22, 1912, Box 1, Fol. 1, Joel and Amy Spingarn Collection/Schomburg Ctr. Res/NYPL.

40. ". . . but not now.": *ibid.* ". . . life of a whole city.": *ibid.*

41. ". . . race has given the world.": Du Bois, *Dusk*, p. 255. ". . . may become a threat to Jews.": Benjamin B. Ringer, "Jews and the Desegregation Crisis," in Charles Herbert

Stember, ed., *Jews in the Mind of America* (New York: Basic Books, 1966), pp. 197–207 (pp. 197–98); Kellogg, *NAACP*, p. 62.

42. Jewish philanthropy in Black America: see Louis R. Harlan, "Booker T. Washington's Discovery of Jews," in J. Morgan Kousser and James McPherson, eds., *Race, Region, and Reconstruction: Essays in Honor of C. Vann Woodward* (New York: Oxford University Press, 1982), pp. 267–279; Harlan, *Booker T. Washington*, II, pp. 140–42; David Levering Lewis, "Parallels and Divergences: Assimilationist Strategies of Afro-American and Jewish Elites from 1910 to the Early Thirties," *Journal of American History*, 7 (Dec. 1984): 543–64 [reprinted in Jack Salzman et al., eds., *Bridges and Boundaries: African Americans and Jews* (New York: Braziller, Inc., 1992), pp. 17–35 (pp. 25–26)]; Hasia Diner, *In the Almost Promised Land: American Jews and Blacks, 1915–1935* (Westport, Conn.: Greenwood Press, 1977), p. 171; Lenora E. Berson, *The Negroes and the Jews* (New York: Random House, 1971), pp. 70–71. Russian pogroms and racial segregation: Lewis, *Vogue*, p. 102; and see Lewis, "Parallels and Divergences"; Arthur Goren, "Jews," in Stephan Thernstrom, *Harvard Encyclopedia of American Ethnic Groups* (Boston: Belknap Press, 1980). ". . . I mean the Negro problem."—Herzl, quoted: Lewis, *Vogue*, p. 102.

43. Collaboration motives: Diner, *The Almost Promised Land*, pp. 75–81, 120–125; Yonathan Shapiro, *Leadership of the American Zionist Organization, 1987–1930* (Urbana: University of Illinois Press, 1971), pp. 55–62; Lewis, "Parallels and Divergences," p. 546; Harlan, "Washington Discovers Jews," pp. 271–74; Kellogg, *NAACP*, p. 44. Lewis, *Vogue*, p. 102; Berson, *Negroes and Jews*, pp. 81–82.

44. Anti-Semitism: Thernstrom, *Harvard Encyclopedia*, pp. 585–86; Herbert L. Feingold, *Zion in America: The Jewish Experience from Colonial Times to the Present* (New York: Twayne Publishers, 1974), pp. 140–45; John Higham, "American Anti-Semitism Historically Reconsidered," in Stember, *Jews in the Mind of America*, pp. 237–58, esp. pp. 250–51; and Higham, *Strangers in the Land: Patterns of American Nativism, 1860–1925* pp. 66–67, 160–61, 185–86.

45. ". . . and are disloyal."—Brandeis, quoted: Shapiro, *Leadership of the American Zionist Organization*, pp. 61–62; Feingold, *Zion in America*, pp. 195–219; Moses Rischin, *The Promised City, New York's Jews, 1870–1914* (Boston: Harvard University Press, 1962), pp. 97–98; Irving Howe, *The World of Our Fathers* (New York: Schocken Books, 1989; orig. pub. 1976), pp. 50–53.

46. ". . . effect of that knowledge.": Oswald Garison Villard to Jacob Schiff, Oct. 21, 1913; Jacob Schiff to Oswald Garrison Villard, Oct. 16, 1913, Fol. Schiff, Jacob, Oswald Garrison Villard Papers/Houghton/Harvard. Villard was not an anti-Semite. In fact, he was an outspoken, if insensitive, supporter of Jewish causes—and this notwithstanding his wife's alleged racial and religious prejudices; see D. Joy Humes, *Oswald Garrison Villard, Liberal of the 1920s*, p. 96.

47. Scapegoating and Leo Frank: Higham, *Strangers in the Land*, pp. 66–67; Lucy Dawidowicz, *The Jewish Presence, Essays on Identity and History* (New York: Holt, Rinehart and Winston, 1960), p. 127; Feingold, *Zion in America*, pp. 145–155; Leonard Dinnerstein, *The Leo Frank Case* (Athens: University of Georgia Press, 1987), p. 134.

48. Kishinev and East St. Louis: see Diner, *Almost Promised Land*, p. 76.

49. Du Bois, "World War and the Color Line," *The Crisis*, 9 (Nov. 1914): 28–30, in Aptheker, *Correspondence*, I, pp. 83–85; "The Children's Number," 8 (Oct. 1914).

50. ". . . an illusion . . .": Joel E. Spingarn to W.E.B. Du Bois, Oct. 24, 1914, Du Bois Papers/U. Mass., p. 201. ". . . extravagant in this matter.": Joel E. Spingarn to W.E.B. Du Bois, Sept. 28, 1914, *ibid.* ". . . Today it is *not* possible.": W.E.B. Du Bois to Joel E. Spingarn, Oct. 24, 1914, in Aptheker, ed., *Correspondence*, I, p. 204. ". . . agents and casual inquiries.": W.E.B. Du Bois to Butler Wilson, July 16, 1915, Du Bois Papers/U. Mass.

51. ". . . unity in our organization.": Joel E. Spingarn to W.E.B. Du Bois, Oct. 24, 1914, in Aptheker, ed., *Correspondence*, I, p. 202.

52. . . . no longer wanted him "associated with us.": Mary White Ovington to Joel E. Spingarn, Nov. 7, 1914, Box M-R, Fol. Ovington, Mary White/Joel E. Spingarn Papers/NYPL. ". . . connection with the general work.": W.E.B. Du Bois to Joel E. Spingarn, Oct. 28, 1914, in Aptheker, ed., *Correspondence*, I, p. 205. *The Crisis* first: "Report of the Department of Publications and Research," Nov. 1913–Oct. 1914, Du Bois Papers/U. Mass.; "Minutes of the Board of Directors," Nov. 4, 1914, NAACP Papers/LC; Meier and Rudwick, *Color Line*, p. 102.

53. ". . . have made fewer mistakes?": W.E.B. Du Bois to Joel E. Spingarn, Oct. 28, 1914, Aptheker, *Correspondence*, I, p. 203.

54. . . . insolence and distrust . . .": *ibid*., p. 206. (". . . made a dozen times."): *ibid*., p. 207.

55. ". . . enough to justify his effort.": *ibid*., p. 207.

56. . . . relinquish his NAACP salary.: W.E.B. Du Bois to George Crawford, Nov. 23, 1914, Du Bois Papers/U. Mass. . . . the July executive committee: Meier and Rudwick, *Color Line*, p. 103. ". . . insubordinate . . .": Mary White Ovington to Joel E. Spingarn, Nov. 7, 1914. ". . . if others couldn't.": Mary White Ovington to Joel E. Spingarn, Nov. 7, 1914/Joel E. Spingarn Papers/NYPL; Kellogg, *NAACP*, p. 103.

57. ". . . over the affairs of the Association . . .": W.E.B. Du Bois to George Crawford, Nov. 23, 1914, Du Bois Papers/U. Mass. ". . . black men can work together.": Joel E. Spingarn to Mary White Ovington, Nov. 5, 1914, Box 1, Fol. 1-37/Mary White Ovington Papers/Wayne State University.

58. ". . . any real power.": W.E.B. Du Bois to George Crawford, Nov. 23, 1914, Du Bois Papers/U. Mass. ". . . break along the color line.": W.E.B. Du Bois to Joel E. Spingarn, Oct. 28, 1914, in Aptheker, ed., *Correspondence*, I, p. 207.

59. "Proposals Drafted by Paul Kennaday," Nov. 24, 1914, Du Bois Papers/U. Mass.; Mary White Ovington to W.E.B. Du Bois, Nov. 21, 1914, Du Bois Papers/U. Mass.; Meier and Rudwick, *Color Line*, pp. 102–3; Kellogg, *NAACP*, p. 104. Spingarn recovers full powers: "Minutes of the Board of Directors," Dec. 1, 1914, NAACP Papers/LC. Villard's "nest egg.": Kellogg, *NAACP*, p. 106.

60. ". . . formulate the policy of *The Crisis*.": "Proposals Drafted by Paul Kennaday," Nov. 24, 1914.

61. *Star of Ethiopia* controversy: W.E.B. Du Bois to Joel E. Spingarn, Nov. 3, 1915, Du Bois Papers/U. Mass. Cover, *The Crisis*, 9 (Nov. 1915). "simply shocking.": Oswald Garrison Villard to Joel E. Spingarn, Nov. 23, 1915, Box 12, Fol. 1/Joel E. Spingarn Papers/NYPL; ". . . a single cent for the publication . . .": Du Bois, "We Come of Age," *The Crisis*, 11 (Nov. 1915): 25–28, in Aptheker, ed., *Selections from The Crisis*, I, pp. 107–10, p. 107; Kellogg, *NAACP*, p. 107; "Document of the Board of Directors," Dec. 6, 1915, Du Bois Papers/U. Mass. ". . . FIFTY THOUSAND subscribers . . .": Du Bois, "We Come of Age," *The Crisis*, 11 (Nov. 1915): 25–28, in Aptheker, ed., *Selections from The Crisis*, I, pp. 107–10 (p. 109). ". . . all connection with it.": Oswald Garrison Villard to Joel E. Spingarn, Nov. 3, 1915, Box S-Z, Fol. Villard, Oswald Garrison/Joel E. Spingarn Papers/Moorland-Spingarn Res. Ctr./Howard.

62. Du Bois, "A Statement," Dec. 1915, Du Bois Papers/U. Mass. ". . . appease all parties.": ". . . convenience of the Board.": *ibid*. ". . . nine hundred and ninety nine times."—Nerney quoted: Kellogg, *NAACP*, p. 108; Oswald Garrison Villard to Joel E. Spingarn, Dec. 10, 1915, Box 12, Fol. 1/Joel E. Spingarn Papers/NYPL; Meier and Rudwick, *Color Line*, p. 104.

63. ". . . quite unable to cope with her.": W.E.B. Du Bois to Archibald Grimké, Dec.

23, 1915, Box 143, Fol. Du Bois/Archibald Grimké Papers/Moorland-Spingarn Res. Ctr./Howard. ". . . organizing branches . . .": "Board of Directors Document," Dec. 6, 1915, Du Bois Papers/U. Mass.; May Childs Nerney to Joel E. Spingarn, Jan. 6, 1916, Box M-R, Fol. Nerney/Joel E. Spingarn Papers/Moorland-Spingarn Res. Ctr./Howard. ". . . infinitely superior to my own.": May Childs Nerney to Joel E. Spingarn [n.d. holograph], Box M-R, Fol. Nerney, May Childs/Joel E. Spingarn Papers/Moorland-Spingarn Res. Ctr./Howard.

64. ". . . glad to have her go.": W.E.B. Du Bois to John Hope, Jan. 26, 1916, Du Bois Papers/U. Mass.; Kellogg, *NAACP*, pp. 79–80.

65. ". . . one of the most attractive offers . . .": John Hope to Joel E. Spingarn, Oct. 21, 1916, Box G-L, Fol. Hope, John/Joel E. Spingarn Papers/Moorland-Spingarn Res. Ctr./Howard; John Hope to W.E.B. Du Bois, Feb. 2, 1916, Du Bois Papers/U. Mass.

18. The Perpetual Dilemma

1. ". . . his usual style": Oswald Garrison Villard to Joel E. Spingarn, Nov. 18, 1915, Box V-Z: Joel E. Spingarn Papers/New York Public Library. Washington monument: see L. Albert Scipio, II, *Pre-War Days at Tuskegee: Historical Essays on Tuskegee Institute (1881–1943)*, pp. 89–95. On Washington's terminal illness: Louis R. Harlan, *Booker T. Washington, II*, pp. 444–52; and see New York *Tribune*, Nov. 10, 1915. ". . . buried in the South."—Washington quoted: *ibid.*, p. 454.

2. ". . . silently rejecting all else.": Du Bois, "Booker T. Washington," *The Crisis*, 11 (Dec. 1915): 82; in Herbert Aptheker, ed., *Selections from the Crisis, 1911–1925*, I, p. 113.

3. ". . . friends both black and white.": Du Bois, "Booker T. Washington," *Selections from The Crisis*, I, p. 113. " '. . . the first of rights.' ": Du Bois, "An Open Letter to Robert Russa Moton," *The Crisis*, 12 (July 1916): 136–37, in *ibid.*, I, pp. 119–20 (p. 120).

4. ". . . and you really see?": Du Bois, "Of the Children of Peace," 8 (Oct. 1914): 289–90; in Aptheker, ed., *Creative Writings*, pp. 99–100. ". . . civilization of the East.": Du Bois, "The Battle of Europe," *The Crisis*, 12 (Sept. 1916): 216–17, in Aptheker, ed., *Selections from The Crisis*, I, p. 126.

5. On Du Bois's anticipation of Lenin: see Peter Duignan and L. H. Gann, *The United States and Africa: A History*, p. 266; and for an excellent exposition of theories of imperial expansion, consult Winifred Baumgart, *Imperialism: The Idea and Reality of British and French Colonial Expansion, 1880–1914* (New York: Oxford University Press, 1982); and William Roger Louis, ed., *Imperialism: The Robinson and Gallagher Controversy* (New York: London: Franklin Watts, 1976), esp. pp. 162–72, 188–95. ". . . name for bestiality and barbarism.": *ibid.*, p. 97. ". . . the world at Algeciras.": Du Bois, "The African Roots of War," *Atlantic Monthly*, 115 (May 1915): 707–14, in Aptheker, ed., *Writings by W.E.B. Du Bois in Periodicals Edited by Others, 1910–1934*, II, pp. 96–104 (p. 98).

6. ". . . exploiting 'chinks and niggers.' ": Du Bois, "African Roots of War," p. 98; also refer to Lance E. Davis and Robert A. Huttenback, *Mammon and the Pursuit of Empire: The Economics of British Imperialism* (Cambridge and New York: Cambridge University Press, 1988; abridged ed.), p. 32. ". . . cost of war abroad.": "African Roots of War," p. 101; see Marable Manning, *W.E.B. Du Bois: Black Radical Democrat*, p. 94. ". . . brown, and black peoples.": Du Bois, "African Roots of War," p. 102.

7. ". . . because you are honest.": John Hope to W.E.B. Du Bois, June 5, 1915, Du Bois Papers/U. Mass.; in Aptheker, *Correspondence*, I, pp. 210–11 (p. 211). ". . . cigar is not too bad.": W.E.B. Du Bois to Garrett Distributing Co., Aug. 29, 1917; Garrett Distributing Co. to W.E.B. Du Bois, Aug. 20, 1917, Du Bois Papers/U. Mass.; also

Aptheker, ed., *The Correspondence [Selected] of W.E.B. Du Bois, 1877–1934*, I, p. 223. ". . . placed it in his coffin.": Dorothy Pohle to W.E.B. Du Bois, Jan. 5, 1916; W.E.B. Du Bois to Dorothy Pohle, June 2, 1916, Du Bois Papers/University of Massachusetts at Amherst.

8. ". . . delivered at St. Mark's Hall. . . .": Marcus Garvey to W.E.B. Du Bois, Apr. 25, 1916, Du Bois Papers/U. Mass.; in Aptheker, ed., *Correspondence*, I, pp. 214–15. "a racial calamity.": William Henry Crogman to W.E.B. Du Bois, Jan. 29, 1917, Du Bois Papers/U. Mass.

9. "Negro" capitalized: Walter Lippmann to W.E.B. Du Bois, Jan. 17, 1916, Du Bois Papers/U. Mass.; in Aptheker, ed., *Correspondence*, I, p. 214. Du Bois was a member of the *New Republic* editorial board. His "That Capital 'N' " appeared in *The Crisis*, 11 (Feb. 1916): 184—"We cannot refuse to capitalize Negro when we capitalize Caucasian, Malay, Indian, Chinese, etc." Du Bois, "The World Problem of the Color Line," Manchester (N.H.) *Leader*, Nov. 16, 1914; in Aptheker, ed., *Annotated Bibliography of the Published Writings of W.E.B. Du Bois*, p. 38; also Du Bois, "World War and the Color Line," *The Crisis*, 9 (Nov. 1914): 28–30, in Aptheker, ed., *Selections from The Crisis*, I, pp. 83–85.

10. The film's debut: Du Bois, "The Clansman," *The Crisis*, 10 (May 1915): 33, in *Selections from The Crisis*, I, pp. 98–99; and Thomas Cripps, *Slow Fade to Black: The Negro in American Film* (New York: Oxford University Press, 1977), pp. 45–52; Florette Henri, *Black Migration: Movement North, 1900–1920*, pp. 228–30. ". . . all so terribly true."—Wilson quoted: Cripps, *Slow Fade*, p. 52; also Joel Williamson, *The Crucible of Race: Black-White Relations in the American South since Emancipation*, p. 176.

11. Reactions of Peabody and White: Cripps, *Slow Fade*, pp. 42, 52. "8 Months in the Making.": *ibid.*, p. 54.

12. ". . . a minority of nine persons": Du Bois, "The Clansman," p. 98.

13. ". . . for a mulatto mistress." *ibid.*, p. 99.

14. Violence surrounding the film: Charles Flint Kellogg, *NAACP: A History of the National Association for the Advancement of Colored People*, p. 143. ". . . for more than a decade.": Du Bois, *Dusk of Dawn*, p. 240.

15. Censorship controversy: Booker Washington, Milholland, Du Bois, Spingarn: Harlan, *B. T. Washington*, II, p. 434; Du Bois, *Dusk*, p. 240; Kellogg, *NAACP*, p. 143. ". . . admittedly notable merits.": Du Bois, *Dusk*, p. 240.

16. Censorship maneuvers—New York, Chicago, elsewhere: Du Bois, *Dusk of Dawn*, p. 239; Cripps, *Slow Fade*, pp. 57, 59; Kellogg, *NAACP*, p. 144; Harold F. Gosnell, *Negro Politicians, The Rise of Negro Politics in Chicago* (Chicago: University of Chicago Press, 1967; orig. pub. 1935), pp. 55–59; James R. Grossman, *Land of Hope: Chicago, Black Southerners and the Great Migration*, p. 176; Harlan, *B. T. Washington*, II, p. 433.

17. ". . . or changed materially.": Harlan, *B. T. Washington*, II, p. 433. *Birth* shown at Hampton: Aptheker, *Annotated Bibliography*, p. 183.

18. Boston demonstrations: Mary White Ovington, *The Walls Came Tumbling Down*, p. 129; Cripps, *Slow Fade*, pp. 59–60. ". . . My God to Thee.": William D. Brigham to W.E.B. Du Bois, May 26, 1915, Du Bois Papers/U. Mass.

19. Peabody and Wilson reconsider: Cripps, *Slow Fade*, pp. 61, 62. ". . . names of small organizations.": W.E.B. Du Bois to William D. Brigham, June 5, 1915, Du Bois Papers/U. Mass.

20. *Lincoln's Dream*: Mary White Ovington to Oswald Garrison Villard, June 6, 1915, Du Bois Papers/U. Mass.; Cripps, *Slow Fade*, p. 71; Neal Gabler, *An Empire of Their Own: How the Jews Invented Hollywood* (New York: Crown Publishers, 1988), p. 91.

21. Grimké's *Rachel*: see the intriguing discussion of this drama in Claudia Tate,

Domestic Allegories of Political Desire: The Black Heroine's Text at the Turn of the Century (New York: Oxford University Press, 1992), pp. 210, 218–19; also Gloria T. Hull, *Color, Sex and Poetry: Three Women Writers of the Harlem Renaissance* (Bloomington: University of Indiana Press, 1987), pp. 119; Kellogg, *NAACP*, p. 145. *Birth of a Race*: Cripps, *Slow Fade*, pp. 71–75; Du Bois, "The Drama Among Black Folk," *The Crisis*, 12 (Aug. 1916): 169–731, in Aptheker, ed., *Selections from The Crisis*, I, 121–23.

22. Trotter's petition: Stephen R. Fox, *The Guardian of Boston: William Monroe Trotter*, p. 175.

23. Racial segregation under Wilson: see Ray Stannard Balker, *Woodrow Wilson: Life and Letters* (New York: Greenwood Press, 1968; orig. pub. 1927–37), 6 vols., IV (1913–1914), pp. 220–25; Arthur S. Link, *Woodrow Wilson: A Brief Biography* (Cleveland and New York: The World Publishing Co., 1963), p. 80; Link, *Woodrow Wilson and the Progressive Era, 1910–1917* (New York: Harper & Bros., 1954), p. 66; Henri, *Black Migration*, p. 252; Rayford W. Logan, *The Betrayal of the Negro: From Rutherford B. Hayes to Woodrow Wilson*, p. 362; Jan Willem Schulte Nordholt, *Woodrow Wilson: A Life for World Peace*, p. 99.

24. ". . . Blease or Hoke Smith.": Du Bois, "Another Open Letter to Woodrow Wilson," *The Crisis*, 6 (Sept. 1913): 232–36, in Aptheker, ed., *Selections from The Crisis*, I, pp. 64–66 (p. 65); and Du Bois, "An Open Letter to Woodrow Wilson," *The Crisis*, 5 (Mar. 1913): 236–37, in *ibid.*, 51–52; Arthur S. Link, "The Negro as a Factor in the Campaign of 1912," *Journal of Negro History*, 32 (Jan. 1947): 81–99.

25. ". . . to solve this thing."—Wilson, quoted: Oswald Garrison Villard, *Fighting Years: Memoirs of a Liberal Editor*, p. 240; Fox, *Guardian of Boston*, pp. 171–72; Nordholt, *Wilson*, p. 99.

26. Racial nadir: John Hope Franklin, *From Slavery to Freedom*, p. 324; Kellogg, *NAACP*, p. 176. ". . . express its opinion": George Foster Peabody to Hollis Frissell, Dec. 11, 1914, Principals and Presidents: Hollis Burke Frissell, 1893–1917/Hampton University Archives.

27. ". . . to escape something."—Wilson, quoted: Fox, *Guardian of Boston*, p. 180.

28. Details of Trotter-Wilson interview: Du Bois, "William Monroe Trotter," *The Crisis*, 9 (Dec. 1914): 82; Du Bois, "Mr. Trotter and Mr. Wilson," *The Crisis*, 9 (Jan. 1915): 119–27; Fox, *Guardian of Boston*, pp. 181–82; John Milton Cooper, Jr., *The Warrior and the Priest: Woodrow Wilson and Theodore Roosevelt* (Cambridge: The Belknap Press of Harvard University Press, 1983), p. 274; Nordholt, *Wilson*, pp. 99–100; Harlan, *B. T. Washington*, II, p. 411.

29. ". . . unfortunate incident of Mr. Trotter."—Moton, quoted: Harlan, *B. T. Washington*, II, p. 413; Henri, *Black Migration*, p. 255. ". . . inaction in a moral crisis."—*World* and *New Republic* cited: Du Bois, "Mr. Trotter and Mr. Wilson," pp. 121–23; Harlan, *B. T. Washington*, II, p. 410.

30. NAACP protests to Wilson: Kellogg, *NAACP*, pp. 164, 167; Elliott Rudwick, *W.E.B. Du Bois: Propagandist of the Negro Protest*, pp. 162–63.

31. ". . . depth of feeling": Du Bois, "William Monroe Trotter," p. 82; W.E.B. Du Bois to Nina Du Bois, Nov. 30, 1914, Du Bois Papers/U. Mass.; Du Bois, "Mr. Trotter and Mr. Wilson," pp. 119–27; Fox, *Guardian of Boston*, p. 178.

32. ". . . you were never mistaken": Joel E. Spingarn to W.E.B. Du Bois, Oct. 24, 1914, Du Bois Papers/U. Mass., in Aptheker, *Correspondence*, II, pp. 200–2 (p. 200).

33. ". . . freedom and efficiency.": Du Bois, "The Immediate Program of the American Negro," *The Crisis*, 9 (Apr. 1915): 310–12, in Apetheker, ed., *Selections from The Crisis*, I, pp. 93–96, p. 95; Du Bois, "Men of the Month," *The Crisis*, 8 (May 1914): 13–15; also Kellogg, *NAACP*, p. 173.

34. *Crisis* circulation: "Minutes of the Meeting of the Board of Directors," Apr. 10, 1916, Du Bois Papers/U. Mass. Consolidating forces: Rudwick, *Du Bois*, p. 184.

35. Gossip about personal life: W.E.B. Du Bois to Major Charles Young, Jan. 21, 1916, Du Bois Papers/U. Mass.

36. ". . . impertinence by the "philanthropoids.": Du Bois, "To the United States Commission on Industrial Education" [dated 1913 and 1915], Du Bois Papers/U. Mass.; consult document, "Conference of the General Education Board of the Rockefeller Foundation on 'Negro Education,'" Nov. 29, 1915, Series 7: General Education Board Papers/ Rockefeller Archive/Pocantico Hills, N.Y.; James D. Anderson. *The Education of Blacks in the South, 1860–1935*, pp. 256–57; John H. Stanfield, *Philanthropy and Jim Crow in American Social Science*, pp. 7–9, 28–30. . . . scorned black intellectual: George Foster Peabody to Edgar Gardner Murphy, Oct. 10, 1911/Principals and Presidents: Hollis Burke Frissell, 1893–1917/Hampton University Archives.

37. Marginal-man typology: *ibid.*; Robert E. Park, *Race and Culture* (Glencoe, Il.: The Free Press, 1950); and see H. F. Dickie-Clark, *The Marginal Situation: A Sociological Study of a Coloured Group* (London: Routledge & Kegan Paul, 1966), pp. 10–20—(p. 171) "simply being in an objectively marginal situation was not enough to make an individual psychologically marginal." Leo Spitzer, *Lives in Between: Assimilation and Marginality in Australia, Brazil, West Africa, 1780–1945* (Cambridge: Cambridge University Press, 1989), esp. pp. 3–15; W. Lloyd Warner et al., *Color and Human Nature: Negro Personality Development in a Northern City*, esp. ch. 4, "Voluntary Negroes and Other Passable People."

38. ". . . moral leadership of the world.": Du Bois, "The Lynching Industry," *The Crisis*, 9 (Feb. 1915): 198, in Aptheker, ed., *Selections from The Crisis*, I, pp. 88–90 (p. 90).

39. Du Bois, "The Waco Horror," *The Crisis*, 12 (June 1916); Du Bois, "The Waco Horror" (Supplement to *The Crisis*), 12 (July 1916). . . . deletions . . . consented to make.: Roy F. Nash to Joel E. Spingarn, June 14, 1916, Box M-R: Joel E. Spingarn Papers/ Moorland-Spingarn Research Center/Howard University.

40. Beyond Waco: Du Bois, "The World Last Month," *The Crisis*, 13 (Jan. 1917); Du Bois, "The Battle of Europe," *The Crisis*, 12 (Sept. 1916): 217–18; Du Bois, "Consolations," *The Crisis*, 12 (June 1916): 81. ". . . feeling of world apprehension.": Du Bois, "England," *The Crisis*, 19 (Jan. 1920): 107–08, in Aptheker, *Crisis Selections*, I, pp. 251–52 (p. 251); additional quotations about Germany, "World War and the Color Line," *The Crisis*, 9 (Nov. 1914): 28–30; in Aptheker, *Crisis Selections*, I, pp. 83–84 (p. 84). Hegel and Hindenburg.: Dewy and Veblen, cited in: Morton G. White, *Social Thought in America: The Revolt Against Formalism* (New York: Viking Press, 1949), pp. 146–47; also, for Dewey's surprising polemical attack on Immanuel Kant, see, Robert B. Westbrook, *John Dewey and American Democracy* (Ithaca and London: Cornell University Press, 1991), pp. 198–99.

41. "All this is past.": Du Bois, "Ireland," *The Crisis*, 12 (Aug. 1916): 166–67. "Someone has blundered.": Du Bois, "Sir Roger Casement—Patriot, Martyr," *The Crisis*, 12 (Sept. 1916): 215–16, in Aptheker, ed., *Selections from The Crisis*, I, pp. 124–25 (p. 125).

42. Du Bois, "Migration and Help," *The Crisis*, 13 (Jan. 1917): 115; "The Elections," *The Crisis*, 13 (Dec. 1916): 59–60. ". . . as every Negro knows.": Du Bois, *ibid.*, p. 59.

43. Outmigration: Du Bois, "Migration," 12 (Oct. 1916): 270; Du Bois, "Editorials," *The Crisis*, 13 (Dec. 1916): 59–60.

44. ". . . large intelligent calibre.": W.E.B. Du Bois to Paul H. Hanus, June 19, 1916; Paul H. Hanus to W.E.B. Du Bois, May 15, 1916, Du Bois Papers/U. Mass., in Aptheker,

Correspondence, I, pp. 215–16 (p. 216). Du Bois, "The Migration of Negroes," *The Crisis*, 14 (June 1917): 63–66, in *Selections from The Crisis*, I, 139–42.

45. Random selections from *Annotated Bibliography*: pp. 183–84.

46. ". . . for Negroes in Jamaica.": Du Bois, "Along the Color Line," *The Crisis*, 12 (May 1916): 9. Aptheker, *Annotated Bibliography*, pp. 183, 187.

47. Young in *The Crisis*: Photo of Major Charles Young, *The Crisis*, 11 (Jan. 1916); Du Bois, "Editorials," *The Crisis*, 11 (Mar. 1916): 240–44; Du Bois, "Men of the Month," *The Crisis*, 12 (Oct. 1916): 278–81. Young's Army service—Wood, quoted: Major General Leonard Wood to Joel E. Spingarn, Jan. 18, 1916, Du Bois Papers/U. Mass. Col. Charles Young (ACP 000214), Record Group 94/National Archives; Bernard C. Nalty, *Strength for the Fight: A History of Black Americans in the Military*, pp. 60–61, 98–99, 110–11.

48. ". . . and the beginning.": Du Bois, *The Amenia Conference, An Historic Negro Gathering*. Troutbeck Leaflet No. 8 (Amenia, N.Y.: Privately printed at Troutbeck Press, 1925), in Aptheker, ed., *Pamphlets and Leaflets by W.E.B. Du Bois*, pp. 210–16 (quote, p. 214); Du Bois, *Dusk*, p. 244.

49. ". . . and quiet of Amenia.": Du Bois, *The Amenia Conference*, p. 214; Rudwick, *Du Bois*, p. 184.

50. Invitations to Troutbeck: Du Bois, *Dusk*, p. 244; Du Bois, *The Amenia Conference*, p. 213. Nash's competence: Kellogg, *NAACP*, p. 113. ". . . mattresses up there.": Roy F. Nash to Joel E. Spingarn, Aug. 15, 1916, Box M-R: Joel E. Spingarn Papers/Moorland-Spingarn Res. Ctr.

51. ". . . into two hard groups.": Roy F. Nash to Joel E. Spingarn, Aug. 16, 1916, Box M-R: Joel E. Spingarn Papers/Moorland-Spingarn Res. Ctr.; Du Bois, "Notes on Amenia Conference" [n.d.], Du Bois Papers/U. Mass.

52. "Lynch, John Roy (1847–1939)," *DANB*, pp. 407–409: Lynch was the author of *The Facts of Reconstruction* (1913) and of a work edited by John Hope Franklin and not published until 1970, *Reminiscences of an Active Life: The Autobiography of John Roy Lynch*; see also John Hope Franklin, "John Roy Lynch: Republican Stalwart from Mississippi," in Howard N. Rabinowitz, ed., *Southern Black Leaders of the Reconstruction Era*, pp. 39–58. ". . . than his fair share": Roy F. Nash to Joel E. Spingarn, Aug. 16, Box M-R: Joel E. Spingarn Papers/Moorland-Spingarn Res. Ctr.

53. Amenia regrets: Samuel Gompers to Joel E. Spingarn, Aug. 2, 1916, Box G-L; George Foster Peabody to Joel E. Spingarn, Aug. 19, 1916, Box M-R; Mary White Ovington to Joel E. Spingarn, Aug. 22, 1916, Box M-R; Ray Stannard Baker to Joel E. Spingarn, July 21, 1916, Box A-C; Florence Kelly to Joel E. Spingarn, July 27, 1916, Box G-L: Joel E. Spingarn Papers/Moorland-Spingarn Res. Ctr.

54. Moton and Trotter: W.E.B. Du Bois to Robert Russa Moton, July 17, 1916, Du Bois Papers/U. Mass.; Du Bois, "An Open Letter to Robert Russa Moton," *The Crisis*, 12 (July 1916): 136–37, in Aptheker, ed., *Selections from The Crisis*, I, pp. 119–20 (p. 119); William Monroe Trotter to Joel E. Spingarn, Aug. 23, 1916, Box S-Z: Spingarn Papers/Moorland-Spingarn Res. Ctr.; Fox, *Guardian of Boston*, p. 202.

55. Amenia invitees: Charles Anderson to Joel E. Spingarn, Aug. 9, 1916, Box A-C; Roscoe Conkling Bruce to Joel E. Spingarn, Aug. 19, 1916, Box A-C; Francis N. Cardozo to Joel E. Spingarn, July 21, 1916, Box D-F: Joel E. Spingarn Papers/Moorland-Spingarn Res. Ctr.

56. ". . . *only 1000 subscribers*.": Du Bois, "The Journal of Negro History," *The Crisis*, 13 (Dec. 1916): 61, in Aptheker, ed., *Selections from The Crisis*, I, p. 129. Tent occupants: Spingarn, Amenia Conference Notes, 95–13 Joel E. Spingarn Papers/Moorland-Spingarn.

57. ". . . own Berkshire Hills.": Du Bois, *Amenia Conference*, p. 210.

58. ". . . a dampness all about.": *ibid.*, p. 213.

59. ". . . her young womanhood": *ibid.*, p. 214; see Doris Stevens, *Jailed for Freedom* (New York: Schocken Books, 1976), pp. 43, 76.

60. ". . . a very short time": Charles W. Chesnutt to Joel E. Spingarn, Sept. 1, 1916, Box D-F: Joel E. Spingarn Papers/Moorland-Spingarn Res. Ctr.

61. ". . . problems of the world.": Du Bois, *Dusk of Dawn*, p. 245. Du Bois, *Amenia Conference*, p. 214.

62. ". . . wellnigh fatal loss of time.": Du Bois, "Hampton," *The Crisis*, 15 (Nov. 1917): 10–12, in Aptheker, ed., *Selections from The Crisis*, I, pp. 146–48 (p. 147).

63. ". . . American race prejudice.": Du Bois, "Notes on Amenia Conference," Du Bois Papers/U. Mass. ". . . dreamers and farmers.": Du Bois, *Dusk of Dawn*, p. 245.

64. ". . . little to choose.": Du Bois, "The Negro Party," *The Crisis*, 12 (Oct. 1916): 268–69, in *Selections from The Crisis*, I, p. 127. " 'despised and rejected of men.' ": Du Bois, "Brandeis," *The Crisis*, 11 (Mar. 1916): 243, in *ibid.*, I, 118. ". . . tried to live up to them . . ."—Wilson quoted: J. Tumulty, secretary to the president, to W.E.B. Du Bois, Oct. 17, 1916, Du Bois Papers/U. Mass., also Aptheker, ed., *Correspondence*, I, 219; W.E.B. Du Bois to president of the United States, Oct. 10, 1916, Fol. 1912–54: Du Bois Collection/Fisk University, also *Correspondence*, I, p. 218.

65. ". . . It will be a crime.": Du Bois, "Mexico," *The Crisis*, 8 (June 1914): 79, in Aptheker, ed., *Selections from The Crisis*, I, 78. ". . . civilized today than Texas.": Du Bois, "Hayti," *The Crisis*, 10 (Oct. 1915): 291, in *ibid.*, I, p. 106; W.E.B. Du Bois to president of the United States, Aug. 3, 1915, Du Bois Papers/U. Mass.

66. ". . . recently formed Woman's Party.": Du Bois, "The Negro Party," *The Crisis*, 12 (Oct. 1916): 268–69, in *Selections from The Crisis*, I, p. 127. Du Bois, "Editorials," *The Crisis*, 13 (Nov. 1916): 59–63; Du Bois, "Josiah Royce," *The Crisis*, 13 (Nov. 1916): 10–11; Du Bois, "The Presidential Campaign," *The Crisis*, 12 (Oct. 1916): 267–71, p. 268; "The Negro Party," *The Crisis*, 12 (Oct. 1916): 268–69.

67. Garvey at the NAACP: Amy Jacques-Garvey, ed., *Philosophy and Opinions of Marcus Garvey* (New York: Atheneum, 1969), p. 57.

68. "Johnson, James Weldon (1871–1938)," *DANB*: 353–57; see James Weldon Johnson, *Along This Way: The Autobiography of James Weldon Johnson* (New York: Viking, 1961; orig. pub. 1933); and Eugene Levy, *James Weldon Johnson, Black Leader, Black Voice* (Chicago: University of Illinois Press, 1973); Jean Wagner, *Black Poets of the United States: From Paul Laurence Dunbar to Langston Hughes*, ch. 9, pp. 351–84.

69. "secret organization": W.E.B. Du Bois to James Weldon Johnson, Nov. 1, 1916, Du Bois Papers/U. Mass., also Aptheker, *Correspondence*, I, 219–20, p. 219.

70. ". . . appeals to me very strongly." James Weldon Johnson to Joel E. Spingarn, Nov. 5, 1916, Box G-L; John Hope to Joel E. Spingarn, Oct. 21, 1916, Box G-L: Joel E. Spingarn Papers/Moorland-Spingarn Res. Ctr.

71. ". . . the main organization": W.E.B. Du Bois to James Weldon Johnson, Nov. 1, 1916, Du Bois Papers/U. Mass., in *Correspondence*, I, pp. 219–20 (p. 219).

72. ". . . the shadow of death.": Du Bois, *Dusk of Dawn*, p. 245.

73. ". . . own peace of mind . . .": Joel E. Spingarn to W.E.B. Du Bois, Dec. 12, 1916, Du Bois Papers/U. Mass.; Secretary to W.E.B. Du Bois to Nina Du Bois, Dec. 14, 1916, Du Bois Papers/U. Mass. Letters written during convalescence: W.E.B. Du Bois to Joel E. Spingarn, Jan. 2, 1917, Box 95-2: Joel E. Spingarn Papers/Moorland-Spingarn Res. Ctr.; W.E.B. Du Bois to Frances Hoggan, Jan. 29, 1917, Du Bois Papers/U. Mass. Dill, Ovington, Spingarn editorials: consult Aptheker, *Annotated Bibliography*, p. 185.

74. ". . . glad I am here.": Du Bois, "The Curtains of Pain," *The Crisis*, 13 (Feb. 1917): 163, in Aptheker, ed., *Selections from The Crisis*, I, p. 130.

75. ". . . racial calamity.": W. H. Crogman to W.E.B. Du Bois, Jan. 29, 1917; Sadie Conyers to W.E.B. Du Bois, Feb. 4, 1917 (also in Apetheker, ed., *Correspondence*, I, p. 221); Mary Church Terrell to W.E.B. Du Bois, Jan. 29, 1917, Du Bois Papers/U. Mass. ". . . feeling quite well.": W.E.B. Du Bois to Joel E. Spingarn, Jan. 20, 1917, Box 95-2: Joel E. Spingarn Papers/Moorland-Spingarn Res. Ctr. ". . . how important I am.": W.E.B. Du Bois to Carrie W. Clifford, Jan. 29, 1917, Du Bois Papers/U. Mass.

76. ". . . Africa and the tropics.": Du Bois, "The Battle of Europe," *The Crisis*, 12 (Sept. 1916): 216–17, in Aptheker, ed., *Selections from The Crisis*, I, p. 126.

77. ". . . civilization on to the natives.": Du Bois, "The Problem of Problems," *Intercollegiate Socialist* (Dec.–Jan. 1918): 5–9, in Aptheker, ed., *Writings in Periodical Literature*, II, pp. 114–20 (p. 119).

78. "forward-looking and radical": Du Bois, "A Field for Socialists," *New Review* (Jan. 11, 1913): 54–57, in *Periodical Literature*, II, pp. 80–84 (p. 83).

79. . . . matter of intense discussion.: Carter G. Woodson, *A Century of Negro Migration* (New York: Ames Press, 1918), p. 180; George Edmund Haynes, *Negro New-Comers in Detroit, Michigan: A Challenge to Christian Statesmanship: A Preliminary Survey* (New York, 1918). NUL-NAACP meeting: L. Hollingsworth Wood to Joel E. Spingarn, Oct. 7, 1916, Box S-Z: Joel E. Spingarn Papers/Moorland-Spingarn Res. Ctr.; Kellogg, *NAACP*, p. 223. ". . . their political rights."—Wilson, quoted: Kellogg, *NAACP*, p. 223.

80. ". . . best athletic record . . .": Du Bois, "The South," *The Crisis*, 13 (Apr. 1917): 268–70, in Aptheker, ed., *Selections from The Crisis*, I, 131–33, p. 131.

81. ". . . substituted for English.": *ibid.*, p. 122; consult "Bethune, Mary Jane McLeod (1875–1955)," *DANB*, pp. 41–43.

82. "Turks teaching Armenians.": Du Bois, "The South," p. 270; see also Willard B. Gatewood, *Aristocrats of Color: The Black Elite, 1880–1920*, p. 282.

83. Joel E. Spingarn to W.E.B. Du Bois, Feb. 26, 1917, Du Bois Papers/U. Mass.; Marable, *Du Bois*, p. 95. Spingarn's training camp: Leonard Wood to Joel E. Spingarn, Jan. 9, 1917: Joel E. Spingarn Papers/Moorland-Spingarn Res. Ctr.; B. Joyce Ross, *J. E. Spingarn and the Rise of the NAACP, 1911–1939*, p. 84.

84. ". . . however . . . this training may be obtained.": Ross, *Spingarn*, p. 85. Promoting the camp: Roy F. Nash to Joel E. Spingarn (telegram), Apr. 11, 1917, Box M-R; Roy F. Nash to Joel E. Spingarn, Apr. 12, 1917, Box M-R; Roy F. Nash to Joel E. Spingarn, Apr. 12, 1917, Box M-R; Roy F. Nash and Archibald Grimké to Secretary of War Newton D. Baker, Apr. 19, 1917, Box M-R: Joel E. Spingarn Papers/Moorland-Spingarn Res. Ctr.; George E. Brice to Joel E. Spingarn, Mar. 14, 1917, Box A-C; George E. Brice to Joel E. Spingarn, Mar. 16, 1917; George E. Brice to Joel E. Spingarn, Mar. 24, 1917, Box A-C; George E. Brice to Joel E. Spingarn, Apr. 26, 1917, Box A-C—Brice letters in Joel E. Spingarn Papers/Moorland-Spingarn Res. Ctr.; Ross, *Spingarn*, p. 92.

85. Opposition to African-American commissions: Jack D. Foner, *Blacks in the Military in American History* (New York: Praeger, 1974), ch. 6; Henri, *Black Migration*, p. 273; and see George S. Schuyler, *Black and Conservative: The Autobiography of George S. Schuyler* (New Rochelle, New York: Arlington House, 1966), p. 87.

86. ". . . already dawning tomorrow.": Du Bois, "The Conservation of Races," *Pamphlets and Leaflets*, p. 1; Du Bois, *Dusk*, p. 249. ". . . absorb ten million Negro Americans . . . ?": Du Bois, "The Niagara Movement. Address to the Country," *Pamphlets and Leaflets*, p. 65.

87. Black camp advocates and opponents: George W. Cook to W.E.B. Du Bois, July 3, 1918, Du Bois Folder/Moorland-Spingarn Res. Ctr.; Richard R. Wright to Joel E. Spingarn, Apr. 3, 1917: Joel E. Spingarn Papers/Moorland-Spingarn Res. Ctr.; George W.

Crawford to Joel E. Spingarn, Mar. 3, 1917: Joel E. Spingarn Papers/Moorland-Spingarn Res. Ctr.; Ross, *Spingarn*, pp. 90–96; Charles Young to Harry Smith, Mar. 23, 1917: Joel E. Spingarn Papers/Moorland-Spingarn Res. Ctr.

88. On military conscription: Roy F. Nash to Joel E. Spingarn (telegram), Apr. 11, 1917, Box M-R: Joel E. Spingarn Papers/Moorland-Spingarn Res. Ctr.; John Whiteclay Chambers III, *To Raise an Army: The Draft Comes to Modern America* (New York: The Free Press, 1987), pp. 157–58, 222–26. "even to be segregated.": Du Bois, *Dusk*, p. 250.

89. ". . . Give us the camp.": Du Bois, "The Perpetual Dilemma," *The Crisis*, 13 (Apr. 1917): 270–71, in Aptheker, ed., *Selections from The Crisis*, I, pp. 137–38 (p. 138).

90. ". . . betrayed the cause of his race." Fox, *Guardian of Boston*, p. 219. ". . . Write us for information.": Du Bois, "Officers," *The Crisis*, 14 (June 1917): 60–61, in *Selections from The Crisis*, I, p. 138.

91. ". . . reactionary Negro leadership"—Randolph and Owen quoted: John Tebbell and Mary Ellen Zuckerman, *The Magazine in America, 1741–1990* (New York: Oxford University Press, 1991), p. 139. For early history of *Messenger*, see *ibid.*, p. 139; Jervis Anderson, *A. Philip Randolph: A Biographical Portrait* (New York: Harcourt Brace Jovanovich, 1972), pp. 76–82; Theodore Kornweibel, Jr., *No Crystal Stair: Black Life and the Messenger* (Westport, Conn.: Greenwood Press, 1975), pp. 3–41; Theodore Vincent, ed., *Voices of a Black Nation: Political Journalism in the Harlem Renaissance* (San Francisco: Ramparts Press, 1973), pp. 43–50.

92. ". . . idealism of the cause."—Young, quoted: David Levering Lewis, *When Harlem Was in Vogue*, p. 9.

93. On Young's military service record: Colonel Charles Young, Record Group 94 NMRM/Nat. Archives; Henri, *Black Migration*, p. 280; Nalty, *Strength for the Fight*, p. 98; Schuyler, *Black and Conservative*, p. 87. John Hope Franklin, *From Slavery to Freedom*, p. 236. ". . . general in the army by 1918.": Du Bois, *Dusk*, p. 250.

94. ". . . head in sudden emergencies.": "Efficiency Report," Fort Huachuca, Arizona, Mar. 31, 1917: Col. Young, R.G. 94/Nat. Archives. This assessment is strikingly analogous to stereotypical claims made of recent date about the performance of women in the military and in other situations of stress. Army racial policy: see Henri, *Black Migration*, p. 281; Nalty, *Strength for the Fight*, pp. 108–110; John Hope Franklin, *Slavery to Freedom*, p. 326.

95. ". . . two or three weeks.": President Woodrow Wilson to Senator John Sharp Williams, June 29, 1917—cited from Newton D. Baker Papers, Manuscript Division/ Library of Congress, in Henri, *Black Migration*, p. 282—Henri erroneously concludes (p. 282) that "the reasonable, if ugly inference, is that the President of the United States, the Secretary of War, the General Staff, and the staff of Letterman General Hospital conspired to relieve Colonel Young of his command," because Wilson advised Senator Williams of Young's disabling infirmity "three days" after learning of the lieutenant colonel's hospitalization. But, in fact, the medical information contained in Young's service record at the National Archives establishes that the army surgeon general, based on examination of Young at Letterman General Hospital, had already recommended (June 25, 1917) that Young be sent before a retirement board. The authorities at Letterman General Hospital had determined in mid-June, 1917, that Young suffered from chronic nephritis. Therefore, while high authorities in the army may have entered into a conspiracy to force Colonel Young's retirement, there were valid grounds for Wilson and Baker to reach the conclusions they did—even if these conclusions were politically expedient.

96. ". . . colored officers into shape.": Charles Young to W.E.B. Du Bois, June 20, 1917, Du Bois Papers/U. Mass., in *Correspondence*, I, pp. 222–23 (p. 222). ". . . a miserable ruse.": Du Bois, *Dusk*, p. 250.

97. ". . . telegrams to the White House.": Charles Young to Joel E. Spingarn, Aug. 15, 1917: Joel E. Spingarn Papers/Moorland-Spingarn Res. Ctr.; W.E.B. Du Bois to Walter Lippmann, June 29, 1917, Du Bois Papers/U. Mass. "in suspense.": Memorandum from Adjutant General H.-P. McCain to General Tasker Bliss, Army Chief of Staff, July 26, 1917; General Tasker H. Bliss, Army Chief of Staff, to General H.-P. McCain, Adjutant General, July 26, 1917/Col. Charles Young/R.G. 94/Nat. Archives.

98. ". . . are not acted upon.": Memorandum from Colonel W. Greaves, Army General Staff, to General Tasker H. Bliss, Army Chief of Staff, July 27, 1917: Col. Charles Young, R.G. 94/Nat. Archives. See Henri, *Black Migration*, pp. 281–83. ". . . I have ever seen.": Oswald Garrison Villard to Francis P. Keppel, Jan. 30, 1918; Francis P. Keppel to Oswald Garrison Villard, Feb. 2, 1918: Oswald Garrison Villard Papers/Houghton Library/ Harvard University.

99. Charles Young to Joel E. Spingarn, Feb. 5, 1918: Joel E. Spingarn Papers/ Moorland-Spingarn Res. Ctr.

19. "The Wounded World"

1. ". . . more trouble.": W.E.B. Du Bois, *The Autobiography: A Soliloquy on Viewing My Life from the Last Decade of Its First Century*, p. 267; Jack D. Foner, *Blacks and the Military* (New York: Praeger, 1974), pp. 113, 117–22, 123–24.

2. African-American inductees and officers: Jack D. Foner, *Blacks and the Military in American History*, p. 117–22; Florette Henri, *Black Migration: Movement North, 1900–1920*, p. 284; Bernard C. Nalty, *Strength for the Fight: A History of Black Americans in the Military*, pp. 108–10; John Hope Franklin, *From Slavery to Freedom: A History of Negro Americans*, p. 326.

3. ". . . provoke race animosity."—General Ballou, quoted: Nalty, *Strength for the Fight*, p. 113; Du Bois, *Dusk*, p. 250; Franklin, *Slavery to Freedom*, p. 329. ". . . whirlwind struck us again": Du Bois, *Dusk*, p. 251.

4. "own travel and observation": Du Bois, *Dusk*, p. 252; Du Bois, "The Migration of Negroes," *The Crisis*, 14 (June 1917): 63–66, in Aptheker, ed., *Selections from The Crisis*, I, pp. 139–42 (p. 139). East St. Louis: Elliott Rudwick, *Race Riot in East St. Louis: July 2, 1917* (New York: Atheneum, 1972), pp. 8–10; Henri, *Black Migration*, pp. 266–67.

5. East St. Louis unions: Rudwick, *East St. Louis*, pp. 15–17.

6. East St. Louis riot: Du Bois, *Dusk*, p. 252; Henri, *Black Migration*, p. 265; Rudwick, *East St. Louis*, pp. 50, 52, 67.

7. Du Bois and Gruening in East St. Louis: William English Walling to W.E.B. Du Bois, July 28, 1917, W.E.B. Du Bois Papers/Special Collections/University of Massachusetts at Amherst; "Memorandum to the Anti-Lynching Committee of W.E.B. Du Bois on East St. Louis" [n.d.], Du Bois Papers/U. Mass.; Minutes of the Meeting of the Board of Directors of the NAACP, Sept. 17, 1917, Du Bois Papers/U. Mass.; Charles Flint Kellogg, *NAACP: A History of the National Association for the Advancement of Colored People*, p. 224; Rudwick, *East St. Louis*, p. 116.

8. ". . . a nation's democracy.": Jessie Fauset, "A Negro in East St. Louis [to the Editor]," *Survey*, 38 (Aug. 18, 1917): 448. ". . . safe, lucrative employment.": Du Bois, "The Problem of Problems," *Intercollegiate Socialist*, 6 (Dec.–Jan. 1918): 5–9, in Aptheker, ed., *Writings of W.E.B. Du Bois in Periodicals Edited by Others*, II, pp. 114–20 (p. 117).

9. Roosevelt and Wilson react: Aptheker, ed., *Annotated Bibliography of the Published Writings of W.E.B. Du Bois*, p. 190; Rudwick, *East St. Louis*, pp. 133–34.

10. Planning the parade: Kellogg, *NAACP*, p. 226. ". . . FULL OF BLOOD.": Franklin, *Slavery to Freedom*, p. 342; Lewis, *When Harlem Was in Vogue*, p. 10.

11. Du Bois and Gruening, "The Massacre of East St. Louis," The Crisis, 14 (Sept. 1917): 215–16. ". . . hosts of Almighty God.": Du Bois, "Awake America," *The Crisis*, 14 (Sept. 1917): 216–17, in *Selections from The Crisis*, I, p. 144.

12. Rudwick, *East St. Louis*, p. 65.

13. ". . . eagerly with the mob.": Du Bois, *Darkwater: Voices from Within the Veil*, p. 95; Rudwick, *East St. Louis*, p. 55.

14. Houston: Robert V. Haynes, *A Night of Violence: The Houston Riot of 1917* (Baton Rouge: Louisiana State University Press, 1976), pp. 90–114; Nalty, *Strength for the Fight*, pp. 103, 105.

15. ". . . whether right or wrong.": Du Bois, "Houston," *The Crisis*, 14 (Oct. 1917): 284–85, in Aptheker, ed., *Selections from The Crisis*, I, p. 145.

16. ". . . not an ordinary outburst.": Du Bois, "Houston," p. 145. ". . . dead men in that regiment.": Du Bois, *Autobiography*, p. 268; Nalty, *Strength for the Fight*, p. 72; Kellogg, *NAACP*, p. 261.

17. ". . . editorial referring to him.": Emmett J. Scott to W.E.B. Du Bois, Dec. 1, 1917, Du Bois Papers/U. Mass.; Du Bois, "The Spingarn Camp," *The Crisis*, 15 (Dec. 1917): 61; "Baker," *The Crisis*, 15 (Dec. 1917): 61–62. ". . . be done about it?": W.E.B. Du Bois to Emmett J. Scott, Dec. 31, 1917; W.E.B. Du Bois to Newton D. Baker, Dec. 6, 1917; Newton D. Baker to W.E.B. Du Bois, Dec. 13, 1917, all in Du Bois Papers/U. Mass.; also (Du Bois to Baker, Baker to Du Bois) in Aptheker, ed., *The Correspondence [Selected] of W.E.B. Du Bois*, I, pp. 224–25. Exchange with Scott also found in Box 115, Fol. 1917–19: The Emmett J. Scott Collection Papers/Special Collections/Morgan State University Library. See Henri, *Black Migration*, pp. 295–96. ". . . the colored candidates.": Schuyler, *Black and Conservative: The Autobiography of George S. Schuyler*, p. 87.

18. ". . . with winning the war.": Du Bois, *Dusk*, p. 251; W.E.B Du Bois to Archibald Grimké, Sept. 26, 1917, W.E.B. Du Bois Folder/Moorland-Spingarn Research Center/Howard University. Des Moines officers: Du Bois, *Dusk*, p. 251.

19. ". . . to save Belgium.": Du Bois, "The Negro's Fatherland," *Survey*, 39 (Nov. 10, 1917): 141, in Aptheker, ed., *Periodical Literature*, II, pp. 111–13 (pp. 112, 111).

20. ". . . from handing it back.": *ibid.*, p. 112.

21. Achievements enumerated: Minutes of the Meeting of the Board of Directors of the NAACP, Jan. 14, 1918, Du Bois Papers/U. Mass.; Kellogg, *NAACP*, p. 114.

22. Spingarn lobbies for a commission: Joel E. Spingarn to General Leonard Wood, Feb. 3, 1917; Edward Platt, U.S. Congress, to Joel E. Spingarn, Feb. 27, 1917; Theodore Roosevelt to Adjutant General, U.S. Army, Mar. 8, 1917, Box 7 LAM-Military 1917–8 (Incomplete), Fol. 4: Joel E. Spingarn Papers/New York Public Library; and see B. Joyce Ross, *J. E. Spingarn and the Rise of the NAACP, 1911–1939*, pp. 96–97; and Kellogg, *NAACP*, p. 114.

23. Villard's candidate, Baldwin: Kellogg, *NAACP*, pp. 114–15.

24. Minutes of the Meeting of the Board of Directors of the NAACP, Jan. 6, 1918, Du Bois Papers/U. Mass. ". . . President of the United States.": Du Bois, "Thirteen," *The Crisis*, 15 (Jan. 1918): 114; Kellogg, *NAACP*, p. 115.

25. ". . . not merely FOR US.": Du Bois, "Editorial," *The Crisis*, 15 (Jan. 1918): 112. Hope, quoted in Du Bois, *The Autobiography*, p. 287; Sophonisba P. Breckinridge to W.E.B. Du Bois, Feb. 9, 1918; Frank A. Hosmer to W.E.B. Du Bois, Feb. 16, 1918; Albert Bushnell Hart to W.E.B. Du Bois, Feb. 24, 1918; W.E.B. Du Bois to Albert Bushnell Hart, Apr. 15, 1918; Herbert Croly to John R. Shillady, Feb. 13, 1918; Simon Flexner to John R. Shillady, Feb. 18, 1918; Ray Stannard Baker to John R. Shillady, Feb. 19, 1918, all in

Du Bois Papers/U. Mass. ". . . opportunity to be Dr. Du Bois.": Bessie Taylor Page to W.E.B. Du Bois, Mar. 4, 1918, Du Bois Papers/U. Mass.

26. ". . . But it was not my time.": Du Bois, "The Shadow of Years," *The Crisis*, 15 (Feb. 1918): 167–71, in Aptheker, ed., *Selections from The Crisis*, II, pp. 150–55 (pp. 155, 150).

27. ". . . of Negro descent.": Du Bois, "The Black Man and the Unions," *The Crisis*, 15 (Mar. 1918): 216–17, in Aptheker, ed., *Selections from The Crisis*, II, pp. 157–58 (p. 157).

28. ". . . at your invitation.": Du Bois, "Hampton," *The Crisis*, 15 (Nov. 1917): 10–12, in Aptheker, ed., *Selections from The Crisis*, II, pp. 146–48 (p. 148); Du Bois, "Three Dead Workers [Frissell]," *The Crisis*, 14 (Oct. 1917): 295–97, p. 295.

29. Jones and his report: See James D. Anderson, *The Education of Blacks in the South, 1860–1935*, pp. 250–51; Robert A. Margo, *Race and Schooling in the South, 1880–1950: An Economic History*, pp. 18–24; John H. Stanfield, *Philanthropy and Jim Crow in American Social Science*, pp. 28–30; Thomas Jesse Jones, ed., *Negro Education: A Study of the Private and Higher Schools for Colored People in the United States* (New York: Arno Press and the New York Times, 1969; orig. pub. 1917), 2 vols. Du Bois, "Negro Education," *The Crisis*, 15 (Feb. 1918): 173–78, reproduced in Daniel B. Walden, ed., *W.E.B. Du Bois: The Crisis Writings*, pp. 146–158.

30. ". . . high sounding courses."—Davis, quoted: Anderson, *Education of Blacks*, p. 142.

31. ". . . Greek for the B.A. degree.": Mary E. Spence to W.E.B. Du Bois [n.d. 1915], Du Bois Papers/U. Mass. Charles H. Thompson, "The Socio-Economic Status of Negro College Students," *Journal of Negro Education*, 2 (Jan. 1933): 26–27; Anderson, *Education of Blacks*, pp. 28–29, 134–35; Raymond Wolters, *The New Negro on Campus: Black Colleges and Rebellions in the 1920s* (Princeton, N.J.: Princeton University Press, 1975), p. 15 and p. 59.

32. ". . . difficult, if not impossible.": Du Bois, "Negro Education," p. 147; and see Du Bois, "The Two Sorts of Schooling" [n.d. 1909?], Du Bois Papers, and *Periodical Literature*, I, pp. 83–85; and Du Bois, "The Training of Negroes for Social Power," *Outlook*, 75 (Oct. 17, 1905): 409–14, in *Periodical Literature*, I, pp. 179–85. ". . . predicted that it would."—Washington, quoted: Jones, *Negro Education*, p. 21.

33. ". . . foundations working among Negroes.": Du Bois, "Negro Education," p. 147.

34. GEB meeting: "Conference of the General Education Board of the Rockefeller Foundation on 'Negro Education,'" Nov. 29, 1915 [typed verbatim transcript, unpaginated], Series 7: General Education Board Papers/Rockefeller Archive/Pocantico Hills, N.Y. Biographical and professional evaluations of Dillard, Flexner, Rose, Sage, inter alia: see indexed references in Anderson, *Education of Blacks*; Raymond B. Fosdick, *Adventures in Giving: The Story of the General Education Board*; Gerald Jonas, *The Circuit Riders: Rockefeller Money and the Rise of Modern Science* (New York and London: W. W. Norton & Co., 1989); Stanfield, *Philanthropy and Jim Crow*.

35. ". . . even with a small salary.": Frissell, Jones, Hope, Moton, Flexner quoted: "Conference of the General Education Board".

36. ". . . to that at all."—Hope quoted: *ibid*.

37. ". . . really met their needs.": *ibid*. On the prevalence of Flexner's ideas and early controversy about coeducation, see Helen Lefkowitz Horowitz, *Alma Mater: Design and Experience in Women's Colleges from Their Nineteenth-Century Beginnings to the 1930s* (New York: Alfred A. Knopf, 1984); Rosalind Rosenberg, *Beyond Separate Spheres: Intellectual Roots of Modern Feminism* (New Haven and London: Yale University Press, 1982), pp. xiii–xxii, and pp. 1–27, 43–51; and Sheila Rothman, *Woman's Proper Place: A History of*

Changing Ideals and Practices, 1870 to the Present (New York: Basic Books, 1978), pp. 23–24, 49.

38. ". . . live without insult.": Du Bois, "The Black Soldier," *The Crisis*, 16 (June 1918): 60. Du Bois, "Report of Director of Publications and Research," July 8, 1918, Du Bois Papers/U. Mass.—re *Crisis* circulation of 78,500 for June. "two German girls": Du Bois, "Justice," *The Crisis*, 14 (July 1917): 112, in Aptheker, ed., *Selections from The Crisis*, II, p. 143. Charles Studin to W.E.B. Du Bois, May 1, 1918, Du Bois Papers/U. Mass.—mentions letter from U.S. attorney general (April 29, 1918) protesting "tone" of the magazine.

39. On government surveillance and investigation: Ellis, " 'Closing Ranks,' and 'Seeking Honors': W.E.B. Du Bois in World War I," *Journal of American History*, 79 (June 1992): 96–124, pp. 101–02; Kenneth O'Reilly, *"Racial Matters": The FBI's Secret File on Black America, 1960–1972* (New York and London: The Free Press, 1989), pp. 12–14; and Patrick S. Washburn, A *Question of Sedition: The Federal Government's Investigation of the Black Press during World War II* (New York: Oxford University Press, 1986), esp. pp. 11–19. ". . . winning of the war."—Spingarn quoted: Mark Ellis, " 'Closing Ranks,' " p. 105. Joel E. Spingarn to C.O., General 78th Division, Apr. 20, 1918, Box 7 LAM-Military (Incomplete), Fol. 4: Joel E. Spingarn Papers/NYPL; also Walter H. Loving to Chief, MIB, Executive Branch, Subj.: 'The Crisis,' May 30, 1918: Walter H. Loving Papers/Moorland-Spingarn Res. Ctr; Ovington, *Walls Came Tumbling Down*, p. 133.

40. Spingarn at MIB:—Creel Committee—antilynching bill "Negro Subversion": Bolton Smith to Joel E. Spingarn, July 20, 1918, Box 7-LAM: Joel E. Spingarn Papers/NYPL; Washburn, *Question of Sedition*, pp. 15–16; Robert L. Zangrando, *The NAACP Crusade Against Lynching, 1909–1950* (Philadelphia: Temple University Press, 1980), pp. 44–45.

41. ". . . offering him a commission.": Joel E. Spingarn to Amy Spingarn [Sunday n.d.], Fol. Amy Spingarn Corr.; Joel E. Spingarn Papers/Moorland-Spingarn Res. Ctr./ Howard University. ". . . things to be accomplished.": *ibid*.

42. Spingarn's suasion: Ellis, " 'Closing Ranks,' " p. 106; Kellogg, *NAACP*, pp. 271–72; Washburn, *Sedition*, p. 19.

43. ". . . become dangerous after all.": Joel E. Spingarn to Amy Spingarn, June 26, 1918, Fol. Spingarn, Joel—1918–1922: Joel E. Spingarn Papers/Moorland-Spingarn Res. Ctr.; W.E.B. Du Bois to Col. Marlborough Churchill, Chief, Military Intelligence Branch, Executive Division, General Staff, June 24, 1918, Box 4, Fol. "Black Man in Wounded World"/W.E.B. Du Bois Collection/Fisk University. Although dissenting from several of his conclusions about motives behind Du Bois's wartime editorial decisions, I am exceedingly grateful for the opportunity to consult the thoroughly researched, provocative, unpublished article by Mr. William Jordan of the Department of History, University of New Hampshire, "A Damnable Dilemma: African-American Accommodation in World War One" [typescript, 1993].

44. Editors' conference: Washburn, *Sedition*, p. 16; see the confidential report on this conference prepared by Loving for Major Nicholas Biddle, MIB, New York City, "Conditions among Negroes in the United States," July 22, 1918: Walter H. Loving Papers/ Moorland-Spingarn Res. Ctr.; also Stephen R. Fox, *The Guardian of Boston: William Monroe Trotter*, p. 219. ". . . seek an opportunity to do"—Wilson, quoted: Fox, *Guardian of Boston*, p. 219; see also Ray Stannard Baker, *Woodrow Wilson: Life and Letters, 1913–1914* (New York: Greenwood Press, 1968), pp. 221–25. ". . . efficient fighter for victory."—Du Bois, quoted: Fox, *Guardian of Boston*, p. 220; Du Bois, "A Philosophy in Time of War," *The Crisis*, 16 (Aug. 1918): 164–65.

45. ". . . before or since.": Du Bois, *Dusk*, pp. 256–57.

46. ". . . during the World War.": *ibid.*, p. 252; W.E.B. Du Bois to F. M. Young, Aug. 8, 1918, Du Bois Papers/U. Mass.

47. ". . . lifted to the hills.:" Du Bois, "Close Ranks," *The Crisis*, 16 (July 1918): 111, in *Selections from The Crisis*, I, p. 159.

48. Reactions to "Close Ranks": Du Bois, *Dusk*, p. 254; George W. Crawford to W.E.B. Du Bois, July 3, 1918, Du Bois Papers/U. Mass.; George W. Cook to W.E.B. Du Bois, July 3, 1918: W.E.B. Du Bois Collection Folder/Moorland-Spingarn Res. Ctr.; "Dr. Du Bois Draws Fire," *Pittsburgh Courier*, July 20, 1918, p. 1; The *Messenger*—cited: Washburn, *Sedition*, p. 21.

49. "my present income.": Du Bois, "To the Board of Directors of the NAACP," July 2, 1918: W.E.B. Du Bois Collection Folder/Moorland-Spingarn Res. Ctr. More debate: Ross, *Spingarn*, pp. 99–100; Neval H. Thomas to Oswald Garrison Villard, Sept. 13, 1918: Oswald Garrison Villard Papers/Houghton Library/Harvard University; Kellogg, *NAACP*, p. 273.

50. ". . . Before Time was . . .": Du Bois, "A Philosophy in Time of War," *The Crisis*, 16 (Aug. 1918): 164–65, in *Selections from The Crisis*, I, pp. 160–61 (p. 160). Du Bois on racial gains: Du Bois, "Our Special Grievances," *The Crisis*, 16 (Sept. 1918): 216–17, in Aptheker, ed., *Selections from The Crisis*, I, 162–63; Joel E. Spingarn to Woodrow Wilson, July 17, 1918, Box 7: Joel E. Spingarn Papers/NYPL; and Zangrando, *NAACP Crusade*, p. 45.

51. ". . . opportunity slip by.": Joel E. Spingarn to W.E.B. Du Bois, July 16, 1918; W.E.B. Du Bois to Joel E. Spingarn, July 12, 1918, Du Bois Papers/U. Mass.; Ross, *Spingarn*, p. 100.

52. ". . . pure and simple?": John Hope to W.E.B. Du Bois, July 22, 1918; W.E.B. Du Bois to John Hope, July 12, 1918, Du Bois Papers/U. Mass.

53. "probably glad": Mary White Ovington to W.E.B. Du Bois, July 10, 1918, Du Bois Papers/U. Mass.; Charles H. Studin to Joel E. Spingarn, July 17, 1918, Box 11, Fol. Studin: Joel E. Spingarn Papers/NYPL; John R. Shillady to Joel E. Spingarn, July 30, 1918, Box 9, Fol. NAACP Papers/LC.

54. ". . . the best result.": Du Bois, *Dusk*, p. 258, and p. 257.

55. ". . . antagonistic in tone": Ellis, " 'Closing Ranks'," p. 114. ". . . results of race prejudice.": Nicholas Biddle, Major, N.A., to Col. Marlborough Churchill, Chief, MIB, Executive Division, General Staff, July 22, 1918: Walter H. Loving Papers/Moorland-Spingarn Res. Ctr.

56. ". . . first interview with him.": Walter H. Loving to Chief, MIB, Executive Branch, Subj., Kelly Miller of Howard University, Mar. 14, 1918; Walter H. Loving to Chief, MIB, Executive Division, General Staff, Subj.: Archibald Grimké, Mar. 5, 1918; Walter H. Loving to Chief, MIB, Executive Division, General Staff, Subj.: Negro Subversion, Mar. 5, 1918; Walter H. Loving to Major Nicholas Biddle, Subj.: C. C. Payne, Negro Soap Box Orator, June 1, 1918: Walter H. Loving Papers/Moorland-Spingarn Res. Ctr.

57. Loving's death, biographical information: Walter H. Loving Papers/Moorland-Spingarn Res. Ctr.

58. Walter H. Loving to Major Nicholas Biddle, MIB, New York City, Subj.: "Conditions among Negroes in the United States, July 22, 1918": Walter H. Loving Papers/Moorland-Spingarn Res. Ctr. The lucidity and scope of Loving's report strongly suggests to me the probability that it served as grist (much distorted) for the infamous, career-enhancing document on African-American subversion prepared by the young J. Edgar Hoover, "Radicalism and Sedition among Negroes as Reflected in Their Publications," presented by Attorney General A. Mitchell Palmer to the U.S. Senate in November 1919. An appreciation of the lower-middle-class, intolerant Protestant cultural formation of Hoover along with quite brief but suggestive observations about his Negrophobia are found in Richard Gid

Powers, *Secrecy and Power: The Life of J. Edgar Hoover* (New York: The Free Press, 1987), esp. pp. 68–72, 128; also Washburn, *Sedition*, p. 27. ". . . unqualified support.": Colonel Marlborough Churchill to Joel E. Spingarn, Aug. 24, 1918; Col. Marlborough Churchill to Joel E. Spingarn, July 30, 1918: Joel E. Spingarn Papers/NYPL; Col. Marlborough Churchill, Chief, MIB, Executive Division, to W.E.B. Du Bois, July 30, 1918, Box 2, Fol. Corr. 1921–30: W.E.B. Du Bois Collection/Fisk University.

59. Aboard the *Orizaba*: Du Bois, "Letter from Dr. Du Bois," *The Crisis*, 17 (Feb. 1919): 163–66, in *Selections from The Crisis*, I, pp. 166–69, p. 169; Du Bois, *Dusk*, p. 261; Emmett J. Scott to George Creel, Director of Committee on Public Information, Nov. 30, 1918, Box 115: Emmett J. Scott Collection Papers/Morgan State University Library. List of members of the press aboard the *Orizaba*, Dec. 8, 1918, Du Bois Papers/U. Mass.

60. ". . . out of a clear sky . . .": Du Bois, *Dusk*, p. 260; and Minutes of the Meeting of the Board of Directors, Dec. 9, 1918, Du Bois Papers/U. Mass.

61. NAACP disinterest in Pan-Africanism: Du Bois, *Autobiography*, p. 289; *Dusk*, p. 263; Kellogg, *NAACP*, pp. 279–80. . . . charade . . . in Washington.: Du Bois, *Dusk*, pp. 260–61; Du Bois to President Wilson, *The Autobiography*, p. 271; Clarence G. Contee, "Du Bois, The NAACP, and the Pan-African Congress of 1919," *Journal of Negro History*, 57 (Jan. 1972): 13–28, esp. pp. 15–17. ". . . collection of facts and documents.": W.E.B. Du Bois to Emmett J. Scott, Nov. 10, 1918; Emmett J. Scott to W.E.B. Du Bois, Nov. 10, 1918; "Correspondence with Mr. Scott, Memoranda," Sunday, Nov. 3, 1918, all in Du Bois Papers/U. Mass.; Du Bois, "War History" *The Crisis*, 17 (Dec. 1918), 61–62. Scott wrote Peabody that he had planned to write a war history long before he learned of Du Bois's project. Scott added, "Let me say in passing that I had talked with Dr. Woodson about my program and plan at least six or eight weeks before the matter was brought forward by these gentlemen.": Emmett Scott to George Foster Peabody, Nov. 25, 1918, Cont. 108/Emmett J. Scott Papers/Morgan State University Library. To Brawley, Scott declared, "I have made an earnest and sincere attempt to cooperate with Dr. Du Bois, but unhappily he does not seem to wish anybody to cooperate with him except upon terms which are belittling.": Emmett Scott to Benjamin Brawley, June 16, 1919, Cont. 102/ Emmett J. Scott Papers/MSU. I thank my former student, Maceo Dailey, formerly of the faculty of Boston College and now professor of history at Spelman College, for sharing these two letters from the Scott collection, now no longer open to researchers. Du Bois, "The Black Man and the Wounded World" [outline of 12—chapter book], (reel 84) Du Bois Papers/U. Mass. Board's actions on war history and Pan-African Congress: Minutes of the NAACP Board, Sept. 9, 1918; Nov. 1, 1918; Dec. 9, 1918; and Feb. 10, 1919, Box A-8 (Group I, Series A, NAACP Board Minutes)/NAACP Papers/LC. Board minutes for Feb. 10 reveal some displeasure on the part of Joseph Loud about Du Bois's expenses and plan to return to USA via North Africa, South America, and the West Indies. It was decided that an additional $300 would be appropriated to cover the Pan-African Congress, but at Loud's insistence, the board cabled Du Bois "to incur no expenditure over the initial $2000, and that no more money is available." Kellogg, *NAACP*, p. 281.

62. Failure to collaborate: Du Bois, "Report of the Director of Publications and Research" [n.d. 1919], Du Bois Papers/U. Mass.

63. Henri, *Black Migration*, p. 300. Report of the Director of Publications and Research [n.d. 1919], Du Bois Papers/U. Mass. ". . . to resuscitate him.": Joel E. Spingarn to Amy Spingarn [an undated, single sheet of stationery from the New Willard Hotel, Washington, D.C.], Box 1: Joel and Amy Spingarn Collection/Schomburg Ctr. for Res.

64. "SOS" units: Du Bois, "An Essay Toward a History of the Black Man in the Great

War," *The Crisis*, 18 (June 1919): 63–87, [*Crisis Selections*, I, p. 208]; Henri, *Black Migration*, p. 296.

65. Wilson aboard the *George Washington*: Jan Willem Schulte Nordholt, *Woodrow Wilson: A Life for World Peace*, p. 284; John Morton Blum, *Wilson and the Politics of Morality*, pp. 23–37.

66. ". . . Make no mistake . . .": Du Bois, "My Mission," *The Crisis*, 18 (May 1919): 7–9, in Aptheker, ed., *Selections from The Crisis*, I, pp. 186–88 (p. 186).

67. ". . . a surging crowd.": Du Bois, "Letters from Dr. Du Bois," *The Crisis*, 17 (Feb. 1919): 163–64, in *Selections from the Crisis*, I, 166–69.

68. Lippmann: Du Bois, "Letters from Dr. Du Bois," p. 167.

69. Wilson's Fourteen points: Gary B. Nash et al., eds., *The American People: Creating a Nation and a Society* (New York: Harper & Row, 1990, 2nd ed.), p. 773. ". . . throughout the world.": Du Bois, "Letters from Dr. Du Bois," pp. 169, 168.

70. Delegates and addresses: Du Bois Papers/U. Mass.; Du Bois, "Vive la France!" *The Crisis*, 17 (Mar. 1919): 215–16, in Aptheker, ed., *Selections from The Crisis*, I, pp. 170–71.

71. ". . . at least embarrassed.": Du Bois, *Dusk*, pp. 259, 260.

72. ". . . we call 'Nigger-hatred.' ": Du Bois, "For What?" *The Crisis*, 17 (Apr. 1919): 268, in *Selections from The Crisis*, I, p. 180. ". . . swing of the Champs-Elysées.": Du Bois, "In France, 1918," *The Crisis*, 17 (Mar. 1919): 215–16, p. 216.

73. ". . . stood to his right.": Du Bois, "Vive la France!" p. 170.

74. On Archinard and de Brazza: a competent English-language treatment is David Levering Lewis's *The Race to Fashoda: European Colonialism and African Resistance in the Scramble for Africa* (New York: Weidenfeld and Nicolson, 1987), pp. 39–47, and 73–84; also Richard West, *Brazza of the Congo: European Exploration and Exploitation in French Equatorial Africa* (London: Jonathan Cape, 1972). Excellent French-language monographs are Catherine Coquery-Vidrovitch, *Brazza et la prise de possession du Congo: La Mission de l'Ouest Africain* (Paris: Mouton, 1969); Marc Michel, *Mission Marchand, 1895–1899* (Paris: Mouton, 1972); Henri Brunschwig's *Mythes et réalités de l'impérialisme colonial français, 1871–1914* (Paris: A. Colin, 1960) remains a staple. ". . . should speak French . . .": Du Bois, "French and Spanish," *The Crisis*, 17 (Apr. 1919): 269–270, in *Crisis Selections*, I, 181.

75. Pan-African difficulties in Paris: Du Bois, "My Mission," *The Crisis*, 18 (May 1919): 7–9, in Aptheker, ed., *Selections from The Crisis*, I, pp. 186–88 (p. 187); and see the perceptive observations of Elliott P. Skinner, *African Americans and U.S. Policy Toward Africa, 1850–1924* (Washington, D.C.: Howard University Press, 1992), p. 404; also Arthur Walworth, *Wilson and His Peacemakers: American Diplomacy at the Paris Peace Conference, 1919* (New York and London: W. W. Norton, 1986), p. 37; Manning Marable, *W.E.B. Du Bois: Black Radical Democrat*, p. 100.

76. ". . . the French Parliament.": Du Bois, *Dusk*, p. 261. See Du Bois, "The Pan-African Movement," in *History of the Pan-African Congress edited by George Padmore* (Manchester: Pan-African Federation, n.d.), pp. 13–17, p. 15.

77. On Diagne's checkered career: see Janet G. Vaillant, *Black, French, and African: A Life of Leopold Sedar Senghor* (Cambridge, Mass., and London: Harvard University Press, 1990), pp. 46–47. Diagne's wartime special title was that of High Commissioner for the Republic and he was given co-equal power with that of the Governor-General of French West Africa. See Michael Crowder, *West Africa under Colonial Rule* (Evanston, IL: Northwestern University Press, 1968), pp. 264–65.

78. ". . . Africa for the Africans.": Du Bois, "Memorandum to M. Diagne and Others on a Pan-African Congress to be Held in Paris in February, 1919," *The Crisis*, 17 (Mar. 1919): 224–25, in Aptheker, ed., *Selections from The Crisis*, I, pp. 178–79 (p. 178); and

Du Bois, *The World and Africa* (Millwood, N.Y.: Kraus-Thomson, 1976; orig. pub. 1947), pp. 8–12; Skinner, *African Americans and U.S. Policy*, p. 404. Skinner (p. 408) notes that Maurice Delafosse, the French colonial official and Africanist attending the Pan-African Congress, observed that his government had no reason to be concerned and that Diagne could be relied upon to keep the agenda safely moderate.

79. ". . . charming woman": Du Bois, *Dusk*, p. 262. Du Bois, "Memorandum to M. Diagne," p. 179. Ida Hunt: "Hunt, Ida Alexander Gibbs (1862–1957)," *DANB*, pp. 336–37. "Bills and Receipts," Box 1, Fol. 6: W.E.B. Du Bois Collection/Fisk.

80. ". . . Chief of Staff, G-2.": F. Schoonmaker, Maj. Gen., H.Q., 92d Div. of A.E.F., to Intelligence Officers, Jan. 1, 1919, Du Bois Papers/U. Mass.; Du Bois, "An Essay Toward a History of the Black Man in the Great War," p. 213.

81. ". . . we learned about it.": Louis Portlock to W.E.B. Du Bois, Apr. 26, 1919, Du Bois Papers/U. Mass.; Du Bois, "The Negro Soldier in Service Abroad During the First World War," *Journal of Negro Education*, 12 (Summer 1943): 324–34, p. 325; Du Bois, "Robert Russa Moton," *The Crisis*, 18 (May 1919): 9–10, in Aptheker, ed., *Selections from The Crisis*, I, pp. 189–90 (p. 189). Also Nalty, *Strength for the Fight*, pp. 123–24; and Foner, *Blacks and the Military*, pp. 123–24. . . . Marseillaise . . . living room.: Du Bois, "Black Man in the Great War," p. 206. . . . City of Metz.: Du Bois, "In France, 1918," *The Crisis*, 17 (Mar. 1919): 215–16, p. 216.

82. 92nd Division: Du Bois, "The Black Man in the Revolution of 1914–1918," *The Crisis*, 17 (Mar. 1919): 218–23, in Aptheker, ed., *Selections from The Crisis*, I, 198–205, pp. 199–200; Du Bois, "Black Man in the Great War," [*Crisis Selections*, I] pp. 211–13; Du Bois, "Negro Soldiers in Service Abroad," pp. 329–30; Henri, *Black Migration*, p. 300.

83. Bullard and Ballou: Du Bois, "Black Man in the Great War," p. 213, and p. 223; Henri, *Black Migration*, p. 300. A Bullard diary entry complained, "Poor Negroes, they are hopelessly inferior." Bullard was dismayed by African-American officers under his command, but his feelings ran to apoplexy about General Ballou, whom he considered sending to an SOS division. Ballou reciprocated, and he wavered between blaming his own men for his troubles and sighing over the feral racism of American senior officers who "will never give the negro the square deal that is his just due."

84. ". . . cause a bad impression.": Du Bois, "Negro Soldiers in Service Abroad," p. 325; Du Bois, *Dusk*, p. 262. ". . . and *esprit de corps*.": Du Bois, "Documents of the War," p. 199.

85. ". . . and the chaplain.": Du Bois, "Black Man in the Great War," p. 216; see Emmett J. Scott, *Scott's Official History of the American Negro in the World War* (Chicago: Homewood Press, 1919), p. 213; Henri, *Black Migration*, p. 300; Lewis, *When Harlem Was in Vogue*, p. 4.

86. Eighth Illinois: Du Bois, "Black Man in the Great War," pp. 221, 222.

87. On postal suppression of *Crisis*: "Chronology," Library of America, *W.E.B. Du Bois*, pp. 1293–94. ". . . appear intolerable.": Du Bois, "Documents of the War," p. 198.

88. ". . . they were withdrawn.": *ibid*.

89. Moton's inspection tour: see William Hardin Hughes and Frederick D. Patterson, eds., *Robert Russa Moton of Hampton and Tuskegee* (Chapel Hill: University of North Carolina Press, 1956), pp. 123–27. Meuse-Argonne debacle: Du Bois, "Black Man in the Great War," pp. 224–25; Louis Portlock to W.E.B. Du Bois, Apr. 26, 1919, Du Bois Papers/U. Mass. ". . . of the Regular Army.": Du Bois, "Black Man in the Great War," p. 211 and p. 214.

90. Addie W. Hunton and Kathryn M. Johnson, *Two Colored Women with the American Expeditionary Forces* (Brooklyn: Brooklyn Eagle Press, n.d.), p. 17. Record of the

369th: Du Bois, "Black Man in the Great War," pp. 216–17; Scott, *Negro in the World War*, pp. 94, 200–13; Nalty, *Strength for the Fight*, pp. 118–21. Henri, *Black Migration*, pp. 279–99.

91. The black regiments: Du Bois, "Black Man in the Great War," pp. 217–27; Nalty, *Strength for the Fight*, pp. 120–21.

92. ". . . either a doctor or a nurse.": Hunton and Johnson, *Two Colored Women*, pp. 24 and 31. Moton's conduct abroad: Du Bois, "Robert Russa Moton," pp. 189–90; full text of Moton's address, in Hardin and Patterson, *Moton*, pp. 126–27; "Moton" [documents relating to Moton's tour of the 92d Division and meeting with African-American officers of the 317th Ammunition Train], Dec. 16, 1918, Du Bois Papers/U. Mass.—"no opportunity was given to the officers to inform him of conditions that had existed in France, and he did not seek any information relative to same from any of the officers after the conference ended."

93. ". . . what did he do about it?": Du Bois, "Our Success and Failure," *The Crisis*, 18 (July 1919): 127–30, in Aptheker, ed., *Selections from The Crisis*, I, pp. 234–37 (p. 236).

94. Du Bois–Scott imbroglio: "Du Bois Draws Fire," Pittsburgh *Courier*, July 20, 1918, p. 1; "Scott Answers Dr. Du Bois," Boston *Chronicle*, May 24, 1919. Letters supporting Scott in Scott Collection Papers/Morgan State University Library—Benjamin Brawley (June 3, 1919); Archibald Grimké (May 10, 1919); J. C. Napier (May 23, 1919); Lester Walton (June 4, 1919); John E. Bruce (Bruce Grit) (June 5, 1919). Also censuring Du Bois was Neval H. Thomas to Joel E. Spingarn, May 3, 1919, Box D-F 95-2: Joel E. Spingarn Papers/Moorland-Spingarn Res. Ctr. See letter from from a serviceman who claimed to have personally informed Scott of deplorable facilities and training program foisted on African-American soldiers—Lafayette S. Hankins to W.E.B. Du Bois, June 3, 1919, Box 4/Du Bois Papers/Fisk University Library; but consult typical aggressive rebuttal by Scott of Du Bois's charges—"Makes 'Red-Hot' Reply to Editor of Crisis," Boston *Chronicle*, May 24, 1919.

95. ". . . throughout the entire world.": Du Bois, "The Pan-African Congress," *The Crisis*, 17 (Apr. 1919): 271–74, in Aptheker, ed., *Selections from The Crisis*, I, pp. 182–85 (pp. 183–84). British opposition: Skinner, *African Americans and U.S. Policy*, pp. 407–8, suggests that Lloyd George eventually displayed moderate sympathy for Du Bois's efforts.

96. No passports: Du Bois, "The Pan-African Movement," p. 15.

97. ". . . less than $10,000.": Du Bois, "My Mission," p. 187, p. 186.

98. ". . . some influence.": Du Bois, *Dusk*, p. 262.

99. ". . . rights and liberties.": Du Bois, "The Pan-African Congress," pp. 183–84.

100. ". . . very much interested . . .": Walter Lippmann to W.E.B. Du Bois, Feb. 20, 1919, Du Bois Papers/U. Mass.; in Aptheker, *Correspondence*, I, p. 233; Du Bois, "The Pan African Movement," p. 15; Du Bois and Beer: see Clarence G. Contee, "Du Bois, the NAACP, and the Pan African Congress of 1919," *Journal of Negro History*, 57 (Jan. 1972): 13–28, pp. 25–26; and William Roger Lewis, "The United States and the African Peace Settlement: The Pilgrimage of George Louis Beer," *Journal of African History*, 4 (1963): 413–33. The mandates: Du Bois, "The Pan African Movement," p. 17; Kellogg, *NAACP*, p. 283; Skinner, *African Americans and U.S. Policy*, p. 408, states, correctly, as I believe, that "it is doubtful whether they [Pan African Congress resolutions] had any impact on the final decisions at Paris, especially on the mandate system that was to loom so large in the future history of the Continent."

101. Pan-African Congress resolutions: Du Bois, "The Pan African Movement," pp. 16–17; and Du Bois, "Adopted Resolutions of the Pan-African Congress," in Aptheker, ed., *Periodical Literature*, II, pp. 125–26.

102. Walworth, *Wilson and His Peacemakers*, p. 33, notes that Clemenceau limited

the amount of press coverage accorded to the Pan-African Congress. ". . . nevertheless interesting.": *Chicago Tribune*, Jan. 19, 1919; and New York *Herald*, cited in Du Bois, "The Pan African Movement," pp. 13–14, 17.

103. Du Bois meets House: Du Bois, "Robert R. Moton," p. 190; Skinner, *African Americans and U.S. Policy*, p. 407; Walworth, *Wilson*, p. 37.

104. ". . . the reason why.": Du Bois, "Returning Soldiers," *The Crisis*, 18 (May 1919): 13–14, in Aptheker, ed., *Selections from The Crisis*, I, pp. 196–97 (p. 197). Du Bois had originally planned to return to the United States via Algeria and Haiti, but the NAACP board cabled its objections: Kellogg, *NAACP*, pp. 281–82.

105. ". . . of modern civilization.": Du Bois, "To the Nations of the World," *Report of the Pan-African Conference, held on 23rd, 24th, and 25th of July 1900 at Westminster Town Hall, Westminster, S.W.*, in *Non-Periodical Literature*, pp. 11–12 (p. 11). ". . . they have been subjected."—Storey quoted: Lewis, *Vogue*, p. 15.

106. The "Red Summer": see Arthur I. Waskow, *From Race Riot to Sit-In: 1919 and the 1960s* (Garden City, N.Y.: Anchor Books, 1966), ch. 2; William Tuttle, Jr., *Race Riot: Chicago in the Red Summer of 1919* (New York: Atheneum, 1970), p. 23; Lewis, *Vogue*, pp. 17–23. ". . . sunlight of real manhood."—*Whip* cited: Robert T. Kerlin, *The Voice of the Negro, 1919* (New York: Arno Press, 1968; orig. pub. 1920), pp. 66–67 (p. 67). ". . . 'Where do we come in?' ": Du Bois, "Causes of Discontent," New York *Sun*, Oct. 12, 1919, pp. 5 and 7, in Aptheker, ed., *Periodical Literature*, II, pp. 130–36 (p. 132).

107. ". . . an American, a Negro": Du Bois, *Souls of Black Folk*, p. 3.

108. ". . . to Freedom or Death.": Du Bois, "Let Us Reason Together," *The Crisis*, 18 (Sept. 1919): 231, in Aptheker, ed., *Selections from The Crisis*, I, p. 240.

Selected Writings of W.E.B. DuBois

Books by W.E.B. Du Bois

The Suppression of the African Slave Trade to the United States of America, 1638–1870; Harvard Historical Studies Number 1 (1896)
The Philadelphia Negro: A Social Study (1899)
The Souls of Black Folk: Essays and Sketches (1903)
John Brown (1909)
The Quest of the Silver Fleece: A Novel (1911)
The Negro (1915)
Darkwater: Voices from Within the Veil (1920)
The Gift of Black Folk: Negroes in the Making of America (1924)
Dark Princess: A Romance (1928)
Africa, Its Geography, People and Products (1930)
Africa—Its Place in Modern History (1930)
Black Reconstruction in America: An Essay Toward a History of the Part Which Black Folk Played in the Attempt to Reconstruct Democracy in America, 1860–1880 (1935)
Black Folk Then and Now: An Essay in the History and Sociology of the Negro Race (1939)
Dusk of Dawn: An Essay Toward an Autobiography of a Race Concept (1940)
Color and Democracy: Colonies and Peace (1945)
The World and Africa: An Inquiry into the Part Which Africa Has Played in World History (1947)
In Battle for Peace: The Story of My 83rd Birthday, with Comment by Shirley Graham (1952)
The Black Flame: A Trilogy
The Ordeal of Mansart (1957)
Mansart Builds a School (1959)
Worlds of Color (1961)
Africa: An Essay Toward a History of the Continent of Africa and Its Inhabitants (1961)
An ABC of Color: Selections from Over a Half Century of the Writings of W.E.B. Du Bois (1963)
The Autobiography of W.E.B. Du Bois: A Soliloquy on Viewing My Life from the Last Decade of its First Century (Moscow, 1962; USA, 1968)

Articles and essays by W.E.B. Du Bois, written before 1920 and selected by the author for their utility, typicality, and/or poignancy

"Tom Brown at Fisk in Three Chapters," *Fisk Herald*, 5 (December 1887): 5–7; 5 (January 1888): 6–7; 5 (March 1888): 5–7.
"The Conservation of Races," *American Negro Academy Occasional Papers*, no. 2 (1897).
"Strivings of the Negro People," *Atlantic Monthly*, 80 (August 1897): 194–98.
"The Negroes of Farmville, Virginia: A Social Study." U.S. Department of Labor, *Bulletin*, no. 14 (January 1898).
"Careers Open to College-Bred Negroes," *Two Addresses Delivered by Alumni of Fisk University . . . June, 1898* (Fisk University, 1898).
"The Storm and Stress in the Black World," *Dial*, 30 (April 16, 1901): 262–64.
"The Evolution of Negro Leadership," *Dial*, 31 (July 16, 1901): 53–55.
"The Talented Tenth," in [editor unknown] *The Negro Problem: A Series of Articles by Representative American Negroes of Today* (1903).
"Credo," *The Independent*, 57 (October 6, 1904): 787.
"Debit and Credit: "The American Negro . . . in Account with . . . the Year of Grace Nineteen Hundred and Four," *Voice of the Negro*, 2, no. 1 (January 1905): 677.
"The Parting of the Ways," *World Today*, 6 (April 1904): 521–23.
"A Litany of Atlanta," *The Independent*, 61 (October 11, 1906): 856–58.
"Reconstruction and Its Benefits," *American Historical Review*, 15 (July 1910): 781–99.
"The Souls of White Folk," *The Independent*, 69 (August 18, 1910): 339–42.
"Socialism and the Negro Problem," *New Review* (February 1, 1913): 138–41.
"The Negro in Literature and Art," *Annals of the American Academy of Political and Social Science*, 49 (September 1913): 233–37.
"The African Roots of War," *Atlantic Monthly*, 115 (May 1915): 707–14.

The Moon Illustrated Weekly
(*December 1905 to July-August? 1906*)

"The New Dispensation," n.d.
"Then and Now," ca. May 1906.
"The Niagara Movement," 1, no. 30 (June 23, 1906): 12.

The Horizon:
A Journal of the Color Line
(*January 1907 to July 1910*)

"India," 1, no. 1 (January 1907): 8.
"The Song and the Smoke," 1, no. 2 (February 1907): 7.
"Socialist of the Path," 1, no. 2 (February 1907): 7.
"Hearken Theodore Roosevelt," 1, no. 3 (March 1907): 7–8.
"Africa," 1, no. 4 (April 1907): 6–7.
"The Lash," 1, no. 5 (May 1907): 5–6.
"Brownsville," 1, no. 6 (June 1907): 8–9.
"A Rebuke," 2, no. 2 (August 1907): 4.

"Niagara," 2, no. 3 (September 1907): 4–6.
"The Burden of Black Women," 2, no. 5 (November 1907): 3–5.
"My Country 'Tis of Thee," 2, no. 5 (November 1907): 5–7.
"Peonage," 3, no. 1 (January 1908): 5–6.
"A Day in Africa," 3, no. 1 (January 1908): 5–6.
"To Black Voters," 3, no. 2 (February 1908): 17–18.
"Ida Dean Bailey," 3, no. 3 (March 1908): 2–5.
"Bryan," 3, no. 3 (March 1908): 7.
"Taft," 3, no. 6 (June 1908): 2–5.
"The Negro Voter," 4, no. 1 (July 1908): 4.
"Niagara Movement," 4, no. 3 (September 1908): 1–3.
"The Negro Vote—Talk Number Four," 4, no. 3 (September 1908): 4–6.
"National Negro Conference," 5, no. 1 (November 1909): 1–2.
"Women," 5, no. 2 (December 1909): 2.
"J'Accuse," 5, no. 4 (February 1910): 1–2.
"The Universal Races Congress," 5, no. 6 (May 1910): 1–2.
"The National Association for the Advancement of Colored People," 6, no. 2 (July 1910): 1–2.
"Atlanta University," 6, no. 2 (July 1910): 2–3.

The Crisis:
A Record of the Darker Races
(*November 1910 to June 1919*)

"Editorial," 1 (November 1910): 10–11.
"Agitation," 1 (November 1910): 11.
"Social Equality," 1 (January 1911): 20–21.
"Pink Franklin," 1 (February 1911): 17.
"The Blair Bill," 1 (March 1911): 16–17.
"Easter," 1 (April 1911): 20.
"Starvation and Prejudice," 2 (June 1911): 62–64.
"Lynching," 2 (August 1911): 158–59.
"Triumph," 2 (September 1911): 195.
"Forward, Backward," 2 (October 1911): 243–44.
"I Am Resolved," 3 (January 1912): 113.
"Alexander Walters," 3 (February 1912): 146.
"Captain Charles Young, U.S.A.," 3 (February 1912): 146–47.
"The Negro Church," 4 (May 1912): 24–25.
"Education," 4 (May 1912): 25–26.
"Lynching Again," 4 (May 1912): 27.
"Suffering Suffragettes," 4 (June 1912): 76–77.
"Organized Labor," 4 (July 1912): 131.
"Politics," 4 (August 1912): 180–81.
"Votes for Women," 4 (September 1912): 234.
"Mr. Roosevelt," 4 (September 1912): 235–36.
"A Great Advocate," 5 (November 1912): 15–16.
"The Election," 5 (December 1912): 75.
"Intermarriage," 5 (February 1913): 180–81.
"An Open Letter to Woodrow Wilson," 5 (March 1913): 236–37.

"Resolutions at Cooper Union on Lincoln's Birthday," 5 (April 1913): 292.
"Hail Columbia," 5 (April 1913): 289–90.
"Woman's Suffrage," 6 (May 1913): 29.
"The Democrats," 6 (June 1913): 79.
"I Go A-Talking," 6 (July 1913): 130–32.
"Another Open Letter to Woodrow Wilson," 6 (September 1913): 232–33, 236.
"The Princess of the Hither Isles," 6 (October 1913): 285, 288–91.
"The National Emancipation Exposition—New York City, October 22–31, 1913," 7 (November 1913): 339–41.
"The Episcopal Church," 7 (December 1913): 83–84.
"The Exposition," 7 (December 1913): 84.
" 'Free, White and Twenty-One,' " 7 (January 1914): 134.
"The Year 1913 in Account with Black Folk," 7 (January 1913): 135.
"Oswald Garrison Villard," 7 (February 1914): 188–89.
"Migration," 7 (February 1914): 190.
"The SURVEY," 7 (March 1914): 240–41.
"Does Organization Pay?" 7 (April 1914): 285.
"Brazil," 7 (April 1914): 286–87.
"The Philosophy of Mr. Dole," 8 (May 1914): 24–26.
"American Civilization," 8 (June 1914): 76.
"Three Members of Parliament," 8 (August 1914): 170.
"Votes for Women," 8 (August 1914): 179–80.
"World War and the Color Line," 9 (November 1914): 28–30.
"William Monroe Trotter," 9 (December 1914): 82.
"The President," 9 (February 1915): 181.
"Segregation in Washington," 9 (February 1915): 182–83.
"The Lynching Industry," 9 (February 1915): 196, 198.
"Woman Suffrage," 9 (April 1915): 285.
"The Immediate Program of the American Negro," 9 (April 1915): 296–97.
"The Clansman," 10 (May 1915): 33.
"An Amazing Island," 10 (June 1915): 80–81.
"Lusitania," 10 (June 1915): 81.
"A Pageant," 10 (September 1915): 230–31.
"Hayti," 10 (September 1915): 232.
"We Come of Age," 11 (November 1915): 25.
"The CRISIS and the N.A.A.C.P.," 11 (November 1915): 25–26.
"Benson," 11 (December 1915): 79–80.
"Booker T. Washington," 11 (December 1915): 82.
" 'The Star of Ethiopia,' " 11 (December 1915): 91–93.
"That Capital 'N'," 11 (February 1916): 184.
"Germany," 11 (February 1916): 186–87.
"Drew," 11 (March 1916): 227.
"Young," 11 (March 1916): 240, 242.
"Brandeis," 11 (March 1916): 243.
"The Church," 11 (April 1916): 302.
"An Open Letter to Robert Russa Moton," 12 (July 1916): 136–37.
"The Drama Among Black Folk," 12 (August 1916): 169, 171–72.
"Sir Roger Casement—Patriot, Martyr," 12 (September 1916): 215–16.
" 'The Battle of Europe,' " 12 (September 1916): 215–18.

"Officers," 14 (June 1917): 60–61.
"The Negro Party," 12 (October 1916): 268–69.
"Migration," 12 (October 1916): 270.
"Cowardice," 12 (October 1916): 270–71.
"Josiah Royce," 13 (November 1916): 9–12.
"Amenia," 13 (November 1916): 19.
"Migration and Help," 13 (January 1917): 115.
"The Curtains of Pain," 13 (February 1917): 163.
"The Perpetual Dilemma," 13 (April 1917): 270–71.
"A Letter to the President," 13 (April 1917): 284.
"The Migration," 14 (May 1917): 8.
"Resolutions of the Washington Conference," 14 (June 1917): 59–60.
" 'We Should Worry,' " 14 (June 1917): 61–62.
"Extract from an Open Letter to the President," 14 (August 1917): 164–65.
"East St. Louis," 14 (September 1917): 215–16.
"Awake America," 14 (September 1917): 216–17.
"Houston," 14 (October 1917): 10–12.
"Hampton," 15 (November 1917): 10–12.
"The Second Coming," 15 (December 1917): 74.
"East St. Louis," 15 (December 1917): 62.
"The Elections," 15 (December 1917): 62.
"The Year of God 1917 in Account with the American Negro," 15 (January 1918): 111.
"The Shadow of Years," 15 (February 1918): 167–71.
"Negro Education," 15 (February 1918): 173–78.
"The Black Man and the Unions," 15 (March 1918): 216–17.
"Colonel Young," 15 (March 1918): 218.
"Houston and East St. Louis," 15 (April 1918): 269.
"Safe for Democracy: Russia—America," 15 (April 1918): 270.
"The Black Soldier," 16 (June 1918): 60.
"Close Ranks," 16 (July 1918): 111.
"Awake, Put on Thy Strength, O Zion," 16 (July 1918): 114.
"Help Us to Help," 16 (August 1918): 163–64.
"A Philosophy in Time of War," 16 (August 1918): 164–65.
"Our Special Grievances," 16 (September 1918): 216–17.
"The Slaughter of the Innocents," 16 (October 1918): 267.
"Blease, Hardwick and Company," 16 (October 1918): 268–69.
"Houston," 16 (October 1918): 269.
" 'Now or Never!' " 17 (November 1918): 11.
"In France," 17 (December 1918): 60–61.
"Vive La France!" 17 (March 1919): 215–16.
"The Black Man in the Revolution of 1914–1918," 17 (March 1919): 218–23.
"Memorandum to M. Diagne and Others on a Pan-African Congress to be Held in Paris in February 1919," 17 (March 1919): 224–25.
"Easter 1919," 17 (April 1919): 267–68.
"The Fields of Battles," 17 (April 1919): 268–69.
"The Pan-African Congress," 17 (April 1919): 271, 273–74.
"My Mission," 18 (May 1919): 7–9.
"To Mr. Emmett Scott," 18 (May 1919): 10.
"The League of Nations," 18 (May 1919): 10–11.

"Returning Soldiers," 18 (May 1919): 13–14.
"Documents of the War," 18 (May 1919): 16–21.
"The History of the Great War," 18 (June 1919): 59–60.
"An Essay Toward a History of the Black Man in the Great War," 18 (June 1919): 63–87.
"Our Success and Failure," 18 (July 1919): 127–30.
"Let Us Reason Together," 18 (September 1919): 231.

INDEX